T0202657

Lecture Notes in Computer Science 14438

The series Lecture Notes in Computer Science (LNCS), including its subseries Lecture Notes in Artificial Intelligence (LNAI) and Lecture Notes in Bioinformatics (LNBI), has established itself as a medium for the publication of new developments in computer science and information technology research, teaching, and education.

LNCS enjoys close cooperation with the computer science R & D community, the series counts many renowned academics among its volume editors and paper authors, and collaborates with prestigious societies. Its mission is to serve this international community by providing an invaluable service, mainly focused on the publication of conference and workshop proceedings and postproceedings. LNCS commenced publication in 1973.

Jian Guo · Ron Steinfeld
Editors

Advances in Cryptology – ASIACRYPT 2023

29th International Conference on the Theory
and Application of Cryptology and Information Security
Guangzhou, China, December 4–8, 2023
Proceedings, Part I

 Springer

Editors
Jian Guo 🆔
Nanyang Technological University
Singapore, Singapore

Ron Steinfeld 🆔
Monash University
Melbourne, VIC, Australia

ISSN 0302-9743   ISSN 1611-3349 (electronic)
Lecture Notes in Computer Science
ISBN 978-981-99-8720-7   ISBN 978-981-99-8721-4 (eBook)
https://doi.org/10.1007/978-981-99-8721-4

This Springer imprint is published by the registered company Springer Nature Singapore Pte Ltd.
The registered company address is: 152 Beach Road, #21-01/04 Gateway East, Singapore 189721, Singapore

Paper in this product is recyclable.

Preface

The 29th Annual International Conference on the Theory and Application of Cryptology and Information Security (Asiacrypt 2023) was held in Guangzhou, China, on December 4–8, 2023. The conference covered all technical aspects of cryptology, and was sponsored by the International Association for Cryptologic Research (IACR).

We received an Asiacrypt record of 376 paper submissions from all over the world, and the Program Committee (PC) selected 106 papers for publication in the proceedings of the conference. Due to this large number of papers, the Asiacrypt 2023 program had 3 tracks.

The two program chairs were supported by the great help and excellent advice of six area chairs, selected to cover the main topic areas of the conference. The area chairs were Kai-Min Chung for Information-Theoretic and Complexity-Theoretic Cryptography, Tanja Lange for Efficient and Secure Implementations, Shengli Liu for Public-Key Cryptography Algorithms and Protocols, Khoa Nguyen for Multi-Party Computation and Zero-Knowledge, Duong Hieu Phan for Public-Key Primitives with Advanced Functionalities, and Yu Sasaki for Symmetric-Key Cryptology. Each of the area chairs helped to lead discussions together with the PC members assigned as paper discussion lead. Area chairs also helped to decide on the submissions that should be accepted from their respective areas. We are very grateful for the invaluable contribution provided by the area chairs.

To review and evaluate the submissions, while keeping the load per PC member manageable, we selected a record size PC consisting of 105 leading experts from all over the world, in all six topic areas of cryptology. The two program chairs were not allowed to submit a paper, and PC members were limited to submit one single-author paper, or at most two co-authored papers, or at most three co-authored papers all with students. Each non-PC submission was reviewed by at least three reviewers consisting of either PC members or their external sub-reviewers, while each PC member submission received at least four reviews. The strong conflict of interest rules imposed by IACR ensure that papers are not handled by PC members with a close working relationship with the authors. There were approximately 420 external reviewers, whose input was critical to the selection of papers. Submissions were anonymous and their length was limited to 30 pages excluding the bibliography and supplementary materials.

The review process was conducted using double-blind peer review. The conference operated a two-round review system with a rebuttal phase. After the reviews and first round discussions the PC selected 244 submissions to proceed to the second round and the authors were then invited to participate in an interactive rebuttal phase with the reviewers to clarify questions and concerns. The remaining 131 papers were rejected, including one desk reject. The second round involved extensive discussions by the PC members. After several weeks of additional discussions, the committee selected the final 106 papers to appear in these proceedings.

The eight volumes of the conference proceedings contain the revised versions of the 106 papers that were selected. The final revised versions of papers were not reviewed again and the authors are responsible for their contents.

The PC nominated and voted for two papers to receive the Best Paper Awards, and one paper to receive the Best Early Career Paper Award. The Best Paper Awards went to Thomas Espitau, Alexandre Wallet and Yang Yu for their paper "On Gaussian Sampling, Smoothing Parameter and Application to Signatures", and to Kaijie Jiang, Anyu Wang, Hengyi Luo, Guoxiao Liu, Yang Yu, and Xiaoyun Wang for their paper "Exploiting the Symmetry of Z^n: Randomization and the Automorphism Problem". The Best Early Career Paper Award went to Maxime Plancon for the paper "Exploiting Algebraic Structure in Probing Security". The authors of those three papers were invited to submit extended versions of their papers to the Journal of Cryptology. In addition, the program of Asiacrypt 2023 also included two invited plenary talks, also nominated and voted by the PC: one talk was given by Mehdi Tibouchi and the other by Xiaoyun Wang. The conference also featured a rump session chaired by Kang Yang and Yu Yu which contained short presentations on the latest research results of the field.

Numerous people contributed to the success of Asiacrypt 2023. We would like to thank all the authors, including those whose submissions were not accepted, for submitting their research results to the conference. We are very grateful to the area chairs, PC members and external reviewers for contributing their knowledge and expertise, and for the tremendous amount of work that was done with reading papers and contributing to the discussions. We are greatly indebted to Jian Weng and Fangguo Zhang, the General Chairs, for their efforts in organizing the event and to Kevin McCurley and Kay McKelly for their help with the website and review system. We thank the Asiacrypt 2023 advisory committee members Bart Preneel, Huaxiong Wang, Kai-Min Chung, Yu Sasaki, Dongdai Lin, Shweta Agrawal and Michel Abdalla for their valuable suggestions. We are also grateful for the helpful advice and organization material provided to us by the Eurocrypt 2023 PC co-chairs Carmit Hazay and Martijn Stam and Crypto 2023 PC co-chairs Helena Handschuh and Anna Lysyanskaya. We also thank the team at Springer for handling the publication of these conference proceedings.

December 2023   Jian Guo
                                                      Ron Steinfeld

Organization

General Chairs

Jian Weng   Jinan University, China
Fangguo Zhang   Sun Yat-sen University, China

Program Committee Chairs

Jian Guo   Nanyang Technological University, Singapore
Ron Steinfeld   Monash University, Australia

Program Committee

Behzad Abdolmaleki   University of Sheffield, UK
Masayuki Abe   NTT Social Informatics Laboratories, Japan
Miguel Ambrona   Input Output Global (IOHK), Spain
Daniel Apon   MITRE Labs, USA
Shi Bai   Florida Atlantic University, USA
Gustavo Banegas   Qualcomm, France
Zhenzhen Bao   Tsinghua University, China
Andrea Basso   University of Bristol, UK
Ward Beullens   IBM Research Europe, Switzerland
Katharina Boudgoust   Aarhus University, Denmark
Matteo Campanelli   Protocol Labs, Denmark
Ignacio Cascudo   IMDEA Software Institute, Spain
Wouter Castryck   imec-COSIC, KU Leuven, Belgium
Jie Chen   East China Normal University, China
Yilei Chen   Tsinghua University, China
Jung Hee Cheon   Seoul National University and Cryptolab Inc,
                             South Korea
Sherman S. M. Chow   Chinese University of Hong Kong, China
Kai-Min Chung   Academia Sinica, Taiwan
Michele Ciampi   University of Edinburgh, UK
Bernardo David   IT University of Copenhagen, Denmark
Yi Deng   Institute of Information Engineering, Chinese
                             Academy of Sciences, China

Patrick Derbez	University of Rennes, France
Xiaoyang Dong	Tsinghua University, China
Rafael Dowsley	Monash University, Australia
Nico Döttling	Helmholtz Center for Information Security, Germany
Maria Eichlseder	Graz University of Technology, Austria
Muhammed F. Esgin	Monash University, Australia
Thomas Espitau	PQShield, France
Jun Furukawa	NEC Corporation, Japan
Aron Gohr	Independent Researcher, New Zealand
Junqing Gong	ECNU, China
Lorenzo Grassi	Ruhr University Bochum, Germany
Tim Güneysu	Ruhr University Bochum, Germany
Chun Guo	Shandong University, China
Siyao Guo	NYU Shanghai, China
Fuchun Guo	University of Wollongong, Australia
Mohammad Hajiabadi	University of Waterloo, Canada
Lucjan Hanzlik	CISPA Helmholtz Center for Information Security, Germany
Xiaolu Hou	Slovak University of Technology, Slovakia
Yuncong Hu	Shanghai Jiao Tong University, China
Xinyi Huang	Hong Kong University of Science and Technology (Guangzhou), China
Tibor Jager	University of Wuppertal, Germany
Elena Kirshanova	Technology Innovation Institute, UAE and I. Kant Baltic Federal University, Russia
Eyal Kushilevitz	Technion, Israel
Russell W. F. Lai	Aalto University, Finland
Tanja Lange	Eindhoven University of Technology, Netherlands
Hyung Tae Lee	Chung-Ang University, South Korea
Eik List	Nanyang Technological University, Singapore
Meicheng Liu	Institute of Information Engineering, Chinese Academy of Sciences, China
Guozhen Liu	Nanyang Technological University, Singapore
Fukang Liu	Tokyo Institute of Technology, Japan
Shengli Liu	Shanghai Jiao Tong University, China
Feng-Hao Liu	Florida Atlantic University, USA
Hemanta K. Maji	Purdue University, USA
Takahiro Matsuda	AIST, Japan
Christian Matt	Concordium, Switzerland
Tomoyuki Morimae	Kyoto University, Japan
Pierrick Méaux	University of Luxembourg, Luxembourg

Mridul Nandi	Indian Statistical Institute, Kolkata, India
María Naya-Plasencia	Inria, France
Khoa Nguyen	University of Wollongong, Australia
Ryo Nishimaki	NTT Social Informatics Laboratories, Japan
Anca Nitulescu	Protocol Labs, France
Ariel Nof	Bar Ilan University, Israel
Emmanuela Orsini	Bocconi University, Italy
Adam O'Neill	UMass Amherst, USA
Morten Øygarden	Simula UiB, Norway
Sikhar Patranabis	IBM Research, India
Alice Pellet-Mary	CNRS and University of Bordeaux, France
Edoardo Persichetti	Florida Atlantic University, USA and Sapienza University, Italy
Duong Hieu Phan	Telecom Paris, Institut Polytechnique de Paris, France
Josef Pieprzyk	Data61, CSIRO, Australia and ICS, PAS, Poland
Axel Y. Poschmann	PQShield, UAE
Thomas Prest	PQShield, France
Adeline Roux-Langlois	CNRS, GREYC, France
Amin Sakzad	Monash University, Australia
Yu Sasaki	NTT Social Informatics Laboratories, Japan
Jae Hong Seo	Hanyang University, South Korea
Yaobin Shen	UCLouvain, Belgium
Danping Shi	Institute of Information Engineering, Chinese Academy of Sciences, China
Damien Stehlé	CryptoLab, France
Bing Sun	National University of Defense Technology, China
Shi-Feng Sun	Shanghai Jiao Tong University, China
Keisuke Tanaka	Tokyo Institute of Technology, Japan
Qiang Tang	University of Sydney, Australia
Vanessa Teague	Thinking Cybersecurity Pty Ltd and the Australian National University, Australia
Jean-Pierre Tillich	Inria, Paris, France
Yosuke Todo	NTT Social Informatics Laboratories, Japan
Alexandre Wallet	University of Rennes, Inria, CNRS, IRISA, France
Meiqin Wang	Shandong University, China
Yongge Wang	UNC Charlotte, USA
Yuyu Wang	University of Electronic Science and Technology of China, China
Qingju Wang	Telecom Paris, Institut Polytechnique de Paris, France

Benjamin Wesolowski	CNRS and ENS Lyon, France
Shuang Wu	Huawei International, Singapore, Singapore
Keita Xagawa	Technology Innovation Institute, UAE
Chaoping Xing	Shanghai Jiao Tong University, China
Jun Xu	Institute of Information Engineering, Chinese Academy of Sciences, China
Takashi Yamakawa	NTT Social Informatics Laboratories, Japan
Kang Yang	State Key Laboratory of Cryptology, China
Yu Yu	Shanghai Jiao Tong University, China
Yang Yu	Tsinghua University, Beijing, China
Yupeng Zhang	University of Illinois Urbana-Champaign and Texas A&M University, USA
Liangfeng Zhang	ShanghaiTech University, China
Raymond K. Zhao	CSIRO's Data61, Australia
Hong-Sheng Zhou	Virginia Commonwealth University, USA

Additional Reviewers

Amit Agarwal	Pedro Branco
Jooyoung Lee	Lauren Brandt
Léo Ackermann	Alessandro Budroni
Akshima	Kevin Carrier
Bar Alon	André Chailloux
Ravi Anand	Suvradip Chakraborty
Sarah Arpin	Debasmita Chakraborty
Thomas Attema	Haokai Chang
Nuttapong Attrapadung	Bhuvnesh Chaturvedi
Manuel Barbosa	Caicai Chen
Razvan Barbulescu	Rongmao Chen
James Bartusek	Mingjie Chen
Carsten Baum	Yi Chen
Olivier Bernard	Megan Chen
Tyler Besselman	Yu Long Chen
Ritam Bhaumik	Xin Chen
Jingguo Bi	Shiyao Chen
Loic Bidoux	Long Chen
Maxime Bombar	Wonhee Cho
Xavier Bonnetain	Qiaohan Chu
Joppe Bos	Valerio Cini
Mariana Botelho da Gama	James Clements
Christina Boura	Ran Cohen
Clémence Bouvier	Alexandru Cojocaru
Ross Bowden	Sandro Coretti-Drayton

Anamaria Costache
Alain Couvreur
Daniele Cozzo
Hongrui Cui
Giuseppe D'Alconzo
Zhaopeng Dai
Quang Dao
Nilanjan Datta
Koen de Boer
Luca De Feo
Paola de Perthuis
Thomas Decru
Rafael del Pino
Julien Devevey
Henri Devillez
Siemen Dhooghe
Yaoling Ding
Jack Doerner
Jelle Don
Mark Douglas Schultz
Benjamin Dowling
Minxin Du
Xiaoqi Duan
Jesko Dujmovic
Moumita Dutta
Avijit Dutta
Ehsan Ebrahimi
Felix Engelmann
Reo Eriguchi
Jonathan Komada Eriksen
Andre Esser
Pouria Fallahpour
Zhiyong Fang
Antonio Faonio
Pooya Farshim
Joël Felderhoff
Jakob Feldtkeller
Weiqi Feng
Xiutao Feng
Shuai Feng
Qi Feng
Hanwen Feng
Antonio Flórez-Gutiérrez
Apostolos Fournaris
Paul Frixons

Ximing Fu
Georg Fuchsbauer
Philippe Gaborit
Rachit Garg
Robin Geelen
Riddhi Ghosal
Koustabh Ghosh
Barbara Gigerl
Niv Gilboa
Valerie Gilchrist
Emanuele Giunta
Xinxin Gong
Huijing Gong
Zheng Gong
Robert Granger
Zichen Gui
Anna Guinet
Qian Guo
Xiaojie Guo
Hosein Hadipour
Mathias Hall-Andersen
Mike Hamburg
Shuai Han
Yonglin Hao
Keisuke Hara
Keitaro Hashimoto
Le He
Brett Hemenway Falk
Minki Hhan
Taiga Hiroka
Akinori Hosoyamada
Chengan Hou
Martha Norberg Hovd
Kai Hu
Tao Huang
Zhenyu Huang
Michael Hutter
Jihun Hwang
Akiko Inoue
Tetsu Iwata
Robin Jadoul
Hansraj Jangir
Dirmanto Jap
Stanislaw Jarecki
Santos Jha

Ashwin Jha
Dingding Jia
Yanxue Jia
Lin Jiao
Daniel Jost
Antoine Joux
Jiayi Kang
Gabriel Kaptchuk
Alexander Karenin
Shuichi Katsumata
Pengzhen Ke
Mustafa Khairallah
Shahram Khazaei
Hamidreza Amini Khorasgani
Hamidreza Khoshakhlagh
Ryo Kikuchi
Jiseung Kim
Minkyu Kim
Suhri Kim
Ravi Kishore
Fuyuki Kitagawa
Susumu Kiyoshima
Michael Klooß
Alexander Koch
Sreehari Kollath
Dimitris Kolonelos
Yashvanth Kondi
Anders Konring
Woong Kook
Dimitri Koshelev
Markus Krausz
Toomas Krips
Daniel Kuijsters
Anunay Kulshrestha
Qiqi Lai
Yi-Fu Lai
Georg Land
Nathalie Lang
Mario Larangeira
Joon-Woo Lee
Keewoo Lee
Hyeonbum Lee
Changmin Lee
Charlotte Lefevre
Julia Len

Antonin Leroux
Andrea Lesavourey
Jannis Leuther
Jie Li
Shuaishuai Li
Huina Li
Yu Li
Yanan Li
Jiangtao Li
Song Song Li
Wenjie Li
Shun Li
Zengpeng Li
Xiao Liang
Wei-Kai Lin
Chengjun Lin
Chao Lin
Cong Ling
Yunhao Ling
Hongqing Liu
Jing Liu
Jiahui Liu
Qipeng Liu
Yamin Liu
Weiran Liu
Tianyi Liu
Siqi Liu
Chen-Da Liu-Zhang
Jinyu Lu
Zhenghao Lu
Stefan Lucks
Yiyuan Luo
Lixia Luo
Jack P. K. Ma
Fermi Ma
Gilles Macario-Rat
Luciano Maino
Christian Majenz
Laurane Marco
Lorenzo Martinico
Loïc Masure
John McVey
Willi Meier
Kelsey Melissaris
Bart Mennink

Charles Meyer-Hilfiger

Victor Miller

Chohong Min

Marine Minier

Arash Mirzaei

Pratyush Mishra

Tarik Moataz

Johannes Mono

Fabrice Mouhartem

Alice Murphy

Erik Mårtensson

Anne Müller

Marcel Nageler

Yusuke Naito

Barak Nehoran

Patrick Neumann

Tran Ngo

Phuong Hoa Nguyen

Ngoc Khanh Nguyen

Thi Thu Quyen Nguyen

Hai H. Nguyen

Semyon Novoselov

Julian Nowakowski

Arne Tobias Malkenes Ødegaard

Kazuma Ohara

Miyako Ohkubo

Charles Olivier-Anclin

Eran Omri

Yi Ouyang

Tapas Pal

Ying-yu Pan

Jiaxin Pan

Eugenio Paracucchi

Roberto Parisella

Jeongeun Park

Guillermo Pascual-Perez

Alain Passelègue

Octavio Perez-Kempner

Thomas Peters

Phuong Pham

Cécile Pierrot

Erik Pohle

David Pointcheval

Giacomo Pope

Christopher Portmann

Romain Poussier

Lucas Prabel

Sihang Pu

Chen Qian

Luowen Qian

Tian Qiu

Anaïs Querol

Håvard Raddum

Shahram Rasoolzadeh

Divya Ravi

Prasanna Ravi

Marc Renard

Jan Richter-Brockmann

Lawrence Roy

Paul Rösler

Sayandeep Saha

Yusuke Sakai

Niels Samwel

Paolo Santini

Maria Corte-Real Santos

Sara Sarfaraz

Santanu Sarkar

Or Sattath

Markus Schofnegger

Peter Scholl

Dominique Schröder

André Schrottenloher

Jacob Schuldt

Binanda Sengupta

Srinath Setty

Yantian Shen

Yixin Shen

Ferdinand Sibleyras

Janno Siim

Mark Simkin

Scott Simon

Animesh Singh

Nitin Singh

Sayani Sinha

Daniel Slamanig

Fang Song

Ling Song

Yongsoo Song

Jana Sotakova

Gabriele Spini

Marianna Spyrakou

Lukas Stennes

Marc Stoettinger

Chuanjie Su

Xiangyu Su

Ling Sun

Akira Takahashi

Isobe Takanori

Atsushi Takayasu

Suprita Talnikar

Benjamin Hong Meng Tan

Ertem Nusret Tas

Tadanori Teruya

Masayuki Tezuka

Sri AravindaKrishnan Thyagarajan

Song Tian

Wenlong Tian

Raphael Toledo

Junichi Tomida

Daniel Tschudi

Hikaru Tsuchida

Aleksei Udovenko

Rei Ueno

Barry Van Leeuwen

Wessel van Woerden

Frederik Vercauteren

Sulani Vidhanalage

Benedikt Wagner

Roman Walch

Hendrik Waldner

Han Wang

Luping Wang

Peng Wang

Yuntao Wang

Geng Wang

Shichang Wang

Liping Wang

Jiafan Wang

Zhedong Wang

Kunpeng Wang

Jianfeng Wang

Guilin Wang

Weiqiang Wen

Chenkai Weng

Thom Wiggers

Stella Wohnig

Harry W. H. Wong

Ivy K. Y. Woo

Yu Xia

Zejun Xiang

Yuting Xiao

Zhiye Xie

Yanhong Xu

Jiayu Xu

Lei Xu

Shota Yamada

Kazuki Yamamura

Di Yan

Qianqian Yang

Shaojun Yang

Yanjiang Yang

Li Yao

Yizhou Yao

Kenji Yasunaga

Yuping Ye

Xiuyu Ye

Zeyuan Yin

Kazuki Yoneyama

Yusuke Yoshida

Albert Yu

Quan Yuan

Chen Yuan

Tsz Hon Yuen

Aaram Yun

Riccardo Zanotto

Arantxa Zapico

Shang Zehua

Mark Zhandry

Tianyu Zhang

Zhongyi Zhang

Fan Zhang

Liu Zhang

Yijian Zhang

Shaoxuan Zhang

Zhongliang Zhang

Kai Zhang

Cong Zhang

Jiaheng Zhang

Lulu Zhang

Zhiyu Zhang

Chang-An Zhao
Yongjun Zhao
Chunhuan Zhao
Xiaotong Zhou
Zhelei Zhou

Zijian Zhou
Timo Zijlstra
Jian Zou
Ferdinando Zullo
Cong Zuo

Sponsoring Institutions

- Gold Level Sponsor: Ant Research
- Silver Level Sponsors: Sansec Technology Co., Ltd., Topsec Technologies Group
- Bronze Level Sponsors: IBM, Meta, Sangfor Technologies Inc.

Invited Talks

Lattice-Based Cryptography: From Theory to Practice

Xiaoyun Wang

Institute for Advanced Study, Tsinghua University, Beijing, China

Abstract. Nowadays, post-quantum cryptography (PQC) mainly refers to the public-key cryptosystems built on mathematical hard problems in computational complexity theory, resisting the attacks from imaginary quantum computers. In the last 30 years, substantial contributions have been made in PQC research. Among the PQC families, lattice-based cryptography is popularly regarded as a promising candidate; its security relies on the hardness of computational mathematical problems in lattice theory with high-dimension. In this talk, I will recap the mathematical background of lattice-based cryptography. Then I will introduce the recent progress on the practical designs of lattice-based cryptosystems, as well as a quick look at an amazing area called fully homomorphic encryption (FHE) which has interesting applications in privacy computing and federated learning, etc.

Mathematical Problems Arising from Timing Attacks on Signatures and Their Countermeasures

Mehdi Tibouchi

NTT Social Informatics Laboratories, Japan

Abstract. One of the aspects of cryptology that make it such an exciting field to work in is the great variety of people's backgrounds, and of the reasons that brought them in to begin with. I personally arrived in cryptology looking for interesting mathematical problems to solve. I did find lots of interesting problems, that I mostly could not solve.

Side-channel attacks, and timing attacks in particular, are of course an important challenge to the deployment of real-world cryptographic systems. In this talk, however, I would like to discuss them from the perspective of a mathematical problem solver. Based on several examples from the analysis of signature schemes, I would like to argue that they are, both on the offensive and on the defensive side, a great source of non-trivial yet tractable mathematical problems.

Contents – Part I

Threshold Cryptography

Secure Multi-party Computation

Breaking the Size Barrier: Universal Circuits Meet Lookup Tables

Yann Disser[ID], Daniel Günther[✉][ID], Thomas Schneider[ID], Maximilian Stillger,
Arthur Wigandt, and Hossein Yalame[ID]

Technical University of Darmstadt, Darmstadt, Germany
disser@mathematik.tu-darmstadt.de,
{guenther,schneider,yalame}@encrypto.cs.tu-darmstadt.de,
maximilian.stillger@arcor.de, arthur.wigandt@protonmail.com

Abstract. A Universal Circuit (UC) is a Boolean circuit of size $\Theta(n \log n)$ that can simulate any Boolean function up to a certain size n. Valiant (STOC'76) provided the first two UC constructions of asymptotic sizes $\sim 5n \log n$ and $\sim 4.75n \log n$, and today's most efficient construction of Liu et al. (CRYPTO'21) has size $\sim 3n \log n$. Evaluating a public UC with a secure Multi-Party Computation (MPC) protocol allows efficient Private Function Evaluation (PFE), where a private function is evaluated on private data.

Previously, most UC constructions have only been developed for circuits consisting of 2-input gates. In this work, we generalize UCs to simulate circuits consisting of $(\rho \to \omega)$-Lookup Tables (LUTs) that map ρ input bits to ω output bits. Our LUT-based UC (LUC) construction has an asymptotic size of $1.5\rho\omega n \log \omega n$ and improves the size of the UC over the best previous UC construction of Liu et al. (CRYPTO'21) by factors $1.12\times$–$2.18\times$ for common functions. Our results show that the greatest size improvement is achieved for $\rho = 3$ inputs, and it decreases for $\rho > 3$.

Furthermore, we introduce Varying Universal Circuits (VUCs), which reduce circuit size at the expense of leaking the number of inputs ρ and outputs ω of each LUT. Our benchmarks demonstrate that VUCs can improve over the size of the LUC construction by a factor of up to $1.45\times$.

Keywords: universal circuit · private function evaluation · multi-party computation

1 Introduction

A *Universal Circuit* (UC) $\mathcal{U}$ is a Boolean circuit that can simulate any Boolean circuit C consisting of n_i inputs, n_g gates, and n_o outputs. The UC $\mathcal{U}$ takes, in addition to the function's input x, a set of programming bits p^C defining the circuit C that $\mathcal{U}$ simulates, i.e., the UC computes $\mathcal{U}(x, p^C) = C(x)$.

Valiant [51] proposed the first two UC constructions known as *2-way* and *4-way* split UCs with asymptotically optimal size $\Theta(n \log n)$ and depth $\mathcal{O}(n)$, where $n = n_i + n_g + n_o$ is the size of the simulated circuit C. Kolesnikov and

© International Association for Cryptologic Research 2023
J. Guo and R. Steinfeld (Eds.): ASIACRYPT 2023, LNCS 14438, pp. 3–37, 2023.
https://doi.org/10.1007/978-981-99-8721-4_1

Schneider [34] gave the first practical implementation of a UC of non-optimal asymptotic size $\mathcal{O}(n \log^2 n)$. A line of work [7,22,31,36,57] followed with the common goal to minimize the size of Valiant's UC construction. Recently, Liu et al. [37] provided today's most efficient UC construction of size $\sim 3n \log n$.

All of these works designed UCs to simulate Boolean gates with 2 inputs and 1 output. However, Valiant's UC construction can be generalized to simulate circuits with $(\rho \rightarrow 1)$-LUT, namely *Lookup-Tables* with ρ inputs $x_1, \ldots, x_\rho$ and one output y and can compute arbitrary functionalities f as $y = f(x_1, \ldots, x_\rho)$ [48].

In this work, we propose LUT-based UCs (LUC) that evaluate circuits composed of $(\rho \rightarrow \omega)$-LUTs having ω output bits $y_1, \ldots, y_\omega$ and are programmed to compute $y_i = f^i(x_1, \ldots, x_\rho)$ for $1 \leq i \leq \omega$ and an arbitrary functionality f^i. In addition, we introduce *Varying UCs (VUCs)* that can simulate circuits consisting of $(\rho \rightarrow \omega)$-LUTs with varying numbers of inputs ρ and outputs ω, thereby leaking the number of in- and outputs of each LUT. VUCs have various applications (summarized in Sect. 1.1) like logic locking [55], which enables the designer to provide the foundry of a chip with a "locked" version of the original circuit. Once the locked circuit on the chip is fabricated, authorized users can regain access to the original functionality by using a secret key.

On top of our new UC constructions, we provide implementations of our constructions and analyze the size optimization of simulating LUT-based circuits with LUCs and VUCs compared to using traditional Boolean circuit-based UCs.

1.1   Applications of (Varying) Universal Circuits

The most prominent application for UCs is **Private Function Evaluation (PFE)** [6], which can be seen as a generalization of *Secure Multi-Party Computation* (MPC) [20,54]. In MPC, a set of k parties $\mathcal{P}_1, \ldots, \mathcal{P}_k$ jointly compute a publicly known circuit C on their respective private inputs $x_1, \ldots, x_k$ and obtain nothing but the result $C(x_1, \ldots, x_k)$. In PFE, the circuit C that shall be computed is private information as well, i.e., party $\mathcal{P}_1$ with circuit input C and parties $\mathcal{P}_{2 \leq i \leq k}$ with data inputs $x_2, \ldots, x_k$ run a protocol that yields nothing but $C(x_2, \ldots, x_k)$ and parties $\mathcal{P}_{2 \leq i \leq k}$ do not learn any information about the circuit C.

PFE can be implemented via MPC by means of UCs as follows: The parties $\mathcal{P}_1, \ldots, \mathcal{P}_k$ run an MPC protocol that evaluates the universal circuit $\mathcal{U}$ as public circuit on the secret inputs p^C of party $\mathcal{P}_1$ and $x_2, \ldots, x_k$ of parties $\mathcal{P}_2, \ldots, \mathcal{P}_k$, resulting in $\mathcal{U}(p^C, x_2, ..., x_k) = C(x_2, ..., x_k)$. In summary, PFE based on UCs is a very generic approach. It can simply be plugged into arbitrary MPC frameworks without any modification to the underlying MPC protocol, resulting in the same security level (semi-honest, covert, or malicious) as the underlying MPC framework. In addition, PFE is completely compatible with the features included in MPC like *secure outsourcing* [27] and *non-interactive computation* [36]. PFE is applicable for situations where customers aim to use a service from companies who want to hide *how* they perform the computation and do not learn the customer's data.[1]

---

[1] UC-based PFE, unlike PFE based on Fully Homomorphic Encryption (FHE) [19,32], relies primarily on symmetric encryption and involves far less computation.

As a trade-off between privacy and efficiency, a variant of PFE called **Semi-Private Function Evaluation (SPFE)** was proposed [21,43]. Unlike PFE, SPFE does not hide the entire function, but leaks the topology of certain sub-functions. SPFE can be applied in PFE scenarios where specific function components are known publicly. This approach is particularly useful in cases where certain function details have already been disclosed, often for promotional purposes. An example of this is car insurance companies offering discounts to experienced drivers.

Beyond (S)PFE, UCs have many applications like hiding policy circuits in attribute-based encryption [8,18], multi-hop homomorphic encryption [19], verifiable computation [16], program obfuscation [58], and hardware logic locking [40].

In this work, we introduce **Varying Private Function Evaluation (VPFE)** whose privacy-guarantee lies in between PFE and SPFE. Similar to PFE, our Varying UCs (VUCs) for VPFE hide the topology and functionality of the LUTs in the circuit, but leak their number of in- and outputs. This has applications in logic obfuscation techniques called logic locking, as demonstrated in prior studies such as LUT-Lock [26] and eFPGA [11]. These techniques proposed using LUTs to achieve secure logic locking on Application-Specific Integrated Circuit (ASIC) designs by removing critical elements and mapping them to custom LUTs. As shown in [11, Fig. 3], the adversary can only determine the number of inputs and outputs of a LUT, while the LUT's configuration bits are hidden, which is exactly our setting for VPFE using VUCs. Without this knowledge, there is no adversarial information leakage [11, Tab. 5]. Therefore, our VUCs can be used for secure logic locking while additionally hiding the topology of the circuit.

1.2 Outline and Our Contributions

So far, UC-based PFE research considered synthesis of the input circuit (to generate a small number of 2-input gates) and construction of the UC (to minimize its size) as independent tasks. In our work, we show that using multi-input/output LUTs these two tasks can be combined to yield a better size. After giving the preliminaries in Sect. 2 and summarizing the two UC constructions of Valiant [51] (Sect. 3.2) and Liu et al. [37] (Sect. 3.3), we contribute the following:

LUT-based UC (LUC) Construction (Sect. 4). Valiant's UC construction can be generalized to support the evaluation of $(\rho \to 1)$-LUT-based circuits by merging for the ρ inputs ρ instances of its basic building block called edge-universal graph [48, App. A]. This leads to a total size of $\sim 1.5\rho n \log n$ using Liu et al.'s [37] UC construction. In our work, we extend this into a novel UC construction to simulate for the first time functions composed of $(\rho \to \omega)$-LUTs with ρ inputs and ω outputs. Our construction is general, can be applied to all UC constructions based on Valiant's framework [51] and improvements by Liu et al. [37], and fits into the definition of UCs (cf. Definition 1 on page 6).

Size Improvements of LUCs for Basic Primitives (Sect. 4.3). Table 1 shows the history of improvements in UC sizes. Taking (V)PFE as our greatest motivation for improving UC sizes, we study three basic building blocks that

Table 1. Asymptotic sizes of various UC constructions and improvements over previous works. Previous UCs were for 2-input gates, whereas our LUC construction is generalized to p-input LUTs.

Universal Circuit	Asymptotic Size	Improvement over previous work	Fanin
Valiant's 2-way [51]	$5n \log n$	-	2
Valiant's 4-way [51]	$4.75n \log n$	$1.05\times$	2
Zhao et al.'s 4-way [57]	$4.5n \log n$	$1.06\times$	2
Liu et al.'s 2-way [37]	$3n \log n$	$1.5\times$	2
Our LUC	$\mathbf{1.5}\rho n \log n$	$\mathbf{1.12 - 2.18\times}$	ρ

can be used to construct more complex functionalities for common PFE applications: We compare the asymptotic circuit sizes when evaluating our new LUC construction with UCs for equivalent binary gates (cf. Table 2) and achieve size improvements of factor $1.67\times$ for full adders, $2.67\times$ for comparisons, and $2\times$ for multiplexers.

Varying UC (VUC) Construction (Sect. 5). In several applications (cf. Sect. 1.1, Sect. 5.2) only the programming of the LUTs needs to be hidden, but not their dimensions, i.e., we can leak their number of in- and outputs. For this, we introduce *Varying Universal Circuits* (VUC) which are circuits that can simulate other LUT-based circuits while hiding their topology and the LUT programmings, but leak the LUTs' number of in- and outputs. We give the first VUC construction that eliminates the leading ρ factor of our LUC construction (cf. Table 1), while still maintaining its general design, i.e., we can transform all UC constructions to our new VUC construction.

Implementation (Sect. 6.1). We provide the first implementation of today's most efficient UC construction of Liu et al. [37] which is of independent interest and our LUC and VUC constructions.[2] Moreover, we integrate these three UC implementations into the MPC framework ABY [13] for PFE. To create LUT-based circuits, we used the hardware circuit synthesis tool Yosys-ABC [10,53] and Synopsis Design Compiler [5] for LUT-Mapping. We optimize LUT-based PFE by combining LUTs with overlapping inputs and multiple outputs. However, hardware synthesis tools do not by default support mapping to multiple output LUTs. To address this, we post-process the single-output LUT circuits produced by the synthesis tool to convert them to multi-output LUT circuits.

Evaluation (Sect. 6.3). We experimentally evaluate our LUC and VUC constructions for various LUT sizes, and compare them with the previous best construction of Liu et al. [37]. The asymptotic UC sizes and improvements over previous works are given in Table 4 for LUC and in Table 6 for VUC. Our new LUC constructions outperform the state-of-the-art UC [37] in terms of circuit sizes by up to $2.18\times$.

---

[2] Our code is published under the MIT license at: https://encrypto.de/code/LUC.

1.3 Related Work

Universal Circuits (UCs). Valiant [51] defined universal circuits, showed that they have a lower bound of size $\Omega(n \log n)$, and proposed two asymptotically size-optimal constructions using a 2-way or a 4-way recursive structure of sizes $\sim 5n \log n$ and $\sim 4.75n \log n$, respectively. Hence, relevant research challenges left are reducing the prefactor and the concrete UC sizes. Valiant's constructions can be generalized to simulate circuits composed of $(\rho \rightarrow 1)$-LUTs as shown by Sadeghi and Schneider [48, App. A] which is summarized in Sect. 4.1.

A modular UC construction of non-optimal size $\sim 1.5n \log^2 n + 2.5n \log n$ was proposed and implemented by Kolesnikov and Schneider [34]. Their construction beats Valiant's construction for small circuits thanks to small prefactors. Motivated to provide more efficient PFE, Kiss and Schneider [31] implemented Valiant's 2-way split construction and proposed a more efficient hybrid construction combining the 2-way split construction with the modular construction of [34]. Lipmaa et al. [36] generalized Valiant's construction to a k-way split construction and proved that the optimal value for k is 3.147, i.e., $k \in \{3, 4\}$ when k is an integer. Günther et al. [22] modularized Valiant's construction, implemented the more efficient 4-way split construction, gave a generic edge-embedding algorithm for k-way split constructions, and showed that the 3-way split construction with Valiant's framework is less efficient than the 2-way split construction. Zhao et al. [57] improved Valiant's 4-way split construction to size $\sim 4.5n \log n$, which is today's most efficient asymptotic size for UCs in Valiant's framework. Alhassan et al. [7] proposed and implemented a scalable hybrid UC construction combining Valiant's 2-way and 4-way split constructions with Zhao et al.'s improvements [57]. Most recently, Liu et al. [37] reduced redundancies in Valiant's framework and provided today's most efficient UC construction of size $\sim 3n \log n$ based on Valiant's 2-way split construction, showed that $k = 2$-way split is the most efficient in their new UC framework, and already almost reached their computed lower bound of $\sim 2.95n \log n$. We provide the first implementation of their construction and use it as a basis for our UC constructions for LUT-based circuits.

Private Function Evaluation (PFE). Katz and Malka [30] designed a constant-round two-party PFE protocol with linear communication complexity based on homomorphic public-key encryption. Holz et al. [24] optimized and implemented the protocol of [30], demonstrating its superiority over the hybrid UC implementation of Alhassan et al. [7] already for circuits with a few thousand gates. Liu et al. [38] provide a constant-round actively secure two-party PFE protocol with linear complexity. However, all these protocols are not generic and hence not directly compatible with arbitrary MPC frameworks, which makes them less flexible. For instance, these protocols cannot easily be extended to multiple parties. Ji et al. [25] demonstrated the evaluation of private RAM programs using four servers, building the first PFE of non-Boolean and non-arithmetic functions. In fact, recent PFE applications relied on so-called Semi-Private Function Evaluation (SPFE) where not necessarily the whole function needs to be hidden from the other parties, but selected parts of the function can be leaked. The first SPFE construction and implementation was proposed by Paus et al. [43] who provided several building blocks that can be programmed with one function out of a class of functions (e.g., ADD/SUB whose circuits have the same topology). Recently, Günther et al. [21] built an SPFE framework that allows to split the function into public and private components, embed the private components into UCs, and merge them into one Boolean circuit that is evaluated via MPC. They demonstrated their framework on computing car insurance tariffs and observed that some information of the function is public, e.g., that experienced drivers usually get discounts.

MPC on LUTs. In the area of secure multi-party computation (MPC), prior work noticed that 2-input/1-output gates can be extended into multi-input/multi-output gates to reduce the circuit evaluation overhead [14,23,39,41, 45]. In Yao's Garbled Circuit (GC) setting, Fairplay [39] implemented MPC protocols to evaluate gates with up to 3-input gates. The TASTY framework [23] implemented ρ-input garbled gates using the garbled row reduction optimization [44]. Recently, [45] proposed an MPC protocol that works on circuits with multi-input/multi-output gates instead of working on circuits with 2-input gates. Another line of work in the secret-sharing setting aims to optimize the rounds and communication of the online phase without using Yao's GC protocol: [14] extended 2-input AND gates to the general N-input case using LUTs. Recently, ABY2.0 [41] extended AND gates from the 2-input to the multi-input setting with a constant online communication complexity at the cost of exponential offline communication in the number of inputs. In addition, Syncirc [42] handles the circuit generation with multi-input gates by using industry-grade hardware synthesis tools [10,53].

2   Preliminaries

We refer to the size of a circuit n as the sum of its number of inputs n_i, gates n_g, and outputs n_o: $n = n_i + n_g + n_o$.

Definition 1 (Universal Circuit [7,51]). *A Universal Circuit $\mathcal{U}$ for n_i inputs, n_g gates, and n_o outputs is a Boolean circuit that can be programmed to compute any Boolean circuit C with n_i inputs, n_g gates, and n_o outputs by defining programming bits p^C such that $\mathcal{U}(x, p^C) = C(x)$ for any input $x \in \{0,1\}^{n_i}$.*

2.1   Graph Theory

Let $G = (V, E)$ be a directed graph and $v \in V$. The indegree (resp. outdegree) of v which is the number of incoming (resp. outgoing) edges is denoted by $\deg^+(v)$ (resp. $\deg^-(v)$). G has fanin (resp. fanout) ρ if $\deg^+(v) \le \rho$ (resp. $\deg^-(v) \le \rho$) for all $v \in V$. We denote by $\Gamma_\rho(n)$ all directed acyclic graphs with at most n nodes and fanin/fanout ρ for $\rho, n \in \mathbb{N}$. For $U \subset V$, $G[U] := \{U, \{e = (u, v) \in$

$E : u, v \in U\}\}$ denotes the subgraph induced by U. We omit the index G in the above definitions if G is clear from the context.

Let $G = (V, E) \in \Gamma_\rho(n)$. A topological order for G is a map $\eta_G \colon V \to \{1, ..., |V|\}$ such that $\forall(u, v) \in E : \eta_G(u) < \eta_G(v)$.

We represent Boolean circuits as directed acyclic graph $G \in \Gamma_\rho(n)$ for some $\rho > 1$. However, almost all previous works [22, 31, 36, 37, 51, 57] restricted the circuits, that are simulated via UCs, to fanin/fanout $\rho = 2$. The reason for this restriction can be found in the structure of universal circuits according to Valiant's [51] and Liu et al.'s [37] constructions. On a high level, a universal circuit (UC) for simulating circuits $C \in \Gamma_\rho(n)$ is composed of ρ so-called *Edge-Universal Graphs* (EUGs) each of size $\mathcal{O}(n \log n)$, i.e., the total size of the UC grows linearly with the maximum fanin/fanout ρ of the gates in the simulated circuit C.

Definition 2 (Edge-Embedding [7,36,37,51]). *Let $G = (V, E)$ and $G' = (P, E')$ be directed graphs with $P \subset V$ and G' acyclic. An edge-embedding from G' into G is a map $\psi\colon E' \to \mathcal{P}_G$, where $\mathcal{P}_G$ denotes the set of all paths in G, with the following properties:*

- *$\psi(e')$ is a u-v-path (in G) for all $e' = (u, v) \in E'$,*
- *$\psi(e')$ and $\psi(\tilde{e}')$ are edge-disjoint paths for all $e', \tilde{e}' \in E'$ with $e' \neq \tilde{e}'$.*

Definition 3 (Edge-Universal Graph [7,36,37,51]). *A directed graph $G = (V, E)$, denoted as $\mathcal{U}_\rho(n)$ with ordered pole set $P \coloneqq \{p_1, ..., p_n\} \subset V$ is called an Edge-Universal Graph for $\Gamma_\rho(n)$ if:*

- *G is acyclic,*
- *Every acyclic $G' = (P, E') \in \Gamma_\rho(n)$ that is order-preserving, i.e., $\forall e = (p_i, p_j) \in E' \Rightarrow i < j$, can be edge-embedded into G.*

On a high level, the graph $G' = (P, E')$ in Definitions 2 and 3 represents a Boolean function that is embedded into the graph $G = (V, E)$, which represents the UC, where $P \subset V$ is the pole set of size $|P| = n$, which represents the inputs, gates, and outputs of the function represented in G'. As an EUG requires that every $G' \in \Gamma_\rho(n)$ can be edge-embedded into G, the UC built by the EUG can compute any function represented by a graph in the set $\Gamma_\rho(n)$.

EUGs for $\Gamma_2(n)$ graphs were constructed by merging two EUGs for $\Gamma_1(n)$ graphs (cf. Definition 4 and Fig. 1) [7, 22, 31, 36, 37, 51, 57]. Thus, research focused on minimizing the size of general EUGs for $\Gamma_1(n)$ graphs as these can be merged to EUGs for arbitrary $\Gamma_\rho(n)$ graphs by merging ρ instances of $\Gamma_1(n)$ EUGs (cf. Corollary 1).

Definition 4 (Merging of EUG). *Let $G = (V, E)$ and $\bar{G} = (\bar{V}, \bar{E})$ be two EUG for $\Gamma_\rho(n)$ and $\Gamma_{\bar{\rho}}(n)$ with the same pole order and $V \cap \bar{V} = P$. Then $\hat{G} = (V \cup \bar{V}, E \cup \bar{E})$ is called the merging of G and $\bar{G}$ with pole set P.*

Proposition 1. *The merging of a $\Gamma_\rho(n)$ and a $\Gamma_{\bar{\rho}}(n)$ EUG is a $\Gamma_{\rho+\bar{\rho}}(n)$ EUG.*

We prove Proposition 1 in Appendix A of the full version [15].

10   Y. Disser et al.

Corollary 1 ([51, Corollary 2.2]). *An EUG for $\Gamma_\rho(n)$ can be constructed by merging ρ EUGs for $\Gamma_1(n)$.*

Proof. Let $G = (V, E)$ be a $\Gamma_1(n)$ EUG with pole set P. Create $\rho - 1$ copies of G with the same pole set and merge these graphs successively. Correctness follows directly by applying Proposition 1 ρ times. □

We call the UCs that are constructed according to Corollary 1 *LUT-based UCs* (LUCs) and this construction was first mentioned in [48, App. A]. In Sect. 5, we introduce our so-called *Varying UC (VUC) construction* that is constructed by two instances of $\Gamma_1(n)$ EUGs but still allows to edge-embed graphs with arbitrary fanin ρ.

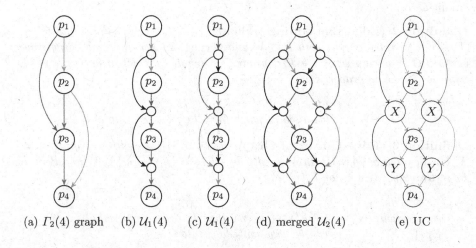

(a) $\Gamma_2(4)$ graph   (b) $\mathcal{U}_1(4)$ (c) $\mathcal{U}_1(4)$ (d) merged $\mathcal{U}_2(4)$ (e) UC

Fig. 1. (a) shows the $\Gamma_2(4)$ graph with already partitioned edge sets E_1 and E_2, (b) and (c) show the EUGs in which the edge sets E_1 resp. E_2 are embedded, (d) shows the merged EUG with all edges embedded, (e) shows the resulting UC, where p_1 is an input, and p_2, p_3, p_4 are translated to universal gates.

2.2   Building Universal Circuits from Edge-Universal Graphs

Boolean Circuits. A Boolean circuit is a directed acyclic graph whose nodes are Boolean inputs, (binary) gates, and outputs, with directed edges representing the wires. A Boolean gate is a function $z: \{0,1\}^k \to \{0,1\}$ for $k \in \mathbb{N}$. However, we can always divide a k-input gate into $\mathcal{O}(2^k)$ binary gates using Shannon's expansion theorem [49]. Unfortunately, we cannot avoid an exponential blow-up of the number of gates by this transformation [52, Theorem 2.1]. The two most prominent minimization methods for Boolean circuits are due to Karnaugh [29] and Quine-McCluskey [46]. As already mentioned, the UC constructions by Valiant [51] and Liu et al. [37] are designed to embed $\Gamma_\rho(n)$ graphs, thus we possibly need to reduce the outdegree of the gates to ρ by using so-called copy gates which just copy their inputs [51, Corollary 3.1].[3]

From Edge-Universal Graphs to Universal Circuits. The translation from an EUG $G = (V, E)$ into a UC is depicted in Fig. 1 and works as follows. First, the nodes of circuit C to be embedded in G are considered as the poles $P \subset V$ of the EUG. A pole $p \in P$ is translated into an input or output wire, if p corresponds to an input or output in C, or into a so-called *Universal Gate*, if p corresponds to a gate in C. Universal gates take k inputs ($k = 2$ in the previous works [7,37,51]), 2^k programming bits, compute one output, and can be programmed to simulate any k input Boolean gate by specifying the truth table with the programming bits. We can implement universal gates with a binary tree of $2^k - 1$ multiplexers (Y-switches) spanned over the 2^k programming bits, where the correct programming bit specified by the k inputs is forwarded to the output (more details in [7,37]).[4]

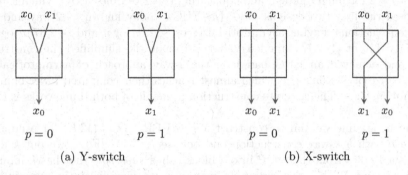

(a) Y-switch   (b) X-switch

Fig. 2. Switching blocks with programming bit p (from [34]).

The remaining nodes in the set $V \setminus P$ are for connecting the routes between the poles. A node $v \in V \setminus P$ is translated as follows:

- if v has two incoming edges and one outgoing edge, it is translated into a multiplexer/Y-switch (cf. Fig. 2a). A multiplexer has two inputs x_0 and x_1 and a programming bit p and outputs one bit, namely x_p. It is implemented with 1 AND gate and 2 XOR gates [34].
- if v has two incoming edges and two outgoing edges, it is translated into an X-switch (cf. Fig. 2b). An X-switch has two inputs x_0 and x_1, one programming bit p and outputs two bits, namely (x_p, x_{1-p}). It is implemented with 1 AND gate and 3 XOR gates [34].

---

[3] Note that a Universal Circuit can also compute circuits with less than the specified number of inputs, gates, and outputs by using dummy values with no functionality.

[4] In Yao's garbled circuit protocol [54], the UC's universal gates can be implemented as garbled tables when the function holder takes over the garbling part.

– if v has one incoming wire, it is replaced by a single wire that connects all of the outgoing edges.

The programming bits of the nodes are derived from the edge-embedding.

3   UC Constructions

In this section, we summarize the general guidelines for constructing edge-universal graphs (Sect. 3.1), present the original idea of Valiant [51] (Sect. 3.2), and describe the state-of-the-art construction of Liu et al. [37] (Sect. 3.3).

3.1   General EUG Constructions

The strategy for building UCs via EUGs is to construct $\Gamma_1(n)$ EUGs of smallest size, merging ρ instances of these (cf. Corollary 1) to construct a $\Gamma_\rho(n)$ EUG ($\rho = 2$ for binary gates), and translating this EUG into a UC. Valiant [51] proposed the first two designs for $\Gamma_1(n)$ EUGs, today known as 2-way and 4-way constructions, having asymptotic sizes of $\sim 2.5n \log n$ and $\sim 2.375n \log n$. Recently, Liu et al. [37] extended Valiant's framework, simplified the construction, and achieved an EUG based on the 2-way approach of asymptotically optimal size of $\sim 1.5n \log n$, which almost reaches their computed lower bound of $\sim 1.475n \log n$. The concrete construction principle of both frameworks is the same.

Let us assume we aim to construct a $\Gamma_1(n)$ EUG $G = (V, E)$ for a circuit of size n with a k-way construction and pole set $P \subset V$. First, we put k distinguished poles from the set P into a block called *superpole* that has k inputs and k outputs. Within this superpole, we can route edge-disjointly between its inputs and poles, and between its poles and outputs. In total, we have $\lceil n/k \rceil$ superpoles built by the poles set P. The k inputs and outputs of each superpole then can be used as poles for k instances of a $\Gamma_1(\lceil n/k \rceil - 1)$ nested EUG, which on a high level allows to find edge-disjoint paths between the superpoles of G.[5]

More formally, a superpole shall be able to edge-embed any so-called *augmented k-way block* (similar to an augmented DAG in [37]). An augmented k-way block is a map that defines the routes between the inputs and poles of the superpole, and between poles and other poles and outputs.

Definition 5 (Augmented k-way Block). *An augmented k-way block $G = (V, E)$ for pole set P, superpole inputs I, and superpole outputs O is a directed graph such that*

- $V = P \cup I \cup O$, $P \cap I = P \cap O = \emptyset$ and $|I| = |O| = k$,
- $G[P] := (P, E^P)$ *has fanin/fanout 1,*
- $E = E^P \cup E^{io}$ *with E^{io} satisfying*

---

[5] We distinguish between EUGs and nested EUGs as the recursively constructed nested EUGs differ from its first EUG in Liu et al.'s construction [37].

- *(Soundness) Every $e \in E^{io}$ satisfies either $e = (in, p)$ or $e = (p, out)$ for $p \in P, in \in I, out \in O$,*
- *(Completeness) For every source (resp. sink) $p \in P$, there exists at most one $in \in I$ (resp. $out \in O$) such that $(in, p) \in E^{io}$ (resp. $(p, out) \in E^{io}$).*

The set of all augmented k-way blocks for P, I, O is denoted by $\mathcal{B}_k(P, I, O)$.

Definition 6 (k-way Superpole). *A k-way superpole $SP(k)$ is a tuple $SP(k) = (G = (V, E), P, \mathcal{P}, \mathcal{I}, \mathcal{O})$ with pole set $P \subset V$, with following conditions:*

- *$P = \mathcal{P} \cup \mathcal{I} \cup \mathcal{O}$ with $|\mathcal{I}| = |\mathcal{O}| = k$ and $\mathcal{P} \cap \mathcal{I} = \mathcal{P} \cap \mathcal{O} = \emptyset$,*
- *G can edge-embed every $G' \in \mathcal{B}_k(\mathcal{P}, \mathcal{I}, \mathcal{O})$.*

We denote the input recursion points $\mathcal{I}$ of a k-way superpole as $\{in_1, in_2, ..., in_k\}$ and the output recursion points $\mathcal{O}$ as $\{out_1, out_2, ..., out_k\}$. These nodes serve as the inputs and outputs to the superpole and will be the poles of the next recursion, i.e., of the next nested EUG. We neither require the sets $\mathcal{I}$ and $\mathcal{O}$ to be disjoint nor that the recursion points of different superpoles must be disjoint. In fact, Valiant [51] merges the output recursion points of the i-th superpole with the input recursion points of the $(i+1)$-th superpole. On a high level, a

---

Algorithm 1: Valiant(P, k)

Input : Poles $P := \{p_1, ..., p_n\}$, split parameter k
Output : $\Gamma_1(n)$ EUG $G = (V, E)$, pole set P, sub-graphs $G^*, G^1, ..., G^k$

1 $V \leftarrow \emptyset$, $E \leftarrow \emptyset$, $G^* \leftarrow \emptyset$
2 $\mathcal{O}_0 \leftarrow$ *create k dummy nodes*
3 **for** $i \leftarrow 1$ **to** $\lceil \frac{n}{k} \rceil$ **do**
4       $\mathcal{P}_i \leftarrow \{p_{k(i-1)+1}, ..., p_{ki}\}$
       // Use $\mathcal{O}_{i-1}$ as input recursion points to this superpole (cf. Fig. 3b)
5       $SP(k)_i = (G_i = (V_i, E_i), P_i, \mathcal{P}_i, \mathcal{I}_i, \mathcal{O}_i) \leftarrow$ Createsuperpole($\mathcal{P}_i, \mathcal{O}_{i-1}, k$);
       $G^* \leftarrow G^* \cup \{G_i\}$
6       $V \leftarrow V \cup V_i, E \leftarrow E \cup E_i$

7 **for** $i \leftarrow 1$ **to** k **do**
8   **if** $n \leq k$ **then**
9         $G^i \leftarrow (\emptyset, ..., \emptyset)$ // Recursion base
10   **else**
         // Take the i-th output recursion point of each superpole (but the last) as the poles for the next sub EUG
11        $P^i \leftarrow \{\mathcal{O}_1[i], \mathcal{O}_2[i], ..., \mathcal{O}_{\lceil \frac{n}{k} \rceil - 1}[i]\}$
12        $(G^i = (V^i, E^i), ...) \leftarrow$ Valiant(P^i, k)
13        $V \leftarrow V \cup V^i, E \leftarrow E \cup E^i$

14 **return** $G = (V, E), P, G^*, G^1, ..., G^k$

superpole in a nested EUG U^1, i.e., an EUG that is derived as a recursion from a larger EUG U, has k entry points to an input of k distinguished superpoles in U as well as k exit points from an output of k distinguished superpoles.

3.2   Valiant's EUG Construction [51]

Definition 7 (Valiant EUG). *A Valiant EUG* $G = (V, E)$ *with pole set* $P \subset V$ *and sub-graphs* $G^*, G^1, ..., G^k$ *is created by Algorithm 1 (*Valiant*). We also use the notation* Valiant$_k(n)$ *for a Valiant EUG with n poles and split parameter k.*

Valiant's k-way EUG construction is built recursively as depicted in Fig. 3a. A $\Gamma_1(n)$ EUG is a chain of $\lceil n/k \rceil$ superpoles $SP(k)_1 = (G_1 = (V_1, E_1), P_1, \mathcal{P}_1, \mathcal{I}_1, \mathcal{O}_1),\ \ldots,\ SP(k)_{\lceil n/k \rceil} = (G_{\lceil n/k \rceil} = (V_{\lceil n/k \rceil}, E_{\lceil n/k \rceil}), P_{\lceil n/k \rceil}, \mathcal{P}_{\lceil n/k \rceil}, \mathcal{I}_{\lceil n/k \rceil}, \mathcal{O}_{\lceil n/k \rceil})$ (lines 3–6 in Algorithm 1). Createsuperpole$(P, \mathcal{O}, k)$ creates a superpole with poles P, input recursion points $\mathcal{O}$, and split parameter k, e.g., Valiant's $k = 2$-way superpole $SP(2)$ (Fig. 3b). The sets $\mathcal{O}_1, \ldots, \mathcal{O}_{\lceil n/k-1 \rceil}$, each of size k, then recursively build the poles of the nested EUGs in the next recursion step (lines 7–13 in Algorithm 1), i.e., we build k nested EUGs $G^1 = (V^1, E^1), \ldots, G^k = (V^k, E^k)$ with pole sets $P^1, \ldots, P^k$, where $G^i \in \Gamma_1(\lceil n/k \rceil - 1)$ and $P^i = (\mathcal{O}_1[i], \ldots, \mathcal{O}_{\lceil n/k-1 \rceil}[i])$. Note that $\mathcal{I}_i := \mathcal{O}_{i-1}$ for all $1 < i \leq \lceil n/k \rceil$ as the k outputs of $G_i \in SP(k)_i$ are pairwise merged with the respective k inputs of $G_{i+1} \in SP(k)_{i+1}$. The creation of the first output recursion points $\mathcal{O}_0$ is a technical trick, and not needed because these nodes will never be used, but it simplifies the definition of the algorithm by avoiding a case distinction. An

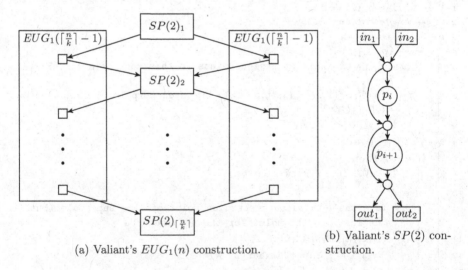

(a) Valiant's $EUG_1(n)$ construction.

(b) Valiant's $SP(2)$ construction.

Fig. 3. (a) shows Valiant's 2-way split construction of $EUG_1(n)$ using two instances of $EUG_1(\lceil \frac{n}{k} \rceil - 1)$. (b) shows the corresponding superpole $SP(2)$ construction for the EUG.

advantage of this recursive method is that we can also recursively reduce the edge-embedding problem to finding paths between poles of the nested EUGs. Assuming we can easily edge-embed paths from inputs to poles and from poles to outputs within the superpoles, we can reduce finding a path from a pole located in $SP(k)_i$ to a pole in $SP(k)_j$ to the problem of finding a path from $\mathcal{O}_i[x]$ to $\mathcal{O}_{j-1}[x]$ for $i, j \in [[n/k]]$, $i < j$, where x is the index of the target output of the superpoles' internal edge-embedding for the concrete poles. Existing UC implementations [7,22] split the edge-embedding into two sub-tasks: (a) the superpole edge-embedding that takes care that the paths within a superpole are defined in a correct manner, and (b) the recursion-point edge-embedding which chooses the correct paths at the recursion points. We define the following theorem and refer to [7,37] for its proof:

Theorem 1. *Let $G = (V, E)$ be a Valiant EUG with pole set $P \subset V$ of size $|P| = n$ and sub-graphs $G^*, G^1, ..., G^k$. Then G is an EUG for $\Gamma_1(n)$.*

3.3 Liu et al.'s EUG Construction [37]

Definition 8 (Liu$^+$ EUG). *A Liu$^+$ EUG $G = (V, E)$ with pole set $P \subset V$ and sub-graphs $G^*, G^1, ..., G^k$ is created by Algorithm 2 (Liu$^+$). We also use the notation $\mathtt{Liu}_k^+(n)$ for a Liu$^+$ EUG with n poles and split parameter k.*

We refer to Appendix B of the full version [15] for a complete description of the construction of Liu et al. [37] including Algorithm 2. In the subsequent sections of this work, we leverage the following theorem and refer to [37] for its proof:

Theorem 2 cf. [37, Theorem 4]). *Let $G = (V, E)$ be a Liu$^+$ EUG with pole set $P \subset V$ of size $|P| = n$ and sub-graphs $G^*, G^1, ..., G^k$. Then G is an EUG for $\Gamma_1(n)$ with size bounded by*

$$\frac{|SP(k)| - k}{k \log_2(k)} n \log_2(n) + \mathcal{O}(n).$$

4 Evaluating LUTs with UCs

In this section, we extend the UC constructions from Sect. 3 to be able to simulate $(\rho \to \omega)$-LUT-based circuits. In Sect. 4.1, we first review the construction of [34,51] to evaluate $(\rho \to 1)$-LUT-based circuits, i.e., circuits that consist of LUTs with ρ inputs and one output. Then, in Sect. 4.2, we extend this to our LUT-based UCs (LUCs) that allows the UC to simulate $(\rho \to \omega)$-LUT-based circuits. Finally, in Sect. 4.3, we analyze the most important building blocks for PFE applications, describe how to implement them with LUTs, and show their theoretical improvement over evaluating the same building blocks with Boolean circuits.

4.1   UCs for LUTs with Multiple Inputs [48,51]

Valiant [51] proposed a method to integrate LUTs with more than two inputs into UCs and its size has been computed in [48].

We can get a UC with n copies of $(\rho \to 1)$-LUT from a $\Gamma_\rho(n)$ EUG that is merged by ρ instances of $\Gamma_1(n)$ EUGs according to Corollary 1. Each pole of U that is not an input or an output can then be implemented as a LUT with ρ inputs.

Corollary 2. *An EUG for $\Gamma_\rho(n)$ for $\rho \in \mathbb{N}_{\geq 2}$ can be constructed with size at most $1.5\rho n \log_2(n) + \mathcal{O}(n)$.*

Proof. Construct ρ instances of $\mathtt{Liu}_2^+(n)$ and merge them. By Corollary 1, this yields an EUG for $\Gamma_\rho(n)$ with size bounded by $1.5\rho n \log_2(n) + \mathcal{O}(n)$.   □

4.2   UCs for LUTs with Multiple In- and Outputs

In order to support $(\rho \to \omega)$-LUTs with $\omega > 1$ outputs in UCs, we propose a general solution that is compatible with the original UC constructions of Valiant [51] and Liu et al. [37]. The high level idea is as follows: For every $(\rho \to \omega)$-LUT that is represented by pole v_i, we add $\omega - 1$ so-called *auxiliary* poles to the EUG and the real pole v_i forwards its inputs directly to these auxiliary poles. The real pole and its auxiliary poles each compute and output one of the LUT's output. Concretely, the first pole takes the ρ inputs of the LUT using any of the above UC constructions and computes the first output of the LUT. The remaining poles copy the ρ inputs of the first poles by direct connections and compute the remaining outputs of the LUT, resulting in a chain of ω poles.

We define the class of $\Gamma_{\rho,\omega}(n)$ graphs that is used to map n $(\rho \to \omega)$-LUTs to a graph $G \in \Gamma_{\rho,\omega}(n)$. As the poles of the EUG are the nodes of G, we need to add for each additional output of the i-th LUT (denoted as pole $v_{i,1}$ in G) in total $\omega - 1$ additional poles (denoted as $v_{i,2}, \ldots, v_{i,\omega}$). These added poles $v_{i,j>1}$ use the inputs from pole $v_{i,1}$ and thus, they all have in-degree 0 (cf. condition 3 in Definition 9). We define $\Gamma_{\rho,\omega}(n)$ as follows:

Definition 9 ($\Gamma_{\rho,\omega}(n)$). *Let $G = (V, E)$ be a directed acyclic graph with topologically ordered $V := \{v_{1,1}, \ldots, v_{1,\omega}, v_{2,1}, \ldots, v_{2,\omega}, \ldots, v_{n,1}, \ldots, v_{n,\omega}\}$ and $\rho, \omega \in \mathbb{N}$. Then $G \in \Gamma_{\rho,\omega}(n)$ if:*

- $|V| \leq n\omega$,
- $|\{v_{i,j} \in V\}| \leq \omega \; \forall i \in [n]$,
- $deg^+(v_{i,1}) \leq \rho \wedge deg^+(v_{i,2}) = \cdots = deg^+(v_{i,\omega}) = 0$,
- $deg^-(v_{i,j}) \leq \rho \; \forall i \in [n] \; \forall j \in [\omega]$.

To easily build an EUG with only marginal modifications, we show that $\Gamma_{\rho,\omega}(n)$ is also a $\Gamma_\rho(n\omega)$ graph:

Proposition 2. *Let $G \in \Gamma_{\rho,\omega}(n)$. Then $G \in \Gamma_\rho(n\omega)$.*

Algorithm 2: $\mathrm{Liu}^+(P, k)$

Input : Poles $P := \{p_1, ..., p_n\}$, split parameter k
Output : $\Gamma_1(n)$ EUG $G = (V, E)$, pole set P, sub-graphs $G^*, G^1, ..., G^k$

1   $V \leftarrow \emptyset, E \leftarrow \emptyset, G^* \leftarrow \emptyset$
2   **for** $i \leftarrow 1$ **to** $\lceil \frac{n}{k} \rceil$ **do**
3      $\mathcal{P}^i \leftarrow \{p_{k(i-1)+1}, ..., p_{ki}\}$
4      $SP(k)_i = (G_i = (V_i, E_i), P_i, \mathcal{P}_i, \mathcal{I}_i, \mathcal{O}_i) \leftarrow \texttt{Createsuperpole}(\mathcal{P}_i, k)$
5      $G^* \leftarrow G^* \cup \{G_i\}$
6      $V \leftarrow V \cup V_i, E \leftarrow E \cup E_i$

7   **for** $i \leftarrow 1$ **to** k **do**
8   **if** $n \leq k$ **then**
9        $G^i \leftarrow (\emptyset, ..., \emptyset)$ // Recursion base
10   **else**
         // Take the i-th output recursion point of each superpole as
         the poles for the next sub EUG
11        $P^i \leftarrow \{\mathcal{O}_1[i], \mathcal{O}_2[i], ..., \mathcal{O}_{\lceil \frac{n}{k} \rceil - 1}[i], \mathcal{O}_{\lceil \frac{n}{k} \rceil}[i]\}$
12        $(G^i = (V^i, E^i), ...) \leftarrow \mathrm{Liu}^+(P^i, k)$
13        $V \leftarrow V \cup V^i, E \leftarrow E \cup E^i$

14   **foreach** $(u, v) \in E$ **do**
15   **if** $u \in s$ and v is recursion point for some superpole $s \in G^*$ **then**
16        $G^x \leftarrow$ the EUG in which v is a pole
17        $E \leftarrow E \setminus \{(u, v)\}$
18        $w \leftarrow \Gamma_{G^x}^-(v)$
19        $E \leftarrow E \setminus \{(v, w)\}$
20        $E \leftarrow E \cup \{(u, w)\}$

21   **else if** u is recursion point for some superpole $s \in G^*$ and $v \in s$ **then**
22        $G^x \leftarrow$ the EUG in which u is a pole
23        $E \leftarrow E \setminus \{(u, v)\}$
24        $w \leftarrow \Gamma_{G^x}^+(u)$
25        $E \leftarrow E \setminus \{(w, u)\}$
26        $E \leftarrow E \cup \{(w, v)\}$

27   *remove all recursion points from V*
28   **return** $G = (V, E), P, G^*, G^1, ..., G^k$

Proof. Let $G = (V, E) \in \Gamma_{\rho, \omega}(n)$. Obviously, it holds that $|V| \leq n\omega$ (condition 1 in Definition 9). Further, for all $v \in V$ it holds that $\deg^+(v) \leq \rho$ and $\deg^-(v_{i,j}) \leq \rho$ from conditions 3 and 4 in Definition 9. Thus, $G \in \Gamma_\rho(n\omega)$.   □

Now, we can build EUGs for multi-input and multi-output LUTs.

Corollary 3. *Let $\rho, \omega \in \mathbb{N}$. Then there exists a EUG for $\Gamma_{\rho, \omega}(n)$ with size bounded by*

$$1.5\rho n\omega \log_2(n\omega) + \mathcal{O}(n\omega).$$

Proof. **Step 1:** Create a $\Gamma_\rho(n\omega)$ EUG $\mathcal{U} = (V^{\mathcal{U}}, E^{\mathcal{U}})$ with a topologically ordered pole set $P \subset V^{\mathcal{U}}$ that has the form $(..., v_{i-1,\omega}, v_{i,1}, ..., v_{i,\omega}, v_{i+1,1}, ...)$ for all $i \in [n]$, i.e., the original pole $v_{i,1}$ directly preceding the auxiliary poles $v_{i,j}$ for $1 < j \leq \omega$: We do this by creating a Liu$^+$ EUG $\mathcal{U}$ with pole set P and split parameter $k = 2$. Then we merge ρ instances of it. By Theorem 2 with $|SP(2)| = 5$ [37] and Corollary 1, this yields a $\Gamma_\rho(n\omega)$ EUG of size at most $1.5\rho n\omega \log_2(n\omega) + \mathcal{O}(n\omega)$.

Step 2: Adjust $\mathcal{U}$ to get the final EUG $\bar{\mathcal{U}} = (V^{\bar{\mathcal{U}}}, E^{\bar{\mathcal{U}}})$ with pole set $P \subset V^{\bar{\mathcal{U}}}$: Let $v_{i,j}$ be an auxiliary pole of $v_{i,1}$ for $i \in [n], 1 < j \leq \omega$. Remove all of its incoming edges and replace each of them with an edge connecting the original pole $v_{i,1}$ with the auxiliary pole $v_{i,j}$, i.e., remove $(w, v_{i,j}) \in E^{\mathcal{U}}$ for $w \in V^{\mathcal{U}}$ and replace it by $(v_{i,1}, v_{i,j})$. This yields ρ edges $(v_{i,1}, v_{i,j})$ per auxiliary pole $v_{i,j}$ (one for each EUG instance). Thus, $E^{\mathcal{U}}$ becomes a multi set. The graph that results from modifying $\mathcal{U}$ in the just described way is denoted by $\bar{\mathcal{U}}$ and its pole set is denoted by P.

Step 3: Embed any graph $G = (P, E) \in \Gamma_{\rho,\omega}(n)$ into $\bar{\mathcal{U}}$: To show that $\bar{\mathcal{U}}$ is a EUG for $\Gamma_{\rho,\omega}(n)$, we need to define an edge-embedding ψ from G into $\bar{\mathcal{U}}$. Thanks to Proposition 2, it holds that $G \in \Gamma_\rho(n\omega)$. Note that the "relative topological order" is maintained, i.e., $\eta_G(v_i) < \eta_G(v_{i+1})$ for $i \in [n]$. However, although $\bar{\mathcal{U}}$ has $n\omega$ poles, it is not an EUG for all $\Gamma_\rho(n\omega)$ graphs as all poles $v_{i,j>1}$ are directly connected to pole $v_{i,1}$ via the edge $(v_{i,1}, v_{i,j>1})$ for $i \in [n], j \in [\omega]$. Thus,

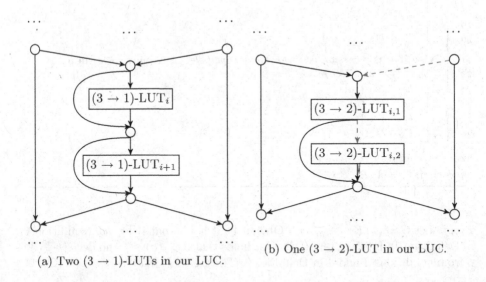

(a) Two $(3 \rightarrow 1)$-LUTs in our LUC.

(b) One $(3 \rightarrow 2)$-LUT in our LUC.

Fig. 4. Embedding of $(3 \rightarrow 1)$-LUTs (a) and $(3 \rightarrow 2)$-LUTs (b) in a single superpole of our LUC construction. The blue line in (b) indicates that the inputs of the first LUT part are forwarded to the second LUT part. Each of the LUT parts in (b) generate one output with the same inputs, thus building together a $(3 \rightarrow 2)$-LUT. The red edge is optional and can be removed as only one input in the superpole is needed.

we cannot find edge-disjoint paths from any pole $v_{k<i,l}$ to $v_{i,j>1}$ for $k \in [n]$, $l \in [\omega]$, as these would all use an ingoing edge of pole $v_{i,1}$. So, we need to show that all nodes $v_{i,j>1} \in G$ have indegree 0 to ensure that no edge-disjoint path needs to end up at pole $v_{i,j>1} \in \bar{\mathcal{U}}$. This, however, is fulfilled due to condition 3 of Definition 9, i.e., there exists no edge $e = (v_{k<i,l}, v_{i,j>1}) \in G$ for which an embedding $\psi(e)$ needs to be defined (the same argument holds for edges $e = (v_{i,l<j}, v_{i,j}) \in G$).

So far, we showed that G only contains edges $e = (v_{k<i,l}, v_{i,1}) \in G$, which are the only ones to edge-embed into $\bar{\mathcal{U}}$. However, as we just added additional edges to poles $v_{i,1}$ and no outgoing edges from any poles in $\bar{\mathcal{U}}$ have been removed, we can get the edge-embedding ψ directly from Corollary 2.   □

In Fig. 4, we present our LUC construction for the embedding of both $(3 \rightarrow 1)$-LUTs and $(3 \rightarrow 2)$-LUTs within a single superpole. Specifically, in Fig. 4a, a superpole consists of two $(3 \rightarrow 1)$-LUTs, each having three individual inputs and one output. In contrast, in Fig. 4b, a $(3 \rightarrow 2)$-LUT requires two poles, limiting the embedding capacity to a single $(3 \rightarrow 2)$-LUT within one superpole. We achieve this by implementing each pole as a $(3 \rightarrow 1)$-LUT in our LUC construction, effectively combining them to form a $(3 \rightarrow 2)$-LUT. The second part of the LUT shares the same inputs as the first part (indicated by the blue edge in Fig. 4b), eliminating the need for an additional node between the two poles. The two outputs of the $(3 \rightarrow 2)$-LUT are forwarded to the lower node and can then propagate to the nested EUGs through this node. As an optimization, we can remove one incoming edge from the superpole (indicated by the red edge in Fig. 4b) since only one outer input is utilized.

4.3   Improvement

In this section, we show improvements of our LUC for several basic building blocks like full adder (FA), comparator (CMP), and multiplexer (MUX). As summarized in Table 2, our basic building blocks are smaller than the previous constructions [7,22,31,37] in UC size by factor $\approx 1.67\times$–$2.67\times$. Note that we compute improvement factors based only on the prefactor. The actual enhancements will be greater as also the logarithmic term is improved. This UC size reduction is achieved by merging 2-input gates into larger multi-input LUTs.

Full Adder (FA): The optimized implementation of a FA uses four 2-input XOR gates and one 2-input AND gate (cf. [33, Fig. 2]). We can implement a FA using only one $(3 \rightarrow 2)$-LUT, resulting in an improvement by $\approx 1.67\times$ in LUC size (cf. Table 2). The embedding of a $(3 \rightarrow 2)$-LUT in our LUC is depicted in Fig. 4b.

Comparator (CMP): The 1-bit comparator consists of three 2-input XOR gates and one 2-input AND gate (cf. [33, Fig. 6]). Our improved LUT-based instantiating for CMP uses only one $(3 \rightarrow 1)$-LUT, resulting in an improvement of $\approx 2.67\times$ in LUC size (cf. Table 2). The embedding of a $(3 \rightarrow 1)$-LUT in our LUC is depicted in Fig. 4a.

Multiplexer (MUX): The MUX block can be instantiated with two 2-input XOR gates and one 2-input AND gate (cf. [35, Fig. 2]). In our approach, MUX can be instantiated with only one $(3 \rightarrow 1)$-LUT, resulting in an improvement of $\approx 2\times$ in the LUC size (cf. Table 2). The embedding of a $(3 \rightarrow 1)$-LUT in our LUC is depicted in Fig. 4a.

Complex Building Blocks. We now present several motivating examples that benefit from improvements of our basic building blocks.

Addition and Subtraction. An l-bit addition is composed of a chain of l Full Adders (FA) (cf. [33, Fig. 1]. An l-bit subtraction is defined as $x - y = x + y + 1$ and can be constructed similarly to an addition circuit using l FAs (cf. [33, Fig. 3]. Using our FA construction, the LUC size of the addition and subtraction is improved by $\approx 1.67\times$.

Table 2. LUC sizes for basic building blocks which can be used to construct more complex functionalities. b denotes the frequency of occurrence of the specific building blocks within the circuit.

Building Block (BB)	Boolean Circuit		LUT-based Circuit		Improvement
	# Gates	Asympt. UC Size	LUT type	Asympt. LUC Size	
FA	4 XOR 1 AND	$15b \log_2 5b + \mathcal{O}(b)$	$(3 \rightarrow 2)$-LUT	$9b \log_2 b + \mathcal{O}(b)$	$1.67\times$
CMP	3 XOR 1 AND	$12b \log_2 4b + \mathcal{O}(b)$	$(3 \rightarrow 1)$-LUT	$4.5b \log_2 b + \mathcal{O}(b)$	$2.67\times$
MUX	2 XOR 1 AND	$9b \log_2 3b + \mathcal{O}(b)$	$(3 \rightarrow 1)$-LUT	$4.5b \log_2 b + \mathcal{O}(b)$	$2\times$

Multiplication. Multiplication of two l-bit numbers can be composed of l^2 of 2-input AND gates $((2 \rightarrow 1)$-LUT) and $(l-1)$ l-bit adders [33]. Using the efficient implementation for LUT-based adders, the LUC size of the multiplication circuit is improved by $\approx 1.67\times$.

Multiplexer. An l-bit multiplexer circuit can be composed of l parallel MUX blocks (cf. [35, Fig. 9]) to select one of the l-bit inputs. So, using our LUT-based MUX has $\approx 2\times$ improvement for an l-bit multiplexer.

Comparison. An l-bit comparison circuit can be composed of a chain of l CMP blocks (cf. [33, Fig. 5]). Thus, our CMP construction improves the LUC size of the comparison circuit by $\approx 2.67\times$. A minimum circuit which selects the minimum value of a list of m l-bit values is composed of l-bit comparison and multiplexer circuits (cf. [33, Fig. 8]) and hence is improved by $\approx 2.3\times$.

5 Our Varying UC (VUC) Construction

In many applications, sub-functionalities are naturally implemented by LUTs with higher dimension, e.g., Sboxes in AES. In this case, we aim to put single LUTs with a higher dimension (e.g., $\rho = 8$) into the UC. Using our LUC construction for this concrete example, we would need to compose the UC of 8 instances of $\Gamma_1(n)$ EUGs, even if we only need the full $(8 \rightarrow 1)$-LUT few times in the whole circuit.[6] Thus, our aim is to find a way to use single LUTs with input dimension of $\rho > 3$ without a massive influence on the total circuit size.

In this section, we present our Varying UC (VUC) construction, which deviates from the conventional universal circuits (UCs) that have been widely studied [7,22,31,34,36,37,51]. Traditionally, UCs have been designed to conceal both the topology and the gate functionality of the simulated function, and have relied on the use of fixed computational units, namely universal 2-input gates or, like in our work, $(\rho \rightarrow \omega)$-LUTs with a globally fixed number of inputs ρ and outputs ω. A VUC, however, allows for the use of different programmable computational units, thereby leaking information about the types of units used. In particular, we focus on VUCs built using $(\rho \rightarrow \omega)$-LUTs with varying numbers of inputs and outputs, thereby revealing the dimensions of the individual LUTs.

Definition 10 (Varying Universal Circuit (VUC)). *A Varying Universal Circuit V for n_i inputs, the ordered list of n_g gates $\mathcal{G} = (\mathcal{G}_1, \ldots, \mathcal{G}_{n_g})$ of varying input and output dimensions, and n_o outputs is a Boolean circuit that can be programmed to compute any Boolean circuit C with n_i inputs, n_o outputs, and n_g gates that can be topologically ordered into $\mathcal{G}$ by defining a set of programming bits p^C such that $V(x, p^C) = C(x)$ for all possible input values $x \in \{0,1\}^{n_i}$.*

In Sect. 5.2, we discuss several applications of VUCs as well as their leakage.

5.1 The VUC Construction

First, we show how to build our VUC for evaluating different $(\rho \rightarrow 1)$-LUTs with varying input dimensions ρ. Later in this section, we show how to extend this construction to evaluate any $(\rho \rightarrow \omega)$-LUTs with varying input and output dimensions ρ and ω. In our VUC construction, we keep building our UC from only two instances of a $\Gamma_1(n)$ EUG, independent of the LUT sizes. This reduces the overhead of our LUT-based UC construction that merges ρ instances of the

---

[6] An alternative would be to decompose the larger LUTs into multiple smaller ones using Shannon expansion [49].

large $\Gamma_1(n)$ EUG for $(\rho \to 1)$-LUT. We do this by adding auxiliary poles u to the EUG whose task is to collect up to two inputs and forward these inputs via direct edges to a real pole v to push the indegree of v to ρ. Definition 11 defines $\Gamma_{\mathrm{P}^+,\mathrm{P}^-}(n)$ graphs, which classify the graphs that can be edge-embedded into our VUC construction, namely, the vectors P^+ and P^- specify the maximum indegree and outdegree of each LUT in our circuit that we aim to evaluate with the UC. Our VUC design additionally allows the evaluation of functions that only use a single type of ρ input LUTs by setting $\mathrm{P}^+ = \mathbb{1}\rho$,[7] i.e., each LUT in the circuit can have at most ρ inputs and the resulting VUC implements each universal gate as a $(\rho \to 1)$-LUT. In this case, the VUC is a real LUT-based UC (LUC) and can be used for PFE. In the case for VPFE, the universal gates of the UC have different implementations and therefore leak the specific input sizes of all LUTs.

Definition 11 ($\Gamma_{\mathrm{P}^+,\mathrm{P}^-}(n)$). *Let $G = (V, E)$ be a directed acyclic graph with topologically ordered $V := \{v_1, ..., v_n\}$ and $\mathrm{P}^+, \mathrm{P}^- \in \mathbb{N}^n$. Then $G \in \Gamma_{\mathrm{P}^+,\mathrm{P}^-}(n)$ if:*

- *$|V| \leq n$,*
- *$deg^+(v_i) \leq \mathrm{P}_i^+ \wedge deg^-(v_i) \leq \mathrm{P}_i^- \; \forall i \in [n]$.*

If $\mathrm{P}^{+/-} = \mathbb{1}\rho$ for some $\rho \in \mathbb{N}$, we write ρ instead of $\mathbb{1}\rho$.

In this sense, Corollary 2 yields a $\Gamma_{\rho,\rho}(n)$ EUG. In the following, we describe our VUC construction. An example of the whole EUG creation and the embedding process is depicted in Fig. 5. The explicit creation of the used auxiliary graph is given by Algorithm 3.

The key observation for our VUC construction is that, when merging two instances of $\Gamma_1(n)$ EUGs, each of the n poles (excluding inputs and outputs) can take two inputs, and *can*, but not necessarily need to, compute one output. We can use this observation to merge poles in order to collect $\rho > 2$ inputs for our LUT. For example, looking at Fig. 5, a $(5 \to 1)$-LUT consists of the three poles p_6, p_7, and p_8, where pole p_6 (resp. p_7) just collects two (resp. one) inputs, but does not compute any output. Instead, the ingoing edges are forwarded to pole p_8 (dashed lines) and the outgoing edges (dotted gray lines) are removed. Pole p_8 now has, in addition to its two regular ingoing edges, three additional ingoing edges that come directly from poles p_6 and p_7. On a high level, we can merge $\lceil \rho/2 \rceil$ poles into one $(\rho \to 1)$-LUT, while the first $\lceil \rho/2 \rceil - 1$ so-called *auxiliary poles* each collect up to two inputs for the LUT which are then directly forwarded to the last pole, which takes the last two inputs of the LUT and computes the output.

---

[7] $\mathbb{1}$ denotes the vector where each entry is 1.

More formally, we begin by constructing an auxiliary graph $\bar{G}$. For each pole p that has $\rho > 2$ incoming edges, we create an auxiliary pole for each two additional inputs, i.e., $\lceil \rho/2 - 1 \rceil$ auxiliary poles. Then, we replace all except two edges from pole p by edges to the auxiliary poles. The purpose of the auxiliary poles is to forward their inputs to the original multi-input pole. The resulting

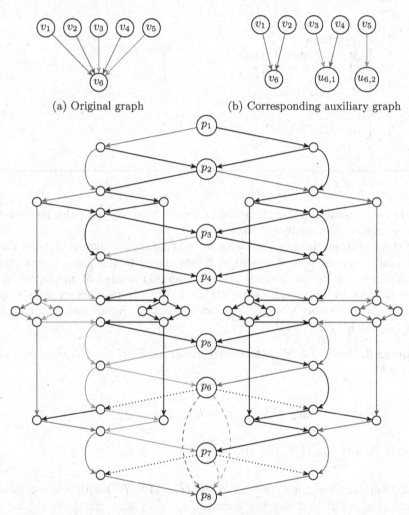

(a) Original graph   (b) Corresponding auxiliary graph

(c) Edge-embedding of the original graph. First, the edges from the auxiliary graph are embedded. Then, dotted gray edges are removed from the EUG, while dashed edges are added to the EUG, resp. to the edge-embedding. The result is an edge-embedding for the original graph. Now we can replace the ingoing edges to p_6 by directed edges to the multi-input pole p_8. The auxiliary pole p_7 becomes a Y-Switch that only forwards the orange wire.

Fig. 5. Our varying UC construction for $\rho = 5$ inputs.

Algorithm 3: AuxiliaryGraph(G)

   Input   : $G = (V, E) \in \Gamma_{\text{P+},2}(n)$

   Output: $\bar{G} = (\bar{V}, \bar{E}) \in \Gamma_2(n + \Delta)$ with $\Delta = \sum_{i=0}^{n} \max\{\lceil \frac{\text{P}_i^+ - 2}{2} \rceil, 0\}$

1   $\bar{G} = (\bar{V}, \bar{E}) \leftarrow (V, \emptyset)$
2   **foreach** $v_i \in V$ **do**
3   $\quad$ $j \leftarrow 0$
4   $\quad$ **foreach** $e = (w, v_i) \in E$ **do**
5   $\quad\quad$ **if** $j \geq 2$ **then**
6   $\quad\quad\quad$ **if** $j \equiv 0 \pmod 2$ **then**
7   $\quad\quad\quad\quad$ $\bar{V} \leftarrow \bar{V} \cup \{u_{i,\frac{j}{2}}\}$
8   $\quad\quad\quad$ $\bar{E} \leftarrow \bar{E} \cup \{(w, u_{i,\lceil \frac{j}{2} \rceil})\}$

9   $\quad\quad$ **else**
10 $\quad\quad\quad$ $\bar{E} \leftarrow \bar{E} \cup \{e\}$
11 $\quad\quad$ $j \leftarrow j + 1$

EUG $\mathcal{U}$ then guarantees that there can be a path from any pole with lower order to the corresponding auxiliary poles.

If there is a multi-input gate with an odd number of inputs ρ, then there will be one auxiliary pole in $\bar{G}$ with only one input. In this case, we can share this auxiliary pole for two poles if both have an odd number of inputs (which is always the case in the special case of PFE). This concrete auxiliary pole is then later translated into an X-switching block so that the inputs can be forwarded to the correct LUT.

Theorem 3. *Let* $\text{P}^+ \in \mathbb{N}^n$. *Then there exists an EUG for* $\Gamma_{\text{P+},2}(n)$ *with size bounded by*

$$3(n + \Delta) \log_2(n + \Delta) + \mathcal{O}(n + \Delta),$$

where $\Delta := \sum_{i=1}^{n} \max\{\lceil \frac{\text{P}_i^+ - 2}{2} \rceil, 0\}$.

Proof. **Step 1:** Create a $\Gamma_2(n + \Delta)$ EUG $\mathcal{U} = (V^{\mathcal{U}}, E^{\mathcal{U}})$ with a topologically ordered pole set P that has the form $(..., v_{i-1}, u_{i,1}, ..., u_{i, \lceil \frac{\text{P}_i^+ - 2}{2} \rceil}, v_i, ...)$ for all $i \in [n]$, i.e., the auxiliary poles $u_{i,j}$ for $j \in [[\lceil \frac{\text{P}_i^+ - 2}{2} \rceil]]$ are directly preceding the original pole v_i: We do this by creating a Liu$^+$ EUG $\mathcal{U}$ with pole set P and split parameter 2. Then we merge two instances of it. By Theorem 2 and Corollary 1, this yields a $\Gamma_2(n + \Delta)$ EUG of size at most $3(n + \Delta) \log_2(n + \Delta) + \mathcal{O}(n + \Delta)$.

Step 2: Adjust $\mathcal{U}$ to get the final EUG $\bar{\mathcal{U}} = (V^{\bar{\mathcal{U}}}, E^{\bar{\mathcal{U}}})$ with pole set $P \subset V^{\bar{\mathcal{U}}}$: Let $u_{i,j}$ be an auxiliary pole of v_i for $i \in [n], j \in [[\lceil \frac{\text{P}_i^+ - 2}{2} \rceil]]$. Remove all of its outgoing edges and replace each of them with an edge connecting the auxiliary pole to the original multi-input pole, i.e., remove each $(u_{i,j}, w) \in E^{\mathcal{U}}$ for $w \in V^{\mathcal{U}}$ and replace it by $(u_{i,j}, v_i)$. This yields two edges $(u_{i,j}, v_i)$ per auxiliary pole $u_{i,j}$. Thus, $E^{\mathcal{U}}$ becomes a multi set. If P_i^+ is odd and $j = 1$, add only one of these edges instead of two (otherwise, v_i would have too many ingoing edges). The graph that results from modifying $\mathcal{U}$ in the just described way is denoted by $\bar{\mathcal{U}}$.

Step 3: Embed any graph $G = (P, E) \in \Gamma_{\mathrm{P}^+,2}(n)$ into $\bar{\mathcal{U}}$: For this, we construct a $\Gamma_2(n+\Delta)$ graph using auxiliary poles for nodes with indegree higher than 2 by setting $\bar{G} = (\bar{V}, \bar{E}) = \texttt{auxiliaryGraph(G)} \in \Gamma_2(n+\Delta)$ (Algorithm 3). Note that the "relative topological order" is maintained, i.e., $\eta_{\bar{G}}(v_i) < \eta_{\bar{G}}(v_{i+1}) \; \forall i \in [n]$. Edge-embedding $\bar{G}$ into $\bar{\mathcal{U}}$ yields $\psi \colon \bar{E} \to \mathcal{P}_{\bar{\mathcal{U}}}$. To show that $\bar{\mathcal{U}}$ is a $\Gamma_{\mathrm{P}^+,2}(n)$ EUG, we need to define an edge-embedding $\bar{\psi}$ from G into $\bar{\mathcal{U}}$: Note that for edges $e = (v_i, v_l) \in G \setminus \bar{G}$, i.e., edges whose endpoints are not auxiliary poles, ψ already yields edge-disjoint v_i-v_l-paths and we can set $\bar{\psi}(e) = \psi(e)$ for those edges.

Now consider edges $e = (v_i, v_l) \in G \cap \bar{G}$, i.e., the endpoints of those edges are transformed into an auxiliary pole in $\bar{G}$. For each e, there is exactly one $\bar{e} = (v_i, u_{l,j}) \in \bar{G}$ for $j \in [[\lceil \frac{\deg^+(v_l)-2}{2} \rceil]]$ (line 8 in Algorithm 3). Now set $\bar{\psi}(e) = \psi(\bar{e}) + (u_{l,j}, v_l)$ for one of the possibly two edges $(u_{l,j}, v_l)$ that were added to $\bar{\mathcal{U}}$ before. Obviously, this yields a v_i-v_l-path. Since there are at most two edges connecting to an auxiliary pole, we can choose a unique last edge for each path. Because the paths in the image of ψ were already edge-disjoint, also the paths in the image of $\bar{\psi}$ are edge-disjoint. Thus, $\bar{\psi}$ is an edge-embedding of G into $\bar{\mathcal{U}}$.   □

Theorem 3 gives us an EUG that can be used to build VUCs for $(\rho \to 1)$-LUTs with varying parameter ρ and can thus be used for VPFE. Next, we consider VUCs for a fixed constant ρ which yields classical PFE.

Corollary 4. *Let* $\mathrm{P}^+ = \mathbb{1}\rho \in \mathbb{N}^n$ *for* $\rho > 2$. *Then there exists a EUG for* $\Gamma_{\mathrm{P}^+,2}(n)$ *with size bounded by*

$$3\lceil \tfrac{\rho}{2}n \rceil \log_2(\lceil \tfrac{\rho}{2}n \rceil) + \mathcal{O}(\lceil \tfrac{\rho}{2}n \rceil).$$

Proof. We follow the proof of Theorem 3 and highlight the differences.

Step 1: Create a $\Gamma_2(\lceil \tfrac{\rho}{2}n \rceil)$ EUG $\mathcal{U}$ with topologically ordered pole set P that has the form $(..., v_{i-1}, u_{i,1}, ..., u_{i,\lceil \frac{\rho-2}{2} \rceil}, v_i, u_{i+1,1}, ..., u_{i+1,\lfloor \frac{\rho-2}{2} \rfloor}, v_{i+1}, ...)$ as described in step 1 in the proof of Theorem 3.

Step 2: Adjust $\mathcal{U}$ to get the final EUG $\bar{\mathcal{U}} = (V^{\mathcal{U}}, E^{\mathcal{U}})$ with pole set $P \subset V^{\mathcal{U}}$ as described in step 2 in the proof of Theorem 3 with one difference: If ρ is odd, we share one auxiliary pole $u_{i,1}$ for two consecutive original poles v_i and v_{i+1}, i.e., we add the two edges $(u_{i,1}, v_i)$ and $(u_{i,1}, v_{i+1})$.

Step 3: Edge-embed G into $\bar{\mathcal{U}}$ as described in step 3 in the proof of Theorem 3 with one difference: If ρ is odd, the auxiliary graph $\bar{G} = (\bar{V}, \bar{E})$ shares one auxiliary pole $u_{i,1}$ for two consecutive original poles v_i and v_{i+1}, i.e., $u_{i+1,1}$ is removed from $\bar{V}$ and the edge $(w, u_{i+1,1})$ is replaced by the edge $(w, u_{i,1})$. As $u_{i,1}$ and $u_{i+1,1}$ both have indegree 1, $u_{i,1}$ now has indegree 2. $\qquad\Box$

Multi-output Support for VUCs. An auxiliary graph that represents multi-output LUTs is a $\Gamma_{\mathrm{P}^+,\mathrm{P}^-,\Omega^-}(n)$ graph as defined in Definition 12, i.e., $\Gamma_{\mathrm{P}^+,\mathrm{P}^-,\Omega^-}(n)$ classifies the graphs that can be edge-embedded into our UC construction. Here, P^+ is a vector of size n that specifies the indegree of each node in the auxiliary graph and thus represents the maximum number of inputs of each LUT in the UC. P^- is a constant that specifies the maximum outdegree of each node in the auxiliary graph/of each LUT in our circuit that we aim to evaluate with the UC. Similarly, Ω^- describes the number of distinguished outputs of the LUTs, i.e., P^- specifies the number of copies we have for each output of a LUT in our circuit, while Ω^- sets the number of outputs for each LUT.

As later, when embedding G into the EUG, each output of a LUT represents a separate value, i.e., we need to put each output into an individual pole. As the poles of the EUG are the nodes of the auxiliary graph, we need to add for each additional output of the i-th LUT in total $\Omega_i^- - 1$ additional poles. In Definition 12, we denote the outputs of the i-th LUT with $v_{i,1}, \ldots, v_{i,\Omega_i^-}$.

Definition 12 $(\Gamma_{\mathrm{P}^+,\mathrm{P}^-,\Omega^-}(n))$**.** *Let $G = (V, E)$ be a directed acyclic graph with topologically ordered $V := \{v_{1,1}, \ldots, v_{1,\Omega_1^-}, v_{2,1}, \ldots, v_{2,\Omega_2^-}, \ldots, v_{n,1}, \ldots, v_{n,\Omega_n^-}\}$ and $\mathrm{P}^+, \mathrm{P}^-, \Omega^- \in \mathbb{N}^n$. Then $G \in \Gamma_{\mathrm{P}^+,\mathrm{P}^-,\Omega^-}(n)$ if:*

$$- |V| \le \sum_{i=1}^n \Omega_i^-,$$
$$- |\{v_{i,j} \in V\}| \le \Omega_i^- \ \forall i \in [n],$$
$$- deg^+(v_{i,1}) \le \mathrm{P}_i^+ \wedge deg^+(v_{i,2}) = \cdots = deg^+(v_{i,\Omega_i^-}) = 0,$$
$$- deg^-(v_{i,j}) \le \mathrm{P}_i^- \ \forall i \in [n] \ \forall j \in [\Omega_i^-].$$

To easily build an EUG with only marginal modifications, we show that a $\Gamma_{\mathrm{P}^+,\mathrm{P}^-,\Omega^-}$ is also a $\Gamma_{\mathrm{P}^+,\mathrm{P}^-}$ graph:

Proposition 3. *Let $G \in \Gamma_{\mathrm{P}^+,\mathrm{P}^-,\Omega^-}(n)$. Then $G \in \Gamma_{\mathrm{P}^+,\mathrm{P}^-}(n + \Delta)$, where $\Delta :=$* $\sum_{i=1}^n \Omega_i^- - 1$.

Proof. Let $G = (V, E) \in \Gamma_{\mathrm{P}^+,\mathrm{P}^-,\Omega^-}(n)$. It holds that $|V| \le \sum_{i=1}^n \Omega_i^- = n + \Delta$ where $\Delta = \sum_{i=1}^n \Omega_i^- - 1$ (condition 1 in Definition 12). Further, for all $v \in V$ it holds that $deg^+(v) \le \mathrm{P}_i^+$ and $deg^-(v_{i,j}) \le \mathrm{P}_i^-$ from conditions 3 and 4 in Definition 12. $\qquad\Box$

We can build VUCs using Corollary 5 and UCs with constant ρ and ω using Corollary 6, whose prove directly follows from Corollarys 4 and 5.

Corollary 5. *Let* $\mathrm{P}^+, \Omega^- \in \mathbb{N}^n$. *Then there exists a EUG for* $\Gamma_{\mathrm{P}^+,2,\Omega^-}(n)$ *with size bounded by*

$$3(n + \Delta)\log_2(n + \Delta) + \mathcal{O}(n + \Delta),$$

where $\Delta := \sum_{i=1}^{n}(\max\{\lceil \frac{\mathrm{P}_i^+ - 2}{2}\rceil, 0\} + \Omega_i^- - 1)$.

Proof. Let $G = (P, E) \in \Gamma_{\mathrm{P}^+,2,\Omega^-}(n)$ be the graph to be embedded in an EUG with $P = \{v_{1,1}, \ldots, v_{1,\Omega_1^-}, v_{2,1}, \ldots, v_{2,\Omega_2^-}, \ldots, v_{n,1}, \ldots, v_{n,\Omega_n^-}\}$. We can transform G into a $\Gamma_{\mathrm{P}^+,2}(n + \Delta')$ graph where $\Delta' := \sum_{i=1}^{n} \Omega_i^- - 1$. Using Theorem 3, we get an EUG for $\Gamma_{\mathrm{P}^+,2}(n + \Delta')$ that is bounded by

$$3(n + \Delta' + \Delta'')\log_2(n + \Delta' + \Delta'') + \mathcal{O}(n + \Delta' + \Delta''),$$

where $\Delta'' := \sum_{i=1}^{n} \max\{\lceil \frac{\mathrm{P}_i^+ - 2}{2}\rceil, 0\}$ and setting $\Delta := \Delta' + \Delta''$ yields an EUG of the given size.

We need to add some more edges to the resulting EUG $\bar{\mathcal{U}} = (V^{\bar{\mathcal{U}}}, E^{\bar{\mathcal{U}}})$ with pole set $P \subset V^{\bar{\mathcal{U}}}$, namely the inputs of the first pole associated with the LUT need to be forwarded to all remaining output poles of the same LUT as follows: $\forall i \in [n] : \forall v_{i,1} \in P : \forall (u, v_{i,1}) \in E^{\bar{\mathcal{U}}} : \forall v_{i,j} \in P, j > 1 : E^{\bar{\mathcal{U}}} = E^{\bar{\mathcal{U}}} \cup (u, v_{i,j})$. □

Corollary 6. *Let* $\mathrm{P}^+ = \rho \in \mathbb{N}^n$ *for* $\rho > 2$ *and* $\Omega^- = \mathbb{1}\omega \in \mathbb{N}^n$ *for* $\omega > 1$. *Then there exists an EUG for* $\Gamma_{\mathrm{P}^+,2,\Omega^-}(n)$ *with size bounded by*

$$3(\lceil(\frac{\rho}{2} + \omega - 1)n\rceil)\log_2(\lceil(\frac{\rho}{2} + \omega - 1)n\rceil) + \mathcal{O}(\lceil(\frac{\rho}{2} + \omega - 1)n\rceil).$$

5.2   Applications of Varying UCs (VUCs)

If we use a VUC instead of a UC in MPC-based PFE, we get Varying Private Function Evaluation (VPFE). VPFE allows a set of k parties $\mathcal{P}_1, \ldots, \mathcal{P}_k$, to jointly compute a circuit C held by $\mathcal{P}_1$ on private data $x_2, \ldots, x_k$ held by $\mathcal{P}_{i \geq 2}$ to obtain nothing but $C(x_2, \ldots, x_k)$, and $\mathcal{P}_{i \geq 2}$ learn nothing about C but the dimensions of all its LUTs. Thus, VPFE does not leak the whole topology of sub-circuits like SPFE (cf. Sect. 1.1), but leaks more information than PFE.

We can reduce the leakage by randomly changing the sequence of LUTs according to the topological order of the simulated circuit. In this way, building blocks (e.g., full adders) do not occur as a whole block of consecutive LUTs of the same dimension in the VUC. The function would be mapped to different sequences of dimensions and thus we would remove fingerprints of certain functions. So, even multiple building blocks of different circuit layers can be mixed in a sequence. This technique, however, still allows to exclude certain functions when they cannot be mapped to the given sequence of dimensions.

Some applications, such as logic locking (cf. [11, Fig. 3] and Sect. 1.1) do not require full privacy of the evaluated function and allow for the leakage of the sequence of dimensions of the used LUTs. However, in general PFE applications, even knowledge of the LUT sizes may reveal too much information about the protected function. Our analysis (cf. Sect. 4.3) and our benchmarks (cf. Sect. 6.3) demonstrate that many functionalities can be reduced to 3-input LUTs. Consequently, we benefit from using LUCs with 3-input LUTs in most cases. This observation is not surprising, as most arithmetic operations can be reduced to full adders (3-input LUTs), and only a small number of sub-functionalities benefit from using LUTs with more than 3 inputs. However, when adding only one of these larger LUTs, the overall size of the LUC would be significantly increased, as a complete EUG graph would need to be added to the circuit for each additional input of all LUTs, even if the higher dimension is used only once. Therefore, VUCs are well-suited for embedding circuits with a limited number of various LUT combinations, such as $(3 \rightarrow 1)$-LUT and $(8 \rightarrow 8)$-LUT, resulting in significant size improvements. By implementing simple functionalities with $(3 \rightarrow 1)$-LUTs and allowing complex functionalities with $(8 \rightarrow 8)$-LUTs, a wide range of possible functions can be achieved without compromising critical information (which can always be implemented using a single LUT type). The $(8 \rightarrow 8)$-LUTs offer a vast set of 256 combinations, enabling the implementation of a large and diverse collection of functionalities. Despite the inclusion of these additional combinations, the resulting leakage remains limited.

There are many PFE applications that benefit from such a setting, including credit checking [17], user-specific tariff calculations [21], and medical diagnosis [9]. All these applications rely on sub-functionalities such as classifiers. A classifier utilizes a mapping table to look up a class based on input data, and then outputs the determined class. To illustrate, a car insurance tariff calculator may use a classifier to establish a basic price based on the type of car a potential customer drives. Multi-input LUTs, such as $(8 \rightarrow 8)$-LUTs, can efficiently implement these classifiers as they provide exactly such a table lookup. By incorporating individually tailored multi-input LUTs in a VUC, we can benefit from overall size improvements over the LUC construction, while still maintaining the internal implementation of the classifier, including the computation performed to obtain the address of the lookup whose topology is hidden.

6   Implementation and Evaluation

We implement our proposed UC constructions using the MPC framework ABY [13] to provide a fair comparison to previous PFE works on UCs [7,22,31]. MPC frameworks supporting multi-input garbled circuits [39] reduce the communication of evaluating a single ρ input LUT to $2^\rho - 1$ ciphertexts. In ABY, we implement ρ input LUTs as a multiplexer tree consisting of $2^\rho - 1$ 2-input AND gates, requiring $2(2^\rho - 1)$ ciphertexts using half-gates [56]. This could be further reduced to $1.5(2^\rho - 1)$ ciphertexts using three-halves garbling [47].

We benchmark our LUC construction (cf. Sect. 4) and compare it with the most recent UC of Liu et al. [37] that simulates circuits with binary gates. Moreover, we evaluate our VUC construction (cf. Sect. 5) to show the improvement over Liu et al.'s UC [37] and our LUC construction. All results in this section use the EUG construction by Liu et al. [37] to construct the underlying Γ_1 EUGs. We discuss the LUT generation in Sect. 6.1, details about our UC compilation in Sect. 6.2, and experimental results in Sect. 6.3.

6.1 LUT Generation

Hardware synthesis is a crucial process in electronic design automation that involves converting an abstract function description into a functionally equivalent logic implementation. This transformation is achieved through the utilization of various optimization and technology mapping algorithms. These algorithms have been extensively researched and developed over the course of many years. The resulting circuit implementation is typically dependent on the target hardware platform and the manufacturing technology employed. The two most common target hardware platforms are Application Specific Integrated Circuits (ASICs) and Field Programmable Gate Arrays (FPGAs).

This work specifically focuses on exploiting multi-input LUTs, which are fundamental components of FPGAs (which consist of logic cells containing programmable LUTs) and their corresponding synthesis tools. Although ASIC synthesis tools can also map to multi-input gates, this process is laborious, impractical, and necessitates the creation of large libraries to accommodate all possible LUTs for each input size. Thus, we chose FPGA synthesis tools. The market offers commercial FPGA synthesis tools like Intel Quartus Prime [1], VTR [2], XST [4], and Vivado Synthesis tools by Xilinx [3]. However, these tools synthesize LUT-based circuits tailored to the specific features of their respective devices. For instance, most current FPGA devices support a maximum of 6-input LUTs. In our work, we aim to generate circuits with up to 8-input LUTs, which, to the best of our knowledge, is not supported by mainstream commercial tools.

In this work, similar to [12,14], we leverage the mapping capabilities of the open-source tools Yosys [53] and ABC [10]. Yosys allows us to transform the circuit descriptions into a network of low-level logic operations represented in an intermediate format. Subsequently, ABC [10] organizes this network into a Directed Acyclic Graph (DAG) and maps it to a depth-optimized circuit composed of LUTs. It is worth noting that ABC [10] does not inherently support mapping to multi-output LUTs. To overcome this limitation, we perform post-processing on the single-output LUT circuits generated by ABC [10] and convert them into multi-output LUT circuits. Additionally, we use integrated Intellectual Property (IP) libraries within the commercial ASIC synthesis tool Synopsys Design Compiler (DC) [5], to generate circuit netlists for more complex functionalities such as floating-point operations. These circuits are initially created as Boolean netlists by Synopsys DC [5], and we subsequently remap them to LUT-based representations using the Yosys-ABC toolchain [10,53].

6.2   UC Compilation

Let C denote the circuit to be embedded and ρ the maximum fan-in of the circuit.

1. Parsing the circuit: The circuit is input in the Secure Hardware Definition Language (SHDL) [39] and parsed into the internal graph representation. We reduce the fan-out of the graph to the allowed fan-in ρ for LUCs (cf. Sect. 4) and 2 for VUCs (cf. Sect. 5) by using copy gates. For VUCs, the auxiliary graph (cf. Theorem 3) is generated. Here, we denote the auxiliary graph by G and the former graph with possibly reduced fan-out by $\bar{G}$.

2. Splitting G into Γ_1 graphs and creating Γ_1 EUGs: Using the LUC construction yields ρ Γ_1 graphs. For each Γ_1 graph, we create a Γ_1 EUG. Possible EUGs are Valiant's EUG [51] and the 2-way split EUG of Liu et al. [37]. If we use the VUC construction, we get two Γ_1 graphs.

3. Edge-embedding the Γ_1 graphs and merging them: Each Γ_1 graph is edge-embedded into the corresponding Γ_1 EUG. This edge-embedding is coded directly into the control bits of the X- and Y-Switches of the EUG. The concrete algorithm uses a slightly modified version of the edge-embedding algorithm in [22]. Then, the Γ_1 EUGs are merged into a Γ_ρ EUG (LUC) or into a Γ_2 EUG (VUC).

4. Basic optimizations and correctness checking: We remove edges connecting to an input pole as they will never be used and replace copy gates with wires. Then we remove isolated nodes or change X- to Y-Switching nodes if one edge was removed before. We check the correctness of the edge-embedding by checking for each edge (u, v) in G, if there is a path leading from u to v.

5. Setting the gates of the EUG: In the VUC construction, we replace the auxiliary poles with wires connecting directly to the actual pole or a Y-Switch if only one input is forwarded. Analogously to step 4, we check the correctness of the edge-embedding to $\bar{G}$. For each node in G, we set the programming bits of the corresponding EUG pole. We determine the order of inputs and then set the programming bits accordingly. This also involves padding the programming bits if the gate has more inputs. Note that these additional inputs are likely to occur since each Universal Gate outputs ρ (in LUC construction) or 2 (in VUC construction) wires, independent of whether they are used in G or not. We pad the programming bits such that additional and undesired inputs are ignored.

6. Transforming the EUG into an ABY compatible UC: As a final step, we topologically order the EUG and output it in the UC format compatible with ABY [13]. Then, each node, along with its incoming and outgoing wires, is written into a circuit file. At the same time, the programming bits are written into a separate programming bits file.

6.3 Experimental Results

Setup. Like previous works [22,31,37], we benchmark a set of real-world circuits from [50]. In addition, we consider other useful functions like Karatsuba multiplication [28], Manhattan and Euclidean distance [14], and floating-point operations [14]. For each functionality, we give the sizes of the resulting circuit, as well as communication and runtime complexity when the UC is evaluated with an MPC protocol. In order to show the improvement of our work, we use two identical machines with a LAN connection of 10 Gbit/s bandwidth and a round-trip time of 1 ms. Each machine is equipped with an Intel Core i9-7960X@2.8 GHz with 128GB DDR4 RAM. All measurements are averaged over 10 executions.

Table 3. Number of AND and XOR gates per building block in our UCs.

Building block	AND gates	XOR gates
X-switching block [35]	1	3
Y-switching block [35]	1	2
Universal Gate with $k \geq 2$ inputs	$2^k - 1$	$2^{k+1} - 2$

LUC Improvement. As we have Universal Gates of different sizes, we cannot just count the number of nodes in the EUG to compare the implementations. As underlying MPC protocol for UC-based PFE we use Yao's protocol [56] using free XORs [35], so XOR gates can be evaluated without communication. Therefore, we count the number of non-free AND gates to instantiate the building blocks of the UC (cf. Table 3). We experimentally compared our implementations with the best existing UC-based PFE construction of Liu et al. [37]. We provide our results for our LUT-based UC constructions in Table 4. In our circuit generation, we vary possible choices for $(\rho \rightarrow \omega)$-LUTs and select the ones with highest improvement. We can see from Table 4 that our LUT-based UC construction is always smaller than that of [37] by $1.12 - 2.18\times$.

For a comparison of the improvements in PFE, we securely evaluate our generated UCs with the GMW-based SP-LUT protocol [14] and Yao's GC protocol [56]. In Table 5, we show the runtime and communication of our LUT-based UC construction (LUC) compared to the most recent UC construction of Liu et al. [37] as baseline using Yao [56] and GMW [20]. Our new UC construction is the fastest implementation: Compared to the baseline using Yao [56], the total

Table 4. Comparison of the sizes of our LUT-based UC construction (LUC, cf. Sect. 4) and the best previous UC construction of Liu et al. [37] as baseline (in number of AND gates) measured with our implementations. The smallest size is marked in **bold** and always achieved by our UCs. The sizes for our UC is the best combinations for ($\rho \to \omega$)-LUT for $\rho \in \{2, ..., 8\}$ inputs and $\omega \in \{1, ..., 8\}$ outputs for the benchmarked circuit.

Circuit	Circuit size (# AND gates)		Improvement ($\times$)	LUT sizes ($\rho \to \omega$)
	UC of [37]	Our LUC		
AES	**1,779,105**	**1,779,105**	1.00	$2 \to 1$
DES	1,269,537	**1,130,037**	1.12	$3 \to 1$
MD5	3,293,262	**1,724,221**	1.91	$3 \to 1$
SHA-1	4,872,501	**2,559,602**	1.90	$3 \to 1$
SHA-256	10,652,234	**5,351,972**	1.99	$3 \to 1$
Add_32	6,926	**3,907**	1.77	$3 \to 2$
Add_64	17,006	**8,963**	1.90	$3 \to 2$
Comp_32	2,519	**1,278**	1.97	$3 \to 1$
Mult_32x32	347,274	**177,081**	1.96	$3 \to 3$
Karatsuba_32x32	286,933	**156,888**	1.83	$3 \to 3$
MD256	327,203	**150,046**	2.18	$3 \to 2$
ED64	1,852,419	**947,679**	1.95	$3 \to 3$
FP-Add_32	113,620	**90,964**	1.25	$3 \to 1$
FP-Mul_32	293,125	**247,859**	1.18	$3 \to 1$
FP-Exp2_32	2,008,269	**1,548,079**	1.30	$3 \to 1$
FP-Div_32	372,101	**236,300**	1.57	$3 \to 1$
FP-Sqrt_32	176,176	**118,873**	1.48	$3 \to 1$
FP-Comp_32	6,387	**5,628**	1.13	$4 \to 4$
FP-Log_32	1,936,813	**1,499,538**	1.29	$3 \to 1$

runtime for our sample circuits is faster by a factor of $1.14-2\times$. The communication improvements over the baseline using Yao [56] are $1.12-2.25\times$. The runtime of Yao's protocol is $3.83-11.5\times$ faster than that of the LUT-based protocols which can be explained by the constant round complexity of Yao's protocol. The SP-LUT protocol [14] always has the lowest communication, achieving factor $1.19-2.44\times$ less communication than Yao's protocol. In Table 5, it is evident that the baseline employing Yao [56] exhibits superior runtime performance and lower total communication overhead than the baseline employing the GMW protocol [20].

Table 5. Runtime and communication for our LUT-based UC construction (cf. Sect. 4) compared to the state-of-the-art UC of [37] when evaluated with ABY [13]. We include the LAN evaluation time (in seconds) and the total communication (in Megabytes) between the parties in LUT-based [14], Yao sharing [56], as well as in GMW sharing [20]. The best values are marked in **bold**.

UC construction	UC of [37]				Our LUT-based UC (LUC)			
MPC protocol	Yao [56]		GMW [20]		Yao [56]		SP-LUT [14]	
Circuit	Time (s)	Comm. (MB)	Time (s)	Comm. (MB)	Time (s)	Comm. (MB)	Time (s)	Comm. (MB)
AES	**1.811**	80.315	142.193	96.845	**1.811**	80.315	13.187	**28.427**
DES	1.282	57.271	101.645	68.071	**1.124**	50.570	9.233	**24.311**
MD5	3.471	148.348	238.847	168.991	**1.832**	76.638	26.642	**46.013**
SHA1	5.184	220.065	343.344	246.708	**2.756**	113.859	27.268	**58.641**
SHA-256	11.571	481.412	722.650	528.122	**5.878**	238.364	54.082	**123.045**
Add_32	0.018	0.314	1.139	0.594	**0.009**	0.177	0.224	**0.148**
Add_64	0.026	0.770	2.323	1.230	**0.017**	0.404	0.452	**0.319**
Comp_32	0.008	0.117	0.265	0.203	**0.004**	0.062	0.139	**0.055**
Mult_32x32	0.350	15.626	31.497	19.650	**0.212**	7.300	4.144	**4.531**
Karatsuba_32x32	0.292	12.901	27.214	16.597	**0.191**	6.469	3.685	**4.020,1**
MD256	0.337	14.801	29.037	18.326	**0.193**	6.592	4.234	**4.544**
ED64	1.924	83.552	142.147	97.558	**1.046**	39.704	17.524	**24.572**
FP-Add_32	0.164	5.105	11.780	6.859	**0.139**	4.003	2.903	**2.426**
FP-Mul_32	0.350	13.178	28.215	16.988	**0.308**	10.949	6.217	**4.579**
FP-Exp2_32	2.292	90.555	155.881	106.023	**1.612**	68.651	21.531	**38.330**
FP-Div_32	0.458	16.743	33.686	21.024	**0.296**	10.443	5.918	**6.528**
FP-Sqrt_32	0.223	7.915	18.910	10.433	**0.168**	5.237	3.417	**3.442**
FP-Comp_32	0.014	0.290	1.066	0.553	**0.012**	0.235	0.226	**0.118**
FP-Log_32	2.083	87.330	151.423	102.369	**1.600**	66.510	20.198	**36.287**

VUC Improvement. Table 6 shows that our VUC construction which – other than LUC – leaks the fanin of the individual LUTs is up to 2.90× smaller than Liu et al.'s UC [37] when evaluated with Yao's protocol [56], the total runtime for our sample circuits is faster by 1.1 − 2.85× and the communication is improved by 1.06 − 2.96×. This shows that significant speedups can be achieved when giving up some function privacy.

Note that during the process of compiling our VUC construction, our tool conducts an initial verification to determine whether the LUC construction results in a better size than VUC, and, if so, proceeds to compile a LUC. Nonetheless, in the majority of cases, VUC yields a better size by a factor of up to 1.45×. The superiority of VUC over LUC is strongly influenced by the circuit design. Specifically, if the circuit can primarily be constructed using Look-Up Tables (LUTs) with identical input dimensions, the overall size is better than VUC. However, if the circuit can be effectively constructed using LUTs with differing input dimensions, VUC performs better.

Table 6. Sizes, runtime, and communication for our VUC construction (cf. Sect. 5). We include LAN evaluation times (in seconds) and total communications (in Megabytes) between the parties in LUT-based [14] as well as in Yao sharing [56]. We show the size improvement of VUC over the UC of [37] and LUC construction (cf. Sect. 4) in the last two columns. Note that VUCs reveal the LUTs' dimensions, showcasing the enhancements obtained by sacrificing some circuit privacy.

Circuit	Size	Yao [56]		SP-LUT [14]		Size Improv.($\times$) VUC/UC of [37]	Size Improv.($\times$) VUC/LUC
		Time	Comm.	Time	Comm.		
AES	1,584,047	1.724	71.753	142.221	2.607	1.13	1.13
DES	960,854	0.98	43.441	93.79	1.66	1.32	1.17
MD5	1,191,566	1.22	52.89	23.01	42.77	2.76	1.45
SHA-1	2,559,602	2.76	113.86	27.27	58.64	1.90	1.00
SHA-256	4,591,982	4.91	201.98	52.22	108.43	2.32	1.17
Add_32	3,907	0.01	0.18	0.23	0.15	1.77	1.00
Add_64	8,963	0.02	0.40	0.45	0.32	1.90	1.00
Comp_32	1,188	0.01	0.05	0.04	0.04	2.12	1.08
Mult_32x32	130,053	0.14	5.51	1.42	4.06	2.67	1.36
Karatsuba_32x32	112,829	0.12	5.01	1.41	3.41	2.54	1.40
MD256	112,829	0.13	5.01	1.37	4.09	2.90	1.33
ED64	947,679	1.05	39.70	17.52	24.58	1.95	1.00
FP-Add_32	90,964	0.14	4.00	2.90	2.43	1.25	1.00
FP-Mul_32	185,968	0.18	8.11	2.04	3.65	1.58	1.33
FP-Exp2_32	1,265,869	1.34	55.72	19.38	25.16	1.59	1.22
FP-Div_32	181,904	0.18	7.89	1.91	5.27	2.05	1.30
FP-Sqrt_32	89,311	0.10	3.84	1.07	2.70	1.97	1.33
FP-Comp_32	5,269	0.01	0.22	0.11	0.093	1.21	1.07
FP-Log_32	1,230,530	1.31	54.16	16.17	24.69	1.57	1.22

Acknowledgements. This project received funding from the ERC under the European Union's Horizon 2020 research and innovation program (grant agreement No. 850990 PSOTI). It was co-funded by the DFG within SFB 1119 CROSSING/236615297 and GRK 2050 Privacy & Trust/251805230.

References

1. Intel Quartus Prime Software. https://www.intel.com/content/www/us/en/products/details/fpga/development-tools/quartus-prime.html
2. Verilog to Routing. https://verilogtorouting.org/
3. Vivado 2023.1 - Logic Synthesis. https://www.xilinx.com/support/documentation-navigation/design-hubs/dh0018-vivado-synthesis-hub.html
4. XST Synthesis. https://www.xilinx.com/products/design-tools/xst.html
5. Synopsys Inc., Design Compiler (2010). http://www.synopsys.com/Tools/Implementation/RTLSynthesis/DesignCompiler

6. Abadi, M., Feigenbaum, J.: Secure circuit evaluation. JoC (1990)
7. Alhassan, M.Y., Günther, D., Kiss, Á., Schneider, T.: Efficient and Scalable Universal Circuits. JoC (2020)
8. Attrapadung, N.: Fully Secure and Succinct Attribute Based Encryption for Circuits from Multi-linear Maps. Cryptology ePrint Archive, Report 2014/772 (2016)
9. Barni, M., Failla, P., Kolesnikov, V., Lazzeretti, R., Sadeghi, A.-R., Schneider, T.: Secure evaluation of private linear branching programs with medical applications. In: Backes, M., Ning, P. (eds.) ESORICS 2009. LNCS, vol. 5789, pp. 424–439. Springer, Heidelberg (2009). https://doi.org/10.1007/978-3-642-04444-1_26
10. Berkeley Logic Synthesis and Verification Group: ABC: A system for sequential synthesis and verification. http://www.eecs.berkeley.edu/alanmi/abc/
11. Bhandari, J., et al.: Not All Fabrics Are Created Equal: Exploring eFPGA Parameters For IP Redaction. CoRR: abs/2111.04222 (2021)
12. Brüggemann, A., Hundt, R., Schneider, T., Suresh, A., Yalame, H.: FLUTE: fast and secure lookup table evaluations. In: S&P (2023)
13. Demmler, D., Schneider, T., Zohner, M.: ABY - a framework for efficient mixed-protocol secure two-party computation. In: NDSS (2015)
14. Dessouky, G., Koushanfar, F., Sadeghi, A., Schneider, T., Zeitouni, S., Zohner, M.: Pushing the communication barrier in secure computation using lookup tables. In: NDSS (2017)
15. Disser, Y., Günther, D., Schneider, T., Stillger, M., Wigandt, A., Yalame, H.: Breaking the Size Barrier: Universal Circuits meet Lookup Tables. Cryptology ePrint Archive, Report 2022/1652 (2022)
16. Fiore, D., Gennaro, R., Pastro, V.: Efficiently verifiable computation on encrypted data. In: CCS (2014)
17. Frikken, K.B., Atallah, M.J., Zhang, C.: Privacy-preserving credit checking. In: ACM Conference on Electronic Commerce (2005)
18. Garg, S., Gentry, C., Halevi, S., Sahai, A., Waters, B.: Attribute-based encryption for circuits from multilinear maps. In: Canetti, R., Garay, J.A. (eds.) CRYPTO 2013. LNCS, vol. 8043, pp. 479–499. Springer, Heidelberg (2013). https://doi.org/10.1007/978-3-642-40084-1_27
19. Gentry, C., Halevi, S., Vaikuntanathan, V.: i-hop homomorphic encryption and rerandomizable yao circuits. In: Rabin, T. (ed.) CRYPTO 2010. LNCS, vol. 6223, pp. 155–172. Springer, Heidelberg (2010). https://doi.org/10.1007/978-3-642-14623-7_9
20. Goldreich, O., Micali, S., Wigderson, A.: How to play any mental game or a completeness theorem for protocols with honest majority. In: STOC (1987)
21. Günther, D., Kiss, Á., Scheidel, L., Schneider, T.: Poster: framework for semi-private function evaluation with application to secure insurance rate calculation. In: CCS (2019)
22. Günther, D., Kiss, Á., Schneider, T.: More efficient universal circuit constructions. In: Takagi, T., Peyrin, T. (eds.) ASIACRYPT 2017. LNCS, vol. 10625, pp. 443–470. Springer, Cham (2017). https://doi.org/10.1007/978-3-319-70697-9_16
23. Henecka, W., Kögl, S., Sadeghi, A., Schneider, T., Wehrenberg, I.: TASTY: Tool for Automating Secure Two-Party Computations. In: CCS (2010)
24. Holz, M., Kiss, Á., Rathee, D., Schneider, T.: Linear-complexity private function evaluation is practical. In: Chen, L., Li, N., Liang, K., Schneider, S. (eds.) ESORICS 2020. LNCS, vol. 12309, pp. 401–420. Springer, Cham (2020). https://doi.org/10.1007/978-3-030-59013-0_20
25. Ji, K., Zhang, B., Lu, T., Ren, K.: Multi-party private function evaluation for RAM. IEEE Trans. Inf. Forensics Secur. **18**, 1252–1267 (2023)

26. Kamali, H.M., Azar, K.Z., Gaj, K., Homayoun, H., Sasan, A.: LUT-lock: a novel LUT-based logic obfuscation for FPGA-bitstream and ASIC-hardware protection. In: ISVLSI (2018)
27. Kamara, S., Raykova, M.: Secure outsourced computation in a multi-tenant cloud. In: IBM Workshop on Cryptography and Security in Clouds (2011)
28. Karatsuba, A.A., Ofman, Y.P.: Multiplication of many-digital numbers by automatic computers. In: SSSR Academy of Sciences (1962)
29. Karnaugh, M.: The map method for synthesis of combinational logic circuits. Trans. Am. Inst. Electrical Eng. **72**, 593–599 (1953)
30. Katz, J., Malka, L.: Constant-round private function evaluation with linear complexity. In: Lee, D.H., Wang, X. (eds.) ASIACRYPT 2011. LNCS, vol. 7073, pp. 556–571. Springer, Heidelberg (2011). https://doi.org/10.1007/978-3-642-25385-0_30
31. Kiss, Á., Schneider, T.: Valiant's universal circuit is practical. In: Fischlin, M., Coron, J.-S. (eds.) EUROCRYPT 2016. LNCS, vol. 9665, pp. 699–728. Springer, Heidelberg (2016). https://doi.org/10.1007/978-3-662-49890-3_27
32. Kluczniak, K.: Circuit privacy for FHEW/TFHE-style fully homomorphic encryption in practice. Cryptology ePrint Archive, Report 2022/1459 (2022)
33. Kolesnikov, V., Sadeghi, A.R., Schneider, T.: Improved garbled circuit building blocks and applications to auctions and computing minima. In: CANS (2009)
34. Kolesnikov, V., Schneider, T.: A practical universal circuit construction and secure evaluation of private functions. In: FC (2008)
35. Kolesnikov, V., Schneider, T.: Improved garbled circuit: free XOR gates and applications. In: Aceto, L., Damgård, I., Goldberg, L.A., Halldórsson, M.M., Ingólfsdóttir, A., Walukiewicz, I. (eds.) ICALP 2008. LNCS, vol. 5126, pp. 486–498. Springer, Heidelberg (2008). https://doi.org/10.1007/978-3-540-70583-3_40
36. Lipmaa, H., Mohassel, P., Sadeghian, S.S.: Valiant's Universal Circuit: Improvements, Implementation, and Applications. Cryptology ePrint Archive, Report 2016/017 (2016)
37. Liu, H., Yu, Yu., Zhao, S., Zhang, J., Liu, W., Hu, Z.: Pushing the limits of valiant's universal circuits: simpler, tighter and more compact. In: Malkin, T., Peikert, C. (eds.) CRYPTO 2021. LNCS, vol. 12826, pp. 365–394. Springer, Cham (2021). https://doi.org/10.1007/978-3-030-84245-1_13
38. Liu, Y., Wang, Q., Yiu, S.: Making private function evaluation safer, faster, and simpler. In: Hanaoka, G., Shikata, J., Watanabe, Y. (eds.) PKC 2022. LNCS, vol. 13177, pp. 349–378. Springer, Cham (2022). https://doi.org/10.1007/978-3-030-97121-2_13
39. Malkhi, D., Nisan, N., Pinkas, B., Sella, Y.: Fairplay - secure two-party computation system. In: USENIX Security (2004)
40. Masserova, E., Garg, D., Mai, K., Pileggi, L., Goyal, V., Parno, B.: Logic Locking-Connecting Theory and Practice. Cryptology ePrint Archive, Report 2022/545 (2022)
41. Patra, A., Schneider, T., Suresh, A., Yalame, H.: ABY2.0: improved mixed-protocol secure two-party computation. In: USENIX Security (2021)
42. Patra, A., Schneider, T., Suresh, A., Yalame, H.: SynCirc: efficient synthesis of depth-optimized circuits for secure computation. In: HOST (2021)
43. Paus, A., Sadeghi, A.-R., Schneider, T.: Practical secure evaluation of semi-private functions. In: Abdalla, M., Pointcheval, D., Fouque, P.-A., Vergnaud, D. (eds.) ACNS 2009. LNCS, vol. 5536, pp. 89–106. Springer, Heidelberg (2009). https://doi.org/10.1007/978-3-642-01957-9_6

44. Pinkas, B., Schneider, T., Smart, N.P., Williams, S.C.: Secure two-party computation is practical. In: Matsui, M. (ed.) ASIACRYPT 2009. LNCS, vol. 5912, pp. 250–267. Springer, Heidelberg (2009). https://doi.org/10.1007/978-3-642-10366-7_15

45. Pohle, E., Abidin, A., Preneel, B.: Poster: fast evaluation of S-boxes in MPC. In: NDSS (2022)

46. Quine, W.V.: The problem of simplifying truth functions. The American Mathematical Monthly (1952)

47. Rosulek, M., Roy, L.: Three halves make a whole? Beating the half-gates lower bound for garbled circuits. In: Malkin, T., Peikert, C. (eds.) CRYPTO 2021. LNCS, vol. 12825, pp. 94–124. Springer, Cham (2021). https://doi.org/10.1007/978-3-030-84242-0_5

48. Sadeghi, A.R., Schneider, T.: Generalized universal circuits for secure evaluation of private functions with application to data classification. In: ICISC (2008)

49. Shannon, C.E.: The synthesis of two-terminal switching circuits. Bell Syst. Tech. J. **28**, 59–98 (1949)

50. Smart, N., Tillich, S.: Bristol Fashion MPC circuits. https://homes.esat.kuleuven.be/nsmart/MPC/old-circuits.html

51. Valiant, L.G.: Universal Circuits (Preliminary Report). In: STOC (1976)

52. Wegener, I.: The Complexity of Boolean Functions. Wiley, New York (1987)

53. Wolf, C., Glaser, J., Kepler, J.: Yosys - a free Verilog synthesis suite. In: Austrian Workshop on Microelectronics (2013)

54. Yao, A.C.: How to generate and exchange secrets (Extended Abstract). In: FOCS (1986)

55. Yasin, M., Sengupta, A., Nabeel, M.T., Ashraf, M., Rajendran, J., Sinanoglu, O.: Provably-secure logic locking: from theory to practice. In: CCS (2017)

56. Zahur, S., Rosulek, M., Evans, D.: Two halves make a whole - reducing data transfer in garbled circuits using half gates. In: Oswald, E., Fischlin, M. (eds.) EUROCRYPT 2015. LNCS, vol. 9057, pp. 220–250. Springer, Heidelberg (2015). https://doi.org/10.1007/978-3-662-46803-6_8

57. Zhao, S., Yu, Yu., Zhang, J., Liu, H.: Valiant's universal circuits revisited: an overall improvement and a lower bound. In: Galbraith, S.D., Moriai, S. (eds.) ASIACRYPT 2019. LNCS, vol. 11921, pp. 401–425. Springer, Cham (2019). https://doi.org/10.1007/978-3-030-34578-5_15

58. Zimmerman, J.: How to obfuscate programs directly. In: Oswald, E., Fischlin, M. (eds.) EUROCRYPT 2015. LNCS, vol. 9057, pp. 439–467. Springer, Heidelberg (2015). https://doi.org/10.1007/978-3-662-46803-6_15

Amortized NISC over $\mathbb{Z}_{2^k}$ from RMFE

Fuchun Lin$^{(\boxtimes)}$, Chaoping Xing, Yizhou Yao, and Chen Yuan

Shanghai Jiao Tong University, Shanghai, China
{linfuchun,xingcp,yaoyizhou0620,chen_yuan}@sjtu.edu.cn

Abstract. Reversed multiplication friendly embedding (RMFE) amortization has been playing an active role in the state-of-the-art constructions of MPC protocols over rings (in particular, the ring $\mathbb{Z}_{2^k}$). As far as we know, this powerful technique has NOT been able to find applications in the crown jewel of two-party computation, the non-interactive secure computation (NISC), where the requirement of the protocol being non-interactive constitutes a formidable technical bottle-neck. We initiate such a study focusing on statistical NISC protocols in the VOLE-hybrid model. Our study begins with making the *decomposable affine randomized encoding (DARE)* based semi-honest NISC protocol compatible with RMFE techniques, which together with known techniques for forcing a malicious sender Sam to honestly follow DARE already yield a secure amortized protocol, assuming both parties follow RMFE encoding. Achieving statistical security in the full malicious setting is much more challenging, as applying known techniques for enforcing compliance with RMFE incurs interaction. To solve this problem, we put forward a new notion dubbed non-malleable RMFE (NM-RMFE), which is a randomized RMFE such that, once one party deviates from the encoding specification, the randomness injected by the other party will randomize the output, preventing information from being leaked. NM-RMFE simultaneously forces both parties to follow RMFE encoding, offering a desired *non-interactive* solution to amortizing NISC. We believe that NM-RMFE is on its own an important primitive that has applications in secure computation and beyond, interactive and non-interactive alike. With an asymptotically good instantiation of our NM-RMFE, we obtain the first *statistical* reusable NISC protocols in the VOLE-hybrid model with *constant communication overhead* for arithmetic branching programs over $\mathbb{Z}_{2^k}$.

As side contributions, we consider computational security and present two concretely efficient NISC constructions in the random oracle model from conventional RMFEs.

1 Introduction

Non-interactive secure computation (NISC) [20] is referring, in particular, to a two-message secure *two-party computation* (2-PC), where the receiver Rachel publishes a message encrypting her private input x and a sender Sam, at any

---

Yizhou Yao is the first author as well as the main contributor of this paper.

J. Guo and R. Steinfeld (Eds.): ASIACRYPT 2023, LNCS 14438, pp. 38–70, 2023.
https://doi.org/10.1007/978-981-99-8721-4_2

time, can use Rachel's message to complete a secure computation of $f(x, y)$, where y is his private input, by sending a single message to Rachel, which contains no information about y beyond $f(x, y)$. The importance of NISC is vividly illustrated by application scenarios such as profile matching in a dating website or DNA data comparing in an algorithm that tells whether two persons are related. In these application scenarios, both Sam's and Rachel's inputs contain sensitive personal information and are to be kept private, hence a secure 2-PC protocol should be implemented to complete the tasks. However, conventional 2-PC protocols require interaction, which means that Sam and Rachel need to be online at the same time and possibly exchange messages in multiple rounds. The synchronization, for one thing, and intolerance to communication latency, for another, put solutions involving *interactive* 2-PC protocols out of consideration. On the other hand, NISC (especially those allow Rachel's message to be reused by multiple senders, called *reusable NISC*, or rNISC for short) enables "public-key" variants of *secure computation* in the fashion that a public-key encryption scheme enables *secure transmission* of messages among strangers.

Without efficiency concerns, the problem can be solved in a simple two-step approach: one begins with any two-message 2-PC protocol secure against *semi-honest* parties, e.g. Yao's garbled circuit (GC) [27] or fully homomorphic encryption (FHE) [16], and then have both parties include a non-interactive zero-knowledge (NIZK) proof showing that their respective messages are honestly prepared. The caveat of this simple approach is that the statements to be proved involve cryptographic operations on secrets, which is in general inefficient.

NISC from oblivious transfer. In order to build NISC protocols for general functions in the oblivious transfer (OT)-hybrid model, Ishai et. al. [17,20] started with the semi-honest GC protocol. They used a statistical NISC for $\mathbf{NC}^0$ circuits to prove that Sam participates in the GC protocol honestly, avoiding the inefficient non-black-box use of NIZK and only making a black-box use of a pseudo-random generator (PRG). For $\mathbf{NC}^0$ circuits, there is an efficient statistical semi-honest two-message 2-PC in the OT-hybrid model using the so-called *decomposable affine randomized encoding* (DARE) [2,19]. The DARE allows to transform a circuit evaluation into parallel calls to an OT functionality, which in fact leaves no room for a malicious NISC receiver (as OT receiver) to cheat. And the desired statistical NISC for $\mathbf{NC}^0$ circuits can be obtained by applying the so-called *certified* OT [20] mechanism that allows Rachel to verify that Sam's inputs to these parallel OTs are honestly prepared. Though the asymptotic efficiency of the above protocol is rather appealing, it contains several ingredients that could incur large hidden constant in the concrete efficiency estimation. The followup work [1] devised a clever way to squash the interactive cut-and-choose to a single round, and obtained a concretely efficient NISC construction. With more sophisticated manipulations, this cut-and-choose approach was extended to yield amortized NISC protocols that allow to simultaneously evaluate multiple instances of the same circuit in order to reduce the cost [23]. This amortization technique seems to be very task-specific and not likely to be applied elsewhere.

Reusable NISC. An impossibility result concerning statistical *reusable* NISC in the OT-hybrid model was shown in [10], casting such protocols in the setting of parallel calls to a string OT, where Sam provides the input pair and Rachel provides the choice bit. The main observation is that such protocols satisfy that Rachel's message can be separated into bits where each bit is interacting with only a small part of Sam's message. This allows a malicious Sam to apply the so-called *selective failure attack*. For instance, Sam honestly follows the protocol specification, except that, in one call to string OT, he replaces one of the two input strings by a uniform string and is caught cheating only when Rachel selects the tampered string, which occurs with probability $1/2$. The authors of [10] then proposed a countermeasure through replacing OT with *oblivious linear function evaluation* (OLE), and constructed efficient statistical rNISC protocols in the OLE-hybrid model for branching programs over finite fields, which has high-level resemblance to the statistical NISC for $\mathbf{NC}^0$ circuits in [20]. The OLE functionality over a ring $\mathcal{R}$ allows Sam to input $a, b \in \mathcal{R}$ and Rachel to input $\alpha \in \mathcal{R}$, after which the functionality outputs $a \cdot \alpha + b$ to Rachel. Intuitively, replacing OT with OLE has the advantage that, the *selective failure attack* succeeds with probability related to the ring size (e.g. $1/|\mathcal{R}|$, if $\mathcal{R}$ is a finite field), which may be negligible by setting the ring to be sufficiently large. For implementing the rNISC protocols, a two-message reusable OLE protocol under the Paillier assumption was also presented in [10]. Informally, a reusable OLE protocol has the property that it is difficult for Sam to construct a partially correct message: any answer message Sam provides to Rachel is either accepted or rejected except with a negligible probability.

The followup work [13] improved the state-of-the-art of statistical rNISC through a new statistical proof system for circuit satisfiability called line-point zero-knowledge (LPZK) by a single Vector-OLE (VOLE) invocation. Another optimization comes from the implementation aspect through an efficient *pseudorandom correlation generator* (PCG) [5] construction for VOLE (similar to OT extension) based on a variant of learning parity with noise (LPN) [3] assumption. Instantiated with the reusable VOLE construction in [10] and the two-round PCG construction in [6], the resulting VOLE protocol has good concrete efficiency.

A very recent work [18] bypassed the impossibility result of [10], through making a black-box use of a secure two-message OT protocol. The authors of [18] followed the framework of [20], instead of extending the VOLE-hybrid framework, and showed a compiler that constructs an rNISC in the *random oracle model* for any Boolean function f, via a black-box use of any non-reusable NISC protocol that computes a related function f'. The non-reusable NISC protocol for f' was then instantiated with the construction of [20]. The main drawbacks are that their compiler is not statistical and incurs at least quadratic communication overhead in the security parameter[1].

rNISC over integer rings. Focusing on statistical security and concerning recent progress on rNISC for branching programs over fields, it is natural to ask

---

[1] We remark that for some simple function f, e.g. branching programs, it seems that the non-reusable NISC can be instantiated with a lightweight NISC protocol, and the overhead is then optimized to linear in the security parameter.

whether these schemes can be *efficiently* adapted to work over arbitrary rings (in particular, the ring $\mathbb{Z}_{2^k}$, as the models of computation in real-life programming and the computer architectures are formulated as operations over $\mathbb{Z}_{2^{32}}$ or $\mathbb{Z}_{2^{64}}$).

More specifically, we are interested in finding out if it is possible to have a statistical rNISC protocol over the ring $\mathbb{Z}_{2^k}$ that matches the benchmarks of statistical rNISC protocols over large fields.

Given a branching program over a sufficiently large field, the statistical rNISC protocols for branching programs in [10,13] have constant communication overhead, compared to the semi-honest NISC (from DARE). We note that naively taking the above rNISC protocols over a field and replacing the field with a ring $\mathbb{Z}_{2^k}$ will ruin the security, due to the fact that the ring $\mathbb{Z}_{2^k}$ contains too many zero divisors (one half). This results in that the soundness error will keep a constant, no matter how large the ring $\mathbb{Z}_{2^k}$ is.

Similar problems have been under scrutiny in the study of arithmetic circuit MPC protocols throughout the last decade, yielding a plethora of important results. We highlight an extremely successful technique, the *reversed multiplication friendly embedding* (RMFE) [7,12]. Informally, an RMFE includes two maps ϕ, ψ, which allows to efficiently transform computations over a small field $\mathbb{F}_p$ (ring $\mathbb{Z}_{2^k}$) into its extension field $\mathbb{F}_{p^d}$ (extension ring $\mathrm{GR}(2^k, d)^2$) through ϕ, and the results over $\mathbb{F}_p$ can be efficiently recovered from the result of computations over the large field $\mathbb{F}_{p^d}$ (Galois ring $\mathrm{GR}(2^k, d)$) through ψ. Here we remark that the naive embedding (e.g. $\mathbb{F}_p \hookrightarrow \mathbb{F}_{p^d}$) is a special case of RMFE ($\mathbb{F}_p^m \hookrightarrow \mathbb{F}_{p^d}$). On the one hand, the RMFE technique provides amortization benefits (compared to naive embedding). On the other hand, non-trivial efforts should be made to force parties to follow the RMFE encoding honestly. As far as we know, RMFEs have been applied into honest majority MPC [7,9,12], dishonest majority MPC [15], VOLE-based ZK [21], and zk-SNARKs [4,8], etc. However, RMFEs have not been applied in the NISC setting yet.

1.1 Our Contributions

We put forward a new and novel RMFE technique that strengthens RMFEs, called *non-malleable RMFE* (NM-RMFE). We initiate the study of NISC over $\mathbb{Z}_{2^k}$ as well. With our NM-RMFE technique, we give the first asymptotically efficient statistical rNISC/VOLE for arithmetic branching programs over $\mathbb{Z}_{2^k}$. We also explore computational approaches to realize more concretely efficient NISC constructions for arithmetic branching programs over $\mathbb{Z}_{2^k}$ from RMFEs.

(1) The NM-RMFE is essentially a randomized variant of RMFE such that, when used in amortizing a secure 2-PC protocol, the randomness injected by the honest party prevents information about his/her private input from being leaked to the malicious party who cheats by providing an element not in the image of the map ϕ. NM-RMFE offers a conceptually simpler (removing the proofs) and, more importantly, *non-interactive* solution to forcing correct RMFE encoding: Rachel can directly implement a check mechanism in NM-RMFE to

---

^{2} see definition in Sect. 2.

abort a cheating Sam, while simultaneously an honest Sam's input is not leaked to Rachel when Rachel is cheating. We believe that NM-RMFE is of independent interest in amortizing secure computation, interactive and non-interactive alike. We give an NM-RMFE construction (in Sect. 3.2) with the following features.

Theorem (informal). *There exists a family of $(m, d; D)$-NM-RMFE's from $\mathbb{Z}_{2^k}^m$ to $\mathrm{GR}(2^k, d)$, supporting multiplication for $D - 1$ times, with d/m asymptotically close to a constant.*

For instance, we construct a family of $(m, d; 2)$-NM-RMFEs over $\mathbb{Z}_{2^k}$ with $\frac{d}{m} \to 29.13, m \to \infty$ and a family of $(m, d; 3)$-NM-RMFEs over $\mathbb{Z}_{2^k}$ with $\frac{d}{m} \to 80.15, m \to \infty$.

(2) Regarding NISC protocols over $\mathbb{Z}_{2^k}$, we have the following informal theorem (induced by Theorem 4).

Theorem (informal). *There exists a statistical rNISC protocol computing branching programs over $\mathbb{Z}_{2^k}$ with communication overhead close to a constant.*

The above theorem indicates that the amortized efficiency of our construction asymptotically matches the state-of-the-art statistical rNISC protocol over large fields [13]. Though our exposition highlights the most useful special cases of arithmetic circuits over $\mathbb{Z}_{2^k}$, all protocols straightforwardly extend to $\mathbb{F}_{p^k}$ and $\mathbb{Z}_{p^k}$ for arbitrary prime p. Before this work, statistical rNISC over small fields [10,13] had to pay overhead at least linear in the security parameter (which are realized by rNISC over large fields). More importantly, there was no efficient constructions for $\mathbb{Z}_{2^k}$. Our results bridge the gaps left behind by the difference between computation domains in an amortized sense (asymptotic nature).

(3) As side contributions, we present a maliciously secure rNISC construction for computing branching programs over $\mathbb{Z}_{2^k}$ from a random oracle aided cut-and-choose, through making a black-box use of any two-message reusable VOLE protocol over $\mathrm{GR}(2^k, d)$ (inspired by the approach of [18]). We also present a highly efficient maliciously secure NISC construction for computing branching programs over $\mathbb{Z}_{2^k}$ in the OT-hybrid model.

1.2 Technical Overview

The challenge for constructing NM-RMFE lies in the fact that the notion itself demands the coexistence of two conflicting properties: multiplication friendliness (malleability for valid multiplicands) and non-malleability (against one invalid multiplicand). There was no cryptographic primitive of this flavor in the literature, as far as we know. One must turn to known constructions for each property separately for inspirations and hope that they can be combined. The RMFE concatenation technique plays an important role in constructing binary RMFE by concatenating two RMFE's. On the other hand, the Fujisaki-Okamoto (FO) transform (widely used in e.g. post-quantum cryptography NIST submissions) uses two encryption schemes, one encrypting the payload while the other one encrypting the random key of the first to enable a consistency check via checking whether the ciphertext of the second encryption scheme is valid. We import the core idea of the FO transformation into RMFE concatenation by injecting randomness into the first RMFE and use the its encoding relation for FO style "cipher text" check.

For rNISC/VOLE constructions, we begin with recalling the construction of rNISC/VOLE for branching programs in [13]. The semi-honest protocol is an execution of t parallel VOLE's over a large enough Galois field $\mathbb{F}$, where t is the number of components in Rachel's input $x \in \mathbb{F}^t$. Rachel's inputs to the VOLE's are simply the t components of x. Sam's inputs to the VOLE's are generated using a *decomposable affine randomized encoding (DARE)* scheme that, given y, the branching program $f(\cdot, \cdot)$ and Sam's private randomness, produces t pairs of vectors (each pair of such vectors define an *affine line*, hence the name DARE). Note that the semi-honest protocol already leaves a malicious Rachel no room to cheat. The malicious protocol only needs to make sure that Sam's t input lines to the VOLE's in the semi-honest protocol are indeed the result of running the DARE scheme using $f(\cdot, \cdot)$, some secret y and some secret randomness. If one adds a new VOLE to the semi-honest protocol and let Sam describe the DARE scheme specification as an arithmetic circuit C to invoke the LPZK proof system using his t input lines as witness, then the only room for Sam to cheat in this intermediate protocol is to fake the consistency of the t lines and LPZK witness encoded in the new VOLE instance. The above consistency check problem boils down to a mechanism called *VOLE with equality constraint (eVOLE)* that allows Sam to prove equivalence of an arbitrary component in the two vectors defining one line and some component in the two vectors defining the other line. To complete the malicious rNISC/VOLE protocol, one more instance of VOLE is then added where Rachel's input is a uniform point $\beta \in \mathbb{F}$ (input randomizer for eVOLE construction), and eVOLE is invoked to prove consistency of Sam's input lines between this copy of VOLE (serving as a bridge) and all other copies of VOLE's.

We are now in good position to describe our constructions for rNISC/VOLE over $\mathbb{Z}_{2^k}$. Our exposition begins with an observation that the Galois ring $\mathrm{GR}(2^k, d)$ behaves very similarly to the Galois field $\mathbb{F}_{2^d}$ with respect to constructing building blocks LPZK and eVOLE in the recalled malicious protocol. This suggests that we could view the inputs of Sam and Rachel as consisting of elements in $\mathrm{GR}(2^k, d)$ and try to design a rNISC/VOLE over $\mathrm{GR}(2^k, d)$. But this idea alone does not give us the desired efficiency, as the choice of the extension degree d depends on the security parameter (we need 2^d to be roughly the size of $\mathbb{F}$ in the recalled protocol). To circumvent this caveat, we embed multiple elements of $\mathbb{Z}_{2^k}$ into a single element of $\mathrm{GR}(2^k, d)$ and make sure that computation (in particular, multiplication) is still "preserved" under this embedding. If we could make the RMFE techniques work with the recalled rNISC/VOLE framework, the cost of operating over a large ring $\mathrm{GR}(2^k, d)$ will be amortized by executing $\Omega(d)$ copies of computation over $\mathbb{Z}_{2^k}$ and we are done.

The first challenge comes from the DARE scheme in the semi-honest protocol. Unlike the conventional masking approach to privacy (adding a one-time-pad to the sensitive value before computing on it and remove the pad afterwards), the DARE scheme hides information through multiplying the sensitive matrix by two random structured matrices from the left and the right, respectively (effectively hiding the sensitive matrix among the set of such matrices that have the same determinant, hence destroying other information about the matrix than its determinant). This subtle difference already causes big troubles in the semi-honest model when naively compiling the DARE scheme with RMFE. Recall that an RMFE over $\mathbb{Z}_{2^k}$ includes two $\mathbb{Z}_{2^k}$-linear maps, the embedding map ϕ and the decoding map ψ. Note that ϕ is not surjective (being an embedding) and the embedding only preserves multiplication for $\mathrm{GR}(2^k, d)$ elements that lie in the image of ϕ. Therefore, one needs to carefully analyze the effect of this fact on the correctness and privacy of the DARE scheme. If we were to sample entries of the structured random matrices over the entire $\mathrm{GR}(2^k, d)$, we could encounter multiplication by a $\mathrm{GR}(2^k, d)$ element that does not lie in the image of ϕ, which would damage the correctness of the DARE scheme. From now on, assume we sample entries of the structured random matrices over the image of ϕ only. The DARE scheme involves computing matrix multiplication for two times (for correctness we can use Degree-3 RMFEs [14]). We next analyze whether the privacy of the DARE scheme is affected by RMFE. We remark that the product of two elements in the image of ϕ may no longer remain in the image of ϕ, which may reveal more information than we expect. We solve this by masking with a random element in the kernel of ψ.

The second challenge comes from making malicious Sam follow the RMFE encoding in our semi-honest protocol and making malicious Rachel correctly encode her input using RMFE, simultaneously. Jumping ahead, note that once the correct RMFE encoding is guaranteed, the rest of the security proof against a malicious adversary follows straightforwardly using analogy to the recalled protocol over fields (we include a self-contained exposition of the building blocks LPZK and eVOLE over $\mathrm{GR}(2^k, d)$ in Sect. 4.2 for completeness). This second challenge is a huge bottle-neck because none of the known RMFE techniques come close to suggesting a workable idea. The standard RMFE techniques for constructing interactive secure computation protocols do have a (V)OLE-based variant [21], where elements in $\mathrm{GR}(2^k, d)$ are restricted in image of ϕ (see the exposition in Sect. 5.1, where we do use it in our two side contributions). The difficulties lie in removing the interaction that is liberally in use and seemingly inherent. For one thing, sacrifice is used to generate correlated randomness that enables the re-embedding VOLE functionality. This can be made non-interactive at the cost of using a random oracle, hence settling for computational security. More seriously, the above process of correlated randomness generation is only capable of allowing one party (VOLE sender) to prove correct RMFE encoding to the other party (VOLE receiver). This means that we would not be able to prove correct RMFE encoding for Sam and Rachel simultaneously without interaction. We put forward the notion of NM-RMFE and propose a statistical instantiation of NM-RMFE that solves this bottle-neck problem. In a high level, strengthening RMFE to NM-RMFE allows for "extraction" in the simulation, which means that the simulation will go through no matter how the adversary deviates from the NM-RMFE encoding. Combining all pieces together, we obtain a statistical rNISC/VOLE for computing branching programs over $\mathbb{Z}_{2^k}$ with asymptotic efficiency as the rNISC/VOLE over large fields.

Computational NISC. Finally, we explore standard computationally secure techniques for forcing both parties to follow the RMFE encoding honestly. For the malicious sender side, we augment the above Galois ring analogue *certified* VOLE by substituting the VOLE-hybrid model with the re-embedding VOLE-hybrid model following the idea of [21]. For the malicious receiver side, we define a variant of VOLE over $\text{GR}(2^k, d)$, where the receiver's inputs are restricted in the image of ϕ, and provide two instantiations. The former instantiation (inspired by [18]) uses the random oracle to realize a non-interactive cut-and-choose such that Rachel "proves" to Sam her input is in the image of ϕ. The latter construction comes from an observation that for a correlated OT-based VOLE construction, since the image of ϕ is actually a linear space over $\mathbb{Z}_{2^k}$, the bits that Rachel sends to correlated OTs one-to-one correspond to an element in the image of ϕ as long as the number of correlated OTs is restricted to the size of the image of ϕ.

2 Preliminaries

Notations. In this paper, bold letters (e.g. $\boldsymbol{a}, \boldsymbol{b}$) are used to denote vectors. We use x_i to denote the i_{th}-component of the vector $\boldsymbol{x}$ (similarly $x_{i,j}$ for the j_{th}-component of $\boldsymbol{x}_i$). We use $[a, b]$ (or $[a, b + 1]$ sometimes) to denote the set of integers in the range from a to b. If $a = 1$, it is simplified by $[b]$. We also use $\boldsymbol{x}|_J$ to denote the set $\{x_i \mid i \in J\}$. We use $x \xleftarrow{\$} \mathcal{R}$ to denote that x is uniformly sampled from a ring $\mathcal{R}$ and denote the uniform distribution over $\mathcal{R}$ by $U_\mathcal{R}$. For a map $\phi : \mathcal{R}_1 \to \mathcal{R}_2$, we naturally extend it to be defined over vector space $\mathcal{R}_1^n$ and matrix space $\mathcal{R}_1^{m \times n}$. Let $\text{Im}(\phi)$ denote the set $\{\phi(x) \mid x \in \mathcal{R}_1\}$ and $\text{Ker}(\phi)$ denote the set $\{x \in \mathcal{R}_1 \mid \phi(x) = 0\}$. For a commitment scheme, we use the notation $[\![\alpha]\!]$ to denote the commitment of α. For two distributions $\mathcal{D}_1, \mathcal{D}_2$, we use the notation $\mathcal{D}_1 \overset{s}{\approx} \mathcal{D}_2$ to denote that they are statistically close.

Galois Rings. Let p be a prime, and $k, d \geq 1$ be integers. Let $f(X) \in \mathbb{Z}_{p^k}[X]$ be a monic polynomial of degree d such that $\overline{f(X)} := f(X) \bmod p$ is irreducible over $\mathbb{F}_p$. A Galois ring over $\mathbb{Z}_{p^k}$ of degree d denoted by $\text{GR}(p^k, d)$ is a ring extension $\mathbb{Z}_{p^k}[X]/(f(X))$ of $\mathbb{Z}_{p^k}$. We refer to the textbook [26] for a friendly exposition. Same as the special case of Galois fields, there is a bound on the number of roots for a nonzero polynomial over $\text{GR}(p^k, d)$.

Lemma 1 ([26]). *A nonzero degree-r polynomial over $\text{GR}(p^k, d)$ has at most $rp^{(k-1)d}$ roots.*

Lemma 1 immediately gives that for any nonzero degree-r polynomial $f(x)$ over $\text{GR}(p^k, d)$, we have that

$$\Pr\left[f(\alpha) = 0 \ \middle|\ \alpha \xleftarrow{\$} \text{GR}(p^k, d) \right] \leq rp^{-d}.$$

In particular, we have that $1/p^d$ fraction of elements are zero divisors in $\text{GR}(p^k, d)$.

Degree-D RMFE. The reverse Multiplicative Friendly Embedding (RMFE for short) was first introduced in [7], which packs multiple multiplications over a field $\mathbb{F}_q$ to one multiplication over its extension $\mathbb{F}_{q^d}$. It was further shown in [12] that RMFEs over Galois fields ($\mathbb{F}_{p^r}^m \to \mathbb{F}_{p^{rd}}$) induce RMFEs over Galois rings $(\mathtt{GR}(p^k, r)^m \to \mathtt{GR}(p^k, rd))$. Degree-$D$ RMFE [14] is a natural generalization of RMFE, which supports multiplication for upto $D - 1$ times.

Definition 1. *Let p be a prime, $k, r, m, d, D \geq 1$ be integers. A pair (ϕ, ψ) is called an $(m, d; D)$-RMFE over $\mathtt{GR}(p^k, r)$, if $\phi : \mathtt{GR}(p^k, r)^m \to \mathtt{GR}(p^k, rd)$ and $\psi : \mathtt{GR}(p^k, rd) \to \mathtt{GR}(p^k, r)^m$ are two $\mathtt{GR}(p^k, r)$-linear maps such that*

$$\psi(\phi(\boldsymbol{x}_1) \cdot \phi(\boldsymbol{x}_2) \cdots \phi(\boldsymbol{x}_D)) = \boldsymbol{x}_1 * \boldsymbol{x}_2 * \cdots * \boldsymbol{x}_D$$

for all $\boldsymbol{x}_1, \boldsymbol{x}_2, ..., \boldsymbol{x}_D \in \mathtt{GR}(p^k, r)^m$, where $*$ denotes the entry-wise multiplication.

Standard RMFEs are essentially degree-2 RMFEs. Degree-D RMFEs have the following properties, which are generalized from the degree-2 case.

Lemma 2 ([21]). *Let (ϕ, ψ) be an $(m, d; D)$-RMFE over Galois ring $\mathtt{GR}(p^k, r)$. We have that $\mathtt{GR}(p^k, rd)$ is the direct sum of $\mathrm{Ker}(\psi), \phi(\boldsymbol{1})^{D-1} \cdot \mathrm{Im}(\phi)$, where $\boldsymbol{1}$ denotes the vector of all 1's. That is $\mathtt{GR}(p^k, rd) = \mathrm{Ker}(\psi) \oplus (\phi(\boldsymbol{1})^{D-1} \cdot \mathrm{Im}(\phi))$.*

As shown in [14], there always exists an $(m, d; D)$-RMFE over Galois ring $\mathtt{GR}(p^k, r)$ with $\phi(\boldsymbol{1}) = 1$. Thus, we always assume $\phi(\boldsymbol{1}) = 1$ for the rest of this paper. Then, the above lemma indicates that ψ introduces a bijection when restricted on $\mathrm{Im}(\phi)$. We have the following lemma that indicates the asymptotic behavior of degree-D RMFEs.

Lemma 3 ([14]). *There exists a family of $(m, d; D)$-RMFE over $\mathbb{Z}_{2^k}$ for all $k \geq 1$ with $m \to \infty$ and $\frac{d}{m} \to \frac{1+2D}{3}(D + \frac{D(3+1/(2^D-1))}{2^{D+1}-1})$.*

For instance, when $m \to \infty$, there exists a family of $(m, d; 2)$-RMFEs over $\mathbb{Z}_{2^k}$ with $\frac{d}{m} \to 4.92$ and a family of $(m, d; 3)$-RMFEs over $\mathbb{Z}_{2^k}$ with $\frac{d}{m} \to 8.47$.

VOLE. The (random) vector oblivious linear function evaluation (VOLE) is a two-party primitive that allows two parties P_S, P_R to obtain random correlated values. In more detail, the sender P_S obtains two random vectors $\boldsymbol{a}, \boldsymbol{b}$, while the receiver P_R obtains a random scalar α and a random vector $\boldsymbol{v}$ such that $\boldsymbol{v} = \boldsymbol{a} \cdot \alpha + \boldsymbol{b}$ holds. We formalize the ideal VOLE functionality over arbitrary ring $\mathcal{R}$ in Fig. 1. We also use the chosen-input variant of VOLE in this paper, where $(\boldsymbol{a}, \boldsymbol{b}), \alpha$ are provided by the sender and the receiver, respectively. The above VOLE correlation can be viewed as a linear homomorphic Message Authentication Code (MAC) that authenticates $\boldsymbol{a}$ using the MAC key α, denoted by $[\boldsymbol{a}]_\alpha$.

Non-Interactive Secure Computation. We follow the VOLE-based reusable Non-interactive Secure Computation (rNISC) definition in [13]. In a high level, the sender P_S encodes its input as multiple lines (P_S's VOLE inputs) and the receiver P_R encodes its input as multiple points (P_R's VOLE inputs), one for each line. In reusable security, a malicious sender $\mathcal{A}$ can learn whether the receiver rejects its possibly illegal messages after each execution. We give the formal definition of rNISC as follows.

Functionality $\mathcal{F}^{\mathcal{R}}_{\text{VOLE}}$

Parameterized by a ring $\mathcal{R}$, length parameters $l_1, ..., l_n \in \mathbb{N}$.

Setup phase: Upon receiving $(sid; \texttt{initialize})$ from P_S and $P_{\mathcal{R}}$, sample $\alpha \xleftarrow{\$} \mathcal{R}$ and store $(sid; \alpha)$, and ignore any further inputs from P_S and $P_{\mathcal{R}}$ with the same session identifier sid. Send α to $P_{\mathcal{R}}$.

Send phases: Upon receiving $(sid; \texttt{send}; l_i)$ from P_S and $P_{\mathcal{R}}$, verify that there are stored values $(sid; \alpha)$; else, ignore that message. Sample $\boldsymbol{a}, \boldsymbol{b} \xleftarrow{\$} \mathcal{R}^{l_i}$, and store $(sid; \boldsymbol{a}, \boldsymbol{b}; l_i)$, and ignore any further inputs from P_S and $P_{\mathcal{R}}$ with the same session identifier sid. Send $(\boldsymbol{a}, \boldsymbol{b})$ to P_S and $\boldsymbol{v} := \boldsymbol{a} \cdot \alpha + \boldsymbol{b}$ to $P_{\mathcal{R}}$.

Fig. 1. Ideal functionality for random VOLE over $\mathcal{R}$.

Definition 2 (rNISC). *An VOLE-based reusable non-interactive secure computation (NISC) protocol for an arithmetic function $f : \mathcal{R}^{n_1} \times \mathcal{R}^{n_2} \to \mathcal{R}^t$ consists of a triple of algorithms $(R1, S, R2)$ defined as follows:*

- *$R1(\mathcal{R}, \boldsymbol{x})$ is a PPT algorithm that, given an input $\boldsymbol{x} \in \mathcal{R}^{n_1}$, outputs points $(\alpha_1, ..., \alpha_{n'}) \in \mathcal{R}^{n'}$ and auxiliary information $\texttt{aux}$.*
- *$S(\mathcal{R}, \boldsymbol{y})$ is a PPT algorithm that, given an input $\boldsymbol{y} \in \mathcal{R}^{n_2}$, outputs n' pairs of vectors $\boldsymbol{a}_i, \boldsymbol{b}_i \in \mathcal{R}^{l_i}$, each specifying an affine line $\boldsymbol{v}_i(\alpha) := \boldsymbol{a}_i \cdot \alpha + \boldsymbol{b}_i$.*
- *$R2(\mathcal{R}, (\boldsymbol{v}_1, ..., \boldsymbol{v}_{n'}), \texttt{aux})$ is a polynomial-time algorithm, such that given n' evaluations $\boldsymbol{v}_i \in \mathcal{R}^{l_i}$ and auxiliary information $\texttt{aux}$, outputs either $\boldsymbol{z} \in \mathcal{R}^t$ or $\perp$.*

We say the algorithms $(R1, S, R2)$ has reusable malicious security, if the following security requirements hold:

- ***Completeness.*** *As long as $R2$ takes inputs $\boldsymbol{v}_i = \boldsymbol{v}_i(\alpha_i)$, for $i \in [n']$, where $\boldsymbol{v}_i(\alpha)$ and α_i are given by S and $R1$, respectively, we have that $R2$ outputs $\boldsymbol{z} = f(\boldsymbol{x}, \boldsymbol{y})$.*
- ***Reusable ε-security against malicious sender.*** *There exists a polynomial-time extractor Ext such that given n' lines $\boldsymbol{v}_i^*(t) := \boldsymbol{a}_i^* \cdot \alpha + \boldsymbol{b}_i^*$ with vectors $\boldsymbol{a}_i^*, \boldsymbol{b}_i^* \in \mathcal{R}^{l_i}$, outputs $\boldsymbol{y}^* \in \mathcal{R}^{n_2}$ or $\perp$ with the following holds: for every honest receiver's input $\boldsymbol{x} \in \mathcal{R}^{n_1}$, the receiver's output $\boldsymbol{z} := R2(\mathcal{R}, (\boldsymbol{v}_1^*, ..., \boldsymbol{v}_{n'}^*), \texttt{aux})$ is equal to $f(\boldsymbol{x}, \boldsymbol{y}^*)$ except with $\leq \varepsilon$ probability over the receiver's randomness. The random-input variant of the above definition is also used in this paper, where the probability is over both the receiver's randomness and an $\boldsymbol{x}$ sampled from $\mathcal{R}^{n_1}$ uniformly at random.*
- ***Statistical security against malicious receiver.*** *There exist a polynomial-time extractor algorithm Ext and PPT simulator algorithm Sim such that, given points $\alpha_1^*, ..., \alpha_{n'}^* \in \mathcal{R}$, Ext outputs effective $\boldsymbol{x}^* \in \mathcal{R}^{n_1}$ with the following holds: for every honest sender's input $\boldsymbol{y} \in \mathcal{R}^{n_2}$, the output distribution of $\mathsf{Sim}(\mathcal{R}, f(\boldsymbol{x}^*, \boldsymbol{y}))$ is statistically close to $\{(\boldsymbol{v}_1(\alpha_1^*), ..., \boldsymbol{v}_{n'}(\alpha_{n'}^*)) \mid (\boldsymbol{v}_1(\alpha), ..., \boldsymbol{v}_{n'}(\alpha)) \leftarrow S(\mathcal{R}, \boldsymbol{y})\}$.*

Branching Program. In this paper, we mainly consider arithmetic functions that can be represented by branching programs [19].

Definition 3 (Branching Program over $\mathcal{R}$). *A branching program (BP) over $\mathcal{R}$ is defined by a quadruple* $BP = (G, \varphi, v, t)$, *where* $G = (V, E)$ *is a directed acyclic graph, φ is an edge labeling function assigning each edge a degree-1 polynomial in a single input variable x_i, and v, t are two special vertices. The size of BP is the number of vertices in G. Each input assignment $\boldsymbol{x} = (x_1, ..., x_n) \in \mathcal{R}^n$ induces an assignment $G_{\boldsymbol{x}}$ of a value from $\mathcal{R}$ to each $e \in E$. The output $BP(\boldsymbol{x})$ is defined as the sum of the weights of all directed paths from v to t in $G_{\boldsymbol{x}}$, where the weight of a path is the product of the values of its edges.*

Let $BP = (G, \varphi, v, t)$ be a BP of size $s + 1$ over $\mathcal{R}$, computing a function $f : \mathcal{R}^n \to \mathcal{R}$. Fix some topological ordering of the vertices of G, where the source vertex v is labeled 1 and the terminal vertex t is labeled $s + 1$. For any input $\boldsymbol{x}$, let $A_{\boldsymbol{x}}$ be the $(s+1) \times (s+1)$ matrix over $\mathcal{R}$ whose (i, j) entry contains the value assigned by φ to the edge (i, j) (or 0 if there is no such edge). Define $L(\boldsymbol{x})$ as the submatrix of $A_{\boldsymbol{x}} - I$ obtained by deleting column v and row t (i.e. the first column and the last row). Note that each entry of $L(\boldsymbol{x})$ has degree (at most) 1 in the inputs $\boldsymbol{x}$; moreover, $L(\boldsymbol{x})$ contains the constant -1 in each entry of its second diagonal (the one below the main diagonal) and the constant 0 below this diagonal. We have the fact that $f(\boldsymbol{x}) = det(L(\boldsymbol{x}))$, and we say $L(\boldsymbol{x})$ is induced by a BP that computes f.

We briefly introduce the so-called "Decomposable Affine Randomized Encoding" (DARE) for branching programs [2,19]. We begin by a simple randomization lemma.

Lemma 4 ([19]). *Let $\mathcal{H}$ be a set of square matrices over $\mathcal{R}$, and $\mathcal{G}_1, \mathcal{G}_2$ be multiplicative groups of matrices of the same dimension as $\mathcal{H}$. Denote by '$\sim$' the equivalence relation on $\mathcal{H}$ defined by: $H \sim H'$ iff there exists $G_1 \in \mathcal{G}_1, G_2 \in \mathcal{G}_2$ such that $H = G_1 H' G_2$. Let R_1, R_2 be uniformly and independently distributed matrices from $\mathcal{G}_1, \mathcal{G}_2$, respectively. Then, for any H, H' such that $H \sim H'$, the random variables $R_1 H R_2$ and $R_1 H' R_2$ are identically distributed.*

The above lemma can be instantiated with the following matrix sets:

- $\mathcal{H}^s$ consists of all $s \times s$ matrices over $\mathbb{Z}_{2^k}$ with -1's in the second diagonal (the diagonal below the main diagonal), and 0's below the second diagonal.
- $\mathcal{G}_1^s$ consists of all $s \times s$ matrices over $\mathbb{Z}_{2^k}$ with 1's on the main diagonal and 0's below the main diagonal.
- $\mathcal{G}_2^s$ consists of all $s \times s$ matrices over $\mathbb{Z}_{2^k}$ with 1's on the main diagonal and 0's in all of the remaining entries except those of the rightmost column.

Let $L(\boldsymbol{x})$ be a matrix induced by a size $(s + 1)$ BP over $\mathbb{Z}_{2^k}$ computing $f : \mathbb{Z}_{2^k}^n \to \mathbb{Z}_{2^k}$. We have the following corollary.

Corollary 1. *Let R_1, R_2 be uniformly and independently distributed matrices from $\mathcal{G}_1^s, \mathcal{G}_2^s$, respectively. We have that $R_1 L(\boldsymbol{x}) R_2$ reveals nothing about $L(\boldsymbol{x})$ but $det(L(\boldsymbol{x}))$.*

Essentially, $R_1 L(\boldsymbol{x}) R_2$ in Corollary 1 is a randomized encoding of $L(\boldsymbol{x})$, and the above procedure is referred as DARE.

3   Non-Malleable RMFE

Before we show how to construct NISC/VOLE over $\mathbb{Z}_{2^k}$, we first introduce our main innovation separately, as we believe it is of independent interest. We start with introducing the conception of NM-RMFE, followed by a construction.

3.1   Non-Malleable RMFE

To better illustrate the benefits of upgrading RMFEs to NM-RMFEs, let us first consider a simple NISC/VOLE task as a warm-up, where P_S has inputs $\boldsymbol{a}_i, \boldsymbol{b}_i \in \mathbb{Z}_{2^k}^l$, $P_{\mathcal{R}}$ has inputs α_i, and $P_{\mathcal{R}}$ wants to obtain $\boldsymbol{v}_i := \boldsymbol{a}_i \cdot \alpha_i + \boldsymbol{b}_i$, for $i \in [m]$, i.e. the task for parallel VOLE over $\mathbb{Z}_{2^k}$. This can be done with the help of an $(m, d; 2)$-RMFE (ϕ, ψ) over $\mathbb{Z}_{2^k}$ and a VOLE functionality $\mathcal{F}_{\text{VOLE}}^{\text{GR}(2^k,d)}$. We show what would go wrong if RMFE encodings are not honestly computed through this example.

In more detail, P_S picks $\boldsymbol{r} \xleftarrow{\$} \text{Ker}(\psi)^l$ and sends $\phi(\boldsymbol{a}_1, ..., \boldsymbol{a}_m)$, $\phi(\boldsymbol{b}_1, ..., \boldsymbol{b}_m) + \boldsymbol{r}$ to $\mathcal{F}_{\text{VOLE}}^{\text{GR}(2^k,d)}$, while $P_{\mathcal{R}}$ sends $\phi(\alpha_1, ..., \alpha_m)$. Finally, $P_{\mathcal{R}}$ receives $\boldsymbol{v}$ from $\mathcal{F}_{\text{VOLE}}^{\text{GR}(2^k,d)}$, and outputs $(\boldsymbol{v}_1, ..., \boldsymbol{v}_m) := \psi(\boldsymbol{v})$. We remark that the mask $\boldsymbol{r}$ is necessary and sufficient for the privacy of P_S's private inputs. In fact, we only want $P_{\mathcal{R}}$ to obtain $\psi(\boldsymbol{v})$, but $P_{\mathcal{R}}$ actually receives $\boldsymbol{v}$. The potential leakage then is prevented by masking with $\boldsymbol{r}$, by Lemma 2.

The above protocol achieves semi-honest security, but not malicious security. The main obstacle is that, for example, if a malicious receiver takes an input $Y \notin \text{Im}(\phi)$, the simulator cannot "extract" a $\boldsymbol{y}'$ from Y (the simulation will go through in the semi-honest model, by setting $\boldsymbol{y}' := \psi(Y)$). Existing works [9, 15, 21] have developed methods to solve this issue, by letting the adversary to prove that $Y \in \text{Im}(\phi)$. However, these approaches are either not statistical or interactive. Instead, we solve the issue statistically by putting forward the notion of Non-Malleable RMFE, which conceptually allows $Y \notin \text{Im}(\phi)$. For the sake of generality, we define Degree-D Non-Malleable RMFE as follows:

Definition 4 (Degree-D NM-RMFE). *Let* $\text{GR}(p^k, r)$ *be a Galois ring and* κ *be the statistical security parameter. A pair of maps* (ϕ, ψ) *is called an* $(m, d; D)$-*NM-RMFE over* $\text{GR}(p^k, r)$, *if it has the following properties:*

1. $\phi : \text{GR}(p^k, r)^m \times \{0, 1\}^{\mathcal{O}(\kappa)} \to \text{GR}(p^k, rd)$, $\psi : \text{GR}(p^k, rd) \to \text{GR}(p^k, r)^m \cup \{\bot\}$ *are* $\text{GR}(p^k, r)$-*linear maps*[3]*, satisfying*

$$\psi(\phi(\boldsymbol{x}_1, r_1) \cdot \phi(\boldsymbol{x}_2, r_2) \cdots \phi(\boldsymbol{x}_D, r_D)) = \boldsymbol{x}_1 * \boldsymbol{x}_2 * \cdots * \boldsymbol{x}_D,$$

   for any $\boldsymbol{x}_1, ..., \boldsymbol{x}_D \in \text{GR}(p^k, r)^m$ *and* $r_1, ..., r_D \xleftarrow{\$} \{0, 1\}^{\kappa}$.

---

[3] More precisely, ϕ is $\text{GR}(p^k, r)$-linear on $\text{GR}(p^k, r)^m$.

2. *if $Y \notin \text{Im}(\phi)$, there exists a constant $\boldsymbol{y} \in \text{GR}(p^k, r)^m$, such that for any* $\boldsymbol{x}_1, ..., \boldsymbol{x}_{D-1} \in \text{GR}(p^k, r)^m$, *we have*

$$\psi(\phi(\boldsymbol{x}_1) \cdots \phi(\boldsymbol{x}_{D-1}) \cdot Y) = \boldsymbol{x}_1 * \cdots * \boldsymbol{x}_{D-1} * \boldsymbol{y} + \boldsymbol{\delta},$$

where $\boldsymbol{\delta} \sim \mathcal{D}_{\boldsymbol{x},Y} \overset{s}{\approx} \mathcal{D}_Y$ and $\mathcal{D}_Y$ is a PPT-sampleable distribution over $\text{GR}(p^k, r)^m \cup \{\bot\}$ determined only by Y. We use the convention that for any $\boldsymbol{z} \in \text{GR}(p^k, r)^m$, $\boldsymbol{z} + \bot = \bot$ to make ψ well-defined.

Note that the above definition includes Degree-D NM-RMFE over Galois fields, as $\text{GR}(p^k, r)$ is a field when $k = 1$. According to property 1, we can specify the distribution $\mathcal{D}_Y$ for $Y \in \text{Im}(\phi)$, such that $\boldsymbol{\delta} \leftarrow^s \mathcal{D}_Y$, $\Pr[\boldsymbol{\delta} = \boldsymbol{0}] = 1$. We remark that in a high level, NM-RMFE allows for "extraction". Using an $(m, d; 2)$-NM-RMFE (ϕ, ψ) over $\mathbb{Z}_{2^k}$ instead of $(m, d; 2)$-RMFEs over $\mathbb{Z}_{2^k}$, we immediately obtain a reusable malicious secure VOLE scheme over $\mathbb{Z}_{2^k}$ in the $\mathcal{F}_{\text{VOLE}}^{\text{GR}(2^k,d)}$-hybrid model without any additional cryptographic primitives (see Fig. 2). We have the following theorem.

Protocol $\Pi_{\text{VOLE}}^{\mathbb{Z}_{2^k}}$

Parameterized by $\text{GR}(2^k, d)$, length l. Suppose $P_{\mathcal{R}}$ has her private inputs $\boldsymbol{\alpha} \in \mathbb{Z}_{2^k}^m$, P_S has his private inputs $\boldsymbol{a}_i, \boldsymbol{b}_i \in \mathbb{Z}_{2^k}^l$, for $i \in [m]$. Let (ϕ, ψ) be an $(m, d; 2)$-NM-RMFE over $\mathbb{Z}_{2^k}$.

1. The receiver $P_{\mathcal{R}}$: Compute $\Delta := \phi(\boldsymbol{\alpha})$. Send Δ to $\mathcal{F}_{\text{VOLE}}^{\text{GR}(2^k,d)}$.
2. The sender P_S: Compute $A := \phi(\boldsymbol{a}_1, ..., \boldsymbol{a}_m)$ and $B := \phi(\boldsymbol{b}_1, ..., \boldsymbol{b}_m)$. Sample $C \overset{\$}{\leftarrow} \text{Ker}(\psi)^l$. Send $A, B + C$ to $\mathcal{F}_{\text{VOLE}}^{\text{GR}(2^k,d)}$.
3. The receiver $P_{\mathcal{R}}$: Upon receiving Z from $\mathcal{F}_{\text{VOLE}}^{\text{GR}(2^k,d)}$. Compute $(\boldsymbol{z}_1, ..., \boldsymbol{z}_m) := \psi(Z)$. Output $\boldsymbol{z}_1, ..., \boldsymbol{z}_l$.

Fig. 2. A reusable malicious secure VOLE construction over $\mathbb{Z}_{2^k}$ in the $\mathcal{F}_{\text{VOLE}}^{\text{GR}(2^k,d)}$-hybrid model

Theorem 1. *The protocol $\Pi_{\text{VOLE}}^{\mathbb{Z}_{2^k}}$ realizes $\mathcal{F}_{\text{VOLE}}^{\mathbb{Z}_{2^k}}$ with reusable malicious security in the $\mathcal{F}_{\text{VOLE}}^{\text{GR}(2^k,d)}$-hybrid model.*

Proof. We first consider the situation that P_S is corrupted and then turn to the situation that $P_{\mathcal{R}}$ is corrupted. Messages with a hat are from the simulator and messages with a prime are from the adversary.

If P_S is corrupted. When the simulator Sim_S extracts the messages $A', B' + C'$ sent to the ideal functionality $\mathcal{F}_{\text{VOLE}}^{\text{GR}(2^k,d)}$ by the adversary $\mathcal{A}$, he computes $\hat{\boldsymbol{a}}_1, ..., \hat{\boldsymbol{a}}_m \in \mathbb{Z}_{2^k}^l$ such that for any $\boldsymbol{\alpha} \in \mathbb{Z}_{2^k}^m$, $\psi(A' \cdot \phi(\boldsymbol{\alpha})) = (\hat{\boldsymbol{a}}_1 \cdot \alpha_1, ..., \hat{\boldsymbol{a}}_m \cdot \alpha_m) + \boldsymbol{\delta}$, where the i-th row of $\boldsymbol{\delta}$ satisfies the distribution $\mathcal{D}_{A'_i}^{\text{T}}$, and picks $(\hat{\boldsymbol{b}}_1, ..., \hat{\boldsymbol{b}}_m) \leftarrow$

$\psi(\boldsymbol{B}'+\boldsymbol{C}')+\mathcal{D}_{\boldsymbol{A}'}{}^4$. $S_\mathcal{S}$ sends $\hat{\boldsymbol{a}}_i$, $\hat{\boldsymbol{b}}_i$ for $i \in [m]$ to the ideal functionality $\mathcal{F}^{\mathbb{Z}_{2^k}}_{\text{VOLE}}$. The indistinguishability comes from that $\psi(\boldsymbol{A}' \cdot \Delta + \boldsymbol{B}' + \boldsymbol{C}')$ in the real world and $(\hat{\boldsymbol{a}}_1 \cdot \alpha_1 + \hat{\boldsymbol{b}}_1, ..., \hat{\boldsymbol{a}}_m \cdot \alpha_1 + \hat{\boldsymbol{b}}_m)$ in the ideal world are statistically-close by the definition of $(m, d; 2)$-NM-RMFE.

If $P_\mathcal{R}$ is corrupted. When $Sim_\mathcal{R}$ extracts the message Δ' sent to the ideal functionality $\mathcal{F}^{\text{GR}(2^k,d)}_{\text{VOLE}}$ by the adversary $\mathcal{A}$, he computes a $\hat{\alpha}$ such that for any $\boldsymbol{a}_1, ..., \boldsymbol{a}_m \in \mathbb{Z}^l_{2^k}$, $\psi(\phi(\boldsymbol{a}_1, ..., \boldsymbol{a}_m) \cdot \Delta') = (\boldsymbol{a}_1 \cdot \hat{\alpha}_1, ..., \boldsymbol{a}_m \cdot \hat{\alpha}_m) + \boldsymbol{\delta}$, where $\boldsymbol{\delta}$ satisfies the distribution $(\mathcal{D}^{\text{T}}_{\Delta'})^l$. $Sim_\mathcal{R}$ sends $\hat{\alpha}$ to the ideal functionality $\mathcal{F}^{\mathbb{Z}_{2^k}}_{\text{VOLE}}$. Upon receiving $\boldsymbol{z}_1, ..., \boldsymbol{z}_m \in \mathbb{Z}^l_{2^k}$ from $\mathcal{F}^{\mathbb{Z}_{2^k}}_{\text{VOLE}}$, $Sim_\mathcal{R}$ picks $(\hat{\boldsymbol{d}}_1, ..., \hat{\boldsymbol{d}}_m) \leftarrow (\mathcal{D}^{\text{T}}_{\Delta'})^l$, $\hat{\boldsymbol{C}} \xleftarrow{\$} \text{Ker}(\psi)^l$, and computes $\hat{\boldsymbol{Z}} := \phi(\boldsymbol{z}_1 + \hat{\boldsymbol{d}}_1, ..., \boldsymbol{z}_m + \hat{\boldsymbol{d}}_m) + \hat{\boldsymbol{C}}$. Then $Sim_\mathcal{R}$ sends $\hat{\boldsymbol{Z}}$ to $\mathcal{A}$. The adversary $\mathcal{A}$ receives $\boldsymbol{Z} = \phi(\boldsymbol{a}_1, ..., \boldsymbol{a}_m) \cdot \Delta' + \phi(\boldsymbol{b}_1, ..., \boldsymbol{b}_m) + \boldsymbol{C}$ in the real world, where $\psi(\boldsymbol{Z})$ and $\psi(\hat{\boldsymbol{Z}})$ are statistically-close by the definition of $(m, d; 2)$-NM-RMFE. Further, as $\boldsymbol{Z}$'s projection on $\text{Ker}(\psi)$ is perfectly masked by $\boldsymbol{C}$, $\mathcal{A}$ can not distinguish $\boldsymbol{Z}$ and $\hat{\boldsymbol{Z}}$ as well. Thus, we conclude the proof. $\square$

3.2 Constructing NM-RMFE

In this section, we present an asymptotically good instantiation, that realizes a slightly weaker variant of NM-RMFE, where the Property 2 in Definition 4 holds for any $\boldsymbol{x}_1, ..., \boldsymbol{x}_D \in (\text{GR}(p^k, r)^*)^m$. We argue that this weaker variant is as good as the standard one when applied in our NISC/VOLE protocol later in Sect. 4.

For convenience and w.l.o.g., we construct NM-RMFE over Galois fields. In a high level, our construction consists of two layers of RMFEs, one is a standard RMFE, and the other is a so-called Extended RMFE. We define degree-D Extended RMFE as follows:

Definition 5 (Degree-D Extended RMFE). Let $\mathbb{F}_q$ be a finite field of q elements, $n > d > m \geq 1$ and $D \geq 1$ be integers. A pair of maps (ϕ, ψ) is called an $(m, d, n; D)_q$-Extended RMFE if $\phi : \mathbb{F}^m_q \times \mathbb{F}_{q^d} \to \mathbb{F}_{q^n}$ and $\psi : \mathbb{F}_{q^n} \to \mathbb{F}^m_q \times \mathbb{F}_{q^d}$ are two $\mathbb{F}_q$-linear maps satisfying

$$\psi(\phi(\boldsymbol{x_1}, y_1) \cdot \phi(\boldsymbol{x_2}, y_2) \cdots \phi(\boldsymbol{x_D}, y_D)) = (\boldsymbol{x_1} * \boldsymbol{x_2} * \cdots * \boldsymbol{x_D}, y_1 y_2 \cdots y_D),$$

for any $\boldsymbol{x}_i \in \mathbb{F}^m_q$, $\boldsymbol{y}_i \in \mathbb{F}_{q^d}$, $i \in [D]$.

The degree-D Extended RMFE is a natural extension of degree-D RMFEs, and the construction is straightforward. Thus it is omitted here.

Let (ϕ_1, ψ_1) be an $(m+k, d; D)_q$-RMFE, and (ϕ_2, ψ_2) be an $(m+k, d, n; D)_q$-extended RMFE. We construct an $(m, n; D)_q$-NM-RMFE (ϕ, ψ) as follows.

- $\phi : \mathbb{F}^m_q \to \mathbb{F}_{q^n}$ is an $\mathbb{F}_q$-linear map, such that $\phi : \boldsymbol{x} \mapsto \phi_2(\boldsymbol{x}, \boldsymbol{r}, \phi_1(\boldsymbol{x}, \boldsymbol{r}))$, where $\boldsymbol{r} \xleftarrow{\$} \mathbb{F}^k_q$.

---

[4] We define $\mathcal{D}_{\boldsymbol{A}'} := (\mathcal{D}_{A'_1}, ..., \mathcal{D}_{A'_l})^{\text{T}}$.

– For a $Y \in \mathbb{F}_{q^n}$, let $(\boldsymbol{y}, \boldsymbol{s}, e) := \psi_2(Y)$, where $\boldsymbol{y} \in \mathbb{F}_q^m$, $\boldsymbol{s} \in \mathbb{F}_q^k$ and $e \in \mathbb{F}_{q^d}$. $\psi : \mathbb{F}_{q^n} \to \mathbb{F}_q^m$ is defined as follows:

$$\psi(Y) = \begin{cases} \boldsymbol{y}, & if\ \psi_1(e) = (\boldsymbol{y}, \boldsymbol{s})\ , \\ \bot, & otherwise. \end{cases}$$

W.l.o.g. and for simplicity, we take $D = 2$, and assume $\phi_1(1) = 1$ and $\phi_2(1,1) = 1$. Let $\mathcal{V}_\bot$ denote the set $\{\phi_2(\boldsymbol{0}, \boldsymbol{0}, \phi_1(\boldsymbol{x}, \boldsymbol{r})) \mid \boldsymbol{x} \in \mathbb{F}_q^m, \boldsymbol{r} \in \mathbb{F}_q^k\}$. We have the following observations (which can be naturally extended to $D > 2$ cases).

Proposition 1. *Let (ϕ, ψ) be defined as above, there exists q^{n-d} solutions for $Y \in \mathbb{F}_{q^n}$, such that $\psi(Y) \neq \bot$.*

Proof. Assume there exist $\boldsymbol{z} \in \mathbb{F}_q^m, \boldsymbol{t} \in \mathbb{F}_q^k$ satisfying $\psi_2(\phi(Y) = (\boldsymbol{z}, \boldsymbol{t}, \phi_1(\boldsymbol{z}, \boldsymbol{t}))$. Then, we have that

$$Y \in \psi_2^{-1}(\{(\boldsymbol{z}, \boldsymbol{t}, \phi_1(\boldsymbol{z}, \boldsymbol{t})) \mid \boldsymbol{z} \in \mathbb{F}_q^m, \boldsymbol{t} \in \mathbb{F}_q^k\}).$$

By Lemma 2, we have that $\psi_2^{-1}(\{(\boldsymbol{z}, \boldsymbol{t}, \phi_1(\boldsymbol{z}, \boldsymbol{t})) \mid \boldsymbol{z} \in \mathbb{F}_q^m, \boldsymbol{t} \in \mathbb{F}_q^k\}) = \mathrm{Ker}(\psi_2) \oplus \mathrm{Im}(\phi)$. Since $|\mathrm{Ker}(\psi_2)| = \frac{q^n}{q^{m+k} \cdot q^d}$ and $|\mathrm{Im}(\phi)| = q^{m+k}$, there are q^{n-d} solutions for Y such that $\psi(Y) \neq \bot$. □

Proposition 2. *Let (ϕ, ψ) be defined as above, then $\mathbb{F}_{q^n} = \mathrm{Im}(\phi) \oplus \mathcal{V}_\bot \oplus \mathrm{Ker}(\psi)$.*

Proof. We show that for any $Y \in \mathbb{F}_{q^n}$, Y can be uniquely written as the additions of the projections on the above sets, respectively. Define $\tau_1 := \phi_1 \circ \psi_1$. Assume $(\boldsymbol{y}, \boldsymbol{s}, e) := \psi_2(Y)$. Let $A := \phi_2(\boldsymbol{y}, \boldsymbol{s}, \phi_1(\boldsymbol{y}, \boldsymbol{s}))$ and $B := \phi_2(\boldsymbol{0}, \boldsymbol{0}, \tau_1(e) - \phi_1(\boldsymbol{y}, \boldsymbol{s}))$. By definition, we have that $A \in \mathrm{Im}(\phi)$ and $B \in \mathcal{V}_\bot$. It can be verified that $\psi_2(Y - A - B) = (\boldsymbol{0}, \boldsymbol{0}, e - \tau_1(e))$. Thus, $(Y - A - B) \in \mathrm{Ker}(\psi)$ and we complete the proof. □

As the adversary can carefully select a $Y \notin \mathrm{Im}(\phi)$, we need to find the distribution $\mathcal{D}_Y$ for each Y. From now on we consider the specific polynomial-based construction of RMFE[5], which allows us to provide an explicit description of $\mathcal{D}_Y$[6].

Let $\alpha_1, \alpha_2, ..., \alpha_m$ and $\beta_1, \beta_2, ..., \beta_k$ be $m + k$ pair-wise distinct elements in $\mathbb{F}_q$. There exists a unique polynomial $f \in \mathbb{F}_q[x]$ with $\deg(f) \leq m + k - 1$, such that $f(\alpha_i) = x_i, i \in [m]$ and $f(\beta_j) = r_j, j \in [k]$. Let $d = 2(m + k) - 1$ and $n \geq 2(m + k + d) - 1$. There exist a degree-d irreducible polynomial $p \in \mathbb{F}_q[x]$ and a degree-n irreducible polynomial $g \in \mathbb{F}_q[x]$ such that $\mathbb{F}_{q^d} \cong \mathbb{F}_q[x]/(p)$ and $\mathbb{F}_{q^n} \cong \mathbb{F}_q[x]/(g)$. Therefore, elements in the extension field can be viewed as polynomials. In particular, we pick $g(x) = x^n + ax + b$, where $a, b \in \mathbb{F}_q$ (such irreducible $g(x)$ exists, if q is a prime and $(n, d) = 1$, see [24]). Let Y be a polynomial over $\mathbb{F}_q$ with degree $\leq n - 1$.

---

[5] In the RMFE literature [7,12,14], known RMFEs are constructed from algebraic geometry curves. Polynomials are essentially genus-0 curves and in most cases, RMFEs constructed from genus-0 curves have a lower ratio $\frac{d}{m}$.

[6] In fact, similar results can be obtained for general constructions of RMFE, also for RMFEs over Galois rings.

– For $\boldsymbol{x} \in \mathbb{F}_q^m$, ϕ is defined as

$$\phi : \boldsymbol{x} \mapsto f, \ where \ f \xleftarrow{\$} \mathbb{F}_q[x]_{\leq m+k-1}, \ satisfying \ f(\alpha_i) = x_i, i \in [m].$$

– For $f \in \mathbb{F}_q[x]_{\leq n-1}$, let $\hat{f} := f \mod p$. ψ is defined as

$$\psi : f \mapsto \begin{cases} (f(\alpha_1), ..., f(\alpha_m)), & if \ \hat{f}(\alpha_i) = f(\alpha_i), \hat{f}(\beta_j) = f(\beta_j), i \in [m], j \in [k], \\ \perp, & otherwise. \end{cases}$$

First we give the following lemma.

Lemma 5. *Given a $\boldsymbol{x} \in \mathbb{F}_q^m$, $\alpha_1, ..., \alpha_m$ and $\beta_1, ..., \beta_k$ are $m+k$ pair-wise distinct elements in $\mathbb{F}_q$, then there are q^i solutions of $\boldsymbol{r} \in \mathbb{F}_q^k$, such that $\boldsymbol{x}, \boldsymbol{r}$ interpolate a polynomial f with degree $\leq m - 1 + i$, $i = 0, 1, ..., k$.*

Proof. Since the evaluation map $\sigma : f \mapsto (f(\alpha_1), ..., f(\alpha_m), f(\beta_1), ..., f(\beta_k))$ induces a bijection from $\mathbb{F}_q[x]_{\leq m+k-1} := \{f \in \mathbb{F}_q[x] \mid \deg(f) \leq m + k - 1\}$ to $\mathbb{F}_q^m \times \mathbb{F}_q^k$, there are at most q^{m+i} solutions of $\boldsymbol{x}, \boldsymbol{r}$ such that $\boldsymbol{x}, \boldsymbol{r}$ interpolate a polynomial f with degree $\leq m - 1 + i$, $i = 0, 1, ..., k$. On the other hand, for a given $\boldsymbol{x} \in \mathbb{F}_q^m$, let the first i positions of $\boldsymbol{r}$ be random, thus $\boldsymbol{x}$ along with $\boldsymbol{r}|_{[i]}$ interpolate a polynomial f with degree $\leq m - 1 + i$. Set the remaining $k - i$ positions of $\boldsymbol{r}$ lie on f. Thus, there are at least q^i solutions of $\boldsymbol{r} \in \mathbb{F}_q^k$ for a given $\boldsymbol{x}$. Combining together, we conclude the proof. $\square$

We have the following theorem.

Theorem 2. *Let ϕ, ψ be defined above. For any $Y \in \mathbb{F}_{q^n}$, $\boldsymbol{x} \in (\mathbb{F}_q^*)^m$ and sufficiently large k, there exists a distribution $\mathcal{D}_Y$ such that $\mathcal{D}_{\boldsymbol{x},Y} \overset{\text{s}}{\approx} \mathcal{D}_Y$.*

Proof. Let us consider the degree of Y. We remark that the result holds for any $\boldsymbol{x} \in \mathbb{F}_q^m$ if not pointed out explicitly.

i. If $\deg(Y) \leq m + k - 1$. We have that

$$\begin{aligned} \psi(\phi(\boldsymbol{x}) \cdot Y) = \psi(f \cdot Y) &= (f \cdot Y(\alpha_1), ..., f \cdot Y(\alpha_m)) \\ &= (f(\alpha_1), ..., f(\alpha_m)) * (Y(\alpha_1), ..., Y(\alpha_m)) \\ &= \boldsymbol{x} * \psi(Y), \end{aligned}$$

as $\deg(f \cdot Y) \leq d - 1$. So in this condition, $\mathcal{D}_{\boldsymbol{x},Y} = \mathcal{D}_Y : \Pr[\boldsymbol{\delta} = \boldsymbol{0}] = 1$.

ii. If $m + k - 1 < \deg(Y) \leq m + 2k - 1$. Since $\deg(\phi(\boldsymbol{x} \cdot Y)) \leq d + k - 1$, $\psi(\phi(\boldsymbol{x}) \cdot Y) = \perp$ if $\deg(\phi(\boldsymbol{x}) \cdot Y) \geq d$. On the other hand, the equation $\psi(\phi(\boldsymbol{x}) \cdot Y) = \boldsymbol{x} \star \psi(Y)$ holds if $\deg(\phi(\boldsymbol{x}) \cdot Y) \leq d - 1$. By Lemma 5, we have that for all possible values of $\boldsymbol{x}$,

$$\mathcal{D}_{\boldsymbol{x},Y} : \begin{cases} \Pr[\boldsymbol{\delta} = \boldsymbol{0}] = 1/q^{\deg(Y)-m-k+1}, \\ \Pr[\boldsymbol{\delta} = \perp] = 1 - 1/q^{\deg(Y)-m-k+1}. \end{cases}$$

So in this condition, $\mathcal{D}_{\boldsymbol{x},Y} = \mathcal{D}_Y$.

iii. If $m + 2k - 1 < \deg(Y) \leq 2(m + k - 1)$. Similarly, since $\deg(\phi(\boldsymbol{x} \cdot Y)) \leq d + m + k - 2$, we have that $\psi(\phi(\boldsymbol{x}) \cdot Y) = \perp$ if $\deg(\phi(\boldsymbol{x}) \cdot Y) \geq d$, and $\psi(\phi(\boldsymbol{x}) \cdot Y) = \boldsymbol{x} \star \psi(Y)$ holds if $\deg(\phi(\boldsymbol{x}) \cdot Y) \leq d - 1$. There are only $q^{2(m+k)-1-\deg(Y)}$ possible values of $\boldsymbol{x}$ such that $\boldsymbol{x}$ interpolates a polynomial f with degree $\leq 2(m+k-1) - \deg(Y)$, as there are exactly $q^{2(m+k)-1-\deg(Y)}$ choices of such f. For these $\boldsymbol{x}$, let $\boldsymbol{r}$ lie on f, and we have that

$$\mathcal{D}_{\boldsymbol{x},Y} : \begin{cases} \Pr[\boldsymbol{\delta} = \boldsymbol{0}] = 1/q^k, \\ \Pr[\boldsymbol{\delta} = \perp] = 1 - 1/q^k. \end{cases}$$

For the remaining $q^m - q^{2(m+k)-1-\deg(Y)}$ possible values of $\boldsymbol{x}$, there are no solutions for $\boldsymbol{r} \in \mathbb{F}_q^k$, and we have $\mathcal{D}_{\boldsymbol{x},Y} = \mathcal{D}$. So in this condition, $\mathcal{D}_{\boldsymbol{x},Y} \overset{s}{\approx} \mathcal{D}$ for sufficient large k.

iv. If $2(m + k) - 1 \leq \deg(Y) \leq n - m - k$. Let $\hat{Y} := Y \mod p$, and we can find $\boldsymbol{r} \in \mathbb{F}_q[x]$ satisfying $Y = \hat{Y} + p \cdot \boldsymbol{r}$. Let $a(x) := \prod_{i=1}^{m}(x - \alpha_i)$, and $b(x) := \prod_{i=1}^{k}(x - \beta_i)$. Since $\deg(\phi(\boldsymbol{x} \cdot Y)) \leq n - 1$, we have that if $\deg(\hat{Y}) \leq m + k - 1$, $a(x) \mid r(x)$, and $r(\beta_j) = 0$ for $j \in J \subseteq [k]$,

$$\mathcal{D}_{\boldsymbol{x},Y} : \begin{cases} \Pr[\boldsymbol{\delta} = \boldsymbol{0}] = 1/q^{k-|J|}, \\ \Pr[\boldsymbol{\delta} = \perp] = 1 - 1/q^{k-|J|}. \end{cases}$$

However, we remark that if $\deg(\hat{Y}) \leq m + k - 1$, $b(x) \mid r(x)$ and $a(x) \nmid r(x)$, we have that $\psi(\phi(\boldsymbol{0}) \cdot Y) = \boldsymbol{0}$ but $\psi(\phi(\boldsymbol{x}) \cdot Y) = \perp$, for $\boldsymbol{x} \in (\mathbb{F}_q^*)^m$. Thus for the remaining choices of Y, $\mathcal{D}_{\boldsymbol{x},Y} = \mathcal{D}$ holds for $\boldsymbol{x} \in (\mathbb{F}_q^*)^m$. So, in this condition, $\mathcal{D}_{\boldsymbol{x},Y} = \mathcal{D}_Y$ for $\boldsymbol{x} \in (\mathbb{F}_q^*)^m$.

v. If $\deg(Y) \geq n - m - k + 1$. If $\deg(\phi(\boldsymbol{x}) \cdot Y) \leq n - 1$, the discussion is similar to the previous one, and we have that $\mathcal{D}_{\boldsymbol{x},Y} = \mathcal{D}_Y$ for $\boldsymbol{x} \in (\mathbb{F}_q^*)^m$. If $\deg(\phi(\boldsymbol{x}) \cdot Y) \geq n$, $\deg(\phi(\boldsymbol{x}) \cdot Y \mod g)$ will exceed $d - 1$ and lead to $\perp$ overwhelmingly, as we take $g(x)$ of the form $g(x) = x^n + ax + b$, $a, b \in \mathbb{F}_q$. So in this condition, $\mathcal{D}_{\boldsymbol{x},Y} \overset{s}{\approx} \mathcal{D}_Y$ for $\boldsymbol{x} \in (\mathbb{F}_q^*)^m$.

From above discussions, we conclude the proof. □

As the above NM-RMFE construction contains two layers of RMFEs, we remark that the asymptotic behavior of NM-RMFE is not as good as RMFE (though still constant). For instance, by Lemma 3, there exists a family of $(m, d; 2)$-NM-RMFEs over $\mathbb{F}_2(\mathbb{Z}_{2^{32}}, \mathbb{Z}_{2^{64}})$ with $m \to \infty$ and $\frac{d}{m} \to 29.13$ and a family of $(m, d; 3)$-NM-RMFEs over $\mathbb{F}_2(\mathbb{Z}_{2^{32}}, \mathbb{Z}_{2^{64}})$ with $m \to \infty$ and $\frac{d}{m} \to 80.15$. For the concrete efficiency of $(m, d; 3)$-NM-RMFEs over $\mathbb{Z}_{2^{32}}$, according to the results in [14], there exists a $(3m, 7(3m+4); 3)$-RMFE over $\mathbb{Z}_{2^{32}}$ for any $m \leq 150$. We obtain that the NM-RMFE ratio $\frac{d}{m+k}$ is 56 approximately, where k is related to the statistical security parameter κ. Assume $\kappa = 80$, by setting $m = 150$, the ratio d/m is 87.3. Note that for a given κ, the ratio d/m is close to a constant (56 in this case), as long as m is relatively large compared to k.

4 Amortized rNISC/VOLE

In this section, we first show how to construct a semi-honest secure NISC/VOLE for computing branching programs over $\mathbb{Z}_{2^k}$. Then we show how to obtain a reusable malicious secure one.

4.1 Amortized NISC/VOLE with Semi-honest Security

Let $L(\boldsymbol{x})$ be a matrix induced by a size $(s+1)$ BP over $\mathbb{Z}_{2^k}$ computing $f : \mathbb{Z}_{2^k}^n \to \mathbb{Z}_{2^k}$, i.e. $det(L(\boldsymbol{x})) = f(\boldsymbol{x})$. Suppose $\boldsymbol{x}_1, ..., \boldsymbol{x}_m \in \mathbb{Z}_{2^k}^n$. We consider the case of computing $f(\boldsymbol{x}_1), ..., f(\boldsymbol{x}_m)$ in parallel[7], where we can amortize the cost by using RMFEs. In a high level, we present a variant of DARE for BP over $\mathtt{GR}(2^k, d)$, which, in effect, computes parallel DAREs for BP over $\mathbb{Z}_{2^k}$ (i.e. reveals nothing but $f(\boldsymbol{x}_1), ..., f(\boldsymbol{x}_m)$).

Let (ϕ, ψ) be an $(m, d; 3)$-RMFE over $\mathbb{Z}_{2^k}$, and $\tau := \phi \circ \psi$. We generalize these maps to perform on matrices in a natural way. As ϕ is a $\mathbb{Z}_{2^k}$-linear map, it can be observed that $\phi(L(\boldsymbol{x}_1), ..., L(\boldsymbol{x}_m)) = L(\phi(\boldsymbol{x}_1, ..., \boldsymbol{x}_m))$. We define following matrix sets over $\mathtt{GR}(2^k, d)$:

$$\hat{\mathcal{H}}^s := \{\phi(H_1, ..., H_m) \mid H_i \in \mathcal{H}^s, i \in [m]\},$$
$$\hat{\mathcal{G}}_1^s := \{\phi(G_1, ..., G_m) \mid G_i \in \mathcal{G}_1^s, i \in [m]\},$$
$$\hat{\mathcal{G}}_2^s := \{\phi(G_1, ..., G_m) \mid G_i \in \mathcal{G}_2^s, i \in [m]\},$$

where $\mathcal{H}^s, \mathcal{G}_1^s, \mathcal{G}_2^s$ are defined in Corollary 1.

We observe that the encoding of $L(\phi(\boldsymbol{x}_1, ..., \boldsymbol{x}_m))$ (i.e. $R_1 L(\phi(\boldsymbol{x}_1, ..., \boldsymbol{x}_m)) R_2$, where R_1, R_2 are sampled uniformly at random from $\hat{\mathcal{G}}_1^s, \hat{\mathcal{G}}_2^s$, respectively) reveals not only $det(L(\boldsymbol{x}_1)), ..., det(L(\boldsymbol{x}_m))$ but also $det(L(\phi(\boldsymbol{x}_1, ..., \boldsymbol{x}_m)))$, which we do not desire. To solve this issue, we mask the encoding by random values over $\mathrm{Ker}(\psi)$. Therefore, we define a matrix group $\mathcal{I}^s$ for this purpose.

Definition 6. *Let $\mathcal{I}^s$ be the set of all $s \times s$ matrices over $\mathrm{Ker}(\psi)$ with 0's below the main diagonal.*

We have the following proposition, which indicates that parallel DAREs over $\mathbb{Z}_{2^k}$ can be implemented at one time via RMFE.

Proposition 3. *Let R_1, R_2, R_3 be uniformly and independently distributed matrices from $\hat{\mathcal{G}}_1^s, \hat{\mathcal{G}}_2^s, \mathcal{I}^s$, respectively. We have that $M := R_1 L(\phi(\boldsymbol{x}_1, ..., \boldsymbol{x}_m)) R_2 + R_3$ reveals no information about $L(\boldsymbol{x}_1), ..., L(\boldsymbol{x}_m)$ but $det(L(\boldsymbol{x}_1)), ..., det(L(\boldsymbol{x}_m))$.*

Proof. The map $\psi : \mathtt{GR}(2^k, d) \to \mathbb{Z}_{2^k}^m$ induces m $\mathbb{Z}_{2^k}$-linear maps $\psi_i : \mathtt{GR}(2^k, d) \to \mathbb{Z}_{2^k}$, for $i \in [m]$, i.e. $(\psi_1, ..., \psi_m) := \psi$. By the definition of $(m, d; 3)$-RMFEs, we have that $\psi_i(R_1 L(\phi(\boldsymbol{x}_1, ..., \boldsymbol{x}_m)) R_2 + R_3) = \psi_i(R_1) L(\boldsymbol{x}_i) \psi_i(R_2)$, for $i \in [m]$.

---

[7] It remains interesting and open whether a branching program can be transformed into copies of a sub branching program.

Since R_1, R_2 are uniformly and independently distributed from $\hat{\mathcal{G}}_1^s, \hat{\mathcal{G}}_2^s$, and ψ conditioned on $\mathrm{Im}(\phi)$ is a bijection, $\psi_i(R_1), \psi_i(R_2)$ are uniformly and independently distributed from $\mathcal{G}_1^s, \mathcal{G}_2^s$ for $i \in [m]$, respectively. Thus, by Corollary 1, $\psi_i(R_1)L(\boldsymbol{x}_i)\psi_i(R_2)$ reveals nothing about $L(\boldsymbol{x}_i)$ but $det(L(\boldsymbol{x}_i))$, for $i \in [m]$. Finally, we claim that $R_1 L(\phi(\boldsymbol{x}_1,...,\boldsymbol{x}_m))R_2 + R_3$ reveals no more information than $\psi(R_1 L(\phi(\boldsymbol{x}_1,...,\boldsymbol{x}_m))R_2 + R_3)$. Since, by Lemma 2, we have that $\mathrm{GR}(2^k, d) = \mathrm{Im}(\phi) \oplus \mathrm{Ker}(\psi)$ (assuming $\phi(\mathbf{1}) = 1$) and $R_1 L(\phi(\boldsymbol{x}_1,...,\boldsymbol{x}_m))R_2$'s projection on $\mathrm{Ker}(\psi)$ is perfectly masked by R_3. This completes the proof. □

Given the above proposition, now we proceed to construct our semi-honest NISC protocol over $\mathbb{Z}_{2^k}$. We consider a slightly more general framework with t branching programs BP_i of size (s_i+1) over $\mathbb{Z}_{2^k}$, computing $f_i : \mathbb{Z}_{2^k}^{n_1} \times \mathbb{Z}_{2^k}^{n_2} \to \mathbb{Z}_{2^k}$, for $i \in [t]$. Let $f(\boldsymbol{x}, \boldsymbol{y})$ be a two-party sender-receiver functionality, taking inputs $\boldsymbol{x} \in \mathbb{Z}_{2^k}^{n_1}, \boldsymbol{y} \in \mathbb{Z}_{2^k}^{n_2}$ from the receiver $P_\mathcal{R}$ and the sender $P_\mathcal{S}$, respectively, and sends $f(\boldsymbol{x}, \boldsymbol{y}) \in \mathbb{Z}_{2^k}^t$ to $P_\mathcal{R}$, where $f := (f_1, ..., f_t)$. Let $L_i(\boldsymbol{x}, \boldsymbol{y})$ be the $s_i \times s_i$ matrix induced by BP_i, for $i \in [t]$. Suppose $f(\boldsymbol{x}, \boldsymbol{y})$ will be invoked m times, with inputs $(\boldsymbol{x}_1, \boldsymbol{y}_1), ..., (\boldsymbol{x}_m, \boldsymbol{y}_m) \in \mathbb{Z}_{2^k}^{n_1} \times \mathbb{Z}_{2^k}^{n_2}$, respectively. We present the amortized NISC protocol in Fig. 3 and we have the following theorem.

Protocol Π_{NISC}

The function $f : \mathbb{Z}_{2^k}^{n_1} \times \mathbb{Z}_{2^k}^{n_2} \to \mathbb{Z}_{2^k}^t$ is described as above. Suppose $P_\mathcal{R}$ has input $\boldsymbol{x}_1, ..., \boldsymbol{x}_m \in \mathbb{Z}_{2^k}^{n_1}$, and $P_\mathcal{S}$ has input $\boldsymbol{y}_1, ..., \boldsymbol{y}_m \in \mathbb{Z}_{2^k}^{n_2}$. Let (ϕ, ψ) be an $(m, d; 3)$-RMFE over $\mathbb{Z}_{2^k}$.

1. The receiver $P_\mathcal{R}$ computes $\boldsymbol{X} := \phi(\boldsymbol{x}_1, ..., \boldsymbol{x}_m)$. For $j \in [n_1]$, $P_\mathcal{R}$ sends $(j; X_j)$ to $\mathcal{F}_{\mathrm{VOLE}}^{\mathrm{GR}(2^k, d)}$.

2. The sender $P_\mathcal{S}$ computes $\boldsymbol{Y} := \phi(\boldsymbol{y}_1, ..., \boldsymbol{y}_m)$. For $i \in [t]$, $P_\mathcal{S}$ computes $M_i(\cdot) := R_{1,i} L_i(\cdot, \boldsymbol{Y}) R_{2,i} + R_{3,i}$, where $R_{1,i} \xleftarrow{\$} \hat{\mathcal{G}}_1^{s_i}, R_{2,i} \xleftarrow{\$} \hat{\mathcal{G}}_2^{s_i}, R_{3,i} \xleftarrow{\$} \mathcal{I}^{s_i}$. Since each entry of $M_i(\boldsymbol{X})$ is a linear polynomial on variables $X_1, ..., X_{n_1}$, $P_\mathcal{S}$ sends messages to $\mathcal{F}_{\mathrm{VOLE}}^{\mathrm{GR}(2^k, d)}$ according to $M_i(\cdot)$, for $i \in [t]$.

3. For $i \in [t]$, $P_\mathcal{R}$ obtains $M_i(\boldsymbol{X})$ from $\mathcal{F}_{\mathrm{VOLE}}^{\mathrm{GR}(2^k, d)}$, and then computes $(L_i(\boldsymbol{x}_1, \boldsymbol{y}_1), ..., L_i(\boldsymbol{x}_m, \boldsymbol{y}_m)) := \psi(M_i(\boldsymbol{X}))$. For $j \in [m]$, $P_\mathcal{R}$ computes and outputs $f(\boldsymbol{x}_j, \boldsymbol{y}_j) := (det(L_1(\boldsymbol{x}_j, \boldsymbol{y}_j)), ..., det(L_t(\boldsymbol{x}_j, \boldsymbol{y}_j)))$.

Fig. 3. Protocol for semi-honest NISC over $\mathbb{Z}_{2^k}$ in the (chosen-input) $\mathcal{F}_{\mathrm{VOLE}}^{\mathrm{GR}(2^k, d)}$-hybrid model.

Theorem 3 (Semi-honest NISC/VOLE over $\mathbb{Z}_{2^k}$). *Protocol Π_{NISC} realizes a two-party sender-receiver functionality that computes $f : \mathbb{Z}_{2^k}^{n_1} \times \mathbb{Z}_{2^k}^{n_2} \to \mathbb{Z}_{2^k}^t$ with semi-honest security in the $\mathcal{F}_{\mathrm{VOLE}}^{\mathrm{GR}(2^k, d)}$-hybrid model. In particular, Π_{NISC} invokes n_1 instances of VOLE, and the length of the j-th VOLE instance is $S_j := \sum_{i \in D(j)} \binom{s_i}{2}$, where $D(j)$ is the set of output entries that depend on X_j.*

Proof. If $P_{\mathcal{R}}$ is corrupted, the simulator $Sim_{\mathcal{R}}$ receives $X_1, ..., X_{n_1}$ from the adversary $\mathcal{A}$. Then, $Sim_{\mathcal{R}}$ computes $(\boldsymbol{x}_1, ..., \boldsymbol{x}_m) := \psi(\boldsymbol{X})$, and sends them to the ideal functionality that computes f. For $j \in [m]$, $Sim_{\mathcal{R}}$ receives $\boldsymbol{z}_j \in \mathbb{Z}_{2^k}^t$ from the ideal functionality, and for $i \in [t]$, $Sim_{\mathcal{R}}$ samples random matrix $L_{j,i}$ over $\mathbb{Z}_{2^k}$ with -1's in the second diagonal and 0's below the second diagonal such that $\det(L_{j,i}) = z_{j,i}$. For $i \in [t]$, $Sim_{\mathcal{R}}$ samples $R_{3,i} \xleftarrow{\$} \mathcal{I}^{s_i}$ and computes $M_i := \phi(L_{1,i}, ..., L_{m,i}) + R_{3,i}$. Finally, $Sim_{\mathcal{R}}$ delivers $M_1, ..., M_t$ to $\mathcal{A}$ emulated as VOLE outputs (n_1 instances of VOLE, with total length $\sum_{j=1}^{n_1} S_j$). We remark that this procedure can be done without the knowledge of $\boldsymbol{Y}$, since the function f is public. The correctness is easy to verify and the indistinguishability is directly obtained by Proposition 3.

If P_S is corrupted, the simulator Sim_S receives VOLE inputs from the adversary $\mathcal{A}$, which conveys the matrices $M_1(\cdot), ..., M_t(\cdot)$ over $\mathrm{GR}(2^k, d)$. For $i \in [t]$, Sim_S computes $(M_{1,i}(\cdot), ..., M_{m,i}(\cdot)) := \psi(M_i(\cdot))$. Recall that for each $M_{j,i}(\cdot)$, there exist $R_{1,j,i} \in \mathcal{G}_1^{s_i}$ and $R_{2,j,i} \in \mathcal{G}_2^{s_i}$ such that $R_{1,j,i} L_i(\cdot, \boldsymbol{y}_j) R_{2,j,i} = M_{j,i}(\cdot)$. It can be observed that each entry of $R_{1,j,i}, R_{2,j,i}$ can be computed from the VOLE messages. (This depends crucially on the structure of $R_{1,j,i}, L_i(\cdot, \boldsymbol{y}_j), R_{2,j,i}$; we refer the reader to [19] for more details.) Since $R_{1,j,i}, R_{2,j,i}$ are invertible, S_S can extract $\boldsymbol{y}_j$ for all $j \in [m]$. Finally, Sim_S sends $\boldsymbol{y}_1, ..., \boldsymbol{y}_m$ to the ideal functionality that computes f. The indistinguishability is obtained by the correct extraction of $\boldsymbol{y}_1, ..., \boldsymbol{y}_m$. This completes the proof. $\square$

4.2 Amortized rNISC/VOLE with Malicious Security

We first consider an intermediate security model where both the malicious sender and the malicious receiver follow the RMFE part specifications[8] (e.g., computes $X := \phi(\boldsymbol{x}_1, ..., \boldsymbol{x}_m), Y := \phi(\boldsymbol{y}_1, ..., \boldsymbol{y}_m)$) and we only need to enforce the malicious sender's compliance with the DARE part specifications (e.g., sends messages to the VOLE functionality according to $M_i(\cdot)$). Then, we consider the full malicious security model and show how to construct maliciously secure rNISC/VOLE for computing branching programs over $\mathbb{Z}_{2^k}$.

We generalize the certified VOLE (cVOLE) method (for Galois fields) [13] to Galois ring analogue as the first step. The cVOLE is a special case of NISC/VOLE, where the sender's inputs sent to multiple instances of VOLE need to satisfy some arithmetic constraints (formulated by a circuit $\mathcal{C}$), which allows for forcing the malicious sender to follow the (Π_{NISC}) protocol specifications honestly (see Fig. 4). Similar to its Galois field counterpart [13], constructing a cVOLE protocol over Galois rings involves two main ingredients, a certified VOLE with equality constraint (eVOLE for short) over Galois rings and a statistical NIZK protocol for proving circuit satisfiability over Galois rings.

eVOLE. The eVOLE is a weak variant of cVOLE, which only restricts some given positions of the sender's inputs to multiple instances of VOLE to being

---

[8] In fact, the malicious receiver can only cheat by deviating from the RMFE encoding. Namely, we assume a semi-honest receiver.

Functionality $\mathcal{F}_{\text{cVOLE}}^{\text{GR}(2^k,d)}$

Parameterized by a Galois ring $\text{GR}(2^k,d)$, a sequence of n positive integers $l_1,...,l_n$, for $i \in [n]$, and an arithmetic circuit $\mathcal{C}$ over $\text{GR}(2^k,d)$ on $q \leq 2\sum_{i=1}^{n} l_i$ inputs. Suppose $P_\mathcal{S}$ has input $\boldsymbol{a}_i, \boldsymbol{b}_i \in \text{GR}(2^k,d)^{l_i}$, and $P_\mathcal{R}$ has input $\alpha_i \in \text{GR}(2^k,d)$, for $i \in [n]$.

1. Receive $(\alpha_1,...,\alpha_n)$ from $P_\mathcal{R}$, and $(\boldsymbol{a}_1,...,\boldsymbol{a}_n,\boldsymbol{b}_1,...,\boldsymbol{b}_n)$ from $P_\mathcal{S}$.
2. Verify that $(\boldsymbol{a}_1,...,\boldsymbol{a}_n,\boldsymbol{b}_1,...,\boldsymbol{b}_n)$ is a satisfying assignment for circuit $\mathcal{C}$. If the check fails, send $\bot$ to $P_\mathcal{R}$. Otherwise, compute $\boldsymbol{v}_i := \boldsymbol{a}_i \cdot \alpha_i + \boldsymbol{b}_i$ for $i \in [n]$ and send $(\boldsymbol{v}_1,...,\boldsymbol{v}_n)$ to $P_\mathcal{R}$. If $P_\mathcal{S}$ is corrupted, and receive **aborting** from $\mathcal{S}$, send $\bot$ to $P_\mathcal{R}$.

Fig. 4. Certified VOLE with a general arithmetic constraint

Functionality $\mathcal{F}_{\text{eVOLE}}^{\text{GR}(2^k,d)}$

$\mathcal{F}_{\text{eVOLE}}^{\text{GR}(2^k,d)}$ extends the (chosen-input) VOLE functionality $\mathcal{F}_{\text{VOLE}}^{\text{GR}(2^k,d)}$. **Setup phase, Send phases,** and **Deliver phases** are identical to those in $\mathcal{F}_{\text{VOLE}}^{\text{GR}(2^k,d)}$, respectively. Parameterized by a Galois ring $\text{GR}(2^k,d)$, length parameters $l_1,...,l_n \in \mathbb{N}$.

Verify phases:

1. Upon receiving $(sid_1, sid_2; \textsf{Verify}\dagger; l_{i_1}, l_{i_2}, j_1, j_2)$ from $P_\mathcal{R}$, where $i_1, i_2 \in [n], j_1 \in [l_{i_1}], j_2 \in [l_{i_2}]$ and sid_1, sid_2 are two session identifiers, verify that there are stored inputs $(sid_1; \boldsymbol{a}_1, \boldsymbol{b}_1; l_{i_1})$ and $(sid_2; \boldsymbol{a}_2, \boldsymbol{b}_2; l_{i_2})$ from $P_\mathcal{S}$; else ignore the message. Then, verify that $a_{1,j_1} = a_{2,j_2}$. If the check fails, send $\bot$ to $P_\mathcal{R}$.
2. Upon receiving $(sid_1, sid_2; \textsf{Verify}\ddagger; l_{i_1}, l_{i_2}, j_1, j_2)$ from $P_\mathcal{R}$, where $i_1, i_2 \in [n], j_1 \in [l_{i_1}], j_2 \in [l_{i_2}]$ and sid_1, sid_2 are two session identifiers, verify that there are stored inputs $(sid_1; \boldsymbol{a}_1, \boldsymbol{b}_1; l_{i_1})$ and $(sid_2; \boldsymbol{a}_2, \boldsymbol{b}_2; l_{i_2})$ from $P_\mathcal{S}$; else ignore the message. Then, verify that $b_{1,j_1} = a_{2,j_2}$. If the check fails, send $\bot$ to $P_\mathcal{R}$.

Fig. 5. Distributional certified VOLE with equality constraints.

equal (rather than satisfying a general arithmetic constraint). We formalize the eVOLE functionality in Fig. 5. The eVOLE construction[9] (presented in Fig. 6) shares similarity with the eVOLE construction for Galois fields [13], and is built upon random VOLE. We address the main difference and sketch how to construct eVOLE from chosen-input VOLE for simplicity (the reduction of chosen-input VOLE to random VOLE is straightforward).

---

[9] We remark that for convenience, the construction proves one equality constraint, which can be naturally extended to prove an arbitrary number of equality constraints.

Protocol $\Pi_{\text{eVOLE}}^{\text{GR}(2^k,d)}$

Parameterized by a Galois ring $\text{GR}(2^k,d)$, length parameters $l_1, l_2 \in \mathbb{N}$. P_S has inputs $\boldsymbol{a}_t, \boldsymbol{b}_t \in \text{GR}(2^k,d)^{l_t}$, $t \in [2]$. P_R has (random) inputs $\alpha_1, \alpha_2 \in \text{GR}(2^k,d)$.

1. The sender P_S and the receiver P_R invoke the **Setup phase** of $\mathcal{F}_{\text{VOLE}}^{\text{GR}(2^k,d)}$ with P_R's inputs (α_1, α_2).

2. For $t \in [2]$, P_S and P_R invoke the **Send phases** of $\mathcal{F}_{\text{VOLE}}^{\text{GR}(2^k,d)}$ with inputs $(t; l_t + 1)$. The sender P_S receives $\hat{\boldsymbol{a}}_t, \hat{\boldsymbol{b}}_t \in \text{GR}(2^k,d)^{l_t+1}$, while P_R receives $\hat{\boldsymbol{v}}_t \in \text{GR}(2^k,d)^{l_t+1}$, such that $\hat{\boldsymbol{v}}_t = \hat{\boldsymbol{a}}_t \cdot \alpha_t + \hat{\boldsymbol{b}}_t$.

3. For $t \in [2]$, P_S sends $\boldsymbol{u}_t := \boldsymbol{a}_t - \hat{\boldsymbol{a}}_t|_{[l_t]}$, $\boldsymbol{w}_t := \boldsymbol{b}_t - \hat{\boldsymbol{b}}_t|_{[l_t]}$ to P_R.

Verify†: On input i, j.

(i) The sender P_S sends $u_{1,l_1+1} := b_{2,j} - \hat{a}_{1,l_2+1}$, $u_{2,l_1+1} := b_{1,i} - \hat{a}_{2,l_2+1}$ and $\hat{b}_{1,l_1+1} - \hat{b}_{2,l_2+1}$ to P_R.

(ii) For $t \in [2]$, P_R computes $\boldsymbol{v}_t := \hat{\boldsymbol{v}}_t + \boldsymbol{u}_t \cdot \alpha_t + (\boldsymbol{w}_t \parallel 0)$, where $\boldsymbol{v}_t|_{[l_t]} = \boldsymbol{a}_t \cdot \alpha_t + \boldsymbol{b}_t$. Note that $v_{1,l_1+1} = b_{2,j} \cdot \alpha_1 + \hat{b}_{1,l_1+1}$, $v_{2,l_2+1} = b_{1,i} \cdot \alpha_2 + \hat{b}_{2,l_2+1}$.

(iii) The receiver P_R checks that $\alpha_2 \cdot v_{1,i} - \alpha_1 \cdot v_{2,j} + v_{1,l_1+1} - v_{2,l_2+1} = \hat{b}_{1,l_1+1} - \hat{b}_{2,l_2+1}$. If the check fails, P_R aborts.

Verify‡: On input i, j.

(i) The sender P_S sends $w_{1,l_1+1} := b_{2,j} - \hat{b}_{1,l_1+1}$, $u_{2,l_2+1} := a_{1,i} - \hat{a}_{2,l_2+1}$ and $\hat{b}_{2,l_2+1} - \hat{a}_{1,l_1+1}$ to P_R.

(ii) The receiver P_R computes $\boldsymbol{v}_1 := \hat{\boldsymbol{v}}_1 + (\boldsymbol{u}_1 \parallel 0) \cdot \alpha_1 + \boldsymbol{w}_1$ and $\boldsymbol{v}_2 := \hat{\boldsymbol{v}}_2 + \boldsymbol{u}_2 \cdot \alpha_2 + (\boldsymbol{w}_2 \parallel 0)$, where $\boldsymbol{v}_t|_{[l_t]} = \boldsymbol{a}_t \cdot \alpha_t + \boldsymbol{b}_t$, for $t \in [2]$. Note that $v_{1,l_1+1} = \hat{a}_{1,l_1+1} \cdot \alpha_1 + b_{2,j}$ and $v_{2,l_2+1} = a_{1,i} \cdot \alpha_2 + \hat{b}_{2,l_2+1}$.

(iii) The receiver P_R checks that $v_{2,j} - v_{1,l_1+1} - v_{1,i} \cdot \alpha_2 + v_{2,l_2+1} \cdot \alpha_1 = \alpha_1 \cdot (\hat{b}_{2,l_2+1} - \hat{a}_{1,l_1+1})$. If the check fails, P_R aborts.

Fig. 6. Protocol for eVOLE over $\text{GR}(2^k,d)$ in the $\mathcal{F}_{\text{VOLE}}^{\text{GR}(2^k,d)}$-hybrid model.

Suppose $\boldsymbol{a}_1, \boldsymbol{b}_1 \in \text{GR}(2^k,d)^{l_1}$, $\boldsymbol{a}_2, \boldsymbol{b}_2 \in \text{GR}(2^k,d)^{l_2}$ are P_S's inputs and α_1, α_2 are P_R's inputs to two VOLE instances, respectively. For proving the equality constraint of some $a_{1,i} = a_{2,j}$, where $i \in [l_1], j \in [l_2]$, we apply a Galois ring analogue of the check mechanism [13]. By P_S setting $a_{1,l_1+1} := b_{2,j}$, $a_{2,l_2+1} := b_{1,i}, b_{1,l_1+1}, b_{2,l_2+1} \xleftarrow{\$} \text{GR}(2^k,d)$ and sending $b_{1,l_1+1} - b_{2,l_2+1}$ to P_R, we have that

$$\alpha_2 \cdot v_{1,i} - \alpha_1 \cdot v_{2,j} + v_{1,l_1+1} - v_{2,l_2+1} = b_{1,l_1+1} - b_{2,l_2+1} \tag{1}$$

holds if $a_{1,i} = a_{2,j}$. If $a_{1,i} \neq a_{2,j}$ and α_1, α_2 are uniformly and independently distributed, by Lemma 1, Eq. (1) holds with probability at most $1/2^{d-1}$.

For proving the equality constraint of some $b_{1,i} = a_{2,j}$, we cannot reduce it to the above case like [13][10]. We use another equation for the check. By P_S

---

[10] In more detail, we cannot reduce $v_{1,i} = a_{1,i} \cdot \alpha_1 + b_{1,i}$ to $v_{1,i} \cdot \alpha_1^{-1} = b_{1,i} \cdot \alpha_1^{-1} + a_{1,i}$, as $1/2^d$ fraction of elements in $\text{GR}(2^k,d)$ are zero divisors.

setting $b_{1,l_1+1} := b_{2,j}$, $a_{2,l_2+1} := a_{1,i}$, $b_{2,l_2+1}, a_{1,l_1+1} \xleftarrow{\$} \mathrm{GR}(2^k, d)$ and sending $b_{2,l_2+1} - a_{1,l_1+1}$ to $P_{\mathcal{R}}$, we have that

$$v_{2,j} - v_{1,l_1+1} - v_{1,i} \cdot \alpha_2 + v_{2,l_2+1} \cdot \alpha_1 = \alpha_1 \cdot (b_{2,l_2+1} - a_{1,l_1+1}) \qquad (2)$$

holds if $b_{1,i} = a_{2,j}$. Similarly, by Lemma 1, Eq. (2) holds with probability at most $1/2^{d-1}$ if $b_{1,i} \neq a_{2,j}$ and α_1, α_2 are uniformly and independently distributed.

We have the following proposition (see the proof in Appendix B.2 of the full version [22]).

Proposition 4. $\Pi_{\mathrm{eVOLE}}^{\mathrm{GR}(2^k,d)}$ *realizes* $\mathcal{F}_{\mathrm{eVOLE}}^{\mathrm{GR}(2^k,d)}$ *in the* $\mathcal{F}_{\mathrm{VOLE}}^{\mathrm{GR}(2^k,d)}$*-hybrid model.*

NIZK. The authors of [13] introduced a simple kind of information-theoretic proof system for proving circuit satisfiability called *line point zero knowledge* (LPZK). Informally, in an LPZK proof, the prover $\mathcal{P}$ generates from the witness w and the circuit $\mathcal{C}$ an affine line $\boldsymbol{v}(x) := \boldsymbol{a} \cdot x + \boldsymbol{b}$ over a field $\mathbb{F}_q$. The verifier $\mathcal{V}$ queries a single point α and obtains the evaluation $\boldsymbol{v}(\alpha)$, then $\mathcal{V}$ decides whether to accept the proof or reject. The LPZK proof system is statistical in the VOLE-hybrid model and can be realized by a single invocation of VOLE. We naturally extend the LPZK-NIZK construction for fields of [13] to Galois rings, by simply replacing the field $\mathbb{F}_q$ with a Galois ring $\mathrm{GR}(2^k, d)$. We remark that the soundness error is decreased from $\mathcal{O}(1/q)$ to $\mathcal{O}(1/2^d)$, which can be negligible in the security parameter for a sufficiently large d. The construction communicates 3 elements over $\mathrm{GR}(2^k, d)$ per multiplication gate and is "free" for addition gates. We refer to Appendix B.1 of the full version [22] for more details.

cVOLE. We next provide a high-level overview of the construction of cVOLE from eVOLE and LPZK-NIZK. The eVOLE is used to move the sender's inputs to multiple VOLE instances (n_1 lines, on fixed points $\alpha_1, ..., \alpha_{n_1}$) to another VOLE instance (another line, on a random point γ), where an LPZK-NIZK over Galois rings can be performed.

When substituting parallel VOLE instances in the semi-honest protocol Π_{NISC} with the above cVOLE construction, the eVOLE requirement should be satisfied (i.e. $P_{\mathcal{R}}$'s inputs need to be uniformly and independently distributed). However, $P_{\mathcal{R}}$ has fixed inputs in the NISC setting. To solve this, $n_1 + 2$ VOLE instances with $P_{\mathcal{R}}$'s corresponding inputs $(\alpha_1 + \beta, ..., \alpha_{n_1} + \beta, \beta, \gamma)$ are required, where $\alpha_1, ..., \alpha_n \in \mathrm{Im}(\phi)$ and $\beta, \gamma \xleftarrow{\$} \mathrm{GR}(2^k, d)$, and the equality constraints are proven between VOLE instances corresponding to $(\alpha_i + \beta, \gamma)$ and (β, γ). The cVOLE protocol is presented in Fig. 7, and we have the following corollary with a deferred proof in Appendix B.2 of the full version [22].

Corollary 2. $\Pi_{\mathrm{cVOLE}}^{\mathrm{GR}(2^k,d)}$ *realizes* $\mathcal{F}_{\mathrm{cVOLE}}^{\mathrm{GR}(2^k,d)}$ *in the* $(\mathcal{F}_{\mathrm{VOLE}}^{\mathrm{GR}(2^k,d)}, \mathcal{F}_{\mathrm{eVOLE}}^{\mathrm{GR}(2^k,d)})$*-hybrid model.*

In particular, if instantiating $\mathcal{F}_{\mathrm{eVOLE}}^{\mathrm{GR}(2^k,d)}$ with $\Pi_{\mathrm{eVOLE}}^{\mathrm{GR}(2^k,d)}$, we obtain a cVOLE/VOLE construction, which essentially admits a NISC/VOLE protocol with reusable malicious security for branching programs over $\mathrm{GR}(2^k, d)$. If we

---

Protocol $\Pi_{\text{cVOLE}}^{\text{GR}(2^k,d)}$

Parameterized by a Galois ring $\text{GR}(2^k, d)$, a sequence of n positive integers $l_1, ..., l_n$, and an arithmetic circuit $\mathcal{C}$ over $\text{GR}(2^k, d)$ on $q_a + q_b = q \leq 2\sum_{i=1}^{n} l_i$ inputs with t multiplication gates. Let $L_1 = 0$ and for $i = 2, 3, ..., n+1$, let $L_i = l_1 + ... + l_{i-1}$. Let (ϕ, ψ) be an $(m, d; 3)$-RMFE over $\mathbb{Z}_{2^k}$. The receiver $P_{\mathcal{R}}$ has inputs $\alpha_i \in \text{GR}(2^k, d)$ and the sender $P_{\mathcal{S}}$ has inputs $\boldsymbol{a}_i, \boldsymbol{b}_i \in \text{GR}(2^k, d)^{l_i}$, for $i \in [n]$. Suppose $\mathcal{C}$ takes q_a inputs from $\boldsymbol{a}$ entries and q_b inputs from $\boldsymbol{b}$ entries.

1. The two parties invoke the **Setup phase** of $\mathcal{F}_{\text{eVOLE}}^{\text{GR}(2^k,d)}$ with $P_{\mathcal{R}}$'s inputs $(\alpha_1 + \beta, ..., \alpha_n + \beta, \beta, \gamma)$, where $\beta, \gamma \xleftarrow{\$} \text{GR}(2^k, d)$.

2. For $i \in [n]$, $P_{\mathcal{S}}$ picks $\boldsymbol{e}_i \xleftarrow{\$} \text{GR}(2^k, d)^{l_i}$ and sends $(\boldsymbol{a}_i, \boldsymbol{b}_i + \boldsymbol{e}_i)$ with session id i to $\mathcal{F}_{\text{eVOLE}}^{\text{GR}(2^k,d)}$. For the $(n+1)$-st instance of VOLE, $P_{\mathcal{S}}$ computes $\boldsymbol{a}_{n+1} := \boldsymbol{a}_1 \| ... \| \boldsymbol{a}_n$, $\boldsymbol{b}_{n+1} := \boldsymbol{e}_1 \| ... \| \boldsymbol{e}_n$ and sends $(n+1; \boldsymbol{a}_{n+1}, \boldsymbol{b}_{n+1}; L_{n+1})$ to $\mathcal{F}_{\text{eVOLE}}^{\text{GR}(2^k,d)}$. For the $(n+2)$-nd instance of VOLE, if $a_{i,j}$ is the k-th input from $\boldsymbol{a}$ entries to circuit $\mathcal{C}$, set $a_{n+2,k} := a_{i,j}$; else if $b_{i,j}$ is the k-th input from $\boldsymbol{b}$ entries to circuit $\mathcal{C}$, set $a_{n+2,q_a+k} := b_{i,j}$ and $a_{n+2,q+k} := b_{n+1,L_i+j}$. Additionally, $P_{\mathcal{S}}$ picks $\boldsymbol{b}_{n+2} \xleftarrow{\$} \text{GR}(2^k, d)^{q+q_b}$. Then, $P_{\mathcal{S}}$ sends $(n+2; \boldsymbol{a}_{n+2}, \boldsymbol{b}_{n+2}; q+q_b)$ to $\mathcal{F}_{\text{eVOLE}}^{\text{GR}(2^k,d)}$. The receiver $P_{\mathcal{R}}$ receives $\boldsymbol{v}_1, ..., \boldsymbol{v}_{n+2}$ from $\mathcal{F}_{\text{eVOLE}}^{\text{GR}(2^k,d)}$.

3. By invoking the **Verify phases** of $\mathcal{F}_{\text{eVOLE}}^{\text{GR}(2^k,d)}$, $P_{\mathcal{R}}$ verifies that
   (i) $a_{i,j} = a_{n+2,k}$ and $a_{n+1,L_i+j} = a_{n+2,k}$, if $a_{i,j}$ is the k-th input from $\boldsymbol{a}$ entries to circuit $\mathcal{C}$, for $k \in [q_a]$.
   (ii) $b_{i,j} = a_{n+2,q_a+k}$ and $b_{n+1,L_i+j} = a_{n+2,q+k}$, if $b_{i,j}$ is the k-th input from $\boldsymbol{b}$ entries to circuit $\mathcal{C}$, for $k \in [q_b]$. Recompute v_{n+2,q_a+k} by subtracting $v_{n+2,q+k}$.

4. Invoke the subprotocol $\Pi_{\text{NIZK}}^{q,t}$ with inputs $\{[a_{n+2,i}]_\gamma\}_{i \in [q]}$ to verify that $\{[a_{n+2,i}]_\gamma\}_{i \in [q]}$ is a satisfying assignment for $\mathcal{C}$. If any of above verifications fails, $P_{\mathcal{R}}$ aborts.

Fig. 7. Protocol for Certified VOLE with a general arithmetic constraint in the $\mathcal{F}_{\text{eVOLE}}^{\text{GR}(2^k,d)}$-hybrid model

further assume both parties follow RMFE encoding honestly, the protocol can securely compute branching programs over $\mathbb{Z}_{2^k}$.

Putting all pieces together. Recall that NM-RMFE allows for "extraction" when the adversary does not follow the NM-RMFE encoding honestly. The final step is upgrading standard RMFE to NM-RMFE and we do not need to assume both parties follow NM-RMFE encoding honestly. For NISC tasks that compute BPs over $\mathbb{Z}_{2^k}$, using the cVOLE technique[11] and substituting Degree-3 RMFEs by an $(m, d; 3)$-NM-RMFE (ϕ, ψ) in Π_{NISC}, we have the following theorem.

---

[11] The circuit $\mathcal{C}$ (specifies the arithmetic constraints in DARE) is of size $S := \sum_{j=1}^{n_1} S_j + \sum_{i=1}^{t} s_i^3$ according to naive matrix multiplication (S_j, s_i are defined as in Theorem 3).

Theorem 4 (rNISC/VOLE from NM-RMFE). *Suppose $f : \mathbb{Z}_{2^k}^{n_1} \times \mathbb{Z}_{2^k}^{n_2} \to \mathbb{Z}_{2^k}^t$ is a sender-receiver functionality whose i-th output can be computed by an arithmetic branching program over $\mathbb{Z}_{2^k}$ of size $s_i + 1$ that depends on d_i inputs. Let (ϕ, ψ) be an $(m, d; 3)$-NM-RMFE over $\mathbb{Z}_{2^k}$ and κ be the statistical security parameter. Then f admits an rNISC/VOLE protocol with the following features:*

- *The protocol takes $n_1 + 2$ parallel VOLE instances over $\mathrm{GR}(2^k, d)$, and outputs m executions of f.*
- *The protocol is secure against a malicious sender and a malicious receiver.*
- *Assume the branching program admits a verification circuit $\mathcal{C}$ that takes q_a inputs from $\boldsymbol{a}$ entries, q_b inputs from $\boldsymbol{b}$ entries. The circuit $\mathcal{C}$ has $S := \sum_{i=1}^{t} (d_i \binom{s_i}{2} + s_i^3)$ multiplication gate. The total length of VOLE instances is $2S + 6q_a + 7q_b + \sum_{i=1}^{t} d_i \binom{s_i}{2}$, and $3S + 1 + 8q_a + 9q_b + 2\sum_{i=1}^{t} d_i \binom{s_i}{2}$ elements over $\mathrm{GR}(2^k, d)$ are communicated.*
- *The simulation error is $\varepsilon = \mathcal{O}\left(1/2^d + 1/2^\kappa\right)$.*

Proof. The construction is obtained by replacing RMFE with NM-RMFE and VOLE with cVOLE in Π_{NISC}. Similar to that in Theorem 1, NM-RMFE allows for simulating the cheating behavior of not following NM-RMFE encoding, thus the resulting NISC protocol has reusable malicious security in the $\mathcal{F}_{\mathrm{cVOLE}}^{\mathrm{GR}(2^k,d)}$-hybrid model. With a statistical secure instantiation of $\mathcal{F}_{\mathrm{cVOLE}}^{\mathrm{GR}(2^k,d)}$ in the $\mathcal{F}_{\mathrm{VOLE}}^{\mathrm{GR}(2^k,d)}$-hybrid model, the resulting NISC protocol has reusable malicious security in the $\mathcal{F}_{\mathrm{VOLE}}^{\mathrm{GR}(2^k,d)}$-hybrid model. The simulation error is computed by the union bound of the soundness of cVOLE and that of NM-RMFE. For the communication complexity, recall that in cVOLE we require two additional entries of VOLE for an $a_{i,j}$ entry that is an input to $\mathcal{C}$, and three additional entries of VOLE for an $b_{i,j}$ entry that is an input to $\mathcal{C}$. Thus, we can obtain the above results. ∎

Recall that by Theorem 2, we realize a slightly weaker variant of NM-RMFE, where $\boldsymbol{x} \in (\mathbb{Z}_{2^k}^*)^m$. We argue that this imperfect construction is still sufficient for building rNISC/VOLE. When instantiating NM-RMFE with our construction in the above rNISC/VOLE, intuitively the adversary $\mathcal{A}$ is allowed to query some positions of the honest party's inputs to VOLEs, and he learns whether they are all in $\mathbb{Z}_{2^k}^*$ (through observing the validity of VOLE outputs). More precisely, if the receiver is corrupted, recall that when we implement parallel DAREs, $P_{\mathcal{S}}$'s input $\boldsymbol{Y}$ will never be put into $\boldsymbol{a}$ entries, thus this attack can be avoided by instantiating Lemma 4 with $\bar{\mathcal{G}}_1^s \le \mathcal{G}_1^s, \bar{\mathcal{G}}_2^s \le \mathcal{G}_2^s$ such that their entries are even (i.e. zero divisors) except for the main diagonal. If the sender is corrupted, we let $P_{\mathcal{R}}$ sample the mask α from $\phi((\mathbb{Z}_{2^k}^*)^m)^{12}$, then applying this attack will always lead to $P_{\mathcal{R}}$ aborting.

5   Amortized Computationally Secure NISC

Our NM-RMFE approach admits rNISC/VOLE with good asymptotic efficiency and practical concrete efficiency for a relative large batch size m. To achieve

---

[12] This would slightly affect the eVOLE soundness.

better concrete efficiency (especially for small m), we consider weaker security models and explore computationally secure solutions to constructing (reusable) NISC protocols for BPs over $\mathbb{Z}_{2^k}$.

In this section, we first show how to force the sender to follow RMFE encoding efficiently. Then, we present two approaches to forcing the receiver to follow RMFE encoding honestly. The former approach is based on cut-and-choose and makes black-box use of any two-round reusable VOLE protocol. The latter OT-based approach is highly efficient but unfortunately not reusable. Combining all together, we obtain two NISC protocols, a concrete efficient reusable NISC construction with communication overhead $\mathcal{O}(\lambda)$, where λ is the computational security parameter, and a highly efficient NISC construction with communication overhead close to a constant.

5.1 Forcing the Sender to Follow RMFE Encoding

A naive solution is to augment the NIZK subprotocol in cVOLE to include a proof for correct RMFE encoding. However, this would lead to proving circuit satisfiability on a circuit of large size, which is inefficient. To this end, we use a more efficient technique, re-embedding VOLE (embVOLE) [21] that was originally designed for ZK protocols and allows to "prove" RMFE constraints before NIZK is applied. We slightly generalize the random embVOLE functionality to fit NISC settings (see $\mathcal{F}_{\text{embVOLE}}^{\text{GR}(2^k,d)}$ in Fig. 8), which then allows the receiver $P_{\mathcal{R}}$ to query $\hat{a}|_J$'s projection on $\text{Ker}(\psi)$, for some $J \subseteq [l]$. For some $i \in J$, to obtain $[a_i]_\alpha$ from a random $[\hat{a}_i]_\alpha$, P_S is supposed to send $u_i := a_i - \hat{a}_i$ to $P_{\mathcal{R}}$, then $P_{\mathcal{R}}$ can verify whether $u_i = \tau(\hat{a}_i) - \hat{a}_i$ ($P_{\mathcal{R}}$ learns $\tau(\hat{a}_i) - \hat{a}_i$ from querying $\hat{a}_i$'s projection on $\text{Ker}(\psi)$). If the check fails, $a_i \notin \text{Im}(\phi)$ and $P_{\mathcal{R}}$ will abort, which forces P_S's inputs to satisfy RMFE constraints.

We present the random embVOLE protocol $\Pi_{\text{embVOLE}}^{\text{GR}(2^k,d)}$ in Appendix B.3 of the full version [22], which can be made non-interactive by Fiat-Shamir heuristic. We remark that $\Pi_{\text{embVOLE}}^{\text{GR}(2^k,d)}$ has communication overhead close to a constant, when the length l is relatively large.

Functionality $\mathcal{F}_{\text{embVOLE}}^{\text{GR}(2^k,d)}$

$\mathcal{F}_{\text{embVOLE}}^{\text{GR}(2^k,d)}$ extends the random VOLE functionality $\mathcal{F}_{\text{VOLE}}^{\text{GR}(2^k,d)}$ (Figure 1). **Setup phase** and **Send phases** are identical to those in $\mathcal{F}_{\text{VOLE}}^{\text{GR}(2^k,d)}$, respectively. Parameterized by a Galois ring $\text{GR}(2^k,d)$, length parameters $l_1, ..., l_n \in \mathbb{N}$. Let (ϕ, ψ) be an $(m, d; 3)$-RMFE over $\mathbb{Z}_{2^k}$, and $\tau := \phi \circ \psi$.

Deliver phases: Upon receiving $(sid; \texttt{Delivery}; l_i; J)$ from the adversary where $i \in [n]$, $J \subseteq [l_i]$ and sid is a session identifier, verify that there are stored values $(sid; \alpha)$ and $(sid; \boldsymbol{a}, \boldsymbol{b}; l_i)$; else ignore that message. Next, compute $\boldsymbol{\eta} := (\tau(\boldsymbol{a}) - \boldsymbol{a})|_J \in \text{Ker}(\psi)^{|J|}$, and send $(sid; \boldsymbol{\eta}; l_i; J)$ to $P_{\mathcal{R}}$, and ignore further messages $(sid; \texttt{Delivery}; l_i; J)$ from the adversary with the same session identifier sid.

Fig. 8. Ideal functionality for random re-embedding VOLE over $\text{GR}(2^k, d)$.

Functionality $\mathcal{F}_{\phi\text{VOLE}}^{\text{GR}(2^k,d)}$

Let (ϕ, ψ) be an $(m, d; 3)$-RMFE over $\mathbb{Z}_{2^k}$. Parameterized by a ring $\text{GR}(2^k, d)$, length parameters $l_1, ..., l_n \in \mathbb{N}$ and the RMFE map ϕ.

Setup phase: Upon receiving input $(sid; \alpha)$ from $P_{\mathcal{R}}$ where $\alpha \in \text{Im}(\phi)$ and sid is a session identifier, store $(sid; \alpha)$, send $(sid; \texttt{initialized})$ to the adversary and ignore any further inputs from $P_{\mathcal{R}}$ with the same session identifier sid.

Send phases: Upon receiving input $(sid; \boldsymbol{a}; \boldsymbol{b}; l_i)$ from $P_{\mathcal{S}}$, where $(\boldsymbol{a}, \boldsymbol{b}; l_i) \in \text{GR}(2^k, d)^{l_i} \times \text{GR}(2^k, d)^{l_i} \times \mathbb{N}$ and sid is a session identifier, store $(sid; \boldsymbol{a}; \boldsymbol{b}; l_i)$, send $(sid; \texttt{sent}; l_i)$ to the adversary, and ignore any further inputs from $P_{\mathcal{S}}$ with the same session identifier sid.

Deliver phases: Upon receiving a message $(sid; \texttt{Delivery}; l_i)$ from the adversary where $l_i \in \mathbb{N}$ and sid is a session identifier, verify that there are stored inputs $(sid; \alpha)$ from $P_{\mathcal{R}}$ and $(sid; \boldsymbol{a}, \boldsymbol{b}; l_i)$ from $P_{\mathcal{S}}$; else ignore that message. Next, compute $\boldsymbol{v} := \boldsymbol{a} \cdot \alpha + \boldsymbol{b}$, send $(sid; \boldsymbol{v}; l_i)$ to $P_{\mathcal{R}}$, and ignore further messages $(sid; \texttt{Delivery}; l_i)$ from the adversary with the same session identifier sid.

Fig. 9. Ideal functionality for chosen-input ϕVOLE over $\text{GR}(2^k, d)$.

We slightly modify functionalities $\mathcal{F}_{\text{eVOLE}}^{\text{GR}(2^k,d)}$, $\mathcal{F}_{\text{cVOLE}}^{\text{GR}(2^k,d)}$ to include checking RMFE constraints (yielding $\mathcal{F}_{\ddot{e}\text{VOLE}}^{\text{GR}(2^k,d)}$, $\mathcal{F}_{\ddot{c}\text{VOLE}}^{\text{GR}(2^k,d)}$, respectively). We construct an $\ddot{e}$VOLE protocol $\Pi_{\ddot{e}\text{VOLE}}^{\text{GR}(2^k,d)}$, which is the same as $\Pi_{\text{eVOLE}}^{\text{GR}(2^k,d)}$, except that $\Pi_{\ddot{e}\text{VOLE}}^{\text{GR}(2^k,d)}$ is built upon $\mathcal{F}_{\text{embVOLE}}^{\text{GR}(2^k,d)}$. We also construct an $\ddot{c}$VOLE protocol $\Pi_{\ddot{c}\text{VOLE}}^{\text{GR}(2^k,d)}$, which is the same as $\Pi_{\text{cVOLE}}^{\text{GR}(2^k,d)}$, except that $\Pi_{\ddot{c}\text{VOLE}}^{\text{GR}(2^k,d)}$ is built upon $\mathcal{F}_{\ddot{e}\text{VOLE}}^{\text{GR}(2^k,d)}$. We refer to Appendix B.4 of the full version [22] for more details.

5.2   Forcing the Receiver to Follow RMFE Encoding

In this section, we consider the remaining issue of forcing the receiver to follow RMFE encoding. We remark again that the malicious receiver in the Π_{NISC} protocol can only cheat by deviating from RMFE encoding. Therefore, in Fig. 9 we define a variant of VOLE, called ϕVOLE, where the receiver's inputs are restricted in the image of a RMFE map ϕ (this leaves no room for the malicious receiver to cheat when building Π_{NISC} upon it). In general, we construct computationally secure NISC protocols following the roadmap below,

$$\mathcal{F}_{\phi\text{VOLE}}^{\text{GR}(2^k,d)} \implies \Pi_{\text{embVOLE}}^{\text{GR}(2^k,d)} \implies \Pi_{\ddot{e}\text{VOLE}}^{\text{GR}(2^k,d)} \overset{+\Pi_{\text{NIZK}}^{q,t}}{\implies} \Pi_{\ddot{c}\text{VOLE}}^{\text{GR}(2^k,d)} \implies \text{NISC}.$$

Recall that in $\ddot{c}$VOLE, there are $n + 2$ VOLE instances, and the first $n + 1$ VOLE instances correspond to $P_{\mathcal{R}}$'s inputs $\alpha_1 + \beta, ..., \alpha_n + \beta, \beta$, respectively. We remark that $\alpha_1 + \beta, ..., \alpha_n + \beta, \beta$ will be restricted in $\text{Im}(\phi)$, the $\ddot{e}$VOLE soundness is $1/2^d + 1/2^m$ rather than $1/2^{d-1}$. We present two ϕVOLE constructions with different features as follows.

The ϕVOLE construction based on cut-and-choose. We are initially inspired by the approach of the concurrent work [18], where they bypassed the impossible result of OT-based rNISC [10] via making a black-box use of OT protocols with random oracles. Making a black-box use of OT (VOLE) protocols instead of assuming black-box access to an ideal OT (VOLE) functionality allows for "connecting" the inputs that the parties use to compute OT messages with the other cryptographic primitives, e.g. commitments. Let $(\Pi_{P_{\mathcal{R}},1}^{\mathrm{GR}(2^k,d)}, \Pi_{P_{\mathcal{S}},1}^{\mathrm{GR}(2^k,d)}, \Pi_{P_{\mathcal{R}},2}^{\mathrm{GR}(2^k,d)})$ be a two-message reusable VOLE protocol over $\mathrm{GR}(2^k,d)$, where $P_{\mathcal{R}}$ runs $\Pi_{P_{\mathcal{R}},1}^{\mathrm{GR}(2^k,d)}$ on her private input and random tape to obtain the first round message π_1, then $P_{\mathcal{S}}$ computes the second round message π_2 by running $\Pi_{P_{\mathcal{S}},1}^{\mathrm{GR}(2^k,d)}$ on π_1 and his private input, and finally $P_{\mathcal{R}}$ obtains the result by evaluating $\Pi_{P_{\mathcal{R}},2}^{\mathrm{GR}(2^k,d)}$ on π_2 and her random tapes. Recall that our goal here is to guarantee that $P_{\mathcal{R}}$'s inputs are restricted in the image of an RMFE map, and intuitively our high-level idea is cut-and-choose. The receiver $P_{\mathcal{R}}$ commits to inputs and random tapes used for generating her first VOLE messages (several copies), and reveals some of them according to queries to a random oracle. The sender $P_{\mathcal{S}}$ then can check whether $P_{\mathcal{R}}$'s inputs are valid and the VOLE messages are correctly computed. However, there is still a gap since $P_{\mathcal{R}}$'s inputs are private (for computing rNISC/VOLE tasks) and none of them could be revealed. We overcome this issue by observing that in cVOLE, $P_{\mathcal{R}}$'s inputs to multiple VOLE instances are masked with a random β (suppose $P_{\mathcal{R}}$ has inputs $\alpha_1, ..., \alpha_n$), thus one of these commitments $[\![\alpha_1 + \beta]\!], ..., [\![\alpha_n + \beta]\!], [\![\beta]\!]$ can be opened. Repeating the procedure for a sufficient number of times and $P_{\mathcal{S}}$ will believe that $P_{\mathcal{R}}$ behaves honestly with an overwhelming probability. The final problem is that a malicious $P_{\mathcal{R}}$ may not provide consistent inputs in different iterations. We show that if further assuming the commitment scheme (Com, Open) is linearly homomorphic over Galois rings, we can apply a random linear combination check on the committed inputs, where the random coefficients can be obtained by querying a random oracle as well. Since RMFEs over $\mathbb{Z}_{2^k}$ are $\mathbb{Z}_{2^k}$-linear maps, these random coefficients can be sampled from $\mathbb{Z}_{2^k}$. We present the desired protocol in Fig. 10, which has $\mathcal{O}(\lambda)$ communication overhead due to cut-and-choose.

We have the following theorem (see the proof in Appendix B.6 of the full version [22]).

Theorem 5. *Assuming a two-message reusable VOLE protocol over* $\mathrm{GR}(2^k,d)$, *and a linearly-homomorphic commitment scheme over* $\mathrm{GR}(2^k,d)$, $\Omega_{\phi\mathrm{VOLE}}^{\mathrm{GR}(2^k,d)}$ *realizes* $\mathcal{F}_{\phi\mathrm{VOLE}}^{\mathrm{GR}(2^k,d)}$ *in the random oracle model.*

Combining all pieces together, we obtain an rNISC protocol (for computing BPs over $\mathbb{Z}_{2^k}$) that makes black-box use of any two-message reusable VOLE protocol in the random oracle model. We note that, for constructing an rNISC computing a general function f, the work [18] provides a compiler that lifts a non-reusable (malicious secure) NISC protocol (computes a related function f') to a reusable one. We observe that their tool is strong, but quite heavy and expensive for general functions, while for some simple f, the efficiency can

Protocol $\Omega_{\phi\text{VOLE}}^{\text{GR}(2^k,d)}$

Parameterized by a Galois ring $\text{GR}(2^k, d)$, length parameter l, computational security parameter λ and cut-and-choose parameter $t = \mathcal{O}(\lambda)$. Let (ϕ, ψ) be an $(m, d; 3)$-RMFE over $\mathbb{Z}_{2^k}$. Let $(\Pi_{P_\mathcal{R},1}^{\text{GR}(2^k,d)}, \Pi_{P_S,1}^{\text{GR}(2^k,d)}, \Pi_{P_\mathcal{R},2}^{\text{GR}(2^k,d)})$ be a two-message reusable VOLE protocol over $\text{GR}(2^k, d)$. Let $H_1 : \{0,1\}^* \to (\{0,1\}^{s_t})^{(n+1)\times t}$ and $H_2 : \{0,1\}^* \to \mathbb{Z}_{2^k}^{n \times t}$ be two hash functions, where s_t is the number of bits needed to toss a biased coin (used for interpreting the hash values as matrices with a special form). Let $(\text{Com}, \text{Open})$ be a commitment scheme. Suppose $P_\mathcal{R}$ has input $\boldsymbol{\alpha} \in \text{Im}(\phi)^n$, and P_S has input $\boldsymbol{a}_i, \boldsymbol{b}_i \in \text{GR}(2^k, d)^l$ for $i = 0, 1, ..., n$.

1. **Round-1:**
   (a) For $j \in [t]$, $P_\mathcal{R}$ samples $\beta_j \xleftarrow{\$} \text{Im}(\phi)$. For $i = 0, 1, ..., n$ and $j \in [t]$, $P_\mathcal{R}$ samples random tape $r_{i,j}$ to be used in the protocol $\Pi_{P_\mathcal{R},1}^{\text{GR}(2^k,d)}$.
   (b) For $i \in [n]$, $P_\mathcal{R}$ computes $[\![\alpha_i]\!] := \text{Com}(\alpha_i)$. For $j \in [t]$, $P_\mathcal{R}$ computes $\pi_{0,j,1} := \Pi_{P_\mathcal{R},1}^{\text{GR}(2^k,d)}(\beta_j; r_{0,j})$, $[\![\beta_j]\!] := \text{Com}(\beta_j)$, and $[\![r_{0,j}]\!] := \text{Com}(r_{0,j})$. For $i \in [n]$ and $j \in [t]$, $P_\mathcal{R}$ computes $\pi_{i,j,1} := \Pi_{P_\mathcal{R},1}^{\text{GR}(2^k,d)}(\alpha_i + \beta_j; r_{i,j})$, $[\![\alpha_i + \beta_j]\!] := \text{Com}(\alpha_i + \beta_j)$ and $[\![r_{i,j}]\!] := \text{Com}(r_{i,j})$. Denote the sequence of values $(\{[\![\alpha_i]\!]\}_{i\in[n]}, \{\pi_{0,j,1}, [\![\beta_j]\!], [\![r_{0,j}]\!]\}_{j\in[t]}, \{\pi_{i,j,1}, [\![\alpha_i + \beta_j]\!], [\![r_{i,j}]\!]\}_{i\in[n],j\in[t]})$ by msg.
   (c) The receiver $P_\mathcal{R}$ computes $S = H_1(\text{msg})$, and interprets S as a $(n+1)\times t$ matrix such that each column contains at most one 1 and zeros everywhere else (we require S has at least one column with all zeros). Then, $P_\mathcal{R}$ computes $\{\chi_{i,j}\}_{i\in[n],j\in[t]} := H_2(\text{msg})$, where $\chi_{i,j} \in \mathbb{Z}_{2^k}$.
   (d) The receiver $P_\mathcal{R}$ computes $\text{unv} := \text{Open}(\sum_{i\in[n],j\in[t]} \chi_{i,j} \cdot ([\![\alpha_i + \beta_j]\!] - [\![\alpha_i]\!] - [\![\beta_j]\!]))$.
   (e) The receiver $P_\mathcal{R}$ sends $(\{\text{msg}, \text{unv}, \{\text{Open}([\![\alpha_i + \beta_j]\!]), \text{Open}([\![r_{i,j}]\!])\}_{S_{i,j}=1})$ as the first message.

2. **Round-2:**
   (a) The sender P_S recomputes S and $\{\chi_{i,j}\}_{i\in[n],j\in[t]}$ as in step-(c) of Round-1 and checks whether the openings are valid. In particular, P_S checks whether unv is an opening of $[\![0]\!]$.
   (b) For $i \in [n], j \in [t]$ such that $S_{i,j} = 1$, P_S checks whether $\alpha_i + \beta_j \in \text{Im}(\phi)$. For $j \in [t]$ such that $S_{0,j} = 1$, P_S checks whether $\beta_j \in \text{Im}(\phi)$.
   (c) For $i \in [n], j \in [t]$ such that $S_{i,j} = 1$, P_S checks whether $\pi_{i,j,1} = \Pi_{P_\mathcal{R},1}^{\text{GR}(2^k,d)}(\alpha_i + \beta_j; r_{i,j})$. For $j \in [t]$ such that $S_{0,j} = 1$, P_S checks whether $\pi_{0,j,1} = \Pi_{P_\mathcal{R},1}^{\text{GR}(2^k,d)}(\beta_j; r_{0,j})$.
   (d) If any of above checks fail, P_S aborts. Otherwise, P_S randomly picks j satisfying the j-th column of S are all 0's.
   (e) P_S computes $\pi_{i,2} := \Pi_{P_S,1}^{\text{GR}(2^k,d)}(\boldsymbol{a}_i, \boldsymbol{b}_i, \pi_{i,j,1})$ for $i = 0, 1, ..., n$. P_S sends $(\pi_{0,2}, ..., \pi_{n,2}, j)$ to $P_\mathcal{R}$.

3. **Output Computation:** The receiver $P_\mathcal{R}$ computes $\boldsymbol{v}_i := \Pi_{P_\mathcal{R},2}^{\text{GR}(2^k,d)}(\pi_{i,2}, r_{i,j})$, for $i = 0, 1, ..., n$.

Fig. 10. Protocol for ϕVOLE making black-box use of VOLE over $\text{GR}(2^k, d)$.

be significantly improved. To optimize the efficiency, we can use their rNISC compiler to obtain a reusable VOLE protocol over Galois rings from black-box use of OT[13], which is expected to have good concrete efficiency.

The ϕVOLE construction from OT. We start with an observation on RMFEs. Let (ϕ, ψ) be an $(m, d; D)$-RMFE over $\mathbb{Z}_{2^k}$. We have that $\mathrm{GR}(2^k, d)$ can be viewed as a linear space over $\mathbb{Z}_{2^k}$ with dimension d. As ϕ, ψ are $\mathbb{Z}_{2^k}$-linear maps, $\mathrm{Im}(\phi)$ can be viewed as a linear space over $\mathbb{Z}_{2^k}$ with dimension m, which is a subspace of $\mathrm{GR}(2^k, d)$ as well. Therefore, there exist a basis $\gamma_1, ..., \gamma_m \in \mathrm{GR}(2^k, d)$ such that

$$\phi : \mathbb{Z}_{2^k}^m \to \mathrm{GR}(2^k, d), \quad (a_1, ..., a_m) \mapsto a_1\gamma_1 + ... + a_m\gamma_m.$$

We call such $\gamma_1, ..., \gamma_m$ an RMFE-basis. Let $\boldsymbol{\alpha} \in \mathbb{Z}_{2^k}^m$, and $\boldsymbol{a}, \boldsymbol{b}_1, ..., \boldsymbol{b}_m \in \mathrm{GR}(2^k, d)^l$. Denote $\boldsymbol{a} \cdot \alpha_i + \boldsymbol{b}_i$ by $\boldsymbol{v}_i$, for $i \in [m]$. We have that

$$\sum_{i=1}^m \boldsymbol{v}_i \cdot \gamma_i = \sum_{i=1}^m (\boldsymbol{a} \cdot \alpha_i + \boldsymbol{b}_i) \cdot \gamma_i = \boldsymbol{a} \cdot \left(\sum_{i=1}^m \alpha_i\gamma_i \right) + \sum_{i=1}^m \boldsymbol{b}_i \cdot \gamma_i$$

$$= \boldsymbol{a} \cdot \phi(\alpha_1, ..., \alpha_m) + \sum_{i=1}^m \boldsymbol{b}_i \cdot \gamma_i.$$

Denoting $\sum_{i=1}^m \boldsymbol{v}_i \cdot \gamma_i$ by $\boldsymbol{v}$ and $\sum_{i=1}^m \boldsymbol{b}_i \cdot \gamma_i$ by $\boldsymbol{b}$, we obtain an VOLE instance $\boldsymbol{v} = \boldsymbol{a} \cdot \phi(\boldsymbol{\alpha}) + \boldsymbol{b}$. From above discussions, we define the (chosen-input) reverse subring VOLE (rsVOLE) functionality over $\mathrm{GR}(2^k, d)$, where the receiver $P_{\mathcal{R}}$'s inputs are over $\mathbb{Z}_{2^k}$. We refer to Appendix B.5 of the full version [22] for the functionality and a straightforward construction based on OT (similar to the way that SPDZ_{2^k} [11] implements VOLE over $\mathbb{Z}_{2^k}$).

Then in Fig. 11, we present a semi-honest secure ϕVOLE construction over $\mathrm{GR}(2^k, d)$ in the $\mathcal{F}_{\mathrm{rsVOLE}}^{\mathrm{GR}(2^k, d)}$-hybrid model. To enable perfect simulation, we further require that γ_1 is invertible in $\mathrm{GR}(2^k, d)$. Such RMFE-basis $\gamma_1, ..., \gamma_m \in \mathrm{GR}(2^k, d)$ always exists, for an $(m, d; D)$-RMFE (ϕ, ψ) with $\phi(\boldsymbol{1}) = 1$. Intuitively, if $\boldsymbol{b}_1$ is uniformly random, then $\boldsymbol{b}$ is uniformly random as well. We have the following theorem (see the proof in Appendix B.6 of the full version [22]).

Theorem 6. *Protocol* $\Pi_{\phi\mathrm{VOLE}}^{\mathrm{GR}(2^k, d)}$ *realizes* $\mathcal{F}_{\phi\mathrm{VOLE}}^{\mathrm{GR}(2^k, d)}$ *with semi-honest security.*

Our OT-based rsVOLE construction essentially admits a ϕVOLE protocol with semi-honest security (mk OTs involved in total). For such OT-based constructions, the malicious security can be naturally obtained if upgrading OTs to Correlated OTs (COTs) (we can use the COT construction in [25]), as there is no room for a malicious $P_{\mathcal{R}}$ to cheat and a malicious $P_{\mathcal{S}}$ can only cheat by providing inconsistent inputs to OTs. This leads to an efficient malicious secure ϕVOLE construction (the cost is even cheaper than constructing standard VOLE from COT), and further an efficient malicious secure NISC construction for computing BPs over $\mathbb{Z}_{2^k}$.

---

[13] VOLE is essentially a simple NISC task, therefore the inner protocol of the rNISC compiler can be an OT-based (non-reusable) VOLE protocol. The specific construction is beyond the scope of this work, thus omitted.

Protocol $\Pi_{\phi\text{VOLE}}^{\text{GR}(2^k,d)}$

Parameterized by a Galois ring $\text{GR}(2^k,d)$, length parameter l. Let (ϕ,ψ) be an $(m,d;3)$-RMFE over $\mathbb{Z}_{2^k}$, and $\gamma_1,...,\gamma_m \in \text{GR}(2^k,d)$ be an RMFE-basis such that γ_1 is invertible. Suppose $P_{\mathcal{R}}$ has input $\boldsymbol{\alpha} \in \mathbb{Z}_{2^k}^m$, and $P_{\mathcal{S}}$ has input $\boldsymbol{a},\boldsymbol{b} \in \text{GR}(2^k,d)^l$.

1. For $i = 1,...,m$, $P_{\mathcal{R}}$ sends $(i;\alpha_i)$ to $\mathcal{F}_{\text{rsVOLE}}^{\text{GR}(2^k,d)}$.
2. For $i = 2,...,m$, $P_{\mathcal{S}}$ picks random $\boldsymbol{b}_i \in \text{GR}(2^k,d)^l$. $P_{\mathcal{S}}$ sets $\boldsymbol{b}_1 = \gamma_1^{-1} \cdot (\boldsymbol{b} - \sum_{i=2}^m \boldsymbol{b}_i \cdot \gamma_i)$. $P_{\mathcal{S}}$ sends $(i;\boldsymbol{a},\boldsymbol{b}_i;l)$ to $\mathcal{F}_{\text{rsVOLE}}^{\text{GR}(2^k,d)}$, for $i \in [m]$.
3. Upon receiving $(i;\boldsymbol{v}_i;l)$ from $\mathcal{F}_{\text{rsVOLE}}^{\text{GR}(2^k,d)}$, where $\boldsymbol{v}_i = \boldsymbol{a} \cdot \alpha_i + \boldsymbol{b}_i$, for $i \in [m]$, $P_{\mathcal{R}}$ computes $\boldsymbol{v} := \sum_{i=1}^m \boldsymbol{v}_i \cdot \gamma_i$.

Fig. 11. Protocol for ϕVOLE over $\text{GR}(2^k,d)$ in the $\mathcal{F}_{\text{rsVOLE}}^{\text{GR}(2^k,d)}$-hybrid model.

Acknowledgements. The authors would like to thank the anonymous reviewers for their insightful comments, which greatly improved the presentation of this work. The work was supported in part by the National Key Research and Development Project under Grant 2022YFA1004900, in part by the National Natural Science Foundation of China under Grant 12031011.

References

1. Afshar, A., Mohassel, P., Pinkas, B., Riva, B.: Non-interactive secure computation based on cut-and-choose. In: Nguyen, P.Q., Oswald, E. (eds.) EUROCRYPT 2014. LNCS, vol. 8441, pp. 387–404. Springer, Heidelberg (2014). https://doi.org/10.1007/978-3-642-55220-5_22

2. Applebaum, B., Ishai, Y., Kushilevitz, E.: How to garble arithmetic circuits. SIAM J. Comput. **43**(2), 905–929 (2014)

3. Blum, A., Furst, M., Kearns, M., Lipton, R.J.: Cryptographic primitives based on hard learning problems. In: Stinson, D.R. (ed.) CRYPTO 1993. LNCS, vol. 773, pp. 278–291. Springer, Heidelberg (1994). https://doi.org/10.1007/3-540-48329-2_24

4. Bootle, J., Chiesa, A., Guan, Z., Liu, S.: Linear-time probabilistic proofs with sublinear verification for algebraic automata over every field. IACR Cryptol. ePrint Arch., p. 1056 (2022). https://eprint.iacr.org/2022/1056

5. Boyle, E., Couteau, G., Gilboa, N., Ishai, Y.: Compressing vector OLE. In: CCS 2018, pp. 896–912. ACM (2018)

6. Boyle, E., et al.: Efficient two-round OT extension and silent non-interactive secure computation. In: CCS 2019, pp. 291–308. ACM (2019)

7. Cascudo, I., Cramer, R., Xing, C., Yuan, C.: Amortized complexity of information-theoretically secure MPC revisited. In: Shacham, H., Boldyreva, A. (eds.) CRYPTO 2018. LNCS, vol. 10993, pp. 395–426. Springer, Cham (2018). https://doi.org/10.1007/978-3-319-96878-0_14

8. Cascudo, I., Giunta, E.: On interactive oracle proofs for Boolean R1CS statements. In: Financial Cryptography and Data Security - 26th International Conference, FC 2022, Grenada, May 2–6, 2022, Revised Selected Papers. LNCS, vol. 13411, pp. 230–247. Springer, Cham (2022). https://doi.org/10.1007/978-3-031-18283-9_11

9. Cascudo, I., Gundersen, J.S.: A secret-sharing based MPC protocol for Boolean circuits with good amortized complexity. In: Pass, R., Pietrzak, K. (eds.) TCC 2020. LNCS, vol. 12551, pp. 652–682. Springer, Cham (2020). https://doi.org/10.1007/978-3-030-64378-2_23
10. Chase, M., et al.: Reusable non-interactive secure computation. In: Boldyreva, A., Micciancio, D. (eds.) CRYPTO 2019. LNCS, vol. 11694, pp. 462–488. Springer, Cham (2019). https://doi.org/10.1007/978-3-030-26954-8_15
11. Cramer, R., Damgård, I., Escudero, D., Scholl, P., Xing, C.: SPD$\mathbb{Z}_{2^k}$: efficient MPC mod 2^k for dishonest majority. In: Shacham, H., Boldyreva, A. (eds.) CRYPTO 2018. LNCS, vol. 10992, pp. 769–798. Springer, Cham (2018). https://doi.org/10.1007/978-3-319-96881-0_26
12. Cramer, R., Rambaud, M., Xing, C.: Asymptotically-good arithmetic secret sharing over $\mathbb{Z}/p^\ell\mathbb{Z}$ with strong multiplication and its applications to efficient MPC. In: Malkin, T., Peikert, C. (eds.) CRYPTO 2021. LNCS, vol. 12827, pp. 656–686. Springer, Cham (2021). https://doi.org/10.1007/978-3-030-84252-9_22
13. Dittmer, S., Ishai, Y., Ostrovsky, R.: Line-point zero knowledge and its applications. In: 2nd Conference on Information-Theoretic Cryptography, ITC 2021, July 23–26, 2021, Virtual Conference. LIPIcs, vol. 199, pp. 5:1–5:24. Schloss Dagstuhl - Leibniz-Zentrum für Informatik (2021)
14. Escudero, D., Liu, H., Xing, C., Yuan, C.: Degree-D reverse multiplication-friendly embeddings: Constructions and applications. IACR Cryptol. ePrint Arch., 173 (2023). https://eprint.iacr.org/2023/173
15. Escudero, D., Xing, C., Yuan, C.: More efficient dishonest majority secure computation over $\mathbb{Z}_{2^k}$ via galois rings. In: CRYPTO 2022. LNCS, vol. 13507, pp. 383–412. Springer (2022). https://doi.org/10.1007/978-3-031-15802-5_14
16. Gentry, C.: Fully homomorphic encryption using ideal lattices. In: Proceedings of the 41st Annual ACM Symposium on Theory of Computing, STOC 2009, Bethesda, MD, USA, May 31 - June 2, 2009, pp. 169–178. ACM (2009)
17. Hazay, C., Ishai, Y., Venkitasubramaniam, M.: Actively secure garbled circuits with constant communication overhead in the plain model. J. Cryptol. **36**(3), 26 (2023)
18. Ishai, Y., Khurana, D., Sahai, A., Srinivasan, A.: Black-box reusable NISC with random oracles. In: EUROCRYPT 2023. LNCS, vol. 14005, pp. 68–97. Springer, Cham (2023). https://doi.org/10.1007/978-3-031-30617-4_3
19. Ishai, Y., Kushilevitz, E.: Perfect constant-round secure computation via perfect randomizing polynomials. In: Widmayer, P., Eidenbenz, S., Triguero, F., Morales, R., Conejo, R., Hennessy, M. (eds.) ICALP 2002. LNCS, vol. 2380, pp. 244–256. Springer, Heidelberg (2002). https://doi.org/10.1007/3-540-45465-9_22
20. Ishai, Y., Kushilevitz, E., Ostrovsky, R., Prabhakaran, M., Sahai, A.: Efficient non-interactive secure computation. In: Paterson, K.G. (ed.) EUROCRYPT 2011. LNCS, vol. 6632, pp. 406–425. Springer, Heidelberg (2011). https://doi.org/10.1007/978-3-642-20465-4_23
21. Lin, F., Xing, C., Yao, Y.: More efficient zero-knowledge protocols over $\mathbb{Z}_{2^k}$ via galois rings. IACR Cryptol. ePrint Arch., 150 (2023). https://eprint.iacr.org/2023/150
22. Lin, F., Xing, C., Yao, Y., Yuan, C.: Amortized nisc over $\mathbb{Z}_{2^k}$ from rmfe. Cryptology ePrint Archive (2023). https://eprint.iacr.org/2023/1363
23. Mohassel, P., Rosulek, M.: Non-interactive secure 2PC in the offline/online and batch settings. In: EUROCRYPT 2017, LNCS, vol. 10212, pp. 425–455 (2017)
24. Ree, R.: Proof of a conjecture of S. Chowla. J. Number Theory **3**(2), 210–212 (1971)

25. Scholl, P.: Extending oblivious transfer with low communication via key-homomorphic PRFs. In: Abdalla, M., Dahab, R. (eds.) PKC 2018. LNCS, vol. 10769, pp. 554–583. Springer, Cham (2018). https://doi.org/10.1007/978-3-319-76578-5_19
26. Wan, Z.X.: Lectures on finite fields and Galois rings. World Scientific Publishing Company (2003)
27. Yao, A.C.: How to generate and exchange secrets (extended abstract). In: 27th Annual Symposium on Foundations of Computer Science, Toronto, Canada, 27–29 October 1986, pp. 162–167. IEEE Computer Society (1986)

Two-Round Concurrent 2PC
from Sub-exponential LWE

Behzad Abdolmaleki[1]([✉]), Saikrishna Badrinarayanan[2], Rex Fernando[3],
Giulio Malavolta[4,5], Ahmadreza Rahimi[5], and Amit Sahai[6]

[1] University of Sheffield, Sheffield, UK
behzad.abdolmaleki@sheffield.ac.uk
[2] LinkedIn, Mountain View, USA
[3] Carnegie Mellon University, Pittsburgh, USA
[4] Bocconi University, Milan, Italy
[5] Max Planck Institute for Security and Privacy, Bochum, Germany
{giulio.malavolta,ahmadreza.rahimi}@mpi-sp.org
[6] UCLA, Los Angeles, USA
sahai@cs.ucla.edu

Abstract. Secure computation is a cornerstone of modern cryptography and a rich body of research is devoted to understanding its round complexity. In this work, we consider two-party computation (2PC) protocols (where both parties receive output) that remain secure in the realistic setting where many instances of the protocol are executed in parallel (concurrent security). We obtain a two-round *concurrent-secure* 2PC protocol *based on a single, standard, post-quantum* assumption: The subexponential hardness of the learning-with-errors (LWE) problem. Our protocol is in the plain model, i.e., it has no trusted setup, and it is secure in the super-polynomial simulation framework of Pass (EUROCRYPT 2003). Since two rounds are minimal for (concurrent) 2PC, this work resolves the round complexity of concurrent 2PC from standard assumptions.

As immediate applications, our work establishes feasibility results for interesting cryptographic primitives, such as the first two-round password authentication key exchange (PAKE) protocol in the plain model and the first two-round concurrent secure computation protocol for quantum circuits (2PQC).

1 Introduction

Secure computation is a fundamental primitive in cryptography which allows two or more parties, all of whom have private inputs, to collectively compute some function over their inputs securely without revealing the inputs themselves. In recent years, significant attention has been devoted to the round-complexity of secure computation in the setting of two parties, as well as in the multi-party

---

S. Badrinarayanan and R. Fernando—Part of the work was done while the author was affiliated with UCLA.

J. Guo and R. Steinfeld (Eds.): ASIACRYPT 2023, LNCS 14438, pp. 71–105, 2023.
https://doi.org/10.1007/978-981-99-8721-4_3

setting (MPC). This has culminated in recent work of [5,11,23,28,35,41], which give protocols that run in four rounds, known to be the least amount of rounds possible for full security in the plain model[1].

The results above achieve security in the *standalone* setting, where all parties are assumed to participate in only one instance of the protocol.

The Concurrent Setting. A more realistic setting allows parties to participate *concurrently* in arbitrarily many instances. Unfortunately, Barak, Prabhakaran and Sahai [14] show that achieving the standard definition of concurrent security is impossible *in any rounds* in the plain model, without a trusted setup. In an effort to overcome the above mentioned impossibility results, many recent works have focused on proving concurrent security for two-party computation (2PC) in alternative models, e.g., in the bounded concurrent model [59], in the multiple ideal-query model [38], and for input-indistinguishable computation [55].

One standard relaxation of simulation security, which is widely used to circumvent many lower-bound results, is the notion of *super-polynomial simulation*, or SPS [58]. With this notion, for any real-world adversary, we require an ideal-world simulator that runs in super-polynomial time. More precisely, in this scenario, the simulator in the ideal world is allowed to run in (fixed) super-polynomial time. Informally, the SPS security guarantees that any polynomial-time attack in the real execution can also be mounted in the ideal world execution, albeit in super-polynomial time. This is directly applicable in settings where ideal world security is guaranteed statistically or information-theoretically and it is known to imply input-indistinguishable computation [55]. There has been a fruitful line of research devoted to understanding the power of SPS security for secure computations in the concurrent setting [26,33,48–50,54,60] [12,34,40].

The Round Complexity. In the concurrent setting, a series of works [33,49] constructed constant-round protocols (approximately 20 rounds) in the simultaneous message exchange model. Later, Garg *et al.* [34] decreased the round complexity to 5 rounds with SPS security from standard sub-exponential assumptions. In 2017, the work of Badrinarayanan et al. [12] used this notion to circumvent both the impossibility of concurrent MPC and the four-round lower-bound, giving a protocol that works in three rounds and satisfies concurrent security. For several years, this result was the best-known result regarding the round complexity of MPC in the plain model. Until very recently, no two-round protocols were known. This was the case even in the restricted setting of two-party computation (where both parties receive output).

Recently two new works improved the state of the art in this area:

– The work of [2] gave a two-round MPC protocol for general functionalities which achieves standalone security in the plain model without setup and with a

---

[1] It is also known how to achieve two-round MPC that satisfies a much weaker notion of *semi-malicious* security, where the adversary is assumed to follow the honest protocol specification. [36] Alternately, achieving full security in two rounds is possible if we allow for a trusted setup. In this paper, we focus on achieving full malicious security in the plain model, without setup.

super-polynomial simulator, assuming subexponential non-interactive witness-indistinguishable arguments, the subexponential SXDH assumption, and the existence of a special type of non-interactive non-malleable commitment.[2]
- The work of [31] gave a concurrent, highly-reusable[3] two-round MPC protocol for general functionalities, assuming subexponential quantum hardness of the learning-with-errors (LWE) problem, subexponential classical hardness of SXDH, the existence of a subexponentially-secure (classically-hard) indistinguishability obfuscation (iO) scheme, and time-lock puzzles.

Assumptions for Two-Party Secure Computation. The goal of our work is to focus on secure computation in the two-party setting and to explore the assumptions under which two-round secure protocols are possible. Even in this more specific setting, the two above results are the only known protocols that achieve two-round protocols for general two-party functionalities.[4] Both of the previously mentioned works on two-round protocols use powerful primitives which are only known from strong assumptions. More specifically, the work of [2] requires a strong version of non-interactive non-malleable commitments, which are only known from strong, non-standard assumptions, such as adaptive one-way functions [57], or keyless hash functions along with a subexponential variant of the "hardness amplifiability" assumption of [19]. The work of [31] is able to avoid using these strong commitments, instead using (a modified version of) the one-round NMC of [46], which relies on the existence of sub-exponential indistinguishability obfuscation (iO).

We briefly discuss the assumptions under which iO exists. Our understanding of these assumptions has vastly improved in recent years, culminating in the work of [44,45], which showed that iO can be built on well-founded assumptions, namely hardness of LPN over $\mathbb{F}_p$, hardness of DLIN, and the existence of PRGs in NC^0. However, our understanding of the assumptions necessary for *quantum-secure* iO is much less stable. We note that besides the above-mentioned work, all other constructions of iO rely on ad-hoc hardness assumptions which were specifically invented for the purpose of proving the security of iO [3,4,6–8,13, 16,21,22,24,27,29,32,37,43,51,52,56,61,64]. Although some of the most recent of these constructions rely on lattice-based assumptions which ostensibly could be quantum-secure [22,37,64], there are already preliminary attacks on some versions of these new assumptions [42]. Thus, in this setting, our understanding is much more limited than in the classical case.

In addition to iO, both of the constructions of the two-round MPC above use other assumptions (i.e., SXDH) which, while standard, are quantum-broken. With all of this in mind, it is interesting to ask the following question:

---

[2] The protocol of [2] is given in the form of a compiler that transforms a two-round semi-malicious-secure MPC protocol into a malicious-secure one.
[3] See [31] for the exact definition of reusability obtained.
[4] If we restrict ourselves to functionalities where only one party receives output, then it is known how to achieve two-round secure computation from much simpler assumptions [10], in the setting of standalone security.

Can we achieve two-round concurrently secure two-party computation under simple, post-quantum assumptions, in the plain model?

As mentioned above, this question is interesting even if we restrict ourselves to the case of two parties, since up to this point the only known results even in this subcase are the two discussed above, which both require strong, potentially quantum-unsafe assumptions.

1.1   Our Contributions

In this work, we make a significant process in answering the above question. In this particular case, we show how to build a two-round, *concurrent-secure*, two-party secure computation protocol *based on a single, standard, post-quantum* assumption, namely sub-exponential the hardness of the learning-with-errors (LWE) problem. We state our main theorem now.

Theorem 1. *Assuming the sub-exponential hardness of the learning-with-errors (LWE) problem, there exists a two-round two-party computation protocol for any polynomial-time functionality f where both parties receive outputs, in the plain model with super-polynomial simulation.*

We note that our protocol is the first two-round concurrent-secure 2PC the protocol that does not require the existence of a one-round non-malleable commitment (NMC). Instead, we are able to use the two-round NMCs of [47], which is instantiable from sub-exponential LWE. Our protocol is also the first such protocol that does not require the existence of non-interactive witness indistinguishable arguments or time-lock puzzles. Here, we briefly mention two of the applications of our protocol.

Application: Round-Optimal PAKE. In a password-authenticated key exchange (PAKE) [18] protocol, two users hold passwords (x_1, x_2) and want to exchange a high-entropy secret if $x_1 = x_2$, otherwise, they learn nothing about the other user's inputs. Our concurrent 2PC protocol directly yields the first two-round PAKE scheme in the plain model, resolving a long-standing open problem in the area. Our protocol achieves the standard game-based security notion, as defined by Bellare *et al.* [17].

Application: Concurrent Quantum Computation. As another application of our protocol, we show how it immediately yields the first concurrent 2PC for quantum functionalities (in the plain model) with classical inputs and outputs. In fact, we show that our classical 2PC provides us with the necessary building block to instantiate the recent compiler of Bartusek *et al.* [15], which we then show how to lift to the concurrent settings.

1.2   Technical Overview

To introduce the techniques used in our concurrent 2PC construction, we start by summarizing a discussion in the work of [12], which gives an intuition for why two-round secure computation protocols seem difficult to achieve. In particular, they argue that such a protocol seems to necessarily imply non-interactive non-malleable commitments (NMCs).

Difficulties in Constructing Concurrent 2PC. We focus our summary on the case of two parties since our paper addresses this case. The authors of [12] note that any such two-round 2PC protocol should have some sort of input commitment in the first round, and then the second round should be used to compute the output. They then make the following important observation: Since we are working in the SPS model without setup, zero knowledge requires at least two rounds. This means that an honest party must send its second message *without knowing if the adversary's first-round message is honest*. The example given in [12] to illustrate this is as follows. Consider a case where the honest party's input is x, and where there is a "rushing" adversary which waits to send its first message until after seeing the honest party's first message. If this adversary "mauls" the other party's message and sends a first-round message which also encodes x, then the honest party cannot detect this before sending out its second message. Ostensibly, this would cause both the honest party and the adversary to learn $f(x, x)$, thus breaking SPS security of the protocol. Because of this, it seems at first glance that non-interactive NMCs are necessary to prevent such "mauling" attacks in two-round protocols.

Avoiding Non-interactive NMCs. As discussed earlier, we want to avoid non-interactive NMCs, since contrary to two-round NMCs all non-interactive constructions require strong assumptions. To do so, we must understand why the intuition above is incorrect. One implicit assumption we have made in this argument is that the adversary always learns the same output that the honest party learns after the second round. This is indeed the case in *public-output* protocols, where anyone can compute the output given just the transcript of the protocol and no other information. However, what about the case of *private-output* protocols, where each party must use private information in order to reconstruct the output? In such protocols, when proving security, it is easier to separate the adversary's output (or more generally, its view) from the output of the honest party. Notice that in the example above, the adversary sends its first message without even knowing the input x which it is encoding. (In order to prove security, at the very least, we must assume the honest party's first-round message does not leak its input.) If we could somehow guarantee that the adversary can only unlock the protocol output if it knows its own input, this would prevent the adversary from learning $f(x, x)$.

Our Approach. We use all these observations in order to obtain our construction. We will use four main tools in our construction: (1) a two-round non-malleable commitment, (2) a two-round statistically-sender-private oblivious transfer protocol (SSP OT), (3) a two-round strong SPS zero-knowledge protocol, and (4) garbled circuits. We will require each party P_i to publish two different types of commitments to its input, one using the NMC and the other using an OT_1 message. Roughly, the OT_1 message will be used by party P_i

in reconstructing its own output and the NMC will be used to help P_{1-i} to reconstruct its output. Crucially, we will show that the non-malleability of the NMC *is not needed for the privacy of the protocol*, i.e., it is not needed to prevent the adversary from learning $f(x,x)$. Rather, it is only needed *in order to prevent the honest party from learning "mauled" outputs such as $f(x,x)$.* Note that although the (rushing) adversary's output must be decided before receiving the adversary's second-round NMC message, the honest party's output can be decided after seeing the entire transcript of the protocol. Thus two-round non-malleability is easily sufficient to prevent mauling in terms of the honest party's output. How do we prevent the adversary from learning $f(x,x)$, then? At a high level, we rely on the SSP oblivious transfer, which satisfies exactly the property we hinted at above: an adversary can only unlock the protocol output if it knows the input of its OT_1 message.

Putting these ideas into practice involves several technical issues. We discuss a few here. One obvious issue is that we must somehow connect the NMC with the OT_1. Otherwise, it would be possible for the adversary to learn $f(x_1, y)$ whereas the honest party learns $f(x_2, y)$. To do this, we observe that it is possible to construct a *simultaneous-message* two-round NMC scheme, where both the committer and receiver send a message in the first round, and where the first round is *binding*. That is, the first round defines a unique x such that after the second round, either the transcript commits non-malleably to x, or the transcript is invalid and cannot be opened. With that in mind, we require that in addition to committing to its input in its OT_1 message, P_i must also commit to the randomness used for its NMC1 message. P_{1-i} then can construct its garbled circuit to only reveal the output if this randomness is correct.

Security Analysis. Although this solution to the problem seems simple, it introduces some subtleties to the proof of security. One such subtlety is in the hybrid order when moving from the real world to the ideal world. Namely, we must switch the OT_1 of the honest party to be an OT_1 of 0 before we switch the honest party's NMC to commit to 0. Since in the real world, the honest party gets its output by opening the adversary's OT_2 message, and in the ideal world it gets its output by extracting the adversary's NMC, this causes there to be several intermediate hybrids where there is no way for the honest party to compute its output. We must carefully prove that during these hybrids, although the honest party cannot compute its output, the output is well-defined and does not change in any computationally distinguishable way across these hybrids. We refer to Sect. 3.3 for details.

One other issue arises in the use of zero-knowledge to prove the honest generation of the garbled circuits with respect to the inputs committed to in the NMCs. That is, at some point during the hybrids, we must switch the honest party from using real proofs to using the SPS zero-knowledge simulator. Once we do this, we must somehow guarantee that the adversary (who now is receiving simulated proofs) cannot somehow use them to behave dishonestly. The work of [12] offers techniques to solve this issue, which is highly related to the notion of *simulation-soundness* [62]. Their main idea involves using *strong* SPS-zero-knowledge arguments in conjunction with non-malleable commitments. In strong SPS-ZK arguments, the zero-knowledge the property holds even against adversaries who are powerful enough to run the simulator. We are able to use the same techniques, although they require careful work to adapt to our setting and security proof. We again refer to Sect. 3.3 for more details on this and other technical issues.

Applications. We highlight two applications of our newly developed concurrent 2PC protocol.

(i) Round-optimal PAKE[5]*:* In Password-Authenticated Key-Exchange (PAKE) two parties want to exchange a session key if their (low-entropy) passwords match. This functionality is a special case of general 2PC, so it is clear that any 2PC protocol immediately yields a PAKE scheme. However, the de-facto security notion for PAKE [17] models security in the presence of concurrent sessions. Thus, only concurrently secure 2PC properly generalizes PAKE to all functionalities. As a corollary of our main theorem, we obtain the first round-optimal PAKE without a trusted setup. This settles a long-standing question in the area.

(ii) Quantum computation (Sect. 5): Observe that we can lift our result to the quantum setting by plugging in our concurrent 2PC protocol in the construction of [15]. At the high level, the protocol of [15] converts any quantum-secure 2PC to a quantum 2PC, where parties wish to securely compute a quantum circuit on their input. In each round, parties compute the encoding of their quantum inputs, and in parallel, they run a classical concurrent secure 2PC to compute the classical description of the quantum garbled circuit. In the end of the second round, the sender can evaluate the circuit and get the output. [15] requires a 2PC with a straight-line simulator (which we can instantiate with our protocol) and a quantum garbling scheme [25]. One subtlety in the proof is that we need to adjust the security parameter for the quantum garbled circuits, as our simulator has sub-exponential run-time (i.e., we use complexity leveraging).

2   Preliminaries

In the following, we write $T_1 \ll T_2$ for functions T_1 and T_2 if for all polynomials p, $p(T_1(\lambda))$ is asymptotically smaller than $T_2(\lambda)$. We denote with $\mathcal{G}(x; r)$ the execution of a probabilistic algorithm $\mathcal{G}$, where x is the input to the algorithm and r is the string of random coins. When we do not need to explicitly deal with the random coins of $\mathcal{G}$, we write $\mathcal{G}(x)$ and assume that the coins r are chosen uniformly at random. Additional definitions are given in the full version of the paper [1].

2.1   Two-Round SPS Strong Zero Knowledge

We define the notion of two-round strong zero knowledge with super-polynomial simulation first given in [47]. Here *strong* means that the zero-knowledge property holds even against adversaries which themselves are strong enough to run the simulator.

---
[5] See the full version of the paper [1].

We consider zero-knowledge protocols with the following syntax. All algorithms below are polynomial-time.

- $\mathsf{ZK}_1(1^\lambda; r) \to \mathsf{zk}_1$ takes as input the security parameter 1^λ along with randomness r and produces the verifier's message.
- $\mathsf{ZK}_2(1^\lambda, x, w, \mathsf{zk}_1; r') \to \mathsf{zk}_2$ takes as input security parameter, the statement x and the witness w along with the verifier's message and randomness r' and produces the prover's message.
- $\mathsf{ZK}_{\mathsf{verify}}(x, \mathsf{zk}_2, r) \to 0/1$ is a deterministic algorithm which takes the statement x along with the prover's message and the randomness used to generate the verifier's message and accepts or rejects.

Definition 1 (($T_{\mathsf{sound}}, T_{\mathsf{Sim}}, T_{\mathsf{zk}}, T_{\mathcal{L}}, \epsilon_{\mathsf{sound}}, \epsilon_{\mathsf{zk}}$)-**SPSS   Zero-Knowledge Arguments**)

Let $\mathcal{L}$ be a language in NP which is decidable in time $T_{\mathcal{L}}$, with a polynomial-time computable relation $\mathcal{R}_{\mathcal{L}}$. Let $T_{\mathsf{sound}}, T_{\mathsf{Sim}}, T_{\mathsf{zk}}$ be superpolynomial functions where $T_{\mathsf{sound}} \ll T_{\mathsf{Sim}} \ll T_{\mathsf{zk}} \ll T_{\mathcal{L}}$, and $\epsilon_{\mathsf{zk}}, \epsilon_{\mathsf{sound}}$ negligible functions. A protocol between a prover P and a verifier V is a $(T_{\mathsf{sound}}, T_{\mathsf{Sim}}, T_{\mathsf{zk}}, T_L, \epsilon_{\mathsf{sound}}, \epsilon_{\mathsf{zk}})$-strong zero-knowledge argument for $\mathcal{L}$ if it satisfies the following properties:

- **Perfect Completeness.** For every security parameter 1^λ and NP statement x and witness w where $(x, w) \in R_{\mathcal{L}}$, it holds that

$$\Pr\left[\mathsf{ZK}_{\mathsf{verify}}(x, \mathsf{zk}_2, r)\right] = 1,$$

where $\mathsf{zk}_1 \leftarrow \mathsf{ZK}_1(1^\lambda; r)$ and $\mathsf{zk}_2 \leftarrow \mathsf{ZK}_2(1^\lambda, x, w, \mathsf{zk}_1; r')$ and the probability is taken over the randomness of r and r'.

- ($T_{\mathsf{sound}}, \epsilon_{\mathsf{sound}}$)-**Adaptive Soundness.** For every polynomial $p(\lambda)$ and every prover P^* that works in time T_{sound} and is given 1^λ and an honest verifier message zk_1; If P^* chooses an input length 1^p for some polynomial $p \in \mathsf{poly}(\lambda)$, and then chooses $x \in \{0,1\}^p \setminus \mathcal{L}$ and outputs (x, zk_2), it holds that

$$\Pr\left[\mathsf{ZK}_{\mathsf{verify}}(x, \mathsf{zk}_2, r) = 1\right] \leq \epsilon_{\mathsf{sound}}(\lambda),$$

where r is the randomness used to generate zk_1 and the probability is over the random coins of V.

- ($T_{\mathsf{Sim}}, T_{\mathsf{zk}}, \epsilon_{\mathsf{zk}}$)-**Strong Zero-Knowledge.** There exists a (uniform) simulator Sim which runs in time T_{Sim} which takes as input the round-one transcript zk_1 and a statement x such that the following holds. Consider an adversary V^* which runs in time T_{zk} that takes as input 1^λ and advice z and outputs a verifier's first round message zk_1^*. Then, for all $(x, w) \in R_{\mathcal{L}}$, distinguishers $\mathcal{D}$ which run in time T_{zk}, and advice z,

$$\left|\Pr\left[\mathcal{D}(x, z, r, \mathsf{ZK}_2(1^\lambda, x, w, \mathsf{zk}_1^*)) = 1\right] - \Pr\left[\mathcal{D}(x, z, r, \mathsf{Sim}(1^\lambda, x, \mathsf{zk}_1^*)) = 1\right]\right|$$
$$< \epsilon_{\mathsf{zk}}(\lambda),$$

where r is the private randomness of V^*.

2.2 Two-Round Statistically-Sender-Private Oblivious Transfer

We give the formal definition of two-round oblivious transfer, where the receiver's security is computational, and there exists a (possibly computationally unbounded) extractor for the receiver's first-round message such that statistical security holds for the sender. The Oblivious Transfer scheme consists of the following polynomial-time algorithms:

- $\mathsf{OT}_1(1^\lambda, b; r) \to \mathsf{ot}_1$: The receiver's OT_1 algorithm takes a choice bit b and produces the receiver's OT message.
- $\mathsf{OT}_2(1^\lambda, \ell_0, \ell_1, \mathsf{ot}_1; r') \to \mathsf{ot}_2$: The sender's OT_2 algorithm takes a pair of strings to choose from along with the receiver's OT message and produces the sender's OT message.
- $\mathsf{OT}_3(\mathsf{ot}_2; r) \to \ell_b$: The receiver's OT_3 takes the sender's OT message and outputs ℓ_b.

Definition 2. *A tuple* $(\mathsf{OT}_1, \mathsf{OT}_2, \mathsf{OT}_3)$ *is a* $(T_R, \epsilon_R, \epsilon_S)$-*statistically-sender-private oblivious transfer algorithm if the following properties hold:*

- **Correctness.** *For all* λ, b, ℓ_0, ℓ_1,

$$\Pr\left[\mathsf{OT}_3(\mathsf{ot}_2; r) = \ell_b \,\middle|\, \begin{array}{l} \mathsf{ot}_1 \leftarrow \mathsf{OT}_1(1^\lambda, b; r) \\ \mathsf{ot}_2 \leftarrow \mathsf{OT}_2(1^\lambda, \ell_0, \ell_1, \mathsf{ot}_1) \end{array}\right] = 1.$$

- (T_R, ϵ_R)-**Computational Receiver Privacy.** *For all machines* $\mathcal{D}$ *running in time at most* $T_R(\lambda)$,

$$\left|\Pr\left[\mathcal{D}(1^\lambda, \mathsf{ot}_{1,0}) = 1\right] - \Pr\left[\mathcal{D}(1^\lambda, \mathsf{ot}_{1,1}) = 1\right]\right| < \epsilon_R(\lambda),$$

where $\mathsf{ot}_{1,b} \leftarrow \mathsf{OT}_1(1^\lambda, b)$ *for* $b \in \{0,1\}$, *and the probability is taken over the coins of* OT_1 *and* $\mathcal{D}$.
- ϵ_S-**Statistical Sender Privacy.** *There exists a (possibly unbounded-time) extractor such that the following holds. For any sequence* $\{\mathsf{ot}_{1,\lambda}, \ell_{0,\lambda}, \ell_{1,\lambda}\}_\lambda$, *define the distribution ensembles* $\{D_{0,\lambda}\}_\lambda$ *and* $\{D_{1,\lambda}\}_\lambda$, *where* $D_{b,\lambda}$ *is defined as follows:*
  1. *Run* $\mathsf{OT}_{\mathsf{extract}}(\mathsf{ot}_{1,\lambda})$ *to obtain* μ.
  2. *If* $b = 0$, *output* $\mathsf{OT}_2(1^\lambda, \ell_{0,\lambda}, \ell_{1,\lambda}, \mathsf{ot}_{1,\lambda})$.
  3. *If* $b = 1$, *set* $\ell'_b = \ell_{b,\lambda}$ *and* $\ell'_{1-b} = 0$ *and output* $\mathsf{OT}_2(1^\lambda, \ell'_0, \ell'_1, \mathsf{ot}_{1,\lambda})$.
  The two ensembles $\{D_{0,\lambda}\}_\lambda$ *and* $\{D_{1,\lambda}\}_\lambda$ *have statistical distance at most* ϵ_S.

In the body of our paper, we will use the following syntax, which reduces trivially to the syntax above.

- $\mathsf{OT}_1(1^\lambda, x; r) \to \mathsf{ot}_1$: The receiver's OT_1 algorithm takes a string of choice bits x and produces the receiver's OT message.
- $\mathsf{OT}_2(1^\lambda, \mathsf{lab}, \mathsf{ot}_1; r') \to \mathsf{ot}_2$: The sender's OT_2 algorithm takes a list $\mathsf{lab} = \{\mathsf{lab}_{i,b}\}_{i \in [|x|], b \in \{0,1\}}$ of pairs of strings to choose from of length $|x|$ along with the receiver's OT message and produces the sender's OT message.
- $\mathsf{OT}_3(\mathsf{ot}_2; r)$: The receiver's OT_3 takes the sender's OT message and outputs $\{\mathsf{lab}_{i,x_i}\}_{i \in [|x|]}$.

2.3   Definition of Concurrent MPC

In this section, we present the definition of concurrent secure multi-party computation. The definition below is a generalization of the definition of concurrent secure multi/two-party computation [53,59]. Parts of this section are taken verbatim from [59], where the main modifications are due to the fact that we allow the simulator to run in super-polynomial time.

Multi-party Computation. Consider an n-party quantum functionality specified by a family of circuits $\mathcal{F} = \{\mathcal{F}_\lambda\}_\lambda$ where $\mathcal{F}_\lambda$ has $m_1(\lambda) + \cdots + m_n(\lambda)$ input bits and $\ell_1(\lambda) + \cdots + \ell_n(\lambda)$ output bits. Let Π be an n-party protocol for computing $\mathcal{F}$. For security parameter λ and any collection of inputs $(\mathbf{x}_1, \ldots, \mathbf{x}_n)$, where $\mathbf{x}_i \in \{0,1\}^{m_i(\lambda)}$. We denote the output of the functionality by $\mathcal{F}_\lambda(\mathbf{x}_1, \ldots, \mathbf{x}_n) \to (\mathbf{y}_1, \ldots, \mathbf{y}_n)$, where $\mathbf{y}_i \in \{0,1\}^{\ell_i(\lambda)}$ and $\mathbf{x}_i$ is P_i's input.

Concurrent Execution in the Ideal Model. Next, we describe the concurrent execution of the protocol in the ideal world. Unlike the stand-alone setting, here the trusted party computes the functionality many times, each time upon different inputs. Let $\Pi := (P_1, \ldots, P_n)$ be an MPC protocol for computing an n-ary circuit $\mathcal{F}$ and λ be the security parameter. We consider adversaries that corrupt any subset of the parties, where the subset is pre-determined before the beginning of the execution, and we denote by $I \subset [n]$ the subset of corrupted parties. An ideal execution with an adversary who controls the parties I proceeds as follows:

- **Inputs**: The inputs of the parties $P_1, \ldots, P_n$ are determined by input-selecting machines $M := M_1, \ldots, M_n$, where each M_i sends $\mathbf{x}_{i,j}$ to each party P_i and for each session j, at the beginning of the experiment.
- **Session initiation**: When the adversary initiates the session number j by sending a (*start-session*, i) to the trusted party. If $i \in [n] - I$ (means P_i is an honest party) the trusted party sends (*start-session*, j) to P_i, where $i \in [n]$, and j is the index of the session (i.e., this is the j-th session to be started by P_i).
- **Honest parties send inputs to trusted party:** Upon receiving the activation message (*start-session*, i) from the trusted party, each honest party P_i sends $(j, \mathbf{x}_{i,j})$ to the trusted party.
- **Corrupted parties send inputs to trusted party:** Whenever the adversary wishes, it may ask a corrupted party P_i to send a message $(j, \mathbf{x}'_{i,j})$ to the trusted third party, for any $\mathbf{x}'_{i,j}$ of its choice. A corrupted party P_i can send the pairs $(j, \mathbf{x}'_{i,j})$ in any order it wishes. The only limitation is that for any j, at most one pair indexed by j can be sent to the trusted party.
- **Trusted party answers corrupted parties:** When the trusted third party has received messages $(j, \mathbf{x}'_{i,j})$ from all parties (both honest and corrupted) it computes $\mathcal{F}(\mathbf{x}'_{1,j}, \ldots, \mathbf{x}'_{n,j}) \to (\mathbf{y}_{1,j}, \ldots, \mathbf{y}_{n,j})$ and sends $(j, \mathbf{y}_{i,j})$ to every corrupted P_i.
- **Adversary instructs the trusted party to answer honest parties:** When the adversary sends a message of the type (*send-output*, j, i) to the trusted party, the trusted party directly sends $(j, \mathbf{y}_{i,j})$ to the honest party P_i.

If all inputs for session j have not yet been received by the trusted party the message is ignored. If the output has already been delivered to the honest party, or i is the index so that P_i is a corrupted party, the message is ignored as well.

- **Outputs:** Each honest party always outputs the vector of outputs that it received from the trusted party. The corrupted parties may output an arbitrary state and the messages obtained from the trusted party.

Let $\mathcal{S}$ be a PPT algorithm (representing the ideal-model adversary) and let $I \subset [n]$ be the set of corrupted parties. The adversary takes as an input an auxiliary information $\mathbf{z}$. Then the ideal execution of $\mathcal{F}$, denoted by the random variable

$$IDEAL_{\mathcal{F},I,\mathcal{S},M}(\lambda, \mathbf{z})$$

is defined as the outputs of the ideal functionality and the output of $\mathcal{S}$, from the ideal process described above.

Execution in the Real Model. We next consider the execution of Π in the real world. We assume that the parties communicate through an asynchronous fully connected and authentic point-to-point channel but without guaranteed delivery of messages. Let $\mathcal{F}, I$ be as above, and let Π be a multi-party protocol for computing the corresponding circuit. Furthermore, let $\mathcal{A}$ be a PPT machine such that for every $i \in I$, the adversary $\mathcal{A}$ controls P_i. Then, the real concurrent execution of Π with security parameter λ, and auxiliary input $\mathbf{z}$ to $\mathcal{A}$, is denoted

$$REAL_{\Pi,I,\mathcal{A}}(\lambda, \mathbf{z})$$

and it is defined as the output vector of the honest parties and the adversary $\mathcal{A}$ resulting from the following process. The parties run concurrent executions of the protocol, where every party initiates a new session whenever it receives a start-session from the adversary. The honest parties use the string provided by the attacker as their input for this session. The scheduling of all messages throughout the executions is controlled by the adversary.

Security. The security of Π under composition is defined by saying that for every real-model adversary there exists an ideal model adversary that can simulate the execution of the secure real-model protocol. We parametrize the definition by the runtime of the simulator T. Formally:

Definition 3 (Concurrent Security in the Malicious Model). *let $\mathcal{F}, n, \lambda$ and Π be as above. Protocol Π is said to T-securely realize $\mathcal{F}$ under concurrent composition if for every real-model PPT adversary $\mathcal{A}$, there exists an ideal-model adversary $\mathcal{S}$ with runtime bounded by T, such that every state $\mathbf{z}$ and every $I \subset [n]$ it holds that*

$$\{IDEAL_{\mathcal{F},I,\mathcal{S}}(\lambda, \mathbf{z})\}_{n \in \mathbb{N}} \approx_c \{REAL_{\Pi,I,\mathcal{A}}(\lambda, \mathbf{z})\}_{n \in \mathbb{N}},$$

where the notation $\approx_c$ denotes computational indistinguishability.

Remark 1. We shall pointed out that the above definition can be also generalized to real-world adversaries $\mathcal{A}$ beyond polynomial-time. Furthermore, our proof in Sect. 3.3 can be adapted to establish security for a real-world adversary whose runtime is bounded by $\tilde{T}$, and the simulator is bounded by some $T \gg \tilde{T}$.

Quantum Circuits. We can modify our definition to work with quantum circuits, how ever we keep the inputs and outputs classical. In particular, we only allow inputs $\boldsymbol{x}_i \in \{0,1\}^{m_i(\lambda)}$ and outputs $\boldsymbol{y}_i \in \{0,1\}^{\ell_i(\lambda)}$. The only differences are:

1. $\mathcal{F}$ is a family of quantum circuits.
2. $\mathcal{A}$ is a quantum circuit with auxiliary (quantum) state $\boldsymbol{z}$.
3. $\mathcal{S}$ runs in quantum polynomial time.

We leave it as an open problem to study the definition of quantum concurrent multiparty computation with inputs and outputs as quantum states.

Remark 2. We remark that our definition assumes that the honest parties' outputs are only revealed to the distinguisher at the end of the experiment and that it cannot adaptively choose honest parties' inputs in subsequent sessions based on previous honest outputs. Such a definition suffices for many applications concurrent 2PC, although we remark that stronger variants exist [26].

3 The Construction

In this section, we prove the following theorem.

Theorem 2. *Assuming the existence of subexponentially-secure versions of the following primitives:*

- *A two-round SPSS zero-knowledge argument system*
- *A two-message concurrent NMC scheme*
- *A two-round statistically-sender private oblivious transfer scheme*
- *A garbled circuit scheme*

there exists a two-round two-party computation protocol for any polynomial-time functionality f, in the plain model with super-polynomial simulation.

We note that each primitive is known from the subexponential hardness of LWE. In particular, [20] show the existence of two-round Statistically-Sender-Private OT from LWE, and both the SPSS zero-knowledge argument and the NMC scheme of [47] can be instantiated using LWE (see Sect. 4 for details). Finally, garbled circuits can be instantiated using any one-way function, which is known from LWE. Thus we have Theorem 2 as a corollary.

We now describe the construction of two-round two-party computation where both parties receive outputs.

3.1   Required Primitives

First, we review the syntax of all the primitives we will use.

Let λ be the security parameter, and we assume 1^λ is an implicit parameter in all the following algorithms.

– A two-round $(T_{\sf sound}, T_{\sf Sim}, T_{\sf zk}, T_{\mathcal{L}}, \epsilon_1, \epsilon_2)$-SPSS ZK argument system

$$(\mathsf{ZK}_1, \mathsf{ZK}_2, \mathsf{ZK}_{\sf verify}, \mathsf{ZK}_{\sf sim}),$$

where $T_{\sf sound}, T_{\sf Sim}, T_{\sf zk}, T_{\mathcal{L}}$ are specified below and ϵ_1, ϵ_2 are any negligible functions.

– A two-round $(T_{\sf nmc}, \epsilon)$-fully-concurrent non-malleable commitment scheme

$$(\mathsf{NMC}_1^{\sf send}, \mathsf{NMC}_1^{\sf recv}, \mathsf{NMC}_2^{\sf send}),$$

where $T_{\sf nmc}$ is specified below and ϵ is any negligible function. In addition, we assume that the extraction algorithm $\mathsf{NMC}_{\sf extract}$ runs in time $T_{\sf NMC_{extract}}$.

– A (T_G, ϵ)-garbled circuit scheme $(\mathsf{Garble}, \mathsf{Eval}, \mathsf{Sim}_{\sf Garble})$, where T_G is specified below and ϵ is any negligible function.

– A two-round $(T_R, \epsilon_1, \epsilon_2)$-statistically-sender-private OT scheme $(\mathsf{OT}_1, \mathsf{OT}_2, \mathsf{OT}_3, \mathsf{OT}_{\sf extract})$, where T_R is specified below and ϵ_1, ϵ_2 are any negligible functions. Additionally, we assume the extraction algorithm $\mathsf{OT}_{\sf extract}$ runs in time $T_{\sf OT_{extract}}$.

For the zero-knowledge system, we define a language $L_{i \to j}$ in NP which will be proved by both parties during the 2PC protocol (Fig. 1).

Complexity Hierarchy. We require the primitives above satisfy the following complexity hierarchy:

$$\mathsf{poly}(\lambda) \ll T_{\sf sound} \ll T_{\sf Sim} \ll T_{\sf nmc} \ll T_{\sf NMC_{extract}} \ll T_{\sf zk} \ll T_R \ll T_{\sf OT_{extract}} \ll T_G \ll T_L.$$

$(\mathbf{nmc}_1^{P_i,\sf send}, \mathbf{nmc}_1^{P_j,\sf recv}, \mathbf{nmc}_1^{P_j,\sf send}, \mathbf{nmc}_2^{P_i,\sf send}, \tilde{C}_i^{\sf P}, \mathbf{ot}_1^{P_j}, \mathbf{ot}_2^{P_i}) \in L_{i \to j}$ **iff:**

There exists $(\mathbf{x}_i, r_c^{P_i,\sf send}, r_{gc}^{P_i}, r_{ot}^{P_i,\sf send})$ where

– $\mathbf{nmc}_1^{P_i,\sf send} = \mathsf{NMC}_1^{\sf send}(1^\lambda, val; r^{P_i,\sf send})$ for the value $val = (\mathbf{x}_i, r_{gc}^{P_i}, r_{ot}^{P_i,\sf send})$,

– $\mathbf{nmc}_2^{P_i,\sf send} = \mathsf{NMC}_2^{\sf send}(1^\lambda, val, \mathbf{nmc}_1^{P_j,\sf recv}, r_c^{P_i,\sf send})$,

– $(\tilde{C}_i^{\sf P}, \mathsf{lab}) = \mathsf{Garble}(C, r_{gc}^{P_i})$ for the circuit C defined below, with the hardcoded value set to $(\mathbf{x}_i, \mathbf{nmc}_1^{P_j,\sf send})$, and

– $\mathbf{ot}_2^{P_i} = \mathsf{OT}_2(\mathsf{lab}, \mathbf{ot}_1^{P_j}, r_{ot}^{P_i,\sf send})$, where lab is the family of labels obtained from Garble.

Fig. 1. Description of the language $\mathcal{L}_{i \to j}$

Additionally, we require that the language above is decidable in time T_L.

Some Final Notation. Let $\mathsf{onlychoices}(x, \mathsf{lab})$ take a string x and a list $\mathsf{lab} = \{\mathsf{lab}_{i,b}\}_{i \in [|x|], b \in \{0,1\}}$ of strings as input and produce the list $\{\mathsf{lab}'_{i,b}\}_{i \in [|x|], b \in \{0,1\}}$, where for each i $\mathsf{lab}'_{i,x_i} = \mathsf{lab}_{i,x_i}$, and $\mathsf{lab}'_{i,1-x_i} = 0$.

3.2 The Protocol

We now describe the protocol for two-round 2PC. Without loss of generality, we describe the actions of Party 1.

2-round 2PC protocol:

In each round, Party 1 performs the following actions.

Round 1:

1. Choose random strings $r_c^{\mathsf{P}_1,\mathsf{send}}, r_c^{\mathsf{P}_1,\mathsf{recv}}, r_{gc}^{\mathsf{P}_1}, r_{\mathsf{ot}}^{\mathsf{P}_1,\mathsf{recv}}, r_{\mathsf{ot}}^{\mathsf{P}_1,\mathsf{send}}$, and $r_{zk}^{\mathsf{P}_1}$ of appropriate sizes.
2. Compute a ZK verifier's message $\mathsf{zk}_1^{\mathsf{P}_1} \leftarrow \mathsf{ZK}_1(1^\lambda; r_{zk}^{\mathsf{P}_1})$.
3. Compute a round-one committer's NMC message

$$\mathbf{nmc}_1^{\mathsf{P}_1,\mathsf{send}} \leftarrow \mathsf{NMC}_1^{\mathsf{send}}(1^\lambda, \mathit{val}; r_c^{\mathsf{P}_1,\mathsf{send}}),$$

where the committed value $\mathit{val} = (\mathbf{x}_1, r_{gc}^{\mathsf{P}_1}, r_{\mathsf{ot}}^{\mathsf{P}_1,\mathsf{send}})$ consists of P_1's input along with the randomness which P_1 will use to generate the garbled circuit and OT2 messages in round 2.
4. Compute a round-one receiver's NMC message

$$\mathbf{nmc}_1^{\mathsf{P}_1,\mathsf{recv}} \leftarrow \mathsf{NMC}_1^{\mathsf{recv}}(1^\lambda; r_c^{\mathsf{P}_1,\mathsf{recv}}).$$

5. Compute an OT receiver's message

$$\mathbf{ot}_1^{\mathsf{P}_1} \leftarrow \mathsf{OT}_1(1^\lambda, (\mathbf{x}_1, r_c^{\mathsf{P}_1,\mathsf{send}}, r_{gc}^{\mathsf{P}_1}, r_{\mathsf{ot}}^{\mathsf{P}_1,\mathsf{send}}); r_{\mathsf{ot}}^{\mathsf{P}_1,\mathsf{recv}}),$$

where the choice bits $(\mathbf{x}_1, r_c^{\mathsf{P}_1,\mathsf{send}}, r_{gc}^{\mathsf{P}_1}, r_{\mathsf{ot}}^{\mathsf{P}_1,\mathsf{send}})$ consist of the randomness $r_c^{\mathsf{P}_1,\mathsf{send}}$ used to generate the round-one sender's NMC message along with the committed values $\mathbf{x}_1, r_{gc}^{\mathsf{P}_1}, r_{\mathsf{ot}}^{\mathsf{P}_1,\mathsf{send}}$.
6. Send $(\mathsf{zk}_1^{\mathsf{P}_1}, \mathbf{nmc}_1^{\mathsf{P}_1,\mathsf{send}}, \mathbf{nmc}_1^{\mathsf{P}_1,\mathsf{recv}}, \mathbf{ot}_1^{\mathsf{P}_1})$ to P_1.

Round 2:

After receiving the first-round message $(\mathsf{zk}_1^{\mathsf{P}_2}, \mathbf{nmc}_1^{\mathsf{P}_2,\mathsf{send}}, \mathbf{nmc}_1^{\mathsf{P}_2,\mathsf{recv}}, \mathbf{ot}_1^{\mathsf{P}_2})$ from party 2, party 1 does the following:

---

1. Compute the sender's second-round NMC message

$$\mathbf{nmc}_2^{\mathsf{P}_1,\mathsf{send}} \leftarrow \mathsf{NMC}_2^{\mathsf{send}}(1^\lambda, val, \mathbf{nmc}_1^{\mathsf{P}_2,\mathsf{recv}}, r_c^{\mathsf{P}_1,\mathsf{send}}),$$

where the committed value $val = (\mathbf{x}_1, r_{gc}^{\mathsf{P}_1}, r_{\mathsf{ot}}^{\mathsf{P}_1,\mathsf{send}})$ is as in round 1.

2. Compute the garbled circuit $(\tilde{C}^{\mathsf{P}_1}, \mathsf{lab}) \leftarrow \mathsf{Garble}(1^\lambda, C, r_{gc}^{\mathsf{P}_1})$, where C is the circuit defined below, and the hardcoded values are $(\lambda, \mathbf{x}_1, \mathbf{nmc}_1^{\mathsf{P}_2,\mathsf{send}})$.

3. Compute the sender's OT message

$$\mathbf{ot}_2^{\mathsf{P}_1} \leftarrow \mathsf{OT}_2(1^\lambda, \mathsf{lab}, \mathbf{ot}_1^{\mathsf{P}_2}; r_{\mathsf{ot}}^{\mathsf{P}_1,\mathsf{send}}),$$

with the labels lab obtained from the garbling algorithm in the previous step.

4. Compute the prover's ZK message $\mathsf{zk}_2^{\mathsf{P}_1} \leftarrow \mathsf{ZK}_2(1^\lambda, \phi, w, \mathsf{zk}_1^{\mathsf{P}_2})$ for the language $L_{1\to2}$ with the statement

$$\phi = (\mathbf{nmc}_1^{\mathsf{P}_1,\mathsf{send}}, \mathbf{nmc}_1^{\mathsf{P}_2,\mathsf{recv}}\mathbf{nmc}_1^{\mathsf{P}_2,\mathsf{send}}, \mathbf{nmc}_2^{\mathsf{P}_1,\mathsf{send}}, \tilde{C}^{\mathsf{P}_1}, \mathbf{ot}_1^{\mathsf{P}_2}, \mathbf{ot}_2^{\mathsf{P}_1})$$

and witness $w = (\mathbf{x}_1, r_c^{\mathsf{P}_1,\mathsf{send}}, r_{gc}^{\mathsf{P}_1}, r_{\mathsf{ot}}^{\mathsf{P}_1,\mathsf{send}})$.

5. Send $(\mathbf{nmc}_2^{\mathsf{P}_1,\mathsf{send}}, \tilde{C}^{\mathsf{P}_1}, \mathbf{ot}_2^{\mathsf{P}_1}, \mathsf{zk}_2^{\mathsf{P}_1})$ to P_2.

Output Computation:

After receiving party 2's second-round message $(\mathbf{nmc}_2^{\mathsf{P}_2,\mathsf{send}}, \tilde{C}^{\mathsf{P}_2}, \mathbf{ot}_2^{\mathsf{P}_2}, \mathsf{zk}_2^{\mathsf{P}_2})$, party 1 does the following to compute its output:

1. If the NMC verification algorithm $\mathsf{NMC}_{\mathsf{verify}}(1^\lambda, \tau, r_c^{\mathsf{P}_1,\mathsf{recv}})$ fails with respect to P_2's commitment transcript

$$\tau = (\mathbf{nmc}_1^{\mathsf{P}_2,\mathsf{send}}, \mathbf{nmc}_1^{\mathsf{P}_1,\mathsf{recv}}, \mathbf{nmc}_2^{\mathsf{P}_1,\mathsf{send}}),$$

then abort and output $\perp$.

2. Let

$$\phi' = (\mathbf{nmc}_1^{\mathsf{P}_2,\mathsf{send}}, \mathbf{nmc}_1^{\mathsf{P}_1,\mathsf{recv}}\mathbf{nmc}_1^{\mathsf{P}_1,\mathsf{send}}, \mathbf{nmc}_2^{\mathsf{P}_2,\mathsf{send}}, \tilde{C}^{\mathsf{P}_2}, \mathbf{ot}_1^{\mathsf{P}_1}, \mathbf{ot}_2^{\mathsf{P}_2})$$

be the statement which party 2 proves via $\mathsf{zk}_2^{\mathsf{P}_2}$, with respect to language $L_{2\to1}$. If $\mathsf{ZK}_{\mathsf{verify}}(\phi', \mathsf{zk}_2^{\mathsf{P}_2}, r_{zk}^{\mathsf{P}_1}) = 0$ then abort and output $\perp$.

3. Compute the output labels $\mathsf{lab}' \leftarrow \mathsf{OT}_3(\mathbf{ot}_2^{\mathsf{P}_2}, r_{\mathsf{ot}}^{\mathsf{P}_1,\mathsf{recv}})$ of the OT protocol.

4. Output the evaluation $\mathsf{Eval}(\tilde{C}^{\mathsf{P}_2}, \mathsf{lab}')$ of the garbled circuit $\tilde{C}^{\mathsf{P}_2}$ sent by P_2, using the labels lab' obtained in the previous step.

The circuit C which is garbled by Party 1 is as follows.

Circuit C:

Input: $(\mathbf{x}_2, r_c^{\mathsf{P}_2,\mathsf{send}}, r_{gc}^{\mathsf{P}_2}, r_{\mathsf{ot}}^{\mathsf{P}_2,\mathsf{send}})$

Hardcoded: $(\lambda, \mathbf{x}_1, \mathsf{nmc}_1^{P_2,\mathsf{send}})$

1. **If** $\mathsf{nmc}_1^{P_2,\mathsf{send}} = \mathsf{NMC}_1^{\mathsf{send}}(1^\lambda, (\mathbf{x}_2, r_{gc}^{P_2}, r_{ot}^{P_2,\mathsf{send}}); r_c^{P_2,\mathsf{send}})$, **then:**
   (a) Return $f(\mathbf{x}_1, \mathbf{x}_2)$
2. **Else:**
   (a) Return $\perp$.

3.3 Security

We now prove Theorem 2 by showing that the protocol above satisfies the definition of concurrent MPC security given in Sect. 2.3.

Let there be n parties, with a subset of corrupted parties $\mathcal{C} \in [n]$. Consider a PPT adversary $\mathcal{A}$ which spawns a polynomial number of sessions of the protocol described above, where for each session at most one party is corrupt, and schedules messages across the different sessions in an arbitrary order, controlling the inputs and messages of the corrupted parties. At the end of the experiment, $\mathcal{A}$ receives the outputs of all parties in all sessions. We show the existence of an ideal-world adversary (called the "simulator") which produces an interaction with $\mathcal{A}$ that is indistinguishable from the real-world interaction of $\mathcal{A}$.

We describe the behavior of the simulator below. In the following, we denote a session by (s, i, j), where s is the session number, and parties P_i and P_j run the 2PC protocol during this session. Without loss of generality we assume P_i is honest and P_j is corrupt, and that $\mathcal{A}$ always asks for the message of P_i in both rounds before sending the message of P_j for that round.

The Concurrent-Secure Simulator:

At the beginning of the experiment, the simulator invokes $\mathcal{A}$. The simulator also initializes a database where it will store, for each session (s, i, j), the messages and extracted values of P_j, the simulator's private state for this session, along with the ideal functionality output for the session. The simulator then responds to $\mathcal{A}$ in the following manner.

Whenever $\mathcal{A}$ initializes session (s, i, j), do the following to simulate P_i's message to P_j:

1. Choose random strings $r_c^{P_i,\mathsf{send}}, r_c^{P_i,\mathsf{recv}}, r_{gc}^{P_i}, r_{ot}^{P_i,\mathsf{recv}}, r_{ot}^{P_i,\mathsf{send}}$, and $r_{zk}^{P_i}$ of appropriate sizes. Store all strings as the simulator's private state for session (s, i, j).
2. Compute a ZK verifier's message $\mathsf{zk}_1^{P_i} \leftarrow \mathsf{ZK}_1(1^\lambda; r_{zk}^{P_i})$.
3. Compute a round-one committer's NMC message

$$\mathsf{nmc}_1^{P_i,\mathsf{send}} \leftarrow \mathsf{NMC}_1^{\mathsf{send}}(1^\lambda, val; r_c^{P_i,\mathsf{send}})$$

   for the value $val = (0, 0, 0)$.
4. Compute a round-one receiver's NMC message

$$\mathsf{nmc}_1^{P_i,\mathsf{recv}} \leftarrow \mathsf{NMC}_1^{\mathsf{recv}}(1^\lambda; r_c^{P_i,\mathsf{recv}}).$$

5. Compute an OT receiver's message $\mathsf{ot}_1^{P_i} \leftarrow \mathsf{OT}_1(1^\lambda, (0,0,0,0); r_{ot}^{P_i,\mathsf{recv}})$, where the choice bits are $(0,0,0,0)$.
6. Send $(\mathsf{zk}_1^{P_i}, \mathbf{nmc}_1^{P_i,\mathsf{send}}, \mathbf{nmc}_1^{P_i,\mathsf{recv}}, \mathsf{ot}_1^{P_i})$ to P_j on behalf of P_i.

Whenever $\mathcal{A}$ sends a first-round message m on behalf of P_j in session (s,i,j), do the following:

1. Parse m as $(\mathsf{zk}_1^{P_j}, \mathbf{nmc}_1^{P_j,\mathsf{send}}, \mathbf{nmc}_1^{P_j,\mathsf{recv}}, \mathsf{ot}_1^{P_j})$. Store m as P_j's first-round message in session (s,i,j).
2. Compute the extracted values $(\mathbf{x}_j, r_c^{P_j,\mathsf{send}}, r_{gc}^{P_j}, r_{ot}^{P_j,\mathsf{send}}) \leftarrow \mathsf{OT}_{\mathsf{extract}}(\mathsf{ot}_1^{P_j})$ from P_j's OT receiver's message, and save $(\mathbf{x}_j, r_c^{P_j,\mathsf{send}}, r_{gc}^{P_j}, r_{ot}^{P_j,\mathsf{send}})$ as P_j's OT receiver value in session (s,i,j).
3. If $\mathbf{nmc}_1^{P_j,\mathsf{send}} = \mathsf{NMC}_1^{\mathsf{send}}(1^\lambda, (\mathbf{x}_j, r_{gc}^{P_j}, r_{ot}^{P_j,\mathsf{send}}); r_c^{P_j,\mathsf{send}})$, then send $\mathbf{x}_j$ to the ideal functionality and receive back the evaluation $y = f(\mathbf{x}_i, \mathbf{x}_j)$. If $\mathbf{nmc}_1^{P_j,\mathsf{send}} \neq \mathsf{NMC}_1^{\mathsf{send}}(1^\lambda, (\mathbf{x}_j, r_{gc}^{P_j}, r_{ot}^{P_j,\mathsf{send}}); r_c^{P_j,\mathsf{send}})$, set $y = \perp$.
4. Store y as the ideal-world output for P_j in session (s,i,j).

Whenever $\mathcal{A}$ requests a second-round message from honest party P_i in session (s,i,j), do the following:

1. Retrieve P_j's first-round message $m = (\mathsf{zk}_1^{P_j}, \mathbf{nmc}_1^{P_j,\mathsf{send}}, \mathbf{nmc}_1^{P_j,\mathsf{recv}}, \mathsf{ot}_1^{P_j})$ for session (s,i,j).
2. Compute a round-two NMC sender's message

$$\mathbf{nmc}_2^{P_i,\mathsf{send}} \leftarrow \mathsf{NMC}_2^{\mathsf{send}}(1^\lambda, val, \mathbf{nmc}_1^{P_j,\mathsf{recv}}, r_c^{P_i,\mathsf{send}})$$

for the value $val = (0,0,0)$.
3. Compute a simulated garbled circuit $(\tilde{C}_i^P, \mathsf{lab}) \leftarrow \mathsf{Sim}_{\mathsf{Garble}}(1^\lambda, |C|, y; r_{gc}^{P_i})$ using the output y saved previously for session (s,i,j).
4. Compute an OT sender's message $\mathsf{ot}_2^{P_i} \leftarrow \mathsf{OT}_2(1^\lambda, \mathsf{onlychoices}(c, \mathsf{lab}), \mathsf{ot}_1^{P_j}, r_{ot}^{P_i,\mathsf{send}})$, where $c = (\mathbf{x}_j, r_c^{P_j,\mathsf{send}}, r_{gc}^{P_j}, r_{ot}^{P_j,\mathsf{send}})$ is the saved OT receiver's value for round (s,i,j). Recall that $\mathsf{onlychoices}$ sets all non-chosen labels to 0.
5. Compute a simulated prover's ZK message $\mathsf{zk}_2^{P_i} \leftarrow \mathsf{ZK}_{\mathsf{sim}}(1^\lambda, \phi, \mathsf{zk}_1^{PTwo}, r')$ using the statement

$$\phi = (\mathbf{nmc}_1^{P_1,\mathsf{send}}, \mathbf{nmc}_1^{P_2,\mathsf{recv}}\mathbf{nmc}_1^{P_2,\mathsf{send}}, \mathbf{nmc}_2^{P_1,\mathsf{send}}, \tilde{C}^{P_1}, \mathsf{ot}_1^{P_2}, \mathsf{ot}_2^{P_1})$$

and r' is random.
6. Send $(\mathbf{nmc}_2^{P_i,\mathsf{send}}, \tilde{C}_i^P, \mathsf{ot}_2^{P_i}, \mathsf{zk}_2^{P_i})$ to P_j on behalf of P_i.

Whenever $\mathcal{A}$ sends a second-round message m on behalf of P_j for session (s,i,j), do the following:

1. Parse m as $(\mathbf{nmc}_2^{P_j,\mathsf{send}}, \tilde{C}_j^P, \mathsf{ot}_2^{P_j}, \mathsf{zk}_2^{P_j})$.
2. If the NMC verification algorithm $\mathsf{NMC}_{\mathsf{verify}}(1^\lambda, \tau, r_c^{P_i,\mathsf{recv}})$ fails with respect to P_j's commitment transcript $\tau = (\mathbf{nmc}_1^{P_j,\mathsf{send}}, \mathbf{nmc}_1^{P_i,\mathsf{recv}}, \mathbf{nmc}_2^{P_i,\mathsf{send}})$, then instruct the ideal functionality to deliver $\perp$ to P_i.
3. If $\mathsf{ZK}_{\mathsf{verify}}(\phi', \mathsf{zk}_2^{P_i}, r_{zk}^{P_j}) = 0$ then instruct the ideal functionality to deliver $\perp$ to P_i.

4. Extract the committed values

$$(\mathbf{x}_j, r_{gc}^{P_j}, r_{ot}^{P_j,\text{send}}) \leftarrow \mathsf{NMC}_{\text{extract}}(\mathbf{nmc}_1^{P_j,\text{send}}, \mathbf{nmc}_1^{P_i,\text{recv}}, \mathbf{nmc}_2^{P_j,\text{send}})$$

from P_j's NMC transcript. If we haven't already queried the ideal functionality, send $\mathbf{x}_j$ to the ideal functionality. Note that because the NMC is perfectly binding after round 1, the value $\mathbf{x}_j$ is identical to the value extracted by $\mathsf{OT}_{\text{extract}}$ during round 2 as long as the identity checked in C holds.

5. Use the values obtained in the previous step to check if the conditions in statement ϕ hold with respect to language $L_{j\to i}$. If they do not hold, output "special abort".

6. If we have not yet aborted, instruct the ideal functionality to deliver the output to P_i.

We show the view in the real world is indistinguishable from the view in the ideal world via a series of hybrid games, where the first hybrid $\mathcal{H}_0$ corresponds to the real world and the last hybrid $\mathcal{H}_6$ corresponds to the ideal world. The hybrids are as follows.

Hybrid $\mathcal{H}_0$: In this hybrid, the simulator plays the role of all honest parties in all sessions, and behaves identically to the real-world executions of the protocol.

Hybrid $\mathcal{H}_1$: Here the simulator acts in the same way as in $\mathcal{H}_0$ except that for each honest party P_i's round 2 message during session (s, i, j) it simulates the ZK proof it sends to $\mathcal{A}$. This hybrid now runs in time $\mathsf{poly}(T_{\text{Sim}})$.

Hybrid $\mathcal{H}_2$: The simulator acts in the same way as $\mathcal{H}_1$, except that when computing each honest party P_i's round 1 message during session (s, i, j), it sends the chooser's OT message with choice bits $(0, 0, 0, 0)$ instead of $(\mathbf{x}_i, r_c^{P_i,\text{send}}, r_{gc}^{P_i}, r_{ot}^{P_i,\text{send}})$. This hybrid still runs in time $\mathsf{poly}(T_{\text{Sim}})$.

Hybrid $\mathcal{H}_3$: The simulator acts in the same way as $\mathcal{H}_2$, except for each session (s, i, j), during rounds 1 and 2 it commits to $(0, 0, 0)$ on behalf of P_i instead of $(\mathbf{x}_i, r_{gc}^{P_i}, r_{ot}^{P_i,\text{send}})$. This hybrid still runs in time $\mathsf{poly}(T_{\text{Sim}})$.

Hybrid $\mathcal{H}_4$: The simulator acts in the same way as $\mathcal{H}_3$, except that after receiving P_j's round 2 message during session (s, i, j) it breaks $\mathbf{nmc}_1^{P_j,\text{send}}$ to obtain $(\mathbf{x}_j, r_{gc}^{P_j}, r_{ot}^{P_j,\text{send}})$ and during the output computation phase outputs "special abort" if the conditions in statement ϕ don't hold. This hybrid now runs in time $\mathsf{poly}(T_{\mathsf{NMC}_{\text{extract}}})$.

Hybrid $\mathcal{H}_5$: The simulator acts in the same way as $\mathcal{H}_4$, except that after receiving P_j's round 1 message during session (s, i, j), it runs $\mathsf{OT}_{\text{extract}}$ on P_j's OT receiver message to obtain the values $(\mathbf{x}_j, r_c^{P_j,\text{send}}, r_{gc}^{P_j}, r_{ot}^{P_j,\text{send}})$. If $\mathbf{nmc}_1^{P_j,\text{send}} = \mathsf{NMC}_1^{\text{send}}(1^\lambda, (\mathbf{x}_j, r_{gc}^{P_j}, r_{ot}^{P_j,\text{send}}); r_c^{P_j,\text{send}})$, the simulator sends $\mathbf{x}_j$ to the ideal functionality to obtain $f(\mathbf{x}_i, \mathbf{x}_j)$. On the other hand, if $\mathbf{nmc}_1^{P_j,\text{send}} \neq \mathsf{NMC}_1^{\text{send}}(1^\lambda, (\mathbf{x}_j, r_{gc}^{P_j}, r_{ot}^{P_j,\text{send}}); r_c^{P_j,\text{send}})$, the simulator sends the value $\mathbf{x}_j$ extracted using $\mathsf{NMC}_{\text{extract}}$ after receiving P_j's round 2 message to the ideal functionality. It tells the ideal functionality to deliver the output to P1 at the end of session (s, i, j) as long as the session did not abort. This hybrid now runs in time $\mathsf{poly}(T_{\mathsf{OT}_{\text{extract}}})$.

Hybrid $\mathcal{H}_6$: The simulator acts in the same way as $\mathcal{H}_5$, except that for every honest party P_i's second-round message during session (s, i, j), it simulates the generation of the garbled circuit using the saved value y received from the ideal functionality instead of generating it honestly. This final hybrid runs in time $\mathsf{poly}(T_{\mathsf{OT}_{\mathsf{extract}}})$, which is the running time of the ideal-world simulator.

We want to use these hybrids to show the view of $\mathcal{A}$ is indistinguishable between the real and ideal worlds. There is a problem, though: in $\mathcal{H}_2$ and $\mathcal{H}_3$, the honest parties have no way to obtain its output. This is because the simulator switches the honest parties' ot_1 messages to 0 in $\mathcal{H}_2$, which means the real-world method of running the garbled circuit to obtain the output will not work, and the simulator is not yet powerful enough to break the commitment.

Despite this, it is still possible to use this ordering of hybrids to prove indistinguishability. Consider the pair $(s, \mathbf{x}_j, b_i)$, where $\mathbf{x}_j$ is the input committed to by corrupt party P_j during session (s, i, j), and b_i is a bit which denotes whether or not honest party P_i accepts P_j's NMC and zero knowledge proof during the same session. Assuming $\mathcal{A}$ cannot generate a proof for a false statement, this pair determines the output of P_i in session (s, i, j) regardless of whether we are in the real or the ideal world. So to make the proof work, during certain steps we will argue indistinguishability of the tuple $(v, \{(s, \mathbf{x}_j, b_i)\}_s)$ between hybrids, where v is the view of $\mathcal{A}$.

The proof is organized as follows.

We first argue computational indistinguishability between each successive pair of hybrids. Afterwards we argue indistinguishablity of the combined view of $\mathcal{A}$ along with the output of P_1. Before starting, define a "bad" event $\mathcal{E}$ which will be useful in our proofs.

Definition 4. *We define event $\mathcal{E}$ to occur if there exists a session (s, i, j) where both of the following happen:*

1. *P_i accepts P_j's ZK proof*
2. *one of the conditions of the statement ϕ' do not hold w.r.t. $L_{j \to i}$.*

Lemma 1. *$\mathcal{E}$ occurs with negligible probability in $\mathcal{H}_0$.*

Proof. This follows from the adaptive soundness of the SPSS ZK argument system for languages decidable in time T_L and the fact that $L_{j \to i}$ is decidable in time T_L. □

Lemma 2. *Assuming the zero-knowledge property of the SPSS ZK argument system, the view of $\mathcal{A}$ between $\mathcal{H}_0$ and $\mathcal{H}_1$ are computationally indistinguishable.*

Proof. We prove the claim via a sequence of subhybrids for each session (s, i, j), where in each subhybrid we switch to a simulated ZK2 message for P_i.

Assume there is a PPT adversary $\mathcal{A}$ who can interact with the simulator and then, given P_1's output, distinguish between real and simulated for session (s, i, j). Then we construct a PPT adversary $\mathcal{A}'$ which contradicts the zero-knowledge property of the ZK system.

Fix the randomness used by the adversary, and by the simulator to generate all honest parties' messages before P_i's second-round message. There must be at least one way to fix this randomness such that the advantage of $\mathcal{A}$ is still nonnegligible. This also fixes the statement ϕ (and the witness w for s) which P_i should prove in round 2.

Now we construct $\mathcal{A}'$ to run the experiment with this fixed randomness, and to forward $\mathsf{zk}_1^{P_j}$ to the ZK challenger. Then $\mathcal{A}'$ receives $\mathsf{zk}_2^{P_i}$ which is either a valid proof of s or a simulated one. $\mathcal{A}'$ uses $\mathsf{zk}_2^{P_i}$ as the proof to send to $\mathcal{A}$ instead of generating one itself when generating the second-round message for P_i. It then outputs whatever $\mathcal{A}$ outputs.

$\mathcal{A}$ distinguishes the real and simulated for (s, i, j) even with the round 1 randomness fixed, and this is identical to the experiment described above with the new $\mathcal{A}'$. So $\mathcal{A}'$ is a distinguisher for the zero-knowledge property of the ZK system. $\qquad\square$

Lemma 3. *Assuming the zero-knowledge property of the SPSS ZK argument system, $\mathcal{E}$ occurs with negligible probability in $\mathcal{H}_1$.*

Proof. Assume there is an adversary $\mathcal{A}$ which causes $\mathcal{E}$ to happen with nonnegligible probability in $\mathcal{H}_1$. Note that by Lemma 1 $\mathcal{A}$ cannot cause $\mathcal{E}$ to happen with nonnegligible probability in $\mathcal{H}_0$. We can extract the committed value in time $T_{\mathsf{NMC}_{\mathsf{extract}}}$ for each session to check whether or not $\mathcal{E}$ holds, thus creating a $\mathsf{poly}(T_{\mathsf{NMC}_{\mathsf{extract}}})$-time distinguisher for $\mathcal{H}_0$ and $\mathcal{H}_1$, contradicting Lemma 2, since $\mathsf{poly}(T_{\mathsf{NMC}_{\mathsf{extract}}}) \ll T_{\mathsf{zk}}$. $\qquad\square$

Lemma 4. *Assuming the chooser's security of the OT scheme, the tuple $(v, \{(s, \mathbf{x}_j, b_i)\}_s)$ between $\mathcal{H}_1$ and $\mathcal{H}_2$ is computationally indistinguishable.*

Proof. We prove the claim via a sequence of subhybrids for each session (s, i, j), where in each subhybrid we switch P_i's $\mathbf{ot}_1$ message to 0.

Assume there is a PPT adversary $\mathcal{A}$ who can interact with the simulator and then, given $\{(s, \mathbf{x}_j, b_i)\}_s$ in addition to its view v at the end of the interaction, distinguishes between the subhybrid for some (s, i, j) and the previous subhybrid with nonnegligible probability. We use $\mathcal{A}$ to build an adversary $\mathcal{A}'$ for the OT chooser's security game. For simplicity of exposition, we first assume that $\mathcal{A}$ distinguishes only given its view v. Once we have established the reduction in this case, we extend it to the case where $\mathcal{A}$ also receives $(v, \{(s, \mathbf{x}_j, b_i)\}_s)$.

Fix the randomness $(r_c^{P_i,\mathsf{send}}, r_{gc}^{P_i}, r_{ot}^{P_i,\mathsf{send}})$ generated on behalf of P_i for session (s, i, j). There must be at least one such fixed value for which $\mathcal{A}$ still distinguishes with nonnegligible probability. Let $\mathcal{A}'$ run the experiment identically to the previous subhybrid with the randomness above fixed to this particular value, except that instead of computing $\mathbf{ot}_1^{P_i}$ directly it receives this value from the OT challenger. The challenger either computes the OT with choice bits $(r_c^{P_i,\mathsf{send}}, r_{gc}^{P_i}, r_{ot}^{P_i,\mathsf{send}})$ or $(0, 0, 0, 0)$.

Assuming $(r_c^{P_i,\mathsf{send}}, r_{gc}^{P_i}, r_{ot}^{P_i,\mathsf{send}})$ is fixed, this experiment is identical to the previous subhybrid in the first case and the subhybrid for (s, i, j) in the second case. So if $\mathcal{A}$ successfully distinguishes then $\mathcal{A}'$ does as well. This contradicts chooser's security of the OT, since $T_{\mathsf{Sim}} \ll T_R$.

To extend to the case where $\mathcal{A}$ also receives $\{(s, \mathbf{x}_j, b_i)\}_s$, note that we can break the commitments of each of the corrupted parties in time $T_{\mathsf{NMC}_{\mathsf{extract}}}$ to retrieve each corrupted input $\mathbf{x}_j$, and b_i is known already by the experiment. Passing these to the adversary we obtain a $\mathsf{poly}(T_{\mathsf{NMC}_{\mathsf{extract}}})$-time distinguisher, which still contradicts chooser's security of the OT, since $\mathsf{poly}(T_{\mathsf{NMC}_{\mathsf{extract}}}) \ll T_R$.

$\square$

Lemma 5. *Assuming $\mathcal{E}$ occurs with negligible probability in $\mathcal{H}_1$, $\mathcal{E}$ occurs with negligible probability in $\mathcal{H}_2$.*

Proof. Assume there is an adversary $\mathcal{A}$ which causes $\mathcal{E}$ to happen with nonnegligible probability in $\mathcal{H}_2$. Note that by Lemma 3 $\mathcal{A}$ cannot cause $\mathcal{E}$ to happen with nonnegligible probability in $\mathcal{H}_1$. We can break the corrupted parties' commitments each in time $T_{\mathsf{NMC}_{\mathsf{extract}}}$ to create a $\mathsf{poly}(T_{\mathsf{NMC}_{\mathsf{extract}}})$-time distinguisher for $\mathcal{H}_1$ and $\mathcal{H}_2$, contradicting Lemma 4, since $\mathsf{poly}(T_{\mathsf{NMC}_{\mathsf{extract}}}) \ll T_R$. $\square$

Lemma 6. *Assuming the non-malleability of the commitment scheme, the tuple $(v, \{(s, \mathbf{x}_j, b_i)\}_s)$ between $\mathcal{H}_2$ and $\mathcal{H}_3$ is computationally indistinguishable.*

Proof. We prove the claim via a sequence of subhybrids for each session (s, i, j), where, in each subhybrid we switch to an NMC of 0 for P_i.

Assume there is a PPT adversary $\mathcal{A}$ who can interact with the simulator and then, given $\{(s, \mathbf{x}_j, b_i)\}_s$ in addition to its view v at the end of the interaction, distinguishes between the previous hybrid and the hybrid for (s, i, j) with non-negligible advantage. Then we create a T_{Sim}-time $\mathcal{A}'$ which contradicts the non-malleability property of the commitment scheme. Note that $\{(s, \mathbf{x}_j, b_i)\}_s$ is computable directly from the output of the non-malleability game, since each corrupted party P_j commits to x_j (i.e., these are part of the RHS committed values).

Fix the randomness $r_{gc}^{P_i}$ and $r_{ot}^{P_i,\mathsf{send}}$ generated for P_i in session (s, i, j). There must be some such fixed values where $\mathcal{A}$ still distinguishes between the two subhybrids with non-negligible advantage. We create $\mathcal{A}'$ as follows. $\mathcal{A}'$ runs the experiment identically to the previous subhybrid, except that the values $r_{gc}^{P_i}$ and $r_{ot}^{P_i,\mathsf{send}}$ are fixed to maximize the probability of distinguishing, and the following changes are made to the non-malleable commitment interactions. When computing P_i's round 1 message, instead of computing $\mathbf{nmc}_1^{P_i,\mathsf{send}}$, it receives this value from the challenger for the NMC game and forwards it to $\mathcal{A}$. It forwards $\mathbf{nmc}_1^{P_j,\mathsf{recv}}$ which it receives from $\mathcal{A}$ to the challenger as well. When computing P_i's round 2 message, it receives $\mathbf{nmc}_2^{P_i,\mathsf{send}}$ from the challenger and forwards it to $\mathcal{A}$ again. The NMC challenger commits to either $(\mathbf{x}_i, r_{gc}^{P_i}, r_{ot}^{P_i,\mathsf{send}})$ or $(0, 0, 0)$.

If the challenger commits to $(\mathbf{x}_i, r_{gc}^{P_i}, r_{ot}^{P_i,\mathsf{send}})$ then the experiment is identical to the subhybrid directly preceding the subhybrid for session (s, i, j), and if the challenger commits to $(0, 0, 0)$ then the experiment is identical to the subhybrid for (s, i, j) (with some fixed randomness, as described above). Thus $\mathcal{A}'$

wins the non-malleability game of the commitment scheme with non-negligible probability, contradicting the non-malleability of the commitment scheme, since $\mathsf{poly}(T_{\mathsf{Sim}}) \ll T_{\mathbf{nmc}}$. □

Lemma 7. *Assuming $\mathcal{E}$ occurs with negligible probability in $\mathcal{H}_2$ and the non-malleability of the commitment scheme, $\mathcal{E}$ occurs with negligible probability in $\mathcal{H}_3$.*

Proof. Assume that $\mathcal{E}$ occurs with non-negligible probability in $\mathcal{H}_3$. We can construct an adversary $\mathcal{A}'$ in the same way as in Lemma 6, playing the role of the adversary in a full nonmalleability game. By the nonmalleability property of the commitment scheme, the joint view of $\mathcal{A}'$ combined with the values it committed to are indistinguishable regardless of what the challenger commits to. If we have both the view of $\mathcal{A}'$ along with the values committed to it is easy to check if $\mathcal{E}$ occurred. If $\mathcal{E}$ occurs with nonnegligible probability in $\mathcal{H}_2$ then by checking $\mathcal{E}$ we have a $\mathsf{poly}(T_{\mathsf{Sim}})$-time distinguisher which contradicts non-malleability of the NMC. □

Lemma 8. *Assuming $\mathcal{E}$ occurs with negligible probability in $\mathcal{H}_3$, then the tuple $(v, \{(s, \mathbf{x}_j, b_i)\}_s)$ between $\mathcal{H}_3$ and $\mathcal{H}_4$ are computationally indistinguishable.*

Proof. The only difference between $\mathcal{H}_3$ and $\mathcal{H}_4$ is that we break all corrupted parties' commitments and output "special abort" if at any point $\mathcal{E}$ occurred. So the only time the two hybrids are distinguishable is if $\mathcal{E}$ occurs. Thus indistinguishability follows from Lemma 7. □

Note that from this point onward, proving hybrid indistinguishability is sufficient for proving $\mathcal{E}$ occurs with negligible probability, since every hybrid now checks $\mathcal{E}$ explicitly.

Lemma 9. *The tuple $(v, \{(s, \mathbf{x}_j, b_i)\}_s)$ between $\mathcal{H}_4$ and $\mathcal{H}_5$ are computationally indistinguishable.*

Proof. This follows trivially from the fact that the view of $\mathcal{A}$ is identical between $\mathcal{H}_4$ and $\mathcal{H}_5$. □

Lemma 10. *Assuming $\mathcal{E}$ happens with negligible probability in $\mathcal{H}_1$ and $\mathcal{H}_5$, the view of the adversary $\mathcal{A}$ between $\mathcal{H}_1$ and $\mathcal{H}_5$ is computationally indistinguishable.*

Proof. By the previous claims the tuple $(v, \{(s, \mathbf{x}_j, b_i)\}_s)$ is indistinguishable between these hybrids. Assuming $\mathcal{E}$ did not happen, in both hybrids the output of each honest party P_i during session (s, i, j) is $f(\mathbf{x}_i, \mathbf{x}_j)$ if $b = 1$ and $\perp$ if $b = 0$. To see why this is the case when $b = 1$, note that the value $\mathbf{x}_j$ extracted by

$OT_{extract}$ after round 1 is identical to the value extracted for $\mathbf{x}'_j$ by $NMC_{extract}$ after round 2. Assuming $\mathcal{E}$ does not occur, P1 outputs $\mathbf{x}'_j$ in $\mathcal{H}_1$, and P1 outputs $\mathbf{x}_j$ in $\mathcal{H}_5$.

Thus the claim follows from the fact that $\mathcal{E}$ occurs with negligible probability in $\mathcal{H}_5$, which follows from Lemma 9.   □

Lemma 11. *Assuming security of the garbled circuit scheme and statistical sender's security of the OT, the view of $\mathcal{A}$ between $\mathcal{H}_5$ and $\mathcal{H}_6$ is computationally indistinguishable.*

Proof. We consider a subhybrid $\mathcal{H}'_5$ which acts similarly to $\mathcal{H}_5$ except that when generating the second-round message for each honest P_i during session (s,i,j), it uses onlychoices to zero out the labels given by the honest party in ot_2 which do not correspond to the adversary's input.

This claim then follows from the next two claims.   □

Lemma 12. *Assuming statistical sender's security of the OT, the view of the adversary $\mathcal{A}$ between $\mathcal{H}_5$ and $\mathcal{H}'_5$ are statistically indistinguishable.*

Proof. We prove the claim via a sequence of subhybrids for each session (s,i,j), where in each subhybrid we switch the ot_2 message of P_i to zero out non-chosen labels. Assume there is an adversary $\mathcal{A}$ who can interact with the simulator and then distinguish between the subhybrid for some session (s,i,j) and the preceding subhybrid with nonnegligible probability. We use $\mathcal{A}$ to build an adversary $\mathcal{A}'$ for the OT sender's security game.

Fix the randomness $r_{gc}^{P_i}$ used to generate P_i's garbled circuit which it sends as part of its second-round message. There must be at least one such fixed value for which $\mathcal{A}$ still distinguishes with nonnegligible probability. Let $\mathcal{A}'$ run the experiment identically to the subhybrid preceding (s,i,j) with $r_{gc}^{P_i}$ fixed to this value, except that it passes the ot_1 message $ot_1^{P_j}$ generated by $\mathcal{A}$ to the OT challenger. The OT challenger then either responds with an $ot_2^{P_i}$ corresponding to the same labels in $\mathcal{H}_5$, or breaks $ot_1^{P_j}$ and zeros out the labels which do not correspond to the adversary's input. $\mathcal{A}'$ then outputs the output of $\mathcal{A}$.

Assuming $r_{gc}^{P_i}$ is fixed, this experiment is identical to the preceding hybrid in the first case and the subhybrid for (s,i,j) in the second case. So if $\mathcal{A}$ successfully distinguishes then $\mathcal{A}'$ does as well.   □

Lemma 13. *Assuming security of the garbled circuit scheme, the views induced by $\mathcal{H}'_5$ and $\mathcal{H}_6$ are computationally indistinguishable.*

Proof. We prove the claim via a sequence of subhybrids for each session (s,i,j), where in each subhybrid we switch the garbled circuit of P_i to be simulated.

Assume there is an adversary $\mathcal{A}$ who distinguishes between the subhybrid directly preceding the one for some session (s,i,j) and the subhybrid for (s,i,j) with nonnegligible probability. We use $\mathcal{A}$ to build a $poly(T_{OT_{extract}})$-time adversary $\mathcal{A}'$ that contradicts security of the garbled circuit.

Fix the randomness used by $\mathcal{A}$ and the randomness used by the simulator in generating all rounds preceding P_i's second-round message during session (s,i,j).

There must be some such fixed randomness such that $\mathcal{A}$ still distinguishes with nonnegligible probability. This also fixes the circuit which the honest party P_i garbles along with P_j's ot_1 input in session (s, i, j).

Let $\mathcal{A}'$ work in the same way as the subhybrid preceding (s, i, j) except that it receives a garbled circuit and labels $(\tilde{C}^{P_1}, labels)$ from the challenger, which it uses as the garbled circuit and labels for P_i in session (s, i, j). The challenger either computes the garbled circuit honestly or simulates using the output $f(\mathbf{x}_i, \mathbf{x}_j)$, which is fixed because of the fixed randomness. $\mathcal{A}'$ finally outputs the output of $\mathcal{A}$. Based on what the challenger does, the experiment is either identical to the subhybrid preceding (s, i, j) or the (s, i, j) subhybrid (with the adversary's randomness fixed). This means that $\mathcal{A}$ distinguishes with nonnegligible probability and thus so does $\mathcal{A}'$, contradicting security of the garbled circuit, since $\mathsf{poly}(T_{\mathsf{OT}_{\mathsf{extract}}}) \ll T_G$.   □

4 Instantiating the Non-Malleable Commitment of [47] Using LWE

In this section, we list all primitives used in each part of the construction of fully concurrent non-malleable commitments of [47], along with how to instantiate each primitive using subexponential hardness of LWE.

Two-round extractable commitments are constructed using the following primitives:
- A non-interactive perfectly binding commitment. *Can be obtained from LWE using one of the LWE-based PKE schemes.*
- Two-round statistically-sender-private oblivious transfer. *Known from LWE* [20].
- Yao's garbled circuits. *Symmetric-key encryption is known from LWE.*
- Two-round zero knowledge with super-polynomial simulation. *Known from LWE* [9,39].

Two-round SPS strong zero knowledge arguments are constructed using the following primitives:
- A zap. *Known from LWE* [9,39].
- The two-round extractable commitment. *See above.*
- A trapdoor for the prover to use. *Can use an instance of SIS.*

Two-round constant-tag non-malleable commitments are constructed using the following primitives:
- The two-round extractable commitment. *See above.*
- A non-interactive perfectly binding commitment. *Can be obtained from LWE using one of the LWE-based PKE schemes.*

One-one non-malleable commitments in two rounds are constructed using the following primitives:
- The two-round constant-tag non-malleable commitment. *See above.*
- The two-round SPS strong ZK. *See above.*

One-one simulation-sound zero knowledge in two rounds is constructed using the following primitives:

- The one-one non-malleable commitment. *See above.*
- A zap. *Known from LWE* [9,39].
- A trapdoor for the prover to use. *Can use an instance of SIS.*

Fully-concurrent non-malleable commitments in two rounds are constructed using the following primitives:

- The one-one simulation-sound zero knowledge argument. *See above.*
- The constant-tag non-malleable commitment. *See above.*

5   Quantum Computation

We conclude by observing that the simulator for our two-party computation protocol is straight-line, i.e., it does not resort to rewinding the adversary to generate a simulated transcript, and black-box. It is shown in [63] that any such protocol remains secure also against quantum attackers (i.e., it is post-quantum secure) and furthermore in [15] it is shown that any post-quantum two-round 2PC with a straight-line black-box simulator can be generically compiled into a secure 2PC for quantum circuits without adding any round. In [15] they proposed an instantiation of the classical 2PC in the common reference string model. Plugging our protocol (with a suitable instantiation of the underlying building blocks) into their result we obtain the following new implication.

Theorem 3. *Assuming the quantum sub-exponential hardness of the LWE problem, there exists a two-round concurrent 2PC for all quantum circuits, with classical inputs and outputs, in the plain model.*

5.1   Quantum Concurrent 2PC

For completeness, we describe our construction of concurrently secure two-round 2PC with respect to quantum functionalities. Our protocol is essentially identical to the three-message two-party protocol described in [15], except that we substitute our (classical) 2PC protocol from Sect. 3 and we only require one party to know the output. Hence we drop the third round from the protocol described in [15]. Before describing the protocol, we need bring some definitions of the quantum primitives and we take them in verbatim from [15].

Definition 5 (Clifford + Measurement Circuit). *A Clifford + Measurement circuit with parameters $n_i + k_{i i \in [d]}$ operates on $n_1 + k_1$ input qubits and applies d alternating layers of Clifford unitary and computational basis measurements, during which a total of $k_1 + \cdots + k_d$ of the input qubits are measured. It is specified by $(F_0, f_1, \ldots, f_d)$, where F_0 us a Clifford unitary, and each f_i is a classical circuit which takes as input the result of computational basis measurements on the i-th layer, and outputs a Clifford unitary F_i. In layer $i \in [d]$, k_i qubits are measured and n_i qubits are left over. The circuit is evaluated by first applying F_0 to the $n_1 + k_1$ input qubits, then the following steps are performed for $i = 1, \ldots d$:*

– *Measure the remaining k_i qubits in the computational basis, resulting in outcomes $m_i \in \{0,1\}^{k_1}$.*
– *Evaluate $f_i(m_i)$ to obtain a classical description of a Clifford $F_i \in \mathfrak{C}_{n_i}$.*
– *Apply F_i to the first n_i registers.*

The output of the circuit is the result of applying F_d to the final n_d registers.

Definition 6. (Garbling scheme for $\mathsf{C}+\mathsf{M}$ Circuits). *A garbling scheme for $\mathsf{C}+\mathsf{M}$ circuits consists of three procedures $(\mathtt{QGarble}, \mathtt{QGEval}, \mathtt{QGSim})$ with the following syntax.*

– $(E_0, \tilde{Q}) \leftarrow \mathtt{QGarble}(1^\lambda, Q)$: *A classical PPT procedure that takes as input the security parameter and a $\mathsf{C}+\mathsf{M}$ circuit and outputs a Clifford input garbling matrix E_0 and a quantum garbled circuit $\tilde{Q}$.*
– $\mathbf{x}_{out} \leftarrow \mathtt{QGEval}(\tilde{\mathbf{x}}_{inp}, \tilde{Q})$: *A QPT procedure that takes as input a garbled input $\tilde{\mathbf{x}}_{inp}$ and a garbled $\mathsf{C}+\mathsf{M}$ circuit $\tilde{Q}$, and outputs a quantum state $\mathbf{x}_{out}$.*
– $(\tilde{\mathbf{x}}_{inp}, \tilde{Q}) \leftarrow \mathtt{QGSim}(1^\lambda, \{n_i, k_i\}_{i \in [d]}, \mathbf{x}_{out})$: *A QPT procedure that takes as input the security parameter, parameters for a $\mathsf{C}+\mathsf{M}$ circuit, and an output state, and outputs a simulated garbled input and garbled circuit.*

Correctness. For any $\mathsf{C}+\mathsf{M}$ circuit Q with parameters $\{n_i + k_i\}_{i \in [d]}$ and n_0-qubit input state $\mathbf{x}_{\text{inp}}$ along with (potentially entangled) auxiliary information z, we have:

$$\{(\mathtt{QGEval}(E_0(\mathbf{x}_{\text{inp}}, 0^{k\lambda}), \tilde{Q}), z) : (E_0, \tilde{Q}) \leftarrow \mathtt{QGarble}(1^\lambda, Q)\} \approx_s (Q(\mathbf{x}_{\text{inp}}), z)).$$

Security. For any $\mathsf{C}+\mathsf{M}$ circuit Q with parameters $\{n_i + k_i\}_{i \in [d]}$ and n_0-qubit input state x_{inp} along with (potentially entangled) auxiliary information z, we have:

$$\{(E_0(\mathbf{x}_{\text{inp}}, 0^{k\lambda}), \tilde{Q}, z) : (E_0, \tilde{Q}) \leftarrow \mathtt{QGarble}(1^\lambda, Q)\}$$
$$\approx_c (\mathtt{QGSim}(1^\lambda, \{n_i, k_i\}_{i \in [d]}, Q(\mathbf{x}_{\text{inp}})), z).$$

The rest of this section assumes familiarity with basic notions of quantum computation, and quantum garbled circuits as we defined above and were initially introduced in [25]. For a comprehensive background, we refer the reader to [15]. For the construction of our protocols, we need the following building blocks:

i A post-quantum secure concurrent two-round two-party protocol for classical computation c2PC (let T_{c2PC} denote the runtime of the simulator).
ii A quantum garbling scheme for $\mathsf{C}+\mathsf{M}$ gates $(\mathtt{QGarble}, \mathtt{QGEval}, \mathtt{QGSim})$, secure against adversaries running in time T_{QGC}.

We denote by T_{c2PC} the runtime of the simulator of the classical two party computation and by T_{QGC} the maximum runtime of the distinguisher allowed by the security of the quantum garbled circuit. We require that $\mathrm{poly}(\lambda) \ll T_{\text{c2PC}} \ll$

T_{QGC}. In our protocol, parties P_1 and P_2 each having inputs $\mathbf{x}_0$ and $\mathbf{x}_1$ want to compute a quantum circuit Q on their inputs and only P_1 gets outputs out_1 while P_2 receives no output in a way that they do not reveal anything about their inputs and only one party gets the output of the computation. We assume that Q is a Clifford+Measurement quantum circuit and takes input $(\mathbf{x}_0, \mathbf{x}_1, \mathbf{T}^k, \mathbf{0}^k)$, where $\mathbf{T}$ denotes a *magic state* $\mathbf{T} = 1/\sqrt{2} \cdot (|0\rangle + e^{i\pi/4} |1\rangle)$.

At a high level, the quantum two-party protocol between parties P_1, P_2 runs in two parallel phases, one is for the parties to jointly encode their quantum inputs and simultaneously they run a two-message classical 2PC that outputs a classical description of a quantum garble circuit to P_1 according to the functionality $f[Q]$ which is described in Fig. 2; which allows P_1 to later evaluate the garbled circuit to get his own output.

To make the protocol secure against a malicious P_2 we use the "cut and choose" technique from [30] and we refer to [15, §2,5] where they explained how this technique would be applied on their two-party protocol to make it secure against malicious P_2. The cut-and-choose technique is done by the Clifford unitary $U_{\text{dec-check-enc}}$ in the functionality of our c2PC that is used in the computation phase of our protocol below. Now we describe our protocol in more detail:

Quantum two party computation protocol

Common information: security parameter λ, and C + M circuit Q to be computed with $n_1 + n_2$ input qubits, $m_1 + m_2$ output qubits, n_Z auxiliary **0** states, and n_T auxiliary T states. let
$s = n_2 + (n_1 + \lambda) + (2n_Z + \lambda) + (n_T + 1)\lambda$.
P_1's **Input:** $\mathbf{x}_1$ (Parsed as a computational basis state)
P_2's **Input:** $\mathbf{x}_2$ (Parsed as a computational basis state)

- **Round 1 P_1 :**
  - Samples a random Clifford $C_1 \leftarrow \mathfrak{C}_{n_1+\lambda}$ and uses it to encrypt and authenticate his input $\mathbf{x}_1$ as $\mathbf{m}_1 := C_1(\mathbf{x}_1, \mathbf{0}^\lambda)$.
  - Computes the first round message m_1, of the c2PC using C_1 as his input.
  - Sends $(m_1, \mathbf{m}_1)$ to P_2.
- **Round 2 P_2 :**
  - Samples random Cliffords $C_2 \leftarrow \mathfrak{C}_s$ and $C_{out} \leftarrow \mathfrak{C}_{m_2+\lambda}$ uses C_2 to encrypt and authenticate his own input $\mathbf{x}_2$ alongside with encoding of his quantum state $\mathbf{m}_2 := C_2(\mathbf{x}_2, \mathbf{m}_1, \mathbf{0}^{2n_Z}, T^{(n_T+1)\lambda})$.
  - Computes the second round message m_2 for the classical c2PC computation using (C_2, C_{out}) as their input.
  - Sends $(m_2, \mathbf{m}_2)$ to P_1.
- **Computation Phase P_1** does the following computation:
  - Using m_2 he can compute the output of the classical c2PC that is $(U_{\text{dec-check-enc}}, D, \tilde{g}_1, \ldots, \tilde{g}_d)$.
  - Compute $(\mathbf{m}_{\text{inp}}, \mathbf{z}_{\text{check}}, \text{trap}_2, T_{\text{inp}}, t_{\text{check}}) \leftarrow U_{\text{dec-check-enc}}(\mathbf{m}_2)$

- Measure each qubit of $(\mathbf{z}_{\text{check}}, \text{trap})$ in the standard basis and abort if any measurement is not zero.
- Measure each qubit of $\mathbf{t}_{\text{check}}$ and the T-basis and abort if any measurement is not zero.
- Compute $\text{out}_1 \leftarrow \texttt{QGEval}(D_0, \tilde{g}_1, \ldots, \tilde{g}_d, \mathbf{m}_{\text{inp}})$.

We note that, in step 2 of Fig. 2, given a $\mathsf{C} + \mathsf{M}$ circuit Q, and a Clifford $C_{\text{out}} \in \mathfrak{C}_{m_1+\lambda}$, the circuit $Q_{\text{dist}}(C_{\text{out}})$ is defined as follows: it takes as input $(n_1 + n_2 + n_Z + \lambda + n_T\lambda)$ qubits $(\mathbf{x}_1 + \mathbf{x}_2 + z_{\text{inp}} + trap_A, t_{\text{inp}})$ on registers $(A, B, Z_{\text{inp}}, Trap_A, T_{\text{inp}})$, it will first apply the magic state distillation circuit from Lemma 3.3 of [15] with parameters $(n_T\lambda, \lambda)$ to t_{inp} to produce QRV t of size n_T, then it will run Q on $(\mathbf{x}_1, \mathbf{x}_2, z_{\text{inp}}, t)$ to produce (y_1, y_2), and in the end, it outputs $(C_{\text{out}}(y_2, trap_A), y_1)$.

5.2 Security Proof of Quantum Concurrent 2PC

In this section, we prove Lemma 14 that is similar to the proof of Theorem 5.1 in [15]. For the sake of completeness, we write out the proof in its entirety.

Lemma 14. *Assuming two-round concurrently secure 2PC protocol with black-box super-polynomial simulation running in time T_{c2PC} and sub-exponentially secure quantum garbled circuit with simulation running time T_{QGC}, where $\text{poly}(\lambda) \ll T_{\text{c2PC}} \ll T_{QGC}$, there exists a concurrent two-round 2PC for all quantum circuits in the plain model.*

Proof. For the sake of simplicity, we prove it in the following two cases when

1. A quantum polynomial-time adversary $\mathcal{A}$ corrupting party P_1.
2. A quantum polynomial-time adversary $\mathcal{A}$ corrupting party P_2.

For the ideal functionality, we use the Classical functionality in Fig. 2.

Case 1: Consider any quantum PT adversary $\mathcal{A}$ corrupting party P_1. The simulator $\text{Sim}(\mathbf{x}_1, \text{aux}_{\mathcal{A}})$ is defined as follows:

- Receive $(m_1, \mathbf{m}_1)$ from $\mathcal{A}$ and compute $\text{inp} \leftarrow \texttt{c2PC.Sim}(1^\lambda, m_1)$. If $\text{inp} = \bot$ the abort, else parse inp as C_1 and compute $(\mathbf{x}'_1, \text{trap}_1) := C_1^\dagger(\mathbf{m}_1)$.
- Query ideal functionality and compute simulated round 2 message as follows:
  - Compute $(\tilde{\mathbf{m}}_{\text{inp}}, D, \tilde{g}_1, \ldots, \tilde{g}_d)$ by running $\texttt{QGSim}(1^\lambda, \{n_i, k_i\}_{i \in [d]}, \text{out}_1)$ where where $\tilde{\mathbf{m}}_{\text{inp}}$ is the simulated quantum garbled input and $\{n_i, k_i\}_{i \in [d]}$ are the parameters of $\mathsf{C} + \mathsf{M}$ circuit $Q_{\text{dist}}(C_{\text{out}})$.
  - Sample a random $U_{\text{dec-check-enc}}$ and compute $\mathbf{m}_2 := U_{\text{dec-check-enc}}^\dagger (\tilde{\mathbf{m}}_{\text{inp}}, \mathbf{0}, \text{trap}_1, T^\lambda)$.
  - Compute $m_2 \leftarrow \texttt{c2PC.Sim}(1^\lambda, U_{\text{dec-check-enc}}, D, \tilde{g}_1, \ldots, \tilde{g}_d)$.
  - Send $(m_2, \mathbf{m}_2)$ to $\mathcal{A}$.

Classical functionality $f[Q]$

Common Information: security parameter λ, and $\mathsf{C} + \mathsf{M}$ circuit Q to be computed with $n_1 + n_2$ input qubits, $m_1 + m_2$ output qubits, n_Z auxiliary $\mathbf{0}$ states, and n_T auxiliary T states. let $s = n_2 + (n_1 + \lambda) + (2n_Z + \lambda) + (n_T + 1)\lambda$.

P_1's **Input:** Classical description of $C_1 \in \mathfrak{C}_{n_1+\lambda}$
P_2's **Input:** Classical description of $C_2 \in \mathfrak{C}_s$ and $C_{\text{out}} \in \mathfrak{C}_{m_2+\lambda}$

1. Sample the unitary U_{check} as follows:
   - sample random permutation π on $(n_T + 1)\lambda$ elements.
   - Sample random element $M \leftarrow \text{GL}(2n_T, \mathbb{F}_2)$.
   - Compute a description of the Clifford U_{check} that operates as follows on registers $(\mathsf{A}, \mathsf{B}, \text{Trap}_{\mathsf{B}}, \mathsf{Z}_{\mathsf{A}}, \text{Trap}_{\mathsf{A}}, \mathsf{T}_{\mathsf{A}})$.
     - Rearrange the registers of T_{A} according to the permutation π and then partition the registers into $(\mathsf{T}_{\text{inp}}, \mathsf{T}_{\text{check}})$.
     - Apply the inner map M to the registers Z_{A} and then partition the registers into $(\mathsf{Z}_{\text{inp}}, \mathsf{Z}_{\text{check}})$.
     - Rearrange the registers to $(\mathsf{A}, \mathsf{B}, \mathsf{Z}_{\text{inp}}, \text{Trap}_{\mathsf{A}}, \mathsf{T}_{\text{inp}}, \mathsf{Z}_{\text{check}}, \text{Trap}_{\mathsf{B}}, \mathsf{T}_{\text{check}})$.
   - Define $U_{\text{dec-check}}$ as:

   $$U_{\text{dec-check}} := U_{\text{check}}(\mathbb{I}^{n_A} \otimes C_B^\dagger \otimes \mathbb{I}^{(2n_Z + \lambda) + (n_T+1)\lambda})C_2^\dagger$$

2. Sample $(E_0, D_0, \tilde{g}_1, \cdots, \tilde{g}_d) \leftarrow \texttt{QGarble}(1^\lambda, Q_{\text{dist}}(C_{\text{out}}))$.
3. Compute the description of $\mathsf{U}_{\text{dec-check-enc}} := (E_0 \otimes \mathbb{I}^{(n_Z+\lambda)\lambda})U_{\text{dec-check}}^\dagger$.

P_1 **Output:**

1. A unitary $\mathsf{U}_{\text{dec-check-enc}}$ on s qubits.
2. A quantum garbled circuit $(D, \tilde{g}_1, \ldots, \tilde{g}_n)$

Fig. 2. Classical functionality $\mathcal{F}[Q]$ to be used in the quantum c2PC protocol

We now show that the simulation strategy is successful against all malicious QPT adversaries. That is, the view of the adversary $\mathcal{A}(\mathbf{x}_2, \text{aux}_{\mathcal{A}})$ along with the output of the honest parties is computationally indistinguishable in the real and ideal worlds. We show this via a series of computationally indistinguishable hybrids where the first world $\mathcal{H}_0$ corresponds to the real world and the last game corresponds to the ideal world.

1. $\mathcal{H}_1$: In this game, Sim runs c2PC.Sim$_{\mathsf{P}_1}$ in time T_{c2PC} and simulates the c2PC scheme, using c2PC.Sim to extract $\mathcal{A}$'s input, C_1, and runs c2PC.Sim to computes party P_2's message m_2. Use C_1 and freshly sampled (C_2, C_{out}) to sample the output of the classical functionality that is given to c2PC.Sim.
   The (computational) indistinguishability of $\mathcal{H}_0$ and $\mathcal{H}_1$ comes directly from the security against corrupted c2PC scheme.

2. $\mathcal{H}_2$: Now, we make a (perfectly indistinguishable) switch in how $\mathbf{m}_2$ is computed and how $U_{\text{dec-check-enc}}$ (part of the classical c2PC output) is sampled. Define $(\mathbf{x}_1', \text{trap}_1) := C_1^\dagger(m_1)$, where C_1 was extracted from m_1. As here exists a Clifford unitary U such that $U_{\text{dec-check-enc}} = UC_2^\dagger$, where C_2 was randomly sampled. Thus, since the Clifford matrices form a group, an equivalent sampling procedure would be to sample $U_{\text{dec-check-enc}}$ and define

$$\mathbf{m}_2 := U_{\text{dec-check-enc}}^\dagger(E_0(\mathbf{x}_1', \mathbf{x}_2, \mathbf{0}^{n_z+\lambda}, T^{n_T\lambda}), \mathbf{0}^{n_z}, \text{trap}_1, T^\lambda).$$

Notice that, in $\mathcal{H}_1$, we have that,

$$U_{\text{dec-check-enc}}(\mathbf{m}_2) := (E_0(\mathbf{x}_1', \mathbf{x}_2, \mathbf{0}^{n_z+\lambda}, T^{n_T\lambda}), \mathbf{0}^{n_z}, \text{trap}_1, T^\lambda).$$

This hybrid runs in time T_{c2PC}. We observe that $\mathcal{H}_1$ and $\mathcal{H}_2$ are equivalent.

3. $\mathcal{H}_3$: In this game, we simulate the quantum garbled circuit. In particular, compute

$$\text{out}_1 \leftarrow \mathsf{Q}_{\text{dist}}[C_{\text{out}}](\mathbf{x}_1', \mathbf{x}_2, \mathbf{0}^{n_z+\lambda}, T^{n_T\lambda})$$

and then compute $\hat{\mathbf{m}}_{\text{inp}}$ by running QGSim and the substitute $\hat{\mathbf{m}}_{\text{inp}}$ for $E_0(\mathbf{x}_1', \mathbf{x}_2, \mathbf{0}^{n_z+\lambda}, T^{n_T\lambda})$ in the computation of $\mathbf{m}_2$, so that $\mathbf{m}_2 := U_{\text{dec-check-enc}}^\dagger(E_0(\mathbf{x}_1', \mathbf{x}_2, \mathbf{0}^{n_z+\lambda}, T^{n_T\lambda}), \mathbf{0}^{n_z}, \text{trap}_1, T^\lambda)$. This hybrid runs in time T_{c2PC}. The (computational) indistinguishability of $\mathcal{H}_2$ and $\mathcal{H}_3$ comes directly from the sub-exponential security of the QGC.

4. $\mathcal{H}_4$: Finally, instead of directly computing out_1 from the first stage of Q_{dist}, query the ideal functionality with $\mathbf{x}_1'$ and receive back out_1. Now, during party P_2's output reconstruction step, if the check passes, send "accept" to the ideal functionality, and otherwise send "abort" to the ideal functionality. This game is now same as the ideal world. This hybrid runs in T_{c2PC}.
We observe that $\mathcal{H}_4$ and $\mathcal{H}_5$ are equivalent.

Case 2: Consider any quantum PT adversary $\mathcal{A}$ corrupting party P_2. The simulator Sim is defined as follows. Whenever we say that the simulator aborts, we mean that it sends $\bot$ to the ideal f'The simulator $\text{Sim}(\mathbf{x}_2, \text{aux}_\mathcal{A})$ works as follows:

- Compute $m_1 \leftarrow$ c2PC.Sim(1^λ), samples a random Clifford C_1, and compute $\mathbf{m}_1 := C_1(\mathbf{0}^{n_1}, \mathbf{0}^\lambda)$. Send $(m_1, \mathbf{m}_1)$ to $\mathcal{A}(\mathbf{x}_2, \text{aux}_\mathcal{A})$.
- Receive $(m_2, \mathbf{m}_2)$ from $\mathcal{A}$ and compute out $\leftarrow$ c2PC.Sim($1^\lambda, m_2$). Abort if out $= \bot$, otherwise, parse out as (C_2, C_{out}).
- Using (C_1, C_2) sample $U_{\text{dec-check}}$ and compute $(\mathbf{x}_1', \mathbf{x}_2', \mathbf{m}_{\text{inp}}, \text{trap}_2, \mathbf{z}_{\text{check}}, \text{trap}_1, T_{\text{inp}}, \mathbf{t}_{\text{check}}) \leftarrow U_{\text{dec-check}}(\mathbf{m}_2)$. Measure each qubit of $\mathbf{z}_{\text{check}}$ and trap_2 in the standard basis and each qubit of $\mathbf{t}_{\text{check}}$ in the T-basis. If any measurement is non-zero, then abort.

We observe that the simulation strategy is successful against all malicious QPT adversaries. That is, the view of the adversary along with the output of the honest parties is computationally indistinguishable in the real and ideal worlds. For this, we consider the following hybrids where $\mathcal{H}_0$ is the real word.

1. $\mathcal{H}_1$ In this world we run c2PC.Sim to compute the first message of the c2PC as m_1 and extract (C_2, C_{out}) (or abort). This hybrid runs in time T_{c2PC}. This world is computationally indistinguishable from the real world by the security of the c2PC scheme against the malicious P_2.
2. $\mathcal{H}_2$ In this world, we compute $\mathbf{m}_1$ as $C_1(\mathbf{0}^{n_B}, \mathbf{0}^\lambda)$ and substitute $\mathbf{x}_1$ with $\mathbf{x}'_1$ before computing $Q_{dist}(C_{out})$. This hybrid runs in time T_{c2PC} This world is statistically indistinguishable from $\mathcal{H}_1$ from the security of the Clifford authentication code.

$\square$

Acknowledgements. Giulio Malavolta was supported by the German Federal Ministry of Education and Research BMBF (grant 16KISK038, project 6GEM). Behzad Abdolmaleki was supported by the German Federal Ministry of Education and Research BMBF (grant 16KISK038, project 6GEM) and most of the work was done while he was affiliated with the Max Planck Institute for Security and Privacy. Rex Fernando was supported by the Algorand Centres of Excellence (ACE) Programme, the Defense Advanced Research Projects Agency under award number HR001120C0086, the Office of Naval Research under award number N000142212064, and the National Science Foundation under award numbers 2128519 and 2044679. The views and conclusions contained in this document are those of the author and should not be interpreted as representing the official policies, either expressed or implied, of any sponsoring institution, the U.S. government or any other entity.

References

1. Abdolmaleki, B., Badrinarayanan, S., Fernando, R., Malavolta, G., Rahimi, A., Sahai, A.: Two-round concurrent 2pc from sub-exponential LWE. Cryptology ePrint Archive, Paper 2022/1719 (2022). https://eprint.iacr.org/2022/1719
2. Agarwal, A., Bartusek, J., Goyal, V., Khurana, D., Malavolta, G.: Two-round maliciously secure computation with super-polynomial simulation. In: Nissim, K., Waters, B. (eds.) TCC 2021. LNCS, vol. 13042, pp. 654–685. Springer, Cham (2021). https://doi.org/10.1007/978-3-030-90459-3_22
3. Agrawal, S.: Indistinguishability obfuscation without multilinear maps: new methods for bootstrapping and instantiation. In: Ishai, Y., Rijmen, V. (eds.) EUROCRYPT 2019, Part I. LNCS, vol. 11476, pp. 191–225. Springer, Cham (2019). https://doi.org/10.1007/978-3-030-17653-2_7
4. Agrawal, S., Pellet-Mary, A.: Indistinguishability obfuscation without maps: attacks and fixes for noisy linear FE. In: Canteaut, A., Ishai, Y. (eds.) EUROCRYPT 2020, Part I. LNCS, vol. 12105, pp. 110–140. Springer, Cham (2020). https://doi.org/10.1007/978-3-030-45721-1_5
5. Ananth, P., Choudhuri, A.R., Jain, A.: A new approach to round-optimal secure multiparty computation. In: Katz, J., Shacham, H. (eds.) CRYPTO 2017, Part I. LNCS, vol. 10401, pp. 468–499. Springer, Cham (2017). https://doi.org/10.1007/978-3-319-63688-7_16
6. Ananth, P., Jain, A., Sahai, A.: Indistinguishability obfuscation without multilinear maps: iO from LWE, bilinear maps, and weak pseudorandomness. Cryptology ePrint Archive, Report 2018/615 (2018). https://eprint.iacr.org/2018/615

7. Ananth, P., Sahai, A.: Projective arithmetic functional encryption and indistinguishability obfuscation from degree-5 multilinear maps. In: Coron, J.-S., Nielsen, J.B. (eds.) EUROCRYPT 2017, Part I. LNCS, vol. 10210, pp. 152–181. Springer, Cham (2017). https://doi.org/10.1007/978-3-319-56620-7_6
8. Ananth, P.V., Gupta, D., Ishai, Y., Sahai, A.: Optimizing obfuscation: avoiding Barrington's theorem. In: Ahn, G.-J., Yung, M., Li, N. (eds.) ACM CCS 2014, pp. 646–658. ACM Press, November 2014
9. Badrinarayanan, S., Fernando, R., Jain, A., Khurana, D., Sahai, A.: Statistical ZAP arguments. In: Canteaut, A., Ishai, Y. (eds.) EUROCRYPT 2020, Part III. LNCS, vol. 12107, pp. 642–667. Springer, Cham (2020). https://doi.org/10.1007/978-3-030-45727-3_22
10. Badrinarayanan, S., Garg, S., Ishai, Y., Sahai, A., Wadia, A.: Two-message witness indistinguishability and secure computation in the plain model from new assumptions. In: Takagi, T., Peyrin, T. (eds.) ASIACRYPT 2017, Part III. LNCS, vol. 10626, pp. 275–303. Springer, Cham (2017). https://doi.org/10.1007/978-3-319-70700-6_10
11. Badrinarayanan, S., Goyal, V., Jain, A., Kalai, Y.T., Khurana, D., Sahai, A.: Promise zero knowledge and its applications to round optimal MPC. In: Shacham, H., Boldyreva, A. (eds.) CRYPTO 2018, Part II. LNCS, vol. 10992, pp. 459–487. Springer, Cham (2018). https://doi.org/10.1007/978-3-319-96881-0_16
12. Badrinarayanan, S., Goyal, V., Jain, A., Khurana, D., Sahai, A.: Round optimal concurrent MPC via strong simulation. In: Kalai, Y., Reyzin, L. (eds.) TCC 2017, Part I. LNCS, vol. 10677, pp. 743–775. Springer, Cham (2017). https://doi.org/10.1007/978-3-319-70500-2_25
13. Badrinarayanan, S., Miles, E., Sahai, A., Zhandry, M.: Post-zeroizing obfuscation: new mathematical tools, and the case of evasive circuits. In: Fischlin, M., Coron, J.-S. (eds.) EUROCRYPT 2016, Part II. LNCS, vol. 9666, pp. 764–791. Springer, Heidelberg (2016). https://doi.org/10.1007/978-3-662-49896-5_27
14. Barak, B., Prabhakaran, M., Sahai, A.: Concurrent non-malleable zero knowledge. In: 47th FOCS, pp. 345–354. IEEE Computer Society Press, October 2006
15. Bartusek, J., Coladangelo, A., Khurana, D., Ma, F.: On the round complexity of secure quantum computation. Cryptology ePrint Archive, Report 2020/1471 (2020). https://ia.cr/2020/1471
16. Bartusek, J., Ishai, Y., Jain, A., Ma, F., Sahai, A., Zhandry, M.: Affine determinant programs: a framework for obfuscation and witness encryption. In: Vidick, T. (ed.) ITCS 2020, vol. 151, pp. 82:1–82:39. LIPIcs, January 2020
17. Bellare, M., Pointcheval, D., Rogaway, P.: Authenticated key exchange secure against dictionary attacks. In: Preneel, B. (ed.) EUROCRYPT 2000. LNCS, vol. 1807, pp. 139–155. Springer, Heidelberg (2000). https://doi.org/10.1007/3-540-45539-6_11
18. Bellovin, S.M., Merritt, M.: Encrypted key exchange: password-based protocols secure against dictionary attacks. In: 1992 IEEE Symposium on Security and Privacy, pp. 72–84. IEEE Computer Society Press, May 1992
19. Bitansky, N., Lin, H.: One-message zero knowledge and non-malleable commitments. In: Beimel, A., Dziembowski, S. (eds.) TCC 2018, Part I. LNCS, vol. 11239, pp. 209–234. Springer, Cham (2018). https://doi.org/10.1007/978-3-030-03807-6_8
20. Brakerski, Z., Döttling, N.: Two-message statistically sender-private OT from LWE. In: Beimel, A., Dziembowski, S. (eds.) TCC 2018, Part II. LNCS, vol. 11240, pp. 370–390. Springer, Cham (2018). https://doi.org/10.1007/978-3-030-03810-6_14

21. Brakerski, Z., Döttling, N., Garg, S., Malavolta, G.: Candidate iO from homomorphic encryption schemes. In: Canteaut, A., Ishai, Y. (eds.) EUROCRYPT 2020, Part I. LNCS, vol. 12105, pp. 79–109. Springer, Cham (2020). https://doi.org/10.1007/978-3-030-45721-1_4

22. Brakerski, Z., Döttling, N., Garg, S., Malavolta, G.: Factoring and pairings are not necessary for iO: circular-secure LWE suffices. Cryptology ePrint Archive, Report 2020/1024 (2020). https://eprint.iacr.org/2020/1024

23. Brakerski, Z., Halevi, S., Polychroniadou, A.: Four round secure computation without setup. In: Kalai, Y., Reyzin, L. (eds.) TCC 2017, Part I. LNCS, vol. 10677, pp. 645–677. Springer, Cham (2017). https://doi.org/10.1007/978-3-319-70500-2_22

24. Brakerski, Z., Rothblum, G.N.: Virtual black-box obfuscation for all circuits via generic graded encoding. In: Lindell, Y. (ed.) TCC 2014. LNCS, vol. 8349, pp. 1–25. Springer, Heidelberg (2014). https://doi.org/10.1007/978-3-642-54242-8_1

25. Brakerski, Z., Yuen, H.: Quantum garbled circuits (2020)

26. Canetti, R., Lin, H., Pass, R.: Adaptive hardness and composable security in the plain model from standard assumptions. In: 51st FOCS, pp. 541–550. IEEE Computer Society Press, October 2010

27. Cheon, J.H., Han, K., Lee, C., Ryu, H., Stehlé, D.: Cryptanalysis of the multilinear map over the integers. In: Oswald, E., Fischlin, M. (eds.) EUROCRYPT 2015, Part I. LNCS, vol. 9056, pp. 3–12. Springer, Heidelberg (2015). https://doi.org/10.1007/978-3-662-46800-5_1

28. Rai Choudhuri, A., Ciampi, M., Goyal, V., Jain, A., Ostrovsky, R.: Round optimal secure multiparty computation from minimal assumptions. In: Pass, R., Pietrzak, K. (eds.) TCC 2020, Part II. LNCS, vol. 12551, pp. 291–319. Springer, Cham (2020). https://doi.org/10.1007/978-3-030-64378-2_11

29. Coron, J.-S., et al.: Zeroizing without low-level zeroes: new MMAP attacks and their limitations. In: Gennaro, R., Robshaw, M. (eds.) CRYPTO 2015, Part I. LNCS, vol. 9215, pp. 247–266. Springer, Heidelberg (2015). https://doi.org/10.1007/978-3-662-47989-6_12

30. Dulek, Y., Grilo, A.B., Jeffery, S., Majenz, C., Schaffner, C.: Secure multi-party quantum computation with a dishonest majority. In: Canteaut, A., Ishai, Y. (eds.) EUROCRYPT 2020, Part III. LNCS, vol. 12107, pp. 729–758. Springer, Cham (2020). https://doi.org/10.1007/978-3-030-45727-3_25

31. Fernando, R., Jain, A., Komargodski, I.: Maliciously-secure mrnisc in the plain model. Cryptology ePrint Archive, Report 2021/1319 (2021). https://ia.cr/2021/1319

32. Garg, S., Gentry, C., Halevi, S., Raykova, M., Sahai, A., Waters, B.: Candidate indistinguishability obfuscation and functional encryption for all circuits. In: 54th FOCS, pp. 40–49. IEEE Computer Society Press, October 2013

33. Garg, S., Goyal, V., Jain, A., Sahai, A.: Concurrently secure computation in constant rounds. In: Pointcheval, D., Johansson, T. (eds.) EUROCRYPT 2012. LNCS, vol. 7237, pp. 99–116. Springer, Heidelberg (2012). https://doi.org/10.1007/978-3-642-29011-4_8

34. Garg, S., Kiyoshima, S., Pandey, O.: On the exact round complexity of self-composable two-party computation. In: Coron, J.-S., Nielsen, J.B. (eds.) EUROCRYPT 2017, Part II. LNCS, vol. 10211, pp. 194–224. Springer, Cham (2017). https://doi.org/10.1007/978-3-319-56614-6_7

35. Garg, S., Mukherjee, P., Pandey, O., Polychroniadou, A.: The exact round complexity of secure computation. In: Fischlin, M., Coron, J.-S. (eds.) EUROCRYPT 2016, Part II. LNCS, vol. 9666, pp. 448–476. Springer, Heidelberg (2016). https://doi.org/10.1007/978-3-662-49896-5_16

36. Garg, S., Srinivasan, A.: Garbled protocols and two-round MPC from bilinear maps. In: Umans, C. (ed.) 58th FOCS, pp. 588–599. IEEE Computer Society Press, October 2017
37. Gay, R., Pass, R.: Indistinguishability obfuscation from circular security. Cryptology ePrint Archive, Report 2020/1010 (2020). https://eprint.iacr.org/2020/1010
38. Goyal, V., Jain, A.: On concurrently secure computation in the multiple ideal query model. In: Johansson, T., Nguyen, P.Q. (eds.) EUROCRYPT 2013. LNCS, vol. 7881, pp. 684–701. Springer, Heidelberg (2013). https://doi.org/10.1007/978-3-642-38348-9_40
39. Goyal, V., Jain, A., Jin, Z., Malavolta, G.: Statistical zaps and new oblivious transfer protocols. In: Canteaut, A., Ishai, Y. (eds.) EUROCRYPT 2020, Part III. LNCS, vol. 12107, pp. 668–699. Springer, Cham (2020). https://doi.org/10.1007/978-3-030-45727-3_23
40. Goyal, V., Lin, H., Pandey, O., Pass, R., Sahai, A.: Round-efficient concurrently composable secure computation via a robust extraction lemma. In: Dodis, Y., Nielsen, J.B. (eds.) TCC 2015. LNCS, vol. 9014, pp. 260–289. Springer, Heidelberg (2015). https://doi.org/10.1007/978-3-662-46494-6_12
41. Halevi, S., Hazay, C., Polychroniadou, A., Venkitasubramaniam, M.: Round-optimal secure multi-party computation. In: Shacham, H., Boldyreva, A. (eds.) CRYPTO 2018, Part II. LNCS, vol. 10992, pp. 488–520. Springer, Cham (2018). https://doi.org/10.1007/978-3-319-96881-0_17
42. Hopkins, S., Jain, A., Lin, H.: Counterexamples to circular security-based IO. In: CRYPTO (2021)
43. Jain, A., Lin, H., Matt, C., Sahai, A.: How to leverage hardness of constant-degree expanding polynomials over $\mathbb{R}$ to build $i\mathcal{O}$. In: Ishai, Y., Rijmen, V. (eds.) EUROCRYPT 2019, Part I. LNCS, vol. 11476, pp. 251–281. Springer, Cham (2019). https://doi.org/10.1007/978-3-030-17653-2_9
44. Jain, A., Lin, H., Sahai, A.: Indistinguishability obfuscation from LPN over $\mathbb{F}_p$, DLIN, and PRGs in NC^0. IACR Cryptology ePrint Archive (2021)
45. Jain, A., Lin, H., Sahai, A.: Indistinguishability obfuscation from well-founded assumptions. In: STOC, pp. 60–73. ACM (2021)
46. Khurana, D.: Non-interactive distributional indistinguishability (NIDI) and non-malleable commitments (2021)
47. Khurana, D., Sahai, A.: How to achieve non-malleability in one or two rounds. In: Umans, C. (ed.) 58th FOCS, pp. 564–575. IEEE Computer Society Press, October 2017
48. Kiyoshima, S.: Round-efficient black-box construction of composable multi-party computation. In: Garay, J.A., Gennaro, R. (eds.) CRYPTO 2014, Part II. LNCS, vol. 8617, pp. 351–368. Springer, Heidelberg (2014). https://doi.org/10.1007/978-3-662-44381-1_20
49. Kiyoshima, S., Manabe, Y., Okamoto, T.: Constant-round black-box construction of composable multi-party computation protocol. In: Lindell, Y. (ed.) TCC 2014. LNCS, vol. 8349, pp. 343–367. Springer, Heidelberg (2014). https://doi.org/10.1007/978-3-642-54242-8_15
50. Lin, H., Pass, R.: Black-box constructions of composable protocols without set-up. In: Safavi-Naini, R., Canetti, R. (eds.) CRYPTO 2012. LNCS, vol. 7417, pp. 461–478. Springer, Heidelberg (2012). https://doi.org/10.1007/978-3-642-32009-5_27
51. Lin, H., Tessaro, S.: Indistinguishability obfuscation from trilinear maps and block-wise local PRGs. In: Katz, J., Shacham, H. (eds.) CRYPTO 2017, Part I. LNCS, vol. 10401, pp. 630–660. Springer, Cham (2017). https://doi.org/10.1007/978-3-319-63688-7_21

52. Lin, H., Vaikuntanathan, V.: Indistinguishability obfuscation from DDH-like assumptions on constant-degree graded encodings. In: Dinur, I. (ed.) 57th FOCS, pp. 11–20. IEEE Computer Society Press, October 2016

53. Lindell, Y.: Lower bounds for concurrent self composition. In: Naor, M. (ed.) TCC 2004. LNCS, vol. 2951, pp. 203–222. Springer, Heidelberg (2004). https://doi.org/10.1007/978-3-540-24638-1_12

54. Malkin, T., Moriarty, R., Yakovenko, N.: Generalized environmental security from number theoretic assumptions. In: Halevi, S., Rabin, T. (eds.) TCC 2006. LNCS, vol. 3876, pp. 343–359. Springer, Heidelberg (2006). https://doi.org/10.1007/11681878_18

55. Micali, S., Pass, R., Rosen, A.: Input-indistinguishable computation. In: 47th FOCS, pp. 367–378. IEEE Computer Society Press, October 2006

56. Miles, E., Sahai, A., Zhandry, M.: Annihilation attacks for multilinear maps: cryptanalysis of indistinguishability obfuscation over GGH13. In: Robshaw, M., Katz, J. (eds.) CRYPTO 2016, Part II. LNCS, vol. 9815, pp. 629–658. Springer, Heidelberg (2016). https://doi.org/10.1007/978-3-662-53008-5_22

57. Pandey, O., Pass, R., Vaikuntanathan, V.: Adaptive one-way functions and applications. In: Wagner, D. (ed.) CRYPTO 2008. LNCS, vol. 5157, pp. 57–74. Springer, Heidelberg (2008). https://doi.org/10.1007/978-3-540-85174-5_4

58. Pass, R.: Simulation in quasi-polynomial time, and its application to protocol composition. In: Biham, E. (ed.) EUROCRYPT 2003. LNCS, vol. 2656, pp. 160–176. Springer, Heidelberg (2003). https://doi.org/10.1007/3-540-39200-9_10

59. Pass, R.: Bounded-concurrent secure multi-party computation with a dishonest majority. In: Babai, L. (ed.) 36th ACM STOC, pp. 232–241. ACM Press, June 2004

60. Pass, R., Lin, H., Venkitasubramaniam, M.: A unified framework for UC from only OT. In: Wang, X., Sako, K. (eds.) ASIACRYPT 2012. LNCS, vol. 7658, pp. 699–717. Springer, Heidelberg (2012). https://doi.org/10.1007/978-3-642-34961-4_42

61. Pass, R., Seth, K., Telang, S.: Indistinguishability obfuscation from semantically-secure multilinear encodings. In: Garay, J.A., Gennaro, R. (eds.) CRYPTO 2014, Part I. LNCS, vol. 8616, pp. 500–517. Springer, Heidelberg (2014). https://doi.org/10.1007/978-3-662-44371-2_28

62. Sahai, A.: Non-malleable non-interactive zero knowledge and adaptive chosen-ciphertext security. In: 40th FOCS, pp. 543–553. IEEE Computer Society Press, October 1999

63. Song, F.: A note on quantum security for post-quantum cryptography. In: Mosca, M. (ed.) PQCrypto 2014. LNCS, vol. 8772, pp. 246–265. Springer, Cham (2014). https://doi.org/10.1007/978-3-319-11659-4_15

64. Wee, H., Wichs, D.: Candidate obfuscation via oblivious LWE sampling. Cryptology ePrint Archive, Report 2020/1042 (2020). https://eprint.iacr.org/2020/1042

Degree-D Reverse Multiplication-Friendly Embeddings: Constructions and Applications

Daniel Escudero[1]([⊠]), Cheng Hong[2], Hongqing Liu[3], Chaoping Xing[3], and Chen Yuan[3]

[1] J.P. Morgan AI Research & J.P. Morgan AlgoCRYPT CoE, New York, USA
daniel.escudero@protonmail.com
[2] Ant Group, Hangzhou, China
[3] Shanghai Jiao Tong University, Shanghai, China

Abstract. In the recent work of (Cheon & Lee, Eurocrypt'22), the concept of a *degree-D packing method* was formally introduced, which captures the idea of embedding multiple elements of a smaller ring into a larger ring, so that element-wise multiplication in the former is somewhat "compatible" with the product in the latter. Then, several optimal bounds and results are presented, and furthermore, the concept is generalized from one multiplication to degrees larger than two. These packing methods encompass several constructions seen in the literature in contexts like secure multiparty computation and fully homomorphic encryption.

One such construction is the concept of reverse multiplication-friendly embeddings (RMFEs), which are essentially degree-2 packing methods. In this work we generalize the notion of RMFEs to *degree-D RMFEs* which, in spite of being "more algebraic" than packing methods, turn out to be essentially equivalent. Then, we present a general construction of degree-D RMFEs by generalizing the ideas on algebraic geometry used to construct traditional degree-2 RMFEs which, by the aforementioned equivalence, leads to explicit constructions of packing methods. Furthermore, our theory is given in a unified manner for general Galois rings, which include both rings of the form $\mathbb{Z}_{p^k}$ and fields like $\mathbb{F}_{p^k}$, which have been treated separately in prior works. We present multiple concrete sets of parameters for degree-D RMFEs (including $D = 2$), which can be useful for future works.

Finally, we discuss interesting applications of our RMFEs, focusing in particular on the case of non-interactively generating high degree correlations for secure multiparty computation protocols. This requires the use of Shamir secret sharing for a large number of parties, which requires large-degree Galois ring extensions. Our RMFE enables the generation of such preprocessing data over small rings, without paying for the multiplicative overhead incurred by using Galois ring extensions of large degree. For our application we also construct along the way, as a side contribution of potential independent interest, a pseudo-random secret-sharing solution for non-interactive generation of packed Shamir-sharings

© International Association for Cryptologic Research 2023
J. Guo and R. Steinfeld (Eds.): ASIACRYPT 2023, LNCS 14438, pp. 106–138, 2023.
https://doi.org/10.1007/978-981-99-8721-4_4

over Galois rings with structured secrets, inspired by the PRSS solutions from (Benhamouda *et al.*, TCC 2021).

1   Introduction

Several cryptographic constructions are designed to work over finite discrete structures. For example, encryption schemes, digital signatures, or message authentication codes, all widely used in day-to-day digital systems, are designed to manipulate bit strings of certain length. The same holds for cryptographic hash functions, or key exchange protocols. However, there is a large body of cryptographic constructions that, on top of working over a finite discrete structure, require certain minimal algebraic properties, either for the definition of the primitive itself or for their construction. For example, Diffie-Hellman key exchange [18] makes use of a finite group where the discrete logarithm problem is hard. Similarly, encryption schemes such as Paillier [28] or RSA [30] make use of group of invertible integers modulo N^2 and N respectively, where N is the product of two large primes.

On the other hand, other cryptographic primitives not only make use of algebraic structures underneath, but their security definition is actually tied to some algebraic structure. For example, in fully homomorphic encryption two messages over some finite ring can be encrypted, and the two corresponding ciphertexts can be added/multiplied together to obtain encryptions of the sum/product of the two underlying plaintexts. Also, functional encryption for dot products (*cf.* [1]) is a primitive that enables the encryption of a message under some public key so that, having certain special secret key, only the dot product between the plaintext and the secret key can be recovered. Again, such definition is tied to a specific algebraic structure in order for the notion of a "dot product" to be well defined. Finally, another good example is secure multiparty computation, where different parties compute a given function securely without leaking their inputs. Such function is typically defined as an arithmetic circuit over some finite algebraic structure.

Typically, the most general algebraic structure that underpins many cryptographic primitives, including the ones exemplified above, is that of a *finite ring*. This is a finite set where a product and addition operation are defined, and these satisfy certain basic properties such as commutativity of addition, associativity, or distributivity. Unfortunately, not all cryptographic primitives can be instantiated under any arbitrary finite ring. For example, most homomorphic encryption techniques work over rings of the form $\mathbb{Z}_N$ for very specific integers N, lattice-based construction typically makes use of polynomial rings extensions of a very structured form [27], and most secure multiparty computation protocols are designed to work over finite fields, which are a subset of finite rings where every non-zero element has a multiplicative inverse, and in some cases this finite field cannot be small. Only recently the case of MPC over rings of the form $\mathbb{Z}_N$ for more general N was considered (*cf.* [13]), and in [20] the case of MPC over a (possibly non-commutative) arbitrary finite ring was studied. In addition, zero-knowledge proofs are typically designed for arithmetic circuits over finite fields, with the case of more general rings only being explored recently [33].

The Use of Ring Extensions. As we mentioned above, ring extensions—which are rings of polynomials reduced modulo some fixed polynomials—appear naturally in the context of lattice-based cryptography. However, that is not the only context where this type of extension rings are used. An interesting and relevant algebraic structure is the ring of integers $\mathbb{Z}_{p^k}$ modulo a prime power p^k. The relevance of this structure is two-fold. On the one hand, it contains as a particular case the integers modulo powers of two, like 2^{64} or 2^{128}, which are good for many applications since they are closer to hardware implementations and they are more "compatible" with binary circuits [16]. On the other hand, having constructions that work over $\mathbb{Z}_{p^k}$ for any arbitrary prime power p^k typically lead, with the help of the Chinese remainder theorem, to constructions that work over $\mathbb{Z}_N$ for *any* positive integer N. It has been identified in many different works (*e.g.* [20]) that the main property required by the underlying ring $\mathbb{Z}_{p^k}$ in order for certain cryptographic primitive (*e.g.* MPC or ZKP) to be instantiable over $\mathbb{Z}_{p^k}$ is that the *Lenstra constant* of the ring, which is the size of the largest subset where every non-zero pairwise difference is invertible, has to be large enough. Since the Lenstra constant of $\mathbb{Z}_{p^k}$ is p, this means that p cannot be very small, which rules out important cases such as $\mathbb{Z}_{2^k}$.

To address the complication above, multiple works such as [2,5,7,8,21] have made use of ring extensions of $\mathbb{Z}_{p^k}$ to ensure the Lenstra constant of the resulting ring is large enough, hence enabling the construction of the specific cryptographic primitive at hand. Such ring extensions are known as *Galois rings*, and they have the form $\mathbb{Z}_{p^k}[X]/(f(X))$, where $f(X)$ is some polynomial of degree d over $\mathbb{Z}_{p^k}$ that is irreducible when taken modulo p. This ring is denoted by $\mathsf{GR}(p^k, d)$, and it is known to have a Lenstra constant of p^d, which increases exponentially as the extension degree d grows. Because of this, works in the context of secure multiparty computation (*cf.* [2]) and more recently zero-knowledge proofs [10,26] have made use of such extensions in order to instantiate these cryptographic primitives over $\mathbb{Z}_{p^k}$.

Packing Methods. As we have mentioned above, ring extensions are required in contexts such as fully homomorphic encryption, which is typically based on lattices, or secure multiparty computation and zero-knowledge proofs over rings of the form $\mathbb{Z}_{p^k}$. However, most applications do not make use of these ring extensions directly, but rather they are better suited for the underlying base ring. In the context of lattice-based FHE, this has been addressed by making use of ring extensions that are ring-isomorphic to multiple copies of the underlying base ring via CRT. These extensions require the quotient polynomial to split completely into linear factors, and in particular it cannot be invertible.

For MPC and ZKPs, the quotient polynomial has to be irreducible in order to guarantee a large-enough Lenstra constant, so in particular packing elements using CRT-based techniques is not possible. To address this complication, a tool named *reverse multiplication-friendly embeddings*, or RMFEs for short, was introduced in [9]. At a high level, an RMFE is a pair of additive homomorphisms from/to a Galois ring to/from $\mathbb{Z}_{p^k}^r$ that map polynomial product in the Galois ring to element-wise product in $\mathbb{Z}_{p^k}^r$. More precisely, an RMFE is a pair of

$\mathbb{Z}_{p^k}$-linear homomorphisms ($\phi : \mathbb{Z}_{p^k}^r \to \mathsf{GR}(p^k, d), \psi : \mathsf{GR}(p^k, d) \to \mathbb{Z}_{p^k}^r$) such that $\psi(\phi(\boldsymbol{x}) \cdot \phi(\boldsymbol{y})) = \boldsymbol{x} \star \boldsymbol{y}$ for every $\boldsymbol{x}, \boldsymbol{y} \in \mathbb{Z}_{p^k}^r$, where $\cdot$ denotes product in $\mathsf{GR}(p^k, d)$ and $\star$ denotes component-wise product in $\mathbb{Z}_{p^k}^r$. This is less ideal than the CRT-based packing techniques used in lattice-based cryptography since it does not hold that the product of *any* two ring extension elements $x \cdot y$ somehow "encodes" multiple products over $\mathbb{Z}_{p^k}$, but rather, if $x = \phi(\boldsymbol{x})$ and $y = \phi(\boldsymbol{y})$, then $x \cdot y$ can be "decoded" to the products $\boldsymbol{x} \star \boldsymbol{y}$ by mapping this value with ψ. Furthermore, very importantly, unlike CRT-based techniques it is not possible to multiply more than two values before "decoding" with ψ, since it is not necessarily the case that $\psi(\phi(\boldsymbol{x}) \cdot \phi(\boldsymbol{y}) \cdot \phi(\boldsymbol{z})) = \boldsymbol{x} \star \boldsymbol{y} \star \boldsymbol{z}$. As a result, for multiple products all existing cryptographic constructions making use of RMFEs must follow a pattern that somewhat resembles "encode $\to$ multiply $\to$ decode $\to$ repeat". In contrast, CRT-based packing can follow the pattern "encode $\to$ multiply $\to \cdots \to$ multiply $\to$ decode".

RMFEs have played a major role in enabling multiple recent results in the literature. In the work where they were introduced [9], they were used in order to achieve honest majority MPC without the $\log n$ overhead stemming from the use of field extensions. This only works for SIMD circuits, a restriction that was later removed in [29] again by using RMFEs. The work of [11] uses RMFEs to improve the state-of-the-art in dishonest majority MPC over $\mathbb{Z}_2$, and [21] uses again RMFEs, this time over more general Galois rings—which are constructed in [15]—to improve the communication of SPDZ$_{2^k}$ [13], the state-of-the-art protocol for dishonest majority MPC over $\mathbb{Z}_{2^k}$. RMFEs have also found applications in the zero-knowledge domain: [10] improves the Aurora and Ligero proof systems by using RMFEs; and in [26] a *concretely efficient* post-quantum signature scheme based on MPC-in-the-Head is proposed, Helium, which makes use of RMFEs in order to increase the field size, which improves the soundness of the proof and hence reduces signature size), while reducing the penalty of using a larger field.

Finally, in the recent work of [12], the concept of a *packing method* was introduced, with the aim of unifying and generalizing the notion of RMFEs and CRT-based packings, already used in the literature. A packing method is similar to an RMFE in that it is comprised of packing ("encoding", ϕ) and unpacking ("decoding", ψ) methods, but: (1) their additive homomorphism property is more relaxed, (2) they can be randomized, (3) unpacking/decoding can lead to an error and, crucially, (4) they allow for more than one multiplication to be carried out before decoding (and in fact there could be different packing/unpacking methods depending on the degree of the multiplication being decoded). In [12], the authors show how packing methods generalize existing approaches in the literature, and they show lower and upper bounds on the parameters of these constructions. We discuss in much more detail the work of [12] in Sect. 1.2.

1.1 Our Contribution

The packing methods defined in [12] allow for several multiplications to be carried out before decoding, while as we discussed above, RMFEs only allow for one single multiplication. On the other hand, RMFEs have better properties than packing methods in that they are $\mathbb{Z}_{p^k}$-homomorphisms that do not output errors and are not randomized. This is important for their applications to MPC and ZKPs. This is the motivation of our work, which includes the following contributions.

Degree-D RMFEs. In this work, we extend the important notion of RMFEs by introducing the concept of *Degree-D Reverse Multiplication-Friendly Embeddings*, which is a generalization of RMFEs that enable $D - 1$ multiplications to be carried out before "decoding". In more detail, a degree-D RMFE is a pair of $\mathbb{Z}_{p^k}$-linear homomorphisms $(\phi : \mathbb{Z}_{p^k}^r \to \mathsf{GR}(p^k, d), \psi : \mathsf{GR}(p^k, d) \to \mathbb{Z}_{p^k}^r)$ such that $\psi(\phi(\boldsymbol{x}_1) \cdot \phi(\boldsymbol{x}_2) \cdots \phi(\boldsymbol{x}_D)) = \boldsymbol{x}_1 \star \boldsymbol{x}_2 \star \cdots \star \boldsymbol{x}_D$ for every $\boldsymbol{x}_1, \ldots, \boldsymbol{x}_D \in \mathbb{Z}_{p^k}^r$.[1] We call $\frac{r}{d}$ the ratio of RMFE. Fix p to be a constant, we call a RMFE asymptotically good if this ratio is a constant for growing r and d. In our work we put forward the study of these objects and make substantial progress in this direction by presenting a construction of an asymptotically good degree-D RMFE for Galois rings over $\mathbb{Z}_{p^k}$ for any r, D, p and k, where the rate is roughly $\frac{3}{D(2D+1)}$, which is *constant* in the length r.

To illustrate how such objects may be constructed, let us first present a simple example of degree-D RMFE which is *not* asymptotically good. Given a vector $\boldsymbol{x} = (x_1, \ldots, x_r) \in \mathbb{Z}_{p^k}^r$ with $p > r$, we define the map ϕ as $\phi(\boldsymbol{x}) = f(x) \in \mathsf{GR}(p^k, (r-1)D + 1) \cong \mathbb{Z}_{p^k}/(g(x))$ with $f(i) = x_i$ and degree-$((r-1)D + 1)$ irreducible polynomial $g(x)$ over $\mathbb{Z}_{p^k}$. The map ψ is defined as $\psi(f(x)) = (f(1), \ldots, f(r))$. The multiplication relation holds as the product of any D degree-$(r-1)$ polynomials is a polynomial of degree at most $D(r-1)$. Since the degree of this polynomial is less than $\deg(g(x)) = D(r-1) + 1$, we can recover r evaluations of this polynomial. The construction of this degree-D RMFE is simple and effective, and its ratio is $\frac{r}{(r-1)D+1}$, which is optimal. However, the length r of the vector $\boldsymbol{x}$ is upper bounded by p, while instead, we would like a single RMFE construction that works for *any* choice of r.[2] Inspired by the approach taken in the original work on (degree-2) RMFEs [9], in order to obtain an asymptotically good degree-D RMFEs we resort to the theory of *function fields*. By applying certain "concatenation" method to the asymptotically good RMFEs derived from these mathematical objects, we are then able to obtain our asymptotically good degree-D RMFEs over $\mathbb{Z}_{2^k}$.

Our results on degree-D RMFEs generalize these in [9] from $D = 2$ to $D > 2$, showing that the techniques in that work are a particular case of a more general framework. This improves our understanding on these important tools, and furthermore, we believe our work opens an interesting direction of study in terms of constructing even better degree-D RMFEs, and expanding the set of applications that can benefit from them.

---

[1] In our actual definition, as in the definition of traditional (degree-2) RMFEs, the domain of ϕ/codomain of ψ can be a Galois ring as well instead of $\mathbb{Z}_{p^k}$.

[2] It is possible to improve this basic construction via certain concatenation techniques. However, any construction based on this polynomial evaluation cannot achieve constant ratio, which can be seen as an analogue of the concatenation of Reed-Solomon codes in the classic coding theory.

Relations to the Packing Methods from [12]. We show that degree-D RMFEs are particular cases of packing methods, but in the general case the converse direction does not hold, that is, not every degree-D packing method is a degree-D RMFE. In fact, we are able to prove that packing methods that satisfy certain *additional* linearity properties can be turned into degree-D RMFEs. Crucially, degree-D RMFEs satisfy the following highly relevant properties not held by packing methods:

– Degree-D RMFEs are actual $\mathbb{Z}_{p^k}$-homomorphisms, so unlike the packing methods from [12], they are not randomized, they are fully linear and they do not output errors.
– A degree-D packing method consists of different packing/unpacking methods, one for every "level" $\ell \in \{1, \ldots, D\}$. In contrast, degree-$D$ RMFEs consist of only *one* "packing/unpacking" pair (ϕ, ψ), which works for all levels.

The relations between packing methods and our degree-D RMFEs are explored in detail in Sect. 3. We show that a degree-D RMFE is actually a degree-D packing method. This means the lower bound on the ratio in [12] can be applied to degree-D RMFE. We provide several constructions of degree-D RMFE which can be directly transformed to degree-D packing method. Unlike the construction in [12], our packing methods obtained from RMFEs are $\mathbb{Z}_{p^k}$-homomorphism. Our construction of RMFE implies that there exists degree-D packing method of density roughly $\frac{3}{D(1+2D)}$ over $\mathbb{Z}_{2^\ell}$ for any D and ℓ, which is *constant* in the length. On the other hand, if we add an extra requirement on the packing method that the packing algorithm in the packing method is deterministic and linear, then a degree-D packing method is a degree-D RMFE as well.

Applications of Degree-D RMFEs. As discussed previously, RMFEs have found multiple theoretical and practical applications across different domains such as MPC and zero-knowledge proofs. From this, our degree-D RMFEs can be used as a drop-in replacement in settings that currently use traditional (degree-2) RMFEs, but require large degree evaluation. For example, it can be used to amortize the communication of securely computing the product of, say, three secrets, or proving in zero-knowledge the correctness of a, say, product of three witnesses. Unfortunately, some of these applications do not benefit directly from products of more than two terms, essentially because of the fact that single multiplication is "complete" to represent a more general computation, and aspects such as interaction enable weaker notions such as traditional degree-2 RMFEs to be sufficient. In Sect. 5 we add a thorough discussion on potential applications of this type, where existing RMFE-based solutions are "enhanced" by enabling larger degree.

In this work we identify a concrete application that benefits extensively by the use of degree-D RMFEs for $D > 2$. This corresponds to delegating the generation of preprocessing material for certain secure computation (*e.g.* authenticated multiplication triples) to a large committee, which is in charge of generating said correlations in order to later re-share them for the target MPC execution. Since the larger the committee the better the ratio of honest parties, it is good if such a protocol for correlation generation scales well as the number of parties grows. We model this by requiring *no interaction* among the parties in the large committee, which can be enabled by means of pseudo-random Shamir secret-sharing techniques and local multiplications with low-enough threshold. However, when the target ring structure has a small Lenstra constant, such techniques do not work, and hence require a large ring extension.

This is precisely where our degree-D RMFEs prove themselves useful: they enable the use of ring extensions while non-interactively multiplying several secrets in order to generate the desired correlations, but without paying the "penalty" of using said large degree extensions. As a result, we obtain efficient delegation of correlations of degree ≥ 2, while avoiding communication among the generating committee (which enables larger and hence more trustworthy quorums). This application, however, is not a simple "plug-and-play" of our degree-D RMFEs, and we introduce several techniques of potential independent interest to tackle this. The main challenge lies in ensuring that pseudo-random secret-sharing techniques can be adapted to generate the concrete type of sharings we need in our context, given that the underlying secrets will have to belong to a particular submodule. In Sect. 5, where we describe this application in detail, we show how such PRSS constructions can be instantiated, drawing inspiration from the techniques in [3] in order to improve the storage complexity by exploiting a small corruption threshold.

We fully prove the security of our PRSS construction, and then we use it in conjunction with our degree-D RMFEs to efficiently instantiate the application above. We refer to the full version [19] for a more detailed overview on this application.

1.2 Related Work

The first constructions of (degree-2) RMFEs appeared in [9], although some ideas were already present in [4]. After these works, there is a large body of research that has applied RMFEs for different settings such as secure multiparty computation or zero-knowledge proofs, with a non-exhaustive list including [2, 10, 21, 26].

Given the traction achieved by the concept of RMFEs, and also given the use of other forms of packing in domains such as lattice-based homomorphic encryption [32], the work of [12] aimed at presenting a unified framework that captures these different packing notions. The resulting concept, *packing methods*, constitutes a generalization of both (degree-2) RMFEs and the CRT-based packing used in lattice-based cryptography. The authors then present a survey of existing techniques that fit their framework, and present bounds and impossibility result on the existence and the efficiency of their packing methods. Our degree-D RMFEs constitute a generalization of degree-2 RMFEs, and, as we show in Sect. 3, they turn out to be particular instances of the packing methods from [12]. Furthermore, with a minor extra condition, packing methods turn out to be equivalent to our degree-D RMFEs. The relation between these two notions is explored in detail in Sect. 3.

Regarding delegation of correlation generation for MPC, the work of [24], which introduces an MPC protocol based on packed secret-sharing that is particularly suitable for parallel computation, presents an application where this protocol is used by a committee $\mathcal{P}$ to generate multiplication triples to another committee $\mathcal{Q}$. We note that their protocol requires communication among the parties in committee $\mathcal{P}$, whereas our solution is fully non-interactive. Even more—and very importantly for our application of degree-D RMFEs—our techniques are used to generate arbitrary degree-D correlations, while in [24] only multiplication triples, a particular case of degree-2 correlations, is considered. However, the non-interactivity aspect of our solution is achieved at the expense of using pseudo-random secret-sharing (which requires exponential storage for some parameter choices), and the high degree aspect requires tolerating a smaller threshold. Furthermore, the techniques in [24] support an active adversary, while our solution in Sect. 5 is only passively secure.

Finally, in terms of pseudo-random secret-sharing, earlier techniques [14,23] required an exponential amount of seeds to be held by each party, and they were only suitable for Shamir secret-sharing over fields where the underlying secret is uniformly random in the field. In the recent work of [3] this was generalized by making use of covering designs, and instantiations of PRSS solutions for sharings of higher-degree with more structured underlying secrets were proposed. These techniques serve as the basis for our PRSS from Sect. 5.2, but we cannot use it directly since (1) they are designed for use over finite fields while in our case we have a Galois ring, and most importantly, (2) the type of correlations we need to generate are not included in the ones proposed in [3]. The first issue is easily addressed by making use of the fact that Galois rings have a large enough Lenstra constant. On the other hand, the second complication requires us to propose from scratch a new PRSS solution for our correlations at hand, based on the covering design approach from [3].

2 Preliminaries

Notation. We let p be a prime, and d, k, m, n be positive integers. Generally, p^k will be the characteristic of the rings we consider, d, m will be the degree of certain ring extensions, and n will be the dimension of the vectors that will be packed. Vectors are denoted with bold characters, and, following the notation in [12], element-wise multiplication of vectors is denoted by $a \star b$.

Galois Rings. Let $\mathsf{Irr}(\mathtt{X})$ be a polynomial over $\mathbb{Z}_{p^k}$ of degree d, such that reducing its coefficients modulo p leads to an irreducible polynomial over the field $\mathbb{Z}_p$. Consider the quotient ring $\mathbb{Z}_{p^k}[\mathtt{X}]/(\mathsf{Irr}(\mathtt{X}))$. This is a *Galois ring* of degree d and characteristic p^k, and we denote it by $\mathsf{GR}(p^k, d)$. As particular cases, we have that $\mathsf{GR}(p^k, 1)$ equals $\mathbb{Z}_{p^k}$, the ring of integers modulo p^k, and $\mathsf{GR}(p, d)$ equals $\mathbb{F}_{p^d}$, the finite field with p^d elements.

A crucial fact of Galois rings is that their non-invertible elements are exactly the elements that are multiples of p. From this, it can be proven that one can do polynomial interpolation over Galois rings in essentially the same way similarly as in the finite field case, as the following proposition shows.

Proposition 1. ([2,35]). *Assume that $p^d \geq n$. There exists n elements $\alpha_1, \ldots, \alpha_n$ in $\mathsf{GR}(p^k, d)$ such that given any $x_1, \ldots, x_n \in \mathsf{GR}(p^k, d)$, there is a unique polynomial of degree $n - 1$, $f(\mathsf{X}) \in \mathsf{GR}(p^k, d)[\mathsf{X}]$, with $f(\alpha_i) = x_i$. We call such $\{\alpha_1, \ldots, \alpha_n\}$ an exceptional set.*

Using Proposition 1, all of the results from finite fields regarding interpolation and polynomial evaluation carry over to the Galois ring setting. For example, Schwartz-Zippel lemma holds, and also Shamir secret-sharing can be constructed.

Function Fields. Let us briefly recall some background on algebraic function fields, which will play a crucial role in our constructions. The reader may refer to [34] for the details.

A function field F over $\mathbb{F}_q$ is a field extension over $\mathbb{F}_q$ in which there exists an element z of F that is transcendental over $\mathbb{F}_q$ such that $F/\mathbb{F}_q(z)$ is a finite extension. $\mathbb{F}_q$ is called the full constant field of F if the algebraic closure of $\mathbb{F}_q$ in F is $\mathbb{F}_q$ itself. In this paper, we always assume that $\mathbb{F}_q$ is the full constant field of F, denoted by $F/\mathbb{F}_q$.

Each discrete valuation ν from F to $\mathbb{Z} \cup \{\infty\}$ defines a local ring $O = \{f \in F : \nu(f) \geq 0\}$. The maximal ideal P of O is called a *place*. We denote the valuation ν and the local ring O corresponding to P by ν_P and O_P, respectively. The residue class field O_P/P, denoted by F_P, is a finite extension of $\mathbb{F}_q$. The extension degree $[F_P : \mathbb{F}_q]$ is called *degree* of P, denoted by $\deg(P)$. For a place P and a function $f \in O_P$, we denote by $f(P)$ the evaluation of f at place P if $f \in O_P$. We note that $f(P) \in F_p$.

A divisor G is a formal sum of places, $G = \sum c_P P$, such that $c_P \in \mathbb{Z}$ and $c_P = 0$ except for a finite number of P.[3] We call this set of places where $c_P \neq 0$ the support of G, denoted by $\mathrm{supp}(G)$. The degree of G is $\deg G := \sum c_P \deg P \in \mathbb{Z}$. The Riemann-Roch space $\mathcal{L}(G)$ is the set of all functions in F with certain prescribed poles and zeros depending on G (together with the zero function). More precisely if $G = \sum c_P P$, every function $f \in \mathcal{L}(G)$ must have a zero of order at least $|c_P|$ in the places P with $c_P < 0$, and f can have a pole of order at most c_P in the places with $c_P > 0$. The space $\mathcal{L}(G)$ is a vector space over $\mathbb{F}_q$. Its dimension is governed by certain laws (given by the so-called Riemann-Roch theorem). A weaker version of that theorem called Riemann's theorem states that if $\deg G \geq 2\mathfrak{g} - 1$ then $\dim \mathcal{L}(G) = \deg(G) - \mathfrak{g} + 1$. On the other hand, if $\deg G < 0$, then $\dim \mathcal{L}(G) = 0$. Let $P_1, \ldots, P_n$ be $n > \deg(G)$ rational places of F that is disjoint from the support of divisor G. Then, $(f(P_1), \ldots, f(P_n))$ has at most $\deg(G)$'s 0 components as $f \in \mathcal{L}(G - \sum_{f(P_i)=0} P_i)$ implying $\dim \mathcal{L}(G - \sum_{f(P_i)=0} P_i) > 0$. Moreover, if $f, g \in \mathcal{L}(G)$, then $fg \in \mathcal{L}(2G)$ as fg has the pole of order at most $2c_P$ in the place P with $G = \sum c_P P$. This property can be seen as the generalization of the polynomials in the function field.

---

[3] c_P is only used for expressing divisor G explicitly so as to present the basic property of the function field. The explicit construction of G is not the focus of this paper. Thus, c_p will not appear in our construction.

Packing Methods. Now we present the notion of packing methods, as introduced in [12, Definition 3.1], together with some results given in that work. The definition in [12], however, considers arbitrary rings, while we adapt it here to focus only on Galois rings. This is not restrictive: as we have mentioned, important rings such as $\mathbb{Z}_{p^k}$ or $\mathbb{F}_{p^d}$ are particular cases, and these are the only types of structures considered in [12] ultimately.

Definition 1 (Packing Methods). *Consider two Galois rings* $\mathsf{GR}(p^k, d)$ *and* $\mathsf{GR}(p^k, m)$. *We call a pair of algorithms* (Pack, Unpack) *a packing method for* n $\mathsf{GR}(p^k, d)$-*messages into* $\mathsf{GR}(p^k, m)$, *if it satisfies the following.*

- Pack *is an algorithm (possibly probabilistic) which, given* $\boldsymbol{a} \in \mathsf{GR}(p^k, d)^n$ *as an input, outputs an element of* $\mathsf{GR}(p^k, m)$.
- Unpack *is a deterministic algorithm which, given* $a \in \mathsf{GR}(p^k, m)$ *as an input, outputs an element of* $\mathsf{GR}(p^k, d)^n$ *or* $\perp$ *denoting a failure.*
- Unpack(Pack($\boldsymbol{a}$)) $= \boldsymbol{a}$ *holds for all* $\boldsymbol{a} \in \mathsf{GR}(p^k, d)^n$ *with probability 1.*

The notion of a packing method does not capture how the packing and unpacking algorithms should behave with respect to the operations of the two involved rings. This is captured by the concept of a degree-D packing, which in essence, requires that these methods must be additively homomorphic, and they must be compatible with "up to D multiplications".

Definition 2. (Degree-D Packing,   Definition   3.1   in   [12]). *Let* (Pack$_i$, Unpack$_i$)$_{i=1}^{D}$ *be a collection of packing methods of* $\mathsf{GR}(p^k, d)^n$ *into* $\mathsf{GR}(p^k, m)$. *We call this collection a degree-D packing method, if it satisfies the following: for any* $1 \le i \le D$, *then*

- Unpack$_i(a \pm b) = \boldsymbol{a} \pm \boldsymbol{b}$, *if* $a, b \in \mathsf{GR}(p^k, m)$ *satisfy* Unpack$_i(a) = \boldsymbol{a} \neq \perp$ *and* Unpack$_i(b) = \boldsymbol{b} \neq \perp$;
- *If* $s, t \in \mathbb{Z}^+$ *are such that* $s + t = i \le D$, *then* Unpack$_i(a \cdot b) = \boldsymbol{a} \star \boldsymbol{b}$ *holds, where* $a, b \in \mathsf{GR}(p^k, m)$ *satisfy* Unpack$_s(a) = \boldsymbol{a} \neq \perp$ *and* Unpack$_t(b) = \boldsymbol{b} \neq \perp$.

These definitions imply that Unpack$_i(c \cdot a) = c \cdot$ Unpack$_i(a)$ for any $c \in \mathbb{Z}_{p^k}$, and in particular Unpack$_i(0) = \boldsymbol{0}$.

We define the *packing density* of a packing method to be the ratio $n \cdot d/m$. Notice that, even though the Pack algorithm of a packing method can be probabilistic, we can make this algorithm deterministic by fixing the random coins. This will not affect Definition 2, and the packing density does not decrease. In what follows, we focus on the deterministic packing algorithms.

3   Degree-D RMFEs and Relations to Packing Methods

We now introduce the novel concept of a degree-D reverse multiplication-friendly embedding, or RMFE, for short. For $D = 2$, the notion of an RMFE was introduced in [9], where explicit constructions based on techniques from algebraic geomtry were given. Here we consider a natural generalization for $D \geq 2$.

Definition 3. (Degree-D Reverse Multiplication-Friendly Embedding).
Consider two Galois rings $\mathsf{GR}(p^k, d)$ and $\mathsf{GR}(p^k, rd)$. Let $\phi : \mathsf{GR}(p^k, d)^n \to \mathsf{GR}(p^k, rd)$ and $\psi : \mathsf{GR}(p^k, rd) \to \mathsf{GR}(p^k, d)^n$ be two group homomorphisms (i.e. they are additively homomorphic). The pair (ϕ, ψ) is a degree-D reverse multiplication-friendly embedding, or degree-D RMFE for short, if, for any $\boldsymbol{a}_1 \ldots, \boldsymbol{a}_D \in \mathsf{GR}(p^k, d)^n$, it holds that $\psi(\phi(\boldsymbol{a}_1) \cdot \phi(\boldsymbol{a}_2) \cdots \phi(\boldsymbol{a}_D)) = \boldsymbol{a}_1 \star \boldsymbol{a}_2 \star \cdots \star \boldsymbol{a}_D$. We call such RMFE a $(n, r; D)$-RMFE over $\mathsf{GR}(p^k, d)$.

Some important direct consequences of this definition are presented in the following propositions.

Proposition 2. *Let (ϕ, ψ) be a degree-D RMFE. Then ϕ is injective and ψ is surjective.*

Proof. To see that ϕ is injective it suffices to show that $\phi(\boldsymbol{a}) = 0$ implies that $\boldsymbol{a} = \boldsymbol{0}$. Indeed, if $\phi(\boldsymbol{a}) = 0$ then $\boldsymbol{0} = \psi(0) = \psi(\phi(\boldsymbol{a}) \star \phi(\boldsymbol{1}) \cdots \phi(\boldsymbol{1})) = \boldsymbol{a} \star \boldsymbol{1} \star \cdots \star \boldsymbol{1} = \boldsymbol{a}$. Similarly, given $\boldsymbol{a} \in \mathsf{GR}(p^k, d)^n$, it can be verified that a preimage of $\boldsymbol{a}$ under ψ is given by $\phi(\boldsymbol{a}) \cdot \phi(\boldsymbol{1}) \cdots \phi(\boldsymbol{1})$, which shows that ψ is surjective. □

Lemma 1. *Both ϕ and ψ are $\mathbb{Z}_{p^k}$-linear maps.*

Proof. The proof is quite straightforward. Due to the fact that ϕ is group homomorphism, we have $\phi(h\boldsymbol{a}) = \phi(\sum_{i=1}^{h} \boldsymbol{a}) = \sum_{i=1}^{h} \phi(\boldsymbol{a}) = h\phi(\boldsymbol{a})$ for any $h \in \mathbb{Z}_{p^k}$ and $\boldsymbol{a} \in \mathsf{GR}(p^k, d)^n$. The same argument can be applied to ψ as well. □

Lemma 2. *Let $(\phi : \mathsf{GR}(p^k, d)^n \to \mathsf{GR}(p^k, m), \ \psi : \mathsf{GR}(p^k, m) \to \mathsf{GR}(p^k, d)^n)$ be a degree-D RMFE. Then there exists a degree-D RMFE $(\phi' : \mathsf{GR}(p^k, d)^n \to \mathsf{GR}(p^k, m), \ \psi' : \mathsf{GR}(p^k, m) \to \mathsf{GR}(p^k, d)^n)$ with $\phi'(\boldsymbol{1}) = 1$.*

Proof. We begin by claiming that $\phi(\boldsymbol{1}) \in \mathsf{GR}(p^k, m)$ is invertible. Assume not, and thus $p \mid \phi(\boldsymbol{1})$. As ϕ is a $\mathbb{Z}_{p^k}$-linear map, we have $\phi(p^{k-1}\boldsymbol{1}) = p^{k-1}\phi(\boldsymbol{1}) = 0$ which contradicts to Proposition 2. Now, we define $\phi' : \mathsf{GR}(p^k, d)^n \to \mathsf{GR}(p^k, m)$ and $\psi' : \mathsf{GR}(p^k, m) \to \mathsf{GR}(p^k, d)^n$ as follows: $\phi'(\boldsymbol{a}) = \phi(\boldsymbol{a}) \cdot \phi(\boldsymbol{1})^{-1}$ for $\boldsymbol{a} \in \mathsf{GR}(p^k, d)^n$, and $\psi'(a) = \psi(a \cdot \phi(\boldsymbol{1})^D)$ for $a \in \mathsf{GR}(p^k, m)$. It is easy to verify that these functions are additively homomorphic. We can also see that $\phi'(\boldsymbol{1}) = \phi(\boldsymbol{1}) \cdot \phi(\boldsymbol{1})^{-1} = 1$, as required. It is only left to check then that (ϕ', ψ') is indeed a degree-D RMFE. To see this, consider $\boldsymbol{a}_1 \ldots, \boldsymbol{a}_D \in \mathsf{GR}(p^k, d)^n$, then $\psi'(\phi'(\boldsymbol{a}_1) \cdot \phi'(\boldsymbol{a}_2) \cdots \phi'(\boldsymbol{a}_D)) = \psi'(\phi(\boldsymbol{a}_1) \cdots \phi(\boldsymbol{a}_D) \cdot \phi(\boldsymbol{1})^{-D}) = \psi(\phi(\boldsymbol{a}_1) \cdots \phi(\boldsymbol{a}_D) \cdot \phi(\boldsymbol{1})^{-D} \cdot \phi(\boldsymbol{1})^D) = \psi(\phi(\boldsymbol{a}_1) \cdots \phi(\boldsymbol{a}_D)) = \boldsymbol{a}_1 \star \boldsymbol{a}_2 \star \cdots \star \boldsymbol{a}_D$. □

A degree-D RMFE (ϕ, ψ) that satisfies $\phi(\boldsymbol{1}) = 1$ has several interesting properties, and due to the previous lemma, we assume this to be the case from now on. First, the composition $\psi \circ \phi$ is the identity function $\mathsf{GR}(p^k, d)^n \to \mathsf{GR}(p^k, d)^n$, which follows from $\psi(\phi(\boldsymbol{a})) = \psi(\phi(\boldsymbol{a}) \cdot \boldsymbol{1} \cdots \boldsymbol{1}) = \psi(\phi(\boldsymbol{a}) \cdot \phi(\boldsymbol{1}) \cdots \phi(\boldsymbol{1})) = \boldsymbol{a} \star \boldsymbol{1} \star \cdots \star \boldsymbol{1} = \boldsymbol{a}$.

In addition, such a degree-D RMFE is also a degree-D' RMFE for any $D' \le D$ (a property that does not necessarily hold for a more general RMFE). Indeed, given $\boldsymbol{a}_1 \ldots, \boldsymbol{a}_{D'} \in \mathsf{GR}(p^k, d)^n$, we have that $\psi(\phi(\boldsymbol{a}_1) \cdots \phi(\boldsymbol{a}_{D'})) =$

$\psi(\phi(\boldsymbol{a}_1)\cdots\phi(\boldsymbol{a}_{D'})\cdot 1\cdots 1) = \psi(\phi(\boldsymbol{a}_1)\cdots\phi(\boldsymbol{a}_{D'})\cdot\phi(1)\cdots\phi(1)) = \boldsymbol{a}_1\star\cdots\star\boldsymbol{a}_{D'}\star$
$1\star\cdots\star 1 = \boldsymbol{a}_1\star\cdots\star\boldsymbol{a}_{D'}$.

These properties will be used later. In what follows, we discuss the equivalence between the degree-D RMFEs introduced here, and the packing methods from [12], discussed in Sect. 2.

3.1 From Degree-D RMFEs to Packing Methods

In this section, we show that every degree-D RMFE is a packing method of degree-D. Let $(\phi : \mathsf{GR}(p^k,d)^n \to \mathsf{GR}(p^k,m),\ \psi : \mathsf{GR}(p^k,m) \to \mathsf{GR}(p^k,d)^n)$ be a degree-D RMFE. From Proposition 2, we can assume without loss of generality that $\phi(1) = 1$.

Theorem 1 (from RMFEs to Packing Methods). *Let* $(\mathsf{Pack}_i, \mathsf{Unpack}_i)_{i=1}^{D}$ *be defined as follows:*

- $\mathsf{Pack}_i = \phi$ *for* $i = 1,\ldots,D$.
- *For each* $i = 1,\ldots,D$, $\mathsf{Unpack}_i(a) = \psi(a)$ *if* $a \in \mathrm{span}_{\mathbb{Z}_{p^k}}(M_i)$ *and* $\mathsf{Unpack}_i(a) = \perp$ *otherwise, where* $\mathrm{span}_{\mathbb{Z}_{p^k}}(M_i)$ *is the* $\mathbb{Z}_{p^k}$-*module generated by* $M_i = \{\prod_{j=1}^{i}\phi(\boldsymbol{x}_j) : \boldsymbol{x}_j \in \mathsf{GR}(p^k,d)^n\}$.

Then, this constitutes a degree-D packing method.

Proof. It is easy to check that $\mathsf{Unpack}_i(a \pm b) = \boldsymbol{a} \pm \boldsymbol{b}$ whenever $a, b \in \mathsf{GR}(p^k,m)$ satisfy $\mathsf{Unpack}_i(a) = \boldsymbol{a} \neq \perp$ and $\mathsf{Unpack}_i(b) = \boldsymbol{b} \neq \perp$, which follows from the fact that ψ is additively homomorphic and from the linearity of the $\mathbb{Z}_{p^k}$-module M_i.

It remains to be checked that, if $s, t \in \mathbb{Z}^+$ are such that $s + t = i$, then $\mathsf{Unpack}_i(a \cdot b) = \boldsymbol{a} \star \boldsymbol{b}$ holds, where $\mathsf{Unpack}_s(a) = \boldsymbol{a} \neq \perp$ and $\mathsf{Unpack}_t(b) = \boldsymbol{b} \neq \perp$. To see this, first we notice that, since $\boldsymbol{a} \neq \perp$ and $\boldsymbol{b} \neq \perp$, it must be that $a \in \mathrm{span}_{\mathbb{Z}_{p^k}}(M_s)$ and $b \in \mathrm{span}_{\mathbb{Z}_{p^k}}(M_t)$, so we can write a and b in the form $a = \sum_{j=1}^{\ell_a}\alpha_j m_j^{(a)}$ and $b = \sum_{j=1}^{\ell_b}\beta_j m_j^{(b)}$, where each $m_j^{(a)}$ is in M_s, each $m_j^{(b)}$ is in M_t, and each α_j, β_j is in $\mathbb{Z}_{p^k}$. Furthermore, we write $m_j^{(a)} = \prod_{q=1}^{s}\phi(\boldsymbol{x}_q^{(j)})$, and $m_j^{(b)} = \prod_{q=1}^{t}\phi(\boldsymbol{y}_q^{(j)})$. Now, we prove some claims that will be useful.

Claim. It holds that $\mathsf{Unpack}_s(a) = \sum_{j=1}^{\ell_a}\alpha_j \prod_{q=1}^{s}\boldsymbol{x}_q^{(j)}$, and similarly $\mathsf{Unpack}_t(b) = \sum_{j=1}^{\ell_b}\beta_j \prod_{q=1}^{s}\boldsymbol{y}_q^{(j)}$.

Proof (of Claim). We prove this for a only, as the proof of b is similar. First, notice that $\psi(m_j^{(a)}) = \psi(\prod_{q=1}^{s}\phi(\boldsymbol{x}_q^{(j)})) = \prod_{q=1}^{s}\boldsymbol{x}_q^{(j)}$, which follows from the fact that (ϕ,ψ) is not only a degree-D RMFE, but also a degree-s RMFE. The claim then holds because of the linearity of ψ.

Claim. For each j it holds that $\psi((\prod_{q=1}^{s}\phi(\boldsymbol{x}_q^{(j)})) \cdot (\prod_{q=1}^{t}\phi(\boldsymbol{y}_q^{(j)}))) = (\prod_{q=1}^{s}\boldsymbol{x}_q^{(j)}) \star (\prod_{q=1}^{t}\boldsymbol{y}_q^{(j)})$.

Proof (of Claim). This follows directly from the fact that (ϕ, ψ) is a degree-D' RMFE for any $D' \leq D$, and the fact that $s + t = i \leq D$.

It is easy to see that $a \cdot b \in \mathsf{span}_{\mathbb{Z}_{p^k}}(M_i)$. With this, and the two claims above at hand, we can compute the following:

$$\mathsf{Unpack}_i(a \cdot b) = \psi(a \cdot b)$$

$$= \psi\left(\left(\sum_{j=1}^{\ell_a} \alpha_j m_j^{(a)}\right) \cdot \left(\sum_{h=1}^{\ell_b} \beta_h m_h^{(b)}\right)\right)$$

$$= \psi\left(\sum_{j,h} \alpha_j \beta_h \cdot m_j^{(a)} m_h^{(b)}\right)$$

$$= \sum_{j,h} \alpha_j \beta_h \cdot \psi(m_j^{(a)} m_h^{(b)}) \qquad \text{linearity of } \psi$$

$$\doteq \sum_{j,h} \alpha_j \beta_h \cdot \left(\left(\prod_{q=1}^{s} \boldsymbol{x}_q^{(j)}\right) \star \left(\prod_{q=1}^{t} \boldsymbol{y}_q^{(j)}\right)\right) \qquad \text{second claim}$$

$$= \left(\sum_{j=1}^{\ell_a} \alpha_j \prod_{q=1}^{s} \boldsymbol{x}_q^{(j)}\right) \star \left(\sum_{h=1}^{\ell_b} \beta_h \prod_{q=1}^{t} \boldsymbol{y}_q^{(j)}\right)$$

$$= \mathsf{Unpack}_s(a) \star \mathsf{Unpack}_t(b). \qquad \text{first claim}$$

This concludes the proof of the theorem. □

3.2   From Degree-D Packing to Degree-D RMFEs

In general, not every degree-D packing is a degree-D RMFE. First, a degree-D packing is a *family* of pairs $(\mathsf{Pack}_i, \mathsf{Unpack}_i)_{i=1}^{D}$, while a degree-$D$ RMFE is only made of one pair of functions. In addition, packing methods do not need to be deterministic or linear, which are properties satisfied by RMFEs. Finally, the Unpack algorithm of a packing method can result in $\perp$ while RMFEs, being homomorphisms, do not. In this direction, consider the following example.

Example 1. Consider a packing method for n $\mathsf{GR}(p^k, d)$-messages into a $\mathsf{GR}(p^k, 2 \cdot n \cdot d)$ message for $p^d \geq n$. From Proposition 1, we can find n distinct elements $\alpha_1, \ldots, \alpha_n \in \mathsf{GR}(p^k, d)$ to do interpolation on. The packing algorithm is defined as follows: given $(x_1, \ldots, x_n) \in \mathsf{GR}(p^k, d)^n$, we randomly select a polynomial $f(x)$ of degree n over $\mathsf{GR}(p^k, d)$ such that $f(\alpha_i) = x_i$. Note that this $f(x)$ is not unique as we only interpolate f at n points. Then, the pack algorithm is defined as $\mathsf{Pack}((x_1, \ldots, x_n)) = f(x) \in \mathsf{GR}(p^k, 2nd)$ as $\mathsf{GR}(p^k, 2nd) \cong \mathsf{GR}(p^k, d)/(g(x))$ with a degree-$2n$ irreducible polynomial $g(x)$ over $\mathsf{GR}(p^k, d)$. The unpack algorithm is also clear as we define $\mathsf{Unpack}(f(x)) = (f(\alpha_1), \ldots, f(\alpha_n))$. One can also easily show that this packing method is a degree-2 packing. However, it is not a degree-2 RMFE as the packing method is not deterministic.

In this section, we show that being deterministic and linear is not only necessary for a degree-D packing to be a degree-D RMFE, but they are in fact *sufficient*. In other words, we show that a degree-D RMFE can be derived from any degree-D packing $(\mathsf{Pack}_i, \mathsf{Unpack}_i)_{i=1}^D$, as long as each Pack_i is $\mathbb{Z}_{p^k}$-linear and deterministic. This is proven in Theorem 2 below. However, we first present Proposition 3 and Lemma 3, which are useful tools for proving the claimed result.

Proposition 3. *Let* $(\mathsf{Pack}_i, \mathsf{Unpack}_i)_{i=1}^D$ *be a degree-D packing method. Then, for any* $a_1 \ldots, a_D \in \mathrm{GR}(p^k, d)^n$, *we have that* $\mathsf{Unpack}_D(\mathsf{Pack}_1(a_1) \cdots \mathsf{Pack}_1(a_D)) = a_1 \star \cdots \star a_D$.

Proof. We prove it by induction. For $D = 2$, it is clear that $\mathsf{Unpack}_D(\mathsf{Pack}_1(a_1) \cdot \mathsf{Pack}_1(a_2)) = a_1 \star a_2$ as we let $i = 2, s = t = 1$ in Definition 2. We proceed to the case D. Let $a = \mathsf{Pack}_1(a_1) \cdots \mathsf{Pack}_1(a_{D-1})$ and $b = \mathsf{Pack}_1(a_D)$ in Definition 2, we have $\mathsf{Unpack}_D(a \cdot b) = \mathsf{Unpack}_{D-1}(a) \star \mathsf{Unpack}_1(b) = \mathsf{Unpack}_{D-1}(a) \star a_D$. The proof is completed by applying the induction $\mathsf{Unpack}_{D-1}(\mathsf{Pack}_1(a_1) \cdots \mathsf{Pack}_1(a_{D-1})) = a_1 \star \cdots \star a_{D-1}$. □

From the proposition above, the following observation holds. Let $a \in M_D = \{\prod_{j=1}^D \mathsf{Pack}_1(x_j) : x_j \in \mathrm{GR}(p^k, d)^n\}$, then $\mathsf{Unpack}_D(a) = \prod_{j=1}^D x_j$, and in particular, $\mathsf{Unpack}_D(a) \neq \bot$. Furthermore, this also extends naturally to the case in which $a \in \mathrm{span}_{\mathbb{Z}_{p^k}}(M_D)$ by using the linearity of Unpack_1. In particular, Unpack_1 restricted to $\mathrm{span}_{\mathbb{Z}_{p^k}}(M_D)$ is a $\mathbb{Z}_{p^k}$-linear homomorphism, and therefore, the following lemma can be applied to it.

Lemma 3. *Let* $f : M \to \mathrm{GR}(p^k, d)^n$ *be a $\mathbb{Z}_{p^k}$-linear function, where M is a $\mathbb{Z}_{p^k}$-submodule of $\mathrm{GR}(p^k, m)$. Then, f can be extended to a $\mathbb{Z}_{p^k}$-linear function* $g : \mathrm{GR}(p^k, m) \to \mathrm{GR}(p^k, d)^n$.

Proof. As M is $\mathbb{Z}_{p^k}$-submodule of $\mathrm{GR}(p^k, m)$, by the fundamental decomposition theorem, we write $M = \sum_{i=1}^a S_i \beta_i$ with $S_1 \subseteq \cdots \subseteq S_a$ are the ideal of $\mathbb{Z}_{p^k}$ and $\beta_i \in \mathrm{GR}(p^k, m)$. To extend f, it suffices to decide the value of $g(\beta_i)$. Assume $S_i = p^{\alpha_i} \mathbb{Z}_{p^k}$. As $g(x)$ is $\mathbb{Z}_{p^k}$-linear, we have $f(p^{\alpha_i} \beta_i) = g(p^{\alpha_i} \beta_i) = p^{\alpha_i} g(\beta_i)$. This implies that $g(\beta_i) = p^{-\alpha_i} f(p^{\alpha_i} \beta_i)$. Thus, we extend the domain of f from M to a free module $M' := \bigoplus_{i=1}^a \mathbb{Z}_{p^k} \beta_i$. As we can write $\mathrm{GR}(p^k, m) = M' \oplus N$ where $N = \bigoplus_{i=1}^{m-a} \mathbb{Z}_{p^k} \gamma_i$, define the value $g(\gamma_i) \in \mathrm{GR}(p^k, d)^n$ in an arbitrary manner and the proof is completed. □

With this lemma at hand we can finally construct our degree-D RMFE from the degree-D packing method $(\mathsf{Pack}_i, \mathsf{Unpack}_i)_{i=1}^D$.

Theorem 2 (from Packing Methods to RMFEs). *Consider the following functions* $\phi : \mathrm{GR}(p^k, d)^n \to \mathrm{GR}(p^k, m)$ *and* $\psi : \mathrm{GR}(p^k, m) \to \mathrm{GR}(p^k, d)^n$:

- $\phi(a) = \mathsf{Pack}_1(a)$ *for* $a \in \mathrm{GR}(p^k, d)^n$;
- ψ *is defined by applying Lemma 3 to* $f = \mathsf{Unpack}_D$ *and* $M = \mathrm{span}_{\mathbb{Z}_{p^k}}(M_D)$. *In a bit more detail,* $\psi(a) = \mathsf{Unpack}_D(a)$ *for* $a \in \mathrm{span}_{\mathbb{Z}_{p^k}}(M_D)$, *and for* $a \notin \mathrm{span}_{\mathbb{Z}_{p^k}}(M_D)$ $\psi(a)$ *is defined as to preserve linearity.*

Then, (ϕ, ψ) is a degree-D RMFE.

Proof. First, from Lemma 3, we know that ψ is a $\mathbb{Z}_{p^k}$-linear map. The linearity of ϕ is followed by the fact that Pack_1 is $\mathbb{Z}_{p^k}$-linear. Since both Pack_1 and Unpack_D are deterministic, ϕ and ψ are well defined.

Finally, we prove the required multiplicative relation. Let $\boldsymbol{a}_1 \ldots, \boldsymbol{a}_D \in \mathsf{GR}(p^k, d)^n$, then, from Proposition 3, we have that

$$\psi(\phi(\boldsymbol{a}_1) \cdots \phi(\boldsymbol{a}_D)) = \mathsf{Unpack}_D(\mathsf{Pack}_1(\boldsymbol{a}_1) \cdots \mathsf{Pack}_1(\boldsymbol{a}_D))$$
$$= \boldsymbol{a}_1 \star \cdots \star \boldsymbol{a}_D,$$

as required. This completes the proof. $\qquad\qquad\qquad\qquad\qquad\qquad\qquad\quad\square$

4   Constructing Degree-D RMFEs

This section is devoted to the explicit construction of degree-D RMFEs over Galois rings. The organization of this section is the following. First, in Sect. 4.1 we provide a series of results that will be useful in our general construction. Then, in Sect. 4.2 we begin with the particular case of $D = 2$, presenting explicit constructions of degree-2 RMFEs over Galois rings. This serves two purposes. First, even though the results of [15] show that degree-2 RMFEs over Galois rings can be obtained by *lifting* existing RMFE constructions over fields (like, for example, the constructions from [9]), no explicit constructions or explicit parameters were provided. Second, we generalize the ideas in our degree-2 constructions in Sect. 4.3 to obtain our main result: degree-D RMFE constructions for $D \geq 2$.

4.1   Lemmata

We first provide a composition lemma that shows that composing two degree-D RMFEs results in a degree-D RMFE. Such lemma can be seen as an analogue of concatenation in classical coding theory. The composition lemma of RMFEs over fields in [9] can reduce the task of designing an RMFE over a general field extension to the case of a prime field. Here we present a version of this lemma over Galois rings. Generally speaking, given one RMFE of large dimension over a big Galois ring and another RMFE of small dimension over a small Galois ring, the composition of these two RMFEs gives rise to an RMFE of large dimension over the small Galois ring.

Lemma 4 (Composition Lemma). *Assume that (ϕ_1, ψ_1) is an $(n_1, k_1; D)$-RMFE over $\mathsf{GR}(p^\ell, k_2 r)$ and (ϕ_2, ψ_2) is an $(n_2, k_2; D)$-RMFE over $\mathsf{GR}(p^\ell, r)$. Then $\phi : \mathsf{GR}(p^\ell, r)^{n_1 n_2} \to \mathsf{GR}(p^\ell, r k_1 k_2)$ given by*

$$(\mathbf{x}_1, \ldots, \mathbf{x}_{n_1}) \mapsto (\phi_2(\mathbf{x}_1), \ldots, \phi_2(\mathbf{x}_{n_1})) \in \mathsf{GR}(p^\ell, r k_2)^{n_1} \mapsto \phi_1(\phi_2(\mathbf{x}_1), \ldots, \phi_2(\mathbf{x}_{n_1}))$$

and $\psi : \mathsf{GR}(p^\ell, r k_1 k_2) \to \mathsf{GR}(p^\ell, r)^{n_1 n_2}$ given by

$$\alpha \mapsto \psi_1(\alpha) = (\mathbf{u}_1, \ldots, \mathbf{u}_{n_1}) \in \mathsf{GR}(p^\ell, r k_2)^{n_1} \mapsto (\psi_2(\mathbf{u}_1), \ldots, \psi_2(\mathbf{u}_{n_1}))$$

define an $(n_1 n_2, k_1 k_2; D)$-RMFE over $\mathsf{GR}(p^\ell, r)$.

Proof. It is clear that both ϕ and ψ are $\mathsf{GR}(p^\ell, r)$-linear. For any $\mathbf{x}^{(1)}, \mathbf{x}^{(2)}, \cdots, \mathbf{x}^{(D)} \in \mathsf{GR}(p^\ell, r)^{n_1 n_2}$, we have

$$\psi(\prod_{i=1}^D \phi(\mathbf{x}^{(i)})) = \psi_2 \circ \psi_1(\phi_1(\prod_{i=1}^D(\phi_2(\mathbf{x}_1^{(i)}), \ldots, \phi_2(\mathbf{x}_{n_1}^{(i)}))))$$

$$= \psi_2((\phi_2(\mathbf{x}_1^{(1)}), \ldots, \phi_2(\mathbf{x}_{n_1}^{(1)})) * \cdots * (\phi_2(\mathbf{x}_1^{(D)}), \ldots, \phi_2(\mathbf{x}_{n_1}^{(D)})))$$

$$= (\psi_2(\phi_2(\mathbf{x}_1^{(1)}) * \cdots * \phi_2(\mathbf{x}_1^{(D)})), \ldots, \psi_2(\phi_2(\mathbf{x}_{n_1}^{(1)}) * \cdots * \phi_2(\mathbf{x}_{n_1}^{(D)})))$$

$$= (\mathbf{x}_1^{(1)} * \cdots * \mathbf{x}_1^{(D)}, \ldots, \mathbf{x}_{n_1}^{(1)} * \cdots * \mathbf{x}_{n_1}^{(D)})$$

$$= \mathbf{x}^{(1)} * \cdots * \mathbf{x}^{(D)}.$$

This completes the proof. $\qquad\square$

It will be important for our constructions to establish a relation between RMFEs and function fields. This is achieved by the following lemma.

Lemma 5. *Let q be a power of a prime. Let $F/\mathbb{F}_q$ be a function field of genus $\mathfrak{g}$ with n distinct rational places $P_1, P_2, \ldots, P_n$. Let G be a divisor of F such that $\mathrm{supp}(G) \cap \{P_1, \ldots, P_n\} = \emptyset$ and $\dim_{\mathbb{F}_q} \mathcal{L}(G) - \dim_{\mathbb{F}_q} \mathcal{L}(G - \sum_{i=1}^n P_i) = n$. If there is a place R of degree k with $k > D \deg(G)$, then there exists an $(n, k; D)$-RMFE over $\mathbb{F}_q$.*

Proof. Consider the map $\pi : \mathcal{L}(G) \to \mathbb{F}_q^n; \; f \mapsto (f(P_1), \ldots, f(P_n))$. Then the kernel of π is $\mathcal{L}(G - \sum_{i=1}^n P_i)$. Since $\dim_{\mathbb{F}_q} \mathrm{Im}(\pi) = \dim_{\mathbb{F}_q} \mathcal{L}(G) - \dim_{\mathbb{F}_q} \mathcal{L}(G - \sum_{i=1}^n P_i) = n$, π is surjective. Choose a subspace V of $\mathcal{L}(G)$ of dimension n such that π induces an isomorphism between V and $\mathbb{F}_q^n$.

We identify $\mathbb{F}_{q^k}$ with the residue field F_R of R. We write by $\mathbf{c}_f$ (and f_R, respectively) the vector $(f(P_1), \ldots, f(P_n))$ (and the residue class of f in F_R, respectively) for a function $f \in \mathcal{L}(D \cdot G)$. Define the linear map $\phi : \pi(V) = \mathbb{F}_q^n \to F_R = \mathbb{F}_{q^k}; \mathbf{c}_f \mapsto f_R \in \mathbb{F}_{q^k}$. Note that the above $f \in V$ is uniquely determined by $\mathbf{c}_f$. It is clear that ϕ is $\mathbb{F}_q$-linear and injective since $\deg(R) > \deg(G)$.

Define $\tau : \mathcal{L}(D \cdot G) \to F_R = \mathbb{F}_{q^k}; f \mapsto f_R \in \mathbb{F}_{q^k}$. Then τ is $\mathbb{F}_q$-linear and injective since $\deg(R) > D \deg(G) = \deg(D \cdot G)$.

Define the map $\psi : \mathrm{Im}(\tau) \subseteq F_R \to \mathbb{F}_q^n; f_R \mapsto (f(P_1), \ldots, f(P_n)) \in \mathbb{F}_q^n$. Note that the above $f \in \mathcal{L}(D \cdot G)$ is uniquely determined by f_R. ψ is $\mathbb{F}_q$-linear and surjective (but not injective). We extend ψ from $\mathrm{Im}(\tau)$ to F_R linearly. We obtain the pair (ϕ, ψ).

For any $\mathbf{c}_{f^{(1)}}, \ldots, \mathbf{c}_{f^{(D)}} \in \mathbb{F}_q^n$ with uniquely determined $f^{(1)}, \ldots, f^{(D)} \in V$, we have

$$\psi(\prod_{i=1}^D \phi(\mathbf{c}_{f^{(i)}})) = \psi(\prod_{i=1}^D f_R^{(i)}) = \psi((\prod_{i=1}^D f^{(i)})_R) = \mathbf{c}_{\prod_{i=1}^D f^{(i)}} = \mathbf{c}_{f^{(1)}} * \cdots * \mathbf{c}_{f^{(D)}}.$$

Note that $(\prod_{i=1}^D f^{(i)})_R$ belongs to $\mathrm{Im}(\tau)$ since $\prod_{i=1}^D f^{(i)} \in \mathcal{L}(DG)$. We conclude that (ϕ, ψ) defined above is an $(n, k; D)$-RMFE over $\mathbb{F}_q$. $\qquad\square$

Note that Galois rings are a generalization of finite fields. In [15], the authors manage to show that one can explicitly construct RMFEs over the Galois ring $GR(p^\ell, k)$ if there exists a explicit construction of RMFEs over the finite field $\mathbb{F}_{p^k}$. This is captured by the lifting result in Theorem 18 of [15], adapted below to our setting.

Lemma 6. *Let $q = p^r$ for a prime p. Then the $(n, k; D)$-RMFE over $\mathbb{F}_q$ constructed in Lemma 5 can be lifted to an $(n, k; D)$-RMFE over $GR(p^\ell, r)$ for any $\ell \geq 1$.*

Note that although Theorem 18 of [15] only proves the above lemma for the case where $D = 2$, it can be easily generalized to arbitrary D. Let us explain this briefly. The map ϕ in the proof of Lemma 5 is injective, thus by Lemma 9 of [15] it can be lifted to a map ϕ' from $GR(p^\ell, r)^n$ to $F_R = GR(p^\ell, kr)$ for any $\ell \geq 1$ and ϕ' is also injective. As the map τ in the proof of Lemma 5 is also injective, we can apply Lemma 9 of [15] again to get a map τ' from $\mathcal{L}(D \cdot D)$ to $F_R = GR(p^\ell, kr)$. Finally, the map ψ' can be defined by sending $f_R \in F_R = GR(p^\ell, kr)$ to $(f(P_1), \ldots, f(P_n)) \in GR(p^\ell, r)^n$. Thus, the pair (ϕ', ψ') is the desired RMFE.

Corollary 1. *If $p \geq n$, then there exists an $(n, k = D(n-1) + 1; D)$-RMFE over $GR(p^\ell, r)$ for any $\ell \geq 1$.*

Proof. We take the rational function field $\mathbb{F}_p(x)$ and a divisor G of degree $n-1$, a place of degree $D \deg(G) + 1 = D(n-1) + 1$, we obtain an $(n, k = D(n-1)+1; D)$-RMFE over $\mathbb{F}_p$ by Lemma 5. The desired result follows from Lemma 6.   □

4.2 Construction of Degree-2 RMFEs

In this subsection, we provide some explicit constructions of degree-2 RMFEs. We begin with an RMFE of bounded length. This RMFE is derived from rational function fields, or function fields of small genus. Then, we provide the asymptotic construction of degree-2 RMFE based on function field towers. This will be useful to settle ideas that will be generalized in Sect. 4 when we construct degree-D RMFEs. Furthermore, we observe that even though degree-2 RMFEs over Galois rings were first proposed in [15], in that work the authors only presented asymptotic constructions of degree-2 RMFEs. These objects have found many applications in recent cryptographic constructions (*cf.* [2,5,7,8,21]), which motivates the task of finding explicit constructions with clear and well determined parameters. We achieve this in this section by providing explicit degree-2 RMFE constructions over Galois rings, with a wide variety of parameters. We remark that these constructions have not appeared in the literature before.

Example 2 (Concrete Degree-2 RMFEs of Bounded Dimension). Consider the rational function field over $\mathbb{F}_2$. Take $n = 2$. Choose a divisor G of degree 1 and a place of degree 2, we obtain a $(2, 3; 2)$-RMFE over $\mathbb{F}_2$ by Lemma 5. Hence, by Lemma 6, there is a $(2, 3; 2)$-RMFE over $\mathbb{Z}_{2^\ell}$ for all $\ell \geq 1$. With a divisor G of degree 2 and a place of degree 5, we obtain a $(3, 5; 2)$-RMFE over $\mathbb{F}_2$ by Lemma 5. Hence, by Lemma 6, there is a $(3, 5; 2)$-RMFE over $\mathbb{Z}_{2^\ell}$ for all $\ell \geq 1$.

Now, consider a function field over $\mathbb{F}_8$ with n rational places and genus $\mathfrak{g}$. Then for any $m \leq n$, we choose m distinct points and a divisor of degree $m+2\mathfrak{g}-1$. Let $k = 2(m+2\mathfrak{g}-1)+1 = 2m+4\mathfrak{g}-1$. Then we have an $(m, k = 2m+4\mathfrak{g}-1; 2)$-RMFE over $\mathbb{F}_8$. Hence, we obtain a $(2m, 6m + 12\mathfrak{g} - 3; 2)$-RMFE over $\mathrm{GR}(2^\ell, 3)$. Hence, by Lemma 5, there is a $(2m, 6m+12\mathfrak{g}-3; 2)$-RMFE over $\mathbb{Z}_{2^\ell}$ for all $\ell \geq 1$. As particular cases:

- Taking $(\mathfrak{g}, m) = (0, 9)$, we get a $(2m, 6m-3; 2)$-RMFE over $\mathbb{Z}_{2^\ell}$ for any $m \leq 9$. For instance, we have a $(8, 21; 2)$-RMFE, $(10, 27; 2)$-RMFE, $(18, 51; 2)$-RMFE over $\mathbb{Z}_{2^\ell}$ for all $\ell \geq 1$.
- Taking $(\mathfrak{g}, m) = (1, 14)$, we get a $(2m, 6m + 9; 2)$-RMFE over $\mathbb{Z}_{2^\ell}$ for any $m \leq 14$. For instance, we have a $(28, 93; 2)$-RMFE over $\mathbb{Z}_{2^\ell}$ for all $\ell \geq 1$.
- Taking $(\mathfrak{g}, m) = (2, 18)$, we get a $(2m, 6m + 21; 2)$-RMFE over $\mathbb{Z}_{2^\ell}$ for any $m \leq 18$. For instance, we have a $(36, 129; 2)$-RMFE over $\mathbb{Z}_{2^\ell}$ for all $\ell \geq 1$.

Finally, consider a function field over $\mathbb{F}_{32}$ with n rational places and genus $\mathfrak{g}$. Then for any $m \leq n$, we choose m distinct points and a divisor of degree $m+2\mathfrak{g}-1$. Let $k = 2(m+2\mathfrak{g}-1)+1 = 2m+4\mathfrak{g}-1$. Then we have an $(m, k = 2m+4\mathfrak{g}-1; 2)$-RMFE over $\mathbb{F}_{32}$. Hence, we obtain a $(3m, 10m+20\mathfrak{g}-5; 2)$-RMFE over $\mathrm{GR}(2^\ell, 5)$. Hence, by Lemma 6, there is a $(3m, 10m + 20\mathfrak{g} - 5; 2)$-RMFE over $\mathbb{Z}_{2^\ell}$ for all $\ell \geq 1$.

- Taking $(\mathfrak{g}, m) = (0, 33)$, we get a $(3m, 10m - 5; 2)$-RMFE over $\mathbb{Z}_{2^\ell}$ for any $m \leq 33$. For instance, we have a $(99, 325; 2)$-RMFE over $\mathbb{Z}_{2^\ell}$ for all $\ell \geq 1$.
- Taking $(\mathfrak{g}, m) = (1, 44)$, we get a $(3m, 10m + 15; 2)$-RMFE over $\mathbb{Z}_{2^\ell}$ for any $m \leq 44$. For instance, we have a $(132, 455; 2)$-RMFE over $\mathbb{Z}_{2^\ell}$ for all $\ell \geq 1$.
- Taking $(\mathfrak{g}, m) = (2, 53)$, we get a $(3m, 10m + 35; 2)$-RMFE over $\mathbb{Z}_{2^\ell}$ for any $m \leq 53$. For instance, we have a $(159, 565; 2)$-RMFE over $\mathbb{Z}_{2^\ell}$ for all $\ell \geq 1$.
- Taking $(\mathfrak{g}, m) = (3, 64)$, we get a $(3m, 10m + 55; 2)$-RMFE over $\mathbb{Z}_{2^\ell}$ for any $m \leq 64$. For instance, we have a $(192, 695; 2)$-RMFE over $\mathbb{Z}_{2^\ell}$ for all $\ell \geq 1$.

Asymptotic Construction of Degree-2 RMFEs. Now we consider the task of constructing degree-2 RMFEs of unbounded dimension. We begin by considering two function field towers. The first tower was introduced in [22]. Let $q = r^2$, where r is a prime power. For $t \geq 1$, let $F_t = \mathbb{F}_q(x_1, x_2, \ldots, x_t)$ with

$$x_{i+1}^r + x_{i+1} = \frac{x_i^r}{x_i^{r-1} + 1} \tag{1}$$

for $i = 1, 2, \ldots, t - 1$. Then the genus $\mathfrak{g}(F_t)$ of F_t is at most r^t and the number $N(F_t)$ of rational places is at least $1 + r^t(r - 1)$.

We proceed to the second tower. Let $q = p^{2m+1}$, where p is a prime and $m \geq 1$ is an integer. For $t \geq 1$, let $F_t = \mathbb{F}_q(x_1, x_2, \ldots, x_t)$ with

$$\mathrm{Tr}_m\left(\frac{x_{i+1}}{x_i^{q^{m+1}}}\right) + \mathrm{Tr}_{m+1}\left(\frac{x_{i+1}^{q^m}}{x_i}\right) = 1 \tag{2}$$

for $i = 1, 2, \ldots, t-1$, where $\mathrm{Tr}_a(T) = T + T^q + \cdots + T^{q^{a-1}}$. Then $\lim_{t \to \infty} \mathfrak{g}(F_t) = \infty$. Furthermore, for all $t \geq 1$, we have $\frac{N(F_t)}{\mathfrak{g}(F_t)-1} \geq \frac{2(p^{m+1}-1)}{p+1+\epsilon}$ with $\epsilon = \frac{p-1}{p^m-1}$, where $\mathfrak{g}(F_t)$ and $N(F_t)$ stands for the genus and the number rational places of F_t, respectively. Coupling these observations with our previous results, we obtain Corollary 2, which shows the existence of degree-D RMFEs over Galois rings for any dimension and any characteristic q. Then, in Corollary 3 we apply this to the relevant case of Galois rings over $\mathbb{Z}_{2^k}$.

Corollary 2. *Let $F/\mathbb{F}_q$ be a function field of genus $\mathfrak{g}$ with n distinct rational places and a place of degree $k \geq 2n + 4\mathfrak{g} - 1$. Then there exists an $(n, k; 2)$-RMFE over $\mathbb{F}_q$. In particular,*

(i) *if q is a square, there is a constructive family of $(n, k; 2)$-RMFE over $\mathbb{F}_q$ with $n \to \infty$ and $\frac{k}{n} \to 2 + \frac{4}{\sqrt{q}-1}$;*

(ii) *if $q = p^{2m+1}$ for a prime p, there is a constructive family of $(n, k; 2)$-RMFE over $\mathbb{F}_q$ with $n \to \infty$ and $\frac{k}{n} \to 2 + \frac{2(p+1+\epsilon)}{p^{m+1}-1}$, where $\epsilon = \frac{p-1}{p^m-1}$.*

Proof. One can take a divisor of degree $n + 2\mathfrak{g} - 1$. Then by the Riemann-Roch Theorem, we have $\dim_{\mathbb{F}_q} \mathcal{L}(G) - \dim_{\mathbb{F}_q} \mathcal{L}(G - \sum_{i=1}^{n}) = \deg(G) - \mathfrak{g} + 1 - (\deg(G) - \mathfrak{g} + 1 - n) = n$. Take $k = 1 + 2\deg(G) = 1 + 2(n + 2\mathfrak{g} - 1) = 2n + 4\mathfrak{g} - 1$. Then $k > 2\deg(G)$. Thus, by Lemma 5, we have an $(n, k; 2)$-RMFE over $\mathbb{F}_q$.

(i) Applying to the first tower with n being the number $N(F_t)$, we have $\frac{k}{n} = \frac{2n+4\mathfrak{g}-1}{n} = 2 + \frac{4\mathfrak{g}}{n} - \frac{1}{n} \to 2 + \frac{4}{\sqrt{q}-1}$.

(ii) Applying to the second tower with n being the number $N(F_t)$, we have $\frac{k}{n} = \frac{2n+4\mathfrak{g}-1}{n} = 2 + \frac{4\mathfrak{g}}{n} - \frac{1}{n} =\to 2 + \frac{2(p+1+\epsilon)}{p^{m+1}-1}$.

$\square$

Corollary 3. *There exists a constructive family of $(n, k; 2)$-RMFE over $\mathbb{Z}_{2^\ell}$ for all $\ell \geq 1$ with $n \to \infty$ and $\frac{k}{n} \to 4.92$.*

Proof. Consider the rational function field over $\mathbb{F}_2$. Choose a divisor G of degree 2 and a place of degree 5, we obtain a $(3, 5; 2)$-RMFE over $\mathbb{F}_2$. Hence, by Lemma 6, there is a $(3, 5; 2)$-RMFE over $\mathbb{Z}_{2^\ell}$ for all $\ell \geq 1$.

By Corollary 2(ii), there is a constructive family of $(N, K; 2)$-RMFE over $\mathbb{F}_{32}$ with $\frac{K}{N} \to 2 + \frac{20}{21} = \frac{62}{21}$. Thus, we obtain $(N, K; 2)$-RMFE over $\mathrm{GR}(2^\ell, 5)$ with $\frac{K}{N} \to 2 + \frac{20}{21} = \frac{62}{21}$.

By Lemma 4, we obtain a constructive family of $(n = 3N, k = 5K; 2)$-RMFE over $\mathbb{Z}_{2^\ell}$ with $n \to \infty$ and $\frac{k}{n} \to \frac{62}{21} \times \frac{5}{3} \approx 4.92$. $\square$

4.3 Construction of Degree-D RMFEs

Finally, in this section we provide some explicit constructions of degree-D RMFEs for $D \geq 2$. As before, we begin by considering RMFEs of bounded dimension, which are obtained from function fields with small genus. Then, we provide degree-D RMFEs with unbounded dimension, which are obtained by making use of certain function field towers. We remark that these constructions are entirely new, considering that the notion of degree-D RMFEs is introduced in our work.

Example 3 (Concrete Degree-D RMFEs of Bounded Dimension). Consider the rational function field over $\mathbb{F}_2$. Choose a divisor G of degree 2 and a place of degree $1 + 2t$ for all $t \geq 2$, we obtain a $(3, 1 + 2t; t)$-RMFE over $\mathbb{F}_2$ by Lemma 5. Hence, by Lemma 6, there is a $(3, 1 + 2t; t)$-RMFE over $\mathbb{Z}_{2^\ell}$ for all $\ell \geq 1$.

Consider a function field over $\mathbb{F}_{2^{2t+1}}$ with n rational places and genus $\mathfrak{g}$. Then for any $m \leq n$, we choose m distinct points and a divisor of degree $m + 2\mathfrak{g} - 1$. Let $k = t(m + 2\mathfrak{g} - 1) + 1 = tm + 2t\mathfrak{g} - t + 1$. Then we have an $(m, k = tm + 2t\mathfrak{g} - t + 1; t)$-RMFE over $\mathbb{F}_{2^{2t+1}}$. Hence, by Lemma 4, we obtain a $(3m, (1 + 2t)(tm + 2t\mathfrak{g} - t + 1); t)$-RMFE over $\mathbb{F}_2$ by composing the $(3, 1 + 2t; t)$-RMFE above and $(m, tm + 2t\mathfrak{g} - t + 1; t)$-RMFE. Hence, by Lemma 6, there is a $(3m, (1 + 2t)(tm + 2t\mathfrak{g} - t + 1); t)$-RMFE over $\mathbb{Z}_{2^\ell}$ for all $\ell \geq 1$.

- Taking $(\mathfrak{g}, m) = (0, 1 + 2^{2t+1})$, we get a $(3m, (1 + 2t)(tm - t + 1); t)$-RMFE over $\mathbb{Z}_{2^\ell}$ for any $m \leq 1 + 2^{2t+1}$. For instance, we have a $(3(1 + 2^{2t+1}), (1 + 2t)(t(1 + 2^{2t+1}) - t + 1); t)$-RMFE over $\mathbb{Z}_{2^\ell}$ for all $\ell \geq 1$.
- Taking $(t, \mathfrak{g}, m) = (3, 1, 150)$, we get a $(3m, 7(3m + 4); 3)$-RMFE over $\mathbb{Z}_{2^\ell}$ for any $m \leq 150$. For instance, we have a $(450, 3178; 3)$-RMFE over $\mathbb{Z}_{2^\ell}$ for all $\ell \geq 1$.
- Taking $(t, \mathfrak{g}, m) = (3, 2, 172)$, we get a $(3m, 7(3m + 10); 3)$-RMFE over $\mathbb{Z}_{2^\ell}$ for any $m \leq 172$. For instance, we have a $(516, 3682; 3)$-RMFE over $\mathbb{Z}_{2^\ell}$ for all $\ell \geq 1$.

Asymptotic Construction of Degree-D RMFEs. We now proceed to the asymptotic construction of degree-D RMFEs of unbounded dimension. The construction makes use of the same function field tower we use in the asymptotic construction of degree-2 RMFE. Our results are presented in the following two corollaries. As with the degree-2 case, Corollary 4 shows the existence of degree-D RMFEs over Galois rings for any dimension and any characteristic q, while Corollary 5 is a particular case for the relevant setting of Galois rings over $\mathbb{Z}_{2^k}$.

Corollary 4. *Let $F/\mathbb{F}_q$ be a function field of genus $\mathfrak{g}$ with n distinct rational places and a place of degree k. Then there exists an $(n, k; D)$-RMFE over $\mathbb{F}_q$ as follows.*

(i) *if q is a square, there is a constructive family of $(n, k; D)$-RMFE over $\mathbb{F}_q$ with $n \to \infty$ and $\frac{k}{n} \to D + \frac{2D}{\sqrt{q}-1}$;*

(ii) *if $q = p^{2m+1}$ for a prime p, there is a constructive family of $(n, k; D)$-RMFE over $\mathbb{F}_q$ with $n \to \infty$ and $\frac{k}{n} \to D + \frac{D(p+1+\epsilon)}{p^{m+1}-1}$, where $\epsilon = \frac{p-1}{p^m-1}$.*

Proof. One can take a divisor of degree $n + 2\mathfrak{g} - 1$. Then by the Riemann-Roch Theorem, we have $\dim_{\mathbb{F}_q} \mathcal{L}(G) - \dim_{\mathbb{F}_q} \mathcal{L}(G - \sum_{i=1}^n) = \deg(G) - \mathfrak{g} + 1 - (\deg(G) - \mathfrak{g} + 1 - n) = n$. Take $k = 1 + D \deg(G) = 1 + D(n + 2\mathfrak{g} - 1)$. Then $k > D \deg(G)$. Thus, by Lemma 5, we have an $(n, k; D)$-RMFE over $\mathbb{F}_q$.

(i) Applying to the first tower in (1) with n being the number $N(F_D)$, we have
$\frac{k}{n} = \frac{tn+2D\mathfrak{g}-D}{n} = D + \frac{2D\mathfrak{g}}{n} - \frac{D}{n} \to D + \frac{2D}{\sqrt{q}-1}$.

(ii) Applying to the second tower in (2) with n being the number $N(F_D)$, we have $\frac{k}{n} = \frac{Dn+2D\mathfrak{g}-D}{n} = D + \frac{2D\mathfrak{g}}{n} - \frac{D}{n} \to D + \frac{D(p+1+\epsilon)}{p^{m+1}-1}$.   □

Corollary 5. *There exists a constructive family of $(n, k; D)$-RMFE over $\mathbb{Z}_{2^\ell}$ for all $\ell \geq 1$ with $n \to \infty$ and $\frac{k}{n} \to \frac{1+2D}{3} \times \left(D + \frac{D(3+1/(2^D-1))}{2^{D+1}-1} \right)$.*

Proof. Consider the rational function field over $\mathbb{F}_2$. Choose a divisor G of degree 2 and a place of degree $1 + 2D$, we obtain a $(3, 1+2D; D)$-RMFE over $\mathbb{F}_2$. Hence, by Lemma 6, there is a $(3, 1 + 2D; D)$-RMFE over $\mathbb{Z}_{2^\ell}$ for all $\ell \geq 1$.

By Corollary 4(ii), there is a constructive family of $(N, K; D)$-RMFE over $\mathbb{F}_{2^{1+2D}}$ with $\frac{K}{N} \to D + \frac{D(3+1/(2^D-1))}{2^{D+1}-1}$. Thus, we obtain $(N, K; D)$-RMFE over $R_\ell(2, 1 + 2D)$ with $\frac{K}{N} \to D + \frac{D(3+1/(2^D-1))}{2^{D+1}-1}$.

By Lemma 4, we obtain a constructive family of $(n = 3N, k = (1 + 2D)K)$-RMFE over $\mathbb{Z}_{2^\ell}$ with $n \to \infty$ and $\frac{k}{n} \to \left(D + \frac{D(3+1/(2^D-1))}{2^{D+1}-1} \right) \times \frac{1+2D}{3}$.   □

Remark 1. The degree-D RMFE over $\mathbb{Z}_{2^\ell}$ presented in Corollary 5 achieves the ratio $\frac{k}{n} \approx \frac{D(1+2D)}{3}$. By Theorem 1, this also means there exists degree-D packing method of density roughly $\frac{3}{D(1+2D)}$ over $\mathbb{Z}_{2^\ell}$.

5   Applications of Degree-D RMFEs

Having established the relations between our novel degree-D RMFEs and the degree-D packing methods from [12] in Sect. 3, and after showing explicit constructions of degree-D RMFEs in Sect. 4, we now proceed to discuss settings in which degree-D RMFEs can prove useful. At a high level, degree-D RMFEs find applications in settings where (1) the goal is to operate over a Galois ring $\mathsf{GR}(p^k, d)$ of small degree d, but the underlying machinery requires a Galois ring extension $\mathsf{GR}(p^k, m)$ of a large degree m; and (2) degree-D computation is needed.

Examples of scenarios that meet these conditions include somewhat homomorphic encryption (SHE), secure multiparty computation (MPC), and even zero knowledge proofs (ZKPs). However, finding *direct* applications of our novel degree-D RMFEs for $D > 2$ to these settings is not trivial since, as we discuss in the full version [19], degree-2 computation seems to be enough for many use-cases. Fortunately, there are certain "less direct" scenarios that benefit from computation of higher degree, and after our initial discussion below we will focus this section on one of these applications, which have to do with generating correlated randomness *non-interactively* for use in secure multiparty computation protocols.

We refer to the full version [19] for a detailed discussion of *potential* applications to SHE and MPC, but here we focus on the following.

Our Main Application: Non-interactive Correlation Generation. Here, we consider an application to MPC where high degree computation is required, but interaction is less desired. Instead of aiming at directly improving the efficiency of MPC protocols, we consider the different but closely related problem of generating preprocessing material used for secure computation. To provide context, we observe that it is a common practice to divide the execution of an MPC protocol into two phases: an *offline phase* (also known as *preprocessing phase*) that is independent of the inputs and hence can be executed by the parties before the inputs are known, and an *online phase*, which depends on the inputs and tends to be much lighter and more efficient than the offline phase, on top of using in some cases less computational assumptions and simpler tools. The motivation behind such separation is to push most of the complexities and inefficiencies to the offline phase which, being independent of the inputs, can be in principle executed by the parties before the inputs are known (say, overnight before a computation that will happen next day). This way, the latency from input provision to output computation, which is dictated by the efficiency of the online phase, can be minimized.

The role of the offline phase is to establish certain *correlated randomness* among the parties (which is, again, independent of the inputs for the computation), which is then "consumed" in the online phase by the parties in order to securely compute the given function. An alternative to letting the parties run the offline phase to generate this correlated randomness themselves, which could be expensive or prohibitive in some settings where no "overnight" computation is available, is to let the parties receive this correlated randomness from some external source. For example, a trusted dealer could be in charge of distributing such randomness [25], using trusted hardware [17], or using PCGs [6].

Another approach to generating the required correlated randomness consists of replacing the trusted dealer with a different set of parties who run an MPC protocol among themselves to generate the required correlations. This way, there is no single point of failure such as a trusted dealer. This approach can be regarded as some form of "correlations-as-a-service", which is a model that has been considered before in the literature [24,31]. In our application, we require minimal interaction among the set of parties in charge of generating the correlated randomness for other committees.

5.1 Degree-D Correlations

We denote by $\mathcal{P} = \{P_1, \ldots, P_n\}$ the parties in the *preprocessing committee*, *i.e.* the parties that will generate the required correlations, and we denote by $\mathcal{Q} = \{Q_1, \ldots, Q_N\}$ the parties in the *online committee*, *i.e.* the parties who will "consume" these correlations to securely compute the desired functionality on their private inputs. We consider an adversary that *passively* corrupts t out of the n parties in $\mathcal{P}$. For simplicity we consider correlations over $\mathbb{Z}_{p^k}$, although this can be easily generalized to Galois rings of arbitrary degree. In its more general form, a correlation is a distribution over vectors of the form $(\boldsymbol{y}^{(1)}, \ldots, \boldsymbol{y}^{(N)}) \in (\mathbb{Z}_{p^k})^N$, where, in the MPC context, each party Q_i is intended to receive $\boldsymbol{y}^{(i)}$. However, in this work we focus on a particular case of high relevance, which is the case in which the parties obtain *sharings* of m values $(y_1, \ldots, y_m) \in \mathbb{Z}_{p^k}$ following certain distribution computable from degree-D polynomials. The sharings are done using some target linear secret-sharing scheme over $\mathbb{Z}_{p^k}$, which we denote by $\langle \cdot \rangle$. That is, the correlation consists of the parties in $\mathcal{Q}$ receiving sharings $(\langle y_1 \rangle, \ldots, \langle y_m \rangle)$.

Definition 4. (Degree-D Correlations). *Consider a degree-D function F : $(\mathbb{Z}_{p^k})^\ell \to (\mathbb{Z}_{p^k})^m$, meaning that, if $(y_1, \ldots, y_m) = F(x_1, \ldots, x_\ell)$, then each y_i is the evaluation of a multivariate polynomial $F_i(x_1, \ldots, x_\ell)$ of degree at most D. A degree-D correlation is a list of sharings of the form $(\langle y_1 \rangle, \ldots, \langle y_m \rangle)$, where $(y_1, \ldots, y_m) = F(\boldsymbol{x})$ for some uniformly random $\boldsymbol{x} \in \mathbb{Z}_{p^k}^\ell$.*

We present several examples of useful degree-D correlations in the full version [19], which include multiplication triples, authenticated triples, and generalizations.

Overview of Our Correlation Generation Techniques. From now onwards, let $F : (\mathbb{Z}_{p^k})^\ell \to (\mathbb{Z}_{p^k})^m$ be a degree-D function given by $\boldsymbol{y} = F(\boldsymbol{x})$, with $y_i = F_i(\boldsymbol{x})$ for $i \in \{1, \ldots, m\}$. At a high level, our approach for the parties in $\mathcal{P}$ to generate the degree-D correlations derived from F towards committee $\mathcal{Q}$ consist of the following steps.

1. Parties in $\mathcal{P}$ generate Shamir sharings $([\![x_1]\!], \ldots, [\![x_\ell]\!])$, where each $x_i \in \mathbb{Z}_{p^k}$ is uniformly random.
2. Parties in $\mathcal{P}$ securely compute $([\![y_1]\!], \ldots, [\![y_m]\!])$, where $y_i = F_i(\boldsymbol{x})$ for $i \in \{1, \ldots, m\}$.
3. Parties in $\mathcal{P}$ reshare $([\![y_1]\!], \ldots, [\![y_m]\!])$ towards $\mathcal{Q}$, which enable the latter committee to obtain $(\langle y_1 \rangle, \ldots, \langle y_m \rangle)$.

Recall that our main goal is to achieve the above while maintaining *no interaction* among the parties in $\mathcal{P}$. The rest of this section is devoted to describing these ideas in detail, and overcoming the following challenges:

- The parties in $\mathcal{P}$ must generate $([\![x_1]\!], \ldots, [\![x_\ell]\!])$ non-interactively. This is done with the help of pseudo-random secret-sharing (PRSS), as described in Sect. 5.2. We build on top of the techniques from [3], adapting to the case of Galois rings, and considering certain extensions we will need for our concrete use-case.
- The parties in $\mathcal{P}$ must compute $([\![y_1]\!], \ldots, [\![y_m]\!])$ non-interactively. This is achieved by requiring the initial threshold in Shamir secret-sharing to be low enough, so that D sequential multiplications can be carried out locally without losing the ability to reconstruct the underlying secrets.
- In our case where the ring is $\mathbb{Z}_{p^k}$, Shamir secret-sharing does not work directly, and instead a Galois ring extension $\mathsf{GR}(p^k, \delta)$ of large enough degree $\delta = \Theta(\log(n))$ must be used. This is exactly where our degree-D RMFEs come into the picture: we make use of our RMFEs to remove asymptotically the overhead caused by this extension, achieving zero overhead and enabling

efficient correlation generation. The use of RMFEs and the use of Galois rings introduce some changes with respect to the PRSS from [3]. This is discussed below.

5.2 Pseudo-Random Secret-Sharing

Let $R = \mathsf{GR}(p^k, \delta)$. Committee $\mathcal{P}$ generates the Shamir sharings $(\llbracket x_1 \rrbracket, \ldots, \llbracket x_\ell \rrbracket)$ where $x_i \in_R R$ for $i \in \{1, \ldots, \ell\}$ using pseudo-random secret sharing, or PRSS for short, which is a technique that enables the parties in $\mathcal{P}$ to generate Shamir shares of random values without interaction, assuming only a setup phase where the parties receive certain "seeds" that are used to feed pseudo-random functions that will determine the corresponding shares. Recall that t is the number of corrupted parties in $\mathcal{P}$, and D is the degree of the correlation. We assume that $t \cdot D < n$, and we let $d = \lfloor \frac{n-1}{D} \rfloor \geq t$, which is the largest integer such that $d \cdot D < n$. The Shamir sharings that we generate will have degree d, which is in principle larger than the corruption threshold t.

We use $\llbracket x \rrbracket_d = (z_1, \ldots, z_n)$ to denote packed secret-sharing of a vector $x \in R^\kappa$, meaning that there exists a polynomial $f(X)$ over R of degree at most d such that $z_i = f(\alpha_i)$ for $i \in \{1, \ldots, n\}$ and $x_j = f(\beta_j)$ for $j \in \{1, \ldots, \kappa\}$, where $\{\alpha_1, \ldots, \alpha_n, \beta_1, \ldots, \beta_\kappa\}$ is an exceptional set over R. It is well known that the secret x is determined by any $d + 1$ shares, but given any t of these shares, the secret vector x is kept private. For our construction we will actually need $\{\beta_0\} \cup \{\alpha_1, \ldots, \alpha_n, \beta_1, \ldots, \beta_\kappa\}$ to be an exceptional set, which requires $1 + n + \kappa \leq p^\delta$.

Recall that $R = \mathsf{GR}(p^k, \delta)$. From now on we fix a degree-D RMFE $(\phi : \mathbb{Z}_{p^k}^r \to R, \psi : R \to \mathbb{Z}_{p^k}^r)$. In our work, we make use of PRSS to non-interactively generate sharings of the form $\llbracket x \rrbracket_d$, where $x = (x_1, \ldots, x_\kappa)$ with $x_i \in \mathsf{Im}(\phi)$ for $i \in \{1, \ldots, \kappa\}$. Inspired by the approach in [3], we construct a PRSS solution suited for our algebraic structure R, which is in general not a field, and also ensuring the underlying secrets are uniformly random in the $\mathbb{Z}_{p^k}$-submodule $(\mathsf{Im}(\phi))^\kappa$, rather than just being uniformly random in R^κ.

Covering Designs. The main insight in [3] is that any PRSS solution is closely tied to the notion of a covering design, and that the latter become more efficient as the gap between the adversarial threshold t and the desired degree d increases. We begin by reusing the definition of a covering design from [3].

Definition 5 (Covering Design, Definition 3.2 in [3]). *Fix integers* $0 < t \leq m \leq n$, *and let* $\mathcal{C} = (S_1, \ldots, S_\ell)$ *be a collection of* ℓ *different subsets* $S_j \subseteq \{1, \ldots, n\}$, *all of size* $|S_j| = m$. $\mathcal{C}$ *is said to be an* (n, m, t)-*cover if for every size-t subset* $T \subseteq \{1, \ldots, n\}$, $|T| = t$, *there is a set* $S_j \in \mathcal{C}$ *that covers it, i.e.* $T \subseteq S_j$.

The goal of pseudo-random secret-sharing (PRSS) as we use it in our work is to enable n parties $\mathcal{P} = \{P_1, \ldots, P_n\}$ to generate a large amount of sharings $\llbracket r \rrbracket_d$, where r is uniformly random in the $\mathbb{Z}_{p^k}$-module $(\mathsf{Im}(\phi))^\kappa$. This was first considered in [14] for the case $d = t$ (*i.e.* the degree d equals the desired threshold t, and $\kappa = 1$ so only one secret can be stored), and the secret lies in R with $k = 1$

(*i.e.* the algebraic structure is a finite field and the secret is uniform in the field itself, not in a subset of it). These traditional solutions require the parties to hold an exponential amount of different seeds, or more precisely, each party must hold $\binom{n}{t}$ seeds, which is exponential in n for parameter ranges of interest. In the recent work of [3], a generalization of the techniques in [14] was presented, where the authors considered the case in which $t < d$, or in other words, the case where there is a gap between the threshold and the degree, which enables for packing more than one secret using packed secret-sharing. In [3], the authors show that such gap can be used to drastically reduce the amount of seeds required to achieve PRSS. We draw inspiration from their construction to design our PRSS solution.

PRSS Construction. Now we are ready to describe our PRSS solution. Recall that the goal is to let the parties obtain a large amount of sharings $[\![x]\!]_d$ where each x_i is uniformly random in $\mathsf{Im}(\phi)$. Also, recall that the packing parameter is $1 \leq \kappa \leq (d-t)+1$. Let $\mathcal{C}' = \{S'_1, \ldots, S'_{\ell'}\}$ be a $(n, d-\kappa+1, t)$-cover. Consider the collection $\overline{\mathcal{C}} = \{S' \setminus \{j\} : S' \in \mathcal{C}', j \in S'\} = \{\overline{S}_1, \ldots, \overline{S}_\ell\}$, which contains $\ell \leq \ell'(d-\kappa+1)$ different subsets, each of size $d-\kappa$. Let us denote $S_i = \{1, \ldots, n\} \setminus \overline{S}_i$, for each $i \in \{1, \ldots, \ell\}$. Notice that $|S_i| = n - (d-\kappa)$.

PRSS Construction

Setup: The parties start with the following setup.

1. For each S_i as defined above, sample a uniformly random key $k_i \in \{0,1\}^\kappa$ for a PRF, which we denote by $\mathsf{PRF}_{k_i}(\cdot)$.
2. Each party P_j for $j \in \{1, \ldots, n\}$ receives the seeds k_i for every $i \in \{1, \ldots, \ell\}$ such that $P_j \in S_i$.

Share generation: In order to *non-interactively* generate shares $[\![r]\!]_d$ where r is uniformly random in the $\mathbb{Z}_{p^k}$-module $(\mathsf{Im}(\phi))^\kappa \subseteq R^\kappa$, the parties proceed as follows.

1. For each $\overline{S}_i = \{1, \ldots, n\} \setminus S_i$, consider the polynomial $P_{\overline{S}_i}(\mathrm{X})$ obtained by interpolating the following conditions: $P_{\overline{S}_i}(X)$ equals 0 if $X = \alpha_h$ with $h \in \overline{S}_i$, it equals r_{ij} if $X = \beta_j \in \{\beta_1, \ldots, \beta_\kappa\}$, and it equals s_i if $X = \beta_0$, where $(r_{i1}, \ldots, r_{i\kappa} \| s_i) = \mathsf{PRF}_{k_i}(\mathtt{id}, j) \in (\mathsf{Im}(\phi))^\kappa \oplus R$, where $\mathtt{id}$ is some common identifier corresponding to the current PRSS run (*e.g.* a counter). Note that:
   - This polynomial has degree at most d since there are $(d-\kappa)+\kappa+1 = d+1$ conditions above given that $|\overline{S}_i| = d - \kappa$.
   - Each party $P_j \in S_i$ can compute the polynomial $P_{\overline{S}_i}(\mathrm{X})$ (and in particular $P_{\overline{S}_i}(\alpha_j)$).
   - Each party $P_j \notin S_i$ can trivially compute $P_{\overline{S}_i}(\alpha_j)$, since this value is equal to zero.
2. Define the polynomial $Q(\mathrm{X}) := \sum_{i=1}^\ell P_{\overline{S}_i}(\mathrm{X})$, which has degree at most d. From the observations above, each party P_j can compute $Q(\alpha_j)$.

3. The parties output the shares $[\![r]\!]_d = (Q(\alpha_1), \ldots, Q(\alpha_n))$, where $r = (Q(\beta_1), \ldots, Q(\beta_\kappa))$.

Theorem 3. *Fix integers $0 < t \le d \le n$ and $1 \le \kappa \le (d-t)+1$. Given a size-ℓ' $(n, d - \kappa + 1, t)$-cover, the construction above is a PRSS solution for t-secure distribution of sharings $[\![r]\!]_d$ where $r \in_R (\mathsf{Im}(\phi))^\kappa$, with the following complexity measures:*

- *The total number of different PRSS seeds is $\ell \le \ell'(d - \kappa + 1)$, and*
- *Each key is received by $|S_i| = n - (d - \kappa)$ parties.*
- *In average, each party in $\mathcal{P}$ stores $\frac{\sum_{i=1}^{\ell} |S_i|}{n} \le \frac{\ell'(d-\kappa+1)(n-(d-\kappa))}{n}$.*

Proof. The claimed complexities can be verified by inspection. For the purpose of the proof we assume that the values $(r_{i1}, \ldots, r_{i\kappa} \| s_i)$ are *uniformly random* (instead of pseudo-random) in $(\mathsf{Im}(\phi))^\kappa \oplus R$. The general case is achieved by a standard reduction to the security of the PRF.

Let $T \subseteq \{1, \ldots, n\}$ be any set with $|T| = t$. Such set determines t shares $Q(\alpha_j)$ for $j \in T$. To see that the PRSS construction is secure we need to show that, even with the knowledge of the seeds of parties P_i for $i \in T$, the output polynomial $Q(\mathsf{X})$ is uniformly random subject to its shares for indices $j \in T$ being equal to $Q(\alpha_j)$, and its secrets being uniformly random in $\mathsf{Im}(\phi)$. Clearly, $Q(\mathsf{X})$ has degree $\le d$. From this, it suffices to show that, even with knowledge of $(r_{i1}, \ldots, r_{i\kappa} \| s_i)$ for i such that $S_i \cap T \ne \emptyset$ (*i.e.* knowledge of k_i), $Q(\mathsf{X})$ satisfies the following:

1. $Q(\alpha_j) = \sum_{S_i \cap T \ne \emptyset} P_{\overline{S}_i}(\alpha_j)$ for $j \in T$ (these are the shares corresponding to the indices in T, which are computable from $(r_{i1}, \ldots, r_{i\kappa} \| s_i)$ for S_i with $S_i \cap T \ne \emptyset$).
2. $(Q(\beta_1), \ldots, Q(\beta_\kappa)) \in_R (\mathsf{Im}(\phi))^\kappa$.
3. $Q(\mathsf{X})$ evaluated at *any other* $\lambda := d + 1 - \kappa - t \ge 0$ points is uniformly random in R^λ.

Now, observe that, since $\mathcal{C}' = \{S_1', \ldots, S_{\ell'}'\}$ is a $(n, d-\kappa+1, t)$-cover, we have that there exists $S' \in \mathcal{C}'$ such that $T \subseteq S'$. Notice that $|S' \backslash T| = (d-\kappa+1) - t = \lambda$. Let us write $S' \backslash T = \{\mu_1, \ldots, \mu_\lambda\}$. By definition of $\overline{\mathcal{C}}$, for each $j \in \{1, \ldots, \lambda\}$ there exists $i_j \in \{1, \ldots, \ell\}$ such that $\overline{S}_{i_j} = S' \backslash \{\mu_j\}$. Notice that $T \subseteq \bigcap_{j=1}^{\lambda} \overline{S}_{i_j}$.

Let us write $Q(\mathsf{X}) = Q'(\mathsf{X}) + Q''(\mathsf{X})$, where $Q'(\mathsf{X}) = \sum_{i \in \{i_1, \ldots, i_\lambda\}} P_{\overline{S}_i}(\mathsf{X})$ and $Q''(\mathsf{X}) = \sum_{i \in \{1, \ldots, \ell\} \backslash \{i_1, \ldots, i_\lambda\}} P_{\overline{S}_i}(\mathsf{X})$. Property (1) above follows directly from the definition of $Q(\mathsf{X})$. Notice that the polynomials Q' and Q'' follow independent distributions, so to prove properties (2) and (3) it suffices to show they hold for the polynomial $Q'(\mathsf{X})$. Also, importantly, notice that for every $j \in \{1, \ldots, \lambda\}$, it holds that $S_{i_j} \cap T = \emptyset$ and therefore $(r_{i_j 1}, \ldots, r_{i_j \kappa} \| s_{i_j})$ are uniformly random in $(\mathsf{Im}(\phi))^\kappa \oplus R$. Due to this, $(P_{\overline{S}_{i_j}}(\beta_1), \ldots, P_{\overline{S}_{i_j}}(\beta_\kappa)) = (r_{i_j 1}, \ldots, r_{i_j \kappa}) \in_R (\mathsf{Im}(\phi))^\kappa$, which proves property (2).

For property (3), we claim that $(Q'(\mu_1), \ldots, Q'(\mu_\lambda))$ is uniformly random in R^λ. It is useful to observe that we can write each $P_{\overline{S}_{i_j}}(\mathbf{X})$ as $P_{\overline{S}_{i_j}}(\mathbf{X}) = s_{i_j} \cdot H_{i_j}(\mathbf{X}) + \sum_{a=1}^\kappa r_{i_j a} \cdot G_{\overline{S}_{i_j},a}(\mathbf{X})$. where all $G_{\overline{S}_{i_j},a}(\alpha_h) = H_{i_j}(\alpha_h) = 0$ for $h \in \overline{S}_i$, but also $H_{i_j}(\beta_h) = 0$ for $h \in \{1, \ldots, \kappa\}$, and equals 1 if $h = 0$; and finally $G_{\overline{S}_{i_j},\ell}(\beta_h) = 0$ for $h \in \{0, 1, \ldots, \kappa\} \setminus \{j\}$, and $G_{\overline{S}_{i_j},a}(\beta_j) = 1$. Notice that $\deg(G_{\overline{S}_{i_j},a}), \deg(H_{i_j}) \leq d+1$ as we only interpolate $G_{\overline{S}_{i_j},a}(\mathbf{X})$ and $H_{i_j}(\mathbf{X})$ at $d - \kappa + 1 + \kappa + 1 = d + 2$ points.

In addition to the above, we observe that for every $j, j' \in \{1, \ldots, \lambda\}$ it holds that $\mu_{j'} \in \overline{S}_{i_j}$ if $j \neq j'$ and, otherwise $\mu_{j'} \in S_{i_j}$. Therefore, $P_{\overline{S}_{i_j}}(\alpha_{\mu_{j'}}) = 0$ if $j \neq j'$. Otherwise, if $j = j'$, we have that $P_{\overline{S}_{i_j}}(\alpha_{\mu_j}) = s_{i_j} \cdot H_{i_j}(\alpha_{\mu_j}) + z_j$, where $z_j = \sum_{h=1}^\kappa r_{i_j h} \cdot G_{\overline{S}_{i_j},h}(\alpha_{\mu_j})$.

Importantly, since z_j is independent of s_{i_j}, and s_{i_j} is uniformly random, for Property (3) it suffices to show that $H_{i_j}(\alpha_{\mu_j})$ is invertible in R. By the definition of $H_{i_j}(\mathbf{X})$, we have $H_{i_j}(\mathbf{X}) = c_{i_j} \cdot \prod_{h \in \overline{S}_{i_j}}(x - \alpha_h) \cdot \prod_{h=1}^\kappa (x - \beta_h)$ with $H_{i_j}(\beta_0) = c_{i_j} \cdot \prod_{h \in \overline{S}_{i_j}}(\beta_0 - \alpha_h) \cdot \prod_{h=1}^\kappa (\beta_0 - \beta_h) = 1$. This implies that c_{i_j} is invertible in R. Combining with the fact that $\{\alpha_1, \ldots, \alpha_n, \beta_0, \beta_1, \ldots, \beta_\kappa\}$ is an exceptional set over R and $\mu_j \notin \overline{S}_{i_j}$ implies that

$$H_{i_j}(\alpha_{\mu_j}) = c_{i_j} \prod_{h \in \overline{S}_{i_j}} (\alpha_{\mu_j} - \alpha_h) \prod_{h=1}^\kappa (\alpha_{\mu_j} - \beta_h)$$

is invertible in R. This leads to the claim that $P_{\overline{S}_{i_j}}(\alpha_{\mu_j})$ distributes uniformly at random over R.

Putting the pieces together, we see then that $(Q(\alpha_{\mu_1}), \ldots, Q(\alpha_{\mu_\lambda}))$ is equal to $(s_{i_j} \cdot H_{i_j}(\alpha_{\mu_j}) + z_j)_{j=1}^\lambda$, which is in a 1-1 correspondence with $(s_{i_1}, \ldots, s_{i_\lambda})$, which is uniformly random in R^λ. This concludes the proof. $\square$

On the Amount of Seeds. An important metric for the efficiency of a PRSS solution is the amount of seeds that every party should hold. In our case, this corresponds to $(\ell'(d - \kappa + 1)(n - d + \kappa))/n$, where ℓ' is the size of the smallest $(n, d - \kappa + 1, t)$-cover. As noted in [3], there is not a closed expression for ℓ', but concrete lower and upper bounds are known in several cases. First, recall that $1 \leq \kappa \leq d - t + 1$. In the case in which $\kappa = d - t + 1$, we have that $d - \kappa + 1 = t$, and in this case the smallest (n, t, t)-cover is comprised of all possible subsets of size t, so $\ell' = \binom{n}{t}$.

For the case in which $\kappa < d - t + 1$, smaller covering designs can be obtained. For example, if $n = 72$, $t = 6$ and $d = 23$ (as we will see in Sect. 5.3, taking $d = 23 < 72/3 = n/3$ enables us to handle degree-3 correlations) and $d - \kappa + 1 = 18$ (so $\kappa = 6$), the best known size of a $(72, 18, 6)$-cover is $\ell' = 10092$.[4] Assuming 128-bit seeds, the average seed size per party becomes only ≈ 2.2Mb.

---

[4] Such covering design sizes can be found in https://www.dmgordon.org/cover/.

5.3   Non-interactive Correlation Generation

With the building blocks presented previously, we are ready to present our end-to-end protocol for the committee $\mathcal{P}$ to generate a sample from the degree-D correlation towards committee $\mathcal{Q}$. Recall that $R = \mathsf{GR}(p^k, \delta)$, and that $(\phi : \mathbb{Z}_{p^k}^r \to R, \psi : R \to \mathbb{Z}_{p^k}^r)$ is a degree-D RMFE. The correlation we aim at generating is $(\langle y_1 \rangle, \ldots, \langle y_m \rangle)$, where $y_i = F_i(\boldsymbol{x}) \in \mathbb{Z}_{p^k}$ for some degree-D polynomial F_i over $\mathbb{Z}_{p^k}$, and $\boldsymbol{x} \in \mathbb{Z}_{p^k}^\ell$ is uniformly random. Jumping ahead, due to the use of RMFEs and packed secret-sharing, our method not only produces one single sample from such distribution, but it actually generates multiple samples $(\langle y_{1jl} \rangle, \ldots, \langle y_{mjl} \rangle)$ for $j \in \{1, \ldots, \kappa\}$ and $l \in \{1, \ldots, r\}$.

We first introduce some preliminaries. Recall that $t < n/D$ is the number of corrupted parties in $\mathcal{P}$, and $d = \lfloor \frac{n-1}{D} \rfloor$, so $t \le d < n$. Also recall that $1 \le \kappa \le (d-t)+1$ is the amount of secrets packed. We denote by $\pi : R \to (\mathbb{Z}_{p^k})^\delta$ the natural bijection between R and δ-dimensional vectors over $\mathbb{Z}_{p^k}$. As before, we use $[\![\boldsymbol{x}]\!]_d = (z_1, \ldots, z_n)$ to denote Shamir secret-sharing of degree d of a secret $\boldsymbol{x} = (x_1, \ldots, x_\kappa) \in R^\kappa$, meaning there is a polynomial $f(\mathbf{X})$ over R of degree at most d such that $z_i = f(\alpha_i)$ for $i \in \{1, \ldots, n\}$ and $x_j = f(\beta_j)$ for $j \in \{1, \ldots, \kappa\}$, where $\{\alpha_1, \ldots, \alpha_n, \beta_1, \ldots, \beta_\kappa\}$ is an exceptional set over R. A simple but important property of packed secret-sharing we will make use of is that, if $[\![\boldsymbol{x}]\!]_{d_1} = (z_1, \ldots, z_n)$ and $[\![\boldsymbol{y}]\!]_{d_2} = (w_1, \ldots, w_n)$, then $[\![\boldsymbol{x} \star \boldsymbol{y}]\!]_{d_1+d_2} = (z_1 \cdot w_1, \ldots, z_n \cdot w_n)$, where $\star$ denotes component-wise product. This implies that, when the parties in $\mathcal{P}$ hold packed sharings, they can *locally* compute their product of their shares to obtain shares of the product of the underlying secrets, albeit with a larger degree.

For $j \in \{1, \ldots, \kappa\}$ and $h \in \{1, \ldots, q+1\}$ for some q, we let $\lambda_{q,j,h} \in R$ be the coefficient such that, for every polynomial $f(\mathbf{X})$ over R of degree at most q, it holds that $f(\beta_j) = \sum_{h=1}^{d+1} \lambda_{q,j,h} f(\alpha_h)$. These correspond to standard Lagrange coefficients used in polynomial interpolation. Given $c \in R$, we denote by $M_c \in \mathbb{Z}_{p^k}^{\delta \times \delta}$ the matrix that represents multiplication by c over $\mathbb{Z}_{p^k}^\delta$, that is, for every $x \in R$ it holds that $\pi(c \cdot x) = M_c \cdot \pi(x)$. Finally, we use $M_\phi \in \mathbb{Z}_{p^k}^{\delta \times r}$ and $M_\psi \in \mathbb{Z}_{p^k}^{r \times \delta}$ to denote the matrices representing the linear transformations $\pi \circ \phi : \mathbb{Z}_{p^k}^r \to \mathbb{Z}_{p^k}^\delta$ and $\psi \circ \pi^{-1} : \mathbb{Z}_{p^k}^\delta \to \mathbb{Z}_{p^k}^r$, respectively. In other words, $M_\phi \cdot \boldsymbol{x} = \pi(\phi(\boldsymbol{x}))$ for every $\boldsymbol{x} \in \mathbb{Z}_{p^k}^r$ and $M_\psi \cdot \boldsymbol{y} = \psi(\pi^{-1}(\boldsymbol{y}))$ for every $\boldsymbol{y} \in \mathbb{Z}_{p^k}^\delta$.

With this notation at hand, we are ready to introduce our protocol to generate the desired correlation.

Degree-D correlation generation

The following protocol enables the parties in $\mathcal{Q}$ to receive $\kappa \cdot r$ degree-D correlations $(\langle y_{1jl} \rangle, \ldots, \langle y_{mjl} \rangle)$ for $j \in \{1, \ldots, \kappa\}$ and $l \in \{1, \ldots, r\}$, generated non-interactively by the parties in $\mathcal{P}$. Assume $t \le d$. Let $d = \lfloor \frac{n-1}{D} \rfloor$, and $\kappa = (d-t)+1$. Let $F_i : \mathbb{Z}_{p^k}^\ell \to \mathbb{Z}_{p^k}$ be a polynomial over $\mathbb{Z}_{p^k}$ of degree $D_i \le D$.

Setup: The parties in $\mathcal{P}$ have the PRSS seeds from Thm 3.
Protocol: The parties proceed as follows:

1. The parties in $\mathcal{P}$ use PRSS to obtain non-interactively $([\![u_1]\!]_d, \ldots, [\![u_\ell]\!]_d)$, where each u_i is equal to $(u_{i1}, \ldots, u_{i\kappa}) \in R^\kappa$, with $u_{ij} = \phi(x_{ij}) \in R$, where $x_{ij} = (x_{ij1}, \ldots, x_{ijr}) \in (\mathbb{Z}_{p^k})^r$.
2. The parties in $\mathcal{P}$ locally compute $([\![v_1]\!]_{d \cdot D_1}, \ldots, [\![v_m]\!]_{d \cdot D_m})$, where $v_{ij} = F_i(u_{1j}, \ldots, u_{\ell j}) \in R$ for every $i \in \{1, \ldots, m\}$ and $j \in \{1, \ldots, \kappa\}$. Notice that here, F_i is treated as a polynomial over R. We denote $d_i = d \cdot D_i$ and $[\![v_i]\!]_{d_i} = (v_i^{(1)}, \ldots, v_i^{(n)})$.
3. For each $i \in \{1, \ldots, m\}$, each $P_h \in \mathcal{P}$ with $h \in \{1, \ldots, d_i + 1\}$ computes $w_i^{(h)} = \pi(v_i^{(h)}) \in (\mathbb{Z}_{p^k})^\delta$. Then P_h distributes shares $(\langle w_{i1}^{(h)} \rangle, \ldots, \langle w_{i\delta}^{(h)} \rangle)$ to the parties in $\mathcal{Q}$.
4. For each $i \in \{1, \ldots, m\}$, and for each $j \in \{1, \ldots, \kappa\}$, the parties in $\mathcal{Q}$ compute locally $(\langle z_{ij1} \rangle, \ldots, \langle z_{ij\delta} \rangle)^\mathsf{T} = \sum_{h=1}^{d_i+1} M_{\lambda_{d_i,j,h}} \cdot (\langle w_{i1}^{(h)} \rangle, \ldots, \langle w_{i\delta}^{(h)} \rangle)^\mathsf{T}$.
5. The parties in $\mathcal{Q}$ compute locally $(\langle y_{ij1} \rangle, \ldots, \langle y_{ijr} \rangle)^\mathsf{T} = M_\psi \cdot (\langle z_{ij1} \rangle, \ldots, \langle z_{ij\delta} \rangle)^\mathsf{T}$. Finally, the parties in $\mathcal{Q}$ output the $r \cdot \kappa$ correlations $(\langle y_{1jl} \rangle, \ldots, \langle y_{mjl} \rangle)$ for $j \in \{1, \ldots, \kappa\}$ and $l \in \{1, \ldots, r\}$.

Theorem 4. *At the end of the protocol above, the $r \cdot \kappa$ correlations $\{(\langle y_{1jl} \rangle, \ldots, \langle y_{mjl} \rangle)\}_{j=1,l=1}^{\kappa,r}$ that the parties in $\mathcal{Q}$ obtain follow the desired correlation distribution. Moreover, a passive adversary corrupting at most t parties in $\mathcal{Q}$ does not learn anything about the underlying secrets.*

Proof. Privacy follows straightforwardly from the properties of the PRSS construction, discussed in Sect. 5.2. Therefore, it only remains to be seen that the sharings output by the parties in $\mathcal{Q}$ follow the correct distribution.

We begin by observing that $(w_{i1}^{(h)}, \ldots, w_{i\delta}^{(h)}) = \pi(v_i^{(h)})$ by definition. Then, for each $i \in \{1, \ldots, m\}$ and $j \in \{1, \ldots, \kappa\}$, the definition of the matrix $M_{\lambda_{d_i,j,h}}$ implies that

$$
\begin{aligned}
(z_{ij1}, \ldots, z_{ij\delta})^\mathsf{T} &= \sum_{h=1}^{d_i+1} M_{\lambda_{d_i,j,h}} \cdot (w_{i1}^{(h)}, \ldots, w_{i\delta}^{(h)})^\mathsf{T} && \text{(by definition)} \\
&= \sum_{h=1}^{d_i+1} M_{\lambda_{d_i,j,h}} \cdot \pi(v_i^{(h)}) && \text{(observation above)} \\
&= \sum_{h=1}^{d_i+1} \pi(\lambda_{d_i,j,h} \cdot v_i^{(h)}) && \text{(definition of } M_{\lambda_{d_i,j,h}}) \\
&= \pi\left(\sum_{h=1}^{d_i+1} \lambda_{d_i,j,h} \cdot v_i^{(h)}\right) && \text{(linearity of } \pi)
\end{aligned}
$$

$$= \pi(v_{ij}) \qquad\qquad \text{(definition of } \{\lambda_{d_i,j,h}\}).$$

Now, notice that since $(y_{ij1}, \dots, y_{ijr})^\intercal = M_\psi \cdot (z_{ij1}, \dots, z_{ij\delta})^\intercal$ and $(z_{ij1}, \dots, z_{ij\delta}) = \pi(v_{ij})$ from the analysis above, the definition of M_ψ implies that $(y_{ij1}, \dots, y_{ijr}) = \psi(v_{ij})$. Furthermore, each $v_{ij} \in R$ for $i \in \{1, \dots, m\}$ and $j \in \{1, \dots, \kappa\}$ satisfies $v_{ij} = F_i(u_{1j}, \dots, u_{\ell j}) = F_i(\phi(\boldsymbol{x}_{1j}), \dots, \phi(\boldsymbol{x}_{\ell j}))$. Since F_i has degree $D_i \le D$, the properties of the degree-D RMFE (ϕ, ψ) imply that, for each $l \in \{1, \dots, r\}$, it holds that

$$\underbrace{(\psi(v_{ij}))_l}_{l\text{-th coordinate of } \psi(v_{ij}) \in \mathbb{Z}_{p^k}^r} = (\psi(F_i(\phi(\boldsymbol{x}_{1j}), \dots, \phi(\boldsymbol{x}_{\ell j}))))_l = F_i(x_{1jl}, \dots, x_{\ell jl}).$$

However, recall that $(y_{ij1}, \dots, y_{ijr}) = \psi(v_{ij})$. This implies that $(\psi(v_{ij}))_l$ is precisely equal to y_{ijl}, so $y_{ijl} = F_i(x_{1jl}, \dots, x_{\ell jl})$.

The above leads us to conclude that the outputs $(\langle y_{1jl}\rangle, \dots, \langle y_{mjl}\rangle)$ for $j \in \{1, \dots, \kappa\}$ and $l \in \{1, \dots, r\}$ follow the correct correlation. This is because, for every j, l, each y_{ijl} is equal to $F_i(\boldsymbol{r})$, where $\boldsymbol{r} = (x_{1jl}, \dots, x_{\ell jl}) \in \mathbb{Z}_{p^k}^\ell$, and by the properties of the PRSS, the distribution of this $\boldsymbol{r}$ is uniformly random over $\mathbb{Z}_{p^k}^\ell$, as required by the correlation. $\qquad\square$

Communication Complexity. In step 3 of our correlation generation protocol, for every $i \in \{1, \dots, m\}$, each party $P_h \in \mathcal{P}$ with $h \in \{1, \dots, D_i \cdot n + 1\}$ must distribute a total of δ shares to each of the N parties in $\mathcal{Q}$. Denoting by s the size in bits of each $\langle \cdot \rangle$-sharing corresponding to each party in $\mathcal{Q}$, this communication sums up to $\delta \cdot N \cdot s \cdot \sum_{i=1}^m (D_i \cdot d + 1)$. Since $\kappa \cdot r$ correlation samples are produced in total, and taking into account that $D_i \le D$ and $\kappa = (d-t)+1$ with $d = \lfloor \frac{n-1}{D} \rfloor$, the amortized total cost per correlation is

$$Ns \cdot \left(\frac{\delta \sum_{i=1}^m (D_i \cdot d + 1)}{\kappa r} \right) = O\left(Ns \left(\frac{\delta}{r} \right) \left(\frac{d}{\kappa} \right) (mD) \right) = O\left(Ns \left(\frac{\delta}{r} \right) \left(\frac{n}{\kappa} \right) m \right).$$

Notice now that we use the construction of degree-D RMFE (ϕ, ψ) in Corollary 5. This map yields $\frac{\delta}{r} \approx \frac{(1+2D)D}{3}$, which crucially, is *constant* in the number of parties n. In contrast, if we did not use our degree-D RMFEs, there would be an overhead that is logarithmic in n. For the factor n/κ, recall that κ is a term such that $1 \le \kappa \le \lfloor \frac{n-1}{D} \rfloor - t + 1$. In the extreme case in which $\kappa = 1$, the factor n/κ equals n, so we get a communication complexity that is *quadratic* in n, but we get the smallest possible covers. We can achieve *linear* communication complexity by taking $\kappa = \Omega(n)$, although this would increase the cover sizes. We refer the reader to the discussion in [3] for more details on known cover sizes.

Acknowledgments. The work of Hongqing Liu was supported in part by the National Key Research and Development Program under the grant 2022YFA1004900. The work of Chaoping Xing was supported in part by the National Key Research and Development Project under the Grant 2021YFE0109900 and by the National Natural Science

Foundation of China (NSFC) under the Grant 12031011. The work of Chen Yuan was supported in part by the National Natural Science Foundation of China under Grant 12101403.

References

1. Abdalla, M., Bourse, F., De Caro, A., Pointcheval, D.: Simple functional encryption schemes for inner products. In: Katz, J. (ed.) PKC 2015. LNCS, vol. 9020, pp. 733–751. Springer, Heidelberg (2015). https://doi.org/10.1007/978-3-662-46447-2_33

2. Abspoel, M., Cramer, R., Damgård, I., Escudero, D., Yuan, C.: Efficient information-theoretic secure multiparty computation over $\mathbb{Z}/p^k\mathbb{Z}$ via galois rings. In: Hofheinz, D., Rosen, A. (eds.) TCC 2019. LNCS, vol. 11891, pp. 471–501. Springer, Cham (2019). https://doi.org/10.1007/978-3-030-36030-6_19

3. Benhamouda, F., Boyle, E., Gilboa, N., Halevi, S., Ishai, Y., Nof, A.: Generalized pseudorandom secret sharing and efficient straggler-resilient secure computation. In: Nissim, K., Waters, B. (eds.) TCC 2021. LNCS, vol. 13043, pp. 129–161. Springer, Cham (2021). https://doi.org/10.1007/978-3-030-90453-1_5

4. Block, A.R., Maji, H.K., Nguyen, H.H.: Secure computation based on leaky correlations: high resilience setting. In: Katz, J., Shacham, H. (eds.) CRYPTO 2017. LNCS, vol. 10402, pp. 3–32. Springer, Cham (2017). https://doi.org/10.1007/978-3-319-63715-0_1

5. Boneh, D., Boyle, E., Corrigan-Gibbs, H., Gilboa, N., Ishai, Y.: Zero-knowledge proofs on secret-shared data via fully linear PCPs. In: Boldyreva, A., Micciancio, D. (eds.) CRYPTO 2019. LNCS, vol. 11694, pp. 67–97. Springer, Cham (2019). https://doi.org/10.1007/978-3-030-26954-8_3

6. Boyle, E., Couteau, G., Gilboa, N., Ishai, Y., Kohl, L., Scholl, P.: Efficient pseudorandom correlation generators: silent OT extension and more. In: Boldyreva, A., Micciancio, D. (eds.) CRYPTO 2019. LNCS, vol. 11694, pp. 489–518. Springer, Cham (2019). https://doi.org/10.1007/978-3-030-26954-8_16

7. Boyle, E., Gilboa, N., Ishai, Y., Nof, A.: Practical fully secure three-party computation via sublinear distributed zero-knowledge proofs. In: Proceedings of the 2019 ACM SIGSAC Conference on Computer and Communications Security, pp. 869–886 (2019)

8. Boyle, E., Gilboa, N., Ishai, Y., Nof, A.: Efficient fully secure computation via distributed zero-knowledge proofs. In: Moriai, S., Wang, H. (eds.) ASIACRYPT 2020. LNCS, vol. 12493, pp. 244–276. Springer, Cham (2020). https://doi.org/10.1007/978-3-030-64840-4_9

9. Cascudo, I., Cramer, R., Xing, C., Yuan, C.: Amortized complexity of information-theoretically secure MPC revisited. In: Shacham, H., Boldyreva, A. (eds.) CRYPTO 2018. LNCS, vol. 10993, pp. 395–426. Springer, Cham (2018). https://doi.org/10.1007/978-3-319-96878-0_14

10. Cascudo, I., Giunta, E.: On interactive oracle proofs for Boolean R1CS statements. In: Eyal, I., Garay, J. (eds.) Financial Cryptography and Data Security: 26th International Conference, FC 2022, Grenada, 2–6 May 2022, Revised Selected Papers, pp. 230–247. Springer, Cham (2022). https://doi.org/10.1007/978-3-031-18283-9_11

11. Cascudo, I., Gundersen, J.S.: A secret-sharing based MPC protocol for boolean circuits with good amortized complexity. In: Pass, R., Pietrzak, K. (eds.) TCC 2020. LNCS, vol. 12551, pp. 652–682. Springer, Cham (2020). https://doi.org/10.1007/978-3-030-64378-2_23

12. Cheon, J.H., Lee, K.: Limits of polynomial packings for $\mathbb{Z}_{p^k}$ and $\mathbb{F}_{p^k}$. In: Dunkelman, O., Dziembowski, S. (eds.) Advances in Cryptology – EUROCRYPT 2022: 41st Annual International Conference on the Theory and Applications of Cryptographic Techniques, Trondheim, 30 May– 3 June 2022, Proceedings, Part I, pp. 521–550. Springer, Cham (2022). https://doi.org/10.1007/978-3-031-06944-4_18

13. Cramer, R., Damgård, I., Escudero, D., Scholl, P., Xing, C.: SPD $\mathbb{Z}_{2^k}$: Efficient MPC mod 2^k for dishonest majority. In: Shacham, H., Boldyreva, A. (eds.) CRYPTO 2018. LNCS, vol. 10992, pp. 769–798. Springer, Cham (2018). https://doi.org/10.1007/978-3-319-96881-0_26

14. Cramer, R., Damgård, I., Ishai, Y.: Share conversion, pseudorandom secret-sharing and applications to secure computation. In: Kilian, J. (ed.) TCC 2005. LNCS, vol. 3378, pp. 342–362. Springer, Heidelberg (2005). https://doi.org/10.1007/978-3-540-30576-7_19

15. Cramer, R., Rambaud, M., Xing, C.: Asymptotically-good arithmetic secret sharing over $\mathbb{Z}/p^\ell\mathbb{Z}$ with strong multiplication and its applications to efficient MPC. In: Malkin, T., Peikert, C. (eds.) CRYPTO 2021. LNCS, vol. 12827, pp. 656–686. Springer, Cham (2021). https://doi.org/10.1007/978-3-030-84252-9_22

16. Damgård, I., Escudero, D., Frederiksen, T., Keller, M., Scholl, P., Volgushev, N.: New primitives for actively-secure MPC over rings with applications to private machine learning. In: 2019 IEEE Symposium on Security and Privacy (SP), pp. 1102–1120. IEEE (2019)

17. Demmler, D., Schneider, T., Zohner, M.: {Ad-Hoc} secure {Two-Party} computation on mobile devices using hardware tokens. In: 23rd USENIX Security Symposium (USENIX Security 14), pp. 893–908 (2014)

18. Diffie, W., Hellman, M.E.: New directions in cryptography. IEEE Trans. Inf. Theory **22**(6) (1976)

19. Escudero, D., Liu, H., Xing, C., Yuan, C.: Degree-d reverse multiplication-friendly embeddings: constructions and applications. Cryptology ePrint Archive, Paper 2023/173 (2023). https://eprint.iacr.org/2023/173

20. Escudero, D., Soria-Vazquez, E.: Efficient information-theoretic multi-party computation over non-commutative rings. In: Malkin, T., Peikert, C. (eds.) CRYPTO 2021. LNCS, vol. 12826, pp. 335–364. Springer, Cham (2021). https://doi.org/10.1007/978-3-030-84245-1_12

21. Escudero, D., Xing, C., Yuan, C.: More efficient dishonest majority secure computation over $\mathbb{Z}_{2^k}$ via Galois rings. In: Dodis, Y., Shrimpton, T. (eds.) Advances in Cryptology – CRYPTO 2022: 42nd Annual International Cryptology Conference, CRYPTO 2022, Santa Barbara, 15–18 August 2022, Proceedings, Part I, pp. 383–412. Springer, Cham (2022). https://doi.org/10.1007/978-3-031-15802-5_14

22. Garcia, A., Stichtenoth, H.: A tower of Artin-Schreier extensions of function fields attaining the Drinfeld-Vladut bound. Invent. Math. **121**, 211–222 (1995)
23. Gilboa, N., Ishai, Y.: Compressing cryptographic resources. In: Wiener, M. (ed.) CRYPTO 1999. LNCS, vol. 1666, pp. 591–608. Springer, Heidelberg (1999). https://doi.org/10.1007/3-540-48405-1_37
24. Gordon, S.D., Starin, D., Yerukhimovich, A.: The more the Merrier: reducing the cost of large scale MPC. In: Canteaut, A., Standaert, F.-X. (eds.) EUROCRYPT 2021. LNCS, vol. 12697, pp. 694–723. Springer, Cham (2021). https://doi.org/10.1007/978-3-030-77886-6_24
25. Huang, Y.: Practical secure two-party computation (2012)
26. Kales, D., Zaverucha, G.: Efficient lifting for shorter zero-knowledge proofs and post-quantum signatures. IACR Cryptol. ePrint Arch, p. 588 (2022)
27. Lyubashevsky, V., Peikert, C., Regev, O.: On ideal lattices and learning with errors over rings. In: Gilbert, H. (ed.) EUROCRYPT 2010. LNCS, vol. 6110, pp. 1–23. Springer, Heidelberg (2010). https://doi.org/10.1007/978-3-642-13190-5_1
28. Paillier, P.: Public-key cryptosystems based on composite degree residuosity classes. In: Stern, J. (ed.) EUROCRYPT 1999. LNCS, vol. 1592, pp. 223–238. Springer, Heidelberg (1999). https://doi.org/10.1007/3-540-48910-X_16
29. Polychroniadou, A., Song, Y.: Constant-overhead unconditionally secure multi-party computation over binary fields. In: Canteaut, A., Standaert, F.-X. (eds.) EUROCRYPT 2021. LNCS, vol. 12697, pp. 812–841. Springer, Cham (2021). https://doi.org/10.1007/978-3-030-77886-6_28
30. Rivest, R.L., Shamir, A., Adleman, L.: A method for obtaining digital signatures and public-key cryptosystems. Commun. ACM **21**(2), 120–126 (1978)
31. Smart, N.P., Tanguy, T.: TAAS: commodity MPC via triples-as-a-service. In: Proceedings of the 2019 ACM SIGSAC Conference on Cloud Computing Security Workshop, pp. 105–116 (2019)
32. Smart, N.P., Vercauteren, F.: Fully homomorphic encryption with relatively small key and ciphertext sizes. In: Nguyen, P.Q., Pointcheval, D. (eds.) PKC 2010. LNCS, vol. 6056, pp. 420–443. Springer, Heidelberg (2010). https://doi.org/10.1007/978-3-642-13013-7_25
33. Soria-Vazquez, E.: Doubly efficient interactive proofs over infinite and non-commutative rings. Cryptology ePrint Archive (2022)
34. Stichtenoth, H.: Algebraic Function Fields and Codes. Universitext, Springer (1993)
35. Wan, Z.-X.: Lectures on Finite Fields and Galois Rings. World Scientific Publishing Company (2003)

Adaptive Distributional Security for Garbling Schemes with $\mathcal{O}(|x|)$ Online Complexity

Estuardo Alpírez Bock[1] , Chris Brzuska[2], Pihla Karanko[2],
Sabine Oechsner[3(✉)] , and Kirthivaasan Puniamurthy[2]

[1] Xiphera, Espoo, Finland
[2] Aalto University, Espoo, Finland
[3] University of Edinburgh, Edinburgh, UK
s.oechsner@ed.ac.uk

Abstract. Garbling schemes allow to garble a circuit C and an input x such that $C(x)$ can be computed while hiding both C and x. In the context of adaptive security, an adversary specifies the input to the circuit *after* seeing the garbled circuit, so that one can pre-process the garbling of C and later only garble the input x in the *online phase*. Since the online phase may be time-critical, it is an interesting question how much information needs to be transmitted in this phase and ideally, this should be close to $|x|$. Unfortunately, Applebaum, Ishai, Kushilevitz, and Waters (AIKW, *CRYPTO 2013*) show that for some circuits, specifically PRGs, achieving online complexity close to $|x|$ is impossible with simulation-based security, and Hubáček and Wichs (HW, *ITCS 2015*) show that online complexity of maliciously secure 2-party computation needs to grow with the incompressibility entropy of the function. We thus seek to understand under which circumstances optimal online complexity is feasible despite these strong lower bounds.

Our starting point is the observation that lower bounds (only) concern *cryptographic* circuits and that, when an embedded secret is not known to the adversary (distinguisher), then the lower bound techniques do not seem to apply. Our main contribution is *distributional simulation-based security* (DSIM), a framework for capturing weaker, yet meaningful simulation-based (adaptive) security which does not seem to suffer from impossibility results akin to AIKW. We show that DSIM can be used to prove security of a distributed symmetric encryption protocol built around garbling. We also establish a bootstrapping result from DSIM-security for NC^0 circuits to DSIM-security for arbitrary polynomial-size circuits while preserving their online complexity.

1 Introduction

The garbled circuits approach to secure two-party computation goes back to a seminal work of Yao [44] and allows two parties to evaluate a circuit C on their private inputs. Bellare, Hoang and Rogaway (BHR) [12] suggest to abstract

© International Association for Cryptologic Research 2023
J. Guo and R. Steinfeld (Eds.): ASIACRYPT 2023, LNCS 14438, pp. 139–171, 2023.
https://doi.org/10.1007/978-981-99-8721-4_5

out the central building block behind this approach into a *garbling scheme*. A garbling scheme allows a party (called garbler) to *garble* a circuit C and input x into $\tilde{C}$ and $\tilde{x}$ such that another party (called evaluator) can derive $C(x)$ from $\tilde{C}$ and $\tilde{x}$. Selective (simulation-based) security of a garbling scheme is defined as comparison between real and simulated garbling: A garbling scheme is secure if no adversary can distinguish real garbling from the output of a simulator who is given only $C(x)$ and some leakage $\Phi(C)$ on C.

BHR further point out [11] that in some settings, a stronger adaptive security notion is needed, in which the adversary chooses the input x adaptively after seeing the garbled circuit $\tilde{C}$. In particular, the simulator works in two stages now and has to produce $\tilde{C}$ first given only $\Phi(C)$, and produces $\tilde{x}$ only after seeing $C(x)$. The second *adaptive* phase is often referred to as *online phase*, and the size of $|\tilde{x}|$ as the online complexity.

In the selective setting, the size of the garbled input $\tilde{x}$ can be linear in the size of x and independent of any other circuit dimension, e.g. $\lambda|x|$ in the case of Yao's garbling scheme and many of its variants (for security parameter λ). Ideally, the online complexity of adaptively secure garbling schemes would match this bound. Unfortunately, Applebaum, Ishai, Kushilevitz and Waters (AIKW [7]) show that adaptively secure garbling schemes for PRGs need online complexity $|C(x)|$, and adaptively secure constructions for general circuits indeed match this bound [4,11,24,29,32,34].

Circumventing the AIKW Lower Bound. Approaches to circumvent the AIKW lower bound include complexity leveraging over all possible values of x (with a superpolynomial-time simulator) and proving security in the programmable random oracle model [11]. Another line of work shows how to construct adaptively secure garbling schemes with low online complexity for restricted circuit classes [4,33,37] which contained in the class of all invertible circuits and, therefore, unfortunately exclude garbling most cryptographic functions with adaptive simulation-security.

Relaxing Garbling Scheme Security. In this work, we explore a new approach which seems suitable for cryptographic circuits. Concretely, we identify a relaxed (simulation-based) garbling scheme security notion that is not affected by the same lower bound and ask which circuit classes can be securely garbled with respect to it. Specifically, when garbling *cryptographic* circuits, some inputs are typically generated *honestly* and *secretly* and thus, in this case, the adversary does not know them, and the standard definition of adaptive simulation-based security seems too strong

1.1 Summary of Contributions

Generalizing Adaptive Garbling Scheme Security. Our main contribution is a security framework for garbling schemes, called *distributional simulation-based security (DSIM)* which relaxes the existing simulation-based adaptive security notion. The idea is to model realistic restrictions on the knowledge of adversary and simulator such as partially hiding the circuit (or inputs) that is garbled from the adversary. DSIM security bypasses the AIKW lower bound and our generalization of it as they are specific to the adversary's and simulator's (lack of) knowledge in the adaptive simulatability game.

We then show relations between DSIM and existing adaptive security notions, in particular that adaptive simulatability implies DSIM when suitably restricting the DSIM parameters. We further show how use a DSIM-secure garbling scheme to turn an authenticated encryption scheme (AE) into a two-party distributed encryption protocol. The AE scheme needs to be additionally secure under linear related-key (RK) attacks. PRFs secure under RK attacks can be achieved, e.g., based on key-homormorphic PRFs [16].

Bootstrapping Distributional Security. Moreover, we show a bootstrapping result for circuits which are *output indistinguishable*, i.e. for which there exists an efficient circuit sampler producing C such that $C(x)$ and $C(0^{|x|})$ are computationally indistinguishable for arbitrary adversarially chosen inputs x.

Theorem 1 (Informal). *Assume that garbling scheme* Gb *is DSIM-secure for garbling the class of output indistinguishable NC^0 circuits with online complexity α and assume IND-CPA secure symmetric encryption exists. Then, there exists a garbling scheme that is DSIM-secure for garbling the class of all polynomial size output indistinguishable circuits with online complexity α.*

Note that the bootstrapping result preserves the online complexity of the garbling scheme, and hence it suffices to construct a DSIM-secure garbling scheme for the class of output indistinguishable NC^0 circuits with online complexity $\mathcal{O}(|x|)$ to obtain a DSIM-secure garbling scheme for the class *all* output indistinguishable circuits with online complexity $\mathcal{O}(|x|)$. The construction of such a garbling scheme remains a very interesting open problem.

Further Results About Standard Simulation-Based Security. To complement our main contribution, we also include two smaller results within the context of the standard adaptive security notion. We generalize the AIKW lower bound and provide small improvements regarding the online complexity for garbling NC^1 circuits.

Bounding Online Complexity in Terms of (Pseudo-)entropy. AIKW show that garbling a pseudorandom generator (PRG) with adaptive security requires the online complexity of the garbling scheme to grow with the output size $|C(x)|$. Using a similar, more general idea, Hubácek and Wichs (HW [31]) show that the online complexity of maliciously 2-party computation is lower bounded by the Yao incompressibility entropy [42,45] of the computed function. HW also translates into a (slightly worse) analogous lower bound for the online complexity of adaptively secure garbling schemes: Assume that the 2PC protocol is realized by a garbling scheme combined with a maliciously secure two-party computation protocol to securely evaluate the input garbling (e.g., an oblivious transfer protocol in the case of a projective garbling scheme), one can deduct the communication complexity of the latter and obtains a lower bound for the online complexity of the garbling scheme.

We apply the HW approach to lower bound the online complexity of a garbling scheme by the Yao incompressibility entropy of the outputs of the garbled circuit and thereby obtain a direct proof of this result as well as slightly improved bounds compared to HW. The lower bound includes cryptographic functions such as PRGs, pseudorandom functions, and encryption schemes, all of which (when using suitable parameters) have higher incompressibility entropy than their input size. Note that the more standard notion of HILL pseudo-entropy (indistinguishabililty from a distribution with k bits of true entropy), if high, also implies high incompressibility entropy, but the converse is not necessarily true [27,30], whence HW and we state our results in terms of incompressibility entropy.

Theorem (Informal). *Let $C \leftarrow\$ \mathsf{Sam}_C(1^\lambda)$ be a distribution over circuits and $x \leftarrow\$ \mathsf{Sam}_x(C, 1^\lambda)$ be a distribution over inputs, depending on C. Then if Gb is a SIM_Φ-secure garbling scheme, its online complexity $|\tilde{x}|$ is greater or equal to the Yao incompressibility-entropy of $C(x)$ (minus a small constant) conditioned on $\Phi(C)$, where Φ is some function on the circuit.*

Here Φ is a function that depends on the flavour of SIM security we want to capture. Typically, Φ is just the topology of the circuit C, which would not contribute to the entropy, but it can also be a less trivial function.

Garbling Schemes with (almost) Optimal Online Complexity. Our final result revisits the question of constructing garbling schemes with (almost) optimal online complexity under existing security notions. To circumvent the AIKW lower bound, various works considered the weaker notion of *indistinguishability-based* adaptive security [11]. (For brevity, we will call this notion adaptive indistinguishability or adaptive IND security.) Table 1 summarizes the existing results, the circuit class they apply to, their online complexity and security assumptions. Note that any circuit with constant treewidth can be simulated in NC^1 [36], and that there exist NC^1 circuits that do not have low treewidth, e.g. Goldreich's PRG [26] is in $NC^0 \subseteq NC^1$ [5] but has high expansion and hence high treewidth. In fact, low treewidth already implies invertibility [14,15,22][1].

Concretely, we revisit the adaptively indistinguishable garbling scheme by Jafargholi, Scafuro and Wichs (JSW) [33] for garbling NC^1 circuits. The JSW construction has an online complexity that includes a small linear overhead in the *circuit depth*. We show how to modify the construction to remove this overhead.

Theorem (Informal). *Assuming the existence of one-way functions, there exists an adaptively indistinguishable garbling scheme for NC^1 circuits with online complexity $2\lambda|x|$.*

---

[1] See full version for details.

Table 1. Overview of adaptively indistinguishable garbling schemes with online complexity linear in the input size $|x|$, by circuit class for which security is known. d denotes the circuit depth and λ the security parameter.

	Circuit class	online complexity	assumption
Ananth & Sahai [4]	Arbitrary	$\mathsf{poly}(\lambda, |x|)$	iO + OWF
Kamath, Klein & Pietrzak [37]	Constant tw	$\lambda|x|$	OWF
Jafargholi, Scafuro & Wichs [33]	NC^1	$2\lambda|x| + 2\lambda^2 d$	OWF
this work	NC^1	$2\lambda|x|$	OWF

Jafargholi, Scafuro and Wichs further observed that an adaptively indistinguishable garbling scheme (IND) is also adaptively simulatable when restricting the garbling scheme to *efficiently invertible functions*. Adaptive IND security ensures that garblings of (C_0, x_0) and (C_1, x_1) are indistinguishable, even when x_0 and x_1 are chosen adaptively, as long as $C_0(x_0) = C_1(x_1)$. Since this equality requirement is rather restrictive, it is not obvious how to use IND security for cryptographic circuits in general. However, IND secure garbling should be useful to use with all techniques that are compatible with indistinguishability obfuscation (iO)as well, because iO requires that for all x, $C_0(x) = C_1(x)$ which implies the condition $C_0(x_0) = C_1(x_1)$ for $x = x_0 = x_1$. Therefore, IND security should be useful, e.g., for puncturable PRFs. We show the following:

Corollary (Informal). *Assuming the existence of one-way functions, there exists an adaptively simulatable garbling scheme for efficiently invertible NC^1 circuits with online complexity $2\lambda|x|$.*

1.2 Outline

In Sect. 2, we provide a technical overview over our main results. Section 3 provides background on garbling schemes and cryptographic primitives. Section 4 introduces our notion of distributional simulation-based security (DSIM). We show how to use the notion in Sect. 5 on the example of distributed symmetric encryption and prove a bootstrapping results for DSIM-secure garbling schemes in Sect. 6. Our adaptation of the HW incompressibility approach to generalize the AIKW lower bound is presented in Sect. 7. Finally, we show how to garble efficiently invertible NC^1 circuits with online complexity $2\lambda|x|$ based on one-way functions in Sects. 8.

2 Technical Overview

This section provides an overview of our core contribution, a relaxed simulation-based security notion for garbling schemes.

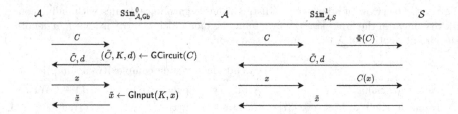

Fig. 1. Simulation-based security games $\mathrm{Sim}^0_{\mathcal{A},\mathsf{Gb}}$ and $\mathrm{Sim}^1_{\mathcal{A},\mathcal{S}}$ for garbling scheme Gb, adversary $\mathcal{A}$ and simulator $\mathcal{S}$, and circuit leakage function Φ.

2.1 Definining Distributional Simulation-Based (DSIM) Security

A quick recap of the existing adaptive simulation-based security notion [11]: Fig. 1 shows the real and ideal security games as interaction between adversary $\mathcal{A}$, the security game, and a simulator $\mathcal{S}$. In the ideal game $\mathrm{Sim}^1_{\mathcal{A},\mathcal{S}}$, $\mathcal{A}$ chooses (and hence knows) the circuit C and input x to be garbled, while the simulator has to simulate given leakage $\Phi(C)$ and output $C(x)$ only. Intuitively, this simultaneously captures strong privacy guarantees on the circuit and input.

This security notion gives the adversary the power to choose and learn the full circuit C *and* the input x to be garbled. The AIKW lower bound and our generalization effectively exploit an attack vector that is specific to this security notion: Since the adversary knows both C and x, they can compute the output $C(x)$ themselves and then compare it to the result of the garbled circuit evaluation. A simulator on the other hand is asked to simulate the garbled input given only $C(x)$. As AIKW and HW show, this simulation can simply not succeed if $C(x)|\Phi(C)$ produces too much (pseudo-)entropy. However, the main purpose of using a garbling scheme is to hide at least some information about either C or x, else one could evaluate $C(x)$ in the clear. For example when garbling a cryptographic function such as an encryption function $enc(k, \cdot)$ for secret key k, the key is typically sampled as part of the outer protocol. Hence only the garbler knows k. Thus when defining and proving security against a malicious evaluator, it suffices to prove security against an adversary (i.e. the evaluator) who does not know k and thus does not know the entire circuit C. As it suffices to consider a weaker adversary, we introduce two modifications to games $\mathrm{Sim}^0_{\mathcal{A},\mathsf{Gb}}$ and $\mathrm{Sim}^1_{\mathcal{A},\mathcal{S}}$:

Modification 1: Partially Hiding the Circuit from $\mathcal{A}$. Instead of $\mathcal{A}$ choosing C, the game is parameterized by a sampler Sam whose description is known to the adversary, leading to a *distributional* definition style. The sampler outputs a circuit C and circuit leakage lkg_C. The latter is given to both adversary and simulator and captures the partial information that $\mathcal{A}$ receives about C. An adversary may for instance be allowed to choose and learn which *class* of functions is garbled, e.g. the particular encryption scheme, but not the random choice of key. If on the other hand Sam samples from a distribution containing a single fixed circuit, then the adversary's knowledge is the same as in the existing security notion. We further augment the leakage so that it outputs a PPT oracle

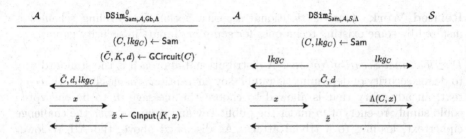

Fig. 2. Distributional simulation-based security games $\text{DSim}^0_{\text{Sam},\mathcal{A},\text{Gb},\Lambda}$ and $\text{DSim}^1_{\text{Sam},\mathcal{A},\mathcal{S},\Lambda}$ for garbling scheme Gb, sampler Sam, adversary $\mathcal{A}$, simulator $\mathcal{S}$, and simulator leakage Λ.

$\mathcal{O}$ which depends on the (secret) state of Sam. Oracle $\mathcal{O}$ models, e.g., encryption queries which depend on a secret key k that is also used in a circuit. Allowing such oracles supports composability, as we will see in Sect. 5, and it is similar to the interface which the ideal functionality exposes to the simulator in Canetti's universal composability framework [19]. For example, in our case this allows us to prove meaningful security of garbling an $-RK-AE secure encryption scheme; here the $-RK-AE security allows the adversary to make multiple queries to the encryption oracle, which would be impossible to model without our "free-form" oracle $\mathcal{O}$ that can contain the encryption oracle in this example use-case.

Modification 2: Relaxing the Consistency Requirement on $\mathcal{S}$. The relaxation to partial adversarial knowledge of C then makes it also natural to relax simulation requirements: If the partial knowledge an adversary gains about C and x does not allow to infer $C(x)$ but only some distribution of a possible output, then simulation may be with respect to this distribution instead of a particular output. We capture this observation through a new leakage function $\Lambda(C,x)$ which as before, is applied to obtain the simulator's input in the game's online phase. This leakage could be $C(x)$ (as in SIM), or empty (the other extreme) or anything in between, depending on what models the situation best (the less information we give to the simulator, the stronger the security guarantee by DSIM). In our $-RK-AE encryption example $\Lambda(C,x) = \emptyset$, since as long as the key remains unknown to the adversary, a uniformly random output is indistinguishable from $enc(k,x)$ for any x. So, the simulator can model the output as a uniformly random string, without knowing the actual output. Interestingly, this gives the security notion a semi-adaptive flavour as the simulator does not depend on the input x at all.

DSIM Security Games. Figure 2 shows a slightly simplified version of our new security games as interaction between adversary $\mathcal{A}$, the security game, and a simulator $\mathcal{S}$. Note that, while consistency is relaxed in the security definition, the garbling scheme is still expected to provide the usual correctness guarantees.

Related Work. Our distributional security notion for garbling schemes is inspired by some existing techniques for sampling inputs in security games.

Distributional Security Notions. A distributional approach is the standard way to define security of deterministic public-key encryption schemes [9]. In this context, an adversary that is allowed to choose the message m to be encrypted could simply re-encrypt m under the public key and compare with the challenge ciphertext, leading to a trivial attack. As discussed above, the AIKW lower bound is derived from a similar attack where the adversary can compare $C(x)$ to the output of the simulation. In both cases, the solution is to limit the adversary's knowledge, and define and prove security only for the scenario where the adversary knows the input *distribution*.

Another context where distributional security notions have been used before is zero knowledge [21,25,35,38]. Distributional zero knowledge and related notions relax the zero knowledge property by choosing the statement, i.e. the verifier's input to the computation, from an efficiently samplable distribution instead of universally quantifying over it. In the context of garbling schemes on the other hand, existing notions give the adversary the power to choose *all* inputs to the computation, and our relaxation to distributional security allows to hide some of the inputs from the adversary while maintaining a relaxed form of adversarial control over them.

Circuits Samplers. Our definitional style uses a circuit sampler which is reminiscent of the treatment of Universal Computational Extractors (UCE) as abstraction of keyed hash functions by Bellare, Hoang and Keelveedhi [10]. When using the DSIM definition with respect to the class of *output indistinguishable* circuits, one can view the DSIM notion as a notion of garbling schemes for *probabilistic functionalities* which is somewhat similar to the concept of probabilistic indistinguishability obfuscation (piO), a notion put forward by Canetti, Lin, Tessaro and Vaikuntanathan [20], where one should not be able to distinguish obfuscations of two computationally indistinguishable distributions $\mathcal{D}_0$ and $\mathcal{D}_1$. Our DSIM variant is different from piO in that DSIM is simulation-based and, since we study garbling schemes, the adversary only gets to see a *single* sample of the distribution.

2.2   Application: Distributed Symmetric Encryption

A distributed symmetric encryption protocol (DSE) allows multiple servers to jointly perform symmetric encryption of a message, such that each server holds only a *share* of the key. The notion was formally introduced by Agrawal, Mohassel, Mukherjee and Rindal (AMMR [2]) and a construction for an arbitrary number of parties based on distributed PRFs was proposed.

Distributed Symmetric encryption for arbitrary encryption schemes. For efficiency reasons, existing constructions have focused on distributed version of special-purpose encryption schemes [1,40]. AMMR point out that while DSE can in principle be achieved from general-purpose MPC (which would allow to distribute any existing encryption scheme), this approach would be prohibitively expensive. Nevertheless, such a construction would be preferable when the encryption scheme to be used in an application is already fixed. In this case, efficiency can be improved in other ways, e.g. through a message-independent preprocessing phase.

In Sect. 5, we show a construction for the two-server case based on a garbling scheme. The idea is to split encryption into two phases: First (and possibly in advance), the encryption circuit is garbled. Then in the online phase, only the message needs to be garbled. This preprocessing strategy means that the garbling scheme needs some flavour of adaptive security and we show that our new distributional simulation-based security notion suffices.

Remark. Encryption is typically length-preserving, so one could use a garbling scheme whose online complexity is proportional to its output length also. However, if the same message was, say, encrypted under t keys into t ciphertexts, then we would have a length-expanding circuit whose pseudo-entropy grows with t. For simplicity of exposition, we will focus on the single-key version.

We show security in a simplified and more restricted model in comparison to AMMR: We assume a two-server setting where only server S_2 makes encryption queries. Server S_2 acts as evaluator in the garbling scheme, and we focus on showing security against a corrupt S_2 as this is the more difficult case. Decryption is assumed to be performed by a trusted party. Finally, we restrict the adversary to multiple indirect encryption queries but only a single direct encryption query in the terminology of AMMR.

Protocol Overview. For two servers S_1 and S_2, the construction works as follows. Assume a symmetric authenticated encryption scheme se, a garbling scheme Gb with DSIM security with respect to output indistinguishable samplers such as authenticated encryption, and ideal oblivious transfer. In the basic construction, each server S_i holds an additive share k_i of the symmetric encryption key $k = k_1 \oplus k_2$. To encrypt a message m under se and k and randomness $r = r_1 \oplus r_2$, the servers act as follows: Server S_1 samples r_1 and garbles $\text{enc}(k_1 \oplus \cdot, \cdot; r_1 \oplus \cdot)$. Both servers then run an OT protocol to garble the missing inputs k_2, m, and r_2. We show that the AE security of the symmetric encryption scheme se still holds against a malicious server S_2. We need to assume related-key security of the AE against linear functions since the malicious server can choose an arbitrary key k_1 to be xored on k_2.

For the case of encrypting the message under t different keys $k^1, \ldots, k^t$, the output of the circuit would consist of t ciphertexts. To compress the size of S_2's input, the key shares k_2^j can be computed by a PRG as $k_2^j = \text{PRG}(s^j)$, and similarly for S_2's randomness. Then in the online phase, we only need to garble the two PRG seeds and the message, both of which are *independent* in size of t and hence the output size. See Sect. 5 for details on the single-key version of the protocol.

2.3   Bootstrapping NC⁰ to Polynomial-Size Circuits

In the realm of obfuscation, *bootstrapping* is an established technique to turn positive results for a *limited* class of circuits into a positive result for arbitrary polynomial-size circuits. The bootstrapping techniques in the context of obfuscation follow the randomized encoding approach by Applebaum, Ishai, Kushilevitz [6], see e.g. [3,23] for examples. Assume we can obfuscate low-depth circuits. Instead of directly obfuscating a given high-depth circuit $C(x)$ for inputs x, a randomized encoding function is applied to the circuit. The result $\tilde{C}(x;r)$ is a new circuit that outputs a randomized encoding of $C(x)$. $\tilde{C}(x;r)$ uses additional randomness r and is chosen such that for random r, $\tilde{C}(x;r)$ does not leak more information than $y = C(x)$. If the encoding function itself has low depth, then $\tilde{C}(x;r)$ can now be obfuscated, and y can be recovered from $\tilde{C}(x;r)$ via a (high-depth, public) decoding function Dec.

Since randomized encodings and garbling schemes are different abstractions of the same underlying idea, it is natural to ask if the randomized encodings bootstrapping technique can be used to bootstrap adaptive security of garbling schemes from low-depth circuits to arbitrary polynomial-size circuits. That is, instead of directly garbling a circuit $C(x)$, we could try to (outer) garble the (inner) garbling function $\tilde{C}(x;r) := [\mathsf{GCircuit}(C(\cdot);r), \mathsf{GInput}(x)]$ with explicit hardcoded randomness r. Now, if the inner garbling scheme produces a low depth circuit $\tilde{C}$, the outer garbling scheme only needs to be secure for low-depth circuits, and, the inner garbling scheme only needs to be selectively secure, not adaptively. Now, the inner garbling scheme $\tilde{C}$ can be simply, e.g., Yao's garbling scheme, which is useful for two reasons: (1) Yao can be proven selectively secure assuming it uses \$-IND-CPA symmetric encryption [12,18,39] and (2) Yao's garbling can be implemented in constant depth (see Lemma 1 for details).

However, proving SIM security in this setting is infeasible for the following reason. When we try to reduce the SIM security of the combined (garbling of garbling) garbling scheme to the SIM security of the outer garbling scheme, the adversarial evaluator chooses the circuit to be garbled, in this case, the inner garbling function $\tilde{C}(.;r)$ *with the hardcoded randomness r*. Adversary knowing r trivially compromises the security of the inner garbling.

Luckily, our DSIM security notion precisely allows to circumvent the randomness issue by dividing the adversary into two parts that do not share a state: first part samples the circuit from a suitable *output indistinguishable* distribution (e.g. \$-IND-CPA secure encryption with a uniformly random key, see Definition 8 for how exactly we define the natural property of output indistinguishability) and the second adversary interacts with the garbler. Hence, we can prove Theorem 1.

3   Preliminaries

All algorithms take as input the security parameter 1^λ. We write it explicitly for some algorithms, but leave it implicit for most algorithms. $a \leftarrow \mathsf{A}(x)$ assigns the result of an execution of the deterministic algorithm A on input x to variable *a. a ←\$ A(x)* denotes the execution of a *randomized* algorithm. *a||b* denotes the concatenation of two bit strings *a* and *b*. $A_2 \circ A_1$ denotes the composition of two algorithms in the form $A_2(A_1(.))$. We often write $\mathcal{A}^{O_1, O_2}$ for an adversary accessing oracle O_1 and O_2 and sometimes write $\mathcal{A}^{O_1}_{O_2}$ for conciseness. We sometimes use the notation $\mathcal{A} \overset{O_1,..,O_t}{\rightsquigarrow} G^b$ inspired from state-separating proofs [17] to say that the adversary $\mathcal{A}$ is the main procedure who has access to oracles $O_1, .., O_t$ of a distinguishing game G^b. $\Pr\left[1 = \mathcal{A} \overset{O_1,..,O_t}{\rightsquigarrow} G^b\right]$ then refers to the probability that the adversary $\mathcal{A}$, after interacting with the oracles $O_1, .., O_t$ of G^b returns 1. We like this notation, because it makes both the name of the game and the adversary's oracle explicit, while the standard oracle subscript notation $\mathcal{A}^{O_1,...,O_t}$ only contains the oracles (but not the name of the game), and the experiment notation $G^b_{\mathcal{A}}$ only contains the name of the game (but not the oracles).

3.1   Cryptographic Primitives

For a symmetric encryption scheme se, \$-IND-CPA-security captures that ciphertexts are indistinguishable from random strings of the same length. The related-key authenticated encryption security game \$-RK-AE provides decryption queries in addition and allows adversarially chosen linear offsets on the key. Related-key security has been introduced by Bellare and Kohno [13].

$\text{\$-IND-CPA}^b_{se}(1^\lambda)$	$\text{\$-RK-AE}^b_{se}(1^\lambda)$	
$\text{ENC}(m)$	$\text{ENC}(m, \Delta)$	$\text{DEC}(c, \Delta)$
if $k = \bot$	if $k = \bot$	if $b = 1$
$\quad k \leftarrow\text{\$} \{0,1\}^\lambda$	$\quad k \leftarrow\text{\$} \{0,1\}^\lambda$	$\quad$ **return** $\bot$
$c \leftarrow\text{\$} \text{enc}(k, m)$	$c \leftarrow\text{\$} \text{enc}(k \oplus \Delta, m)$	if $k = \bot$
	$S \leftarrow S \cup \{c\}$	$\quad k \leftarrow\text{\$} \{0,1\}^\lambda$
if $b = 1$	if $b = 1$	**assert** $c \notin S$
$\quad c \leftarrow\text{\$} \{0,1\}^{|c|}$	$\quad c \leftarrow\text{\$} \{0,1\}^{|c|}$	$m \leftarrow \text{dec}(k \oplus \Delta, c)$
return c	**return** c	**return** m

Fig. 3. Games $\text{\$-IND} - \text{CPA}^b_{se}(1^\lambda)$ and $\text{\$-RK} - \text{AE}^b_{se}(1^\lambda)$.

Definition 1 (\$-IND-CPA and \$-RK-AE Security). *A symmetric encryption scheme* se = (enc, dec) *is indistinguishable under chosen plaintext attacks (\$-IND-CPA) if for all PPT adversaries* $\mathcal{A}$*, the advantage* $\text{Adv}^{\text{\$-IND}-\text{CPA}}_{se,\mathcal{A}}(1^\lambda) :=$

$$\left|\Pr\left[1 = \mathcal{A}(1^\lambda) \overset{\text{ENC}}{\longrightarrow} \text{\$-IND} - \text{CPA}^0(1^\lambda)\right] - \Pr\left[1 = \mathcal{A}(1^\lambda) \overset{\text{ENC}}{\longrightarrow} \text{\$-IND} - \text{CPA}^1(1^\lambda)\right]\right|$$

is negligible in λ*.* se *is authenticated encryption under linear related key attacks if for all PPT adversaries* $\mathcal{A}$*, the advantage* $\text{Adv}^{\text{\$-RK}-\text{AE}}_{se,\mathcal{A}}(1^\lambda) :=$

$$\left|\Pr\left[1 = \mathcal{A}(1^\lambda) \overset{\text{ENC,DEC}}{\longrightarrow} \text{\$-RK} - \text{AE}^0(1^\lambda)\right] - \Pr\left[1 = \mathcal{A}(1^\lambda) \overset{\text{ENC,DEC}}{\longrightarrow} \text{\$-RK} - \text{AE}^1(1^\lambda)\right]\right|$$

is negligible in λ*. See Fig. 3 for the security games.*

3.2 Garbling Schemes

Definition 2 (Garbling scheme). *A Garbling scheme* Gb *consists of three PPT algorithms* (GCircuit, GInput, GEval) *with the following syntax:*

- $(\tilde{C}, K, d) \leftarrow_\$ \mathsf{GCircuit}(C)$: *the garbling algorithm takes as input a circuit* $C : \{0,1\}^n \rightarrow \{0,1\}^m$, *and outputs a garbled circuit* $\tilde{C}$, *keys* K *and output decoding information* d. *m and n are polynomials in λ.*
- $\tilde{x} \leftarrow_\$ \mathsf{GInput}(K, x)$: *the input garbling algorithm takes an input* $x \in \{0,1\}^n$ *and the keys K and outputs an encoding of the input $\tilde{x}$.*
- $y \leftarrow \mathsf{GEval}(\tilde{C}, \tilde{x}, d)$: *the evaluation algorithm takes as input the garbled circuit, a garbled input, the output encoding information d and returns a value* $y \in \{0,1\}^m$, *where m is the output length of C.*

Correctness of the garbling scheme holds if for any λ, any circuit C and any input $x \in \{0,1\}^n$ we have

$$\Pr\Big[C(x) = \mathsf{GEval}(\tilde{C}, \tilde{x}, d)\Big] = 1 - \mathsf{negl}(\lambda),$$

where $(\tilde{C}, K, d) \leftarrow_\$ \mathsf{GCircuit}(C)$, $\tilde{x} \leftarrow_\$ \mathsf{GInput}(K, x)$.

We first define *selective simulation security*, where the adversary chooses circuit C and input x at the same time. We define adaptive garbling scheme security in Sect. 4, where we compare it to the DSIM definition, which we propose.

$$\underline{\mathsf{SelSim}^0_{\mathcal{A},\mathsf{Gb}}(1^\lambda)}$$
$(C, x, \mathsf{st}) \leftarrow_\$ \mathcal{A}(1^\lambda)$
$(\tilde{C}, K, d) \leftarrow_\$ \mathsf{GCircuit}(C)$
$\tilde{x} \leftarrow_\$ \mathsf{GInput}(K, x)$
$b' \leftarrow_\$ \mathcal{A}(\tilde{C}, \tilde{x}, d, \mathsf{st})$
return b'

$$\underline{\mathsf{SelSim}^1_{\mathcal{A},\mathcal{S}}(1^\lambda)}$$
$(C, x, \mathsf{st}) \leftarrow_\$ \mathcal{A}(1^\lambda)$
$(\tilde{C}, \tilde{x}, d) \leftarrow_\$ \mathcal{S}(\Phi(C), C(x))$
$b' \leftarrow_\$ \mathcal{A}(\tilde{C}, \tilde{x}, d, \mathsf{st})$
return b'

Fig. 4. Experiments $\mathsf{SelSim}^0_{\mathcal{A},\mathsf{Gb}}$ and $\mathsf{SelSim}^1_{\mathcal{A},\mathcal{S}}$.

Definition 3 (SelSim security). *Let Φ be a leakage function. We say that* Gb *is **selectively simulation secure** (SelSim) if for any PPT adversary $\mathcal{A}$ there exists a PPT simulator $\mathcal{S}$ such that*

$$\mathsf{Adv}^{\mathsf{SelSim}}_{\mathcal{A},\mathcal{S},\mathsf{Gb}}(1^\lambda) := |\Pr[1 = \mathsf{SelSim}^0_{\mathcal{A},\mathcal{S},\mathsf{Gb}}] - \Pr[1 = \mathsf{SelSim}^1_{\mathcal{A},\mathcal{S}}]| = \mathsf{negl}(\lambda),$$

where experiments $\mathsf{SelSim}^0_{\mathcal{A},\mathsf{Gb}}$ *and* $\mathsf{SelSim}^1_{\mathcal{A},\mathcal{S}}$ *are specified in Fig. 4.*

4 Distributional Simulation-Based Security (DSIM)

In this section, we first define the simulation-based and indistinguishability flavours of adaptive security and then present our new definition of adaptive distributional simulation-based security (DSIM) for garbling schemes.

$\mathrm{Sim}^0_{\mathcal{A},\mathsf{Gb}}(1^\lambda)$	$\mathrm{Sim}^1_{\mathcal{A},\mathcal{S}}(1^\lambda)$	$\mathrm{Ind}^b_{\mathcal{A},\mathsf{Gb}}(1^\lambda)$
$(C,\mathrm{st}) \leftarrow\!\!\$\ \mathcal{A}(1^\lambda)$	$(C,\mathrm{st}) \leftarrow\!\!\$\ \mathcal{A}(1^\lambda)$	$(C_0,C_1,\mathrm{st}) \leftarrow\!\!\$\ \mathcal{A}(1^\lambda)$
$(\tilde{C},K,d) \leftarrow\!\!\$\ \mathsf{GCircuit}(C)$	$(\tilde{C},d,\mathrm{st}_\mathcal{S}) \leftarrow\!\!\$\ \mathcal{S}(\Phi(C))$	$(\tilde{C},K,d) \leftarrow\!\!\$\ \mathsf{GCircuit}(C_b)$
$(x,\mathrm{st}') \leftarrow\!\!\$\ \mathcal{A}(\tilde{C},d,\mathrm{st})$	$(x,\mathrm{st}') \leftarrow\!\!\$\ \mathcal{A}(\tilde{C},d,\mathrm{st})$	$(x_0,x_1,\mathrm{st}') \leftarrow\!\!\$\ \mathcal{A}(\tilde{C},d,\mathrm{st})$
$\tilde{x} \leftarrow\!\!\$\ \mathsf{GInput}(K,x)$	$\tilde{x} \leftarrow\!\!\$\ \mathcal{S}(C(x),\mathrm{st}_\mathcal{S})$	$\tilde{x} \leftarrow\!\!\$\ \mathsf{GInput}(K,x_b)$
$b' \leftarrow\!\!\$\ \mathcal{A}(\tilde{x},\mathrm{st}')$	$b' \leftarrow\!\!\$\ \mathcal{A}(\tilde{x},\mathrm{st}')$	$b' \leftarrow\!\!\$\ \mathcal{A}(\tilde{x},\mathrm{st}')$
return b'	**return** b'	**return** b'

$\mathrm{DSim}^0_{\mathsf{Sam},\mathcal{A},\mathsf{Gb},\Lambda,\mathsf{Filter}}(1^\lambda)$	$\mathrm{DSim}^1_{\mathsf{Sam},\mathcal{A},\mathcal{S},\Lambda,\mathsf{Filter}}(1^\lambda)$
$(C,\mathrm{lkg}_C,\mathcal{O}) \leftarrow\!\!\$\ \mathsf{Sam}(1^\lambda)$	$(C,\mathrm{lkg}_C,\mathcal{O}) \leftarrow\!\!\$\ \mathsf{Sam}(1^\lambda)$
$(\tilde{C},K,d) \leftarrow\!\!\$\ \mathsf{GCircuit}(C)$	$(\tilde{C},d,\mathrm{st}_\mathcal{S}) \leftarrow\!\!\$\ \mathcal{S}^{\mathcal{O}}(\mathsf{Filter}(\mathrm{lkg}_C))$
$(x,\mathrm{st}_\mathcal{A}) \leftarrow\!\!\$\ \mathcal{A}^{\mathcal{O}}(\tilde{C},d,\mathrm{lkg}_C)$	$(x,\mathrm{st}_\mathcal{A}) \leftarrow\!\!\$\ \mathcal{A}^{\mathcal{O}}(\tilde{C},d,\mathrm{lkg}_C)$
$\tilde{x} \leftarrow\!\!\$\ \mathsf{GInput}(K,x)$	$\tilde{x} \leftarrow\!\!\$\ \mathcal{S}^{\mathcal{O}}(\Lambda(\mathrm{st}_\mathcal{A}),\mathrm{st}_\mathcal{S})$
$b' \leftarrow\!\!\$\ \mathcal{A}^{\mathcal{O}_{C(x)}}(\tilde{x},\mathrm{st}_\mathcal{A})$	$b' \leftarrow\!\!\$\ \mathcal{A}^{\mathcal{O}_{\tilde{C}(\tilde{x})}}(\tilde{x},\mathrm{st}_\mathcal{A})$
return b'	**return** b'

Fig. 5. Experiments $\mathrm{Ind}^b_{\mathcal{A},\mathsf{Gb}}$, $\mathrm{Sim}^0_{\mathcal{A},\mathsf{Gb}}$, $\mathrm{Sim}^1_{\mathcal{A},\mathcal{S}}$, $\mathrm{DSim}^0_{\mathsf{Sam},\mathcal{A},\mathsf{Gb},\Lambda,\mathsf{Filter}}(1^\lambda)$ and $\mathrm{DSim}^1_{\mathsf{Sam},\mathcal{A},\mathcal{S},\Lambda,\mathsf{Filter}}(1^\lambda)$.

Definition 4 (Adaptive SIM security). *Let Φ be a leakage function. We say that* Gb *is adaptively SIM$_\Phi$-secure if for any PPT adversary $\mathcal{A}$ there exists a PPT simulator $\mathcal{S}$ such that*

$$\mathsf{Adv}^{\mathsf{Sim}}_{\mathcal{A},\mathcal{S},\mathsf{Gb}}(1^\lambda) := |\Pr[1 = \mathrm{Sim}^0_{\mathcal{A},\mathcal{S},\mathsf{Gb}}] - \Pr[1 = \mathrm{Sim}^1_{\mathcal{A},\mathcal{S}}]| = \mathsf{negl}(\lambda),$$

where experiments $\mathrm{Sim}^0_{\mathcal{A},\mathsf{Gb}}$ and $\mathrm{Sim}^1_{\mathcal{A},\mathcal{S}}$ are specified in Fig. 5.

Definition 5 (Adaptive IND security). *We say that* Gb *is **adaptively IND-secure** if for any PPT adversary $\mathcal{A}$ which queries circuits C_0 and C_1 with equal input length and inputs x_0 and x_1 such that $C_0(x_0) = C_1(x_1)$ and $\Phi(C_0) = \Phi(C_1)$, there exists a negligible function $\mathsf{negl}(\lambda)$ such that:*

$$\mathsf{Adv}^{\mathsf{Ind}}_{\mathcal{A},\mathsf{Gb}}(1^\lambda) := |\Pr[1 = \mathrm{Ind}^0_{\mathcal{A},\mathsf{Gb}}] - \Pr[1 = \mathrm{Ind}^1_{\mathcal{A},\mathsf{Gb}}]| = \mathsf{negl}(\lambda),$$

where the experiment $\mathrm{Ind}^b_{\mathcal{A},\mathsf{Gb}}$ is specified in Fig. 5.

Definition 6 (Sampler classes). *A class of samplers $\mathcal{C}$ is a set of PPT adversaries* Sam *such that $(C, lkg_C, \mathcal{O}) \leftarrow\!\!\$\ \mathsf{Sam}(1^\lambda)$.*

Definition 7 (Adaptive distributional SIM security (DSIM).) *Let $\mathcal{C}$ be a sampler class and Λ be a leakage-function. Garbling scheme* Gb *is $DSim_{\Lambda,\mathsf{Filter}}[\mathcal{C}]$-secure if for any PPT* Sam $\in \mathcal{C}$ *and any PPT $\mathcal{A}$, there exists a PPT simulator $\mathcal{S}$ such that* $\mathsf{Adv}^{\mathsf{DSim}}_{\mathsf{Sam},\mathcal{A},\mathcal{S},\mathsf{Gb}}(1^\lambda) :=$

$$\left|\Pr\left[1 = \text{DSim}^0_{\text{Sam},\mathcal{A},\text{Gb},\Lambda,\text{Filter}}(1^\lambda)\right] - \Pr\left[1 = \text{DSim}^1_{\text{Sam},\mathcal{A},\mathcal{S},\Lambda,\text{Filter}}(1^\lambda)\right]\right|$$

is negligible, where Fig. 5 defines the experiments $\text{DSim}^0_{\text{Sam},\mathcal{A},\text{Gb},\Lambda,\text{Filter}}(1^\lambda)$ *and* $\text{DSim}^1_{\text{Sam},\mathcal{A},\mathcal{S},\Lambda,\text{Filter}}(1^\lambda)$.

In the above DSIM definition lkg_C could be e.g. the topology of the circuit C (to match the SIM definition). Alternatively, if we are garbling e.g. an encryption scheme with the key hardcoded in the circuit C, then lkg_C could be the circuit C without the hardcoded random key. $\mathcal{O}$ is a (possibly stateful) PPT oracle which might be, for example, an encryption oracle which depends on the key k embedded into C, $\mathcal{O}_{C(x)}$ might additionally depend on $C(x)$, e.g., when forbidding to send $C(x)$ to a decryption oracle, see Sect. 5 for an example. See Sect. 2.1 for more intuition behind the different parameters.

In the DSIM definition, the grey parameters (Λ, Filter) are optional and can be ignored (i.e. Filter can be thought of as identity and Λ as empty) when reading this paper, that is, they are not needed for understanding the bootstrapping proof or DENC example. They are included just as an example on how to extend the definition and to draw connection to SIM definition.

Remark on the Optional Parameters. W.l.o.g. we consider that $\text{st}_\mathcal{A}$ contains variables for lkg_C and x, and, if lkg_C allows to compute C, then we also assume that w.l.o.g., lkg_C and $\text{st}_\mathcal{A}$ contain a variable for C which contains the correct value. This will later allow us to discuss specific leakage functions.

In the special case when the sampler leaks $\text{lkg}_C := C$ and $\Lambda(\text{st}_\mathcal{A}) = C(x)$, SIM implies DSIM, because the adversary has slightly less information in DSIM than in SIM (since it does not know the randomness used for sampling), and additionally, the simulator $\mathcal{S}$ is stronger in DSIM.

Theorem 2 (SIM implies DSIM). *Let Φ be a polynomial-time computable leakage function. If a garbling scheme* Gb *is* SIM_Φ-*secure, then* Gb *is* $DSim_{\Lambda,\text{Filter}}[\mathcal{C}]$-*secure, where* $\mathcal{C} = \{PPT\ \text{Sam} : (C, lkg_C := C) \leftarrow\!\!\$\ \text{Sam}\}$, $\Lambda(\text{st}_\mathcal{A}) = C(x)$ *and* Filter(lkg_C) *is such that* $\Phi(lkg_C)$ *can be computed given* Filter(lkg_C).

Proof. Let Gb be a SIM_Φ-secure garbling scheme. Assume towards contradiction that there is Sam $\in \mathcal{C}$ and PPT $\mathcal{A}$ s.t. for all PPT $\mathcal{S}$ $\text{Adv}^{\text{DSim}}_{\text{Sam},\mathcal{A},\mathcal{S},\text{Gb}}(1^\lambda)$ is non-negligible. Define the first stage of the SIM-adversary as $\mathcal{A}'(1^\lambda) := \text{Sam}(1^\lambda)$ and $\mathcal{A}'$ is $\mathcal{A}$ for all further stages. Let $\mathcal{S}'$ be the simulator ensured by SIM-security such that $\text{Adv}^{\text{Sim}}_{\mathcal{A}',\mathcal{S}',\text{Gb}}(1^\lambda)$ is negligible.

Now, define the first stage simulator as $\mathcal{S}(\text{Filter}(\text{lkg}_C)) = \mathcal{S}'(\Phi(\text{lkg}_C))$ and the second stage simulator as $\mathcal{S}(\cdot,\cdot) := \mathcal{S}'(\cdot,\cdot)$ and $\mathcal{A}'$ is $\mathcal{A}$ for all other inputs. Now $\text{Adv}^{\text{Sim}}_{\mathcal{A}',\mathcal{S}',\text{Gb}}(1^\lambda) = \text{Adv}^{\text{DSim}}_{\text{Sam},\mathcal{A},\mathcal{S},\text{Gb}}(1^\lambda)$, and we reached a contradiction. □

We can also recover the other direction, DSIM implies SIM, if we choose lkg_C to be the sampler's full state and choose Filter$(\text{lkg}_C) = \Phi(C)$ and $\Lambda(\text{st}_\mathcal{A}) = C(x)$.

Note however, that the core difference between SIM and DSIM is the idea of *sampler classes* which *restrict* the information lkg which is passed from Sam to $\mathcal{A}$.[2] Recall that this restriction models that in garbling scheme applica-tion such as private func-

$$
\begin{array}{l}
\underline{\mathsf{Sam}(1^\lambda)} \\[4pt]
r \leftarrow\!\!\$\, \{0,1\}^{p(\lambda)} \\
C_r \leftarrow C_\lambda(.,r) \\
(\mathrm{lkg}_{C_r}, \mathcal{O}) \leftarrow \mathsf{Sam}_{\mathrm{leak}}(r) \\
\mathbf{return}\ C_r, \mathrm{lkg}_{C_r}, \mathcal{O}
\end{array}
$$

$$
\begin{array}{l}
\underline{\mathsf{Out}^b_{\mathsf{Sam},\mathcal{D}}(1^\lambda)} \\[4pt]
C_r, \mathrm{lkg}_{C_r}, \mathcal{O} \leftarrow\!\!\$\, \mathsf{Sam}(1^\lambda) \\
(x_0, \mathrm{st}) \leftarrow\!\!\$\, \mathcal{D}^{\mathcal{O}}(1^\lambda, \mathrm{lkg}_{C_r}) \\
x_1 \leftarrow 0^{|x_0|} \\
b^* \leftarrow\!\!\$\, \mathcal{D}^{\mathcal{O}_{C_r(x_b)}}(C_r(x_b), \mathrm{st}) \\
\mathbf{return}\ b^*
\end{array}
$$

Fig. 6. Output indistinguishability

tion evaluation, the party choosing the input might have *some* information about the function to be evaluated, but not *all* information—otherwise one party could simply send its function to the other party. Of particular interest to us are circuits with embedded *cryptographic keys* which make the output of the evaluated circuit *indistinguishable* from a distribution which could have been chosen *independently* of the input to the circuit, as, e.g., in IND-CPA-secure encryption where an encryption of a message m is indistinguishable from an encryption of $0^{|m|}$. To be useful for garbling security, we need the indistinguishable distribution to be generated by a circuit of the same size. Therefore, we demand that the function distribution consists of a fixed circuit C for which only the *randomness* is sampled, i.e., $C := C(\cdot; r)$ is a circuit with randomness r hardcoded into it.

Definition 8 (Output Indistinguishable Sampler). *We define the class $\mathcal{C}^{out}$ of output indistinguishable samplers as the set of PPT Sam such that*

Fixed circuit *there exists a circuit $C = (C_\lambda)_\lambda$, polynomial p and PPT Sam_{leak} such that Sam can be written as in Fig. 6 (left), and*
Output indistinguishability *for all PPT distinguishers $\mathcal{D}$, the advantage*

$$
\mathsf{Adv}^{\mathsf{Out}}_{\mathsf{Sam},\mathcal{D}}(1^\lambda) := |\Pr[1 = \mathsf{Out}^0_{\mathsf{Sam},\mathcal{D}}(1^\lambda)] - \Pr[1 = \mathsf{Out}^1_{\mathsf{Sam},\mathcal{D}}(1^\lambda)]| = \mathsf{negl}(\lambda),
$$

where Fig. 6 defines $\mathsf{Out}^0_{\mathsf{Sam},\mathcal{D}}(1^\lambda)$ and $\mathsf{Out}^1_{\mathsf{Sam},\mathcal{D}}(1^\lambda)$.

Remark. Note that $\mathcal{D}$ does not need to receive any leakage about C since the circuit is fixed. We use the notation lkg_{C_r} just to be consistent with definition of DSIM.

5   Distributed Symmetric Encryption (DSE)

This section shows that DSIM security with respect to admissible samplers implies useful security properties on the example of distributed encryption that was introduced in Sect. 2. For simplicity of exposition, we focus on the case of two servers and a single message. See Sect. 2 for further introduction to our example and a discussion on extending the example into a length-expanding case

---

[2] hence, in most cases where DSIM is a meaningful notion, Filter should just be identity.

while maintaining the same online complexity. See the full version for a discussion on how to replace the ENC queries in the protocol by further garblings. In a nutshell, self-composition requires careful consideration regarding the order of quantifiers of the sampler Sam, the adversary $\mathcal{A}$ and the simulator $\mathcal{S}$ in the DSIM security notion, and additionally, a straightforward approach only allows for the self-composition of a constant number of garblings.

Remember that we are in a setting with two servers who hold secret shares k_1, k_2 of a symmetric key $k = k_1 \oplus k_2$, and who wish to perform distributed encryptions under k. One way to implement such a protocol is by combining a garbling scheme with an oblivious transfer protocol to obtain a two-party computation protocol for evaluating $\mathsf{enc}(k_1 \oplus k_2, x)$ for message $x \in \{0,1\}^\lambda$.

Below, we describe the protocol between two stateful servers. We keep state implicit for concise notation and we abstract away the OT protocol. The symmetric key k is assumed to be generated and secret shared by a trusted party in a setup phase. We refer to the protocol below as *distributed symmetric encryption protocol (DSE)*, using a symmetric encryption scheme se and a garbling scheme Gb.

Phase I	Phase II	
Server 1	Server 2	Server 2
Input: $k_1, 1^\lambda$	Input: $k_2, \mathsf{msg}, \tilde{C}, d, 1^\lambda$	Input: $\tilde{x}, \tilde{C}, d, 1^\lambda$
$r_1 \leftarrow\!\!\$ \{0,1\}^\lambda$	$r_2 \leftarrow\!\!\$ \{0,1\}^\lambda$	$x' \leftarrow \mathsf{Gb.GEval}(\tilde{C}, \tilde{x}, d)$
$C \leftarrow \mathsf{se.enc}(k_1 \oplus \cdot, \cdot; r_1 \oplus \cdot)$	$x \leftarrow k_2\|\|\mathsf{msg}\|\|r_2$	**return** x'
$(\tilde{C}, K, d) \leftarrow\!\!\$ \mathsf{Gb.GCircuit}(C)$	**return** x	
return $(\tilde{C}, d)$		

Security. The protocol shall provide security in a setting where the adversary obtains the key of one of the two servers. We here focus on corruption of the key of Server 2 and model security in this case. The security notion we consider is $-AE security in the presence of the above distributed protocol under the same key. In this toy example, we consider only a single corrupted execution of the protocol.

Security is defined as indistinguishability of $\mathsf{Denc}_{\mathcal{A}}^0(1^\lambda)$ and $\mathsf{Denc}_{\mathcal{A}}^1(1^\lambda)$ in Fig. 7. The game starts by sampling key shares k_1 and k_2 and computing a garbled circuit $\tilde{C}$ and d, either honestly or via simulator $\mathcal{S}$. The adversary $\mathcal{A}$, acting as corrupted Server 2, is then given $\tilde{C}$, d and k_2 and outputs a message msg to be encrypted. The game proceeds by garbling this message together with encryption randomness r_2 and providing this $\tilde{x}$ to $\mathcal{A}$. At every step, $\mathcal{A}$ has access to encryption and decryption oracles, modeling honest executions run concurrently. Finally, $\mathcal{A}$ outputs a guess b'.

Definition 9 (Distributed Encryption Security (DENC)). *Let* se *be a symmetric encryption scheme where ciphertexts are twice as long as the plaintexts. Let* Gb *be a garbling scheme. Then, the DSE protocol using* se *and* Gb *is DENC-secure if for all PPT adversaries* $\mathcal{A}$, *there exists a PPT simulator* $\mathcal{S}$ *such that*

$$|\Pr[1 = \text{Denc}^0_{\mathcal{A}}(1^\lambda)] - \Pr[1 = \text{Denc}^1_{\mathcal{A},\mathcal{S}}(1^\lambda)]|$$

is negligible, where Fig. 7 defines $\text{Denc}^0_{\mathcal{A}}(1^\lambda)$ *and* $\text{Denc}^1_{\mathcal{A}}(1^\lambda)$.

$\text{Denc}^0_{\mathcal{A}}(1^\lambda)$	$\text{Denc}^1_{\mathcal{A},\mathcal{S}}(1^\lambda)$	$\text{Hybrid}_{\mathcal{A}}(1^\lambda)$
$k_1 \leftarrow\!\!\$\ \{0,1\}^\lambda$	$k_1 \leftarrow\!\!\$\ \{0,1\}^\lambda$	$k_1 \leftarrow\!\!\$\ \{0,1\}^\lambda$
$k_2 \leftarrow\!\!\$\ \{0,1\}^\lambda$	$k_2 \leftarrow\!\!\$\ \{0,1\}^\lambda$	$k_2 \leftarrow\!\!\$\ \{0,1\}^\lambda$
$k \leftarrow k_1 \oplus k_2$	$k \leftarrow k_1 \oplus k_2$	$k \leftarrow k_1 \oplus k_2$
$r_1 \leftarrow\!\!\$\ \{0,1\}^\lambda$		
$C \leftarrow \text{enc}(k_1 \oplus \cdot, \cdot; r_1 \oplus \cdot)$		
$(\tilde{C}, K, d) \leftarrow\!\!\$\ \text{GCircuit}(C)$	$(\tilde{C}, d) \leftarrow\!\!\$\ \mathcal{S}(1^\lambda)$	$(\tilde{C}, d) \leftarrow\!\!\$\ \mathcal{S}^{\text{ENC,DEC}}_{\text{hybrid}}(1^\lambda)$
$\text{msg} \leftarrow\!\!\$\ \mathcal{A}^{\text{ENC}}_{\text{DEC}}(1^\lambda, k_2, \tilde{C}, d)$	$\text{msg} \leftarrow\!\!\$\ \mathcal{A}^{\text{ENC}}_{\text{DEC}}(1^\lambda, k_2, \tilde{C}, d)$	$\text{msg} \leftarrow\!\!\$\ \mathcal{A}^{\text{ENC}}_{\text{DEC}}(1^\lambda, k_2, \tilde{C}, d)$
$r_2 \leftarrow\!\!\$\ \{0,1\}^\lambda$		
$x \leftarrow k_2 \|\text{msg}\| r_2$		
$\tilde{x} \leftarrow\!\!\$\ \text{GInput}(K, x)$	$\tilde{x} \leftarrow\!\!\$\ \mathcal{S}(1^\lambda)$	$\tilde{x} \leftarrow\!\!\$\ \mathcal{S}^{\text{ENC,DEC}}_{\text{hybrid}}(1^\lambda)$
$S \leftarrow S \cup \{\tilde{C}(\tilde{x})\}$		$S \leftarrow S \cup \{\tilde{C}(\tilde{x})\}$
$b' \leftarrow\!\!\$\ \mathcal{A}^{\text{ENC}}_{\text{DEC}}(1^\lambda, \tilde{x})$	$b' \leftarrow\!\!\$\ \mathcal{A}^{\text{ENC}}_{\text{DEC}}(1^\lambda, \tilde{x})$	$b' \leftarrow\!\!\$\ \mathcal{A}^{\text{ENC}}_{\text{DEC}}(1^\lambda, \tilde{x})$
return b'	**return** b'	**return** b'

$\text{ENC}(m)$	$\text{ENC}(m)$	$\text{ENC}(m)$
assert $|m| = \lambda$	**assert** $|m| = \lambda$	**assert** $|m| = \lambda$
$c \leftarrow\!\!\$\ \text{enc}(k, m)$	$c \leftarrow\!\!\$\ \{0,1\}^{2\lambda}$	$c \leftarrow\!\!\$\ \text{enc}(k, m)$
$S \leftarrow S \cup \{c\}$		$S \leftarrow S \cup \{c\}$
return c	**return** c	**return** c

$\text{DEC}(c)$	$\text{DEC}(c)$	$\text{DEC}(c)$
assert $c \notin S$		**assert** $c \notin S$
$m \leftarrow \text{dec}(k, c)$		$m \leftarrow \text{dec}(k, c)$
return m	**return** $\bot$	**return** m

Fig. 7. Security games (left and middle) for DENC-security and hybrid game (right) for Theorem 3. The adversary $\mathcal{A}$ and simulators $\mathcal{S}$ and $\mathcal{S}_{\text{hybrid}}$ are *stateful*. We leave their state implicit for conciseness of notation.

$\mathsf{Sam}(1^\lambda)$	$\mathcal{O}_{C(x)}$	$\mathcal{C}^{\mathcal{O}}(\tilde{C}, d, \mathrm{lkg}_C)$
$k_1 \leftarrow\!\!\$ \{0,1\}^\lambda$	$\underline{\mathsf{ENC}(m)}$	$k_2 \leftarrow \mathrm{lkg}_C$
$k_2 \leftarrow\!\!\$ \{0,1\}^\lambda$	$\mathbf{assert}\ |m| = \lambda$	$\mathrm{msg, st} \leftarrow\!\!\$ \mathcal{A}^{\mathcal{O}}(1^\lambda, k_2, \tilde{C}, d)$
$k \leftarrow k_1 \oplus k_2$	$c \leftarrow\!\!\$ \mathsf{enc}(k, m)$	$x \leftarrow \mathrm{msg}$
$r_1 \leftarrow\!\!\$ \{0,1\}^\lambda$	$S \leftarrow S \cup \{c\}$	$\mathbf{return}\ (x, \mathrm{st})$
$C \leftarrow \mathsf{enc}(k_1 \oplus \cdot, \cdot; r_1 \oplus \cdot)$	$\mathbf{return}\ c$	
$\mathrm{lkg}_C \leftarrow k_2$		$\underline{\mathcal{C}^{\mathcal{O}_{C(x)}}(\tilde{x}, \mathrm{st})}$
$\mathcal{O} \leftarrow \mathsf{ENC}, \mathsf{DEC}$	$\underline{\mathsf{DEC}(c)}$	$b' \leftarrow\!\!\$ \mathcal{A}^{\mathcal{O}_{C(x)}}(\tilde{x}, \mathrm{st})$
$\mathbf{return}\ (C, \mathrm{lkg}_C, \mathcal{O})$	$\mathbf{assert}\ |m| = \lambda$	$\mathbf{return}\ b'$
	$\mathbf{assert}\ c \notin S \cup \{C(x)\}$	
	$m \leftarrow\!\!\$ \mathsf{dec}(k, c)$	
	$\mathbf{return}\ m$	

Fig. 8. Sampler Sam that emulates the sampling of $\mathsf{Denc}^0(1^\lambda)$ and a distinguisher $\mathcal{C}$ which just runs $\mathcal{A}$.

Theorem 3. *If se is an authenticated encryption scheme in the presence of linear related-key attacks ($-RK-AE-secure) and Gb is DSim[$\mathcal{C}^{Out}$]-secure, then DSE is DENC-secure.*

Remark. We write DSim[$\mathcal{C}^{Out}$] to denote DSim$_{\Lambda, \mathsf{Filter}}$[$\mathcal{C}^{Out}$] where Λ is empty and Filter is identity. That is, the parameters Λ and Filter are not needed for this section.

Proof. The proof of Theorem 3 proceeds via two high-level game-hops, see Fig. 7 (right) for the hybrid game between $\mathsf{DENC}^0_{\mathcal{A}}(1^\lambda)$ and $\mathsf{DENC}^1_{\mathcal{A},\mathcal{S}}(1^\lambda)$. The first game hop from $\mathsf{DENC}^0_{\mathcal{A}}(1^\lambda)$ to $\mathsf{Hybrid}_{\mathcal{A}}(1^\lambda)$ reduces t to $\mathsf{DSim}[\mathcal{C}^{Out}]$-security, and the second game-hop from $\mathsf{Hybrid}_{\mathcal{A}}(1^\lambda)$ to $\mathsf{DENC}^1_{\mathcal{A},\mathcal{S}}(1^\lambda)$ reduces to RK-AE security. We first provide the reduction for the 2nd game-hop, since it is easier than the first game-hop.

$\mathsf{Hybrid}_{\mathcal{A}}(1^\lambda)$ to $\mathsf{DENC}^1_{\mathcal{A},\mathcal{S}}(1^\lambda)$: For any PPT simulator $\mathcal{S}_{\mathrm{hybrid}}$, we define a PPT simulator $\mathcal{S}$ as follows: The simulator $\mathcal{S}$ runs $\mathcal{S}_{\mathrm{hybrid}}$, but answers its ENC queries with random strings of length 2λ and its DEC queries with $\perp$. Now, to reduce the indistinguishability of $\mathsf{Hybrid}_{\mathcal{A}}(1^\lambda)$ and $\mathsf{DENC}^1_{\mathcal{A},\mathcal{S}}(1^\lambda)$ to $-RK-AE, observe that k_1 is not used and thus, k_1 is perfectly random as required. Now, assume toward contradiction that there exists a pair of PPT algorithms $(\mathcal{A}, \mathcal{S}_{\mathrm{hybrid}})$ such that the difference between $\Pr[1 = \mathsf{Hybrid}_{\mathcal{A}}(1^\lambda)]$ and $\Pr[1 = \mathsf{DENC}^1_{\mathcal{A},\mathcal{S}}(1^\lambda)]$ is non-negligible, where $\mathcal{S}$ is derived from $\mathcal{S}_{\mathrm{hybrid}}$ as previously described. Then, we can construct the following adversary $\mathcal{B}$ against $-RK-AE: $\mathcal{B}$ emulates $\mathsf{Hybrid}_{\mathcal{A}}(1^\lambda)$, except for all ENC and DEC queries which it forwards to its $-RK-AE-game (with Δ being the all-zeroes string). $\mathcal{B}$ outputs whatever $\mathcal{A}$ outputs. By construction, we have that

$$\Pr\left[1 = \mathcal{A}(1^\lambda) \stackrel{\mathsf{ENC},\mathsf{DEC}}{\longrightarrow} \$\text{-}\mathsf{RK} - \mathsf{AE}^0(1^\lambda)\right] = \Pr\left[1 = \mathtt{Hybrid}_\mathcal{A}(1^\lambda)\right].$$

Additionally, we claim that

$$\Pr\left[1 = \mathcal{A}(1^\lambda) \stackrel{\mathsf{ENC},\mathsf{DEC}}{\longrightarrow} \$\text{-}\mathsf{RK} - \mathsf{AE}^1(1^\lambda)\right] = \Pr\left[1 = \mathtt{DENC}^1_{\mathcal{A},\mathcal{S}}(1^\lambda)\right].$$

Namely, in both cases, the ENC queries of $\mathcal{A}$ are answered by random strings of length 2λ, and the DEC queries are answered by $\perp$, and the game is *stateless*, as there is no set S of previously obtained ciphertexts. Therefore, it does not matter whether queries to ENC and DEC are forwarded to the $\$\text{-}\mathsf{RK} - \mathsf{AE}^1$ game (as done by $\mathcal{B}$) or simulated as random answers and $\perp$ answers, respectively, without forwarding (as done by $\mathcal{S}$). Thus, we can conclude $\mathsf{Adv}^{\$\text{-}\mathsf{RK}-\mathsf{AE}}_{\mathsf{se},\mathcal{A}}(1^\lambda)$ is non-negligible and reach a contradiction.

$\mathtt{DENC}^0_\mathcal{A}(1^\lambda)$ to $\mathtt{Hybrid}_\mathcal{A}(1^\lambda)$: Assume towards contradiction that $\mathcal{A}$ is a PPT adversary which has non-negligible advantage in distinguishing between $\mathtt{DENC}^0_\mathcal{A}(1^\lambda)$ and $\mathtt{Hybrid}_{\mathcal{A},\mathcal{S}_{\text{hybrid}}}(1^\lambda)$, regardless of how we instantiate $\mathcal{S}_{\text{hybrid}}$. Now, we construct an adversary $(\mathsf{Sam}(1^\lambda),\mathcal{C})$ against $\mathsf{DSim}[\mathcal{C}^{\mathsf{Out}}]$-security. $(\mathsf{Sam}(1^\lambda),\mathcal{C})$ is shown in Fig. 8. We first prove that Sam is output indistinguishable.

Claim 1. *If* se *is an* $\$\text{-}RK\text{-}AE$, *then* $\mathsf{Sam} \in \mathcal{C}^{\mathsf{Out}}$.

Written with explicit randomness $r := k_1 \| k_2 \| r_1$ of length $p(\lambda) := 3\lambda$, circuit $C_\lambda(.,r) := \mathsf{enc}(k_1 \oplus \cdot, \cdot; r_1 \oplus \cdot)$ and $\mathsf{Sam}_{\text{leak}}(r)$ which returns $\mathsf{lkg}_C \leftarrow k_2$ and $\mathcal{O} \leftarrow \mathsf{ENC}, \mathsf{DEC}$, we can re-write Sam as in Fig. 9, as required to prove output indistinguishability. We now prove that for all PPT $\mathcal{D}$,

$\mathsf{Sam}(1^\lambda)$	$\mathsf{Out}^b_{\mathsf{Sam},\mathcal{D}}(1^\lambda)$
$r \leftarrow\!\!\$\ \{0,1\}^{p(\lambda)}$	$C_r, \mathsf{lkg}_{C_r}, \mathcal{O} \leftarrow\!\!\$\ \mathsf{Sam}(1^\lambda)$
$C_r \leftarrow C_\lambda(.,r)$	$(x_0, \mathsf{st}) \leftarrow\!\!\$\ \mathcal{D}^\mathcal{O}(1^\lambda, \mathsf{lkg}_{C_r})$
$(\mathsf{lkg}_{C_r}, \mathcal{O}) \leftarrow \mathsf{Sam}_{\text{leak}}(r)$	$x_1 \leftarrow 0^{\|x_0\|}$
$\mathbf{return}\ C_r, \mathsf{lkg}_{C_r}, \mathcal{O}$	$b^* \leftarrow\!\!\$\ \mathcal{D}^{\mathcal{O}_{C_r(x_b)}}(C_r(x_b), \mathsf{st})$
	$\mathbf{return}\ b^*$

Fig. 9. Rewritten version of Sam.

$$\left|\Pr\left[1 = \mathsf{Out}^0_{\mathsf{Sam},\mathcal{D}}(1^\lambda)\right] - \Pr\left[1 = \mathsf{Out}^1_{\mathsf{Sam},\mathcal{D}}(1^\lambda)\right]\right|$$

is negligible, via a sequence of game hops shown in Fig. 10.

We inline the code of Sam, move computations downwards when variables are not used before, and inline the code of the circuit C_r. We also write $S \leftarrow S \cup \{c^*\}$ as an explicit state update instead of writing $c^* = C(x_b)$ as oracle subscript. The encryption process in the grey line uses fresh and uniform randomness since r_1 is uniformly random and so is r_1 xored with an adversarially chosen value.

We now reduce to $\$\text{-}\mathsf{RK}\text{-}\mathsf{AE}$ security (Definition 1) in order to replace the ENC oracle by one that returns random strings of length 2λ, the string c^* by a random string of length 2λ and the DEC oracle by an oracle that always returns $\perp$. After the reduction to $\$\text{-}\mathsf{RK}\text{-}\mathsf{AE}$ security, since c^* does not depend on b anymore, we have that $\Pr[b = b^*] = \frac{1}{2}$.

$\mathrm{Out}^b_{\mathrm{Sam},\mathcal{D}}(1^\lambda)$	$\mathrm{Out}^b_{\mathrm{Sam},\mathcal{D}}(1^\lambda)$	$\mathrm{ENC}(m)$
$k_1 \leftarrow\!\!\$\ \{0,1\}^\lambda$	$k_1 \leftarrow\!\!\$\ \{0,1\}^\lambda$	**assert** $\|m\| = \lambda$
$k_2 \leftarrow\!\!\$\ \{0,1\}^\lambda$	$k_2 \leftarrow\!\!\$\ \{0,1\}^\lambda$	$c \leftarrow\!\!\$\ \mathrm{enc}(k,m)$
$k \leftarrow k_1 \oplus k_2$	$k \leftarrow\!\!\$\ \{0,1\}^\lambda$	$S \leftarrow S \cup \{c\}$
$r_1 \leftarrow\!\!\$\ \{0,1\}^\lambda$		**return** c
$C \leftarrow \mathrm{enc}(k_1 \oplus \cdot, \cdot; r_1 \oplus \cdot)$		
$(x_0, \mathrm{st}) \leftarrow\!\!\$\ \mathcal{D}^{\mathrm{ENC,DEC}}(1^\lambda, k_2)$	$(x_0, \mathrm{st}) \leftarrow\!\!\$\ \mathcal{D}^{\mathrm{ENC,DEC}}(1^\lambda, k_2)$	$\mathrm{DEC}(c)$
$x_1 \leftarrow 0^{\|x_0\|}$	$x_1 \leftarrow 0^{\|x_0\|}$	**assert** $\|m\| = \lambda$
	$\mathrm{msg}\|\|\Delta\|\|r' \leftarrow x_b$	**assert** $c \notin S$
$c^* \leftarrow C(x_b)$	$c^* \leftarrow\!\!\$\ \mathrm{enc}(k_1 \oplus \Delta, \mathrm{msg})$	$m \leftarrow\!\!\$\ \mathrm{dec}(k,c)$
$S \leftarrow S \cup \{c^*\}$	$S \leftarrow S \cup \{c^*\}$	**return** m
$b^* \leftarrow\!\!\$\ \mathcal{D}^{\mathrm{ENC,DEC}}(c, \mathrm{st})$	$b^* \leftarrow\!\!\$\ \mathcal{D}^{\mathrm{ENC,DEC}}(c, \mathrm{st})$	
return b^*	**return** b^*	

Fig. 10. Game hops to show Claim 1.

The reduction $\mathcal{B}$ to \$-RK-AE security can answer all ENC queries m by a query $(m, \Delta = 0^\lambda)$ to its own encryption oracle, and it can compute the ciphertext c by choosing $\Delta' := \Delta \oplus k_2$, since then,

$$k \oplus \Delta' = (k_1 \oplus k_2) \oplus (\Delta \oplus k_2) = k_1 \oplus \Delta,$$

which $\mathcal{B}$ expects. Analogously, the reduction proceeds with decryption queries. This concludes the proof of Claim 1 that $\mathrm{Sam} \in \mathcal{C}^{\mathrm{Out}}$.

Hence, by $\mathrm{DSim}[\mathcal{C}^{\mathrm{Out}}]$-security, there exists a simulator $\mathcal{S}_{\mathrm{DSIM}}$ for $(\mathrm{Sam}, \mathcal{B})$ such that

$$|\Pr[1 = \mathrm{DSim}^0_{\mathrm{Sam},\mathcal{B},\mathrm{Gb},\Lambda}(1^\lambda)] - \Pr[1 = \mathrm{DSim}^1_{\mathrm{Sam},\mathcal{B},\mathcal{S}_{\mathrm{DSIM}},\Lambda}(1^\lambda)]|$$

is negligible. Given $\mathcal{S}_{\mathrm{DSIM}}$, the simulator $\mathcal{S}_{\mathrm{hybrid}}$ with oracle access to ENC and DEC runs

$$(\tilde{C}, d, \mathrm{st}_S) \leftarrow\!\!\$\ \mathcal{S}^{\mathrm{ENC,DEC}}_{\mathrm{DSIM}}(\mathrm{lkg}_C) \text{ and } \tilde{x} \leftarrow\!\!\$\ \mathcal{S}^{\mathrm{ENC,DEC}}_{\mathrm{DSIM}}([], \mathrm{st}_S)$$

and returns $(\tilde{C}, d, \tilde{x})$.

Since $|\Pr[1 = \mathrm{DSim}^0_{\mathrm{Sam},\mathcal{C},\mathrm{Gb}}(1^\lambda)] - \Pr[1 = \mathrm{DSim}^1_{\mathrm{Sam},\mathcal{C},\mathcal{S}_{\mathrm{DSIM}}}(1^\lambda)]|$

$$= |1 = \Pr[\mathrm{DENC}^0_{\mathcal{A}}(1^\lambda)] - \Pr[1 = \mathrm{Hybrid}_{\mathcal{A},\mathcal{S}_{\mathrm{hybrid}}}(1^\lambda)]|$$

and the former is negligible and the latter non-negligible, we reached a contradiction.

$\square$

$\mathsf{GCircuit_{comb}}(C)$	$\mathsf{GInput_{comb}}(K, x)$	$\mathsf{GEval_{comb}}(\tilde{C}, \tilde{x}, d)$
$r_{\mathrm{in}} \leftarrow_\$ \{0,1\}^{12\lambda|C|}$	$\tilde{x} \leftarrow \mathsf{GInput_{outer}}(K, x)$	$\tilde{C}_{\mathrm{in}}, \tilde{x}_{\mathrm{in}}, d_{\mathrm{in}} \leftarrow \mathsf{GEval_{outer}}(\tilde{C}, \tilde{x}, d)$
$\tilde{C}_{\mathrm{in}}, K_{\mathrm{in}}, d_{\mathrm{in}} \leftarrow \mathsf{GCircuit_{in}}(C(\cdot); r_{\mathrm{in}})$	$\textbf{return } \tilde{x}$	$y \leftarrow \mathsf{GEval_{in}}(\tilde{C}_{\mathrm{in}}, \tilde{x}_{\mathrm{in}}, d_{\mathrm{in}})$
$C_{\mathrm{in}}(\cdot) \leftarrow [\tilde{C}_{\mathrm{in}}, \mathsf{GInput_{in}}(\cdot, K_{\mathrm{in}}), d_{\mathrm{in}}]$		$\textbf{return } y$
$\tilde{C}, K, d \leftarrow_\$ \mathsf{GCircuit_{outer}}(C_{\mathrm{in}})$		
$\textbf{return } \tilde{C}, K, d$		

Fig. 11. Garbling scheme $\mathsf{Gb_{comb}}$. Length of r_{in} is chosen s.t. it is compatible with Yao's garbling scheme, however, the same results apply to any projective garbling scheme, just $|r_{\mathrm{in}}|$ might need to be adjusted.

6 Bootstrapping for Output Indistinguishable Samplers

In this section, we bootstrap DSIM security for output indistinguishable samplers returning NC^0 circuits to output indistinguishable samplers returning arbitrary polynomial-size circuits. Let us denote the class of output indistinguishable samplers by $\mathcal{C}^{\mathrm{Out}}$ and output indistinguishable samplers which only return circuits in NC^0 by $\mathcal{C}^{\mathrm{Out,NC}^0} \subseteq \mathcal{C}^{\mathrm{Out}}$. Based on a $\mathsf{DSim}_{\Lambda,\mathsf{Filter}}[\mathcal{C}^{\mathrm{Out,NC}^0}]$-secure garbling scheme (for NC^0 circuits), we construct a $\mathsf{DSim}_{\Lambda,\mathsf{Filter}}[\mathcal{C}^{\mathrm{Out}}]$-secure garbling scheme (for arbitrary poly-size circuits): The new garbling scheme $\mathsf{Gb_{comb}} = (\mathsf{GCircuit_{comb}}, \mathsf{GInput_{comb}}, \mathsf{GEval_{comb}})$ which we construct (cf. Fig. 11) combines two garbling schemes, the *inner* SelSim-secure garbling scheme $\mathsf{Gb_{in}} = (\mathsf{GCircuit_{in}}, \mathsf{GInput_{in}}, \mathsf{GEval_{in}})$ for arbitrary polynomial-size circuits and an *outer* garbling scheme $\mathsf{Gb_{outer}} = (\mathsf{GCircuit_{outer}}, \mathsf{GInput_{outer}}, \mathsf{GEval_{outer}})$ for NC^0 circuits which is $\mathsf{DSim}_{\Lambda,\mathsf{Filter}}[\mathcal{C}^{\mathrm{Out,NC}^0}]$-secure, to obtain a *combined* garbling scheme $\mathsf{Gb_{comb}}$ which is $\mathsf{DSim}_{\Lambda,\mathsf{Filter}}[\mathcal{C}^{\mathrm{Out}}]$-secure. $\mathsf{Gb_{comb}}$ garbles a circuit $C(\cdot)$ and input x as depicted in Fig. 11, where C_{in} is a circuit that takes as input x and produces as output the (selectively secure) garbling of C, i.e., $\tilde{C}_{\mathrm{in}}$, a garbling of x and the decoding information d_{in}. $\mathsf{Gb_{in}}$ could be any SelSim-secure, projective[3] garbling scheme, e.g., $\mathsf{Gb_{in}} = (\mathsf{GCircuit_{in}}, \mathsf{GInput_{in}}, \mathsf{GEval_{in}}) := (\mathsf{GCircuit_{yao}}, \mathsf{GInput_{yao}}, \mathsf{GEval_{yao}})$ is a valid choice (Yao's garbling is provably SelSim secure, assuming only the existence of \$-IND-CPA secure symmetric encryption scheme). We need to show that the circuit C_{in} is indeed in NC^0 and that $\mathsf{Gb_{comb}}$ is $\mathsf{DSim}_{\Lambda,\mathsf{Filter}}[\mathcal{C}^{\mathrm{Out}}]$-secure.

Section 6.1 shows the (easy) statement that the circuit C_{in} is in NC^0. In a nutshell, this follows from $\mathsf{Gb_{in}}$ being a projective garbling scheme and $\tilde{C}_{\mathrm{in}}$ and the decoding information d_{in} being just some constant bitstring in C_{in}.

Section 6.2 proves that if the sampler for circuit $C(x)$ is in $\mathcal{C}^{\mathrm{Out}}$, then the sampler for circuit $\tilde{C}(x; r)$ is in $\mathcal{C}^{\mathrm{Out,NC}^0}$. Section 6.3 then states and proves our main bootstrapping theorem.

---

[3] A garbling scheme is projective, if for each input bit x_i, the input garbling is one out of two possible strings $K_0(i)$ and $K_1(i)$. For example, Yao's garbling scheme is projective.

6.1 C_{in} is low-depth

Recall that C_{in} is defined as $C_{\text{in}}(\cdot) := [\tilde{C}_{\text{in}}, \mathsf{GInput}_{\text{in}}(\cdot, K_{\text{in}}), d_{\text{in}}]$ where $\tilde{C}_{\text{in}}, d_{\text{in}}$ and K_{in} are constant values (constant bitstrings). Hence, in order to show that the function C_{in} can be implemented as a constant depth circuit, it is enough to show the following lemma.

Lemma 1 (Low-depth Projective Input Garbling). *If* Gb_{in} *is a projective garbling scheme, then* $\mathsf{GInput}_{\text{in}}(\cdot; K_{in}) : x \mapsto \mathsf{GInput}_{\text{in}}(x; K_{in})$ *can be described by a constant-depth circuit.*

Proof. Denote by x_i the ith bit of the input x. Now K_{in} consists of key pairs k_0^i, k_1^i for each bit of x. W.l.o.g., we can assume that K_{in} is a concatenation of all the key pairs in order. The input garbling of x, i.e. $\mathsf{GInput}_{\text{in}}(x; K_{\text{in}})$, outputs $k_{x_1}^1||...||k_{x_\lambda}^\lambda$. This can clearly be done in constant depth by a circuit that just checks each bit of x one by one (in parallel) and outputs the corresponding key k_{x_i} for each bit. $\qquad\square$

6.2   Output Indistinguishable Sampling

We now prove that the above circuit transformation, when applied to a circuit sampler $\mathsf{Sam}_{\text{comb}}(1^\lambda)$ in $\mathcal{C}^{\mathsf{Out}}$ yields a circuit sampler $\mathsf{Sam}_{\text{outer}}(1^\lambda)$ in $\mathcal{C}^{\mathsf{Out},\mathsf{NC}^0}$. Since $\mathsf{Sam}_{\text{comb}}$ is output indistinguishable, there exists a polynomial $p(\lambda)$ and a circuit $C = (C_\lambda)_{\lambda\in\mathbb{N}}$ such that $\mathsf{Sam}_{\text{comb}}(1^\lambda)$ can be written as below (left). Then, we define the circuit sampler $\mathsf{Sam}_{\text{outer}}(1^\lambda)$ (with randomness $r||r_{\text{in}}$) as follows (right):

$\mathsf{Sam}_{\text{comb}}(1^\lambda)$	$\mathsf{Sam}_{\text{outer}}(1^\lambda)$
$r \leftarrow\!\!{\scriptstyle\$}\ \{0,1\}^{p(\lambda)}$	$r \leftarrow\!\!{\scriptstyle\$}\ \{0,1\}^{p(\lambda)}$
$C_r(.) \leftarrow C(\cdot, r)$	$r_{\text{in}} \leftarrow\!\!{\scriptstyle\$}\ \{0,1\}^{12\lambda|C_r|}$
return $C_r, \mathrm{lkg}_{C_r}, \mathcal{O}$	$\tilde{C}_{\text{in}}, K_{\text{in}}, d_{\text{in}} \leftarrow \mathsf{GCircuit}_{\text{in}}(C_r(\cdot); r_{\text{in}})$
	$C_{\text{in}}(\cdot) \leftarrow [\tilde{C}_{\text{in}}, \mathsf{GInput}_{\text{in}}(\cdot, K_{\text{in}}), d_{\text{in}}]$
	return $C_{\text{in}}, \mathrm{lkg}_{C_r}, \mathcal{O}$

Lemma 2 (Output indististinguishability). *Let* $\mathsf{Sam}_{\text{comb}} \in \mathcal{C}^{\mathsf{Out}}$. *If Yao's garbling scheme is selectively secure, then* $\mathsf{Sam}_{\text{outer}}(1^\lambda) \in \mathcal{C}^{\mathsf{Out},\mathsf{NC}^0}$.

Proof. Firstly, by Lemma 1, $\mathsf{Sam}_{\text{outer}}$ produces circuits in NC^0. Hence remains to show that $\mathsf{Sam}_{\text{outer}}$ is output indistinguishable, i.e., we prove that for all PPT adversaries $\mathcal{D}_{\text{outer}}$,

$$|\Pr[1 = \mathsf{Out}^0_{\mathsf{Sam}_{\text{outer}},\mathcal{D}_{\text{outer}}}(1^\lambda)] - \Pr[1 = \mathsf{Out}^1_{\mathsf{Sam}_{\text{outer}},\mathcal{D}_{\text{outer}}}(1^\lambda)]| = \mathsf{negl}(\lambda).$$

We prove indistinguishability of $\mathsf{Out}^0_{\mathcal{D}_{\mathrm{outer}}}(1^\lambda)$ and $\mathsf{Out}^1_{\mathcal{D}_{\mathrm{outer}}}(1^\lambda)$ via several hybrids. The games $\mathsf{Out}^b_{\mathcal{D}_{\mathrm{outer}}}(1^\lambda)$ and H^b are perfectly equivalent; we only inline the definition of circuit $\mathsf{Sam}_{\mathrm{outer}}$ and reorder some lines, whose order does not affect the functionality.

From $H^b(1^\lambda)$ to $H^{b+2}_{\mathcal{S}}$, we reduce to the selective simulation-based security of $\mathsf{Gb}_{\mathrm{in}}$. The highlighted lines in H^b refer to the SelSim adversary (who first chooses circuit, input and its state, C_r, x_b, st, and then receives garbling and returns its guess). Note that the SelSim adversary knows r and can hence compute the algorithm $\mathcal{O}$ and pass it in st, so $\mathcal{D}_{\mathrm{outer}}{}^{\mathcal{O}}$ can be replaced by a code equivalent and efficient algorithm that does not make oracle queries to $\mathcal{O}$ (but simply runs the algorithm $\mathcal{O}$).

From $H^{0+2}_{\mathcal{S}}$ to $H^{1+2}_{\mathcal{S}}$, we reduce to the output indistinguishability of $\mathsf{Sam}_{\mathrm{comb}}$, note that the two first lines of $H^{b+2}_{\mathcal{S}}$ are code equivalent to $\mathsf{Sam}_{\mathrm{comb}}$ and the highlighted lines refer to the output indistinguishability adversary (note that the topology $\Phi(C_r)$ can be computed when you know C and C is constant). For this game hop we switch back to $\mathcal{O}$ being an oracle algorithm (as opposed to emulating $\mathcal{D}_{\mathrm{outer}}{}^{\mathcal{O}}$ by running the actual algorithm $\mathcal{O}$).

$$\underline{\mathsf{Out}^b_{\mathsf{Sam}_{\mathrm{outer}},\mathcal{D}_{\mathrm{outer}}}(1^\lambda)}$$

$C_{\mathrm{in}}, \mathrm{lkg}_{C_r}, \mathcal{O} \twoheadleftarrow\!\$ \ \mathsf{Sam}_{\mathrm{outer}}$

$(x_0, \mathsf{st}) \twoheadleftarrow\!\$ \ \mathcal{D}_{\mathrm{outer}}{}^{\mathcal{O}}(1^\lambda, \mathrm{lkg}_{C_r})$

$x_1 \leftarrow 0^{|x_0|}$

$b^* \twoheadleftarrow\!\$ \ \mathcal{D}_{\mathrm{outer}}{}^{\mathcal{O}_{C_r}(x_b)}(C_{\mathrm{in}}(x_b), \mathsf{st})$

return b^*

$\underline{H^b}$	$\underline{H^{b+2}_{\mathcal{S}}}$
$r \twoheadleftarrow\!\$ \ \{0,1\}^{p(\lambda)}$	$r \twoheadleftarrow\!\$ \ \{0,1\}^{p(\lambda)}$
$C_r, \mathrm{lkg}_{C_r} \leftarrow C(\cdot, r), \mathrm{lkg}_{C_r}$	$C_r, \mathrm{lkg}_{C_r} \leftarrow C(\cdot, r), \mathrm{lkg}_{C_r}$
$(x_0, \mathsf{st}) \twoheadleftarrow\!\$ \ \mathcal{D}_{\mathrm{outer}}{}^{\mathcal{O}}(1^\lambda, \mathrm{lkg}_{C_r})$	$(x_0, \mathsf{st}) \twoheadleftarrow\!\$ \ \mathcal{D}_{\mathrm{outer}}{}^{\mathcal{O}}(1^\lambda, \mathrm{lkg}_{C_r})$
$x_1 \leftarrow 0^{|x_0|}$	$x_1 \leftarrow 0^{|x_0|}$
$r_{\mathrm{in}} \twoheadleftarrow\!\$ \ \{0,1\}^{12\lambda|C_r|}$	
$\tilde{C}_{\mathrm{in}}, K_{\mathrm{in}}, d_{\mathrm{in}} \leftarrow \mathsf{GCircuit}_{\mathrm{in}}(C_r(\cdot); r_{\mathrm{in}})$	
$C_{\mathrm{in}}(\cdot) \leftarrow [\tilde{C}_{\mathrm{in}}, \mathsf{GInput}_{\mathrm{in}}(\cdot, K_{\mathrm{in}}), d_{\mathrm{in}}]$	
$(\tilde{C}, \tilde{x}, d) \leftarrow C_{\mathrm{in}}(x_b)$	$(\tilde{C}, \tilde{x}, d) \leftarrow \mathcal{S}(\Phi(C_r), C_r(x_b))$
$b^* \twoheadleftarrow\!\$ \ \mathcal{D}_{\mathrm{outer}}{}^{\mathcal{O}_{C_r}(x_b)}((\tilde{C}, \tilde{x}, d), \mathsf{st})$	$b^* \twoheadleftarrow\!\$ \ \mathcal{D}_{\mathrm{outer}}{}^{\mathcal{O}_{C_r}(x_b)}((\tilde{C}, \tilde{x}, d), \mathsf{st})$
return b^*	**return** b^*

$\square$

6.3   Main Theorem

We now prove our main bootstrapping theorem.

Theorem 4 (Bootstrapping RIND from NC^0 to poly). *If the garbling scheme* $\mathsf{Gb}_{\mathrm{outer}} = (\mathsf{GCircuit}_{\mathrm{outer}}, \mathsf{GInput}_{\mathrm{outer}}, \mathsf{GEval}_{\mathrm{outer}})$ *is* $DSim_{\Lambda, \mathsf{Filter}}[\mathcal{C}^{Out,NC^0}]$-*secure and if* $\mathsf{Gb}_{\mathrm{in}} = (\mathsf{GCircuit}_{\mathrm{in}}, \mathsf{GInput}_{\mathrm{in}}, \mathsf{GEval}_{\mathrm{in}})$ *is a projective SelSim-secure* *garbling scheme, then the garbling scheme* $\mathsf{Gb}_{\mathsf{comb}} = (\mathsf{GCircuit}_{\mathsf{comb}}, \mathsf{GInput}_{\mathsf{comb}},$ $\mathsf{GEval}_{\mathsf{comb}})$ *achieves* $DSim_{\Lambda,\mathsf{Filter}}[\mathcal{C}^{Out}]$ *security.*

Proof. For all PPT $\mathsf{Sam}_{\mathsf{comb}} \in DSim_{\Lambda,\mathsf{Filter}}[\mathcal{C}^{Out}]$ and for all PPT $\mathcal{A}$, we want to construct a simulator $\mathcal{S}_{\mathsf{comb}}$ such that the following advantage

$$|\Pr[1 = \mathsf{DSim}^0_{\mathsf{Sam}_{\mathsf{comb}},\mathcal{A},\mathsf{Gb}_{\mathsf{comb}},\Lambda}(1^\lambda)] - \Pr[1 = \mathsf{DSim}^1_{\mathsf{Sam}_{\mathsf{comb}},\mathcal{A},\mathcal{S}_{\mathsf{comb}},\Lambda}(1^\lambda)]| \quad (1)$$

is negligible.

$\underline{\mathsf{DSim}^0_{\mathsf{Sam}_{\mathsf{comb}},\mathcal{A},\mathsf{Gb}_{\mathsf{comb}},\Lambda}(1^\lambda)}$	$\underline{H^0}$
	$r \leftarrow\!\!{\scriptstyle\$} \{0,1\}^{p(\lambda)}$
$C_r, \mathrm{lkg}_{C_r}, \mathcal{O} \leftarrow\!\!{\scriptstyle\$} \mathsf{Sam}_{\mathsf{comb}}(1^\lambda)$	$C_r(.) \leftarrow C(\cdot, r)$
	$r_{\mathrm{in}} \leftarrow\!\!{\scriptstyle\$} \{0,1\}^{12\lambda|C|}$
	$\tilde{C}_{\mathrm{in}}, K_{\mathrm{in}}, d_{\mathrm{in}} \leftarrow \mathsf{GCircuit}_{\mathrm{in}}(C_r(\cdot); r_{\mathrm{in}})$
	$C_{\mathrm{in}}(\cdot) \leftarrow [\tilde{C}_{\mathrm{in}}, \mathsf{GInput}_{\mathrm{in}}(\cdot, K_{\mathrm{in}}), d_{\mathrm{in}}]$
$(\tilde{C}, K, d) \leftarrow\!\!{\scriptstyle\$} \mathsf{GCircuit}_{\mathsf{comb}}(C_r)$	$\tilde{C}, K, d \leftarrow\!\!{\scriptstyle\$} \mathsf{GCircuit}_{\mathrm{outer}}(C_{\mathrm{in}})$
$(x, \mathrm{st}_\mathcal{A}) \leftarrow\!\!{\scriptstyle\$} \mathcal{A}^{\mathcal{O}}(\tilde{C}, d, \mathrm{lkg}_{C_r})$	$(x, \mathrm{st}_\mathcal{A}) \leftarrow\!\!{\scriptstyle\$} \mathcal{A}^{\mathcal{O}}(\tilde{C}, d, \mathrm{lkg}_{C_r})$
$\tilde{x} \leftarrow\!\!{\scriptstyle\$} \mathsf{GInput}_{\mathsf{comb}}(K, x)$	$\tilde{x} \leftarrow\!\!{\scriptstyle\$} \mathsf{GInput}_{\mathrm{outer}}(K, x)$
$b' \leftarrow\!\!{\scriptstyle\$} \mathcal{A}^{\mathcal{O}_{C_r(x)}}(\tilde{x}, \mathrm{st}_\mathcal{A})$	$b' \leftarrow\!\!{\scriptstyle\$} \mathcal{A}^{\mathcal{O}_{\tilde{C}_r(\tilde{x})}}(\tilde{x}, \mathrm{st}_\mathcal{A})$
return b'	**return** b'

$\underline{\mathsf{DSim}^1_{\mathsf{Sam}_{\mathsf{comb}},\mathcal{A},\mathcal{S}_{\mathsf{comb}},\Lambda}(1^\lambda)}$	$\underline{H^1}$
	$r \leftarrow\!\!{\scriptstyle\$} \{0,1\}^{p(\lambda)}$
$C_r, \mathrm{lkg}_{C_r}, \mathcal{O} \leftarrow\!\!{\scriptstyle\$} \mathsf{Sam}_{\mathsf{comb}}(1^\lambda)$	$C_r(.) \leftarrow C(\cdot, r)$
	$r_{\mathrm{in}} \leftarrow\!\!{\scriptstyle\$} \{0,1\}^{12\lambda|C|}$
	$\tilde{C}_{\mathrm{in}}, K_{\mathrm{in}}, d_{\mathrm{in}} \leftarrow \mathsf{GCircuit}_{\mathrm{in}}(C_r(\cdot); r_{\mathrm{in}})$
	$C_{\mathrm{in}}(\cdot) \leftarrow [\tilde{C}_{\mathrm{in}}, \mathsf{GInput}_{\mathrm{in}}(\cdot, K_{\mathrm{in}}), d_{\mathrm{in}}]$
$(\tilde{C}, d, \mathrm{st}_S) \leftarrow\!\!{\scriptstyle\$} \mathcal{S}^{\mathcal{O}}(\mathsf{Filter}(\mathrm{lkg}_{C_r}))$	$\tilde{C}, d, \mathrm{st}_S \leftarrow\!\!{\scriptstyle\$} \mathcal{S}_{\mathrm{outer}}{}^{\mathcal{O}}(\mathsf{Filter}(\mathrm{lkg}_{C_r}))$
$(x, \mathrm{st}_\mathcal{A}) \leftarrow\!\!{\scriptstyle\$} \mathcal{A}^{\mathcal{O}}(\tilde{C}, d, \mathrm{lkg}_{C_r})$	$(x, \mathrm{st}_\mathcal{A}) \leftarrow\!\!{\scriptstyle\$} \mathcal{A}^{\mathcal{O}}(\tilde{C}, d, \mathrm{lkg}_{C_r})$
$\tilde{x} \leftarrow\!\!{\scriptstyle\$} \mathcal{S}^{\mathcal{O}}(\Lambda(\mathrm{st}_\mathcal{A}), \mathrm{st}_S)$	$\tilde{x} \leftarrow\!\!{\scriptstyle\$} \mathcal{S}_{\mathrm{outer}}{}^{\mathcal{O}}(\Lambda(\mathrm{st}_\mathcal{A}), \mathrm{st}_S)$
$b' \leftarrow\!\!{\scriptstyle\$} \mathcal{A}^{\mathcal{O}_{\tilde{C}_r(\tilde{x})}}(\tilde{x}, \mathrm{st}_\mathcal{A})$	$b' \leftarrow\!\!{\scriptstyle\$} \mathcal{A}^{\mathcal{O}_{\tilde{C}_r(\tilde{x})}}(\tilde{x}, \mathrm{st}_\mathcal{A})$
return b'	**return** b'

The experiments $\mathsf{DSim}^0_{\mathsf{Sam}_{\mathsf{comb}},\mathcal{A},\mathsf{Gb}_{\mathsf{comb}},\Lambda}(1^\lambda)$ and the hybrid game H^0 are code equivalent by inlining the code of $\mathsf{Sam}_{\mathsf{comb}}$, $\mathsf{GCircuit}_{\mathsf{comb}}$ and $\mathsf{GInput}_{\mathsf{comb}}$. Now, observe that the lines highlighted in grey in H^0 describe $\mathsf{Sam}_{\mathrm{outer}}(1^\lambda)$ and thus, H^0 is also equivalent to $\mathsf{DSim}^0_{\mathsf{Sam}_{\mathrm{outer}},\mathcal{A},\mathsf{Gb}_{\mathrm{outer}},\Lambda}(1^\lambda)$, as required for the reduction.

Analogously, the hybrid game H^1 is equivalent to $\mathsf{DSim}^1_{\mathsf{Sam}_{\mathsf{outer}},\mathcal{A},\mathsf{Gb}_{\mathsf{outer}},\Lambda}(1^\lambda)$ with $\mathsf{Sam}_{\mathsf{outer}} \in \mathcal{C}^{\mathsf{Out},\mathsf{NC}^0}$ (Lemma 2) and thus, by $\mathsf{DSim}_{\Lambda,\mathsf{Filter}}[\mathcal{C}^{\mathsf{Out},\mathsf{NC}^0}]$-security of $\mathsf{Gb}_{\mathsf{outer}}$ (assumption), there is a simulator $\mathcal{S}_{\mathsf{outer}}$ s.t. H^0 is indistinguishable from H^1. If we define simulator $\mathcal{S}$ according to grey lines in H^1, we notice that H^1 is also code equivalent to $\mathsf{DSim}^1_{\mathsf{Sam}_{\mathsf{comb}},\mathcal{A},\mathsf{Gb}_{\mathsf{comb}},\Lambda}(1^\lambda)$, which concludes the proof. $\qquad\square$

7   Large Yao-Incompressibility Entropy Implies Large Online Complexity

HW lower-bound the online complexity of 2-party computation with security against malicious parties by the *incompressibility entropy* of the output distribution induced by the function to be computed, i.e., the shortest possible encoding of the output. Their lower bound also induce lower bounds on the online complexity of a SIM-secure garbling scheme, albeit with slightly worse parameters, see Sect. 1.1 for more discussion. In this section, we adapt the HW approach and lower bound the online complexity of a SIM-secure garbling scheme directly.

To explain our approach conceptually, let us revisit the AIKW lower bound which shows that SIM-secure garbling of a PRG requires an online complexity equal to the output length of the PRG. Namely, AIKW consider $C := \mathsf{PRG}$ and by correctness of the garbling scheme, we have $\tilde{C}(\tilde{x}) = \mathsf{PRG}(x)$. Therefore, the simulator who first creates a garbled circuit $\tilde{C}$ and then gets $y = \mathsf{PRG}(x)$ also needs to create $\tilde{x}$ such that $\tilde{C}(\tilde{x}) = y$. Now, the check that $\tilde{C}(\tilde{x})$ evaluates to y can be performed only knowing y, and since the simulator gets only y, we can run the simulator on a *random* y instead of a PRG output—by PRG security, the simulator should be as successful in creating a simulated input $\tilde{x}$ such that $\tilde{C}(\tilde{x}) = y$. However, if $|\tilde{x}| < |y|$ the simulator has an impossible task, because y has more entropy than $\tilde{x}$. Therefore, $|\tilde{x}|$ should be proportional to the *computational entropy* of $C(x)$.

In this paper, following HW, we measure computational entropy of a distribution $\mathcal{D}$ by its smallest efficient encoding, known as *Yao incompressibility entropy* (or Yao pseudo-entropy). This way, our result extends also to the entropy of all distributions which are indistinguishable from $\mathcal{D}$ and thus the *HILL pseudo-entropy* of $\mathcal{D}$. This is because high HILL pseudo-entropy implies high Yao incompressibility entropy (see e.g. [43]).

Definition 10 (Yao Incompressibility Entropy [42]). *Let Φ be a leakage function and $(C,x) \leftarrow\!\!\$\, \mathcal{D}(1^\lambda)$ be an efficiently sampleable distribution. The distribution $\mathcal{D}$ is k_λ-incompressible, if for every polynomial-size circuit family pair of a compression algorithm $\mathsf{Cmpr}_\lambda(\cdot,\cdot)$ and a decompression function $\mathsf{Decmpr}_\lambda(\cdot,\cdot)$ s.t. for all x: $\mathsf{Decmpr}(\mathsf{Cmpr}(C(x),\Phi(C)),\Phi(C)) = C(x)$ it holds that*

$$\mathbb{E}_{(C,x)\leftarrow\$\mathcal{D}(1^\lambda)}[|\mathsf{Cmpr}(C(x),\Phi(C))|] \geq k_\lambda,$$

where $|.|$ measures the output of Cmpr in bits.

Theorem 5 (Lower Bound, generalized AIKW). *Let* Gb *be a SIM-secure garbling scheme with leakage function* Φ, *and let* $(C, x) \leftarrow_{\$} \mathcal{D}(1^\lambda)$ *be an efficiently samplable distribution with incompressibility-entropy* $\geq k_\lambda$.

Then, the expected online complexity is

$$\mathbb{E}_{(C,x)\leftarrow_{\$}\mathcal{D}(1^\lambda),\tilde{x}\leftarrow_{\$}\text{Gb.GInput}}[|\tilde{x}|] \geq k_\lambda - 2.$$

We assume that the online complexity $|\tilde{x}|$ *is uniquely determined by* $\Phi(C)$.

Remark. Previous works [8, 28, 31, 42] define (conditional) Yao and HILL pseudo-entropy in different flavors with respect to using (im)perfect correctness of compression as well as Shannon entropy vs. min-entropy. In the full version, we discuss their relation and prove a variant of Theorem 5 for each of them.

Proof. Assume towards contradiction that

$$\mathbb{E}_{(C,x)\leftarrow_{\$}\mathcal{D}(1^\lambda),\tilde{x}\leftarrow_{\$}\text{Gb.GInput}}[|\tilde{x}|] < k_\lambda - 2, \tag{2}$$

Since the garbling scheme Gb is SIM-secure, there exists a PPT simulator $\mathcal{S}$, s.t.

$$\Pr\left[\begin{array}{c}\text{Gb.GEval}(\tilde{C}, \tilde{x}, d) = C(x) \\ |\tilde{x}| = |\text{Gb.GInput}(x)|\end{array} \middle| \begin{array}{c}(C, x) \leftarrow_{\$} \mathcal{D}(1^\lambda) \\ \tilde{C}, d, \text{st} \leftarrow_{\$} \mathcal{S}(1^\lambda, \Phi(C)) \\ \tilde{x} \leftarrow_{\$} \mathcal{S}(1^\lambda, C(x), \text{st})\end{array}\right] \geq 1 - \mu(\lambda),$$

where μ is negligible. The garbled input that the simulator returns must (almost always) have the correct online complexity, since otherwise we can use the length of the garbled input to distinguish real garbling from simulated garbling. We now use the simulator $\mathcal{S}$ to build a pair of efficient algorithms compressor Cmpr and decompressor Decmpr. Let $\mathcal{S}_\lambda^{\text{det}}$ be a *deterministic* version of the simulator, i.e., $\mathcal{S}_\lambda^{\text{det}}$ is equal to the simulator $\mathcal{S}(1^\lambda, \cdot; r_\lambda)$, where r_λ is the internal randomness that maximizes the above probability. We here use that [42] allow Cmpr and decompressor Decmpr to be a non-uniform circuit family. Then, we define compressor Cmpr and decompressor Decmpr as follows, writing lkg_Φ for a supposed output of $\Phi(C)$.

Cmpr(y, lkg_Φ)	Decmpr$(b\|z, \text{lkg}_\Phi)$
$\tilde{C}, d, \text{st} \leftarrow \mathcal{S}_\lambda^{\text{det}}(\text{lkg}_\Phi)$ // 1st stage of simulator	**if** $b = 1$
$\tilde{x} \leftarrow \mathcal{S}_\lambda^{\text{det}}(y, \text{st})$ // 2nd stage of simulator	**return** z
if GEval$(\tilde{C}, \tilde{x}, d) = y$ AND $|\tilde{x}| = |\text{Gb.GInput}(x)|$	$\tilde{C}, d, \text{st} \leftarrow \mathcal{S}_\lambda^{\text{det}}(\text{lkg}_\Phi)$
return $0\|\tilde{x}$	// 1st stage of simulator
return $1\|y$	**return** GEval$(\tilde{C}, z, d)$
return $\tilde{x}_{1,\dots,k-2}$	

The if-clause in the compressor is false only with negligible probability, because by averaging argument, we can show that there is simulator's randomness r_λ that achieves at least success probability $1 - 2\mu(\lambda)$. Hence,

$$\mathbb{E}_{\mathcal{D}}[|\mathsf{Cmpr}(C(x), \Phi(C))|] = \sum_{C,x \in \mathcal{D}, \text{if true}} \Pr_{\mathcal{D}}[C, x] \underbrace{|\mathsf{Cmpr}(C(x), \Phi(C))|}_{=|\mathsf{Gb.GInput}(x)|+1}$$

$$+ \underbrace{\sum_{C,x \in \mathcal{D}, \text{if false}} \Pr_{\mathcal{D}}[C, x] \underbrace{|\mathsf{Cmpr}(C(x), \Phi(C))|}_{\text{polynomial (WLOG)}}}_{\text{negl}(\lambda)}$$

$$\underbrace{}_{\text{negl}(\lambda)}$$

$$\leq \mathbb{E}_{\mathcal{D}}[|\mathsf{Gb.GInput}(x)| + 1] + \text{negl}(\lambda)$$

$$= \underbrace{\mathbb{E}_{\mathcal{D}}[|\mathsf{Gb.GInput}(x)|]}_{\leq k-2 \text{ by (2)}} + 1 + \text{negl}(\lambda) < k - 1 + \text{negl}(\lambda)$$

which is a contradiction with incompressibility.

$\square$

8   Garbling NC^1 Circuits with Online Complexity $\mathcal{O}(|x|)$

In this section we construct a garbling scheme with online complexity $2n\lambda$ and prove that it is adaptively indistinguishable for NC^1circuits. Our construction can thus be seen as JSW [33] instantiated just with Yao's garbling scheme and without the somewhere equivocal encryption layer. In a nutshell, the JSW construction garbles a circuit C by first constructing a new circuit C' consisting of two copies of C connected through selector gates that each forward the output of one of the copies of C. The circuit C' is then garbled using Yao's garbling scheme and the resulting garbled circuit is encrypted with a somewhere equivocal encryption scheme [29]. The somewhere equivocal encryption scheme contributes to the online complexity as decryption keys need to be transmitted in the online phase. We show through a new security analysis that the final encryption step can actually be omitted, thus reducing the online complexity to $2\lambda|x|$.

We now present the construction and then discuss how our proof differs from JSW and then provide the proof in the supplementary material.

8.1   Yao's Garbling Scheme

Let $\mathsf{se} = (\mathsf{enc}, \mathsf{dec})$ be a symmetric encryption scheme with key space $\{0,1\}^\lambda$. Yao's garbling scheme $\mathsf{Gb}_{\mathsf{yao}}$ [44,46] consists of algorithms $\mathsf{GCircuit}_{\mathsf{yao}}$, $\mathsf{GInput}_{\mathsf{yao}}$ and $\mathsf{GEval}_{\mathsf{yao}}$ that are shown in Fig. 12. For each wire, two uniformly random keys are sampled and assigned values 0 and 1, respectively. To garble a gate g, its left and right predecessor and the corresponding wire keys are determined, and four ciphertexts are computed according to gate operation $op(g)$.

$\mathsf{GCircuit}_{\mathsf{yao}}(C)$

for $g \in \mathrm{Gates}(C)$
  $K_g(0) \leftarrow\!\!\$\ \{0,1\}^{\lambda}$
  $K_g(1) \leftarrow\!\!\$\ \{0,1\}^{\lambda}$
for $g \in \mathrm{Gates}(C)$:
  $K_{\mathrm{left}} \leftarrow K_{\mathsf{LeftPred}}(g, C)$
  $K_{\mathrm{right}} \leftarrow K_{\mathsf{RightPred}}(g, C)$
  $K_{\mathrm{output}} \leftarrow K_g$
  for $(b_{\mathrm{left}}, b_{\mathrm{right}}) \in \{0,1\}^2$:
    $d \leftarrow (op(g))(b_{\mathrm{left}}, b_{\mathrm{right}})$
    $c_{\mathrm{in}} \leftarrow\!\!\$\ \mathsf{enc}(K_{\mathrm{left}}(b_{\mathrm{left}}), K_{\mathrm{out}}(d))$
    $c_{\mathrm{out}} \leftarrow\!\!\$\ \mathsf{enc}(K_{\mathrm{right}}(b_{\mathrm{right}}), c_{\mathrm{in}})$
    $\tilde{g} \leftarrow \tilde{g} \cup \{c_{\mathrm{out}}\}$
  $\tilde{C}[g] \leftarrow \tilde{g}$
$K \leftarrow \{(K_g, g), g \in \mathrm{InputGates}(C)\}$
$K_{\mathrm{out}} \leftarrow \{(\mathrm{sort}(K_g(0), K_g(1)), g),$
        $g \in \mathrm{OutputGates}(C)\}$
for $g \in \mathrm{OutputGates}(C)$:
  if $K_{\mathrm{out}}(g) = (K_g(0), K_g(1))$
  then $\mathrm{out}_g \leftarrow 0$
  else $\mathrm{out}_g \leftarrow 1$
$d \leftarrow \{(\mathrm{out}_g, g) : g \in \mathrm{OutputGates}(C)\}$
return $((\tilde{C}, K_{\mathrm{out}}), K, d)$

$\mathsf{GInput}_{\mathsf{yao}}(K, x)$

for $g \in \mathrm{InputGates}(C)$:
  $d_g \leftarrow g\text{-th pos. of } x$
  $\tilde{x}[g] \leftarrow K_g(d_g)$
return $\tilde{x}$

$\mathsf{GEval}_{\mathsf{yao}}(\tilde{C}', \tilde{x}, d)$

$(\tilde{C}, K_{\mathrm{out}}) \leftarrow \tilde{C}'$
for $g \in \mathrm{InputGates}(C)$: $k_g \leftarrow \tilde{x}[g]$
for $g \in \mathrm{Gates}(C) \setminus \mathrm{InputGates}(C)$:
  $k_{\mathrm{left}} \leftarrow k_{\mathsf{LeftPred}}(g, \Phi(C))$
  $k_{\mathrm{right}} \leftarrow k_{\mathsf{RightPred}}(g, \Phi(C))$
  for $c \in \tilde{C}[g]$:
    $m_{\mathrm{out}} \leftarrow \mathsf{dec}(k_{\mathrm{right}}, c)$
    $m_{\mathrm{in}} \leftarrow \mathsf{dec}(k_{\mathrm{lef}}, m_{\mathrm{out}})$
    if $m_{\mathrm{in}} \neq \bot$ **then** $k_g \leftarrow m_{\mathrm{in}}$
for $g \in \mathrm{OutputGates}(C)$:
  $\mathrm{map}_g \leftarrow d(g)$
  if $k_g = K_{\mathrm{out}}(g)(\mathrm{map}_g)$
  then $y[g] = 0$
  if $k_g = K_{\mathrm{out}}(g)(1 - \mathrm{map}_g)$
  then $y[g] = 1$
return y

Fig. 12. Yao's garbling scheme $\mathsf{Gb}_{\mathsf{yao}}$ with split output map.

Our description differs slightly from the literature in the split between garbled circuit and output decoding information: Instead of the more traditional view that treats the whole output map (consisting of wire keys and their mapping to bits) as part of the output decoding information, we separate the wire keys K_{out} (sorted lexicographically to hide their association with bits) from the actual map d (pointing now to entries in the key list). The wire keys then become part of the garbled circuit. This is in line with what JSW called *output-key security* in their construction: Yao's garbling scheme is actually adaptively simulatable even when the output wire keys (without the mapping to bits) are sent with the garbled gates in the offline phase. We refer to this version as *weak online Yao*. Interestingly, this is reminiscent of the point-and-permute technique [41] applied only to the output wires, and reduces the

$(\mathsf{Sel}_0 \circ C \| C)\ (x)$

$y_0 \leftarrow C(x)$
$y_1 \leftarrow C(x)$
$y \leftarrow y_0$
return y

Fig. 13. Circuit C'.

online complexity to $n\lambda + m$ (assuming a suitable encoding of gate indices). Note that this change does not affect the combined information contained in the garbled circuit and output decoding information, we simply redistribute it.

8.2   Our Construction

For $b \in \{0,1\}$, a *selector gate* Sel_b takes as input two bits u_0 and u_1 and outputs u_b. We define our garbling scheme $\mathsf{Gb} = (\mathsf{GCircuit}, \mathsf{GInput}, \mathsf{GEval})$ as

- $\mathsf{GCircuit}(C) := \mathsf{GCircuit}_{\mathsf{yao}}(C')$, where $C' := \mathsf{Sel}_0 \circ C || C$ (Fig. 13) is a circuit consisting of two copies of C connected by m selector gates Sel_0.
- $\mathsf{GInput}(K, x) := \mathsf{GInput}_{\mathsf{yao}}(K, x||x)$.
- $\mathsf{GEval}(\tilde{C}, \tilde{x}, d) := \mathsf{GEval}_{\mathsf{yao}}(\tilde{C}, \tilde{x}, d)$

The input size of C' is twice that of C, and hence the input encoding size is twice that of Yao's garbling scheme.

Comparison to JSW Construction. JSW additionally encrypt the garbled circuit with a layer of somewhere equivocal encryption (SEE) where the simulator can revoke at pebbling complexity many ciphertexts. The overall construction has an online complexity independent of the output size of the circuit. However, the online complexity of JSW is affected by the SEE decryption key, which is sent together with the garbled input. The decryption key removes the layer of somewhere equivocal encryption and then the garbled circuit can be evaluated on the garbled input. By the formula in [29] (Table 1), the size of the decryption key is $t \cdot s \cdot \lambda \cdot \log n$, where for JSW, t is the number of gates to be revoked and s is the size of a garbled gate, which is effectively linear in λ. Since the number of gates to revoked is either the *width* w or the *depth* d of the circuit, the size of the decryption key is either $\mathcal{O}(d\lambda^2)$ or $\mathcal{O}(w\lambda^2)$.

8.3   Security

Theorem 6. *Assuming IND-CPA security of symmetric encryption scheme* se, *the garbling scheme* Gb *is IND-secure (Definition 5) for* NC^1 *circuits and has an online complexity of* $2n\lambda$.

   Our proof of Theorem 6 follows JSW and HJOSW [29], except when moving from left selectors to right selectors. Here, we observe that under the condition that $C_0(x_0) = C_1(x_1)$, selector gates do not need to be garbled in an input-dependent way. The reason is that switching from left selectors to right selectors preserves the encryption of the zero output key under the left and right zero input key as well as the encryption of the one output key under the left and right one key. Since $C_0(x_0) = C_1(x_1)$, these decryptions always yield the correct output key, no matter whether the output gate was pebbled according to the left or right selector. Only the content of "mixed" ciphertexts changes depending on whether we garble a left or right selector, but mixed ciphertexts are never decrypted since $C_0(x_0) = C_1(x_1)$. We provide the proof of Theorem 6 in the full version.

Acknowledgments. We thank Christoph Egger, Pierre Meyer, the cryptography group at ENS Paris and the anonymous reviewers of Asiacrypt 2023 for the interesting discussion, and for pointing us towards the work of Hubáček and Wichs [31].

This work was supported by the Research Council of Finland, Blockchain Technology Laboratory at the University of Edinburgh and Input Output Global.

References

1. Agrawal, S., Dai, W., Luykx, A., Mukherjee, P., Rindal, P.: ParaDiSE: efficient threshold authenticated encryption in fully malicious model. In: Isobe, T., Sarkar, S. (eds.) LNCS. INDOCRYPT 2022, vol. 13774, pp. 26–51. Springer, Cham (2022). https://doi.org/10.1007/978-3-031-22912-1_2
2. Agrawal, S., Mohassel, P., Mukherjee, P., Rindal, P.: DiSE: distributed symmetric-key encryption. In: Lie, D., Mannan, M., Backes, M., Wang, X.F., (eds.), ACM CCS 2018: 25th Conference on Computer and Communications Security, pp. 1993–2010. ACM Press, October 2018
3. Agrawal, S.: Indistinguishability obfuscation without multilinear maps: new methods for bootstrapping and instantiation. In: Ishai, Y., Rijmen, V. (eds.) EUROCRYPT 2019. LNCS, vol. 11476, pp. 191–225. Springer, Cham (2019). https://doi.org/10.1007/978-3-030-17653-2_7
4. Ananth, P., Sahai, A.: Functional encryption for Turing machines. In: Kushilevitz, E., Malkin, T. (eds.) TCC 2016. LNCS, vol. 9562, pp. 125–153. Springer, Heidelberg (2016). https://doi.org/10.1007/978-3-662-49096-9_6
5. Applebaum, B.: Cryptography in Constant Parallel Time. ISC, Springer, Heidelberg (2014). https://doi.org/10.1007/978-3-642-17367-7
6. Applebaum, B., Ishai, Y., Kushilevitz, E.: Cryptography in NC^0. In: 45th Annual Symposium on Foundations of Computer Science, pp. 166–175. IEEE Computer Society Press, October 2004
7. Applebaum, B., Ishai, Y., Kushilevitz, E., Waters, B.: Encoding functions with constant online rate or how to compress garbled circuits keys. In: Canetti, R., Garay, J.A. (eds.) CRYPTO 2013. LNCS, vol. 8043, pp. 166–184. Springer, Heidelberg (2013). https://doi.org/10.1007/978-3-642-40084-1_10
8. Barak, B., Shaltiel, R., Wigderson, A.: Computational analogues of entropy. In: Arora, S., Jansen, K., Rolim, J.D.P., Sahai, A. (eds.) APPROX/RANDOM -2003. LNCS, vol. 2764, pp. 200–215. Springer, Heidelberg (2003). https://doi.org/10.1007/978-3-540-45198-3_18
9. Bellare, M., Boldyreva, A., O'Neill, A.: Deterministic and efficiently searchable encryption. In: Menezes, A. (ed.) Advances in Cryptology - CRYPTO 2007. Lecture Notes in Computer Science, vol. 4622, pp. 535–552. Springer, Heidelberg (2007). https://doi.org/10.1007/978-3-540-74143-5_30
10. Bellare, M., Hoang, V.T., Keelveedhi, S.: Instantiating random oracles via UCEs. In: Canetti, R., Garay, J.A. (eds.) CRYPTO 2013. LNCS, vol. 8043, pp. 398–415. Springer, Heidelberg (2013). https://doi.org/10.1007/978-3-642-40084-1_23
11. Bellare, M., Hoang, V.T., Rogaway, P.: Adaptively secure garbling with applications to one-time programs and secure outsourcing. In: Wang, X., Sako, K. (eds.) ASIACRYPT 2012. LNCS, vol. 7658, pp. 134–153. Springer, Heidelberg (2012). https://doi.org/10.1007/978-3-642-34961-4_10
12. Bellare, M., Hoang, V.T., Rogaway, P.: Foundations of garbled circuits. In: Yu, T., Danezis, G., Gligor, V.D. (eds.), ACM CCS 2012: 19th Conference on Computer and Communications Security, pp. 784–796. ACM Press, October 2012

13. Bellare, M., Kohno, T.: A theoretical treatment of related-key attacks: RKA-PRPs, RKA-PRFs, and Applications. In: Biham, E. (ed.) EUROCRYPT 2003. LNCS, vol. 2656, pp. 491–506. Springer, Heidelberg (2003). https://doi.org/10.1007/3-540-39200-9_31

14. Bodlaender, H.L.: Dynamic programming on graphs with bounded treewidth. In: Lepistö, T., Salomaa, A. (eds.) ICALP 1988. LNCS, vol. 317, pp. 105–118. Springer, Heidelberg (1988). https://doi.org/10.1007/3-540-19488-6_110

15. Bodlaender, H.L., Koster, A.M.C.A.: Combinatorial optimization on graphs of bounded treewidth. Comput. J. **51**(3), 255–269 (2008)

16. Boneh, D., Lewi, K., Montgomery, H., Raghunathan, A.: Key homomorphic PRFs and their applications. In: Canetti, R., Garay, J.A. (eds.) CRYPTO 2013. LNCS, vol. 8042, pp. 410–428. Springer, Heidelberg (2013). https://doi.org/10.1007/978-3-642-40041-4_23

17. Brzuska, C., Delignat-Lavaud, A., Fournet, C., Kohbrok, K., Kohlweiss, M.: State separation for code-based game-playing proofs. In: Peyrin, T., Galbraith, S. (eds.) ASIACRYPT 2018. LNCS, vol. 11274, pp. 222–249. Springer, Cham (2018). https://doi.org/10.1007/978-3-030-03332-3_9

18. Brzuska, C., Oechsner, S.: A state-separating proof for YAO's garbling scheme. In: 36th IEEE Computer Security Foundations Symposium - CSF 2023, pp. 137–152. IEEE (2023)

19. Canetti, R.: Universally composable security: a new paradigm for cryptographic protocols. In: 42nd Annual Symposium on Foundations of Computer Science, pp. 136–145. IEEE Computer Society Press, October 2001

20. Canetti, R., Lin, H., Tessaro, S., Vaikuntanathan, V.: Obfuscation of probabilistic circuits and applications. In: Dodis, Y., Nielsen, J.B. (eds.) TCC 2015. LNCS, vol. 9015, pp. 468–497. Springer, Heidelberg (2015). https://doi.org/10.1007/978-3-662-46497-7_19

21. Dwork, C., Naor, M., Reingold, O., Stockmeyer, L.J.: Magic functions. In: 40th Annual Symposium on Foundations of Computer Science, pp. 523–534. IEEE Computer Society Press, October 1999

22. Freuder, E.C.: Complexity of k-tree structured constraint satisfaction problems (1990)

23. Garg, S., Gentry, C., Halevi, S., Raykova, M., Sahai, A., Waters, B.: Candidate indistinguishability obfuscation and functional encryption for all circuits. In: 54th Annual Symposium on Foundations of Computer Science, pp. 40–49. IEEE Computer Society Press, October 2013

24. Garg, S., Srinivasan, A.: Adaptively secure garbling with near optimal online complexity. In: Nielsen, J.B., Rijmen, V. (eds.) EUROCRYPT 2018. LNCS, vol. 10821, pp. 535–565. Springer, Cham (2018). https://doi.org/10.1007/978-3-319-78375-8_18

25. Goldreich, O.: A uniform-complexity treatment of encryption and zero-knowledge. J. Cryptol. **6**(1), 21–53 (1993)

26. Goldreich, O.: Candidate one-way functions based on expander graphs. In: Goldreich, O. (ed.) Studies in Complexity and Cryptography. Miscellanea on the Interplay between Randomness and Computation. LNCS, vol. 6650, pp. 76–87. Springer, Heidelberg (2011). https://doi.org/10.1007/978-3-642-22670-0_10

27. Haitner, I., Mazor, N., Silbak, J.: Incompressiblity and next-block pseudoentropy. In: Kalai, Y.T. (ed.), 14th Innovations in Theoretical Computer Science Conference, ITCS 2023, vol. 251, LIPIcs, pp. 66:1–66:18. Schloss Dagstuhl - Leibniz-Zentrum für Informatik (2023)

28. Håstad, J., Impagliazzo, R., Levin, L.A., Luby, M.: A pseudorandom generator from any one-way function. SIAM J. Comput. **28**(4), 1364–1396 (1999)

29. Hemenway, B., Jafargholi, Z., Ostrovsky, R., Scafuro, A., Wichs, D.: Adaptively secure garbled circuits from one-way functions. In: Robshaw, M., Katz, J. (eds.) CRYPTO 2016. LNCS, vol. 9816, pp. 149–178. Springer, Heidelberg (2016). https://doi.org/10.1007/978-3-662-53015-3_6

30. Hsiao, C.-Y., Lu, C.-J., Reyzin, L.: Conditional computational entropy, or toward separating pseudoentropy from compressibility. In: Naor, M. (ed.) EUROCRYPT 2007. LNCS, vol. 4515, pp. 169–186. Springer, Heidelberg (2007). https://doi.org/10.1007/978-3-540-72540-4_10

31. Hubacek, P., Wichs, D.: On the communication complexity of secure function evaluation with long output. In: Roughgarden, T. (ed.) ITCS 2015: 6th Conference on Innovations in Theoretical Computer Science, pp. 163–172. Association for Computing Machinery, January 2015

32. Jafargholi, Z., Oechsner, S.: Adaptive security of practical garbling schemes. In: Bhargavan, K., Oswald, E., Prabhakaran, M. (eds.) INDOCRYPT 2020. LNCS, vol. 12578, pp. 741–762. Springer, Cham (2020). https://doi.org/10.1007/978-3-030-65277-7_33

33. Jafargholi, Z., Scafuro, A., Wichs, D.: Adaptively indistinguishable garbled circuits. In: Kalai, Y., Reyzin, L. (eds.) TCC 2017. LNCS, vol. 10678, pp. 40–71. Springer, Cham (2017). https://doi.org/10.1007/978-3-319-70503-3_2

34. Jafargholi, Z., Wichs, D.: Adaptive security of Yao's garbled circuits. In: Hirt, M., Smith, A. (eds.) TCC 2016. LNCS, vol. 9985, pp. 433–458. Springer, Heidelberg (2016). https://doi.org/10.1007/978-3-662-53641-4_17

35. Jain, A., Kalai, Y.T., Khurana, D., Rothblum, R.: Distinguisher-dependent simulation in two rounds and its applications. In: Katz, J., Shacham, H. (eds.) CRYPTO 2017. LNCS, vol. 10402, pp. 158–189. Springer, Cham (2017). https://doi.org/10.1007/978-3-319-63715-0_6

36. Jansen, M.J., Sarma, J.: Balancing bounded treewidth circuits. Theory Comput. Syst. **54**(2), 318–336 (2014)

37. Kamath, C., Klein, K., Pietrzak, K.: On treewidth, separators and Yao's garbling. In: Nissim, K., Waters, B. (eds.) TCC 2021. LNCS, vol. 13043, pp. 486–517. Springer, Cham (2021). https://doi.org/10.1007/978-3-030-90453-1_17

38. Khurana, D.: Non-interactive distributional indistinguishability (NIDI) and non-malleable commitments. In: Canteaut, A., Standaert, F.-X. (eds.) EUROCRYPT 2021. LNCS, vol. 12698, pp. 186–215. Springer, Cham (2021). https://doi.org/10.1007/978-3-030-77883-5_7

39. Lindell, Y., Pinkas, B.: A proof of security of Yao's protocol for two-party computation. J. Cryptol. **22**(2), 161–188 (2009)

40. Mukherjee, P.: Adaptively secure threshold symmetric-key encryption. In: Bhargavan, K., Oswald, E., Prabhakaran, M. (eds.) INDOCRYPT 2020. LNCS, vol. 12578, pp. 465–487. Springer, Cham (2020). https://doi.org/10.1007/978-3-030-65277-7_21

41. Rogaway, P.: The round complexity of secure protocols. Ph.D. thesis, MIT (1991)

42. Trevisan, L., Vadhan, S., Zuckerman, D.: Compression of samplable sources. Comput. Complex. **14**(3), 186–227 (2005)

43. Wee, H.: On pseudoentropy versus compressibility. In: Proceedings of 19th IEEE Annual Conference on Computational Complexity 2004, pp. 29–41 (2004)

44. Yao, A.C.-C.: Protocols for secure computations (extended abstract). In: 23rd Annual Symposium on Foundations of Computer Science, pp. 160–164. IEEE Computer Society Press, November 1982

45. Yao, A.C.-C.: Theory and applications of trapdoor functions (extended abstract). In: 23rd Annual Symposium on Foundations of Computer Science, pp. 80–91. IEEE Computer Society Press, November 1982

46. Yao, A.C.-C.: How to generate and exchange secrets (extended abstract). In: 27th Annual Symposium on Foundations of Computer Science, pp. 162–167. IEEE Computer Society Press, October 1986

MPC with Delayed Parties over Star-Like Networks

Mariana Gama[1]([✉])[ID], Emad Heydari Beni[1,2][ID], Emmanuela Orsini[3][ID],
Nigel P. Smart[1,4][ID], and Oliver Zajonc[1][ID]

[1] COSIC, KU Leuven, Leuven, Belgium
{mariana.botelhodagama,nigel.smart}@kuleuven.be,
oliver.zajonc@esat.kuleuven.be
[2] Nokia Bell Labs, Antwerp, Belgium
emad.heydari_beni@nokia-bell-labs.com
[3] Bocconi University, Milan, Italy
emmanuela.orsini@unibocconi.it
[4] Zama Inc., Paris, France

Abstract. This paper examines multi-party computation protocols in the presence of two major constraints commonly encountered in deployed systems. Firstly, we consider the situation where the parties are connected not by direct point-to-point connections, but by a star-like topology with a few central post-office style relays. Secondly, we consider MPC protocols with a strong honest majority ($t \ll n/2$) in which we have stragglers (some parties are progressing slower than others). We model stragglers by allowing the adversary to delay messages to and from some parties for a given length of time.

We first prove that having only a single honest relay is enough to ensure consensus of the messages sent within a protocol; then, we show that special care must be taken to describe multiplication protocols in the case of relays and stragglers; finally, we present an efficient honest-majority MPC protocol which can be run ontop of the relays and which provides active-security with abort in the case of a strong honest majority, even when run with stragglers. We back up our protocol presentation with both experimental evaluations and simulations of the effect of the relays and delays on our protocol.

1 Introduction

Multi-Party Computation (MPC) allows a set of mutually distrusting parties to compute a function of their joint private inputs, without revealing anything about the inputs bar what can be deduced from any output of the function. MPC is now practical for a number of use-cases, it is becoming increasingly deployed in special niche applications, and much research work is now focused on extending the application space beyond these specific use-cases.

While MPC has been studied in a variety of different settings, most of the protocols are based on strong assumptions, such as the existence of direct fast communication channels between each pair of computing parties, fully synchronous

J. Guo and R. Steinfeld (Eds.): ASIACRYPT 2023, LNCS 14438, pp. 172–203, 2023.
https://doi.org/10.1007/978-981-99-8721-4_6

communication channels and a static set of parties which is progress through the protocol execution at the same speed.

Network Topology. In almost all academic works, and almost all academic implementations of MPC, the computing parties $\{\mathcal{P}_1, \ldots, \mathcal{P}_n\}$ are all connected with each other by dedicated connections, thus if we have n parties, this requires $n \cdot (n-1)$ uni-directional channels, often realised using $n \cdot (n-1)/2$ bi-directional TLS connections. However, in commercial applications this is not practical, as it implies each commercial entity enables $n-1$ external connections per MPC calculation. This can be problematic, as a corporate network is often locked down to an extent that creating new connections on new ports is frowned upon by the IT department.

One solution to this problem is to route all messages via a relay, so that communication operates in a star-like pattern. Indeed, this was proposed by the company ZenGo in their white paper describing the White-City protocol [23]. This protocol proposes a number of such relays (aimed to protect against adversarial behaviour) which maintain consistency via a consensus protocol between them. Each relay $\mathcal{R}$ does not (necessarily) need to be one of the computing parties, it simply acts as a message transmission conduit between $\mathcal{P}_i$ and $\mathcal{P}_j$, for each pair (i, j). This means that each party $\mathcal{P}_i$ only needs to maintain a single connection to the relay $\mathcal{R}$. Communication can be kept private from the relay by end-to-end encryption between $\mathcal{P}_i$ and $\mathcal{P}_j$, and communication on the links between $\mathcal{P}_i$ and $\mathcal{R}$ can be ensured to be authentic via the use of message authentication codes. Other than being more practical, another advantage of having one (or more) relay node is that this provides a business model for companies to supply MPC services to clients: the relay node is providing the MPC service, for clients to connect to, and it can also act as a broker in brokering relationships between parties who desire to compute some joint function on their input. By charging for the usage of the relay node the companies can obtain revenue for providing the service.

In this work, we propose a relay model similar to Amazon SQS (Simple Queue Service) where messages are sent to a server and receivers retrieve and delete them. However, in our model, multiple relays are utilized to ensure security guarantees, whereas Amazon uses multiple servers for quality-of-service purposes in its highly distributed system.

Dynamic Computation with Delays. In common with most secure protocols, one works (ideally) in a Dolev-Yao model [11] in which the adversary is able to control the messages which are sent between parties, for example by replacing, dropping or placing messages out-of-order. In a real network, this is relatively hard for an adversary to do, thus most (practical) MPC work assumes that if party $\mathcal{P}_i$ sends a message to party $\mathcal{P}_j$ then such a message will *eventually* get from the source to the destination, and messages will be delivered in order. In a real computer network, such as the internet, the latter is a valid assumption as the exact route taken by messages is often unknown before the message is sent, and underlying network protocols provide the guarantee that messages arrive in order. However, if the "network" has a single bottleneck of a relay $\mathcal{R}$, then an adversary who controls the relay can mount trivial attacks which break the assumption that a message will always get through. In addition, modelling the system as synchronous, with a publicly known upper bound (*time-out*) on message latency, in practice is either very difficult to achieve or can severely impact communication speed, for example, if a large time-out upper bound is set so to ensure that all the messages from all the parties are delivered.

1.1   Our Contributions

In this work, we consider both these aspects and define an MPC protocol in presence of relay nodes which ensures some kind of robustness against delays, without relying on large time-out bounds. Our goal is to design a concretely efficient protocol based on more realistic network assumptions.

Concretely, we can summarize our main results as follows: 1) We formalize our communication model in the UC framework by giving an ideal functionality, called $\mathcal{F}_{\mathsf{SecureRobustRelay}}$, which defines a network where all communication occurs through relay nodes in a star-like topology and in the presence of a δ-*delaying active adversary* which can arbitrarily delay a party's execution of a command for up to δ rounds. In addition, we provide a protocol implementing this ideal functionality. 2) We give a generic secret sharing based MPC protocol secure against a δ-delaying active adversary that can proceed at the speed of the fastest parties. Our protocol makes use of an ideal functionality $\mathcal{F}_{\mathsf{Mult}}$ to evaluate multiplication gates. 3) We instantiate $\mathcal{F}_{\mathsf{Mult}}$ and show that the efficiency of the resulting protocol is comparable to that of the most efficient protocols in the setting of an honest majority which assume point-to-point channels between each pair of parties and without delays. In particular, our protocol achieves $O(n|C|)$ communication and takes advantage of the star-like network topology which allows to implement broadcast communication essentially for free. In addition, we give a detailed description of related protocols and highlight the differences with our approach. 4) Finally, we implement the communication network with relay nodes in pure Rust and present experimental results comparing its performance to that of direct TLS connections between the parties and showing the practicality of our star-like topology. Additionally, we explore the behaviour of our network under different settings and the performance of the MPC protocol built on top of the relays.

We now describe our contributions and techniques in greater detail.

Relays Nodes/Star-Like Network Topology. We consider a star-like topology network and build a model for relay nodes. We demonstrate that it is possible to remove the problem of adversarial control of the relay node by providing a set of r relay nodes $\{\mathcal{R}_1, \ldots, \mathcal{R}_r\}$, instead of just one, such that quality of service is maintained, after an initial key agreement phase, as long as at *least one* relay node is honest. Compared to the White-City protocol, our setting requires consensus only to set the communication channels (where pairwise keys are distributed), offering a significant advantage compared to other protocols, like White-City, which requires consensus at every interaction. We provide more comparison with [23] is given in the full version.

In practice, the value of r can be much less than the number of MPC parties n. For example, one may allow for $r = 2$ and have the two relay nodes provided by two different companies or servers. In such a situation, the adversary can corrupt one out of the $r = 2$ relay nodes and we still maintain security.

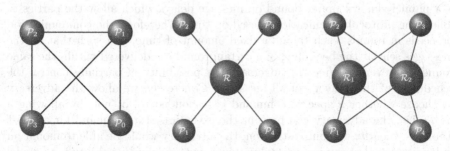

Fig. 1. Comparison between different topology networks with 4 computing parties $\mathcal{P}_1, \mathcal{P}_2, \mathcal{P}_3, \mathcal{P}_4$: a full network topology, a star-like network with 1 relay node and a replicated star-like topology with 2 relays.

More formally, we will model a relay node as an ideal functionality, and have the computing parties $\mathcal{P}_1, \ldots, \mathcal{P}_n$ connected with each other via a *replicated star-like network* with r relays $\mathcal{R}_1, \ldots, \mathcal{R}_r$, such that each $\mathcal{P}_i$ is connected only to the relays. The adversary, in practice, has full control of the communication, through point-to-point, secure authenticated channels, in that it can read (note not modify) messages sent between honest parties. In Fig. 1, we graphically compare our model with a full-network topology and a more classical star-like topology. Notice the relays are not connected to each other and they maintain an internal state that is updated when interacting with parties.

The benefit of this network model is twofold: a more realistic communication model and low communication complexity in the MPC evaluation, since it allows us to reduce the communication between the computing parties, in that they only need to communicate with the central nodes. We will expand on this below.

Modelling Delays. We consider protocols where one could have a large number n of computing parties, some of which may be statically corrupt, over a network topology as described above with $r \ll n$. In such a situation it can be the case that even honest parties $\mathcal{P}_i$ may occasionally drop out of the computation and then come back or be suffering from some kind of delays in the communication. This could be for legitimate reasons, the need for something to be patched in the organization, a simple reboot, or it could be via adversarial behaviour, i.e. the adversary temporarily stops the given party from being part of the computation via a DoS attack, for example. We note that in these situations the adversary does not take control of the party, instead we are still in a static and not adaptive security model, but the adversary can actively make the party drop out of the computation for a while (a time interval we denote by δ).

We ensure that our relays, and the MPC protocol we run on top, can cope with a party dropping out of a computation and then returning to it. This is why we require that the relays must not simply act as a store-and-forward postal service, but must maintain some state in order to allow a party to rejoin and recover messages which they have not received.

More formally, we assume a synchronous network. This means that there is a publicly-known upper bound on message delays which allow the parties to follow the protocol specifications based on time. Therefore, the communication proceeds in rounds, each taking a fixed amount of time, and such that all the messages sent at the beginning of a certain round are delivered within the same round. However, we give the adversary the possibility of partially control the scheduling of the delivery of all messages. Concretely, we allow the adversary to choose whether a specific command is responded to, or not, by allowing a *delay*, i.e., the adversary can prevent the execution of a command for at most δ rounds. Clearly, without restriction, the adversary would be able to mount an indefinite denial of service attack but, since our usage of this ability is to model the situation where a party goes temporarily offline for a short period, we admit only *bounded delays*. In addition, the delays are *local*, i.e., it applies to a single party $\mathcal{P}_i$ and it applies to all the messages passed between $\mathcal{P}_i$ and all the relays $\mathcal{R}_1, \ldots, \mathcal{R}_r$.

We define an ideal functionality $\mathcal{F}_{\mathsf{SecureRobustRelay}}$ modelling such a network with relays and delays and describe a protocol implementing it.

Efficient MPC with Stragglers. A line of research [1–3,8,9,12,15,22], motivated by concrete applications, have proposed MPC protocols supporting a more dynamic form of participation, with parties that can join and/or leave the computation. Most of these protocols rely on committees to carry on the computation.

We describe an MPC protocol which allows for parties to recover from dropped messages without the need for either the relays to maintain a list of *all* messages ever sent, or the parties restart the computation from scratch. However, we adopt a different approach compared to other works. Our protocol will proceed without waiting for all parties' message to be delivered in each round, but rather at the speed of the fastest parties. In particular, a party will progress through the MPC computation at its own pace, essentially stopping if a delay is activated. Thus, it can be the case that different parties progress through the MPC protocol at different rates, a bit like an asynchronous MPC protocol, even though the underlying communication model is synchronous.

Our main goal is to achieve efficiency by reducing the time-out bound of rounds and make the whole protocol proceed at the peace of the fastest parties. We note that a similar approach was also taken by Benhamouda et al. [4]. In this latter paper is defined the notion of *stragglers resilience*. Our security goal is similar, and we will give a detailed comparison both in techniques and efficiency between this and our work in the full version.

MPC Techniques. We describe an MPC protocol with computing parties $\mathcal{P}_1, \ldots,$ $\mathcal{P}_n$ and relays $\mathcal{R}_1, \ldots, \mathcal{R}_r$, where a malicious static adversary can corrupt up to t_p computing parties and t_r relays and control the delays of an *arbitrary number* of computing parties, albeit for a limited number of rounds. We provide active *security with abort* in the case of a strong honest majority, i.e. $t_p/2 \ll n/2$.

Our protocol is based on a degree-t Shamir secret sharing scheme, with $t_p \leq t < n/2$, and can proceed through a computation at the speed of the fastest $2 \cdot t + 1$ parties (which could include the t_p dishonest ones). This is possible as the fast parties can rely on the relays to act as a 'storage' mechanism to allow for the slower parties to catch up. We can also easily bound, and try to limit, the state size which needs to be stored by the relays as a function of the multiplicative width and depth of the function being computed, and the number of computing parties.

We first present a generic secret-shared based protocol which makes use of a multiplication functionality, $\mathcal{F}_{\mathsf{Mult}}$, to evaluate multiplication gates. The functionality $\mathcal{F}_{\mathsf{Mult}}$ can be instantiated with a multiplication protocol that is secure up to additive attacks [14]. As observed in prior work, some of the most efficient passively secure multiplication protocol [10,21] are actually actively secure up to additive attacks in normal networks, or in networks without a super-honest majority. Roughly, this means that the only thing a fully malicious adversary can do is to add fixed values to the output of multiplication gates, and to the output of the computation. We show that our basic protocol is secure up to additive internal attacks (additive attacks mounted on the internal wires of the circuit) in the $\mathcal{F}_{\mathsf{SecureRobustRelay}}$-hybrid. Notice to allow input completeness, i.e. all honest parties' input being included in the computation, we assume that no delays occur in the input phase, or alternatively, we could make all the parties wait until they receive all the $n - 1$ input messages from all the other parties.

We then compile this protocol to achieve active security with abort. A standard strategy to do this is to first run the basic passively secure protocol, then add a verification step aimed to check that all the multiplications were correctly done and finally reconstruct the output if the check passed. However, this would imply storing very large states on our relays. Hence, we use the same approach of Chida et al. [7], also used in Fluid MPC [8] and LeMans [22], and perform two computations of the circuit, one on secret shared values $\langle x \rangle$ and the other one with randomised versions $\langle \Delta \cdot x \rangle$ of the actual values. To avoid maintaining large states, we proceed like in FluidMPC and incrementally compute the checking equation during the computation.

We adopt the framework of circuit compilation [8,14], and compile the circuit C to be evaluated into a new circuit $\tilde{C}$, called a *robust circuit*, such that when $\tilde{C}$ is evaluated using a passively secure MPC protocol which is secure up to additive attacks, it results in a protocol for evaluating the original circuit C which is actively secure with abort. This view point allows us to bound the state which needs to be saved by the relays in our protocol.

We note that our notion of state is different from that in Fluid MPC, where the state needed to be transferred is the entire width of the circuit at any one layer, whereas in our situation the state is only the part of the width related to multiplication gates at that layer. Thus we adopt a slightly different notion of robust circuit, and associated compiler. This also implies that, although keeping small states is an important task, it is not as crucial as in committee-based protocols because we do not need to pass them from one committee to another. This gives rise to trade-offs between communication and state-complexity.

As a last remark, even if the general strategy we adopt in our MPC protocol is similar to that used in other works, adapting it to our setting and trying to maintain low complexity requires a careful design of the basic building blocks. For example, we show in the full version that if we instantiate $\mathcal{F}_{\mathsf{Mult}}$ with the widely used Maurer's multiplication protocol [20], our general construction does not work anymore. Instead, we provide a simple and efficient instantiation of $\mathcal{F}_{\mathsf{Mult}}$ using a variant of the multiplicative protocol given by Damgård and Nielsen [10] (DN protocol), showing that the security of the multiplication and resulting MPC protocol relies on the robustness of $\mathcal{F}_{\mathsf{SecureRobustRelay}}$. In particular, our network allows a single party $\mathcal{P}_i$ to send a value to all the computing parties in a single command, by simply sending the value to all the relays. This means that we can remove the "king" from the DN protocol, and instead utilize a broadcast mechanism to allow all parties to essentially be the king. Since at least one relay is honest, this broadcast mechanism comes "for free" and ensures that corrupt parties are forced to send the same value to all honest parties. This simple observation enables us to prevent the *double dipping attack* [13,17] on the DN protocol.

Notice that the fact that it is simpler – and more efficient – for a party to communicate in a broadcast manner, as opposed to a point-to-point manner, via the relays means that traditional notions of communication complexity of protocols may not apply, since, traditionally a broadcast is considered more expensive than point-to-point communication.

Finally, in the full version, we outline possible optimizations to our basic construction and give an estimation of the complexity of different strategies. In particular, we show that our main approach roughly match the communication complexity of [7], achieving linear communication and a concrete amortized communication cost of 12/13 field elements per multiplication gate per party. If we allow the use of PRGs this costs goes down to 8/9 field elements per party. We also sketch how to further reduce the communication costs to 6 (or 4 with PRGs) field elements per party using techniques from [5,18,19].

Implementation. While the use of relays results in a more realistic network, it might introduce additional communication. To evaluate the performance of our network topology, we implemented protocol $\Pi_{\mathsf{SecureRobustRelay}}$, presented in Fig. 4, in pure Rust, and compared its performance to that of direct communication between two parties. The results in Sect. 7 show that using relays has no noticeable impact on the performance when sending up to 2^{19} 16-byte messages. Note that, a 16-byte message can correspond to a finite field element of around 128 bits in size, and thus can represent native data-type for any MPC computation layered ontop.

In addition, we analyse how to best configure the network in order to optimise the communication runtimes. First, we conclude that although erasing each message in the relays immediately after retrieval results in slower communication, erasing them in batches achieves similar performance to direct communication. On the other hand, never deleting messages not only means the relays might run out of memory, but also turns out to be slower since the relays must iterate through several messages when answering message request. Second, we show that a network with more relays has increased security while adding only a small overhead to the communication time.

A second set of experiments is dedicated to evaluate the performance of the MPC protocol. We measure the number of multiplications performed in one second both when parties all run at the same speed and when some of them are slower than others.

2   Preliminaries

For a set S, we denote by $a \leftarrow S$ the process of drawing a from S with a uniform distribution on the set S. If D is a probability distribution, we denote by $a \leftarrow D$ the process of drawing a with the given probability distribution. For a probabilistic algorithm A, we denote by $a \leftarrow A$ the process of assigning a the output of algorithm A, with the underlying probability distribution being determined by the random coins of A. We use $[n]$ to denote the set $\{1, \ldots, n\}$ and $\mathcal{P} = \{\mathcal{P}_1, \ldots, \mathcal{P}_n\}$ the set of parties.

In the full version we cover the basic definitions of Shamir's secret sharing, encryption and circuit depth/width that we will require.

2.1   Communication and Security Model

We summarize here our settings, as previously described. We assume $\mathcal{P} = \{\mathcal{P}_1, \ldots, \mathcal{P}_n\}$ computing parties and $\{\mathcal{R}_1, \ldots \mathcal{R}_r\}$ relay nodes. Parties are only connected with relays via authenticated, but not necessarily private, channels and not with each other and also the relays are not connected with each other. More formally, we prove security in the *authenticated-links model* (AM) [6], where the adversary can only deliver messages that were sent by parties and must deliver them unmodified. Relays maintain an internal state that is updated when interacting with parties.

We assume a synchronous network with a publicly-known upper bound (timeout) on message delays which allows the parties to follow protocol specifications based on time. Therefore, the communication proceeds in rounds, each taking a fixed amount of time.

We consider δ-*delaying malicious static adversaries* which are allowed to control up to $t_r \leq r - 1$ relays and $t_p \leq t$ parties, where $n \geq 2t + 1$. We also give the adversary the possibility of partially control the scheduling of the delivery of all messages by allowing it to arbitrarily delay parties by up to δ rounds. This means that each party can be delayed more than once during the computation, but each time only by δ rounds.

We consider security with *selective abort*, where the adversary receives the output and determines which honest parties will receive abort and which will receive their correct output.

2.2   Internal Additive Attacks

Intuitively, an additive attack (Definition 1) is an attack which changes the value of a gate's output wire in the circuit by an additive value before the calculation is performed, i.e. blindly changing a wire from $f(x)$ to $f(x) + \delta_a$, where $f(x)$ is the function computed by the gate and δ_a is a value known by the adversary.

We recall the formal definition of an additive attack. One minor modification to the definition from [8,14] is due to the check in our protocol for opening a value, given in Fig. 5, Sect. 4. In particular, since the output wires of a circuit will be checked via the underlying error-detection properties of the Shamir's secret sharing scheme, we restrict to an additive attack only related to the internal wires of a circuit and not to the output wires. We call such an attack "internal additive attack" in order to distinguish it from the standard notion of an additive attack (which also allows the adversary to add a known value to the output wires of the circuit).

Definition 1 (Internal Additive Attack). *Let $C : \mathbb{F}^n \to \mathbb{F}^k$ be a circuit. An additive attack A by an adversary on the evaluation of the circuit C assigns an element of $\mathbb{F}$ to each of the circuits' internal wires, i.e. a wire between two gates g^a and g^b. Let $A_{a,b}$ denote the value assigned by the attack to the internal wire between gates g^a and g^b. The additive attack changes the calculation of the circuit as follows: For each internal wire between gates g^a and g^b, the value $A_{a,b}$ is added to the wires value after the calculation of the output of gate g^a, but before the calculation of the gate g^b.*

3   Relays and Delays

In this section, we present the protocol $\Pi_{\text{SecureRobustRelay}}$, which formally describes how parties and relays securely communicate in presence of bounded delays. The protocol is given in Fig. 4. It implements the ideal functionality $\mathcal{F}_{\text{SecureRobustRelay}}$, given in the full version.

The protocol $\Pi_{\text{SecureRobustRelay}}$ uses two main distinct building blocks, namely the functionalities $\mathcal{F}_{\text{SingleRelay}}$ and $\mathcal{F}_{\text{Delay}}$, that we briefly describe before introducing our main protocol. This approach allows to first introduce the topology of our network with relays and then add the possibility of adversarial delays.

Functionality $\mathcal{F}_{\mathsf{SingleRelay}}(\mathcal{R}, \mathcal{P}_1, \ldots, \mathcal{P}_n)$

This functionality runs with an adversary $\mathcal{S}$, a special party (denoted by $\mathcal{R}$), which is the relay, and n parties (denoted by $\mathcal{P}_1, \ldots, \mathcal{P}_n$). The functionality maintains pairwise counters $\tau_{i,j}$, for all $i \neq j$, and global counters $\tau_{i,\mathcal{P}}$ for all $i \in \mathcal{P}$, and variables $\epsilon_{\tau_{i,j}} \in \{\bot, 0, 1\}$, and $\epsilon_{\tau_{i,\mathcal{P},j}} \in \{\bot, 0, 1\}$.

Upon activation the functionality receives either $(-, \mathcal{P}_I)$ or $(\mathcal{R}, \mathcal{P}_I)$ from the adversary, where $\mathcal{P}_I \subset \{\mathcal{P}_1, \ldots, \mathcal{P}_n\}$ is the set of corrupt parties, indicating in the first case that the relay is honest, and the in second case that the relay is dishonest. We assume $|\mathcal{P}_I| \leq t_p$.

Init: On input (init) from all parties the functionality sets all the counters $\tau \leftarrow 0$ and $\epsilon \leftarrow \bot$.

Send: On input $(\mathsf{send}, \mathcal{R}, \mathcal{P}_i, \mathcal{P}_j, m)$ from $\mathcal{P}_i$,
  1. Send (sent, i, j, m) to $\mathcal{R}$ and increment $\tau_{i,j}$ by one.
  2. Set $m_{\tau_{i,j}} \leftarrow m$ and store it. Set $\epsilon_{\tau_{i,j}} \leftarrow 0$.
  3. Delete (i, j, m) from the store.

SendToAll: On input $(\mathsf{sendToAll}, \mathcal{R}, \mathcal{P}_i, \mathcal{P}, m)$ from $\mathcal{P}_i$,
  1. Send $(\mathsf{sendToAll}, i, \mathcal{P}, m)$ to $\mathcal{R}$ and increment $\tau_{i,\mathcal{P}}$ by one.
  2. Set $m_{\tau_{i,\mathcal{P}}} \leftarrow m$ and store it. Set $\epsilon_{\tau_{i,\mathcal{P},j}} \leftarrow 0, \forall j \in \mathcal{P} \setminus i$.
  3. Delete $(i, \mathcal{P}, m)$ from the store.

Erase: On input $(\mathsf{erase}, \mathcal{R}, \mathcal{P}_i, \mathcal{P}_j, \tau_{i,j})$ from $\mathcal{P}_j$.
  1. Send $(\mathsf{erase}, \mathcal{P}_i, \mathcal{P}_j, \tau)$ to $\mathcal{R}$.
  2. Set $\epsilon_{\tau_{i,j}} \leftarrow 1$, and delete $m_{\tau_{i,j}}$ for all $\tau_{i,j} \leq \tau$.

EraseAll: On input $(\mathsf{eraseAll}, \mathcal{R}, \mathcal{P}, \mathcal{P}_j, \tau)$ from $\mathcal{P}_j$, where $\tau = \{\tau_{i,\mathcal{P}}\}_{i \neq j}$
  1. Send $(\mathsf{eraseAll}, \mathcal{P}, \mathcal{P}_j, \{\tau_{i,\mathcal{P}}\}_{i \neq j})$ to $\mathcal{R}$.
  2. Set $\epsilon_{\tau_{i,\mathcal{P},j}} \leftarrow 1, \forall i$
  3. For each i, if $\epsilon_{\tau_{i,\mathcal{P},j}} = 1$ for all $j \in \mathcal{P}$, delete $m_{\tau_{i,\mathcal{P}}}$ for all $\tau_{i,\mathcal{P}} \leq \tau$.

Request: On input $(\mathsf{request}, \mathcal{R}, \mathcal{P}_i, \mathcal{P}_j, \tau_{i,j})$ from $\mathcal{P}_j$,
  1. Send $(\mathsf{request}, \mathcal{P}_i, \mathcal{P}_j, \tau_{i,j})$ to $\mathcal{R}$.
  2. If $\mathcal{R}$ is corrupt, wait for $(\mathsf{Deliver}, \tilde{m})$ from $\mathcal{S}$, send $\tilde{m}$ to $\mathcal{P}_j$.
     Else, if $\epsilon_{\tau_{i,j}} \neq 0$ then return $\bot$ to $\mathcal{P}_j$, else retrieve $m_{\tau_{i,j}}$ and send it to $\mathcal{P}_j$.

RequestFromAll: On input $(\mathsf{requestFromAll}, \mathcal{R}, \mathcal{P}, \mathcal{P}_j, \tau)$ from $\mathcal{P}_j$, where $\tau = \{\tau_{i,\mathcal{P}}\}_{i \neq j}$,
  1. Send $(\mathsf{requestFromAll}, \mathcal{P}, \mathcal{P}_j, \{\tau_{i,\mathcal{P}}^{\mathcal{R}}\}_{i \neq j})$ to $\mathcal{R}$.
  2. If $\mathcal{R}$ is corrupt, wait for $(\mathsf{Deliver}, \tilde{\mathbf{m}})$ from $\mathcal{S}$, send $\tilde{\mathbf{m}}$ to $\mathcal{P}_j$.
     Else, for all $i \neq j$, if $\epsilon_{\tau_{i,\mathcal{P},j}} \neq 0$ then set the ith-coordinate of $\mathbf{m}$ to be equal to $\bot$, otherwise retrieve the ith-message corresponding to $\tau_{i,\mathcal{P}}$. Send the vector $\mathbf{m}$ to $\mathcal{P}_j$.

Figure 2. Functionality modelling a single relay

3.1   A Single Relay

The functionality $\mathcal{F}_{\mathsf{SingleRelay}}$, described in Fig. 2, captures all the interactions between parties $\mathcal{P}_1, \ldots, \mathcal{P}_n$ and a single relay $\mathcal{R}$. The functionality is described by six commands, other than the initialization command Init, as explained below.

Send. In the **send** command we let the adversary see the message being sent even between honest parties and an honest relay. This captures the fact that our connections are only authentic. To manage the **send** commands the functionality maintains pairwise counters, $\tau_{i,j}$, $\forall(i,j)$, that are used to store, retrieve and erase messages sent from party $\mathcal{P}_i$ to $\mathcal{P}_j$. The relay uses the variable $\epsilon_{\tau_{i,j}}$ to indicate whether the $\tau_{i,j}$-th message from $\mathcal{P}_i$ to $\mathcal{P}_j$ needs to be stored for future possible retrievals by party $\mathcal{P}_j$. We have $\epsilon_{\tau_{i,j}} = \perp$ if the specific message associated to counter $\tau_{i,j}$ has not been sent, $\epsilon_{\tau_{i,j}} = 0$ if the associated message is stored for future use, and $\epsilon_{\tau_{i,j}} = 1$ if the associated message is never going to be retrieved.

The variable $\epsilon_{\tau_{i,j}}$ is used to avoid messages being stored indefinitely by the relay. We allow a receiving party to indicate that the network can erase messages, and these will never be requested in the future. To indicate which messages are not going to be retrieved, a receiving party uses the **erase** command.

Request. Parties use the **request** command to retrieve a message. The request is of the form $(i, j, \tau_{i,j})$, where party $\mathcal{P}_j$ is requesting the $\tau_{i,j}$-th message sent to it by party $\mathcal{P}_i$. The adversary is allowed to replace any sent message, which has not been erased, to any value it wants, including $\perp$, as long as the relay is corrupt, via the **request** query. A $\perp$ value is returned by an honest relay if the message has been erased, or it has not yet been received by the relay. Note, the **request** command allows an adversarial relay to send different messages for the same $(i, j, \tau_{i,j})$ tuples for different **request** queries.

SendToAll. Similarly, a party $\mathcal{P}_i$ can also send a message to all the other parties (or even a subset of $\mathcal{P}$), by just sending a single message to the relay. This is captured by the **sendToAll** command. To manage these, the functionality maintains 'global' counters, $\tau_{i,\mathcal{P}}$ and $\epsilon_{\tau_{i,\mathcal{P},j}}$, $\forall i, j \in \mathcal{P}$, used to store, retrieve and erase messages sent from $\mathcal{P}_i$ to all parties in $\mathcal{P} \setminus \mathcal{P}_i$. The **sendToAll** command is paired with **requestFromAll** and **eraseAll** commands in order to manage these sent messages.

RequestToAll. The command **requestFromAll** allows a single party $\mathcal{P}_j$ to retrieve messages from all parties. To ease the exposition, we only allow this command on global messages with counters $\tau_{i,\mathcal{P}}$, for all i. It can be used by $\mathcal{P}_j$ to obtain all the $n - 1$ messages $m_{\tau_{i,\mathcal{P}}}$, for $i \neq j$. This command will retrieve a vector of messages, one from each sending party. If a specific message has not yet been received by the relay, then $\perp$ is returned in this location.

Erase EraseFromAll. The relaying party $\mathcal{R}$ only stores messages for which $\epsilon_{\tau_{i,j}}$ (resp. $\epsilon_{\tau_{i,\mathcal{P},j}}$) is not equal to one. Notice that, the relay $\mathcal{R}$ does not delete the message on retrieval (by setting $\epsilon_{\tau_{i,j}} = 1$) since the receiving party may wish to request it again (in the case of it failing for some reason during the execution of the **request** command). Relays delete messages only when they are instructed to, which happens when either **erase** or **eraseAll** are called.

An implementation of this underlying functionality $\mathcal{F}_{\mathsf{SingleRelay}}$ is immediate, in that the relaying party $\mathcal{R}$ just needs to maintain a list of messages sent, which may be requested in future, and it needs to maintain authenticated links with all parties.

Functionality $\mathcal{F}_{\mathsf{Delay}}(\mathcal{P}_1, \ldots, \mathcal{P}_n, \mathcal{R}_1, \ldots, \mathcal{R}_r, \delta)$

This functionality runs with an adversary $\mathcal{S}$, n parties, denoted by $\mathcal{P}_1, \ldots, \mathcal{P}_n$, and r relays, denoted by $\mathcal{R}_1, \ldots, \mathcal{R}_r$. In addition as input it takes a parameter $\delta \in \mathbb{N}$. Further, it stores $\delta_i \leq \delta$ for each $i \in [n]$.

Init: Set $\delta_i \leftarrow \perp$ for all $i \in [n]$.
Delay: On input $(\mathtt{delay}, \mathcal{P}_i, \mathtt{command})$:
  – If $\delta_i = \perp$: Send $(\mathtt{delay}, i)$ to $\mathcal{S}$ and wait for input.
    – If $\mathcal{S}$ returns $(\mathtt{delay}, D_i)$ and $0 < D_i \leq \delta$, then
       1. Send $(\mathtt{delayed}, D_i)$ to $\mathcal{S}$.
       2. Set $\delta_i \leftarrow D_i$.
    – If $\mathcal{S}$ returns $(\mathtt{delay}, D_i)$ and $D_i \geq \delta$, then
       1. Send $(\mathtt{delayed}, \delta)$ to $\mathcal{S}$.
       2. Set $\delta_i \leftarrow \delta$.
    – Else, send $\mathtt{ok}$ to $\mathcal{P}_i$
  – If $\delta_i \neq \perp$:
     1. Set $\delta_i \leftarrow \delta_i - 1$.
     2. If $\delta_i = 0$: send $\mathtt{ok}$ to $\mathcal{P}_i$

Figure 3. Functionality modelling delays

3.2   Modelling Bounded Delays

We now turn to modelling the bounded-delay communication setting for our main protocol. This is captured by the functionality $\mathcal{F}_{\mathsf{Delay}}$ given in Fig. 3. It is parametrized by a constant δ and it works by querying the adversary, who can then impose a delay bounded by δ. This means that, as soon as a party has been delayed for δ rounds, the next command will proceed. More in details, once the functionality is called with $(\mathtt{delay}, \mathcal{P}_i, \mathtt{command})$, where $\mathtt{command}$ represent a specific action that $\mathcal{P}_i$ is trying to execute, we distinguish two different cases. If $\delta_i = \perp$, it means that $\mathcal{P}_i$ is not currently delayed. Hence, the functionality sends a message $(\mathtt{delay}, i)$ to the ideal adversary $\mathcal{S}$. If $\mathcal{S}$ replies with $(\mathtt{delay}, D_i)$, then the functionality sets $\delta = D_i$, meaning that $\mathcal{P}_i$ will be delayed for D_i rounds, otherwise returns $\mathtt{ok}$ to $\mathcal{P}_i$. If otherwise $\delta_i \neq \perp$, $\mathcal{P}_i$ has been already delayed, so the functionality sets $\delta_i \leftarrow \delta_i - 1$, and if the resulting δ_i is 0, it sends $\mathtt{ok}$ to $\mathcal{P}_i$.

In a real world implementation, as communication is essentially synchronous, if a party does not receive a valid response (e.g. a message or an $\mathtt{ok}$ signal) after a request, then they interpret this as a $\mathtt{delay}$. Note, that the delay is *local* for a party $\mathcal{P}_i$, it does not depend on the specific corresponding party $\mathcal{P}_j$. However, it does apply for all messages passed between $\mathcal{P}_i$ and *all* of the relays $\mathcal{R}_1, \ldots, \mathcal{R}_r$.

In addition, we require that parties are delayed only for a limited number of rounds; if we removed this condition, and set $\delta = \infty$, then the resulting functionality would produce something akin to an asynchronous network, which would result in some changes needed to the resulting MPC protocol which we run on top of our relays.

As remarked, the delays model the fact that parties can execute the protocol at different speeds, and can reboot themselves or go offline for a short period. We give the adversary the ability to control this operation.

3.3   Implementing a Secure Robust Relay Using Multiple Single Relay's

We can now formally describe our star-like topology where n parties, instead of relying on a single relay, rely on a set of relays, assuming at least one of them is honest. We show that, once each party has agreed pair-wise keys for an AEAD encryption scheme with each other party, then a robust relay protocol can be implemented, assuming only one honest relay and without expensive consensus procedures. We could assume these keys are pre-distributed, however for completeness in the full version we present how the parties can execute a key agreement protocol over a set of relays, as just defined. However, to do so requires that a majority of the relays is honest.

We stress that AEAD encryption is only used on point-to-point channels, i.e. with the send command. Looking ahead, our MPC protocol only relies on sendToAll, which works like a public broadcast in a normal MPC protocol and does not require encryption.

Protocol Intuition. The protocol $\Pi_{\text{SecureRobustRelay}}$ has an initialization phase where parties call the key-exchange functionality $\mathcal{F}_{\text{KE}}$. To send a message $m_{i,j}$ to $\mathcal{P}_j$, a party $\mathcal{P}_i$ first encrypts the message and then waits for an ok message from the network. This model the fact that $\mathcal{P}_i$ might be either temporarily offline, for example for a reboot, or delayed by the adversary. When ok is received, it sends the ciphertext $\text{ct}_{i,j} \leftarrow \text{Enc}_{k_{i,j}}(m_{i,j})$ to all the relays. Each relay stores the ciphertext, and makes it available for a later request from $\mathcal{P}_j$. Note that if $\mathcal{P}_i$ is honest, then all the relays have the same ciphertext $\text{ct}_{i,j}$ stored. When $\mathcal{P}_j$ wants to get this message, again it waits for an ok message from the network, and then requests these ciphertexts to all the relays. Intuitively, security is guaranteed by the following argument.

- If both $\mathcal{P}_i$ and $\mathcal{P}_j$ are honest, and $\mathcal{P}_j$ requests a message sent by $\mathcal{P}_i$, it receives $\text{ct}_{i,j}$ from the honest relays, which will decrypt to the input message $m_{i,j}$ sent by $\mathcal{P}_i$. Note that corrupt relays can send arbitrary messages/ciphertexts, however, since they do not know the secret key $k_{i,j}$, these messages are either invalid ciphertexts or $\perp$. For this reason, $\mathcal{P}_j$ will always receive the correct message.
- If $\mathcal{P}_i$ is honest and $\mathcal{P}_j$ is corrupt, then $\mathcal{P}_j$ can output whatever they want. It can also abort after it decrypts the message $m_{i,j}$ sent by $\mathcal{P}_i$.
- The case of $\mathcal{P}_i$, $\mathcal{P}_j$ both corrupt is similar to the previous one.
- If only $\mathcal{P}_i$ is corrupt, then it can send arbitrary values to the relays during the send command. However, if $\mathcal{P}_i$ is colluding with some of the corrupt relays, then it can make an honest $\mathcal{P}_j$ accept a value that was not previously stored. This can happen for example when the honest relays reply $\perp$ on a

Protocol $\Pi_{\text{SecureRobustRelay}}(\mathcal{R}_1, \ldots, \mathcal{R}_r, \mathcal{P}_1, \ldots, \mathcal{P}_n, \delta)$

Let $\mathcal{H}$ be a hash function modelled as a random oracle and $\mathcal{E} = (\text{KeyGen}, \text{Enc}, \text{Dec})$ an AEAD encryption scheme that uses $\mathcal{F}_{\text{KE}}$ as key-exchange functionality.

init: Each pair of parties (i,j) call the functionality $\mathcal{F}_{\text{KE}}$ obtaining $\mathsf{k}_{i,j}$.

send: When $\mathcal{P}_i$ wishes to send a message m to $\mathcal{P}_j$:
1. $\mathcal{P}_i$ computes $\mathsf{ct} \leftarrow \text{Enc}_{\mathsf{k}_{i,j}}(m)$ and sends $(\text{delay}, \mathcal{P}_i, (\text{send}, \mathcal{P}_j))$ to $\mathcal{F}_{\text{Delay}}$ until it receives an **ok** message from the functionality.
2. When $\mathcal{P}_i$ receives **ok**, it calls $(\text{send}, \mathcal{R}_k, \mathcal{P}_i, \mathcal{P}_j, \mathsf{ct})$ on $\mathcal{F}_{\text{SingleRelay}}$, $\forall k \in [r]$.

sendToAll: When $\mathcal{P}_i$ wishes to send a message m to all other parties:
1. $\mathcal{P}_i$ sends the command $(\text{delay}, \mathcal{P}_i, (\text{sendToAll}, \mathcal{P}))$ to $\mathcal{F}_{\text{Delay}}$ until it receives an **ok** message from the functionality.
2. When $\mathcal{P}_i$ receives **ok**, it calls $(\text{send}, \mathcal{R}_k, \mathcal{P}_i, \mathcal{P}, m)$ on $\mathcal{F}_{\text{SingleRelay}}$ $\forall k \in [r]$.

request: When party $\mathcal{P}_j$ wishes to get the message from $\mathcal{P}_i$ with index $\tau_{i,j}$, $\mathcal{P}_j$ sends $(\text{delay}, \mathcal{P}_j, (\text{request}, \mathcal{P}_i))$ to $\mathcal{F}_{\text{Delay}}$ until it receives an **ok** message from the functionality.
1. When $\mathcal{P}_j$ receives **ok**, it calls $(\text{request}, \mathcal{R}_k, \mathcal{P}_i, \mathcal{P}_j, \tau_{i,j})$ on $\mathcal{F}_{\text{SingleRelay}}$, for each $k \in [r]$, obtaining ct_k for $k \in [r]$.
2. **Check:** Party $\mathcal{P}_j$ performs the following check
   - If, for all values of k, $\mathsf{ct}_k = \bot$ then return $\bot$ //it might be that the message has not yet been sent by party $\mathcal{P}_i$.
   - Else, for each k such that $\mathsf{ct}_k \neq \bot$, compute $m_k \leftarrow \text{Dec}_{\mathsf{k}_{i,j}}(\mathsf{ct}_k)$.
     - If there is a *unique* $m_k \neq \bot$ then accept this value.
     - Else, if there is more than one value $m_k \neq \bot$, then **abort**.

requestFromAll: When party $\mathcal{P}_j$ wishes to get $n-1$ messages from $\mathcal{P} \setminus \mathcal{P}_j$ with index $\tau_{i,\mathcal{P}}$, $i \neq j$, $\mathcal{P}_j$ sends $(\text{delay}, \mathcal{P}_j, (\text{requestFromAll}, \mathcal{P}))$ to $\mathcal{F}_{\text{Delay}}$ until it receives an **ok** message from the functionality.
1. When $\mathcal{P}_j$ receives **ok**, it calls $(\text{requestFromAll}, \mathcal{R}_k, \mathcal{P}, \mathcal{P}_j, \boldsymbol{\tau})$, where $\boldsymbol{\tau} = \{\tau_{i,\mathcal{P}}\}_{i \neq j}$, on $\mathcal{F}_{\text{SingleRelay}}$, for each $k \in [r]$, obtaining $\mathbf{m}_k$, $k \in [r]$.
2. **Check:** Party $\mathcal{P}_j$ performs the following check for each coordinate of the received vectors $\mathbf{m}_k = (m_{i,k})_{i \neq j}$.
   - If, for some values of k, $m_{i,k} = \bot$, then set $m_{\tau_{i,\mathcal{P}}} = \bot$.
   - Otherwise, if there is a *unique* $m_{i,k} \neq \bot$, for all k, then accept this value; else, if there is more than one value $m_{i,k}$, for different k, such that $m_{i,k} \neq \bot$, then **abort**.

erase: When $\mathcal{P}_j$ wishes to erase messages from $\mathcal{P}_i$:
1. $\mathcal{P}_j$ sends $(\text{delay}, \mathcal{P}_j, (\text{erase}, \mathcal{P}_i))$ to $\mathcal{F}_{\text{Delay}}$ until it receives an **ok** message from the functionality.
2. When $\mathcal{P}_j$ receives **ok**, it calls $(\text{erase}, \mathcal{R}_k, \mathcal{P}_i, \mathcal{P}_j, \tau_{i,j})$ on $\mathcal{F}_{\text{SingleRelay}}$ $\forall k \in [r]$.

eraseAll: When $\mathcal{P}_j$ wishes to erase messages from $\mathcal{P}$:
1. $\mathcal{P}_j$ sends $(\text{delay}, \mathcal{P}_j, (\text{eraseAll}, \mathcal{P}))$ to $\mathcal{F}_{\text{Delay}}$ until it receives an **ok** message from the functionality.
2. When $\mathcal{P}_j$ receives **ok**, it calls $(\text{eraseAll}, \mathcal{R}_k, \mathcal{P}, \mathcal{P}_j, \boldsymbol{\tau})$ on $\mathcal{F}_{\text{SingleRelay}}$ for each $k \in [r]$, where $\boldsymbol{\tau}$ is a vector of counters $(\tau_{i,\mathcal{P}})_{i \neq j}$.

Figure 4. Protocol $\Pi_{\text{SecureRobustRelay}}$

request command from $\mathcal{P}_j$, while the corrupt ones send valid ciphertexts corresponding to a unique message m. This is possible since in this case the key $k_{i,j}$ is known to the relays in $\mathcal{R}_I$, i.e., the set of corrupt relays. This means that a corrupt sender cannot change a value that was previously stored by the honest relays, but can input a new value if no previous value was stored in $\mathcal{R}_k$, $k \notin \mathcal{R}_I$.

When a party $\mathcal{P}_i$ wants to send a common message to all parties, via sendToAll, it does not encrypt the message but simply sends it to all the relays via authenticated links. Similar to the previous case, we show that, since we assume at least one honest relay, the output of the request step, if the receiving party $\mathcal{P}_j$ is honest, either is the value actually sent and stored in the relays or $\mathcal{P}_j$ outputs abort. Note that this time we do not allow the adversary to send values that are not stored in all the relays, so a message is not accepted unless it is the only valid message stored in all the relays. Similarly, we extend request to requestFromAll allowing a party $\mathcal{P}_j$ to request messages from all other parties. The security of it can be proven by applying the same arguments given for request to each of the messages that $\mathcal{P}_j$ is retrieving. More formally, we prove the following theorem. For the proof see the full version.

Theorem 1. *The protocol* $\Pi_{\mathsf{SecureRobustRelay}}$ *securely with abort realizes* $\mathcal{F}_{\mathsf{SecureRobustRelay}}$ *in the* $\{\mathcal{F}_{\mathsf{SingleRelay}}, \mathcal{F}_{\mathsf{Delay}}, \mathcal{F}_{\mathsf{KE}}\}$-*hybrid model.*

4 MPC Building Blocks

We describe our MPC protocol via a set of standard MPC functionalities and sub-protocols which utilize $\mathcal{F}_{\mathsf{SecureRobustRelay}}$ to implement the communication between the parties. We let $\mathcal{P}_I$ denote the set of computing parties which are adversarially controlled, i.e. $\mathcal{P}_I \subset \{\mathcal{P}_1, \dots, \mathcal{P}_n\}$.

We recall that in our protocols, both parties $\mathcal{P}$ and relays $\mathcal{R}$ maintain pairwise and global counters and variables, as described in the previous section. To ease the exposition, we describe our protocols implicitly assuming that each message is associated with its counter.

In describing our protocols in the $\mathcal{F}_{\mathsf{SecureRobustRelay}}$-hybrid model, we present each command as separate send, sendToAll, request and requestFromAll commands. However, evaluating each layer of the circuit (bar those at depth zero) consists in each party executing a set of send/sendToAll commands followed, by a set of request/requestFromAll commands. In terms of the underlying synchronous communication model upon which the relays are built, a send/sendToAll command passed to the r-relays from party $\mathcal{P}_i$ is executed in one round. This means that, if P_i wants to send a message to P_j and there are no delays, then the send from $\mathcal{P}_i$ to all of the $\mathcal{R}_k$'s terminates within the same communication round. However, two consecutive send commands by party $\mathcal{P}_i$ destined for $\mathcal{P}_j$ and $\mathcal{P}_k$ will take up two rounds in the underlying synchronous communication model.

Sub-protocol Open$(j, \langle x \rangle)$

INPUT: Each party $\mathcal{P}_i$ holds a share x_i of the unknown value x. We denote by ct_{x_i} the ciphertext corresponding to x_i according to an AEAD encryption scheme.
OUTPUT: $\mathcal{P}_j$ obtains x

Open$(j, \langle x \rangle_t)$:
1. For all $i \in [n]$, $j \neq i$ $\mathcal{P}_i$ calls $(\mathbf{send}, \mathcal{P}_i, \mathcal{P}_j)$ on $\mathcal{F}_{\mathsf{SecureRobustRelay}}$, inputting a vector $\mathbf{x}$ after receiving ok, where $\mathbf{x}$ is the vector consisting of r-values ct_{x_i} and r is the number of relays. Let the associated τ value for these messages be $\tau_{i,j}$.
2. $\mathcal{P}_j$ runs the sub-protocol $\mathbf{y} \leftarrow$ Receive$(j, 2t)$ below.
3. $\mathcal{P}_j$ forms the set $\mathcal{M}$ of all indices for which $y_i \neq \perp$, and the vector $\mathbf{x}^{\mathcal{M}}$ of values $y_i \neq \perp$.
4. $\mathcal{P}_j$ computes $P^{\mathcal{M}} \cdot \mathbf{x}^{\mathcal{M}}$ and outputs abort if the result is not equal to $\mathbf{0}$, where $P^{\mathcal{M}}$ is the parity check matrix, restricted to the set of parties $\mathcal{M}$.
5. Party $\mathcal{P}_j$ computes $x \leftarrow \mathbf{r}^{\mathcal{M}} \cdot \mathbf{x}^{\mathcal{M}}$, where $\mathbf{r}^{\mathcal{M}}$ is the recombination vector restricted to the parties in $\mathcal{M}$, and returns this as the output of the procedure.

Figure 5. Procedure to open a sharing $\langle x \rangle$ towards a single party $\mathcal{P}_j$ or to $\mathcal{P}$

We will make use of the following sub-protocols and functionalities.

Sub-protocol Open$(i, \langle x \rangle_t)$. Described in Fig. 5, it takes a shared value $\langle x \rangle_t$ and opens it to $\mathcal{P}_i$.

Sub-protocol Open$(\langle x \rangle_t)$. It takes a shared value $\langle x \rangle_t$ and opens it to all parties $\mathcal{P}$. The cost of Open$(\langle x \rangle_t)$ and Open$(i, \langle x \rangle_t)$ is r field elements per party, where r is the number of relays.

Sub-protocol Receive(i, ι). It is described in Fig. 6 and allows party $\mathcal{P}_i$ to receive a vector $\mathbf{y}$ of shares/values via a number of **request** to $\mathcal{F}_{\mathsf{SecureRobustRelay}}$. The second input parameter ι, indicates the minimum number of shares $\mathcal{P}_i$ needs to receive to complete the command. Notice, in Receive(i, ι) after executing enough **request** commands to complete the recovery of the secret shared value, we then execute **erase** commands for all other parties. Thus data which has been received is deleted on the relays, and data which is not received for this round is not stored by the relays when they do eventually receive it. These **erase** commands could be executed every so often, and not every execution of Receive(i, ι), as they increase the number of underlying rounds needed. However, the less one executes them, the more data needs to be stored by the relays. Thus there is a trade-off, and we settle on executing the **erase** commands for every Receive(i, ι) for expository purposes. It can be modified to obtain the sub-procedure ReceiveFromAll(i, ι) by using the **requestFromAll** to $\mathcal{F}_{\mathsf{SecureRobustRelay}}$. Notice that both variants allow the receiving parties to proceed as soon as they have received $2 \cdot t + 1$ shares, hence they do not need to wait for the full set of n shares.

Sub-protocols Receive($j, \langle x \rangle$) and ReceiveFromAll(j, ι)

Receive(j, ι):
1. Party $\mathcal{P}_j$ initializes a vector **y** of length n containing $\perp$ in each location, bar location j where it places the value x_j.
2. $\mathcal{P}_j$ repeats the following step until the vector **y** contains at least ι non-$\perp$ values:
   (a) For $i \in [n]$, if $y_i = \perp$ then call (**request**, $\mathcal{P}_i, \mathcal{P}_j$) on $\mathcal{F}_{\mathsf{SecureRobustRelay}}$, inputting $\tau_{i,j}$ after receiving ok, to obtain the value x_i. If the functionality return abort, then abort, otherwise place x_i in position i in the vector **y**.
   Note, this may take many iterations since party $\mathcal{P}_j$ may possibly not yet have sent its message yet, or the adversary may be delaying messages.
3. Party $\mathcal{P}_j$ calls (**erase**, $\mathcal{P}_i, \mathcal{P}_j$) on $\mathcal{F}_{\mathsf{SecureRobustRelay}}$, inputting $\tau_{i,j}$ on receiving ok, for all parties $\mathcal{P}_i$.
   This ensures that data on relays is either deleted, or not stored if it is not going to be called for.

ReceiveFromAll(j, ι):
1. Party $\mathcal{P}_j$ initializes a vector **y** of length n containing $\perp$ in each location, bar location j where it places the value x_j.
2. $\mathcal{P}_j$ repeats the following step until it receives at least ι non-$\perp$ values:
   (a) Call (**requestFromAll**, $\mathcal{P}, \mathcal{P}_j$) on $\mathcal{F}_{\mathsf{SecureRobustRelay}}$, inputting $\tau = (\tau_{i,\mathcal{P}})_i$ after receiving ok, to obtain the values $(x_i)_{i \neq j}$. If the functionality return abort, then abort, otherwise place $(x_i)_i$ in position i in the vector **y**, for each i.
   Note, this may take many iterations since party $\mathcal{P}_j$ may possibly not yet have sent its message yet, or the adversary may be delaying messages.
3. Party $\mathcal{P}_j$ calls (**eraseAll**, $\mathcal{P}, \mathcal{P}_j$) on $\mathcal{F}_{\mathsf{SecureRobustRelay}}$, inputting $\tau = (\tau_{i,\mathcal{P}})_i$ on receiving ok, for all parties $\mathcal{P}_i$.
   This ensures that data on relays is either deleted, or not stored if it is not going to be called for.

Figure 6. Sub-Procedures to open a sharing $\langle x \rangle$

Sub-Protocol $\Pi_{\mathsf{Input}(i)}$. It is a data-input sub-protocol given in Fig. 7. It requires that all parties are in consensus about the value broadcast by party $\mathcal{P}_i$, thus we need all parties to terminate Input(i) before proceeding. This is unlike other parts of our MPC scheme, which allow faster parties to continue with the computation, i.e. they do not need to wait for all other parties to terminate the protocol. The communication cost of the protocol is $\approx 2 \cdot r$ field elements per party for each input, where r is the number of relays, plus a call to $\mathcal{F}_{\mathsf{Rand}}$.

Functionalities $\mathcal{F}_{\mathsf{Rand}}$ and $\mathcal{F}_{\mathsf{Coin}}$. When the number of parties is small, we will use the relatively standard functionality $\mathcal{F}_{\mathsf{Rand}}^{\mathsf{NI}}$, described in the full version. It generates a random degree-t Shamir sharing $\langle r \rangle_t$ in a non-interactive manner. In the full version, we also discuss how we proceed for larger values of n and t_p, and describe a protocol Π_{Rand} that implements the interactive functionality $\mathcal{F}_{\mathsf{Rand}}$ in the $\mathcal{F}_{\mathsf{SecureRobustRelay}}$-hybrid model. The amortized communication cost

---

Sub-protocol Input(i)

INPUT: Party $\mathcal{P}_i$ holds a secret value x
OUTPUT: Parties in $\mathcal{P}$ hold $\langle x \rangle_t$
This protocol assumes $\delta = 0$.

1. All the parties call $\mathcal{F}_{\mathsf{Rand}}$ for a new counter value cnt and obtains a sharing $\langle v \rangle$.
2. $\mathcal{P}_i$ runs $\mathsf{Open}(\mathcal{P}_i, \langle v \rangle)$, to obtain the random value v. If the output is abort, then $\mathcal{P}_i$ outputs abort.
3. $\mathcal{P}_i$ computes $w \leftarrow x - v$ and calls $\mathcal{F}_{\mathsf{SecureRobustRelay}}^{\delta=0}$ on $(\mathsf{sendToAll}, \mathcal{P}_i, \mathcal{P})$, inputting a vector **w** consisting of r-ciphertexts ct_w.
4. Each $\mathcal{P}_j$, for $\mathcal{P}_j \neq \mathcal{P}_i$, calls $(\mathsf{request}, \mathcal{P}_i, \mathcal{P}_j)$, inputting τ on receiving ok, for the requisite value of τ.
   - If this returns $\perp$ then party $\mathcal{P}_j$ aborts.
   - If a value w is returned then call $(\mathsf{erase}, \mathcal{P}_i, \mathcal{P}_j)$, inputting τ on receiving ok.
5. The parties set $\langle x \rangle \leftarrow \langle v \rangle + w$.

Figure 7. Sub-protocol Input(i) to enable party $\mathcal{P}_i$ to enter a secret value x into the computation.

of Π_{Rand} is $\frac{n-1}{n-t-1}$. In the full version, we also explain how to produce a protocol implementing a functionality $\mathcal{F}_{\mathsf{DoubleRand}}$, which produces a random double sharing $(\langle r \rangle_t, \langle r \rangle_{2t})$, and a protocol to implement a functionality $\mathcal{F}_{\mathsf{Coin}}$, which generates a common random value.

4.1 Multiplication Protocols

Functionality $\mathcal{F}_{\mathsf{Mult}}$

Let $\mathcal{P}_I$ be the set of corrupt parties and $\mathcal{P}_H = \mathcal{P} \setminus \mathcal{P}_I$ the set of honest parties. On input $(\mathsf{Multiply}, \mathcal{P}', \mathsf{id}_x, \mathsf{id}_y, \mathsf{id}_z)$, where $\mathcal{P}' \subseteq \mathcal{P}$, and $\mathsf{id}_x, \mathsf{id}_y$ are present in memory. Retrieve the values x, y. Send $(\mathsf{Multiply}, \mathcal{P}', \mathsf{id}_x, \mathsf{id}_y)$ to $\mathcal{S}$ along with corrupt shares, and wait for a reply. We can have the following cases:

- If $\mathcal{S}$ sends $(\mathsf{abort}, \hat{H})$, forward abort to $\hat{H} \subseteq \mathcal{P}_H$
- If $\mathcal{S}$ sends $(\mathsf{Done}, \hat{\mathcal{P}}, \delta_a, \{z_i\}_{i \in \mathcal{P}_I})$, compute $x \cdot y + \delta_a$, construct a full sharing $\langle z \rangle_t$ using $x \cdot y + \delta_a$ and $\{z_i\}_{i \in \mathcal{P}_I}$ and distributes it to the honest parties in $\hat{\mathcal{P}}$. Moreover, store $(\mathsf{id}_z, \langle z \rangle_t)$.
- If the adversary sends $(\mathsf{Done}, \hat{H})$, retrieve the $(\mathsf{id}_z, \langle z \rangle)$ and sends $\{z_i\}_{\hat{H}}$ to parties in $\hat{H}$.

Figure 8. The functionality $\mathcal{F}_{\mathsf{Mult}}$ secure up to additive attacks

In our main MPC protocol we will use the ideal functionality $\mathcal{F}_{\mathsf{Mult}}$ (given in Fig. 8) to evaluate multiplication gates. $\mathcal{F}_{\mathsf{Mult}}$ takes two sharing $\langle x \rangle_t$ and $\langle y \rangle_t$

present in memory and outputs a sharing $\langle z \rangle_t = \langle x \cdot y + \delta_a \rangle_t$, where δ_a is a value chosen by the adversary.

$\mathcal{F}_{\mathsf{Mult}}$ is a delayed functionality and it works as follows. It takes as input $\langle x \rangle_t$ and $\langle y \rangle_t$. When a subset $\mathcal{P}' \subseteq \mathcal{P}$ of parties calls the functionality, $\mathcal{F}_{\mathsf{Mult}}$ sends a message to the ideal adversary $\mathcal{S}$. The ideal adversary $\mathcal{S}$ emulates $\mathcal{F}_{\mathsf{SecureRobustRelay}}$ and controls all the communications between the computing parties and relays receiving delay messages from the adversary $\mathcal{A}$. In the simulation, every time a party $\mathcal{P}_i$, or a subset of parties $\hat{\mathcal{P}}$, is able to request enough shares to compute the shared output of the multiplication gate, $\mathcal{S}$ checks if these shares are valid. If this is the case, it extracts the error δ_a that could have been introduced by $\mathcal{A}$ and forward the value δ_a, along with corrupt shares $\{z_i\}_{i \in \mathcal{P}_I}$ to the functionality which constructs a valid sharing of $x \cdot y + \delta_a$ consistent with the corrupt shares obtained by $\mathcal{S}$. In addition, the functionality stores $\langle z \rangle_t$. If $\mathcal{S}$ detects same inconsistency in the output shares, then it sends an abort message to the functionality, together with the set of honest parties that in the simulation received those shares. Finally, when slower parties successfully conclude the evaluation of the multiplication gate, $\mathcal{S}$ just communicates to the functionality the indices of those parties, that will receive their consistent shares from $\mathcal{F}_{\mathsf{Mult}}$.

Crucially, since the $2t + 1$ or more shares used by the "fastest parties" to evaluate the multiplication gate are stored in the relays and used also by the slower parties later in the protocol, these shares fix any (potential) malicious behaviour. Indeed, if the first parties output abort when they reconstruct their shares, also slower parties that are going to use the same shares will output abort; on the other hand, if the fastest parties successfully evaluate the gate, then the shares used by those fix the (potential) additive error, so that the next set of parties concluding the gate evaluation either output the same value (and additive error) or abort.

The protocol Π_{Mult1} (Fig. 9), which we use to implement $\mathcal{F}_{\mathsf{Mult}}$, is an adaptation of [10,16] and requires a communication of only r field elements per party, plus the cost of generating random $\langle r \rangle_t$ and $\langle r \rangle_{2t}$, that can be amortized as we have seen before.

Recall, the DN was proven to be *insecure* (i.e., not private) in the case of MPC protocols with strong honest majority via the double-dipping attack. However, in our setting, the double-dipping attack does not work anymore because corrupt parties have to send the same share (that can be incorrect) to all honest parties and, moreover, we do not have a special computing party playing the role of the king. We will prove this in the next lemma, showing that the view of the adversary controlling up to $t_p \leq t$ parties is independent from honest parties' shares. For the proof see the full version.

Lemma 1. *The protocol Π_{Mult1} described in Fig. 9 securely with abort implements the functionality $\mathcal{F}_{\mathsf{Mult}}$ in the $\{\mathcal{F}_{\mathsf{SecureRobustRelay}}, \mathcal{F}_{\mathsf{Rand}}\}$-hybrid model against a malicious adversary corrupting up to $t < n/2$ computing parties and $r - 1$ relays.*

Protocol Π_{Mult1}

INPUT: $\langle x \rangle_t$ and $\langle y \rangle_t$. Also we need random $\langle r \rangle_t$ and $\langle r \rangle_{2t}$
OUTPUT: $\langle z \rangle_t$, s.t. $z = x \cdot y$

Init: Parties call $\mathcal{F}_{\mathsf{DRand}}$ to obtain $\langle r \rangle_t$ and $\langle r \rangle_{2t}$.
Mult: 1. Each party locally computes $\langle v \rangle_{2t} = \langle x \rangle_t \cdot \langle y \rangle_t + \langle r \rangle_{2t}$
      2. Each $\mathcal{P}_i$ calls $\mathcal{F}_{\mathsf{SecureRobustRelay}}$ on $(\mathsf{sendToAll}, \mathcal{P}_i, \mathcal{P})$.
         After receiving ok, $\mathcal{P}_i$ inputs its share value v_i.
      3. Each party $\mathcal{P}_i$ runs the sub-protocol ReceiveFromAll$(i, 2t+1)$ to obtain the shares $v_j, j \neq i$.
         Note, each party has to receive $2 \cdot t + 1$ shares, $2 \cdot t$ are not enough to ensure the simulation is correct.
      4. Parties reconstruct $v = x \cdot y + r$ and locally compute $\langle z \rangle_t = v - \langle r \rangle_t$.
         Note, on reconstruction the parties may notice that the sharing is not a degree $2 \cdot t$ sharing, in which case they abort.

Figure 9. Protocol Π_{Mult1} to compute $\langle z \rangle_t$.

5 MPC Secure up to an (Internal) Additive Attack Using Secure Robust Relays

In this section, we show how to run an MPC protocol with an honest majority using the network model described in the previous sections, i.e., according to the functionality $\mathcal{F}_{\mathsf{SecureRobustRelay}}$, which is secure up to a form of additive attack. Assuming only adversaries which do not delay messages, this is relatively simple[1], thus our main challenge is to efficiently deal with delays. Our protocol will allow the parties not being delayed, (or being delayed less) to proceed without waiting messages from the slowest parties and as soon as they have the required $2 \cdot t + 1$ values from other parties. Any messages that are sent to the delayed parties will of course be stored in the relays until they are needed. As an extreme example, assuming a large enough number of participating parties, a party could simply send no messages, wait for the other parties to finish the computation, and then request all of the messages from other parties to compute the output for themselves.

5.1 The δ-iaa MPC Protocol in the $\mathcal{F}_{\mathsf{SecureRobustRelays}}$-Hybrid Model

The protocol Π_{PMPC} to securely (up to internal additive attacks) evaluate a randomized arithmetic circuit C over a finite field $\mathbb{F}$ is given in the full version. At a high level the protocol proceeds in three stages: an *input stage*, that is instantiated with the sub-protocol Π_{Input}, described in Fig. 7, and with calls to the ideal functionalities $\mathcal{F}_{\mathsf{Rand}}$ and $\mathcal{F}_{\mathsf{DRand}}$, an *evaluation stage*, consisting in the evaluation of linear and multiplicative gates, and an *output stage*, where

---

[1] No delays means that the relays function like a regular point to point network on which one can run general MPC protocols.

parties call the sub-protocol Open, given in Fig. 5. We start with a protocol Π_{PMPC} that evaluates a (randomized) circuit C in the $\mathcal{F}_{\mathsf{SecureRobustRelay}}$-hybrid model with security against δ-delaying passive adversaries, except for an actively secure input step without delays, i.e. with $\delta = 0$. We show that, when Π_{PMPC} is executed in the presence of an active adversary, it computes a circuit C' that is the same as C up to some internal additive attacks. The key point is that, if the actively secure input protocol completes, then we know that the share values in the input gates are correct and the output gates are self-authenticating in that Π_{Open} will output abort if the input shared value is not a valid Shamir sharing. Thus the only place where the adversary can introduce errors, and avoid an abort, is by transmitting the sharing of the wrong value in the multiplication protocol. This wrong value will equate to the adversary introducing a known error, as per Definition 1.

Note that, whilst the underlying network is synchronous and the underlying MPC protocol proceeds in what looks like "rounds" of interaction, due to the delays, the parties can actually be at different rounds of the MPC protocol at the same point in time.

More formally, we prove in the full version the following theorem.

Theorem 2. *Given a randomized circuit C, the protocol Π_{PMPC} for computing C is secure against any δ-delaying passive adversary controlling up to $t < n/2$ parties and $r - 1$ relays in the $\{\mathcal{F}_{\mathsf{DoubleRand}}, \mathcal{F}_{\mathsf{Rand}}, \mathcal{F}_{\mathsf{Mult}}, \mathcal{F}_{\mathsf{SecureRobustRelay}}\}$-hybrid model. In addition, Π_{PMPC} securely evaluates a circuit C' with abort against δ-delaying active adversaries controlling up to $t. < n/2$ parties and $r - 1$ relays, where C' is a corruptible version of C that additionally takes an input A, which specifies an additive attack on each internal wire of C from the adversary, and outputs the result of the additively corrupted C as specified by A to a subset $\hat{\mathcal{P}} \subseteq \mathcal{P}$ of parties.*

In the full version we also examine the effect of delays on the state size needed to be held by a relay in the best case of no delays, the worst case and the case of random delays. We present a simulation for the case of random delays which models the state size of the relays and the round in which the MPC protocol terminates, when evaluating a circuit of a given multiplicative depth.

6   Actively Secure MPC-with-Abort Using Secure Robust Relays

In Fig. 10, we give our functionality $\mathcal{F}_{\mathsf{DelayedMPC}}$, with the associated implementing protocol $\Pi_{\mathsf{DelayedMPC}}$, being given in Fig. 11. Intuitively, the functionality presents a variant of the standard active-with-abort MPC security definition, modified to the situation where we have delays, so that some subset of parties can conclude the evaluation before others. In the previous section, we presented a protocol Π_{PMPC} which achieves security up to δ-internal additive attacks. In this section, we compile the prior protocol into one which does not allow internal additive attacks. This is done by following the same approach described in [14], in which it was proved that every circuit C can be compiled to a *robust* circuit $\tilde{C}$, i.e., the circuit itself protects the protocol against internal additive attacks. Therefore, we simply apply Π_{PMPC} to a robust circuit and prove that this is enough to achieve our goal.

Functionality $\mathcal{F}_{\mathsf{DelayedMPC}}(\mathcal{P}_1, \ldots, \mathcal{P}_n)$

The functionality runs with parties $\mathcal{P}_1, \ldots, \mathcal{P}_n$ and an adversary $\mathcal{S}$. Let C be a (randomized) arithmetic circuit

Initialise: On input $(\mathtt{init}, \mathbb{F})$ from all parties, if $(\mathtt{init})$ was received before then ignore the command, otherwise store $\mathbb{F}$.

Evaluation: The functionality receives input from parties and adversary. Evaluate the circuit C and compute the output. Send the output to $\mathcal{S}$.

Output: The functionality wait an input from the adversary. When $\mathcal{S}$ sends $(\mathtt{abort}, \hat{H})$, send $\mathtt{abort}$ to honest parties $\hat{H} \subseteq \mathcal{P}_H$; when $\mathcal{S}$ sends $(\mathtt{Done}, \hat{\mathcal{P}})$, send the output to honest parties in $\hat{\mathcal{P}}$.

Figure 10. The delayed MPC functionality

Protocol $\Pi_{\mathsf{DelayedMPC}}$

The protocol takes as input a randomized arithmetic circuit C and the corresponding robust circuit $\tilde{C}$. The protocol executes all the gates at a given depth in parallel. We proceed from depth zero to depth d. The depth zero gates consist of input, random-input and linear gates. At depth greater than zero there are linear, multiplication and output gates.

Evaluation: Parties evaluates the robust circuit $\tilde{C}$ on their private input using Shamir's secret sharing scheme to run the protocol Π_{PMPC}.

Output: This is the final stage of the protocol and parties $\hat{\mathcal{P}} \subseteq \mathcal{P}$ reaching this point hold the output of $\tilde{C}$, i.e. $\langle \mathbf{z} \rangle_t = \langle \mathbf{y} + \mathbf{c} \cdot Z \rangle_t$ and $\langle T \rangle_t = \langle \beta \cdot Z \rangle_t$.

  1. Each $\mathcal{P}_i \in \hat{\mathcal{P}}$ runs $\mathsf{Open}(\langle T \rangle)$ and $\mathsf{Open}(\langle \mathbf{z} \rangle)$ to obtain the values T and $\mathbf{z}$. If either of these protocols outputs $\mathtt{abort}$ then output $\mathtt{abort}$.
  2. If $T \neq 0$ then output $\mathtt{abort}$, otherwise return $\mathbf{z}$.

Figure 11. The protocol $\Pi_{\mathsf{DelayedMPC}}$ for secure delayed MPC

Unlike [14], we do not need to compile into the robust circuit an error correcting code, since this comes "for free" with Shamir's secret sharing. Thus our definition of a robust circuit differs slightly from the one in [14] and it is perhaps closest to the definition given in [8] even if we do not need to preserve each wire value in the state across committees, therefore our definition becomes simpler than that considered in [8].

Definition 2 (Robust Circuit). *Given an arithmetic circuit C for a functionality f of depth d and width $w = \max\{w_1, \ldots, w_d\}$, a robust circuit $\tilde{C}$ corresponding to C is a circuit that realizes the functionality $\tilde{f}$ that computes:*

ORIGINAL OUTPUT: *Compute $\mathbf{y} = C(\mathbf{x})$ for some inputs $\mathbf{x}$.*
RANDOM VALUES: *Sample random values $\Delta, \beta, \alpha_{k,l} \in \mathbb{F}$, where each $\alpha_{k,l}$ is associated to the k-th multiplication gate at depth l, and $\mathbf{c} \in \mathbb{F}^{|\mathbf{y}|}$.*
LINEAR COMBINATIONS: *Computes the following linear combinations*

$$u = \sum_{l=1}^{d} \left(\sum_{k=1}^{w_l} \alpha_{k,l} \cdot z_{k,l} \right),$$

$$v = \sum_{l=1}^{d} \left(\sum_{k=1}^{w_l} \alpha_{k,l} \cdot (\Delta \cdot z_{k,l}) \right),$$

where $z_{k,l}$ corresponds to the output of the k-th multiplication at depth l.
ZERO CHECK VALUE: *Compute $Z = \Delta \cdot u - v$.*
FINAL OUTPUT: *Output $(\mathbf{z}, T) = (\mathbf{y} + \mathbf{c} \cdot Z, \; \beta \cdot Z)$.*

A robust circuit can be computed from a standard circuit with a small increase in depth and a linear increase in the width, as the following lemma demonstrates.

Lemma 2. *Any arithmetic circuit C for functionality f, with input $\mathbf{x}$, output $\mathbf{y}$, depth d and width w, can be transformed into a robust randomized circuit $\tilde{C}$ for functionality $\tilde{f}$ of Definition 2 of depth $d + 4$ and maximum width $4 \cdot w$, assuming $|\mathbf{x}| \leq w$.*

The proof of this lemma and a more intuitive description of how a robust circuit is evaluated is given in the full version. Given this lemma, we can now prove that if we evaluate a robust circuit $\tilde{C}$ corresponding to a (randomized) circuit C using the protocol Π_{PMPC} described in the previous section, we obtain an actively secure protocol with abort implementing the ideal functionality $\mathcal{F}_{\mathsf{DelayMPC}}$ for C, where the communication can be adversarially delayed by the adversary and modelled using relays.

This discussion is formalised in the following theorem, which is proved in the full version. In the full version, we also give an informal intuition of why the final check can be performed even in presence of delays and without requiring additional randomness for slower parties.

Theorem 3. *Let $\tilde{C}$ be the robust circuit over $\mathbb{F}$ corresponding to C (according to Definition 2). The protocol $\Pi_{\mathsf{DelayedMPC}}$ in Fig. 11, computing $\tilde{C}$, securely implements $\mathcal{F}_{\mathsf{DelayedMPC}}$ with abort against a δ-delaying active adversary corrupting up to $t < n/2$ parties and $r - 1$ relays, except with probability $3/|\mathbb{F}|$ in the $\{\mathcal{F}_{\mathsf{Rand}}, \mathcal{F}_{\mathsf{SecureRobustRelay}}, \mathcal{F}_{\mathsf{Mult}}\}$-hybrid model.*

A complete proof can be found in the full version. Intuitively, however, the security of the protocol follows from the security of Π_{PMPC} and the zero-check provided by the robust variant of C. Note that, while corrupt parties can always output abort, if an honest party $\mathcal{P}_i$ outputs abort in the final stage of $\Pi_{\mathsf{DelayedMPC}}$, either they received inconsistent shares in one of the openings or the check did not pass. Since, in both cases, the shares causing abort are stored in the relays and cannot be changed, this means that all honest parties concluding the protocol after $\mathcal{P}_i$ will also output abort. If, on the contrary, the check passed, then finishing parties $\hat{\mathcal{P}}$ open the correct value $\mathbf{y}$ except with negligible probability. An important observation is that, when more parties will finish the circuit evaluation, they are going to use the same shares and randomness used by a previous set of parties in the zero-check, rather than additional shares, which in general could be problematic. However, as noticed in the previous section, a malicious behaviour of $\mathcal{A}$ is somehow fixed by the first $2t + 1$ shares stored in the relays, because these shares cannot be changed any more if at least one of the relays is honest. Therefore, if there is an additive attack on the output of a multiplication gate, this must be reflected in the first $2t + 1$ shares revealed, otherwise when more shares of the output value are sent to the relays, and later to the parties, inconsistencies will be noticed by honest parties. More concretely, this implies that if the first subset of honest parties $\hat{\mathcal{P}}_H$ successfully finish the protocol, then slower honest parties either output the same correct value or they abort the computation. In the full version we also give an estimation of the communication complexity of our protocol and discuss further optimizations.

7   Experiments

We present two forms of experiments. The first evaluates the networking performance of the relays. We investigate the difference multiple relays have on performance, as well as the communication slowdown induced by the relays' existence. The second set of experiments evaluates the performance of the MPC protocol built on top of the relays. Here we measure performance by the number of multiplications per second that can be performed. Precise numerical values for the main results presented in this section are given in the full version.

7.1   Networking Experiments

We now provide a more detailed explanation of our implementation of the protocol $\Pi_{\mathsf{SecureRobustRelay}}$, as well as the results of our experimental evaluations. To maximise the degree of concurrency, asynchronicity and parallelism, we used the `tokio` framework. For high-performance and manageable communications between the parties and relays, we used the `tonic` framework to employ gRPC, which is a remote-procedure-call framework that uses Protocol Buffers (known as `protobuf`) for data serialisation. We used the RustCrypto crate for standard cryptographic primitives, such as the AES256-GCM-SIV authenticated encryption scheme and the CMAC-AES256 message authentication code (MAC) algorithm. We ensure that our deployment takes advantage of AES hardware acceleration, namely AES-NI.

In the following experiments, the relays are run on identical machines with an Intel i9-9900 CPU and a 128 GB RAM. The parties communicating through the relays run machines with an Intel i7-770 CPU and a 32 GB RAM. The ping time between all of the machines is 1.003 ms.

We examine the case of both the send and request commands and the sendToAll and requestFromAll commands; we refer to the former as the "p2p experiments" whereas the latter we refer to as the "broadcast experiments". The send and request commands have potentially more overhead, since the sending party needs to encrypt and the receiving party needs to decrypt.

Data Structures. The data structures used to implement the different message stores in the relays are different depending on whether we are considering p2p or broadcast communication.

For the p2p messages, the relays use multi-value maps to store the messages exchanged between party $\mathcal{P}_i$ and party $\mathcal{P}_j$. At runtime, there are $n \cdot (n-1)$ entry lists in the map for all uni-directional channels. For each entry $(\mathcal{P}_i, \mathcal{P}_j)$, the map stores a list of messages sent by $\mathcal{P}_i$ to $\mathcal{P}_j$. Each message is composed of a round number, an encrypted message payload and a MAC for authentication between parties and relays. Since the relays should be capable of handling many requests concurrently in a multi-threaded setting, the multi-value map should be resilient against the problems caused by concurrent accesses. We used the evmap crate for this purpose. The crate evmap offers lock-free, eventually consistent, and concurrent read handles. Our protocol requires many reads since parties continuously invoke the request command until a new message is retrieved. However, the write handles in a multi-writer setting require a mutex for thread safety. As a result, writing operations will be considerably more expensive than reads.

For the broadcast messages, multi-value maps are again used through the evmap crate, and the messages contain the same information. However, since each message is now meant to be received by all the other parties, messages are no longer stored according to the corresponding $(\mathcal{P}_i, \mathcal{P}_j)$ pair, but to their counter (or round number). Thus, for each counter, the map stores a list of messages sent by the different parties during that same round. Note that every time we erase broadcast messages, we always erase all the messages associated with the same counter. Hence, erasing messages will correspond to deleting entries from the map.

Experiments. We identified four key experimental setups that we wanted to investigate, which we label as *DP*, *E0*, *E1* and *Ek*.

- *DP*: This experiment used no relays between the parties. Parties communicate directly, and all communications are protected by TLS.
- *E0*: This experiment used relays to establish indirect communications between the parties. Parties request messages without removing them from the relays.

- *E1*: This experiment had the same setting as *E0*, but parties immediately remove each message after retrieval, i.e. the removal batch size is one.
- *Ek*: This experiment is similar to *E1*, but parties issue `erase` commands after retrieval of $k > 1$ messages, i.e., the removal batch size is k.

For the p2p experiments we considered the case of only two communicating parties: a sender and a receiver. The sender sends a predetermined number of messages one by one, either directly to the receiver (in *DP*) or to all the relays (in *E0*, *E1* and *Ek*). In *DP*, the receiver passively waits until all the expected messages were received and the runtime is measured on the sender's side as the time taken to send all the messages. In the experiments with relays (*E0*, *E1* and *Ek*), the receiver continuously queries the relays for each message. Once message i is successfully retrieved, queries for message $i+1$ are sent, and so on, until all of the expected messages were sent and received. At the end of the experiment, an acknowledgement of receipt is sent to the sender through the relays (the sender starts querying the relays for the receipt once all messages have been sent). The runtime is measured on the sender's side as the time between starting sending the messages and receiving the acknowledgement of receipt.

For the broadcast experiments we considered the case of three communicating parties, where each party simultaneously acts as a sender and receiver. Parties alternate between sending and receiving messages: after sending message i, they continuously query the relays until they receive message i from the other parties. They then send and request message $i + 1$, and so on, until all the expected messages were received. When this happens, each party broadcasts an acknowledgement of receipt and then waits for the acknowledgement of receipt from the other parties. The runtime is measured by each party as the time between starting sending the messages and receiving the acknowledgement of receipt from every other party.

Relays vs Direct Comm. We seek first to understand the overhead caused by relays compared to a deployment topology wherein parties communicate directly. The graphs in Fig. 12 show the runtimes of the experiments above for an increasing number of 16-byte messages, with three relays and *Ek* with the removal batch size $k = 100$ for both the p2p and broadcast messages. Additionally, runtimes for *Ek* with batch size $k = 100$ and 16 kB messages are also presented. First, it is clear that the results for all experiments are very similar when sending up to 2^{15} messages. For 2^{17} and 2^{19} messages, *E1* has the slowest runtimes, which is due to the receiver invoking the `erase` command after each received message and before requesting the next message. However, erasing messages is necessary to guarantee the relays do not run out of memory. Furthermore, for p2p communications, even though *E0* is faster than *E1*, it is still much slower than *Ek*. This happens because when answering message requests, the relays need to iterate through all of their stored messages until the desired one is found. As the number of stored messages grows, this will substantially affect the performance.

Erasing batches of messages as in the *Ek* experiment prevents running into a memory limit while keeping the runtimes very close to the ones for *DP*. Indeed, batch erasure avoids accumulating large numbers of messages in the relays with-

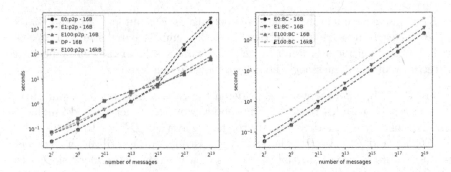

Fig. 12. Runtimes (with logarithmic scale on the y-axis) for experiments *DP*, *E0*, *E1* and *Ek* with $k = 100$ and 16-byte messages, and for *Ek* with $k = 100$ and 16 kB messages, showing: (left) p2p messages; (right) broadcast messages.

out the high cost of repeatedly invoking the **erase** command. Sending larger messages will naturally increase the communication time, but the overhead is insignificant.

Note that the broadcast experiments are always slower than the p2p experiments, which results from the following difference: in the p2p experiments, there is one sender and one receiver; in the broadcast experiments, there are three parties, and all of them send and receive (additionally, each of them needs to receive the messages from the other parties before sending the next message).

One can also see that E0 and E1 behave differently in the broadcast experiments compared to the p2p experiments. This is due to the difference in the way messages are organised in the relays, as was mentioned in Subsect. 7.1. In the p2p experiments, the relays first find the list of messages between two parties and then iterate through the list to obtain the message with the requested counter. In the broadcast experiments, the relays find the list of messages for the requested counter (which will contain at most a message by each party), and return all of them. Therefore, requesting broadcast messages does not become slower even when we never erase them. In both cases erasing in batches is to be preferred anyway, as it prevents an explosion in the memory requirements.

Removal Batch Size. We also wished to determine the influence of the size k of the removal batch in the *Ek* experiment. To do so, we perform this experiment with a fixed number of sent messages (2^{17}) and an increasing batch size k for both the p2p and the broadcast settings. The results are presented in the left graph of Fig. 13.

As seen in the previous experiment, erasing each message after retrieval is considerably slower than batch erasure. However, the batch size $k > 1$ has little influence on the total runtime up until $k = 50000$. For this batch size, because the relays will store up to $k - 1$ messages before deleting, the time required for the relays to iterate through all of the stored messages and retrieve the correct one becomes noticeable in the total communication time. This is, however, only a small increase when compared to lower batch sizes, and still much faster than erasing every message after retrieval.

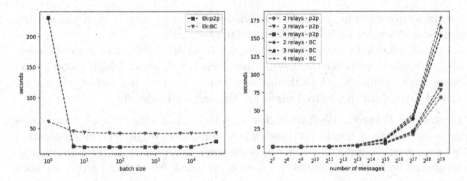

Fig. 13. Communication runtimes, showing for both the p2p and broadcast (BC) communications: (left) experiment Ek with 2^{17} 16-byte messages and increasing batch size k; (right) experiment Ek with $k = 100$ and 16-byte messages with 2, 3 and 4 relays.

In the p2p experiments with $k = 1$, we observe a considerable slowdown because of numerous concurrent write queries (requests and erasures) sent to the relays. The relays employ a pessimistic concurrency control by locking the data items to mitigate conflicting updates. Therefore, such controls offer data safety and integrity at the cost of latency due to resource contention. In our implementation, as explained earlier, the p2p and the broadcast experiments have slightly different data structures impacting the locking mechanisms. Another critical factor for concurrent systems is the resource access pattern. The p2p experiment ($k = 1$) and the broadcast experiments are inherently different. In the latter, the parties send messages to the relays simultaneously and wait until all messages for that round are available within the relays. Afterwards, they issue delete requests concurrently. They do not need to wait for all deletes; the faster parties can continue to the next broadcast round. However, in the former, a sending and a receiving party exchange messages simultaneously via relays (causing contention within the relays). The write queries fight to acquire locks, which is one of the reasons that the larger `erase` batches reduce the number of concurrent write queries, resulting in faster overall runtimes. These experiments are quite different in terms of deployment topology and the order of executions.

Note that when choosing the optimal batch size we must consider our specific setting, e.g., the number of players and the memory of the relays.

Number of Relays. Finally, we analysed the influence of the number of relays on the network performance. In the right graph of Fig. 13 we present results for experiment Ek with $k = 100$ when using 2, 3 and 4 relays (as opposed to the previous experiments which used a fixed number of three relays). On one hand, more relays mean the sender will send each message more times (one for each relay). On the other hand the receiver accepts a message as soon as it decrypts correctly (in the p2p experiments) and hence does not need to wait until all relays reply to the message request. However, requesting and erasing messages from more relays will also increase the communication. We therefore obtain slower communication times when using more relays, even though the overhead of adding each new relay is relatively small.

Recall also that because we only require one honest relay to ensure the overall communication is secure, having more relays will allow a higher corruption percentage within the relays themselves. Thus, the exact number of relays used should depend on the desired performance security trade-off.

Concluding Remarks. We have shown that communicating through relay nodes introduces only a small overhead when compared to direct communication between parties, especially when erasing messages in batches. Our implementation can be further optimized by, e.g., using a lock-free data structure for both reading and writing. For a real-world deployment of this network topology, we do recommend doing application-specific benchmarking to find a (sub)optimal batch size and relay number for the desired settings since there are unlimited possible deployment plans and hardware profiles.

7.2   Multiplication

We now turn to benchmarking our MPC protocol running on top of the relay enabled network. We benchmark the protocol by examining the number of multiplications which can be performed per second by the MPC protocol. Recall that the main communication required in the multiplication protocol is that of each party sending a single broadcast message via the `sendToAll` command, and then each party executing the requisite `requestFromAll` commands. The computation cost on top of this is then the execution of the relevant PRSS and some associated simple arithmetic operations.

We first targeted an MPC protocol with three parties, with at most one corruption; thus the non-interactive version of the PRSS could be utilized. We examined an implementation based on a finite field of 128 bits in size, which fits into the 16 bytes of our earlier experiments. We performed experiments similar to the broadcast experiments mentioned above. In particular, we examined the effect on the throughput (measured in multiplications per second) of varying the number of multiplications which are batched in each execution of the protocol. One can think of the batch size as the number of multiplications at a given depth in the evaluated circuit, since all such multiplications can be batched together.

Then, we examined an MPC protocol with six parties, again with at most one corruption. The setup is similar to the experiment with three parties, except now instead of three relays we have only two, one of them run on one of the faster machines (Intel i9-9900 CPU and 128 GB RAM) and the other on one of the slower machines (Intel i7-770 CPU and 32 GB RAM) - note that in all previous experiments, the relays were always run on the faster machines. Regarding the parties, instead of running all of them on the slower machines as before, three of them are now run on the faster machines. This allows us to simulate a situation where some of the parties participating the protocol are faster and progress in the computation ahead of the others. Indeed, since we assume at most one corruption, it is possible to process multiplications as soon as messages from any three of the parties are available.

The experiments are presented in Fig. 14, where we averaged the execution time over a total of 2^{11} multiplication rounds. For the six party setting, we averaged the run time over the three slow parties, and the three fast parties, separately. We see that for the three party multiplication, our implementation can cope with up to around 300 thousand multiplications per second when the number of parallel multiplications exceeds $2^{16} = 65536$. When considering six parties, the faster parties achieve close to 270 thousand multiplications per second for the same batch size. The effect of having both fast and slow parties is observable in the throughput of multiplications per second shown in Fig. 14, for the average of the three fast and the three slow parties.

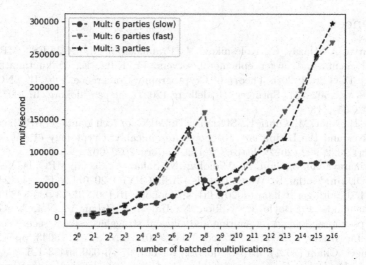

Fig. 14. Number of multiplications per second for increasing size of multiplication batches and erasing messages every 100 multiplication rounds, for 3 parties and 3 relays and for 6 parties and 2 relays.

For sequential multiplication (i.e., batch size 2^0) the difference is less obvious (1165 multiplications per second for slow parties vs 3483 for fast parties) since the slow parties can catch up after every single multiplication. As the batch size increases, the computation and communication to be performed in each multiplication round also increase, resulting in the fast parties computing on average 180 thousand more multiplications per second than the slow ones. This illustrates how the use of relays allows faster parties to progress in the computation, while slower ones are still able to retrieve all the necessary messages at their own pace. We note that one of the slow parties was on average 4 times slower than the other two, which impacts the presented average multiplication rate. There is a small kink in the graph at a batch size of around 2^7 (for the three party case) or around 2^8 (for the six party case) which we could not explain, we think this is an effect of the underlying Rust switching between two different algorithms for data access.

Our code can be significantly improved, as this is just a first implementation, with the multiplications being performed in a single threaded manner. We expect throughputs of around one million multiplications per second could be easily achieved with a fully optimized implementation.

Acknowledgements. This work was supported by CyberSecurity Research Flanders with reference number VR20192203, by the FWO under an Odysseus project GOH9718N, and by the Flemish Government through FWO SBO project SNIPPET S007619N.
The work of the second and third authors was primarily carried out while these authors were affiliated with COSIC.

References

1. Acharya, A., Hazay, C., Kolesnikov, V., Prabhakaran, M.: SCALES - MPC with small clients and larger ephemeral servers. In: Kiltz, E., Vaikuntanathan, V. (eds.) TCC 2022: 20th Theory of Cryptography Conference, Part II. LNCS, vol. 13748, pp. 502–531. Springer, Heidelberg (2022). https://doi.org/10.1007/978-3-031-22365-5_18
2. Alon, B., Naor, M., Omri, E., Stemmer, U.: MPC for tech giants (GMPC): enabling Gulliver and the Lilliputians to cooperate amicably. Cryptology ePrint Archive, Report 2022/902 (2022). https://eprint.iacr.org/2022/902
3. Badrinarayanan, S., Jain, A., Manohar, N., Sahai, A.: Secure MPC: laziness leads to GOD. In: Moriai, S., Wang, H. (eds.) ASIACRYPT 2020. LNCS, vol. 12493, pp. 120–150. Springer, Cham (2020). https://doi.org/10.1007/978-3-030-64840-4_5
4. Benhamouda, F., Boyle, E., Gilboa, N., Halevi, S., Ishai, Y., Nof, A.: Generalized pseudorandom secret sharing and efficient straggler-resilient secure computation. In: Nissim, K., Waters, B. (eds.) TCC 2021. LNCS, vol. 13043, pp. 129–161. Springer, Cham (2021). https://doi.org/10.1007/978-3-030-90453-1_5
5. Boneh, D., Boyle, E., Corrigan-Gibbs, H., Gilboa, N., Ishai, Y.: Zero-knowledge proofs on secret-shared data via fully linear PCPs. In: Boldyreva, A., Micciancio, D. (eds.) CRYPTO 2019. LNCS, vol. 11694, pp. 67–97. Springer, Cham (2019). https://doi.org/10.1007/978-3-030-26954-8_3
6. Canetti, R., Krawczyk, H.: Analysis of key-exchange protocols and their use for building secure channels. In: Pfitzmann, B. (ed.) EUROCRYPT 2001. LNCS, vol. 2045, pp. 453–474. Springer, Heidelberg (2001). https://doi.org/10.1007/3-540-44987-6_28
7. Chida, K., et al.: Fast large-scale honest-majority MPC for malicious adversaries. In: Shacham, H., Boldyreva, A. (eds.) CRYPTO 2018. LNCS, vol. 10993, pp. 34–64. Springer, Cham (2018). https://doi.org/10.1007/978-3-319-96878-0_2
8. Choudhuri, A.R., Goel, A., Green, M., Jain, A., Kaptchuk, G.: Fluid MPC: secure multiparty computation with dynamic participants. In: Malkin, T., Peikert, C. (eds.) CRYPTO 2021. LNCS, vol. 12826, pp. 94–123. Springer, Cham (2021). https://doi.org/10.1007/978-3-030-84245-1_4
9. Damgård, I., Escudero, D., Polychroniadou, A.: Phoenix: secure computation in an unstable network with dropouts and comebacks. Cryptology ePrint Archive, Report 2021/1376 (2021). https://eprint.iacr.org/2021/1376
10. Damgård, I., Nielsen, J.B.: Scalable and unconditionally secure multiparty computation. In: Menezes, A. (ed.) CRYPTO 2007. LNCS, vol. 4622, pp. 572–590. Springer, Heidelberg (2007). https://doi.org/10.1007/978-3-540-74143-5_32

11. Dolev, D., Yao, A.C.C.: On the security of public key protocols (extended abstract). In: 22nd Annual Symposium on Foundations of Computer Science, pp. 350–357. IEEE Computer Society Press, Nashville, TN, USA, 28–30 October 1981. https://doi.org/10.1109/SFCS.1981.32

12. Fitzi, M., Hirt, M., Maurer, U.: Trading correctness for privacy in unconditional multi-party computation. In: Krawczyk, H. (ed.) CRYPTO 1998. LNCS, vol. 1462, pp. 121–136. Springer, Heidelberg (1998). https://doi.org/10.1007/BFb0055724

13. Furukawa, J., Lindell, Y.: Two-thirds honest-majority MPC for malicious adversaries at almost the cost of semi-honest. In: Cavallaro, L., Kinder, J., Wang, X., Katz, J. (eds.) ACM CCS 2019: 26th Conference on Computer and Communications Security, pp. 1557–1571. ACM Press, London, UK, 11–15 November 2019. https://doi.org/10.1145/3319535.3339811

14. Genkin, D., Ishai, Y., Prabhakaran, M., Sahai, A., Tromer, E.: Circuits resilient to additive attacks with applications to secure computation. In: Shmoys, D.B. (ed.) 46th Annual ACM Symposium on Theory of Computing, pp. 495–504. ACM Press, New York, NY, USA, 31 May–3 June 2014. https://doi.org/10.1145/2591796.2591861

15. Gentry, C., et al.: YOSO: you only speak once. In: Malkin, T., Peikert, C. (eds.) CRYPTO 2021. LNCS, vol. 12826, pp. 64–93. Springer, Cham (2021). https://doi.org/10.1007/978-3-030-84245-1_3

16. Goyal, V., Li, H., Ostrovsky, R., Polychroniadou, A., Song, Y.: ATLAS: efficient and scalable MPC in the honest majority setting. In: Malkin, T., Peikert, C. (eds.) CRYPTO 2021. LNCS, vol. 12826, pp. 244–274. Springer, Cham (2021). https://doi.org/10.1007/978-3-030-84245-1_9

17. Goyal, V., Liu, Y., Song, Y.: Communication-efficient unconditional MPC with guaranteed output delivery. In: Boldyreva, A., Micciancio, D. (eds.) CRYPTO 2019. LNCS, vol. 11693, pp. 85–114. Springer, Cham (2019). https://doi.org/10.1007/978-3-030-26951-7_4

18. Goyal, V., Song, Y.: Malicious security comes free in honest-majority MPC. Cryptology ePrint Archive, Report 2020/134 (2020). https://eprint.iacr.org/2020/134

19. Goyal, V., Song, Y., Zhu, C.: Guaranteed output delivery comes free in honest majority MPC. In: Micciancio, D., Ristenpart, T. (eds.) CRYPTO 2020. LNCS, vol. 12171, pp. 618–646. Springer, Cham (2020). https://doi.org/10.1007/978-3-030-56880-1_22

20. Maurer, U.: Secure multi-party computation made simple. In: Cimato, S., Persiano, G., Galdi, C. (eds.) SCN 2002. LNCS, vol. 2576, pp. 14–28. Springer, Heidelberg (2003). https://doi.org/10.1007/3-540-36413-7_2

21. Maurer, U.M.: Secure multi-party computation made simple. Discret. Appl. Math. **154**(2), 370–381 (2006). https://doi.org/10.1016/j.dam.2005.03.020

22. Rachuri, R., Scholl, P.: Le mans: dynamic and fluid MPC for dishonest majority. In: Dodis, Y., Shrimpton, T. (eds.) Advances in Cryptology - CRYPTO 2022, Part I. LNCS, vol. 13507, pp. 719–749. Springer, Heidelberg (2022). https://doi.org/10.1007/978-3-031-15802-5_25

23. ZenGo: White-city: a framework for massive MPC with partial synchrony and partially authenticated channels (2020). https://github.com/ZenGo-X/white-city/blob/master/White-City-Report/whitecity_new.pdf

Ramp Hyper-invertible Matrices
and Their Applications to MPC Protocols

Hongqing Liu[1], Chaoping Xing[1], Yanjiang Yang[2], and Chen Yuan[1(✉)]

[1] Shanghai Jiao Tong University, Shanghai, China
chen_yuan@sjtu.edu.cn
[2] Huawei International, Singapore, Singapore

Abstract. Beerliová-Trubíniová and Hirt introduced hyper-invertible matrix technique to construct the first perfectly secure MPC protocol in the presence of maximal malicious corruptions $\lfloor \frac{n-1}{3} \rfloor$ with linear communication complexity per multiplication gate [5]. This matrix allows MPC protocol to generate correct shares of uniformly random secrets in the presence of malicious adversary. Moreover, the amortized communication complexity of generating each sharing is linear. Due to this prominent feature, the hyper-invertible matrix plays an important role in the construction of MPC protocol and zero-knowledge proof protocol where the randomness needs to be jointly generated. However, the downside of this matrix is that the size of its base field is linear in the size of its matrix. This means if we construct an n-party MPC protocol over $\mathbb{F}_q$ via hyper-invertible matrix, q is at least $2n$.

In this paper, we propose the ramp hyper-invertible matrix which can be seen as the generalization of hyper-invertible matrix. Our ramp hyper-invertible matrix can be defined over constant-size field regardless of the size of this matrix. Similar to the arithmetic secret sharing scheme, to apply our ramp hyper-invertible matrix to perfectly secure MPC protocol, the maximum number of corruptions has to be compromised to $\frac{(1-\epsilon)n}{3}$. As a consequence, we present the first perfectly secure MPC protocol in the presence of $\frac{(1-\epsilon)n}{3}$ malicious corruptions with constant communication complexity. Besides presenting the variant of hyper-invertible matrix, we overcome several obstacles in the construction of this MPC protocol. Our arithmetic secret sharing scheme over constant-size field is compatible with the player elimination technique, i.e., it supports the dynamic changes of party number and corrupted party number. Moreover, we rewrite the public reconstruction protocol to support the sharings over constant-size field. Putting these together leads to the constant-size field variant of celebrated MPC protocol in [5].

We note that although it was widely acknowledged that there exists an MPC protocol with constant communication complexity by replacing Shamir secret sharing scheme with arithmetic secret sharing scheme, there is no reference seriously describing such protocol in detail. Our work fills the missing detail by providing MPC primitive for any applications relying on MPC protocol of constant communication complexity. As an application of our perfectly secure MPC protocol which implies perfect robustness in the MPC-in-the-Head framework, we present the

J. Guo and R. Steinfeld (Eds.): ASIACRYPT 2023, LNCS 14438, pp. 204–236, 2023.
https://doi.org/10.1007/978-981-99-8721-4_7

constant-rate zero-knowledge proof with 3 communication rounds. The previous work achieves constant-rate with 5 communication rounds [32] due to the statistical robustness of their MPC protocol. Another application of our ramp hyper-invertible matrix is the information-theoretic multi-verifier zero-knowledge for circuit satisfiability [44]. We manage to remove the dependence of the size of circuit and security parameter from the share size.

1 Introduction

Secure multiparty computation (MPC) is a technique that allows several parties to jointly compute a public function without disclosing their private inputs even if an adversary corrupts t out of n parties. The MPC protocols can be divided into several classes based on their security levels and threat models. A protocol is perfectly secure if an adversary's view of the protocol can be simulated given only his inputs and outputs, and the simulated view follows exactly the same distribution as the real view. An adversary is called malicious if the corrupted parties he controls can deviate the protocol in an arbitrary manner. It was shown in [6] that the maximal number of corrupted parties is $\lfloor \frac{n-1}{3} \rfloor$ for an n-party MPC protocol perfectly secure against malicious adversary.[1] Since then, there is a great effort to improve the communication complexity of MPC protocol in this adversary model. The first MPC protocol achieving linear communication complexity is due to [5]. They introduced a new technique called hyper-invertible matrices (HIM for short) that can generate a random sharing at the cost of linear communication complexity. They also borrow several ideas from previous works such as player elimination [31], public reconstruction [18]. We note that although they achieve the linear communication complexity, the actual amortized communication complexity of securely evaluating a multiplication gate is $O(n \log n)$ bits regardless of the size of the field. The work in [11] introduced a new technique called reverse multiplication friendly embedding which maps a vector in $\mathbb{F}_q^r$ into an element in extension field $\mathbb{F}_{q^m}$ while the component-wise product of two vectors is preserved by mapping it to a product of two elements(here m is linear in r). This technique enables their MPC protocol to securely evaluate $O(\log n)$ instances over binary field by invoking the protocol in [5] in a "black-box" way and thus they manage to achieve the linear communication complexity for any Boolean circuit. All above protocols use the Shamir secret sharing scheme (SSS) [40] as their building block. Thus, the share sizes of their protocols are least $\Omega(\log n)$.

The arithmetic SSS introduced in [12] generalizes the idea of Shamir SSS. The merit of the generalization is that one can obtain a variant of Shamir SSS over constant-size field while the downside of this variant is that there is an ϵn gap between privacy and reconstruction. Thus, such arithmetic SSS can not handle the maximal number of corruptions $\lfloor \frac{n-1}{3} \rfloor$ but the sub-optimal number of

---

[1] The perfectly secure MPC protocol in this paper is assumed to have guaranteed output delivery since $t < n/3$.

corruptions $\frac{(1-\epsilon)n}{3}$. Due to the Franklin-Yung paradigm [21] and arithmetic SSS, it was widely acknowledged that there exists an MPC protocol over constant-size field perfectly secure against $\frac{(1-\epsilon)n}{3}$ malicious corrupted parties with $O(1)$ amortized communication complexity. However, we are surprised to find that there is no literature seriously describing such a protocol in detail. In this paper, we present such a protocol by deriving constant-size field variant of the celebrated MPC protocol [5]. The first challenge we face is the constant-size field variant of hyper-invertible matrix which we name it ramp hyper-invertible matrix. The idea of ramp hyper-invertible matrix can be dated back to [11]. However, they do not seriously expand such idea by providing efficient constructions of this matrix. Instead, we present the explicit constructions of such matrix in this paper and apply it to MPC protocol. We believe that the applications of ramp hyper-invertible matrix are not limited to MPC protocol and might be of independent interests. Besides, the player elimination technique is not compatible with arithmetic SSS. The player elimination technique remove parties from the preprocessing phase which implies that the number of parties n and the number of corrupted parties t are dynamically changed during the preprocessing phase. Thus, we propose an arithmetic SSS that is compatible with the dynamic changes of n and t. Finally, we rewrite the public reconstruction protocol to make it applicable over constant-size field. Putting everything together, we are able to present the constant-size variant of MPC protocol [5]. As a consequence, we obtain a constant-rate zero-knowledge proof from MPC-in-the-head (MPCitH) framework [32]. We also provide two applications of our ramp hyper-invertible matrices in the zero-knowledge proof.

1.1 Our Contributions

The hyper-invertible matrix was proposed in [5] to amortize the communication complexity of generating random sharings. However, the downside of this matrix is that the size of its base field grows with the size of the matrix. Therefore, any MPC protocol based on hyper-invertible matrix must be defined over a field of size $\Omega(n)$. The motivation of our ramp hyper-invertible matrix is to construct a perfectly secure MPC protocol over constant-size field for n-parties in the presence of almost maximal malicious corruptions $\frac{(1-\epsilon)n}{3}$ such that the amortized communication complexity of evaluating single multiplication gate is $O(1)$. Such an MPC protocol implies a constant-rate zero-knowledge proof [32]. Although such an MPC protocol was assumed to exist by replacing the Shamir secret sharing scheme with the asymptotically good arithmetic secret sharing scheme [12] in the MPC protocol, we note that there are still several technical difficulties to be overcome which were not explored so far. In this work, we consider the constant-size field variant of the celebrated MPC protocol [5]. The first obstacle is the variant of hyper-invertible matrix defined over constant-size field which we believe to be of independent interest. The second obstacle is to construct arithmetic secret sharing scheme compatible with the dynamic change of the number of parties and the number of corrupted parties. This is due to the application of player elimination protocol which removes a pair of parties at a time. The third obstacle is to carry out error correction over constant-size field as our shares are defined over constant-size field. In the rest of this subsection, we will introduce these obstacles in detail and how we overcome them.

Hyper-invertible Matrix. We introduce ramp hyper-invertible matrices which can be seen as a generalization of hyper-invertible matrices. Basically speaking, M is an $n \times n$ hyper-invertible matrix if for any subsets $I, J \subseteq [n]$ with $|I| = |J|$, the submatrix of M indexed by the rows in I and the columns in J is invertible. As a consequence, if $(y_1, \ldots, y_n)^T = M(x_1, \ldots, x_n)^T$, for any subsets $I, J \subseteq [n]$ with $|I| + |J| = n$, there is a linear bijective function $f : \mathbb{F}_q^n \to \mathbb{F}_q^n$ mapping $(x_i)_{i \in I}, (y_j)_{j \in J}$ onto $(x_i)_{i \in [n]/I}, (y_j)_{j \in [n]/J}$. This leads to the following two properties. If I is the set of corrupted parties, $(x_i)_{i \in [n]/I}$ and $(y_j)_{j \in [n]/J}$ uniquely determine $(y_j)_{j \in J}$. Moreover, $(y_j)_{j \in J}$ are distributed uniformly at random by knowing $(x_i)_{i \in I}$ and $(y_j)_{j \in [n]/J}$. The argument in [5] leverages these two properties to generate random double sharings with linear communication complexity. Our ramp hyper-invertible matrices still keep these two properties with slight relaxation. In particular, we require that $|I| + |J| \leq (1 - \epsilon)n$ for the first property to hold and $|I| + |J| \geq (1 + \epsilon)n$ for the second property to hold. We show that this ramp hyper-invertible matrix is closely related to linear code with large distance and dual distance. Such connection allows us to exploit the knowledge from the well-studied coding theory to produce ramp hyper-invertible matrix over any constant-size field.

Asymptotically Good Arithmetic Secret Sharing Scheme and Player Elimination. The player elimination technique was introduced in [31] to divide the preprocessing phase into $\Omega(n)$ segments and in each segment if a party deviates from the protocol, a pair of parties containing this party will be identified and removed from the following computation. This technique can efficiently reduce the communication cost of identifying corrupted parties and thus was adopted in [5] and some follow-ups. To adapt such technique to our MPC protocol, our asymptotically good arithmetic SSS must be compatible with dynamic change of the number of parties and the number of corrupted parties. We note that in contrast to the Shamir SSS, the known construction of asymptotically good arithmetic SSS does not satisfy this dynamic property, i.e., based on algebraic geometry code, one can construct a family of t_i-strongly multiplicative SSS[2] on n_i parties such that $\frac{t_i}{n_i} = \Omega(1)$ and n_i tends to infinity with $\frac{n_i}{n_{i-1}} > 1$ is a constant. In Theorem 4, we show how to construct t'-strongly multiplicative SSS on n' parties for any $n' = n - 2(t - t')$ and $t' \leq t$ from a t-strongly multiplicative SSS on n parties.

Error-Correcting Codes and Public Reconstruction. The public reconstruction in [5] can efficiently and robustly open the secret at the cost of linear

---

[2] We refer the reader to Sect. 4.1 for formal definition.

communication complexity. The first step is to treat k secrets waiting for opening as a message and re-encode such message to a codeword $(c_1, \ldots, c_n)$ via a Reed-Solomon code. In this process, all parties locally compute the share of c_i according to the encoding algorithm. Then, all parties send their shares of c_i to the i-th party and let i-th party reconstruct c_i'. By applying the decoding algorithm to $(c_1', \ldots, c_n')$, all parties can robustly reconstruct the codeword and thus obtain k secrets. To adapt this protocol, we propose an error-correcting code over constant-size field with large distance. Moreover, the encoding and decoding algorithm of our code can be efficiently implemented.

Beaver Triples. The Beaver triples are used to securely evaluate the multiplication gate in the online phase. The Beaver triple consists of two sharings of random elements $[a]_t, [b]_t$ and the share of their product $[ab]_t$ where $[\cdot]_t$ represents sharing of t-threshold Shamir SSS. To produce this triple in [5], the preprocessing phase first prepares two sharings of random element $[r]_t, [r]_{2t}$. Both of them can be efficiently produced via hyper-invertible matrix technique. $[r]_{2t}$ is used to mask the product $[a]_t[b]_t$ and $[r]_t$ is used to re-share the secret ab by computing $ab + r - [r]_t$. One can think of $[\cdot]_t$ as degree-t polynomial. To adapt this technique, we let $[\cdot]_t$ be the sharings of an SSS Σ_t with t-privacy. Since our SSS is t-strongly multiplicative, the product of two sharings belongs to a new SSS Σ_{2t} with $2t$-privacy. The reconstruction of Σ_{2t} is $2r$ if the reconstruction of Σ_t is r.[3]

Perfectly Secure MPC Protocol with Constant Amortized Communication Complexity. With all building blocks above at hand, we are able to present the perfectly secure MPC protocol with constant amortized communication complexity in the presence of $\frac{(1-\epsilon)n}{3}$ corrupted parties. The idea is to replace the building blocks in [5] defined over large field with our new building blocks which can be defined over constant-size field. To do this, we first replace the Shamir SSS with our arithmetic SSS to reduce the share size. Moreover, our new public reconstruction protocol is applicable to secret over constant-size field as we resort to error-correcting code over constant-size field. By replacing hyper-invertible matrix with ramp hyper-invertible matrix, we can generate double-sharings as efficient as in [5]. As a consequence, our new protocol can achieve the linear complexity as the celebrated MPC protocol in [5]. Since the number of corrupted parties $\frac{(1-\epsilon)n}{3}$ is suboptimal, our protocol use the packed arithmetic secret sharing to further reduce the communication complexity. If we simultaneously evaluate $\Omega(n)$ instances of the same circuit, we can reduce linear communication complexity to constant. In this sense, our protocol achieves the constant amortized communication complexity.

Constant-Rate Zero-Knowledge Proof. The communication complexity of constant-rate zero-knowledge proof is linear in circuit size $|C|$. The first construction was presented in [32] as a byproduct of the MPC-in-the-Head framework.

---

[3] In fact, we are only concerned about the reconstruction of Σ_{2t}.

This requires an MPC protocol over constant-size field with perfect or statistical t-robustness (in a malicious model) and t-privacy (in a semi-honest model). In [32], they show that a variant of the MPC protocol given in [16] using arithmetic SSS as the building block can serve this purpose. However, the MPC protocol in [16] only achieves statistical t-robustness. This forces the MPCitH protocol relying on this MPC protocol to be separated into two phases which causes more communication rounds. It is desirable to achieve perfect t-robustness so as to optimize the communication rounds. The building block of our MPCitH protocol is a perfectly secure MPC protocol over constant-size field and thus our MPCitH needs 3 communication rounds.

Joint Sampling of Multiple Verifiers. In information-theoretic multi-verifier zero-knowledge(MVZK), n verifiers jointly generate one challenge for the prover. We consider MVZK for circuit satisfiability in the setting of honest majority verifiers. By applying HIM technique in [5] to generate random secret sharings, the coin-tossing protocol in MVZK [44] achieves communication overhead $O(\lambda + \log|C|)$ where λ is security parameter and $|C|$ is the number of multiplication gates in the circuit. If we relax the number of corrupt parties from $\frac{n-1}{2}$ to $(\frac{1-\epsilon}{2})n$, the ramp HIM can replace HIM to do the same job and reduce the communication overhead of coin-tossing protocol to $O(1)$. Moreover, we propose a new technique to remove the dependence of security parameter from the share size when checking the circuit satisfiability.

1.2 Related Work

The first perfectly secure MPC protocol was proposed in [6] for $t < n/3$. Since then, there are numerous efforts to reduce the communication complexity. The introduction of the hyper-invertible matrix in [5] leads to the first perfectly secure MPC protocol with linear communication complexity which also reaches the theoretical limit. The same linear communication complexity can be achieved for perfectly secure MPC protocol over *any* finite field [11]. The depth related communication complexity in the expression was further removed in [27]. For honest majority setting $t < (n-1)/2$, there are many constructions achieving linear complexity in security-with-abort model [7,14,18,20,24,26,29,37]. In [13], they consider the honest majority MPC protocol tolerating $t < \frac{n(1-\epsilon)}{2}$ corruptions. Compared to the optimal corruption $\frac{n-1}{2}$, their scheme is defined over constant-size field and thus can save a $O(\log n)$ multiplicative factor. We note that once $t > n/3$, MPC protocols can not be zero-error but succeed with high probability with the help of broadcast channel. Thus, it is not comparable with our MPC protocol for $t < n/3$ where the broadcast can be simulated with perfect secure by communicating $O(n^2)$ bits.

The MPC-in-the-head paradigm establishes a close connection between zero-knowledge proof systems and MPC protocols. Its theoretical framework was proposed in [32] and the first practical instantiation was given in [25]. From practical point of view, the MPC protocols based on additive secret sharing play a crucial role in the MPCitH protocol. The reason is that additive secret sharing can be efficiently generated by the pseudo-random generator and thus the MPCitH protocol can commit to the seed instead of sharings. The preprocessing phase was introduced to the MPCitH protocols in [34]. Since then, there are two ways of verification in the preprocessing phase: cut-and-choose (KKW [34]) and sacrificing (BN [4], Limbo [19], Helium [33]). They are practical MPCitH protocols requiring either more communication rounds or larger field size. In this work, we are concerned about the theoretical performance of zero-knowledge proof and thus propose the MPCitH protocol based on ramp HIM. Combined with our perfectly secure MPC protocol against malicious adversary, our MPCitH protocol is a 3-round constant-rate zero-knowledge proof.

MVZK was first proposed in [10] and non-interactive MVZK was instantiated in [1]. Some earlier works [1,30] rely on public-key operations and thus achieve only computational security. In [2], they focus on minimal assumption for MVZK and achieves computational security and everlasting security. There are a few works investigating MVZK in the presence of honest majority verifiers [2,3,44]. The protocol in [3] aims to realize stronger security-with-identifiable-abort at a cost of tolerating a smaller number of corruptions($t < n/3$ or $t < n/4$). In this paper, we aim to reduce the communication overhead by replacing the HIM in [44] with the ramp HIM.

2 Preliminaries

For an integer $n > 1$, denote by $[n]$ the set $\{1, 2, \ldots, n\}$. For two integers a, b with $0 \leq a < b$, denote by $[a, b]$ the set $\{a, a+1, \cdots, b\}$. A finite field of size q is denoted by $\mathbb{F}_q$. Throughout this paper, we use bold face $\mathbf{v}$ to represent a vector. Given a vector $\mathbf{u} = (u_i)_{i \in [n]} \in \mathbb{F}_q^n$ and a subset $J \subset [n]$, we denote by $\mathbf{u}_J = (u_i)_{i \in J}$ the projection of $\mathbf{u}$ at J. The component-wise product of two vectors $\mathbf{c}_1$ and $\mathbf{c}_2$ is denoted by $\mathbf{c}_1 \star \mathbf{c}_2$. $\mathbb{F}_q^r$ is the collection of r-dimensional vectors over $\mathbb{F}_q$ and $\mathbb{F}_q^{r \times n}$ the collection of $r \times n$ matrices over $\mathbb{F}_q$. We assume the circuits evaluated by MPC protocol consist of c_I input gates, c_R random gates and c_M multiplicative gates. The depth of multiplication gates is denoted as D_M. We denote by λ the security parameter in zero-knowledge proof, which implies that soundness error is at most $2^{-\lambda}$.

2.1 Hyper-invertible Matrices

The hyper-invertible matrix was introduced in [5] to amortize the communication complexity of generating random sharings. A prominent feature of hyper-invertible matrix is that every square submatrix of this matrix is invertible.

Definition 1. *A matrix $M \in \mathbb{F}_q^{r \times n}$ is called a hyper-invertible matrix if for any row index set $I \subseteq [r]$ and column index set $J \subseteq [n]$ with $|I| = |J|$, the square submatrix of M formed by rows indexed by I and columns indexed by J is invertible.*

The mapping of a hyper-invertible matrix implies a symmetry property.

Lemma 1 ([5]). *Let M be an $n \times n$ hyper-invertible matrix over $\mathbb{F}_q$. Let $(y_1, \ldots, y_n)^T = M(x_1, \ldots, x_n)^T$. Then for any subset $I, B \subseteq [n]$ with $|I| + |B| = n$, there is a linear bijective function $f : \mathbb{F}_q^n \to \mathbb{F}_q^n$ mapping $((x_i)_{i \in I}, (y_j)_{j \in B})$ onto $((x_i)_{i \in [n]/I}, (y_j)_{j \in [n]/B})$.*

2.2 Linear Codes

A linear code C over $\mathbb{F}_q$ is a linear subspace in $\mathbb{F}_q^n$. The dimension of C is defined to be the $\mathbb{F}_q$-dimension of this subspace and the length of C is defined to be n. One can define Hamming distance for any pair of vectors $\mathbf{v} = (v_i), \mathbf{u} = (u_i)$ in $\mathbb{F}_q^n$, i.e., $d(\mathbf{v}, \mathbf{u}) = |\{i \in [n] : v_i \neq u_i\}|$. The Hamming weight of $\mathbf{u}$ is defined as $wt(\mathbf{u}) = d(\mathbf{u}, \mathbf{0})$, where $\mathbf{0}$ stands for the zero vector. For a linear code C, the minimum distance (distance for short) of C is defined to be the smallest Hamming weight of nonzero codewords. A linear code of length n, dimension k and distance d is denoted by $[n, k, d]$. A generator matrix G of a linear code C is a $k \times n$ matrix whose row vectors form an $\mathbb{F}_q$-basis. The dual code $C^\perp$ of C consists of the solutions to $G\mathbf{x}^T = \mathbf{0}^T$, i.e., $C^\perp = \{\mathbf{x} \in \mathbb{F}_q^n : G\mathbf{x} = \mathbf{0}\}$. We call the minimum distance of $C^\perp$ the dual distance of C. A generator matrix of $C^\perp$ is called a parity-check matrix of C.

2.3 Secret Sharing Scheme

Let us briefly introduce the background of secret sharing scheme.

Definition 2 (Secret sharing scheme). *A secret sharing scheme over $\mathbb{F}_q$ is a vector of random variables $\mathbf{X} = (X_0, X_1, \ldots, X_n)$ with each $X_i \in \mathbb{F}_q$ such that the following holds:*

- *The random variable X_0 is uniform over $\mathbb{F}_q$.*
- *t-privacy: Given any subset $B \subseteq [n]$ with $|B| \leq t$, any $x_0 \in \mathbb{F}_q$ and any $\mathbf{x}_B \in \mathbb{F}_q^{|B|}$ with $\Pr[(X_i)_{i \in B} = \mathbf{x}_B | X_0 = x_0] > 0$, $\Pr[X_0 = x_0 | (X_i)_{i \in B} = \mathbf{x}_B] = 1/q$. That is, the shares in the set B provide no information on the secret.*
- *r-reconstruction: Given any subset $B \subseteq [n]$ with $|B| \geq t+1$ and any $\mathbf{x}_B \in \mathbb{F}_q^{|B|}$ with $\Pr[(X_i)_{i \in B} = \mathbf{x}_B | X_0 = x_0] > 0$, there is a unique $x_0 \in \mathcal{X}_0$ such that $\Pr[X_0 = x_0 | (X_i)_{i \in B} = \mathbf{x}_B] = 1$. That is, the shares in the set B uniquely determine the secret.*

In this paper, we use packed secret sharing scheme to reduce the communication complexity. A packed secret sharing scheme is a secret sharing scheme with its secret defined over a vector space instead of a field.

Definition 3 (Packed secret sharing scheme). *A packed secret sharing scheme over $\mathbb{F}_q$ with secret space $\mathbb{F}_q^s$ is a vector of random variables $\mathbf{X} = (X_0, X_1, \ldots, X_n)$ with each $X_i \in \mathbb{F}_q$ for $i \in [n]$ and $X_0 \in \mathbb{F}_q^s$.*

In most of the cases, a packed secret sharing scheme is obtained by first construct-ing a secret sharing scheme over $\mathbb{F}_q$ with $n + s - 1$ shares $(X_1, \ldots, X_{n+s-1})$ and move $s-1$ shares $(X_{n+1}, \ldots, X_{n+s-1})$ to the secret space. Then, such secret shar-ing scheme has n shares $(X_1, \ldots, X_n)$ and the secret $(X_0, X_{n+1}, \ldots, X_{n+s-1}) \in \mathbb{F}_q^s$. It is easy to show that if the original secret sharing scheme has t-privacy and r-reconstruction, the resulting packed secret sharing scheme has $t - s$-privacy and r-reconstruction.

2.4   Algebraic Curves

Let us briefly introduce some background on algebraic curves and function fields over finite fields. The reader may refer to [42,43] for detail. An algebraic curve $\mathcal{X}$ defined over $\mathbb{F}_q$ is denoted by $\mathcal{X}/\mathbb{F}_q$. We denote by $\mathcal{X}(\mathbb{F}_q)$ the set of all $\mathbb{F}_q$-rational points on $\mathcal{X}$ (informally those points with coordinates belonging to $\mathbb{F}_q$). We denote by $\mathbb{F}_q(\mathcal{X})$ the function field of $\mathcal{X}/\mathbb{F}_q$. An element of $\mathbb{F}_q(\mathcal{X})$ is called a function. For a point P on $\mathcal{X}$, we denote by ν_P the normalized discrete valuation corresponding to the point P.

For a nonzero function x of $\mathbb{F}_q(\mathcal{X})$ and a point P, we denote by $\nu_P(x)$ the valuation of x at P. For $m \in \mathbb{Z}$, we form the vector space

$$\mathcal{L}(mP) = \{x \in \mathbb{F}_q(\mathcal{X})\backslash\{0\} : \nu_P(x) \geq -m; \nu_Q(x) \geq 0 \text{ for all } Q \neq P\}\cup\{0\}. \quad (1)$$

This is a finite-dimensional vector space over $\mathbb{F}_q$. We have the following Riemann-Roch Theorem [42, Chapter 1].

Proposition 1 (Riemann-Roch Theorem). *Let $\mathcal{X}/\mathbb{F}_q$ be an algebraic curve of genus g. Then for any $m \in \mathbb{Z}$ and a point P, one has*

$$\dim_{\mathbb{F}_q} \mathcal{L}(mP) \geq m - g + 1 \quad (2)$$

and equality holds if $m \geq 2g - 1$.

For algebraic geometry codes based on algebraic curves, we usually require curves have many rational points compared with genus. In other words, given an algebraic curve $\mathcal{X}/\mathbb{F}_q$ of genus g, we want the cardinality $|\mathcal{X}(\mathbb{F}_q)|$, denoted by $N(\mathcal{X})$, to be as large as possible. By the Hasse-Weil bound [36,42,43], we know that

$$N(\mathcal{X}) \leq q + 1 + 2g\sqrt{q}. \quad (3)$$

The above Hasse-Weil bound is tight for relatively small genus, i.e., for genus $g \leq q(q-1)/2$. For large genus, we have the following asymptotic Vlăduţ-Drinfeld bound [36,42,43]: for any family $\{\mathcal{X}/\mathbb{F}_q\}$ of algebraic curves with genus $g(\mathcal{X})$ of $\mathcal{X}$ tending to ∞, we have

$$\limsup_{g(\mathcal{X})\to\infty} \frac{N(\mathcal{X})}{g(\mathcal{X})} \leq \sqrt{q} - 1. \quad (4)$$

If q is an even power of a prime, then based on modular curves, Garcia-Stichtenoth [22,23] provided an explicit construction of a family $\{\mathcal{X}/\mathbb{F}_q\}$ of algebraic curves satisfying that $g(\mathcal{X}) \to \infty$ and

$$N(\mathcal{X}) \geq 1 + (\sqrt{q} - 1)g(\mathcal{X})$$

for every curve $\mathcal{X}$ in this family.

2.5 MPC-in-the-Head

The MPC-in-the-Head paradigm was introduced by [32]. It applies an MPC protocol and a commitment scheme to construct a zero-knowledge proof for the witness w of any NP relation R. MPCitH tackles any NP relation $R(x, w)$ as an multiparty computation functionality $f(x, w)$ for input client I, n parties $P_1, \cdots, P_n$ and output client O. Input cient I receives witness w from the prover and shares to n parties, who can execute a protocol to verify the witness with public input x and send result to output client O.

The prover emulates the execution of an MPC protocol with n imaginary parties in his head and commits to the views of all parties. The view of a party consists of its private input, its random tapes, and all its received messages from other parties. The verifier selects a subset containing t parties. Finally, the prover reveals the views of chosen parties and the verifier checks the consistency of views. We say a pair of views V_i, V_j of party P_i, P_j are consistent if all ongoing messages of V_i are identical to the incoming messages in V_j and vice versa.

If we want to instantiate MPCitH paradigm with a concrete MPC protocol, it should satisfy following properties:

Definition 4 (Three properties of an MPC protocol). *Let Π_f be an MPC protocol realizing the function f representing a NP relation R for input client I, n parties $P_1, \cdots, P_n$ and output client O. Let $1 \leq t < n$ and the adversary could corrupt at most input client and t parties. We denote $I \subseteq [n]$ with $|I| \leq t$ as corrupted parties.*

- **Correctness**: *We say Π_f realizes perfect (statistical, respectively) correctness if for any $(x, w_1, \cdots, w_n)$, the probability that the outputs of some parties deviate from $f(x, w_1, \cdots, w_n)$ is 0 (negl(λ), respectively).*
- t-**Privacy**: *We say Π_f realizes statistical (perfect, respectively) t-privacy in the presence of semi-honest adversary if for any input $(x, w_1, \cdots, w_n)$, there exists a PPT algorithm $\mathcal{S}$ such that the distribution of $\mathcal{S}(x, \{w_i\}_{i \in I}, f(x, w_1, \cdots, w_n))$ is statistically(perfectly, respectively) indistinguishable with the distribution of joint views $View_I(x, w_1, \cdots, w_n)$*
- t-**Robustness**: *We say Π_f realizes statistical (perfect, respectively) t-robustness in the presence of malicious adversary if for any input $(x, w_1, \cdots, w_n)$ satisfying $f(x, w_1, \cdots, w_n) = 0$, the probability that all parties outputs 1 and the views of honest parties are consistent is negl(λ) (0, respectively).*

3 Ramp Hyper-Invertible Matrix

In this section, we will introduce the notion of ramp hyper-invertible matrices and their constructions. We also provide an explicit construction via algebraic geometry codes as well as an existence result based on the Gilbert-Varshamov bound.

3.1 Ramp Hyper-Invertible Matrices and Functions

The ramp hyper-invertible matrix (ramp HIM for short) is a generalization of the hyper-invertible matrix. The formal definition is given as follows.

Definition 5. *A matrix $M \in \mathbb{F}_q^{m \times n}$ with $m \leq n$ is called an $(n, m; r, p)_q$-ramp hyper-invertible matrix if*

(i) *For any integers s, t satisfying $0 \leq s \leq m$, $0 \leq t \leq n$ and $s + t \geq r$, every $s \times (n - t)$ submatrix of M has full column rank;*

(ii) *For any integers s, t satisfying $0 \leq s \leq m$, $0 \leq t \leq n$ and $s + t \leq p$, every $s \times (n - t)$ submatrix of M has full row rank.*

Definition 5 implies that an $(n, m; n, n)_q$-ramp HIM is actually an HIM defined in [5]. However, it is not easy to see how to construct a ramp HIM meeting Definition 5. Thus, we propose an equivalence definition, i.e., ramp hyper-invertible function (HIF for short). The ramp HIF is a generalization of hyper-invertible function defined in [5].

Definition 6. *An $\mathbb{F}_q$-linear map from $\mathbb{F}_q^n$ to $\mathbb{F}_q^m$ is called an $(n, m; r, p)_q$-ramp hyper-invertible function if*

(i) *Given every pair $\mathbf{x} \in \mathbb{F}_q^n$ and $\mathbf{y} \in \mathbb{F}_q^m$ with $\mathbf{y} = f(\mathbf{x})$; and any subsets $I \subseteq [n]$ and $J \subseteq [m]$ with $|I| + |J| \geq r$, the vectors $\mathbf{x}_I$ and $\mathbf{y}_J$ uniquely determine $\mathbf{x}_{\bar{I}}$.*

(ii) *Given any subsets $I \subseteq [n]$ and $J \subseteq [m]$ with $|I| + |J| \leq p$, and any vector $\mathbf{u}_I \in \mathbb{F}_q^{|I|}$, the composition map $\pi_J \circ f(\mathbf{u}_I, \mathbf{x}_{\bar{I}})$ is a surjective map from $\mathbb{F}_q^{|\bar{I}|}$ to $\mathbb{F}_q^{|J|}$:*

$$\mathbb{F}_q^{|\bar{I}|} \xrightarrow{f(\mathbf{u}_I, \mathbf{x}_{\bar{I}})} \mathbb{F}_q^m \xrightarrow{\pi_J} \mathbb{F}_q^{|J|},$$

where π_J is the projection map at the index set J.

The following result proves the equivalence between ramp HIMs and ramp HIFs.

Theorem 1. *There exists an $(n, m; r, p)_q$-ramp HIM if and only if there exists an $(n, m; r, p)_q$-ramp hyper-invertible function.*

Proof. We first prove the if direction. Assume that there is an $(n, m; r, p)_q$-ramp hyper-invertible function ϕ. By fixing a basis $\{\mathbf{v}_1, \dots, \mathbf{v}_n\}$ of $\mathbb{F}_q^n$ and a basis $\{\mathbf{u}_1, \dots, \mathbf{u}_m\}$ of $\mathbb{F}_q^m$, we have $\phi(\mathbf{v}_i) = \sum_{j=1}^m a_{ij}\mathbf{u}_j$. Since ϕ is an $\mathbb{F}_q$-linear map, we conclude that $\phi(\mathbf{x}) = A\mathbf{x}^T$, where $A = (a_{ij})$. Next, we show that A is indeed an $(n, m; r, p)$-ramp HIM. Let $I \subseteq [n]$, $J \subseteq [m]$ be any subsets of size t and s respectively.

1. Assume $s + t \geq r$. Recall that the matrix A_{JI} is a submatrix of A whose rows are indexed by J and columns indexed by I. As $\phi(\mathbf{x}) = A\mathbf{x}^T = \mathbf{y}^T$, we have $\mathbf{y}_J^T = A_{JI}\mathbf{x}_I^T + A_{J\bar{I}}\mathbf{x}_{\bar{I}}^T$. By the first condition of a ramp HIF, $\mathbf{y}_J$ and $\mathbf{x}_I$ uniquely determine $\mathbf{x}_{\bar{I}}$. Suppose that $A_{J\bar{I}}$ would not have full column rank, then there exists a nonzero vector $\mathbf{a}$ such that $A_{J\bar{I}}\mathbf{a}^T = \mathbf{0}$. This implies that $A_{J\bar{I}}\mathbf{x}_{\bar{I}}^T = A_{J\bar{I}}(\mathbf{a} + \mathbf{x}_{\bar{I}})^T = \mathbf{y}_J^T - A_{JI}\mathbf{x}_I^T$. This contradicts the first condition of a ramp HIF. Thus, we conclude that any $s \times (n - t)$ submatrix of A has full column rank if $s + t \geq r$.

2. Assume $s + t \leq p$. Similarly, we have $\mathbf{y}_J^T = A_{JI}\mathbf{x}_I^T + A_{J\bar{I}}\mathbf{x}_{\bar{I}}^T$. By fixing $\mathbf{x}_I$ and the second condition of a ramp HIF, the map $\phi_J : \mathbb{F}_q^{|\bar{I}|} \to \mathbb{F}_q^{|J|}$ given by

$$\phi_J(\mathbf{x}_{\bar{I}}) := A_{J\bar{I}}\mathbf{x}_{\bar{I}}^T + A_{JI}\mathbf{x}_I^T$$

is surjective. This implies that $A_{J\bar{I}}$ has full row rank. Thus, we conclude that any $s \times (n - t)$ submatrix of A has full row rank if $s + t \leq p$.

We proceed to prove the only if direction. Given an $[n, m; r, p]_q$-ramp HIM A, we define the linear map $\phi : \mathbb{F}_q^n \to \mathbb{F}_q^m$ given by $\phi(\mathbf{x}) = A\mathbf{x}^T$. Let $I \subseteq [n]$, $J \subseteq [m]$ be any subsets of size t and s respectively.

1. Assume $s + t \geq r$. Given every pair $\mathbf{x} \in \mathbb{F}_q^n$ and $\mathbf{y} \in \mathbb{F}_q^m$ with $\mathbf{y}^T = \phi(\mathbf{x})$, we have $\mathbf{y}_J^T = A_{JI}\mathbf{x}_I^T + A_{J\bar{I}}\mathbf{x}_{\bar{I}}^T$. Since any $s \times (n - t)$ submatrix of A has full column rank, a similar proof in the "if" part shows that $\mathbf{x}_{\bar{I}}$ is uniquely determined by $\mathbf{y}_J$ and $\mathbf{x}_I$.

2. Assume $s + t \leq p$. Observe that $\mathbf{y}_J^T = A_{JI}\mathbf{x}_I^T + A_{J\bar{I}}\mathbf{x}_{\bar{I}}^T$. Fixing any $\mathbf{x}_I \in \mathbb{F}_q^{|I|}$, the map $\pi_J \circ \phi(\mathbf{x}) = \mathbf{y}_J$ is surjective as $A_{J\bar{I}}$ is an $s \times (n - t)$ submatrix of A with full row rank.

The proof is completed.

From Theorem 1, it suffices to construct a ramp HIF so as to construct a ramp HIM. In the following subsection, we show how to construct the ramp HIF from the linear code. This provides a machinery for the constructions of ramp HIMs.

3.2   Connections with Linear Codes

In this subsection, we establish the connection between ramp HIFs and linear codes. We show that a linear code with large distance and dual distance can be used to construct a ramp HIF. Since linear codes are well studied, this provides a very good source for explicitly constructing HIMs. In the following theorem, we prove that a ramp HIF exists if and only if a linear code with certain property exists.

Theorem 2. *There exists an $(n, m; r, p)_q$-ramp HIF if and only if there exists an $[n + m, n, n + m - r + 1]$-linear code C with dual distance $p + 1$ over $\mathbb{F}_q$.*

Proof. We first prove the if direction. Since the dimension of C is n, without loss of generality, we may assume the first n indices of C form an information set, i.e., the first n columns of every generator matrix are linearly independent. We proceed to show how to construct a ramp HIF from C. Define a linear map $\phi : \mathbb{F}_q^n \to \mathbb{F}_q^m$ given by $\phi(c_1, \ldots, c_n) = (c_{n+1}, \ldots, c_{n+m})$ with $(c_1, \ldots, c_{n+m}) \in C$. We first prove that this map is well defined. Note that $[n]$ is an information set of C. This implies that the projection map $\pi_{[n]} : C \to \mathbb{F}_q^n$ is a bijection. For any vector $(c_1, \ldots, c_n) \in \mathbb{F}_q^n$, there exists unique codeword $\mathbf{c} \in \mathbb{F}_q^{n+m}$ such that $\mathbf{c}_{[n]} = (c_1, \ldots, c_n)$. Thus, this map is well defined. It is clear that ϕ is an $\mathbb{F}_q$-linear map. We proceed to show that ϕ is an $(n, m; r, p)_q$-ramp HIF. Let $I \subseteq [n]$, $J \subseteq [m]$ be any subsets of size t and s, respectively.

1. Assume $s + t \geq r$. Given every pair $\mathbf{x} \in \mathbb{F}_q^n$ and $\mathbf{y} \in \mathbb{F}_q^m$ with $\mathbf{y} = \phi(\mathbf{x})$, we have $(\mathbf{x}, \mathbf{y}) \in C$. Since C has minimum distance $n + m - r + 1$, knowing $\mathbf{x}_I$ and $\mathbf{y}_J$, we can uniquely identify a codeword $(\mathbf{x}, \mathbf{y}) \in C$. Otherwise, if there exists another codeword $(\mathbf{x}', \mathbf{y}') \in C$ such that $\mathbf{x}'_I = \mathbf{x}_I$ and $\mathbf{y}'_J = \mathbf{y}$. Due to the linearity of C, $(\mathbf{x} - \mathbf{x}', \mathbf{y} - \mathbf{y}') \in C$ is a nonzero codeword of weight at most $n + m - r$. A contradiction occurs. Since we can uniquely identify a codeword $(\mathbf{x}, \mathbf{y}) \in C$, $\mathbf{x}_{\bar{I}}$ is unique.

2. Assume $s + t \leq p$. Given any vector $\mathbf{u}_I \in \mathbb{F}_q^{|I|}$, we want to prove that the map $\pi_J \circ \phi(\mathbf{u}_I, \mathbf{u}_{\bar{I}})$ is a surjection from $\mathbb{F}_q^{|\bar{I}|} \to \mathbb{F}_q^{|J|}$. To see this, we recall that the dual distance of C is $p + 1$. This implies that for any $\mathbf{u}_I \in \mathbb{F}_q^{|I|}$ and $\mathbf{v}_J \in \mathbb{F}_q^{|J|}$, there exists a codeword $(\mathbf{x}, \mathbf{y}) \in C$ such that $\mathbf{x}_I = \mathbf{u}_I$ and $\mathbf{y}_J = \mathbf{v}_J$ as $|I| + |J| \leq p$. By the definition of the map ϕ, the identity $\pi_J \circ \phi(\mathbf{x}_I, \mathbf{x}_{\bar{I}}) = \mathbf{y}_J$ holds for any $\mathbf{y}_J \in \mathbb{F}_q^{|J|}$.

We proceed to prove the only if direction. Let ϕ be an $(n, m; r, p)_q$-ramp HIF. Thus, by Theorem 1, we have $\phi(\mathbf{x}) = A\mathbf{x}^T$ for some $m \times n$ matrix A over $\mathbb{F}_q$. To define a linear code C, it suffices to define a generator matrix G of C. Let $G = (I_n, A^T)$ be an $n \times (n + m)$ matrix over $\mathbb{F}_q$, where I_n is the identity matrix of size n. We want to show that the linear code with generator matrix G has dimension n, minimum distance at least $n + m - r + 1$ and dual distance at least $p + 1$. The dimension of this code is clear as $rank(G) = n$.

(i) We now show that the minimum distance of C is at least $n + m - r + 1$. Suppose that the minimum distance were less than $n + m - r + 1$. Let $(\mathbf{x}, \mathbf{x}A^T) \in C$ be a codeword of weight at most $n + m - r$. This means there exists two index subsets $I \subseteq [n]$ and $J \subseteq [m]$ with $|I| + |J| \geq r$ such that $\mathbf{x}_I = \mathbf{0}$ and $\pi_J(A\mathbf{x}^T) = A_{JI}\mathbf{x}_I^T + A_{J\bar{I}}\mathbf{x}_{\bar{I}}^T = \mathbf{0}$. This gives $A_{J\bar{I}}\mathbf{x}_{\bar{I}} = \mathbf{0}$. Put $s = |I|$ and $t = |J|$. Since ϕ is an $(n, m; r, p)_q$-ramp HIF, by Theorem 1, any $s \times (n - t)$ submatrix of A has full column rank. This implies $A_{J\bar{I}}$ has full column rank and $\mathbf{x}_{\bar{I}}$ has to be $\mathbf{0}$. Therefore, the distance of C is at least $n + m - r + 1$.

(ii) Finally we show that the dual distance of C is at least $p + 1$. Since the generator matrix G of C is systematic, a generator matrix of dual code $C^\perp$ of C has the form $(-A, I_m)$. We turn to bound the minimum distance of this dual code. Let $\mathbf{c} = (-\mathbf{x}A, \mathbf{x}) \in C^\perp$ be a codeword of weight at most p.

Let $I \subseteq [n]$ and $J \subseteq [m]$ with $s = |I|$ and $t = |J|$ be the support sets of $\mathbf{x}A$ and $\mathbf{x}$, respectively. This implies $\pi_{\bar{I}}(-\mathbf{x}A) = -\mathbf{x}_J A_{J\bar{I}} = \mathbf{0}$. Since ϕ is an $(n, m; r, p)_q$-ramp HIF, by Theorem 1, any $s \times (n-t)$ submatrix of A has full row rank as long as $s + t \leq p$. This forces $\mathbf{x}_J = \mathbf{0}$ and thus $\mathbf{c} = \mathbf{0}$. Therefore, the dual distance of C is at least $p + 1$.

The proof is completed.

By combining Theorem 2 and Theorem 1, we obtain the following corollary.

Corollary 1. *The following are equivalent.*

(i) *There exists an $[n, m; r, p]_q$-ramp HIM.*
(ii) *There exists an $[n, m; r, p]_q$-ramp HIF.*
(iii) *There exists an $[n + m, n, n + m - r + 1]$ linear code C over $\mathbb{F}_q$ with dual distance $p + 1$.*

Moreover, if $G = (I_n, A^T)$ is the generator matrix of C, then A is an $[n, m; r, p]_q$-ramp HIM.

3.3   Construction of q-ary Ramp HIM

By Subsect. 3.2, we know that in order to construct a ramp HIM with smaller reconstruction r and larger privacy p, we need a linear code with both large distance and dual distance. A good candidate for such a code is the algebraic geometry code. Before instantiating our construction of ramp HIMs through linear codes, let us briefly introduce algebraic geometry codes in this subsection. The reader may refer to [42,43] for details. In this subsection, we instantiate the construction of q-ary ramp HIM. The binary ramp HIM is deferred to the Appendix in the full version [35].

Let $\mathcal{X}/\mathbb{F}_q$ be an algebraic curve of genus g with $\ell+1$ pairwise distinct rational points $P_\infty, P_1, \ldots, P_\ell$. Denote by $\mathcal{P}$ the set $\{P_1, \ldots, P_\ell\}$. For an integer κ with $g \leq \kappa < \ell$, define an algebraic geometry code

$$C(\mathcal{P}, \kappa P_\infty) := \{(f(P_1), \ldots, f(P_\ell)) : f \in \mathcal{L}(\kappa P_\infty)\}. \tag{5}$$

Then the code $C(\mathcal{P}, \kappa P_\infty)$ is a linear code over $\mathbb{F}_q$. Furthermore, $C(\mathcal{P}, \kappa P_\infty)$ and its dual $C^\perp(\mathcal{P}, \kappa P_\infty)$ have the following parameters

Proposition 2 (see [42,43]). *Assume $2g - 1 < k < \ell$, then $C(\mathcal{P}, \kappa P_\infty)$ is a q-ary $[\ell, k, d]$-linear code and $C^\perp(\mathcal{P}, \kappa P_\infty)$ is a q-ary $[\ell, k^\perp, d^\perp]$-linear code with the parameters $k, k^\perp, d, d^\perp$ satisfying*

$$k = \kappa - g + 1, \quad k^\perp = \ell - \kappa + g - 1, \quad d \geq \ell - \kappa \quad d^\perp \geq \kappa - 2g + 2.$$

Corollary 2 (via Garcia-Stichtenoth tower). *Assume that q is an even power of a prime. There exists a family of $[n, k, d]$-linear codes over $\mathbb{F}_q$ with efficient encoding and decoding algorithms and $k + d \geq n(1 - \frac{1}{\sqrt{q}-1}) + 1$. Here $g = \frac{n}{\sqrt{q}-1}$.*

If the curve is a projective line, then the genus g is equal to 0 and the algebraic geometry code defined above is a Reed-Solomon code. Now we instantiate the above algebraic geometry code to Corollary 1 to obtain a ramp HIM.

Proposition 3. *Let $\mathcal{X}/\mathbb{F}_q$ be an algebraic curve of genus g with at least $m+n+1$ pairwise distinct rational points. If $g-1 < m \leq n$, then for any κ there exists an $(n, m; r, p)_q$-ramp HIM with $r \leq n + g$ and $p \geq n - g$.*

Proof. Put $\ell = m+n$ and $\kappa = n-g+1$. By Proposition 2, the code $C(\mathcal{P}, \kappa P_\infty)$ is a q-ary $[m+n, n]$-linear code with minimum distance $d \geq m+n-\kappa = m-g+1$ and dual distance $d^\perp \geq \kappa - 2g + 2 = n - g + 1$. By Corollary 1, there is an $(n, m; r, p)$-ramp HIM with $d = n + m - r + 1$ and $p + 1 = d^\perp$. This gives $r = n + m + 1 - d \leq n + g$ and $p = d^\perp - 1 \geq n - g$. This completes the proof.

Note that if the base curve is a projective line, then the genus $g = 0$. Thus, we obtain an $(n, m; n, n)$-ramp HIM, i.e., an $(n, m)_q$-HIM.

Theorem 3. *If $q \geq 4$ is an even power of a prime, then there exists a family of $(n, m; r, p)$-ram HIM with $n \to \infty$, $m \geq \frac{n}{\sqrt{q}-1}$ and*

$$\limsup_{n\to\infty} \frac{r}{n} \leq 1 + \frac{2}{\sqrt{q}-1}, \quad \liminf_{n\to\infty} \frac{p}{n} \geq 1 - \frac{2}{\sqrt{q}-1}.$$

Furthermore, this family can be constructed in time $O(n^3)$.

Proof. Let $\{\mathcal{X}/\mathbb{F}_q\}$ be a family of algebraic curves given in [22]. Then we have $N(\mathcal{X}) \geq 1 + g(\mathcal{X})(\sqrt{q} - 1)$. Put $g = g(\mathcal{X})$ and let $g - 1 < m \leq n$ satisfy $N(\mathcal{X}) = n + m$. By Proposition 3, there exists a family of $(n, m; r, p)_q$-ramp HIMs with $r \leq n + g$ and $p \geq n - g$. As $m \leq n$ and $\frac{g}{m+n} \to \frac{1}{\sqrt{q}-1}$, we have $\frac{g}{n} \leq \frac{2}{\sqrt{q}-1}$. The desired result follows. As the Riemann-Roch space $\mathcal{L}(\kappa P_\infty)$ can be constructed in time $O(\kappa^3)$ [41], A generator matrix of $C(\mathcal{P}, \kappa P_\infty)$ can be constructed in time $O(n^3)$. By Corollary 1, the corresponding ramp HIM can be constructed in time $O(n^3)$ as well.

Corollary 3. *If $q = O(1/\epsilon^2)$ for a real $\epsilon \in (0, 1)$, then there exists a family of $(n, n; (1 + \epsilon)n, (1 - \epsilon)n)$-ramp HIM with $n \to \infty$. Furthermore, this family can be constructed in time $O(n^3)$.*

4   Perfectly Secure MPC for $t < \frac{n(1-\epsilon)}{3}$ over Constant-Size Fields

In this section, we will present a perfectly secure MPC protocol over constant-size fields by modifying the one in [5]. The challenge is to replace each gadget over large field in [5] with the one over constant-size fields. We emphasize that our security proof follows the line of [5]. The missing proof can be found in [5] such as the player elimination and so on. Since our MPC protocol is perfectly secure, most of the efforts are taken to detect the corruptions and remove the corrupted parties.

4.1   Arithmetic Secret Sharing Schemes

Let us briefly explain the downside of the Shamir secret sharing scheme. Since the Shamir secret sharing scheme is derived from polynomial evaluation, the number of parties is at most the size of underlying field. If an n-parties MPC protocol securely evaluates an arithmetic circuit over the constant-size field $\mathbb{F}_q$, then Shamir secret sharing scheme will cause a $\Omega(\log n)$ overhead by embedding this constant field $\mathbb{F}_q$ into $\mathbb{F}_{q^r}$ with $q^r \geq n$. Thus, it is desirable to design secret sharing scheme over constant-size field. Our protocol utilizes the gap ϵn to simultaneously compute $\Omega(n)$ instances. We emphasize that although we present our perfectly secure MPC protocol over field of size $\Omega(\frac{1}{\epsilon^2})$, it is possible to construct perfectly secure MPC protocol over binary field by replacing each gadget with the one over the binary field.

An arithmetic secret sharing scheme [15] is a generalization of the Shamir secret sharing scheme which can be instantiated over any constant-size field. The formal definition of arithmetic secret sharing scheme is tedious and too general for our application. We briefly explain the motivation of this scheme and only provide the necessary definitions for our purpose. We note that the Shamir secret sharing scheme supports multiplication, i.e., the component-wise product of two sharings from t-threshold Shamir secret sharing scheme is a sharing from $2t$-threshold Shamir secret secret sharing scheme. It can be generalized to component-wise product of d sharings. In arithmetic secret sharing scheme, we first have a base scheme called C and let the component-wise product of d sharings consist of a scheme C^{*d}. We require that the sharing in C^{*d} can be used to recover the product of d secrets corresponding to these d sharings. Moreover, the base scheme must have t-privacy and r-reconstruction. These are the properties necessary for MPC protocols. In this sense, the arithmetic secret sharing scheme captures the essence of the Shamir secret sharing scheme for MPC application. The merit of such generalization is that we can find a large number of codes except Reed-Solomon codes meet the definition of arithmetic secret sharing and are applicable to MPC protocol and other cryptography primitives.

Definition 7. *Let $C \subseteq \mathbb{F}_q^s \times \mathbb{F}_q^n$ (packed secret sharing scheme for $s > 1$) be a linear secret sharing scheme whose secret space is $\mathbb{F}_q^s$ and share space is $\mathbb{F}_q^n$.[4] We say C is t-strongly multiplicative secret sharing scheme[5] if*

1. *C has t-privacy: for any subset A of $[n]$ of size at most t, and any pair of secret $\mathbf{s}, \mathbf{s}' \in \mathbb{F}_q^s$, one has that $|\{\mathbf{c} \in C : \mathbf{c}_A = \mathbf{s}\}| = |\{\mathbf{c} \in C : \mathbf{c}_A = \mathbf{s}'\}|$.*
2. *C has $(n - 2t)$-reconstruction: i.e., for any subset A of $[n]$ of size at least $n - 2t$ and $\mathbf{c}, \mathbf{c}' \in C^{*2}$, one has that $\mathbf{c}_A \neq \mathbf{c}'_A$.*
3. *The secret sharing scheme $C^{*2} = span_{\mathbb{F}_q}\{\mathbf{c}_1 \star \mathbf{c}_2 : \mathbf{c}_1, \mathbf{c}_2 \in C\}$ has $(n - t)$-reconstruction, i.e., for any subset A of $[n]$ of size at least $n - t$ and $\mathbf{c}, \mathbf{c}' \in C^{*2}$, one has that $\mathbf{c}_A \neq \mathbf{c}'_A$.*

---

[4] We use 0 to represent the index of the secret and $[n]$ to represent n indices of the shares.

[5] In [15], a t-strongly multiplicative LSSS on n players for $\mathbb{F}_q^k$ over $\mathbb{F}_q$ is also called an $(n, t, 2, t)$-arithmetic secret sharing scheme with secret space $\mathbb{F}_q^k$ and share space $\mathbb{F}_q$.

It is desirable to fix the field size q and let the number of parties n approach infinity. If the ratio $\frac{t}{n}$ is a constant, such t-strongly SSS is asymptotically good. The instantiation of asymptotically good t-strongly multiplicative SSS is based on algebraic geometry code. By applying Garcia-Stichtenoth tower [22], we obtain the following construction.

Proposition 4 (via Garcia-Stichtenoth tower). *Assume q is an even power of a prime. Let $\gamma \in \left(0, \frac{1}{3} - \frac{2}{\sqrt{q}-1}\right)$. Then there exists a sequence $\{C_i\}$ of q-ary LSSS on n_i players with the secret space $\mathbb{F}_{q^{k_i}}$, the share space $\mathbb{F}_q$ such that*

(i) $\lim_{i \to \infty} \frac{k_i}{n_i} = \gamma$.

(ii) C_i *has r_i-reconstruction and t_i-privacy satisfying* $\frac{t_i}{n_i} = \frac{r_i}{n_i} - \frac{2}{\sqrt{q}-1} - \gamma$.

(iii) $C_i^{*2} = \text{span}_{\mathbb{F}_q}\{\mathbf{c}_1 \star \mathbf{c}_2 : \mathbf{c}_1, \mathbf{c}_2 \in C_i\} \subseteq \mathbb{F}_q^{k_i} \times \mathbb{F}_q^{n_i}$ *is a SSS with $2r_i$- reconstruction and $2t_i$-privacy.*

(iv) *The sharing and reconstruction algorithms of C_i and C_i^{*2} can be efficiently implemented.*

(v) *The decoding algorithm of C_i can efficiently correct up to $\frac{n_i - r_i - 1}{2}$ corrupted shares for any sharing in C_i*

If $2r_i \leq n_i - t_i$, then C_i is a t_i-strongly multiplicative LSSS. Let $r_i = \frac{n_i}{3}$ and we obtain the following SSS.

Corollary 4. *Let $q \approx \frac{144}{\epsilon^2} = O(\frac{1}{\epsilon^2})$ and $\gamma = \frac{\epsilon}{6}$. There exists a family of $(\frac{1-\epsilon}{3})n_i$- strongly multiplicative secret sharing scheme $C_i \subseteq \mathbb{F}_q^{\frac{\epsilon n_i}{6}} \times \mathbb{F}_q^{n_i}$ when $n_i \to \infty$. This multiplicative SSS has $\frac{(1-\epsilon)n_i}{3}$-privacy and $\frac{n_i}{3}$-reconstruction.*

The player elimination introduced in [31] is used to transform a non-robust protocol into a robust protocol with no additional costs. Each time the inconsistent sharings are detected, this player elimination protocol is initiated to localize and remove a pair of parties containing at least one corrupted party from the preprocessing phase. To apply this protocol, our arithmetic secret sharing scheme should be compatible with the reduced number of the parties and corrupted parties. In the following theorem, we show how to obtain a t_i'-strongly multiplicative LSSS from a t_i-strongly multiplicative LSSS with $t_i' < t_i$. Then, we can apply Corollary 4 for any privacy t_i and number n_i of parties.

Theorem 4. *Assume that $C_i \subseteq \mathbb{F}_q^s \times \mathbb{F}_q^{n_i}$ is a t_i-strongly multiplicative LSSS on n_i players in Proposition 4. Then, there exists a t_i'-strongly multiplicative LSSS $C' \subseteq \mathbb{F}_q^s \times \mathbb{F}_q^{n_i'}$ with $n_i' = n_i - 2(t_i - t_i')$. Moreover, $r_i' \leq \frac{n_i'}{3}$ and $t_i' \leq \frac{n_i'(1-\epsilon)}{3}$ if $r_i = \frac{n_i}{3}$ and $t_i = \frac{n_i(1-\epsilon)}{3}$.*

Proof. Since C_i is a t_i-strongly multiplicative LSSS, we have $2r_i \leq n_i - t_i$. We first fix the number of parties n_i and the dimension of secret space s_i, and let the privacy be t_i' and reconstruction be $r_i' = r_i - (t_i - t_i')$ in Proposition 4. Such SSS $\hat{C}_i$ exists as

$$\frac{t_i'}{n_i} = \frac{t_i}{n_i} - \frac{(t_i - t_i')}{n_i} = \frac{r_i - (t_i - t_i')}{n_i} - \frac{2}{\sqrt{q}-1} - \gamma = \frac{r_i'}{n_i} - \frac{2}{\sqrt{q}-1} - \gamma$$

We obtain C_i' by puncturing the last $2(t_i - t_i')$ shares of $\hat{C}_i$. The privacy and reconstruction of C_i' are exactly the same as that of $\hat{C}_i$ which are t_i' and $r_i' = r_i - (t_i - t_i')$ respectively. Similarly, the reconstruction of $C_i'^{*2}$ is $2r_i'$. The proof is completed as $2r_i' = 2r_i - 2(t_i - t_i') \leq n_i' - t_i \leq n_i' - t_i'$. It is clear that $r_i' \leq \frac{n_i'}{3}$ and $t_i' \leq \frac{n_i'(1-\epsilon)}{3}$ if $r_i = \frac{n_i}{3}$ and $t_i = \frac{n_i(1-\epsilon)}{3}$.

Remark 1. *Although we only present t-strongly multiplicative SSS over field of size $\Omega(1/\epsilon^2)$, it is possible to construct t-strongly multiplicative SSS over binary field [39]. The same trick in Theorem 4 can be applied to this SSS. The resulting SSS becomes the building block of perfectly secure MPC over the binary field.*

Remark 2. *To check the consistency of this linear secret sharing scheme, we note that it suffices to run the reconstruction algorithm of this linear secret sharing scheme and then compare the shares recovered by this reconstruction algorithm with the shares at hand. Since our secret sharing scheme is obtained from algebraic geometry code with an efficient decoding algorithm, this reconstruction algorithm is in fact the decoding algorithm for this algebraic geometry code.*

4.2   Randomization Based on Ramp Hyper-invertible Matrices

Protocol RandEl(d)

Setup: a set of n' parties $\mathcal{I} = \{P_1, \ldots, P_{n'}\}$ and at most $t' \leq \frac{n'(1-\epsilon)}{3}$ of them are corrupted. Let M be an $(n', n', n'(1+\epsilon), n'(1-\epsilon))$-ramp hyper-invertible matrix over $\mathbb{F}_q$ in Definition 6.

- For $P_i \in \mathcal{I}$, P_i generates a random secret $\mathbf{s}_i \in \mathbb{F}_q^s$ and shares this secret among parties in $\mathcal{I}$ by invoking Σ_d.
- All parties locally compute $([\mathbf{r}_1]_d, \ldots, [\mathbf{r}_{n'}]_d)^T = M([\mathbf{s}_1]_d, \ldots, [\mathbf{s}_{n'}]_d)^T$.
- For $i = T+1, \ldots, n'$ for some $T \leq t'$, all parties open $\mathbf{r}_i$ to P_i. P_i checks the consistency of $[\mathbf{r}_i]_d$ and becomes unhappy if the sharing is not correct.
- Output the remaining unopened sharings $[\mathbf{r}_1]_d, \ldots, [\mathbf{r}_T]_d$.

The secret sharing scheme in Corollary 4 is our building block for our MPC protocol. Our MPC protocol starts with n parties and at most $t = \frac{(1-\epsilon)n}{3}$ of them are corrupted where ϵ can be an arbitrarily small value. In what follows, we fix $t = \frac{(1-\epsilon)n}{3}$. During the preprocessing phase, the player elimination technique introduced in [31] divides the computation into $O(n)$ segments and in each segment the protocol tries to identify the corrupted parties when inconsistent shares are detected. This protocol can locate a pair of parties such that at least one of them is corrupted. Then, this pair of parties are removed from the protocol. The number of parties and the number of corrupted parties are updated to $n - 2$ and $t - 1$ respectively. All remaining parties repeat current segment. Thus, in the preprocessing phase, our protocol assumes that the number of parties and corrupted parties are $n' \leq n$ and $t' \leq t$ respectively.

In what follows, we assume $q = O(\frac{1}{\epsilon^2})$ and our MPC protocol is defined over $\mathbb{F}_q$.

Let $\Sigma_d \in \mathbb{F}_q^s \times \mathbb{F}_q^{n'}$ be an SSS in Theorem 4 with privacy $d \in [t', \frac{n'(1-\epsilon)}{3}]$, reconstruction $r = \frac{n'}{3}$ and $s = \frac{\epsilon n}{6}$. Due to the player elimination protocol, the value of d may decrease throughout the prepocessing protocol. The initial value of d is t. Denote by $[\mathbf{s}]_d = (x_1, \ldots, x_n) \in \Sigma_d$ the packed secret-sharing of $\mathbf{s} \in \mathbb{F}_q^s$.[6] Since our SSS supports multiplication, to open the secret of $[\mathbf{s}_1]_d \star [\mathbf{s}_2]_t$ safely, we need to mask it with $[\mathbf{r}]_{2d}$, a sharing of a random vector $\mathbf{r}$ generated by Σ_{2d}. This is because Σ_{2d} is actually the "squared" Σ_d, i.e., Σ_d corresponds to C_i and Σ_{2d} corresponds to C_i^{*2} by Proposition 4. In this sense, Σ_{2d} has $2d$-privacy and $2r$-reconstruction.

Proposition 5. *Assume that Σ_d in the Protocol **RandEl** has d-privacy with $d \geq t'$. If $T \leq t'$ and all honest parties are happy, then $[\mathbf{r}_1]_d, \ldots, [\mathbf{r}_T]_d$ are correct sharings of uniformly random secrets $\mathbf{r}_1, \ldots, \mathbf{r}_T$ and the adversary learns no information about them. The total communication complexity is $O(n^2)$ for generating $\Omega(n)$ correct sharings.*

Proof. The proof follows the same step in [5] except that we replace hyper-invertible matrix with ramp hyper-invertible matrix in Definition 5. For convenience, we use $[\mathbf{r}_i]$ to represent the sharing $[\mathbf{r}_i]_d$ in the proof. We first consider the robustness, i.e., the unopened sharings $[\mathbf{r}_1], \ldots, [\mathbf{r}_T]$ are correct. Let $S \subseteq \{T+1, \ldots, n'\}$ be the index set of honest parties and $\bar{S} = \{T+1, \ldots, n'\}/S$. Since there are at most t' corrupted parties in $\mathcal{I}$, $|S| \geq n' - T - t' \geq n' - 2t'$. $[\mathbf{r}_i]_{i \in S}$ are correct sharings checked by the honest parties in S as all parties do not complain. Moreover, there are at least $n' - t'$ honest parties in $\mathcal{I}$. Let H be the collection of honest parties in $\mathcal{I}$ and we have $|H| \geq n' - t'$. Observe that $|H| + |S| \geq 2n' - 3t' \geq n + \epsilon n$ as $t' \leq \frac{n'(1-\epsilon)}{3}$. This implies that $n' - t'$ sharings $[\mathbf{s}_i]_{i \in H}$ generated by the honest parties together with $[\mathbf{r}_i]_{i \in S}$ uniquely determine T sharings $[\mathbf{r}_i]_{i \in [T]}$ as M is an $(n', n', n'(1+\epsilon), n'(1-\epsilon))$-ramp HIM. Since $[\mathbf{s}_i]_{i \in H}$ and $[\mathbf{r}_i]_{i \in S}$ are correct sharings, the unopened sharings $[\mathbf{r}_i]_{i \in [T]}$ are correct as well.

We proceed to the privacy argument. The secret sharing scheme Σ has $d \geq t'$-privacy. This implies that the adversary can not obtain $\mathbf{r}_i$ from any t' shares of $[\mathbf{r}_i]$. Moreover, the adversary knows the random vectors $\mathbf{r}_i$ for $i \in \bar{S}$ opening to the corrupted parties and $\mathbf{s}_i$ for $i \in [n'] \setminus H$ generated by the corrupted parties. They are at most $2t'$ vectors in total. If we fix these vectors, as M is an $(n', n', n'(1+\epsilon), n'(1-\epsilon))$-ramp HIM and $|\bar{S} \cup [T]| + |[n] \setminus H| \leq 3t' \leq n'(1-\epsilon)$, there is a surjection from $\mathbf{s}_i, i \in H$ to $\mathbf{r}_i, i \in [T]$. Since $\mathbf{s}_i, i \in H$ are distributed uniformly at random, $\mathbf{r}_i, i \in [T]$ are distributed uniformly at random as well. This means the distribution $\mathbf{r}_i, i \in [T]$ is independent of $\mathbf{r}_i$ for $i \in \bar{S}$ and $\mathbf{s}_i$ for $i \in [n'] \setminus H$.

---

[6] In the Shamir SSS, one can identify this privacy d as the degree of polynomials.

As for the communication complexity, we note that each party sends and receives $n' - 1$ shares. Thus, the total communication complexity is $O(n'^2) = O(n^2)$. If no one complains, invoking **RandEl** can generate $\Omega(n)$ correct sharings and thus each sharing cost $O(n)$ communication complexity. We also note that each sharing belongs to a packed secret sharing scheme and thus the amortized communication complexity is further reduced to constant.

The **RandEl** was invoked in [5] to produce random double sharings. Assume there are t' corrupted parties and n' parties remaining in the preprocessing phase. Instead of using HIM, we use ramp HIM over constant-size field to generate the random double sharings. All parties want to obtain the double sharings $([\mathbf{a}]_d, [\mathbf{a}]_{d'})$ of random vector $\mathbf{a}$ for some $t' \leq d, d' \leq n' - t'$. In order to do that, one can modify **RandEl** protocol as follows. P_i generates random double sharings $[\mathbf{s}_i]_d, [\mathbf{s}_i]_{d'}$ and applies the ramp hyper-invertible matrix to obtain $[\mathbf{r}_i]_d$ and $[\mathbf{r}_i]_{d'}$. For $i = T + 1, \ldots, n$, P_i not only checks the consistency of $[\mathbf{r}_i]_d$ and $[\mathbf{r}_i]_{d'}$ but also makes sure that the opened secrets $\mathbf{r}_i$ are the same. This will force the remaining unopened sharings $[\mathbf{r}_i]_d$ and $[\mathbf{r}_i]_{d'}$ to be correct and associated with the same secret. We call this modified protocol **DoubleSharings**. The same argument implies the following result.

Corollary 5. *Assume that $t' \leq d, d' \leq n' - t'$. If $T \leq t'$ and all honest parties are happy, then **DoubleSharings** will output correct sharings $([\mathbf{r}_1]_d, [\mathbf{r}_1]_{d'}), \ldots, ([\mathbf{r}_T]_d, [\mathbf{r}_T]_{d'})$ with uniformly random secrets $\mathbf{r}_1, \ldots, \mathbf{r}_T$ and the adversary learns no information about them. The total communication complexity is $O(n^2)$ for generating $\Omega(n)$ correct sharings.*

4.3   Public Reconstruction

The public reconstruction protocol is used to efficiently and robustly open the secret [5,18]. The idea is that instead of reconstructing one secret, this protocol allows all parties to simultaneously reconstruct $\Omega(n)$ secrets. Meanwhile, the communication complexity keeps the same $O(n^2)$ and thus the amortized communication complexity is reduced to $O(n)$. To achieve this goal, this protocol treats $k = \Omega(n)$ secrets as a message of length k and re-encodes this message to a codeword of length n' such that this linear code has minimum distance at least $2t' + 1$. Each party reconstructs one secret corresponding to one component of this codeword. Since there are at most t' corrupted parties, this message can be robustly recovered subject to at most t' errors. Our Protocol **ReconPub** is a generalization of the counterpart in [5,18]. Because our protocol is defined over constant-size field, we resort to algebraic geometry codes for error correction.

Theorem 5. *For $d \leq t$, **ReconPub** robustly reconstructs the secrets $\mathbf{a}_1, \ldots, \mathbf{a}_T$ towards all parties in $\mathcal{I}$. For $d \leq 2t'$, **ReconPub** detectably reconstructs the secrets $\mathbf{a}_1, \ldots, \mathbf{a}_T$ towards all parties in $\mathcal{I}$. The total communication complexity is $O(n'^2)$*

Protocol ReconPub$(d, [\mathbf{a}_1]_d, \ldots, [\mathbf{a}_T]_d)$

Setup: a set of n' parties $\mathcal{I} = \{P_1, \ldots, P_{n'}\}$ and at most $t' \leq \frac{n'(1-\epsilon)}{3}$ of them are corrupted. Let $T = n'(1 - \epsilon) - 2t' - 1 = \Omega(n)$ and $M = (m_{ij})_{n' \times T}$ be a generator matrix of a $[n', T, 2t'+1]$ linear code C over $\mathbb{F}_q$ in Corollary 2 as $2t'+1+T = n'(1-\epsilon)$.

Input: T sharings $[\mathbf{a}_1]_d, \ldots, [\mathbf{a}_T]_d \in \Sigma_d$ in Corollary 4.

- For $i = 1, \ldots, n'$, the parties in $\mathcal{I}$ locally compute $[\mathbf{r}_i]_d = \sum_{j=1}^{T} m_{ij} [\mathbf{a}_j]_d$.
- The parties in $\mathcal{I}$ send their shares of $[\mathbf{r}_i]_d$ to P_i.
- P_i checks the consistency of $[\mathbf{r}_i]_d$. If $d \leq t'$, P_i robustly reconstructs the secret $\mathbf{r}_i$ by invoking decoding algorithm of Σ_d and sends them to other parties in $\mathcal{I}$. Otherwise if $d \leq 2t'$, P_i either reconstructs the secret $\tilde{\mathbf{r}}_i$ and sends it to other parties in $\mathcal{I}$ or becomes unhappy if there are inconsistent shares.
- If no one becomes unhappy, the parties in $\mathcal{I}$ robustly reconstruct $\mathbf{a}_1, \ldots, \mathbf{a}_T$ from $\tilde{\mathbf{r}}_1, \ldots, \tilde{\mathbf{r}}_{n'}$. More precisely, write $\tilde{\mathbf{r}}_i = (r_{i1}, \ldots, r_{is}) \in \mathbb{F}_q^s$ and decode the codeword $(r_{1j}, \ldots, r_{n'j}) \in C$ for $j = 1, \ldots, s$ to obtain the message $(a_{1j}, \ldots, a_{Tj})$ for $j = 1, \ldots, s$.

Output: $\mathbf{a}_i = (a_{i1}, \ldots, a_{is}), i = 1, \ldots, T$.

Proof. We prove the first claim. Without loss of generality, we assume $d = t$. For each party $P_i \in \mathcal{I}$, $[\mathbf{r}_i]_d$ consists of at most t' incorrect shares. Since $[\mathbf{r}_i]_d \in \Sigma_d$, by Proposition 4, the reconstruction of Σ_d is $r = t + \epsilon n'/3$ and it can correct up to $\frac{(n'-r)}{2} \geq t'$ errors. Thus, the honest party P_i can robustly reconstruct $\mathbf{r}_i$. After this reconstruction, there are at least $n' - t'$ correct secrets $\mathbf{r}_i$. Thus, the decoding algorithm of C can correct errors and output correct messages.

We proceed to the second claim $d = 2t'$. The argument is divided into two cases.

1. Some honest party P_j receives corrupted shares of $[\mathbf{r}_i]_d$ from the adversary. By Proposition 4 and Corollary 4, the minimum distance of $\Sigma_{2t'}$ is at least $n' - 2r' \geq n'/3$. Since there are at most $t' < n'/3$ corrupted shares, P_j can detect them and become unhappy.
2. All honest parties receive consistent shares. This implies that there are at least $n' - t'$ correct secrets $\mathbf{r}_i$. Thus, the decoding algorithm of C can correct errors and output correct messages.

As for the communication complexity, party P_i sends his share of $[\mathbf{r}_j]_d$ to P_j and the secret $\mathbf{r}_i$ to all other parties. Thus, the total communication complexity is $O(n^2)$ for opening $T = \Omega(n)$ secrets. The proof is completed.

Now we proceed to generate Beaver triples $([\mathbf{a}]_t, [\mathbf{b}]_t, [\mathbf{c}]_t)$ to prepare for multiplication gates. Random sharings $[\mathbf{a}]_t$ and $[\mathbf{b}]_t$ could be generated by invoking **RandEl**. Since arithmetic secret sharing has strong multiplicativity, all parties could locally compute $[\mathbf{c}]_{2t}$. The key of transforming $[\mathbf{c}]_{2t}$ to $[\mathbf{c}]_t$ is degree reduction, which can be done with double sharings generated in **RandEl**.

Protocol Triples

Setup: The set of parties $\mathcal{I} = \{P_1, \ldots, P_{n'}\}$, the number of parties n' and the number of corrupted parties t'.

*– The parties in $\mathcal{I}$ invoke **DoubleSharings** three times to generate $([\mathbf{a}_1]_t, [\mathbf{a}_1]_{t'}), \ldots, ([\mathbf{a}_T]_t, [\mathbf{a}_T]_{t'})$, $([\mathbf{b}_1]_t, [\mathbf{b}_1]_{t'}), \ldots, ([\mathbf{b}_T]_t, [\mathbf{b}_T]_{t'})$ and $([\mathbf{r}_1]_t, [\mathbf{r}_1]_{2t'}), \ldots, ([\mathbf{r}_T]_t, [\mathbf{r}_T]_{2t'})$.
– The parties in $\mathcal{I}$ locally compute $[\mathbf{d}_k]_{2t'} = [\mathbf{a}_i]_{t'} \star [\mathbf{b}_i]_{t'} + [\mathbf{r}_i]_{2t'}$ for $i = 1, \ldots, T$.
– The parties in $\mathcal{I}$ invoke **ReconPub**$(2t', [\mathbf{d}_1]_{2t'}, \ldots, [\mathbf{d}_T]_{2t'})$ to publicly reconstruct $\mathbf{d}_1, \ldots, \mathbf{d}_T$,
– The parties in $\mathcal{I}$ locally compute $[\mathbf{c}_i]_t = \mathbf{d}_i - [\mathbf{r}_i]_t$.

Output: T triples $([\mathbf{a}_1]_t, [\mathbf{b}_1]_t, [\mathbf{c}_1]_t), \ldots, ([\mathbf{a}_T]_t, [\mathbf{b}_T]_t, [\mathbf{c}_T]_t)$.

Theorem 6. *If all honest parties are happy, Protocol **Triples** successfully outputs Beaver triples $([\mathbf{a}_i]_t, [\mathbf{b}_i]_t, [\mathbf{c}_i]_t)_{i \in [T]}$[7] such that $\mathbf{a}_i$ and $\mathbf{b}_i$ are uniformly random vectors and $\mathbf{c}_i = \mathbf{a}_i \star \mathbf{b}_i$. Moreover, the total communication complexity of **Triples** is $O(n^2)$.*

Proof. Corollary 5 shows that if all honest parties are happy, then **Double-Sharings** generates correct sharings $([\mathbf{a}_i]_{t'}, [\mathbf{b}_i]_{t'}, [\mathbf{r}_i]_{2t'})_{i \in [T]}$ such that $\mathbf{a}_i, \mathbf{b}_i, \mathbf{r}_i$ are uniformly random vectors by Corollary 5. Theorem 5 shows that **Recon-Pub** can reconstruct correct secrets towards all parties if all honest parties are happy. It is clear that $\mathbf{c}_i = \mathbf{a}_i \star \mathbf{b}_i$ as our SSS are multiplicative by Proposition 4. The privacy argument is straightforward. **DoubleSharings** does not reveal any information to the adversary by Corollary 5. Moreover, **ReconPub** only opens the random elements which contain no information about $\mathbf{c}_i$. The total communication complexity is the cost of invoking **DoubleSharings** and **ReconPub**, which is $O(n^2)$ due to Corollary 5 and Theorem 5.

4.4   Put Together

In this subsection, we briefly explain how to replace the protocols in [5] with our new protocols so as to obtain perfectly secure MPC for $t < \frac{n(1-\epsilon)}{3}$ over constant-size fields. The prominent feature of our MPC protocol is constant share size. We use the same player elimination protocol in [5] containing fault detection, fault localization and player elimination.

Put everything together, we obtain the following theorem.

Theorem 7. *The protocol **PreprocessingPhase** generates $c_M + c_R + c_I$ independent random Beaver triples $[\mathbf{a}_i]_t, [\mathbf{b}_i]_t, [\mathbf{a}_i \star \mathbf{b}_i]_t$ with independently random vectors $\mathbf{a}_i, \mathbf{b}_i \in \mathbb{F}_q^{\frac{\epsilon n}{6}}$. The total communication complexity is $O((c_I + c_M + c_R)n + n^3)$. The amortized communication complexity of generating one triple is $O(n)$.*[8]

---

[7] Invoking **Triples** once can generate $T = n'(1 - \epsilon) - 2t' - 1 = \Omega(n)$ triples. Each triple contains $\frac{\epsilon n}{6}$ secrets.

[8] Since such triple consists of packed secret sharing scheme, we can further reduce the amortized communication complexity to constant if we evaluates $\Omega(n)$ instances of the same circuit in the online phase.

Proof. The proof is quite straightforward since we have already proven Theorem 6. If every party is happy, then **Triples** guarantees that all the Beaver triples generated in this segment is correct. Otherwise, all parties invoke the player elimination protocol to localize a pair of parties containing at least one corrupt party. The privacy argument can be derived directly from Theorem 6. It remains to compute the communication complexity. We note that we divide the preprocessing phase into t segments. In each segment, we either remove two parties or complete this segment and obtain ℓ Beaver triples. Since there are n parties, we invoke at most $t + \frac{n}{2} = O(t)$ segments. For each segment, we invoke **Triples** $\frac{\ell}{tT}$ times which incurs $O(\frac{\ell n^2}{tT}) = O(\ell)$ communication complexity. The player elimination protocol in Appendix incurs the same amount of communication complexity in this segment plus the cost of three broadcasts $O(n^2)$. Thus, the total communication complexity for preprocessing phase is $O(\ell t + n^3) = O((c_I + c_M + c_R)n + n^3)$.

Protocol PreprocessingPhase

Setup: the set of actual parties is $\mathcal{I} = \{P_1, \ldots, P_{n'}\}$, the number of parties is $n' = n$ and the number of corrupted parties is $t' = t$. The preprocessing phase generates $\ell = c_I + c_M + c_R$ Beaver triples.

- For $1st, \ldots, t$th segment,

  - Each party in $\mathcal{I}$ sets his happy-bit to happy.
  - The party in $\mathcal{I}$ invokes **Triples** $\lfloor \frac{\ell}{tT} \rfloor$ times to generate $\frac{\ell}{t}$ Beaver triples $([\mathbf{a}]_{t'}, [\mathbf{b}]_{t'}, [\mathbf{a} \star \mathbf{b}]_{t'})$.
  - If there is at least one party unhappy, invoke player elimination protocol to localize a pair of parties $P' = \{P_i, P_j\}$.
  - Set $\mathcal{I} = \mathcal{I} \setminus P'$ and $n' = n' - 2, t' = t' - 1$. Repeat this segment.

Theorem 8. *The protocol **OnlinePhase** perfectly securely evaluates a single instruction multiple data (SIMD) circuit with $\frac{\epsilon n c_I}{6}$ input, $\frac{\epsilon n c_M}{6}$ multiplication, $\frac{\epsilon n c_R}{6}$ random gates and D_M depth in the presence of $t = \frac{(1-\epsilon)n}{3}$ actively corrupted parties, given $c_I + c_M + c_R$ pre-shared multiplication triples. The total communication complexity is $O((c_I + c_M + c_R)n + D_M n^2 + n^3)$ and thus the amortized communication complexity of computing each gate is $O(\frac{D_M n + n^2}{c_I + c_M + c_R})$. If $c_I + c_M + c_R$ is bigger than $n^2 + D_M n$, the amortized communication complexity for each gate is a constant.*

Proof. The online phase follows the line of *Computationphase* protocol in [5]. Since our circuit is a SIMD circuit, we use the packed secret sharing obtained in preprocessing phase to compute the *Computationphase* protocol. Each triple in the preprocessing phase can compute $\frac{\epsilon n}{6}$ instances simultaneously. Thus, it suffices to generate $c_I + c_M + c_R$ Beaver triples in the preprocessing phase. The total communication complexity in the preprocessing phase is $O((c_I + c_M + c_R)n + n^3)$ by Theorem 7.

Protocol   OnlinePhase

Input Gate: (P_i input $\mathbf{s}$)

- The parties in $\mathcal{I}$ send their shares of $[\mathbf{r}]_t$ to P_i. P_i robustly reconstructs $\mathbf{r}$ by running decoding algorithm in Proposition 4.
- P_i broadcasts $\mathbf{s} - \mathbf{r}$ and the parties in $\mathcal{I}$ locally compute $[\mathbf{s}]_t = \mathbf{s} - \mathbf{r} + [\mathbf{r}]_t$.

Addition Gate: The parties in $\mathcal{I}$ locally compute $[\mathbf{x} + \mathbf{y}]_t = [\mathbf{x}]_t + [\mathbf{y}]_t$.
Scalar Gate: The parties in $\mathcal{I}$ locally compute $[\lambda \mathbf{x}]_t = \lambda [\mathbf{x}]_t$
Random Gate: Pick a random sharing $[\mathbf{r}]_t$ associated with this gate.
Multiplication Gate: Up to $\frac{T}{2}$ multiplication gates are processed simultaneously. The input of each multiplication gate is $[\mathbf{x}_i]_t, [\mathbf{y}_i]_t$ for $i = 1, \ldots, T/2$. The Beaver triples $([\mathbf{a}_i]_t, [\mathbf{b}_i]_t, [\mathbf{c}_i]_t), i = 1, \ldots, T/2$ are given.

- For $i = 1, \ldots, T/2$, the parties in $\mathcal{I}$ locally compute $[\mathbf{d}_i]_t = [\mathbf{x}_i]_t - [\mathbf{a}_i]_t$ and $[\mathbf{e}_i]_t = [\mathbf{y}_i]_t - [\mathbf{b}_i]_t$.
- Invoke **ReconPub** to robustly reconstruct the secrets $\mathbf{d}_i, \mathbf{e}_i$ for $i = 1, \ldots, T/2$.
- The parties in $\mathcal{I}$ locally compute $[\mathbf{x}_i \star \mathbf{y}_i]_t = \mathbf{d}_i \star \mathbf{e}_i + \mathbf{e}_i \star [\mathbf{x}_i]_t + \mathbf{d}_i \star [\mathbf{y}_i]_t + [\mathbf{c}_i]_t$ for $i = 1, \ldots, T/2$.

Output Gate: (Output $[\mathbf{s}]_t$ to all parties) The parties in $\mathcal{I}$ send their shares of $[\mathbf{s}]_t$ to other parties. All parties robustly reconstruct $\mathbf{s}$ by running decoding algorithm in Proposition 4.

We proceed to the online phase. At the input gate, we use a pre-shared random vector $\mathbf{r}$ to mask the input $\mathbf{s}$ and then broadcast the difference $\mathbf{s} - \mathbf{r}$. Thus, we broadcast n times and each broadcast can be simulated by communicating $O(n^2)$ bits. All parties obtain their shares of the secret $\mathbf{s}$ by locally computing $[\mathbf{r}]_t + \mathbf{s} - \mathbf{r}$. The addition and scalar gate can be done locally. Thus, the total communication complexity for computing input gates is $O(n^3 + c_I n)$. At the multiplication gate, the Beaver triple $([\mathbf{a}]_t, [\mathbf{b}]_t, [\mathbf{a} \star \mathbf{b}]_t)$ is used to securely compute a sharing of a product at the cost of two public reconstructions. The **ReconPub** amortizes the communication complexity of public reconstruction by reconstructing $T = \Omega(n)$ secrets simultaneously. Thus, we can evaluate $\Omega(n)$ multiplication gates by invoking **ReconPub** once. Since the secret space of our SSS has dimension $\frac{\epsilon n}{6}$, this packed secret sharing scheme can evaluate $\frac{\epsilon n}{6}$ instances simultaneously. Each random gate picks a random sharing. Thus, the total communication complexity of random gates is $O(c_R n)$. This means the total communication complexity of computing multiplication gates is $O(c_M n + D_M n^2)$. Therefore, the total communication complexity of **OnlinePhase** is $O((c_I + c_M + c_R)n + D_M n^2 + n^3)$.

We proceed to the robustness argument. At the input gate, all parties use a random sharing generated in the preprocessing phase to generate the sharing of one input. No corruption happens in this stage. At the addition gate and scalar gate, all parties do local computation and no corruption happens. At the multiplication gate, all parties open secrets by invoking **ReconPub**. We note that the the sharings to be opened belong to Σ_t which can be error corrected by Proposition 4. Thus, the corruptions caused by the adversary in this stage will be corrected. At the output gate, we obtain the same conclusion as the sharings to be opened belong to Σ_t as well.

We proceed to the privacy argument. We note that the secret sharing scheme we use has t-privacy and there are $t' \leq t$ corrupted parties in the online phase. At the input gate, the input is masked by a random element and thus the element broadcasted is a random element revealing no information about the input. At the multiplication gate, the opened secrets are random elements which reveal no information. Thus, the adversary learns nothing except the output in the online phase.

Remark 3. *Since our MPC protocol uses the packed secret sharing scheme, to achieve constant amortized communication complexity, our MPC protocol must run over single instruction multiple data (SIMD) circuit which carries out the exact same computation to several inputs simultaneously. However, it is also possible to adapt it to other circuits although the protocol will be more complicated. We briefly explain the modification required for this goal. In [17], they propose a way to reroute the network. We can replace our double sharings with the sharings of random vectors and the permutation of their coordinates in the ramp HIM protocol. When we open the pair of secrets, we compare if the secret and the permutation of the secret are consistent. Thus, we can apply the technique in [17] to modify the circuit to achieve small communication complexity. The technique in [17] is to embed the computation in a special form of a universal circuit based on the so-called Bene's network [9] which requires the sharings with the permutation of their coordinates.*

5   MPC-in-the-Head

5.1   Check Consistency of Shares via Ramp HIM

The application of HIM in zero-knowledge proof was due to [8] where HIM was used to check the consistency of sharings. To check consistency of $n - 2t$ sharings, HIM requires $n + t$ additional sharings. Thus, the overhead of checking one sharing is roughly $\frac{t+n}{n-2t} = O(1)$ field element. The downside is that HIM requires that $|\mathbb{F}| \geq 2n$. As a generalization of HIM, the ramp HIM is defined over constant-size field which can save the communication complexity.

Proposition 6. *Assume at most $t = \frac{1-\epsilon}{3}n$ parties of $P_1, \cdots, P_n$ are corrupted and Σ_d has d-privacy with $d \geq t$. Protocol **CheckConsistency**(d) verify the d-consistency of $2t$ secret sharings with zero error probability. It is t-private in the presence of semi-honest adversary and perfectly t-robust in the presence of malicious adversary.*

Proof. We use $[r_i]$ to represent $[r_i]_d$. We begin by proving that protocol **Check-Consistency**(d) is t-robust in the presence of malicious adversary. Let $H \subseteq [n]$ be the index set of honest parties and $\bar{H} = [n]/H$ be the index set of corrupted parties. Since there are at most t corrupted parties, $|H| \geq n - t$. If no party complains, $[s_i]$ for $i \in H$ are correct sharings. Moreover, $[r_i]$ for $i \in [2t + 1, n]$ provided by the input client can not be corrupted by the adversary. The fact that

$|H| + |[2t+1, n]| \geq 2n - 3t \geq (1+\epsilon)n$ and M is an $(n, n, (1+\epsilon)n, (1-\epsilon)n)$-ramp HIM implies that $[s_i]$ for $i \in H$ and $[r_i]$ for $i \in [2t+1, n]$ uniquely determine the sharings $[r_i]$ for $i \in [2t]$. Since $[r]$ for $i \in [2t]$ and $[s_i]$ for $i \in H$ are correct sharings, $[r_i]$ for $i \in [2t]$ are also correct sharings.

We proceed to the argument of t-privacy in the presence of semi-honest adversary. Since Σ_d has $d \geq t$-privacy, the adversary learns nothing from any t shares of $[s_1], \ldots, [s_n]$. If we fix $[s_i]$ for $i \in H$ and $[r_i]$ for $i \in [2t]$, the fact that M is an $(n, n, (1+\epsilon)n, (1-\epsilon)n)$-ramp HIM and $|\bar{H}| + 2t \leq 3t \leq (1-\epsilon)n$ implies that there is a surjection from $r_i, i \in [2t+1, n]$ to $s_i, i \in \bar{H}$. Since $r_i, i \in [2t+1, n]$ provided by the input client are distributed uniformly at random, $s_i, i \in \bar{H}$ are also distributed uniformly.

Protocol CheckConsistency(d)

Setup: n parties $P_1, \cdots, P_n$ and an input client I

Public input: an $(n, n, (1+\epsilon)n, (1-\epsilon)n)$-ramp HIM M

Private input: P_i obtains corresponding shares of $[r_1]_d, \cdots, [r_{2t}]_d$

- Input client randomly generates $[r_{2t+1}]_d, \cdots, [r_n]_d$ and distributes corresponding shares to $P_1, \cdots, P_n$
- Parties locally compute $([s_1]_d, \cdots, [s_n]_d)^T = M([r_1]_d, \cdots, [r_n]_d)^T$
- Party P_i receives all shares of $[s_i]$ from other parties and checks the consistency. If the sharing is incorrect, P_i complains and the protocol aborts.
- If no party complains, the parties conclude that $[r_1]_d, \cdots, [r_{2t}]_d$ are consistent.

Remark 4. *Protocol **CheckConsistency(d)** is similar to Protocol **RandEl(d)** as ramp HIM is used to guarantee d-consistency. The major difference is input and output. In MPC protocol, preprocessing data come from secret sharings generated by each party including both honest parties and corrupted parties while in MPCitH protocol, preprocessing data are directly provided by the prover.*

5.2   Constant-Rate Zero-Knowledge Proof

The MPC protocol in [5] is perfectly secure against malicious adversary. This MPC protocol has perfect robustness and the MPCitH protocol relying on it thus saves two rounds of communication [32].

The communication cost of the prover consists of commitment and decommitment. According to [32], we need a statistically-binding commitment scheme, whose output length grows linearly in message length. The communication cost of commitment is $O(n|C| \log q)$ bits. The decommitment requires the prover to reveal the views of t parties selected by the verifier which includes witness, preprocessing data and broadcast value, which takes $O(t|C| \log q)$ bits communication. In summary, the communication complexity of MPCitH protocol is $O((n+t)|C| \log q)$ bits, which is equivalent to $O(n|C| \log n)$ as $t = \Omega(n)$ and HIM forces $q \geq 2n$ [8].

We briefly describe how to reduce communication complexity to $O(|C|)$ with the help of ramp HIM. Firstly, we apply a packed secret sharing which batches $\Omega(n)$ evaluations together to remove the multiplicative factor n in the communication complexity. The next step is to apply an MPC protocol over constant-size field in Section 4. By replacing **RandEl**(d) with **CheckConsistency**(d), we obtain an MPC protocol Π_f that has t-privacy and perfect t-robustness due to Proposition 6. Plugging this MPC protocol in [8], finally we obtain a 3-round constant-rate zero-knowledge proof. In contrast, the constant-rate zero-knowledge proof proposed in [32] has 5 communication rounds since it relies on a MPC protocol [16] with statistical robustness and coin tossing between prover and verifier causes more interaction.

Theorem 9. *Given a statistically binding commitment scheme, for any NP relation $R(x,w)$ which can be verified with a circuit with $O(|C|)$ gates, there exists a two-party* **3-round**[9] *constant-rate zero-knowledge proof in the random oracle model. The protocol has communication complexity $O(|C|)$ and soundness error $2^{-\Omega(n)}$.*

6   Information-Theoretic Multi-verifier Zero-Knowledge Proof

In MVZK, the prover $\mathcal{P}$ wants to convince n verifiers $\mathcal{V}_1, \cdots, \mathcal{V}_n$ that regarding to a NP relation R, it holds a witness w for a statement such that $R(x,w) = 1$. In this paper, we focus on a special NP relation:circuit satisfiability, which aims to find a witness $w \in \mathbb{F}_q$ for a circuit C such that $C(w) = 1$. We assume that at most t verifiers are corrupted by the adversary and can collude with the prover. There are two types of communications, the communications between the verifiers and prover and the communications between different verifiers. In [44], they present an efficient MVZK in the presence of honest-majority verifiers.

In the information-theoretic MVZK, the verifiers invoke a coin-tossing functionality $\mathcal{F}_{coin}$ to jointly sample an random element in the challenge set. In this process, HIM plays a central role in producing random sharings. However, due to circuit size and the security parameter, the share size of MVZK has to be large enough. There is another challenge related to the share size which is the verification technique [44]. We briefly introduce this technique and show how to adapt it to our constant-size field later.

1. For a circuit with $|C|$ multiplication gates, the prover distributes corresponding share of $([x_i], [y_i], [z_i])_{i \in [|C|]}$ to n verifiers, which needs communication of $O(n|C|)$ field elements in $\mathbb{F}_q$.
2. All verifiers jointly sample a uniform challenge $\chi \in \mathbb{F}_{q^r}$ and compute the inner-product tuple:

---

[9] If we consider random oracle model, then statistically binding commitment scheme needs only one round [38]. We emphasize that regardless the model, our new MPCitH protocol saves two rounds of communication compared to [32].

$$[\mathbf{x}] = ([x_1], \chi \cdot [x_2], \ldots, \chi^{|C|-1} \cdot [x_{|C|}])$$
$$[\mathbf{y}] = ([y_1], [y_2], \ldots, [y_{|C|}])$$
$$[z] = \sum_{i=1}^{|C|} \chi^{i-1} \cdot [z_i]$$

Note that inner product tuples are Shamir SSS defined over $\mathbb{F}_{q^r}$. In this step, joint sampling communicates $O(n^2)$ field elements in $\mathbb{F}_{q^r}$.

3. All verifiers apply the inner-product checking method in [28,29]. As [28] has analyzed, the verification procedure incurs communication of $O((n\tau + n^2) \log_\tau |C|)$ field elements in $\mathbb{F}_{q^r}$ (Here τ is compress parameter).

We notice that the soundness error is dependent on $\mathbb{F}_{q^r}$. If there exists one incorrect multiplication triple, then the inner-product tuple passes the verification of inner product with probability at most $\frac{|C|-1}{q^r}$. To achieve a soundness error of $2^{-\lambda}$, we have to set $q^r = 2^\lambda(|C|-1)$, which incurs a communication overhead $O(\lambda + \log |C|)$ if our computation is carried out over $\mathbb{F}_q$ instead of $\mathbb{F}_{q^r}$.

It is clear that moving from $\mathbb{F}_q$ to $\mathbb{F}_{q^r}$ increases the communication complexity in Step 2 and Step 3. We can save the communication complexity in Step 2 by introducing ramp secret sharing and ramp HIM. The communication complexity in step 3 can be saved by "batched checking".

Functionality $\mathcal{F}_{coin}$

This functionality runs for n verifiers and an adversary $\mathcal{A}$ as follows:

- Upon receiving $(coin, \mathcal{C})$ from all verifiers where $\mathcal{C}$ is the challenge set, sample $r \leftarrow \mathcal{C}$ and sends $(random, r)$ to $\mathcal{A}$.
- If $\mathcal{A}$ returns the message $(deliver)$, then sends $(random, r)$ to all verifiers. Otherwise $\mathcal{A}$ returns the message $(abort)$, then outputs abort for all verifiers.

To begin with, we instantiate $\mathcal{F}_{coin}$ over constant-size field. The building blocks of our protocol are ramp secret sharing scheme and ramp HIM, i.e., we use the ramp secret sharing scheme over constant-size field with $\frac{1-\epsilon}{2}n$-privacy and $\frac{1}{2}n$-reconstruction. This ramp SSS requires that the number of corrupted verifiers is sub-optimal $t = \frac{(1-\epsilon)n}{2}$ and its secret space is $\mathbb{F}_q^{\Omega(\epsilon n)}$ with $\epsilon = O(\frac{\lambda \log |C|}{n})$.

Protocol Rand

Public input: an $(n, t, a, (1-\epsilon)n)$-ramp HIM M (a can be any number since **Rand** only uses $(1-\epsilon)n$-privacy instead of $(1+\epsilon)n$-reconstruction of ramp HIM).

- Each verifier $\mathcal{V}_i$ samples a random sharing $[s_i]_t$ and distributes corresponding share to other verifiers.
- All verifiers locally compute $([r_1]_t, \ldots, [r_t]_t)^T = M([s_1]_t, \cdots, [s_n]_t)^T$.

Protocol Coin

Setup: The protocol **Rand** generates t random sharings at one time. The protocol **Coin** picks a random sharing $[r]_t$ from these t sharings.

- Each verifier sends his share of $[r]_t$ to all other verifiers. After receiving shares from other $n-1$ verifiers, each verifier checks whether $[r]_t$ is a valid secret sharing.
- If each verifier $\mathcal{V}_i$ concludes that all shares are correct, the secret r are reconstructed and outputted. Otherwise, $\mathcal{V}_i$ broadcasts the message $(abort)$ and the protocol aborts.

Similar to [44], we obtain the following result.

Theorem 10. *The protocol **Coin** realizes $\mathcal{F}_{coin}$ in security-with-abort model in the presence of a malicious adversary corrupting $t = \frac{1-\epsilon}{2}n$ verifiers.*

Proof. The only difference from [44] is that our **Rand** protocol uses ramp HIM instead of HIM. It suffices to prove that the randomness produced by **Rand** protocol is independent of the adversary. Since M is an $(n, t, a, (1-\epsilon)n)$-ramp HIM and $2t = (1-\epsilon)n$, there is a surjection from $(\mathbf{s}_i)_{i \in H}$ to $(\mathbf{r}_i)_{i \in [t]}$ where H is the set of honest parties. This means $(\mathbf{r}_i)_{i \in [t]}$ distributes uniformly at random conditioning on the sharings of the corrupted parties $(\mathbf{s}_i)_{i \in [n]/H}$.

We proceed to the batch checking. Assume that $[x]$ is a sharing over $\mathbb{F}_q$ and $\chi \in \mathbb{F}_{q^r}$. We redefine the inner product in this setting. We note that one can represent $\mathbb{F}_{q^r}$ as a linear subspace over $\mathbb{F}_q$. Let $v_1, \ldots, v_r$ be the basis of $\mathbb{F}_{q^r}$ over $\mathbb{F}_q$. Then, for any element $\lambda \in \mathbb{F}_{q^r}$, we have $\lambda v_i = \sum_{j=1}^{r} m_{ij} v_j$. Thus, λ can be thought of as a linear map $M_\lambda = (m_{ij})_{r \times r}$ from $\mathbb{F}_q^r$ to its self. In this sense, we redefine $\cdot$ as

$$\lambda \cdot (x_1, \ldots, x_r) = M_\lambda (x_1, \ldots, x_r)$$

where $x_1, \ldots, x_r \in \mathbb{F}_q$. We now show how to check circuit satisfiability.

1. For a circuit with $|C|$ multiplication gates, the prover distributes corresponding share of $([x_i], [y_i], [z_i])_{i \in [|C|]}$ over $\mathbb{F}_q$ to n verifiers. Pad $([0], [0], [0])$'s to these $|C|$ sharings so that the number of sharings is divisible by r. We now assume that $|C|$ is divisible by r.

2. All verifiers jointly sample a uniform challenge $\chi \in \mathbb{F}_{q^r}$ and compute the inner-product tuple:

$$[\mathbf{x}] = (([x_1], \ldots, [x_r]), \chi \cdot ([x_{r+1}], \ldots, [x_{2r}]), \ldots, \chi^{|C|/r-1} \cdot [x_{|C|-r+1}], \ldots, [x_{|C|}])$$

$$[\mathbf{y}] = (([y_1], \ldots, [y_r]), ([y_{r+1}], \ldots, [y_{2r}]), \ldots, ([y_{|C|-r+1}], \ldots, [y_{|C|}]))$$

$$[z] = \sum_{i=1}^{|C|/r} \chi^{i-1} \cdot ([z_{(i-1)r+1}], \ldots, [z_{ir}])$$

3. All verifiers apply the inner-product checking method in [28,29].

Therefore, the amortized share size is now independent of the security parameter and circuit size.

Acknowledgments. We thank the anonymous reviewers from ASIACRYPT 2023 for their insightful comments. The work of Chaoping Xing was supported in part by the National Key Research and Development Project under Grant 2022YFA1004900, in part by the National Natural Science Foundation of China under Grant 12031011. The work of Chen Yuan was supported in part by the National Natural Science Foundation of China under Grant 12101403.

A   Player Elimination

Player elimination was first proposed in [31] to transform a non-robust (but detectable) protocol into a robust protocol at essentially no additional costs. This protocol cuts the preprocessing phase into many segments. At the beginning of each segment, all parties are happy. If some party detects the inconsistency, he becomes unhappy in this segment. At the end of this segment, if there is some party unhappy, the protocol enters into fault localization and removes a pair of parties from the rest of the computation. Then, the player elimination protocol repeats this segment. For completeness, we present the player elimination protocol in [5].

Player Eliminiation

Setup: a set of n' parties $\mathcal{I} = \{P_1, \ldots, P_{n'}\}$ and at most $t' \leq \frac{n'(1-\epsilon)}{3}$ of them are corrupted. Divide the computation into several segment and do the following in each segment.

Initialization: All parties set their happy-bit happy.

Fault Detection: Reach agreement whether or not at least one party is unhappy.

Fault Localization: Find a pair of parties E in $\mathcal{I}$ that contain at least one corrupted party.

- Denote the player $P_r \in \mathcal{I}$ with the smallest index r as the referee.
- Every $P_i \in \mathcal{I}$ sends everything he received and all random values he chose during the computation of the actual segment (including fault detection) to P_r.
- Given the value received above, P_r can reproduce all message that should be sent and compare it with the value from the recipient that claims to have. Then, P_r broadcasts (ℓ, i, j, x, x') where ℓ is the index of the message, x is the message sent by P_i and x' is the message received by P_j with $x \neq x'$.
- The accused parties P_i, P_j broadcast whether they agree with P_r. If P_i disagrees, set $E = \{P_r, P_i\}$. If P_j disagrees, set $E = \{P_r, P_j\}$. Otherwise set $E = \{P_i, P_j\}$.

Player Elimination: Set $\mathcal{I} = I \setminus E, n' = n' - 2, t' = t' - 1$ and repeat this segment.

References

1. Abe, M., Cramer, R., Fehr, S.: Non-interactive distributed-verifier proofs and proving relations among commitments. In: Zheng, Y. (ed.) ASIACRYPT 2002. LNCS, vol. 2501, pp. 206–224. Springer, Heidelberg (2002). https://doi.org/10.1007/3-540-36178-2_13
2. Applebaum, B., Kachlon, E., Patra, A.: Verifiable relation sharing and multi-verifier zero-knowledge in two rounds: trading nizks with honest majority. In: Dodis, Y., Shrimpton, T. (eds.) CRYPTO 2022. LNCS, vol. 13510, pp. 33–56. Springer, Heidelberg (2022)
3. Baum, C., Jadoul, R., Orsini, E., Scholl, P., Smart, N.P.: Feta: efficient threshold designated-verifier zero-knowledge proofs. Cryptology ePrint Archive (2022)
4. Baum, C., Nof, A.: Concretely-efficient zero-knowledge arguments for arithmetic circuits and their application to lattice-based cryptography. In: Kiayias, A., Kohlweiss, M., Wallden, P., Zikas, V. (eds.) PKC 2020. LNCS, vol. 12110, pp. 495–526. Springer, Cham (2020). https://doi.org/10.1007/978-3-030-45374-9_17
5. Beerliová-Trubíniová, Z., Hirt, M.: Perfectly-secure MPC with linear communication complexity. In: Canetti, R. (ed.) TCC 2008. LNCS, vol. 4948, pp. 213–230. Springer, Heidelberg (2008). https://doi.org/10.1007/978-3-540-78524-8_13
6. Ben-Or, M., Goldwasser, S., Wigderson, A.: Completeness theorems for non-cryptographic fault-tolerant distributed computation (extended abstract). In: Simon, J. (ed.) Proceedings of the 20th Annual ACM Symposium on Theory of Computing, 2–4 May 1988, Chicago, Illinois, USA, pp. 1–10. ACM (1988)
7. Ben-Sasson, E., Fehr, S., Ostrovsky, R.: Near-linear unconditionally-secure multi-party computation with a dishonest minority. IACR Cryptol. ePrint Arch., p. 629 (2011)
8. Bendlin, R., Damgård, I.: Threshold decryption and zero-knowledge proofs for lattice-based cryptosystems. In: Micciancio, D. (ed.) TCC 2010. LNCS, vol. 5978, pp. 201–218. Springer, Heidelberg (2010). https://doi.org/10.1007/978-3-642-11799-2_13
9. Beneš, V.E.: Optimal rearrangeable multistage connecting networks. Bell Syst. Tech. J. **43**(4), 1641–1656 (1964)
10. Burmester, M., Desmedt, Y.: Broadcast interactive proofs. In: Davies, D.W. (ed.) EUROCRYPT 1991. LNCS, vol. 547, pp. 81–95. Springer, Heidelberg (1991). https://doi.org/10.1007/3-540-46416-6_7
11. Cascudo, I., Cramer, R., Xing, C., Yuan, C.: Amortized complexity of information-theoretically secure MPC revisited. In: Shacham, H., Boldyreva, A. (eds.) CRYPTO 2018. LNCS, vol. 10993, pp. 395–426. Springer, Cham (2018). https://doi.org/10.1007/978-3-319-96878-0_14
12. Chen, H., Cramer, R.: Algebraic geometric secret sharing schemes and secure multi-party computations over small fields. In: Dwork, C. (ed.) CRYPTO 2006. LNCS, vol. 4117, pp. 521–536. Springer, Heidelberg (2006). https://doi.org/10.1007/11818175_31
13. Chen, H., Cramer, R., Goldwasser, S., de Haan, R., Vaikuntanathan, V.: Secure computation from random error correcting codes. In: Naor, M. (ed.) EUROCRYPT 2007. LNCS, vol. 4515, pp. 291–310. Springer, Heidelberg (2007). https://doi.org/10.1007/978-3-540-72540-4_17
14. Chida, K., et al.: Fast large-scale honest-majority MPC for malicious adversaries. In: Shacham, H., Boldyreva, A. (eds.) CRYPTO 2018. LNCS, vol. 10993, pp. 34–64. Springer, Cham (2018). https://doi.org/10.1007/978-3-319-96878-0_2

15. Cramer, R., Damgård, I., Nielsen, J.B.: Secure Multiparty Computation and Secret Sharing. Cambridge University Press, Cambridge (2015)
16. Damgård, I., Ishai, Y.: Scalable secure multiparty computation. In: Dwork, C. (ed.) CRYPTO 2006. LNCS, vol. 4117, pp. 501–520. Springer, Heidelberg (2006). https://doi.org/10.1007/11818175_30
17. Damgård, I., Ishai, Y., Krøigaard, M.: Perfectly secure multiparty computation and the computational overhead of cryptography. In: Gilbert, H. (ed.) EUROCRYPT 2010. LNCS, vol. 6110, pp. 445–465. Springer, Heidelberg (2010). https://doi.org/10.1007/978-3-642-13190-5_23
18. Damgård, I., Nielsen, J.B.: Scalable and unconditionally secure multiparty computation. In: Menezes, A. (ed.) CRYPTO 2007. LNCS, vol. 4622, pp. 572–590. Springer, Heidelberg (2007). https://doi.org/10.1007/978-3-540-74143-5_32
19. de Saint Guilhem, C.D., Orsini, E., Tanguy, T.: Limbo: efficient zero-knowledge mpcith-based arguments. In: Proceedings of the 2021 ACM SIGSAC Conference on Computer and Communications Security, pp. 3022–3036 (2021)
20. Escudero, D., Goyal, V., Polychroniadou, A., Song, Y.: Turbopack: honest majority MPC with constant online communication. In: Yin, H., Stavrou, A., Cremers, C., Shi, E. (eds.) Proceedings of the 2022 ACM SIGSAC Conference on Computer and Communications Security, CCS 2022, Los Angeles, CA, USA, 7–11 November 2022, pp. 951–964. ACM (2022)
21. Franklin, M.K., Yung, M.: Communication complexity of secure computation (extended abstract). In: Kosaraju, S.R., Fellows, M., Wigderson, A., Ellis, J.S. (eds.) Proceedings of the 24th Annual ACM Symposium on Theory of Computing, Victoria, British Columbia, Canada, 4–6 May 1992, pp. 699–710. ACM (1992)
22. Garcia, A., Stichtenoth, H.: A tower of Artin - Schreier extensions of function fields attaining the Drinfeld - Vlâdut bound. Inventiones Mathematicae 121, 211–222 (1995)
23. Garcia, A., Stichtenoth, H.: On the asymptotic behaviour of some towers of function fields over finite fields. J. Numb. Theory 61, 248–273 (1996)
24. Genkin, D., Ishai, Y., Polychroniadou, A.: Efficient multi-party computation: from passive to active security via secure SIMD circuits. In: Gennaro, R., Robshaw, M. (eds.) CRYPTO 2015. LNCS, vol. 9216, pp. 721–741. Springer, Heidelberg (2015). https://doi.org/10.1007/978-3-662-48000-7_35
25. Giacomelli, I., Madsen, J., Orlandi, C.: Zkboo: faster zero-knowledge for Boolean circuits. In: USENIX Security Symposium, vol. 16 (2016)
26. Goyal, V., Li, H., Ostrovsky, R., Polychroniadou, A., Song, Y.: ATLAS: efficient and scalable MPC in the honest majority setting. In: Malkin, T., Peikert, C. (eds.) CRYPTO 2021. LNCS, vol. 12826, pp. 244–274. Springer, Cham (2021). https://doi.org/10.1007/978-3-030-84245-1_9
27. Goyal, V., Liu, Y., Song, Y.: Communication-efficient unconditional MPC with guaranteed output delivery. In: Boldyreva, A., Micciancio, D. (eds.) CRYPTO 2019. LNCS, vol. 11693, pp. 85–114. Springer, Cham (2019). https://doi.org/10.1007/978-3-030-26951-7_4
28. Goyal, V., Song, Y.: Malicious security comes free in honest-majority mpc. Cryptology ePrint Archive (2020)
29. Goyal, V., Song, Y., Zhu, C.: Guaranteed output delivery comes free in honest majority MPC. In: Micciancio, D., Ristenpart, T. (eds.) CRYPTO 2020. LNCS, vol. 12171, pp. 618–646. Springer, Cham (2020). https://doi.org/10.1007/978-3-030-56880-1_22
30. Groth, J., Ostrovsky, R.: Cryptography in the multi-string model. J. Cryptol. 27(3), 506–543 (2014)

31. Hirt, M., Maurer, U., Przydatek, B.: Efficient secure multi-party computation. In: Okamoto, T. (ed.) ASIACRYPT 2000. LNCS, vol. 1976, pp. 143–161. Springer, Heidelberg (2000). https://doi.org/10.1007/3-540-44448-3_12

32. Ishai, Y., Kushilevitz, Ostrovsky, R., Sahai, A.: Zero-knowledge from secure multi-party computation. In Proceedings of the Thirty-Ninth Annual ACM Symposium on Theory of Computing, pp. 21–30 (2007)

33. Kales, D., Zaverucha, G.: Efficient lifting for shorter zero-knowledge proofs and post-quantum signatures. Cryptology ePrint Archive (2022)

34. Katz, J., Kolesnikov, V., Wang, X.: Improved non-interactive zero knowledge with applications to post-quantum signatures. In: Proceedings of the 2018 ACM SIGSAC Conference on Computer and Communications Security, pp. 525–537 (2018)

35. Liu, H., Xing, C., Yang, Y., Yuan, C.: Ramp hyper-invertible matrices and their applications to mpc protocols. Cryptology ePrint Archive, Paper 2023/1369 (2023). https://eprint.iacr.org/2023/1369

36. Niederreiter, H., Xing, C.: Rational Points on Curves over Finite Fields-Theory and Applications. Cambridge University Press, Cambridge (2001)

37. Nordholt, P.S., Veeningen, M.: Minimising communication in honest-majority MPC by batchwise multiplication verification. In: Preneel, B., Vercauteren, F. (eds.) ACNS 2018. LNCS, vol. 10892, pp. 321–339. Springer, Cham (2018). https://doi.org/10.1007/978-3-319-93387-0_17

38. Pass, R.: On deniability in the common reference string and random oracle model. In: Boneh, D. (ed.) CRYPTO 2003. LNCS, vol. 2729, pp. 316–337. Springer, Heidelberg (2003). https://doi.org/10.1007/978-3-540-45146-4_19

39. Cascudo, I., Chen, H., Cramer, R., Xing, C.: Asymptotically good ideal linear secret sharing with strong multiplication over *Any* fixed finite field. In: Halevi, S. (ed.) CRYPTO 2009. LNCS, vol. 5677, pp. 466–486. Springer, Heidelberg (2009). https://doi.org/10.1007/978-3-642-03356-8_28

40. Shamir, A.: How to share a secret. Commun. ACM **22**(11), 612–613 (1979)

41. Shum, K., Aleshnikov, I., Kumar, P.V., Stichtenoth, H., Deolalikar, V.: A low-complexity algorithm for the construction of algebraic-geometric codes better than the Gilbert-Varshamov bound. IEEE Trans. Inf. Theory **47**(6), 2225–2241 (2001)

42. Stichtenoth, H.: Function Fields and Codes. Springer, Heidelberg (2003). https://doi.org/10.1007/978-3-540-76878-4

43. Tsfasman, M.A., Vlăduţ, S.G.: Algebraic-Geometric Codes. Springer, Heidelberg (1991). https://doi.org/10.1007/978-94-011-3810-9

44. Yang, K., Wang, X.: Non-interactive zero-knowledge proofs to multiple verifiers. Cryptology ePrint Archive (2022)

Scalable Multi-party Private Set Union from Multi-query Secret-Shared Private Membership Test

Xiang Liu[1] and Ying Gao[1,2]

[1] School of Cyber Science and Technology, Beihang University, Beijing, China
{lx1234,gaoying}@buaa.edu.cn
[2] Zhongguancun Laboratory, Beijing, China

Abstract. Multi-party private set union (MPSU) allows $k(k \geq 3)$ parties, each holding a dataset of known size, to compute the union of their sets without revealing any additional information. Although two-party PSU has made rapid progress in recent years, applying its effective techniques to the multi-party setting would render information leakage and thus cannot be directly extended. Existing MPSU protocols heavily rely on computationally expensive public-key operations or generic secure multi-party computation techniques, which are not scalable.

In this work, we present a new efficient framework of MPSU from multi-party secret-shared shuffle and a newly introduced protocol called multi-query secret-shared private membership test (mq-ssPMT). Our MPSU is mainly based on symmetric-key operations and is secure against any semi-honest adversary that does not corrupt the leader and clients simultaneously. We also propose new frameworks for computing other multi-party private set operations (MPSO), such as the intersection, and the cardinality of the union and the intersection, meeting the same security requirements.

We demonstrate the scalability of our MPSU protocol with an implementation and a comparison with the state-of-the-art MPSU. Experiments show that when computing on datasets of 2^{10} elements, our protocol is 109× faster than the state-of-the-art MPSU, and the improvement becomes more significant as the set size increases. To the best of our knowledge, ours is the first protocol that reports on large-size experiments. For 7 parties with datasets of 2^{20} elements each, our protocol requires only 46 s.

Keywords: Multi-query secret-shared private membership test ·
Private set union · Multi-party secret-shared shuffle

1 Introduction

Private set union (PSU) allows a group of mutually untrusted parties to compute the union of their sets without revealing any additional information. PSU has

J. Guo and R. Steinfeld (Eds.): ASIACRYPT 2023, LNCS 14438, pp. 237–271, 2023.
https://doi.org/10.1007/978-981-99-8721-4_8

various applications, including cyber risk assessment and management [26,34], privacy-preserving data aggregation [6,8], and computing private DB full join [33]. For example, to assess system risks and deploy corresponding defenses, security practitioners usually want to obtain a joint list of their IP blacklists. However, they are increasingly concerned with the privacy of sensitive data, which may experience disclosure without appropriate computation techniques. One crucial way this can be enhanced is PSU, which can be used to protect the privacy of each organization while computing the union correctly.

In addition, the combination of PSU with other set operations is also greatly in use. For instance, a social service organization needs to determine the cancer patients who are entitled to social welfare, and they would require the patient data from several hospitals to obtain the set of all cancer patients, and then identify those who are eligible for social welfare [30,33]. Using PSU, the organization can securely compute the union of all cancer patients from the hospitals without revealing any raw data to other parties. Subsequently, the organization can obtain the final result while preserving privacy by performing a private set intersection (PSI) calculation between the obtained set and those eligible for social welfare.

PSI and PSU can be classified into two-party and multi-party settings based on the number of participants. Over the last decade, two-party PSI has received considerable research attention [2,7,11,13,14,17,19,22,29,31,38–41,43,44]. The most efficient two-party PSI protocol to date [43] achieves performance comparable to the insecure naive hashing PSI. Multi-party PSI (MPSI) has also benefited from the research on two-party PSI, leading to the development of many efficient constructions [4,9,32,36] suitable for large sets with millions of elements. As for PSU, Kisser and Song initially studied the two-party PSU [30]. Although some subsequent works [5,16,20,25] have been proposed, their constructions rely heavily on additively homomorphic encryption (AHE) or complex circuits, resulting in low efficiency. In 2019, Kolesnikov et al. [33] proposed the first two-party PSU protocol suitable for large sets. Their construction is mainly based on symmetric-key operations combined with oblivious transfer (OT), achieving a three-orders-of-magnitude improvement in speed compared to [16]. In the following years, Garimella et al. [21] and Jia et al. [28] further reduced the communication and computation overhead using oblivious switching. Very recently, [12,24,49] realize linear computation and communication complexity and are more efficient.

1.1 Motivation

Despite growing interest in PSU, there has been no scalable multi-party PSU (MPSU) protocol. Most of the previous protocols [20,23,27,30,47] are not feasible on large datasets, due to non-constant AHE operations that are proportional to the size of the sets. [46] constructed a constant-round protocol from reversed Laurent Series and secret sharing but has a high computation and communication complexity. The protocol proposed in [5] sorts and merges the sets of the participants using general MPC techniques, but it suffers from the significant overhead caused by complex circuits. [48] requires public-key operations proportional to the input domain size of the sets. Although they have optimized the protocol using a divide-and-conquer approach, the number of public-key operations still grows linearly with the size of the set and the number of participants. Currently, most work on MPSU is still in the theoretical stage. Only [5, 48] have implemented and tested their protocols, but their performance is unsatisfactory. These above-mentioned drawbacks limit the applications of MSPU. Therefore, it is sensible to pose the problem:

Can we construct a truly scalable MPSU protocol?

1.2 Contribution

In this paper, we answer this problem affirmatively in the semi-honest setting. In detail, our contributions can be summarized as follows:

1. We analyze the differences between MPSU and MPSI, then discuss the performance gap between them, and point out the difficulties in extending two-party PSU protocols to multi-party settings (cf. Sect. 2.1).
2. We propose a new protocol called multi-query secret-shared private set membership test (mq-ssPMT) to cater for the multi-party setting, and provide an efficient construction of mq-ssPMT based on the multi-query reverse private set membership test (mq-RPMT) proposed in [49]. mq-ssPMT can easily realize mq-RPMT and can be directly used for computing two-party PSI and PSU. Specifically, when constructing a two-party PSU protocol, our mq-ssPMT reduces one round of communication and n bits of communication cost, where n is the size of the set, compared to mq-RPMT in [49] while keeping the same computation cost.
3. We present new frameworks for computing multi-party private set operations (MPSO) based on mq-ssPMT and multi-party secret-shared shuffle. Useful functions include:
   - Computing the union, i.e., MPSU
   - Computing only the cardinality of the union
   - Computing the intersection, i.e., MPSI
   - Computing only the cardinality of the intersection
   Furthermore, we prove that our frameworks are secure against any semi-honest adversary that does not corrupt the leader and clients simultaneously.
4. We demonstrate the scalability of our MPSU protocol with an implementation. As a result, our MPSU protocol is $109\times$ faster in terms of running time on sets of 2^{10} elements than the state-of-the-art MPSU protocol. Moreover, for 7 parties each holding a million-element dataset, our MPSU protocol requires only 4 min on WAN and 46 s on a LAN. Our implementation is released on Github: https://github.com/lx-1234/MPSU.

1.3 Related Work

We review previous MPSU protocols in the semi-honest setting and provide a theoretical comparison among them.

AHE-Based MPSU. Kisser and Song [30] proposed the first MPSU protocol based on polynomial representations and threshold AHE. The core idea is that each participant $\mathcal{P}_i$ represent his set X_i as a polynomial f_i whose roots are the set elements, so the polynomial $\prod_{i=1}^{k} f_i$ represents the union $\bigcup_{i=1}^{k} X_i$. Their protocol requires a large number of AHE operations and high-degree polynomial calculations, which results in inefficiency.

Frikken [20] also uses polynomial representation and threshold AHE. Each $\mathcal{P}_i$ represents his set X_i as a polynomial f_i. $\mathcal{P}_1$ first encrypts f_1 using AHE, and sends to $\mathcal{P}_2$. $\mathcal{P}_2$ computes $(x \cdot \mathsf{Enc}(f_1), \mathsf{Enc}(f_1))$ for each $x \in X_2$. Note that if $x \notin X_1$, then $f_1(x) \neq 0$, and all participants can jointly decrypt the ciphertext and recover x by computing the inverse. Otherwise, both ciphertexts decrypt to 0. Therefore, they can compute the difference set $X_2 \backslash X_1$. Similarly, they compute $X_2 \backslash X_1, \cdots, X_k \backslash (X_1 \cup \cdots \cup X_{k-1})$ separately, which can be merged to get the union. Although the polynomial degree in [20] is lower than [30], the complexity is still of quadratic order in the size of the set due to the need to perform multi-point evaluations on the encrypted polynomials.

Gong et al. [23] proposed a constant-round MPSU protocol based on threshold AHE and Bloom filters (BF). They observed that if a BF has no collisions, then for each element stored in it, at least one of the positions is mapped only by itself. Exploiting this property, they first construct a BF storing the union and then check whether each position in the BF was mapped only by one element. If so, they could figure out that element. Since the length of the BF is related to the statistical security parameter and the union size, their protocol requires a large amount of AHE operations. So the computational overhead is unacceptable.

All these three works use a threshold AHE and when the threshold is set to k, they can resist arbitrary collusion.

Other MPSU. Seo et al. [46] proposed a constant-round MPSU protocol based on secret sharing and reversed Laurent series. Their core idea is that if two sets X and Y are represented by polynomials f_X and f_Y respectively, then the union $X \cup Y$ can be represented by the least common multiple of f_X and f_Y, denoted as $\mathrm{lcm}(f_X, f_Y)$. Note that $\frac{1}{f_X} + \frac{1}{f_Y} = \frac{q(x)}{\mathrm{lcm}(f_X,f_Y)}$, so it suffices to calculate $\frac{1}{f_X} + \frac{1}{f_Y}$. Although this protocol achieves constant-round communication, the operations on high-degree polynomials result in high computation and communication complexity. Additionally, their protocol relies on the honest majority assumption.

Blanton et al. [5] proposed a more efficient MPSU protocol based on oblivious sorting and generic MPC techniques in the honest majority setting. At a high level, they first merge all sets into a large set, then sort it, and remove duplicate elements by comparing adjacent elements to obtain the union. They focused on constructing corresponding circuits and implemented them using generic MPC techniques. Their experimental results show that in the three-party for 32-bit sized elements, computing the union of 2^{10} elements set takes 11.8 s.

Vos et al. [48] convert sets to bit-sets, i.e., a vector of bits is assigned to each dataset X_i in which the ith element of this bit-vector (bit-set) is equal to 1 if the ith element of an ordered universe $\mathcal{U}$ of elements belongs to X_i, and 0 otherwise. They obtain the union by performing a secure OR on the bit-sets. Their secure OR is based on totally public-key operation, and the number of secure OR is linearly related to the size of $\mathcal{U}$, which makes the protocol unsuitable for a large $\mathcal{U}$ such as $|\mathcal{U}| = 2^{32}$. To address this issue, they use a divide-and-conquer approach where each participant divides their bit-set into D parts and uses secure OR to check if each part contains any elements. If so, the part is further divided; otherwise, it is discarded. Nevertheless, each participant in the optimized protocol still needs to perform $O(kn \log |\mathcal{U}|)$ public-key operations, which makes it non-scalable for large sets or a large $\mathcal{U}$.

Other related work contains an MPSU protocol with an untrusted third party's help [47] and an MPSU protocol focus on multiset setting [27], which both rely heavily on AHE and are out of the scope of our consideration.

Table 1 summarizes and compares the theoretical complexity and the ability to resist collusion of existing MPSU protocols and our protocol. Leader refers to the participant who obtains the union result or starts the computation. Client refers to the remaining participants. [5,20,46] can achieve malicious security, but we only compare with their semi-honest protocols here.

It should be noted that [23,30,48] will reveal the union to all participants unavoidably, while in our protocol only the leader gets the result. Moreover, our protocol can be extended to that case in the semi-honest setting, i.e., the leader just broadcasts the output once he receives it. So we could say we achieve a stronger MPSU function in the semi-honest setting.

Table 1. Asymptotic communication (bits) and computation costs of MPSU protocols in the semi-honest setting. Pub: public-key operations; sym: symmetric-key operations. n is the size of input set. k is the number of participants. N is the size of union. $\mathcal{U}$ is the universe of input elements. σ is the bit length of input elements. t is the number of AND gates in the SKE decryption circuit. λ is statistical security parameter. κ is computational security parameter. Generally, $\lambda = 40$. In our protocol, $\kappa = 128$ while in other works κ is the public key length. We ignore the offline phase cost in our protocol. * means that in our protocol the adversary does not corrupt the leader and clients simultaneously.

Protocol	Comm.			Comp. (#Ops sym/pub)		Corruption
	Leader	Client	Rounds	Leader	Client	
[30]	$O(\kappa k^3 n^2)$		$O(k)$	$O(k^2 n^3)$ pub		$< k$
[20]	$O(\kappa k n)$		$O(k)$	$O(k n^2)$ pub		$< k$
[46]	$O(\sigma k^3 n^2)$		$O(1)$	$O(k^4 n^2)$ sym		$< \lfloor (k+1)/2 \rfloor$
[5]	$O(\sigma(\sigma kn \log n + k^2))$		$O(\log k)$	$O(\sigma kn \log n + k^2)$ sym		$< \lfloor (k+1)/2 \rfloor$
[23]	$O(\kappa \lambda k N)$	$O(\kappa \lambda N)$	$O(1)$	$O(\lambda k N)$ pub	$O(\lambda N)$ pub	$< k$
[48]	$O(\kappa k^2 n \log |\mathcal{U}|)$	$O(\kappa kn \log |\mathcal{U}|)$	$O(\log |\mathcal{U}|)$	$O(k^2 n \log |\mathcal{U}|)$ pub	$O(kn \log |\mathcal{U}|)$ pub	$< k$
Ours	$O((t + \kappa + (\sigma + \lambda + \log(kn))k)kn)$	$O((t + \lambda + \kappa)kn)$	$O(\log(\sigma - \log n) + k)$	$O(tkn)$ sym		$< k^*$

2 Overview of Our Techniques

In this section, we provide a high-level technical overview of our MPSU protocol. We first analyze the difficulties in constructing MPSU protocols and then show

how to address these issues using our new techniques. The ideal functionality of MPSU is given in Fig. 1.

PARAMETERS: k parties: $\mathcal{P}_1, \cdots, \mathcal{P}_k$; Set size n; The bit length of set elements σ.

FUNCTIONALITY:

- Wait for input $X_i = \{x_i^1, \cdots, x_i^n\} \subset \mathbb{F}_{2^\sigma}$ from $\mathcal{P}_i$.
- Give output $\bigcup\limits_{i=1}^{k} X_i$ to $\mathcal{P}_1$.

Fig. 1. Multi-party Private Set Union Functionality $\mathcal{F}_{\mathsf{mpsu}}$

2.1 Difficulties in MPSU

The Difference Between MPSU and MPSI. Like MPSI, the security of MPSU requires that the receiver cannot obtain any information except for the union. However, unlike MPSI, the intersection must be a subset of the receiver's set, so we only need to consider the elements in the receiver's set. On the other hand, the union output by MPSU contains all the sets of the participants, so the protocol must involve the transmission of elements from all the participants' sets. And it is necessary to prevent an adversary from distinguishing which participant an element belongs to. Moreover, if different participants have the same element, the duplicates must be removed during the protocol execution to ensure that each element appears only once in the union; otherwise, the adversary will know how many participants have that element. Therefore, the MPSU protocol is more complex in its design than MPSI and has some efficiency gaps.

Difficulties in Extending from Two-Party PSU. In two-party PSI, there is a function called private set membership test (PMT). In the PMT, the sender inputs a set X, and the receiver inputs an element y. The receiver can determine whether y belongs to X, while the sender cannot obtain any information.

However, PMT cannot be applied to two-party PSU. To compute the union, [33] proposed reverse PMT (RPMT), in which the sender inputs an element x, and the receiver inputs a set Y, then the receiver determines whether $x \in Y$. They combine RPMT and oblivious transfer (OT) to construct a PSU protocol. For each element $x \in X$, the sender and the receiver run the OT protocol with input $(x, \perp)$ and the boolean value of the expression $x \in Y$ (i.e., 1 if $x \in Y$ otherwise 0), respectively, where $\perp$ is a special symbol. Note that the receiver can obtain x if and only if $x \notin Y$, so the receiver can obtain $X \backslash Y$, and finally output $(X \backslash Y) \cup Y = X \cup Y$. Figure 2 illustrates this idea.

The core of the existing efficient two-party PSU protocols [12,21,24,28,33,49] is the efficient construction of RPMT. However, if we want to extend this idea to compute $X_1 \cup X_2 \cup \cdots \cup X_k$, which can be split into $X_1 \cup (X_2 \backslash X_1) \cup \cdots \cup (X_k \backslash (X_1 \cup \cdots \cup X_{k-1}))$, two problems arise:

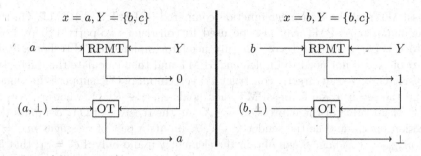

Fig. 2. Illustration of how to use RPMT and OT to perform PSU. The sender's set is $\{a, b\}$ and the receiver's set is $\{b, c\}$. The left-hand side illustrates that the sender computes for his element a, which does not belong to Y. The right-hand side shows that the sender computes for his element $b \in Y$ that belongs to Y.

1. Since the receiver in RPMT knows whether the sender's element belongs to the receiver's set, RPMT leaks the size of the cardinality of the difference set $|X \backslash Y|$ to the receiver, which is not allowed in the multi-party setting.
2. RPMT can only compute the difference between two sets but does not work in the multi-party setting, i.e., computing $X_k \backslash (X_1 \cup \cdots \cup X_{k-1})$ where $k \geq 3$.

Therefore, it is difficult to directly apply the techniques (RPMT) of two-party PSU to the multi-party setting. The construction of efficient MPSU protocols requires stronger functions.

2.2 Multi-Query Secret-Shared Private Membership Test

Based on the analysis in the previous section, the root cause of the first problem is that, in RPMT, the result is directly output to the receiver, which leads to information leakage. If we output the result of RPMT in the form of secret sharing, with each party holding a share of the output, then neither party can obtain any information. This function is called secret-shared RPMT. In this case, the roles of the two parties are completely symmetric, so secret-shared RPMT and secret-shared PMT (ssPMT) are the same function. We will use ssPMT to refer to this function in the following text.

As early as 2018, Ciampi et al. [14] combined PSI with secure two-party computation (2PC) to construct ssPMT. In 2021, Zhao et al. [50] formally defined ssPMT and built it based on the secure comparison protocol in [15]. However, their constructions have high communication overhead. Moreover, since only one element of the sender can be tested each time, multiple repetitions of ssPMT are needed to query all elements, which results in significant overhead.

In this work, we propose multi-query ssPMT (mq-ssPMT), which supports querying multiple elements of the sender simultaneously, thereby reducing the average cost per element. The ideal functionality of mq-ssPMT $\mathcal{F}_{\text{mq-sspmt}}$ is given in Fig. 3. mq-ssPMT can implement PMT(RPMT) simply by having the sender (receiver) send its share to the receiver (sender) to recover the result. Therefore, mq-ssPMT realizes a stronger function compared to PMT and RPMT. On the other hand, mq-ssPMT can also be used to construct two-party PSI or PSU protocols. For a PSI protocol, we only need to implement PMT. For a PSU protocol, we do not need to implement RPMT and then calculate the difference set using OT. We can directly construct a special input of OT: suppose the sender $\mathcal{S}$ and the receiver $\mathcal{R}$ of mq-ssPMT each holds $e_0, e_1 \in \{0, 1\}$, where $e_0 \oplus e_1$ is the boolean value of the expression $y \in X$. As the receiver of OT, $\mathcal{S}$ inputs the selection bit e_0, and as the sender of OT, $\mathcal{R}$ inputs a pair of messages $m_{e_1} = y$ and $m_{e_1 \oplus 1} = \bot$. Then, $\mathcal{S}$ can obtain the element y if and only if $e_0 = e_1$, that is, $y \notin X$, thus completing the computation of the union. Figure 4 illustrates the main idea behind this.

PARAMETERS: Sender $\mathcal{S}$, Receiver $\mathcal{R}$; Set size n; The bit length of set elements σ.

FUNCTIONALITY:

- Wait an input $Y = \{y_1, \cdots, y_n\} \subset \mathbb{F}_{2^\sigma}$ from $\mathcal{R}$.
- Wait an input $X = \{x_1, \cdots, x_n\} \subset \mathbb{F}_{2^\sigma}$ from $\mathcal{S}$.
- For $i \in [n]$: Set $b_i = 1$ if $y_i \in X$, otherwise set $b_i = 0$. Sample $e_0 \leftarrow \{0, 1\}^n$ and compute $e_1 = e_0 \oplus b$. Give e_0 to $\mathcal{S}$ and give e_1 to $\mathcal{R}$.

Fig. 3. Multi-Query Secret-Shared Private Membership Test Functionality $\mathcal{F}_{\text{mq-sspmt}}$

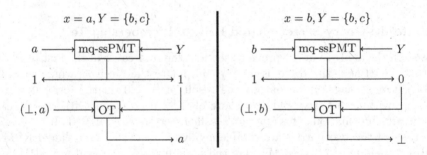

Fig. 4. Illustration of how to use mq-ssPMT and OT to perform PSU. The sender's set is $\{a, b\}$ and the receiver's set is $\{b, c\}$. The left-hand side illustrates that the sender computes for his element a, which does not belong to Y. The right-hand side shows that the sender computes for his element $b \in Y$ that belongs to Y. We remark that the sender can query a, b simultaneously, and we separate a and b only for illustration.

2.3   MPSU Based on mq-ssPMT

We have now solved the first problem discussed in Sect. 2.1 using the new function mq-ssPMT. How can we solve the second problem, namely, how to compute

$X_k \backslash (X_1 \cup \cdots \cup X_{k-1})$? Note that in MPSU, the adversary is not allowed to know any intermediate results $X_i \backslash (X_1 \cup \cdots \cup X_{i-1})(2 \leq i \leq k)$, so we cannot directly compute and output them. They must exist in some form of ciphertexts or secret shares.

Let's consider a simplified setting where three parties $\mathcal{P}_1, \mathcal{P}_2, \mathcal{P}_3$ want to compute $X_3 \backslash (X_1 \cup X_2)$. In Sect. 2.2, we showed how to compute the difference set between two parties directly using mq-ssPMT. If we split $X_3 \backslash (X_1 \cup X_2)$ into $(X_3 \backslash X_1) \cap (X_3 \backslash X_2)$, and send not the element itself but the share of the element in the OT phase, then $\mathcal{P}_1, \mathcal{P}_2, \mathcal{P}_3$ can recover the element x if and only if $x \in X_3 \backslash X_1 \wedge x \in X_3 \backslash X_2$, i.e., $x \in X_3 \backslash (X_1 \cup X_2)$. Specifically, $\mathcal{P}_3$ acts as the receiver and executes the mq-ssPMT separately with $\mathcal{P}_1$ and $\mathcal{P}_2$. For any $x \in X_3$, $\mathcal{P}_3$ and $\mathcal{P}_1$ each hold secret shares $e_{31}^1, e_{31}^0 \in \{0, 1\}$, indicating whether $x \in X_1$, and $\mathcal{P}_3$ and $\mathcal{P}_2$ each hold secret shares $e_{32}^1, e_{32}^0 \in \{0, 1\}$, indicating whether $x \in X_2$. $\mathcal{P}_3$ uses additive secret sharing to split x into $x = x_1 \oplus x_2 \oplus x_3$, and then acts as the sender to execute the OT protocol separately with $\mathcal{P}_1$ and $\mathcal{P}_2$. Taking the OT with $\mathcal{P}_1$ as an example, $\mathcal{P}_3$ inputs $m_{e_{31}^1} = x_1$ and $m_{e_{31}^1 \oplus 1} = r_1$, where r_1 is a random value, and $\mathcal{P}_1$ inputs e_{31}^0. $\mathcal{P}_1$ can obtain the share x_1 if and only if $x \notin X_1$. Similarly, $\mathcal{P}_2$ can obtain the share x_2 if and only if $x \notin X_2$. Therefore, only when $x \notin (X_1 \cup X_2)$, that is, $x \in X_3 \backslash (X_1 \cup X_2)$, can $\mathcal{P}_1, \mathcal{P}_2, \mathcal{P}_3$ recover x, otherwise they can only get a random value.

In the same way, we can compute all $X_i \backslash (X_1 \cup \cdots \cup X_{i-1})(2 \leq i \leq k)$. Since any party always holds a share of his own set, any number of other participants can not collude to obtain his input information. However, if we want to merge all difference sets and output the union to $\mathcal{P}_1$, there are two remaining problems:

1. $\mathcal{P}_1$ knows the correspondence between the shares and the difference sets, so the shares cannot be directly sent to $\mathcal{P}_1$ for recovery.
2. Since $\mathcal{P}_1$ has no knowledge of the elements in the other parties' sets, and these elements do not necessarily have a specific structure. So $\mathcal{P}_1$ cannot distinguish between set elements and random values, i.e., $\mathcal{P}_1$ don't know which element he should add to the union.

To solve the first problem, we use a multi-party secret-shared shuffle (cf. Sect. 3.4) to randomly permute and re-share all the shares held by the parties. Since any $k-1$ parties don't know the information about the permutation and all shares are refreshed, the adversary can not find the correspondence between the difference sets and the shares. To solve the second problem, all parties append the hash value of the element to the end of it when performing secret sharing, i.e., sharing $x \| \mathsf{H}(x)$. When the output length of the hash function H is long enough, the probability that there exists an s satisfying $r = s \| \mathsf{H}(s)$ is negligible. Therefore, $\mathcal{P}_1$ can distinguish the set elements from random values with overwhelming probability.

Note that both mq-ssPMT and multi-party secret-shared shuffle have an efficient online phase, so our MPSU protocol is also efficient in the online phase.

3   Preliminaries

3.1   Notation

We use $\mathcal{P}_i$ to denote participants, X_i to represent the sets they hold, where each set has n σ-bit elements. k denotes the number of participants. We use λ, κ as the statistical and computational security parameters, respectively. $[n]$ denotes the set $1, 2, \cdots, n$. $\mathbb{F}_{2^\sigma}$ denotes the finite field composed of all σ-bit strings. We use $x\|y$ to denote the concatenation of two strings. We denote vectors with bold fonts and individual elements with indices. For example, $\boldsymbol{a}$ is a vector of n elements where each individual element is denoted as a_i. $\boldsymbol{a} \oplus \boldsymbol{b}$ represents $(a_1 \oplus b_1, \cdots, a_n \oplus b_n)$. $\pi(\boldsymbol{a})$ represents $(a_{\pi(1)}, \cdots, a_{\pi(n)})$, where π is a permutation on n items. We use $:=$ to denote assignment. For some set S, the notation $s \leftarrow S$ means that s is assigned a uniformly random element from S. By $\mathsf{negl}(\lambda)$ we denote a negligible function, i.e., a function f such that $f(\lambda) < \frac{1}{p(\lambda)}$ holds for any polynomial $p(\cdot)$ and sufficient large λ. We use the abbreviation PPT to denote probabilistic polynomial-time.

3.2   Symmetric-Key Encryption

Our construction of mq-ssPMT is based on the mq-RPMT in [49], which uses symmetric-key encryption (SKE). We use the standard definition of SKE. To ensure the security of our mq-ssPMT, we require a security notion called *multi-message multi-ciphertext pseudorandomness* like the mq-RPMT in [49]. We give these definitions in Appendix A.

3.3   Oblivious Transfer

OT [42] is a foundational primitive in MPC, the functionality of 1-out-of-2 random OT (ROT) is given in Fig. 5.

PARAMETERS: Sender $\mathcal{S}$, Receiver $\mathcal{R}$; The bit length of message σ.

FUNCTIONALITY:

- Wait an input $b \in \{0, 1\}$ from $\mathcal{R}$.
- Sample $m_0, m_1 \leftarrow \mathbb{F}_{2^\sigma}$. Give (m_0, m_1) to S and give m_b to $\mathcal{R}$.

Fig. 5. 1-out-of-2 Random OT Functionality $\mathcal{F}_{\mathsf{rot}}$

3.4   Multi-party Secret-Shared Shuffle

Multi-party secret-shared shuffle can permute the share vectors of all parties randomly and refresh all shares, and the functionality is given in Fig. 6. Early works [10,35] focused on the construction for the two-party setting, and later,

Eskandarian et al. [18] extended the protocol of [10] to the multi-party setting. Their protocol consists of an offline phase and an online phase. In the offline phase, each party generates a random permutation and a set of correlated vectors called share correlation. In the online phase, each party permutes and refreshes the share vectors efficiently using share correlation. We give the functionality of share correlation and details of their protocol in Appendix B.

PARAMETERS: k parties: $\mathcal{P}_1, \cdots, \mathcal{P}_k$; The dimension of vector n; The bit length of individual element σ.

FUNCTIONALITY:

- Wait an input $\boldsymbol{x}_i = (x_i^1, \cdots, x_i^n) \in \mathbb{F}_{2^\sigma}^n$ from each $\mathcal{P}_i (1 \le i \le k)$.
- Sample a random permutation $\pi : [n] \to [n]$. For $1 \le i \le k$, sample $\boldsymbol{x}_i' \leftarrow \mathbb{F}_{2^\sigma}^n$ satisfying

$$\bigoplus_{i=1}^{k} \boldsymbol{x}_i' = \pi\left(\bigoplus_{i=1}^{k} \boldsymbol{x}_i\right)$$

and give $\boldsymbol{x}_i'$ to $\mathcal{P}_i$.

Fig. 6. Multi-party Secret-Shared Shuffle Functionality $\mathcal{F}_{\mathsf{ms}}$

3.5 Oblivious Key-Value Stores

A key-value store [22,38] is a data structure that stores a map from keys to corresponding values. The definition is as follows:

Definition 1. *A key-value store (KVS) is parameterized by a set $\mathcal{K}$ of keys, a set $\mathcal{V}$ of values, and a random value $r \in \{0,1\}^\kappa$, and consists of two algorithms:*

- Encode($\{(k_1, v_1), \cdots, (k_n, v_n)\}, r$): *takes as input a set of $\{(k_i, v_i)\}_{i \in [n]} \subseteq \mathcal{K} \times \mathcal{V}$ and outputs an object D (or, with statistically small probability, an error indicator $\perp$).*
- Decode: *takes as input an object S, a key k, and outputs a value v.*

Correctness. For all $A \subseteq \mathcal{K} \times \mathcal{V}$ with distinct keys:

$$(k, v) \in A \text{ and } \perp \neq D \leftarrow \mathsf{Encode}(A, r) \Rightarrow \mathsf{Decode}(D, k, r) = v$$

Obliviousness. For all distinct $\{k_1^0, \cdots, k_n^0\}$ and all distinct $\{k_1^1, \cdots, k_n^1\}$, if Encode does not output $\perp$ for $\{k_1^0, \cdots, k_n^0\}$ or $\{k_1^1, \cdots, k_n^1\}$, then the output $\{D | v_i \leftarrow \mathcal{V}, i \in [n], \mathsf{Encode}(\{(k_1^0, v_1), \cdots, (k_n^0, v_n)\}, r)\}$ is computationally indistinguishable to $\{D | v_i \leftarrow \mathcal{V}, i \in [n], \mathsf{Encode}(\{(k_1^1, v_1), \cdots, (k_n^1, v_n)\}, r)\}$.

A KVS is an oblivious KVS (OKVS) if it satisfies the obliviousness property. In addition to the obliviousness, [49] also proposed the randomness property to prove the security of their mq-RPMT protocol. Our mq-ssPMT protocol similarly requires this property.

Randomness. For any $A = \{(k_1, v_1), \cdots, (k_n, v_n)\}$ and $k^* \notin \{k_1, \cdots, k_n\}$, the output of $\mathsf{Decode}(D, k^*, r)$ is statistically indistinguishable to that of uniform distribution over $\mathcal{V}$, where $D \leftarrow \mathsf{Encode}(A, r)$.

Garbled cuckoo table (GCT) is the most efficient construction of KVS, including 2H-GCT in [38] and 3H-GCT in [22]. And 3H-GCT satisfies both obliviousness and randomness. Recently, Raghuraman et al. conducted a thorough theoretical and experimental analysis of the Encode algorithm in GCT, and presented the most efficient Encode algorithm to date within the commonly used parameters range. Due to space limitation, the formal description of their algorithm is given in deffer to Appendix C.

3.6 Security Model

In this work, we consider only the semi-honest model, where adversaries strictly follow the protocol specification but try to learn more than allowed by inspecting the protocol transcript. Furthermore, since our protocol involves multiple parties, we also consider collusion, which means an adversary can corrupt multiple parties and combine their views to infer more information. We adopt the standard definition of semi-honest security as defined in [37].

Definition 2. *Let* $f : (\{0,1\}^*)^k \rightarrow (\{0,1\}^*)^k$ *be an* k-*ary functionality, where* $f_i(x_1, \cdots, x_k)$ *denotes the* ith *element of* $f(x_1, \cdots, x_k)$. *For* $I = \{i_1, \cdots, i_t\} \subseteq [k]$, *let* $f_I(x_1, \cdots, x_k)$ *denote the subsequence* $f_{i_1}(x_1, \cdots, x_k), \cdots, f_{i_t}(x_1, \cdots, x_k)$. *Let* Π *be a* k-*party protocol for computing* f. *The view of the* ith *party* Π *during an execution of* Π *on* $\bar{x} = (x_1, \cdots, x_k)$ *is denoted by* $\mathrm{VIEW}_i^{\Pi}(\bar{x})$. *For any* $I = \{i_1, \cdots, i_t\}$, *we let* $\mathrm{VIEW}_I^{\Pi}(\bar{x}) \overset{\mathrm{def}}{=} (I, \mathrm{VIEW}_{i_1}^{\Pi}(\bar{x}), \cdots, \mathrm{VIEW}_{i_t}^{\Pi}(\bar{x}))$. *We say* Π *privately computes* f *against semi-honest adversaries if there exists a* PPT *algorithm, denoted* Sim, *such that for every* $I \subseteq [k]$, *it holds that*

$$\{\mathsf{Sim}(I, (x_{i_1}, \cdots, x_{i_t}), f_I(\bar{x}))\}_{\bar{x} \in (\{0,1\}^*)^k} \overset{c}{\equiv} \{\mathrm{VIEW}_I^{\Pi}(\bar{x})\}_{\bar{x} \in (\{0,1\}^*)^k}$$

4   Multi-Query Secret-Shared Private Membership Test

In this section, we describe the details of our efficient mq-ssPMT, which securely computes the functionality in Fig. 3 in the presence of semi-honest adversaries. We first revisit the mq-RPMT in [49], then show how to build an mq-ssPMT protocol based on it.

4.1   Revisit mq-RPMT in ZCLZL23

Zhang et al. [49] observe that the reason why the RPMT proposed in [33] cannot support multiple queries is that they use the same indication string s for every element belonging to the receiver $\mathcal{R}$. Specifically, if an element x belongs to $\mathcal{R}$'s set $Y = \{y_1, \cdots, y_n\}$, then S will get s when queries x. Allowing $\mathcal{S}$ to make multiple queries will result in information leakage if S gets the same string when queries distinct elements, which means they belong to the intersection with overwhelming probability. A natural idea to address this issue is that R uses different indication strings for different elements, but this will allow R to know the specific elements from S based on the correspondence between the elements and the indication strings.

To tackle this challenge, in [49], R uses a randomized encryption scheme to encrypt an indication string s n times to get n different ciphertexts $s_1, \cdots, s_n$. Then R uses an OKVS to map each element to a s_i, i.e., compute $D :=$ Encode($\{(y_1, s_1), \cdots, (y_n, s_n)\}, r$), and sends D to S. S queries each element $x_i (1 \leq i \leq n)$ in his set X to get $s_i^* :=$ Decode(D, x_i, r). Then they use a newly introduced function called vector oblivious decryption-then-matching (VODM), where S inputs s^* and R inputs an encryption key and s, and then R knows whether Dec(k, s^*) equals s. Note that if $x_i \in Y$, s_i^* belongs to $\{s_1, \cdots, s_n\}$. If not, s_i^* is a random ciphertext due to the randomness property of OKVS. So their construction realizes mq-RPMT correctly. The security relies on the security of VODM and the randomness of OKVS.

[49] proposed VODM constructions for both public-key encryption (PKE) and SKE. For PKE, they use a re-randomizable PKE. S directly sends the re-randomized ciphertext to R for decryption. For SKE, they use GMW protocol to compute the decryption circuit of SKE. Then S sends the output shares to R, who recovers the final result. They notice that randomized SKE causes ciphertext expansion. To avoid this problem, they proposed new construction for deterministic SKE: R uses a deterministic SKE to encrypt $0, 1, \cdots, n-1$ to obtain n different ciphertexts $s_1, \cdots, s_n$, and adds a comparison circuit at the end of the decryption circuit in VODM to check whether the decryption result is less than n. If it is, the element belongs to Y. Otherwise, it does not.

4.2 Construction of mq-ssPMT

It is worth noting that in [49], the output of mq-RPMT is exactly the output of VODM. If we realize secret-shared VODM (ssVODM), we can achieve mq-ssPMT. The ideal function of ssVODM is given in Fig. 7. In the SKE-based mq-RPMT in [49], GMW is used to implement VODM. However, the output of GMW is already in the form of secret sharing. If we omit the last step of recovering the secret, this construction is actually ssVODM. Therefore, we can directly obtain an efficient mq-ssPMT from the mq-RPMT in [49]. According to the method of constructing the two-party PSU using mq-ssPMT in Sect. 2.2, the SKE-based PSU in [49] can reduce one round of communication and n bits of communication.

Furthermore, the OKVS scheme used in [49] is 3H-GCT in [22]. We use an optimized 3H-GCT in [43] to reduce computation and communication costs. The details of our mq-ssPMT are shown in Fig. 8.

Security. Regarding the security of $\Pi_{\mathsf{mq\text{-}sspmt}}$, we have the following theorem.

PARAMETERS: Sender $\mathcal{S}$, Receiver $\mathcal{R}$; Set size n; An encryption scheme $\mathcal{E} = $ (Setup, KeyGen, Enc, Dec).

FUNCTIONALITY:

- Wait an input k, S from $\mathcal{R}$.
- Wait an input $\{s_1^*, \cdots, s_n^*\} \subset \{0, 1\}^*$ from $\mathcal{S}$.
- For $i \in [n]$, compute $s_i' = \text{Dec}(k, s_i^*)$. Set $b_i = 1$ if $s_i' \in S$, otherwise set $b_i = 0$. Sample $e_0 \leftarrow \{0, 1\}^n$, then compute $e_1 = e_0 \oplus b$. Give e_0 to $\mathcal{S}$. Give e_1 to $\mathcal{R}$.

Fig. 7. Secret-Shared VODM Functionality $\mathcal{F}_{\text{ssvodm}}$

PARAMETERS:

- Sender $\mathcal{S}$, Receiver $\mathcal{R}$.
- A SKE $\mathcal{E} = $ (Setup, KeyGen, Enc, Dec) satisfies multi-message multi-ciphertext pseudorandomness.
- An OKVS scheme (Encode, Decode) and its random value r.
- Ideal functionality $\mathcal{F}_{\text{ssvodm}}$ in Fig. 7.

INPUT OF $\mathcal{S}$: $X = \{x_1, \cdots, x_n\} \subset \mathbb{F}_{2^\sigma}$.
INPUT OF $\mathcal{R}$: $Y = \{y_1, \cdots, y_n\} \subset \mathbb{F}_{2^\sigma}$.

PROTOCOL:

1. $\mathcal{S}$ runs $pp \leftarrow \text{Setup}(1^\kappa)$ and $\text{KeyGen}(pp)$ to get a key k. For $i \in [n]$, computes $s_i = \text{Enc}(k, i - 1)$.
2. $\mathcal{S}$ computes an OKVS $D := \text{Encode}((x_1, s_1), \cdots, (x_n, s_n), r)$ and sends D to $\mathcal{R}$.
3. $\mathcal{R}$ computes $s_i^* := \text{Decode}(D, y_i, r)$ for $i \in [n]$.
4. $\mathcal{S}$ and $\mathcal{R}$ invokes $\mathcal{F}_{\text{ssvodm}}$. $\mathcal{R}$ acts as sender with input $(s_1^*, \cdots, s_n^*)$. $\mathcal{S}$ acts as receiver with input $\{0, 1, \cdots, n - 1\}, k$. $\mathcal{S}$ and $\mathcal{R}$ receive $e_0, e_1 \in \{0, 1\}^n$, respectively.

Fig. 8. mq-ssPMT Protocol $\Pi_{\text{mq-sspmt}}$

Theorem 1. *Assume the SKE scheme $\mathcal{E} = $ (Setup, KeyGen, Enc, Dec) satisfies multi-message multi-ciphertext pseudorandomness. The protocol in Fig. 8 securely computes $\mathcal{F}_{\text{mq-sspmt}}$ against semi-honest adversaries in the $\mathcal{F}_{\text{ssvodm}}$-hybrid model.*

Since $\Pi_{\text{mq-sspmt}}$ is essentially the same as mq-RPMT in [49] except for omitting the last step of secret reconstruction, the security proof of $\Pi_{\text{mq-sspmt}}$ is similar to that of mq-RPMT and is not repeated here. We recommend interested readers to refer to the proof in [49].

5   Protocol Overviews and Details

In this section, we give the details of our MPSU protocol. We also construct multi-party private set union cardinality (MPSU-CA), MPSI, and multi-party private set intersection cardinality (MPSI-CA) protocols based on mq-ssPMT and multi-party secret-shared shuffle.

5.1 MPSU

Our MPSU protocol follows the approach outlined in Sect. 2. Each participant $\mathcal{P}_i$ $(2 \leq i \leq k)$ acts as the receiver and performs the mq-ssPMT protocol with all $\mathcal{P}_j$ $(1 \leq j < i)$. For each element in the set of $\mathcal{P}_i$, $\mathcal{P}_i$ splits it into i shares using additively secret sharing and shares with all $\mathcal{P}_j$. Since each share is a random value, we use random OT to generate each share, and $\mathcal{P}_i$ computes his own share locally to reduce the communication overhead caused by OT. Next, all parties combine their shares of all the difference sets (if there is no corresponding share, set it to 0) to generate a $(k-1) \times n$ dimensional vector and set it as the input to the multi-party secret-shared shuffle protocol. Then, $\mathcal{P}_2, \cdots, \mathcal{P}_k$ send their new shares to $\mathcal{P}_1$, who recovers $\bigcup_{i=2}^{k} X_i \backslash X_1$. Finally, $\mathcal{P}_1$ outputs $\bigcup_{i=1}^{k} X_i = X_1 \cup (\bigcup_{i=2}^{k} X_i \backslash X_1)$. The protocol details are given in Fig. 9.

PARAMETERS:

- k parties: $\mathcal{P}_1, \cdots, \mathcal{P}_k$.
- Ideal functionalities $\mathcal{F}_{\text{mq-sspmt}}$ in Fig. 3, $\mathcal{F}_{\text{rot}}$ in Fig. 5, $\mathcal{F}_{\text{ms}}$ in Fig. 6.
- A collision-resistant hash function $\mathsf{H}(x) : \{0,1\}^* \to \{0,1\}^\ell$.

INPUT OF $\mathcal{P}_i$: $X_i = \{x_i^1, \cdots, x_i^n\} \subset \mathbb{F}_{2^\sigma}$.

PROTOCOL:

1. For $1 \leq i < j \leq k$, $\mathcal{P}_i$ and $\mathcal{P}_j$ invoke $\mathcal{F}_{\text{mq-sspmt}}$. $\mathcal{P}_i$ acts as sender with input X_i. $\mathcal{P}_j$ acts receiver with input X_j. $\mathcal{P}_j, \mathcal{P}_i$ receive $e_{ji}^0, e_{ji}^1 \in \{0,1\}^n$, respectively.
2. For $1 \leq i < j \leq k, 1 \leq t \leq n$:
   - $\mathcal{P}_i$ and $\mathcal{P}_j$ invoke $\mathcal{F}_{\text{rot}}$.
   - $\mathcal{P}_j$ acts as sender with no input.
   - $\mathcal{P}_i$ acts as receiver with input $e_{ji,t}^1$.
   - $\mathcal{P}_j$ receives $r_{ji,t}^0, r_{ji,t}^1 \in \{0,1\}^{\sigma+\ell}$. $\mathcal{P}_i$ receives $r_{ji,t} := r_{ji,t}^{e_{ji,t}^1}$.
3. For $2 \leq j \leq k$, $\mathcal{P}_j$ computes $r_{jj,t} := \left(x_j^t \| \mathsf{H}(x_j^t)\right) \oplus \bigoplus_{i=1}^{j-1} r_{ji,t}^{e_{ji,t}^0}$ for $t \in [n]$.
4. Each $\mathcal{P}_i$ computes $\boldsymbol{sh}_i \in \mathbb{F}_{2^{\sigma+\ell}}^{(k-1)n}$ as follows: for $\max(2,i) \leq j \leq k, 1 \leq t \leq n$, $sh_{i,(j-2)n+t} := r_{ji,t}$. Set all other positions to 0.
5. All $\mathcal{P}_i$ invoke $\mathcal{F}_{\text{ms}}$ with input $\boldsymbol{sh}_i$. $\mathcal{P}_i$ receives $\boldsymbol{sh}_i'$.
6. For $2 \leq i \leq k$, $\mathcal{P}_i$ sends $\boldsymbol{sh}_i'$ to $\mathcal{P}_1$. $\mathcal{P}_1$ recovers $\boldsymbol{z} := \bigoplus_{i=1}^{k} \boldsymbol{sh}_i'$. Set $Y := \emptyset$. For $1 \leq i \leq (k-1)n$, if $z_i = s \| \mathsf{H}(s)$ holds for some $s \in \mathbb{F}_{2^\sigma}$, $\mathcal{P}_1$ computes $Y = Y \cup \{z_i\}$. Outputs $X_1 \cup Y$.

Fig. 9. Multi-party Private Set Union Protocol Π_{mpsu}

Correctness. We first prove $\bigcup_{i=1}^{k} X_i \subseteq X_1 \cup Y$. For any $x \in \bigcup_{i=1}^{k} X_i$, if $x \in X_1$, then $x \in X_1 \cup Y$. Otherwise, there exists a unique j that satisfies $x \in X_j \backslash X_1 \cup \cdots \cup X_{j-1})$. Therefore, when $\mathcal{P}_j$ shares $x \| \mathsf{H}(x)$ to all $\mathcal{P}_i (1 \leq i < j)$ using ROT, all $\mathcal{P}_i$ will choose the share instead of the random value. Because the multi-party secret-shared shuffle does not affect the correctness of the recovery, $\mathcal{P}_1$ will always obtain $x\|H(x)$ and add x to the output.

Then, we prove $(X_1 \cup Y) \subseteq \bigcup_{i=1}^{k} X_i$, which is equivalent to proving $Y \subset \bigcup_{i=1}^{k} X_i$. Since Y is a subset of $\{z_1, \cdots, z_{(k-1)n}\}$, we only need to consider each individual z_i. If there is no $x \in \bigcup_{i=1}^{k} X_i$ that satisfies $z_i \neq x\|H(x)$, then z_i must be a random value due to the randomness of ROT's output. Therefore, $\Pr[z_i = s\|H(s) \text{ for some } s] = 2^{-\ell}$. By a union bound, we have:

$$\Pr\left[X_1 \cup Y \nsubseteq \bigcup_{i=1}^{k} X_i\right] \leq (k-1) \cdot n \cdot 2^{-\ell} = 2^{\log(k-1)+\log n - \ell}$$

When $\ell \geq \lambda + \log(k-1) + \log n$, the probability is negligible.

Security. Now we prove the security of Π_{mpsu} in Fig. 9.

Theorem 2. Π_{mpsu} *in Fig. 9 securely computes* $\mathcal{F}_{\mathsf{mpsu}}$ *against any semi-honest adversary that does not corrupt* $\mathcal{P}_1$ *and any subset of* $\{\mathcal{P}_2, \cdots, \mathcal{P}_k\}$ *simultaneously in the* $(\mathcal{F}_{\mathsf{mq\text{-}sspmt}}, \mathcal{F}_{\mathsf{rot}}, \mathcal{F}_{\mathsf{ms}})$*-hybrid model.*

Proof. Let C and H be a coalition of corrupt and honest parties, respectively. $|C| = \eta$. To show how to simulate C's view in the ideal model, we consider two cases based on whether $\mathcal{P}_1$ is corrupted.

$\mathcal{P}_1$ *is Honest.* In this case, $\mathcal{P}_1 \notin C$. $\mathsf{Sim}_C(X_{i_1}, \cdots, X_{i_\eta})$ runs as follows:

1. For all $\mathcal{P}_i \in C$, Sim_C samples $e'^0_{iu} \leftarrow \{0,1\}^n$ for $1 \leq u < i$ and $e'^1_{vi} \leftarrow \{0,1\}^n$ for $i < v \leq k$, which satisfy for all $\mathcal{P}_i, \mathcal{P}_j \in C(i < j), 1 \leq t \leq n$:
   - $e'^0_{ji,t} \oplus e'^1_{ji,t} = 1$, if $x^t_j \in X_i$
   - $e'^0_{ji,t} \oplus e'^1_{ji,t} = 0$, if $x^t_j \notin X_i$
   Then Sim_C appends all e'^0_{iu}, e'^1_{vi} to the view.
2. For all $P_i \in C$, Sim_C samples $r'^0_{iu}, r'^1_{iu} \leftarrow \mathbb{F}^n_{2^\sigma + \ell}$ for $1 \leq u < i$ and $r'_{vi} \leftarrow \mathbb{F}^n_{2^\sigma + \ell}$ for $i < v \leq k$, which satisfy for all $\mathcal{P}_i, \mathcal{P}_j \in C(i < j)$ and all $1 \leq t \leq n$:

$$\forall 1 \leq t \leq n, r'_{ji,t} = r'^{e'^1_{ji,t}}_{ji,t}$$

   Then Sim_C appends all $r'^0_{iu}, r'^1_{iu}, r'_{vi}$ to the view.
3. For all $\mathcal{P}_i \in C$, Sim_C samples $\boldsymbol{sh}''_i \leftarrow \mathbb{F}^{(k-1)n}_{2^\sigma + \ell}$ and appends is to the view.
4. For all $\mathcal{P}_i \in C$, Sim_C invokes mq-ssPMT simulator $\mathsf{Sim}^{\mathcal{R}}_{\mathsf{mq\text{-}sspmt}}(X_i, e'^0_{iu})$ for $1 \leq u < i$ and $\mathsf{Sim}^{\mathcal{S}}_{\mathsf{mq\text{-}sspmt}}(X_i, e'^1_{vi})$ for $i < v \leq k$. Then appends the output to the view.
5. For all $\mathcal{P}_i \in C$, Sim_C invokes ROT simulator $\mathsf{Sim}^{\mathcal{S}}_{\mathsf{rot}}(r'^0_{iu}, r'^1_{iu})$ for $1 \leq u < i$ and $\mathsf{Sim}^{\mathcal{R}}_{\mathsf{rot}}(e'^1_{vi}, r'_{vi})$ for $i < v \leq k$. Then appends the output to the view.
6. For all $\mathcal{P}_i \in C$, Sim_C creates $\boldsymbol{sh}_i$ as Step 3 and Step 4 of Π_{mpsu}. Then invokes multi-party secret-shared shuffle simulator $\mathsf{Sim}^{\mathcal{P}_i}_{\mathsf{ms}}(\boldsymbol{sh}_i, \boldsymbol{sh}''_i)$ and appends the output to the view.

Now we argue that the view output by Sim_C is indistinguishable from the real one. In the real world, the output e_{ji}^0, e_{ji}^1 of mq-ssPMT, the output r_{ji}^0, r_{ji}^1 of ROT, and the output sh_i' of multi-party secret-shared shuffle are uniformly random from the perspective of a single corrupted party. Even if all the parties in C combine their views, the outputs of the mq-ssPMT and ROT protocols run with the honest parties, i.e., $e_{ji}^0, e_{ji}^1, r_{ji}^0, r_{ji}^1 (\mathcal{P}_i \in H \text{ or } \mathcal{P}_j \in H)$, are uniformly random and mutually independent. Moreover, the outputs of the protocols run with the corrupted parties, i.e., $e_{ji}^0, e_{ji}^1, r_{ji}^0, r_{ji}^1 (\mathcal{P}_i, \mathcal{P}_j \in C)$, are still uniformly random but constrained by the correctness of mq-ssPMT and ROT.

As for the output of multi-party secret-shared shuffle protocol, at least one share sh_h' is unknown because the number of corrupted parties is always less than k. So from the perspective of C, the output $sh_i'(\mathcal{P}_i \in C)$ are uniformly random and independent of each other.

Notice that in the view output by Sim_C, all messages are uniformly random and satisfy the correctness constraints, which is exactly the same as that of real world. So the simulated view is computationally indistinguishable from the real.

$\mathcal{P}_1$ *is Corrupted.* In this case, $C = \{\mathcal{P}_1\}$. So the simulator $\mathsf{Sim}_C(X_1, \bigcup_{i=1}^k X_i)$ needs to simulate $\mathcal{P}_1$'s view. Sim_C runs as follows:

1. Sim_C samples $e_{i1}'^1 \leftarrow \{0,1\}^n$ for $2 \leq i \leq k$ and appends them to the view.
2. Sim_C samples $r_{i1}' \leftarrow \mathbb{F}_{2^{\sigma+\ell}}^n$ for $2 \leq i \leq k$ and appends them to the view.
3. Sim_C computes $Y' := (\bigcup_{i=1}^k X_i) \setminus X_1$, and constructs $z' \in \mathbb{F}_{2^{\sigma+\ell}}^{(k-1)n}$ as follows:
   - for $\forall y_i \in Y'$, $z_i' := y_i \| \mathsf{H}(y_i)$
   - for $|Y'| < i \leq (k-1)n$, samples $z_i' \leftarrow \mathbb{F}_{2^{\sigma+\ell}}$
   Then, Sim_C samples a random permutation $\pi : [(k-1)n] \rightarrow [(k-1)n]$, and computes $z'' := \pi(z')$.
4. For $1 \leq i \leq k$, Sim_C samples $sh_i'' \leftarrow \mathbb{F}_{2^{\sigma+\ell}}^{(k-1)n}$, which satisfies $\bigoplus_{i=1}^k sh_i'' = z''$. Then Sim_C appends all sh_i'' to the view.
5. Sim_C invokes mq-ssPMT simulator $\mathsf{Sim}_{\text{mq-sspmt}}^{\mathcal{S}}(X_1, e_{i1}'^1)$ for $2 \leq i \leq k$. Then appends the output to the view.
6. Sim_C invokes ROT simulator $\mathsf{Sim}_{\text{rot}}^{\mathcal{R}}(e_{i1}'^1, r_{i1}')$ for $2 \leq i \leq k$. Then appends the output to the view.
7. Sim_C constructs sh_1 as Step 3 and Step 4 of Π_{mpsu}. Then invokes multi-party secret-shared shuffle simulator $\mathsf{Sim}_{\text{ms}}^{\mathcal{P}_1}(sh_1, sh_1'')$ and appends the output to the view.

Now we argue that the view output by Sim_C is indistinguishable from the real one. Specifically, we need to prove sh_i' from each $\mathcal{P}_i$ does not leak any other information except for the union. For all $2 \leq j \leq k$, consider an element $x_j^t \in X_j$. If there exists some $X_i(1 \leq i < j)$ that $x_j^t \in X_i$, then $e_{ji,t}^0 \oplus e_{ji,t}^1 = 1, r_{ji,t} = r_{ji,t}^{e_{ji,t}^1} \neq r_{ji,t}^{e_{ji,t}^0}$. So $\bigoplus_{i=1}^k sh_{i,(j-2)n+t} = \bigoplus_{i=1}^j r_{ji,t} = r \oplus r_{ji,t}^{e_{ji,t}^0} \oplus r_{ji,t}^{e_{ji,t}^1}$ is uniformly random from the perspective of $\mathcal{P}_1$, where r is the sum of remaining terms. So in the real world, the individual elements of $\bigoplus_{i=1}^k sh_i'$ are all uniformly random values except for $|\bigcup_{i=2}^k X_i \setminus X_1|$ elements, which is the same as simulated view. So the simulated view is computationally indistinguishable from the real. $\quad\square$

An Efficiency Optimization. In our MPSU protocol, each $\mathcal{P}_i (1 \leq i \leq k - 2)$ acts as sender to execute mq-ssPMT with $\mathcal{P}_{i+1}, \cdots, \mathcal{P}_k$. And in each mq-ssPMT, $\mathcal{P}_i$ needs to encrypt n messages and compute a corresponding OKVS. We observe that $\mathcal{P}_i$ can use the same OKVS in all mq-ssPMT, which could avoid additional computation costs caused by multiple encryptions and Encode without compromising the security of the protocol. The only change required is the length of ciphertexts of SKE, which should be increased from $\lambda + 2 \log n$ to $\lambda + 2 \log n + 2 \log (k - i)$. So we can guarantee that the probability of collisions between the random results of Decode and the ciphertexts of indication strings is negligible. Therefore, we can ensure the correctness of the protocol.

Insecurity Against Arbitrary Collusion. We now illustrate why we need the assumption that $\mathcal{P}_1$ does not collude with others. In our protocol, $\mathcal{P}_1$ reconstructs the vector z in Step 6, which is a permutation of $\bigoplus_{i=1}^{k} sh_i$. So each individual element of z is the form of $\bigoplus_{i=1}^{j} r_{ji,t}$. However, all $r_{ji,t} (1 \leq i < j, 1 \leq t \leq n)$ is known by $\mathcal{P}_j$, which is not uniformly random from the perspective of colluding $\mathcal{P}_1, \mathcal{P}_j$. More specifically, they can recover the output of $\mathcal{P}_i$ in ROT. So they could get the output of $\mathcal{P}_i$ in mq-ssPMT with $\mathcal{P}_j$, which will reveal the information of X_i. We argue that although we require this special assumption, we achieve security against any number of semi-honest clients and significant improvement in efficiency.

MPSU-CA. MPSU-CA is a variant of MPSU, where the receiver is only allowed to know the cardinality of the union. To fill the gap between MPSU and MPSU-CA, we only need to make minor modifications to our MPSU protocol. Each party no longer shares his own elements, but instead, an indication string s agreed on in advance. Finally, $\mathcal{P}_i$ could count the number of s to get the cardinality of the union.

Another difference is that since each party agrees on an indication string, the problem of distinguishing random values and set elements in MPSU does not arise here. So we do not need to append a hash at the end of each element, which could reduce communication costs. The details of our MPSU-CA protocol are given in the full version.

5.2   MPSI

We now discuss MPSI. We first give the functionality in Fig. 10. Since the intersection must be a subset of X_1, we only need to share X_1. So $\mathcal{P}_1$ acts as sender and executes mq-ssPMT with all other $\mathcal{P}_i (2 \leq i < k)$. On the other hand, unlike computing the union, the intersection $\bigcap_{i=1}^{k} X_i$ can be decomposed into $\bigcap_{i=1}^{k} (X_1 \cap X_i)$. Therefore, each $\mathcal{P}_i$ should obtain the share of the intersection $X_1 \cap X_i$ instead of the share of the difference set $X_1 \setminus X_i$. Therefore, $\mathcal{P}_i$ cannot directly use the output of mq-ssPMT as the selection bit in ROT as in the MPSU protocol but should choose the other message. The detailed description is given in Fig. 11.

PARAMETERS: k parties $\mathcal{P}_1, \cdots, \mathcal{P}_k$; Set size n; The bit length of set elements σ.

FUNCTIONALITY:

- Wait for input $X_i = \{x_i^1, \cdots, x_i^n\} \subset \mathbb{F}_{2^\sigma}$ from $\mathcal{P}_i$.
- Give output $\bigcap\limits_{i=1}^{k} X_i$ to $\mathcal{P}_1$

Fig. 10. Multi-party Private Set Intersection Functionality $\mathcal{F}_{\mathsf{mpsi}}$

PARAMETERS:

- k parties: $\mathcal{P}_1, \cdots, \mathcal{P}_k$.
- Ideal functionalities $\mathcal{F}_{\mathsf{mq\text{-}sspmt}}$ in Fig. 3, $\mathcal{F}_{\mathsf{rot}}$ in Fig. 5, $\mathcal{F}_{\mathsf{ms}}$ in Fig. 6.
- The bit length of indication string ℓ.

INPUT OF $\mathcal{P}_i$: $X_i = \{x_i^1, \cdots, x_i^n\} \subset \mathbb{F}_{2^\sigma}$.

PROTOCOL:

1. For $2 \leq i \leq k$, $\mathcal{P}_1$ and $\mathcal{P}_i$ invoke $\mathcal{F}_{\mathsf{mq\text{-}sspmt}}$. $\mathcal{P}_i$ acts as sender with input X_i, $\mathcal{P}_1$ acts as receiver with input X_1. $\mathcal{P}_1, \mathcal{P}_i$ receive $e_{1i}^0, e_{1i}^1 \in \{0,1\}^n$, respectively.
2. For $2 \leq i \leq k, 1 \leq t \leq n$:
   - $\mathcal{P}_1$ and $\mathcal{P}_i$ invoke $\mathcal{F}_{\mathsf{rot}}$.
   - $\mathcal{P}_i$ acts as sender with no input.
   - $\mathcal{P}_1$ acts as receiver with input $e_{1i,t}^0 \oplus 1$.
   - $\mathcal{P}_i$ receives $r_{1i,t}^0, r_{1i,t}^1 \in \{0,1\}^{\sigma+\ell}$. $\mathcal{P}_1$ receives $r_{1i,t} := r_{1i,t}^{e_{1i,t}^0 \oplus 1}$.
3. For $1 \leq t \leq n$, $\mathcal{P}_1$ computes $r_{11,t} := \left(x_1^t \| \mathsf{H}(x_1^t)\right) \oplus \bigoplus_{i=2}^{k} r_{1i,t}$.
4. Each $\mathcal{P}_i (2 \leq i \leq k)$ computes $\boldsymbol{sh}_i \in \mathbb{F}_{2^{\sigma+\ell}}^n$ as follows: for $1 \leq t \leq n$, $sh_t := r_{1i,t}^{e_{1i,t}^1}$. $\mathcal{P}_1$ computes $\boldsymbol{sh}_1 \in \mathbb{F}_{2^{\sigma+\ell}}^n$ as follows: for $1 \leq t \leq n$, $sh_t := r_{11,t}$.
5. All $\mathcal{P}_i (1 \leq i \leq k)$ invoke $\mathcal{F}_{\mathsf{ms}}$ with input $\boldsymbol{sh}_i$. $\mathcal{P}_i$ receives $\boldsymbol{sh}_i'$.
6. For $2 \leq i \leq k$, $\mathcal{P}_i$ sends $\boldsymbol{sh}_i'$ to $\mathcal{P}_1$. $\mathcal{P}_1$ recovers $\boldsymbol{z} := \bigoplus_{i=1}^{k} \boldsymbol{sh}_i'$. Set $Y := \emptyset$. For $1 \leq i \leq n$, if $z_i = x\|\mathsf{H}(x)$ holds for some $x \in X_1$, computes $Y = Y \cup \{z_i\}$. Outputs Y.

Fig. 11. Multi-party Private Set Intersection Protocol Π_{mpsi}

Correctness. Similar to the analysis of MPSU protocol in Sect. 5.1. Since z_i needs to satisfy $z_i = x\|\mathsf{H}(x)$ and $x \in X_1$, the probability of Π_{mpsi} outputting a wrong result does not exceed $n \cdot 2^{-\sigma} \cdot 2^{-\ell} = 2^{\log n - \sigma - \ell}$. If $\sigma - \log n \geq \lambda$, it's not necessary to append $\mathsf{H}(x)$ to the end of x to ensure that the error probability is less than $2^{-\lambda}$. If $\sigma - \log n < \lambda$, we need $\ell \geq \lambda + \log n - \sigma$.

Security. We now prove the security of Π_{mpsi} in Fig. 11.

Theorem 3. *Π_{mpsi} in Fig. 11 securely computes $\mathcal{F}_{\mathsf{mpsi}}$ against any semi-honest adversary that does not corrupt $\mathcal{P}_1$ and any subset of $\{\mathcal{P}_2, \cdots, \mathcal{P}_k\}$ simultaneously in the $(\mathcal{F}_{\mathsf{mq\text{-}sspmt}}, \mathcal{F}_{\mathsf{rot}}, \mathcal{F}_{\mathsf{ms}})$-hybrid model.*

Proof. Since the proof is similar to the Proof of Theorem 2, we leave it to Appendix D.

MPSI-CA. Like our MPSU-CA protocol, we could similarly build MPSI-CA based on our MPSI protocol. In contrast to MPSI, $\mathcal{P}_1$ shares an indication string s instead of his own elements, just like MPSU-CA protocol. The details are given in the full version.

Remark 1. These approaches for MPSI and MPSI-CA are not competitive with the state-of-the-art special-purpose protocols for MPSI and MPSI-CA. In particular, mq-ssPMT and multi-party secret-shared shuffle is unnecessary for them. We include these two protocols merely for illustrative purposes.

6   Complexity Analysis

In this section, we analyze the computation and communication complexity of our four protocols.

6.1   mq-ssPMT

We first analyze the complexity of our mq-ssPMT protocol. The costs of mq-ssPMT can be divided into three parts: the cost of SKE encryption, the cost of OKVS, and the cost of ssVODM. Similar to [49], we use LowMC [1] to initialize SKE and implement ssVODM using 2PC. In addition to the decryption circuit of LowMC, we also need a comparison circuit. In this work, we only consider the case where $n = 2^q$, so we can use the method in [49]: to compare whether a σ-bit string is less than n, we only need to check if one of its first $\sigma - \log n$ bits is 1, so we need a total of $\sigma - \log n - 1$ AND gates. Therefore, the ssVODM protocol requires a total of $n(t + \sigma - \log n - 1) = O(tn)$ AND gates, where t is the number of AND gates in the SKE decryption circuit. We now calculate the cost of each part.

- SKE encryption: The computation complexity of encrypting $0, 1, \cdots, n-1$ is $O(n)$.
- OKVS: We use the optimized 3H-GCT algorithm in [43]. We employ it with a cluster size of 2^{14}, weight $w = 3$. These result in the size of OKVS is $1.28n|c|$ bits, where $|c|$ is the size of a ciphertext of SKE. The computation complexities of Encode, Decode are both $O(n)$. Sending an OKVS to other parties needs one round communication.
- ssVODM: We use GMW to employ 2PC. Notice that we do not need to share the input, i.e., the sender of ssVODM could use 0 as the share of $s_1^*, \cdots, s_n^*$ and the receiver could use 0 as the share of the decryption key k. Therefore, the costs contain only the evaluation of the AND gates. Using Beaver triple [3], each AND gate requires 4 bits communication and $O(1)$ computation. Therefore, the communication costs are $4n(t + \sigma - \log n - 1)$ bits and the computation complexity is $O(n(t + \sigma - \log n))$. Since the round complexity of GMW depends on the depth of AND gates, which is one in each round of LowMC decryption and $\log_2(\sigma - \log n)$ in string comparison, the round complexity is $O(\log(\sigma - \log n))$.

According to the analysis in Sect. 5.1, the length of a ciphertext is no more than $\lambda + 2\log(kn)$. In the scenario we are studying, where $\sigma \leq 128, n \leq 2^{24}, k \leq 20$, we have t is greater than σ and $\log(kn)$. Therefore, we can approximate $O(t + \sigma + \log(kn))$ as $O(t)$. Thus, in mq-ssPMT, the computation complexity is $O(nt)$, the communication complexity is $O(n(t + \lambda))$ bits, and the round complexity is $O(\log(\sigma - \log n))$.

6.2 MPSU and MPSU-CA

MPSU. The costs of our MPSU protocol can be split to four parts, including mq-ssPMT, ROT, multi-party secret-shared shuffle and secret reconstruction. We analyze the costs of these parts, respectively.

- mq-ssPMT: Since $\mathcal{P}_i$ executes mq-ssPMT $k - 1$ times, the communication complexity is $O((t + \lambda)kn)$, and the computation complexity is $O(tkn)$ for all parties. Moreover, $\mathcal{P}_i$ can run mq-ssPMT with others in parallel, so the round complexity is $O(\log(\sigma - \log n))$.
- ROT: $\mathcal{P}_i$ executes ROT $k - 1$ times, so the communication complexity is $O(\kappa kn)$, and the computation complexity is $O(kn)$ for all parties. Since we use a constant-round ROT and execute all ROT in parallel, the round complexity is $O(1)$.
- Multi-party secret-shared shuffle: We use the protocol in [18]. In its offline phase, each pair of parties need to run a share translation protocol in [10]. Omitting message sizes and log factors, the computation complexity and the communication complexity for each party are both $\tilde{O}(k^2 n)$. In the online phase, since we need to shuffle $(\sigma + \ell)$-bits elements, the computation complexity is $O(kn)$ for each party, and the communication complexity is $O((\sigma + \ell)k^2 n)$ for $\mathcal{P}_1$ and $O((\sigma + \ell)kn)$ for $\mathcal{P}_2, \cdots, \mathcal{P}_k$ according to the details described in Appendix B. The round complexity is $O(k)$.
- Secret reconstruction: The communication complexity and computation complexity of $\mathcal{P}_1$ is $O((\sigma + \ell)k^2 n)$ and $O(n)$, respectively. The communication complexity of other parties is $O((\sigma + \ell)kn)$. And it needs one round communication.

Therefore, omitting the costs in the offline phase and taking $\ell = \lambda + \log n + \log(k - 1)$, the computation complexity of all parties is $O(tkn)$. The communication complexity of $\mathcal{P}_1$ is $O((t + \kappa + (\sigma + \lambda + \log(kn))k)kn)$. The communication complexity of $\mathcal{P}_2, \cdots, \mathcal{P}_k$ is $O((t + \lambda + \kappa)kn)$. The round complexity is $O(\log(\sigma - \log n) + k)$.

MPSU-CA. Our MPSU-CA protocol differs from the MPSU protocol only in the elements being shared. In MPSU, the length of the secret being shared is $\sigma + \ell$, while in MPSU-CA it is ℓ. We take $\ell = \lambda + \log n + \log(k - 1)$. The computation complexity of all parties is $O(tkn)$. The communication complexity of $\mathcal{P}_1$ is $O((t + \kappa + (\lambda + \log(kn))k)kn)$. The communication complexity of $\mathcal{P}_2, \cdots, \mathcal{P}_k$ is $O((t + \lambda + \kappa)kn)$. The round complexity is $O(\log(\sigma - \log n) + k)$.

6.3 MPSI and MPSI-CA

MPSI. Our MPSI protocol's costs can also be divided into mq-ssPMT, ROT, multi-party secret-shared shuffle, and secret reconstruction. We analyze the costs of these parts, respectively.

- mq-ssPMT: Since $\mathcal{P}_1$ needs to act as receiver to execute mq-ssPMT with all $\mathcal{P}_2, \cdots, \mathcal{P}_k$, the communication complexity is $O((t + \lambda)kn)$ and the computation complexity is $O(tkn)$ for $\mathcal{P}_1$. The communication complexity is $O((t + \lambda)n)$ and the computation complexity is $O(tn)$ for $\mathcal{P}_2, \cdots, \mathcal{P}_k$.
- ROT: Assume the average communication cost per ROT is $c_{ot} = O(\kappa)$ bits. Since $\mathcal{P}_1$ needs to run ROT with $\mathcal{P}_2, \cdots, \mathcal{P}_k$, the communication complexity and the computation complexity of $\mathcal{P}_1$ is $O(\kappa kn)$ and $O(kn)$, respectively. The communication complexity and the computation complexity of $\mathcal{P}_2, \cdots, \mathcal{P}_k$ is $O(\kappa n)$ and $O(n)$, respectively.
- Multi-party secret-shared shuffle: Same as the analysis in Sect. 6.2, the computation of each party is $O(n)$. The communication complexity of $\mathcal{P}_1$ is $O((\sigma + \ell)kn)$. The communication complexity of $\mathcal{P}_2, \cdots, \mathcal{P}_k$ is $O((\sigma + \ell)n)$.
- Secret reconstruction: The communication complexity and computation complexity of $\mathcal{P}_1$ is $O((\sigma + \ell)kn)$ and $O(n)$, respectively. The communication complexity of other parties is $O((\sigma + \ell)n)$.

Omitting the costs in the offline phase, since $\sigma + \ell = \max\{\lambda + \log n, \sigma\}$, the computation complexity and communication complexity of $\mathcal{P}_1$ is $O(tkn)$ and $O((t + \kappa + \lambda)kn)$, respectively. The computation complexity and communication complexity of $\mathcal{P}_2, \cdots, \mathcal{P}_k$ is $O(tn)$ and $O((t + \kappa + \lambda)n)$, respectively. Similarly, the round complexity is $O(\log(\sigma - \log n) + k)$.

MPSI-CA. The bit length of the secret shared in our MPSI protocol is $\sigma + \ell = \max\{\lambda + \log n, \sigma\}$, which is the same as that of MPSI-CA. Therefore, they have the same complexity.

We conclude the complexity of our four protocols in Table 2.

Table 2. The conclusion and comparison of our MPSU, MPSU-CA, MPSI, and MPSI-CA protocols. n is the set size. k is the number of parties. σ is the bit length of set elements. t is the number of AND gates in an SKE decryption circuit. λ is statistical security parameter. κ is computational security parameter. The computation complexity refers to the number of symmetric-key operations.

Protocol	Comm.			Comp.	
	Leader	Client	Rounds	Leader	Client
MPSU	$O((t + \kappa + (\sigma + \lambda + \log(kn))k)kn)$	$O((t + \lambda + \kappa)kn)$	$O(\log(\sigma - \log n) + k)$	$O(tkn)$	
MPSU-CA	$O((t + \kappa + (\lambda + \log(kn))k)kn)$				
MPSI	$O((t + \lambda + \kappa)kn)$	$O((t + \lambda + \kappa)n)$		$O(tkn)$	$O(tn)$
MPSI-CA					

7   Implementation

In this section, we provide experimental details and test results for MPSU, and compare our results with previous work. We ignore the costs of the offline phase, including the generation of base OTs, share correlations, and Beaver triples. All experimental data are the average of 10 trials under the same environment. We compute the communication costs of a party as the sum of the data he sent and received.

7.1   Experimental Setup

We run all protocols on a single Intel Ice Lake processor at 3.2 GHz with 256 GB RAM. We emulate the two network connections using Linux tc command. For the LAN setting, we set network latency to 0.02 ms and bandwidth of 10 Gbps and for the WAN setting the latency is set to 40 ms and bandwidth 400 Mbps.

7.2   Implementation Details

For concrete analysis we set the computational security parameter $\kappa = 128$ and the statistical security parameter $\lambda = 40$. Our protocol is written in C++ and we use the following libraries in our implementation.

- OKVS and GMW: We use the optimized 3H-GCT in [43] as our OKVS instantiation, and re-use the implementation of 3H-GCT and GMW by the authors of [43][1].
- LowMC: We set both block size and key length to 128 bits, and the number of Sbox to 10, so the number of rounds is 20. Therefore, the number of AND gates in decryption circuit is $t = 600$. The concrete parameters we use are from [49][2]. And we use the implementation of LowMC by the authors of [1][3].
- ROT: We use SoftSpokenOT [45] implemented in libOTe[4], and set field bits to 5 to balance computation and communication costs.
- Others: We utilize the implementations of circuit, PRNG, and hash function provided by cryptoTools[5]. In addition, we adopt Coproto[6] to realize network communication.

7.3   Comparison with Prior Work

Since only [5] and [48] have implemented their protocols so far, we only compare our work with these two works.

---

[1] https://github.com/Visa-Research/volepsi.git.
[2] https://github.com/alibaba-edu/mpc4j/blob/adee91f7966a3166f6e662f6b4a321ea36fc f39d/mpc4j-common-tool/src/main/resources/low_mc/lowmc_128_128_20.txt.
[3] https://github.com/LowMC/lowmc.git.
[4] https://github.com/osu-crypto/libOTe.git.
[5] https://github.com/ladnir/cryptoTools.git.
[6] https://github.com/Visa-Research/coproto.git.

Blanton et al. [5]. Since their implementation is not available, we can only use the experimental results they published in their papers. They implemented the 3-party PSU protocol in C++, assuming an honest majority, and tested it in a LAN with a bandwidth of 1 Gbps on 2.4 GHz AMD Opteron. They tested their protocol with 32-bit elements and set sizes of $2^4, 2^6, 2^8, 2^{10}$, and the running times were 0.13 s, 0.52 s, 2.41 s, and 11.89 s, respectively. In contrast, our protocol, which is secure under the assumption that $\mathcal{P}_1$ does not collude with other parties, runs in a 10 Gbps bandwidth environment in the same setting, taking 0.10 s, 0.10 s, 0.11 s, and 0.14 s, respectively.

Vos et al. [48]. Vos et al.'s protocol employs a divide-and-conquer approach, so the computational cost and communication overhead are related to the distribution of the input set. Precisely, if the input elements are concentrated in neighboring regions of the universe, then most branches can be pruned by the divide-and-conquer algorithm. If the input elements are more dispersed, then more secure OR operations are required. We test their open-source code on random datasets and set the divide-and-conquer parameter $D = 2$ to minimize the number of secure OR operations required. The (expected) communication overhead is calculated using the formula provided in their paper. Finally, since in their implementation parties transmit data directly through memory, which is not affected by bandwidth, we only test our protocol in a LAN and compare it with theirs. The results are shown in Table 3.

We test our protocol for set sizes of $n = \{2^4, 2^6, 2^8, 2^{10}\}$ and different numbers of parties $k = \{3, 4, 5, 7, 10\}$. For each set size, we set the universe size to be $|\mathcal{U}| = 2^{16}$ to make [48] achieve higher efficiency. From the perspective of running time, our protocol shows significant efficiency improvements compared to [48]. Moreover, it gains greater improvements for larger set sizes. In particular, under the condition of a set size of 2^{10}, our protocol achieves a 109× speedup. If the set size is increased to 2^{20}, there will be a remarkable improvement. However, [48] already takes 75 s for 10 parties and a set size of 2^{10}, and testing larger sets will take several tens of minutes or even an hour and require a larger input domain, such as $|\mathcal{U}| = 2^{32}$, which will further decrease the efficiency of [48]. Therefore, we believe that testing for a set size of 2^{10} is sufficient to demonstrate that our protocol is more efficient than [48].

From the perspective of communication overhead, all communication costs in [48] come from secure OR operations, so we should minimize the number of secure OR operations required. Therefore, we chose $D = 2$ as the optimal parameter for the expected communication overhead. Nevertheless, our protocol still achieves 3–4× improvements in communication overhead. Specifically, when $n = 2^{10}$ and $k = 10$, the communication overhead of the leader in their protocol is 25.55 MB, while our protocol only requires 6.30 MB. Moreover, as the universe size increases, the gap becomes even more significant.

Table 3. The comparison of [48] and our MPSU protocol in running time (seconds) and communication cost (MB) in the LAN setting. The bit length of our elements is 64. The output length of H is $\ell = 64$. The size of universe in [48] is set to $|\mathcal{U}| = 2^{16}$. The parameter in divide-and-conquer is $D = 2$. The communication cost refers to Leader's communication cost. In our protocol, each party uses $k - 1$ threads to interact with all other parties separately, and 4 threads are used to perform parallel SKE encryption. In their protocol, the leader uses $k - 1$ threads to interact with all other parties simultaneously. Bold numbers indicate the best results under current conditions. Cells with - means there is almost no improvement.

	Number Parties k	Protocol	Set Size n			
			2^4	2^6	2^8	2^{10}
Time	3	[48]	0.56	1.71	4.84	15.36
		Ours	**0.10**	**0.10**	**0.11**	**0.14**
	4	[48]	0.76	2.36	7.64	20.84
		Ours	**0.15**	**0.16**	**0.17**	**0.19**
	5	[48]	1.08	3.50	10.73	26.43
		Ours	**0.22**	**0.22**	**0.23**	**0.24**
	7	[48]	1.84	4.49	15.29	52.82
		Ours	**0.36**	**0.36**	**0.37**	**0.39**
	10	[48]	3.15	9.12	29.65	75.58
		Ours	**0.58**	**0.62**	**0.63**	**0.68**
	Speedup		5×	12×	41×	109×
Comm.	3	[48]	0.16	0.56	1.82	5.68
		Ours	**0.15**	**0.16**	**0.28**	**0.96**
	4	[48]	0.25	0.84	2.74	8.52
		Ours	**0.22**	**0.24**	**0.45**	**1.54**
	5	[48]	0.33	1.11	3.65	11.36
		Ours	**0.30**	**0.33**	**0.63**	**2.17**
	7	[48]	0.49	1.67	5.47	17.03
		Ours	**0.45**	**0.52**	**1.04**	**3.63**
	10	[48]	0.74	2.51	8.21	25.55
		Ours	**0.69**	**0.83**	**1.77**	**6.30**
	Speedup		-	3×	4×	4×

7.4 Scalability

To demonstrate the scalability and practicality of our protocol, we test our protocol for larger set sizes of $n = 2^{14}, 2^{16}, 2^{18}, 2^{20}$ and different number of parties $k = 3, 4, 5, 7, 10$. For each party, we use $k - 1$ threads to interact with all other parties simultaneously and 4 threads to perform parallel SKE encryption.

Running Time. The running time of our protocol in both LAN and WAN settings are shown in Table 4. Our protocol demonstrates good scalability. In the

LAN setting, the running time of the protocol increases linearly with the set size. Specifically, for the 3-party setting, computing MPSU for small sets ($n = 2^{14}$) takes less than one second; medium-sized sets ($n = 2^{16}, 2^{18}$) can be computed within 10 s; and large sets ($n = 2^{20}$) only require 29.02 s. Moreover, since our protocol can be well parallelized, it also shows good scalability as the number of parties increases. For example, for $n = 2^{18}$, when the number of parties increases from 3 to 10, the running time only increases by 2.8×, and when the number of parties increases from 3 to 7 for $n = 2^{20}$, the running time only increases by 1.6×. On the other hand, our protocol has reasonable communication overhead, making it also efficient in the WAN setting. For example, in the 10-party setting, computing $n = 2^{18}$ takes around 2 min, and in the 7-party setting, computing $n = 2^{20}$ takes around 4 min.

Table 4. Running time (seconds) of our protocol in LAN and WAN settings. Each party holds n 64-bit elements. The output length of H is $\ell = 64$. Cells with - denotes trials that ran out of memory.

Setting	Number Parties k	Set Size n			
		2^{14}	2^{16}	2^{18}	2^{20}
LAN	3	0.55	1.79	7.04	29.02
	4	0.60	1.88	7.46	30.28
	5	0.67	2.01	7.92	34.10
	7	0.88	2.71	10.77	45.68
	10	1.41	4.89	19.90	-
WAN	3	3.36	6.64	15.38	51.81
	4	4.14	8.63	20.28	72.61
	5	5.53	10.56	29.35	111.06
	7	6.91	17.21	60.17	227.75
	10	11.08	33.89	127.71	-

Communication Overhead. The communication overhead of the protocol is shown in Table 5. $\mathcal{P}_1$ has the highest communication overhead, and the communication overhead of $\mathcal{P}_2, \cdots, \mathcal{P}_{k-1}$ is the same, and the communication overhead of $\mathcal{P}_k$ is slightly lower than that of $\mathcal{P}_i (2 \leq i \leq k - 1)$. The communication overhead of all parties is linearly proportional to the set size. The communication overhead of $\mathcal{P}_2, \cdots, \mathcal{P}_k$ is linearly proportional to the number of parties. The communication overhead of $\mathcal{P}_1$ grows quadratically with the number of parties, as it need to reconstruct the secret.

Table 5. Communication (MB) of our protocol for different set sizes and different numbers of parties. Each party holds n 64-bit elements. The output length of H is $\ell = 64$. $\mathcal{P}_i$ denotes $\mathcal{P}_2, \cdots, \mathcal{P}_{k-1}$. Cells with - denotes trials that ran out of memory.

Number Parties k	Set Size n											
	2^{14}			2^{16}			2^{18}			2^{20}		
	$\mathcal{P}_1$	$\mathcal{P}_i$	$\mathcal{P}_k$	$\mathcal{P}_1$	$\mathcal{P}_i$	$\mathcal{P}_k$	$\mathcal{P}_1$	$\mathcal{P}_i$	$\mathcal{P}_k$	$\mathcal{P}_1$	$\mathcal{P}_i$	$\mathcal{P}_k$
3	14.43	13.93	13.43	57.58	55.58	53.58	229.76	221.76	213.76	917	885	853
4	23.14	20.89	20.14	92.38	83.38	80.38	368.64	332.64	320.64	1472	1328	1280
5	32.86	27.86	26.86	131.17	111.17	107.17	523.52	443.52	427.52	2090	1770	1706
7	55.29	41.79	40.29	220.75	166.75	160.75	881.28	665.28	641.28	3519	2655	2559
10	96.43	62.68	60.43	385.13	250.13	241.13	1537.92	997.92	961.92	-	-	-

8 Conclusion

In this work, we introduce a new protocol called mq-ssPMT, which is an effective technique in multi-party private set operations. We also give an efficient construction of mq-ssPMT, which is mainly based on symmetric-key operations. By combining with multi-party secret-shared shuffle and ROT, we propose a multi-party private set operation framework from mq-ssPMT, including MPSU, MPSU-CA, MPSI, and MPSI-CA. We stress that although our protocols require the assumption that the leader does not collude with others, which achieves weaker security, our MPSU protocol is the first protocol that reports on large-size experiments and is truly scalable. We leave the construction of efficient MPSU protocol which resists arbitrary collusion as a future work.

Acknowledgement. We thank all the anonymous reviewers for helpful feedback on the write-up. This work is supported by the National Key Research and Development Program of China (2022YFB2701600), National Natural Science Foundation of China (U21A20467, 61932011, 61972019), and Beijing Natural Science Foundation (M21033, M21031).

A Symmetric-Key Encryption

A SKE scheme is a tuple of four algorithms:

- Setup(1^κ): on input the security parameter κ outputs public parameters pp, which include the description of the message and ciphertext space $\mathcal{M}, \mathcal{C}$.
- KeyGen(pp): on input public parameter pp outputs a key k.
- Enc(k, m): on input a key k and a plaintext $m \in \mathcal{M}$, outputs a ciphertext $c \in \mathcal{C}$.
- Dec(k, c): on input a key k and a ciphertext $c \in \mathcal{C}$, outputs a message $m \in \mathcal{M}$ or an error symbol$\perp$.

Correctness. For any $pp \leftarrow \mathsf{Setup}(1^\kappa)$, any $k \leftarrow \mathsf{KeyGen}(pp)$, any $m \in \mathcal{M}$ and any $c \leftarrow \mathsf{Enc}(k, m)$, it holds $\mathsf{Dec}(k, c) = m$.

Security. To ensure the security of our mq-ssPMT, we require a security notion called *multi-message multi-ciphertext pseudorandomness* like the mq-RPMT in [49]. Formally, a SKE is multi-message multi-ciphertext pseudorandom if for any PPT $\mathcal{A} = (\mathcal{A}_1, \mathcal{A}_2)$:

$$\mathsf{Adv}_{\mathcal{A}}(1^\kappa) = \Pr \left[\beta = \beta' : \begin{array}{l} pp \leftarrow \mathsf{Setup}(1^\kappa); \\ k \leftarrow \mathsf{KeyGen}(pp); \\ (m_1, \cdots, m_n, state) \leftarrow \mathcal{A}_1(pp); \\ \beta \leftarrow \{0,1\}; \\ \text{for } i \in [n] : c_{i,0} \leftarrow \mathsf{Enc}(k, m_i), c_{i,1} \leftarrow \mathcal{C}; \\ \beta' \leftarrow \mathcal{A}_2(pp, state, \{c_{i,\beta}\}_{i \in [n]}) \end{array} \right] - \frac{1}{2}$$

is negligible is κ.

B   Multi-party Secret-Shared Shuffle

The functionality of share correlation is given in Fig. 12. The protocol details of multi-party secret-shared shuffle in [18] are given in Fig. 13.

PARAMETERS: k parties: $\mathcal{P}_1, \cdots, \mathcal{P}_k$; The dimension of vector n; The bit length of individual element σ.

FUNCTIONALITY:

- Wait an input $\pi_i : [n] \to [n]$ from each $\mathcal{P}_i (1 \le i \le k)$.
- Sample $a_i', b_i \leftarrow \mathbb{F}_{2^\sigma}^n$ for $1 \le i \le k-1$ and $a_i \leftarrow \mathbb{F}_{2^\sigma}^n, \Delta \leftarrow \mathbb{F}_{2^\sigma}^n$ for $2 \le i \le k$, which satisfy:

$$\Delta = \pi_k \left(\cdots \left(\pi_2 \left(\pi_1 \left(\bigoplus_{i=2}^{k} a_i \right) \oplus a_1' \right) \oplus a_2' \right) \cdots \oplus a_{k-1}' \right) \oplus \bigoplus_{i=1}^{k-1} b_i$$

Give a_1', b_1 to $\mathcal{P}_1$. Give a_i', a_i, b_i to $\mathcal{P}_i (2 \le i \le k-1)$. Give a_k, Δ_k to $\mathcal{P}_k$.

Fig. 12. Share Correlation Functionality $\mathcal{F}_{\mathsf{sc}}$

PARAMETERS:

- k parties $\mathcal{P}_1, \cdots, \mathcal{P}_k$.
- Ideal functionality $\mathcal{F}_{\mathsf{sc}}$ in Fig. 12.
- The dimension of vector n and the bit length of individual element σ.

INPUT OF $\mathcal{P}_i$: $[\boldsymbol{x}]_i$, a share of $\boldsymbol{x} \in \mathbb{F}_{2^\sigma}^n$ based on addtively secret sharing.

PROTOCOL:

1. Each $\mathcal{P}_i$ samples a random permutation $\pi_i : [n] \to [n]$ and invokes $\mathcal{F}_{\mathsf{sc}}$ with input π_i. $\mathcal{P}_1$ receives $\boldsymbol{a}_1', \boldsymbol{b}_1 \in \mathbb{F}_{2^\sigma}^n$. $\mathcal{P}_i (2 \le i \le k-1)$ receives $\boldsymbol{a}_i', \boldsymbol{a}_i, \boldsymbol{b}_i \in \mathbb{F}_{2^\sigma}^n$. $\mathcal{P}_k$ receives $\boldsymbol{a}_k, \boldsymbol{\Delta}_k \in \mathbb{F}_{2^\sigma}^n$.
2. For $2 \le i \le k$, $\mathcal{P}_i$ computes $\boldsymbol{z}_i := [\boldsymbol{x}]_i \oplus \boldsymbol{a}_i$, and send $\boldsymbol{z}_i$ to $\mathcal{P}_1$.
3. $\mathcal{P}_1$ computes $\boldsymbol{z}_1' := \pi_1 \left(\bigoplus_{i=2}^k \boldsymbol{z}_i \oplus [\boldsymbol{x}]_1 \right) \oplus \boldsymbol{a}_1'$ and send it to $\mathcal{P}_2$. $\mathcal{P}_1$ outputs $\boldsymbol{b}_1$.
4. For $2 \le i \le k-1$, $\mathcal{P}_i$ computes $\boldsymbol{z}_i' := \pi_i(\boldsymbol{z}_{i-1}') \oplus \boldsymbol{a}_i'$ and sends it to $\mathcal{P}_{i+1}$. $\mathcal{P}_i$ output $\boldsymbol{b}_i$.
5. $\mathcal{P}_k$ outputs $\pi_k(\boldsymbol{z}_{k-1}') \oplus \boldsymbol{\Delta}_k$.

Fig. 13. Multi-party Secret-Shared Shuffle Protocol Π_{ms}

C   Garbled Cuckoo Table

The formal description of GCT in [43] is given in Fig. 14.

D   Proof of Theorem 3

Below we give the details of the Proof of Theorem 3.

Proof. Let C and H be a coalition of corrupt and honest parties, respectively. $|C| = \eta$. To show how to simulate C's view in the ideal model, we consider two cases based on whether $\mathcal{P}_1$ is corrupted.

$\mathcal{P}_1$ *is Honest.* In this case, $\mathcal{P}_1 \notin C$. $\mathsf{Sim}_C(X_{i_1}, \cdots, X_{i_\eta})$ runs as follows:

1. For all $\mathcal{P}_i \in C$, Sim_C samples $\boldsymbol{e}_{1i}'^1 \leftarrow \{0,1\}^n, \boldsymbol{r}_{1i}'^0, \boldsymbol{r}_{1i}'^1 \leftarrow \mathbb{F}_{2^{\sigma+\ell}}^n, \boldsymbol{sh}_i'' \leftarrow \mathbb{F}_{2^{\sigma+\ell}}^n$ and appends them to the view.
2. For all $\mathcal{P}_i \in C$, Sim_C invokes mq-ssPMT simulator $\mathsf{Sim}_{\mathsf{mq\text{-}sspmt}}^{\mathcal{S}}(X_i, \boldsymbol{e}_i'^1)$ and appends the output to the view.
3. For all $\mathcal{P}_i \in C$, Sim_C invokes ROT simulator $\mathsf{Sim}_{\mathsf{rot}}^{\mathcal{S}}(\boldsymbol{r}_{1i}'^0, \boldsymbol{r}_{1i}'^1)$ and appends the output to the view.
4. For all $\mathcal{P}_i \in C$, Sim_C creates $\boldsymbol{sh}_i$ as Step 4 of Π_{mpsi}. Then invokes multi-party secret-shared shuffle simulator $\mathsf{Sim}_{\mathsf{ms}}^{\mathcal{P}_i}(\boldsymbol{sh}_i, \boldsymbol{sh}_i'')$ and appends the output to the view.

Now we argue that the view output by Sim_C is indistinguishable from the real one. In the real world, the output $\boldsymbol{e}_{1i}^1$ of mq-ssPMT, the output $\boldsymbol{r}_{1i}^0, \boldsymbol{r}_{1i}^1$ of ROT, and the output $\boldsymbol{sh}_i'$ of multi-party secret-shared shuffle are uniformly random. Moreover, the outputs of mq-ssPMT and ROT of all parties in C are mutually independent.

PARAMETERS:

- Statistical security parameter λ and computational security parameter κ.
- Finite field $\mathbb{F}$ and finite group $\mathbb{G}$.
- Output length $m = m' + \hat{m}$ where $m' = O(n), \hat{m} = O(\lambda)$.

Input: n key-value pairs $\{(k_1, v_1), \cdots, (k_n, v_n)\} \subseteq \mathcal{K} \times \mathcal{V}$.

Encode($\{(k_1, v_1), \cdots, (k_n, v_n)\}, r$) :

(1) **[Sample]** Let $\mathrm{row}' : \mathcal{K} \times \{0,1\}^\kappa \to S_w$ and $\hat{\mathrm{row}} : \mathcal{K} \times \{0,1\}^\kappa \to \mathbb{F}^{\hat{m}}$ be random functions where $S_w \subset \{0,1\}^{m'}$ is the set of all weight w strings. Let $\mathrm{row}(k, r) := \mathrm{row}'(k, r) \| \hat{\mathrm{row}}(k, r)$ and define

$$H := \begin{bmatrix} \mathrm{row}(k_1, r) \\ \cdots \\ \mathrm{row}(k_n, r) \end{bmatrix} \in \mathbb{F}^{n \times m}$$

(2) **[Triangulate]** Let $H' := H, J := \emptyset$. While H' has rows:
   (a) Select $j \in [m]$ such that the jth (sparse) column of H' has the minimum non-zero weight.
   (b) Append index j to the ordered list J. Remove all rows $i \in [n]$ from H' for which $H'_{i,j} \neq 0$.
   Define $\delta := |J|$, the gap as $g := n - \delta$, permutation matrices $\pi^r \in \{0,1\}^{n \times n}, \pi^c \in \{0,1\}^{m \times m}$ such that $\pi^c_{m-k, m-\delta-k} = 1$ for $k \in [0, \hat{m})$, $\pi^c_{J_i, m+1-i} = 1$ and $\pi^r_{n+1-i, i'} = 1$ for some i' where $H_{i', J_i} \neq 0$ and all $i \in [\delta]$. Let

$$T := \pi^r \cdot H \cdot \pi^c = \begin{bmatrix} A & B & C \\ D & E & F \end{bmatrix}$$

   where $F \in \{0,1\}^{\delta \times \delta}$ is lower triangular, $B \in \mathbb{F}^{g \times \hat{m}}, E \in \mathbb{F}^{\delta \times \hat{m}}$ are the dense columns.

(3) **[Zero-C]** Compute $T' := \begin{bmatrix} I & -CF^{-1} \\ 0 & I \end{bmatrix} \cdot T = \begin{bmatrix} A' & B' & 0 \\ D & E & F \end{bmatrix}$.

(4) **[Solve-Dense]** If B' doesn't have full row rank, return $\bot$. Let $B^* := QB'$ be the (lower) reduced row echelon form of B', and

$$T^* := \begin{bmatrix} Q & 0 \\ 0 & I \end{bmatrix} \cdot T' = \begin{bmatrix} A^* & B^* & 0 \\ D & E & F \end{bmatrix}, v^* := \begin{bmatrix} Q & -QCF^{-1} \\ 0 & I \end{bmatrix} \cdot \pi^r \cdot v$$

   where $v = (v_1, \cdots, v_n)^T \in \mathbb{F}^{n \times 1}$.

(5) **[Back-substitution]** Compute $P^* := T^{*-1} \cdot v^*$ via back-substitution and return $P := P^* \cdot \pi^{c-1}$.

Decode(P, k, r) : return$\langle \mathrm{row}(k, r), P \rangle$.

Fig. 14. GCT algorithm in [43]

As for the output of multi-party secret-shared shuffle protocol, the share $\boldsymbol{sh}_1'$ is unknown and uniformly random for corrupted parties because $\mathcal{P}_1$ is honest. So all $\boldsymbol{sh}_i'(\mathcal{P}_i \in C)$ are uniformly random and independent of each other from the perspective of C. Notice that in the simulated view, all messages are uniformly random and mutually independent, so the output view of Sim_C is computationally indistinguishable from real.

$\mathcal{P}_1$ *is Corrupted.* In this case, $C = \{\mathcal{P}_1\}$. So the simulator $\mathsf{Sim}_C(X_1, \bigcap_{i=1}^{k} X_i)$ needs to simulate $\mathcal{P}_1$'s view. Sim_C runs as follows:

1. For $2 \leq i \leq k$, Sim_C samples $\boldsymbol{e}_{1i}'^{0} \leftarrow \{0,1\}^n$ and $\boldsymbol{r}_{1i}' \leftarrow \mathbb{F}_{2^\sigma + \ell}^n$. Then appends all these vectors to the view.
2. Sim_C constructs $\boldsymbol{z}' \in \mathbb{F}_{2^\sigma + \ell}^n$ as follows:
   - Set $\boldsymbol{z}'$ uninitialized. For each $x \in \bigcap_{i=1}^{k} X_i$, Sim_C computes $x\|\mathsf{H}(x)$ and set a random uninitialized position of $\boldsymbol{z}'$ to this value.
   - For all uninitialized positions of $\boldsymbol{z}'$, set a random value from $\mathbb{F}_{2^\sigma + \ell}$.
3. Sim_C samples $\boldsymbol{sh}_i'' \leftarrow \mathbb{F}_{2^\sigma + \ell}^n$ for all $1 \leq i \leq k$, which satisfies $\bigoplus_{i=1}^{k} \boldsymbol{sh}_i'' = \boldsymbol{z}'$. Sim_C appends all $\boldsymbol{sh}_i''$ to the view.
4. Sim_C invokes mq-ssPMT simulator $\mathsf{Sim}_{\mathsf{mq\text{-}sspmt}}^{\mathcal{R}}(X_1, \boldsymbol{e}_{1i}'^{1})$ for $2 \leq i \leq k$. Then appends the output to the view.
5. Sim_C invokes ROT simulator $\mathsf{Sim}_{\mathsf{rot}}^{\mathcal{R}}(\boldsymbol{e}_{1i}'^{0} \oplus 1^n, \boldsymbol{r}_{1i}')$ for $2 \leq i \leq k$. Then appends the output to the view.
6. Sim_C constructs $\boldsymbol{sh}_1$ as Step 3 and Step 4 of Π_{mpsi}. Then invokes multi-party secret-shared shuffle simulator $\mathsf{Sim}_{\mathsf{ms}}^{\mathcal{P}_i}(\boldsymbol{sh}_1, \boldsymbol{sh}_1'')$ and appends the output to the view.

Now we argue that the view output by Sim_C is indistinguishable from the real one. In the real world, the output $\boldsymbol{e}_{1i}^0$ of mq-ssPMT, the output $\boldsymbol{r}_{1i}$ of ROT, and the output $\boldsymbol{sh}_i'$ of multi-party secret-shared shuffle are uniformly random. Moreover, for different i, they are independent of each other. We prove that $\boldsymbol{sh}_i'$ from each $\mathcal{P}_i$ does not leak any other information except for the intersection. For each element x_1^t that belongs to X_1, if there exists $2 \leq i \leq k$ that $x_1^t \notin X_1 \cap X_i$, we have $e_{1i,t}'^{0} \oplus e_{1i,t}'^{1} = 0, r_{1i,t} = r_{1i,t}^{e_{1i,t}^0 \oplus 1} \neq r_{ji,t}^{e_{ji,t}^1}$. Therefore, $\bigoplus_{i=1}^{k} sh_{i,t} = \bigoplus_{i=1}^{k} r_{1i,t} = r \oplus r_{1i,t}^{e_{1i,t}^1} \oplus r_{1i,t}^{e_{1i,t}^0 \oplus 1}$ is uniformly random from the perspective of $\mathcal{P}_1$, where r is the sum of remaining terms. So in the real world, $\bigoplus_{i=1}^{k} \boldsymbol{sh}_i'$ is uniformly random except for $|\bigcap_{i=1}^{k} X_i|$ positions. So the simulated view is computationally indistinguishable from the real. $\square$

References

1. Albrecht, M.R., Rechberger, C., Schneider, T., Tiessen, T., Zohner, M.: Ciphers for MPC and FHE. In: Oswald, E., Fischlin, M. (eds.) EUROCRYPT 2015. LNCS, vol. 9056, pp. 430–454. Springer, Heidelberg (2015). https://doi.org/10.1007/978-3-662-46800-5_17

2. Aranha, D.F., Lin, C., Orlandi, C., Simkin, M.: Laconic private set-intersection from pairings. In: Proceedings of the 2022 ACM SIGSAC Conference on Computer and Communications Security, CCS 2022, pp. 111–124. Association for Computing Machinery, New York (2022). https://doi.org/10.1145/3548606.3560642

3. Beaver, D.: Efficient multiparty protocols using circuit randomization. In: Feigenbaum, J. (ed.) CRYPTO 1991. LNCS, vol. 576, pp. 420–432. Springer, Heidelberg (1992). https://doi.org/10.1007/3-540-46766-1_34

4. Ben-Efraim, A., Nissenbaum, O., Omri, E., Paskin-Cherniavsky, A.: PSImple: practical multiparty maliciously-secure private set intersection. In: Proceedings of the 2022 ACM on Asia Conference on Computer and Communications Security, ASIA CCS 2022, pp. 1098–1112. Association for Computing Machinery, New York (2022). https://doi.org/10.1145/3488932.3523254

5. Blanton, M., Aguiar, E.: Private and oblivious set and multiset operations. Int. J. Inf. Sec. **15**(5), 493–518 (2016). https://doi.org/10.1007/s10207-015-0301-1

6. Brickell, J., Shmatikov, V.: Privacy-preserving graph algorithms in the semi-honest model. In: Roy, B. (ed.) ASIACRYPT 2005. LNCS, vol. 3788, pp. 236–252. Springer, Heidelberg (2005). https://doi.org/10.1007/11593447_13

7. Bui, D., Couteau, G.: Improved private set intersection for sets with small entries. In: Boldyreva, A., Kolesnikov, V. (eds.) Public-Key Cryptography, PKC 2023. LNCS, vol. 13941, pp. 190–220. Springer, Cham (2023). https://doi.org/10.1007/978-3-031-31371-4_7

8. Burkhart, M., Strasser, M., Many, D., Dimitropoulos, X.A.: SEPIA: privacy-preserving aggregation of multi-domain network events and statistics. In: Proceedings of the 19th USENIX Security Symposium, Washington, DC, USA, 11–13 August 2010, pp. 223–240. USENIX Association (2010)

9. Chandran, N., Dasgupta, N., Gupta, D., Obbattu, S.L.B., Sekar, S., Shah, A.: Efficient linear multiparty PSI and extensions to circuit/quorum PSI. In: Proceedings of the 2021 ACM SIGSAC Conference on Computer and Communications Security, CCS 2021, pp. 1182–1204. Association for Computing Machinery, New York (2021). https://doi.org/10.1145/3460120.3484591

10. Chase, M., Ghosh, E., Poburinnaya, O.: Secret-shared shuffle. In: Moriai, S., Wang, H. (eds.) ASIACRYPT 2020. LNCS, vol. 12493, pp. 342–372. Springer, Cham (2020). https://doi.org/10.1007/978-3-030-64840-4_12

11. Chase, M., Miao, P.: Private set intersection in the internet setting from lightweight oblivious PRF. In: Micciancio, D., Ristenpart, T. (eds.) CRYPTO 2020. LNCS, vol. 12172, pp. 34–63. Springer, Cham (2020). https://doi.org/10.1007/978-3-030-56877-1_2

12. Chen, Y., Zhang, M., Zhang, C., Dong, M., Liu, W.: Private set operations from multi-query reverse private membership test. Cryptology ePrint Archive, Paper 2022/652 (2022). https://eprint.iacr.org/2022/652

13. Chongchitmate, W., Ishai, Y., Lu, S., Ostrovsky, R.: Psi from ring-ole. In: Proceedings of the 2022 ACM SIGSAC Conference on Computer and Communications Security, CCS 2022, pp. 531–545. Association for Computing Machinery, New York (2022). https://doi.org/10.1145/3548606.3559378

14. Ciampi, M., Orlandi, C.: Combining private set-intersection with secure two-party computation. In: Catalano, D., De Prisco, R. (eds.) SCN 2018. LNCS, vol. 11035, pp. 464–482. Springer, Cham (2018). https://doi.org/10.1007/978-3-319-98113-0_25

15. Couteau, G.: New protocols for secure equality test and comparison. In: Preneel, B., Vercauteren, F. (eds.) ACNS 2018. LNCS, vol. 10892, pp. 303–320. Springer, Cham (2018). https://doi.org/10.1007/978-3-319-93387-0_16

16. Davidson, A., Cid, C.: An efficient toolkit for computing private set operations. In: Pieprzyk, J., Suriadi, S. (eds.) ACISP 2017. LNCS, vol. 10343, pp. 261–278. Springer, Cham (2017). https://doi.org/10.1007/978-3-319-59870-3_15
17. Dong, C., Chen, L., Wen, Z.: When private set intersection meets big data: an efficient and scalable protocol. In: Proceedings of the 2013 ACM SIGSAC Conference on Computer and Communications Security, CCS 2013, pp. 789–800. Association for Computing Machinery, New York (2013). https://doi.org/10.1145/2508859.2516701
18. Eskandarian, S., Boneh, D.: Clarion: anonymous communication from multiparty shuffling protocols. In: 29th Annual Network and Distributed System Security Symposium, NDSS 2022, San Diego, California, USA, 24–28 April 2022. The Internet Society (2022)
19. Freedman, M.J., Nissim, K., Pinkas, B.: Efficient private matching and set intersection. In: Cachin, C., Camenisch, J.L. (eds.) EUROCRYPT 2004. LNCS, vol. 3027, pp. 1–19. Springer, Heidelberg (2004). https://doi.org/10.1007/978-3-540-24676-3_1
20. Frikken, K.: Privacy-preserving set union. In: Katz, J., Yung, M. (eds.) ACNS 2007. LNCS, vol. 4521, pp. 237–252. Springer, Heidelberg (2007). https://doi.org/10.1007/978-3-540-72738-5_16
21. Garimella, G., Mohassel, P., Rosulek, M., Sadeghian, S., Singh, J.: Private set operations from oblivious switching. In: Garay, J.A. (ed.) PKC 2021. LNCS, vol. 12711, pp. 591–617. Springer, Cham (2021). https://doi.org/10.1007/978-3-030-75248-4_21
22. Garimella, G., Pinkas, B., Rosulek, M., Trieu, N., Yanai, A.: Oblivious key-value stores and amplification for private set intersection. In: Malkin, T., Peikert, C. (eds.) CRYPTO 2021. LNCS, vol. 12826, pp. 395–425. Springer, Cham (2021). https://doi.org/10.1007/978-3-030-84245-1_14
23. Gong, X., Hua, Q.S., Jin, H.: Nearly optimal protocols for computing multi-party private set union. In: 2022 IEEE/ACM 30th International Symposium on Quality of Service (IWQoS), pp. 1–10 (2022). https://doi.org/10.1109/IWQoS54832.2022.9812897
24. Gordon, D., Hazay, C., Le, P.H., Liang, M.: More efficient (reusable) private set union. Cryptology ePrint Archive, Paper 2022/713 (2022). https://eprint.iacr.org/2022/713
25. Hazay, C., Nissim, K.: Efficient set operations in the presence of malicious adversaries. J. Cryptol. **25**(3), 383–433 (2012). https://doi.org/10.1007/s00145-011-9098-x
26. Hogan, K., et al.: Secure multiparty computation for cooperative cyber risk assessment. In: IEEE Cybersecurity Development, SecDev 2016, Boston, MA, USA, 3–4 November 2016, pp. 75–76. IEEE Computer Society (2016). https://doi.org/10.1109/SecDev.2016.028
27. Hong, J., Kim, J.W., Kim, J., Park, K., Cheon, J.H.: Constant-round privacy preserving multiset union. Cryptology ePrint Archive, Paper 2011/138 (2011). https://eprint.iacr.org/2011/138
28. Jia, Y., Sun, S.F., Zhou, H.S., Du, J., Gu, D.: Shuffle-based private set union: faster and more secure. In: 31st USENIX Security Symposium, USENIX Security 2022, August 2022, pp. 2947–2964. USENIX Association, Boston, MA (2022)
29. Kerschbaum, F., Blass, E., Mahdavi, R.A.: Faster secure comparisons with offline phase for efficient private set intersection. In: 30th Annual Network and Distributed System Security Symposium, NDSS 2023, San Diego, California, USA, 27 February–3 March 2023. The Internet Society (2023)

30. Kissner, L., Song, D.: Privacy-preserving set operations. In: Shoup, V. (ed.) CRYPTO 2005. LNCS, vol. 3621, pp. 241–257. Springer, Heidelberg (2005). https://doi.org/10.1007/11535218_15
31. Kolesnikov, V., Kumaresan, R., Rosulek, M., Trieu, N.: Efficient batched oblivious PRF with applications to private set intersection. In: Proceedings of the 2016 ACM SIGSAC Conference on Computer and Communications Security, CCS 2016, pp. 818–829. Association for Computing Machinery, New York (2016). https://doi.org/10.1145/2976749.2978381
32. Kolesnikov, V., Matania, N., Pinkas, B., Rosulek, M., Trieu, N.: Practical multi-party private set intersection from symmetric-key techniques. In: Proceedings of the 2017 ACM SIGSAC Conference on Computer and Communications Security, CCS 2017, pp. 1257–1272. Association for Computing Machinery, New York (2017). https://doi.org/10.1145/3133956.3134065
33. Kolesnikov, V., Rosulek, M., Trieu, N., Wang, X.: Scalable private set union from symmetric-key techniques. In: Galbraith, S.D., Moriai, S. (eds.) ASIACRYPT 2019. LNCS, vol. 11922, pp. 636–666. Springer, Cham (2019). https://doi.org/10.1007/978-3-030-34621-8_23
34. Lenstra, A., Voss, T.: Information security risk assessment, aggregation, and mitigation. In: Wang, H., Pieprzyk, J., Varadharajan, V. (eds.) ACISP 2004. LNCS, vol. 3108, pp. 391–401. Springer, Heidelberg (2004). https://doi.org/10.1007/978-3-540-27800-9_34
35. Mohassel, P., Sadeghian, S.: How to hide circuits in MPC an efficient framework for private function evaluation. In: Johansson, T., Nguyen, P.Q. (eds.) EUROCRYPT 2013. LNCS, vol. 7881, pp. 557–574. Springer, Heidelberg (2013). https://doi.org/10.1007/978-3-642-38348-9_33
36. Nevo, O., Trieu, N., Yanai, A.: Simple, fast malicious multiparty private set intersection. In: Proceedings of the 2021 ACM SIGSAC Conference on Computer and Communications Security, CCS 2021, pp. 1151–1165. Association for Computing Machinery, New York (2021). https://doi.org/10.1145/3460120.3484772
37. Oded, G.: Foundations of Cryptography: Volume 2, Basic Applications, 1st edn. Cambridge University Press, USA (2009)
38. Pinkas, B., Rosulek, M., Trieu, N., Yanai, A.: SpOT-Light: lightweight private set intersection from sparse OT extension. In: Boldyreva, A., Micciancio, D. (eds.) CRYPTO 2019. LNCS, vol. 11694, pp. 401–431. Springer, Cham (2019). https://doi.org/10.1007/978-3-030-26954-8_13
39. Pinkas, B., Rosulek, M., Trieu, N., Yanai, A.: PSI from PaXoS: fast, malicious private set intersection. In: Canteaut, A., Ishai, Y. (eds.) EUROCRYPT 2020. LNCS, vol. 12106, pp. 739–767. Springer, Cham (2020). https://doi.org/10.1007/978-3-030-45724-2_25
40. Pinkas, B., Schneider, T., Zohner, M.: Faster private set intersection based on OT extension. In: 23rd USENIX Security Symposium, USENIX Security 2014, August 2014, San Diego, CA, pp. 797–812. USENIX Association (2014)
41. Pinkas, B., Schneider, T., Zohner, M.: Scalable private set intersection based on OT extension. ACM Trans. Priv. Secur. **21**(2) (2018). https://doi.org/10.1145/3154794
42. Rabin, M.O.: How to exchange secrets with oblivious transfer. IACR Cryptology ePrint Archive, p. 187 (2005). http://eprint.iacr.org/2005/187
43. Raghuraman, S., Rindal, P.: Blazing fast PSI from improved OKVS and subfield VOLE. In: Proceedings of the 2022 ACM SIGSAC Conference on Computer and Communications Security, CCS 2022, pp. 2505–2517. Association for Computing Machinery, New York (2022). https://doi.org/10.1145/3548606.3560658

44. Rindal, P., Schoppmann, P.: VOLE-PSI: fast OPRF and circuit-PSI from vector-OLE. In: Canteaut, A., Standaert, F.-X. (eds.) EUROCRYPT 2021. LNCS, vol. 12697, pp. 901–930. Springer, Cham (2021). https://doi.org/10.1007/978-3-030-77886-6_31
45. Roy, L.: SoftSpokenOT: quieter OT extension from small-field silent VOLE in the Minicrypt model. In: Dodis, Y., Shrimpton, T. (eds.) Advances in Cryptology, CRYPTO 2022. LNCS, vol. 13507, pp. 657–687. Springer, Cham (2022). https://doi.org/10.1007/978-3-031-15802-5_23
46. Seo, J.H., Cheon, J.H., Katz, J.: Constant-round multi-party private set union using reversed Laurent series. In: Fischlin, M., Buchmann, J., Manulis, M. (eds.) PKC 2012. LNCS, vol. 7293, pp. 398–412. Springer, Heidelberg (2012). https://doi.org/10.1007/978-3-642-30057-8_24
47. Shishido, K., Miyaji, A.: Efficient and quasi-accurate multiparty private set union. In: 2018 IEEE International Conference on Smart Computing (SMARTCOMP), pp. 309–314 (2018). https://doi.org/10.1109/SMARTCOMP.2018.00021
48. Vos, J., Conti, M., Erkin, Z.: Fast multi-party private set operations in the star topology from secure ANDs and ORS. Cryptology ePrint Archive, Paper 2022/721 (2022). https://eprint.iacr.org/2022/721
49. Zhang, C., Chen, Y., Liu, W., Zhang, M., Lin, D.: Linear private set union from multi-query reverse private membership test. In: 32st USENIX Security Symposium, USENIX Security 2023 (2023). https://eprint.iacr.org/2022/358
50. Zhao, S., Ma, M., Song, X., Jiang, H., Yan, Y., Xu, Q.: Lightweight threshold private set intersection via oblivious transfer. In: Liu, Z., Wu, F., Das, S.K. (eds.) WASA 2021, Part III. LNCS, vol. 12939, pp. 108–116. Springer, Cham (2021). https://doi.org/10.1007/978-3-030-86137-7_12

Robust Publicly Verifiable Covert Security: Limited Information Leakage and Guaranteed Correctness with Low Overhead

Yi Liu[1], Junzuo Lai[1(✉)], Qi Wang[2], Xianrui Qin[3], Anjia Yang[1], and Jian Weng[1(✉)]

[1] College of Cyber Security, Jinan University, Guangzhou 510632, China
liuyi@jnu.edu.cn, laijunzuo@gmail.com, anjiayang@gmail.com
cryptjweng@gmail.com
[2] Department of Computer Science and Engineering & National Center for Applied Mathematics Shenzhen, Southern University of Science and Technology, Shenzhen 518055, China
wangqi@sustech.edu.cn
[3] Department of Computer Science, The University of Hong Kong, Hong Kong, China
xrqin@cs.hku.hk

Abstract. Protocols with *publicly verifiable covert (PVC) security* offer high efficiency and an appealing feature: a covert party may deviate from the protocol, but with a probability (*e.g.*, 90%, referred to as the *deterrence factor*), the honest party can identify this deviation and expose it using a publicly verifiable certificate. These protocols are particularly suitable for practical applications involving reputation-conscious parties.

However, in the cases where misbehavior goes undetected (*e.g.*, with a probability of 10%), *no security guarantee is provided for the honest party*, potentially resulting in a complete loss of input privacy and output correctness.

In this paper, we tackle this critical problem by presenting a highly effective solution. We introduce and formally define an enhanced notion called *robust PVC security*, such that even if the misbehavior remains undetected, the malicious party can only gain an additional 1-bit of information about the honest party's input while maintaining the correctness of the output. We propose a novel approach leveraging *dual execution* and *time-lock puzzles* to design a robust PVC-secure two-party protocol with *low overhead* (depending on the deterrence factor). For instance, with a deterrence factor of 90%, our robust PVC-secure protocol incurs *only additional* ∼10% *overhead* compared to the state-of-the-art PVC-secure protocol.

Given the stronger security guarantees with low overhead, our protocol is highly suitable for practical applications of secure two-party computation.

Keywords: Secure two-party computation · Robust publicly verifiable covert security · 1-bit leakage · Dual execution

© International Association for Cryptologic Research 2023
J. Guo and R. Steinfeld (Eds.): ASIACRYPT 2023, LNCS 14438, pp. 272–301, 2023.
https://doi.org/10.1007/978-981-99-8721-4_9

1   Introduction

Secure two-party computation (2PC) allows two mutually distrusted parties to jointly evaluate a common function on their inputs while maintaining input privacy. Traditionally, two main security notions for 2PC, *i.e.*, *semi-honest security* and *malicious security*, have been considered [12]. Protocols with *semi-honest security* could be efficient but only protect against passive attackers who strictly adhere to the prescribed protocols. Alternatively, protocols with *malicious security* provide a much stronger guarantee, preventing attackers from gaining any advantage through deviations from protocols. However, despite progress in the past few years, protocols with malicious security remain significantly complex and incur high overhead compared to those with semi-honest security.

The notion of *covert security* [4] is thereby introduced to serve as a compromise between semi-honest and malicious security. Covert security ensures that a party deviating from the protocol will be caught by the honest party with a fixed probability ϵ (*e.g.*, $\epsilon = 90\%$), referred to as the *deterrence factor*. Achieving covert security entails significantly lower overhead than malicious security [4,8,14,22]. Meanwhile, covert security provides a stronger security guarantee than semi-honest security, as it incorporates the risk of being caught, which can serve as a deterrent to potential cheaters.

Nevertheless, in certain scenarios, the deterrent effect of covert security may be insufficient. Merely catching the cheater does not enable the honest party to effectively persuade others and accuse the cheater, as the cheater can still deny their misconduct. To address this limitation, Asharov and Orlandi [2] introduced an enhanced notion called *publicly verifiable covert (PVC) security*. Protocols with PVC security allow the honest party to generate a *publicly verifiable certificate* when cheating is detected. The certificate serves as proof of cheating and can be used to convince all other parties, including external entities. The certificate can be utilized for legal proceedings or incorporated into a smart contract that automatically enforces financial penalties against the cheater. This property is particularly compelling in practice, as it is efficient[1] and can expose the cheater's misbehavior publicly and permanently, thereby imposing a reputational risk and providing stronger accountability measures. In recent years, PVC security has garnered substantial attention, resulting in the development of protocols for both general two-party [2,17,20] and multi-party [3,9,10,31] computation. Furthermore, PVC security model is also widely used in specific scenarios, such as financially backed protocols based on blockchain [11,32], secure computation concerning commitment based on blockchain [1], and private function evaluation [25].

While PVC security offers an effective deterrent when cheating is detected, there is a critical issue when misbehavior remains undetected (e.g., with a probability of 10%). In such cases, *the honest party is left without any security guar-*

---

[1] It has been shown that a two-party PVC protocol with deterrence factor 50% incurs only 20–40% overhead compared to the state-of-the-art semi-honest protocols based on garbled circuits [17].

antees, potentially resulting in a complete loss of input privacy and output correctness. In other words, the cheater may gain complete knowledge of the honest party's input and manipulate the output. This is unacceptable in many scenarios, particularly for parties less concerned about reputation, who may be more inclined to take risks in pursuit of significant gains. An existing countermeasure to address this problem is to increase the deterrence factor to a relatively high level (*e.g.*, 99% or 99.9%). However, it should be noted that the efficiency of protocols with PVC security is directly related to the deterrence factor, and increasing the deterrence factor comes at the cost of reduced efficiency. Worse, existing protocols with PVC security exhibit diminishing marginal benefits when increasing the deterrence factor. For instance, increasing the deterrence factor from 90% to 99% leads to a *tenfold* increase in protocol execution cost, and the same holds for increasing from 99% to 99.9%.

Therefore, there is still a lack of effective approaches to prevent reputation-insensitive parties from deviating from the protocol without incurring significant overhead.

1.1 Our Contributions

In this paper, we present a compelling countermeasure to address the aforementioned problem. Specifically:

New security notion. We introduce an enhanced notion for PVC security named *robust PVC security* to capture the goal. This notion can be seen as making up for the deficiency of covert security in the other direction, focusing on reducing the benefits of malicious behavior when it goes undetected while maintaining the increased cost for cheater when caught provided by PVC security. Protocols with robust PVC security ensure that *even if the misbehavior remains undetected, the malicious party can only obtain an additional 1-bit of information about the honest party's input while simultaneously preserving the correctness of the protocol's output*. By significantly reducing the benefits of successful cheating, our approach goes further to effectively discourages malicious parties from cheating in the protocol.

Protocol with low overhead. We propose a novel approach leveraging *dual execution* and *time-lock puzzles* to design a general *robust PVC-secure* two-party computation protocol with *low overhead* (depending on the deterrence factor). For instance, when the deterrence factor is 90%, our protocol will incur *only additional ~10% overhead compared to the state-of-the-art PVC-secure protocol*.

With its stronger security guarantees and low overhead, our protocol is highly suitable for practical applications of secure two-party computation.

1.2 Technical Overview

In this subsection, we commence by reviewing the *derandomization technique*, which has been employed in prior works for the design of PVC protocols. Notably, this technique will also serve as a key component in our protocol. Then, we briefly explain our robust PVC security notion and present the basic idea for designing protocols with robust PVC security. Finally, we discuss the main intuition behind our novel approach to achieving robust PVC security with low overhead.

Derandomization in PVC Security. Recent general secure computation protocols with PVC security employ the *cut-and-choose* paradigm along with the derandomization technique [3,9,10,17,31], which is simpler and more efficient compared to the signed-OT technique used in earlier work [2,20].

Specifically, in the state-of-the-art PVC-secure two-party computation protocol [17] based on garbled circuits, each party pre-selects a seed for each instance. These seeds determine the randomness used in specific instances, ensuring that the execution of each instance is fully determined by the protocol description and the parties' seeds. At the start of the protocol, the evaluator, who cannot cheat in garbled circuit evaluation, commits to its own seeds and selects one instance for evaluation, leaving the remaining instances for checking. Subsequently, the evaluator, acting as the receiver, engages in classical oblivious transfer (OT) protocols with the garbler to obtain the garbler's seeds for the checking instances. Additionally, the parties sign the transcripts for each instance. Throughout the protocol execution, the evaluator uses the garbler's seeds to verify the correctness of the messages received from the garbler for the checking instances. Upon detecting a deviation from the checking instances, the evaluator combines the previously signed messages and its own seed decommitment to generate the certificate. Any other party can use the seeds to simulate the protocol execution and verify deviations. If no deviation is detected, the evaluator proceeds to evaluate the garbled circuit generated in the evaluation instance.

Importantly, in protocols with PVC security, potential cheaters are unaware of which instances are being checked, making it impossible for them to prevent honest parties from generating certificates. The deterrence factor in these protocols is determined by the number of instances. For example, in the state-of-the-art PVC-secure two-party computation protocol [17], λ instances are involved, with $\lambda - 1$ instances checked by the evaluator and the remaining one instance used for evaluation. Hence, the deterrence factor of this protocol is $\frac{\lambda-1}{\lambda}$. This is the reason why existing protocols exhibit diminishing marginal benefits when increasing the deterrence factor.

Robust PVC Security. In this paper, we introduce a new notion called robust PVC security. Protocols with robust PVC security aim to provide security guarantees inherited from PVC security while simultaneously limiting the benefits for cheaters when their deviations go undetected. We require that in such protocols, cheaters can obtain *at most an additional 1-bit of information about the honest party's input*, while *ensuring the correctness of the protocol output*, i.e., the output remains untampered.

The term "1-bit information" is used here because our approach leverages the idea of *dual execution*. The dual execution technique was initially introduced by

Mohassel and Franklin [27] and later formalized by Huang, Katz, and Evans [18]. This technique has found broad applications in general secure two-party computation with malicious and covert security [16,19,21,28,29] as well as private set intersection (PSI) [30].

The dual execution technique is primarily employed in garbled circuits. The idea behind dual execution is that two parties, P_A and P_B, execute two protocols for the same evaluation circuit and inputs. In one protocol, P_A acts as the garbler, and P_B acts as the evaluator, while in the other protocol, they switch roles, i.e., P_B becomes the garbler, and P_A becomes the evaluator. Finally, the two parties run a secure *equality test* protocol on the outputs of the two garbled circuits to determine the final result. If the test passes, both parties obtain the correct evaluation result; otherwise, it indicates that one party deviated from the protocol, leading to termination. By utilizing this dual execution technique, the malicious party can obtain, at most, an additional 1-bit of information about the honest party's input. The intuition is that even if the malicious party deviates from the protocol as the garbler, it cannot cheat in garbled circuit evaluation as the evaluator. Therefore, the information it can obtain from the maliciously generated garbled circuit is limited to the result of the equality test, *i.e.*, the 1-bit information of either true or false, which may depend on the honest party's inputs.

Therefore, a straightforward approach to achieving robust PVC security is by integrating dual execution into PVC-secure protocols. Specifically, two parties P_A and P_B can execute a PVC-secure protocol, such as the one proposed in [17], to perform garbled circuit checking and obtain a final garbled circuit for evaluation. Simultaneously, these two parties switch roles and execute the protocol again to obtain another garbled circuit for evaluation. Then, each party plays the role of the evaluator and evaluates the garbled circuit they have chosen. Finally, a secure equality test protocol is employed to determine the final result. Although this approach may seem viable, we propose a superior solution in this work.

Our Novel Approach. If the aforementioned approach is based on the state-of-the-art PVC-secure protocol in [17], achieving robust PVC security with a deterrence factor of $\frac{\lambda-1}{\lambda}$ would require the protocol to generate 2λ garbled circuits. Specifically, each party would need to generate $2\lambda - 1$ garbled circuits and evaluate one garbled circuit. This includes λ circuits generated as the garbler, $\lambda - 1$ garbled circuits generated for simulating garbled circuit generation in instance checking, and one garbled circuit that is not generated but needs to be evaluated. Therefore, achieving robust PVC security based on a PVC-secure protocol incurs a cost that is roughly double that of the PVC-secure protocol itself. As emphasized in [17], the cost of generating garbled circuits (unless the circuit is very small) is the efficiency bottleneck of the protocol. Therefore, this approach is not entirely satisfactory.

It happens that this cost can be significantly reduced by leveraging the special protocol framework when integrating dual execution into a PVC-secure protocol. The idea behind our novel approach stems from the following question:

Must each party generate λ garbled circuits as the garbler while generating $\lambda - 1$ different garbled circuits as the evaluator for circuit checking?

Fortunately, we found that the answer is NO, and parties can combine these two circuit generation processes together. The idea of our approach is to let the two parties jointly select $\lambda + 1$ seeds in a blind fashion. Subsequently, each party randomly obtains λ seeds, while one seed remains hidden. When the sets of seeds obtained by the two parties differ, the intersection of their seeds is of size $\lambda - 1$. Importantly, each party remains unaware of the seeds obtained by the other party. They can use their own λ seeds to generate λ garbled circuits and an additional *dummy garbled circuit* for the hidden seed. Since the parties share $\lambda - 1$ common seeds, they can now *reuse* the materials computed for circuit generation when playing the role of the evaluator to perform the circuit checking.

In summary, there are $\lambda + 1$ seeds, and each party obtains λ seeds, resulting in a seed intersection of size $\lambda - 1$. Using their respective λ seeds, the parties generate λ garbled circuits, where $\lambda - 1$ garbled circuits (derived from seeds in the seed intersection) are identical for both parties. Each party can then reuse the materials generated from these common $\lambda - 1$ seeds to check the $\lambda - 1$ garbled circuits generated by the other party. Consequently, each party is left with one unchecked garbled circuit, which can be used for dual execution.

With this insight, to achieve robust PVC security with a deterrence factor of $\frac{\lambda-1}{\lambda}$, each party only needs to generate λ garbled circuits and evaluate one garbled circuit. Notably, the checking of $\lambda - 1$ garbled circuits generated by the other party no longer requires garbled circuit generation. In comparison to the state-of-the-art protocol with PVC security [17], where a total of $2\lambda - 1$ garbled circuits are generated by both parties, and one is evaluated, our approach requires only one additional garbled circuit generation and one additional garbled circuit evaluation. For instance, for the protocol in [17], achieving a deterrence factor of 90% necessitates the garbler to generate 10 garbled circuits, while the evaluator needs to perform 9 garbled circuit generations and one garbled circuit evaluation. In contrast, our approach requires each party to generate 10 garbled circuits and evaluate one garbled circuit. That is, the protocol in [17] requires 20 garbled circuit generations and evaluations, whereas our approach requires 22, and thus the additional overhead in our approach is less than 10% (given that the cost of evaluations is lower than that of generations). Furthermore, the computation of circuit checking for the protocol in [17] must be conducted after circuit generation, while this computation is already performed during the garbled circuit generation in our approach. Thus, as garbled circuit generations and evaluations for each party can be executed in parallel in our approach, the running time of our approach may outperform the PVC protocol in [17].

However, the realization of this insight is highly non-trivial. We omit intricate details and provide a brief illustration of the idea behind our approach as follows. The detailed description of our protocol can be found in Sect. 4.

To generate $\lambda + 1$ seeds, two parties, denoted as P_A and P_B, can each select $\lambda + 1$ seed shares s_i^A and s_i^B, respectively. Subsequently, each party engages in OT protocols with the other party in two directions. As the sender, each party inputs their seed shares, while as the receiver, each party retrieves λ shares, leaving one share unretrieved. To ensure that each party retrieves all-but-one shares, we incorporate random values called *witnesses* as input in the OT protocols, similar to the approach used in [17]. If a receiving party does not retrieve a share, this party must retrieve the corresponding witness. The retrieved shares and witnesses should be provided by the receiver and verified by the sender later to continue the execution of the protocol. The seeds are then defined as $s_i = s_i^A \oplus s_i^B$, and each party will derive λ seeds. A secure equality test is performed by the two parties to ensure that the sets of their seeds are distinct, and if they are found to be identical, the two parties restart the protocol. Step 1 in Fig. 1 illustrates the scenario where 6 seeds are generated.

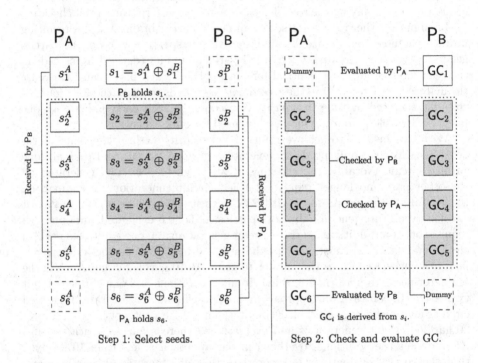

Fig. 1. Seeds generation and garbled circuit evaluation.

Then, each party can utilize the λ seeds they obtained to generate λ garbled circuits. In the case where a party does not obtain a particular seed, a *dummy garbled circuit* is generated in its place. The parties can exchange the commitments of their $\lambda + 1$ garbled circuits, where the randomness of each commitment is also derived from the respective seed. With λ seeds in hand, each party can verify the correct generation of $\lambda - 1$ garbled circuits (from the commitments) while identifying the remaining one as the dummy circuit. Finally, each party can evaluate the garbled circuit corresponding to the seed it does not obtain as dual execution and subsequently perform a secure equality test on the outputs of the garbled circuits to determine the final result. Step 2 in Fig. 1 provides an illustrative depiction of this procedure.

One issue encountered in this approach is the potential identification of the dummy garbled circuit when receiving the commitments. More precisely, a malicious party can discern which instances are being checked by the honest party based on the dummy garbled circuit. If its maliciously generated garbled circuit is checked by the other party, the malicious party can promptly abort and refuse to sign the messages required for generating a publicly verifiable certificate. To address this issue, we must ensure that each party remains unaware of which instances are being checked until the necessary materials for certificate generation are ready.

In our approach, we leverage a verifiable time-lock puzzle scheme [10,26] to tackle this challenge. Using this scheme, the puzzle generator can efficiently create a time-lock puzzle for a message, ensuring that the message remains concealed until a specific time has passed, even against parallel adversaries. Essentially, this efficiently generated time-lock puzzle compels a solver to complete a computational task that takes no less time than the specified duration to recover the message. Moreover, once a puzzle is solved, the solver can effectively convince others that the retrieved message originates from the puzzle. In addition, we also require the option for the puzzle solver to *open the puzzle* at any time, serving as the commitment scheme.

By employing a verifiable time-lock puzzle scheme, each party can generate puzzles for the commitments of the garbled circuits. Therefore, both parties, unaware of the instances being checked, can generate all the necessary materials (*e.g.*, signatures) for generating a publicly verifiable certificate. Afterwards, both parties open their puzzles, verify the garbled circuits, and continue the protocol's execution. If a party refuses to open its puzzles, the other party can solve the puzzle instead. When both parties are honest, no puzzle solving procedure is involved. In the case of detected deviation, the party solving the puzzle can still generate a publicly verifiable certificate as proof of cheating. Given that the puzzle solver can efficiently convince others that the recovered message is derived from the puzzle, the certificate verification process is also efficient. If no deviation is detected, both parties open the respective garbled circuits for evaluation and employ the dual execution approach to evaluate the garbled circuits and determine the evaluation result.

Indeed, similar to the dummy garbled circuit, there exists a potential identification of the dummy instance in the OT protocols for input-wire labels. The solution is also based on time-lock puzzles, but it is more involved (refer to Sect. 4 for the detailed solution). Additionally, to improve efficiency, we generate time-lock puzzle for messages in a batched fashion, allowing each party to generate only one *real* time-lock puzzle (see Sect. 2 and 4 for details).

1.3 Organization

In Sect. 2, we introduce the notations used in this paper and the building blocks that form the foundation of our protocol. Subsequently, in Sect. 3, we present the formal definition of robust PVC security. Based on this definition, in Sect. 4, we propose our robust PVC protocol in detail, leveraging the idea outlined in Sect. 1.2, and provide the security proof. Finally, we discuss the efficiency and potential enhancements of our protocol in Sect. 5.

2 · Preliminaries

We denote the size of a set S as $|S|$ and use the notation $x \leftarrow_{\$} S$ to represent the uniform sampling of an element x from the set S. Additionally, let $[n] = \{1, \ldots, n\}$ for a positive integer n. For a bit string x, the ith bit of x is denoted by $x[i]$. The function $\mathsf{bin}(\cdot)$ returns the bit representation of the input.

Let κ denote the computational security parameter, which is provided in unary format as input to all algorithms. A function f in κ, mapping natural numbers to $[0,1]$, is considered *negligible* if $f(\kappa) = \mathcal{O}(\kappa^{-c})$ for every constant $c > 0$. Conversely, a function $1 - f$ is deemed *overwhelming* if f is negligible.

Given a $\mathsf{seed} \in \{0,1\}^{\kappa}$, we can use a pseudorandom function with seed as the key in the Counter (CTR) mode to derive sufficiently many pseudorandom numbers and use them as random coins for operations in protocols.

We denote a (non-interactive) commitment scheme as Com. The scheme utilizes random coins decom for commitment generation and opening. It should satisfy (computational) binding and hiding properties, while also supporting extraction and equivocation. In our protocol, we implement Com using the random oracle $H: \{0,1\}^{*} \to \{0,1\}^{\kappa}$ by defining $\mathsf{Com}(m) = H(m, \mathsf{decom})$, where $\mathsf{decom} \leftarrow_{\$} \{0,1\}^{\kappa}$. We employ the collision-resistant hash function H in the protocol. Our protocol will use the signature scheme $(\mathsf{KGen}, \mathsf{Sig}, \mathsf{Vf})$ that is existentially unforgeable under chosen-message attacks (EUF-CMA).

For an execution transcript of a two-party protocol $\mathsf{trans} = (m_1, m_2, m_3, \ldots)$, where the parties send their messages alternately, the *transcript hash* of this execution is defined as $\mathcal{H} = (H(m_1), H(m_2), H(m_3), \ldots)$.

Let Π_{OT} be the protocol that securely realizes a parallel version of the OT functionality $\mathcal{F}_{\mathsf{OT}}$ below with perfect correctness [9], such that the receiver (resp. sender) cannot "equivocate" its view by finding a random tape that produces a different output (resp. uses a different input) from the one in the real execution.

Functionality $\mathcal{F}_{\mathsf{OT}}$

Private inputs: $\mathsf{P_A}$ has input $x \in \{0,1\}^{\lambda}$ and $\mathsf{P_B}$ has input $\{(A_{i,0}, A_{i,1})\}_{i \in [\lambda]}$.

Upon receiving $x \in \{0,1\}^{\lambda}$ from $\mathsf{P_A}$ and $\{(A_{i,0}, A_{i,1})\}_{i \in [\lambda]}$ from $\mathsf{P_B}$, send the selected message $\{A_{i,x[i]}\}_{i \in [\lambda]}$ to $\mathsf{P_A}$.

In our protocol, we will use the protocol Π_{Eq} that securely realizes the two-party equality test [7,18] functionality $\mathcal{F}_{\mathsf{Eq}}$ in the following.

Functionality $\mathcal{F}_{\mathsf{Eq}}$

Private inputs: $\mathsf{P_A}$ has input $x \in \{0,1\}^{\kappa}$ and $\mathsf{P_B}$ has input $y \in \{0,1\}^{\kappa}$.

Upon receiving $x \in \{0,1\}^{\kappa}$ from $\mathsf{P_A}$ and $y \in \{0,1\}^{\kappa}$ from $\mathsf{P_B}$, let $b = \mathsf{true}$ if $x = y$, and $b = \mathsf{false}$ otherwise.

- If both parties are honest, send b to both parties.
- If a party is corrupted by the adversary, send b to this corrupted party. Then if continue from the adversary is received, send b to the honest party.

Garbling Scheme. Our protocol uses a circuit garbling scheme $(\mathsf{Gb}, \mathsf{Eval})$ as follows.

- The algorithm Gb takes as input the security parameter 1^{κ} and a circuit $\mathcal{C}$ that has $n = n_A + n_B$ input wires and n_O output wires, and outputs input-wire labels $\{(X_{i,0}, X_{i,1})\}_{i \in [n]}$, a garbled circuit GC, and output-wire labels $\{(Z_{i,0}, Z_{i,1})\}_{i \in [n_O]}$.
- The deterministic algorithm Eval takes as input a set of input-wire labels $\{X_i\}_{i \in [n]}$ and a garbled circuit GC. It outputs a set of output-wire labels $\{Z_i\}_{i \in [n_O]}$.

The correctness of the garbling scheme means that for any circuit $\mathcal{C}$ as above and any input $x \in \{0,1\}^n$, we have

$$\Pr\left[\begin{array}{l} \forall i, Z_i = Z_{i,z[i]} \\ \wedge Z_i \neq Z_{i,1-z[i]} \end{array} : \begin{array}{l} (\{(X_{i,0}, X_{i,1})\}_{i \in [n]}, \mathsf{GC}, \{(Z_{i,0}, Z_{i,1})\}_{i \in [n_O]}) \leftarrow \mathsf{Gb}(1^{\kappa}, \mathcal{C}) \\ \{Z_i\} \leftarrow \mathsf{Eval}(\{X_{i,x[i]}, \mathsf{GC}\}) \end{array} \right]$$

where $z = \mathcal{C}(x)$, except for a negligible probability. We assume that the garbling scheme satisfies the standard security definition [5,23]. We assume that there is a simulator $\mathcal{S}_{\mathsf{Gb}}$ such that for all $\mathcal{C}$ and x, the distribution $\{\mathcal{S}_{\mathsf{Gb}}(1^{\kappa}, \mathcal{C}, \mathcal{C}(x))\}$ is computationally indistinguishable from

$$\left\{ \left(\begin{array}{l} \{X_{i,x[i]}\}_{i \in [n]}, \mathsf{GC}, \\ \{(Z_{i,0}, Z_{i,1})\}_{i \in [n_O]} \end{array} \right) : (\{(X_{i,0}, X_{i,1})\}_{i \in [n]}, \mathsf{GC}, \{(Z_{i,0}, Z_{i,1})\}_{i \in [n_O]}) \leftarrow \mathsf{Gb}(1^{\kappa}, \mathcal{C}) \right\}.$$

Verifiable Time-Lock Puzzle Scheme. We use a verifiable time-lock puzzle scheme in our protocol. We restate its definition in [10] with minor modification[2] as follows.

Definition 1. *A verifiable time-lock puzzle scheme* TLP *consisting of algorithms* $(\mathsf{Setup}, \mathsf{Gen}, \mathsf{Solve}, \mathsf{Verify}, \mathsf{Verify}')$ *with solution space* $\mathbb{S}$ *is as follows.*

- *The algorithm* Setup *takes as input* 1^{κ} *and a hardness parameter* τ, *and outputs public parameters* pp.
- *The algorithm* Gen *takes as input public parameters* pp *and a solution* $s \in \mathbb{S}$ *and then outputs a puzzle* p, *together with an opening* π.

---

[2] In particular, we include the opening π (*e.g.*, randomness) as the output of Gen for later puzzle opening. We add the algorithm Verify to verify the opening of a puzzle from the puzzle generator.

- *The deterministic algorithm* Solve *takes as input public parameters pp and a puzzle* p *and then outputs a solution s and a proof* π'.
- *The deterministic algorithm* Verify *takes as input public parameters pp, a puzzle* p, *a solution s, and an opening* π *and then outputs* true *if the solution s is the valid solution for* p. *Otherwise, the algorithm outputs* false.
- *The deterministic algorithm* Verify' *takes as input public parameters pp, a puzzle* p, *a solution s, and a proof* π' *and then outputs* true *if the solution s is valid. Otherwise, the algorithm outputs* false. *This algorithm must run in total time polynomial in* κ *and* $\log \tau$.

A verifiable time-lock puzzle scheme TLP should satisfy *completeness, correctness for opening and proof, soundness,* and *security.* We provide the definition of these properties and present a verifiable time-lock puzzle scheme [10, 26] in the full version of this paper [24].

In the description of our protocol, we do not explicitly differentiate between puzzle opening and proof, as well as between the algorithms Verify and Verify'. This is because all of these components enable efficient verification of the correctness of a given solution within the protocol.

It is worth noting that we can use a time-lock puzzle scheme to generate time-lock puzzles in a batched manner. Specifically, we can generate a solution $s \in \mathbb{S}$ and a time-lock puzzle p for s. Then, given messages $\{m_i\}$, we can use s as the seed to derive a sufficient number of (symmetric encryption) keys and randomness and encrypt messages $\{m_i\}$ using keys via IND-CPA (or IND-CCA) encryption schemes with generated randomness. For simplicity, we slightly abuse notation and denote the encryption as $\text{Enc}_s(\cdot)$. The puzzle generator can send the puzzle p and the ciphertexts of m_i's to the puzzle receiver. Note that the ciphertexts of m_i's can also be regarded as time-lock puzzles since the puzzle receiver learns nothing about the solution s before p is solved based on the security of the time-lock puzzle and the encryption scheme[3]. After solving p and obtaining s, the receiver can easily derive the messages $\{m_i\}$. In this approach, we refer to the solution s as the *master puzzle key* and the puzzle p as the *master time-lock puzzle.*

In our protocol, we use s as the seed to derive keys, and then use the random oracle with keys in CTR mode to generate enough pseudorandom padding to encrypt messages $\{m_i\}$. We can easily see that the encryption is IND-CPA-secure before s is derived from p. This scheme allows us to program the random oracle to equivocate the encrypted values in the security proof.

Remark 1. We note that given a ciphertext from the ciphertext space and a key, the decryption of the ciphertext always succeeds (although not necessarily yielding the correct result). This property is solely for the convenience of our protocol description. It is very straightforward to modify our protocol to enable honest parties to generate publicly verifiable certificates for decryption failures and attribute blame to malicious parties responsible for generating invalid ciphertexts [26].

---

[3] In this paper, we use "ciphertext" and "puzzle" interchangeably for this setting.

3   Definition of Robust PVC Security

Based on the discussion in Sect. 1.2, we define the ideal functionality $\mathcal{F}_{\mathsf{RobustPVC}}$ for robust PVC security as follows.

Functionality $\mathcal{F}_{\mathsf{RobustPVC}}$ with deterrence ϵ

Public inputs: Both parties agree on a circuit $\mathcal{C}$, which has $n = n_A + n_B$ input wires and n_O output wires.

Private inputs: $\mathsf{P_A}$ has input $x_A \in \{0,1\}^{n_A}$, whereas the other party $\mathsf{P_B}$ has input $x_B \in \{0,1\}^{n_B}$.

Both parties send their inputs to the ideal functionality. If abort from the party corrupted by the adversary is received, send $\perp$ to both parties and terminate.

- If an input of the form (cheat, $\hat{\epsilon}$), where $\hat{\epsilon} \geq \epsilon$, from the party corrupted by the adversary is received:
  - With probability $\hat{\epsilon}$, send (corrupted) to both parties and terminate.
  - With probability $1 - \hat{\epsilon}$, send (undetected) to the corrupted party. Then ignore any input of the form (cheat, ·) or (stupidCheat, ·).
- If an input of the form (stupidCheat, $\hat{\epsilon}$) from the party corrupted by the adversary is received:
  - With probability $\hat{\epsilon}$, send (corrupted) to both parties and terminate.
  - With probability $1 - \hat{\epsilon}$, send $\perp$ to both parties and terminate.
- If input $x_A \in \{0,1\}^{n_A}$ from $\mathsf{P_A}$ and $x_B \in \{0,1\}^{n_B}$ from $\mathsf{P_B}$ has been received:
  1. If both parties are honest, give $C(x_A, x_B)$ to them and terminate.
  2. If any party is corrupted, give $C(x_A, x_B)$ to the corrupted party.
  3. If a boolean function g from the adversary is received and undetected has been sent, give $g(x_A, x_B)$ to the adversary. Then if continue from the adversary is received, give cheating to the honest party if $g(x_A, x_B) = 0$, else give $C(x_A, x_B)$ to the honest party.

In order to align with the security proof, we introduce slight modifications to the definition inherited from PVC security. In the ideal functionality $\mathcal{F}_{\mathsf{RobustPVC}}$, we permit the adversary to cheat with a probability of being caught $\hat{\epsilon}$ that larger than or equal to the specified deterrence factor ϵ, i.e., $\hat{\epsilon} \geq \epsilon$. It is evident that this modification does not compromise security. Additionally, we allow the adversary to engage in *stupid cheating*. With stupid cheating, we do not impose any restrictions on the probability of remaining undetected. In this scenario, even if the adversary is not detected, the ideal functionality will still abort, rendering the adversary unable to gain any advantage. It is also apparent that this modification does not compromise security.

The definition of robust PVC security is given in the following.

Definition 2. *A two-party protocol $\Pi_{\mathsf{RobustPVC}}$ along with algorithms* Blame *and* Judge *achieves robust publicly verifiable covert (PVC) security with deterrence ϵ if the following conditions hold.*

Simulatability *The protocol $\Pi_{\mathsf{RobustPVC}}$, where the honest party might send* cert *to the adversary if cheating is detected, securely realizes $\mathcal{F}_{\mathsf{RobustPVC}}$ with deterrence ϵ.*

Public Verifiability *If the honest party outputs* corrupted *(together with an output certificate* cert*), then the output of* Judge(cert) *is* true, *except for a negligible probability.*

Defamation Freeness *For every* PPT *adversary* $\mathcal{A}$ *corrupting a party, if the other party is honest, the probability that* $\mathcal{A}$ *generates a certificate* cert* *that blames the honest party and leads to* Judge(cert*) *outputting* true *is negligible.*

Remark 2. In the definition above and the protocol description in Sect. 4, it is specified that the honest party sends the certificate to the adversary. This specification in the definition is to ensure that the adversary cannot learn any information about the honest party's input even when the certificate is provided.

Remark 3. We note that public verifiability in the definition also implies that if the honest party outputs corrupted, the malicious party cannot hinder the honest party from generating a valid certificate.

4   Our Robust PVC-Secure Protocol

In this section, we introduce the protocol $\Pi_{\text{RobustPVC}}$ that achieves robust PVC security defined in Sect. 3. This protocol is based on the idea introduced in Sect. 1.2.

The protocol description here employs λ instances instead of $\lambda+1$ in Sect. 1.2 (thus with deterrence factor $\epsilon = \frac{\lambda-2}{\lambda-1}$) for the sake of notation simplicity. The circuit for $\Pi_{\text{RobustPVC}}$ is denoted by $\mathcal{C}$, consisting of $n = n_A + n_B$ input wires and n_O output wires. The input of $\mathsf{P_A}$ is $x_A \in \{0,1\}^{n_A}$ while the input of $\mathsf{P_B}$ is $x_B \in \{0,1\}^{n_B}$.

Seed Preparation. At the beginning of the protocol, each party generates three random κ-bit strings. For example, $\mathsf{P_A}$ generates seed_j^A, seed'^A_j, and $\mathsf{witness}'^A_j$. Here, $(\mathsf{seed}'^A_j, \mathsf{witness}'^A_j)$ represents $\mathsf{P_A}$'s seed share and witness for the jth instance, as discussed in Sect. 1.2, and seed_j^A is used to derive randomness for Π_{OT} when $\mathsf{P_A}$ acts as the receiver. Each party commits to their three random strings, and the commitments will be signed by the other party later. This enables a certificate verifier to simulate the protocols execution based on these seeds/witnesses and verify the deviation of the other party, given the signature and the openings of signed commitments to these seeds/witnesses.

Next, each party executes Π_{OT} and retrieves all-but-one, *i.e.*, $\lambda - 1$, seed shares from the other party. For example, we assume that the index of the garbled circuit $\mathsf{P_A}$ will evaluate is $\hat{\jmath}_A$, then $\mathsf{P_A}$ retrieves $\{\mathsf{seed}'^B_j\}_{j \in [\lambda] \setminus \{\hat{\jmath}_A\}}$ and $\mathsf{witness}'^B_{\hat{\jmath}_A}$. Each seed is defined as $\mathsf{seed}'_j \leftarrow \mathsf{seed}'^A_j \oplus \mathsf{seed}'^B_j$. Subsequently, both parties execute the equality test protocol Π_{Eq} as mentioned in Sect. 1.2 to ensure they do not possess the same set of seeds. Furthermore, parties commit to their retrieved seed shares and witnesses, which should be opened and verified by the other party at a later stage.

Circuit and Input Preparation. After obtaining the $\lambda - 1$ seeds seed'_j's, each party can generate $\lambda - 1$ garbled circuits $\{\mathsf{GC}_j\}$ with randomness derived from $\{\mathsf{seed}'_j\}$. To avoid sending the whole garbled circuits, each party generates a commitment to each GC_j, along with its (randomly permuted) input-wire and output-wire labels, using randomness derived from seed'_j. The input-wire labels in each pair are randomly permuted to hide the semantic values of the labels when the garbled circuit is later opened for evaluation. Additionally, the garbler commits to the index of his/her input-wire labels with respect to the randomly permuted input-wire labels. This step ensures that parties cannot change the input after the instance checking. For the $\hat{\jmath}_A$th (resp. $\hat{\jmath}_B$th) instance where $\mathsf{P_A}$ (resp. $\mathsf{P_B}$) does not possess the seed, dummy materials are generated in their places. As discussed in Sect. 1.2, a party cannot directly send the commitments of the garbled circuits to the other party. Instead, each party uses the verifiable time-lock puzzle scheme to encrypt those commitments and sends them to the other party.

Then each party acting as the sender executes Π_{OT} with the other party to transmit input-wire labels. The inputs to Π_{OT} are the input-wire labels for the other parties. For each checking instance, it is essential to ensure that each party can verify the validity of the input-wire labels provided by the other party. For example, $\mathsf{P_A}$ needs to verify that $\mathsf{P_B}$ acting as the sender in Π_{OT} uses the correct input-wire labels for $\mathsf{P_A}$. Since $\mathsf{P_A}$ knows seed'_j, she knows all the correct input-wire labels. Therefore, if $\mathsf{P_A}$ knows the randomness used by $\mathsf{P_B}$ in Π_{OT}, she can check whether $\mathsf{P_B}$ deviates from the protocol. However, it is important to note that $\mathsf{P_B}$'s randomness cannot simply be derived from seed'_j or seed'^B_j that are known to $\mathsf{P_A}$. The reason is that, given those materials, $\mathsf{P_A}$ can simulate the execution of Π_{OT} and immediately determine which instance is the $\hat{\jmath}_B$th instance, *i.e.*, the dummy instance of $\mathsf{P_B}$, subsequently identify the checking instances. Hence, similar to the problem mentioned in Sect. 1.2, we need to ensure that a party can check the instance, but until all materials for certificate generation are ready. In our protocol, we additionally introduce $\mathsf{seed}^A_{j,\mathsf{OT}}$ and $\mathsf{seed}^B_{j,\mathsf{OT}}$ to address this issue. For each instance, $\mathsf{P_A}$ randomly chooses uniform κ-bit string $\mathsf{seed}^A_{j,\mathsf{OT}}$ and uses the time-lock puzzle to encrypt $\mathsf{seed}^A_{j,\mathsf{OT}}$ and input-wire labels of $\mathsf{P_B}$. Then in the execution of Π_{OT} where $\mathsf{P_A}$ acts as the sender, the inputs are time-lock puzzles for input-wire labels of $\mathsf{P_B}$, and the randomness is derived from $\mathsf{seed}^A_{j,\mathsf{OT}}$ for $\mathsf{P_A}$'s $\hat{\jmath}_A$th instance while $\mathsf{seed}'_j \oplus \mathsf{seed}^A_{j,\mathsf{OT}}$ for other instances.

Each party also acts as the receiver and executes Π_{OT} with the other party. For example, the inputs of $\mathsf{P_A}$ to Π_{OT} is 0^{n_A} for checking instance and $x_A \in [n_A]$ for the evaluation instance with index $\hat{\jmath}_A$. The randomness in each execution is derived from seed^A_j. With knowledge of seed'_j and $\mathsf{seed}^B_{j,\mathsf{OT}}$, $\mathsf{P_A}$ can later simulate the execution of $\mathsf{P_A}$ in Π_{OT} and detect $\mathsf{P_B}$'s deviations.

Publicly Verifiable Evidence Creation. Each party proceeds to sign the messages exchanged in each instance. At this stage, all materials necessary for certificate generation are available. Since all materials related to checking deviations are encrypted using time-lock puzzles, both parties are unable to perform the instance checking at this point. Therefore, we need to set the hardness parameter of the verifiable time-lock puzzle scheme to ensure that the time-lock puzzle cannot be solved until both parties have exchanged their signatures. In our protocol, we let the hardness parameter $\tau > 2\tau_c$, where τ_c is the timeout time for execution of Steps 6 and 7.

Check of Instances. Upon receiving the signature of the other party, each party can open their respective time-lock puzzles, allowing the other party to perform instance checking. If the other party fails to open the puzzles, each party can solve the puzzles themselves. With the commitments of the garbled circuit generated by the other party and the seed for Π_{OT} (*i.e.*, $\mathsf{seed}_{j,\mathsf{OT}}^A$ or/and $\mathsf{seed}_{j,\mathsf{OT}}^B$), both parties can simulate the computation of the other party for their checking instances. Among these instances, one should be a dummy instance, while the remaining instances should be correct. In case a deviation by the other party is detected, the detecting party can generate the certificate based on the signed materials, the openings/proofs for the time-lock puzzles, and the decommitments for the seeds/witnesses used in Π_{OT}.

Circuit Evaluation. Assuming the checking instances are correct, two garbled circuits remain for evaluation. First, both parties open the commitments for the seed shares and the witness they obtained at the beginning of the protocol to demonstrate their honesty. Then, they open their respective garbled circuits, input-wire labels, and the mapping of output-wire labels to each other. Both parties verify the openings provided by the other party and proceed to evaluate the garbled circuit to obtain the output-wire labels and the result. For example, $\mathsf{P_A}$ obtains the output-wire labels $\{Z_{\hat{j}_A,i}\}_{i\in[n_O]}$ and the result $z_{\hat{j}_A}$, where $\hat{j}_A$ represents $\mathsf{P_A}$'s index of instance for evaluation. $\mathsf{P_A}$ then sets $\beta_A \leftarrow \mathsf{H}(\bigoplus_{i=1}^{n_O}(Z_{\hat{j}_A,i} \oplus Z_{\hat{j}_B,i,z_{\hat{j}_A}[i]}))$, where $\{Z_{\hat{j}_B,i,b}\}_{i\in[n_O],b\in\{0,1\}}$ denotes the output-wire labels for the garbled circuit generated by $\mathsf{P_A}$ and evaluated by $\mathsf{P_B}$. Similarly, $\mathsf{P_B}$ evaluates the garbled circuit, obtains the output, and computes β_B. Finally, the two parties use the equality test protocol Π_{Eq} to determine the final evaluation result.

The full description of the protocol $\Pi_{\mathsf{RobustPVC}}$ between two parties $\mathsf{P_A}$ and $\mathsf{P_B}$ is given in the following.

Protocol $\Pi_{\mathsf{RobustPVC}}$

Schemes/Protocols: The signature scheme $(\mathsf{KGen}, \mathsf{Sig}, \mathsf{Vf})$ is EUF-CMA-secure. The verifiable time-lock puzzle scheme TLP is secure with respect to the hardness parameter $\tau > 2\tau_c$, where τ_c is the timeout time for execution of Steps 6 and 7. Com is the computational binding and hiding commitment scheme, H is the collision-resistant hash function, the encryption scheme with respect to TLP is IND-CPA-secure (see Section 2 for more information). Π_{OT} is a perfectly correct protocol that realizes $\mathcal{F}_{\mathsf{OT}}$, and Π_{Eq} is an equality test protocol that realizes $\mathcal{F}_{\mathsf{Eq}}$. The garbling scheme used in this protocol is secure.

Public inputs: Both parties agree on parameters κ, λ, and τ, and a circuit $\mathcal{C}$, which has $n = n_A + n_B$ input wires and n_O output wires. Both parties also agree on the public information (*e.g.*, time for communication rounds, algorithms, parameters, and unique *id* for the execution of this protocol). $\mathsf{P_A}$ and $\mathsf{P_B}$ know keys vk_B and vk_A, respectively, for the signature scheme.

Private inputs: P_A has input $x_A \in \{0,1\}^{n_A}$ and keys $(\mathsf{vk}_A, \mathsf{sigk}_A)$ for the signature scheme. P_B has input $x_B \in \{0,1\}^{n_B}$ and keys $(\mathsf{vk}_B, \mathsf{sigk}_B)$ for the signature scheme.

Seed Preparation

1. P_A goes through the following steps with P_B. In the meantime, they switch their roles to execute the symmetric steps, *i.e.*, P_A plays P_B's role and P_B plays P_A's.
   (a) P_A chooses uniform κ-bit strings for seed_j^A, seed'_j^A, and $\mathsf{witness}'_j^A$, and computes $c_{\mathsf{seed}_j^A} \leftarrow \mathsf{Com}(\mathsf{seed}_j^A)$, $c_{\mathsf{seed}'_j^A} \leftarrow \mathsf{Com}(\mathsf{seed}'_j^A)$, and $c_{\mathsf{witness}'_j^A} \leftarrow \mathsf{Com}(\mathsf{witness}'_j^A)$ for $j \in [\lambda]$, and sends these commitments to P_B. P_B picks $\hat{\jmath}_B \leftarrow_\$ [\lambda]$ and sets $b_{\hat{\jmath}_B} = 1$ and $b_j = 0$ for $j \neq \hat{\jmath}_B$.
   (b) P_A and P_B run λ executions of the protocol Π_{OT}. In the jth execution, P_A uses as input $(\mathsf{seed}'_j^A, \mathsf{witness}'_j^A)$ with randomness derived from seed_j^A, while P_B uses as input b_j with randomness derived from his seed_j^B generated in Step 1a. At the end, P_B has $\{\mathsf{seed}'_j^A\}_{j \neq \hat{\jmath}_B}$ and $\mathsf{witness}'_{\hat{\jmath}_B}^A$. Denote the transcript of the jth execution by trans_j^A.
   Let $\mathsf{CheckSet}_A = [\lambda] \backslash \{\hat{\jmath}_A\}$, $\mathsf{CheckSet}_B = [\lambda] \backslash \{\hat{\jmath}_B\}$, and $\mathsf{ComCheckSet} = [\lambda] \backslash \{\hat{\jmath}_A, \hat{\jmath}_B\}$.

2. P_A computes $\mathsf{seed}'_j \leftarrow \mathsf{seed}'_j^A \oplus \mathsf{seed}'_j^B$ for all $j \in \mathsf{CheckSet}_A$ and $h_A \leftarrow H(\bigoplus_{j \in \mathsf{CheckSet}_A} \mathsf{seed}'_j)$. P_B performs a similar computation to derive $\{\mathsf{seed}'_j\}$ and h_B according to his $\mathsf{CheckSet}_B$. P_A and P_B use the protocol Π_{Eq} to check whether $h_A = h_B$. If it does not hold, they continue the protocol execution. Otherwise, they restart the protocol.

3. P_A computes $c_A \leftarrow \mathsf{Com}(\hat{\jmath}_A, \{\mathsf{seed}'_j^B\}_{j \neq \hat{\jmath}_A}, \mathsf{witness}'_{\hat{\jmath}_A}^B)$ and sends it to P_B. Similarly, P_B computes and sends c_B to P_A.

Circuit and Input Preparation

4. For $j \in \mathsf{CheckSet}_A$, P_A follows the procedure below, where all randomness in the jth instance is derived from seed'_j.
   (a) P_A garbles the circuit C. Denote the jth garbled circuit by GC_j, the input-wire labels of P_A by $\{A_{j,i,b}\}_{i \in [n_A], b \in \{0,1\}}$, the input-wire labels of P_B by $\{B_{j,i,b}\}_{i \in [n_B], b \in \{0,1\}}$, and the output-wire labels by $\{Z_{j,i,b}\}_{i \in [n_O], b \in \{0,1\}}$.
   (b) P_A computes her label commitments $h_{j,i,b}^A \leftarrow \mathsf{Com}(A_{j,i,b})$ for all $i \in [n_A]$ and $b \in \{0,1\}$ and also $h_{j,i,b}^B \leftarrow \mathsf{Com}(B_{j,i,b})$ for all $i \in [n_B]$ and $b \in \{0,1\}$.
   (c) P_A computes the commitment $c_j \leftarrow \mathsf{Com}(GC_j, \{(h_{j,i,\alpha_i^A}^A, h_{j,i,\bar{\alpha}_i^A}^A)\}_{i \in [n_A]}$, $\{(h_{j,i,\alpha_i^B}^B, h_{j,i,\bar{\alpha}_i^B}^B)\}_{i \in [n_B]}, \{(H(Z_{j,i,0}), H(Z_{j,i,1}))\}_{i \in [n_O]})$, in which each pair $(h_{j,i,0}^A, h_{j,i,1}^A)$ is randomly permuted with respect to $\alpha_i^A \leftarrow_\$ \{0,1\}$, while $(h_{j,i,0}^B, h_{j,i,1}^B)$ is also randomly permuted. Denote the index of $h_{j,i,x_A[i]}^A$ with respect to $x_A[i]$ in $(h_{j,i,\alpha_i^A}^A, h_{j,i,\bar{\alpha}_i^A}^A)$ by $\gamma_j^A[i] = \alpha_i^A \oplus x[i]$, and thus the string of indices is denoted by $\gamma_j^A \in \{0,1\}^{n_A}$.
   In parallel, P_B also follows this procedure as P_A for $j \in \mathsf{CheckSet}_B$ using randomness derived from seed'_j.
   Then, P_A lets $c_{\hat{\jmath}_A} = 0$, $\gamma_{\hat{\jmath}_A}^A = 0$, and $B_{\hat{\jmath}_A,i,b} = 0$ for all $i \in [n_B]$ and $b \in \{0,1\}$. Symmetrically, P_B lets $c_{\hat{\jmath}_B} = 0$, $\gamma_{\hat{\jmath}_B}^B = 0$, and $A_{\hat{\jmath}_B,i,b} = 0$ for all $i \in [n_A]$ and $b \in \{0,1\}$.

5. P_A computes and sends $c_{\gamma_j^A} \leftarrow \mathsf{Com}(\gamma_j^A)$ for $j \in [\lambda]$ to P_B. Similarly, P_B computes and sends $c_{\gamma_j^B} \leftarrow \mathsf{Com}(\gamma_j^B)$ for $j \in [\lambda]$ to P_A.

6. For $j \in [\lambda]$, P_A chooses uniform κ-bit string $\mathsf{seed}_{j,\mathsf{OT}}^A$ and a random master puzzle key s_j^A, and generates a master time-lock puzzle $\mathsf{p}_{s_j^A}$ for s_j^A with respect to the hardness parameter τ. She also computes puzzles $\mathsf{p}_{c_j} \leftarrow \mathsf{Enc}_{s_j^A}(c_j)$, $\mathsf{p}_{\mathsf{seed}_{j,\mathsf{OT}}^A} \leftarrow \mathsf{Enc}_{s_j^A}(\mathsf{seed}_{j,\mathsf{OT}}^A)$, and $\mathsf{p}_{B_{j,i,b}} \leftarrow \mathsf{Enc}_{s_j^A}(B_{j,i,b})$ for $i \in [n_B]$ and $b \in \{0,1\}$. Then P_A sends $\mathsf{p}_{s_j^A}$, p_{c_j}, and $\mathsf{p}_{\mathsf{seed}_{j,\mathsf{OT}}^A}$ to P_B.

   P_A and P_B run λ executions of Π_{OT}. In the jth execution, P_A uses as input $\{(\mathsf{p}_{B_{j,i,0}}, \mathsf{p}_{B_{j,i,1}})\}_{i \in [n_B]}$, and P_B uses $x_B \in \{0,1\}^{n_B}$ as input if $j = \hat{j}_B$ and 0^{n_B} otherwise. Here P_A uses $(\mathsf{seed}_j' \oplus \mathsf{seed}_{j,\mathsf{OT}}^A)$ for $j \neq \hat{j}_A$ and $\mathsf{seed}_{j,\mathsf{OT}}^A$ for $j = \hat{j}_A$ to derive her randomness in the jth execution, while P_B uses seed_j^B. Finally, P_B obtains $\{\mathsf{p}_{B_{\hat{j}_B,i,x_B[i]}}\}_{i \in [n_B]}$ for the $\hat{j}_B$th execution. Denote the transcript hash for the jth execution of Π_{OT} by $\mathcal{H}_j^A$.

   Similarly, P_B also follows the same procedure as P_A, *i.e.*, P_B computes and sends $\mathsf{p}_{s_j^B}$, p_{c_j}, and $\mathsf{p}_{\mathsf{seed}_{j,\mathsf{OT}}^B}$ for $j \in [\lambda]$ to P_A. P_B also runs λ executions of Π_{OT} for input $\{(\mathsf{p}_{A_{j,i,0}}, \mathsf{p}_{A_{j,i,1}})\}_{i \in [n_A]}$ with P_A as above. Denote the transcript hash for the jth execution of Π_{OT} by $\mathcal{H}_j^B$.

Publicly Verifiable Evidence Creation

7. For each $j \in [\lambda]$, P_A generates a signature $\sigma_j^A \leftarrow \mathsf{Sig}_{\mathsf{sigk}_A}(id, \mathcal{C}, j, c_{\mathsf{seed}_j^B}, c_{\mathsf{seed}'_j^B}, c_{\mathsf{witness}'_j^B}, \mathsf{trans}_j^A, \mathsf{trans}_j^B, \mathcal{H}_j^A, \mathsf{p}_{s_j^A}, \mathsf{p}_{c_j}, \mathsf{p}_{\mathsf{seed}_{j,\mathsf{OT}}^A}, \tau, \lambda)$ and sends these signatures to P_B. Then P_B checks whether σ_j^A is valid for all $j \in [\lambda]$, and aborts with output $\bot$ if not. Similarly, P_B sends the symmetric signatures σ_j^B for all j to P_A, and P_A checks their validity.

Check of Instances

8. P_A and P_B open the master time-lock puzzle of the master puzzle key to each other. If one party does not open the puzzle, the other party can also solve the puzzle to derive the master puzzle key.

9. For each $j \in [\lambda]$, P_A decrypts P_B's p_{c_j} and $\mathsf{p}_{\mathsf{seed}_{j,\mathsf{OT}}^B}$ using the master puzzle key s_j^B to obtain c_j and $\mathsf{seed}_{j,\mathsf{OT}}^B$. P_A also decrypts $\mathsf{p}_{A_{\hat{j}_A,i,x_A[i]}}$ to obtain $A_{\hat{j}_A,i,x_A[i]}$. Note that for $j \in \mathsf{ComCheckSet}$, honest P_A holds the same seed_j' as honest P_B, and thus the same materials in Step 4. P_A follows the checking procedure below to check P_B's $\{c_j\}$ and $\{\mathcal{H}_j^B\}$. Once a certificate cert is generated during the check, P_A outputs corrupted, sends cert to P_B, and halts immediately.

   (a) For $j \in \mathsf{CheckSet}_A$, if there exists a c_j from P_B that is not equal to P_A's c_j and also $c_j \neq 0$, P_A uniformly chooses such a j and uses $\mathsf{Blame}(\mathsf{BadCom}, j)$ to generate cert.

   (b) For $j \in \mathsf{CheckSet}_A$, if c_j from P_B is equal to P_A's c_j, P_A simulates P_B's computation of $\{\mathsf{p}_{A_{j,i,b}}\}_{i \in [n_A]}$ and the executions of Π_{OT} in Step 6 with P_B's randomness derived from $\{\mathsf{seed}_j' \oplus \mathsf{seed}_{j,\mathsf{OT}}^B\}$ to derive the transcript hash $\hat{\mathcal{H}}_j^B$. If $\hat{\mathcal{H}}_j^B \neq \mathcal{H}_j^B$, P_A uniformly chooses such a j and uses $\mathsf{Blame}(\mathsf{BadOT}, j)$ to generate cert.

   For $j \in \mathsf{CheckSet}_A$, if P_B's $c_j = 0$, P_A simulates P_B's computation of $\{\mathsf{p}_{A_{j,i,b}}\}$, where $A_{j,i,b} = 0$, and the executions of Π_{OT} in Step 6 with P_B's randomness derived from $\mathsf{seed}_{j,\mathsf{OT}}^B$ to derive the transcript hash $\hat{\mathcal{H}}_j^B$. If $\hat{\mathcal{H}}_j^B \neq \mathcal{H}_j^B$, $\mathsf{P_A}$ uniformly chooses such a j and uses $\mathsf{Blame}(\mathsf{BadOT}, j)$ to generate cert.

(c) If there are more than one commitment $c_j = 0$ for $j \in \mathsf{CheckSet}_A$, uniformly choose two of them and let $J = \{j \mid c_j = 0\}$ such that $|J| = 2$. $\mathsf{P_A}$ uses $\mathsf{Blame}(\mathsf{BadNum}, J)$ to generate cert.

(d) If for all $j \in \mathsf{CheckSet}_A$, c_j from $\mathsf{P_B}$ is equal to $\mathsf{P_A}$'s c_j, $\mathsf{P_A}$ aborts with output $\perp$.

Symmetrically, $\mathsf{P_B}$ follows the same procedure to check instances (and generates cert if needed).

Circuit Evaluation

10. $\mathsf{P_A}$ opens the committed message $(\hat{j}_A, \{\mathsf{seed}'^B_j\}_{j \neq \hat{j}_A}, \mathsf{witness}'^B_{\hat{j}_A})$ inside c_A to $\mathsf{P_B}$, while $\mathsf{P_B}$ opens c_B to $\mathsf{P_A}$. If the other party does not open the commitment or the committed message is incorrect, the party aborts with output $\perp$.

11. $\mathsf{P_A}$ sends $\mathsf{GC}_{\hat{j}_B}$, $\{(h_{i,(0)}^A, h_{i,(1)}^A) = (h_{\hat{j}_B,i,\alpha_i^A}^A, h_{\hat{j}_B,i,\bar{\alpha}_i^A}^A)\}$, $\{(h_{j,i,\alpha_i^B}^B, h_{j,i,\bar{\alpha}_i^B}^B)\}$ (in the same permuted order as before), and $\{(\mathsf{H}(Z_{\hat{j}_B,i,0}), \mathsf{H}(Z_{\hat{j}_B,i,1}))\}$, together with $\mathsf{decom}_{c_{\hat{j}_B}}$ to $\mathsf{P_B}$. If $\mathsf{Com}(\mathsf{GC}_{\hat{j}_B}, \{(h_{\hat{j}_B,i,\alpha_i^A}^A, h_{\hat{j}_B,i,\bar{\alpha}_i^A}^A)\}, \{(h_{j,i,\alpha_i^B}^B, h_{j,i,\bar{\alpha}_i^B}^B)\}, \{\mathsf{H}(Z_{\hat{j}_B,i,b})\}; \mathsf{decom}_{c_{\hat{j}_B}}) \neq c_{\hat{j}_B}$ for some i, $\mathsf{P_B}$ aborts with output $\perp$.

    Symmetrically, $\mathsf{P_B}$ sends the corresponding materials with respect to the $\hat{j}_A$th instance to $\mathsf{P_A}$, and $\mathsf{P_A}$ checks the correctness of the materials.

12. $\mathsf{P_A}$ sends $\{A_{\hat{j}_B,i,x_A[i]}\}_{i \in [n_A]}$, $\gamma_{\hat{j}_B}^A$, together with decommitments $\mathsf{decom}_{\gamma_{\hat{j}_B}^A}$ and $\{\mathsf{decom}_{\hat{j}_B,i,x_A[i]}^A\}_{i \in [n_A]}$ to $\mathsf{P_B}$. If $\mathsf{Com}(\gamma_{\hat{j}_B}^A; \mathsf{decom}_{\gamma_{\hat{j}_B}^A}) \neq c_{\gamma_{\hat{j}_B}^A}$ or $\mathsf{Com}(A_{\hat{j}_B,i,x_A[i]};$
    $\mathsf{decom}_{\hat{j}_B,i,x_A[i]}^A) \neq h_{i,\gamma_{\hat{j}_B}^A[i]}^A$ for some i, $\mathsf{P_B}$ aborts with output $\perp$.

    Otherwise, $\mathsf{P_B}$ evaluates $\mathsf{GC}_{\hat{j}_B}$ with input-wire labels $\{A_{\hat{j}_B,i,x_A[i]}\}_{i \in [n_A]}$ and $\{B_{\hat{j}_B,i,x_B[i]}\}_{i \in [n_B]}$ to obtain the output-wire labels $\{Z_{\hat{j}_B,i}\}_{i \in [n_O]}$. $\mathsf{P_B}$ can derive the result $z_{\hat{j}_B}$ from $\{Z_{\hat{j}_B,i}\}_{i \in [n_O]}$ and $\{(\mathsf{H}(Z_{\hat{j}_B,i,0}), \mathsf{H}(Z_{\hat{j}_B,i,1}))\}_{i \in [n_O]}$. If any of the decoded bits is $\perp$, $\mathsf{P_B}$ then lets $z_{\hat{j}_B} = \perp$.

    Symmetrically, $\mathsf{P_B}$ sends the corresponding materials with respect to the $\hat{j}_A$th instance to $\mathsf{P_A}$. Then $\mathsf{P_A}$ checks the correctness of the materials and evaluates the $\hat{j}_A$th garbled circuits to derive the result $z_{\hat{j}_A}$.

13. If $z_{\hat{j}_A} = \perp$, $\mathsf{P_A}$ lets β_A be a random κ-bit value. Otherwise, $\mathsf{P_A}$ sets $\beta_A \leftarrow \mathsf{H}(\bigoplus_{i=1}^{n_O}(Z_{\hat{j}_A,i} \oplus Z_{\hat{j}_B,i,z_{\hat{j}_A}[i]}))$. Symmetrically, $\mathsf{P_B}$ computes his β_B. Then $\mathsf{P_A}$ and $\mathsf{P_B}$ use the equality test protocol Π_{Eq} to check whether $\beta_A = \beta_B$. If it holds, $\mathsf{P_A}$ (resp. $\mathsf{P_B}$) outputs $z_{\hat{j}_A}$ (resp. $z_{\hat{j}_B}$). Otherwise, parties abort with output cheating.

The description of the corresponding algorithm Blame that could output a publicly verifiable certificate for cheating is given in the following.

Algorithm Blame

The party $\mathsf{P_X}$ runs this algorithm to obtain a certificate cert for the malicious behavior of $\mathsf{P_Y}$. We first define the following notations:

- Denote $\mathsf{msg}_j = (id, \mathsf{trans}_j^Y, \mathsf{trans}_j^X, \mathcal{H}_j^Y, \mathsf{p}_{s_j^Y}, \mathsf{p}_{c_j}, \mathsf{p}_{\mathsf{seed}_{j,\mathsf{OT}}^Y}, \tau, \lambda)$, where p_{c_j} is the ciphertext from $\mathsf{P_Y}$.
- Denote the proof/opening with respect to $\mathsf{p}_{s_j^Y}$ for s_j^Y by $\pi_j{}^a$.

– Denote $v_j^X = (\text{seed}_j^X, \text{seed}'^X_j, \text{witness}'^X_j)$ and $\text{decom}_j = (\text{decom}_j^X, \text{decom}'^X_j, \text{decom}^X_{\text{witness}'_j})$.

The algorithm generates a certificate cert as follows depending on the received parameters.

– (BadCom, j): Output cert = $(\text{BadCom}, j, \text{msg}_j, v_j^X, \text{decom}_j, \sigma_j^Y, s_j^Y, \pi_j)$.
– (BadOT, j): Output cert = $(\text{BadOT}, j, \text{msg}_j, v_j^X, \text{decom}_j, \sigma_j^Y, s_j^Y, \pi_j)$.
– (BadNum, J): Output cert = $(\text{BadNum}, \{j, \text{msg}_j, v_j^X, \text{decom}_j, \sigma_j^Y, s_j^Y, \pi_j\}_{j \in J})$.

---

[a] Note that π_j can be provided by P_Y for puzzle opening or generated by P_X if the puzzle is solved by P_X.

In the following, we present the description of the algorithm Judge. The algorithm Judge could take as input a certificate cert generated by the algorithm Blame and output whether the accused party is cheating.

Algorithm Judge

Inputs: A public key vk_Y, a circuit $\mathcal{C}$, and a certificate cert.
Depending on the types of cheating, the algorithm verifies the certificate cert as follows.

– BadCom: Parse the remaining part as $(j, \text{msg}_j, v_j^X, \text{decom}_j, \sigma_j^Y, s_j^Y, \pi_j)$. Verify the correctness of (s_j^Y, π_j) and output false if π_j is incorrect. Derive c_j from p_{c_j}. Use v_j^X and decom_j to re-construct commitments $c_{\text{seed}_j^X}$, $c_{\text{seed}'^X_j}$, and $c_{\text{witness}'^X_j}$. Check the correctness of σ_j^Y using vk_Y, and output false if the signature is invalid. Decrypt p_{c_j} to obtain c_j. Use v_j^X to simulate the executions of Π_{OT} (in two directions) based on trans_j^X and trans_j^Y and derive seed'^Y_j in Step 1a. Verify the simulation of Π_{OT} using trans_j^X and trans_j^Y. If they do not match, output false. Then use $\text{seed}'_j = \text{seed}'^X_j \oplus \text{seed}'^Y_j$ to simulate Step 4 and obtain $\hat{c}_j$. If $c_j \neq \hat{c}_j$ and $c_j \neq 0$, output true. Otherwise, output false.
– BadOT: Parse the remaining part as $(j, \text{msg}_j, v_j^X, \text{decom}_j, \sigma_j^Y, s_j^Y, \pi_j)$. Verify the correctness of (s_j^Y, π_j), and output false if π_j is incorrect. Use v_j^X and decom_j to re-construct commitments $c_{\text{seed}_j^X}$, $c_{\text{seed}'^X_j}$, and $c_{\text{witness}'^X_j}$. Check the correctness of σ_j^Y using vk_Y, and output false if the signature is invalid. Decrypt p_{c_j} and $\mathsf{p}_{\text{seed}^Y_{j,\text{OT}}}$ to obtain c_j and $\text{seed}^Y_{j,\text{OT}}$.
If $c_j = 0$, use $\text{seed}^Y_{j,\text{OT}}$ and the master time-lock puzzle key s_j^Y to simulate the execution of Π_{OT} in Step 6, and verify whether P_Y is the first one whose message hash is different from the one in $\mathcal{H}_j^Y$. If yes, output true. Otherwise, output false.
If $c_j \neq 0$, use v_j^X to simulate the executions of Π_{OT} (in two directions) based on trans_j^X and trans_j^Y and derive seed'^Y_j in Step 1a. Verify the simulation of Π_{OT} using trans_j^X and trans_j^Y. If they do not match, output false. Compute $\text{seed}'_j \leftarrow \text{seed}'^X_j \oplus \text{seed}'^Y_j$. Then use seed'_j, $\text{seed}'_j \oplus \text{seed}^Y_{j,\text{OT}}$, and the master time-lock puzzle key s_j^Y to simulate the executions of Π_{OT} in Step 6, and verify whether P_Y is the first one whose message hash is different from the one in $\mathcal{H}_j^Y$. If yes, output true. Otherwise, output false.

– BadNum: Parse the remaining part as $\{j, \mathsf{msg}_j, \mathsf{v}_j^X, \mathsf{decom}_j, \sigma_j^Y, s_j^Y, \pi_j\}_{j \in J}$. Verify the correctness of $\{(s_j^Y, \pi_j)\}$ and output false if there exists a tuple (s_j^Y, π_j) that is incorrect. Use $\{\mathsf{v}_j^X\}$ and $\{\mathsf{decom}_j\}$ to re-construct commitments $\{\mathsf{c}_{\mathsf{seed}_j^X}\}$, $\{\mathsf{c}_{\mathsf{seed}'_j^X}\}$, and $\{\mathsf{c}_{\mathsf{witness}'_j^X}\}$. Check the correctness of $\{\sigma_j^Y\}$ using vk_Y, and output false if there exists a signature that is invalid. Decrypt $\{\mathsf{p}_{\mathsf{c}_j}\}$ to obtain $\{\mathsf{c}_j\}$. If $\mathsf{c}_j = 0$ for all $j \in J$, output true. Otherwise, output false.

Theorem 1. *The protocol $\Pi_{\mathsf{RobustPVC}}$ along with algorithms Blame and Judge is robust publicly verifiable covert secure with deterrence $\epsilon = 1 - \frac{1}{\lambda - 1}$.*

Proof. We prove the robust PVC security of $\Pi_{\mathsf{RobustPVC}}$ by showing its simulatability, public verifiability, and defamation freeness.

Simulatability. We first prove that $\Pi_{\mathsf{RobustPVC}}$ securely realizes $\mathcal{F}_{\mathsf{RobustPVC}}$ with deterrence $\epsilon = 1 - \frac{1}{\lambda - 1}$. Without loss of generality, we assume that $\mathsf{P_B}$ is honest and $\mathsf{P_A}$ is corrupted by $\mathcal{A}$. Since the roles of $\mathsf{P_A}$ and $\mathsf{P_B}$ in $\Pi_{\mathsf{RobustPVC}}$ is symmetric, the proof for the scenario where $\mathsf{P_B}$ is corrupted is similar.

For an adversary $\mathcal{A}$ corrupting $\mathsf{P_A}$ in the real world, we construct a simulator $\mathcal{S}$ holding vk_A that runs $\mathcal{A}$ as a sub-routine with auxiliary input z and interacts with $\mathcal{F}_{\mathsf{RobustPVC}}$ in the ideal world. The simulation procedure is presented below.

0. $\mathcal{S}$ uses KGen to generate a pair of key $(\mathsf{vk}_B, \mathsf{sigk}_B)$ and sends vk_B to $\mathcal{A}$.
1. $\mathcal{S}$ goes through the following steps with $\mathcal{A}$.
   (a) $\mathcal{S}$ receives $\{\mathsf{c}_{\mathsf{seed}_j^A}, \mathsf{c}_{\mathsf{seed}'_j^A}, \mathsf{c}_{\mathsf{witness}'_j^A}\}_{j \in [\lambda]}$ from $\mathcal{A}$. In the meantime, $\mathcal{S}$ picks uniform κ-bit strings $\{\mathsf{seed}_j^B, \mathsf{seed}'_j^B, \mathsf{witness}'_j^B\}_{j \in [\lambda]}$, computes $\{\mathsf{c}_{\mathsf{seed}_j^B}, \mathsf{c}_{\mathsf{seed}'_j^B}, \mathsf{c}_{\mathsf{witness}'_j^B}\}_{j \in [\lambda]}$, and sends these commitments to $\mathcal{A}$ as in the protocol.
   (b) For all j, $\mathcal{S}$ playing the role of the receiver uses $b_j = 0$ to retrieve seed'_j^A in Π_{OT} with randomness derived from seed_j^B. $\mathcal{S}$ also plays the role of the sender and uses $\{(\mathsf{seed}'_j^B, \mathsf{witness}'_j^B)\}_{j \in [\lambda]}$ as input in Π_{OT} with randomness derived from seed_j^B.
2. $\mathcal{S}$ computes $\mathsf{seed}'_j = \mathsf{seed}'_j^A \oplus \mathsf{seed}'_j^B$ for all $j \in [\lambda]$. Then $\mathcal{S}$ let $h_B^j \leftarrow \mathsf{H}(\bigoplus_{[\lambda]\backslash j} \mathsf{seed}'_j)$ for all $j \in [\lambda]$. For the execution of Π_{Eq}, $\mathcal{S}$ uses the simulator $\mathcal{S}_{\mathsf{Eq}}$, *i.e.*, the corresponding simulator for the protocol Π_{Eq}, to obtain h_A. If there exists h_B^j, such that $h_B^j = h_A$, $\mathcal{S}$ sets $\mathsf{GoodEq} = \mathsf{true}$ and picks $\hat{j}_B \leftarrow_\$ [\lambda]$. If $h_B^{\hat{j}_B} = h_A$, $\mathcal{S}$ returns true for Π_{Eq} to $\mathcal{A}$ and restarts the protocol, and otherwise returns false for Π_{Eq} to $\mathcal{A}$. If there is no h_B^j, such that $h_B^j = h_A$, $\mathcal{S}$ sets $\mathsf{GoodEq} = \mathsf{false}$ and returns false for Π_{Eq} to $\mathcal{A}$.
3. $\mathcal{S}$ computes and sends dummy commitment c_B to $\mathcal{A}$. $\mathcal{S}$ also receives commitment c_A from $\mathcal{A}$.
4. For all $j \in [\lambda]$, $\mathcal{S}$ prepares garbled circuits and input materials as in Step 4 of the protocol.
5. $\mathcal{S}$ computes and sends dummy commitment $\{\mathsf{c}_{\gamma_j^B}\}$ to $\mathcal{A}$. $\mathcal{S}$ also receives $\{\mathsf{c}_{\gamma_j^A}\}$ from $\mathcal{A}$.
6. $\mathcal{S}$ generates the puzzle $\mathsf{p}_{s_j^B}$ for a random chosen master puzzle key s_j^B as in the protocol for $j \in [\lambda]$. $\mathcal{S}$ also generates dummy ciphertexts for his $\mathsf{p}_{\mathsf{c}_j}$ and $\mathsf{p}_{\mathsf{seed}_{j,\mathsf{OT}}^B}$ for $j \in [\lambda]$. Then $\mathcal{S}$ sends these puzzles to $\mathcal{A}$.
   $\mathcal{S}$ receives puzzles $\mathsf{p}_{s_j^A}$, $\mathsf{p}_{\hat{\mathsf{c}}_j}$, and $\mathsf{p}_{\mathsf{seed}_{j,\mathsf{OT}}^A}$ for $j \in [\lambda]$ from $\mathcal{A}$. Since time-lock puzzles can be solved in polynomial time, $\mathcal{S}$ can decrypt these puzzles and derive s_j^A, $\hat{\mathsf{c}}_j$, and $\mathsf{seed}_{j,\mathsf{OT}}^A$ for $j \in [\lambda]$.
   For λ executions of Π_{OT} where $\mathcal{S}$ plays the role of the receiver, $\mathcal{S}$ uses as input 0^{n_B} and randomness derived from seed_j^B and receives $\mathcal{A}$'s $\{\mathsf{p}_{B_{j,i,0}}\}$. Let $\mathcal{H}_j^A$ denote the transcript hash for the jth executions.
   For λ executions of Π_{OT} where $\mathcal{S}$ plays the role of the sender, $\mathcal{S}$ first generates dummy ciphertexts $\{\mathsf{p}_{A_{j,i,b}}\}$ and random κ-bit string seed''_j for all $j \in [\lambda]$. Then $\mathcal{S}$ executes Π_{OT} with $\mathcal{A}$ using $\{(\mathsf{p}_{A_{j,i,0}}, \mathsf{p}_{A_{j,i,1}})\}_{i \in [n_A]}$ as input with randomness derived from seed''_j.
7. $\mathcal{S}$ generates signatures $\{\sigma_j^B\}$ as an honest $\mathsf{P_B}$ and sends them to $\mathcal{A}$.

$\mathcal{S}$ also receives $\{\sigma_j^A\}$ from $\mathcal{A}$. If any of the signatures are invalid, $\mathcal{S}$ executes the *finishing touches* procedure as follows and sends abort to $\mathcal{F}_{\text{RobustPVC}}$ to terminate the execution of the protocol.

(a) Choose $\hat{j}_B \leftarrow_{\$} [\lambda]$ if GoodEq = false, and otherwise use $\hat{j}_B$ chosen in Step 2 in this simulation.

(b) Program the random oracle to let the decryption of $\mathsf{p}_{\mathsf{c}_{\hat{j}_B}}$ be 0, decryption of $\mathsf{p}_{\mathsf{c}_j}$ be c_j for $j \in [\lambda]\backslash\{\hat{j}_B\}$, and decryption of $\{\mathsf{p}_{A_{j,i,b}}\}$ be the correct values as those in the protocol for $j \in [\lambda]\backslash\{\hat{j}_B\}$ and $j = \hat{j}_B$, respectively.

(c) Program the random oracle: for the $\hat{j}_B$th instance, let the decryption of $\mathsf{p}_{\text{seed}^B_{\hat{j}_B},\text{OT}}$ be $\text{seed}^B_{\hat{j}_B,\text{OT}} = \text{seed}''_{\hat{j}_B}$. For $j \in [\lambda]\backslash\{\hat{j}_B\}$, let the decryption of $\mathsf{p}_{\text{seed}^B_{j,\text{OT}}}$ be the decryption of $\mathsf{p}_{\text{seed}^B_{j,\text{OT}}}$ be $\text{seed}^B_{j,\text{OT}} = \text{seed}''_j \oplus \text{seed}'_j$.

Then $\mathcal{S}$ simulates the computation of an honest P_A playing the role of the sender in the executions of Π_{OT} in Step 6 of the protocol and obtain $\hat{\mathcal{H}}^A_j$. If $\hat{\mathsf{c}}_j = 0$, the simulation is based on $\text{seed}^A_{j,\text{OT}}$ as the $\hat{j}_A$th instance in the protocol. If $\hat{\mathsf{c}}_j = \mathsf{c}_j$, the simulation is based on $\text{seed}'_j \oplus \text{seed}^A_{j,\text{OT}}$ as other instances in the protocol. Let J_z be the set of indices that $\hat{\mathsf{c}}_j = 0$ and $\hat{\mathcal{H}}^A_j$ matches the simulation of Π_{OT} for the $\hat{j}_A$th instance as described in the protocol. Let J_s be the set of indices that $\hat{\mathsf{c}}_j = \mathsf{c}_j$ and $\hat{\mathcal{H}}^A_j$ matches the simulation of Π_{OT} for the checking instances.

Hence, there are following cases (let Stupid = false and Type $=\perp$ by default):

- If $|J_s| < \lambda - 2$, $\mathcal{S}$ executes the *finishing touches* procedure as in Step 7a–7c of the simulation, sends (cheat, 1) to $\mathcal{F}_{\text{RobustPVC}}$, receives corrupted, opens the puzzle as in Step 8 of the protocol, generates the certificate cert with respect to j and the inconsistent $\hat{\mathsf{c}}_j$ or $\hat{\mathcal{H}}^A_j$ as in the protocol. $\mathcal{S}$ then sends cert to $\mathcal{A}$ as Step 9 of the protocol to complete the simulation.

- If $|J_s| = \lambda - 2$ and $|J_z| = 2$, $\mathcal{S}$ sets Stupid = true and sends (stupidCheat, $\frac{\lambda-2}{\lambda}$) to $\mathcal{F}_{\text{RobustPVC}}$. If $\mathcal{F}_{\text{RobustPVC}}$ returns corrupted, $\mathcal{S}$ sets caught = ($\frac{\lambda-2}{\lambda}$, true) and Type = BadNum. If $\mathcal{F}_{\text{RobustPVC}}$ returns $\perp$, $\mathcal{S}$ sets caught = ($\frac{\lambda-2}{\lambda}$, false). Then $\mathcal{S}$ continues the simulation.

- If $|J_s| = \lambda - 2$, $|J_z| = 1$, and GoodEq = true, $\mathcal{S}$ sends (cheat, $\frac{\lambda-2}{\lambda-1}$) to $\mathcal{F}_{\text{RobustPVC}}$. If $\mathcal{F}_{\text{RobustPVC}}$ returns corrupted, $\mathcal{S}$ sets caught = ($\frac{\lambda-2}{\lambda-1}$, true) and Type according to the possible certificate with respect to the inconsistent $\hat{\mathsf{c}}_j$ or $\hat{\mathcal{H}}^A_j$. If $\mathcal{F}_{\text{RobustPVC}}$ returns undetected, $\mathcal{S}$ sets caught = ($\frac{\lambda-2}{\lambda-1}$, false). Then $\mathcal{S}$ continues the simulation.

- If $|J_s| = \lambda - 2$, $|J_z| = 1$, and GoodEq = false, $\mathcal{S}$ sends (cheat, $\frac{\lambda-1}{\lambda}$) to $\mathcal{F}_{\text{RobustPVC}}$. If $\mathcal{F}_{\text{RobustPVC}}$ returns corrupted, $\mathcal{S}$ sets caught = ($\frac{\lambda-1}{\lambda}$, true) and Type according to the possible certificate with respect to the inconsistent $\hat{\mathsf{c}}_j$ or $\hat{\mathcal{H}}^A_j$. If $\mathcal{F}_{\text{RobustPVC}}$ returns undetected, $\mathcal{S}$ sets caught = ($\frac{\lambda-1}{\lambda}$, false). Then $\mathcal{S}$ continues the simulation.

- If $|J_s| = \lambda - 2$ and $|J_z| = 0$, $\mathcal{S}$ executes the *finishing touches* procedure as in Step 7a–7c, sends (cheat, 1) to $\mathcal{F}_{\text{RobustPVC}}$, receives corrupted, opens the puzzle as in Step 8 of the protocol, generates the certificate cert with respect to j and the inconsistent $\hat{\mathsf{c}}_j$ or $\hat{\mathcal{H}}^A_j$ as in the protocol, and sends cert to $\mathcal{A}$ as in Step 9 of the protocol to complete the simulation.

- If $|J_s| = \lambda - 1$, $|J_z| = 1$, and GoodEq = true, $\mathcal{S}$ sets caught $=\perp$. Then $\mathcal{S}$ continues the simulation.

- If $|J_s| = \lambda - 1$, $|J_z| = 1$, and GoodEq = false, then $\mathcal{S}$ tosses a coin, which with probability $\frac{1}{\lambda}$ outputs false and $\frac{\lambda-1}{\lambda}$ outputs true. If the output is false, then $\mathcal{S}$ executes the *finishing touches* procedure as follows, opens his puzzle, and sends abort to $\mathcal{F}_{\text{RobustPVC}}$ to terminate the execution of the protocol.

  (a) Let $\hat{j}_B$ be the element in J_z.

  (b) Program the random oracle to let the decryption of $\mathsf{p}_{\mathsf{c}_{\hat{j}_B}}$ be 0, decryption of $\mathsf{p}_{\mathsf{c}_j}$ be c_j for $j \in [\lambda]\backslash\{\hat{j}_B\}$, and decryption of $\{\mathsf{p}_{A_{j,i,b}}\}$ be the correct values as those in the protocol for $j \in [\lambda]\backslash\{\hat{j}_B\}$ and $j = \hat{j}_B$, respectively.

  (c) Program the random oracle: Let the decryption of $\mathsf{p}_{\text{seed}^B_{\hat{j}_B},\text{OT}}$ be $\text{seed}^B_{\hat{j}_B,\text{OT}} = \text{seed}''_{\hat{j}_B}$. For $j \in [\lambda]\backslash\{\hat{j}_B\}$, let the decryption of $\mathsf{p}_{\text{seed}^B_{j,\text{OT}}}$ be $\text{seed}^B_{j,\text{OT}} = \text{seed}''_j \oplus \text{seed}'_j$.

  If the output is true, then $\mathcal{S}$ sets caught $=\perp$ and continues the simulation.

- If $|J_s| = \lambda - 1$ and $|J_z| = 0$, $\mathcal{S}$ sets Stupid = true and then sends the message (stupidCheat, $\frac{\lambda-1}{\lambda}$) to $\mathcal{F}_{\text{RobustPVC}}$. If $\mathcal{F}_{\text{RobustPVC}}$ returns corrupted, $\mathcal{S}$ executes the *finishing touches* by picking $\hat{j}_B \leftarrow_{\$} J_s$, programming the random oracle to let the decryption of $\mathsf{p}_{\mathsf{c}_{\hat{j}_B}}$ be 0, decryption of $\mathsf{p}_{\mathsf{c}_j}$

be c_j for $j \in [\lambda] \backslash \{\hat{j}_B\}$, and decryption of $\{p_{A_{j,i,b}}\}$ be the correct values as those in the protocol for $j \in [\lambda] \backslash \{\hat{j}_B\}$ and $j = \hat{j}_B$, respectively. $\mathcal{S}$ also programs the random oracle: for the $\hat{j}_B$th instance, let the decryption of $p_{\text{seed}_{\hat{j}_B,\text{OT}}^B}$ be $\text{seed}_{\hat{j}_B,\text{OT}}^B = \text{seed}_{\hat{j}_B}''$.

For $j \in [\lambda] \backslash \{\hat{j}_B\}$, let the decryption of $p_{\text{seed}_{j,\text{OT}}^B}$ be $\text{seed}_{j,\text{OT}}^B = \text{seed}_j'' \oplus \text{seed}_j'$. Then $\mathcal{S}$ opens the puzzle as in Step 8 of the protocol, generates the certificate cert with respect to the inconsistent $\hat{c}_j$ or $\hat{\mathcal{H}}_j^A$ as in the protocol. $\mathcal{S}$ then sends cert to $\mathcal{A}$ as Step 9 of the protocol to complete the simulation.

If $\mathcal{F}_{\text{RobustPVC}}$ returns $\perp$, $\mathcal{S}$ executes the *finishing touches* by picking $\hat{j}_B \leftarrow_\$ [\lambda] \backslash J_s$ and programming the random oracle following the same procedure as $\mathcal{F}_{\text{RobustPVC}}$ returns corrupted. Then $\mathcal{S}$ opens his puzzle as in Step 8 of the protocol, and simulates the abortion of the honest P_B to terminate the simulation.

- If $|J_s| = \lambda$, $\mathcal{S}$ executes the *finishing touches* procedure as in Step 7a-7c in this simulation, opens his puzzle, and sends abort to $\mathcal{F}_{\text{RobustPVC}}$ to terminate the execution of the protocol.

Rewind $\mathcal{A}$ and run steps $1' - 7'$ below until[a] $|J_s'| = |J_s|$, $|J_z'| = |J_z|$, caught$'$ = caught, GoodEq$'$ = GoodEq, Stupid$'$ = Stupid, and Type$'$ = Type.

$1'$. $\mathcal{S}$ goes through the following steps with $\mathcal{A}$.

   (a) $\mathcal{S}$ receives the commitments $\{c_{\text{seed}_j^A}, c_{\text{seed}_j'^A}, c_{\text{witness}_j'^A}\}_{j \in [\lambda]}$ from $\mathcal{A}$. In the meantime, $\mathcal{S}$ playing the role of P_B randomly chooses $\hat{j}_B \leftarrow_\$ [\lambda]$ and then picks uniform κ-bit strings $\{\text{seed}_j^B, \text{seed}_j'^B, \text{witness}_j'^B\}_{j \in [\lambda]}$. $\mathcal{S}$ then computes $c_{\text{seed}_j^B}$, $c_{\text{seed}_j'^B}$, and $c_{\text{witness}_j'^B}$ for $j \in [\lambda] \backslash \{\hat{j}_B\}$ as in the protocol and let $c_{\text{seed}_{\hat{j}_B}^B}$, $c_{\text{seed}_{\hat{j}_B}'^B}$, and $c_{\text{witness}_{\hat{j}_B}^B}$ be dummy commitments. Finally, $\mathcal{S}$ sends these commitments to $\mathcal{A}$ as in the protocol.

   (b) For all $j \in [\lambda] \backslash \{\hat{j}_B\}$, $\mathcal{S}$ playing the role of the receiver uses $b_j = 0$ to retrieve $\{\text{seed}_j'^A\}_{j \in [\lambda] \backslash \{\hat{j}_B\}}$ with randomness derived from $\{\text{seed}_j^B\}$. For the $\hat{j}_B$th instance, $\mathcal{S}$ runs the simulator $\mathcal{S}_{\text{OT}}$ for the protocol Π_{OT}, and extracts $(\text{seed}_{\hat{j}_B}'^A, \text{witness}_{\hat{j}_B}'^A)$. $\mathcal{S}$ also plays the role of the sender and uses $\{(\text{seed}_j'^B, \text{witness}_j'^B)\}_{j \in [\lambda]}$ as input with randomness derived from seed_j^B.

$2'$. $\mathcal{S}$ computes $\text{seed}_j' = \text{seed}_j'^A \oplus \text{seed}_j'^B$ for all $j \in [\lambda]$. Then $\mathcal{S}$ let $h_B^j \leftarrow H(\bigoplus_{[\lambda] \backslash j} \text{seed}_j')$ for all $j \in [\lambda]$. $\mathcal{S}$ uses the simulator $\mathcal{S}_{\text{Eq}}$ for Π_{Eq} to obtain h_A. If there exists h_B^j, such that $h_B^j = h_A$, $\mathcal{S}$ sets GoodEq$'$ = true. Then if $h_B^{j_B} = h_A$, $\mathcal{S}$ returns true for Π_{Eq} to $\mathcal{A}$ and restart the protocol, and otherwise returns false for Π_{Eq} to $\mathcal{A}$. If there is no $h_B^j = h_A$, $\mathcal{S}$ sets GoodEq$'$ = false and returns false for Π_{Eq} to $\mathcal{A}$.

$3'$. $\mathcal{S}$ computes and sends commitment c_B to $\mathcal{A}$. $\mathcal{S}$ also receives commitment c_A from $\mathcal{A}$. $\mathcal{S}$ extracts $(\hat{j}_A, \{\text{seed}_j'^B\}_{j \neq \hat{j}_A}, \text{witness}_{\hat{j}_A}'^B)$ from c_A. If this extracted message is correct, store $\hat{j}_A$. Otherwise, let $\hat{j}_A = \perp$.

$4'$. For all $j \in [\lambda]$, $\mathcal{S}$ prepares garbled circuits and input materials as in Step 4 of the protocol.

$5'$. $\mathcal{S}$ computes and sends dummy $\{c_{\gamma_j^B}\}$ to $\mathcal{A}$. $\mathcal{S}$ also receives $\{c_{\gamma_j^A}\}$ from $\mathcal{A}$.

$6'$. $\mathcal{S}$ generates puzzles $p_{s_j^B}$ for a random chosen master puzzle key s_j^B and ciphertexts $p_{\text{seed}_{j,\text{OT}}^B}$ for $j \in [\lambda]$ as in the protocol. $\mathcal{S}$ generates ciphertexts p_{c_j} for computed c_j for $j \in [\lambda] \backslash \{\hat{j}_B\}$ and let the ciphertext $p_{c_{\hat{j}_B}}$ encrypt 0. Then $\mathcal{S}$ sends these puzzles to $\mathcal{A}$.

$\mathcal{S}$ receives puzzles $p_{s_j^A}$, $p_{\hat{c}_j}$, and $p_{\text{seed}_{j,\text{OT}}^A}$ for $j \in [\lambda]$ from $\mathcal{A}$. Since time-lock puzzles can be solved in polynomial time, $\mathcal{S}$ can decrypt these puzzles and derive s_j^A, $\hat{c}_j$, and $\text{seed}_{j,\text{OT}}^A$ for $j \in [\lambda]$.

For all $j \neq \hat{j}_B$, $\mathcal{S}$ playing the role of the receiver runs Π_{OT} with $\mathcal{A}$, using input 0^{n_B} and randomness derived from seed_j^B. In this way, $\mathcal{S}$ receives $\mathcal{A}$'s $\{p_{B_{j,i,0}}\}$. In the $\hat{j}_B$th execution of Π_{OT}, $\mathcal{S}$ playing the role of the receiver uses the simulator $\mathcal{S}_{\text{OT}}$ for Π_{OT} to extract $\{p_{B_{\hat{j}_B,i,b}}\}_{i \in [n_B], b \in \{0,1\}}$. $\mathcal{S}$ can decrypt $\{p_{B_{\hat{j}_B,i,b}}\}_{i \in [n_B], b \in \{0,1\}}$ and obtain $\{B_{\hat{j}_B,i,b}\}_{i \in [n_B], b \in \{0,1\}}$.

If $\hat{j}_A = \perp$, $\mathcal{S}$ first generates ciphertexts for $\{p_{A_{j,i,b}}\}$ for $j \in [\lambda]$ as in the protocol. Then, $\mathcal{S}$ playing the role of the sender executes Π_{OT} with $\mathcal{A}$ using $\{(p_{A_{j,i,0}}, p_{A_{j,i,1}})\}_{i \in [n_A]}$ as input with randomness derived from $\text{seed}_j' \oplus \text{seed}_{j,\text{OT}}^B$ or $\text{seed}_{j,\text{OT}}^B$ as in the protocol. If $\hat{j}_A \neq \perp$, $\mathcal{S}$ generates ciphertexts for $\{p_{A_{j,i,b}}\}$ for $j \in [\lambda] \backslash \{\hat{j}_A\}$ as in the protocol. For $[\lambda] \backslash \{\hat{j}_A\}$, $\mathcal{S}$ playing the role of the sender executes Π_{OT} with $\mathcal{A}$ using $\{(p_{A_{j,i,0}}, p_{A_{j,i,1}})\}_{i \in [n_A]}$ as input with randomness derived from $\text{seed}_j' \oplus \text{seed}_{j,\text{OT}}^B$ or $\text{seed}_{j,\text{OT}}^B$ as in the protocol. For

$j = \hat{\jmath}_A$, $\mathcal{S}$ runs the simulator $\mathcal{S}_{\mathsf{OT}}$ for Π_{OT} to extract the input x_A and returns dummy ciphertexts $\{\mathsf{p}_{A_{\hat{\jmath}_A,i}}\}$ to $\mathcal{A}$.

7′. $\mathcal{S}$ generates $\{\sigma_j^B\}$ as an honest P_B in the protocol and sends them to $\mathcal{A}$. $\mathcal{S}$ also receives $\{\sigma_j^A\}$ from $\mathcal{A}$. If any of the signatures are invalid, then return to Step 1′.

Then $\mathcal{S}$ simulates the computation of an honest P_A playing the role of the sender in the executions of Π_{OT} in Step 6 of the protocol and obtain $\hat{\mathcal{H}}_j^A$. If $\hat{\mathsf{c}}_j = 0$, the simulation is based on $\mathsf{seed}_{j,\mathsf{OT}}^A$ as the $\hat{\jmath}_A$th instance in the protocol. If $\hat{\mathsf{c}}_j = \mathsf{c}_j$, the simulation is based on $\mathsf{seed}_j' \oplus \mathsf{seed}_{j,\mathsf{OT}}^A$ as other instances in the protocol. Let J_z' be the set of indices that $\hat{\mathsf{c}}_j = 0$ and $\hat{\mathcal{H}}_j^A$ matches the simulation of Π_{OT} for the $\hat{\jmath}_A$th instance as described in the protocol. Let J_s' be the set of indices that $\hat{\mathsf{c}}_j = \mathsf{c}_j$ and $\hat{\mathcal{H}}_j^A$ matches the simulation of Π_{OT} for the checking instances.

Hence, there are following cases (let Stupid′ = false and Type′ $=\perp$ by default):

- If $|J_s'| < \lambda - 2$, then return to Step 1′.
- If $|J_s'| = \lambda - 2$ and $|J_z'| = 2$, $\mathcal{S}$ sets Stupid′ = true. If $\hat{\jmath}_B \in J_s'$, $\mathcal{S}$ sets caught′ = $(\frac{\lambda-2}{\lambda}, \text{true})$ and Type′ = BadNum. Otherwise, $\mathcal{S}$ sets caught′ = $(\frac{\lambda-2}{\lambda}, \text{false})$.
- When $|J_s'| = \lambda - 2$, $|J_z'| = 1$, and GoodEq′ = true, if $\hat{\jmath}_B \in J_s'$, $\mathcal{S}$ sets caught′ = $(\frac{\lambda-2}{\lambda-1}, \text{true})$ and Type′ according to the possible certificate with respect to the inconsistent $\hat{\mathsf{c}}_j$ or $\hat{\mathcal{H}}_j^A$. Otherwise, $\mathcal{S}$ sets caught′ = $(\frac{\lambda-2}{\lambda}, \text{false})$.
- When $|J_s'| = \lambda - 2$, $|J_z'| = 1$, and GoodEq′ = false, if $\hat{\jmath}_B \in J_s'$ or $\hat{\jmath}_B \in J_z'$, $\mathcal{S}$ sets caught′ = $(\frac{\lambda-1}{\lambda}, \text{true})$ and Type′ according to the possible certificate with respect to the inconsistent $\hat{\mathsf{c}}_j$ or $\hat{\mathcal{H}}_j^A$. Otherwise, $\mathcal{S}$ sets caught′ = $(\frac{\lambda-1}{\lambda}, \text{false})$.
- If $|J_s'| = \lambda - 2$ and $|J_z'| = 0$, then return to Step 1′.
- If $|J_s'| = \lambda - 1$, $|J_z'| = 1$, and GoodEq′ = true, $\mathcal{S}$ sets caught′ $=\perp$.
- When $|J_s'| = \lambda - 1$, $|J_z'| = 1$, and GoodEq′ = false, if $\hat{\jmath} \in J_s$, then $\mathcal{S}$ sets caught′ $=\perp$. Otherwise, return to Step 1′.
- If $|J_s'| = \lambda - 1$ and $|J_z'| = 0$, then return to Step 1′.
- If $|J_s'| = \lambda$, then return to Step 1′.

8. If $\hat{\jmath}_A \neq \perp$, $\mathcal{S}$ sends x_A to $\mathcal{F}_{\mathsf{RobustPVC}}$ and receives the output z. Then $\mathcal{S}$ regenerates the garbled circuit via

$$(\{A_{\hat{\jmath}_A,i}\}, \{B_{\hat{\jmath}_A,i}\}, \mathsf{GC}_{\hat{\jmath}_A}, \{Z_{\hat{\jmath}_A,i,b}\}) \leftarrow \mathcal{S}_{\mathsf{Gb}}(1^\kappa, \mathcal{C}, z)$$

and recomputes the materials of the $\hat{\jmath}_A$th instance in Step 4b and 4c of the protocol. Since this garbled circuit is simulated, $\mathcal{S}$ uses/programs dummy commitments/values in case of need, e.g., for $\gamma_{\hat{\jmath}_A}^B$. $\mathcal{S}$ also uses the random oracle to program the opening of $\mathsf{c}_{\hat{\jmath}_A}$ and $\{\mathsf{p}_{A_{\hat{\jmath}_A,i}}\}$ with respect to the simulated garbled circuit. Then $\mathcal{S}$ opens his puzzle to $\mathcal{A}$ as in the protocol. $\mathcal{A}$ may also open her puzzle.

9. If caught′ = $(\cdot, \text{true})$, $\mathcal{S}$ generates the corresponding cert and sends it to $\mathcal{A}$ to complete the simulation.

10. $\mathcal{S}$ sends the opening for c_B to $\mathcal{A}$ as in the protocol. $\mathcal{S}$ also receives the opening for c_A from $\mathcal{A}$. If Stupid′ = true, $\mathcal{S}$ simulates the abortion of the honest party to complete the simulation. If the opening $(\hat{\jmath}_A, \{\mathsf{seed}_j'^B\}_{j \neq \hat{\jmath}_A}, \mathsf{witness}_{\hat{\jmath}_A}'^B)$ is not correct, $\mathcal{S}$ sends abort to $\mathcal{F}_{\mathsf{RobustPVC}}$ and simulates the abortion of the honest party to complete the simulation.

11. $\mathcal{S}$ sends the simulated garbled circuit $\mathsf{GC}_{\hat{\jmath}_A}$, together with corresponding label hash values, to $\mathcal{A}$. $\mathcal{S}$ also receives the garbled circuit $\mathsf{GC}_{\hat{\jmath}_B}$ and related materials from $\mathcal{A}$. If they are invalid, $\mathcal{S}$ sends abort to $\mathcal{F}_{\mathsf{RobustPVC}}$ and simulates the abortion of the honest party to complete the simulation.

12. $\mathcal{S}$ sends the simulated labels, $\gamma_{\hat{\jmath}_A}^B$, and corresponding decommitments to $\mathcal{A}$. $\mathcal{S}$ also receives the labels, $\gamma_{\hat{\jmath}_B}^A$, and corresponding decommitments. If the received materials are invalid, $\mathcal{S}$ sends abort to $\mathcal{F}_{\mathsf{RobustPVC}}$ and simulates the abortion of the honest party to complete the simulation.

13. $\mathcal{S}$ uses the simulator $\mathcal{S}_{\mathsf{Eq}}$ for Π_{Eq} to obtain β_A from $\mathcal{A}$. Then $\mathcal{S}$ defines the boolean function g as follows.

(a) On input $x_B \in \{0,1\}^{n_B}$, select the corresponding input labels for x_B in the label tuples $\{(B_{\hat{\jmath}_B,i,0}, B_{\hat{\jmath}_B,i,1})\}_{i \in [n_B]}$.

(b) Evaluate the garbled circuit $\mathsf{GC}_{\hat{\jmath}_B}$ with the input-wire labels $\{A_{\hat{\jmath}_B,i,x_A[i]}\}_{i \in [n_A]}$ and $\{B_{\hat{\jmath}_B,i,x_B[i]}\}_{i \in [n_B]}$ as in the protocol to obtain $\{Z_{\hat{\jmath}_B,i}\}_{i \in [n_O]}$ and $z_{\hat{\jmath}_B}$. In particular, if some error occurs in the evaluation of garbled circuit, some hard-coded random values provided by $\mathcal{S}$ are used for $\{Z_{\hat{\jmath}_B,i}\}_{i \in [n_O]}$ and $z_{\hat{\jmath}_B}$.

(c) Compute $\beta_B \leftarrow \mathsf{H}(\bigoplus_{i=1}^{n_O}(Z_{\hat{\jmath}_A,i,z_{\hat{\jmath}_B}[i]} \oplus Z_{\hat{\jmath}_B,i,z_{\hat{\jmath}_B}[i]}))$.

(d) If $\beta_A = \beta_B$, return true. Otherwise, return false.

$\mathcal{S}$ sends g to $\mathcal{F}_{\text{RobustPVC}}$, receives the output e from $\mathcal{F}_{\text{RobustPVC}}$, and gives e to $\mathcal{A}$. If $\mathcal{A}$ does not abort, $\mathcal{S}$ sends continue to $\mathcal{F}_{\text{RobustPVC}}$ to complete the simulation.

---

[a] We could use standard techniques [13, 15] to ensure that $\mathcal{S}$ runs in expected polynomial time.

Now it remains to show that the joint distribution of the view of $\mathcal{A}$ simulated by $\mathcal{S}$ and the output of P_B in the ideal world is computationally indistinguishable from the joint distribution of the view of $\mathcal{A}$ and the output of P_B in the real world. We provide the detailed proof in the full version of this paper [24].

Public Verifiability. We argue that whenever an honest party P_X outputs the message corrupted, this party should also be capable of producing a valid certificate for the malicious party P_Y corrupted by the adversary. This implies that once the honest party detects the adversary's cheating behavior, the adversary cannot prevent the honest party from generating the certificate.

Note that in Step 7, without receiving a valid signature, the honest party will not continue the execution of the protocol. Alternatively, if the honest party does receive valid signatures, though this party still cannot obtain the solutions for the time-lock puzzles/ciphertexts at this time, it is guaranteed that the adversary has signed the time-lock puzzles/ciphertexts. Meanwhile, the adversary still cannot access the solution for the time-lock puzzles and remains unaware of the indices of the instances chosen by P_X. Therefore, the adversary cannot base her decision to continue or abort on these indices.

When the adversary gains knowledge of the indices of instances chosen by P_X to verify, the honest party has already gathered sufficient evidence to attribute blame to the adversary. The honest party can locally solve the adversary's puzzles to obtain s_j^Y, c_j, and $\text{seed}_{j,\text{OT}}^Y$ sent by the adversary. These messages, combined with the committed seeds and witness, as well as trans_j^X and trans_j^Y, provide enough information for anyone to simulate the execution of the checked instance and obtain $\hat{c}_j$ and $\hat{\mathcal{H}}_j^Y$. Anyone can conduct the same verification on $\hat{c}_j$ and $\hat{\mathcal{H}}_j^Y$ as P_X to determine if malicious P_Y deviated from the protocol execution. Since P_X's signature is provided, the non-repudiation property is ensured.

Defamation Freeness. Assuming an honest party P_X is accused by the adversary corrupting P_Y with a valid certificate, it implies that the adversary will provide valid signature(s) of P_X for the message(s)

$$(\mathcal{C}, j, c_{\text{seed}_j^Y}, c_{\text{seed}_j^{\prime Y}}, c_{\text{witness}_j^Y}, \text{trans}_j^X, \text{trans}_j^Y, \mathcal{H}_j^X, p_{s_j^X}, p_{c_j}, p_{\text{seed}_{j,\text{OT}}^X}, \tau, \lambda).$$

Since P_X is honest, she only signs the puzzles $p_{s_j^X}$, p_{c_j}, and $p_{\text{seed}_{j,\text{OT}}^X}$ she has generated. These puzzles can be decrypted to derive s_j^X, c_j, and $\text{seed}_{j,\text{OT}}^X$. According to the soundness of the verifiable time-lock puzzle scheme, the adversary cannot provide openings/proofs for solutions different from s_j^X, c_j, and $\text{seed}_{j,\text{OT}}^X$.

First, we consider the certificate with type BadCom. In this setting, the adversary aims to demonstrate that c_j does not match the commitment generated from the seed'_j (and $\mathsf{c}_j \neq 0$, which is obvious). Due to the binding property, the adversary can only provide the valid committed values seed_j^Y, seed'^Y_j, and $\mathsf{witness}'^Y_j$ inside $\mathsf{c}_{\mathsf{seed}_j^Y}$, $\mathsf{c}_{\mathsf{seed}'^Y_j}$, and $\mathsf{c}_{\mathsf{witness}'^Y_j}$. A certificate verifier will recompute seed'^X_j from trans_j^X with randomness derived from seed_j^Y. On the one hand, since seed'^X_j is the output of a perfectly correct OT protocol, given the signed transcript of Π_{OT}, there is exactly one valid output for P_Y that is consistent with $\mathsf{trans}^X_{\cdot j}$, regardless of P_Y's randomness and inputs. On the other hand, if the committed values seed'^Y_j and $\mathsf{witness}'^Y_j$ are not the inputs of P_Y playing the role of the sender in the perfectly correct protocol Π_{OT}, these committed values do not match the signed transcript of Π_{OT}. Therefore, $\mathsf{seed}'_j = \mathsf{seed}'^A_j \oplus \mathsf{seed}'^B_j$ should be the same as the one derived by the honest P_X. Consequently, simulation for the computation conducted by P_X always leads to the same c_j, and the algorithm Judge will not output true (except for a negligible probability).

Then we consider the certificate with type BadOT. Similarly, we know that the adversary cannot forge $\mathsf{seed}'_j = \mathsf{seed}'^A_j \oplus \mathsf{seed}'^B_j$, $\mathsf{seed}^X_{j,\mathsf{OT}}$, and s^X_j, and a certificate verifier should derive the same $\{(\mathsf{p}_{Y_{j,i,0}}, \mathsf{p}_{Y_{j,i,1}})\}$ and $\mathsf{seed}'_j \oplus \mathsf{seed}^X_{j,\mathsf{OT}}$. Hence, given the signed $\mathcal{H}^X_j$, the algorithm Judge will not output true except for a negligible probability (when a collision of the hash function is found).

Finally, for the certificate with type BadNum, we know that the adversary cannot forge c_j. Hence, the honest P_X should always have exactly one $\mathsf{c}_j = 0$. Therefore, the algorithm Judge will not output true (except for a negligible probability).

Therefore, the protocol $\Pi_{\mathsf{RobustPVC}}$ along with algorithms Blame and Judge is robust publicly verifiable secure with deterrence $\epsilon = 1 - \frac{1}{\lambda-1}$. $\qquad\square$

5   Discussion

In this section, we discuss the performance and possible enhancement of our protocol $\Pi_{\mathsf{RobustPVC}}$.

5.1   Comparison

The protocol $\Pi_{\mathsf{RobustPVC}}$ is building upon the state-of-the-art secure two-party computation protocol with PVC security [17]. As discussed in Sect. 1.2, our protocol incurs low additional overhead. We can easily observe that, compared to the protocol in [17], our protocol only requires an additional garbled circuit generation and an additional garbled circuit evaluation (see Table 1). Interestingly, as the deterrence factor increases, the additional overhead for garbled circuit generation/evaluation in our protocol compared to the protocol in [17] decreases. As emphasized in [17], the cost of generating garbled circuits (unless the circuit is very small) is the efficiency bottleneck of their protocol, making the number of garbled circuit generations in our protocol highly desirable.

In the following, we argue that each phase of our protocol incurs low additional overhead compared to the protocol in [17].

Table 1. Number of garbled circuit generation and evaluation needed to achieve different deterrence factor ϵ, along with the additional overhead of our $\Pi_{\text{RobustPVC}}$ compared
to the protocol in [17]. Since evaluations should be faster than generations, the additional cost is actually overestimated.

ϵ	PVC-secure protocol [17]			Our protocol $\Pi_{\text{RobustPVC}}$			Additional overhead
	P_A	P_B	Total	P_A	P_B	Total	
80%	$5+0=5$	$4+1=5$	10	$5+1=6$	$5+1=6$	12	20%
87.5%	$8+0=8$	$7+1=8$	16	$8+1=9$	$8+1=9$	18	12.5%
90%	$10+0=10$	$9+1=10$	20	$10+1=11$	$10+1=11$	22	10%
95%	$20+0=20$	$19+1=20$	40	$20+1=21$	$20+1=21$	42	5%

Seed Preparation It is easy to verify that the expected number of executions
for this phase is $2-\epsilon$, where ϵ is the deterrence factor. For $\epsilon=90\%$, the
expected number of executions is only 1.1. For $\epsilon=95\%$, the expected number
is reduced to only 1.05. Additionally, the secure equality test can be completed
very quickly [7,18]. Therefore, the overhead of this phase is low.

Circuit and Input Preparation In our protocol, two parties can perform
garbled circuit generation in parallel during this phase. For the same deterrence factor, the number of garbled circuits generated in [17] is the same as
in $\Pi_{\text{RobustPVC}}$ (for each party). Therefore, the running time for garbled circuit
generation is approximately the same as that of the protocol in [17]. We also
note that time-lock puzzle generation is efficient. Indeed, for *all* instances, a
single master puzzle key (inside a *real* time-lock puzzle) is sufficient. Hence,
the overhead of this phase is low.

Publicly Verifiable Evidence Creation This phase is almost identical to the
protocol in [17].

Check of Instances If both parties are honest and the master time-lock puzzle
is correctly opened, the computation performed by both parties (in parallel)
mainly involves the simulation of Π_{OT}, which incurs a similar running time
as the protocol in [17]. Moreover, compared to the protocol in [17], no simulation of garbled circuit generation is needed. Therefore, our protocol may
outperform the protocol in [17] in this phase.

Circuit Evaluation In this phase, both parties can evaluate the garbled circuit
in parallel. Hence, the running time required for garbled circuit evaluation is
almost the same as that of the protocol in [17]. Additionally, secure equality
tests can be completed quickly. Therefore, the overhead of this phase is low.

The communication cost primarily encompasses the execution of OT protocols
and the transmission of garbled circuits (including input-wire labels) for evaluation. Consequently, the one-way communication is nearly identical to that in [17],
and the two-way communication is twice of that in [17]. Therefore, there is no
additional communication overhead in duplex networks compared to [17].

Based on the implementation presented in [17], as an example, when $\epsilon=$
87.5%, *i.e.*, the number of garbled circuit is 8, the execution time of their PVC-
secure protocol for an SHA-256 circuit is 71.31 ms in LAN and 2436 ms in
WAN. In comparison, the corresponding semi-honest protocol takes 38.04 ms

in LAN and 1080ms in WAN, while the maliciously secure protocol takes 611.7 ms in LAN and 17300 ms in WAN. Given that the performance of our protocol is similar to that of the protocol in [17], it is evident that our $\Pi_{\text{RobustPVC}}$ achieves comparable performance to the semi-honest protocol while significantly outperforming the maliciously secure protocol.

5.2 Size of Certificate

In $\Pi_{\text{RobustPVC}}$, we have chosen not to include the circuit description $\mathcal{C}$ in the certificate. Instead, we make the assumption that the circuit description is commonly known. This practice aligns with the convention followed in PVC-secure protocols [3,9,10,17,31]. Alternatively, one could opt to include the circuit description $\mathcal{C}$ in the certificate. It is worth noting that the description of $\mathcal{C}$ can be significantly shorter than the full circuit, such as representing it in high-level code or utilizing an ID number from a widely used "reference circuits" database.

Due to the exclusion of the circuit description in the certificate, the size of publicly verifiable certificates generated in the $\Pi_{\text{RobustPVC}}$ protocol remains *constant*.

5.3 Potential Enhancements

In our protocol $\Pi_{\text{RobustPVC}}$, we do not aim to prevent an attacker from learning the evaluation result $\mathcal{C}(x_A, x_B)$ even when the honest party outputs cheating at the end of the protocol. This occurs when the attacker generates a malicious garbled circuit but not being caught (with probability $1 - \epsilon$) or when the attacker causes an abortion in the final equality test protocol.

We note this issue is not the focus of our protocol. In fact, it is well known that two-party computation cannot guarantee fairness in general [6]. But there are still some countermeasures that can be readily incorporated into our protocols.

For instance, one approach is to introduce an additional circuit that processes the output-wire labels before they are used in the equality test, effectively concealing the semantic values associated with the garbled circuit's output. Another technique, known as *progressive revelation*, allows for a gradual release of the evaluation result bit-by-bit, preventing the attacker from obtaining the complete input while leaving the honest party with nothing. For more detailed information on these countermeasures, we refer interested readers to the work [18].

Acknowledgments. We would like to express our sincere appreciation to the anonymous reviewers for their valuable comments. Yi Liu was supported by National Natural Science Foundation of China under Grant No. 62302194. Junzuo Lai was supported by National Natural Science Foundation of China under Grant No. U2001205, Guangdong Basic and Applied Basic Research Foundation (Grant No. 2023B1515040020). Qi Wang was supported by Shenzhen Key Laboratory of Safety and Security for Next Generation of Industrial Internet under Grant No. ZDSYS20210623092007023 and Guangdong Provincial Key Laboratory of Brain-inspired Intelligent Computation under Grant No. 2020B121201001. Anjia Yang was supported by National Key

Research and Development Program of China under Grant No. 2021ZD0112802 and National Natural Science Foundation of China under Grant No. 62072215. Jian Weng was supported by National Natural Science Foundation of China under Grant Nos. 61825203, 62332007 and U22B2028, Major Program of Guangdong Basic and Applied Research Project under Grant No. 2019B030302008, Guangdong Provincial Science and Technology Project under Grant No. 2021A0505030033, Science and Technology Major Project of Tibetan Autonomous Region of China under Grant No. XZ202201ZD0006G, National Joint Engineering Research Center of Network Security Detection and Protection Technology, Guangdong Key Laboratory of Data Security and Privacy Preserving, Guangdong Hong Kong Joint Laboratory for Data Security and Privacy Protection, and Engineering Research Center of Trustworthy AI, Ministry of Education.

References

1. Agrawal, N., Bell, J., Gascón, A., Kusner, M.J.: MPC-friendly commitments for publicly verifiable covert security. In: Kim, Y., Kim, J., Vigna, G., Shi, E. (eds.) 2021 ACM SIGSAC Conference on Computer and Communications Security, CCS 2021, Virtual Event, Republic of Korea, 15–19 November 2021, pp. 2685–2704. ACM (2021)

2. Asharov, G., Orlandi, C.: Calling out cheaters: covert security with public verifiability. In: Wang, X., Sako, K. (eds.) ASIACRYPT 2012. LNCS, vol. 7658, pp. 681–698. Springer, Heidelberg (2012). https://doi.org/10.1007/978-3-642-34961-4_41

3. Attema, T., Dunning, V., Everts, M.H., Langenkamp, P.: Efficient compiler to covert security with public verifiability for honest majority MPC. In: Ateniese, G., Venturi, D. (eds.) Proceedings of the 20th International Conference on Applied Cryptography and Network Security, ACNS 2022, Rome, Italy, 20–23 June 2022. LNCS, vol. 13269, pp. 663–683. Springer, Cham (2022). https://doi.org/10.1007/978-3-031-09234-3_33

4. Aumann, Y., Lindell, Y.: Security against covert adversaries: efficient protocols for realistic adversaries. J. Cryptol. **23**(2), 281–343 (2010)

5. Bellare, M., Hoang, V.T., Rogaway, P.: Foundations of garbled circuits. In: Yu, T., Danezis, G., Gligor, V.D. (eds.) The ACM Conference on Computer and Communications Security, CCS 2012, Raleigh, NC, USA, 16–18 October 2012, pp. 784–796. ACM (2012)

6. Cleve, R.: Limits on the security of coin flips when half the processors are faulty (extended abstract). In: Hartmanis, J. (ed.) Proceedings of the 18th Annual ACM Symposium on Theory of Computing, 28–30 May 1986, Berkeley, California, USA, pp. 364–369. ACM (1986)

7. Couteau, G.: New protocols for secure equality test and comparison. In: Preneel, B., Vercauteren, F. (eds.) ACNS 2018. LNCS, vol. 10892, pp. 303–320. Springer, Cham (2018). https://doi.org/10.1007/978-3-319-93387-0_16

8. Damgård, I., Geisler, M., Nielsen, J.B.: From passive to covert security at low cost. In: Micciancio, D. (ed.) TCC 2010. LNCS, vol. 5978, pp. 128–145. Springer, Heidelberg (2010). https://doi.org/10.1007/978-3-642-11799-2_9

9. Damgård, I., Orlandi, C., Simkin, M.: Black-box transformations from passive to covert security with public verifiability. In: Micciancio, D., Ristenpart, T. (eds.) CRYPTO 2020, Part II. LNCS, vol. 12171, pp. 647–676. Springer, Cham (2020). https://doi.org/10.1007/978-3-030-56880-1_23

10. Faust, S., Hazay, C., Kretzler, D., Schlosser, B.: Generic compiler for publicly verifiable covert multi-party computation. In: Canteaut, A., Standaert, F.-X. (eds.) EUROCRYPT 2021, Part II. LNCS, vol. 12697, pp. 782–811. Springer, Cham (2021). https://doi.org/10.1007/978-3-030-77886-6_27

11. Faust, S., Hazay, C., Kretzler, D., Schlosser, B.: Financially backed covert security. In: Hanaoka, G., Shikata, J., Watanabe, Y. (eds.) Public-Key Cryptography - PKC 2022, Part II—25th IACR International Conference on Practice and Theory of Public-Key Cryptography, Proceedings, Virtual Event. LNCS, 8–11 March 2022, vol. 13178, pp. 99–129. Springer, Cham (2022). https://doi.org/10.1007/978-3-030-97131-1_4

12. Goldreich, O.: The Foundations of Cryptography - Volume 2: Basic Applications. Cambridge University Press (2004)

13. Goldreich, O., Kahan, A.: How to construct constant-round zero-knowledge proof systems for NP. J. Cryptol. 9(3), 167–190 (1996)

14. Goyal, V., Mohassel, P., Smith, A.: Efficient two party and multi party computation against covert adversaries. In: Smart, N. (ed.) EUROCRYPT 2008. LNCS, vol. 4965, pp. 289–306. Springer, Heidelberg (2008). https://doi.org/10.1007/978-3-540-78967-3_17

15. Hazay, C., Lindell, Y.: Efficient Secure Two-Party Protocols - Techniques and Constructions. Information Security and Cryptography, Springer, Heidelberg (2010). https://doi.org/10.1007/978-3-642-14303-8

16. Hazay, C., Shelat, A., Venkitasubramaniam, M.: Going beyond dual execution: MPC for functions with efficient verification. In: Kiayias, A., Kohlweiss, M., Wallden, P., Zikas, V. (eds.) PKC 2020, Part II. LNCS, vol. 12111, pp. 328–356. Springer, Cham (2020). https://doi.org/10.1007/978-3-030-45388-6_12

17. Hong, C., Katz, J., Kolesnikov, V., Lu, W., Wang, X.: Covert security with public verifiability: faster, leaner, and simpler. In: Ishai, Y., Rijmen, V. (eds.) EUROCRYPT 2019, Part III. LNCS, vol. 11478, pp. 97–121. Springer, Cham (2019). https://doi.org/10.1007/978-3-030-17659-4_4

18. Huang, Y., Katz, J., Evans, D.: Quid-pro-quo-tocols: strengthening semi-honest protocols with dual execution. In: IEEE Symposium on Security and Privacy, SP 2012, 21–23 May 2012, San Francisco, California, USA, pp. 272–284. IEEE Computer Society (2012)

19. Huang, Y., Katz, J., Evans, D.: Efficient secure two-party computation using symmetric cut-and-choose. In: Canetti, R., Garay, J.A. (eds.) CRYPTO 2013, Part II. LNCS, vol. 8043, pp. 18–35. Springer, Heidelberg (2013). https://doi.org/10.1007/978-3-642-40084-1_2

20. Kolesnikov, V., Malozemoff, A.J.: Public verifiability in the covert model (almost) for free. In: Iwata, T., Cheon, J.H. (eds.) ASIACRYPT 2015, Part II. LNCS, vol. 9453, pp. 210–235. Springer, Heidelberg (2015). https://doi.org/10.1007/978-3-662-48800-3_9

21. Kolesnikov, V., Mohassel, P., Riva, B., Rosulek, M.: Richer efficiency/security trade-offs in 2PC. In: Dodis, Y., Nielsen, J.B. (eds.) TCC 2015, Part I. LNCS, vol. 9014, pp. 229–259. Springer, Heidelberg (2015). https://doi.org/10.1007/978-3-662-46494-6_11

22. Lindell, Y.: Fast cut-and-choose-based protocols for malicious and covert adversaries. J. Cryptol. 29(2), 456–490 (2016)

23. Lindell, Y., Pinkas, B.: A proof of security of Yao's protocol for two-party computation. J. Cryptol. 22(2), 161–188 (2009). https://doi.org/10.1007/s00145-008-9036-8

24. Liu, Y., Lai, J., Wang, Q., Qin, X., Yang, A., Weng, J.: Robust publicly verifiable covert security: limited information leakage and guaranteed correctness with low overhead. Cryptology ePrint Archive, Paper 2023/1392 (2023). https://eprint.iacr.org/2023/1392

25. Liu, Y., Wang, Q., Yiu, S.: Making private function evaluation safer, faster, and simpler. In: Hanaoka, G., Shikata, J., Watanabe, Y. (eds.) Public-Key Cryptography - PKC 2022–25th IACR International Conference on Practice and Theory of Public-Key Cryptography, Virtual Event, 8–11 March 2022, Proceedings, Part I. LNCS, vol. 13177, pp. 349–378. Springer, Cham (2022). https://doi.org/10.1007/978-3-030-97121-2_13

26. Liu, Y., Wang, Q., Yiu, S.: Towards practical homomorphic time-lock puzzles: applicability and verifiability. In: Atluri, V., Pietro, R.D., Jensen, C.D., Meng, W. (eds.) Proceedings of the 27th European Symposium on Research in Computer Security, ESORICS 2022, Copenhagen, Denmark, 26–30 September 2022, Part I. LNCS, vol. 13554, pp. 424–443. Springer, Cham (2022). https://doi.org/10.1007/978-3-031-17140-6_21

27. Mohassel, P., Franklin, M.: Efficiency tradeoffs for malicious two-party computation. In: Yung, M., Dodis, Y., Kiayias, A., Malkin, T. (eds.) PKC 2006. LNCS, vol. 3958, pp. 458–473. Springer, Heidelberg (2006). https://doi.org/10.1007/11745853_30

28. Mohassel, P., Riva, B.: Garbled circuits checking garbled circuits: more efficient and secure two-party computation. In: Canetti, R., Garay, J.A. (eds.) CRYPTO 2013, Part II. LNCS, vol. 8043, pp. 36–53. Springer, Heidelberg (2013). https://doi.org/10.1007/978-3-642-40084-1_3

29. Rindal, P., Rosulek, M.: Faster malicious 2-party secure computation with online/offline dual execution. In: Holz, T., Savage, S. (eds.) 25th USENIX Security Symposium, USENIX Security 16, Austin, TX, USA, 10–12 August 2016, pp. 297–314. USENIX Association (2016)

30. Rindal, P., Rosulek, M.: Malicious-secure private set intersection via dual execution. In: Thuraisingham, B., Evans, D., Malkin, T., Xu, D. (eds.) Proceedings of the 2017 ACM SIGSAC Conference on Computer and Communications Security, CCS 2017, Dallas, TX, USA, 30 October–03 November 2017, pp. 1229–1242. ACM (2017)

31. Scholl, P., Simkin, M., Siniscalchi, L.: Multiparty computation with covert security and public verifiability. Cryptology ePrint Archive, Report 2021/366 (2021). https://ia.cr/2021/366

32. Zhu, R., Ding, C., Huang, Y.: Efficient publicly verifiable 2PC over a blockchain with applications to financially-secure computations. In: Cavallaro, L., Kinder, J., Wang, X., Katz, J. (eds.) Proceedings of the 2019 ACM SIGSAC Conference on Computer and Communications Security, CCS 2019, London, UK, 11–15 November 2019, pp. 633–650. ACM (2019)

LERNA: Secure Single-Server Aggregation via Key-Homomorphic Masking

Hanjun Li[1]([✉]), Huijia Lin[1], Antigoni Polychroniadou[2], and Stefano Tessaro[1]

[1] University of Washington, Seattle, WA, USA
{hanjul,rachel,tessaro}@cs.washington.edu
[2] J.P. Morgan AI Research & AlgoCRYPT CoE, New York, NY, USA
antigoni.polychroniadou@jpmorgan.com

Abstract. This paper introduces LERNA, a new framework for single-server secure aggregation. Our protocols are tailored to the setting where multiple consecutive aggregation phases are performed with the same set of clients, a fraction of which can drop out in some of the phases. We rely on an initial secret sharing setup among the clients which is generated once-and-for-all, and *reused* in all following aggregation phases. Compared to prior works [Bonawitz et al. CCS'17, Bell et al. CCS'20], the reusable setup eliminates one round of communication between the server and clients per aggregation—i.e., we need two rounds for semi-honest security (instead of three), and three rounds (instead of four) in the malicious model. Our approach also significantly reduces the server's computational costs by only requiring the reconstruction of a *single* secret-shared value (per aggregation). Prior work required reconstructing a secret-shared value for each client involved in the computation.

We provide instantiations of LERNA based on both the Decisional Composite Residuosity (DCR) and (Ring) Learning with Rounding ((R)LWR) assumptions respectively and evaluate a version based on the latter assumption. In addition to savings in round-complexity (which result in reduced latency), our experiments show that the server computational costs are reduced by two orders of magnitude in comparison to the state-of-the-art. In settings with a large number of clients, we also reduce the computational costs up to twenty-fold for most clients, while a small set of "heavy clients" is subject to a workload that is still smaller than that of prior work.

Keywords: Secure Aggregation · Reusable Setup · Privacy Preserving Machine Learning

1 Introduction

A secure aggregation protocol allows a set of clients, each holding an input x_i, to interact with one or more servers, so that the latter learns the sum $\sum x_i$, but no additional information. The inputs x_i could be integers, often mod q, or vectors of integers. In contrast to the usual setting of multi-party computation, which

© International Association for Cryptologic Research 2023
J. Guo and R. Steinfeld (Eds.): ASIACRYPT 2023, LNCS 14438, pp. 302–334, 2023.
https://doi.org/10.1007/978-981-99-8721-4_10

assumes point-to-point channels, here communication only occurs between each individual client and the server(s), i.e., there is no *direct* inter-client communication and clients can only communicate indirectly through the server(s).

Secure aggregation protocols are suitable for a broad range of applications, such as privacy-preserving telemetry in browsers [14], analytics in digital contact tracing [2], and Federated Machine Learning [9]. Practical *multi-server* protocols [15,18] are, in fact, already being considered for standardization by IETF [22]. In this paper, however, we target the *single-server* setting. This setting is preferable whenever distributing trust among multiple non-colluding entities is not easily feasible. However, it is also more challenging, as protocols require multiple rounds of interaction and need to accommodate for potential *client dropouts*, whilst ensuring the correctness of aggregation and the privacy of clients' inputs against other colluding clients and/or the server. These protocols have emerged primarily in the context of Federated Machine Learning, starting from Bonawitz et al. [10], which underlies Google's Federated ML system [9], and its recent optimizations and extensions [6,7].

This paper introduces a new general paradigm for single-server secure aggregation, which improves upon the state-of-the-art in terms of round and computational complexities. Our protocols are particularly advantageous in settings where *repeated aggregation* phases are performed with the same set of clients (some of which may drop out) as they only require two rounds per aggregation, in addition to an initial setup round, at the presence of semi-honest colluding clients and/or server. In comparison, prior protocols [7,10] require three rounds per aggregation (without initial setup). In the malicious security model, all protocols require one additional round, namely, three rounds in our protocols and four rounds in prior works. Moreover, our approach also significantly improves the server workload by reducing the number of secret-sharing reconstructions.

Repeated Aggregation. While existing single server aggregation protocols mainly focus on running a single aggregation, many scenarios require running repeated aggregation sessions throughout a period of time, with the same set of clients. A prototypical application involves a number of sensors or nodes in a network reporting telemetry data. For example, a company of Internet of Things (IoT) devices may want to aggregate operation data from a certain area periodically to help understand how the devices are used throughout the day. Other examples include wireless sensor networks (WSN) [21], smart meters [3], and medical devices [23].

Our protocol leverages the repeated aggregation setting by having an initial setup round that generates correlated states among clients to facilitate the many aggregation phases later, reducing both round and computational complexity. The protocol is robust to drop-outs, as long as the fraction of drop-out clients is bounded at any point in time. Our main protocol focuses on the setting with a large number of clients, e.g. $M \geq 20K$. To reduce communication costs, it selects a committee of fixed size $O(\kappa^2)$ in the initial setup round to hold the correlated states. And the committee stays unchanged through out many aggregation phases. The protocol guarantees the privacy of clients' inputs against statically corrupted clients that may collude with the server, provided that the total number of corrupted clients in the setup and all aggregation phases are bounded. Compared to protocols designed for single aggregation, we rely on the more stringent condition that the total number of corrupted clients is bounded across many aggregation sessions. However, one can alleviate this assumption by periodically rerunning the setup phase, generating fresh correlated states among clients. Different applications may refresh at a different frequency, say, every day, every week, or even longer, depending on how likely clients are corrupted. Viewed this way, our protocol offers a new tradeoff between the rate of corruption and efficiency gain.

Alternatively, when the number of client is small, e.g. $M \leq 80$, our protocol can avoid the committee in the initial setup round to guarantee stronger privacy: in this setting, the clients may be *adaptively* corrupted instead of statically as assumed above. (See the full version for details on this variant.)

Existing Single-Server Secure Aggregation. It is helpful to first review the blueprint behind existing single-server aggregation protocols [7,10]. Here, we restrict ourselves to the semi-honest setting for simplicity, but these protocols (along with ours) can be modified to support malicious corruption of server and clients.

The initial idea is to have each client $i \in [M]$ send a *masked* input $z_i = x_i + c_i$ to the server. To generate these masks, every pair of clients i, j establishes a shared key $k_{ij} = k_{ji} = \mathrm{PRG}(g^{s_i s_j})$, where g^{s_i} is a group element which acts as an ephemeral *public key* associated with each client $i \in [M]$, and which is shared in an initial round (through the server) with all other clients. The value s_i is kept secret by client i. Then, each client $i \in [M]$ uses the mask

$$c_i = \sum_{j<i} k_{ij} - \sum_{j>i} k_{ij} .$$

These masks satisfy in particular the *cancellation property* $\sum_i c_i = 0$, and consequently the server can simply output $\sum_i z_i = \sum_i x_i$.

A first concern is that this only works if each client remains alive and indeed submits its own masked input—a term $k_{ij} = k_{ji}$ included in client j's mask c_j is not canceled out without client i's contribution. To handle a dropout, each client additionally secret shares their own secret s_i, which is reconstructed in case they drop out, to then, in turn, derive all k_{ji}'s for $j \neq i$.

A second concern is that a slow client i could be prematurely labeled as a dropout, and their secret s_i reconstructed *before* the masked value z_i reaches the server, thus revealing x_i. To prevent this, each client initially shares a second random mask b_i, along with s_i, and sends instead the masked input $z_i = x_i + b_i + c_i$ to the server. Then, after receiving the masked inputs $\{z_i\}_{i \in I}$ from a subset $I \subseteq [M]$ of the clients, for each $i \in I$, the server reconstructs b_i, thus allowing the inclusion of $(x_i + c_i)$ in the final sum. In contrast, it reconstructs s_i for all $i \notin I$, thus enabling the computation of $\sum_{i \in I} x_i$ as discussed above. For every client $i \notin I$, because b_i remains secret, the value x_i remains protected even if later z_i is obtained by the adversary.

Therefore, the overall protocol needs three rounds. An additional round is needed to tolerate a malicious server, and it forces the server to commit to a single set I of clients which are claimed not to have dropped out.

The Costs of Secret Sharing. The most expensive part in the above blueprint is the initial sharing of s_i and b_i, along with the later reconstruction of (one of) them for each client. This impacts both the round and computational complexity in several ways.

Foremost, secret sharing s_i and b_i takes one additional round of communication. While some initial setup round is somewhat inherent (e.g., to share keys to allow clients to communicate with each other via the server), this becomes a bigger concern in the repeated aggregation setting. Here, it is crucial that the values s_i and b_i are re-generated and re-shared *at each repeated session*, for otherwise dropping out at some later session may compromise the privacy of the inputs from prior sessions.

Moreover, the computation and communication costs due to secret sharing are high – $\Theta(M)$ for each client, and $\Theta(M^2)$ for the server. Crucially, the server needs to reconstruct one secret shared value—either s_i or b_i—for each client. In addition, for every client dropout, the server needs to perform $\Theta(M)$ exponentiations to recover the corresponding values k_{ij}. To reduce costs, Bell et. al. [7] proposed to have clients only secret share in a random neighborhood of size $\Theta(\log M + \kappa)$, where κ is the statistical security parameter. Though this idea reduces the client and server costs to $\Theta(\log M + \kappa)$ and $M(\Theta(\log M + \kappa))$, respectively, the improvement is at the cost of weakening the security guarantees at the presence of maliciously corrupted clients and/or server.[1]

Our Contributions. This paper proposes LERNA, a new lightweight approach to single-server secure aggregation which addresses the aforementioned issues. Foremost, it reduces the round complexity to two respectively three communication rounds for semi-honest and malicious security, respectively, in addition to an initial offline round which establishes a setup that can be re-used across multiple aggregations. Moreover, LERNA also features very small server costs, as the server only needs to perform a single reconstruction of a secret-shared value. We validate the performance of LERNA also by benchmarking a prototype implementation.

An important feature of our implementation is that it identifies a (random) subset of the clients as a *committee*. Our benchmarking shows that the computational costs of committee members are smaller than the client costs of prior solutions. However, LERNA is even more lightweight for clients outside of the committee. Indeed, in addition to participating in an initial setup stage, non-members only need to send a single message to the server to include their input in an aggregation session, and subsequent interaction within the same session only involves committee members. Our benchmarking demonstrates up to twenty-fold performance improvement for these non-committee clients.

---

[1] More specifically, using the protocol of Bell et. al., if the server is malicious, it may recover the sums of inputs of multiple subsets of clients.

A drawback of our solution, as shown in our benchmark, is a relatively heavy communication cost in the initial offline round. This requires participating devices to have sufficient storage and network bandwidth. To amortize this one-time cost, an ideal application for LERNA runs repeated aggregation for large numbers of iterations, T, before rerunning the setup. We envision running LERNA for machine learning from data collected from a large number of relatively powerful devices, e.g. the payment terminals Amazon One, medical imaging devices, weather stations, etc.

Our protocols are built on top of a new primitive, which we call a *key-homomorphic masking* scheme, which allows clients to initially secret share a *re-usable* secret value (i.e., which can be reused across multiple computations) to the committee as part of the initial offline round. We provide two instantiations from, respectively, the DCR assumption [16] and (Ring) LWR assumption [5], with the latter being our main result.

Related Work. The same reduction in round complexity was very recently achieved by Guo et al. [19], also relying on a re-usable secret shared value. However, their solution performs the aggregation in the exponent of a discrete-log hard group, resulting essentially in the sever obtaining the value $g^{\sum_i x_i}$, where g is a group generator. In other words, the actual result can only be extracted by computing the discrete logarithm, which is feasible only if $\sum_i x_i$ is sufficiently small. This forces the computation to be over small domains accommodating Federated learning of models with small weights, such as quantized or compressed models. In contrast, most Federated ML tasks typically involve large values. LERNA does not suffer from this drawback. Our approach differs from [19] in that it relies on different mathematical structures (underlying the LWR and DCR assumptions) to obtain the aggregated sum *in the clear*. This, in turn, requires overcoming a few challenges, in particular, designing special secret-sharing schemes tailored to our requirements – linear reconstruction via small coefficients (for LWR) and working over the integers (for DCR).

The work of [20] proposed a semi-honest protocol, SASH+, using a seed-homomorphic PRG based on LWR similar to our key-homomorphic masking scheme. However, SASH+ exploits the homomorphic property in a different way from LERNA. At high-level, assuming LWR with dimension n, SASH+ reduces the problem of aggregating ℓ-dimension inputs to aggregating n-dimensional homomorphic PRG seeds, which is done using the protocol of [7]. This reduction reduces the computation cost of the server and each client by roughly a factor of (ℓ/n), but at the cost of increasing the round complexity from 3 to 4 per iteration, and introducing an error to the aggregation result that scales linearly with M. In comparison, LERNA reduces the round complexity from 3 to 2, and improves the computation cost at the same time. LERNA also computes the aggregation results exactly without error. As we'll discuss in our benchmarks, LERNA server, and non-committee clients are significantly faster than SASH+'s, while LERNA committee clients become slower than SASH+ clients for very large M.

The work of [25] focuses on the specific application of repeated aggregation in federated machine learning (FL), where the server selects a random subset of clients to aggregate at each iteration. It observes that the usual random client selection strategy in FL causes a leakage of client inputs when the model is close to converged. The paper proposes a new client selection algorithm to mitigate this leakage, assuming an honest server following this new algorithm. We note that LERNA can also be adapted to run repeated aggregation over a different subset of clients at each iteration. The mitigation strategy can then be orthogonally applied to the semi-honest version of LERNA. We stress that the client selection strategy is not to be confused with LERNA's committee selection. Client selection could be added on top of our protocol (but is not included explicitly), and would happen in every iteration, whereas committee selection is within our protocol, and happens only once during its setup phase.

A recent and concurrent work by Bell et al. [6] additionally considers the question of input validation. While this is extremely important, it is orthogonal to the issues studied by this paper. Their system also uses Ring-LWE for efficiency improvement, but still follows broadly the above blueprint without a re-usable setup.

1.1 Overview of LERNA

LERNA's approach differs from the existing protocols in [7,10] whose core idea is hiding each input x_i with a masks that, as described above, satisfies the cancellation property. Instead, LERNA starts with a conceptually simpler solution, where each client i hides its input x_i with a (random) mask c_i as $z_i = x_i + c_i$, and sends the masked value z_i to the server. With the help of the clients, the server first recovers $c_U = \sum_{i \in U} c_i$, for the set of online clients U, and hence the aggregation result $x_U = \sum_{i \in U} z_i - c_U$. The key question we answer is how the clients securely help the server to compute c_U.

Straw Man Solution. The first naïve idea is to let every client secret share its mask c_i with all other clients using a *linear* secret sharing scheme (Share, Recon), such as Shamir's secret-sharing scheme. In particular, the Recon algorithm involves evaluating a linear function on the shares. As in prior works [7,10] each client only has a private and authenticated channel with the server. They can also communicate with each other indirectly through the server. Assuming a PKI setup, such indirect communication can be private and authenticated.

In more detail, each client $i \in [M]$ sends (through the server) the j'th share c_j^i of c_i to each other client $j \in [M]$, before sending their masked input $z_i = c_i + x_i$. The server then finds the set of clients U who have completed both steps, and notifies them of the set U for aggregation. Each client j then locally aggregates the shares it has received from clients $i \in U$, obtaining $c_j^U = \sum_{i \in U} c_j^i$. By the linear homomorphism of the secret sharing, c_j^U is the j'th share of the aggregated mask c_U. As long as enough clients, say $j \in U' \subseteq U$, send their aggregated shares c_j^U to the server, the latter can reconstruct $c_U = \mathsf{Recon}(\{c_j^U\}_{j \in U'})$, and then recover the aggregated input x_U.

This simple solution is, however inefficient: The step where each client i shares its mask c_i with all other clients has overall $\Omega(M^2)$ communication complexity per aggregation. To aggregate T times, the cost grows as $\Omega(M^2 \times T)$.

Key-Homomorphic Masking Scheme. Somewhat informally a key-homomorphic masking scheme involves a pair of algorithms Mask, UnMask. The Mask algorithm takes an input x from some input space $\mathbb{Z}_p$, a masking key k from some key space $\mathcal{K}$, and a tag τ, and computes a masked message $z \leftarrow \mathsf{Mask}(k, \tau, x)$. The UnMask algorithm takes the above z and an "empty" mask $c \leftarrow \mathsf{Mask}(k, \tau, 0)$ under the same key k and tag τ, and recovers the message $x \leftarrow \mathsf{UnMask}(z, c)$.

Importantly, the scheme is *additively key-homomorphic* for masks with the *same* tag τ: $\mathsf{Mask}(k + k', \tau, x + x') \equiv \mathsf{Mask}(k, \tau, x) \boxplus \mathsf{Mask}(k', \tau, x')$, where $\boxplus$ represents homomorphic addition. We can generalize the additive homomorphism to evaluate any linear function L over masks $\{z_i \leftarrow \mathsf{Mask}(k_i, \tau, x_i)\}$:

$$\mathsf{Eval}(L, \{z_i\}) \equiv \mathsf{Mask}(L(\{k_i\}), \tau, L(\{x_i\})),$$

where the linear function L is evaluated respectively over k_i's in the key space $\mathcal{K}$ and over x_i's in the message space $\mathbb{Z}_p$.

Jumping ahead, our instantiation of the masking scheme under LWR will only achieve *approximate* key-homomorphism. We will explain below how we get around this limitation. For now, it is helpful to assume a perfect masking scheme to convey the main idea.

Sketch of the LERNA Protocol. We now describe the semi-honest protocol. Note that the following description depends on a commitment $Q \subseteq [M]$. One can easily think of this committee as containing all clients, although in our concrete instantiation below, we only include a (random) subset of the clients in Q

- Setup phase: The clients agree on a common committee $Q \subseteq [M]$ using public, common randomness. Every client i secret shares a fresh masking key k_i as $\{k_j^i\}_{j \in [Q]}$ and sends the j'th share k_j^i to committee member $j \in Q$.
- Online phase: In the tth aggregation session,
  1. The clients sample a common tag $\tau \leftarrow \mathcal{H}(\mathsf{sid}, t)$ using a hash function $\mathcal{H}$, modeled as a random oracle. Every client P_i then computes a masked input $z_i \leftarrow \mathsf{Mask}(k_i, \tau, x_i)$ and sends z_i to the server.
     The server identifies the set U of online clients. It sends U to all committee members Q, indicating that it wants to aggregate the inputs in U.
  2. Upon receiving U, every committee member P_j aggregates the key shares k_j^i it received from clients $i \in U$, obtaining $k_j^U = \sum_{i \in U} k_j^i$, which by linear homomorphism, equals the j'th share of $k_U = \sum_{i \in U} k_i$. (Therefore, given enough shares $\{k_j^U\}_{j \in U'}$, for a large enough subset U', one can recover k_U.) Then, P_j computes an empty mask $c_j^U \leftarrow \mathsf{Mask}(k_j^U, \tau, 0)$, and sends it back to the server.

Upon receiving enough shares $\{c_j^U\}_{j \in U'}$ from a subset $U' \subseteq U$, the server homomorphically computes the aggregated mask

$$c_U = \mathsf{Eval}(\mathsf{Recon}, \{c_j^U\}_{j \in U'})$$
$$\equiv \mathsf{Mask}(\mathsf{Recon}(\{k_j^U\}_{j \in U'}), \tau, 0) \equiv \mathsf{Mask}(k_U, \tau, 0)$$

where the first equivalence uses the fact that the Recon algorithm is linear. Similarly,

$$z_U = \sum_{i \in U} z_i = \sum_{i \in U} \mathsf{Mask}(k_i, \tau, x_i)$$
$$\equiv \mathsf{Mask}(\sum_{i \in U} k_i, \tau, \sum_{i \in U} x_i) = \mathsf{Mask}(k_U, \tau, x_U)$$

The server can now recover $x_U = \mathsf{UnMask}(z_U, c_U)$.

LWR-Based Instantiation. Our main instantiation of the masking scheme is inspired by the simple seed-homomorphic PRG of [11]. The LWR assumption [5] is associated with two moduli $q > p$, where p is the modulus of the message space. A tag τ is an LWR public vector $\mathbf{a} \in \mathbb{Z}_q^n$, and the masking key k is an LWR secret $\mathbf{s} \in \mathbb{Z}_q^n$. A masked input z is simply an LWR sample rounded to p added with the message x, i.e.,

$$\text{LWR: } \tau = \mathbf{a} \in \mathbb{Z}_q^n, \qquad k = \mathbf{s} \in \mathbb{Z}_q^n, \qquad z = \lfloor \langle \mathbf{s}, \mathbf{a} \rangle \rceil_p + x \in \mathbb{Z}_p.$$

The linear structure of LWR implies the key homomorphism property. However, it only holds *approximately* due to rounding errors. More specifically: *i)* additive key-homomorphism holds approximately with bounded error, and *ii)* linear key-homomorphism holds with bounded error if the linear function L evaluated has *small coefficients*. To see *i)*, consider two masks with keys $k_1 = \mathbf{s}_1, k_2 = \mathbf{s}_2$, inputs x_1, x_2, and a common tag $\tau = \mathbf{a}$. We have

$$z_1 + z_2 = \lfloor \langle \mathbf{s}_1, \mathbf{a} \rangle \rceil_p + x_1 + \lfloor \langle \mathbf{s}_2, \mathbf{a} \rangle \rceil_p + x_2$$
$$= \lfloor \langle \mathbf{s}_1 + \mathbf{s}_2, \mathbf{a} \rangle \rceil_p + x_1 + x_2 + \epsilon,$$

where ϵ is the rounding difference between $\lfloor \langle \mathbf{s}_1, \mathbf{a} \rangle \rceil_p + \lfloor \langle \mathbf{s}_2, \mathbf{a} \rangle \rceil_p$ and $\lfloor \langle \mathbf{s}_1 + \mathbf{s}_2, \mathbf{a} \rangle \rceil_p$, which is bounded by 1. With regard to *ii)*, when evaluating a linear function L over the masks using the above approximate additive homomorphism, the error is scaled by the coefficients of L.

The approximate key homomorphism creates a technical issue in the protocol: when the server evaluates Recon homomorphically, it introduces an additive error in the aggregation result. To remove the error, our solution is to multiply the inputs with a scaling factor Δ, set to be larger than the noise.

If the coefficients of Recon are large – e.g., as in Shamir's secret sharing – then the error induced by homomorphic evaluation, and hence the scaling factor Δ becomes large, causing a significant overhead in the protocol. To minimize this overhead, we will use a linear secret-sharing scheme whose reconstruction function has only $-1, 0, 1$ coefficients – referred to as the *flatness* property. An additional benefit of the flatness property is that Recon becomes computationally cheaper, involving only simple additions and subtractions.

Committee Based Flat Secret Sharing Scheme. As motivated above, we need a secret sharing scheme with small reconstruction coefficients. One solution appears to come from the work of [17], which transforms any monotone Boolean formula for the threshold function into a linear secret-sharing scheme with small coefficients, satisfying flatness. Unfortunately, however, known constructions of Boolean formulae for the threshold function with M inputs has a size $\Omega(M^{5.3})$ [26], which by the transformation of [17] gives a secret sharing consisting of $\Omega(M^{5.3})$ elements in total. This is prohibitively expensive and recent work [4] indicates several challenges in improving this.

Our committee-based construction follows the blueprint of [17], but drastically reduces the total share size from $\Omega(M^{5.3})$ to $\Theta(\kappa^2)$ where κ is the security parameter. Our key observation is that in the setting of secure aggregation, a much weaker secret sharing scheme (than that of [17]) suffices:

1. Instead of using a monotone Boolean formula for threshold functions, it suffices to consider *gap threshold* functions. Such a function outputs 1 if more than ρ fraction of the inputs are 1 and outputs 0 if less than $\gamma < \rho$ fraction of the inputs are 1 (and has no guarantees for inputs in between). The values of ρ and γ correspond to the reconstruction and privacy thresholds in the context of secret sharing.
2. Instead of using a single formula, we use a *distribution* $\mathcal{F}$ of formulae. Our secret-sharing scheme has a setup phase where a formula is sampled $f \leftarrow \mathcal{F}$. As such, the security and correctness of secret sharing only need to hold with overwhelming probability over the random choice of f.

   Sampling $f \leftarrow \mathcal{F}$ directly translates to sampling a committee of share holders in the secret sharing scheme, corresponding to the committee Q chosen in the setup phase of our protocol above.
3. In fact, we do not even need formulae that compute exactly the gap threshold function. Instead, it suffices if for every "promised" input x, a random formula $f \leftarrow \mathcal{F}$ computes the correct output with overwhelming probability. That is,

$$\forall x \text{ with hamming weight } < \gamma M \text{ or } > \rho M,$$
$$\Pr\left[f(x) \text{ correct} \mid f \leftarrow \mathcal{F}\right] > 1 - \mathrm{negl}(\kappa).$$

These relaxations allow us to modify the randomized construction of formulae for threshold function in [26] to obtain a distribution of formulae with sizes $\Theta(\kappa^2)$ satisfying the above. The transformation of [17] then gives a committee based secret sharing consisting of only $\Theta(\kappa^2)$ elements in total, with a $\Theta(\kappa^2)$ size committee.

Server Efficiency. LERNA admits very efficient server computation. Upon collecting all the masked inputs z_i and all the mask shares c_i^U, the server simply computes a sum $\sum_{i \in U} z_i$, reconstruction over shares c_i^U, and finally unmasks. Since our secret sharing has $0/1$ coefficients, reconstruction is also computing a sum. LERNA server is $100\times$ faster than that of prior work [7], where the server needs to perform $\Theta(M)$ reconstruction of Shamir's secret sharing, and $\Theta(M(\log M + \kappa))$ group exponentiations. See Sect. 5 experimental data, and the full version for asymptotic comparisons.

Static vs. Adaptive Corruptions. One consequence of the above approach is that the random choices involved in sampling the formula (i.e., the committee of share holders) need to be independent of corruptions and dropouts in an execution of the protocol, which we expect to be chosen non-adaptively (for dropouts, in fact, we only require an overall set of potential dropouts to be fixed non-adaptively, but when individual parties drop out can be chosen adaptively). We stress that this assumption already inherently underlies the optimized aggregation protocol from [7], which relies on choosing a random graph independently of corruption and dropout patterns.

For the setting where the number of clients is small, e.g. $M \leq 80$, we show an alternative instantiation of LERNA that doesn't involve sampling a committee of share holders in the full version. In this variant, LERNA tolerates adaptive corruption.

2   Preliminaries

In this section, we explain the system and failure models of LERNA, and give an overview of LERNA's security requirements. We provide a formal security definition in the UC framework in the full version.

System Model. LERNA is a framework for secure aggregation involving M clients and a single server. Different from the systems in [7,10], LERNA has a one-time setup phase followed by many, T, online phases (also referred to as aggregation sessions). The setup phase creates correlated secrets $s_1, \ldots, s_M$ among the M clients, which are re-used in all following online phases. During each online phase, the server computes the aggregation over fresh inputs $\mathbf{x}_1, \ldots, \mathbf{x}_M$ from the same set of clients. The inputs to the clients $\mathbf{x}_i \in \mathbb{Z}^\ell$ are large integer vectors from a bounded (but potentially exponentially large) range, and the aggregation results are computed coordinate-wise over the integers.

Communication Model. Similar to prior work, LERNA has a simple communication pattern. During the online phases, each client communicates only with the server through private and authenticated channels. During the setup phase, the clients communicate indirectly with each other through the server, also in a private and authenticated way. This can be achieved by assuming a PKI setup, or, to avoid the PKI setup, the clients can run pairwise key-agreement through the server at the beginning of the setup phase. We need to assume (similarly to [7,10]) the server behave honestly in the key-agreement round.

The LERNA protocol proceeds in rounds. In each round, each client may send one message to the server, and may receive a reply message from the server. For simplicity, we assume synchronized communication channels.

Failure Model. LERNA is designed to be robust against two types of failures, corruption and dropout. For the first type of failure, a subset of the parties, may or may not include the server, collude to try to learn the individual input of the other clients. We further differentiate static and adaptive corruptions. In static corruption, the adversary selects a subset of corrupted parties at the beginning of the protocol execution. In adaptive corruption, the adversary is free to choose which party to corrupt at any stage of the protocol execution. Our main protocol in Sect. 4, suitable for running with large number of clients, tolerates static corruption. The variant described in the full version for running with small number of clients tolerates adaptive corruption. In the semi-honest setting, the adversary learns the inputs and the internal states of the corrupted parties, throughout the setup phase and all online phases. In the malicious setting, the adversary controls the actions of the corrupted parties entirely.

For the second type of failure, a potentially different subset of clients drop out from each online phase (and may come back in the future). We model no clients dropout during the setup phase. This is equivalent to saying only the set of clients who complete the setup phase is considered during the following online phases. More precisely, we model the dropout failure by allowing the adversary to choose a set of potential dropout clients D_t for each online phase t, all at the beginning of the protocol. The adversary is allowed to adaptively decide whether and when each client $P_i \in D_t$ (from the potential set) actually drops out during the online phase t.

Security Definition. The security of LERNA has two aspects: correctness and privacy. They are parameterized by a constant fraction δ, which represents the fraction of dropout clients tolerated by LERNA.

Correctness guarantees that in the semi-honest setting, the server computes the correct result in a session, as long as less than δM clients drop out in that session. In contrast, in the malicious setting, a corrupted client may arbitrarily "pollute" the aggregation result or cause it to be $\perp$, indicating an error.

For privacy, we consider an adversary that *statically* corrupts at most a γ fraction of the clients, before the aggregation protocol begins. We tolerate any fraction $0 \leq \gamma < 1 - \delta$. The adversary may additionally corrupt the server. The following privacy guarantee applies to both the semi-honest and the malicious settings.

In the simpler case, where only clients but not the server are corrupted, the adversary learns only the corrupted clients' inputs in each aggregation session and nothing else. In the case where the server is also corrupted, the adversary learns the corrupted clients' inputs, as well as a single sum of the honest clients' inputs in a sufficiently large set $U \subseteq [M]$, where $|U| > (1 - \delta)M$.

For comparison, the privacy guarantee of [7] is weaker. In the case where both the server and a subset of the clients are corrupted, an adversary may learn *multiple* non-overlapping sums of the honest inputs in each aggregation session. Their security guarantees that each such sum contains at least $\Omega(\log M)$ inputs, which provides a weaker degree of anonymity.

Formally, we define the security of LERNA in the UC framework [13]. Details of the UC framework and our formal security definition are deferred to the full version.

3   Technical Tools

In this section, we construct two technical tools, a key-homomorphic masking scheme and a flat secret sharing scheme. As outlined in the technical overview (Sect. 1.1), the masking scheme is used for hiding clients' input vectors, and the secret sharing scheme is used for sharing each client's secret masking key.

3.1   Key-Homomorphic Masking

We first introduce the syntax of a key-homomorphic masking scheme.

- Setup($1^\lambda, \ell, B_{\mathrm{msg}}$) : takes as inputs the security parameter λ, a message dimension ℓ, and a lower bound B_{msg} on the message modulus. It outputs public parameters pp, which defines a key space $\mathcal{K}$, a message space $\mathbb{Z}_{p_m}^\ell$ with some modulus $p_m \geq B_{\mathrm{msg}}$, and a mask space $\mathbb{Z}_q^\ell$ with some modulus q.

In our framework, we assume every client enters the setup phase (Fig. 1) with common correctly generated public parameters pp. If the Setup algorithm is deterministic, or public-coin, then this assumption is simply a notational convenience, since each client can compute the common pp on its own, using a random oracle to derive common public randomness if necessary.

- KeyGen(pp) : outputs a masking key $k \in \mathcal{K}$.
- TagGen(pp) : outputs a tag τ.

In our framework, each client P_i derives its secret masking key k_i in the setup phase, and re-uses it during all online phases. In contrast, it derives a fresh tag τ for each online phase, using common public randomness. We only require the key-homomorphic property to hold for masks under the same tag τ. While the tag is public to all clients, the masking keys must remain secret.

- Mask(pp, $k, \tau, \mathbf{m}$) : takes as inputs a masking key $k \in \mathcal{K}$, a tag τ, and a message $\mathbf{m} \in \mathbb{Z}_{p_m}^\ell$, and outputs a masked message $\mathbf{c}_m$.
- UnMask(pp, $\mathbf{c}_m, \mathbf{c}_0$) : takes as inputs a masked message $\mathbf{c}_m$, and an "empty" mask $\mathbf{c}_0$ (of message $\mathbf{0}$) under the same key and tag. It recovers a message $\mathbf{m}^*$ or $\perp$.

The UnMask algorithm is a bit unusual, as it doesn't take the masking key k or the tag τ to recover the message. Instead, it asks the caller to first compute an empty mask $\mathbf{c}_0$ using the key k and tag τ, and then feed $\mathbf{c}_0$ to the algorithm. We define such a syntax because in our framework, the caller of UnMask is the server. The clients jointly help the server compute the empty mask $\mathbf{c}_0$, instead of revealing their masking keys, so that the keys remain secret during each online phase.

- Eval(pp, L, $\{\mathbf{c}_i\}$): takes as inputs a linear function L with d integer coefficients and d masks $\{\mathbf{c}_i\}_{i\in[d]}$. It homomorphically evaluates L on the masks and outputs the result $\mathbf{c}_L$.

As mentioned earlier, the input masks $\{\mathbf{c}_i\}$ to the Eval algorithm should be masked under a common tag τ. Evaluating L on the masks roughly translates to evaluating L on both the masking keys, over the key space $\mathcal{K}$, and over the messages, over the message space $\mathbb{Z}_{p_m}^\ell$. We define this property below as key-homomorphism.

Correctness. Formally, we define the correctness and the key-homomorphism requirement as follows.

Definition 1 (correctness). *For all public parameters* pp, *tags* τ, *and keys* k *output by* Setup, TagGen *and* KeyGen, *and for all messages* $\mathbf{m} \in \mathbb{Z}_{p_m}^\ell$, *the following holds.*

$$\Pr\left[\mathsf{UnMask}(\mathsf{pp}, \mathbf{c}_m, \mathbf{c}_0) = \mathbf{m} \,\middle|\, \begin{array}{l} \mathbf{c}_m \leftarrow \mathsf{Mask}(\mathsf{pp}, k, \tau, \mathbf{m}), \\ \mathbf{c}_0 \leftarrow \mathsf{Mask}(\mathsf{pp}, k, \tau, \mathbf{0}). \end{array}\right] = 1.$$

Definition 2 (key-homomorphism). *Consider any linear function* L, *represented by* d *integer coefficients. For all public parameters* pp, *tag* τ, *and keys* $k_1, .., k_\ell$ *output by* Setup, TagGen, *and* KeyGen, *and all messages* $\mathbf{m}_1, ..., \mathbf{m}_d \in \mathbb{Z}_{p_m}^\ell$, *the following holds.*

$$\left\{\tilde{\mathbf{c}}_L \leftarrow \mathsf{Mask}(\mathsf{pp}, L(\{k_i\}), \tau, L(\{\mathbf{m}_i\}))\right\}$$
$$\equiv \left\{\mathbf{c}_L \leftarrow \mathsf{Eval}(\mathsf{pp}, L, \{\mathbf{c}_i\}) \,|\, \mathbf{c}_i \leftarrow \mathsf{Mask}(\mathsf{pp}, k_i, \tau, \mathbf{m}_i)\right\},$$

where $L(\{\mathbf{m}_i\})$ *is evaluated over* $\mathbb{Z}_{p_m}^\ell$ *and* $L(\{k_i\})$, *over the key space* $\mathcal{K}$.

The key-homomorphism definition above requires the evaluated mask $\mathbf{c}_L$ to have the same distribution as the "target" mask $\tilde{\mathbf{c}}_L$. We next introduce a relaxation to this rather strong property. Roughly, the evaluated mask $\mathbf{c}_L$ should be distributed close to the target mask $\tilde{\mathbf{c}}_L$. In other words, through homomorphic evaluation we obtain the target mask with some bounded additive noise.

Our framework requires two additional properties from an approximate key-homomorphic scheme. First, when computing UnMask on a masked input $\mathbf{c}_m$ and an empty mask $\mathbf{c}_0$, any additive noises in them translate to additive noises in the recovered message. Second, when computing Eval on noisy masks, the additive noises translates to an additive noise in the evaluated mask, with bounded magnitude. We formalize the above requirements as follows.

Definition 3 (ϵ-*approximate* key-homomorphism). *Consider any linear function* L, *with* d *integer coefficients whose absolute values are bounded by some* $B_L \in \mathbb{N}$.

- *Let* $\tilde{\mathbf{c}}_L$, $\mathbf{c}_L$ *be the evaluated and the "target" masks as defined in Definition 2. We require*
$$\|\tilde{\mathbf{c}}_L - \mathbf{c}_L\|_\infty \leq \epsilon d B_L.$$

– Let $\mathbf{c}_m, \mathbf{c}_0$ be the masked input and the empty mask as defined in Definition 1. For all integer noise vectors $\mathbf{e}_1, \mathbf{e}_2 \in \mathbb{Z}^\ell$, we require

$$\mathsf{UnMask}(\mathsf{pp}, \mathbf{c}_m + \mathbf{e}_1, \mathbf{c}_0 + \mathbf{e}_2) = \mathbf{m} + \mathbf{e}_1 + \mathbf{e}_2 \bmod p_m.$$

– Let $\mathsf{pp}, \{\mathbf{c}_i\}$ be the public parameters and the masks as defined in Definition 2. For all integer noise vectors $\{\mathbf{e}_i\}$, whose values are bounded by some $B_e \in \mathbb{N}$ we require

$$\|\mathsf{Eval}(\mathsf{pp}, L, \{\mathbf{c}_i\}) - \mathsf{Eval}(\mathsf{pp}, L, \{\mathbf{c}_i + \mathbf{e}_i\})\|_\infty \leq B_e d B_L.$$

Security. For security, we require a mask under a randomly chosen key hides its message. We further require this holds for a polynomial number of adaptive sessions, each with a fresh tag sampled with public randomness, reusing the same key.

Definition 4 (security). *Let λ be the security parameter. The masking scheme is secure if for all input dimension $\ell = \ell(\lambda) \leq \mathrm{poly}(\lambda)$ and message modulus lower bound $B_{msg} = B_{msg}(\lambda) \leq 2^{\mathrm{poly}(\lambda)}$, any efficient adversary $\mathcal{A}$ has negligible advantage in distinguishing the experiments $\mathsf{Exp}_{\mathsf{Mask}}^{\mathcal{A},b}(1^\lambda)$ defined as follows:*

– *The challenger computes* $\mathsf{pp} \leftarrow \mathsf{Setup}(1^\lambda, \ell, B_{msg})$, *and samples a masking key* $k \leftarrow \mathsf{KeyGen}(\mathsf{pp})$. *It launches* $\mathcal{A}(1^\lambda)$, *sends* pp *to* $\mathcal{A}$, *and repeats the following steps until* $\mathcal{A}$ *outputs a bit* b'.
   1. *Run* $\tau \leftarrow \mathsf{TagGen}(\mathsf{pp}; r)$ *using fresh randomness* r, *and send* (τ, r) *to* $\mathcal{A}$. *$\mathcal{A}$ replies with a message* $\mathbf{m} \in \mathbb{Z}_{p_m}^\ell$.
   2. *If $b = 1$, compute* $\mathbf{c}_1 \leftarrow \mathsf{Mask}(\mathsf{pp}, k, \tau, \mathbf{m})$. *Otherwise, compute* $\mathbf{c}_0 \leftarrow \mathsf{Mask}(\mathsf{pp}, k, \tau, \mathbf{0})$. *Send* $\mathbf{c}_b$ *to* $\mathcal{A}$.

Construction Based on LWR. We construct a 1-approximate key-homomorphic masking scheme based on the learning with rounding (LWR) assumption [5]. The construction is a slight modification to the almost seed homomorphic PRG based on LWR in [11].

Definition 5 (LWR [5]). *let λ be the security parameter, $n = n(\lambda)$, $q = q(\lambda)$, $p = p(\lambda)$ be integers. The $LWR_{n,q,p}$ assumption states that for any $m = \mathrm{poly}(n)$ $A \leftarrow \mathbb{Z}_q^{m \times n}$, $\mathbf{s} \leftarrow \mathbb{Z}_q^n$, $\mathbf{u} \leftarrow \mathbb{Z}_q^m$, the following indistinguishability holds:*

$$(A, \lfloor A \cdot \mathbf{s} \rceil_p) \approx^c (A, \lfloor \mathbf{u} \rceil_p),$$

where $\lfloor \cdot \rceil_p$ is the rounding function defined as $\lfloor \cdot \rceil_p : \mathbb{Z}_q \to \mathbb{Z}_p : x \mapsto \lfloor (p/q) \cdot x \rfloor$.

Construction 1 (key-homomorphic masking by LWR).

– $\mathsf{Setup}(1^\lambda, \ell, p_m)$: *deterministically choose a modulus q and dimension n such that LWR_{n,q,p_m} is assumed to be hard. Output* $\mathsf{pp} = (\ell, p_m, q, n)$. *The key space is $\mathcal{K} = \mathbb{Z}_q^n$, the message space, $\mathbb{Z}_{p_m}^\ell$, which is the same as the mask space.*

- KeyGen(pp) : sample a vector $\mathbf{s} \leftarrow \mathbb{Z}_q^n$, and output $k = \mathbf{s}$.
- TagGen(pp) : sample a matrix $A \leftarrow \mathbb{Z}_q^{n \times \ell}$, and output $\tau = A$.
- Mask(pp, $k, \tau, \mathbf{m}$) : parse the key and tag as $k, \tau = \mathbf{s}, A$. Output the masked message $\mathbf{c}_m = \lfloor A \cdot \mathbf{s} \rfloor_{p_m} + \mathbf{m} \in \mathbb{Z}_{p_m}^{\ell}$.
- UnMask(pp, $\mathbf{c}_m, \mathbf{c}_0$) : output the message $\mathbf{m}^* = \mathbf{c}_m - \mathbf{c}_0 \in \mathbb{Z}_{p_m}^{\ell}$.
- Eval(pp, $L, \{\mathbf{c}_i\}$) : parse L as d integer coefficients $u_1, \ldots, u_d$. Output the evaluated mask $\mathbf{c}_L = \sum_{i \in [d]} u_i \mathbf{c}_i \in \mathbb{Z}_{p_m}^{\ell}$.

The idea of the construction is simple. A masking key is an LWR secret $k = \mathbf{s}$, and a tag is a random LWR public matrix $\tau = A$. Given a masking key $\mathbf{s}$, a tag A, and a message $\mathbf{m}$ as inputs, the Mask algorithm hides the message $\mathbf{m}$ with a fresh LWR sample $\lfloor A \cdot \mathbf{s} \rfloor_{p_m}$. We defer the proof of Lemma 1 to the full version.

Lemma 1. *Construction 1 is a 1-approximate key-homomorphic masking scheme under the LWR_{n,q,p_m} assumption.*

Choosing Parameters q, n. It is proved in [5] that under the Learning With Error (LWE) assumption with dimension n, modulus q, and any noise distribution bounded by B, the LWR assumption also holds with dimension n and moduli q, p_m such that $q \geq B p_m n^{\omega(1)}$. It's commonly believed that the LWE assumption holds for sufficiently large $B = \text{poly}(n)$, and sub-exponential modulus-to-noise ratio $\alpha = q/B \leq 2^{\sqrt{n}}$. Therefore, given a message modulus $p_m \in \mathbb{N}$, it suffices to set $n = (\log p_m + \Omega(\lambda))^2$, and $q = B p_m n^{\log \lambda}$.

Extension to Ring LWR. The above scheme can also be instantiated using the Ring LWR assumption introduced together with LWR in [5]. We implement the more computationally efficient version with Ring LWR and present experiment data in Sect. 5.

Construction Based on DCR. Due to limited space, we defer our construction of an exact key-homomorphic masking scheme under the decisional composite residuosity (DCR) assumption to the full version.

3.2   Flat Secret Sharing

A threshold secret-sharing scheme with M parties normally has two algorithms Share, Recon, and is parameterized by privacy and reconstruction thresholds γ, ρ, where $0 < \gamma < \rho < 1$. Running Share on a secret value creates M shares. Running Recon on any subset of more than ρM shares recovers the secret. Any subset of less than γM shares contains no information about the secret.

Secret Sharing in Our Framework. Our framework uses the scheme in an unusual way. In the setup phase, the clients run Share to create shares of their masking keys. In the online phase, the server runs Recon *not* over the key shares, but homomorphically over empty masks created under the key shares. As long as Recon is a linear function, the key-homomorphism property (Definition 2) ensures that running Recon over the masks translates to over the underlying key shares. The two thresholds γ, ρ guarantees the masking keys are hidden when at most γM clients are corrupted, and Recon succeeds when at least ρM clients are online.

This approach creates a technical challenge when the masking scheme has only approximate key-homomorphism (Definition 3). Namely, evaluating Recon homomorphically creates an additive noise, which grows with the magnitude of the coefficients of Recon. The noise then propagates into the aggregation result.

To help remove the noise, each client input is multiplied with a scaling factor Δ, set larger than the noise. To accommodate the factor Δ in the clients inputs, the message modulus of the masking scheme is in turn increased by $\log \Delta$ bits. This overhead motivates us to construct a secret-sharing scheme with small coefficients in Recon, which we call a *flat* secret sharing scheme.

Overview of Our Scheme. Our starting point is the linear secret sharing scheme [17] that has $0, 1$ coefficients. However, using the scheme has a prohibitive overhead: the *total* share size scales polynomially in the population M, namely $\Omega(M^{5.3})$.

A first attempt at reducing the share size is to run the scheme in a small committee, sampled during the setup phase. If client corruption and dropout happen independently to the committee sampling, then the fractions of corruption and dropout in the committee roughly equal the true fractions in the population. This is true in our framework, where the set of corrupted clients, and potential dropout clients are decided statically at the beginning.

That is, we add a Setup algorithm to the scheme, which samples a committee $Q \subseteq [M]$ at random. It can be shown that when the fractions $0 < \gamma < \rho < 1$ has a constant gap, a committee of size $O(\kappa)$ suffices, with a $O(2^{-\kappa})$ statistical error.

Running [17] as a blackbox with a committee of size $O(\kappa)$ reduces the total share size from $O(M^{5.3})$ to $O(\kappa^{5.3})$. But we are able to further improve it to $O(\kappa^2)$, with a $O(\kappa^2)$-size committee, by re-visiting the analysis of [26], and constructing a committee version of [17] in a non-blackbox way. We summarize the syntax of our committee-based scheme for some secret space $\mathcal{M}$ below.

- Setup$(1^\kappa, M)$ takes as inputs the statistical security parameter κ, and the population size M. It outputs a committee Q of share holders, and public parameters pp.
- Share(pp, s) outputs shares $\{s_j\}_{j \in Q}$ computed from $s \in \mathcal{M}$.
- Recon$(pp, W, \{s_j\}_{j \in W})$ takes as inputs a set W indicating which shares are received, and the set of shares $\{s_j\}_{j \in W}$. It outputs a recovered secret s^* or $\perp$.

Correctness and Security. Formally, we define the correctness requirements as follows.

Definition 6 (ρ-reconstruction). *Let κ be the statistical security parameter. For all population size $M \in \mathbb{N}$, secret $s \in \mathcal{M}$, and subset $T \subseteq [M]$ with size $|T| > \rho M$*

the following holds.

$$\Pr\left[\begin{array}{l} \mathsf{Recon}(\mathsf{pp}, W, \{s_j\}_W) \\ \quad = s \end{array} \middle| \begin{array}{l} (Q, \mathsf{pp}) \leftarrow \mathsf{Setup}(1^\kappa, M), \\ \quad W = T \cap Q, \\ \{s_j\}_Q \leftarrow \mathsf{Share}(\mathsf{pp}, s) \end{array} \right] \geq 1 - \mathrm{negl}(\kappa).$$

The usual security requires that, for any corruption set $C \subseteq [M]$ below the threshold, i.e. $|C| \leq \gamma M$, corrupted shares $\{s_j\}_{Q \cap C}$ contain no information about the secret s.

We need a stronger property (which implies the usual one) to prove security of our framework: given corrupted shares $\{s_j\}_{Q \cap C}$ of 0, there is algorithm Ext that "extents" them to a full set of shares $\{s_j\}_Q$ for any secret s. The shares $\{s_j\}_Q$ distribute statistically close to shares of s. This is analogous to the property that, given a corrupted subset of Shamir's shares, one can interpolate the rest of the shares to any secret s. We formalize this requirement as follows.

Definition 7 (γ-simulation-privacy). *Let κ be the statistical security parameter. There exists an efficient deterministic algorithm Ext such that for all population size $M \in \mathbb{N}$, secret $s \in \mathcal{M}$, and subset $C \subseteq [M]$ with size $|C| < \gamma M$ the following two distributions are statistically close.*
They share the same public parameters $(Q, \mathsf{pp}) \leftarrow \mathsf{Setup}(1^\kappa, M)$.

1. *$\{s_j\}_Q$ is computed normally as $\{s_j\}_Q \leftarrow \mathsf{Share}(\mathsf{pp}, s)$.*
2. *$\{\tilde{s}_j\}_Q = \{s'_j\}_{Q \cap C} \cup \{\tilde{s}_j\}_{Q \cap \overline{C}}$ is computed by*
   $\{s'_j\}_Q \leftarrow \mathsf{Share}(\mathsf{pp}, 0)$ and $\{\tilde{s}_j\}_{Q \cap \overline{C}} = \mathsf{Ext}(\mathsf{pp}, C, \{s'_j\}_{Q \cap C}, s)$.

Flatness. As explained in "Secret Sharing in Our Framework", we require the Recon algorithm to have small coefficients as a linear function over the input shares. This minimizes the noise introduced by evaluating Recon homomorphically over empty masks. A similar situation arises in the security proof of our framework, where the simulator needs to evaluate Ext (Definition 7) homomorphically over noisy masks. We therefore additionally require Ext to have small coefficients as a linear function over the input shares and the secret. We summarize the above requirements as "flatness".

Definition 8 (flatness). *Let κ be the statistical security parameter. A flat secret sharing scheme satisfies the following.*

- *The Recon algorithm, when not outputting $\bot$, can be written as a linear function over the input shares, with integer coefficients bounded by $O(1)$.*
- *The Ext algorithm can be written as a linear function over the input shares and the secret, with integer coefficients bounded by $O(\log \kappa)$.*

Construction Details. We start by recalling the result of [8] and [17], summarized in the following theorem.

Theorem 1 (formula to secret sharing [8,17]). *For secrets over $\mathcal{M} = \mathbb{Z}_q$ for any modulus q or $\mathcal{M} = \mathbb{Z}$, there exists an efficient algorithm that translates any monotone Boolean formula $f : \{0,1\}^M \to \{0,1\}$, over variables $x_1, \ldots, x_M$, of size $d = |f|$, to a pair of secret sharing algorithms $\mathsf{Share}_f, \mathsf{Recon}_f$ satisfy the following:*

- $\mathsf{Share}_f(s)$ *computes d share units, each corresponding to a literal in f. For each share holder $i \in [M]$, its share s_i consists of all units corresponding to x_i. $\mathsf{Share}_f(s)$ outputs the shares $\{s_i\}$.*
  If $\mathcal{M} = \mathbb{Z}_q$, each share unit is an element in $\mathbb{Z}_q$. If $\mathcal{M} = \mathbb{Z}$, with secrets bounded by B, each unit is an integer bounded by $B2^\kappa$.
- *For any subset $T \subseteq [M]$, let $\mathbf{a}_T \in \{0,1\}^M$ denote the assignment where $a_i = 1$ iff $i \in T$. For every subset of the shares $\{s_j\}_T$, reconstruction $\mathsf{Recon}(T, \{s_j\}_T)$ succeeds iff $f(\mathbf{a}_T) = 1$.*
  For any subset $\{s_j\}_C$ that fails to reconstruct, there exists a simulation algorithm Ext defined analogously to Definition 7.
- *The algorithms $\mathsf{Share}_f, \mathsf{Recon}_f$ satisfy "flatness" per Definition 8.*

With Theorem 1, constructing a flat secret sharing scheme for any access structure reduces to finding a corresponding formula f:

- Setup constructs a formula f as pp, and defines the committee Q as the set of distinct literals in f.
- Share, Recon simply run $\mathsf{Share}_f, \mathsf{Recon}_f$ given by Theorem 1.

Below we first describe the result of [26], which shows the existence of a formula f_t, of size $O(M^{5.3})$, for any t-threshold function. (Note that for any $\gamma M < t < \rho M$, f_t satisfies our requirement.)

Construction 2 (t-threshold monotone Boolean formula [26]).
In [26], f_t (over M variables) is implicitly constructed through a formulae distribution F_t satisfying the following:

$$\forall \mathbf{a} \in \{0,1\}^M, \quad \Pr\left[f(\mathbf{a}) = \mathsf{Thresh}_t(\mathbf{a}) \mid f \leftarrow F_t\right] > 1 - 2^M, \tag{1}$$

where Thresh_t denotes the t-threshold function. Applying the union bound over all 2^M values for $\mathbf{a}$, we have

$$\Pr\left[\forall \mathbf{a} \in \{0,1\}^M, \ f(\mathbf{a}) = \mathsf{Thresh}_t(\mathbf{a}) \mid f \leftarrow F_t\right] > 0.$$

Hence, there exists a formula f_t in F_t that computes Thresh_t exactly.

Further, note that for any threshold $0 < t < M$, the function Thresh_t over M inputs is equivalent to $\mathsf{Thresh}_{M'/2}$ over $M' = M + D \leq 2M$ inputs, with $D \leq M$ dummy variables always set to 1 or 0, respectively for the case of $t < M/2$ or $t \geq M/2$. For technical reasons, we always choose M' to be odd. Therefore, it remains to construct a formulae distribution $F_{M/2}$, for any *odd* M.

The construction is recursive. In the base case, $F^{(0)}$ is defined as

$$F^{(0)} := \begin{cases} x_j \text{ for a uniform } j \xleftarrow{\$} [M] & \text{w/ prob. } p = 3 - \sqrt{5} \\ 0 & \text{w/ prob. } (1-p). \end{cases}$$

For $i \geq 1$, the formulae distribution F^i is defined inductively

$$F^{(i)} := (F_1^{(i-1)} \vee F_2^{(i-1)}) \wedge (F_3^{(i-1)} \vee F_4^{(i-1)}),$$

where $F_1^{(i-1)}, F_2^{(i-1)}, F_3^{(i-1)}, F_4^{(i-1)}$ are distributions independent and identical to $F^{(i-1)}$. It's shown that after $k = O(1) + 2.65 \log M$ recursion steps, the distribution $F_{M/2} = F^{(k)}$ satisfies Eq. 1.

Correctness and Efficiency of Construction 2. According to Eq. 1, we examine the probability that, for any assignment $\mathbf{a} \in \{0,1\}^M$, a sample $f^{(i)} \leftarrow F^{(i)}$ computes the _incorrect_ result.

- When $\mathbf{a}$ has less than $M/2$ ones, $f^{(i)}(\mathbf{a})$ is supposed to output 0, but instead (incorrectly) outputs 1. Let $p_s^{(i)}$ denote this probability, i.e., $f^{(i)}(\mathbf{a}) = 1$. By construction, we have

$$p_s^{(i)} = \left(1 - (1 - p_s^{(i-1)})^2\right)^2. \tag{2}$$

- When $\mathbf{a}$ has at least $M/2$ ones, let $p_c^{(i)}$ denote the probability that $f^{(i)}(\mathbf{a})$ (incorrectly) outputs 0. Similarly, we have

$$p_c^{(i)} = 1 - \left(1 - (p_c^{(i-1)})^2\right)^2. \tag{3}$$

By construction of $F^{(0)}$, and that M is odd, we also have

$$p_s^{(0)} < p(\frac{1}{2} - \frac{1}{2M}), \quad p_c^{(0)} \leq (1-p) + p(\frac{1}{2} - \frac{1}{2M}).$$

It remains to show that $p_s^{(k)}, p_c^{(k)} < 2^M$ for $k = O(1) + 2.65 \log M$, which follows from the technical claims below, which are taken directly from [26].

Claim 1 (phase 1). _For the recurrence relations specified by Eq. 2, 3 with any initial values satisfying $p_s^{(0)} < p/2 - p/(2M)$, $p_c^{(0)} < 1 - p/2 - p/(2M)$, it holds that $p_s^{(k_1)} \leq p/2 - \Omega(1)$, and $p_c^{(k_1)} \leq 1 - p/2 - \Omega(1)$ for $k_1 = 1.65 \log M$._

Claim 2 (phase 2). _For the recurrence relations specified by Eq. 2, 3 with any initial values satisfying $p_s^{(0)} < p/2 - \Omega(1)$, and $p_c^{(0)} < 1 - p/2 - \Omega(1)$, it holds that $p_s^{(k_2)}, p_c^{(k_2)} < 2^M$ for $k_2 = O(1) + \log M$._

Intuitively, a formula sampled from $F^{(0)}$ fails with probability close to (but less than) $p/2$ and $1 - p/2$ respectively in the two cases. Each recursive step "shifts" them further away from the starting points towards 0. Claim 1 shows that it takes $k_1 = O(\log M)$ steps to start at $\Theta(1/M)$-away and shift to $\Omega(1)$-away from the starting points. Claim 2 shows that it takes additional $k_2 = O(\log M)$ steps to shift exponentially close to 0.

Since each recursive step multiplies the formula size by 4, after $k = k_1 + k_2 = O(1) + 2.65 \log M$ steps, the formulas in $F^{(k)}$ has size $4^{O(1)+2.65 \log M} = O(M^{5.3})$.

Reducing the Size of Construction 2. Our first observation is instead of the formula f_t, we only need a formula $f_{\rho,\gamma}$ that 1) computes 1 if the inputs have $> \rho M$ ones, 2) computes 0 if the inputs have $< \gamma M$ ones, and 3) may otherwise compute either. We denote this (ρ, γ)-threshold function $\mathsf{Thresh}_{\rho,\gamma}$. A similar trick reduces computing $\mathsf{Thresh}_{\rho,\gamma}$ over M variables to $\mathsf{Thresh}_{1/2+\delta,1/2-\delta}$ over $M' \leq 2M$ variables for some constant fraction $\delta = (\rho - \gamma)/4$.

This observation allows us to calculate the initial failure probability for $f^{(0)} \leftarrow F^{(0)}$ differently from above.

- When $\mathbf{a}$ has less than $M(1/2 - \delta)$ ones, $f^{(0)}$ fails (i.e., computes 1) with probability $p_s^{(0)} < p(1/2 - \delta) < p/2 - \Omega(1)$.
- When $\mathbf{a}$ has more than $M(1/2 + \delta)$ ones, $f^{(0)}$ fails with probability $p_c^{(0)} < (1 - p) + p(1/2 + \delta) < 1 - p/2 - \Omega(1)$.

Since the initial values of $p_s^{(0)}, p_c^{(0)}$ already satisfies the condition for Claim 2, we indeed only need $k_2 = O(1) + \log M$ recursive steps! This observation already let us reduce the size of the formula from $4^{O(1)+2.56 \log M} = O(M^{5.3})$ to $4^{O(1)+\log M} = O(M^2)$.

Our second observation is that in the static corruption model, the set of corrupted and the reconstructing share holders C, T_i at each iteration i is fixed before the secret sharing Setup algorithm. Therefore, instead of finding an exact formula $f_{\rho,\gamma}$ that's correct on all assignments, it suffices to sample $f \leftarrow F_{\rho,\gamma}$ during Setup that's correct on the $(\mathsf{poly}(\kappa)$ many) fixed assignments $\mathbf{a}_C$ and $\mathbf{a}_{T_i}$.

In particular, we can avoid taking the union bound over 2^M values for $\mathbf{a}$, and only construct a distribution $F_{\rho,\gamma}$ (equivalently, $F_{1/2+\delta,1/2-\delta}$) such that

$$\forall \mathbf{a} \in \{0,1\}^M, \quad \Pr\left[f(\mathbf{a}) = \mathsf{Thresh}_{\rho,\gamma}(\mathbf{a}) \mid f \leftarrow F_{\rho,\gamma}\right] > 1 - 2^\kappa.$$

By Claim 2, we now only need $k_2' = O(1) + \log \kappa$ recursive steps, which further reduces the formula size to $O(\kappa^2)$!

To summarize, we obtain the following lemma.

Lemma 2 (flat secret sharing). *For any population size $M \in \mathbb{N}$, constant fractions $0 < \gamma < \rho < 1$, integer modulus q and dimension ℓ, there exists a flat secret-sharing scheme $\mathsf{Setup}, \mathsf{Share}, \mathsf{Recon}$ for secrets space $\mathcal{M} = \mathbb{Z}_q^\ell$ or $\mathcal{M} = \mathbb{Z}^\ell$, with privacy and reconstruction thresholds γ, ρ. Furthermore,*

- *It has committee size $|Q| = O(\kappa^2)$, where the constant depends on the thresholds γ, ρ.*
- *The Recon algorithm, when written as a linear function, has $O(\kappa)$ non-zero coefficients, which are 1 or -1.*

Concrete Algorithm for Theorem 1. When sharing a secret according to a formula f, Share$_f$ views f as a tree with AND, OR on the intermediate nodes, and literals x_i on the leaf nodes. It assigns a share to each node of this tree: i) Upon reaching an AND node, split the current share s into two additive shares of s, and assign them to the children. ii) Upon reaching an OR node, duplicate s and assign them to the children. iii) Upon reaching a literal x_i, assign s to share holder i. Reconstruction according to f follows a similar recursive algorithm.

4 The LERNA Framework

In this section, we describe our abstract secure aggregation protocol assuming the existence of the two technical tools introduced in Sect. 3:

- An ϵ-approximate key-homomorphic masking scheme HM = (HM.Setup, KeyGen, TagGen, Mask, UnMask, Eval) setup properly with HM.pp, specifying a message space $\mathbb{Z}_{p_m}^\ell$, mask space $\mathbb{Z}_q^\ell$ and key space $\mathcal{K}$.
- A flat secret sharing scheme SS = (SS.Setup, Share, Recon) for sharing the masking keys in the above key space $\mathcal{K}$.

The protocol additionally assumes a public key encryption scheme and two hash functions $\mathcal{H}_1, \mathcal{H}_2$ modeled as random oracles. We assume the hash functions $\mathcal{H}_1, \mathcal{H}_2$ output exactly the numbers of random bits required by the algorithms SS.Setup, and TagGen.

The protocol runs with M clients $\{P_i\}$ and a single server S for T iterations. During each iteration $t \in [T]$, every client P_i obtains a fresh integer vector $\mathbf{x} \in \mathbb{Z}^\ell$ from a bounded range $[0, B_x]$. To avoid wrap-around in the aggregation results, we setup the masking scheme with a modulus lower bound $B_{\mathrm{msg}} = \Delta M B_x$, where Δ is a message scaling factor introduced in the protocol.

The protocol is further parameterized by two thresholds $\gamma, \delta \in (0,1)$, specifying the maximum fractions of corrupted clients and dropout clients, respectively, under the restriction that $\gamma + \delta < 1$. We set the privacy threshold of the secret sharing scheme to γ, and the reconstruction threshold to $\rho = 1 - \delta$.

In the online phase, the protocol uses a noise bound B_e and a message scaling factor Δ, which we specify in Sect. 4.4 for concrete instantiations under LWR.

4.1 The Semi-honest Protocol

We start with the simpler, semi-honest variant of the protocol, given in Fig. 1, and Fig. 2. We describe the additional steps to obtain the malicious variant next, and defer the more formal (in the UC framework) security proof for the malicious protocol to the full version.

Setup Phase. During the setup phase, the clients first agree on a small committee Q, computed using public common randomness $\mathbf{r}_1$. They each sample a secret masking key k_i, and secret share it to the committee Q, using the server

---

Setup Phase

Inputs to P_i: The session id sid, public keys of other clients, and public parameters of the masking scheme HM.pp.

1. Each client P_i obtains common randomness $r_1 = \mathcal{H}_1(\text{sid})$ for sampling the committee $(Q, \text{SS.pp}) \leftarrow \text{SS.Setup}(; r_1)$.

   Next, P_i samples a masking key $k_i \leftarrow \text{KeyGen}(\text{HM.pp})$ and secret shares it to the committee:

   $$\{k_j^i\}_{j \in Q} \leftarrow \text{Share}(\text{SS.pp}, k_i).$$

   P_i encrypts each share k_j^i with the public key of its target P_j as $\tilde{k}_j^i$, and sends $(\text{sid}, i, j, \{\tilde{k}_j^i\}_{j \in Q})$ to the server S.
2. The server S receives the above encrypted shares from all M clients, and distributes them through messages $(\text{sid}, \{\tilde{k}_j^i\}^{i \in [M]})$ to every committee member $P_j \in Q$.
3. Each committee member $P_j \in Q$ receives encrypted shares, decrypts them, and stores the plain shares $\{k_j^i\}^{i \in [M]}$.

Fig. 1. LERNA protocol for the setup phase.

to distribute those shares. To keep the shares secret from the server, the clients encrypt each share using the public key of its target share-holder.

Note that the clients only run the setup phase once, followed by T online phases. In each online phase, each client P_i uses the same masking key k_i to mask its fresh input vector $\mathbf{x}_i$. Reusing the masking key may seem like a privacy concern. To address this, we ensure that in each online phase, the clients sample a *fresh tag* τ used for computing the mask. The randomness of the tag τ protects the input vector $\mathbf{x}_i$, as long as the masking key remains secret.

Online Phase.

Step 1: Every client runs the key-homomorphic masking scheme HM.Mask to obtain a masked input vector $\mathbf{z}_i$, and sends it to the server S. It's important to note that key-homomorphism only holds for masks computed using the same tag τ. Therefore, the clients sample the tag using public common randomness r_2.

Step 2: The server receives the masked input vectors $\{\mathbf{z}_i\}$ from the online clients, and replies the online set U to each committee member. Note that non-committee member clients don't need to send anything in the rest of the online phase.

Step 3: Every committee member P_j aggregates locally its shares of masking keys from the online set U to obtain an aggregated key share k_j^U, uses it to compute an "empty mask" as its reconstruction vector $\mathbf{w}_j$, and sends it to the server S.

Step 4: The server S receives reconstruction vectors $\{\mathbf{w}_j\}$ from the online committee members. It proceeds to locally recover the aggregation result.

First, it homomorphically aggregates the masked input vectors $\mathbf{z}_i$ to obtain $\mathbf{c}_{\text{sum}}$. By key-homomorphism, the vector $\mathbf{c}_{\text{sum}}$ approximately equals running

---

Online Phase: iteration $t = 1, ..., T$

Inputs to P_i: The session id sid, and an integer vector $\mathbf{x}_i \in \mathbb{Z}^\ell$.

1. Each client P_i obtains common randomness $\mathbf{r}_2 = \mathcal{H}_2(\text{sid}, t)$ for sampling a tag $\tau = \text{TagGen}(\text{HM.pp}; \mathbf{r}_2)$, computes

$$\mathbf{z}_i \leftarrow \text{Mask}(\text{HM.pp}, k_i, \tau, \Delta \cdot \mathbf{x}_i),$$

   and sends a message $(\text{sid}, i, \mathbf{z}_i, t)$ to the server S.

2. The server S receives a masked input vector $\mathbf{z}_i$ from each online client, and records the set of dropout clients D. It computes the "online set" $U = [M] \setminus D$, and sends a message (sid, U, t) to every online committee member $P_j \in (Q \cap U)$.

3. Each online committee member P_j checks that $|U| > (1 - \delta)M$, and computes a reconstruction vector

$$\mathbf{w}_j = \text{Mask}(\text{HM.pp}, \sum_{i \in U} k_j^i, \tau, \mathbf{0}) + \mathbf{e}_j,$$

   where $\mathbf{e}_j \leftarrow [B_e]^\ell$ is a uniformly sampled noise from range B_e. If $|U|$ is too small, P_j sets $\mathbf{w}_j = \bot$. P_j sends a message $(\text{sid}, j, \mathbf{w}_j, t)$ to the server S.

4. The server S receives a reconstruction vector $\mathbf{w}_j$ from every online committee member, ignoring $\bot$. It records the set of valid vectors W. S homomorphically sums over the masked inputs as $\mathbf{c}_{\text{sum}} = \text{Eval}(\text{HM.pp}, +, \{\mathbf{z}_i\}_{i \in U})$, and then homomorphically runs the Recon algorithm over the vectors $\{\mathbf{w}_i\}$

$$\mathbf{c}_0 = \text{Eval}\big(\text{HM.pp}, \text{Recon}(\text{SS.pp}, W, \cdot), \{\mathbf{w}_i\}\big).$$

   If Recon aborts on the set W, then S outputs a message $(\text{sid}, \bot, D, t)$. Otherwise, it uses $\mathbf{c}_0$ as the "empty mask" to recover $\mathbf{x}_U' \leftarrow \text{UnMask}(\text{HM.pp}, \mathbf{c}_{\text{sum}}, \mathbf{c}_0)$, and rounds $\mathbf{x}_U'$ by Δ to obtain $\mathbf{x}_U$. It outputs a message $(\text{sid}, \mathbf{x}_U, D, t)$.

Fig. 2. LERNA protocol for the online phase (semi-honest).

HM.Mask on the scaled aggregation result $\mathbf{x}_U' = \Delta \cdot \sum_U \mathbf{x}_i$ under the key $k_U = \sum_U k_i$. It remains to obtain an "empty mask" $\mathbf{c}_0$ under the same key k_U, with which the server can recover the scaled aggregation result $\mathbf{x}_U'$, and then the actual aggregation result $\mathbf{x}_U = \lfloor \mathbf{x}_U'/\Delta \rceil$ through rounding.

To obtain the empty mask $\mathbf{c}_0$ under the key k_U, the server homomorphically runs the algorithm SS.Recon over the reconstruction vectors $\mathbf{w}_j$. By key-homomorphism, the result indeed approximately equals $\mathbf{c}_0$. Note that approximate key-homomorphism causes some errors in the recovered result $\mathbf{x}_U'$. But we set the scaling factor Δ sufficiently large to make sure such errors are removed by the rounding step.

Alternative to the PKI Setup. The setup phase of our protocol requires the clients to encrypt their secret shares under the public keys of the target share-holders. For simplicity, our protocol assumes a public key infrastructure (PKI), and that each client enters the setup phase knowing every other client's public key.

An alternative approach is to let the clients run pairwise key agreement at the beginning of the setup phase, as described in the "Communication Model" paragraph (Sect. 2).

Committee Members and Non-members. Note that in each online phase, non-member clients only have one task: send masked input vectors to the server. The rest of the reconstruction steps are handled by committee member clients.

This separation of responsibility suggests an alternative aggregation model, where during each phase, only a small, potentially random, subset among the non-member clients is required to provide inputs. Our protocol can be adapted straightforwardly to guarantee: as long as not too many committee members drop out during the session, the server can securely compute the aggregation result. This scenario can be useful for stochastic federated learning algorithms that benefit from a large input population, but only learns from a random subset at each iteration.

4.2 Correctness of LERNA

Below, we illustrate correctness by proving Lemma 3. A formal functionality definition and security proof in the UC framework is in the full version.

Lemma 3 (correctness). *If less than δM clients dropout in an online session t, then the server outputs the correct aggregation result with overwhelming probability in the semi-honest setting.*

Proof (sketch). Looking at the reconstruction step (online step 4), we first argue that the aggregated mask $\mathbf{c}_{\mathrm{sum}}$ is distributed close to a mask over the aggregation result. By ϵ-approximate key homomorphism (Definition 3), we have

$$\|\mathbf{c}_{sum} - \mathsf{Mask}(\mathsf{HM.pp}, \sum_{i \in U} k_i, \tau, \Delta \sum_{i \in U} \mathbf{x}_i)\|_{\infty} \leq \epsilon M.$$

For the UnMask algorithm to work correctly, we need to argue the reconstructed mask $\mathbf{c}_0$ is distributed close to an empty mask under the key $\sum_{i \in U} k_i$. To this end, we first argue that the Recon algorithm succeeds over the shares from the set W with overwhelming probability. By assumption, online set U computed by the server at the online step 2 has size $|U| > (1 - \delta)M$. Therefore, all online committee members send reconstruction vectors $\mathbf{w}_j$ at online step 3. Let the online set at online step 3 be $U' \subseteq U$. The set of valid reconstruction vectors W equals $W = U' \cap Q$. By assumption, we have $|U'| > (1 - \delta)M$. Therefore, by $(1 - \delta)$-reconstruction, the algorithm Recon indeed succeeds with overwhelming probability.

By flatness (Definition 8), the function $\mathsf{Recon}(\mathsf{SS.pp}, W, \cdot)$ is linear with $O(1)$ coefficients. Therefore, by ϵ-approximate key homomorphism, we have

$$\|\mathbf{c}_0 - \mathsf{Mask}(\mathsf{HM.pp}, \sum_{i \in U} \underbrace{\mathsf{Recon}(\mathsf{SS.pp}, W, \{k_j^i\}_{j \in W})}_{k_i}, \tau, \mathbf{0})\|_{\infty}$$
$$\leq O(\epsilon B_e |Q|),$$

where B_e is the bound on the noises $\mathbf{e}_j$ in the vectors $\mathbf{w}_j$.

Finally, we conclude that the UnMask algorithm on masks $\mathbf{c}_{\text{sum}}$ and $\mathbf{c}_0$ returns a noisy result $\mathbf{x}'_U = \Delta \sum_U \mathbf{x}_i + \mathbf{e}$, where the noise has entries bounded by $\|\mathbf{e}\|_\infty = O(\epsilon(M + B_e|Q|))$. As long as the message scaling factor Δ is sufficiently large $\Delta \geq 2\|\mathbf{e}\|_\infty$, the server indeed recovers the correct result through rounding by Δ.   □

4.3 Achieving Malicious Security

To achieve malicious security, we keep the setup phase (Fig. 1) unchanged, and only modify the online phase (Fig. 2) starting from step 2. The modifications follow similar ideas to prior work [7,10]. The modified online phase is given in Fig. 3, where the changes are highlighted in blue.

Online Phase: iteration $t = 1, ..., T$

Inputs to P_i: The session id sid, public keys of other clients, and an integer vector $\mathbf{x}_i \in \mathbb{Z}^\ell$.

2. The server S records the dropout set D and online set $U = [M] \setminus D$ as in Figure 2, and sends a message (sid, U, t) to every online committee member $P_j \in (Q \cap U)$. Additionally, it sends a short hash of U, h_U to every online client.

3. Each client P_i receives a hash h_U from the server S, and sends its signature $\sigma_i(h_U)$ to S.

4. The server S receives a signature from every online client, and sends the set of valid signatures $\{\sigma_i(U)\}$ to every online committee member P_j.

5. Each online committee member P_j checks that at least $(1 + \gamma)M/2$ signatures over the hash h_U are valid. If there are not enough valid signatures, it sets the reconstruction vector $\mathbf{w}_j = \bot$. Otherwise, it proceeds as in Figure 2 step 3 to compute the vector $\mathbf{w}_j$, and sends it to the server S.

6. The server S receives a reconstruction vector $\mathbf{w}_j$ from every online committee member, ignoring invalid vectors like $\bot$. It proceeds as in Figure 2 step 4 to recover the result $\mathbf{x}_U$. In case of any failed step, it outputs a message $(\text{sid}, \bot, D, t)$.

Fig. 3. LERNA protocol for the online phase (malicious). (Color figure online)

To see why we need the additional steps in the malicious setting, consider the following corrupted server. Recall that in the semi-honest online protocol, the server sends an online set U to online committee members to recover an aggregation result $\mathbf{x}_U = \sum_U \mathbf{x}_i$. A corrupted server instead sends different online sets, $U \neq U'$, to two subsets of online committee members. As long as both subsets are large enough, the correctness of the semi-honest protocol guarantees the successful recovery of both results $\mathbf{x}_U$ and $\mathbf{x}_{U'}$ by the server. This obviously violates our security definition, which requires only a single sum of honest inputs is leaked in each online phase.

The additional steps 3–4 in Fig. 3 roughly ask each client, including corrupted ones, to "vote" on an online set U by signing a hash h_U. The server collects those signatures as unforgeable votes and sends them to the committee members. The threshold in step 5 is set such that at most one online set U^* can have enough votes. Therefore, the above attack is prevented.

Preventing Abort Attacks. While setting the threshold for valid signatures in Step 5 to $(1+\gamma)M/2$ guarantees that at most one online set U^* has enough votes, it creates an opportunity for malicious clients to abort the protocol, even when the server is honest, by not sending enough valid signatures. To avoid this issue, we need enough honest clients so that their signatures alone are enough for the threshold. Restricting the corruption and dropout threshold γ, δ such that $(3\gamma + 2\delta) < 1$ suffices.

Claim 3. *Assuming $(3\gamma + 2\delta) < 1$, and the server is honest, then every honest committee member always collects at least $(1+\gamma)M/2$ valid signatures in Step 5.*

Proof. By the assumption, there are at least $(1-\gamma-\delta)M$ honest clients in each iteration that remain online, and will send a valid signature in Step 3 on the hash h_U received from an honest server. Calculation shows $(1-\gamma-\delta)M \geq (1-\gamma)M/2$ iff $1 \geq (3\gamma + 2\delta)$. □

By the above claim, an honest server is guaranteed to receive non-$\perp$ reconstruction messages from all honest online committee members in Step 6. By ρ-reconstruction ($\rho = 1 - \delta$) of the secret sharing, the server succeeds in computing the empty mask c_0.

Finally, the server may still abort if UnMask(HM.pp, c_{sum}, c_0) fails. However, in our LWR masking scheme (Construction 1), the UnMask algorithm simply computes a subtraction modulo p_m, which always succeeds.

Overhead of the Malicious Protocol. As highlighted in Fig. 3, the communication and computation overhead of the malicious variant consists of the server sending valid signatures $\{\sigma_i(U)\}$ in step 4, and each committee member verifying those signatures in step 5, respectively.

For ease of presentation, the variant shown in Fig. 3 requires every client to send a signature in step 3. However, it can be shown that at the cost of a $O(2^{-\kappa})$ statistical error in privacy, only committee members need to send signatures. Note that the number of signatures is at most the committee size $|Q| = O(\kappa^2)$, which is independent of the number of clients M, or the input dimension ℓ. Therefore, when M or ℓ is large, sending and checking those signatures incur only negligible communication and computation overheads over the semi-honest variant.

4.4   Instantiation Under LWR

Concretely, we instantiate the LERNA protocol with the 1-approximate homomorphic masking scheme based on LWR in Construction 1.

We set the noise bound $B_e = O(\log(\kappa)M2^\kappa)$, which is required for security. (See the full version for security proofs.) where κ is the statistical security parameter. We set the message scaling factor $\Delta = O(M + B_e|Q|)$ as required by the correctness proof of Lemma 3, where $|Q| = O(\kappa^2)$ is the committee size of the flat secret sharing scheme, as described in Sect. 3.2. Under these settings, our protocol sets up the LWR-based masking scheme with message modulus (which is the same as the mask modulus) $p_m = \Delta M B_x$, which has bit length $\log p_m < O(1) + 3\log\kappa + \kappa + 2\log M + \log B_x$.

The LWR-based masking scheme has keyspace $\mathcal{K} = \mathbb{Z}_q^n$, where the dimension n and modulus q is chosen such that LWR_{n,q,p_m} is assumed to be hard. We therefore instantiate a flat secret-sharing scheme with secret space $\mathcal{M} = \mathcal{K} = \mathbb{Z}_q^n$.

We present communication and computation efficiency analysis for the LWR instantiation in the full version.

5 Experimental Evaluation

We benchmark the concrete efficiency of the LERNA framework by implementing the semi-honest protocol instantiated under the (Ring) LWR assumption (cf. Sect. 4.4 for a description).

As our baseline, we compare our protocol design with the semi-honest protocol from [7], adapted naturally to the multi-session setting. In particular, the baseline server uses the setup phase to randomly sample a communication graph, and inform each client of its set of neighbors. Baseline clients re-use the same communication graph throughout the following online phases.

Our benchmarks clearly highlight the lightweight server computation during each online phase.

5.1 Implementation Details

Our prototypes are implemented in Python. The protocol simulations are run locally, using the ABIDES simulation framework [12]. Our implementations use the following libraries for heavy computations:

- SEAL [24] and PySEAL [2] for polynomial arithmetics required by Ring LWR.
- Gmpy2[3] for large integer arithmetics.
- M2Crypto[4] as an interface to AES for implementing a PRG and a random oracle.
- PyNaCl[5] for public key encryption and key-agreement.

Setting Parameters. In the LERNA framework, we need to set two security parameters, $\lambda = 128, \kappa = 40$. Computationally secure primitives (e.g., encryption

---

[2] https://github.com/Lab41/PySEAL.
[3] https://gmpy2.readthedocs.io/.
[4] https://m2crypto.readthedocs.io/.
[5] https://pynacl.readthedocs.io/.

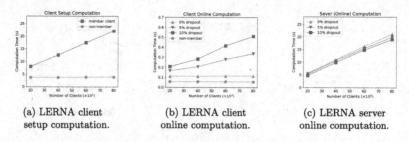

(a) LERNA client setup computation.

(b) LERNA client online computation.

(c) LERNA server online computation.

Fig. 4. LERNA computation time vs. number of clients (M), with fixed input dimension $\ell = 10K$.

and the masking scheme) are set to have $\lambda = 128$ bits of security, and statistically secure primitives (e.g., the flat secret sharing scheme) are set to have $\kappa = 40$ bits of security. The concrete committee size equals $|Q| = 2^{14} = 16384$ for $\kappa = 40$.

In our prototype, the message modulus p_m for the (Ring) LWR based key-homomorphic masking scheme is set as described in Sect. 4.4, which ranges from 142 to 145 bits in our benchmark settings. We set the RLWR dimension to be 2^{11}, and the modulus to $q = p_m \cdot 2^{254}$ to guarantee at least 128 bits of security, according to the hardness estimator[6] of [1].

In the baseline prototype, we set the field size for Shamir's secret sharing to be a 257 bit prime, because the secrets are 256 bit curves used in key-agreement. To set the neighborhood size k and privacy threshold t of Shamir's secret sharing, we follow Theorem 3.10 in [7] (section 3.5). In our settings where the number of parties ranges from $M = 400, \ldots, 80K$, the neighborhood size ranges from $k = 109, \ldots, 126$, and the privacy threshold ranges from $t = 55, \ldots, 63$ to achieve $2^{-\kappa} = 2^{-40}$ statistical error.

5.2 Benchmarks

Our benchmarks are run on a desktop machine with 32 Gigabyte of memory and with a single core CPU speed 3.9 GHz. Our prototype implementations do not take advantage of multiple cores. For computation time measurements, we report an average over 10 experiment runs.

Computation Efficiency. We first benchmark the computation time of our LERNA prototype with increasing numbers of clients $M = 20K \ldots, 80K$. We run the prototype with $\ell = 10K$ dimension inputs vector with random entries from $[0, 2^{64}]$, and fix the corruption threshold at $\gamma = 10\%$. In Fig. 4a, 4b, and 4c, we respectively plot our client runtime during the setup and the online phases, and our server runtime during the online phase. Comparing Fig. 4a and 4b, we observe that the setup phase is much heavier compared to the online phases.

In Fig. 4b, and 4c, we observe that the dropout rate affects the computation time of both committee member clients and the server. This is because our

---

[6] Running code provided at https://lwe-estimator.readthedocs.io.

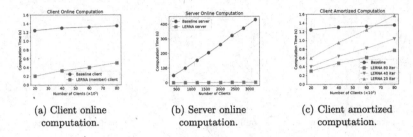

(a) Client online computation.

(b) Server online computation.

(c) Client amortized computation.

Fig. 5. Computation time comparison between LERNA and [7], with fixed input dimension $\ell = 10K$, and dropout rate $\gamma = 10\%$. (b) compares the server computation at a smaller number of clients $M = 400, \ldots, 3200$ due to the high cost of the baseline server. (c) compares the amortized computation time of a single setup phase plus 20/40/80 online phases. Since the baseline client has negligible computation during setup, its amortized time equals that shown in (a).

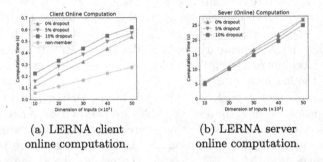

(a) LERNA client online computation.

(b) LERNA server online computation.

Fig. 6. LERNA computation time vs. input dimension (ℓ), with fixed number of clients $M = 20K$. The plot for client setup computation is omitted, as it doesn't depend on ℓ.

committee member needs to aggregate masking key shares over the dropout set, which becomes larger both under higher dropout rates and with a larger number of clients. Our server similarly aggregates masked input vectors over the online set, which becomes smaller under higher dropout rates.

In the full version, we give more detailed numbers about the running time of different components of our protocols.

We next benchmark the computation time of our protocol with increasing input dimensions $\ell = 10K \ldots, 50K$. We run the prototype with $M = 20K$ clients, and fix the corruption threshold again at $\gamma = 10\%$. In Fig. 6a, and Fig. 6b, we respectively plot our client and server during the online phase. Since the clients and the server during the setup phase are independent of input dimensions, we omit their plots.

Communication Efficiency. In Table 1 we report the communication sizes of our client with increasing input dimensions $\ell = 10K \ldots, 50K$. The server communication can be deduced as the sum of all clients. Hence we omit its table. We run the prototype with $M = 20K$ clients, and input entries from $[0, 2^{64}]$. We fix the corruption threshold and the dropout rate both at 10%.

Table 1. Client communication sizes.

Phase	$\ell = 10K$	$\ell = 30K$	$\ell = 50K$
Non-member setup	2.00 (GB)	2.00 (GB)	2.00 (GB)
Member setup	4.44 (GB)	4.44 (GB)	4.44 (GB)
Non-member online	0.18 (MB)	0.54 (MB)	0.91 (MB)
Member online	0.37 (MB)	1.09 (MB)	1.82 (MB)

The total offline communication of our clients is indeed heavy, as reported in Table 1. Each client sends encrypted shares of its masking key to the server. Due to the large Ring LWR dimension (2048) and modulus ($\sim$400 bits), this phase requires large communication (2 GB) from each client. Each committee member additionally receives the encrypted shares from the clients.

Thankfully, the entire offline phase doesn't need to be synchronized, which eases the bandwidth requirement. If needed, each client can send a share of its masking key to a committee member one at a time.

Comparing with the Baseline. To compare with the baseline, we run both prototypes with $10K$ dimension inputs vectors with random entries from $[0, 2^{64}]$. We fix the corruption rate and the dropout rate at $\gamma = 10\%$.

As discussed in the introduction, we assume a statically corrupted set of clients throughout the repeated T sessions. A larger T, means a stronger assumption on the staticness and the fraction of corruption. On the flip side, since our protocol enjoys a re-usable setup across T sessions, a larger T gives better efficiency. In comparing with the baseline, we not only compare the computation time of each online iteration (Fig. 5a, 5b), but also the amortized time over different settings of T (Fig. 5c). The client computation and communication cost of running our setup phase (, where a fresh committee is formed and secret masking keys are shared,) are shown in Fig. 4a and Table 1. The server costs of setup for our server and for the baseline solution are negligible. Hence we omit reporting them here.

From Fig. 5a, we observe that even our slower committee member client runs faster than the baseline during each online iteration for $M = 20K$ to $M = 80K$. As expected, its running time grows faster with M than the baseline because our committee member needs to aggregate masking key shares over the dropout set. If the dropout rate is a non-zero constant, as set in our experiment, then the committee client's work grows linearly in M. In comparison, the computation of the baseline depends linearly in its neighborhood size in the communication graph, which is $O(\log M)$.

In Fig. 5c, we compare the clients' amortized running time (showing the heavy member clients for LERNA) of a single setup phase followed by $T = 20/40/80$

online iterations. Since the baseline client has negligible computation during setup, its amortized time equals its online computation time, which doesn't change with T. We observe an advantage, even for the member clients, over the baseline when amortized over more than $T = 40$ online sessions. For example, at $M = 80K$, the total client computation time of 40 LERNA iterations equals $22 + 0.5 \cdot 40 = 42(s)$. The total time of 40 baseline iterations is at least $1.2 \cdot 40 = 48(s)$, according to the plot.

In Fig. 5b we are only able to compare the server's performance at moderate numbers of clients $M = 400 \ldots 3200$, because the baseline server runs too long when M reaches $10K$. But this is enough to illustrate LERNA's advantage (concretely, more than $100\times$) in server computation times.

Comparing with SASH+ [20]. As mentioned in "Related Work", the protocol SASH+ from [20] reduces aggregating ℓ-dimension inputs to aggregating n-dimensional homomorphic PRG seeds, where n is the LWR dimension. SASH+ then runs [7] for the latter. Asymptotically, SASH+ reduces the computation cost of [20] from $\widetilde{O}(\kappa^2 + \kappa\ell)$ to $\widetilde{O}(\kappa^2 + \kappa n + \ell)$ for the clients, and from $\widetilde{O}(\kappa M\ell + \kappa^2 M)$ to $\widetilde{O}(\kappa Mn + \kappa^2 M + \ell M)$ for the server. We optimistically estimate that SASH+ reduces the computation cost of [7] by a factor of (ℓ/n).

In our benchmarks, $\ell = 10K$, and the LWR dimension $n = 2048$. We estimate the server and client computational costs of SASH+ to be 5x smaller than [7] (in reality, the improvement is smaller due to other computation steps that remain constant). Under this estimation, we observe that the LERNA server (Fig. 5b) and non-committee member clients (Fig. 4b) still significantly outperforms the SASH+ server and SASH+ clients. However, the cost of a LERNA committee member (Fig. 5a) becomes comparable to (when M is relatively small e.g. $20K$) or slower than (when M is larger) a SASH+ client.

Acknowledgement. This paper was prepared in part for information purposes by the Artificial Intelligence Research group and AlgoCRYPT CoE of JPMorgan Chase & Co and its affiliates ("JP Morgan"), and is not a product of the Research Department of JP Morgan. JP Morgan makes no representation and warranty whatsoever and disclaims all liability, for the completeness, accuracy or reliability of the information contained herein. This document is not intended as investment research or investment advice, or a recommendation, offer or solicitation for the purchase or sale of any security, financial instrument, financial product or service, or to be used in any way for evaluating the merits of participating in any transaction, and shall not constitute a solicitation under any jurisdiction or to any person, if such solicitation under such jurisdiction or to such person would be unlawful. 2023 JP Morgan Chase & Co. All rights reserved.

Hanjun Li was supported by a NSF grant CNS-2026774 and a Cisco Research Award.

Huijia Lin was supported by NSF grants CNS-1936825 (CAREER), CNS-2026774, a JP Morgan AI Research Award, a Cisco Research Award, and a Simons Collaboration on the Theory of Algorithmic Fairness.

Stefano Tessaro was supported in part by NSF grants CNS-2026774, CNS-2154174, a JP Morgan Faculty Award, a CISCO Faculty Award, and a gift from Microsoft.

References

1. Albrecht, M.R., Player, R., Scott, S.: On the concrete hardness of learning with errors. Cryptology ePrint Archive, Report 2015/046 (2015). https://eprint.iacr.org/2015/046

2. Apple, Google: Exposure notification privacy-preserving analytics (ENPA) (2021). https://covid19-static.cdn-apple.com/applications/covid19/current/static/contact-tracing/pdf/ENPA_White_Paper.pdf

3. Asghar, M.R., Dán, G., Miorandi, D., Chlamtac, I.: Smart meter data privacy: a survey. IEEE Commun. Surv. Tutorials 19(4), 2820–2835 (2017). https://doi.org/10.1109/COMST.2017.2720195

4. Ball, M., Çakan, A., Malkin, T.: Linear threshold secret-sharing with binary reconstruction. In: Tessaro, S. (ed.) 2nd Conference on Information-Theoretic Cryptography, ITC 2021, 23–26 July 2021, Virtual Conference. LIPIcs, vol. 199, pp. 12:1–12:22. Schloss Dagstuhl - Leibniz-Zentrum für Informatik (2021). https://doi.org/10.4230/LIPIcs.ITC.2021.12

5. Banerjee, A., Peikert, C., Rosen, A.: Pseudorandom functions and lattices. In: Pointcheval, D., Johansson, T. (eds.) EUROCRYPT 2012. LNCS, vol. 7237, pp. 719–737. Springer, Heidelberg (2012). https://doi.org/10.1007/978-3-642-29011-4_42

6. Bell, J., et al.: Acorn: input validation for secure aggregation. Cryptology ePrint Archive, Paper 2022/1461 (2022). https://eprint.iacr.org/2022/1461

7. Bell, J.H., Bonawitz, K.A., Gascón, A., Lepoint, T., Raykova, M.: Secure single-server aggregation with (poly)logarithmic overhead. In: Ligatti, J., Ou, X., Katz, J., Vigna, G. (eds.) ACM CCS 2020, pp. 1253–1269. ACM Press (2020). https://doi.org/10.1145/3372297.3417885

8. Benaloh, J., Leichter, J.: Generalized secret sharing and monotone functions. In: Goldwasser, S. (ed.) CRYPTO 1988. LNCS, vol. 403, pp. 27–35. Springer, New York (1990). https://doi.org/10.1007/0-387-34799-2_3

9. Bonawitz, K.A., et al.: Towards federated learning at scale: system design. In: Talwalkar, A., Smith, V., Zaharia, M. (eds.) Proceedings of Machine Learning and Systems 2019, MLSys 2019, Stanford, CA, USA, 31 March– 2 April 2019. mlsys.org (2019). https://proceedings.mlsys.org/book/271.pdf

10. Bonawitz, K., et al.: Practical secure aggregation for privacy-preserving machine learning. In: Thuraisingham, B.M., Evans, D., Malkin, T., Xu, D. (eds.) ACM CCS 2017, pp. 1175–1191. ACM Press (2017). https://doi.org/10.1145/3133956.3133982

11. Boneh, D., Lewi, K., Montgomery, H., Raghunathan, A.: Key homomorphic PRFs and their applications. In: Canetti, R., Garay, J.A. (eds.) CRYPTO 2013. LNCS, vol. 8042, pp. 410–428. Springer, Heidelberg (2013). https://doi.org/10.1007/978-3-642-40041-4_23

12. Byrd, D., Hybinette, M., Balch, T.H.: ABIDES: towards high-fidelity multi-agent market simulation. In: Proceedings of the 2019 ACM SIGSIM Conference on Principles of Advanced Discrete Simulation, SIGSIM-PADS 2020, Miami, FL, USA, 15–17 June 2020, pp. 11–22 (2020). https://doi.org/10.1145/3384441.3395986

13. Canetti, R.: Universally composable security: a new paradigm for cryptographic protocols. In: 42nd FOCS, pp. 136–145. IEEE Computer Society Press (2001). https://doi.org/10.1109/SFCS.2001.959888

14. Corrigan-Gibbs, H.: Privacy-preserving firefox telemetry with prio (2020). https://rwc.iacr.org/2020/slides/Gibbs.pdf

15. Corrigan-Gibbs, H., Boneh, D.: Prio: private, robust, and scalable computation of aggregate statistics. In: Akella, A., Howell, J. (eds.) 14th USENIX Symposium on Networked Systems Design and Implementation, NSDI 2017, Boston, MA, USA, 27–29 March 2017, pp. 259–282. USENIX Association (2017). https://www.usenix.org/conference/nsdi17/technical-sessions/presentation/corrigan-gibbs

16. Damgård, I., Jurik, M.: A generalisation, a simplification and some applications of Paillier's probabilistic public-key system. In: Kim, K. (ed.) PKC 2001. LNCS, vol. 1992, pp. 119–136. Springer, Heidelberg (2001). https://doi.org/10.1007/3-540-44586-2_9

17. Damgård, I., Thorbek, R.: Linear integer secret sharing and distributed exponentiation. In: Yung, M., Dodis, Y., Kiayias, A., Malkin, T. (eds.) PKC 2006. LNCS, vol. 3958, pp. 75–90. Springer, Heidelberg (2006). https://doi.org/10.1007/11745853_6

18. Gilboa, N., Ishai, Y.: Distributed point functions and their applications. In: Nguyen, P.Q., Oswald, E. (eds.) EUROCRYPT 2014. LNCS, vol. 8441, pp. 640–658. Springer, Heidelberg (2014). https://doi.org/10.1007/978-3-642-55220-5_35

19. Guo, Y., Polychroniadou, A., Shi, E., Byrd, D., Balch, T.: Microfedml: privacy preserving federated learning for small weights. Cryptology ePrint Archive, Paper 2022/714 (2022). https://eprint.iacr.org/2022/714

20. Liu, Z., Chen, S., Ye, J., Fan, J., Li, H., Li, X.: SASH: efficient secure aggregation based on SHPRG for federated learning. In: Cussens, J., Zhang, K. (eds.) Uncertainty in Artificial Intelligence, Proceedings of the Thirty-Eighth Conference on Uncertainty in Artificial Intelligence, UAI 2022, 1–5 August 2022, Eindhoven, The Netherlands. Proceedings of Machine Learning Research, vol. 180, pp. 1243–1252. PMLR (2022). https://proceedings.mlr.press/v180/liu22c.html

21. Özdemir, S., Xiao, Y.: Secure data aggregation in wireless sensor networks: a comprehensive overview. Comput. Netw. **53**(12), 2022–2037 (2009). https://doi.org/10.1016/j.comnet.2009.02.023

22. Patton, C., Barnes, R., Schoppmann, P.: Verifiable Distributed Aggregation Functions. Internet-Draft draft-patton-cfrg-vdaf-01, Internet Engineering Task Force (2022). https://datatracker.ietf.org/doc/html/draft-patton-cfrg-vdaf-01

23. Rieke, N., et al.: The future of digital health with federated learning. CoRR abs/2003.08119 (2020). https://arxiv.org/abs/2003.08119

24. Microsoft SEAL (release 4.0). Microsoft Research, Redmond, WA (2022). https://github.com/Microsoft/SEAL

25. So, J., Ali, R.E., Guler, B., Jiao, J., Avestimehr, S.: Securing secure aggregation: mitigating multi-round privacy leakage in federated learning. arXiv preprint arXiv:2106.03328 (2021)

26. Valiant, L.G.: Short monotone formulae for the majority function. J. Algorithms **5**(3), 363–366 (1984). https://doi.org/10.1016/0196-6774(84)90016-6

Unconditionally Secure Multiparty Computation for Symmetric Functions with Low Bottleneck Complexity

Reo Eriguchi[✉]

National Institute of Advanced Industrial Science and Technology, Tokyo, Japan
eriguchi-reo@aist.go.jp

Abstract. Bottleneck complexity is an efficiency measure of secure multiparty computation (MPC) introduced by Boyle et al. (ICALP 2018) to achieve load-balancing. Roughly speaking, it is defined as the maximum communication complexity required by any player within the protocol execution. Since it was shown to be impossible to achieve sublinear bottleneck complexity in the number of players n for all functions, a prior work constructed MPC protocols with low bottleneck complexity for specific functions. However, the previous protocol for symmetric functions needs to assume a computational primitive of garbled circuits and its unconditionally secure variant has exponentially large bottleneck complexity in the depth of an arithmetic formula computing the function, which limits the class of symmetric functions the protocol can compute with sublinear bottleneck complexity in n. In this work, we make the following contributions to unconditionally secure MPC protocols for symmetric functions with sublinear bottleneck complexity in n.

- We propose for the first time unconditionally secure MPC protocols computing *any* symmetric function with sublinear bottleneck complexity in n. Technically, our first protocol is inspired by the one-time truth-table protocol by Ishai et al. (TCC 2013) but our second and third protocols use a novel technique to express the one-time truth-table as an array of two or higher dimensions and achieve better trade-offs.
- We propose an unconditionally secure protocol tailored to the AND function with lower bottleneck complexity. It avoids pseudorandom functions used by the previous protocol for the AND function, preserving bottleneck complexity up to a logarithmic factor in n.
- By combining our protocol for the AND function with Bloom filters, we construct an unconditionally secure protocol for private set intersection (PSI), which computes the intersection of players' private sets. This is the first PSI protocol with sublinear bottleneck complexity in n and to the best of our knowledge, there has been no such protocol even under cryptographic assumptions.

Keywords: Secure multiparty computation · Bottleneck complexity · Unconditional security

© International Association for Cryptologic Research 2023
J. Guo and R. Steinfeld (Eds.): ASIACRYPT 2023, LNCS 14438, pp. 335–368, 2023.
https://doi.org/10.1007/978-981-99-8721-4_11

1   Introduction

Secure multiparty computation (MPC) [58] is a fundamental cryptographic primitive which enables n players to jointly compute a function $f(x_1, \ldots, x_n)$ without revealing any additional information on their private inputs x_i. Communication complexity, which counts the total number of bits transmitted between players, is considered as the most fundamental metric to measure the efficiency of MPC protocols. A number of works have made significant progresses to minimize communication complexity for various useful functions (e.g., [7, 13, 15, 20, 21, 27, 28, 30, 42]).

However, in practical applications where lightweight devices perform MPC via peer-to-peer communication, the per-party communication cost is a more effective measure than the total cost. For example, consider secure computation on a star interaction pattern, in which a central player interacts with all the other players and computes an output. Then, while total communication cost is possibly scalable (i.e., $O(n)$), the central player must bear communication proportional to the total number of players. In large-scale MPC, these costs quickly become prohibitive. To address these concerns, Boyle et al. [11] introduced a different important efficiency measure, called *bottleneck complexity*. Roughly speaking, the bottleneck complexity of an MPC protocol is defined as the maximum communication required by any player during the execution of the protocol.

To make protocols useful in applications to large-scale secure computation, we aim at designing MPC protocols with sublinear bottleneck complexity in the number of players n. On the negative side, Boyle et al. [11] showed that it is impossible to achieve sublinear bottleneck complexity for all functions — even without any security considerations. On the positive side, they proposed a generic transformation from any (possibly insecure) protocol computing a function f to a secure MPC protocol for f preserving bottleneck complexity (up to polynomial factors in a security parameter). Their results reduce in some sense the above goal to constructing protocols with sublinear bottleneck complexity without any privacy requirements, which is a purely complexity-theoretic question. However, a main drawback of their compiler is that it needs to use fully homomorphic encryption, which can only be instantiated from narrow cryptographic assumptions [25, 56]. Recently, Orlandi, Ravi and Scholl [48] constructed MPC protocols with sublinear bottleneck complexity for specific functions from weaker assumptions of one-way functions or linearly homomorphic encryption. It still remains open whether we can construct *unconditionally secure* MPC protocols with sublinear bottleneck complexity.

1.1   Our Results

In this paper, we propose for the first time unconditionally secure MPC protocols for symmetric functions with sublinear bottleneck complexity in the number of players[1]. We also propose an MPC protocol with lower bottleneck complexity tailored to the functionality of checking if the sum of inputs is zero. As an application, we construct an unconditionally secure protocol for *private set intersection* (PSI), which computes the intersection of players' private sets. This is the first PSI protocol with sublinear bottleneck complexity and to the best of our knowledge, there has been no such protocol even under cryptographic assumptions. Following [48], we assume semi-honest adversaries, who do not deviate from protocols, and the preprocessing model, in which players receive in advance input-independent correlated randomness from a trusted third party. In what follows, we discuss our contributions in more detail.

Protocols for General Symmetric Functions. Orlandi et al. [48] constructed an MPC protocol for a symmetric function $h : \{0,1\}^n \to \{0,1\}$ assuming a garbled circuit [59]. Although their original protocol was computationally secure, it can be made unconditionally secure by replacing the underlying garbled circuit with an information-theoretic one, which is also known as randomized encoding [39]. However, the unconditionally secure variant has exponentially large bottleneck complexity in the depth of an arithmetic formula computing the function $f : \{0, 1, 2, \ldots, n\} \to \{0,1\}$ such that $f(\sum_{i \in [n]} x_i) = h(x_1, \ldots, x_n)$ for all $(x_1, \ldots, x_n) \in \{0,1\}^n$. To achieve bottleneck complexity $O(n^{1-\epsilon})$ for a constant $\epsilon > 0$, the unconditionally secure protocol needs to assume that the related function f is represented by an arithmetic formula of depth $(1-\epsilon) \log n$. Note that such symmetric functions only account for $o(1)$ fraction of all symmetric functions. We propose three kinds of unconditionally secure protocols with sublinear bottleneck complexity for *any* symmetric function. There are trade-offs between online bottleneck complexity, offline bottleneck complexity, i.e., the amount of correlated randomness per party, and the privacy threshold (see Table 1). The first protocol has online bottleneck complexity $O(\log n)$ and offline bottleneck complexity $O(n)$. The second is more balanced and its online and offline bottleneck complexities are both $O(\sqrt{n})$. The third protocol has lower bottleneck complexity $O(n^{1/d} \log n)$ for any constant d but is only secure against adversaries corrupting less than $n/(d-1)$ players. The numbers of rounds of our protocols are $O(n)$, which is the same as [48]. We also show that the round complexity of our protocols can be made $O(\log n)$ by increasing the online complexity by $O(\log n)$ times. Technically, our first protocol is inspired by the one-time truth-table protocol [40] and our second and third protocol use a novel technique to express the truth-table of f as an array of two or higher dimensions (see Sect. 2 for technical details).

Protocol for Checking Equality to Zero. We propose an unconditionally secure MPC protocol realizing the functionality of checking if the sum of players'

---

[1] An independent work [41] show an unconditionally secure MPC protocol for symmetric functions but our second and third protocols achieve better offline bottleneck complexity than [41].

Table 1. Comparison of unconditionally secure MPC protocols for a symmetric function h with sublinear bottleneck complexity in the number of players n.

Reference	Bottleneck complexity			
	Condition on h	Online	Offline	Corruption
[48]	$D_h \leq (1 - \epsilon) \log n$	$O(n^{1-\epsilon})$	$O(n^{1-\epsilon})$	$t < n$
Ours (Theorem 1)	Unnecessary	$O(\log n)$	$O(n)$	$t < n$
Ours (Theorem 2)	Unnecessary	$O(\sqrt{n})$	$O(\sqrt{n})$	$t < n$
Ours (Theorem 3)	Unnecessary	$O(n^{1/d} \log n)$	$O(n^{1/d} \log n)$	$t < n/(d-1)$

The offline bottleneck complexity means the amount of correlated randomness per party and t is the maximum number of players corrupted by adversaries. Let ϵ be a constant and D_h be the minimum depth of arithmetic formulas computing the unique function f such that $f(\sum_{i \in [n]} x_i) = h(x_1, \ldots, x_n)$ for all $(x_1, \ldots, x_n) \in \{0,1\}^n$.

inputs is equal to zero over a finite field $\mathbb{F}$. Since the functionality is symmetric, we can apply the above protocols for general symmetric functions. Our tailored protocol achieves lower bottleneck complexity $O(\max\{\lambda, \log |\mathbb{F}|\})$, where λ is a security parameter. The functionality is a generalization of the AND function if we choose a field whose characteristic is larger than n. As a comparison, the AND protocol in [48] is based on pseudorandom functions and hence only computationally secure. Our protocol avoids their use of pseudorandom functions while preserving bottleneck complexity up to a logarithmic factor in n.

Application to Private Set Intersection. By combining our protocol for checking equality to zero with Bloom filters [9,10], we obtain an unconditionally secure PSI protocol, that is, an MPC protocol for computing $X_1 \cap \cdots \cap X_n$ from private sets $X_1, \ldots, X_n \subseteq U$ each of size at most s. The offline bottleneck complexity is $O_\lambda(s^2 \log n)$ and the online bottleneck complexity is $O_\lambda(s^2 \log n + s \log |U|)$, where we omit a polynomial factor in λ. Note that the bottleneck complexity is sublinear in n. To the best of our knowledge, there has been no such PSI protocol even under cryptographic assumptions (see Sect. 1.2 for a more detailed comparison). The round complexity of our protocol is $O(n)$. It can be decreased to $O(\log n)$ by increasing the online complexity by $O(\log n)$ times.

1.2   Related Work

General MPC. Since the introduction of MPC [58], a rich line of works studied communication complexity in various settings and showed feasibility results and optimizations, e.g., [4,7,8,13,15,17,19–21,27–30,34–36,42,51]. However, protocols in all of the above works require *full interaction* among players, that is, each player may send messages to all the other players in each round of interaction. This feature necessarily results in high bottleneck complexity $\Omega(n)$.

MPC with Restricted Interaction Patterns. Halevi, Lindell and Pinkas [32] initiated the study of MPC which restricts interaction among players. Halevi et al. [31] formalized the notion in the more general setting by representing an interaction pattern as a directed acyclic graph. MPC protocols on a star-based interaction were proposed for general tasks and for specific tasks including symmetric functions [5,23,38]. As we mentioned above, protocols on a star-based interaction require a central player to bear communication proportional to n, which results in $\Omega(n)$ bottleneck complexity. Halevi et al. [31] also studied a chain-based interaction, in which players interact over a simple directed path traversing all players. Protocols on a chain-based interaction possibly achieve low bottleneck complexity since each player communicates with at most two players. However, since the last player on the chain is allowed to evaluate the function on every possible input of his choice, the constructions in [31] cannot achieve the standard security of MPC, which requires that corrupted players learn nothing but the output. The weaker security notion of MPC with restricted interaction is formalized as residual security [31,32].

Private Set Intersection. Private set intersection (PSI) has a wide variety of real-world applications as pointed out in [44]. Although many PSI protocols were constructed unconditionally or based on cryptographic assumptions, to the best of our knowledge, there has been no PSI protocol that achieves sublinear bottleneck complexity in n. Indeed, the protocols in [14,26,37,43–45,47,49,50, 52,53] require full interaction and those in [1,2,6,12,24,33,46,57] assume a star interaction pattern. Thus the bottleneck complexity of these protocols must be at least linear in n. An exception is the protocol in [18], which utilizes a "round table" structure where players are supposed to be nodes in a ring network and each player only communicates with the consecutive players around the table. The bottleneck complexity is thus possibly independent of n. However, their protocol outputs an incorrect intersection with constant probability. Essentially, their protocol securely finds elements $x \in X_n$ on which a polynomial $p(T) := r \cdot \sum_{i \in [n]} f_i(T)$ vanishes, where r is a random element unknown to any player and each $f_i(T)$ is a polynomial which vanishes exactly when evaluated on the elements of the i-th player's input set X_i.[2] It is true that $p(x) = 0$ for all $x \in X_1 \cap \cdots \cap X_n$ but the set of all the roots of $p(T)$ may include elements outside $X_1 \cap \cdots \cap X_n$ since $\sum_{i \in [n]} f_i(x) = 0$ even if x is not a common root of the f_i's. The authors of [18] do not show how to make the probability of this event negligible. This is why we do not consider their protocol for our comparison. Finally, we note that the previous state-of-the-art protocols have better dependency on the maximum size s of players' input sets than ours. Indeed, the best-known communication complexity (e.g., [1]) is linear in s while ours is quadratic in s.

---

[2] We here assume that there is an injective map from the universe U containing all the X_i's to some finite field.

2   Technical Overview

In this section, we provide an overview of our techniques. We give more detailed descriptions and security proofs in the following sections. We call MPC protocols with sublinear bottleneck complexity in the number of players *BC-efficient*.

2.1   BC-Efficient Protocols for General Symmetric Functions

First Protocol. Let $h : \{0,1\}^n \to \{0,1\}$ be a symmetric function. Since the value of h depends only on the sum $\sum_{i\in[n]} x_i$, there is the unique function $f : \{0,1,\ldots,n\} \to \{0,1\}$ such that $h(x_1,\ldots,x_n) = f(\sum_{i\in[n]} x_i)$. Our starting point is the protocol in [48]: In the setup, players receive an additive sharing $(r_i)_{i\in[n]}$ of a random secret r, and a garbled circuit of a circuit computing $g(y) := f(y - r)$ from y, where r is hard-coded. In the online phase, each player broadcasts $y_i = x_i + r_i$, computes $y = \sum_{i\in[n]} y_i$, and evaluates the garbled circuit on y in a threshold manner. Due to the mask r, the value y is random and independent of $\sum_{i\in[n]} x_i$, and the security of the garbled circuit ensures that the evaluation process reveals nothing but the output $g(y) = h(x_1,\ldots,x_n)$. However, to achieve unconditional security, it is necessary to replace the garbled circuit with an information-theoretic one, which results in exponentially large bottleneck complexity in the depth of an arithmetic formula computing g.

Instead, our first protocol uses the idea of one-time truth-tables (OTTT) [40]. Roughly speaking, in an OTTT protocol, players receive in the setup an additive sharing of the truth-table of a (not necessarily symmetric) function h permuted with a random shift $\mathbf{r} = (r_1,\ldots,r_n)$. In the online phase, each player broadcasts $y_i = x_i + r_i$ and sets $\mathbf{y} = (y_1,\ldots,y_n)$. Players recover the $\mathbf{y}$-th component of the permuted truth-table, which is equal to $h(\mathbf{y} - \mathbf{r}) = h(x_1,\ldots,x_n)$. We adapt the OTTT protocol to the setting of h being symmetric. In this case, it is sufficient to prepare an additive sharing of a shifted version of the truth-table of the related function $f : \{0,1,\ldots,n\} \to \{0,1\}$. By receiving an additive sharing of the random shift $r \in \{0,1,\ldots,n\}$ in the setup, players can open $y = \sum_{i\in[n]} x_i + r$ and the y-th component of the table, which is $f(y - r) = f(\sum_{i\in[n]} x_i)$.

Now, remaining problems are how to let players open secrets and broadcast messages in a BC-efficient way. The protocol in [48] used a round-table structure and let each player add his share to the message from the previous player and send the result to the next player around the table. However, the round complexity of this protocol is $O(n)$. We propose a recursive protocol that opens secrets with $O(\log n)$ rounds at the cost of increasing the online bottleneck complexity by $O(\log n)$ times. Assume that players are partitioned into $n/2$ pairs and call the members of each pair as the right and left players of the pair. For every pair, the right player sends his share to the left player, who then adds it to his own share. All of the left players then execute the protocol recursively on $n/2$ inputs, each of which is the sum of shares of each pair. After $O(\log n)$ iterations, the final call of the protocol outputs the aggregation of all shares. In the worst case, a player who is chosen as the left player of a pair in every iteration needs to communicate $O(\log n)$ elements and hence the online bottleneck complexity increases by $O(\log n)$ times. In [48], the broadcast functionality was also realized by a similar round-table structure, in which each player simply relays a message from the previous to the next one. We reduce it to $O(\log n)$ but now with no additional cost for online complexity. Our solution is simple: Represent the set of players by a binary tree whose height is $O(\log n)$ and root is the player who broadcasts a message. We let each player relay the message from his parent to his children in the tree.

Second Protocol. Although the first protocol has polylogarithmic online bottleneck complexity in the number of players n, a drawback is that the offline bottleneck complexity is linear in n. We show a novel technique to extend the above OTTT-based approach and obtain a protocol that balances offline and online bottleneck complexities. The core idea of the first protocol is that players securely obtain the component of the truth table $\mathbf{T} = [f(0), f(1), \ldots, f(n)]$ at position $s = \sum_{i \in [n]} x_i$. This can also be interpreted as securely computing the inner product $\langle \mathbf{T}, \mathbf{e}_s \rangle$, where $\mathbf{e}_s$ is the unit vector whose entry is 1 at position s and 0 otherwise (we identify the set indexing entries with $\{0, 1, \ldots, n\}$).

The key idea of our second protocol is to represent vectors $\mathbf{T}$ and $\mathbf{e}_s$ as arrays of two dimension. Assume that $n+1$ is the product of two distinct primes p, q of almost equal size $O(\sqrt{n})$. We then have a one-to-one correspondence ϕ between $\mathbb{Z}_{n+1} := \{0, 1, \ldots, n\}$ and $\mathbb{Z}_p \times \mathbb{Z}_q$ from the Chinese remainder theorem. The truth-table $\mathbf{T}$ then corresponds to a matrix $\mathbf{M} \in \{0, 1\}^{p \times q}$ whose (k_1, k_2)-th entry is $f(k)$, where $(k_1, k_2) = \phi(k)$ (we identify the set indexing rows and columns with $\mathbb{Z}_p$ and $\mathbb{Z}_q$, respectively). Furthermore, the equation $\langle \mathbf{T}, \mathbf{e}_s \rangle = f(s)$ is rewritten as

$$\langle \mathbf{e}_{s_1}, \mathbf{M} \cdot \mathbf{e}_{s_2} \rangle = f(s), \text{ where } (s_1, s_2) = \phi(s). \tag{1}$$

Importantly, since $\mathbf{M}$ is public, the computation of $\mathbf{M} \cdot \mathbf{e}_{s_2}$ can be locally done and hence the computation players need to interactively perform is only the inner product of vectors of dimension $O(\sqrt{n})$, instead of $O(n)$.

Specifically, we cannot compute the inner product (1) for $(s_1, s_2) = \phi(s)$ directly since we should not reveal s and can only open $y = s - r$ with a random mask r. To unmask s from y, we give players vectors $\mathbf{e}_{u_1} \in \{0, 1\}^p$ and $\mathbf{e}_{u_2} \in \{0, 1\}^q$ as correlated randomness, where $(u_1, u_2) = \phi(r)$. Now, as in our first protocol, players open $y = \sum_{i \in [n]} x_i - r$, express it as $\phi(y) = (z_1, z_2)$, and permutes $\mathbf{e}_{u_1}$ and $\mathbf{e}_{u_2}$ with shifts z_1 and z_2, respectively. They obtain $\mathbf{e}_{u_1 + z_1} = \mathbf{e}_{s_1}$ and $\mathbf{e}_{u_2 + z_2} = \mathbf{e}_{s_2}$, from which $f(s) = h(x_1, \ldots, x_n)$ can be computed via Eq. (1). However, distributing $(\mathbf{e}_{u_1}, \mathbf{e}_{u_2})$ itself reveals r. We instead give players additive shares for $\mathbf{e}_{u_1}$ and $\mathbf{e}_{u_2}$ as correlated randomness. Since permuting vectors with a public shift and multiplying vectors by a constant matrix are linear operations, players can obtain additive shares for $\mathbf{e}_{s_1}$ and $\mathbf{M} \cdot \mathbf{e}_{s_2}$.

A remaining problem is how to compute the inner product of $\mathbf{e}_{s_1}$ and $\mathbf{M} \cdot \mathbf{e}_{s_2}$ in a secret-shared form. Our key observation is that the multiplication protocol based on Beaver triples [3] is BC-efficient. Indeed, assume that players have additive shares of (a, b, c), where a, b are random secrets and $c = ab$. They can compute an additive sharing of xy from those for x and y as follows: (1) players open $u := x - a$ and $v := y - b$; (2) they compute $[\![xy]\!] = uv + v[\![a]\!] + u[\![b]\!] + [\![c]\!]$, where $[\![w]\!]$ means an additive sharing for w. Since the functionality of opening secrets can be realized in a BC-efficient way, this multiplication protocol is also BC-efficient. Therefore, if we additionally distribute $O(\sqrt{n})$ Beaver triples in the setup, we can securely compute $\langle \mathbf{e}_{s_1}, \mathbf{M} \cdot \mathbf{e}_{s_2} \rangle = f(s)$ in a secret-shared form. Although we assume for simplicity that $n + 1$ is the product of two primes of almost equal size, it is straightforward to extend it the general case since we can choose primes such that $\sqrt{n} < p < 2\sqrt{n} < q < 4\sqrt{n}$ thanks to Bertrand's postulate [55].

Third Protocol. In our second protocol, we express the truth-table $\mathbf{T}$ of the function f by a two-dimensional array. We further extend the technique and use an array of higher dimension $d \geq 2$. For simplicity, assume that $n + 1$ is the product of d distinct primes $p_1, p_2, \ldots, p_d$ of almost equal size $O(n^{1/d})$. The general case can be dealt with similarly. From the Chinese remainder theorem, we have a one-to-one correspondence ϕ from $\{0, 1, \ldots, n\}$ to $\mathbb{Z}_{p_1} \times \mathbb{Z}_{p_2} \times \cdots \times \mathbb{Z}_{p_d}$. We can then equivalently express the truth-table $\mathbf{T}$ of f by a p_1-by-q matrix $\mathbf{M}$ over any field $\mathbb{F}$, where $q = p_2 \cdots p_d$. Indeed, fixing a one-to-one correspondence between $k \in \mathbb{Z}_q$ and $(s_2, \ldots, s_d) \in \mathbb{Z}_{p_2} \times \cdots \times \mathbb{Z}_{p_d}$, we embed every value $f(s)$ into the (s_1, k)-th entry of $\mathbf{M}$ for $(s_1, s_2, \ldots, s_d) = \phi(s)$. In other words, we can choose a matrix $\mathbf{M}$ such that the equation $\langle \mathbf{T}, \mathbf{e}_s \rangle = f(s)$ is rewritten as

$$\langle \mathbf{e}_{s_1}, \mathbf{M} \cdot (\mathbf{e}_{s_2} \otimes \cdots \otimes \mathbf{e}_{s_d}) \rangle = f(s), \tag{2}$$

where $(s_1, s_2, \ldots, s_d) = \phi(s)$, $\mathbf{e}_{s_j} \in \mathbb{F}^{p_j}$ is the unit vector whose entry is 1 at position s_j, and $\mathbf{a} \otimes \mathbf{b}$ denotes Kronecker product of $\mathbf{a}$ and $\mathbf{b}$. The problem is now reduced to securely computing the inner product (2). Again, we should not compute (2) for the sum $s = \sum_{i \in [n]} x_i$ itself since we can only open a masked value $y = s - r$. To remove the mask r, we try to distribute vectors $\mathbf{e}_{u_1}, \mathbf{e}_{u_2}, \ldots, \mathbf{e}_{u_d}$ for $(u_1, u_2, \ldots, u_d) = \phi(r)$. Since this trivially reveals r, we give players shares for them. A major difference from the second protocol is that we use the Shamir secret sharing scheme over $\mathbb{F}$ with a threshold $t < n/(d-1)$ [54] instead of the additive one. By opening $\phi(y) = (z_1, z_2, \ldots, z_d)$ and permuting each share vector with a shift z_j, players can compute a Shamir sharing of $\mathbf{e}_{s_1}, \mathbf{e}_{s_2}, \ldots, \mathbf{e}_{s_d}$ without recovering s. Importantly, the homomorphic property of the Shamir scheme enables players to locally compute a Shamir sharing of $\mathbf{e}_{s_2} \otimes \cdots \otimes \mathbf{e}_{s_d}$ with a threshold $(d-1)t$ since the degree of a function to be evaluated is at most $d - 1$. Furthermore, since $(d-1)t < n$, the shares can be locally converted to an additive sharing of $\mathbf{e}_{s_2} \otimes \cdots \otimes \mathbf{e}_{s_d}$ and to an additive sharing of $\mathbf{M} \cdot (\mathbf{e}_{s_2} \otimes \cdots \otimes \mathbf{e}_{s_d})$. Finally, using $p_1 = O(n^{1/d})$ Beaver triples, players interactively computes the inner product $\langle \mathbf{e}_1, \mathbf{M} \cdot (\mathbf{e}_{s_2} \otimes \cdots \otimes \mathbf{e}_{s_d}) \rangle$ in a secret-shared form in a BC-efficient way. For any constant d, the offline and online bottleneck complexities are both $O(n^{1/d})$ field elements if we open secrets in a round-table structure, which requires $O(n)$ rounds. Since the Shamir scheme needs to assume $|\mathbb{F}| > n$, they are $O(n^{1/d} \log n)$ in bits. We can reduce the round complexity from $O(n)$ to $O(\log n)$ if the recursive protocol is used to open secrets, which increases the online bottleneck complexity by $O(\log n)$ times.

2.2 BC-Efficient Protocol for Checking Equality to Zero

We propose an unconditionally secure BC-efficient protocol for checking if the sum of players' inputs is zero over a finite field $\mathbb{F}$. Since the functionality is symmetric, we can apply our protocols for general symmetric functions. Our tailored protocol shown below achieves lower bottleneck complexity $O(\max\{\lambda, \log |\mathbb{F}|\})$, where λ is a security parameter.

First, we show a special case of our protocol, which computes the OR function of players' inputs. Our starting point is the previous protocol for the OR function in [48][3]. In the protocol, players receive an additive sharing $(r_i)_{i \in [n]}$ of a random secret r in the setup. The i-th player sets $y_i \leftarrow r_i$ if he has $x_i = 0$, and otherwise he chooses y_i uniformly at random. Players then open $y = \sum_{i \in [n]} y_i$, which is equal to r if and (essentially) only if $\mathrm{OR}(x_1, \ldots, x_n) = 0$. Note that r should not be revealed since otherwise an adversary can learn the OR of the honest players' inputs by subtracting the inputs and correlated randomness of the corrupted players. It is therefore necessary to check the equality $y = r$ without revealing r. In [48], this is done by using a pseudorandom function (PRF): Players apply the PRF in a nested manner starting from y by using their private keys, and check the final value is equal to the value computed in the same way except that it starts from r. To obtain an unconditionally secure protocol, we propose a different method to check the equality $y = r$. Our key observation is that for two random secrets a and b, the equation $ay + b = ar + b$ is equivalent to $y = r$ except with a small probability that $a = 0$, and the view $(ay + b, ar + b)$ reveals nothing but whether the equality $y = r$ holds in the information-theoretic sense. In our protocol, players receive additive shares $(a_i)_{i \in [n]}$ and $(b_i)_{i \in [n]}$ for a and b, and $r' := ar + b$ in the setup. In the online phase, after opening y, each player computes $y_i' = a_i y + b_i$ and obtains $y' = \sum_{i \in [n]} y_i' = ay + b$. Players then check $y' = r'$ and if so, output 0. The probability of failure can be made negligible in λ if we choose r, a, b and shares for them from sufficiently large sets.

Finally, it is straightforward to extend the above protocol to a protocol for checking whether $\sum_{i \in [n]} x_i = 0$ holds. Let every player compute $y_i = x_i + r_i$ and open $y = \sum_{i \in [n]} x_i + r$. Using the above technique, players can check the equality $y = r$, i.e., $\sum_{i \in [n]} x_i = 0$, without learning any additional information.

2.3 BC-Efficient PSI Protocol

We combine our protocol for checking equality to zero with Bloom filters [9] and construct an unconditionally secure PSI protocol with sublinear bottleneck complexity in n. First, we show a simple protocol whose bottleneck complexity

---

[3] The original protocol in [48] computes the AND function. The functionalities are equivalent since $\mathrm{OR}(x_1, \ldots, x_n) = 1 - \mathrm{AND}(1 - x_1, \ldots, 1 - x_n)$.

is sublinear in n but linear in the cardinality of the universe $U = \{1, 2, \ldots, N\}$ containing all the input sets. In the protocol, each player encodes his input set $X_i \subseteq U$ as the characteristic vector $\mathbf{B}_i \in \{0,1\}^N$ of its complement, i.e., the vector whose entry at position j is 1 if and only if $j \notin X_i$. They compute an additive sharing of the sum $\mathbf{V} = \sum_{i \in [n]} \mathbf{B}_i$ over a finite field. (We suppose that the characteristic of the field is so large that no wrap-around occurs.) This can be done by giving players an additive sharing $(\mathbf{u}_i)_{i \in [n]}$ of the N-dimensional zero vector in the setup and letting them compute $\mathbf{B}_i + \mathbf{u}_i$. Observe that $x \in X_1 \cap \cdots \cap X_n$ if and only if the entry $\mathbf{V}[x]$ at position x is 0. For each element x of the input set of a designated player, players compute the inner product of $\mathbf{V}$ and $\mathbf{e}_x$ in a secret-shared form using N Beaver triples. While the inner products themselves reveal additional information on elements outside $X_1 \cap \cdots \cap X_n$, players use our BC-efficient protocol for checking equality to zero and learn whether $\langle \mathbf{V}, \mathbf{e}_x \rangle = 0$ and nothing else. Finally, $X_1 \cap \cdots \cap X_n$ is securely obtained if the designated player broadcasts the x's for which $\langle \mathbf{V}, \mathbf{e}_x \rangle = 0$ holds.

Since U has typically large size, we aim to achieve better dependency on $|U|$ by making use of Bloom filters, which provide compact encodings of sets. A Bloom filter encodes a set X of elements as an m-bit vector with respect to λ randomly selected hash functions $H_1, \ldots, H_\lambda$. In a Bloom filter for X, all entries are initialized to 0. To insert an element $x \in X$ to the Bloom filter, the entries at positions $H_1(x), \ldots, H_\lambda(x)$ are all set to 1. We can test whether $y \in X$ by checking if the entries at positions $H_1(y), \ldots, H_\lambda(y)$ are all 1. There is a possibility of false positives but its probability can be made negligible in λ if we choose $m = \Theta(s\lambda)$, where s is the maximum size of input sets [10]. Although our PSI protocol bears some similarities with the previous protocols based on Bloom filters [1,46], their protocols are not BC-efficient and assume a computational primitive of homomorphic threshold public-key encryption. In our protocol, each player computes a Bloom filter $\mathbf{BF}(X_i)$ of his input set X_i and inverts it, i.e., $\mathbf{B}_i := \mathbf{1}_m - \mathbf{BF}(X_i)$, where $\mathbf{1}_m$ is the m-dimensional all-ones vector. As above, players compute an additive sharing of $\mathbf{V} = \sum_{i \in [n]} \mathbf{B}_i$ using additive sharings of zeros. For any $x \in X_1 \cap \cdots \cap X_n$, the entries of $\mathbf{B}_i$ at positions $H_1(x), \ldots, H_\lambda(x)$ are all zero and hence so are the corresponding entries of $\mathbf{V}$. The converse is not always true but with overwhelming probability, for $x \notin X_1 \cap \cdots \cap X_n$, at least one entry of $\mathbf{V}$ at positions $H_1(x), \ldots, H_\lambda(x)$ is non-zero due to the property of Bloom filters. Based on that observation, for each element x of the input set of a designated player, we let players compute the inner product of $\mathbf{V}$ and a Bloom filter $\mathbf{BF}(\{x\})$ of the singleton $\{x\}$ in a secret-shared form. The rest is similar to the above: Players check whether $\langle \mathbf{V}, \mathbf{BF}(\{x\}) \rangle = 0$ based on our protocol for checking equality to zero, and the designated player broadcasts the x's for which the equality holds. If we implement the functionality of opening secrets based on a round-table structure, the bottleneck complexity is $O(sm) = O_\lambda(s^2)$ field elements plus $O(s \log |U|)$ bits since we have to compute s inner products of m-dimensional vectors and $m = \Theta(s\lambda)$. Since no wrap-around occurs if the characteristic is larger than $n\lambda$, the bottleneck complexity is $O_\lambda(s^2 \log n + s \log |U|)$ in bits, omitting a polynomial factor in λ. We can

also construct a PSI protocol with $O(\log n)$ rounds if we increase the online
bottleneck complexity by $O(\log n)$ times.

3 Preliminaries

Notations. For $m \in \mathbb{N}$, define $[m] = \{1, \ldots, m\}$ and $[0..m] = [m] \cup \{0\}$. Define
$\mathbb{Z}_m$ as the ring of integers modulo m. We identify $\mathbb{Z}_m$ (as a set) with $\{z \in \mathbb{Z} :$
$0 \le z \le m - 1\}$. We denote the set of all subsets of X by 2^X. For a subset X
of a set Y, we define $Y \setminus X = \{y \in Y : y \notin X\}$ and simply denote it by $\overline{X}$ if Y
is clear from the context. We write $u \leftarrow_\text{s} Y$ if u is chosen uniformly at random
from a set Y. We call a function $f : \mathbb{N} \ni \lambda \mapsto f(\lambda) \in \mathbb{R}$ *negligible* and denote
it by $\mathsf{negl}(\lambda)$ if for any $c > 0$, there exists $\lambda_0 \in \mathbb{N}$ such that $0 \le f(\lambda) < \lambda^{-c}$
for any $\lambda > \lambda_0$. We call f *polynomial* and denote it by $\mathsf{poly}(\lambda)$ if there exists
$c > 0$ and $\lambda_0 \in \mathbb{N}$ such that $0 \le f(\lambda) \le \lambda^c$ for any $\lambda > \lambda_0$. For two random
variables with range U, we define the statistical distance $\mathrm{SD}(X, Y)$ between X
and Y as $\mathrm{SD}(X, Y) = (1/2) \sum_{u \in U} |\Pr[X = u] - \Pr[Y = u]|$. For two sequences
$X = (X_\lambda)_{\lambda \in \mathbb{N}}$, $Y = (Y_\lambda)_{\lambda \in \mathbb{N}}$ of random variables, we write $X \approx Y$ if a function
$f : \lambda \mapsto \mathrm{SD}(X_\lambda, Y_\lambda)$ is negligible in λ. By default, the i-th element of a vector
$\mathbf{u}$ is denoted by u_i or $\mathbf{u}[i]$. For a vector $\mathbf{s} = (s_i)_{i \in \mathbb{Z}_m} \in X^m$ and $r \in \mathbb{Z}_m$,
we define $\mathsf{Shift}_r(\mathbf{s})$ as the vector obtained by shifting elements by r. Formally,
$\mathsf{Shift}_r(\mathbf{s}) = (t_i)_{i \in \mathbb{Z}_m}$ is defined by $t_i = s_{(i-r) \bmod m}$ for all $i \in \mathbb{Z}_m$. Let $\mathbf{0}_m$ be
the zero vector of dimension m and $\mathbf{1}_m$ be the all-ones vector of dimension
m. We simply write $\mathbf{0}$ or $\mathbf{1}$ if the dimension is clear from the context. Let $\mathbf{I}_m$
denote the m-by-m identity matrix and $\mathbf{e}_i$ denote the i-th unit vector. For two
vectors $\mathbf{u}, \mathbf{v}$ over a ring, we define the standard inner product of $\mathbf{u}$ and $\mathbf{v}$ as
$\langle \mathbf{u}, \mathbf{v} \rangle = \sum_i \mathbf{u}[i] \mathbf{v}[i]$. For a tuple of m polynomials $\boldsymbol{\varphi} = (\varphi_j)_{j \in [m]}$ over $\mathbb{F}$ and
$\alpha \in \mathbb{F}$, we write $\boldsymbol{\varphi}(\alpha) = (\varphi_j(\alpha))_{j \in [m]} \in \mathbb{F}^m$. Let g be a deterministic function
on D^n, where D is a set. We denote by $\mathcal{F}_g$ an n-input/n-output functionality
that on input $\mathbf{x} \in D^n$, outputs $\mathcal{F}_g(\mathbf{x}) = (g(\mathbf{x}), \ldots, g(\mathbf{x}))$. We call a function
$h : \{0, 1\}^n \to \{0, 1\}$ *symmetric* if $h(x_{\sigma(1)}, \ldots, x_{\sigma(n)}) = h(x_1, \ldots, x_n)$ for input
$(x_1, \ldots, x_n) \in \{0, 1\}^n$ and any permutation σ on $[n]$. The value of a symmetric
function h is determined only by the Hamming weight w of the input, i.e.,
$w := |\{i \in [n] : x_i = 1\}| = \sum_{i \in [n]} x_i$. Thus, there is the unique function
$f : [0..n] \to \{0, 1\}$ such that $f(\sum_{i \in [n]} x_i) = h(x_1, \ldots, x_n)$ for all $(x_1, \ldots, x_n) \in \{0, 1\}^n$.

3.1 Secure Multiparty Computation

Let n be a polynomial in a security parameter λ. We denote the set of n players
by $\{\mathsf{P}_1, \ldots, \mathsf{P}_n\}$, where P_i is the i-th player. Assume that each player P_i has
a private input x_i from a finite set D. Let g be a deterministic function on
D^n. Consider the functionality $\mathcal{F}_g(\mathbf{x}) = (g(\mathbf{x}), \ldots, g(\mathbf{x}))$ for $\mathbf{x} = (x_1, \ldots, x_n)$.
Let Π be a protocol between n players. We assume the *preprocessing model*.
That is, a protocol includes a joint distribution $\mathcal{D}$ over the Cartesian product
$R_1 \times \cdots \times R_n$ of n sets, and each player P_i receives $r_i \in R_i$ before he decides

his input, where $(r_1, \ldots, r_n)$ is sampled from $R_1 \times \cdots \times R_n$ according to $\mathcal{D}$. We assume computationally unbounded adversaries who passively corrupt up to t players. (We do not consider active adversaries whose corrupted players deviate from protocols arbitrarily.) Let $\mathsf{View}_{\Pi,i}(\mathbf{x})$ denote the view of P_i at the end of the protocol execution on input $\mathbf{x}$, and let $\mathsf{Output}_{\Pi,i}(\mathbf{x})$ be the output of P_i. For a security parameter λ, we say that Π is a t-secure MPC protocol for $\mathcal{F}_g$ if

Correctness. For any input $\mathbf{x}$, $\Pr\left[\exists i \in [n] : \mathsf{Output}_{\Pi,i}(\mathbf{x}) \neq g(\mathbf{x})\right] = \mathsf{negl}(\lambda)$;

Privacy. For any set $T \subseteq [n]$ of size at most t and any pair of inputs $\mathbf{x} = (x_i)_{i \in [n]}$, $\mathbf{w} = (w_i)_{i \in [n]}$ such that $(x_i)_{i \in T} = (w_i)_{i \in T}$ and $g(\mathbf{x}) = g(\mathbf{w})$, it holds that $\{(\mathsf{View}_{\Pi,i}(\mathbf{x}))_{i \in T}\}_{\lambda \in \mathbb{N}} \approx \{(\mathsf{View}_{\Pi,i}(\mathbf{w}))_{i \in T}\}_{\lambda \in \mathbb{N}}$.

We simply say that Π is *fully secure* if it is $(n-1)$-secure.

We denote by $\mathsf{Comm}_i(\Pi)$ the total number of bits sent or received by the i-th player P_i during the execution of a protocol Π with worst-case inputs. We denote by $\mathsf{Rand}_i(\Pi)$ the size of correlated randomness for P_i, i.e., the total number of bits received by P_i in the setup of Π. We define the online (resp. offline) bottleneck complexity of Π as $\mathsf{BC}_{\mathrm{on}}(\Pi) = \max_{i \in [n]}\{\mathsf{Comm}_i(\Pi)\}$ (resp. $\mathsf{BC}_{\mathrm{off}}(\Pi) = \max_{i \in [n]}\{\mathsf{Rand}_i(\Pi)\}$). We say that Π is *BC-efficient* if $\mathsf{BC}_{\mathrm{on}}(\Pi)$ is $o(n)$. We denote by $\mathsf{Round}(\Pi)$ the round complexity of Π, i.e., the number of sequential rounds of interaction.

We defer the simulation-based definition of secure MPC for n-input/n-output randomized functionalities to the full version [22]. We also argue in the full version [22] that a set of protocols in the paper can be composed concurrently.

3.2 Basic Algorithms

Let $\mathbb{G}$ be an abelian group (e.g., a finite field or a ring of integers modulo m). Define $\mathsf{Additive}_\mathbb{G}(s)$ as an algorithm to generate additive shares over $\mathbb{G}$ for a secret $s \in \mathbb{G}$. Formally, on input $s \in \mathbb{G}$, $\mathsf{Additive}_\mathbb{G}(s)$ chooses $(s_1, \ldots, s_n) \in \mathbb{G}^n$ uniformly at random conditioned on $s = \sum_{i \in [n]} s_i$, and outputs it. For a vector $\mathbf{s} \in \mathbb{G}^m$, we define $\mathsf{Additive}_\mathbb{G}(\mathbf{s})$ as $\mathsf{Additive}_\mathbb{G}$ being applied to $\mathbf{s}$ in an element-wise way. We simply write $\mathsf{Additive}$ instead of $\mathsf{Additive}_\mathbb{G}$ if $\mathbb{G}$ is clear from the context.

Let $\mathbb{F}$ be a finite field. Define $\mathsf{MakeBeaver}_\mathbb{F}()$ as an algorithm to generate a Beaver triple [3]. Formally, $\mathsf{MakeBeaver}_\mathbb{F}()$ takes no input and does the following: (1) Let $a, b \leftarrow_{\$} \mathbb{F}$ and $c = ab$; (2) Let $(a_i)_{i \in [n]} \leftarrow \mathsf{Additive}_\mathbb{F}(a)$, $(b_i)_{i \in [n]} \leftarrow \mathsf{Additive}_\mathbb{F}(b)$ and $(c_i)_{i \in [n]} \leftarrow \mathsf{Additive}_\mathbb{F}(c)$; (3) Output $(a_i, b_i, c_i)_{i \in [n]}$.

Suppose that $|\mathbb{F}| \geq n + 1$ and let $\alpha_1, \ldots, \alpha_n$ be pairwise distinct non-zero elements of $\mathbb{F}$. Define $\mathsf{Shamir}_{\mathbb{F},t}(s)$ as an algorithm to generate shares of the (t, n)-Shamir secret sharing scheme for a secret $s \in \mathbb{F}$. Formally, on input $s \in \mathbb{F}$, $\mathsf{Shamir}_{\mathbb{F},t}(s)$ chooses a random polynomial φ over $\mathbb{F}$ of degree at most t such that $\varphi(0) = s$, and then outputs $(\varphi(\alpha_1), \ldots, \varphi(\alpha_n))$. For a vector $\mathbf{s} \in \mathbb{F}^m$, we define $\mathsf{Shamir}_{\mathbb{F},t}(\mathbf{s})$ as $\mathsf{Shamir}_{\mathbb{F},t}$ being applied to $\mathbf{s}$ in an element-wise way.

We can convert consistent shares of the Shamir scheme into additive shares for the same secret. Indeed, there exist constants $\ell_1, \ldots, \ell_n$, which we call *Lagrange coefficients associated with the α_i's*, such that $\ell_1 \cdot \varphi(\alpha_1) + \cdots + \ell_n \cdot$

$\varphi(\alpha_n) = \varphi(0)$ for any polynomial φ of degree at most $n-1$. It immediately implies that $\sum_{i\in[n]} \ell_i v_i = s$ for $(v_i)_{i\in[n]} \leftarrow \mathsf{Shamir}_{\mathbb{F},t}(s)$, which means that $(\ell_i v_i)_{i\in[n]}$ is a tuple of additive shares for s.

Finally, we recall a simple mathematical fact that also follows from the invertibility of Vandermonde matrices: Let $s \in \mathbb{F}$ and $T \subseteq [n]$ be any set of size at most t. Then, there is a polynomial φ of degree at most t such that $\varphi(0) = s$ and $\varphi(\alpha_i) = 0$ for all $i \in T$.

3.3 Bloom Filters

Bloom filters [9] are probabilistic data structures that provide compact encodings of sets. Formally, let U be a set and $\mathcal{H}$ be a set of k independent uniform hash functions $\mathcal{H} = \{H_1, \ldots, H_k\}$ such that each H_i maps elements in U to numbers in $[m]$. To add an element $x \in U$, an algorithm Add takes an m-bit string $\mathbf{BF} = (v^{(h)})_{h\in[m]}$ and an element $x \in U$ as input, and sets $v^{(h)} \leftarrow 1$ for all $h \in \{H_1(x), \ldots, H_k(x)\}$. Let $\mathbf{BF}(\emptyset)$ denote the string whose bits are all zero. For $X \in 2^U$, let $\mathbf{BF}(X)$ denote a string obtained by adding the elements of X. That is, if $X = \{x_1, \ldots, x_s\}$, first construct $\mathbf{BF}_1, \ldots, \mathbf{BF}_s$ as $\mathbf{BF}_j = \mathsf{Add}(\mathbf{BF}_{j-1}, x_j)$ for all $j \in [s]$, where $\mathbf{BF}_0 = \mathbf{BF}(\emptyset)$, and then define $\mathbf{BF}(X) = \mathbf{BF}_s$. Note that the definition of $\mathbf{BF}(X)$ is independent of the order of the elements of X. To query $\mathbf{BF}(X)$ for an element $y \in U$ (i.e., to test whether $y \in X$), a query algorithm Check takes an m-bit string $\mathbf{BF} = (v^{(h)})_{h\in[m]}$ and an element $y \in U$ as input, and checks if $v^{(h)} = 1$ for all $h \in \{H_1(y), \ldots, H_k(y)\}$. If so, the algorithm outputs 1 ("yes") and otherwise it outputs 0 ("no").

It is straightforward to see that if y is indeed in X, Check correctly outputs "yes". On the other hand, the converse is not true. Suppose that $y \notin X$. If the bits at positions $H_1(y), \ldots, H_k(y)$ have by chance been set to 1 during the insertion of the elements of X, the algorithm outputs "yes" incorrectly, resulting in a false positive. We require a Bloom filter to satisfy that the probability of false positives is negligible. Formally, we say that $\mathcal{BF} = (\mathsf{Add}, \mathsf{Check})$ is a Bloom filter for U with parameters m, k and s if for any $X \in 2^U$ with $|X| = s$ and any $y \in U \setminus X$, the probability that $\mathsf{Check}(\mathbf{BF}(X), y) = 1$ is negligible in k, where the probability is taken over the random choice of $\mathcal{H}$.

We can implement $\mathcal{H}$ with a d-universal hash family, which ensures that the hash values of any d distinct inputs are independent and uniformly at random. According to [16], the false positive probability of a Bloom filter is still negligible even when a universal hash family is used instead of truly random functions. More precisely, the analysis [16, Proposition 3.10] shows that if $\mathcal{H}$ is a d-universal hash family for a constant $d \geq 2$, then the false positive probability of the Bloom filter based on $\mathcal{H}$ with parameters m, k, s is upper bounded by

$$\left(1 - \left(1 - \frac{k}{m}\right)^s + \left(\frac{ks}{m}\right)^d\right)^k \leq \left(1 - \left(1 - \frac{ks}{m}\right) + \left(\frac{ks}{m}\right)^d\right)^k = \left(\frac{ks}{m} + \left(\frac{ks}{m}\right)^d\right)^k$$

If we set $m = 2ks$, then $ks/m + (ks/m)^d = 1/2 + 1/2^d$ is a constant less than 1, and hence the probability is negligible in k. We note that an efficient d-universal hash family can be obtained by letting a hash function be a random polynomial p of degree $d-1$ over a field of size at least m, and letting the hash value of x be $p(x)$. Note that such a function can be described in $O(\log m)$ bits if $d = O(1)$.

4 BC-Efficient Protocols for Basic Functionalities

Broadcast. Let $\mathcal{F}_{\mathsf{Broadcast},i}$ be the functionality which receives a non-private input y from the i-th player and gives y to all players (described in Fig. 1). Since we assume that all players are semi-honest, we immediately obtain a BC-efficient protocol realizing $\mathcal{F}_{\mathsf{Broadcast},i}$. Indeed, we just utilize a round table structure where players are supposed to be nodes in a ring network and each player only communicates with the consecutive players around the table. Such a protocol implicitly appears in [48]. However, the round complexity of this protocol is $O(n)$. To reduce it to $O(\log n)$, assume that the set of n players is represented by a binary tree whose height is $O(\log n)$ and root is P_i. Each player sends his two children the element that he received from his parent node. We show the formal description of the protocol $\Pi_{\mathsf{Broadcast},i}$ in Fig. 1. The complexity of $\Pi_{\mathsf{Broadcast},i}$ is $\mathsf{BC}_{\mathsf{on}}(\Pi_{\mathsf{Broadcast},i}) = O(\ell_y)$ and $\mathsf{Round}(\Pi_{\mathsf{Broadcast},i}) = O(\log n)$, where ℓ_y is the bit-length of y. Note that $\mathsf{BC}_{\mathsf{off}}(\Pi_{\mathsf{Broadcast},i}) = 0$.

Functionality $\mathcal{F}_{\mathsf{Broadcast},i}$

Upon receiving y from the i-th player P_i, $\mathcal{F}_{\mathsf{Broadcast},i}$ gives every player y.

Protocol $\Pi_{\mathsf{Broadcast},i}$

Assumption. The set of n players is represented by a binary tree whose height is $h = O(\log n)$ and root is the i-th player P_i. For each $k \in [n]$, let Parent_k be the parent of P_k if $k \neq 1$, and $\{\mathsf{L}_k, \mathsf{R}_k\}$ be at most two children of P_k.

Non-private input. The i-th player P_i has y.

Output. Every player obtains y.

Protocol.
1. P_i sets $y_i = y$ and sends it to L_i and R_i.
2. For each $j = 1, 2, \ldots, h$, every player P_k at the j-th level sets y_k as the element he received from Parent_k, and sends it to L_k and R_k.
3. Each player P_k outputs y_k.

Fig. 1. The functionality $\mathcal{F}_{\mathsf{Broadcast},i}$ and a protocol $\Pi_{\mathsf{Broadcast},i}$ implementing it

---

Functionality $\mathcal{F}_{\mathsf{Sum}}((x_i)_{i \in [n]})$

Upon receiving a group element $x_i \in \mathbb{G}$ from each player P_i, $\mathcal{F}_{\mathsf{Sum}}$ gives every player $s := \sum_{i \in [n]} x_i$.

Sub-Protocol Π_0

Input. Each player P_i has a group element $y_i \in \mathbb{G}$.

Output. Every player obtains $s = \sum_{i \in [n]} y_i$.

Protocol.
1. Partition the set of n players into $\lceil n/2 \rceil$ pairwise disjoint sets $S_1, \ldots, S_{\lceil n/2 \rceil}$, each of size at most 2. Let $S_k = \{\mathsf{P}_{\ell_k}, \mathsf{P}_{r_k}\}$, where $\ell_k < r_k$.
2. For each $k = 1, 2, \ldots, \lceil n/2 \rceil$, P_{r_k} sends his input y_{r_k} to P_{ℓ_k}.
3. For each $k = 1, 2, \ldots, \lceil n/2 \rceil$, P_{ℓ_k} computes $s_k = y_{\ell_k} + y_{r_k}$.
4. Players $\mathsf{P}_{\ell_1}, \ldots, \mathsf{P}_{\ell_{\lceil n/2 \rceil}}$ invoke Π_0 on input $(s_1, \ldots, s_{\lceil n/2 \rceil})$ and obtain s.
5. For each $k = 1, 2, \ldots, \lceil n/2 \rceil$, P_{ℓ_k} sends s to P_{r_k}.
6. Each player P_i outputs s.

Protocol Π'_{Sum}

Input. Each player P_i has a group element $x_i \in \mathbb{G}$.

Output. Every player obtains $s = \sum_{i \in [n]} x_i$.

Setup.
1. Let $(a_i)_{i \in [n]} \leftarrow \mathsf{Additive}_{\mathbb{G}}(0)$.
2. Each player P_i receives a_i.

Protocol.
1. Each player P_i sets $y_i = x_i + a_i$.
2. Players invoke Π_0 on input $(y_1, \ldots, y_n)$ and obtain $s = \sum_{i \in [n]} y_i$.
3. Each player P_i outputs s.

Fig. 2. The functionality $\mathcal{F}_{\mathsf{Sum}}$ and a protocol Π'_{Sum} implementing it

Sum. In Fig. 2, we describe the functionality $\mathcal{F}_{\mathsf{Sum}}$ which receives group elements $x_1, \ldots, x_n \in \mathbb{G}$, each from P_i, and gives $s := \sum_{i \in [n]} x_i$ to all players. There are two incomparable BC-efficient implementations of $\mathcal{F}_{\mathsf{Sum}}$. The former protocol Π_{Sum}, which implicitly appears in [48], utilizes a round table structure and lets each player add his share to the message from the previous player and send the result to the next player around the table. However, the round complexity of Π_{Sum} is $O(n)$. We propose a novel protocol Π'_{Sum} that uses recursion. Assume that players are partitioned into $\lceil n/2 \rceil$ pairs and name the members of each pair as the right and left players of the pair. For every pair, the right player sends his element to the left player, who then computes the sum s_k of their elements. All of the left players then execute the protocol Π'_{Sum} recursively on $\lceil n/2 \rceil$ inputs $s_1, \ldots, s_{\lceil n/2 \rceil}$. After $O(\log n)$ iterations, the final call of the protocol outputs the aggregation of the sum of all elements. In the worst case, a player who is chosen as the left player of a pair in every iteration needs to communicate $O(\log n)$ elements and hence the online bottleneck complexity increases by $O(\log n)$ times. Note that if one naively implements the above procedures, players learn additional information, e.g., a partial sum of inputs. We thus let players mask their inputs with additive shares of 0 in advance. The formal description of Π'_{Sum} is shown in Fig. 2. The complexities are $\mathrm{BC}_{\mathrm{off}}(\Pi_{\mathsf{Sum}}) = \mathrm{BC}_{\mathrm{off}}(\Pi'_{\mathsf{Sum}}) = O(\log |\mathbb{G}|)$,

- $\mathrm{BC}_{\mathrm{on}}(\Pi_{\mathsf{Sum}}) = O(\log |\mathbb{G}|)$ and $\mathrm{Round}(\Pi_{\mathsf{Sum}}) = O(n)$;
- $\mathrm{BC}_{\mathrm{on}}(\Pi'_{\mathsf{Sum}}) = O((\log n)(\log |\mathbb{G}|))$ and $\mathrm{Round}(\Pi'_{\mathsf{Sum}}) = O(\log n)$.

Multiplication. In Fig. 3, we describe the functionality $\mathcal{F}_{\mathsf{Mult}}$ which takes additive shares $(x_i)_{i \in [n]}$, $(y_i)_{i \in [n]}$ for x and y (respectively), and gives additive shares $(z_i)_{i \in [n]}$ for $z = xy$. We obtain a BC-efficient protocol Π_{Mult} for $\mathcal{F}_{\mathsf{Mult}}$ based on the above BC-efficient protocols for sum and a Beaver triple. We show its formal description in Fig. 3. The correctness and security follow from [3]. Since players also need to receive correlated randomness for two executions of a protocol implementing $\mathcal{F}_{\mathsf{Sum}}$, the offline bottleneck complexity is $\mathrm{BC}_{\mathrm{off}}(\Pi_{\mathsf{Mult}}) = O(\log |\mathbb{F}|)$. The protocol has different online bottleneck complexity and round complexity depending on implementation of $\mathcal{F}_{\mathsf{Sum}}$:

- $\mathrm{BC}_{\mathrm{on}}(\Pi_{\mathsf{Mult}}) = O(\log |\mathbb{F}|)$ and $\mathrm{Round}(\Pi_{\mathsf{Mult}}) = O(n)$;
- $\mathrm{BC}_{\mathrm{on}}(\Pi_{\mathsf{Mult}}) = O((\log n)(\log |\mathbb{F}|))$ and $\mathrm{Round}(\Pi_{\mathsf{Mult}}) = O(\log n)$.

Inner Product. Let $\mathbb{F}$ be a finite field. Define a functionality $\mathcal{F}_{\mathsf{IP}}$ as follows (described in Fig. 4): On input $(\mathbf{x}_i, \mathbf{y}_i)_{i \in [n]}$, where $\mathbf{x}_i, \mathbf{y}_i \in \mathbb{F}^m$, $\mathcal{F}_{\mathsf{IP}}$ gives all players $z = \langle \mathbf{x}, \mathbf{y} \rangle$, where $\mathbf{x} = \sum_{i \in [n]} \mathbf{x}_i$ and $\mathbf{y} = \sum_{i \in [n]} \mathbf{y}_i$. We construct a BC-efficient protocol Π_{IP} for $\mathcal{F}_{\mathsf{IP}}$ based on BC-efficient protocols for sum and multiplication. We show the security proof in the full version [22].

Since players need to receive correlated randomness for m executions of a protocol implementing $\mathcal{F}_{\mathsf{Mult}}$ and one execution of a protocol implementing $\mathcal{F}_{\mathsf{Sum}}$, the offline communication complexity is $\mathrm{BC}_{\mathsf{off}}(\Pi_{\mathsf{IP}}) = O(m \log |\mathbb{F}|)$. In the online phase, the protocol Π_{IP} invokes $\mathcal{F}_{\mathsf{Mult}}$ m times and $\mathcal{F}_{\mathsf{Sum}}$ once and thus has different online communication complexity and round complexity depending on implementation of $\mathcal{F}_{\mathsf{Mult}}$ and $\mathcal{F}_{\mathsf{Sum}}$:

- $\mathrm{BC}_{\mathsf{on}}(\Pi_{\mathsf{IP}}) = O(m \log |\mathbb{F}|)$ and $\mathrm{Round}(\Pi_{\mathsf{IP}}) = O(n)$;
- $\mathrm{BC}_{\mathsf{on}}(\Pi_{\mathsf{IP}}) = O((\log n)m \log |\mathbb{F}|)$ and $\mathrm{Round}(\Pi_{\mathsf{IP}}) = O(\log n)$.

We define a variant $\mathcal{F}'_{\mathsf{IP}}$, whose difference from $\mathcal{F}_{\mathsf{IP}}$ is that $\mathcal{F}'_{\mathsf{IP}}$ outputs shares for an inner product z instead of z itself. We can construct a BC-efficient protocol Π'_{IP} for $\mathcal{F}'_{\mathsf{IP}}$ in a similar way. Indeed, Π'_{IP} is the same as Π_{IP} except that it does not reconstruct the inner product z. Thus, the bottleneck communication complexity and round complexity of Π'_{IP} is asymptotically the same as those of Π_{IP}. We defer the formal description to the full version [22].

Functionality $\mathcal{F}_{\mathsf{Mult}}((x_i, y_i)_{i \in [n]})$

1. $\mathcal{F}_{\mathsf{Mult}}$ receives field elements $x_i, y_i \in \mathbb{F}$ from each player P_i.
2. $\mathcal{F}_{\mathsf{Mult}}$ computes $x = \sum_{i \in [n]} x_i$, $y = \sum_{i \in [n]} y_i$ and $z = xy$.
3. $\mathcal{F}_{\mathsf{Mult}}$ runs $(z_i)_{i \in [n]} \leftarrow \mathsf{Additive}_{\mathbb{F}}(z)$.
4. $\mathcal{F}_{\mathsf{Mult}}$ gives z_i to each player P_i.

Protocol Π_{Mult}

Input. Each player P_i has $x_i, y_i \in \mathbb{F}$.

Output. Each player P_i obtains $z_i \in \mathbb{F}$, where $(z_i)_{i \in [n]} \leftarrow \mathcal{F}_{\mathsf{Mult}}((x_i, y_i)_{i \in [n]})$.

Setup.
1. Generate a Beaver triple $(a_i, b_i, c_i)_{i \in [n]} \leftarrow \mathsf{MakeBeaver}_{\mathbb{F}}()$.
2. Each player P_i receives (a_i, b_i, c_i).

Protocol.
1. Each player P_i computes $u_i = x_i - a_i$ and $v_i = y_i - b_i$.
2. Players obtain $u = \mathcal{F}_{\mathsf{Sum}}((u_i)_{i \in [n]})$ and $v = \mathcal{F}_{\mathsf{Sum}}((v_i)_{i \in [n]})$.
3. For each $k = 1, 2, \ldots, n$, P_k does the following:
   - If $k = 1$, output $z_1 = ub_1 + a_1v + c_1 + uv$.
   - If $k \neq 1$, output $z_i = ub_i + a_iv + c_i$.

Fig. 3. The functionality $\mathcal{F}_{\mathsf{Mult}}$ and a protocol Π_{Mult} implementing it

352   R. Eriguchi

Functionality $\mathcal{F}_{\mathsf{IP}}((\mathbf{x}_i, \mathbf{y}_i)_{i \in [n]})$

1. $\mathcal{F}_{\mathsf{IP}}$ receives vectors $\mathbf{x}_i, \mathbf{y}_i \in \mathbb{F}^m$ from each player P_i.
2. $\mathcal{F}_{\mathsf{IP}}$ computes $\mathbf{x} = \sum_{i \in [n]} \mathbf{x}_i$, $\mathbf{y} = \sum_{i \in [n]} \mathbf{y}_i$ and $z = \langle \mathbf{x}, \mathbf{y} \rangle$.
3. $\mathcal{F}_{\mathsf{IP}}$ gives z to every player P_i.

Protocol Π_{IP}

Input. Each player P_i has $\mathbf{x}_i = (x_i^{(j)})_{j \in [m]} \in \mathbb{F}^m$ and $\mathbf{y}_i = (y_i^{(j)})_{j \in [m]} \in \mathbb{F}^m$.

Output. Each player P_i obtains $z = \mathcal{F}_{\mathsf{IP}}((\mathbf{x}_i, \mathbf{y}_i)_{i \in [n]})$.

Protocol.
1. For each $j \in [m]$, players obtain $(w_i^{(j)})_{i \in [n]} \leftarrow \mathcal{F}_{\mathsf{Mult}}((x_i^{(j)}, y_i^{(j)})_{i \in [n]})$.
2. Each player P_i computes $z_i = \sum_{j \in [m]} w_i^{(j)} \in \mathbb{F}$.
3. Players obtain $z = \mathcal{F}_{\mathsf{Sum}}((z_i)_{i \in [n]})$.
4. Each player P_i outputs z.

Fig. 4. The functionality $\mathcal{F}_{\mathsf{IP}}$ and a protocol Π_{IP} implementing it

5 BC-Efficient Protocols for General Symmetric Functions

5.1 First Protocol

First, we show a fully secure protocol that can achieve low online bottleneck complexity $O(\log n)$. Recall that for a function $h : \{0,1\}^n \to \{0,1\}$, we denote the functionality of giving every player $h(x_1, \dots, x_n)$ by $\mathcal{F}_h$.

Theorem 1. *Let* $h : \{0,1\}^n \to \{0,1\}$ *be a symmetric function. The protocol* Π_{Sym} *described in Fig. 5 is a fully secure MPC protocol for* $\mathcal{F}_h$ *in the* $\mathcal{F}_{\mathsf{Sum}}$*-hybrid model. Implementing* $\mathcal{F}_{\mathsf{Sum}}$*, the protocol* Π_{Sym} *achieves either of the following efficiency measures:*

- $\mathrm{BC}_{\mathrm{off}}(\Pi_{\mathsf{Sym}}) = O(n)$, $\mathrm{BC}_{\mathrm{on}}(\Pi_{\mathsf{Sym}}) = O(\log n)$ *and* $\mathrm{Round}(\Pi_{\mathsf{Sym}}) = O(n)$;
- $\mathrm{BC}_{\mathrm{off}}(\Pi_{\mathsf{Sym}}) = O(n)$, $\mathrm{BC}_{\mathrm{on}}(\Pi_{\mathsf{Sym}}) = O((\log n)^2)$ *and* $\mathrm{Round}(\Pi_{\mathsf{Sym}}) = O(\log n)$.

Proof. First, we prove the correctness of Π_{Sym}. Let $\mathbf{x} \in \{0,1\}^n$ be any input. Since $r = \sum_{i \in [n]} r_i$, it holds that $y = r + \sum_{i \in [n]} x_i$. It also holds that

$$z = \sum_{i \in [n]} z_i = \sum_{i \in [n]} (\mathbf{S}_i)_y = (\mathbf{S})_y = T_{(y-r) \bmod (n+1)}$$

where $(\mathbf{S})_y$ is the y-th element of $\mathbf{S}$. Therefore, we have that $z = f(\sum_{i \in [n]} x_i) = h(x_1, \ldots, x_n)$.

Next, we prove the privacy of Π_{Sym}. Let $T \subseteq [n]$ be the set of corrupted players. Let $H = \overline{T}$ be the set of honest players and fix an honest player $j \in H$. Note that corrupted players' view can be simulated from the following elements:

Correlated randomness. $(r_i, \mathbf{S}_i)$ for all $i \in T$;
Online messages. $y_i = x_i + r_i$ and $z_i = (\mathbf{S}_i)_y$ for all $i \in H$.

Let $\mathbf{x}, \mathbf{x}' \in \{0,1\}^n$ be any pair of inputs such that

$$x_i = x_i' \ (\forall i \in T) \text{ and } h(x_1, \ldots, x_n) = h(x_1', \ldots, x_n').$$

It is sufficient to prove that the distribution of the above elements during the execution of Π_{Sym} on input $\mathbf{x}$ is identical to that on input $\mathbf{x}'$. To show the equivalence of the distributions, we show a bijection between the random strings used by Π_{Sym} on input $\mathbf{x}$ and the random strings used by Π_{Sym} on input $\mathbf{x}'$ such that the correlated randomness received by T and the online messages from H

Protocol Π_{Sym}

Notations.
  - Let $h : \{0,1\}^n \to \{0,1\}$ be a symmetric function.
  - Let $f : [0..n] \to \{0,1\}$ be a function such that $h(x_1, \ldots, x_n) = f(\sum_{i \in [n]} x_i)$ for all $(x_1, \ldots, x_n) \in \{0,1\}^n$.
  - Let $\mathbb{F} = \{0,1\}$ be the binary field.

Input. Each player P_i has $x_i \in \{0,1\}$.

Output. Every player obtains $z = h(x_1, \ldots, x_n)$.

Setup.
  1. Let $r \leftarrow_\$ \mathbb{Z}_{n+1}$ and $(r_i)_{i \in [n]} \leftarrow \mathsf{Additive}_{\mathbb{Z}_{n+1}}(r)$.
  2. Define $\mathbf{T} = (T_i)_{i \in \mathbb{Z}_{n+1}} \in \{0,1\}^{n+1}$ by $T_i = f(i)$ for all $i \in \mathbb{Z}_{n+1}$.
  3. Define $\mathbf{S} \in \{0,1\}^{n+1}$ by $\mathbf{S} = \mathsf{Shift}_r(\mathbf{T})$ and let $(\mathbf{S}_i)_{i \in [n]} \leftarrow \mathsf{Additive}_{\mathbb{F}}(\mathbf{S})$.
  4. Each player P_i receives $(r_i, \mathbf{S}_i)$.

Protocol.
  1. Each player P_i computes $y_i = x_i + r_i \bmod (n+1)$.
  2. Players obtain $y = \mathcal{F}_{\mathsf{Sum}}((y_i)_{i \in [n]})$.
  3. Each player P_i sets $z_i = (\mathbf{S}_i)_y$, where $(\mathbf{S}_i)_y$ is the y-th element of $\mathbf{S}_i$. Here, we identify the set indexing the entries of $\mathbf{S}_i$ with $\mathbb{Z}_{n+1}$.
  4. Players obtain $z = \mathcal{F}_{\mathsf{Sum}}((z_i)_{i \in [n]})$.
  5. Each player P_i outputs z.

Fig. 5. The first protocol Π_{Sym} for computing a symmetric function

are the same under this bijection. The set of all random strings is

$$
\mathcal{R} = \left\{ (r_i, \mathbf{S}_i)_{i \in [n]} : \sum_{i \in [n]} \mathbf{S}_i = \mathsf{Shift}_r(\mathbf{T}), \text{ where } r = \sum_{i \in [n]} r_i \right\}.
$$

We denote the randomness of Π_{Sym} on input $\mathbf{x}$ by $(r_i, \mathbf{S}_i)_{i \in [n]}$ and that on input $\mathbf{x}'$ by $(r_i', \mathbf{S}_i')_{i \in [n]}$. The bijection maps the randomness $(r_i, \mathbf{S}_i)_{i \in [n]} \in \mathcal{R}$ to $(r_i', \mathbf{S}_i')_{i \in [n]} \in \mathcal{R}$ in such a way that

$$
r_i' = \begin{cases} r_i, & \text{if } i \in T, \\ r_i + x_i - x_i', & \text{if } i \in H, \end{cases}
$$

$$
\mathbf{S}_i' = \begin{cases} \mathbf{S}_i, & \text{if } i \neq j, \\ \mathbf{S}_j + \mathsf{Shift}_{r'}(\mathbf{T}) - \mathsf{Shift}_r(\mathbf{T}), & \text{if } i = j, \end{cases}
$$

where $r := \sum_{i \in [n]} r_i$ and $r' := \sum_{i \in [n]} r_i' = r + \sum_{i \in H} (x_i - x_i')$. The image is indeed a consistent random string (i.e., $(r_i', \mathbf{S}_i')_{i \in [n]} \in \mathcal{R}$) since $\sum_{i \in [n]} \mathbf{S}_i' = \mathsf{Shift}_{r'}(\mathbf{T})$ if and only if $\sum_{i \in [n]} \mathbf{S}_i = \mathsf{Shift}_r(\mathbf{T})$. The above map is indeed a bijection since it has the inverse

$$
r_i = \begin{cases} r_i', & \text{if } i \in T, \\ r_i' + x_i' - x_i, & \text{if } i \in H, \end{cases}
$$

$$
\mathbf{S}_i = \begin{cases} \mathbf{S}_i', & \text{if } i \neq j, \\ \mathbf{S}_j' + \mathsf{Shift}_r(\mathbf{T}) - \mathsf{Shift}_{r'}(\mathbf{T}), & \text{if } i = j. \end{cases}
$$

Clearly, this bijection does not change the correlated randomness $(r_i, \mathbf{S}_i)_{i \in T}$ of T. It can be seen that $x_i' + r_i' = x_i' + (r_i + x_i - x_i') = x_i + r_i$ for $i \in H$. In particular, the message y is the same in both executions and hence so is $z_i = (\mathbf{S}_i)_y$ for $i \in H \setminus \{j\}$. We see that

$$
\begin{aligned}
(\mathbf{S}_j')_y &= (\mathbf{S}_j)_y + (\mathsf{Shift}_{r'}(\mathbf{T}))_y - (\mathsf{Shift}_r(\mathbf{T}))_y \\
&= (\mathbf{S}_j)_y + f(y - r') - f(y - r) \\
&= (\mathbf{S}_j)_y
\end{aligned}
$$

since $f(y - r') = f(\sum_{i \in [n]} x_i') = f(\sum_{i \in [n]} x_i) = f(y - r)$.

Finally, since players also need to receive correlated randomness for two executions of a protocol implementing $\mathcal{F}_{\mathsf{Sum}}$, the offline communication complexity is $\mathsf{BC}_{\mathsf{off}}(\Pi_{\mathsf{Sym}}) = O(n)$. Depending on implementation of $\mathcal{F}_{\mathsf{Sum}}$, Π_{Sym} has $\mathsf{BC}_{\mathsf{on}}(\Pi_{\mathsf{Sym}}) = O(\log n)$ and $\mathsf{Round}(\Pi_{\mathsf{Sym}}) = O(n)$; or $\mathsf{BC}_{\mathsf{on}}(\Pi_{\mathsf{Sym}}) = O((\log n)^2)$ and $\mathsf{Round}(\Pi_{\mathsf{Sym}}) = O(\log n)$. $\qquad\square$

5.2   Second Protocol

The second protocol reduces the offline bottleneck complexity of the first protocol to $O(\sqrt{n})$ at the cost of increasing the online bottleneck complexity.

Theorem 2. *Let $h : \{0,1\}^n \to \{0,1\}$ be a symmetric function. The protocol Π'_{Sym} described in Fig. 6 is a fully secure MPC protocol for $\mathcal{F}_h$ in the $\{\mathcal{F}_{\mathsf{Sum}}, \mathcal{F}_{\mathsf{IP}}\}$-hybrid model. Implementing $\mathcal{F}_{\mathsf{Sum}}$ and $\mathcal{F}_{\mathsf{IP}}$, the protocol Π'_{Sym} achieves either of the following efficiency measures:*

- $\mathrm{BC}_{\mathrm{off}}(\Pi'_{\mathsf{Sym}}) = O(\sqrt{n})$, $\mathrm{BC}_{\mathrm{on}}(\Pi'_{\mathsf{Sym}}) = O(\sqrt{n})$ and $\mathrm{Round}(\Pi'_{\mathsf{Sym}}) = O(n)$;
- $\mathrm{BC}_{\mathrm{off}}(\Pi'_{\mathsf{Sym}}) = O(\sqrt{n})$, $\mathrm{BC}_{\mathrm{on}}(\Pi'_{\mathsf{Sym}}) = O(\sqrt{n}\log n)$ and $\mathrm{Round}(\Pi'_{\mathsf{Sym}}) = O(\log n)$.

Proof. We prove the correctness of Π'_{Sym}. Since the proof of the privacy bears some similarities with that of Π_{Sym}, we defer it to the full version [22]. Let $\mathbf{x} \in \{0,1\}^n$ be any input. Since $r = \sum_{i\in[n]} r_i$, it holds that $y = \sum_{i\in[n]} x_i - r$. Let $\mathbf{a} := \sum_{i\in[n]} \mathbf{a}_i$ and $\mathbf{b} := \sum_{i\in[n]} \mathbf{b}_i$. Since $\sum_{i\in[n]} \mathbf{c}_i = \mathbf{e}_u$ and $\sum_{i\in[n]} \mathbf{d}_i = \mathbf{e}_v$, we have that

$$z = \langle \mathbf{a}, \mathbf{b}\rangle = \langle \mathsf{Shift}_\sigma(\mathbf{c}_1 + \cdots + \mathbf{c}_n), \mathbf{M}\cdot\mathsf{Shift}_\tau(\mathbf{d}_1 + \cdots + \mathbf{d}_n)\rangle = \mathbf{M}[u+\sigma, v+\tau],$$

where $\mathbf{M}[u', v']$ is the (u', v')-th entry of $\mathbf{M}$. Since $\phi^{-1}(u+\sigma, v+\tau) = y + r = \sum_{i\in[n]} x_i \in [0..n]$, it is equal to $f(y+r) = h(x_1, \ldots, x_n)$.

Finally, since players also need to receive correlated randomness for one execution of a protocol implementing $\mathcal{F}_{\mathsf{IP}}$ and for one execution of a protocol implementing $\mathcal{F}_{\mathsf{Sum}}$, the offline bottleneck complexity is

$$\mathrm{BC}_{\mathrm{off}}(\Pi'_{\mathsf{Sym}}) = O(\log pq) + O((p+q)\log|\mathbb{F}|) + O(p\log|\mathbb{F}|) = O(\sqrt{n}).$$

At Step 1 of the online phase, each player sends a constant number of elements in $\mathbb{Z}_{pq}$. The bottleneck complexity of Step 5 is equal to that of a protocol realizing $\mathcal{F}_{\mathsf{IP}}$. The protocol Π'_{Sym} thus has different online communication complexity and round complexity depending on implementation of $\mathcal{F}_{\mathsf{IP}}$ and $\mathcal{F}_{\mathsf{Sum}}$: $\mathrm{BC}_{\mathrm{on}}(\Pi'_{\mathsf{Sym}}) = O(\sqrt{n})$ and $\mathrm{Round}(\Pi'_{\mathsf{Sym}}) = O(n)$; or $\mathrm{BC}_{\mathrm{on}}(\Pi'_{\mathsf{Sym}}) = O(\sqrt{n}\log n)$ and $\mathrm{Round}(\Pi'_{\mathsf{Sym}}) = O(\log n)$. $\square$

Protocol Π'_{Sym}

Notations.
- Let $h : \{0,1\}^n \to \{0,1\}$ be a symmetric function.
- Let $f : [0..n] \to \{0,1\}$ be a function such that $h(x_1,\ldots,x_n) = f(\sum_{i \in [n]} x_i)$ for all $(x_1,\ldots,x_n) \in \{0,1\}^n$.
- For a prime p, we identify the set indexing the entries of a vector of dimension p with $\mathbb{Z}_p$.
- Let p,q be primes such that $\sqrt{n} < p < q \leq O(\sqrt{n})$. We identify $[0..n]$ with a subset of $\mathbb{Z}_{pq}$.
- Let $\phi : \mathbb{Z}_{pq} \to \mathbb{Z}_p \times \mathbb{Z}_q$ be the ring isomorphism induced by the Chinese remainder theorem.
- Let $\mathbb{F} = \{0,1\}$ be the binary field.
- Define a matrix $\mathbf{M} \in \mathbb{F}^{p \times q}$ as follows: For $(y,z) \in \mathbb{Z}_p \times \mathbb{Z}_q$, the (y,z)-th entry of $\mathbf{M}$ is $f(\phi^{-1}(y,z))$ if $\phi^{-1}(y,z) \in [0..n]$, and 0 otherwise, where we identify the sets indexing the rows and columns of $\mathbf{M}$ as $\mathbb{Z}_p$ and $\mathbb{Z}_q$, respectively.

Input. Each player P_i has $x_i \in \{0,1\}$.

Output. Every player obtains $z = h(x_1,\ldots,x_n)$.

Setup.
1. Let $r \leftarrow_\$ \mathbb{Z}_{pq}$, $(r_i)_{i \in [n]} \leftarrow \mathsf{Additive}_{\mathbb{Z}_{pq}}(r)$ and $(u,v) = \phi(r)$.
2. Let $(\mathbf{c}_i)_{i \in [n]} \leftarrow \mathsf{Additive}_{\mathbb{F}}(\mathbf{e}_u)$ and $(\mathbf{d}_i)_{i \in [n]} \leftarrow \mathsf{Additive}_{\mathbb{F}}(\mathbf{e}_v)$, where $\mathbf{e}_u \in \mathbb{F}^p$ (resp. $\mathbf{e}_v \in \mathbb{F}^q$) is the vector whose entry is 1 at position $u \in \mathbb{Z}_p$ (resp. $v \in \mathbb{Z}_q$), and 0 otherwise.
3. Each player P_i receives $(r_i, \mathbf{c}_i, \mathbf{d}_i)$.

Protocol.
1. Each player P_i computes $y_i = x_i - r_i \bmod pq$.
2. Players obtain $y = \mathcal{F}_{\mathsf{Sum}}((y_i)_{i \in [n]})$.
3. Each player P_i computes $\phi(y) = (\sigma, \tau) \in \mathbb{Z}_p \times \mathbb{Z}_q$.
4. Each player P_i computes $\mathbf{a}_i = \mathsf{Shift}_\sigma(\mathbf{c}_i) \in \mathbb{F}^p$ and $\mathbf{b}_i = \mathbf{M} \cdot \mathsf{Shift}_\tau(\mathbf{d}_i) \in \mathbb{F}^p$.
5. Players obtain $z = \mathcal{F}_{\mathsf{IP}}((\mathbf{a}_i, \mathbf{b}_i)_{i \in [n]})$.
6. Each player P_i outputs z.

Fig. 6. The second protocol Π'_{Sym} for computing a symmetric function

5.3 Third Protocol

The third protocol achieves bottleneck complexity $O(n^{1/d} \log n)$ for any constant d but is only secure against adversaries corrupting less than $n/(d-1)$ players.

To begin with, we prepare some notations. Let $h : \{0,1\}^n \to \{0,1\}$ be a symmetric function and $f : [0..n] \to \{0,1\}$ be a function such that $h(x_1,\ldots,x_n) = f(\sum_{i \in [n]} x_i)$ for all $(x_1,\ldots,x_n) \in \{0,1\}^n$. Let $d \geq 2$ be any constant and choose d pairwise distinct primes $p_1,\ldots,p_d$ such that $n^{1/d} < p_j \leq 2n^{1/d}$ for all $j \in [d]$.

Such primes indeed exist for sufficiently large n since Bertrand's postulate [55, Theorem 5.8] ensures that there are at least $M/(3\log(2M))$ primes between M and $2M$. Set $N := p_1 \cdots p_d$ and $q := N/p_1 = p_2 \cdots p_d$. We identify $[0..n]$ with a subset of $\mathbb{Z}_N$. Let $\phi : \mathbb{Z}_N \to \mathbb{Z}_{p_1} \times \mathbb{Z}_q$ and $\psi : \mathbb{Z}_q \to \mathbb{Z}_{p_2} \times \cdots \times \mathbb{Z}_{p_d}$ be the ring isomorphisms induced by the Chinese remainder theorem. Define projection maps $\pi_1 : \mathbb{Z}_{p_1} \times \mathbb{Z}_q \to \mathbb{Z}_{p_1}$, $\pi_2 : \mathbb{Z}_{p_1} \times \mathbb{Z}_q \to \mathbb{Z}_q$ and $\pi'_j : \mathbb{Z}_{p_2} \times \cdots \times \mathbb{Z}_{p_d} \to \mathbb{Z}_{p_j}$ for $j = 2, \ldots, d$. Also, define

$$\phi_1 = \pi_1 \circ \phi, \ \psi_j = \pi'_j \circ \psi, \text{ and } \phi_j = \psi_j \circ \pi_2 \circ \phi, \tag{3}$$

where $\circ$ means the composition of maps. For $j \in [d]$, we identify the set indexing the entries of a vector $\mathbf{v} \in \mathbb{F}^{p_j}$ (resp. $\mathbf{v} \in \mathbb{F}^q$) with $\mathbb{Z}_{p_j}$ (resp. $\mathbb{Z}_q$). Let $\mathbf{e}_u \in \mathbb{F}^{p_j}$ denote the vector whose entry is 1 at position $u \in \mathbb{Z}_{p_j}$ and 0 otherwise. For vectors $\mathbf{v}_2 \in \mathbb{F}^{p_2}, \ldots, \mathbf{v}_d \in \mathbb{F}^{p_d}$, we define the Kronecker product $\mathbf{v}_2 \otimes \cdots \otimes \mathbf{v}_d \in \mathbb{F}^q$ as

$$(\mathbf{v}_2 \otimes \cdots \otimes \mathbf{v}_d)[k] = \mathbf{v}_2[\psi_2(k)] \cdots \mathbf{v}_d[\psi_d(k)]$$

for all $k \in \mathbb{Z}_q$. Define a matrix $\mathbf{M} \in \mathbb{F}^{p_1 \times q}$ as follows: For each $(j, k) \in \mathbb{Z}_{p_1} \times \mathbb{Z}_q$, the (j, k)-th entry $\mathbf{M}[j, k]$ of $\mathbf{M}$ is

$$\mathbf{M}[j, k] = \begin{cases} f(\phi^{-1}(j, k)), & \text{if } \phi^{-1}(j, k) \in [0..n], \\ 0, & \text{otherwise,} \end{cases}$$

where we identify the sets indexing the rows and columns of $\mathbf{M}$ as $\mathbb{Z}_{p_1}$ and $\mathbb{Z}_q$, respectively. It then holds that for all $x \in [0..n]$,

$$\begin{aligned}
&\langle \mathbf{e}_{\phi_1(x)}, \mathbf{M} \cdot (\mathbf{e}_{\phi_2(x)} \otimes \cdots \otimes \mathbf{e}_{\phi_d(x)}) \rangle \\
&= \sum_{j \in \mathbb{Z}_{p_1}} \mathbf{e}_{\phi_1(x)}[j] \left(\sum_{k \in \mathbb{Z}_q} \mathbf{M}[j, k] \cdot (\mathbf{e}_{\phi_2(x)} \otimes \cdots \otimes \mathbf{e}_{\phi_d(x)})[k] \right) \\
&= \sum_{k \in \mathbb{Z}_q} \mathbf{M}[\phi_1(x), k] \mathbf{e}_{\phi_2(x)}[\psi_2(k)] \cdots \mathbf{e}_{\phi_d(x)}[\psi_d(k)] \\
&= \mathbf{M}[\pi_1 \circ \phi(x), \pi_2 \circ \phi(x)] \\
&= f(x).
\end{aligned} \tag{4}$$

At the third equation, we use the fact that

$$\begin{aligned}
\psi_j(k) = \phi_j(x) \ (\forall j = 2, \ldots, d) &\Rightarrow \pi'_j(\psi(k)) = \pi'_j(\psi \circ \pi_2 \circ \phi(x)) \ (\forall j = 2, \ldots, d) \\
&\Rightarrow \psi(k) = \psi(\pi_2 \circ \phi(x)) \\
&\Rightarrow k = \pi_2 \circ \phi(x).
\end{aligned}$$

Using the above notations, we show the following theorem.

Theorem 3. *Let $h : \{0,1\}^n \to \{0,1\}$ be a symmetric function. Let $d \geq 2$ be any constant. For any $t < n/(d-1)$, the protocol $\Pi_{\mathsf{Sym}}^{(d)}$ described in Fig. 7 is a t-secure MPC protocol $\Pi_{\mathsf{Sym}}^{(d)}$ for $\mathcal{F}_h$ in the $\{\mathcal{F}_{\mathsf{Sum}}, \mathcal{F}_{\mathsf{IP}}\}$-hybrid model. Implementing $\mathcal{F}_{\mathsf{Sum}}$ and $\mathcal{F}_{\mathsf{IP}}$, the protocol $\Pi_{\mathsf{Sym}}^{(d)}$ achieves either of the following efficiency measures:*

- $\mathrm{BC}_{\mathrm{off}}(\Pi_{\mathrm{Sym}}^{(d)}) = O(n^{1/d}\log n)$, $\mathrm{BC}_{\mathrm{on}}(\Pi_{\mathrm{Sym}}^{(d)}) = O(n^{1/d}\log n)$ and $\mathrm{Round}(\Pi_{\mathrm{Sym}}^{(d)}) = O(n)$;
- $\mathrm{BC}_{\mathrm{off}}(\Pi_{\mathrm{Sym}}^{(d)}) = O(n^{1/d}\log n)$, $\mathrm{BC}_{\mathrm{on}}(\Pi_{\mathrm{Sym}}^{(d)}). = O(n^{1/d}(\log n)^2)$ and $\mathrm{Round}(\Pi_{\mathrm{Sym}}^{(d)}) = O(\log n)$.

Proof. First, we prove the correctness of $\Pi_{\mathrm{Sym}}^{(d)}$. Let $\mathbf{x} \in \{0,1\}^n$ be any input. Since $r = \sum_{i\in[n]} r_i$, it holds that $y = \sum_{i\in[n]} x_i - r$. We have that $\phi_j(\sum_{i\in[n]} x_i) = \phi_j(y) + \phi_j(r) = \sigma_j + u_j$ for all $j \in [d]$. At Step 4 of the online phase, we have that for all $j \in [d]$, $(\mathbf{a}_i^{(j)})_{i\in[n]}$ is a tuple of consistent shares whose secret is the unit vector $\mathbf{e}_{u_j+\sigma_j} \in \mathbb{F}^{p_j}$. That is, there is a tuple of degree-t polynomials $(\varphi_k^{(j)})_{k\in\mathbb{Z}_{p_j}}$ such that for all $k \in \mathbb{Z}_{p_j}$,

$$\varphi_k^{(j)}(0) = \mathbf{e}_{u_j+\sigma_j}[k] \text{ and } \varphi_k^{(j)}(\alpha_i) = \mathbf{a}_i^{(j)}[k] \ (\forall i \in [n]).$$

The property of Lagrange coefficients ℓ_i's implies that $(\mathbf{a}_i)_{i\in[n]}$ is a tuple of consistent additive shares for $\mathbf{e}_{u_1+\sigma_1}$. That is,

$$\mathbf{a} := \sum_{i\in[n]} \mathbf{a}_i = \mathbf{e}_{u_1+\sigma_1}.$$

Also, for any $k \in \mathbb{Z}_q$ and any $i \in [n]$, it holds that

$$(\mathbf{a}_i^{(2)} \otimes \cdots \otimes \mathbf{a}_i^{(d)})[k] = \mathbf{a}_i^{(2)}[k_2] \cdots \mathbf{a}_i^{(d)}[k_d] = (\varphi_{k_2}^{(2)} \cdots \varphi_{k_d}^{(d)})(\alpha_i),$$

where $k_j = \psi_j(k) \in \mathbb{Z}_{p_j}$. Since the degree of $\varphi_{k_2}^{(2)} \cdots \varphi_{k_d}^{(d)}$ is at most $t(d-1) \le n-1$, we have that

$$\sum_{i\in[n]} \ell_i \cdot (\mathbf{a}_i^{(2)} \otimes \cdots \otimes \mathbf{a}_i^{(d)})[k] = (\varphi_{k_2}^{(2)} \cdots \varphi_{k_d}^{(d)})(0)$$

$$= \mathbf{e}_{u_2+\sigma_2}[k_2] \cdots \mathbf{e}_{u_d+\sigma_d}[k_d]$$

$$= (\mathbf{e}_{u_2+\sigma_2} \otimes \cdots \otimes \mathbf{e}_{u_d+\sigma_d})[k].$$

Protocol $\Pi_{\text{Sym}}^{(d)}$

Notations.
- Let $h : \{0,1\}^n \to \{0,1\}$ be a symmetric function.
- Let $f : [0..n] \to \{0,1\}$ be a function such that $h(x_1,\ldots,x_n) = f(\sum_{i\in[n]} x_i)$ for all $(x_1,\ldots,x_n) \in \{0,1\}^n$.
- Let $p_1,\ldots,p_d$ be d pairwise distinct primes such that $n^{1/d} < p_j \leq 2n^{1/d}$ for all $j \in [d]$, and set $N = p_1 \cdots p_d$ and $q = N/p_1 = p_2 \cdots p_d$.
- Let $\phi_j : \mathbb{Z}_N \to \mathbb{Z}_{p_j}$ ($j \in [d]$) be the ring homomorphism defined in Eq. (3).
- Let $\mathbf{M} \in \mathbb{F}^{p_1 \times q}$ be a matrix such that

$$\langle \mathbf{e}_{\phi_1(x)}, \mathbf{M} \cdot (\mathbf{e}_{\phi_2(x)} \otimes \cdots \otimes \mathbf{e}_{\phi_d(x)}) \rangle = f(x)$$

  for all $x \in [0..n]$.
- Let $\mathbb{F}$ be the minimum finite field containing n pairwise distinct non-zero elements $\alpha_1,\ldots,\alpha_n$.
- Let $\ell_1,\ldots,\ell_n \in \mathbb{F}$ be Lagrange coefficients associated with the α_i's.

Input. Each player P_i has $x_i \in \{0,1\}$.

Output. Every player obtains $z = h(x_1,\ldots,x_n)$.

Setup.
1. Let $r \leftarrow_\$ \mathbb{Z}_N$, $(r_i)_{i\in[n]} \leftarrow \text{Additive}_{\mathbb{Z}_N}(r)$ and $u_j = \phi_j(r)$ for all $j \in [d]$.
2. For each $j \in [d]$, let $(\mathbf{c}_i^{(j)})_{i\in[n]} \leftarrow \text{Shamir}_{\mathbb{F},t}(\mathbf{e}_{u_j})$, where $\mathbf{e}_{u_j} \in \mathbb{F}^{p_j}$ is the vector whose entry is 1 at position $u_j \in \mathbb{Z}_{p_j}$ and 0 otherwise.
3. Each player P_i receives r_i and $(\mathbf{c}_i^{(j)})_{j\in[d]}$.

Protocol.
1. Each player P_i computes $y_i = x_i - r_i \bmod N$.
2. Players obtain $y = \mathcal{F}_{\text{Sum}}((y_i)_{i\in[n]})$.
3. Each player P_i computes $\phi_j(y) = \sigma_j \in \mathbb{Z}_{p_j}$ for all $j \in [d]$.
4. Each player P_i computes $\mathbf{a}_i^{(j)} = \text{Shift}_{\sigma_j}(\mathbf{c}_i^{(j)}) \in \mathbb{F}^{p_j}$ for all $j \in [d]$.
5. Each player P_i sets $\mathbf{a}_i' := \mathbf{a}_i^{(1)}$ and computes $\mathbf{b}_i' := \mathbf{M} \cdot (\mathbf{a}_i^{(2)} \otimes \cdots \otimes \mathbf{a}_i^{(d)}) \in \mathbb{F}^{p_1}$.
6. Each player P_i computes $\mathbf{a}_i = \ell_i \cdot \mathbf{a}_i'$ and $\mathbf{b}_i = \ell_i \cdot \mathbf{b}_i'$.
7. Players obtain $z = \mathcal{F}_{\text{IP}}((\mathbf{a}_i, \mathbf{b}_i)_{i\in[n]})$.
8. Each player P_i outputs z.

Fig. 7. The third protocol $\Pi_{\text{Sym}}^{(d)}$ for computing a symmetric function

Therefore, we have that

$$\mathbf{b} := \sum_{i\in[n]} \mathbf{b}_i = \mathbf{M} \cdot \sum_{i\in[n]} \ell_i(\mathbf{a}_i^{(2)} \otimes \cdots \otimes \mathbf{a}_i^{(d)}) = \mathbf{M} \cdot (\mathbf{e}_{u_2+\sigma_2} \otimes \cdots \otimes \mathbf{e}_{u_d+\sigma_d}).$$

We obtain that

$$z = \langle \mathbf{a}, \mathbf{b} \rangle = \langle \mathbf{e}_{u_1+\sigma_1}, \mathbf{M} \cdot (\mathbf{e}_{u_2+\sigma_2} \otimes \cdots \otimes \mathbf{e}_{u_d+\sigma_d}) \rangle = f(\sum_{i \in [n]} x_i) = h(x_1, \ldots, x_n).$$

Here, we use the fact that $u_j + \sigma_j = \phi_j(\sum_{i \in [n]} x_i)$ and Eq. (4).

Next, we prove the privacy of $\Pi_{\mathsf{Sym}}^{(d)}$. Let $T \subseteq [n]$ be the set of t corrupted players. Let $H = \overline{T}$ be the set of honest players and fix an honest player $j \in H$. In the $\mathcal{F}_{\mathsf{IP}}$-hybrid model, corrupted players' view at Step 7 (including their correlated randomness for $\mathcal{F}_{\mathsf{IP}}$) only contains their inputs $(\mathbf{a}_i, \mathbf{b}_i)_{i \in T}$ to Π_{IP} and the output $z = h(x_1, \ldots, x_n)$. Since every $(\mathbf{a}_i, \mathbf{b}_i)$ is locally computed from y and $(\mathbf{c}_i^{(j)})_{j \in [d]}$ at Steps 3–6, it is sufficient to show that the joint distribution of the following elements can be simulated from $(x_i)_{i \in T}$ and z:

Correlated randomness. r_i and $(\mathbf{c}_i^{(j)})_{j \in [d]}$ for all $i \in T$;
Online messages. $y_i = x_i - r_i$ for all $i \in H$.

Let $\mathbf{x}, \tilde{\mathbf{x}} \in \{0,1\}^n$ be any pair of inputs such that

$$x_i = \tilde{x}_i \ (\forall i \in T) \text{ and } h(x_1, \ldots, x_n) = h(\tilde{x}_1, \ldots, \tilde{x}_n).$$

It is sufficient to prove that the distribution of the above elements during the execution of $\Pi_{\mathsf{Sym}}^{(d)}$ on input $\mathbf{x}$ is identical to that on input $\tilde{\mathbf{x}}$. To show the equivalence of the distributions, we show a bijection between the random strings used by $\Pi_{\mathsf{Sym}}^{(d)}$ on input $\mathbf{x}$ and the random strings used by $\Pi_{\mathsf{Sym}}^{(d)}$ on input $\tilde{\mathbf{x}}$ such that the above values are the same under this bijection. Note that the randomness of $\Pi_{\mathsf{Sym}}^{(d)}$ on input $\mathbf{x}$ is uniformly distributed over a set $\mathcal{S}$ consisting of all $(r_i, (\mathbf{c}_i^{(j)})_{j \in [d]})_{i \in [n]}$ such that for each $j \in [d]$, $(\mathbf{c}_i^{(j)})_{i \in [n]}$ is a tuple of consistent shares of the (t,n)-Shamir scheme for a secret $\mathbf{e}_{u_j}$, where $u_j = \phi_j(\sum_{i \in [n]} r_i)$.

We recall the fact that for any $\mathbf{c} \in \mathbb{F}^p$, there exists a uniquely determined tuple of p polynomials $\boldsymbol{\theta}(X) \in (\mathbb{F}[X])^p$, each of degree at most t, such that

$$\boldsymbol{\theta}(0) = \mathbf{c} \text{ and } \boldsymbol{\theta}(\alpha_i) = \mathbf{0} \ (\forall i \in T)$$

(see Sect. 3.2). Now, we define a bijection map from the randomness $(r_i, (\mathbf{c}_i^{(j)})_{j \in [d]})_{i \in [n]}$ of $\Pi_{\mathsf{Sym}}^{(d)}$ on input $\mathbf{x}$ to the randomness $(\tilde{r}_i, (\tilde{\mathbf{c}}_i^{(j)})_{j \in [d]})_{i \in [n]}$ of $\Pi_{\mathsf{Sym}}^{(d)}$ on input $\tilde{\mathbf{x}}$ in such a way that

$$\tilde{r}_i = \begin{cases} r_i, & \text{if } i \in T, \\ r_i + \tilde{x}_i - x_i, & \text{if } i \in H, \end{cases}$$

$$\tilde{\mathbf{c}}_i^{(j)} = \begin{cases} \mathbf{c}_i^{(j)}, & \text{if } i \in T, \\ \mathbf{c}_i^{(j)} + \boldsymbol{\theta}^{(j)}(\alpha_i), & \text{if } i \in H, \end{cases}$$

where

$$\tilde{r} := \sum_{i \in [n]} \tilde{r}_i, \ r := \sum_{i \in [n]} r_i, \ \tilde{u}_j := \phi_j(\tilde{r}), \ u_j := \phi_j(r),$$

and $\boldsymbol{\theta}^{(j)}$ is the uniquely determined tuple of p_j polynomials, each of degree at most t, such that $\boldsymbol{\theta}^{(j)}(0) = \mathbf{e}_{\tilde{u}_j} - \mathbf{e}_{u_j}$ and $\boldsymbol{\theta}^{(j)}(\alpha_i) = \mathbf{0}$ for all $i \in T$.

We see that the image is indeed a consistent random string, i.e., $(\tilde{r}_i, (\tilde{\mathbf{c}}_i^{(j)})_{j \in [d]})_{i \in [n]} \in \mathcal{S}$. If $(r_i, (\mathbf{c}_i^{(j)})_{j \in [d]})_{i \in [n]} \in \mathcal{S}$, then $(\mathbf{c}_i^{(j)})_{i \in [n]}$ forms a tuple of consistent shares for $\mathbf{e}_{u_j}$, i.e., there is a tuple of p_j polynomials $\boldsymbol{\varphi}^{(j)}$, each of degree at most t, such that

$$\boldsymbol{\varphi}^{(j)}(0) = \mathbf{e}_{u_j} \text{ and } \boldsymbol{\varphi}^{(j)}(\alpha_i) = \mathbf{c}_i^{(j)} \ (\forall i \in [n]).$$

A tuple of polynomials $\tilde{\boldsymbol{\varphi}}^{(j)} := \boldsymbol{\varphi}^{(j)} + \boldsymbol{\theta}^{(j)}$ satisfies that

$$\tilde{\boldsymbol{\varphi}}^{(j)}(0) = \boldsymbol{\varphi}^{(j)}(0) + \boldsymbol{\theta}^{(j)}(0) = \mathbf{e}_{u_j} + (\mathbf{e}_{\tilde{u}_j} - \mathbf{e}_{u_j}) = \mathbf{e}_{\tilde{u}_j},$$

$$\tilde{\boldsymbol{\varphi}}^{(j)}(\alpha_i) = \mathbf{c}_i^{(j)} + \boldsymbol{\theta}^{(j)}(\alpha_i) = \tilde{\mathbf{c}}_i^{(j)} \ (\forall i \in [n])$$

since $\boldsymbol{\theta}^{(j)}(\alpha_i) = \mathbf{0}$ for any $i \in T$. Thus, we have that $(\tilde{r}_i, (\tilde{\mathbf{c}}_i^{(j)})_{j \in [d]})_{i \in [n]} \in \mathcal{S}$.

The above map is indeed a bijection since it has the inverse

$$r_i = \begin{cases} \tilde{r}_i, & \text{if } i \in T, \\ \tilde{r}_i + x_i - \tilde{x}_i, & \text{if } i \in H, \end{cases}$$

$$\mathbf{c}_i = \begin{cases} \tilde{\mathbf{c}}_i, & \text{if } i \in T, \\ \tilde{\mathbf{c}}_j - \boldsymbol{\theta}^{(j)}(\alpha_i), & \text{if } i \in H, \end{cases}$$

Clearly, this bijection does not change the correlated randomness $(r_i, (\mathbf{c}_i^{(j)})_{j \in [d]})_{i \in T}$ of T. Since $x_i' - r_i' = x_i' - (r_i + x_i' - x_i) = x_i - r_i$ for $i \in H$, it does not change the online messages from H.

Finally, since players also need to receive correlated randomness for one execution of a protocol implementing $\mathcal{F}_{\mathsf{IP}}$ and for one execution of a protocol implementing $\mathcal{F}_{\mathsf{Sum}}$, the offline bottleneck complexity is

$$\mathrm{BC}_{\mathsf{off}}(\Pi_{\mathsf{Sym}}^{(d)}) = O(\log N) + \sum_{j \in [d]} O(p_j \log |\mathbb{F}|) + O(p_1 \log |\mathbb{F}|) = O(n^{1/d} \log n).$$

Here, we use the fact that $d \in O(1)$, $p_j \in O(n^{1/d})$ and $|\mathbb{F}| \in O(n)$. At Steps 1 and 2 of the online phase, each player sends a constant number of elements in $\mathbb{Z}_N$. Players perform local computation at Steps 3–6. The bottleneck complexity of Step 7 is equal to that of a protocol realizing $\mathcal{F}_{\mathsf{IP}}$. The protocol $\Pi_{\mathsf{Sym}}^{(d)}$ thus has different online communication complexity and round complexity depending on implementation of $\mathcal{F}_{\mathsf{IP}}$ and $\mathcal{F}_{\mathsf{Sum}}$: $\mathrm{BC}_{\mathsf{on}}(\Pi_{\mathsf{Sym}}^{(d)}) = O(n^{1/d} \log n)$ and $\mathrm{Round}(\Pi_{\mathsf{Sym}}^{(d)}) = O(n)$; or $\mathrm{BC}_{\mathsf{on}}(\Pi_{\mathsf{Sym}}^{(d)}) = O(n^{1/d}(\log n)^2)$ and $\mathrm{Round}(\Pi_{\mathsf{Sym}}^{(d)}) = O(\log n)$. □

6 BC-Efficient Protocol for Checking Equality to Zero

Let $\mathbb{F}$ be a finite field. Define a functionality $\mathcal{F}_{\mathsf{CheckZero},\mathbb{F}}$ as follows: On input $(x_i)_{i \in [n]} \in \mathbb{F}^n$, $\mathcal{F}_{\mathsf{CheckZero},\mathbb{F}}$ gives all players $b \in \{0,1\}$ such that $b = 0$ if and only if $\sum_{i\in[n]} x_i = 0$ in $\mathbb{F}$. We show a protocol tailored to the functionality that achieves lower bottleneck complexity than our protocols for general symmetric functions. A high-level idea is given in Sect. 2.2. The formal description and security proof are deferred to the full version [22].

Theorem 4. *Let λ be a security parameter. Let $\mathbb{F}$ be a finite field and $\mathbb{K}$ be an extension field of $\mathbb{F}$ such that $|\mathbb{K}| \geq 2^\lambda$. There exists a fully secure MPC protocol $\Pi_{\mathsf{CheckZero},\mathbb{K}}$ for $\mathcal{F}_{\mathsf{CheckZero},\mathbb{F}}$ in the $\mathcal{F}_{\mathsf{Sum}}$-hybrid model. Implementing $\mathcal{F}_{\mathsf{Sum}}$, the protocol $\Pi_{\mathsf{CheckZero},\mathbb{K}}$ achieves either of the following efficiency measures:*

- $\mathrm{BC}_{\mathsf{off}}(\Pi_{\mathsf{CheckZero},\mathbb{K}}) = O(\max\{\lambda, \log|\mathbb{F}|\})$, $\mathrm{BC}_{\mathsf{on}}(\Pi_{\mathsf{CheckZero},\mathbb{K}}) = O(\max\{\lambda, \log|\mathbb{F}|\})$ *and* $\mathrm{Round}(\Pi_{\mathsf{CheckZero},\mathbb{K}}) = O(n)$;
- $\mathrm{BC}_{\mathsf{off}}(\Pi_{\mathsf{CheckZero},\mathbb{K}}) = O(\max\{\lambda, \log|\mathbb{F}|\})$, $\mathrm{BC}_{\mathsf{on}}(\Pi_{\mathsf{CheckZero},\mathbb{K}}) = O((\log n)\max\{\lambda, \log|\mathbb{F}|\})$ *and* $\mathrm{Round}(\Pi_{\mathsf{CheckZero},\mathbb{K}}) = O(\log n)$.

Remark 1. If the characteristic of $\mathbb{F}$ is larger than n, e.g., $\mathbb{F} = \mathbb{Z}_p$ for a prime $p > n$, our protocol $\Pi_{\mathsf{CheckZero},\mathbb{K}}$ implies BC-efficient protocols for computing the AND and OR of players' inputs $x_i \in \{0,1\}$. Indeed, we can compute the OR function due to the fact that if $x_i \in \{0,1\}$, $\sum_{i\in[n]} x_i = 0$ (over $\mathbb{F}$) if and only if $x_i = 0$ for all $i \in [n]$. A protocol for the AND function is immediately follows from the fact that $\mathrm{AND}(x_1,\ldots,x_n) = 1 - \mathrm{OR}(1-x_1,\ldots,1-x_n)$.

7   BC-Efficient Protocol for Private Set Intersection

In this section, we show a BC-efficient protocol for computing the intersection of players' input sets. For now, we assume that players' input sets have the same size s. We will show later that the protocol is extended to the general case.

To begin with, we define a functionality computing the intersection based on a Bloom filter. Let λ be a security parameter. Let U be a finite set. Assume that there exists a Bloom filter $\mathcal{BF} = (\mathsf{Add}, \mathsf{Check})$ for U with parameters $m = m(\lambda)$, $k = \Theta(\lambda)$ and $s = \mathsf{poly}(\lambda)$. For a subset $X \in 2^U$ of size s, let $\mathbf{BF}(X)$ denote an m-bit string obtained after adding the elements of X with Add. Define an n-input/single-output functionality $\mathcal{F}_{\mathsf{PSI},\mathcal{BF}}$ as follows (described in Fig. 8): On input $(X_i)_{i\in[n]}$ such that X_i is a subset of U of size s, $\mathcal{F}_{\mathsf{PSI},\mathcal{BF}}$ gives all players

$$Z_\lambda(X_1,\ldots,X_n) := \{x \in X_n : \forall i \in [n], \mathsf{Check}(\mathbf{BF}(X_i), x) = 1\}. \quad (5)$$

Recall that the property of the Bloom filter $\mathcal{BF}$ ensures that for any (x, X) such that $x \notin X$, the probability that $\mathsf{Check}(\mathbf{BF}(X), x) = 1$ is negligible in k (and hence in λ). For any $x \in X_1 \cap \cdots \cap X_n$, it holds with probability 1 that $x \in Z_\lambda(X_1,\ldots,X_n)$, while for $x \in U \setminus (X_1 \cap \cdots \cap X_n)$, the probability that $x \in Z_\lambda(X_1,\ldots,X_n)$ is negligible in λ since we suppose $n = \mathsf{poly}(\lambda)$. Thus, the probability that $Z_\lambda(X_1,\ldots,X_n) = X_1 \cap \cdots \cap X_n$ is at least $1 - |X_n|\cdot\mathsf{negl}(\lambda) = 1 - s\cdot\mathsf{negl}(\lambda) \geq 1 - \mathsf{negl}(\lambda)$ since we assume $s = \mathsf{poly}(\lambda)$. Therefore, for any input $(X_i)_{i\in[n]}$, the statistical distance between $Z_\lambda(X_1,\ldots,X_n)$ and $\mathrm{Int}_\lambda(X_1,\ldots,X_n)$ is upper bounded by a negligible function. Here, we abuse notation and denote the random variable over 2^U defined in Eq. (5) by $Z_\lambda(X_1, \ldots, X_n)$ and the random variable whose outcome is $X_1 \cap \cdots \cap X_n$ with probability 1 by $\text{Int}_\lambda(X_1, \ldots, X_n)$. In the following, we show a protocol realizing $\mathcal{F}_{\mathsf{PSI},\mathcal{BF}}$. From the above observation, it also securely realizes the functionality that directly computes $\text{Int}_\lambda(X_1, \ldots, X_n) = X_1 \cap \cdots \cap X_n$.

We now show the following theorem. The formal proof is given in the full version [22].

Theorem 5. *Let λ be a security parameter. Assume that there exists a Bloom filter $\mathcal{BF}$ for U with parameters $m = m(\lambda)$, $k = \Theta(\lambda)$ and $s = \mathsf{poly}(\lambda)$. Let $\mathbb{F} = \mathbb{Z}_p$ be a prime field such that $p > nk$. The protocol Π_{PSI} described in Fig. 8 is a fully secure MPC protocol for $\mathcal{F}_{\mathsf{PSI},\mathcal{BF}}$ in the $\{\mathcal{F}_{\mathsf{Broadcast},n}, \mathcal{F}_{\mathsf{CheckZero},\mathbb{F}}, \mathcal{F}'_{\mathsf{IP}}\}$-hybrid model. Implementing $\mathcal{F}_{\mathsf{Broadcast},n}$, $\mathcal{F}_{\mathsf{CheckZero},\mathbb{F}}$, and $\mathcal{F}'_{\mathsf{IP}}$, the protocol Π_{PSI} achieves either of the following efficiency measures:*

- $\mathrm{BC}_{\mathrm{off}}(\Pi_{\mathsf{PSI}}) = O(sm\log(n\lambda) + s\lambda)$, $\mathrm{BC}_{\mathrm{on}}(\Pi_{\mathsf{PSI}}) = O(sm\log(n\lambda) + s\lambda + s\log|U|)$ *and* $\mathrm{Round}(\Pi_{\mathsf{PSI}}) = O(n)$;
- $\mathrm{BC}_{\mathrm{off}}(\Pi_{\mathsf{PSI}}) = O(\max\{\lambda, \log|\mathbb{F}|\})$, $\mathrm{BC}_{\mathrm{on}}(\Pi_{\mathsf{PSI}}) = O((\log n)(sm\log(n\lambda) + s\lambda) + s\log|U|)$ *and* $\mathrm{Round}(\Pi_{\mathsf{PSI}}) = O(\log n)$.

According to the analysis in [16], we can choose a Bloom filter $\mathcal{BF}$ such that $m = \Theta(ks)$. Then, the complexity of Π_{PSI} is $\mathrm{BC}_{\mathrm{off}}(\Pi_{\mathsf{PSI}}) = O(s^2\lambda\log(n\lambda))$,

- $\mathrm{Round}(\Pi_{\mathsf{PSI}}) = O(n)$ *and* $\mathrm{BC}_{\mathrm{on}}(\Pi_{\mathsf{PSI}}) = O(s^2\lambda\log(n\lambda) + s\log|U|)$; *or*
- $\mathrm{Round}(\Pi_{\mathsf{PSI}}) = O(\log n)$ *and* $\mathrm{BC}_{\mathrm{on}}(\Pi_{\mathsf{PSI}}) = O(s^2\lambda(\log\lambda)(\log n)^2 + s\log|U|)$

Finally, we deal with the general case where the sizes of players' input sets are upper bounded by s. Let $V_1, \ldots, V_n$ be n sets, each of size s, such that they are pairwise disjoint and also disjoint from U, i.e., $|V_i \cap V_j| = |V_i \cap U| = \emptyset$ for any $i \neq j$. Set $U' = U \cup V_1 \cup \cdots \cup V_n$. Each player P_i pads his input set X_i with $s - |X_i|$ elements in V_i if $|X_i| < s$, and lets X'_i be the resulting set of size exactly s. Since $X'_1 \cap \cdots \cap X'_n = X_1 \cap \cdots \cap X_n$, players can compute the intersection by running Π_{PSI} on input $X'_1, \ldots, X'_n \subseteq U'$. Since $|U'| = |U| + ns$, this reduction only incurs an additive factor of $\log(ns)$ to online bottleneck complexity. In particular, the complexity is asymptotically the same as given above.

Functionality $\mathcal{F}_{\mathsf{PSI},\mathcal{BF}}((X_i)_{i\in[n]})$

1. $\mathcal{F}_{\mathsf{PSI},\mathcal{BF}}$ receives a subset $X_i \in 2^U$ of size s from each player P_i.
2. $\mathcal{F}_{\mathsf{PSI},\mathcal{BF}}$ gives every player

$$Z_\lambda(X_1,\dots,X_n) := \{x \in X_n : \forall i \in [n],\ \mathsf{Check}(\mathbf{BF}(X_i),x) = 1\}.$$

Protocol Π_{PSI}

Notations.
- Let U be a set.
- Let $\mathcal{BF} = (\mathsf{Add}, \mathsf{Check})$ be a Bloom filter for U with parameters m, k and s.
- For a subset $X \in 2^U$ of size s, let $\mathbf{BF}(X)$ denote an m-bit string obtained after adding the elements of X with Add.
- Let $\mathbb{F} = \mathbb{Z}_p$ be a prime field such that $p > nk$.

Input. Each player P_i has a subset $X_i \in 2^U$ of size s.

Output. Every player obtains $Z = \mathcal{F}_{\mathsf{PSI},\mathcal{BF}}((X_i)_{i\in[n]})$.

Setup.
1. Let $(\mathbf{u}_i)_{i\in[n]} \leftarrow \mathsf{Additive}_\mathbb{F}(\mathbf{0}_m)$ and $(\mathbf{w}_i^{(j)})_{i\in[n]} \leftarrow \mathsf{Additive}_\mathbb{F}(\mathbf{0}_m)$ for $j \in [s]$.
2. Each player P_i receives $\mathbf{u}_i$ and $(\mathbf{w}_i^{(j)})_{j\in[s]}$.

Protocol.
1. Each player P_i computes $\mathbf{B}_i = \mathbf{1}_m - \mathbf{BF}(X_i) \in \{0,1\}^m$.
2. Each player P_i computes $\mathbf{V}_i = \mathbf{B}_i + \mathbf{u}_i$, which is the i-th additive share of $\mathbf{V} := \sum_{i\in[n]} \mathbf{B}_i \in \mathbb{F}^m$.
3. P_n permutes the elements of X_n uniformly at random and lets $x^{(1)},\dots,x^{(s)}$ be the permuted elements of X_n.
4. Each player P_i does the following:
   - If $i \neq n$, P_i sets $\mathbf{W}_i^{(j)} = \mathbf{w}_i^{(j)}$ for all $j \in [s]$.
   - If $i = n$, P_n computes $\mathbf{W}_n^{(j)} = \mathbf{BF}(\{x^{(j)}\}) + \mathbf{w}_n^{(j)}$ for all $j \in [s]$.
5. For each $j \in [s]$, players obtain $(y_i^{(j)})_{i\in[n]} \leftarrow \mathcal{F}'_{\mathsf{IP}}((\mathbf{V}_i, \mathbf{W}_i^{(j)})_{i\in[n]})$.
6. For each $j \in [s]$, players obtain $z^{(j)} = \mathcal{F}_{\mathsf{CheckZero},\mathbb{F}}((y_i^{(j)})_{i\in[n]})$.
7. P_n computes $Z = \{x^{(j)}\}_{j\in[s]:z^{(j)}=0}$ and invoke $\mathcal{F}_{\mathsf{Broadcast},n}$ with input Z.
8. Each player P_i outputs Z.

Fig. 8. The functionality $\mathcal{F}_{\mathsf{PSI},\mathcal{BF}}$ and a protocol Π_{PSI} implementing it

Acknowledgements. We thank anonymous reviewers of ASIACRYPT 2023 for their helpful comments. Especially, one of the reviewers kindly showed us a more round-efficient protocol for computing the sum. This optimization reduces the round complexity of our protocols to $O(\log n)$, which appears in the full version [22]. We really appreciate his or her great solution. We also thank Koji Nuida and Takahiro Matsuda for helpful discussions and suggestions. This work was partially supported by JST AIP Acceleration Research JPMJCR22U5, Japan and JST CREST Grant Number JPMJCR22M1, Japan.

References

1. Bay, A., Erkin, Z., Hoepman, J.H., Samardjiska, S., Vos, J.: Practical multi-party private set intersection protocols. IEEE Trans. Inf. Forensics Secur. **17**, 1–15 (2022)
2. Bay, A., Erkin, Z., Alishahi, M., Vos, J.: Multi-party private set intersection protocols for practical applications. In: Proceedings of the 18th International Conference on Security and Cryptography - SECRYPT, pp. 515–522 (2021)
3. Beaver, D.: Efficient multiparty protocols using circuit randomization. In: Feigenbaum, J. (ed.) CRYPTO 1991. LNCS, vol. 576, pp. 420–432. Springer, Heidelberg (1992). https://doi.org/10.1007/3-540-46766-1_34
4. Beerliová-Trubíniová, Z., Hirt, M.: Perfectly-secure MPC with linear communication complexity. In: Theory of Cryptography, pp. 213–230 (2008)
5. Beimel, A., Gabizon, A., Ishai, Y., Kushilevitz, E., Meldgaard, S., Paskin-Cherniavsky, A.: Non-interactive secure multiparty computation. In: Garay, J.A., Gennaro, R. (eds.) CRYPTO 2014, Part II. LNCS, vol. 8617, pp. 387–404. Springer, Heidelberg (2014). https://doi.org/10.1007/978-3-662-44381-1_22
6. Ben-Efraim, A., Nissenbaum, O., Omri, E., Paskin-Cherniavsky, A.: PSimple: practical multiparty maliciously-secure private set intersection. In: Proceedings of the 2022 ACM on Asia Conference on Computer and Communications Security. ASIA CCS 2022, pp. 1098–1112 (2022)
7. Ben-Or, M., Goldwasser, S., Wigderson, A.: Completeness theorems for non-cryptographic fault-tolerant distributed computation. In: Proceedings of the Twentieth Annual ACM Symposium on Theory of Computing, pp. 1–10 (1988)
8. Ben-Sasson, E., Fehr, S., Ostrovsky, R.: Near-linear unconditionally-secure multiparty computation with a dishonest minority. In: Safavi-Naini, R., Canetti, R. (eds.) CRYPTO 2012. LNCS, vol. 7417, pp. 663–680. Springer, Heidelberg (2012). https://doi.org/10.1007/978-3-642-32009-5_39
9. Bloom, B.H.: Space/time trade-offs in hash coding with allowable errors. Commun. ACM **13**(7), 422–426 (1970)
10. Bose, P., et al.: On the false-positive rate of bloom filters. Inf. Process. Lett. **108**(4), 210–213 (2008)
11. Boyle, E., Jain, A., Prabhakaran, M., Yu, C.H.: The bottleneck complexity of secure multiparty computation. In: 45th International Colloquium on Automata, Languages, and Programming (ICALP 2018). Leibniz International Proceedings in Informatics (LIPIcs), vol. 107, pp. 24:1–24:16 (2018)
12. Chandran, N., Dasgupta, N., Gupta, D., Obbattu, S.L.B., Sekar, S., Shah, A.: Efficient linear multiparty psi and extensions to circuit/quorum psi. In: Proceedings of the 2021 ACM SIGSAC Conference on Computer and Communications Security. CCS 2021, pp. 1182–1204 (2021)
13. Chaum, D., Crépeau, C., Damgard, I.: Multiparty unconditionally secure protocols. In: Proceedings of the Twentieth Annual ACM Symposium on Theory of Computing. STOC 1988, pp. 11–19 (1988)
14. Cheon, J.H., Jarecki, S., Seo, J.H.: Multi-party privacy-preserving set intersection with quasi-linear complexity. IEICE Trans. Fundam. Electron. Commun. Comput. Sci. **95**(8), 1366–1378 (2012)

15. Chida, K.: Fast large-scale honest-majority MPC for malicious adversaries. In: Shacham, H., Boldyreva, A. (eds.) CRYPTO 2018, Part III. LNCS, vol. 10993, pp. 34–64. Springer, Cham (2018). https://doi.org/10.1007/978-3-319-96878-0_2

16. Chung, K.M., Mitzenmacher, M., Vadhan, S.: Why simple hash functions work: exploiting the entropy in a data stream. Theory Comput. 9(30), 897–945 (2013)

17. Cramer, R., Damgård, I., Maurer, U.: General secure multi-party computation from any linear secret-sharing scheme. In: Preneel, B. (ed.) EUROCRYPT 2000. LNCS, vol. 1807, pp. 316–334. Springer, Heidelberg (2000). https://doi.org/10.1007/3-540-45539-6_22

18. Dachman-Soled, D., Malkin, T., Raykova, M., Yung, M.: Secure efficient multiparty computing of multivariate polynomials and applications. In: Applied Cryptography and Network Security, pp. 130–146 (2011)

19. Damgård, I., Ishai, Y., Krøigaard, M.: Perfectly secure multiparty computation and the computational overhead of cryptography. In: Gilbert, H. (ed.) EUROCRYPT 2010. LNCS, vol. 6110, pp. 445–465. Springer, Heidelberg (2010). https://doi.org/10.1007/978-3-642-13190-5_23

20. Damgård, I., Nielsen, J.B.: Scalable and unconditionally secure multiparty computation. In: Menezes, A. (ed.) CRYPTO 2007. LNCS, vol. 4622, pp. 572–590. Springer, Heidelberg (2007). https://doi.org/10.1007/978-3-540-74143-5_32

21. Damgård, I., Pastro, V., Smart, N., Zakarias, S.: Multiparty computation from somewhat homomorphic encryption. In: Safavi-Naini, R., Canetti, R. (eds.) CRYPTO 2012. LNCS, vol. 7417, pp. 643–662. Springer, Heidelberg (2012). https://doi.org/10.1007/978-3-642-32009-5_38

22. Eriguchi, R.: Unconditionally secure multiparty computation for symmetric functions with low bottleneck complexity (2023). https://eprint.iacr.org/2023/662

23. Feige, U., Kilian, J., Naor, M.: A minimal model for secure computation (extended abstract). In: Proceedings of the Twenty-Sixth Annual ACM Symposium on Theory of Computing. STOC 1994, pp. 554–563 (1994)

24. Freedman, M.J., Nissim, K., Pinkas, B.: Efficient private matching and set intersection. In: Cachin, C., Camenisch, J.L. (eds.) EUROCRYPT 2004. LNCS, vol. 3027, pp. 1–19. Springer, Heidelberg (2004). https://doi.org/10.1007/978-3-540-24676-3_1

25. Gentry, C.: Fully homomorphic encryption using ideal lattices. In: Proceedings of the Forty-First Annual ACM Symposium on Theory of Computing. STOC 2009, pp. 169–0178 (2009)

26. Ghosh, S., Nilges, T.: An algebraic approach to maliciously secure private set intersection. In: Ishai, Y., Rijmen, V. (eds.) EUROCRYPT 2019, Part III. LNCS, vol. 11478, pp. 154–185. Springer, Cham (2019). https://doi.org/10.1007/978-3-030-17659-4_6

27. Goldreich, O., Micali, S., Wigderson, A.: How to play any mental game. In: Proceedings of the Nineteenth Annual ACM Symposium on Theory of Computing. STOC 1987, pp. 218–229 (1987)

28. Goyal, V., Li, H., Ostrovsky, R., Polychroniadou, A., Song, Y.: ATLAS: efficient and scalable MPC in the honest majority setting. In: Malkin, T., Peikert, C. (eds.) CRYPTO 2021, Part II. LNCS, vol. 12826, pp. 244–274. Springer, Cham (2021). https://doi.org/10.1007/978-3-030-84245-1_9

29. Goyal, V., Liu, Y., Song, Y.: Communication-efficient unconditional MPC with guaranteed output delivery. In: Boldyreva, A., Micciancio, D. (eds.) CRYPTO 2019, Part II. LNCS, vol. 11693, pp. 85–114. Springer, Cham (2019). https://doi.org/10.1007/978-3-030-26951-7_4

30. Goyal, V., Song, Y., Zhu, C.: Guaranteed output delivery comes free in honest majority MPC. In: Micciancio, D., Ristenpart, T. (eds.) CRYPTO 2020. LNCS, vol. 12171, pp. 618–646. Springer, Cham (2020). https://doi.org/10.1007/978-3-030-56880-1_22

31. Halevi, S., Ishai, Y., Jain, A., Kushilevitz, E., Rabin, T.: Secure multiparty computation with general interaction patterns. In: Proceedings of the 2016 ACM Conference on Innovations in Theoretical Computer Science. ITCS 2016 (2016)

32. Halevi, S., Lindell, Y., Pinkas, B.: Secure computation on the web: computing without simultaneous interaction. In: Rogaway, P. (ed.) CRYPTO 2011. LNCS, vol. 6841, pp. 132–150. Springer, Heidelberg (2011). https://doi.org/10.1007/978-3-642-22792-9_8

33. Hazay, C., Venkitasubramaniam, M.: Scalable multi-party private set-intersection. In: Fehr, S. (ed.) PKC 2017. LNCS, vol. 10174, pp. 175–203. Springer, Heidelberg (2017). https://doi.org/10.1007/978-3-662-54365-8_8

34. Hirt, M., Maurer, U.: Robustness for free in unconditional multi-party computation. In: Kilian, J. (ed.) CRYPTO 2001. LNCS, vol. 2139, pp. 101–118. Springer, Heidelberg (2001). https://doi.org/10.1007/3-540-44647-8_6

35. Hirt, M., Maurer, U., Przydatek, B.: Efficient secure multi-party computation. In: Okamoto, T. (ed.) ASIACRYPT 2000. LNCS, vol. 1976, pp. 143–161. Springer, Heidelberg (2000). https://doi.org/10.1007/3-540-44448-3_12

36. Hirt, M., Tschudi, D.: Efficient general-adversary multi-party computation. In: Sako, K., Sarkar, P. (eds.) ASIACRYPT 2013, Part II. LNCS, vol. 8270, pp. 181–200. Springer, Heidelberg (2013). https://doi.org/10.1007/978-3-642-42045-0_10

37. Inbar, R., Omri, E., Pinkas, B.: Efficient scalable multiparty private set-intersection via garbled bloom filters. In: Security and Cryptography for Networks, pp. 235–252 (2018)

38. Ishai, Y., Kushilevitz, E.: Private simultaneous messages protocols with applications. In: Proceedings of the Fifth Israeli Symposium on Theory of Computing and Systems, pp. 174–183 (1997)

39. Ishai, Y., Kushilevitz, E.: Randomizing polynomials: a new representation with applications to round-efficient secure computation. In: Proceedings 41st Annual Symposium on Foundations of Computer Science, pp. 294–304 (2000)

40. Ishai, Y., Kushilevitz, E., Meldgaard, S., Orlandi, C., Paskin-Cherniavsky, A.: On the power of correlated randomness in secure computation. In: Theory of Cryptography, pp. 600–620 (2013)

41. Keller, H., Orlandi, C., Paskin-Cherniavsky, A., Ravi, D.: MPC with low bottleneck-complexity: Information-theoretic security and more. In: 4th Information-Theoretic Cryptography (ITC) Conference (2023). https://eprint.iacr.org/2023/683

42. Keller, M.: MP-SPDZ: a versatile framework for multi-party computation. In: Proceedings of the 2020 ACM SIGSAC Conference on Computer and Communications Security. CCS 2020, pp. 1575–1590 (2020)

43. Kissner, L., Song, D.: Privacy-preserving set operations. In: Shoup, V. (ed.) CRYPTO 2005. LNCS, vol. 3621, pp. 241–257. Springer, Heidelberg (2005). https://doi.org/10.1007/11535218_15

44. Kolesnikov, V., Matania, N., Pinkas, B., Rosulek, M., Trieu, N.: Practical multiparty private set intersection from symmetric-key techniques. In: Proceedings of the 2017 ACM SIGSAC Conference on Computer and Communications Security. CCS 2017, pp. 1257–1272 (2017)

45. Li, R., Wu, C.: An unconditionally secure protocol for multi-party set intersection. In: Katz, J., Yung, M. (eds.) ACNS 2007. LNCS, vol. 4521, pp. 226–236. Springer, Heidelberg (2007). https://doi.org/10.1007/978-3-540-72738-5_15
46. Miyaji, A., Nishida, S.: A scalable multiparty private set intersection. In: NSS 2015. LNCS, vol. 9408, pp. 376–385. Springer, Cham (2015). https://doi.org/10.1007/978-3-319-25645-0_26
47. Nevo, O., Trieu, N., Yanai, A.: Simple, fast malicious multiparty private set intersection. In: Proceedings of the 2021 ACM SIGSAC Conference on Computer and Communications Security. CCS 2021, pp. 1151–1165 (2021)
48. Orlandi, C., Ravi, D., Scholl, P.: On the bottleneck complexity of MPC with correlated randomness. In: Hanaoka, G., Shikata, J., Watanabe, Y. (eds.) Public-Key Cryptography - PKC 2022, Part I. LNCS, vol. 13177, pp. 194–220. Springer, Cham (2022). https://doi.org/10.1007/978-3-030-97121-2_8
49. Patra, A., Choudhary, A., Rangan, C.P.: Information theoretically secure multi party set intersection re-visited. In: Jacobson, M.J., Rijmen, V., Safavi-Naini, R. (eds.) SAC 2009. LNCS, vol. 5867, pp. 71–91. Springer, Heidelberg (2009). https://doi.org/10.1007/978-3-642-05445-7_5
50. Patra, A., Choudhary, A., Rangan, C.P.: Round efficient unconditionally secure MPC and multiparty set intersection with optimal resilience. In: Roy, B., Sendrier, N. (eds.) INDOCRYPT 2009. LNCS, vol. 5922, pp. 398–417. Springer, Heidelberg (2009). https://doi.org/10.1007/978-3-642-10628-6_26
51. Rabin, T., Ben-Or, M.: Verifiable secret sharing and multiparty protocols with honest majority. In: Proceedings of the Twenty-First Annual ACM Symposium on Theory of Computing. STOC 1989, pp. 73–85 (1989)
52. Sang, Y., Shen, H.: Privacy preserving set intersection protocol secure against malicious behaviors. In: Eighth International Conference on Parallel and Distributed Computing, Applications and Technologies (PDCAT 2007), pp. 461–468 (2007)
53. Sang, Y., Shen, H.: Privacy preserving set intersection based on bilinear groups. In: Proceedings of the Thirty-First Australasian Conference on Computer Science. ACSC 2008, vol. 74, pp. 47–54 (2008)
54. Shamir, A.: How to share a secret. Commun. ACM **22**(11), 612–613 (1979)
55. Shoup, V.: A Computational Introduction to Number Theory and Algebra. Cambridge University Press, Cambridge (2009)
56. van Dijk, M., Gentry, C., Halevi, S., Vaikuntanathan, V.: Fully homomorphic encryption over the integers. In: Gilbert, H. (ed.) EUROCRYPT 2010. LNCS, vol. 6110, pp. 24–43. Springer, Heidelberg (2010). https://doi.org/10.1007/978-3-642-13190-5_2
57. Vos, J., Conti, M., Erkin, Z.: Fast multi-party private set operations in the star topology from secure ANDs and ORs. Cryptology ePrint Archive, Paper 2022/721 (2022). https://eprint.iacr.org/2022/721
58. Yao, A.C.: Protocols for secure computations. In: Proceedings of the 23rd Annual Symposium on Foundations of Computer Science. SFCS 1982, pp. 160–164 (1982)
59. Yao, A.C.: How to generate and exchange secrets. In: 27th Annual Symposium on Foundations of Computer Science (SFCS 1986), pp. 162–167 (1986)

Threshold Cryptography

Simple Threshold (Fully Homomorphic) Encryption from LWE with Polynomial Modulus

Katharina Boudgoust$^{(\boxtimes)}$ and Peter Scholl

Aarhus University, Aarhus, Denmark
{katharina.boudgoust,peter.scholl}@cs.au.dk

Abstract. The learning with errors (LWE) assumption is a powerful tool for building encryption schemes with useful properties, such as plausible resistance to quantum computers, or support for homomorphic computations. Despite this, essentially the only method of achieving threshold decryption in schemes based on LWE requires a modulus that is superpolynomial in the security parameter, leading to a large overhead in ciphertext sizes and computation time.

In this work, we propose a (fully homomorphic) encryption scheme that supports a simple t-out-of-n threshold decryption protocol while allowing for a polynomial modulus. The main idea is to use the Rényi divergence (as opposed to the statistical distance as in previous works) as a measure of distribution closeness. This comes with some technical obstacles, due to the difficulty of using the Rényi divergence in decisional security notions such as standard semantic security. We overcome this by constructing a threshold scheme with a weaker notion of one-way security and then showing how to transform any one-way (fully homomorphic) threshold scheme into one guaranteeing indistinguishability-based security.

1 Introduction

In a public key encryption (PKE) scheme, one needs the secret key sk to decrypt an encrypted message. Giving one single party control of the whole secret key can be seen as a single point of failure. The study of PKE with threshold decryption aims to mitigate this by splitting the secret key into n key shares $sk_1, \ldots, sk_n$, such that several key shares are needed to be able to decrypt ciphertexts. This is known as threshold public key encryption (ThPKE). In the common t-out-of-n setting, any set of t parties or fewer learns no information about encrypted messages, while any set of $t + 1$ parties can jointly decrypt ciphertexts. To decrypt, the parties first compute their own partial decryption shares and then combine them together to recover the encrypted message. When $t = n - 1$, we call it full-threshold decryption.

Recently, NIST announced the standardization of the first cryptosystems to provide security even in the presence of quantum computers.[1] Among the finalists

---

[1] https://csrc.nist.gov/projects/post-quantum-cryptography.

© International Association for Cryptologic Research 2023
J. Guo and R. Steinfeld (Eds.): ASIACRYPT 2023, LNCS 14438, pp. 371–404, 2023.
https://doi.org/10.1007/978-981-99-8721-4_12

to be standardized, a majority base their security on the presumed hardness of
(structured) lattice problems, such as Dilithium [Lyu+20] and Kyber [Sch+20]
based on the (module) learning with errors problem (M-LWE) [LS15]. NIST
also just began a project on threshold cryptography, which aims to produce
guidelines and recommendations for implementing threshold cryptosystems.

It is thus a very important research question to study the possibility of
thresholdizing lattice-based PKE schemes. This line of research has been initiated by [BD10], where they proposed a threshold key generation and decryption starting from Regev's encryption scheme [Reg05]. To split the secret key
they use replicated secret sharing, which has a complexity that scales with $\binom{n}{t}$.
Later, it has been shown that we can even build full-threshold decryption for
fully homomorphic encryption (FHE) schemes [Ash+12]. A threshold fully homomorphic encryption scheme (ThFHE) allows to perform arbitrary computations
on encrypted data and afterwards to partially decrypt the outcome of the computations. Their results have then been extended to t-out-of-n threshold and
other access structures [Bon+18].

All works above have in common that they use a technique called *noise flooding* to guarantee that partial decryption shares do not leak any information on
the underlying secret key. More precisely, each party first computes a "noiseless"
partial decryption of a ciphertext using their secret key share. The noiseless
partial decryptions allow recovering the message, but also reveal a small noise
term e_{ct} that depends on the given ciphertext and the secret key. To prevent
this leakage, every party locally adds some fresh noise on their decryption share
before they jointly combine the necessary number of shares to recover the mes-
sage. After decryption, the revealed noise term becomes $e_{ct}+e'$, where $e' \leftarrow \mathcal{D}_{\text{flood}}$
is a noise term that is hidden to the adversary. When proving security, the real
partial decryption shares are replaced by simulated ones which do not depend on
the secret key, and instead reveal noise terms of the form $e' \leftarrow \mathcal{D}_{\text{flood}}$. By arguing that the statistical distance between both ways of deriving partial decryption
shares is negligible, one can argue security. While this approach has the advantage of being rather simple, it has the drawback of requiring the ratio between
the flooding noise and the size of the ciphertext noise e_{ct} to be superpolynomial in the security parameter. This in turn requires the LWE problem to be
secure with a superpolynomial modulus-to-noise ratio, which weakens security
and requires larger LWE parameters to compensate.

Recently, multi-party reusable non-interactive secure computation (MrNISC)
was constructed from LWE with a polynomial modulus [Ben+21,Shi22]. This
leads to a construction of full-threshold (multi-key) FHE with a polynomial
modulus. It seems plausible that their construction can also be extended to
build t-out-of-n threshold FHE with polynomial modulus; however, their techniques are very complex, due to a non-black-box "round-collapsing" technique
based on garbled circuits, so unlikely to be practical. We thus started our work
asking the following research question:

> Is it possible to construct a fully homomorphic encryption scheme that
> supports a *simple t-out-of-n* threshold decryption while allowing for a *poly-
> nomial modulus*?

Our Results. We give a positive answer to this question. On a high level, we show that the simple threshold decryption technique from previous works [BD10,Bon+18] can be significantly improved by replacing the noise flooding analysis with respect to the statistical distance by one with respect to the Rényi divergence (RD). Doing so comes with the benefit of only requiring a polynomial ratio between ciphertext noise and flooding noise, hence allowing for the desired polynomial modulus. However, it comes with several additional challenges. First, the Rényi divergence fits well in search-based security notions, such as OW-CPA security[2], but does not work well with decision-based security notions, such as the standard IND-CPA security.[3] Furthermore, it is especially difficult to apply the Rényi divergence to obtain simulation-based security, as required for typical notions of threshold decryption, since a small RD between two distributions does not imply a small statistical distance.

To overcome these challenges, we define new game-based notions of OW-CPA and IND-CPA security for threshold homomorphic cryptosystems, which are compatible with Rényi divergence-based proofs, whilst also giving desirable security guarantees for applications. Then, we give general transformations from OW-CPA to IND-CPA security for ThPKE and ThFHE schemes, and finally also show how to construct OW-CPA schemes based on the (module) LWE assumption with a polynomial modulus. For our transformation to go through, we also need the OW-CPA scheme to be *circuit private*; while this property is often achieved using noise flooding techniques that require a large modulus, it is also possible to use bootstrapping [DS16] or GSW-style FHE [Bou+16] to obtain circuit privacy with a polynomial modulus.

Put together, these techniques lead to our main result of ThFHE from (module) LWE with a polynomial modulus. More precisely, in our construction the modulus q scales as $O(\sqrt{\ell})$, where ℓ is the number of partial decryption queries made by an adversary within the security game, so q is polynomial as long as ℓ is polynomially-bounded in advance.

What About IND-CCA *Security?* We could likely upgrade our construction (for PKE) to be IND-CCA secure using non-interactive zero-knowledge proofs, similarly to [Dev+21a]. However, note that (adaptive) IND-CCA security is not possible for homomorphic encryption, and IND-CPA is still useful for standard PKE; indeed, [HV22] showed that an IND-CPA secure KEM suffices to prove security of TLS-1.3. Furthermore, when running TLS with ephemeral keys and no key re-use, the adversary only ever sees a single ciphertext under any public key—this is an ideal use-case for using our ThPKE construction in a threshold post-quantum TLS setting (e.g. for hardening security of a TLS server), since we only need to choose the parameters to be secure against a single decryption query.

---

[2] OW-CPA security for PKE roughly says that given the public key and an encryption of a random message m, it is hard to guess m.

[3] Unless a property called *public sampleability* is fulfilled [Bai+18].

1.1 Overview of Techniques

Defining IND-CPA *security for* ThFHE *(Sect. 3).* Most of the previous IND-CPA security definitions of ThFHE required the underlying FHE scheme to be IND-CPA secure and the partial decryptions to be statistically simulatable, e.g. [Bon+18]. When replacing the statistical distance by the Rényi divergence, however, we cannot prove the statistical simulation anymore and instead have to move to a game-based notion that combines the IND-CPA game and the partial decryption queries together into one single game. Here, to support homomorphic computations, we consider a game where in each partial decryption query, first some homomorphic evaluation is performed on a set of ciphertexts, before giving decryptions of the result to the adversary. *When* and *how* the adversary gets access to the partial decryption oracle within the IND-CPA game crucially impacts the strength of the achieved security. For example, one can allow the adversary to only query partial decryptions *before* seeing the challenge ciphertext. This was done in a previous version of ThFHE [Cho+22a], which also uses a Rényi divergence based analysis. A more realistic setting, which has first been defined in [JRS17] and is now used in the updated version of [Cho+22b], is to allow the adversary to query partial decryptions even *after* having seen the challenge ciphertext *and* to allow queries that involve the challenge ciphertext. Note that [JRS17] split the IND-CPA game into sequential phases, where the adversary first sends all messages to be encrypted at once and in a second phase sends all circuits to be evaluated and then partially decrypted, again at once. We strengthen the security notion by giving the adversary adaptive access to both the encryption and the partial decryption oracles simultaneously. Of course, to prohibit trivial attacks, the partial decryption oracle refuses to answer to queries which would directly leak which message has been encrypted when computing the challenge ciphertext. This flavour of security notion, while lacking simulation-based security, still offers a strong guarantee in the form of *input indistinguishability*: given partial decryptions for an evaluation $f(x_1, x_2)$, where x_1 is known to the adversary and x_2 is hidden, our security game implies that the adversary cannot distinguish whether the input x_2 was used, or some other input x_2' such that $f(x_1, x_2) = f(x_1, x_2')$. Similar notions have been used in secure multi-party computation [MPR06, CPP16].

To further motivate our definition, we highlight that allowing partial decryption queries that involve the challenge ciphertext is critical to achieving a meaningful notion of security. In a typical use-case, the goal of using ThFHE is to compute some function $f(x_1, \ldots, x_n)$, the result of which only reveals a small amount of information compared to the inputs x_i. However, in a security game it is always the challenge ciphertext that contains the hidden information, so disallowing this in partial decryption queries does not capture the desired goals. Indeed, consider the following ThFHE scheme that is obviously insecure in this setting: firstly, modify the evaluation algorithm to output not only an encryption of $f(x_1, \ldots, x_n)$, but also the encryption of x_1; secondly, modify the partial decryption algorithm to also output partial decryptions for x_1. Given a set of partial decryptions for $f(x_1, \ldots, x_n)$, the parties will also learn x_1 which is exactly what we want to avoid. Going back to the definition of IND-CPA security for ThFHE, as the security game of [Cho+22b] only allows for partial decryption queries before seeing the challenge ciphertext, the above obviously insecure construction could actually be shown secure using their definition.

Defining OW-CPA *Security for* ThFHE *(Sect. 3)*. As mentioned above, the Rényi divergence is hard to use in the context of decision-based security notions, such as IND-CPA. We give some intuition on why this is the case in the following. The probability preservation property of RD allows us to reason about the probability of a bad event happening in two different games. Roughly speaking, this says that if D_1, D_2 are distributions such that the Rényi divergence of D_1 from D_2 is at most δ, then for any event E, it holds that $\Pr[D_1(E)] \leq (\Pr[D_2(E)] \cdot \delta)^c$, for some constant c close to 1. If the event E occurs with negligible probability in game D_2, then we can get by with a polynomial-sized δ to argue the same holds in D_1. However, this is inherently hard to make use of in distinguishing games like IND-CPA, where probabilities of winning are close to $1/2$.

Instead of IND-CPA security, therefore we first aim for OW-CPA security, which is easier to prove with the Rényi divergence. When defining OW-CPA in the (fully homomorphic) threshold setting, the main changes are that the adversary also obtains t shares of the secret key and has access to a bounded number of partial decryption queries. In order to avoid trivial attacks, the partial decryption oracle refuses to answer to queries which would leak too much information on the challenge messages which the adversary tries to recover. As a measurement of *too much information* we use conditional min-entropy [Dod+08]. In other words, the oracle only answers to queries if the min-entropy of the challenge message conditioned on all the previously queried circuits and circuit evaluations is not much smaller then the original min-entropy of the challenge message.

Constructing Full-Threshold OW-CPA-*Secure* ThFHE *(Sect. 5)*. To simplify the presentation in the introduction, we first describe our construction in the full-threshold setting and then explain how to get t-out-of-n threshold. As a starting point, we take any encryption scheme whose decryption function is nearly linear, as is the case for most LWE-based encryption schemes (including FHE). That is, for a given ciphertext ct on a message m with respect to a key pair (sk, pk), it holds that $\langle \mathsf{sk}, \mathsf{ct} \rangle = m + e_{\mathsf{ct}}$, where e_{ct} is what we earlier called decryption noise and depends on the ciphertext and the secret key.[4]

To achieve threshold decryption, we use standard additive secret sharing to split the secret key into $\mathsf{sk}_1, \ldots, \mathsf{sk}_n$ in a setup phase. By linearity, we could simply set the partial decryption shares as $\tilde{d}_i = \langle \mathsf{ct}, \mathsf{sk}_i \rangle$. However, after summing all shares together, the parties recover e_{ct}, which leaks information on sk. As in previous threshold solutions for lattice-based schemes, to compute their decryption share d_i every party now locally adds to $\tilde{d}_i$ a noise term e_i which is sampled from the noise flooding distribution $\mathcal{D}_{\mathsf{flood}}$. When summing those partial decryption shares together, the parties learn $m + e_{\mathsf{ct}} + \sum_{i=1}^{n} e_i$.

---

[4] Actually, it only reveals an encoding of m, which is easy to decode as long as parameters are set accordingly.

To prove the OW-CPA security of our construction, we modify the security experiment such that in a first step, the answers to the partial decryption queries no longer depend on the underlying secret key sk (reflected by e_{ct}), and in a second step the secret key shares are also independent of sk. In this case, OW-CPA security of the threshold scheme is implied by the OW-CPA security of the underlying standard encryption scheme. We simulate the partial decryption noise term $e_{\mathsf{ct}} + \sum_{i=1}^{n} e_i$ by sampling some independent noise $e' \leftarrow \mathcal{D}_{\mathsf{sim}}$. As long as the Rényi divergence between the two noise distributions is bounded by a constant, we can appeal to the probability preservation property, and the negligible probability of some PPT adversary guessing the message is preserved in both games. Note that previous works always chose $\mathcal{D}_{\mathsf{sim}} = \mathcal{D}_{\mathsf{flood}}$, but we later exploit in Sect. 6 that choosing a different $\mathcal{D}_{\mathsf{sim}}$ can lead to better parameters.

From Full-Threshold to t-Out-of-n Threshold (Sect. 5). When moving to the t-out-of-n setting, a natural choice is to use Shamir secret sharing. However, this leads to the problem that reconstruction is no longer addition, and instead requires multiplying the partial decryptions with Lagrange interpolation coefficients. These coefficients may be large, which in turn blows up the noise, breaking correctness. We offer two different solutions to this issue.

First, as in [Bon+18], we can use a special type of linear secret sharing scheme with binary coefficients, so that reconstruction is always a simple sum. Efficient threshold schemes with this property exist, for any n, t. We also consider a second method based on *pseudorandom secret sharing* [CDI05], which allows the parties to generate sharings of bounded, pseudorandom values without interaction. This uses replicated secret sharing, which is more expensive, but on the other hand, allows the partial decryptions to be converted into Shamir sharings before reconstruction. This leads to smaller partial decryptions, slightly better parameters and gives a form of robustness via Shamir error correction.

The high level idea is to encrypt a message m of δ bits, is to sample a random message x and to encrypt it using the OW-CPA-secure scheme. Then, the message bits are hidden by δ hard-core bits coming from a concatenation of δ Goldreich-Levin extractors. We use the notion of unpredictable entropy [HLR07] to give a bound on how many pseudorandom bits can be extracted from this construction. We say that a message x has unpredictability entropy k if for any PPT adversary $\mathcal{A}$ the probability of finding x given $\mathsf{Enc}(\mathsf{pk}, x)$ is at most 2^{-k}. We can then use existing results that show that a concatenation of δ Goldreich-Levin extractors can be used to extract $k - O(\log(1/\varepsilon))$ pseudorandom bits, where ε is the desired distinguishing advantage. Those pseudorandom bits then allow us to encrypt a message such that the ciphertexts of two given messages are computationally indistinguishable.

To prove this construction IND-CPA secure, we additionally need to assume circuit privacy of the underlying OW-CPA secure FHE scheme. Intuitively, this is necessary because the IND-CPA security definition says that an adversary should not be able to distinguish between the partial decryptions of a ciphertext encrypting $f(x_1, x_2)$ and those for a ciphertext encrypting $f(x_1, x_2')$ for some $x_2' \neq x_2$ where $f(x_1, x_2) = f(x_1, x_2')$. If, for instance, $x_2' = x_2 \oplus 1$, this is equivalent to distinguishing between ciphertexts for $f(x_1, x_2)$ and $g(x_1, x_2)$, where the function g is defined as $g(x, y) = f(x, y \oplus 1)$. This can be seen as a circuit privacy problem, thus, intuitively, it seems that some form of circuit privacy is necessary to build IND-CPA-secure FHE.

Sample Parameters and Security Analysis (Sect. 6). We conclude our work by discussing how to choose concrete sample parameters for our threshold PKE scheme, when instantiating it with the lattice-based scheme Kyber [Sch+20].

As an example, to obtain 1-out-of-2 threshold decryption with a single query (e.g. for ephemeral key exchange), we can use the same parameters as Kyber1024 with a modulus increased only by a factor of 5, while supporting > 100 bits of classical hardness from our reduction. In a setting with up to 2^{32} queries, we need to use a 39-bit modulus and slightly larger module rank; this increases the ciphertext size by around 5x.

1.2 Related Work

Similarly to our work, [Cho+22b] used the Rényi divergence to obtain threshold FHE from LWE with a polynomial modulus-to-noise ratio. By arguing that the public sampleability property applies in their setting, they directly used the Rényi divergence to prove IND-CPA security. However, their definition of IND-CPA security is weaker than ours with respect to several aspects: First, they only allow for static access to the different queries, e.g., the adversary has to send the full list of circuits to the partial decryption oracle at once. In our case, those queries are adaptive, i.e., the adversary can adapt their next query to the partial decryption oracle based on the outcome of the previous query. Second, their adversary has to query challenge encryptions *before* querying partial decryptions. Moreover, their work focuses on a specific construction of ThFHE based on Torus-FHE, whereas our results are phrased generically for all encryption schemes with nearly linear decryption. Lastly, they focus on linear integer secret sharing schemes, whereas we additionally propose pseudorandom secret sharing and different ways of achieving robustness.

The Rényi divergence has seen widespread use in security proofs in lattice-based cryptography, since [Bai+18]. Replacing statistical noise flooding by Rényi noise flooding has led to a significant improvement in parameters for security reductions, for instance when proving the hardness of (structured) LWE with a binary secret [Bou+20], when designing multi-key FHE [DWF22], or more recently, in the context of lattice-based threshold signatures [ASY22]. The latter work of [ASY22] is quite similar to ours, since they also apply Rényi noise flooding to threshold FHE; however, they do not directly prove security of the threshold FHE scheme, and instead analyze the resulting threshold signature scheme directly (which is based on a search problem, so amenable to a Rényi divergence analysis). They additionally show the optimality of their noise flooding by providing an attack when a smaller noise flooding ratio is used. As the attack uses that their signature scheme is deterministic, it does not directly apply to our randomized encryption scheme. Previous works [Dev+21b, Nae+20] have already observed that OW-CPA allows to bypass the issues caused by the Rényi divergence. However, both are in the PKE setting, whereas our work focused on the FHE setting. This required some care: it is not straightforward to define a OW-CPA notion in the fully-homomorphic setting and the standard transformation used in [Dev+21b,Nae+20] to lift one-way security to indistinguishability is not suited for the fully-homomorphic setting neither.

In an independent line of work, another noise flooding technique, called gentle noise flooding, has been studied in order to avoid the superpolynomial parameter blow-up [BD20a]. It was first used in theoretical hardness results on entropic (structured) LWE [BD20a,BD20b]. Later, a similar technique was used in [Cas+22] for improving parameters in additively homomorphic encryption with circuit privacy. The setting of [Cas+22] is quite different to ours, however, since with circuit privacy, the challenge is to deal with leakage on a plaintext rather than the secret key. This is handled via gentle noise flooding by applying a randomized encoding to the plaintext, so that leaking a constant fraction of its coordinates does not reveal anything about the plaintext. A similar technique does not seem to work in the threshold setting, with leakage on the secret key.

From a high level perspective, our notion of IND-CPA security has some similarities to the notion of IND-CPA^D security introduced in [LM21] in the context of approximate FHE. For instance, partial decryption queries in our setting correspond to decryption queries in their setting. Our security notion further matches with the game-based input-indistinguishability notion in the context of secure multi-party computation from [MPR06,CPP16], when realizing the latter with the help of ThFHE.

Another approach to build threshold key generation and decryption protocols is to use general multi-party computation tools like garbled circuits. This was done in [Kra+19] for a Ring-LWE based scheme. Their solution does not need any noise flooding or increased parameters of the underlying scheme, however, it relies on generic multi-party computation techniques like garbled circuits, and the partial decryption shares are generated using an expensive, interactive protocol rather than non-interactively as in our setting.

2   Preliminaries

For any positive integer q, we denote by $\mathbb{Z}_q$ the integers modulo q and for any positive integer n, we denote by $[n]$ the set $\{1, \ldots, n\}$. Vectors are denoted in bold lowercase and matrices in bold capital letters. The identity matrix of order m is denoted by $\mathbf{I}_m$. The concatenation of two matrices $\mathbf{A}$ and $\mathbf{B}$ with the same number of rows is denoted by $[\mathbf{A}|\mathbf{B}]$. The abbreviation PPT stands for probabilistic polynomial-time. When we split a PPT adversary $\mathcal{A}$ in several sub algorithms $(\mathcal{A}_i)_i$, we implicitly assume that $\mathcal{A}_i$ outputs a state that is passed to the next $\mathcal{A}_{i+1}$. We call a function $\mathsf{negl}(\cdot)$ negligible in λ if $\mathsf{negl}(\lambda) = \lambda^{-\omega(1)}$, i.e., it decreases faster towards 0 than the inverse of any polynomial.

Throughout the paper we make use of the random oracle model (ROM), where we assume the existence of perfectly random functions, realized by oracles. For a random oracle $\mathsf{F}: \{0,1\}^n \to \{0,1\}^m$ it holds that $\Pr[\mathsf{F}(x) = y] = 2^{-m}$ and that $\Pr[\mathsf{F}(x) = \mathsf{F}(x') = y : x \neq x'] = \Pr[\mathsf{F}(x) = y] \cdot \Pr[\mathsf{F}(x') = y] = 2^{-2m}$. Hence, random oracles are per definition collision resistant. For $x, y \in \{0,1\}^n$ we denote by $x \oplus y$ the bit-wise XOR operator.

2.1   Probability and Entropy

For a finite set S, we denote its cardinality by $|S|$ and the uniform distribution over S by $U(S)$. The operation of sampling an element $x \in S$ according to a distribution D over S is denoted by $x \leftarrow D$, where the set S is implicit.

For standard deviation $\sigma > 0$ and mean $c \in \mathbb{R}$, we define the continuous Gaussian distribution $D_{\sigma,c} : \mathbb{R} \rightarrow (0,1]$ by $D_{\sigma,c}(x) = 1/(\sigma\sqrt{2\pi}) \cdot \exp(-(x-c)^2/(2\sigma^2))$. We also define the rounded Gaussian distribution over $\mathbb{Z}$, by rounding the result to the nearest integer, and denote this by $\lfloor D_{\sigma,c} \rceil$.

A random variable X over $\mathbb{R}$ is called τ-subgaussian for some $\tau > 0$ if for all s it holds $\mathbb{E}[\exp(sX)] \leq \exp(\tau^2 s^2/2)$. A τ-subgaussian random variable satisfies $\mathbb{E}[X] = 0$ and $\mathbb{E}[X^2] \leq \tau^2$. We associate to X the width $\sigma = \sqrt{\mathbb{E}[X^2]}$. The continuous Gaussian distribution D_σ and its rounded version $\lfloor D_\sigma \rceil$ are σ-subgaussian. Further, the uniform distribution over $[-a, a] \cap \mathbb{Z}$ is a-subgaussian.

The statistical distance between two probability distributions X and Y, denoted by $\mathsf{sdist}(X, Y)$, is defined as $\max_T |\Pr[T(X) = 1] - \Pr[T(Y) = 1]|$, where T is any test function. The computational distance with respect to size s circuits, denoted by $\mathsf{cdist}_s(X, Y)$, limits T to be any circuit of size s. For any event E, the probability preservation property of sdist (resp. cdist_s) states that $X(E) \leq Y(E) + \mathsf{sdist}(X, Y)$ (resp. $X(E) \leq Y(E) + \mathsf{cdist}_s(X, Y)$).

The notion of unpredictable entropy has been introduced and studied in [HLR07] in the context of conditional computational entropy.

Definition 1 (Unpredictable Entropy). *For a distribution (X, Z), we say that X has unpredictable entropy at least k conditioned on Z, if there exists a collection of distributions Y_Z (giving rise to a joint distribution (Y, Z)) such that $\mathsf{cdist}_s((X, Z), (Y, Z)) \leq \varepsilon$, and for all circuits C of size s,*

$$\Pr[C(Z) = Y] \leq 2^{-k}.$$

We write $H^{\mathsf{unp}}_{\varepsilon,s}(X|Z) \geq k$.

Definition 2 (Concatenated Goldreich-Levin Extractor). *Fix $n, \delta \in \mathbb{N}$. We define the* concatenated Goldreich-Levin extractor $\mathcal{E} : \{0,1\}^n \times (\{0,1\}^n)^\delta \rightarrow \{0,1\}^\delta \times (\{0,1\}^n)^\delta$ *as*

$$\mathcal{E}(x, s_1, \ldots, s_\delta) := (\langle x, s_1 \rangle \bmod 2, \ldots, \langle x, s_\delta \rangle \bmod 2, s_1, \ldots, s_\delta).$$

By analyzing a *reconstruction property* of the Goldreich-Levin extractor and applying a result of [HLR07], we get the following concrete bound on the number of pseudorandom bits that can be extracted.

Lemma 1 ([HLR07], Lemma 6). *Let X be a distribution with unpredictable entropy $H^{\mathsf{unp}}_{\varepsilon,s}(X|Z) \geq k$ and let $\mathcal{E}$ be the concatenated Goldreich-Levin extractor for some $n, \delta \in \mathbb{N}$. If $k = \delta + \log_2 2n + 3\log_2 1/\varepsilon$, then $\mathcal{E}$ extracts δ pseudorandom bits, i.e.,*

$$\mathsf{cdist}_{s'} \left((Z, \mathcal{E}(X, U(\{0,1\}^{n\delta}))), (Z, U(\{0,1\}^\delta \times \{0,1\}^{n\delta})) \right) \leq 5\delta\varepsilon,$$

where $s' = O(sn^{-3}\varepsilon^4)$.

Let $\mathbf{x}$ follow a distribution on a set X, and $\mathbf{z}$ follow a possibly correlated distribution on a set Z. The *average conditional min-entropy* [Dod+08] of $\mathbf{x}$ given $\mathbf{z}$ is defined by

$$\widetilde{H}_{\infty}(\mathbf{x}|\mathbf{z}) = -\log_2\left(E_{\mathbf{z}'}\left[\max_{\mathbf{x}'\in X}\Pr[\mathbf{x}=\mathbf{x}'|\mathbf{z}=\mathbf{z}']\right]\right).$$

Lemma 2 ([Dod+08], Lem. 2.2). *Let* $\mathbf{x},\mathbf{y},\mathbf{z}$ *be three random variables, where* $\mathbf{z}$ *takes at most* 2^{λ} *values. Then*

$$\widetilde{H}_{\infty}(\mathbf{x}|\mathbf{y},\mathbf{z}) \geq \widetilde{H}_{\infty}(\mathbf{x}|\mathbf{y}) - \lambda.$$

The Rényi divergence (RD) defines an alternative measure of distribution closeness. We follow [Bai+18] and use a definition of the RD which is the exponential of the classical definition. We restrict the order a to be in $(1,\infty)$.

Definition 3 (Rényi Divergence). *Let* P *and* Q *be two discrete probability distributions such that* $\mathrm{Supp}(P) \subseteq \mathrm{Supp}(Q)$. *For* $a \in (1,\infty)$ *the Rényi divergence of order a is defined by*

$$\mathrm{RD}_a(P,Q) = \left(\sum_{x\in\mathrm{Supp}(P)}\frac{P(x)^a}{Q(x)^{a-1}}\right)^{\frac{1}{a-1}}.$$

The definitions are extended in the natural way to continuous distributions. We recall some useful properties of the RD. The first two were proven in [EH14] and the last one was proven in [Ros20, Prop. 2].

Lemma 3. *Let* P,Q *be two discrete probability distributions with* $\mathrm{Supp}(P) \subseteq \mathrm{Supp}(Q)$. *For* $a \in (1,\infty)$, *it yields:*

Data Processing Inequality: $\mathrm{RD}_a(g(P)\|g(Q)) \leq \mathrm{RD}_a(P\|Q)$ *for any function* g, *where* $g(P)$ *(resp.* $g(Q)$*) denotes the distribution of* $g(y)$ *induced by sampling* $y \leftarrow P$ *(resp.* $y \leftarrow Q$*).*

Probability Preservation: *Let* $E \subset \mathrm{Supp}(Q)$ *be an event, then for* $a \in (1,\infty)$

$$Q(E) \cdot \mathrm{RD}_a(P\|Q) \geq P(E)^{\frac{a}{a-1}}.$$

Multiplicativity: *Let* P,Q *be two probability distributions of a pair of random variables* (Y_1,Y_2). *For* $i \in \{1,2\}$, *let* P_i *(resp.* Q_i*) denote the marginal distribution of* Y_i *under* P *(resp.* Q*), and let* $P_{2|1}(\cdot|y_1)$ *(resp.* $Q_{2|1}(\cdot|y_1)$*) denote the conditional distribution of* Y_2 *given that* $Y_1 = y_1$. *Then for* $a \in (1,\infty)$

$$\mathrm{RD}_a(P\|Q) \leq \mathrm{RD}_a(P_1\|Q_1) \cdot \max_{y_1\in Y_1}\mathrm{RD}_a(P_{2|1}(\cdot|y_1)\|Q_{2|1}(\cdot|y_1)).$$

The Rényi divergence of two shifted Gaussians is given below. This also allows us to bound the RD of rounded Gaussians by the data processing inequality.

Lemma 4 ([GAL13]). *Let σ be a positive real number and $c \in \mathbb{Z}$. Then for a $\in$ $(1, \infty)$ it yields*

$$\mathrm{RD}_a(D_{\sigma,c} \| D_\sigma) = \exp\left(\frac{ac^2}{2\sigma^2}\right).$$

We provide the proof of the following lemma in the full version [BS23, Sec. 2].

Lemma 5. *Let D_1, D_2 be two probability distributions over $\mathbb{Z}$ and $e_1, \ldots, e_N$ be (possibly dependent) random variables over $\mathbb{Z} \cap [-B, B]$ for some $B \in \mathbb{Z}$, for which there exist $a \in (1, \infty)$ and $\rho \geq 1$ such that for all β with $|\beta| \leq B$, it holds that $\mathrm{Supp}(D_1 + \beta) \subseteq \mathrm{Supp}(D_2)$, and furthermore, $\mathrm{RD}_a(D_1 + \beta \| D_2) \leq \rho$. Then,*

$$\mathrm{RD}_a((D_1 + e_N, \ldots, D_1 + e_1) \| D_2^N) \leq \rho^N.$$

2.2 Linear Secret Sharing

We use linear secret sharing schemes (LSSS) for monotone access structures with a special $\{0, 1\}$-reconstruction property, as follows.

Definition 4 (Monotone Access Structure). *Let $\mathcal{P} = \{P_1, \ldots, P_n\}$ be a set of parties and $2^{\mathcal{P}}$ its power set. A monotone access structure is a collection of sets $\mathbb{A} \subset 2^{\mathcal{P}}$, such that for any $S \in \mathbb{A}$, if $T \supset S$ then $T \in \mathbb{A}$. We say that $\mathbb{A}$ is efficient if membership of $\mathbb{A}$ can be verified in time $\mathsf{poly}(\lambda)$, where $\mathbb{A}$ is viewed as a function of λ.*

In this work, we only consider efficient access structures. To ease notation, we identify a party P_i with its index i, viewing each set $S \in \mathbb{A}$ as a subset of $[n]$. For any $S \subset [n]$ and vector $\mathbf{v} = (\mathbf{v}_1, \ldots, \mathbf{v}_n)$, we let $\mathbf{v}|_S$ denote the vector of shares restricted to $\mathbf{v}_i$ for indices $i \in S$.

Definition 5 (Linear Secret Sharing Scheme). *Let q, L, n be positive integers and $\mathbb{A}$ a monotone access structure. A linear secret sharing scheme LSSS for $\mathbb{A}$ is defined by a randomized algorithm $\mathsf{Share} : \mathbb{Z}_q \to (\mathbb{Z}_q^L)^n$ and a family of deterministic algorithms $\mathsf{Rec}_S : (\mathbb{Z}_q^L)^{|S|} \to \mathbb{Z}_q$, for $S \subseteq [n]$, which satisfy:*

Privacy: *For any set $S \notin \mathbb{A}$, any $x, x' \in \mathbb{Z}_q$ and $\mathbf{v} \in \mathbb{Z}_q^{L|S|}$, it holds that $\Pr[\mathsf{Share}(x)|_S = \mathbf{v}] = \Pr[\mathsf{Share}(x')|_S = \mathbf{v}]$.*
Reconstruction: *For any set $S \in \mathbb{A}$, any $x \in \mathbb{Z}_q$ and $\mathbf{v} = \mathsf{Share}(x)$, the reconstruction algorithm outputs $\mathsf{Rec}_S(\mathbf{v}|_S) = x$.*
Linearity: *For any $\alpha, \beta \in \mathbb{Z}_q$, any set S with $|S| > t$ and any share vectors $\mathbf{u}, \mathbf{v}$, it holds that $\mathsf{Rec}_S(\alpha\mathbf{u}|_S + \beta\mathbf{v}|_S) = \alpha\mathsf{Rec}_S(\mathbf{u}|_S) + \beta\mathsf{Rec}(\mathbf{v}|_S)$.*

When the set of shares is $S = [n]$, we write Rec instead of $\mathsf{Rec}_{[n]}$.

We need the following notion of valid and invalid share sets [Bon+18].

Definition 6. *Let $x \in \mathbb{Z}_q$, $(\mathbf{v}_1, \ldots, \mathbf{v}_n) = \mathsf{Share}(x)$, and write $\mathbf{v}_i = (\mathbf{v}_{i,1}, \ldots, \mathbf{v}_{i,L})$. A set of pairs of indices $T \subseteq [n] \times [L]$ is an invalid set of share elements if the corresponding shares $(\mathbf{v}_{i,j})_{(i,j) \in T}$ reveal no information about x. Otherwise, we say that T is a valid set of share elements. We additionally say:*

- $T \subseteq [n] \times [L]$ *is a* maximal invalid set of share elements *if it is invalid, but for any* $(i,j) \in [n] \times [L] \setminus T$, *the set* $T \cup \{(i,j)\}$ *is a valid set of share elements.*
- $T \subseteq [n] \times [L]$ *is a* minimal valid set of share elements *if it is valid, but for any* $T' \subsetneq T$, *the set* T' *is an invalid set of share elements.*

Note that in any LSSS, a valid set as defined above always allows reconstruction of the secret x. This is because an LSSS can equivalently be defined by a matrix M, such that each share element $\mathbf{v}_{i,j}$ is computed as the inner product of some row of M and $(x, r_1, \ldots, r_{n-1})$, where r is the randomness used in Share. Reconstruction is possible for a given set of share elements iff the corresponding set of rows of M span the target vector $(1, 0, \ldots, 0)$. This definition implies that any set of rows is either invalid—and reveals nothing about x—or valid, and allows full reconstruction. For further details, see e.g. [Bei96, Chapter 4].

Our main construction requires that the reconstruction function Rec_S takes a $0/1$ combination of its inputs. In the following, we require this to hold not only for any set of shares corresponding to a valid set of parties in $\mathbb{A}$, but for any valid set of share elements. This property is equivalent to the notion of a derived $\{0,1\}$-LSSS, used in [JRS17].[5]

Definition 7 (Strong $\{0,1\}$-Reconstruction). *We say that a LSSS has* strong $\{0,1\}$-reconstruction *if for any secret* x *and* $(\mathbf{v}_1, \ldots, \mathbf{v}_n) = \mathsf{Share}(x)$, *for any valid set of share elements* $T \subseteq [n] \times [L]$, *there exists a subset* $T' \subseteq T$ *such that* $\sum_{(i,j) \in T'} \mathbf{v}_{i,j} = x$, *where* $\mathbf{v}_i = (\mathbf{v}_{i,1}, \ldots, \mathbf{v}_{i,L})$.

Sharing Values in R_q. In our constructions, we share $\mathbf{x} \in R_q^r$, where $R_q = \mathbb{Z}_q[X]/f(X)$, instead of just in $\mathbb{Z}_q$. We do this coefficient-wise, by separately sharing each coefficient of the r polynomials in $\mathbf{x}$. Each party's share then lies in $(R_q^r)^L$, and the parties can perform R_q-linear operations on these shares.

Example Linear Secret Sharing Schemes. In Table 1, we detail a few example secret sharing schemes we consider. The schemes are for t-out-of-n access structures, where any $t+1$ parties can reconstruct, and they all have strong $\{0,1\}$-reconstruction. In the table, we show two quantities $\tau_{\max}, \tau_{\min}$, which are relevant for choosing parameters in our constructions of Sect. 5 and we will refer to later. By $\tau_{\max}$ we denote the size of the smallest maximal invalid set of share elements, while $\tau_{\min}$ is the size of the largest minimal valid set of share elements.

---

[5] [Bon+18] only assumed a weaker property for their threshold FHE construction. However, this is a mistake introduced when merging the two works [JRS17] and [Bon+17] (and has been confirmed by the authors of [JRS17]).

Table 1. Example t-out-of-n linear secret sharing schemes with strong $\{0,1\}$-reconstruction. Details for the last row are omitted, due to their complexity.

Scheme	Sharing method	P_i's share	L	τ_{max}	τ_{min}
Additive	$x = \sum\limits_{i=1}^{n} x_i$	x_i	1	$n-1$	n
Replicated	$x = \sum\limits_{A, \lvert A \rvert = t} x_A$	$\{x_A\}_{i \notin A}$	$\binom{n-1}{t}$	$(n-t)(\binom{n}{t}-1)$	$\binom{n}{t}$
Naive	$x = \sum\limits_{i \in A} x_{A,i}, \lvert A \rvert = t+1$	$\{x_{A,i}\}_{i \in A}$	$\binom{n-1}{t}$	$t\binom{n}{t+1}$	$t+1$
Monotone Boolean formula for threshold fn. [Val84]			$O(n^{4.3})$	$O(n^{5.3})$	$O(n^{5.3})$

2.3 Learning with Errors

In the following, we recall the definitions of the decision (module) LWE problem [Reg05,LS15], formulated with a bounded uniform secret and noise. Let $R_q = \mathbb{Z}_q[X]/f(X)$ for some irreducible $f(X)$ of degree d. Further, we define $S_\beta = \{a \in R : \lVert a \rVert_\infty \leq \beta\}$ with $\beta \in \mathbb{N}$.

Definition 8 (M-LWE). *Let $m, r, \beta, q \in \mathbb{N}$. The Module Learning With Errors problem M-LWE$_{q,m,r,\beta}$ is defined as follows. Given $\mathbf{A} \leftarrow U(R_q^{m \times r})$ and $\mathbf{t} \in R_q^m$. Decide whether $\mathbf{t} \leftarrow U(R_q^m)$ or if $\mathbf{t} = [\mathbf{A} \vert \mathbf{I}_m] \cdot \mathbf{s}$, where $\mathbf{s} \leftarrow U(S_\beta^{m+r})$.*

The special case of $d = 1$, where the ring R is isomorphic to $\mathbb{Z}$, is simply denoted LWE (and is historically the one that has been introduced first).

3 Threshold Fully Homomorphic Encryption

3.1 Syntax and Basic Properties of Threshold FHE/PKE

We first recall the syntax of a fully homomorphic threshold public key encryption scheme. We implicitly assume that after Setup, all algorithms are given the public parameters as input. We omit the partial verification algorithm used in previous works (e.g., [BBH06]), which was only used to model stronger notions of robustness that also capture CCA attacks.

Definition 9 (ThFHE). *A fully homomorphic threshold public key encryption scheme (ThFHE) for a message space $\mathcal{M}$ and circuits of depth κ is a tuple of PPT algorithms ThFHE = (Setup, Enc, Eval, PartDec, Combine) defined as follows:*

Setup($1^\lambda, 1^\kappa, n, t$) $\rightarrow$ (pp, pk, sk$_1$, ..., sk$_n$): *On input the security parameter λ, a bound on the circuit depth κ, the number of parties n and a threshold value $t \in \{1, \ldots, n-1\}$, the setup algorithm outputs the public parameters pp, a public key pk and a set of secret key shares sk$_1$, ..., sk$_n$.*

Enc(pk, m) $\rightarrow$ ct: *On input the public key pk and a message $m \in \mathcal{M}$, the encryption algorithm outputs a ciphertext ct.*

Eval(pk, C, ct_1, ..., ct_k) → ct: *On input the public key* pk, *a circuit* $C\colon \mathcal{M}^k \to \mathcal{M}$ *of depth at most* κ *and a set of ciphertexts* $\text{ct}_1, \ldots, \text{ct}_k$, *the evaluation algorithm outputs a ciphertext* ct.

PartDec(sk_i, ct) → d_i: *On input a key share* sk_i *for some* $i \in [n]$ *and a ciphertext* ct, *the partial decryption algorithm outputs a partial decryption share* d_i.

Combine($\{d_i\}_{i \in S}$, ct) → m': *On input a set of decryption shares* $\{d_i\}_{i \in S}$ *and a ciphertext* ct, *where* $S \subset [n]$ *is of size at least* $t + 1$, *the combining algorithm outputs a message* $m' \in \mathcal{M} \cup \{\bot\}$.

The above can be seen as a generalization encompassing non-threshold and threshold PKE and FHE.

Definition 10 (ThPKE). *A threshold public key encryption scheme* (ThPKE) *for a message space* $\mathcal{M}$ *is a* ThFHE *scheme, where* $k = 1$ *and the only allowed circuit* $C\colon \mathcal{M} \to \mathcal{M}$ *is the identity. In this case, we drop the trivial evaluation algorithm* Eval *and the parameter* κ *in the scheme's specifications.*

Definition 11 (FHE). *A fully homomorphic public key encryption scheme* (FHE) *for a message space* $\mathcal{M}$ *is a* ThFHE *scheme, where* $n = 1$. *In this case, we drop the parameters* n *and* t *in the scheme's specifications. To simplify notations, we merge* PartDec *and* Combine *into one single algorithm that we denote* Dec. *Hence, the algorithm* Dec *takes* sk *and* ct *as input and outputs* $m' \in \{\mathcal{M} \cup \{\bot\}\}$.

We require compactness and correctness, whose definitions we recall in the full version [BS23, App. A]. There, we also define two notions of robustness [BS23, Sec. 3.2].

In Sect. 4, we also need FHE schemes which are circuit private, defined below. This can be instantiated under LWE with a polynomial modulus [DS16].

Definition 12 (Circuit Privacy). *Let* $s, \varepsilon > 0$. *A* ThFHE *scheme with message space* $\mathcal{M}$ *and maximal circuit depth* κ *fulfills* (s, ε)-*circuit privacy if for every circuit* C *of depth at most* κ *it yields*

$$\text{cdist}_s\left(((\text{sk}_i)_{i \in n}, \text{Eval}(\text{pk}, C, \text{ct}_1, \ldots, \text{ct}_k)), ((\text{sk}_i)_{i \in [n]}, \text{Enc}(\text{pk}, C(m_1, \ldots, m_k)))\right) \le \varepsilon,$$

where $m_i \in \mathcal{M}$ *and* $\text{ct}_i \leftarrow \text{Enc}(\text{pk}, m_i)$ *for all* $i \in [k]$ *and for honestly generated keys* $(\text{pk}, \text{sk}_1, \ldots, \text{sk}_n)$.

3.2 One-Wayness

We now present our definition of OW-CPA security for ThFHE schemes.

The high level idea of the security game is the following. At the beginning, the adversary decides on the parties they want to corrupt and receives the corresponding secret key shares. We call this the static corruption setting. Then the adversary has access to three different oracles. The first, OEnc, allows them to obtain honestly generated, fresh ciphertexts on messages of their choice. Through the second oracle, OChallEnc, the adversary obtains encryptions of unknown, randomly chosen messages, which we call the challenge messages and challenge ciphertexts. Finally, they can query up to ℓ times the last oracle, OPartDec, by inputting a circuit and a list of indices referring to previous encryption *and* challenge encryption queries, and receiving the corresponding partial decryption shares of all parties (after the evaluation algorithm has been applied). However, the partial decryption oracle aborts if for one of the challenge messages the conditional min-entropy has decreased more than an allowed amount ν, after having learned the circuit evaluation. Note that we do not condition the information-theoretical min-entropy on ChallCT as it uniquely defines ChallM. Implicitly, we assume that the entropy condition can be efficiently verified for the circuits input to OPartDec. One way to practically implement this, is to ask the adversary to input an algorithm which verifies the entropy condition when querying the oracle. We stress that in the transformation of Sect. 4 we only query circuits for which the entropy condition can be checked efficiently. To highlight the query bound ℓ and the entropy loss bound ν, we write (ℓ, ν)-OW-CPA.

Definition 13 ((ℓ, ν)-OW-CPA for ThFHE). *We call a ThFHE scheme (ℓ, ν)-OW-CPA secure for the security parameter λ, the circuit depth bound κ, the threshold parameters n, t, the query bound ℓ and the entropy bound ν, if for all PPT adversaries $\mathcal{A} = (\mathcal{A}_1, \mathcal{A}_2)$*

$$\mathsf{Adv}_{\mathsf{ThFHE}}^{(\ell, \nu)\text{-OW-CPA}}(\mathcal{A}) := \Pr[\mathsf{Expt}_{\mathcal{A}, \mathsf{ThFHE}}^{(\ell, \nu)\text{-OW-CPA}}(1^\lambda, 1^\kappa, n, t) = 1] = \mathsf{negl}(\lambda),$$

where $\mathsf{Expt}_{\mathcal{A}, \mathsf{ThFHE}}^{(\ell, \nu)\text{-OW-CPA}}$ is the experiment in Fig. 1 with $\mathsf{ctr} = 0$, $\mathsf{idx} = 0$ and $\mathsf{L} = \emptyset$ at the beginning.

3.3 Indistinguishability

In the following, we present our definition of IND-CPA security for ThFHE.

As for the OW-CPA security, we allow for static corruptions and access to three different oracles. The first, OEnc, is the same as in the OW-CPA game. To the second oracle, OChallEnc, the adversary inputs two messages and obtains the encryption of one of it. Finally, they can again query up to ℓ times OPartDec, by inputting a circuit and a list of indices and receiving the corresponding partial decryption shares of all parties. This time, the partial decryption oracle aborts if the circuit evaluates to different values on the corresponding input messages to the OChallEnc oracle. To highlight the query bound ℓ, we write ℓ-IND-CPA.

By allowing adaptive access to all three oracles, our definition can be seen as a strengthening of Definition 14 in [JRS17].

Definition 14 (ℓ-IND-CPA for ThFHE). *We call a ThFHE scheme ℓ-IND-CPA secure for the security parameter λ, the circuit depth bound κ, the threshold parameters n, t and the query bound ℓ, if for all PPT adversaries $\mathcal{A} = (\mathcal{A}_1, \mathcal{A}_2)$*

$$\mathsf{Adv}_{\mathsf{ThFHE}}^{\ell\text{-IND-CPA}}(\mathcal{A}) := \left| \Pr[\mathsf{Expt}_{\mathcal{A}, \mathsf{ThFHE}}^{\ell\text{-IND-CPA}}(1^\lambda, 1^\kappa, n, t) = 1] - \frac{1}{2} \right| = \mathsf{negl}(\lambda),$$

$$\mathsf{Expt}_{\mathcal{A},\mathsf{ThFHE}}^{(\ell,\nu)\text{-OW-CPA}}(1^\lambda, 1^\kappa, n, t)$$

1 : $(\mathsf{pp}, \mathsf{pk}, \mathsf{sk}_1, \ldots, \mathsf{sk}_n) \leftarrow \mathsf{Setup}(1^\lambda, 1^\kappa, n, t)$

2 : $S \leftarrow \mathcal{A}_1(\mathsf{pp}, \mathsf{pk}) : S \subset [n] \wedge |S| \le t$

3 : $(m', j) \leftarrow \mathcal{A}_2^{\mathsf{OEnc}, \mathsf{OChallEnc}, \mathsf{OPartDec}}(\mathsf{pk}, \{\mathsf{sk}_i\}_{i \in S})$

4 : $(b_j, m_j, \mathsf{ct}_j) := \mathsf{L}[j]$

5 :   **return** $m_j = m' \wedge b_j = 1$

OEnc(m)	OChallEnc()
1 : **if** $m \notin \mathcal{M}$ **then return** $\bot$	1 : $\mathsf{idx} = \mathsf{idx} + 1$
2 : $\mathsf{idx} = \mathsf{idx} + 1$	2 : $m \leftarrow \mathcal{M}$
3 : $\mathsf{ct} \leftarrow \mathsf{Enc}(\mathsf{pk}, m)$	3 : $\mathtt{ChallM} = \mathtt{ChallM} \cup \{m\}$
4 : $\mathtt{CT} = \mathtt{CT} \cup \{\mathsf{ct}\}$	4 : $\mathsf{ct} \leftarrow \mathsf{Enc}(\mathsf{pk}, m)$
5 : $\mathsf{L}[\mathsf{idx}] := \{(0, m, \mathsf{ct})\}$	5 : $\mathtt{ChallCT} = \mathtt{ChallCT} \cup \{\mathsf{ct}\}$
6 : **return** ct	6 : $\mathsf{L}[\mathsf{idx}] := \{(1, m, \mathsf{ct})\}$
	7 : **return** ct

OPartDec($C, \iota_1, \ldots, \iota_k$)

1 : $\mathsf{ctr} = \mathsf{ctr} + 1$

2 :   **if** $\mathsf{ctr} > \ell$ **then return** $\bot$

3 :   **if** $\exists j \in [k] : \iota_j > |\mathsf{L}|$ **then return** $\bot$

4 :   **if** $\mathsf{depth}(C) > \kappa$ **then return** $\bot$

5 : $(b_j, m_j, \mathsf{ct}_j) := \mathsf{L}[\iota_j], \quad j \in [k]$

6 : $\mathsf{ct} \leftarrow \mathsf{Eval}(\mathsf{pk}, C, \mathsf{ct}_1, \ldots, \mathsf{ct}_k)$

7 : $d_i \leftarrow \mathsf{PartDec}(\mathsf{sk}_i, \mathsf{ct}), \quad i \in [n]$

8 : $\mathbf{d} = (d_i)_{i \in [n]}$

9 :   **for** $m \in \mathtt{ChallM}$

10 :   **if** $\tilde{H}_\infty(m | \mathtt{E} \cup \{(C, C(m_1, \ldots, m_k))\}) < \tilde{H}_\infty(m) - \nu$ **then**

11 :   **return** $\bot$

12 : $\mathtt{E} = \mathtt{E} \cup \{(C, C(m_1, \ldots, m_k))\}$

13 : $\mathtt{PartD} = \mathtt{PartD} \cup \{\mathbf{d}\}$

14 :   **return** $\mathbf{d}$

Fig. 1. Experiments for (ℓ, ν)-OW-CPA security of ThFHE schemes.

where $\mathsf{Expt}_{\mathcal{A},\mathsf{ThFHE}}^{\ell\text{-IND-CPA}}$ is the experiment in Fig. 2 with $\mathsf{ctr} = 0$ and $\mathsf{L} = \emptyset$ at the beginning.

$$\mathsf{Expt}_{\mathcal{A},\mathsf{ThFHE}}^{\ell\text{-IND-CPA}}(1^\lambda, 1^\kappa, n, t)$$

1 : $(\mathsf{pp}, \mathsf{pk}, \mathsf{sk}_1, ..., \mathsf{sk}_n) \leftarrow \mathsf{Setup}(1^\lambda, 1^\kappa, n, t)$

2 : $S \leftarrow \mathcal{A}_1(\mathsf{pp}, \mathsf{pk}) \colon S \subset [n] \wedge |S| \le t$

3 : $b \leftarrow \{0, 1\}$

4 : $b' \leftarrow \mathcal{A}_2^{\mathsf{OEnc},\mathsf{OChallEnc},\mathsf{OPartDec}}(\mathsf{pk}, \{\mathsf{sk}_i\}_{i \in S})$

5 : **return** $b = b'$

$\mathsf{OEnc}(m)$	$\mathsf{OChallEnc}(m^{(0)}, m^{(1)})$
1 : **if** $m \notin \mathcal{M}$ **then return** $\perp$	1 : **if** $(m^{(0)}, m^{(1)}) \notin \mathcal{M} \times \mathcal{M}$ **then return** $\perp$
2 : $\mathsf{idx} = \mathsf{idx} + 1$	2 : $\mathsf{idx} = \mathsf{idx} + 1$
3 : $\mathsf{ct} \leftarrow \mathsf{Enc}(\mathsf{pk}, m)$	3 : $\mathsf{ct}_b \leftarrow \mathsf{Enc}(\mathsf{pk}, m^{(b)})$
4 : $\mathsf{L}[\mathsf{idx}] := \{(m, m, \mathsf{ct})\}$	4 : $\mathsf{L}[\mathsf{idx}] := \{(m^{(0)}, m^{(1)}, \mathsf{ct}_b)\}$
5 : **return** ct	5 : **return** ct_b

$\mathsf{OPartDec}(C, \iota_1, \ldots, \iota_k)$

1 : $\mathsf{ctr} = \mathsf{ctr} + 1$

2 : **if** $\mathsf{ctr} > \ell$ **then return** $\perp$

3 : **if** $\exists j \in [k] \colon \iota_j > |\mathsf{L}|$ **then return** $\perp$

4 : **if** $\mathsf{depth}(C) > \kappa$ **then return** $\perp$

5 : $(m_j^{(0)}, m_j^{(1)}, \mathsf{ct}_j) := \mathsf{L}[\iota_j], \quad j \in [k]$

6 : **if** $C(m_1^{(0)}, \ldots, m_k^{(0)}) \ne C(m_1^{(1)}, \ldots, m_k^{(1)})$ **then return** $\perp$

7 : $\mathsf{ct} \leftarrow \mathsf{Eval}(\mathsf{pk}, C, \mathsf{ct}_1, \ldots, \mathsf{ct}_k)$

8 : $d_i \leftarrow \mathsf{PartDec}(\mathsf{sk}_i, \mathsf{ct}), \quad i \in [n]$

9 : **return** $(d_i)_{i \in [n]}$

Fig. 2. Experiments for ℓ-IND-CPA security of ThFHE schemes.

4 From One-Wayness to Indistinguishability

In the following, we describe a generic way of transforming a OW-CPA secure ThFHE scheme into an IND-CPA secure one in the standard model, via hardcore bits.

The Construction. The transformation is parameterized by $\delta, \gamma \in \mathbb{N}$. Given $\mathsf{ThFHE} = (\mathsf{Setup}, \mathsf{Enc}, \mathsf{Eval}, \mathsf{PartDec}, \mathsf{Combine})$ with message space $\mathcal{M} = \{0, 1\}^\gamma$ being OW-CPA secure, we define $\mathsf{ThFHE}' = (\mathsf{Setup}', \mathsf{Enc}', \mathsf{Eval}', \mathsf{PartDec}', \mathsf{Combine}')$ with message space $\mathcal{M}' = \{0, 1\}^\delta$, which fulfills IND-CPA security, as follows.

Setup': On input $(1^\lambda, 1^\kappa, n, t)$, it outputs $(\mathsf{pp}, \mathsf{pk}, \mathsf{sk}_1, \ldots, \mathsf{sk}_n) \leftarrow \mathsf{Setup}(1^\lambda, 1^\kappa, n, t)$.

Enc': On input (pk, m) with $m = (m_j)_{j \in [\delta]} \in \mathcal{M}'$, it samples $x \leftarrow U(\mathcal{M})$ and computes $c_0 \leftarrow \mathsf{Enc}(\mathsf{pk}, x)$. For $j \in [\delta]$, it samples $s_j \leftarrow U(\mathcal{M})$ and computes $c_j = \langle x, s_j \rangle + m_j \bmod 2$. It outputs $\mathsf{ct} = (c_0, s_1, \ldots, s_\delta, c_1, \ldots, c_\delta)$.

Eval': On input $I := (\mathsf{pk}, C, \mathsf{ct}_1, \ldots, \mathsf{ct}_k)$, where $\mathsf{ct}_i = (c_{i0}, s_{i1}, \ldots, s_{i\delta}, c_{i1}, \ldots, c_{i\delta})$ such that $c_{i0} \leftarrow \mathsf{Enc}(\mathsf{pk}, x_i)$ for $i \in [k]$ and $C : (\mathcal{M}')^k \to \mathcal{M}'$, it first defines a circuit $\widetilde{C} : (\mathcal{M})^k \to \mathcal{M}$ as follows:

  - $\widetilde{C}$ takes as input $(x_1, \ldots, x_k)$ and has the information I hard-coded
  - It computes $m_{ij} = c_{ij} + \langle x_i, s_{ij} \rangle \bmod 2$, for $j \in [\delta]$ and $i \in [k]$
  - It outputs $C(m_1, \ldots, m_k)$, where $m_i = (m_{ij})_{j \in [\delta]}$

It then outputs $\mathsf{ct}' = \mathsf{Eval}(\mathsf{pk}, \widetilde{C}, c_{10}, \ldots, c_{k0})$.

PartDec': On input $(\mathsf{sk}_i, \mathsf{ct}')$, it outputs $d_i = \mathsf{PartDec}(\mathsf{sk}_i, \mathsf{ct}')$.

Combine': On input $(\{d_i\}_{i \in S}, \mathsf{ct}')$, it outputs $m = \mathsf{Combine}(\{d_i\}_{i \in S}, \mathsf{ct}')$.

Ciphertext Expansion. The ratio between the bit size of the plaintext and the ciphertext is give by

$$\frac{|\mathsf{ct}|}{|m|} = \frac{|c_0| + \delta(\gamma + 1)}{\delta},$$

where c_0 is the OW-CPA ciphertext encrypting γ bits coming from ThFHE. We can see that with larger δ the ciphertext expansion gets better.

We prove compactness and decryption correctness in the full version [BS23, App. B].

Remark 1. One way to reduce the size of the ciphertext to $|c_0| + \gamma + \delta$ (and hence to improve the ciphertext expansion) is to replace the δ random seeds $s_1, \ldots, s_\delta$ by one single seed and a random oracle F. More precisely, one could define $s_j := \mathsf{F}(r, j)$ for a random seed $r \leftarrow U(\mathcal{M})$ and $j \in [\delta]$. As a result, the transformation wouldn't be in the standard, but in the random oracle model. As the random oracle is only used to derive the seeds, not when masking the message, this transformation still applies to the threshold FHE setting.

Theorem 1 (Security). *Fix $\ell, \delta, \gamma, \lambda, s \in \mathbb{N}$ and $\varepsilon > 0$. Let q_c denote the number of provided challenge ciphertexts, i.e., the number of queries to OChallEnc. Let ThFHE be an $(\ell + q_c, \delta)$-OW-CPA secure scheme with $\mathcal{M} = \{0, 1\}^\gamma$, such that any adversary $\mathcal{B}$ of circuit size s has advantage $\mathsf{Adv}_{\mathsf{ThFHE}}^{(\ell + q_c, \delta)\text{-OW-CPA}}(\mathcal{B}) \leq 2^{-\lambda}$, where $\lambda \geq 3 \log_2(1/\varepsilon) + \log_2(2\gamma) + \delta$. Further, we assume that ThFHE fulfills (s', ε')-circuit privacy, where $s' = O(s\gamma^3 \varepsilon^{-4})^6$ and $\varepsilon' = 5 q_c \delta \varepsilon / \ell$ and $\varepsilon' = 5 q_c \delta \varepsilon / \ell$. Then, ThFHE' is ℓ-IND-CPA secure with $\mathcal{M}' = \{0, 1\}^\delta$; concretely, for any adversary $\mathcal{A}$ of circuit size s' it yields*

$$\mathsf{Adv}_{\mathsf{ThFHE}'}^{\ell\text{-IND-CPA}}(\mathcal{A}) \leq \frac{25 q_c \delta \varepsilon + 1}{2}.$$

---

[6] The hidden constant in the $O(\cdot)$ notation is the same as that in the proof of Lemma 1, which can be derived from the Goldreich-Levin theorem.

Choosing the Parameters. To ensure a small enough advantage, since q_c, δ are relatively small, it suffices to choose a small enough ε, which we denote $\varepsilon = 2^{-\lambda'}$. We then require $\lambda = \delta + 3\lambda' + \log_2(2\gamma)$, which determines the required security level of the original OW-CPA scheme. There's therefore a tradeoff between the increased security requirement and the value δ, which improves ciphertext expansion. For instance, if $\lambda' = 128$ then by choosing $\delta = 118, \gamma = 512$, we can pack 118 message bits into each FHE ciphertext, which must encrypt 512 actual bits using the OW-CPA scheme. In this case, to achieve security according to the reduction, the parameters of the OW-CPA scheme would need to be chosen for $\lambda = 512$-bit security. We note that this way of setting parameters may be overly conservative, since our reduction is not tight—unlike with the number of queries ℓ and the matching attack, we are not aware of any weaknesses from choosing smaller values of λ.

Proof. Recall that we are given an OW-CPA secure threshold decryption scheme ThFHE = (Setup, Enc, Eval, PartDec, Combine) with message space $\mathcal{M} = \{0,1\}^\gamma$ and we want to construct a new threshold scheme ThFHE' = (Setup', Enc', Eval', PartDec', Combine') with message space $\mathcal{M}' = \{0,1\}^\delta$, which fulfills IND-CPA security. In the IND-CPA security game (Definition 14), the adversary has access to three different oracles, OEnc', OChallEnc' and OPartDec'. In the following, we define a sequence of games which modify how the different oracles are implemented. The first game consists of the IND-CPA security game, where $b = 1$. The last game consists of the IND-CPA security game, where $b = 0$.

Game$_0$:

Queries to OEnc': On input the message $m = (m_i)_{i \in [\delta]} \in \{0,1\}^\delta = \mathcal{M}'$, sample $x, s_1, \ldots, s_\delta \leftarrow U(\mathcal{M})$, compute $c_0 \leftarrow \text{Enc}(\text{pk}, x)$, and set $c_i = \langle x, s_i \rangle + m_i \bmod 2$ for all $i \in [\delta]$. Set $m^{(0)} = m^{(1)} = m$. Output the ciphertext $\text{ct} = (c_0, s_1, \ldots, s_\delta, c_1, \ldots, c_\delta)$ and store $(m^{(0)}, m^{(1)}, \text{ct})$ in the list L.

Queries to OChallEnc': On input messages $m^{(0)}, m^{(1)} \in \{0,1\}^\delta = \mathcal{M}'$, sample $x, s_1, \ldots, s_\delta \leftarrow U(\mathcal{M})$, compute $c_0 \leftarrow \text{Enc}(\text{pk}, x)$, and set $c_i = \langle x, s_i \rangle + m_i^{(1)}$ for all $i \in [\delta]$. Output $\text{ct} = (c_0, s_1, \ldots, s_\delta, c_1, \ldots, c_\delta)$ and store $(m^{(0)}, m^{(1)}, \text{ct})$ in the list L.

Queries to OPartDec': On input a circuit C and indices $\iota_1, \ldots, \iota_k$, find the corresponding ciphertexts $\text{ct}_1, \ldots, \text{ct}_k$ in the list L. First compute $\text{ct} \leftarrow \text{Eval}'(\text{pk}, C, \text{ct}_1, \ldots, \text{ct}_k)$ (by internally calling Eval on associated circuit $\widetilde{C}$) and then $d_i \leftarrow \text{PartDec}'(\text{sk}_i, \text{ct})$ (by internally calling PartDec) for all $i \in [n]$. Output $\mathbf{d} = (d_i)_{i \in [n]}$.

Game$_1$:

Queries to OEnc' and to OChallEnc': as in Game$_0$

Queries to OPartDec': On input a circuit C and indices $\iota_1, \ldots, \iota_k$, find the corresponding messages $m_1^{(1)}, \ldots, m_k^{(1)}$ in the list L. Define the constant circuit $\widetilde{C}$ which, on any input simply outputs $C(m_1^{(1)}, \ldots, m_k^{(1)})$. First compute $\text{ct} \leftarrow \text{Enc}(\text{pk}, \widetilde{C}(x_1^{(1)}, \ldots, x_k^{(1)}))$ (on arbitrary input $x_i^{(1)}$) and then $d_i \leftarrow \text{PartDec}(\text{sk}_i, \text{ct})$ for all $i \in [n]$. Output $\mathbf{d} = (d_i)_{i \in [n]}$.

Game$_2$:

Queries to OEnc$'$ and to OPartDec$'$: as in Game$_1$
Queries to OChallEnc$'$: On input messages $m^{(0)}, m^{(1)} \in \{0,1\}^\delta = \mathcal{M}'$, sample $x, s_1, \ldots, s_\delta \leftarrow U(\mathcal{M})$ and compute $c_0 \leftarrow \mathsf{Enc}(\mathsf{pk}, x)$. Further, sample $r_1, \ldots, r_\delta \leftarrow U(\{0,1\})$ and set $c_i = r_i + m_i^{(1)} \bmod 2$ for all $i \in [\delta]$. Output $\mathsf{ct} = (c_0, s_1, \ldots, s_\delta, c_1, \ldots, c_\delta)$ and store $(m^{(0)}, m^{(1)}, \mathsf{ct})$ in L.

Game$_3$:

Queries to OEnc$'$ and to OPartDec$'$: as in Game$_2$
Queries to OChallEnc$'$: On input messages $m^{(0)}, m^{(1)} \in \{0,1\}^\delta = \mathcal{M}'$, sample $x, s_1, \ldots, s_\delta \leftarrow U(\mathcal{M})$ and compute $c_0 \leftarrow \mathsf{Enc}(\mathsf{pk}, x)$. Further, sample $r_1, \ldots, r_\delta \leftarrow U(\{0,1\})$ and set $c_i = r_i + m_i^{(0)} \bmod 2$ for all $i \in [\delta]$. Output $\mathsf{ct} = (c_0, s_1, \ldots, s_\delta, c_1, \ldots, c_\delta)$ and store $(m^{(0)}, m^{(1)}, \mathsf{ct})$ in L.

Game$_4$:

Queries to OEnc$'$ and to OPartDec$'$: as in Game$_3$
Queries to OChallEnc$'$: On input messages $m^{(0)}, m^{(1)} \in \{0,1\}^\delta = \mathcal{M}'$, sample $x, s_1, \ldots, s_\delta \leftarrow U(\mathcal{M})$, compute $c_0 \leftarrow \mathsf{Enc}(\mathsf{pk}, x)$ and set $c_i = \langle x, s_i \rangle + m_i^{(0)} \bmod 2$ for all $i \in [\delta]$. Output $\mathsf{ct} = (c_0, s_1, \ldots, s_\delta, c_1, \ldots, c_\delta)$ and store $(m^{(0)}, m^{(1)}, \mathsf{ct})$ in L.

Game$_5$:

Queries to OEnc$'$ and to OChallEnc$'$: as in Game$_4$
Queries to OPartDec$'$: On input a circuit C and indices $\iota_1, \ldots, \iota_k$, find the corresponding ciphertexts $\mathsf{ct}_1, \ldots, \mathsf{ct}_k$ in the list L. First compute $\mathsf{ct} \leftarrow \mathsf{Eval}'(\mathsf{pk}, C, \mathsf{ct}_1, \ldots, \mathsf{ct}_k)$ and then $d_i \leftarrow \mathsf{PartDec}'(\mathsf{sk}_i, \mathsf{ct})$ for all $i \in [n]$. Output $\mathbf{d} = (d_i)_{i \in [n]}$.

Claim. Assume there is an adversary $\mathcal{A}$ of circuit size s' who wins the ℓ-IND-CPA game against ThFHE' with probability at least p. Then, there exists an $i \in \{0, \ldots, 4\}$ such that $\mathrm{cdist}_{s'}(\mathsf{Game}_i, \mathsf{Game}_{i+1}) > (2p-1)/5 := \tilde{\varepsilon}$.

Next, we argue for all $i \in \{0, \ldots, 4\}$, if $\mathrm{cdist}_{s'}(\mathsf{Game}_i, \mathsf{Game}_{i+1}) > \tilde{\varepsilon}$, it either breaks one-way security of ThFHE or circuit privacy of ThFHE'. Note that the modifications from Game$_0$ to Game$_1$ are the same (in reverse order) as from Game$_4$ to Game$_5$. Similarly, the modifications from Game$_1$ to Game$_2$ are the same as from Game$_3$ to Game$_4$. Moreover, Game$_2$ and Game$_3$ are information-theoretically close to each other, because the challenge messages $m^{(0)}$ or $m^{(1)}$ are hidden by truly random bits. We thus focus on the step from Game$_0$ to Game$_1$ and the step from Game$_1$ to Game$_2$ in the following. The step from Game$_0$ to Game$_1$ is necessary to correctly apply the Goldreich-Levin extractor argument in the next step. By replacing the evaluation algorithm with the direct encryption of the evaluated circuit, we make sure that partial decryptions do not leak any information on the challenge bit $b = 1$.[7]

---

[7] We have overseen this subtlety in an earlier version of this paper and thank the Asiacrypt reviewers for pointing it out to us.

Claim (Game$_0$ to Game$_1$). Assuming that cdist$_{s'}$(Game$_0$, Game$_1$) > $\widetilde{\varepsilon}$ contradicts the $(s', \widetilde{\varepsilon}/\ell)$-circuit privacy of ThFHE'.

Proof. Recall that ℓ denotes the maximal number of allowed queries to OPartDec'. As Game$_0$ and Game$_1$ only differ on how queries to OPartDec' are answered, it yields

$$\widetilde{\varepsilon} < \text{cdist}_{s'}(\text{Game}_0, \text{Game}_1) \leq \ell \cdot \text{cdist}_{s'}(\mathbf{d}, \widetilde{\mathbf{d}}),$$

where $\mathbf{d}$ is a vector of partial decryptions output by the oracle in Game$_0$ and $\widetilde{\mathbf{d}}$ a vector of partial decryptions output by the oracle in Game$_1$. Using that applying the randomized function PartDec'$(\text{sk}_i, \cdot)$ does not increase the computational distance and using the definitions of PartDec' and Eval' (through PartDec and Eval, respectively), we observe that $\widetilde{\varepsilon}/\ell$ is bounded above by

$$\text{cdist}_{s'}\left(((\text{sk}_i)_i, \text{Eval}(\text{pk}, \widetilde{C}, \text{ct}_1, \dots, \text{ct}_k)), ((\text{sk}_i)_i, \text{Enc}(\text{pk}, \widetilde{C}(x_1^{(1)}, \dots, x_k^{(1)})))\right),$$

contradicting the $(s', \widetilde{\varepsilon}/\ell)$-circuit privacy of ThFHE (cf. Definition 12). We later link $\widetilde{\varepsilon}$ to ε' as in the theorem statement. ∎

Claim (Game$_1$ to Game$_2$). Assuming that cdist$_{s'}$(Game$_1$, Game$_2$) > $\widetilde{\varepsilon}$ contradicts the $(\ell + q_c, \delta)$-OW-CPA security assumption of ThFHE.

Proof. Let q_c denote the number of allowed queries to OChallEnc'. As Game$_1$ and Game$_2$ only differ on how queries to OChallEnc' are answered, it yields

$$\widetilde{\varepsilon} < \text{cdist}_{s'}(\text{Game}_1, \text{Game}_2) \leq q_c \cdot \text{cdist}_{s'}(\text{ct}, \widetilde{\text{ct}}),$$

where ct is an encryption output by the oracle in Game$_1$ and $\widetilde{\text{ct}}$ is an encryption output by the oracle in Game$_2$. We can rewrite ct using the concatenated Goldreich-Levin extractor $\mathcal{E}$ from Definition 2. We define $m := (0, \dots, 0, m^{(1)}) \in \mathcal{M}^\delta \times \mathcal{M}'$, $X := U(\mathcal{M})$ and $Z := (\text{Enc}(\text{pk}, X), (\text{sk}_i)_{i \in S}, \text{E}, \text{PartD})$, the latter being the random variable defined by the randomized encryption algorithm for uniform random messages, the corrupted secret key shares, the circuit evaluations and the partial decryptions given by the partial decryption queries in the security game. Furthermore, we set $Y = X$, such that cdist$_{s'}((X, Z), (Y, Z)) \leq \varepsilon$ for all $s', \varepsilon > 0$. We observe that $\text{ct} = (Z, \mathcal{E}(X, U(\mathcal{M}^\delta) + m)$ and $\widetilde{\text{ct}} = (Z, U(\mathcal{M}^\delta \times \mathcal{M}') + m)$. It holds that

$$\widetilde{\varepsilon}/q_c < \text{cdist}_{s'}(\text{ct}, \widetilde{\text{ct}}) \leq \text{cdist}_{s'}\left((Z, \mathcal{E}(X, U(\mathcal{M}^\delta))), (Z, U(\mathcal{M}^\delta \times \mathcal{M}'))\right).$$

Applying Lemma 1 implies an upper bound on the unpredictability entropy, i.e., $H_{\varepsilon, s}^{\text{unp}}(X|Z) < \lambda$, where $\varepsilon = \frac{\widetilde{\varepsilon}}{5 q_c \delta}$, $s = O(s' \gamma^{-3} \varepsilon^4)$ and $\lambda = \delta + \log_2 2\gamma + 3 \log_2 1/\varepsilon$. To conclude the proof of the claim, we link the unpredictability entropy of X given Z to the OW-CPA security of ThFHE via a reduction. In the following, we explain how the corresponding oracle queries for ThFHE' (which define X and Z) can be answered by having access to the three analogue oracles (denoted OEnc, OChallEnc and OPartDec) from the OW-CPA security game, cf. Definition 13.

Reduction to OW-CPA Game.

Queries to OEnc′: On input the message $m = (m_i)_{i \in [\delta]} \in \{0,1\}^\delta = \mathcal{M}'$, sample $x, s_1, \ldots, s_\delta \leftarrow U(\mathcal{M})$ and query OEnc on input x. Take the received $c_0 = \mathsf{Enc}(\mathsf{pk}, x)$ and compute $c_i = \langle x, s_i \rangle + m_i \bmod 2$ for all $i \in [\delta]$. Set $m^{(0)} = m^{(1)} = m$. Output the ciphertext $\mathsf{ct} = (c_0, s_1, \ldots, s_\delta, c_1, \ldots, c_\delta)$ and store $(m^{(0)}, m^{(1)}, \mathsf{ct})$ in the list L.

Queries to OChallEnc′: On input $m^{(0)}, m^{(1)} \in \{0,1\}^\delta = \mathcal{M}'$, query OChallEnc (on no input) and get back an encryption $c_0 = \mathsf{Enc}(\mathsf{pk}, x)$ for an unknown x. For $i \in [\delta]$, sample $s_i \leftarrow U(\mathcal{M})$. Define the circuit $\tilde{C}$ which takes as input x and computes $\langle x, s_i \rangle + m_i^{(1)} \bmod 2$ for every $i \in [\delta]$. Then query OPartDec on c_0 and the circuit $\tilde{C}$. For every $i \in [\delta]$, the partial decryption oracle outputs all partial decryption shares that can be combined to $c_i = \langle x, s_i \rangle + m_i^{(1)}$. Output the ciphertext $\mathsf{ct} = (c_0, s_1, \ldots, s_\delta, c_1, \ldots, c_\delta)$ and store $(m^{(0)}, m^{(1)}, \mathsf{ct})$ in L.

Queries to OPartDec′: On input a circuit C and indices $\iota_1, \ldots, \iota_k$, find the corresponding messages $m_1^{(1)}, \ldots, m_k^{(1)}$ in the list L. Define the constant circuit $\tilde{C}$ which, on any input, simply outputs $C(m_1^{(1)}, \ldots, m_k^{(1)})$. Query OPartDec on the circuit $\tilde{C}$ and the indices $\iota_1, \ldots, \iota_k$ as input. On output $\mathbf{d} = (d_i)_{i \in [n]}$ of the oracle OPartDec, output $\mathbf{d}$.

Queries to OPartDec done within OChallEnc′ and within OPartDec′ do pass the entropy-check with the entropy bound δ (cf. line 10 of Fig. 2). Regarding the first case, by Lemma 2, every inner product $\langle x, s_i \rangle \bmod 2$ leaks at most one bit of x. Hence, at most δ bits are leaked in total when querying OPartDec on circuit $\tilde{C}$. A similar argument holds for OPartDec′: The circuit C' leaks at most δ bits for every x_i with $i \in [k]$. Note that every query to OChallEnc′ leads to one query to OPartDec. Similarly, every query to OPartDec′ leads to one query to OPartDec. Thus, the OW-CPA scheme has to allow for $\ell + q_c$ partial decryption queries in total. To conclude the proof, we observe that $H_{\varepsilon,s}^{\mathsf{unp}}(X|Z) < \lambda$ implies that for any adversary $\mathcal{B}$ of circuit size s

$$2^{-\lambda} < \Pr[\mathcal{B}(Z) = X] \le \mathsf{Adv}_{\mathsf{ThFHE}}^{(\ell+q_c,\delta)\text{-OW-CPA}}(\mathcal{B}).$$

∎

Regarding the parameters from the theorem statement, we observe from the above two sub proofs that $\varepsilon' = \tilde{\varepsilon}/\ell = \varepsilon 5 q_c \delta / \ell$ and $s' = O(s\gamma^3 \varepsilon^{-4})$ as stated. □

5 Threshold Fully Homomorphic Encryption from LWE with Polynomial Modulus

We now present our construction of a t-out-of-n ThFHE scheme with OW-CPA security. First, we describe and analyze our main construction based on any LSSS with strong $\{0,1\}$-reconstruction. Then, in Sect. 5.5, we give an alternative construction that combines pseudorandom secret sharing with Shamir sharing to improve efficiency when $\binom{n}{t}$ is small.

By applying the OW-CPA to IND-CPA transformation for ThFHE from Sect. 4, we hence obtain an IND-CPA secure scheme. When we restrict ourselves to standard PKE, our construction gives us a standard ThPKE scheme (cf. Definition 10). We can then also apply the alternative transformation which additionally achieves some form of robustness.

5.1   Nearly Linear Decryption of FHE

We use the following abstraction of LWE-based encryption schemes, where decryption is viewed as a linear function of the secret key that outputs a "noisy" version of the correct message. Similar notions were used in [BKS19, Bra+19].

Definition 15 (FHE with (β, ε)-linear decryption). *Let* FHE $:=$ (Setup, Enc, Dec, Eval) *be a fully homomorphic encryption scheme (as in Definition 11) with message space* $\mathcal{M} \subseteq R_p$ *and ciphertext space* R_q^r. *Suppose that* Setup *outputs a secret key* sk $\in R_q^r$ *which has the form* $(1, \mathbf{s})$ *for some* $\mathbf{s} \in R_q^{r-1}$.

Let $\beta = \beta(\lambda) \in \mathbb{N}, \varepsilon = \varepsilon(\lambda) \in [0,1]$. *We say that* FHE *has* (β, ε)*-linear decryption if for any* $\lambda, \kappa \in \mathbb{N}$, (pp, pk, sk) $\leftarrow$ Setup$(1^\lambda, 1^\kappa)$, *depth-*κ *circuit* $C \colon \mathcal{M}^k \to \mathcal{M}$, *messages* $m_1, \ldots, m_k \in R_p$, *ciphertexts* $\mathbf{c}_i \leftarrow$ Enc(pk, m_i) $\in R_q^r$ *and* ct $\leftarrow$ Eval(pk, $\mathbf{c}_1, \ldots, \mathbf{c}_k$), *it holds that*

$$\langle \mathsf{sk}, \mathsf{ct} \rangle = \lfloor q/p \cdot C(m_1, \ldots, m_k) \rceil + e \mod q,$$

for some $e \in R_q$ *such that* $\Pr[\|e\|_\infty \leq \beta] \geq 1 - \varepsilon$ *(where the probability is taken over the randomness of* Setup, Enc *and* Eval*).*

In standard (Module)-LWE based constructions, it's possible to securely set the parameters such that the ratio β/q can be made arbitrarily small, and as long as we have $\beta/q = 1/\mathsf{poly}(\lambda)$, then q is $\mathsf{poly}(\lambda)$.

For security, we require that FHE is IND-CPA secure.[8] This can be instantiated under the Module-LWE assumption to obtain (leveled) FHE using, for instance, the BGV scheme [BGV12] (with superpolynomial q). For $p = 2, d = 1$ and $R = \mathbb{Z}$, we also get (leveled) FHE under the standard LWE assumption with a polynomial modulus q [BV14].

5.2   Construction from LSSS with Strong $\{0, 1\}$-Reconstruction

Our construction works over the ring $R = \mathbb{Z}[X]/f(X)$ for some degree-d irreducible polynomial f, and uses the following main ingredients:

- $\mathcal{D}_{\mathsf{flood}}$: a noise distribution over $\mathbb{Z}_q$ with magnitude bounded by β_{flood},
- $\mathcal{D}_{\mathsf{sim}}$: a noise distribution over $\mathbb{Z}_q$, where $\mathrm{RD}_a(\mathcal{D}_{\mathsf{sim}} \| \mathcal{D}_{\mathsf{flood}} + B) \leq \varepsilon_{\mathrm{RD}_a}$, for some $a \in (1, \infty), \varepsilon_{\mathrm{RD}_a} > 1$ and for all B with $|B| \leq \beta_{\mathsf{fhe}}$,
- LSS: a t-out-of-n linear secret sharing scheme LSS = (Share, (Rec$_S$)$_{S \subset [n]}$) with strong $\{0, 1\}$-reconstruction, associated parameters $L, \tau_{\max}, \tau_{\min}$ and shares in $\mathbb{Z}_q^L$ (cf. Definition 6),

---

[8] In our main construction, we assume $\mathcal{M}$ is large and only rely on OW-CPA security of FHE. When extending to smaller $\mathcal{M}$ in Sect. 5.3, we instead need IND-CPA security.

- FHE: a OW-CPA secure FHE = (Setup′, Enc, Eval, Dec) scheme with message space $\mathcal{M} \subseteq R_p$, ciphertext space R_q^r, and $(\beta_{\mathsf{fhe}}, \varepsilon)$-linear decryption for some $\beta_{\mathsf{fhe}} < q/(2p) - \tau_{\min}\beta_{\mathsf{flood}}$ and some negligible ε.

We now define the scheme ThFHE := (Setup, Enc, Eval, PartDec, Combine) by using Enc and Eval from the underlying FHE scheme and setting Setup, PartDec and Combine as specified in Fig. 3. We prove its correctness in the full version [BS23].

For now, we assume the plaintext space $\mathcal{M} \subseteq R_p$ is superpolynomial in the security parameter, so that FHE is OW-CPA secure. In Sect. 5.3, we show how to extend this to use FHE with any plaintext space, which allows instantiating from LWE with polynomial modulus.

We write $\mathcal{D}_{\mathsf{flood}, R_q^r}$ (resp. $\mathcal{D}_{\mathsf{sim}, R_q^r}$) to refer to the distribution consisting of rd independent $\mathcal{D}_{\mathsf{flood}}$ (resp. $\mathcal{D}_{\mathsf{sim}}$) random variables, used to sample the coefficients of r elements of R_q.

We show security in the following.

Theorem 2 (Security). *For any adversary $\mathcal{A}$ against the (ℓ, ν)-OW-CPA property of the ThFHE scheme in Fig. 3 with message space $\mathcal{M}$, there exists an adversary $\mathcal{B}$ against the IND-CPA property of FHE, such that*

$$\mathsf{Adv}_{\mathsf{ThFHE}}^{(\ell,\nu)\text{-OW-CPA}}(\mathcal{A}) \leq \left[|\mathtt{ChallM}|\left(\mathsf{Adv}_{\mathsf{FHE}}^{\mathsf{IND\text{-}CPA}}(\mathcal{B}) + 2^{-\log_2(|\mathcal{M}|)+\nu}\right)\cdot \varepsilon_{\mathsf{RD}_a}^{\ell d(nL-\tau_{\max})}\right]^{(a-1)/a} + \ell\varepsilon,$$

where L and $\tau_{\max}$ are parameters from the LSS and $|\mathtt{ChallM}|$ is the number of challenge ciphertexts the adversary queried.

Proof. The high-level idea is to modify the (ℓ, ν)-OW-CPA game (Fig. 2) such that the t secret shares and the answers to the ℓ partial decryption queries provided to the adversary no longer depend on the underlying secret key sk. This is reflected by the sequence of games from G_0 to G_4. In the new game G_4,

---

Setup($1^\lambda, 1^\kappa, n, t$)

1: $(\mathsf{pp}, \mathsf{pk}, \mathsf{sk}) \leftarrow \mathsf{Setup}'(1^\lambda, 1^\kappa)$
2: // $\mathsf{sk} \in R_q^r, \mathsf{sk}_i \in (R_q^r)^L$
3: $(\mathsf{sk}_1, \ldots, \mathsf{sk}_n) \leftarrow \mathsf{LSS.Share}(\mathsf{sk})$
4: **return** $(\mathsf{pp}, \mathsf{pk}, \mathsf{sk}_1, \ldots, \mathsf{sk}_n)$

PartDec($\mathsf{sk}_i, \mathsf{ct}$)

1: $\mathbf{e}_{i,j} \leftarrow \mathcal{D}_{\mathsf{flood}, R_q}$ for $j \in [L]$
2: // $\mathsf{sk}_i = (\mathsf{sk}_{i,1}, \ldots, \mathsf{sk}_{i,L}) \in (R_q^r)^L$
3: $\mathbf{d}_{i,j} \leftarrow \langle \mathsf{ct}, \mathsf{sk}_{i,j}\rangle + \mathbf{e}_{i,j}$
4: **return** $\mathbf{d}_i \leftarrow (\mathbf{d}_{i,1}, \ldots, \mathbf{d}_{i,L})$

Combine($\{\mathbf{d}_i\}_{i\in S}, \mathsf{ct}$)

1: $y \leftarrow \mathsf{Rec}_S((\mathbf{d}_i)_{i\in S})$
2: **return** $\lfloor (p/q)\cdot y\rceil$

Fig. 3. Setup, partial decrypt and combine algorithms for OW-CPA secure ThFHE. The Enc and Eval algorithms are the same as for FHE.

the adversary still learns the circuit evaluations, stored in the set E, which might leak some information on the challenge messages, stored in ChallM. In a final step, when going to G_5, we make those circuit evaluations independent of the challenge ciphertexts, by tweaking the oracle OChallEnc to output random ciphertexts (independent of the challenge messages). Here we need to assume the IND-CPA security of the underlying non-threshold FHE scheme. By arguing that the circuit evaluations coming from the partial decryption queries do not leak too much information on the challenge messages, we can bound the advantage of the resulting adversary in the last game G_5 to be negligible.

Game G_0: This is the real threshold (ℓ, ν)-OW-CPA experiment as in Fig. 2. The view of $\mathcal{A}$ is given by

$$\mathcal{V} = (\text{pp}, \text{pk}, \{\text{sk}_i\}_{i \in S}, \text{CT}, \text{ChallCT}, \text{E}, \text{PartD}),$$

where pp are the public parameters, pk is the public key, $\{\text{sk}_i\}_{i \in S}$ are the secret key shares given to the adversary, CT and ChallCT contain the (challenge) ciphertexts the adversary has queried, E and PartD store the results of up to ℓ adaptive circuit evaluations and partial decryption queries. In each partial decryption query, $\mathcal{A}$ inputs a circuit C and list of indices $(i_1, \dots, i_k)$, and receives $(\mathbf{d}_i)_{i \in [n]}$, where $\mathbf{d}_i$ is the partial decryption of $\text{ct} \leftarrow \text{Eval}(\text{pk}, C, \text{ct}_{i_1}, \dots, \text{ct}_{i_k})$ under sk_i. Once the adversary knows all the partial decryption shares, they can reconstruct the circuit evaluation $C(m_{i_1}, \dots, m_{i_k})$. It yields, $\text{Adv}_{\text{ThFHE}}^{(\ell, \nu)\text{-OW-CPA}}(\mathcal{A}) = \text{Adv}_{\text{ThFHE}}^{G_0}(\mathcal{A})$.

Game G_1: In this game, we redefine how the partial decryptions are computed. After the adversary chooses the set $S \subset [n]$ of corrupt parties, let $S_L = \{(i, j)\}_{i \in S, j \in [L]}$ be the corresponding set of share elements. Fix $T \supseteq S_L$ to be a maximal invalid set of share elements. Then, compute the partial decryptions $\mathbf{d}_i$ for a ciphertext ct as follows:

1. For $(i, j) \in T$, let $\tilde{\mathbf{d}}_{i,j} = \langle \text{ct}, \text{sk}_{i,j} \rangle$;
2. For $(i, j) \in ([n] \times [L]) \setminus T$, let $T_{i,j} \subseteq T \cup \{(i, j)\}$ be a minimal valid set of share elements, and compute $\tilde{\mathbf{d}}_{i,j} = \langle \text{ct}, \text{sk} \rangle - \sum_{(k,l) \in T_{i,j} \setminus \{(i,j)\}} \tilde{\mathbf{d}}_{k,l}$;
3. Sample $\mathbf{e}_i \leftarrow \mathcal{D}_{\text{flood}, R_q^L}$ and compute $\mathbf{d}_i = \tilde{\mathbf{d}}_i + \mathbf{e}_i$, for $i \in [n]$.

Game G_2: In this game, before outputting the partial decryptions for a ciphertext ct, we first check that $\langle \text{ct}, \text{sk} \rangle = \lfloor q/p \rceil \cdot C(m_1, \dots, m_k) + e$ for some e with $\|e\|_\infty \le \beta_{\text{fhe}}$. If not, the game aborts.

Game G_3: We replace the partial decryptions corresponding to shares outside of T with simulated ones. Firstly, in step (2) above, for $(i, j) \in ([n] \times [L]) \setminus T$, we now compute $\tilde{\mathbf{d}}_{i,j}$ as $\tilde{\mathbf{d}}_{i,j} = \lfloor q/p \cdot C(m_1, \dots, m_k) \rceil - \sum_{(k,l) \in T_{i,j} \setminus \{(i,j)\}} \tilde{\mathbf{d}}_{k,l}$. Secondly, in step (3), instead of always sampling $\mathbf{e}_{i,j} \leftarrow \mathcal{D}_{\text{flood}, R_q}$, we only sample $\mathbf{e}_{i,j} \leftarrow \mathcal{D}_{\text{flood}, R_q}$ if $(i, j) \in T$, and $\mathbf{e}_{i,j} \leftarrow \mathcal{D}_{\text{sim}, R_q}$ otherwise.

Game G_4. In the next game, we change how the secret key shares are sampled: pick $(\text{sk}_1', \dots, \text{sk}_n') \leftarrow \text{LSS.Share}(0)$ and give to $\mathcal{A}$ the shares $\{\text{sk}_i'\}_{i \in S}$.

Game G_5. In the last game, we replace the oracle OChallEnc by OChallEnc′, as defined in Fig. 4. In the new oracle, two independent m and m' are sampled. Whereas m is added to the challenge message list ChallM, the encryption of m' is added to the challenge ciphertext list ChallCT.

OChallEnc′()

1: $\mathsf{idx} = \mathsf{idx} + 1$

2: $m, m' \leftarrow \mathcal{M}$

3: $\mathsf{ChallM} = \mathsf{ChallM} \cup \{m\}$

4: $\mathsf{ct} \leftarrow \mathsf{Enc}(\mathsf{pk}, m')$

5: $\mathsf{ChallCT} = \mathsf{ChallCT} \cup \{\mathsf{ct}\}$

6: $\mathsf{L}[\mathsf{idx}] := \{(1, m, \mathsf{ct})\}$

7: **return** ct

Fig. 4. Modified OChallEnc′ oracle.

The theorem then follows from the following lemmata relating the advantages between the different games and showing that the final advantage in the last game is negligibly small.

Lemma 6. *For any* PPT *adversary* $\mathcal{A}$ *in Games* G_0 *and* G_1, *it holds that*

$$\mathsf{Adv}^{G_0}_{\mathsf{ThFHE}}(\mathcal{A}) = \mathsf{Adv}^{G_1}_{\mathsf{ThFHE}}(\mathcal{A}).$$

Proof. Note that the view of $\mathcal{A}$ in G_1 is identical to that in G_0, due to the strong $\{0,1\}$-reconstruction property of LSS. This is because every share belonging to the maximally invalid set T is computed the same way as in G_0, using the shares sk_i, while each share outside this set is deterministically fixed to be a sharing of the correct secret $\langle \mathsf{ct}, \mathsf{sk} \rangle$, plus noise sampled from $\mathcal{D}_{\mathsf{flood}}$, as in G_0. Hence, $\mathsf{Adv}^{G_0}_{\mathsf{ThFHE}}(\mathcal{A}) = \mathsf{Adv}^{G_1}_{\mathsf{ThFHE}}(\mathcal{A})$. ∎

Lemma 7. *For any* PPT *adversary* $\mathcal{A}$ *in Games* G_1 *and* G_2, *it holds that*

$$\mathsf{Adv}^{G_1}_{\mathsf{ThFHE}}(\mathcal{A}) \leq \mathsf{Adv}^{G_2}_{\mathsf{ThFHE}}(\mathcal{A}) + \ell\varepsilon.$$

Proof. Due to the $(\beta_{\mathsf{fhe}}, \varepsilon)$-linear decryption property of FHE, and applying a union bound over the ℓ queries, we have that $\mathsf{Adv}^{G_1}_{\mathsf{ThFHE}}(\mathcal{A}) \leq \mathsf{Adv}^{G_2}_{\mathsf{ThFHE}}(\mathcal{A}) + \ell\varepsilon$. ∎

Lemma 8. *For any* PPT *adversary* $\mathcal{A}$ *in Games* G_2 *and* G_3, *it holds that*

$$\mathsf{Adv}^{G_2}_{\mathsf{ThFHE}}(\mathcal{A}) \leq \left(\mathsf{Adv}^{G_3}_{\mathsf{ThFHE}}(\mathcal{A}) \cdot \varepsilon^{\ell d(nL - \tau_{\max})}_{\mathsf{RD}_a}\right)^{(a-1)/a},$$

where $\tau_{\max}$ *is the size of the smallest maximal invalid share set in* LSS.

Proof. We compute the Rényi divergence between the views of the adversary in each game. Each view consists of the adversary's random tape and

$$\mathcal{V} = (\mathsf{pp}, \mathsf{pk}, \{\mathsf{sk}_i\}_{i \in S}, \mathsf{CT}, \mathsf{ChallCT}, \mathsf{E}, \mathsf{PartD}),$$

where CT and $\mathsf{ChallCT}$ store the (challenge) ciphertexts and E and PartD the circuit evaluations and partial decryption shares after the ℓ partial decryption queries. For simpler notation, we set $\mathbf{i}^\eta := (i_1^\eta, \dots, i_k^\eta)$ and $\mathbf{m}^\eta := (m_{i_1}^\eta, \dots, m_{i_k}^\eta)$ for the index list and corresponding message vector of the η-th query. Let D_2 and D_3 denote the distributions of $\mathcal{V}$ in games G_2 and G_3, respectively. Since the partial decryption queries are adaptive, note that, the circuit C^η and the index list $\mathbf{i}^\eta$ input during the η-th query depend on the previous queries to OEnc, OChallEnc and OPartDec and the corresponding responses. However, since each $(C^\eta, \mathbf{i}^\eta)$ is a deterministic function of the other values in the view (including the random tape), by the data processing inequality (Lemma 3), $\mathrm{RD}_a(D_2 \| D_3) \le \mathrm{RD}_a(D_2' \| D_3')$, where D_2', D_3' are the distributions with the $C^\eta, \mathbf{i}^\eta$ values removed. D_2' are D_3' are now defined identically, except in the way the partial decryption components $\mathbf{d}_{i,j}^\eta$ are computed for indices $(i,j) \notin T$. In G_2, $\mathbf{d}_{i,j}^\eta$ is computed using (amongst other values) $\langle \mathsf{ct}^\eta, \mathsf{sk} \rangle + \mathcal{D}_{\mathsf{flood}, R_q}$, whereas G_3 instead uses $\lfloor q/p \cdot C(\mathbf{m}^\eta) \rceil + \mathcal{D}_{\mathsf{sim}, R_q}$. Since $\langle \mathsf{ct}^\eta, \mathsf{sk} \rangle = \lfloor q/p \cdot C(\mathbf{m}^\eta) \rceil + e_\eta$ for some e_η with $\|e_\eta\|_\infty \le \beta_{\mathsf{fhe}}$, and the view contains $nL - |T|$ pairs $(i,j) \notin T$ where the sampling of $\mathbf{d}_{i,j}^\eta$ changes from G_2 to G_3, to compute $\mathrm{RD}_a(D_2' \| D_3')$, it suffices to compute

$$\mathrm{RD}_a\left(((e_1 + \mathcal{D}_{\mathsf{flood}, R_q})^{nL - |T|}, \dots, (e_\ell + \mathcal{D}_{\mathsf{flood}, R_q})^{nL - |T|}) \| \mathcal{D}_{\mathsf{sim}, R_q}^{\ell(nL - |T|)} \right).$$

Applying Lemma 5 with $N = d\ell(nL - |T|)$, $D_1 = \mathcal{D}_{\mathsf{flood}}, D_2 = \mathcal{D}_{\mathsf{sim}}$, we get

$$\mathrm{RD}_a(D_2' \| D_3') \le \varepsilon_{\mathrm{RD}_a}^{d\ell(nL - |T|)}.$$

Applying the probability preservation property of Rényi divergence, we bound the success probability of the adversary as required. ∎

Lemma 9. *For any* PPT *adversary* $\mathcal{A}$ *in Games* G_3 *and* G_4, *it holds that*

$$\mathsf{Adv}_{\mathsf{ThFHE}}^{G_3}(\mathcal{A}) = \mathsf{Adv}_{\mathsf{ThFHE}}^{G_4}(\mathcal{A}).$$

Proof. Note that the view of $\mathcal{A}$ in G_4 is perfectly indistinguishable from the one in G_3 by the perfect privacy property of LSS. Hence, $\mathsf{Adv}_{\mathsf{ThFHE}}^{G_3}(\mathcal{A}) = \mathsf{Adv}_{\mathsf{ThFHE}}^{G_4}(\mathcal{A})$. ∎

Lemma 10. *For any* PPT *adversary* $\mathcal{A}$ *in Games* G_4 *and* G_5, *it holds that*

$$\mathsf{Adv}_{\mathsf{ThFHE}}^{G_4}(\mathcal{A}) \le \mathsf{Adv}_{\mathsf{ThFHE}}^{G_5}(\mathcal{A}) + |\mathsf{ChallM}| \cdot \mathsf{Adv}_{\mathsf{FHE}}^{\mathsf{IND\text{-}CPA}}(\mathcal{A}).$$

Proof. The view of $\mathcal{A}$ in G_5 and G_4 are computationally indistinguishable assuming the IND-CPA security of the non-threshold FHE scheme for every query to OChallEnc'. In total, there are $|\mathsf{ChallM}|$ many such queries. Hence, we obtain $\mathsf{Adv}_{\mathsf{ThFHE}}^{G_4}(\mathcal{A}) \le \mathsf{Adv}_{\mathsf{ThFHE}}^{G_5}(\mathcal{A}) + |\mathsf{ChallM}| \cdot \mathsf{Adv}_{\mathsf{FHE}}^{\mathsf{IND\text{-}CPA}}(\mathcal{A})$. ∎

Lemma 11. *For any* PPT *adversary* $\mathcal{A}$ *in Game* G_5, *it yields that*

$$\mathsf{Adv}^{G_5}_{\mathsf{ThFHE}}(\mathcal{A}) \leq q_c \cdot 2^{-\log_2(|\mathcal{M}|)} \cdot 2^{\nu},$$

where $\mathcal{M}$ *is the message space,* ν *the bound on the entropy leakage guaranteed in the* (ℓ, ν)-OW-CPA *game and* $q_c := |\mathtt{ChallM}|$ *the number of queried ciphertext challenges. If* ν *is logarithmic,* $|\mathcal{M}|$ *exponential and* q_c *polynomial in* λ, *the advantage is negligible in* λ.

Proof. Let $\mathcal{V}$ denote the views of $\mathcal{A}$ in Game G_5. It is given by

$$\mathcal{V} = (\mathsf{pp}, \mathsf{pk}, \{\mathsf{sk}_i\}_{i \in S}, \mathtt{CT}, \mathtt{ChallCT}, \mathtt{E}, \mathtt{PartD}).$$

Note that in Game G_5, all challenge messages in $\mathtt{ChallM}$ are independent of the challenge ciphertexts in $\mathtt{ChallCT}$. Furthermore, the secret key shares $\{\mathsf{sk}_i\}_{i \in S}$ are independent of the secret key sk and hence also independent of the challenge messages in $\mathtt{ChallM}$. The same is true for the simulated partial decryption shares stored in $\mathtt{PartD}$. The public parameters pp, public key pk and normal ciphertexts stored in $\mathtt{CT}$, are trivially independent of $\mathtt{ChallM}$. Thus, $\tilde{H}_\infty(m|\mathcal{V}) = \tilde{H}_\infty(m|\mathtt{E})$. Overall, it yields

$$\mathsf{Adv}^{G_5}_{\mathsf{ThFHE}}(\mathcal{A}) \leq \sum_{m \in \mathtt{ChallM}} 2^{-\tilde{H}_\infty(m|\mathcal{V})} = \sum_{m \in \mathtt{ChallM}} 2^{-\tilde{H}_\infty(m|\mathtt{E})}$$

$$\leq \sum_{m \in \mathtt{ChallM}} 2^{-\tilde{H}_\infty(m)+\nu},$$

where we used that the leakage is guaranteed to be bounded above by ν. Finally, we use that every $m \in \mathtt{ChallM}$ is sampled uniformly at random over $\mathcal{M}$, thus $\tilde{H}_\infty(m) = \log_2(|\mathcal{M}|)$, leading to $\mathsf{Adv}^{G_5}_{\mathsf{ThFHE}}(\mathcal{A}) \leq |\mathtt{ChallM}| \cdot 2^{-\log_2(|\mathcal{M}|)} \cdot 2^{\nu}$. ∎

5.3 Supporting a Larger Plaintext Space

The above construction works for a plaintext space $\mathcal{M} \subseteq R_p$. Since we only obtain one-way security, this requires $|R_p|$ to be superpolynomial in λ to give a meaningful security guarantee. If R_p is small, we can easily modify our threshold scheme to still be secure by using several ciphertexts to encrypt larger messages with the underlying FHE scheme. Note that this change is necessary to obtain an instantiation from LWE with polynomial modulus, since $\mathcal{M} = R_p = \mathbb{Z}_2$.

Concretely, suppose that FHE is IND-CPA secure and has small message space $\mathcal{M}$. Define FHE′ with message space $\mathcal{M}^k$, such that $|\mathcal{M}^{-k}|$ is negligible, by encrypting each of the k message components separately under FHE. We then instantiate our threshold scheme using FHE′ instead of FHE, where during the partial decrypt and combine steps, we run the algorithms for the previous construction on each component separately. If FHE is IND-CPA secure, then so is FHE′, and the proof carries over in the same way, except that the ℓ values in the statement of Theorem 2 will be replaced with $k\ell$, to account for the fact that each of the ℓ decryption queries involves k decryptions of ciphertexts from FHE.

5.4   Bounding the Rényi Divergence

We now analyze parameters and instantiate the distributions $\mathcal{D}_{\text{flood}}$ and $\mathcal{D}_{\text{sim}}$. For now, we simply choose them both to be rounded Gaussian distributions $\lfloor D_\sigma \rceil$ with the same standard deviation σ. In Sect. 6.1, we obtain tighter parameters by carefully optimizing the choice of distributions. If FHE has a maximum ciphertext noise bound of β_{fhe}, then using Lemma 4 with our choice of distributions, we get $\varepsilon_{\text{RD}_a} = \text{RD}_a(\mathcal{D}_{\text{flood}} + \beta_{\text{fhe}} \| \mathcal{D}_{\text{sim}}) \leq \exp\left(\frac{a\beta_{\text{fhe}}^2}{2\sigma^2}\right)$. If FHE has λ_{FHE} bits of security, then from Theorem 2, the resulting ThFHE scheme is λ_{ThFHE}-bit secure, such that

$$\lambda_{\text{ThFHE}} \geq (\lambda_{\text{FHE}} - \ell d(nL - \tau_{\max}) \log_2 \varepsilon_{\text{RD}_a}) \frac{a-1}{a} \tag{1}$$

Combining the above two equations, we obtain $\lambda_{\text{ThFHE}} \geq \frac{a-1}{a}\lambda_{\text{FHE}} - \ell d(nL - \tau_{\max})(a-1)\frac{\beta_{\text{fhe}}^2}{2\sigma^2} \log_2 e$. Setting for instance $a = \lambda_{\text{ThFHE}}$, and choosing $\sigma, q, \beta_{\text{fhe}}$ such that $\sigma = O(\beta_{\text{fhe}}\sqrt{\ell d(nL - \tau_{\max})(a-1)})$ while decryption is still correct, the loss in security is only a constant factor. Smaller values of a give different tradeoffs between the size of σ and the security loss. Note that in any case, if ℓ and nL are polynomially bounded then both σ and the modulus q can be also.

5.5   Alternative Construction Using Pseudorandom Secret Sharing

In the full version of this paper [BS23], we also give a different construction based on pseudorandom secret sharing (PRSS), which improves upon the previous one in some aspects. Instead of having each party perturb their share by an independent, random noise term, we will use PRSS [GI99, CDI05]. This allows them to jointly sample replicated secret sharings of small noise terms, without interaction, after a one-time setup that distributes PRF keys. We also exploit the fact that replicated secret shares can be locally converted to any other LSS, and convert the secret shared noise terms into Shamir sharings before using them for partial decryption. This means that the partial decryptions are Shamir shares, which are much smaller, consisting of only 1 element over R_q each. Furthermore, this leads to improved parameters in the security reduction (by avoiding the $nL - \tau_{\max}$ term in Eq. 1), and we can additionally take advantage of the error-correction capability of Shamir to achieve strong robustness when $t < n/3$. This offers a way of getting robustness for ThFHE instead of only ThPKE with our previous transformations, with the drawback that we require $\binom{n}{t}$ to be not too large, due to using replicated secret sharing.

To sum up, PRSS is a lightweight tool for achieving robustness with a small number of parties.

6   Sample Parameters and Security Estimates

In this section, we discuss how to choose concrete parameters for our OW-CPA secure threshold construction, where we take as a starting point the lattice-based scheme Kyber [Sch+20]. Hence, we are not in the fully homomorphic case, but in the standard PKE case and thus obtain a standard ThPKE scheme. We denote the thresholdized version of Kyber by TKyber.

The relevant parameters for Kyber are the ring degree d, the rank r, the modulus q and the width η of the secret key and encryption randomness distributions. Whereas the specifications of Kyber only consider three parameter sets, called Kyber512, Kyber768 and Kyber1024, we additionally consider three more parameter sets, that we subsequently call Kyber1280, Kyber1536 and Kyber1792. As the name suggest, they are obtained in a similar manner as the previous parameter sets, simply by increasing the rank by +1.

6.1   Security from the Reduction

Let λ_{PKE} (resp. λ_{ThPKE}) denote the security level of the starting PKE (resp. the resulting ThPKE) from Theorem 2. Further, we set $\Delta_\lambda := \lambda_{\mathsf{PKE}} - \lambda_{\mathsf{ThPKE}}$, which describe the security loss in our reduction. Instantiating Eq. 1 in the standard PKE setting yields

$$\lambda_{\mathsf{ThPKE}} \geq \frac{a-1}{a} \cdot \left(\lambda_{\mathsf{PKE}} - \ell d(nL - \tau_{\mathsf{max}}) \log_2 \varepsilon_{\mathrm{RD}_a} \right), \tag{2}$$

where ℓ is the number of partial decryption queries, d the degree of the ring R, L and τ_{max} parameters of the underlying LSSS and $\varepsilon_{\mathrm{RD}_a}$ an upper bound on the Rényi divergence $\mathrm{RD}_a(\mathcal{D}_{\mathsf{sim}} \| \mathcal{D}_{\mathsf{flood}} + \beta_{\mathsf{pke}})$ of order a. Here, $\mathcal{D}_{\mathsf{sim}}$ (resp. $\mathcal{D}_{\mathsf{flood}}$) denotes the simulating (resp. flooding) noise distribution and β_{pke} is a bound on the decryption noise that depends on the concrete parameters of Kyber, in particular on the ring degree d, the module rank r and the parameter η, as well as the maximal failure probability ε we want to achieve. For concreteness we set λ_{PKE} as the core-SVP classical hardness, i.e., the resulting BKZ block estimated from the Lattice Estimator [APS15] size multiplied by 0.292.

Table 2 and Table 3 present some sample parameters. The relevant difference between the two is that in the first table, we focus on larger numbers of parties n and samples ℓ while accepting a modulus of up to 39 bits. For simplicity, we assume that both $\mathcal{D}_{\mathsf{flood}}$ and $\mathcal{D}_{\mathsf{sim}}$ follow a Gaussian distribution of width σ.

Table 2. Sample parameters and security estimates following the reduction from Theorem 2 using a generic approach.

Set	$(\beta_{\mathsf{pke}}, \varepsilon)$	n	t	ℓ	$\lceil \log_2 \sigma \rceil$	$\lceil \log_2 q \rceil$	λ_{PKE}	λ_{ThPKE}	Δ_λ
TKyber1024	$(390, 2^{-60})$	2	1	1	17	23	120	117	3
TKyber1024	$(934, 2^{-300})$	2	1	1	18	24	111	108	3
TKyber1024	$(390, 2^{-60})$	10	9	1	17	25	105	102	3
TKyber1280	$(435, 2^{-60})$	10	5	1	21	29	120	117	3
TKyber1536	$(476, 2^{-60})$	20	10	10	27	36	112	109	3
TKyber1792	$(513, 2^{-60})$	2	1	2^{32}	33	39	123	120	3

Table 3. Sample parameters and security estimates following the reduction from Theorem 2 obtained from a hand-tuned Python program.

Set	q	n	t	ℓ	$\mathcal{D}_{\text{flood}}$	$\mathcal{D}_{\text{sim}}$	λ_{ThPKE}	Δ_λ
TKyber1024	$5 \cdot 3329$	2	1	1	947	1087	100	111
TKyber1024	$10 \cdot 3329$	2	1	2	1994	2034	104	91
TKyber1024	$9 \cdot 3329$	3	2	1	1197	1297	106	92

In contrast, in the second table we fine-tuned the flooding and simulation distributions so that we can allow for very small q (only multiplying the original Kyber modulus by small constants up to 10).

Acknowledgments. We would like to thank Ivan Damgård and Aayush Jain for helpful discussions on secret sharing, and the anonymous reviewers for pointing out a flaw in an earlier version of this work, and other valuable feedback.

This work has been supported by the Independent Research Fund Denmark (DFF) under project number 0165-00107B (C3PO), the Protocol Labs Research Grant Program RFP-013 and the Aarhus University Research Foundation.

References

[APS15] Albrecht, M.R., Player, R., Scott, S.: On the concrete hardness of learning with errors. Cryptology ePrint Archive, Report 2015/046 (2015). https://eprint.iacr.org/2015/046

[Ash+12] Asharov, G., Jain, A., López-Alt, A., Tromer, E., Vaikuntanathan, V., Wichs, D.: Multiparty computation with low communication, computation and interaction via threshold FHE. In: Pointcheval, D., Johansson, T. (eds.) EUROCRYPT 2012. LNCS, vol. 7237, pp. 483–501. Springer, Heidelberg (2012). https://doi.org/10.1007/978-3-642-29011-4_29

[ASY22] Agrawal, S., Stehle, D., Yadav, A.: Round-optimal lattice-based threshold signatures, revisited. Cryptology ePrint Archive, Report 2022/634 (2022). https://eprint.iacr.org/2022/634

[Bai+18] Bai, S., Lepoint, T., Roux-Langlois, A., Sakzad, A., Stehlé, D., Steinfeld, R.: Improved security proofs in lattice-based cryptography: using the Rényi divergence rather than the statistical distance. J. Cryptol. **31**(2), 610–640 (2018)

[BBH06] Boneh, D., Boyen, X., Halevi, S.: Chosen ciphertext secure public key threshold encryption without random oracles. In: Pointcheval, D. (ed.) CT-RSA 2006. LNCS, vol. 3860, pp. 226–243. Springer, Heidelberg (2006). https://doi.org/10.1007/11605805_15

[BD10] Bendlin, R., Damgård, I.: Threshold decryption and zero-knowledge proofs for lattice-based cryptosystems. In: Micciancio, D. (ed.) TCC 2010. LNCS, vol. 5978, pp. 201–218. Springer, Heidelberg (2010). https://doi.org/10.1007/978-3-642-11799-2_13

[BD20a] Brakerski, Z., Döttling, N.: Hardness of LWE on general entropic distributions. In: Canteaut, A., Ishai, Y. (eds.) EUROCRYPT 2020, Part II. LNCS, vol. 12106, pp. 551–575. Springer, Cham (2020). https://doi.org/10.1007/978-3-030-45724-2_19

[BD20b] Brakerski, Z., Döttling, N.: Lossiness and entropic hardness for ring-LWE. In: Pass, R., Pietrzak, K. (eds.) TCC 2020, Part I. LNCS, vol. 12550, pp. 1–27. Springer, Cham (2020). https://doi.org/10.1007/978-3-030-64375-1_1

[Bei96] Beimel, A.: Secure schemes for secret sharing and key distribution. Ph.D. thesis, Technion, Haifa, Israel (1996)

[Ben+21] Benhamouda, F., Jain, A., Komargodski, I., Lin, H.: Multiparty reusable non-interactive secure computation from LWE. In: Canteaut, A., Standaert, F.-X. (eds.) EUROCRYPT 2021, Part II. LNCS, vol. 12697, pp. 724–753. Springer, Cham (2021). https://doi.org/10.1007/978-3-030-77886-6_25

[BGV12] Brakerski, Z., Gentry, C., Vaikuntanathan, V.: (Leveled) fully homomorphic encryption without bootstrapping. In: Goldwasser, S. (ed.) ITCS 2012, pp. 309–325. ACM (2012)

[BKS19] Boyle, E., Kohl, L., Scholl, P.: Homomorphic secret sharing from lattices without FHE. In: Ishai, Y., Rijmen, V. (eds.) EUROCRYPT 2019, Part II. LNCS, vol. 11477, pp. 3–33. Springer, Cham (2019). https://doi.org/10.1007/978-3-030-17656-3_1

[Bon+17] Boneh, D., Gennaro, R., Goldfeder, S., Kim, S.: A lattice-based universal thresholdizer for cryptographic systems. Cryptology ePrint Archive, Report 2017/251 (2017). https://eprint.iacr.org/2017/251

[Bon+18] Boneh, D., et al.: Threshold cryptosystems from threshold fully homomorphic encryption. In: Shacham, H., Boldyreva, A. (eds.) CRYPTO 2018, Part I. LNCS, vol. 10991, pp. 565–596. Springer, Cham (2018). https://doi.org/10.1007/978-3-319-96884-1_19

[Bou+16] Bourse, F., Del Pino, R., Minelli, M., Wee, H.: FHE circuit privacy almost for free. In: Robshaw, M., Katz, J. (eds.) CRYPTO 2016, Part II. LNCS, vol. 9815, pp. 62–89. Springer, Heidelberg (2016). https://doi.org/10.1007/978-3-662-53008-5_3

[Bou+20] Boudgoust, K., Jeudy, C., Roux-Langlois, A., Wen, W.: Towards classical hardness of module-LWE: the linear rank case. In: Moriai, S., Wang, H. (eds.) ASIACRYPT 2020, Part II. LNCS, vol. 12492, pp. 289–317. Springer, Cham (2020). https://doi.org/10.1007/978-3-030-64834-3_10

[Bra+19] Brakerski, Z., Döttling, N., Garg, S., Malavolta, G.: Leveraging linear decryption: rate-1 fully-homomorphic encryption and time-lock puzzles. In: Hofheinz, D., Rosen, A. (eds.) TCC 2019, Part II. LNCS, vol. 11892, pp. 407–437. Springer, Cham (2019). https://doi.org/10.1007/978-3-030-36033-7_16

[BS23] Boudgoust, K., Scholl, P.: Simple threshold (fully homomorphic) encryption from LWE with polynomial modulus. Cryptology ePrint Archive (2023)

[BV14] Brakerski, Z., Vaikuntanathan, V.: Lattice-based FHE as secure as PKE. In: Naor, M. (ed.) ITCS 2014, pp. 1–12. ACM (2014)

[Cas+22] de Castro, L., Hazay, C., Ishai, Y., Vaikuntanathan, V., Venkitasubramaniam, M.: Asymptotically quasi-optimal cryptography. In: Dunkelman, O., Dziembowski, S. (eds.) EUROCRYPT 2022. LNCS, vol. 13275, pp. 303–334. Springer, Cham (2022). https://doi.org/10.1007/978-3-031-06944-4_11

[CDI05] Cramer, R., Damgård, I., Ishai, Y.: Share conversion, pseudorandom secret-sharing and applications to secure computation. In: Kilian, J. (ed.) TCC

2005. LNCS, vol. 3378, pp. 342–362. Springer, Heidelberg (2005). https://doi.org/10.1007/978-3-540-30576-7_19

[Cho+22a] Chowdhury, S., et al.: Efficient FHE with threshold decryption and application to real-time systems. Cryptology ePrint Archive. Version 2023-01-23 (2022)

[Cho+22b] Chowdhury, S., et al.: Efficient FHE with threshold decryption and application to real-time systems. Cryptology ePrint Archive. Version 2023-06-01 (2022)

[CPP16] Couteau, G., Peters, T., Pointcheval, D.: Encryption switching protocols. In: Robshaw, M., Katz, J. (eds.) CRYPTO 2016, Part I. LNCS, vol. 9814, pp. 308–338. Springer, Heidelberg (2016). https://doi.org/10.1007/978-3-662-53018-4_12

[Dev+21a] Devevey, J., Libert, B., Nguyen, K., Peters, T., Yung, M.: Non-interactive CCA2-secure threshold cryptosystems: achieving adaptive security in the standard model without pairings. In: Garay, J.A. (ed.) PKC 2021, Part I. LNCS, vol. 12710, pp. 659–690. Springer, Cham (2021). https://doi.org/10.1007/978-3-030-75245-3_24

[Dev+21b] Devevey, J., Sakzad, A., Stehlé, D., Steinfeld, R.: On the integer polynomial learning with errors problem. In: Garay, J.A. (ed.) PKC 2021, Part I. LNCS, vol. 12710, pp. 184–214. Springer, Cham (2021). https://doi.org/10.1007/978-3-030-75245-3_8

[Dod+08] Dodis, Y., Ostrovsky, R., Reyzin, L., Smith, A.D.: Fuzzy extractors: how to generate strong keys from biometrics and other noisy data. SIAM J. Comput. 38(1), 97–139 (2008)

[DS16] Ducas, L., Stehlé, D.: Sanitization of FHE ciphertexts. In: Fischlin, M., Coron, J.-S. (eds.) EUROCRYPT 2016, Part I. LNCS, vol. 9665, pp. 294–310. Springer, Heidelberg (2016). https://doi.org/10.1007/978-3-662-49890-3_12

[DWF22] Dai, X., Wu, W., Feng, Y.: Summation rather than concatenation: a more efficient MKFHE scheme in the plain model. Cryptology ePrint Archive, Report 2022/055 (2022). https://eprint.iacr.org/2022/055

[EH14] van Erven, T., Harremoës, P.: Rényi divergence and kullback-leibler divergence. IEEE Trans. Inf. Theory 60(7), 3797–3820 (2014)

[GAL13] Gil, M., Alajaji, F., Linder, T.: Rényi divergence measures for commonly used univariate continuous distributions. Inf. Sci. 249, 124–131 (2013)

[GI99] Gilboa, N., Ishai, Y.: Compressing cryptographic resources. In: Wiener, M. (ed.) CRYPTO 1999. LNCS, vol. 1666, pp. 591–608. Springer, Heidelberg (1999). https://doi.org/10.1007/3-540-48405-1_37

[HLR07] Hsiao, C.-Y., Lu, C.-J., Reyzin, L.: Conditional computational entropy, or toward separating pseudoentropy from compressibility. In: Naor, M. (ed.) EUROCRYPT 2007. LNCS, vol. 4515, pp. 169–186. Springer, Heidelberg (2007). https://doi.org/10.1007/978-3-540-72540-4_10

[HV22] Huguenin-Dumittan, L., Vaudenay, S.: On IND-qCCA security in the ROM and its applications - CPA security is sufficient for TLS 1.3. In: Dunkelman, O., Dziembowski, S. (eds.) EUROCRYPT 2022, Part III. LNCS, vol. 13277, pp. 613–642. Springer, Heidelberg (2022). https://doi.org/10.1007/978-3-031-07082-2_22

[JRS17] Jain, A., Rasmussen, P.M.R., Sahai, A.: Threshold fully homomorphic encryption. Cryptology ePrint Archive, Report 2017/257 (2017). https://eprint.iacr.org/2017/257

[Kra+19] Kraitsberg, M., Lindell, Y., Osheter, V., Smart, N.P., Talibi Alaoui, Y.: Adding distributed decryption and key generation to a ring-LWE based CCA encryption scheme. In: Jang-Jaccard, J., Guo, F. (eds.) ACISP 2019. LNCS, vol. 11547, pp. 192–210. Springer, Cham (2019). https://doi.org/10.1007/978-3-030-21548-4_11

[LM21] Li, B., Micciancio, D.: On the security of homomorphic encryption on approximate numbers. In: Canteaut, A., Standaert, F.-X. (eds.) EUROCRYPT 2021, Part I. LNCS, vol. 12696, pp. 648–677. Springer, Cham (2021). https://doi.org/10.1007/978-3-030-77870-5_23

[LS15] Langlois, A., Stehlé, D.: Worst-case to average-case reductions for module lattices. Des. Codes Cryptogr. **75**(3), 565–599 (2015)

[Lyu+20] Lyubashevsky, V., et al.: CRYSTALS-DILITHIUM. Technical report, National Institute of Standards and Technology (2020). https://csrc.nist.gov/projects/post-quantum-cryptography/post-quantum-cryptography-standardization/round-3-submissions

[MPR06] Micali, S., Pass, R., Rosen, A.: Input-indistinguishable computation. In: 47th FOCS, pp. 367–378. IEEE Computer Society Press (2006)

[Nae+20] Naehrig, M., et al.: FrodoKEM. Technical report, National Institute of Standards and Technology (2020). https://csrc.nist.gov/projects/post-quantum-cryptography/post-quantum-cryptography-standardization/round-3-submissions

[Reg05] Regev, O.: On lattices, learning with errors, random linear codes, and cryptography. In: Gabow, H.N., Fagin, R. (eds.) 37th ACM STOC, pp. 84–93. ACM Press (2005)

[Ros20] Rossi, M.: Extended security of lattice-based cryptography. (Sécurité étendue de la cryptographie fondée sur les réseaux euclidiens). Ph.D. thesis, Paris Sciences et Lettres University, France (2020)

[Sch+20] Schwabe, P., et al.: CRYSTALS-KYBER. Technical report, National Institute of Standards and Technology (2020). https://csrc.nist.gov/projects/post-quantum-cryptography/post-quantum-cryptography-standardization/round-3-submissions

[Shi22] Shiehian, S.: mrNISC from LWE with polynomial modulus. In: Galdi, C., Jarecki, S. (eds.) SCN 2022. LNCS, vol. 13409, pp. 481–493. Springer, Cham (2022)

[Val84] Valiant, L.G.: Short monotone formulae for the majority function. J. Algorithms **5**(3), 363–366 (1984)

VSS from Distributed ZK Proofs
and Applications

Shahla Atapoor[1], Karim Baghery[1]([⊠]), Daniele Cozzo[1,2],
and Robi Pedersen[1]

[1] COSIC, KU Leuven, Leuven, Belgium
{shahla.atapoor,karim.baghery,daniele.cozzo,robi.pedersen}@kuleuven.be
[2] IMDEA Software Institute, Madrid, Spain

Abstract. Non-Interactive Verifiable Secret Sharing (NI-VSS) is a technique for distributing a secret among a group of individuals in a verifiable manner, such that shareholders can verify the validity of their received share and only a specific number of them can access the secret. VSS is a fundamental tool in cryptography and distributed computing. In this paper, we present an extremely efficient NI-VSS scheme using Zero-Knowledge (ZK) proofs on secret shared data. While prior VSS schemes have implicitly used ZK proofs on secret shared data, we specifically use their formal definition recently provided by Boneh et al. in CRYPTO 2019. The proposed NI-VSS scheme uses a quantum random oracle and a quantum computationally hiding commitment scheme in a black-box manner, which ensures its ease of use, especially in post-quantum threshold protocols. Implementation results further solidify its practicality and superiority over current constructions. With the new VSS scheme, for parameter sets $(n,t) = (128, 63)$ and $(2048, 1023)$, a dealer can share a secret in less than 0.02 and 2.0 s, respectively, and shareholders can verify their shares in less than 0.4 and 5.0 ms. Compared to the well-established Pedersen VSS scheme, for the same parameter sets, at the cost of $2.5\times$ higher communication, the new scheme is respectively $22.5\times$ and $3.25\times$ faster in the sharing phase, and notably needs $271\times$ and $479\times$ less time in the verification. Leveraging the new NI-VSS scheme, we revisit several classic and PQ-secure threshold protocols and improve their efficiency. Our revisions led to more efficient versions of both the Pedersen DKG protocol and the GJKR threshold signature scheme. We show similar efficiency enhancements and improved resilience to malicious parties in isogeny-based DKG and threshold signature schemes. We think, due to its remarkable efficiency and ease of use, the new NI-VSS scheme can be a valuable tool for a wide range of threshold protocols.

Keywords: Verifiable Secret Sharing · ZK Proofs on Secret Shared Data · Shamir Secret Sharing · DKG · Threshold Signatures · Isogenies

1 Introduction

Secret sharing schemes are fundamental tools in the field of threshold cryptography and secure multi-party computation. Such schemes consist of a sharing

© International Association for Cryptologic Research 2023
J. Guo and R. Steinfeld (Eds.): ASIACRYPT 2023, LNCS 14438, pp. 405–440, 2023.
https://doi.org/10.1007/978-981-99-8721-4_13

phase, where a dealer shares a secret among the shareholders, followed by a reconstruction phase where qualified shareholders collaborate to reconstruct the original secret. Standard secret sharing schemes, such as Shmair's protocol [33], assume the presence of honest parties but do not provide security against malicious participants. Verifiable Secret Sharing (VSS) schemes [15,20] have been developed to address the challenges posed by malicious players. These schemes aim to withstand various attacks, including incorrect share distribution by the dealer and malicious behavior by the shareholders (e.g., using incorrect shares) during the reconstruction phase. Depending on the communication model, to incorporate verifiability, typically interaction among the dealer and shareholders is required. It can however be shown that, assuming the dealer has a broadcast channel, a single message from the dealer to the shareholders can be sufficient. This is known as a Non-Interactive VSS (NI-VSS).

Most existing constructions of VSS schemes are based on regular secret-sharing schemes, often starting with Shamir's scheme [33], and then adding verifiability features on top [5,15,20,23–25,29,32]. The known discrete-logarithm (DL) based VSS schemes such as those by Feldman [20], Pedersen [29], Schoenmakers [32], and their variants, utilize Shamir secret sharing and achieve verifiability by having the dealer publish the shares and coefficients of the underlying secret polynomial in the group. Then, they leverage the homomorphic property of the group to convince the shareholders [20,29], or an external verifier [32], that the secret sharing is performed correctly. DL-based VSS schemes are typically non-interactive and support public verifiability, allowing both shareholders and external verifiers to verify the validity of the shares without interaction. However, due to the threat posed by Shor's algorithm [34], discrete logarithm based VSS schemes are not suitable for cryptographic protocols (e.g., distributed key generation schemes, threshold signatures, etc.), that require post-quantum security. Gentry, Halevi, and Lyubashevsky [24] recently proposed a practical non-interactive publicly VSS scheme that relies on lattice-based and DL-based problems at the same time, unfortunately making it unsuitable for use in post-quantum secure threshold protocols. Given the limitations and vulnerabilities of existing NI-VSS schemes, it becomes imperative to develop an efficient post-quantum secure VSS scheme that can also address challenges of scalability and computational overhead. Such VSS schemes can pave the way for the realization of more efficient post-quantum threshold protocols.

In the VSS scheme proposed by Ben-or, Goldwasser, and Wigderson (BGW) [5], a dealer employs a distributed Zero-Knowledge (ZK) proof scheme based on bivariate polynomials to add (designated) verifiability to the Shamir secret sharing scheme. The BGW VSS scheme achieves Information-Theoretical (IT) security and can be employed in both classical and post-quantum secure threshold protocols. However, in their (non-interactive) ZK proof scheme the verifiers need to interact two-by-two for share validation and to achieve (perfect) soundness their scheme requires at least two-thirds of the designated verifiers to be honest.

In Crypto 2019, Boneh et al. [11] provided a formal definition for ZK proofs over secret shared data and presented several feasibility and infeasibility results.

In a ZK proof scheme over secret shared data, there is a single prover P and n (designated) verifiers $\{V_i\}_{i=1}^n$, and each verifier V_i holds a piece (share) x_i of an input (statement) x, which is distributed among n participants. The prover's task is to convince the (designated) verifiers that the main input x belongs to a specific language L. Essentially, the prover P possesses full knowledge of x, while each verifier V_i possesses a secret share denoted as x_i. In their best feasibility (and positive) result, Boneh et al. [11] demonstrated that, in the majority honest setting, using a robust encoding scheme, any multi-round public-coin linear Interactive Oracle Proof (IOP) for a non-distributed relation R_L can be compiled into a secure ZK proof scheme over secret shared data. The resulting distributed ZK proof scheme satisfies (computational) soundness against the prover and $t < n/2$ malicious verifiers. Moreover, it guarantees ZK even if t of the verifiers collude [11, Section 6.3], where t represents a threshold parameter in the underlying encoding scheme. Boneh et al. [11] coined the term "Strong zero-knowledge" to describe this variant of ZK, which ensures that even if up to t verifiers collude, they learn nothing about the witness. We will refer to this notion as "threshold zero-knowledge" (TZK) in this paper.[1] Based on the formal definitions, we can restate that the BGW VSS scheme [5] has been proven to achieve TZK and (perfect) soundness against the prover, given that at least two-thirds of the (designated) verifiers are honest.

Consequently, a generic approach for constructing a ZK proof scheme over secret shared data for n-distributed relations R_i involves first developing a multi-round public-coin IOP for the non-distributed relation R. Subsequently, Boneh et al.'s compiler can be utilized to transform it into a distributed ZK proof scheme, featuring a single prover P and n designated verifiers $\{V_i\}_{i=1}^n$. However, it is worth noting that generic approaches are typically less efficient compared to ad-hoc constructions tailored for specific purposes in practical implementations.

Our Contributions. We summarize the contributions of this paper as follows:

An Efficient Post-Quantum Secure NI-TZK for the Shamir Relation. Considering the feasibility result of Boneh et al. [11], we directly (without using their compiler [11]) construct an efficient Non-Interactive TZK (NI-TZK) proof scheme for the n-distributed relations $R_1, \ldots, R_n$, where

$$R_i = \{(x_i, f(X)) | f(i) = x_i\}. \tag{1}$$

Here $f(X) \in \mathbb{Z}_N[X]_t$ is a secret polynomial in X of degree (at most) t and with coefficients defined over the ring $\mathbb{Z}_N$. The proposed construction is built in the majority honest setting (i.e., the majority of the verifiers are honest) and utilizes a quantum computationally hiding commitment scheme. We prove (in Theorem 1) that in the Quantum Random Oracle Model (QROM), the proposed

---

[1] This choice is done for two main reasons. First, *strong* ZK might lead to misunderstandings, as the majority of verifiers is actually honest in our cases. Second, we risk confusion by using the abbreviation SZK, which usually stands for *statistical* zero-knowledge.

NI-TZK proof scheme satisfies completeness, TZK, and soundness against the prover and t malicious verifiers, as formally defined in [11].

Table 1. A comparison among BGW [5], Pedersen [29] and the new NI-VSS schemes.

BGW VSS [5]	Pedersen VSS [29]	This Work
uses bivariate polynomials (lightweight operations)	based on discrete logarithm (heavy operations)	based on hash functions (lightweight operations)
achieves Information Theoretical (IT) security	achieves IT and classic (computational) security	achieves post-quantum (computational) security
needs $\geq \frac{2}{3}$ honest parties	needs $\geq \frac{1}{2}$ honest parties	needs $\geq \frac{1}{2}$ honest parties
verification is designated and to verify the shares the verifiers <u>need</u> to interact two-by-two, which induces $O(n)$ communication for each shareholder	verification is designated (but can also be made public) and to verify the shares the verifiers <u>do not need</u> to interact two-by-two	verification is designated and to verify the shares the verifiers <u>do not need</u> to interact two-by-two

NI-VSS Schemes from NI-TZK Proofs and a Quantum Secure Scheme. We further show how one can use a secure NI-TZK proof scheme for the n-distributed relations given in Eq. (1), and build a *computationally secure* NI-VSS scheme based on Shamir secret sharing in the majority honest setting. Building upon that, we use the proposed NI-TZK proof scheme and present an extremely efficient computationally secure NI-VSS scheme that works over general rings, and is proven to be secure in the QROM. One notable factor contributing to the efficiency of new VSS scheme is using lightweight cryptographic operations such as hashing and polynomial evaluation, in the underlying NI-TZK proof scheme. Within the new VSS scheme, we introduce a novel reconstruction approach that, in scenarios where the dealer is one of the parties (e.g., as in the DKG protocols and threshold signatures), can lead to the development of more efficient threshold protocols.

Our resulting NI-VSS scheme serves as a post-quantum secure alternative to the classical Pedersen VSS scheme [29] (or Feldman's VSS scheme [20]) when public verifiability is unnecessary. We later show that this scenario often occurs in various threshold protocols. It can also be considered an alternative to the Information-Theoretically (IT) secure BGW VSS [5] in cases where quantum computational security suffices and there is a desire to reduce communication between parties, or when assuming two-thirds of the parties are honest among the shareholders is challenging. Table 1 provides a comprehensive summary of the key features of our proposed NI-VSS scheme, comparing it to the well-known Pedersen [29] and BGW [5] VSS schemes from various perspectives.

To assess the empirical performance of new VSS scheme, we implemented a prototype of it alongside the Pedersen scheme [29] using SageMath. Implementation results show that using the new NI-VSS scheme a dealer can share a secret with 2048 parties in 2 s, and shareholders can verify the validity of their shares in less than 5 ms. When considering the same number of parties and aiming for 128-bit quantum security, the dealer broadcasts a proof of approximately 130 KB and privately sends less than 32B to each shareholder. Our empirical analysis affirm the superiority of our NI-VSS scheme over the well-known Pedersen scheme in both sharing and verification steps, in addition to post-quantum security. The new NI-VSS scheme demonstrates significant efficiency improvements in the verification phase, achieving speedups of approximately 271×, 437×, and 498× compared to the Pedersen scheme for (n, t) values of $(128, 63)$, $(512, 255)$, and $(8194, 4095)$, respectively. In the sharing phase under the same settings, our scheme is about 22.6×, 9.3×, and 1.57× faster than the Pedersen scheme. In terms of communication cost, compared to Pedersen scheme, our VSS scheme increases the dealer's broadcast by a factor of 2.5.

We believe, the simplicity and efficiency of our new NI-VSS scheme can make it an attractive choice for various large-scale threshold protocols, especially those that require post-quantum security.

Application Examples of New NI-VSS Scheme. As our next major contribution, we leverage the new NI-VSS scheme and revisit several threshold protocols based on discrete logarithm and isogenies, and improve their efficiency, and in some cases also decrease the lower bound on the number of honest parties.

More Efficient Threshold Protocols in the DL Setting. As mentioned previously, the new VSS scheme serves as a more efficient alternative to the well-established Pedersen VSS scheme [29] when public verifiability is not required. Our observations indicate that this scenario commonly arises in Distributed Key Generation (DKG) protocols and threshold signatures. In light of this insight, we revisit Pedersen's DKG protocol [28] in conjunction with the robust threshold signature scheme proposed by Gennaro, Jarecki, Krawczyk, and Rabin (GJKR) [22], which employs Schnorr's signature for signing and Pedersen's DKG protocol for the generation of (secret, public, and ephemeral) keys. To this end, we first build an NI-TZK proof scheme for the following set of n-distributed relations,

$$R_i = (y, x_i, f(X))|y = g^{f(0)} \wedge f(i) = x_i, \quad i = 1, \ldots, n \qquad (2)$$

where $f(X) \in \mathbb{Z}_q[X]_t$ is a secret polynomial in X of degree (at most) t with coefficients defined over the field $\mathbb{Z}_q$. This NI-TZK proof scheme serves as the main component for our revisions and holds potential interest in other DL-based threshold protocols that utilize Shamir secret sharing. Subsequently, we present a new DKG protocol and a Schnorr-based threshold signature scheme, which can be considered as more efficient alternatives to Pedersen's DKG protocol [28] and the GJKR threshold signature [22].

When comparing our resulting variants to the original schemes, there are certain trade-offs. While our variants slightly increase communication costs, they improve computational efficiency in both schemes. In summary, in our proposed DKG protocol, each party needs to perform approximately $2n$ exponentiations in the group, $5n$ (short) hashes, and $3n$ degree-t polynomial evaluations in the field.

This represents a factor of $t \approx n/2$ improvement compared to the secure version of Pedersen DKG protocol [22], which demands roughly $2tn+2n$ exponentiations in the group and $2n$ degree-t polynomial evaluations in the field. While incurring slightly higher communication costs, our new threshold signature scheme offers similar improvements over the GJKR threshold signature scheme [22]. The detailed comparisons are provided in Sect. 4 (and Table 4).

More Efficient Threshold Protocols from Isogenies. As previously discussed, the new NI-VSS scheme can also be integrated into various post-quantum secure threshold protocols. Notably, it can serve as an alternative to the BGW VSS [5] in certain scenarios. By adopting the new VSS scheme in place of BGW, it becomes possible to reduce communication costs and improve tolerance for malicious parties, albeit at the expense of transitioning from information-theoretic (IT) security to quantum computational security. Taking this into consideration, we revisit the isogeny-based DKG protocol developed by Atapoor, Baghery, Cozzo, and Pedersen [2], alongside the CSI-FiSh-based threshold signature scheme introduced by Campos and Muth [13].

Currently, their DKG protocol [2] stands as the most efficient scheme in terms of isogeny computations within the CSIDH (Commutative Supersingular Isogeny Diffie-Hellman) setting [14]. We show that by integrating the new NI-VSS scheme into the VSS step of their DKG protocol, we can address two bottlenecks present in their scheme. Specifically, we reduce the requirement from needing at least $2/3$ honest shareholders to a more practical threshold of just $1/2$. Additionally, we eliminate the need for pairwise interactive verification, which was a primary reason to the high communication overhead in the VSS step of their DKG protocol. While these enhancements do come at the cost of sacrificing IT security in the VSS step in favor of quantum computational security, it's worth noting that the DKG protocols proposed in [2] rely on quantum computational security from the outset. These improvements can make the revisited DKG protocol highly appealing for use in CSIDH-based threshold settings. The resulting DKG protocol retains the same efficiency in terms of isogeny computations.

The threshold signature scheme proposed by Campos and Muth [13] is based on the basic version of the CSI-FiSh signature [9], which features shorter public keys but longer signature sizes, as well as slower signing and verification algorithms. To enhance the efficiency of their threshold signature, we introduce two key modifications. First, we adapt their scheme to work with the CSI-SharK signature [1], which has been demonstrated to outperform CSI-FiSh in the threshold setting. This modification enables us to leverage our revisited DKG protocol, resulting in more efficient key generation for the resulting robust threshold signature scheme. Furthermore, we apply a similar strategy used in the construction of the revisited DKG protocol to improve the efficiency of ephemeral key generation in the resulting threshold signature. This further enhances the efficiency of the distributed signing protocol, leading to the development of a new and more efficient isogeny-based threshold robust signature scheme.

Outline. In Sect. 2, we provide an overview of some preliminary concepts. In Sect. 3, we first present our NI-VSS scheme, and then evaluate its performance through a prototype implementation. Leveraging the proposed NI-VSS scheme, in Sect. 4, we revisit the well-known Pedersen DKG protocol [29] and the GJKR threshold signature scheme [22], introducing new variants that offer improved efficiency. Similarly, in Sect. 5, we revisit two isogeny-based DKG protocols [2] and a threshold signature scheme [13], and present two new versions that offer improved efficiency. Finally, in Sect. 6, we conclude the paper.

2   Preliminaries

Notation. We let λ denote a security parameter. A function is called *negligible in* X, written $\mathsf{negl}(X)$, if for any constant c, there exists some X_0, such that $f(X) < X^{-c}$ for $X > X_0$. A function that is negligible in the security parameter λ is simply called negligible. We use the assignment operator $\leftarrow$ to denote uniform sampling from a set Ξ, e.g. $x \leftarrow \Xi$. We write $\mathbb{Z}_N := \mathbb{Z}/N\mathbb{Z}$ and $\mathbb{Z}_N[X]_t$ for polynomials of degree t in the variable X and with coefficients in $\mathbb{Z}_N$. For $n \in \mathbb{N}$, we write $[n] = \{1, \ldots, n\}$. Finally all logarithms are in base 2.

We also introduce the notion of *exceptional sets*, which occur naturally when working over rings $\mathbb{Z}_N$.

Definition 1 (Exceptional set [4,10,16]). *An exceptional set (modulo N) is a set $\Xi_k = \{c_1, \ldots, c_k\} \subseteq \mathbb{Z}_N$, where the pairwise difference of all distinct elements is invertible modulo N. If further the pairwise sum of all elements is invertible modulo N, Ξ_k is called a* superexceptional set *(modulo N).*

2.1   Zero-Knowledge Proofs on Secret Shared Data

In typical NIZK (non-interactive zero-knowledge) arguments for NP languages, there is a single prover P and a single verifier V, where P knows both a statement x and witness for the statement w, while V only knows the statement x. In CRYPTO 2019, Boneh et al. [11], presented formal definitions for distributed ZK proofs which a prover interacts with several verifiers $\{V_i\}_{i=1}^n$ over a network that includes secure point-to-point channels. In such a model, each verifier V_j holds a piece (share) $x^{(j)} \in \mathbb{F}^{l_j}$ of an input (statement) x, and the prover's task is to convince the verifiers that the main input x is in some language $L \subseteq \mathbb{F}^l$.

Similar to the typical cases, such proof systems must be complete, meaning that if $x \in L$, an honest prover will be able to convince honest verifiers. Similarly, they should satisfy soundness, meaning that if $x \notin L$, then all verifiers will reject the verification except for a negligible probability. However, in certain settings, including ours, a limited number of verifiers may be malicious and collude with the adversarial prover. In such cases, the malicious verifiers might accept a fake proof. Finally, the proof system must satisfy a variant of ZK, so called *threshold ZK*, as introduced (as strong ZK) by Boneh et al. [11]. TZK implies that any subset of the verifiers up to a certain bound should learn no additional information about statement x, beyond their own shares and the fact that $x \in L$. Note that in standard ZK, the verifier learns the statement x and the fact that $x \in L$, but in threshold ZK, a single verifier only learns his share of x and the fact that $x \in L$. In other words, a set of verifiers only learn that they are jointly holding pieces (shares) of $x \in L$.

Definition 2 (Distributed Inputs, Languages, and Relations [11]). *Let n be a number of parties, $\mathbb{F}$ be a finite field, and $l, l_1, l_2, \cdots, l_n \in \mathbb{N}$ be length parameters, where $l = l_1 + l_2 + \cdots + l_n$. An n-distributed input over $\mathbb{F}$ (or just distributed input) is a vector $x = x^{(1)} \parallel x^{(2)} \parallel \cdots \parallel x^{(n)} \in \mathbb{F}^l$ where $x^{(i)} \in \mathbb{F}^{l_i}$, and it refers to a piece (or share) of x. An n-distributed language L is a set of n-distributed inputs. A distributed NP relation with witness length h is a binary relation $R(x, w)$ where x is an n-distributed input and $w \in \mathbb{F}^h$. We assume that all x in L and $(x, w) \in R$ share the same length parameters. Finally, we let $L_R = \{x : \exists w (x, w) \in R\}$.*

Next, we recall the formal definition provided by Boneh et al. [11] for ZK proofs over shared data which originally are defined over a field. In some cases, we employ an extended version of their definitions that naturally encompasses rings. In this model, parties can have synchronous communication over secure point-to-point channels.

Definition 3 (n-Verifier Interactive Proofs [11]). *An n-Verifier Interactive Proof protocol over $\mathbb{F}$ is an interactive protocol $\Pi = (P, V_1, V_2, \cdots, V_n)$ involving a prover P and n verifiers $\{V_i\}_{i=1}^n$. The protocol proceeds as follows.*

- *In the beginning of the protocol the prover P holds an n-distributed input $x = x^{(1)} \parallel x^{(2)} \parallel \cdots \parallel x^{(n)} \in \mathbb{F}^l$, a witness $w \in \mathbb{F}^h$, and each verifier V_j holds an input piece (or share) $x^{(j)}$.*
- *The protocol allows the parties to communicate in synchronous rounds over secure point-to-point channels. While honest parties send messages according to Π, malicious parties (i.e., adversary) can send arbitrary messages.*
- *At the end, each verifier outputs either 1 (accept) or 0 (reject) based on its view, where the view of V_j consists of its input piece $x^{(j)}$, random input $r^{(j)}$, and messages it received during the protocol execution.*

In the rest, $\Pi(x, w)$ denotes running Π on shared input x and witness w, and says that $\Pi(x, w)$ accepts (respectively, rejects) if at the end all verifiers output 1 (resp., 0). $View_{\Pi,T}(x, w)$ denotes the (joint distribution of) views of verifiers $\{V_j\}_{j \in T}$ in the execution of Π on the distributed input x and witness w.

Let $R(x, w)$ be a k-distributed relation over finite field $\mathbb{F}$. We say that an n-verifier interactive proof protocol $\Pi = (P, V_1, \cdots, V_n)$ is a distributed threshold ZK proof protocol for R with t-security against malicious prover *and* malicious verifiers, and with soundness error ϵ, if Π satisfies the following properties [11]:

Definition 4 (Completeness). *For every n-distributed input $x = x^{(1)} \parallel x^{(2)} \parallel \cdots \parallel x^{(n)} \in \mathbb{F}^l$, and witness $w \in \mathbb{F}^h$, such that $(x, w) \in R$, the execution of $\Pi(x^{(1)} \parallel x^{(2)} \parallel \cdots \parallel x^{(n)}, w)$ accepts with probability 1.*

Definition 5 (Soundness Against Prover and t Verifiers). *For every $T \subseteq [n]$ of size $|T| \leq t$, an $\mathcal{A}$ controlling the prover P and verifiers $\{V_j\}_{j \in T}$, n-distributed input $x = x^{(1)} \parallel x^{(2)} \parallel \cdots \parallel x^{(n)} \in \mathbb{F}^l$, and witness $w \in \mathbb{F}^h$ the following holds. If there is no n-distributed input $x' \in L_R$ such that $x'_H = x_H$, where $H = [n]/T$, the execution of $\Pi^*(x, w)$ rejects except with at most ϵ probability, where here Π^* denotes the interaction of $\mathcal{A}$ with the honest verifiers.*

Definition 6 (Threshold ZK). *For every $T \subseteq [n]$ of size $|T| \leq t$ and an $\mathcal{A}$ controlling $\{V_j\}_{j \in T}$, there exists a simulator S such that for every n-distributed input $x = x^{(1)} \parallel x^{(2)} \parallel \cdots \parallel x^{(n)} \in \mathbb{F}^l$, and witness $w \in \mathbb{F}^h$ such that $(x, w) \in R$, we have $\mathcal{S}((x^{(j)})_{j \in T}) \equiv View_{\Pi^*, T}(x, w)$. Here, Π^* denotes the interaction of adversary $\mathcal{A}$ with the honest prover P and the honest verifiers $\{V_j\}_{j \in T}$.*

Remark 1 (Threshold Honest-Verifier ZK). In the context of Threshold ZK, one may consider a relaxed definition, Threshold *Honest-Verifier* ZK, that retains the same properties as the original definition, with the added requirement that the subset of verifiers, $\{V_j\}_{j \in T}$, is stipulated to follow the protocol honestly.

2.2 Verifiable Secret Sharing

Secret sharing is a technique for securely distributing a secret among a group of parties, where no single party can learn the secret individually. However, when a sufficient number of parties come together and combine their 'shares', the original secret can be reconstructed. Throughout the paper, our studied protocols use Shamir Secret Sharing [33] for securely sharing a secret, which we review below.

Shamir Secret Sharing. A $(t+1, n)$-Shamir secret sharing scheme [33] allows n parties to individually hold a share x_i of a common secret x_0, such that any subset of t parties or less are not able to learn any information about the secret x_0, while any subset of at least $t+1$ parties are able to efficiently reconstruct the common secret x_0. In more detail, this is achieved via polynomial interpolation over the ring $\mathbb{Z}_N$. A common polynomial $f(x) \in \mathbb{Z}_N[x]_t$ is chosen, such that the secret x_0 is set to be its constant term, namely $x_0 = f(0)$. Each party P_i for $i \in \{1, \cdots, n\}$ is assigned the secret share $x_i = f(i)$. Then any subset $Q \subseteq \{1, \ldots, n\}$ of at least t parties can reconstruct the secret x_0 via Lagrange interpolation by computing $x_0 = f(0) = \sum_{i \in Q} x_i \cdot L_{0,i}^Q$, where

$$L_{0,i}^Q := \prod_{j \in Q \setminus \{i\}} \frac{j}{j-i} \pmod{N}.$$

are the Lagrange basis polynomials evaluated at 0. Any subset of less than t parties are not able to find $x_0 = f(0)$, as this is information theoretically hidden from the other shares. In the case where $\mathbb{Z}_N$ is a ring, the difference of any elements in $\{1, \ldots, n\}$ must be invertible modulo N, thus $\{1, \ldots, n\}$ must be an exceptional set. This is only the case if n is smaller than the smallest prime divisor q of N. In the case where more than q parties want to participate in the protocol, we would have to work in a subgroup $\mathbb{Z}_{N'} \subset \mathbb{Z}_N$ such that the smallest divisor of N' is larger than q.

Verifiable Secret Sharing (VSS). A standard secret sharing scheme is designed to be resilient against passive attacks. In many applications, a secret sharing scheme needs to be secure against the malicious dealer or parties with active attacks. This is achieved through VSS schemes, which were first introduced in 1985 [15]. Shamir secret sharing scheme by default does not qualify as a VSS scheme, as it does not provide protection against malicious participants (i.e., the dealer and shareholders).

2.3   Threshold Signatures

A threshold signature scheme enables a group of authorized parties to collectively sign a message m, generating a signature σ that can be verified using a single public key pk. Specifically, a threshold signature scheme, in terms of an $(t+1, n)$-threshold access structure, is defined as follows:

Definition 7. *A* threshold digital signature scheme *consists of three probabilistic algorithms:* KeyGen, Sign, *and* Verify.

- KeyGen (1^λ)*: Given the security parameter as input and returns the public key* pk *along with a set of secret keys* sk_i *- one secret key per party. (For simplicity, we limit ourselves to the case where each party has a single share of the secret, focusing on Shamir and full-threshold secret sharing.)*
- Sign $(\{sk_i\}_{i \in Q}, m)$*: Given as input a* qualified set *of private keys and a message and returns a signature on the message.*
- Verify $(pk, (\sigma, m))$*: Given* pk *and a signature* σ *on a message* m*, and outputs a bit that is equal to one if and only if the signature on* m *is valid.*

In essence, security for a threshold signature scheme means that an unqualified group of parties cannot forge a signature on a new message. In addition, for distributed signatures, we require that a valid output signature is indistinguishable from the signature produced by the signing algorithm of the underlying non-thresholdized scheme with the same public key.

3   VSS from ZK Proofs over Shared Data

In this section, we propose a novel Non-Interactive Verifiable Secret Sharing (NI-VSS) scheme that utilizes ZK proofs over secret shared data [8,11] to prove the validity and consistency of the individual shares. The proposed scheme does not rely on a concrete cryptographic hard problem, rather than a random oracle and a collapsing (quantum) computationally hiding commitment scheme.

To build the NI-VSS scheme, we first construct a non-interactive proof scheme which allows a single prover to convince a set of verifiers that they have each received a distinct evaluation of a polynomial $f(X) \in \mathbb{Z}_N[X]_t$.[2] It is worth noting

---

[2] In general $\mathbb{Z}_N$ will constitute a ring. In later applications, we sometimes choose N to be a prime, so that $\mathbb{Z}_N$ becomes a field.

that to achieve soundness, the number of honest verifiers is supposed to exceed t. On the other hand, to achieve threshold zero-knowledge, we assume that an adversarial prover can corrupt at most t verifiers. Thus, we assume the number of verifiers to be greater than or equal to $2t+1$. We then demonstrate that our proposed scheme satisfies completeness (Definition 4), soundness against the prover and t malicious verifiers (Definition 5), and threshold ZK (Definition 6). We subsequently use the resulting Non-Interactive Threshold ZK (NI-TZK) proof scheme and build an efficient NI-VSS scheme based on Shamir secret sharing.

3.1   A NI-TZK Proof Protocol for Shamir Secret Sharing

As the key building block for our novel NI-VSS scheme, in this section, we present an efficient NI-TZK proof scheme that can be used to build a NI-VSS based on Shamir secret sharing. The new NI-TZK proof scheme is built for a collection of relations $R_1, \ldots, R_n$ with the same witness space, where each statement can be verified independently by individual verifiers. Given the shared input $x = x_1 \parallel x_2 \parallel \ldots \parallel x_n$, the prover proves the existence of a witness w that satisfies $(x_i, w) \in R_i$ for every $i \in 1, \ldots, n$. The proof includes proof pieces $\{\pi_i\}_{i \in 1, \ldots, n}$, where π_i allows the verifier V_i to check the validity of x_i in relation to R_i. The prover has a secret polynomial $f(X) \in \mathbb{Z}_N[X]_t$, and wants to prove the following n-distributed relations,

$$R_i = \{(x_i, f(X)) | f(i) = x_i\}, \tag{3}$$

where $i = 1, \ldots, n$. For the sake of convenience, we will refer to the relation mentioned above as the Shamir relation throughout the rest of the paper.

Prover: Given, a witness polynomial $f(X) \in \mathbb{Z}_N[X]_t$, an input $x = (x_1, \cdots, x_n)$, proceed as follows and output a proof π of the relations in eq. (3).
1. Sample $b(X) \leftarrow \mathbb{Z}_N[X]_t$ uniformly at random;
2. For $i = 1, \ldots, n$: Sample $y_i, y_i' \leftarrow \{0,1\}^\lambda$ uniformly at random; Set $\mathsf{C}_i \leftarrow \mathcal{C}(b(i), y_i)$ and $\mathsf{C}_i' \leftarrow \mathcal{C}(x_i, y_i')$;
3. Set $d \leftarrow \mathcal{H}(\mathsf{C}, \mathsf{C}')$, where $\mathsf{C} = (\mathsf{C}_1, \ldots, \mathsf{C}_n)$, $\mathsf{C}' = (\mathsf{C}_1', \ldots, \mathsf{C}_n')$;
4. Set $r(X) \leftarrow b(X) - d \cdot f(X) \mod N$;
5. Set $\pi := (\mathsf{C}, \mathsf{C}', r(X), \{\pi_i\}_{i=1}^n)$, where $\pi_i = (y_i, y_i')$;
6. Publish $(\mathsf{C}, \mathsf{C}', r(X))$; Send individual proof $\{\pi_i = (y_i, y_i')\}_{i=1}^n$ to verifier V_i.

Verification: For $i = 1, \cdots, n$, each verifier (shareholder) i has a statement $x_i \in \mathbb{Z}_N$, and a proof $((\mathsf{C}, \mathsf{C}', r(X)), (y_i, y_i'))$. Given the set of statements and proofs for $i \in 1, \ldots, n$ the verifiers (i.e., shareholders) proceed as follows:
1. Verifier i acts as below and outputs **true** or **false**.
    (a) If $\mathsf{C}_i' \neq \mathcal{C}(x_i, y_i')$ return **false**;
    (b) Set $d \leftarrow \mathcal{H}(\mathsf{C}, \mathsf{C}')$;
    (c) If $\mathsf{C}_i == \mathcal{C}(r(i) + d \cdot x_i, y_i)$ return **true**; otherwise **false**;
2. Return **true** if *all* the verifiers return **true**; otherwise returns **false**.

Fig. 1. A NI-TZK Proof Scheme for Shamir Secret Sharing.

Figure 1 describes the proof generation and verification of the new NI-TZK proof scheme for the Shamir relation given in Eq. (3), where $\mathcal{H} : \{0,1\}^* \to \Xi_k$ is a random oracle with Ξ_k an exceptional set of size k,[3] and $\mathcal{C} : \{0,1\}^* \times \{0,1\}^\lambda \to \{0,1\}^{2\lambda}$ is a commitment scheme that is collapsing [37, Def. 12] and quantum computationally hiding. Next, we show the proposed NI-TZK proof scheme (given in Fig. 1) satisfies the key security requirements of a ZK proof protocol over shared data, as defined in Sect. 2.1.

Remark 2. The challenge space of the protocol in Fig. 1 is $|\Xi_k| = k$. When $\mathbb{Z}_N$ is a cryptographically sized field, we can easily choose $\Xi_k = \mathbb{Z}_N$ to achieve a negligible soundness error, i.e. below $2^{-\lambda}$. In the case where $\mathbb{Z}_N$ is a ring, we might have the case that the largest exceptional set has size $k < 2^\lambda$. In that case the protocol from Fig. 1 would have to be repeated in the standard fashion: defining $S = \lceil \lambda / \log k \rceil$, we would have to sample S different $b_j(X)$ and construct S responses $r_j(X) = b_j(X) - d_j f(X)$, sampling the d_j using the hash function $\mathcal{H} : \{0,1\}^* \to (\Xi_k)^S$.

Theorem 1 (NI-TZK Proof Scheme for Shamir Secret Shares). *Let L be an n-distributed language for the list of relations given in Eq. (3), $t \geq 0$ be a security threshold such that $n \geq 2t + 1$, and $h = n - t$. Assuming that the commitment scheme $\mathcal{C}$ is collapsing and quantum computationally hiding, for any potential set $I \subseteq [n]$ of size $|I| \geq h$, the protocol given in Fig. 1 is a non-interactive distributed proof scheme for L that satisfies completeness, threshold ZK, and soundness against the prover and t malicious verifiers in the QROM.*

Completeness. If the protocol is followed honestly and if the input was a valid statement-witness pair $(x, w) \in R$, where each verifier V_i, $1 \leq i \leq n$, has an input piece (share) x_i, then the verification will always accept the proof. Note that, the prover commits to the evaluations of $f(i)$ and $b(i)$ for $i = 1, \cdots, n$, and given x_i and $r(X) = b(X) - d \cdot f(X)$, the verifier V_i computes $r(i) + dx_i = b(i) - df(i) + dx_i = b(i)$, if $x_i = f(i)$. So if the witness is valid, then the commitments C_i and C_i' match and the verification (i.e., all the shareholders) will return **true** and accept the proof.

Soundness Against the Prover and t Malicious Verifiers. The NI-TZK scheme presented in Fig. 1 is made non-interactive using a variant of Fiat-Shamir transform which is proposed by Boneh et al. [11] for proofs on distributed data, and its security is also proven formally in [8] for a particular protocol. The commonly used transform of Fiat-Shamir [21], which is analysed in the (Quantum) Random Oracle model [19,38], is applied on a public coin interactive proof systems. Such that, instead of getting the challenge from the verifier, in the non-interactive protocol the prover applies a random oracle $\mathcal{H}$ to the concatenation of the input (i.e., the statement), and the communication transcript up to that point. In the case of sigma protocols the communication transcript is the commitment made

---

[3] Such a hash function can easily be implemented by hashing into a set $\{1, \ldots, k\}$ and then using the output value $i \in \{1, \ldots, k\}$ as an index in Ξ_k, i.e. $c_i \in \Xi_k$.

in the first round. But in this variant of the Fiat-Shamir transform, the challenge is public, but the input (i.e., the statement) is shared among the verifiers and cannot be revealed to any single verifier. To deal with this concern, the idea is to generate the random challenge using the joint view of the verifiers in previous rounds [11]. Namely, the prover obtains the random challenge value as the hash of concatenation of n public commitments to the individual shares (i.e., shares of statement), and n public commitments produced in the initial round of the sigma protocol. Note that in this variant, each individual secret share is linked to a public commitment which satisfies (perfect) binding and (computational) hiding and can be verified by the corresponding shareholder.

The following Lemma is proven in [8], which proves the soundness of a NI-TZK argument that is built using the above variant of Fiat-Shamir transform.

Lemma 1. *Suppose $\Sigma = (P_1, V_1, P_2, V_2)$ is a sigma protocol for the relation R with super-polynomially sized challenge space Ch, special soundness, and quantum computationally unique responses. Let $\Sigma' = (P_1', V_1', P_2', V_2')$ be the following sigma protocol:*

$$P_1'(x, w) : y \leftarrow \{0, 1\}^\lambda, \ \mathsf{C}_x \leftarrow \mathcal{C}(x, y),$$
$$com \leftarrow P_1(x, w), \ com' = (\mathsf{C}_x, com)$$
$$V_1'(com') : ch \leftarrow Ch$$
$$P_2'(ch) : rsp \leftarrow P_2(ch), rsp' \leftarrow (x, y, rsp)$$
$$V_2'(x, com', ch, rsp') : accept \ if \ \mathsf{C}_x = \mathcal{C}(x, y) \ and \ V_2(x, com, ch, rsp) = 1$$

Then the non-interactive version of Σ', transformed by the mentioned variant of Fiat-Shamir transform is a non-interactive quantum proof of knowledge for the same relation R, assuming that $\mathcal{C}$ is a collapsing commitment.

In the rest, we prove the protocol (given in Fig. 1) satisfies soundness against an adversarial prover and t malicious verifiers. Note that we structure our proof along the lines of [8, Theorem 2], but do this for a different relation, which has very different implications.

Lemma 2. *The proof system given in Fig. 1 constitutes a NI-TZK argument in the QROM for the list of relations of Eq. (3) if the deployed commitment scheme is collapsing.*

Proof. The results from Boneh et al. [11] show that in a NI-TZK proof scheme over secret shared data, the best combination of soundness and ZK that we can achieve is threshold zero-knowledge combined with soundness against prover and t malicious verifiers. To achieve this, we require to have at least $t+1$ honest parties among $n \geq 2t+1$ verifiers, i.e. be in the honest majority setting. Achieving these combinations means that in the target NI-TZK proof scheme, the prover can collude with t malicious verifiers to break the soundness, and at most t verifiers are allowed to collude to break the ZK and learn about the witness.

As a result, we need to prove that for any set $I \subset \{1, \cdots, n\}$ of honest parties where $|I| > t$ and any poly-time quantum adversary $\mathcal{A}^{RO}$, the following advantage is negligible:[4]

$$\mathsf{Adv}^{\mathsf{sound}}_{\mathcal{A},I}(\lambda) = \Pr \left[\begin{matrix} \forall i \in I : V^{RO}(i, x_i, \widetilde{\pi}, \pi_i) = 1 \\ \not\exists w \forall i : (x_i, w) \in R_i \end{matrix} \middle| \{(x_i, \pi_i)\}_{i \in I} \leftarrow \mathcal{A}^{RO}(1^\lambda) \right].$$

For compactness, we use the index I to denote the set of elements with index $i \in I$, e.g. $x_I = \{x_i\}_{i \in I}$. We further define the function F, which on the input of the data available to the set I, outputs the commitments as follows.

$$F : \Xi_k \times \mathbb{Z}_N^{|I|} \times \{0,1\}^{\lambda|I|} \times \mathbb{Z}_N[X]_{\leq t} \to \{0,1\}^{2\lambda}$$
$$(d, x_I, y_I, r(X)) \mapsto \{\mathcal{C}(r(i) + dx_i, y_i)\}_{i \in I},$$

Let us define the following protocol $\Sigma' = (P_1', V_1', P_2', V_2')$.

$$P_1'(x_I, w) : \forall i \in I : y_i, y_i' \leftarrow \{0,1\}^\lambda, \ \mathsf{C}_i' \leftarrow \Xi(x_i, y_i')$$
$$b(X) \leftarrow \mathbb{Z}_N[X]_{\leq t}, \ \mathsf{C}_I = F(0, x_I, y_I, b(X))$$
$$V_1'(\mathsf{C}_I, \mathsf{C}_I') : d \leftarrow \Xi_k$$
$$P_2'(\mathbf{c}) : r(X) = b(X) - dw, \ rsp' = (y_I, y_I', r(X))$$
$$V_2'(rsp) : \text{accept if } \mathsf{C}_I' = \mathcal{C}(x_I, y_I) \text{ and } \mathsf{C}_I = F(d, x_I, y_I, r(X)).$$

It is clear that, if $F(RO(\mathsf{C}, \mathsf{C}'), x_I, y_I, r(X)) = \mathsf{C}_I$ and $\mathsf{C}_I' = \mathcal{C}(x_I, y_I')$, then $V^{RO}(I, x_I, \widetilde{\pi}, \pi_I) = 1.$[5] This implies that $\mathsf{Adv}^{\mathsf{sound}}_{\mathcal{A},I}(\lambda)$ is indeed negligible if the previously discussed variant of the Fiat-Shamir transform of Σ' is a (quantum) computationally sound proof of R_I as per [19, Definition 9]. This, in turn, is implied by proving that the transformed protocol is a quantum proof of knowledge as per [19, Definition 14]. We prove this last step by using Lemma 1, which implies the soundness of our protocol from Fig. 1, when the following protocol has super-polynomially sized challenge space Ξ_k, special soundness, and quantum computationally unique responses.

$$P_1(x_I, w) : \forall i \in I : y_i \leftarrow \{0,1\}^\lambda,$$
$$b(X) \leftarrow \mathbb{Z}_N[X]_{\leq t}, \mathsf{C}_I = F(0, x_I, y_I, b(X))$$
$$V_1(\mathsf{C}_I) : d \leftarrow \Xi_k$$
$$P_2(\mathbf{c}) : r(X) = b(X) - dw, \ rsp' \leftarrow (y_I, r(X))$$
$$V_2(rsp) : \text{accept if } \mathsf{C}_I = F(d, x_I, y_I, r(X))$$

We end this proof by discussing that these three properties are satisfied.

- **Challenge space:** In the case where $\mathbb{Z}_N$ is a field, the exceptional set Ξ_k is simply the field itself, which by definition has size superpolynomial in λ. Otherwise, the maximal size of Ξ_k is limited by the smallest divisor of N. In that case, as mentioned in Remark 2 we can amplify the challenge space size to above 2^λ by repeating the protocol $\lceil \lambda / \log k \rceil$ times.

---

[4] For $|I| \leq t$, there always exists a witness that satisfies the relation.
[5] Read component-wise, e.g. $\forall i \in I : \mathsf{C}_i' = \mathcal{C}(x_i, y_i')$.

- **Special Soundness**: Let $(x_I, C_I, d, r(X))$ and $(x_I, C_I, d', r'(X))$ with $d \neq d'$ be two accepting transcripts. Now, if for some $i \in I$, we have $r(i) + dx_i \neq r'(i) + d'x_i$, then we have found a collision in $\mathcal{C}$. Otherwise, we can compute a witness for x_I via $\frac{r(X) - r'(X)}{d' - d}$. Note that $d' - d$ is invertible because they are distinct elements from an exceptional set Ξ_k.
- **Unique responses**: Using the results from [8, Section A.2], this property is guaranteed in case $\mathcal{C}$ is collapsing and that $r(X)$ are unique. The latter follows from the fact that the function $(r, d, x) \mapsto r + dx$ is injective if d is an element from an exceptional set. □

Threshold zero-knowledge. We begin this section by stating the following Lemma.

Lemma 3. *The protocol in Fig. 1 satisfies the TZK property in the QROM for the list of relations of (3) if the used commitment scheme is quantum computationally hiding and collapsing, and if the underlying sigma protocol has honest-verifier zero-knowledge, completeness, and unpredictable commitments.*

We skip the proof of Lemma, as it immediately follows from the discussion in [8, Section A.3]. There, the authors show that it suffices to show zero-knowledge for any $I \subset \{0, \dots, n\}$.[6] The case $i = 0$ is not relevant in this work and for the cases $i = 1, \dots, n$, we can readily apply the results of their Lemmas 4 and 5 to our protocol. By definition, our commitment is quantum computationally hiding and collapsing. We can therefore finish the proof by showing that the sigma protocol underlying Fig. 1 is complete, HVZK, and has unpredictable commitments.

- **Completeness**: It follows from the completeness of our protocol.
- **HVZK**: We can define a simulator that samples $y_I, y_I' \leftarrow \{0,1\}^\lambda$, $r(X) \leftarrow \mathbb{Z}_N[X]_t$ and $d \leftarrow \Xi_k$ uniformly at random, then sets $C_I = F(d, x_I, y_i, r(X))$ and $C_I' = \mathcal{C}(x_I, y_I')$. Since these sampled elements are also uniformly random in the real execution of the protocol, the transcripts are indistinguishable.
- **Unpredictable commitments**: By [38, Definition 4], unpredictable commitments imply that for every $(x_I, w) \in R_I$, finding two different commitments $(C_I^{(1)}, C_I'^{(1)})$ and $(C_I^{(2)}, C_I'^{(2)})$ that satisfy the probability

$$\Pr\left[(C_I^{(1)}, C_I'^{(1)}) = (C_I^{(2)}, C_I'^{(2)}) \,\middle|\, \begin{matrix} (C_I^{(1)}, C_I'^{(1)}) \leftarrow P_1(x_I, w) \\ (C_I^{(2)}, C_I'^{(2)}) \leftarrow P_1(x_I, w) \end{matrix}\right]$$

is negligible in the security parameter λ. There are two options to get such a collision, either the inputs to $\mathcal{C}$ are equal, or we find a collision in $\mathcal{C}$. The former happens with negligible probability, since the inputs to $\mathcal{C}$ are uniformly distributed in $\mathbb{Z}_N \times \{0,1\}^\lambda$ and the latter is prevented by the fact that $\mathcal{C}$ is collapsing. □

This completes the proof of Theorem 1.

---

[6] Actually, the authors implicitly prove TZK, but do not call it as such.

3.2   A NI-VSS Scheme from NI-TZK Proofs

Next, we use the NI-TZK proof scheme proposed in the last subsection and construct a NI-VSS scheme based on Shamir secret sharing. Our scheme operates on the assumption that each shareholder has a secure communication channel with the dealer, which can be achieved through a public key infrastructure. Therefore, the shares will only be hidden computationally. The proposed scheme works in the majority honest setting, and the validity of secret shares cannot be publicly verified (as in [5,32]), and it requires (non-interactive) collaboration among the shareholders to verify them. We demonstrate later that this is sufficient in many Shamir-based threshold protocols (e.g. DKGs, threshold signatures, etc.) that also work in the majority-honest setting.

Our Definitions. Before going through the proposed construction to build a NI-VSS scheme, we review our formal definitions of VSS schemes which are a minimally modified version of the ones from previous works [29,32].

Definition 8. *An (n, t, x_0) non-interactive VSS consists of four PPT Algorithms of (Initialization, Share, Verification, Reconstruction) as follows:*

1. *Initialization: In this phase, the system parameters are generated and shared with the parties.*
2. *Share$(n, t, x_0) \rightarrow (x_1, \cdots, x_n, \pi)$: Given the number of parties n, threshold t, and the secret x_0, the algorithm secret shares x_0 and outputs the shares $\{x_1, \cdots, x_n\}$ and a proof π to prove that it has done the sharing correctly.*
3. *Verification$(n, t, x_1, \cdots, x_n, \pi) \rightarrow$ true/false: Given the number of parties n, threshold t, and the shares $x_1, \cdots, x_n$ (or encryption of them), and the proof π, generated by Share, the algorithm outputs either true or false.*
4. *Reconstruction$(n, t, x_1, \cdots, x_{t+1}) \rightarrow x_0/\{$true/false$\}$: Given any $t + 1$ of the shares, e.g., $\{x_1, \cdots, x_{t+1}\}$, it reconstructs and returns x_0. Alternatively, given a candidate value for x_0 (or in general a function of it) and t (or in general $t+1$) of the shares, the algorithm confirms the validity of the candidate secret x_0 (or the function of it), and returns either $\{$true/false$\}$.*

A verifiable secret sharing scheme further has two requirements as follows [32].

- **Verifiability constraint**: A shareholder must be able to determine whether a share of the secret is valid or not. If it is valid, then Reconstruction should produce a unique secret x_0 when run on any $t + 1$ distinct valid shares. Alternatively any t (or in general $t + 1$) shareholders should be able to check the validity of a potential value of x_0 (or in general a function of it).
- **Unpredictability**: The protocol must be unpredictable, meaning that there is no strategy for selecting t shares of the secret that would enable someone to predict the secret x_0 with a significant advantage.

We highlight that our definition of VSS differs slightly from current ones [29, 32]. Our definitions utilize a ZK proof scheme over secret shared data for proving the validity of the shares, ensures the existence of a polynomial-time verification algorithm that can validate the shares, and also introduces a *novel approach* for reconstruction of the main secret. The first two features already are implicitly built in any VSS scheme, however the third one is new in our framework. In our Reconstruction algorithm, in addition to enabling the reconstruction of the secret x_0 using Largange interpolation by any $t + 1$ shareholders, we also consider a scenario where the dealer disclose a candidate value for x_0 (or in general a function of it) and t (or in general $t + 1$) of the shareholders can validate the validity of the disclosed secret (or the correctness of a computation performed on x_0). Later, we demonstrate that the new reconstruction approach is commonly used in practice, and shareholders typically do not reconstruct the plain value of x_0. Instead, each shareholder acts as a dealer once and subsequently employs their shared secret to perform certain computations. They then provide a ZK proof to prove the correctness of their actions. In some cases, these proofs may only be verifiable by the shareholders themselves.

Our Construction. In a VSS scheme, a dealer aims to distribute shares of a secret x_0 among n parties $P_1, \ldots, P_n$. Such that depending on the underlying access structure, a subset of shareholders are qualified to recover the secret x_0. In our case, which is based on Shamir secret sharing, the secret can be recovered by any subset of more than t shareholders, where $t < n$. On the other hand, any subset of size $\leq t$ will not gain any information about x_0, unless the security of underlying NI-TZK proof scheme is broken. The complexity of our VSS scheme is linear in the security parameter and also linear in the number of shareholders which is essentially optimal, but notably our scheme only uses lightweight operations (such as hashing and polynomial evaluations). It achieves computational security, which is proven in the (Q)ROM, using a secure commitment scheme. We present our protocol in Fig. 2.

It is important to note that in the *Reconstruction* with the new approach, unlike the Lagrange interpolation based approaches, the parties do not perform any decryption or proof generation to show the correctness of their actions. Instead, the dealer calculates and publishes the reconstructed secret value $f(0) = x_0$ (or a function thereof) along with a NI-TZK proof for the distributed relation $R_i = \{(x_i, f(X)) | f(i) = x_i\}$, for $i = 0, 1, \ldots, n$. Then, any t (or in general $t + 1$ if a function of x_0 is reconstructed) shareholders use their secret shares to verify the validity of the disclosed secret value x_0 (or a function of it). If the verification process returns true, this confirms that the disclosed value x_0 (or a function of it) represents the main secret $f(0)$ (or a function thereof). Note that as in other schemes, if we have $t + 1$ shares, we only can achieve a reconstruction with *abort*, while with n shares we can have a *robust* reconstruction phase.

It's important to highlight that, similar to the first reconstruction approach, where any subset of qualified sets can recover the secret $f(0)$ and fewer than a threshold number of them gain no knowledge about $f(0)$, the new reconstruction approach also allows only a qualified subset of the shareholders to confirm the soundness of the underlying NI-TZK proof scheme and the validity of the disclosed value x_0. Conversely, relaying on the TZK property of the underlying NI-TZK proof scheme, any group of parties that is smaller than the threshold value will be unable to confirm the authenticity of the revealed value x_0 (or any function derived from it) and gain information about the original secret $f(0)$ (or any computation involving the original secret $f(0)$).

Initialization: Parties $P_1, \cdots, P_n$ generate system parameters and each one registers a PK to facilitate secure communications.

Share: Given n and t, to share x_0, the dealer proceeds as follows:

1. Sample a uniformly random polynomial $f(X)$ of degree t with coefficients in a ring R, subject to $f(0) = x_0$.
2. For $i = 1, 2, \cdots, n$: set $x_i := f(i)$.
3. Given $f(X)$ and $x = (x_1, \cdots, x_n)$, run the prover of NI-TZK scheme in Fig. 1, and obtain the proof $\pi := (\mathsf{C}, \mathsf{C}', r(X), \{\pi_i\}_{i=1}^n)$.
4. Send the share and the individual proof (x_i, π_i) privately to party P_i and broadcast the elements $(\mathsf{C}, \mathsf{C}', r(X))$ as the proof.

Verification: To verify the received shares, $P_1, \cdots, P_n$ utilize their shares $\{x_i\}_{i=1}^n$ and run the verifier of the NI-TZK proof scheme given of Fig. 1. If the verification of P_i fails, then P_i broadcasts a complain against the dealer. If more than t shareholders complain against the dealer, then the *Verification* returns `false`. If P_i complains that his part of proof does not verify, the dealer broadcasts $(x_i, \pi_i := (y_i, y_i'))$ so that everyone can verify it using the verification algorithm of the NI-TZK scheme. If it passed the verification, the protocol continues as normal, otherwise the parties disqualify the dealer and *Verification* returns `false`. Since disqualifying the dealer or parties happens on the basis of only broadcasted information, at the end all the honest shareholders will agree on the same set of qualified parties $Q \subseteq \{1, 2, \cdots, n\}$ or will reject the final verification. At the end, if the verification returns `true`, all honest shareholders are sure that they have received a valid share of $x_0 = f(0)$, and any subset of size larger than t of them can retrieve the secret x_0.

Reconstruction: This can be done through two approaches: either by using Lagrange interpolation as in previous works or by employing a novel approach outlined below. In the new approach, the dealer reconstructs (i.e., reveals) the secret x_0 and also proves its validity, and for that the process proceeds as follows:

1. Given the witness $f(X)$, the dealer computes (reconstructs) $x_0 = f(0)$.
2. Using $f(X)$ and $x = (x_0, x_1, \cdots, x_n)$, run the prover of the NI-TZK scheme in Fig. 1 for $i = 0, 1, \ldots, n$, to prove that $f(0) = x_0 \wedge f(i) = x_i$ for $i = 1, \ldots, n$, and obtain $(x_0, y_0, y_0', \{\mathsf{C}_i, \mathsf{C}_i'\}_{i=0}^n, r(X), \{\pi_i\}_{i=1}^n)$. This allows the dealer to convince the shareholders that their shares come from a polynomial of degree t with free term $x_0 = f(0)$.
3. Send the individual proof $\pi_i := (y_i, y_i')$ privately to party P_i, and broadcast the elements $(x_0, y_0, y_0', \{\mathsf{C}_i, \mathsf{C}_i'\}_{i=0}^n, r(X))$.
4. Each shareholder P_i has secret values $(x_i, \pi_i := (y_i, y_i'))$, and a public proof $(x_0, y_0, y_0', \{\mathsf{C}_i, \mathsf{C}_i'\}_{i=0}^n, r(X))$. Given the set of statements and proofs, the shareholders run the verification of the NI-TZK scheme in Fig. 1 and return either `true` or `false`. Note that in this case, each shareholder P_i additionally checks if $\mathsf{C}_0' = \mathcal{C}(x_0, y_0') \wedge \mathsf{C}_0 == \mathcal{C}(r(0) + d \cdot x_0, y_0)$.
5. At the end, the algorithm **return true** if *all* the shareholders return `true`; otherwise **return false**. Returning `true`, confirms that the value x_0 is the reconstruction of the main secret value $f(0)$.

Fig. 2. The proposed NI-VSS scheme.

In practical distributed protocols, the dealer typically does not reveal the main secret $f(0)$. Instead, they disclose the results of specific computations carried out with it, such as $h_0 = g^{f(0)}$ in the context of distributed generation of a DL tuple. In these cases, the dealer is required to publish a proof that the computation was conducted using $f(0)$, e.g., $h_0 = g^{f(0)} \wedge f(i) = x_i$ in the context of distributed key generation for signature schemes such as Schnorr and BLS. At first glance, this may seem unconventional. However, as we will show later, it is actually sufficient and common practice in many threshold protocols, e.g., DKGs and threshold signatures. In the upcoming section, we will explore some applications and types of NI-TZK proof systems that one might need in the *Reconstruction* phase.

Theorem 2 (VSS from NI-TZK Proof Schemes). *If the proof scheme given in Fig. 1 is a secure NI-TZK protocol for the relations in Eq. (3), then, the non-interactive VSS scheme (given in Fig. 2) is secure. That is, (i) the Reconstruction protocol results in the secret distributed by the dealer for any qualified set of shareholders, (ii) any non-qualified set of shareholders is unable to recover the secret (i.e., unpredictability).*

Proof. In Theorem 1, we showed that the protocol presented in Fig. 1 is a NI-TZK scheme for L, that is an n-distributed language for the list of relations given in Eq. (3), satisfies completeness, threshold ZK, and soundness against the prover and t malicious verifiers in the QROM.

Completeness of the NI-TZK scheme implies that if the parties $P_1, \cdots, P_n$ follow the protocol, then at the end of the *Sharing* phase, each of them obtain a distinct evaluation of a polynomial degree t, where $t < n$. Relaying on the fact that any degree t polynomial is uniquely determined by $t+1$ distinct evaluations, any $t+1$ of n shareholders can use Lagrange interpolation and reconstruct $f(X)$ and retrieve the value $f(0)$, which is the secret value in the NI-VSS scheme. Similarly, any t (or in general any $t+1$) shareholders can also verify the proof given by dealer in the *Reconstruction* phase, and ensure that the secret value x_0 revealed by the dealer, is equal to the secret shared value $f(0)$.

The NI-TZK scheme's soundness against prover and t malicious verifiers implies that if there is no n-distributed input $x' \in L_R$ such that $x_i = x'_i$, for all honest parties P_i, then the protocol (honest verifiers) will reject the proof except with negligible probability. Therefore, a malicious dealer would have to either break the soundness of the underlying NI-TZK proof scheme or it will be caught with an overwhelming probability. It is important to note that, during the verification process any conflicts between the dealer and shareholders are resolved using the method outlined in the Verification algorithm. In the scenario where the majority of shareholders are honest, this enables the parties to achieve robustness within the resulting NI-VSS scheme.

For unpredictability, the threshold ZK property of the underlying NI-TZK scheme guarantees that any polynomial-time adversary $\mathcal{A}$ that controls up to t verifiers cannot learn anything about the secret polynomial $f(x)$, including the value $f(0)$. As a result, any non-qualified set of shareholders is unable to recover the secret $x_0 = f(0)$. In other words, if an adversary who controls a non-qualified set of shareholders can learn about the secret value $f(0)$, they can be used as an adversary against the threshold ZK property of the NI-TZK proof scheme.   □

3.3 Asymptotic Costs and Empirical Performance

Next, we first summarize the efficiency metrics for our proposed NI-VSS scheme, and then assess its empirical performance through a prototype implementation. To gauge the efficiency of new scheme, we also conduct a comparative analysis with the widely used VSS scheme of Pedersen [29].

Asymptotic Costs. As in Shamir secret sharing, to share a secret x_0 among n parties with threshold value t, the dealer first computes n evaluations of a degree-t polynomial $f(X)$. Then, it runs the prover of NI-TZK scheme outlined in Fig. 1 and generates a proof for the correctness of the shearing phase. To this end, the dealer needs to compute n evaluations of a new degree-t polynomial $b(X)$, compute $2n$ commitments, query one time to the RO, and perform t subtractions between the coefficients of $f(X)$ and $b(X)$. To verify their shares, the shareholders participate in the verification of the NI-TZK proof system (outlined in Fig. 1) and disseminate the final output to the network. As part of this process, each shareholder must compute two commitments, one evaluation of a random oracle, one polynomial evaluation of degree t, and one addition over $\mathbb{Z}_N$. In terms of communication, the dealer broadcasts $(\mathsf{C}, \mathsf{C}', r(X))$ to the network, which consists of $2n$ commitments and t polynomial coefficients. It also sends the individual proof (x_i, π_i) privately to party P_i, which consists of 3 $\mathbb{Z}_N$ elements.

Table 2. Asymptotic costs in Pedersen [29] and our proposed NI-VSS schemes. DL: Discrete Logarithm, BC: Broadcast, n: Number of parties, $E_{\mathbb{G}}$: Exponentiation in group $\mathbb{G}$, $M_{\mathbb{G}}$: Multiplication in group $\mathbb{G}$, $\mathcal{PE}$: degree-t Polynomial Evaluation, $\mathcal{H}$: Hashing, $|\mathbb{G}|$: $\mathbb{G}$ element size, $|\mathbb{Z}_q|$: $\mathbb{Z}_q$ element size, $|\mathbb{Z}_N|$: $\mathbb{Z}_N$ element size, $|\mathcal{H}|$: Output size of $\mathcal{H}$, DV: Designated Verifier, FS: Fiat-Shamir.

VSS Scheme	Assumption	Sharing	Dealer's Communication	Verification (DV)
Pedersen [29]	DL-based (IT & Classic)	$1n\ E_{\mathbb{G}}$ $2n\ \mathcal{PE}$	Private: $2n\ |\mathbb{Z}_q|$ BC: $t \approx 0.5n\ |\mathbb{G}|$	$t \approx 0.5n\ E_{\mathbb{G}}$
This work Sect. 3.2	Hash-based (PQ)	$2n\ \mathcal{H}$ $2n\ \mathcal{PE}$	Private: $1n\ |\mathbb{Z}_N|$ BC: $2n\ |\mathcal{H}| + 0.5n\ |\mathbb{Z}_N|$	$1\ \mathcal{PE} + 3\ \mathcal{H}$ ($1\ \mathcal{H}$ is for FS)

In Pedersen VSS scheme, to share a secret, a dealer needs to evaluate a degree-t polynomial $2n$ times (i.e., n times with $f(X)$ and n times with $b(X)$), compute n exponentiations and $t \approx n/2$ multiplications in the underlying group $\mathbb{G}$. Then, the dealer needs to broadcast $t \approx n/2$ group elements as the commitments, and also privately send 2 field elements to each party P_i, as their shares. Then, to verify the shares, each verifier needs to compute $t \approx n/2$ exponentiations in the group $\mathbb{G}$. Table 2, summarizes the asymptotic costs of our proposed protocol and compares it with Pedersen's scheme [29]. As a crucial optimization in our scheme, we eliminate the need for additional randomness, represented as y_i and y_i' within the hashes (i.e., the commitments). This optimization results in shorter private communication from the dealer to the parties in the table.

Empirical Performance. To assess the practical performance of the new VSS scheme, we implemented a prototype of it alongside the Pedersen scheme using SageMath. In the new VSS scheme, we employed a SHA256 hash function for instantiating the commitment scheme $\mathcal{C}$ and the random oracle $\mathcal{H}$. For the Pedersen scheme implementation, we utilized `Curve 25519`, and optimized the implementation through Montgomery x-arithmetic. Additionally, we relied on SageMath's built-in functions for handling polynomials and hash operations.

To evaluate their performance, we conducted experiments where we varied the number of parties and the threshold value. Specifically, we report the run times of the *Sharing* and *Verification* phases, along with the communication size for different numbers of parties, i.e., n, and threshold values, i.e., t. To conduct these experiments, we ran our code on a laptop with Ubuntu 22.04 LTS, a 11th Gen Intel(R) Core(TM) i9-11950H at base frequency 2.60 GHz, and 64 GB of memory. All the operations in the sharing and verification phases are done in a single-thread mode. The performance results with different values of (n, t), ranging from $(32, 15)$ to $(16384, 8191)$ are summarized in Table 3.

Table 3. Empirical performance of NI-VSS schemes Pedersen [29] and our proposed scheme for various numbers of parties and threshold values (n, t). n: Number of parties, t: Threshold value, BC: Broadcast, $|\mathbb{Z}_q| = |\mathbb{Z}_N| = 252$, $|\mathbb{G}| = 510$, $|\mathcal{H}| = 256$ bits.

(n, t)	Scheme	Sharing	Dealer's Communication	Verification
(32, 15)	Pedersen [29]	78.1 msec	Private: 1.97 KB + BC: 1.00 KB	10.2 msec
	This Work	2.40 msec	Private: 0.98 KB + BC: 2.49 KB	0.12 msec
(128, 63)	Pedersen [29]	310 msec	Private: 7.87 KB + BC: 3.98 KB	97.6 msec
	This Work	13.7 msec	Private: 3.93 KB + BC: 9.96 KB	0.36 msec
(512, 255)	Pedersen [29]	1.310 sec	Private: 31.5 KB + BC: 15.9 KB	525 msec
	This Work	0.140 sec	Private: 15.7 KB + BC: 39.9 KB	1.20 msec
(2048, 1023)	Pedersen [29]	6.53 sec	Private: 126 KB + BC: 63.74 KB	2.35 sec
	This Work	2.00 sec	Private: 63 KB + BC: 129.5 KB	4.90 msec
(8192, 4095)	Pedersen [29]	48.1 sec	Private: 504 KB + BC: 255 KB	9.47 sec
	This Work	30.6 sec	Private: 252 KB + BC: 638 KB	0.019 sec
(16384, 8191)	Pedersen [29]	153.6 sec	Private: 1008 KB + BC: 510 KB	19.2 sec
	This Work	121.7 sec	Private: 504 KB + BC: 1276 KB	0.039 sec

The implementation results solidify the advantage of our NI-VSS scheme over the Pedersen scheme in both sharing and verification phases, in addition to post-quantum security. Specifically, our NI-VSS scheme demonstrates a remarkable speedup in the verification phase, achieving 271×, 437×, and 498× faster verification times than the Pedersen scheme for (n, t) equal to $(128, 63)$, $(512, 255)$, and $(8194, 4095)$, respectively. Similarly, in the sharing phase, for the same settings, our scheme is approximately 22.6×, 9.3×, and 1.57× faster than the Pedersen scheme. Regarding communication cost, our scheme incurs a broadcast cost for the dealer that is 2.5× higher than that of the Pedersen scheme. These implementation results also affirm the practicality and scalability of the new NI-VSS scheme for deployment in various threshold protocols. One notable factor contributing to our improvements in the sharing and verification phases is using lightweight cryptographic operations such as hashing and polynomial evaluation, in the underlying NI-TZK proof scheme.

We highlight that our implementation remains relatively naive, operating in a single-threaded fashion without specific optimizations. A potential optimization strategy could involve adopting algorithms from [36], which offer improved computational complexity for evaluating a polynomial at multiple points, thus improving the efficiency of the sharing (and also verification in some cases).

4   More Efficient Threshold Protocols in the DL Setting

In this section, we leverage our new VSS scheme from Sect. 3 and revisit the well-known Pedersen DKG protocol [28] along with the threshold signature of Gennaro, Jarecki, Krawczyk, and Rabin [22], which uses Schnorr's signature [31] for signing and Pedersen's DKG protocol for generating the (ephemeral) keys.

4.1   An Efficient DKG Protocol for DL

Pedersen DKG protocol [28] allows a group of parties to generate a DL instance, e.g., $\mathsf{pk} = g^{\mathsf{sk}}$, in a fully distributed manner, where g is the generator of the DL group, and $(\mathsf{sk}, \mathsf{pk})$ are a pair of secret and public keys, respectively.

In the following, we present an efficient robust DKG protocol for distributed generation of a DL instance, which can outperform Pedersen's protocol. To this end, we first construct an efficient NI-TZK proof scheme for the DL problem that acts as a building block in our proposed DKG protocol (and threshold signature). The NI-TZK proof scheme allows a prover to convince a set of verifiers (i.e., shareholders) that $h = g^{f(0)} \wedge f(i) = x_i$, for the shared input $x = x_1 \parallel x_2 \parallel \cdots \parallel x_n$, a secret polynomial $f(X) \in \mathbb{F}_p[X]_t$ and a secret input $x_0 = f(0)$. One usually can face with a similar scenario in the DL-based threshold protocols (e.g., threshold variants of El Gamal, ECDSA, etc.). The new NI-TZK proof scheme is built for the following n-distributed relations,

$$R_i = \{(g, h, x_i, f(X)) | h = g^{f(0)} \wedge f(i) = x_i\}, \tag{4}$$

where $i = 1, \ldots, n$. Figure 3 describes the algorithms of our proposed NI-TZK proof scheme for the DL relation, where $\mathcal{H}$ is a random oracle and $\mathcal{C}$ is a computationally hiding commitment scheme. Roughly speaking, the protocol is obtained by slightly modifying the conjunction of the Schnorr ID protocol with the NI-TZK scheme presented in Fig. 1. This is another instance of different NI-TZK proof schemes that one may need in the *Reconstruction* phase of the new VSS scheme, where parties reconstruct a function of the main secret $f(0)$, namely $h = g^{f(0)}$, rather than the plain value of it.

Prover: Given, $f(X) \in \mathbb{F}_p[X]_t$, and the input $x = (g, h := g^{f(0)}, x_1, \cdots, x_n)$, proceed as follows and output a proof π of the relations in equation (4).

1. Sample $b(X) \leftarrow \mathbb{F}_p[X]_t$ uniformly at random;
2. For $i = 1, \ldots, n$: Sample $y_i, y_i' \leftarrow \{0,1\}^\lambda$ uniformly at random and set $\mathsf{C}_i = \mathcal{C}(b(i), y_i)$ and $\mathsf{C}_i' = \mathcal{C}(x_i, y_i')$;
3. Sample $y_0, y_0' \leftarrow \{0,1\}^\lambda$ and set $\mathsf{C}_0 = \mathcal{C}(g^{b(0)}, y_0), \mathsf{C}_0' = \mathcal{C}(g\|h, y_0')$
4. Set $d \leftarrow \mathcal{H}(\mathsf{C}, \mathsf{C}')$, where $\mathsf{C} = (\mathsf{C}_0, \mathsf{C}_1, \ldots, \mathsf{C}_n), \mathsf{C}' = (\mathsf{C}_0', \mathsf{C}_1', \ldots, \mathsf{C}_n')$;
5. Set $r(X) \leftarrow b(X) - d \cdot f(X) \mod p$;
6. Return $\pi := (g, h, \mathsf{C}, \mathsf{C}', r(X), y_0, y_0', \{\pi_i\}_{i=1}^n)$, where $\pi_i = (y_i, y_i')$;

Verification: Given $\pi := (g, h, \mathsf{C}, \mathsf{C}', r(X), y_0, y_0', \{\pi_i := (y_i, y_i')\}_{i=1}^n)$, the verifiers $\{V_i\}_{i=1}^n$ use their shares and individual proofs (x_i, π_i), and the verification proceeds as follows:

1. Verifier i acts as below and outputs **true** or **false**.
   (a) If $\mathsf{C}_i' \neq \mathcal{C}(x_i, y_i')$ or $\mathsf{C}_0' \neq \mathcal{C}(g\|h, y_0')$ return **false**
   (b) Set $d' \leftarrow \mathcal{H}(\mathsf{C}, \mathsf{C}')$;
   (c) Compute $h' = g^{r(0)} \cdot h^d$.
   (d) If $\mathsf{C}_i == \mathcal{C}(r(i) + d \cdot x_i, y_i) \wedge \mathsf{C}_0 == \mathcal{C}(h', y_0)$ return **true**; otherwise **false**;
2. Return **true** if *all* the verifiers return **true**; otherwise returns **false**.

Fig. 3. A NI-TZK proof scheme for discrete logarithm.

Theorem 3 (NI-TZK Proofs for DL). *Let L be an n-distributed language for the list of relations given in Eq. (4), $t \geq 1$ be a security threshold such that $n \geq 2t + 1$. Assuming that the commitment scheme $\mathcal{C}$ is computationally hiding, for any potential set $I \subseteq [n]$ of size $|I| \geq n - t$, the protocol described in Fig. 3 is a non-interactive distributed threshold ZK protocol for L that satisfies completeness, threshold ZK, and soundness against the prover and t malicious verifiers in the ROM.*

Proof. The proof is analogous to the proof of Theorem 1 which is omitted. We highlight that in this case, in the soundness proof, one reduces the security of scheme to the DL problem, thus this scheme only achieves classical security.   □

Now, we can use the general NI-VSS of Fig. 2 and the NI-ZSK proof scheme given in Fig. 3, and construct a DKG protocol with designated verifiers for DL. The resulting DKG is described in Fig. 5 and can be considered as an adaption of the Pedersen DKG protocol version from [22] to work with NI-TZK proofs and the new VSS scheme.

Theorem 4. *Under the DL assumption, the protocol in Fig. 4 is a secure DKG protocol, namely it satisfies the correctness and secrecy properties against a malicious adversary corrupting up to t parties, with $t < n/2$.*

Proof. The proof is analogous to the ones in [8,22], but in this case the simulator of DKG scheme runs the simulator of NI-TZK proof scheme as a subroutine.   □

Round 1 (VSS and Committing): Each party P_i proceed as follows:

1. Sample $f^{(i)}(X) \leftarrow \mathbb{F}_p[X]_t$ subject to $f^{(i)}(0) = x_i$ and set $x_{ij} = f^{(i)}(j)$
2. Using $(g, h_i := g^{x_i}, \{x_{ij}\}_{j=1}^n)$, run the prover of NI-TZK proof scheme in Fig. 3, and obtain $\pi := (g, h_i, \mathsf{C}, \mathsf{C}', r(X), y_{i0}, y'_{i0}, \{\pi_{ij}\}_{j=1}^n)$, where $\pi_{ij} = (y_{ij}, y'_{ij})$.
3. Publish $(g, \mathsf{C}, \mathsf{C}', r(X))$ and store $(h_i, y_{i0}, y'_{i0}, \{x_{ij}, \pi_{ij}\}_{j=1}^n)$ for next round.

Round 2 (Opening, Verification, PK Computation):

1) **Opening:** Each party $\{P_i\}_{i=1}^n$ broadcasts $(h_i = g^{x_i}, y_{i0}, y'_{i0})$ and sends (x_{ij}, π_{ij}) privately to party P_j. If a party refuses to open a commitment, then that party is disqualified.

2) **Verification:** Each party $\{P_j\}_{j=1}^n$ uses $(\pi_{ij}, y_{i0}, y'_{i0})$ and verifies the correctness of the share x_{ij} it got from P_i with respect to $g, h_i = g^{x_i}$ for $i \neq j$, by running the verifier of NI-TZK proof scheme given in Fig. 1. If the verification fails, then P_j broadcasts a complaint against P_i. Any player with at least $t+1$ complaints is disqualified. If P_j complains that P_i's proof does not verify, then P_i broadcasts $(x_{ij}, y_{ij}, y'_{ij})$, so that everyone can verify it using the verification algorithm of NI-TZK scheme. If this verification succeeds, the protocol continues as normal, otherwise P_i is disqualified. Since disqualifying the parties happens on the basis of only broadcasted information, at the end, all parties will agree on the same set of qualified parties $Q \subseteq \{1, \ldots, n\}$ such that $x = \sum_{i \in Q} L_{0,i}^Q x_i$, where $L_{0,i}^Q = \prod_{j \in Q, \, j \neq i} \frac{j}{j-i}$ is a Lagrange coefficient.

3) **PK Computation:** Parties compute the public key as $g^x = \prod_{i \in Q} g^{L_{0,i}^Q x_i}$.

Fig. 4. Designated verifier DKG protocol for DL-based schemes.

KeyGen: Parties run the DKG protocol of Fig. 4. At the end, each party holds a verified secret share x_i of x. The resulting public key is g^x. We assume $Q_0 = \{1, \ldots, n\}$ to be the qualified set at the end of this step.

Sign$(m, \langle x_i \rangle)$: To sign a message m, the parties in Q_0 act as follows.
1. Parties run the DKG protocol of Fig. 4 to compute g^b. Malicious parties might be disqualified, so we end up with a set $Q_1 \subseteq Q_0$. Only the parties in Q_1 continue the protocol. Each party P_i in Q_1 holds a share b_i of b.
2. The parties compute the challenge $d \leftarrow H(g^b \| m)$.
3. Parties in Q_1 behave as follows.
   (a) Each party P_i computes and broadcasts $r^{(i)}(X) = b^{(i)}(X) - ds^{(i)}(X)$.
   (b) Using the shared values from VSS phase, each other party P_j verifies
   $$r^{(i)}(j) \stackrel{?}{=} b^{(i)}(j) - ds^{(i)}(j).$$
   (c) Whenever one of these checks fails, P_j broadcasts a complaint against P_i. When a player P_i has $t+1$ or more complaints against them, they are disqualified. The remaining players can then construct $r^{(i)}(0)$ by reconstructing both $b^{(i)}(0)$ and $s^{(i)}(0)$. This is always possible when there are at least $t+1$ honest parties.
   (d) For each party P_i in $Q = Q_0 \backslash Q_1$, set and reconstruct $r_l^{(i)}(0) = s_{d_l}^{(i)}(0)$.
   (e) Using $\{r^{(i)}(0)\}_{i=1,\ldots,n}$, parties build the response $r = \sum_{i \in Q} r^{(i)}(0)$.
4. Finally, parties output the signature $((r, d), m)$.

Verify$((r, d), m, \text{pk})$: To verify a signature (r, d) on m using the public key $\text{pk} = g^x$, the verifier proceeds as follows.
1. Compute $h = g^r \cdot (g^x)^{-d}$.
2. Compute $d' \leftarrow H(h \| m)$.
3. If $d = d'$, return valid, otherwise invalid.

Fig. 5. A novel robust threshold signature scheme based on GJKR scheme [22].

4.2 More Efficient Threshold Signatures from Schnorr's Scheme

Next, using the DKG protocol given in Fig. 4, we modify the Schnorr-based threshold signature scheme of Gennaro, Jarecki, Krawczyk, and Rabin [22], and present a new variant of it that can be more efficient in practice. Figure 5 represents the description of our proposed robust threshold signature scheme that uses Fig. 4 for the DKG and the distributed generation of the ephemeral key g^b.

Theorem 5. *Under the DL problem the threshold signature described in Fig. 5, is secure against a static adversary corrupting up to t parties, with $t < n/2$.*

We refer to the full version of paper [3] for the security proof of the scheme.

Security Against Wagner's Attack. The threshold signature in Fig. 5 is secure against the concurrent attack using Wagner's algorithm [6,40]. Intuitively, the attack crucially relies on the fact that an adversary can open ℓ sessions of the protocol in parallel, that is in the same round. At each session r the adversary gets g^{b_i} from the honest parties and computes its commitment shares g^{b_j}, $j \in A$, based on the honest parties' commitment shares, before submitting g^b to the RO. For big enough ℓ this is enough for the adversary to forge a signature [6]. As mentioned in the same paper [6], a countermeasure is to let parties commit to the shares g^{b_i} and only after a round of broadcast they open them. This clearly prevents the adversary to compute his shares adaptively. A typical way for implementing this is using PK-based commitments such as Pedersen's, as done for example in [22,27]. We have a similar approach in our protocol, and reveal the commitments and opening at the beginning of the second round.

4.3 Efficiency of New Protocols

Next, we summarize the efficiency of the proposed DKG protocol (Fig. 4) and the threshold signature (Fig. 5) and compare them with the ones proposed by Pedersen [29] and Gennaro et al. [22].

Comparing our DKG protocol to the variant of Pedersen DKG presented in [22], we observe asymptotic improvements in computational cost of parties. In our DKG protocol, each party is required to perform approximately $2n$ exponentiations within the group, conduct $3n$ evaluations of degree-t polynomials in the field, and execute $5n$ hash operations for commitment purposes. While, in the Pedersen DKG each party needs to compute $(2tn+n)$ exponentiations in the group, $2n$ degree-t polynomial evaluations in the field, and a single hash operation. Regarding communication, our DKG protocol entails each party privately sending n field elements to other participants, along with broadcasting approximately $2n$ images generated through hash functions (i.e., the commitments) and t field elements (i.e., coefficients of $r(X)$). Conversely, in the Pedersen DKG protocol, each party privately sends $2n$ field elements to the other participants and then broadcast $2t$ group elements. We refer Table 4 for a summarized comparison of the asymptotic costs in both DKG protocols.

When evaluating the efficiency of threshold signatures, as outlined in our protocol (described in Fig. 5), in addition to executing our DKG protocol with associated costs summarized in Table 4, each participants is required to perform n evaluations of degree-t polynomials in the field (for the verification of partial openings) and broadcast t field elements (representing the coefficients of the polynomial $r^{(i)}(X)$). In the GJKR [22] signature, alongside the Pedersen DKG protocol with its cost breakdown provided in Table 4, each party must conduct $2n$ group exponentiations and broadcast a single field element (for the opening).

In line with the efficiency trends observed in the VSS and DKG protocols, we anticipate that our threshold signature scheme can have significantly improved performance compared to the construction presented by Gennaro et al. [22].

Table 4. Asymptotic costs in the GJKR [22] variant of Pedersen DKG [29] and our proposed scheme. DL: Discrete Logarithm, BC: Broadcast, n: Number of parties, $t \approx n/2$: Threshold value, $E_{\mathbb{G}}$: Exponentiation in group $\mathbb{G}$, $\mathcal{PE}$: degree-t Polynomial Evaluation, $\mathcal{H}$: Hashing, $|\mathbb{G}|$: $\mathbb{G}$ element size, $|\mathbb{Z}_q|$: $\mathbb{Z}_q$ element size, $|\mathcal{H}|$: $\mathcal{H}$ image size.

DKG Scheme	Assumption	Parties' Computation	Communication
GJKR [22] (Pedersen [29])	DL-based	$(2nt + n)\,E_{\mathbb{G}} + 2n\,\mathcal{PE} + 1\,\mathcal{H}$ ($2nt\,E_{\mathbb{G}}$ is for verify)	Private: $2n\,|\mathbb{Z}_q|$ BC: $2t \approx n\,|\mathbb{G}|$
This work Sect. 4.1	DL & Hash-based	$2n\,E_{\mathbb{G}} + 3n\,\mathcal{PE} + 5n\,\mathcal{H}$ ($2n\,E_{\mathbb{G}} + n\,\mathcal{PE} + 3n\,\mathcal{H}$ is for verify)	Private: $1n\,|\mathbb{Z}_q|$ BC: $2n\,|\mathcal{H}| + t\,|\mathbb{Z}_q|$

5 More Efficient Threshold Protocols from Isogenies

Our VSS construction from Sect. 3 can be seamlessly integrated into current isogeny-based DKG protocols and threshold signatures present in the literature [1,2,8,13]. The resulting protocols outperform the current state-of-the-art in terms of communication and/or computational cost.

In the interest of clarity and conciseness, we defer a brief introduction to isogenies and of the state-of-the-art protocols to the full version of paper [3]. Here, we only present the modifications to these protocols to achieve the better performance results.

5.1 More Efficient DKG Protocols for CSIDH

In this section, we revisit the DKG protocols recently proposed in [2] for CSIDH-based primitives, which can be considered variants of CSI-RAShi [1,8] and Structured CSI-RAShi [1]. We only focus on the structured case (i.e. where the target public key has the structure $\{E_i = [c_i x_0]E_0\}_{i=1}^k$ for public integers $\{c_i\}_{i=1}^k$), as it is generally more efficient and a single public key is a special case of this (for $k = 1$). The extended (non-structured) case (i.e. public keys of the type $\{E_i = [x_i]E_0\}_{i=1}^k$) can be inferred from the latter.

Structured CSI-RAShi++ DKG Protocol. Both DKG protocols proposed in [2] are new variants of the protocols in [1,8] with lower computational cost which in terms of isogeny computations. This is achieved at the cost of higher communication complexity, a reduced number of corrupted parties to $n/3$, and an interactive share verification in the final DKG protocols.

We revisit these protocols in in the full version of paper [3, Fig. 10]. They consist of two stages: a VSS step and a computationally secure public key computation step. During the VSS step, the parties engage in the BGW VSS scheme [5] and share a secret x_0 (i.e., the secret key) among themselves. Then, in the (public key) computation step, they use their shares obtained from the first step and compute the target public key $\{E_i = [c_i x_0]E_0\}_{i=1}^k$ in a round-robin fashion.

In this section, we show that by integrating our new NI-VSS scheme into the VSS step of their DKG protocols, we can resolve all of the drawbacks mentioned above at the same time. Our protocols achieve lower communication, allow $n/2$ corrupted parties and are non-interactively verifiable, while achieving the same computational complexity as the fastest protocols from [2].

In Fig. 6, we present a new variant of the structured DKG protocol from [2, Section 4], by replacing the BGW VSS scheme used in their protocol with our NI-VSS scheme. This replacement results in a reduction of IT security in the VSS step to computational security, but overall, as in the original case, the resulting DKG protocol achieves quantum computational security.

We discuss security below. For formal definitions of the security properties of DKGs, we refer to [8, 22].

Theorem 6 (Structured CSI-RAShi++ DKG Protocol). *If the VSS scheme given in Fig. 2 is a secure verifiable secret sharing scheme in the QROM, then the DKG protocol of Fig. 6 is secure in the QROM. That is correct, robust, and satisfies the secrecy property.*

Verifiable Secret Sharing Step: This is done using the NI-VSS scheme presented in Fig. 2 in a standard distributed manner. Namely, each party P_i one time plays the role of the dealer in Fig. 2, samples $f^{(i)}(X)$, and then in a verifiable manner shares $f^{(i)}(0)$ with other parties. In the end, all the shareholders get a share of the joint secret key x_0, where implicitly is defined as $x_0 = \sum_{i \in Q} f^{(i)}(0)$ for a qualified set Q. Each party P_j obtains its share of x_0 as $x_j = \sum_{i \in Q} f^{(i)}(j)$.

SPK Computation Step: This is done as in the structured public key computation step of the DKG protocol presented in [2, Section 4], which is reviewed in [3, Fig. 10]. At the end, the parties return the structured public key $\{E_i = [c_i x_0] E_0\}_{i=1}^{k}$.

Fig. 6. Structured CSI-RAShi++: an efficient DKG protocol for a structured public key $\{E_i = [c_i x_0] E_0\}_{i=1}^{k}$.

Proof. The proof is almost identical to the proof of [2, Theorem 4.1], except that in this case we will rely on the security of the new NI-VSS, proven in Theorem 2, rather than the security of the BGW VSS scheme [5] which is employed in the secret sharing step of their DKG protocol.   □

Efficiency of the Revised DKG Protocols. In Tables 5 and 6, we summarize the computational and communication costs of our proposed DKG protocols, CSI-RASHI++ and Structured CSI-RAShi++ (both from Fig. 6, the former for the choice $k = 1$), and compare them with current DKG protocols in the CSIDH setting. To have a fair comparison we express the computational cost as the sequential runtime of the protocol steps, i.e. the total runtime from start to finish, including when some of the parties are idle. We quantify the communication cost as the amount of outgoing communication per party. Our cost analysis methodology builds on that of [2] with some optimizations from [1].

Table 5. Sequential computational costs (including idle time) of the different DKGs from [2] and from this work, in terms of polynomial evaluations, isogeny computations and calls to the commitment scheme and random oracle. For compactness, we assume $\gcd(k,n) = \min\{k,n\}$ and do not explicitly write down the gains through the twist trick. See [2] for more details.

	Polynomial Eval.	Isogenies	Commitments	RO queries
Basic DKG [2]	$2(n-1)^2 + n\lambda(n+2)$	$2n\lambda + n$	$2n(n+3)$	$2n$
Extended DKG [1,2]	$2(n-1)^2 k + n\lambda(n\lceil\frac{k}{n}\rceil + k)$	$n(n\lambda+1)\lfloor\frac{k}{n}\rfloor$	$2n((n-1)\lceil\frac{k}{n}\rceil + 2k)$	nk
Structured DKG [2]	$2(n-1)^2 + n\lambda(2n+1)$	$n(n\lambda+1)\lfloor\frac{k}{n}\rfloor$	$2n(3n-1)$	n^2
Our Basic DKG	$(3n-1) + n\lambda(n+2)$	$2n\lambda + n$	$2n(n+5) - 2$	$3n$
Our Extended DKG	$(3n-1)k + n\lambda(n\lceil\frac{k}{n}\rceil + k)$	$n(n\lambda+1)\lfloor\frac{k}{n}\rfloor$	$2n((n-2)\lceil\frac{k}{n}\rceil + 4k) - 2k$	$2nk$
Our Structured DKG	$(3n-1) + 2n^2\lambda$	$n(n\lambda+1)\lfloor\frac{k}{n}\rfloor$	$2n(3n+1) - 2$	$n(n+1)$

Table 6. Communication costs of different DKGs from [2] and this work, in terms of elements in $\mathbb{Z}_N$ and $\mathcal{E}$, and the number of commitments and proof pieces (i.e. elements of size 2λ). The cost represents the outgoing cost per party. The cost of the basic DKG follows by setting $k = 1$.

	Element of $\mathbb{Z}_N$	Element of $\mathcal{E}$	Commitment/Proof Piece
Extended DKG [1,2]	$2k(n-1)(n+t-1) + kn\lambda(t+1)$	nk	$nk(3n+2)$
Structured DKG [2]	$2(n-1)(n+t-1) + n\lambda(t+1)$	nk	$n(3n+2)$
Our Extended DKG	$k(n\lambda(t+1) + n + t)$	nk	$k(n(3n+5) - 1)$
Our Structured DKG	$n\lambda(t+1) + n + t$	nk	$n(3n+5) - 1$

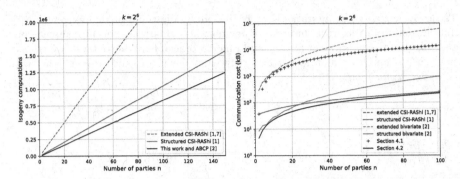

Fig. 7. Computational and communication costs of the DKG protocols [1,2,8] for the CSIDH-512 parameter set, shown as a function of the number of parties for $k = 2^6$.

In Fig. 7, we further plot the computational and communication costs of our protocols and compare them to the literature. We note that the number of isogeny computations coincides exactly with [2], currently the fastest in the literature. In terms of communication, both the extended and structured versions of our protocols outperform their counterparts from the literature. For asymptotically large n, the communication cost of our protocols tend towards the communication cost of CSI-RAShi, as the commmunication cost of underlying NI-TZK proof schemes starts to dominate in these regions.

5.2   Threshold, Efficient, and Robust CSI-SharK

Next, we revisit the CSI-FiSh-based threshold signing protocol of Campos and Muth [13], and construct *ThreshER SharK*, which is a **T**hreshold, **E**fficient and **R**obust signature scheme based on CSI-**SharK** [1]. Campos-Muth threshold signature [13] is based on the basic version of CSI-FiSh [9], with its public key and the ephemeral keys being sampled by the CSI-RAShi DKG protocol [8]. The basic version of CSI-FiSh is based on an ID scheme that has a binary challenge space, leading to long signing and verification times. By using larger public keys (e.g. extended or structured ones) of k elements, less repetitions are needed and the signatures become faster and smaller.

KeyGen: Given an integer k, as the design parameter in CSI-SharK signature, the parties first agree on a public exceptional set $\Xi_k = \{c_0 = 0, c_1 = 1, c_2, \ldots, c_{k-1}\}$. Then, they engage in the $\mathsf{DKG}^{\text{Structured CSI-RAShi++}}$ protocol (refer to Fig. 6) to sample the public key $\mathsf{pk} := (E_0, \ldots, E_{k-1})$, where $E_i = [c_i x]E_0$. At the end, we have a qualified set, which w.l.o.g. we assume to be $Q_0 := \{P_1, P_2, \ldots, P_n\}$.

Sign$(m, \langle x_i \rangle)$: To generate a signature on m, the parties in Q_0 act as follows.

1. For $l = 1, \ldots, t_k$, parties run $(b_l, F_l, B_l) \leftarrow \mathsf{DKG}^{\text{CSI-RAShi++}}(E_0)$. Note that at each invocation, malicious parties might be disqualified. We assume to end every step with a set $Q_l \subseteq Q_{l-1}$. Only the parties in Q_{t_k} continue the protocol.

2. The parties compute the challenge $d_1, \ldots, d_{t_k} \leftarrow H(F_1, \ldots, F_{t_k} \| m)$.

3. For $l = 1, \ldots, t_k$, the parties in Q_{t_k} behave as follows.

   (a) each party P_i computes $r_l^{(i)}(X) = b_l^{(i)}(X) - d_l s^{(i)}(X)$.

   (b) using their secret values shared during the NI-VSS protocol, namely $s^{(i)}$ and $b_l^{(i)}$, each other party P_j verifies
   $$r_l^{(i)}(j) \overset{?}{=} b_l^{(i)}(j) - d_l s^{(i)}(j)$$

   (c) Whenever one of these checks fails, P_j broadcasts a complaint against P_i. When a player P_i has $t+1$ or more complaints against them, they are disqualified. The remaining players can then construct $r_l^{(i)}(0)$ by reconstructing both $b_l^{(i)}(0)$ and $s^{(i)}(0)$ using the information from the DKGs. This is always possible when there are at least $t+1$ honest parties.

   (d) For each party P_i in $Q_l \backslash Q_{t_k}$, reconstruct $r_l^{(i)}(0)$ in the same way.

   (e) For each party P_i in $Q_0 \backslash Q_l$, set and reconstruct $r_l^{(i)}(0) = s^{(i)}(0)$.

   (f) Using $\{r_l^{(i)}(0)\}_{i=1,\ldots,n}$, parties build the responses $r_l = \sum_{i \in Q} r_l^{(i)}(0)$.

4. Finally, parties output the signature (r, d), where $r = (r_1, \ldots, r_{t_k})$.

Verify$((r, d_1, \ldots, d_{t_k}), m, \mathsf{pk})$: To verify a signature $(r, d_1, \ldots, d_{t_k})$ on m using the public key $\mathsf{pk} = (E_1, \ldots, E_{k-1})$, the verifier proceeds as follows.

1. For $l = 1, \ldots, t_k$, compute $F_l = [r_l]E_{d_l}$, where

2. Compute $d_1', \ldots, d_{t_k}' \leftarrow H(F_1, \ldots, F_{t_k} \| m)$

3. If $d_1 = d_1' \wedge \cdots \wedge d_{t_k} = d_{t_k}'$, return valid, otherwise invalid.

Fig. 8. ThreshER SharK: a Threshold, Efficient, and Robust signature scheme based on CSI-SharK.

Similarly, one can extend the robust threshold signing protocol of Campos and Muth to work with the extended version of CSI-FiSh [9] or its structured counterpart CSI-SharK [1]. Based on the comparisons presented in Tables 5,6 and Fig. 7, we know that the latter has faster DKG protocols to generate the public key. Considering this, we propose two modifications to enhance the efficiency of Campos and Muth's robust threshold signature scheme [13]. First, we adapt their threshold signature scheme to work with CSI-SharK [1]. Consequently, the parties can use the Structured CSI-RAShi++ DKG protocol to sample the keys and need to store only a single secret key. As the second modification, we employ the (non-structured) extended variant of our proposed CSI-RAShi++ DKG protocol to sample the ephemeral keys for the revised threshold signature scheme. Figure 8 describes the algorithms of the resulting robust threshold signature, which is called ThreshER SharK. In the figure, $\mathcal{H} : \{0,1\}^* \to (\Xi_k)^{t_k}$ is a random oracle which returns t_k elements from an exceptional set $\Xi_k = \{c_0 = 0, c_1 = 1, c_2, \ldots, c_{k-1}\}$ of size k. ThreshER SharK uses the new NI-VSS scheme in both the key generation and singing protocols.

Efficiency. ThreshER SharK, utilizing an SPK, benefits from the ability to sample keys more efficiently using Structured CSI-RAShi++. While it is possible to extend Campos and Muth's robust threshold signature scheme [13] to accommodate the extended version of CSI-FiSh and gain efficiency through our proposed DKG protocols, it should be noted that the result would be less efficient than ThreshER SharK (We refer to Tables 5-6 for a detailed comparison).

Security. We discuss security of our scheme in the full version of paper [3].

6 Conclusion

In this paper, we presented a general construction for building a NI-VSS scheme using a ZK proof scheme over secret shared data, as formally defined by Boneh et al. [11]. Leveraging this construction, we proposed a practical post-quantum secure NI-VSS scheme based on Shamir secret sharing.

The proposed NI-VSS scheme can be viewed as a modification of the variant of the Pedersen VSS scheme used in the GJKR DKG protocol [22], where we replace the Pedersen commitment with a hash-based commitment scheme. The later modification pushes the protocol to the designated verifier setting, requires a ZK proof over secret shared data, but enables the attainment of Post-Quantum (PQ) security and notably improved efficiency. Consequently, our NI-VSS scheme presents a more efficient and PQ-secure alternative to the Pedersen [29] (or Feldman [20]) VSS scheme in scenarios where public verifiability is not necessary. This holds true for various (post-quantum secure) threshold protocols such as DKG schemes and threshold signatures. To assess the performance of the new NI-VSS scheme alongside the well-established Pedersen scheme, we conducted a prototype implementation, yielding promising results. Compared to the Pedersen scheme, while incurring a $2.5\times$ higher broadcast cost for the dealer, our scheme demonstrates significantly faster sharing times, ranging from $32.5 - 3.25\times$ faster for different values of (n,t), spanning from $(32,15)$ to $(2048,1023)$. Moreover, verification times are substantially reduced, with the new scheme requiring $85 - 479\times$ less time. Using our scheme, a dealer can share a secret with 2048 parties in approximately 2 sec, while parties can verify their shares in less than 5 msec.

A key advantage of new PQ-secure NI-VSS scheme, when compared to the IT-secure BGW VSS scheme [5], is its reduced communication overhead and improved robustness. Specifically, our scheme requires half of the shareholders to be honest, as opposed to two-thirds in the BGW VSS scheme.

Leveraging the new NI-VSS scheme we revisited and improved various classic and PQ-secure DKG and threshold signing protocols [1,2,8,13,22]. Through our revisions, we have not only improved their performance but also relaxed the requirements on the number of honest parties in some cases. We have introduced a new variants of the Pedersen DKG [29] combined with the GJKR threshold signature scheme [22] that can outperform the original versions in terms of computational cost. One notable factor contributing to these improvements is the practical advantage of using a hash function for commitment, which often outperforms the Pedersen commitment. Our results show that, in practice, DKG and threshold signing protocols with designated verifiers suffice for constructing a threshold signature scheme with public-verifier. Our revisions also have led to the development of two DKG protocols and a threshold signature scheme based on isogenies that surpass the state-of-the-art constructions [2,13]. Our isogeny-based threshold signature scheme builds upon the CSI-SharK signature [1], but it can also be adapted to work with the CSI-FiSh [9], although with lower efficiency in the key generation phase.

The remarkable efficiency and simplicity of the NI-VSS scheme render it a valuable tool for various classic and PQ-secure threshold protocols, extending beyond those revisited in this paper. Future research can explore the integration of the new NI-VSS scheme and the revised protocols into other settings and threshold protocols, while evaluating their impact on overall efficiency.

Acknowledgments. We would like to express our gratitude to the anonymous reviewers for their valuable insights and suggestions. We also extend our thanks to Navid Ghaedi Bardeh for his valuable assistance during the implementation of VSS schemes.

This work has been supported in part by the Defense Advanced Research Projects Agency (DARPA) under contract No. HR001120C0085, by the FWO under an Odysseus project GOH9718N, by the European Research Council (ERC) under the European Union's Horizon 2020 research and innovation programme (Grant agreement No. 101020788 - Adv-ERC-ISOCRYPT), by CyberSecurity Research Flanders with reference number VR20192203, by the European Research Council (ERC) under the European Union's Horizon 2020 research and innovation program under project PICOCRYPT (grant agreement No. 101001283), by the Spanish Government under projects PRODIGY (TED2021-132464B-I00) and ESPADA (PID2022-142290OB-I00). The last two projects are co-funded by European Union EIE, and NextGenerationEU/PRTR funds.

References

1. Atapoor, S., Baghery, K., Cozzo, D., Pedersen, R.: CSI-SharK: CSI-FiSh with Sharing-friendly Keys. In: Simpson, L., Rezazadeh Baee, M.A. (eds.) Information Security and Privacy. ACISP 2023. LNCS, vol. 13915. Springer, Cham (2023). https://doi.org/10.1007/978-3-031-35486-1_21
2. Atapoor, S., Baghery, K., Cozzo, D., Pedersen, R.: Practical robust DKG protocols for CSIDH. In: Tibouchi, M., Wang, X., (eds.) Applied Cryptography and Network Security. ACNS 2023. LNCS, vol. 13906. Springer, Cham (2023). https://doi.org/10.1007/978-3-031-33491-7_9
3. Atapoor, S., Baghery, K., Cozzo, D., Pedersen, R.: VSS from distributed ZK proofs and applications. Cryptology ePrint Archive, Paper 2023/992 (2023). https://eprint.iacr.org/2023/992

4. Baghery, K., Cozzo, D., Pedersen, R.: An isogeny-based ID protocol using structured public keys. In: Paterson, M.B. (ed.) IMACC 2021. LNCS, vol. 13129, pp. 179–197. Springer, Cham (2021). https://doi.org/10.1007/978-3-030-92641-0_9

5. Ben-Or, M., Goldwasser, S., Wigderson, A.: Completeness theorems for non-cryptographic fault-tolerant distributed computation (extended abstract). In: 20th Annual ACM Symposium on Theory of Computing, pp. 1–10, Chicago, IL, USA, 2–4 May 1988. ACM Press (1988)

6. Benhamouda, F., Lepoint, T., Loss, J., Orrù, M., Raykova, M.: On the (in)security of ROS. In: Canteaut, A., Standaert, F.-X. (eds.) Advances in Cryptology – EUROCRYPT 2021. EUROCRYPT 2021. LNCS, vol. 12696. Springer, Cham (2021). https://doi.org/10.1007/978-3-030-77870-5_2

7. Bernstein, D., De Feo, L., Leroux, A., Smith, B.: Faster computation of isogenies of large prime degree. arXiv preprint arXiv:2003.10118 (2020)

8. Beullens, W., Disson, L., Pedersen, R., Vercauteren, F.: CSI-RAShi: distributed key generation for CSIDH. In: Cheon, J.H., Tillich, J.-P. (eds.) PQCrypto 2021 2021. LNCS, vol. 12841, pp. 257–276. Springer, Cham (2021). https://doi.org/10.1007/978-3-030-81293-5_14

9. Beullens, W., Kleinjung, T., Vercauteren, F.: CSI-FiSh: efficient isogeny based signatures through class group computations. In: Galbraith, S.D., Moriai, S. (eds.) ASIACRYPT 2019. LNCS, vol. 11921, pp. 227–247. Springer, Cham (2019). https://doi.org/10.1007/978-3-030-34578-5_9

10. Bishnoi, A., Clark, P.L., Potukuchi, A., Schmitt, J.R.: On zeros of a polynomial in a finite grid. Combinat. Probab. Comput. **27**(3), 310–333 (2018)

11. Boneh, D., Boyle, E., Corrigan-Gibbs, H., Gilboa, N., Ishai, Y.: Zero-knowledge proofs on secret-shared data via fully linear PCPs. In: Boldyreva, A., Micciancio, D. (eds.) CRYPTO 2019. LNCS, vol. 11694, pp. 67–97. Springer, Cham (2019). https://doi.org/10.1007/978-3-030-26954-8_3

12. Bonnetain, X., Schrottenloher, A.: Quantum security analysis of CSIDH. In: Canteaut, A., Ishai, Y. (eds.) EUROCRYPT 2020. LNCS, vol. 12106, pp. 493–522. Springer, Cham (2020). https://doi.org/10.1007/978-3-030-45724-2_17

13. Campos, F., Muth, P.: On actively secure fine-grained access structures from isogeny assumptions. In: Cheon, J.H., Johansson, T., (eds.) Post-Quantum Cryptography. PQCrypto 2022. LNCS, vol. 13512. Springer, Cham (2022). https://doi.org/10.1007/978-3-031-17234-2_18

14. Castryck, W., Lange, T., Martindale, C., Panny, L., Renes, J.: CSIDH: an efficient post-quantum commutative group action. In: Peyrin, T., Galbraith, S. (eds.) ASIACRYPT 2018. LNCS, vol. 11274, pp. 395–427. Springer, Cham (2018). https://doi.org/10.1007/978-3-030-03332-3_15

15. Chor, B., Goldwasser, S., Micali, S., Awerbuch, B.: Verifiable secret sharing and achieving simultaneity in the presence of faults (extended abstract). In 26th Annual Symposium on Foundations of Computer Science, pp. 383–395. Portland, Oregon, 21–23 October 1985. IEEE Computer Society Press (1985)

16. Dalskov, A., Lee, E., Soria-Vazquez, E.: Circuit amortization friendly encodings and their application to statistically secure multiparty computation. In: Moriai, S., Wang, H. (eds.) ASIACRYPT 2020. LNCS, vol. 12493, pp. 213–243. Springer, Cham (2020). https://doi.org/10.1007/978-3-030-64840-4_8

17. De Feo, L.: Mathematics of isogeny based cryptography. arXiv preprint arXiv:1711.04062 (2017)

18. Feo, L.D., et al.: SCALLOP: scaling the CSI-FiSh. In: Boldyreva, A., Kolesnikov, V. (eds.) Public-Key Cryptography – PKC 2023. PKC 2023. LNCS, vol. 13940. Springer, Cham (2023). https://doi.org/10.1007/978-3-031-31368-4_13

19. Don, J., Fehr, S., Majenz, C., Schaffner, C.: Security of the Fiat-Shamir transformation in the quantum random-oracle model. In: Boldyreva, A., Micciancio, D. (eds.) CRYPTO 2019. LNCS, vol. 11693, pp. 356–383. Springer, Cham (2019). https://doi.org/10.1007/978-3-030-26951-7_13

20. Feldman, P.: A practical scheme for non-interactive verifiable secret sharing. In: 28th Annual Symposium on Foundations of Computer Science, pp. 427–437. Los Angeles, CA, USA, 12–14 October 1987. IEEE Computer Society Press (1987)

21. Fiat, A., Shamir, A.: How to prove yourself: practical solutions to identification and signature problems. In: Odlyzko, A.M. (ed.) CRYPTO 1986. LNCS, vol. 263, pp. 186–194. Springer, Heidelberg (1987). https://doi.org/10.1007/3-540-47721-7_12

22. Gennaro, R., Jarecki, S., Krawczyk, H., Rabin, T.: Secure distributed key generation for discrete-log based cryptosystems. J. Cryptol. **20**(1), 51–83 (2007)

23. Gennaro, R., Rabin, M.O., Rabin, T.: Simplified VSS and fast-track multiparty computations with applications to threshold cryptography. In: Coan, B.A., Afek, Y. (eds.) 17th ACM Symposium Annual on Principles of Distributed Computing, pp. 101–111. Puerto Vallarta, Mexico, 28 June - 2 July 1998. Association for Computing Machinery (1988)

24. Gentry, C., Halevi, S., Lyubashevsky, V.: Practical non-interactive publicly verifiable secret sharing with thousands of parties. In: Dunkelman, O., Dziembowski, S., (eds.) Advances in Cryptology – EUROCRYPT 2022. EUROCRYPT 2022. LNCS, vol. 13275. Springer, Cham (2022). https://doi.org/10.1007/978-3-031-06944-4_16

25. Groth, J.: Non-interactive distributed key generation and key resharing. Cryptology ePrint Archive, Report 2021/339 (2021). https://eprint.iacr.org/2021/339

26. Kitaev, A.Y.: Quantum measurements and the abelian stabilizer problem. Electron. Colloquium Comput. Complex. **TR96-003**, 22 (1996)

27. Komlo, C., Goldberg, I.: FROST: flexible round-optimized Schnorr threshold signatures. In: Dunkelman, O., Jacobson, Jr., M.J., O'Flynn, C. (eds.) SAC 2020. LNCS, vol. 12804, pp. 34–65. Springer, Cham (2021). https://doi.org/10.1007/978-3-030-81652-0_2

28. Pedersen, T.P.: A threshold cryptosystem without a trusted party. In: Davies, D.W. (ed.) EUROCRYPT 1991. LNCS, vol. 547, pp. 522–526. Springer, Heidelberg (1991). https://doi.org/10.1007/3-540-46416-6_47

29. Pedersen, T.P.: Non-interactive and information-theoretic secure verifiable secret sharing. In: Feigenbaum, J. (ed.) CRYPTO 1991. LNCS, vol. 576, pp. 129–140. Springer, Heidelberg (1992). https://doi.org/10.1007/3-540-46766-1_9

30. Peikert, C.: He gives C-Sieves on the CSIDH. In: Canteaut, A., Ishai, Y. (eds.) EUROCRYPT 2020. LNCS, vol. 12106, pp. 463–492. Springer, Cham (2020). https://doi.org/10.1007/978-3-030-45724-2_16

31. Schnorr, C.P.: Efficient identification and signatures for smart cards. In: Brassard, G. (ed.) CRYPTO 1989. LNCS, vol. 435, pp. 239–252. Springer, New York (1990). https://doi.org/10.1007/0-387-34805-0_22

32. Schoenmakers, B.: A simple publicly verifiable secret sharing scheme and its application to electronic voting. In: Wiener, M. (ed.) CRYPTO 1999. LNCS, vol. 1666, pp. 148–164. Springer, Heidelberg (1999). https://doi.org/10.1007/3-540-48405-1_10

33. Shamir, A.: How to share a secret. Commun. ACM **22**(11), 612–613 (1979)

34. Shor, P.W.: Algorithms for quantum computation: discrete logarithms and factoring. In: 35th Annual Symposium on Foundations of Computer Science, pp. 124–134. Santa Fe, NM, USA, 20–22 November 1994. IEEE Computer Society Press (1994)

35. Silverman, J.H.: The Arithmetic of Elliptic Curves. GTM, vol. 106. Springer, New York (2009). https://doi.org/10.1007/978-0-387-09494-6

36. Tomescu, A., et al.: Towards scalable threshold cryptosystems. In: 2020 IEEE Symposium on Security and Privacy, pp. 877–893, San Francisco, CA, USA, 18–21 May 2020. IEEE Computer Society Press (2020)

37. Unruh, D.: Computationally binding quantum commitments. In: Fischlin, M., Coron, J.-S. (eds.) EUROCRYPT 2016. LNCS, vol. 9666, pp. 497–527. Springer, Heidelberg (2016). https://doi.org/10.1007/978-3-662-49896-5_18

38. Unruh, D.: Post-quantum security of Fiat-Shamir. In: Takagi, T., Peyrin, T. (eds.) ASIACRYPT 2017. LNCS, vol. 10624, pp. 65–95. Springer, Cham (2017). https://doi.org/10.1007/978-3-319-70694-8_3

39. Vélu, J.: Isogénies entre courbes elliptiques. CR Acad. Sci. Paris, Séries A **273**, 305–347 (1971)

40. Wagner, D.: A generalized birthday problem. In: Yung, M. (ed.) CRYPTO 2002. LNCS, vol. 2442, pp. 288–304. Springer, Heidelberg (2002). https://doi.org/10.1007/3-540-45708-9_19

Threshold Linear Secret Sharing
to the Rescue of MPC-in-the-Head

Thibauld Feneuil[1,2]([✉]) [iD] and Matthieu Rivain[1] [iD]

[1] CryptoExperts, Paris, France
thibauld.feneuil@cryptoexperts.com
[2] Sorbonne Université, CNRS, INRIA, Institut de Mathématiques
de Jussieu-Paris Rive Gauche, Ouragan, Paris, France

Abstract. The MPC-in-the-Head paradigm is a popular framework to build zero-knowledge proof systems using techniques from secure multi-party computation (MPC). While this paradigm is not restricted to a particular secret sharing scheme, all the efficient instantiations for small circuits proposed so far rely on additive secret sharing.

In this work, we show how applying a threshold linear secret sharing scheme (threshold LSSS) can be beneficial to the MPC-in-the-Head paradigm. For a general *passively-secure* MPC protocol model capturing most of the existing MPCitH schemes, we show that our approach improves the soundness of the underlying proof system from $1/N$ down to $1/\binom{N}{\ell}$, where N is the number of parties and ℓ is the privacy threshold of the sharing scheme. While very general, our technique is limited to a number of parties $N \leq |\mathbb{F}|$, where $\mathbb{F}$ is the field underlying the statement, because of the MDS conjecture.

Applying our approach with a low-threshold LSSS also boosts the performance of the proof system by making the MPC emulation cost independent of N for both the prover and the verifier. The gain is particularly significant for the verification time which becomes logarithmic in N (while the prover still has to generate and commit the N input shares). We further generalize and improve our framework: we show how linearly-homomorphic commitments can get rid of the linear complexity of the prover, we generalize our result to any quasi-threshold LSSS, and we describe an efficient batching technique relying on Shamir's secret sharing.

We finally apply our techniques to specific use-cases. We first propose a variant of the recent SDitH signature scheme achieving new interesting trade-offs. In particular, for a signature size of 10 KB, we obtain a verification time lower than 0.5 ms, which is competitive with SPHINCS⁺, while achieving much faster signing. We further apply our batching technique to two different contexts: batched SDitH proofs and batched proofs for general arithmetic circuits based on the Limbo proof system. In both cases, we obtain an amortized proof size lower than 1/10 of the baseline scheme when batching a few dozen statements, while the amortized performances are also significantly improved.

© International Association for Cryptologic Research 2023
J. Guo and R. Steinfeld (Eds.): ASIACRYPT 2023, LNCS 14438, pp. 441–473, 2023.
https://doi.org/10.1007/978-981-99-8721-4_14

1   Introduction

Zero-knowledge proofs are an important tool for many cryptographic protocols and applications. Such proofs enable a *prover* to prove a statement by interacting with a *verifier* without revealing anything more than the statement itself. Zero-knowledge proofs find applications in many contexts: secure identification and signature, (anonymous) credentials, electronic voting, blockchain protocols, and more generally, privacy-preserving cryptography.

Among all the possible techniques to build zero-knowledge proofs, the MPC-in-the-Head framework introduced by Ishai, Kushilevitz, Ostrovsky and Sahai in [IKOS07] has recently gained popularity. This framework relies on secure multi-party computation (MPC) techniques: the prover emulates "in her head" an ℓ-private MPC protocol with N parties and commits each party's view independently. The verifier then challenges the prover to reveal the views of a random subset of ℓ parties. By the privacy of the MPC protocol, nothing is revealed about the plain input, which implies the zero-knowledge property. On the other hand, a malicious prover needs to cheat for at least one party, which shall be discovered by the verifier with high probability, hence ensuring the soundness property.

The MPC-in-the-Head (MPCitH) paradigm provides a versatile way to build (candidate) quantum-resilient proof systems and signature schemes. This approach has the advantage to rely on security assumptions that are believed to be robust in the quantum setting, namely the security of commitment schemes and/or hash functions. Many recent works have proposed new MPCitH techniques which can be applied to general circuits and/or specific problems, some of them leading to efficient candidate post-quantum signature schemes, see for instance [GMO16, CDG+17, AHIV17, KKW18, DDOS19, KZ20b, BFH+20, BN20, BD20, BDK+21, DOT21, DKR+21, KZ22, FJR22, FMRV22]. Proof systems built from the MPCitH paradigm can be divided in two categories:

- Schemes targeting small circuits (*e.g.* to construct efficient signature schemes), such as [KKW18, BN20, KZ22]. In these schemes, the considered MPC protocol only needs to be secure in the *semi-honest model*, enabling efficient constructions, but the resulting proof is linear in the circuit size. Previous schemes in this category are all based on additive secret sharing.
- Schemes such as [AHIV17, GSV21] in which the considered MPC protocol is secure in the *malicious model* and the proof is *sublinear* in the circuit size (in $O(\sqrt{|C|})$ with $|C|$ being the circuit size). Due to their sublinearity, these schemes are more efficient for *middle-size circuits* (while the former remain more efficient for smaller circuits arising *e.g.* in signature schemes).

We note that other quantum-resilient proof systems exist (a.k.a. SNARK, STARK) which do not rely on the MPCitH paradigm and which achieve polylogarithmic proof size (w.r.t. the circuit size), see *e.g.* [BCR+19, BBHR19]. These schemes are hence better suited for *large circuits*.

Our work belongs to the first category of MPCitH-based schemes (*i.e.* targeting small circuits). Currently, the best MPCitH-based schemes in this scope rely on $(N - 1)$-private passively-secure MPC protocols with N parties [KKW18, BN20, DOT21, KZ22], where the parameter N provides different trade-offs between communication (or signature size) and execution time. In these schemes, the proof is composed of elements of size solely depending on the target security level λ (the "incompressible" part) and other elements of size $\mathcal{O}(\lambda^2/\log N)$ bits (the "variable" part). To obtain short proofs or signatures, one shall hence take a large number of parties N. On the other hand, the prover and verifier running times scale linearly with N (because of the MPC emulation) and hence quickly explode while trying to minimize the proof size.

In this paper, we improve this state of affairs. While previous efficient instantiations of the MPCitH paradigm for small circuits all rely on additive secret sharing, we show how to take advantage of using threshold linear secret sharing. Using our approach, we can decrease the soundness error from $1/N$ to $1/\binom{N}{\ell}$ (still using passively-secure protocols), for a small constant ℓ, while making the cost of the MPC emulation independent of N, for both the prover and the verifier. The prover running time remains globally linear in N (because of the initial sharing and commitment phase) but is still significantly improved in practice. On the other hand, the verification time becomes logarithmic in N and is hence drastically reduced (both asymptotically and in practice).

Our Contribution. We first describe a general model of multiparty computation protocol (with additive secret sharing) which captures a wide majority of the protocols used in the MPCitH context. (To the best of our knowledge, our model applies to all the MPCitH schemes except those derived from ZKBoo or Ligero.) Given a statement x and a relation $\mathcal{R}$, these MPC protocols aim to evaluate a randomized function f on a secret witness w such that f outputs ACCEPT when $(x, w) \in \mathcal{R}$ and REJECT with high probability otherwise. The *false-positive rate* of the MPC protocol corresponds to the probability that f outputs ACCEPT even if $(x, w) \notin \mathcal{R}$. We further recall the general transformation of such a protocol into a zero-knowledge proof which achieves a soundness error of

$$\frac{1}{N} + p \cdot \left(1 - \frac{1}{N}\right)$$

where N is the number of parties and p is the false-positive rate of the MPC protocol. We then show how to apply an arbitrary threshold linear secret sharing scheme (LSSS) to our general MPC model and how to transform the obtained MPC protocol into a zero-knowledge proof achieving the following soundness error:

$$\frac{1}{\binom{N}{\ell}} + p \cdot \frac{\ell \cdot (N - \ell)}{\ell + 1},$$

where ℓ is the threshold of the LSSS (any ℓ shares leak no information while the secret can be reconstructed from any $\ell + 1$ shares). Our theorems cover all the MPC protocols complying with our general model, and for any threshold LSSS (covering additive sharing as a particular case).

Besides improving soundness, using an LSSS with a small threshold implies significant gains in terms of timings. Indeed, the prover and the verifier do not need to emulate all the N parties anymore, but only a small number of them ($\ell+1$ for the prover and ℓ for the verifier). For instance, when working with Shamir's secret sharing [Sha79] with polynomials of degree $\ell = 1$, the prover only needs to emulate 2 parties (instead of N) and the verifier only needs to emulate 1 party (instead of $N-1$) while keeping a soundness error about $\frac{1}{N}$ (assuming a small false positive rate p). On the other hand, the proof size is slightly larger than in the standard case (with additive sharing) since one needs to use a Merkle tree for the commitments (and include authentication paths for the opened commitments in the proof). Overall, our approach provides better trade-offs between proof size and performances for MPCitH schemes while drastically reducing the verification time in particular.

We further improve and generalize our approach in different ways. We first show how using linearly-homomorphic commitments can make both the prover and verifier times independent of N (which opens the doors to efficient schemes with large N). The main issue with this approach given the context of application of MPCitH is the current absence of post-quantum candidates for homomorphic commitment schemes. We also generalize our approach to quasi-threshold LSSS, for which a gap Δ exists between the number of parties ℓ which leak no information and the number of parties $\ell + 1 + \Delta$ necessary to reconstruct the secret. We particularly analyze algebraic geometric quasi-threshold schemes [CC06] but our result is mostly negative: we show that using such schemes does not bring a direct advantage to our framework. We then show that our result on quasi-threshold schemes is still useful in the context of batched proofs (*i.e.* proving simultaneously several statements with a single verification process). We propose a batching technique based on Shamir's secret sharing which enables to efficiently batch proofs in our framework (for a subset of the existing MPCitH schemes).

Finally, we describe some applications of our techniques. We first adapt the SDitH signature scheme [FJR22] to our framework with Shamir's secret sharing. We obtain a variant of this scheme that achieves new interesting size-performance trade-offs. For instance, for a signature size of 10 KB, we obtain a signing time of around 3 ms and a verification time lower than 0.5 ms, which is competitive with SPHINCS+ [ABB+22] in terms of size and verification time while achieving much faster signing. We further apply our batching technique to two different contexts: batched proofs for the SDitH scheme and batched proofs for general arithmetic circuits based on the Limbo proof system [DOT21]. In both cases and for the considered parameters, we obtain an amortized proof size lower than $1/10$ of the baseline scheme when batching a few dozen statements, while the amortized performances are also significantly improved (in particular for the verifier).

Related Works. The MPC-in-the-Head paradigm was introduced in the seminal work [IKOS07]. The authors propose general MPCitH constructions relying on MPC protocols in the *semi-honest model* and in the *malicious model*. In the former case (semi-honest model), they only consider 2-private MPC protocols using an additive sharing as input (they also propose an alternative construction with 1-private protocols). In the latter case (malicious model), they are not restricted to any type of sharing. The exact security of [IKOS07] is analyzed in [GMO16]. As other previous works about the MPCitH paradigm, our work can be seen as a specialization of the IKOS framework. In particular, we restrict the considered MPC model, optimize the communication in this model and provide a refined analysis for the soundness (in the exact security setting) to achieve good practical performances.

To the best of our knowledge, besides [IKOS07], the only previous work which considers MPCitH without relying on an additive secret sharing scheme is Ligero [AHIV17]. Ligero is a practical MPCitH-based zero-knowledge proof system for generic circuits which uses Shamir's secret sharing (or Reed-Solomon codes). The authors consider a particular type of MPC protocol in the *malicious model* and analyze the soundness of the resulting proof system. Ligero achieves sublinear communication cost by packing several witness coordinates in one sharing which is made possible by the use of Shamir's secret sharing.

In comparison, our work formalizes the MPC model on which many recent MPCitH-based schemes (with additive sharing) rely and shows how using LSSS in this model can be beneficial. We consider a slightly more restricted MPC model than the one of Ligero: we impose that the parties only perform linear operations on the sharings. On the other hand, we only need the MPC protocol to be secure in the *semi-honest model* and not in the malicious model as Ligero. In fact, this difference of settings (semi-honest versus malicious) makes our techniques and Ligero's different in nature. While Ligero makes use of proximity tests to get a robust MPC protocol, we can use lighter protocols in our case (since we do not need robustness). Moreover, for a given number of parties and a given privacy threshold, the soundness error of our work is smaller than the one of [AHIV17]. On the other hand, we consider MPC protocols which only performs linear operations on shares which, in the current state of the art, cannot achieve sublinearity. For this reason, our work targets proofs of knowledge for small circuits (for example, to build efficient post-quantum signature schemes) while Ligero remains better for middle-size circuits (thanks to the sublinearity).

Finally, let us cite [DOT21] which is another article providing a refined analysis for the transformation of a general MPC model. The scope of the transformation differs from ours, since it covers $(N-1)$-private MPC protocols using broadcast.

In Table 1, we sum up all the MPC models considered in the state of the art of the MPC-in-the-Head paradigm with the soundness errors and limitations of the general schemes.

Concurrent Work. A concurrent and independent work [AGH+23] proposes an optimization of the MPCitH-based schemes based on additive secret sharing. The authors propose a "hypercube" technique which enables the prover to emulate the entire MPC protocol by performing the computation of only $\log_2 N + 1$ parties instead of N, while keeping the same communication cost. While both

Table 1. Existing general transformations of an MPC protocol into a zero-knowledge proof, with associated MPC model and resulting soundness error. The column "Priv." indicates the privacy threshold of the MPC protocol, while the column "Rob." indicates its robutness threshold. N denotes the number of parties in the MPC protocol, δ denotes the robustness error, and p denotes the false positive rate as defined in this work.

Construction	SharingScheme	Priv.	Rob.	Soundness	Restriction
[IKOS07, Sect. 3]	Additive	2	0	$1 - \frac{1}{\binom{N}{2}}$	-
[IKOS07, Sect. 4]	Any	t	t	When $N = \Omega(t), 2^{-\Omega(t)}$	-
[GMO16]	Any	t	r	$\max\left\{\frac{\binom{r}{t}}{\binom{N}{t}}, \sum_{j=0}^{k} 2^j \frac{\binom{t}{j}\binom{N-2k}{t-j}}{\binom{N}{t}}\right\}$ with $k = \lfloor r/2 \rfloor + 1$	-
[AHIV17]	Any	t	r	$\left(1 - \frac{r}{N}\right)^t + \delta$	Broadcast
[DOT21]	Additive	$N-1$	0	$\frac{1}{N} + p\left(1 - \frac{1}{N}\right)$	Broadcast
Our work, Sect. 4	LSSS	ℓ	0	$\frac{1}{\binom{N}{\ell}} + p\frac{\ell(N-\ell)}{\ell+1}$	BroadcastLinear operations
Our work, Sect. 5.2	LSSS withthresholdgap $\Delta + 1$	ℓ	0	$\frac{\binom{\ell+\Delta}{\ell}}{\binom{N}{\ell}} + p \cdot \frac{\ell}{\ell+\Delta+1} \cdot \binom{N-\ell}{\Delta+1}$	BroadcastLinear operations

the hypercube approach and our approach enables to significantly speed up MPCitH-based schemes, they provide different interesting trade-offs and their relative performances shall depend on the context.

2 Preliminaries

Throughout the paper, $\mathbb{F}$ shall denote a finite field. For any $m \in \mathbb{N}^*$, the integer set $\{1, \ldots, m\}$ is denoted $[m]$. For a probability distribution D, the notation $s \leftarrow D$ means that s is sampled from D. For a finite set S, the notation $s \leftarrow S$ means that s is uniformly sampled at random from S. For an algorithm $\mathcal{A}$, $out \leftarrow \mathcal{A}(in)$ further means that out is obtained by a call to $\mathcal{A}$ on input in (using uniform random coins whenever $\mathcal{A}$ is probabilistic). Along the paper, probabilistic polynomial time is abbreviated PPT.

In this paper, we shall use the standard cryptographic notions of indistinguishability, secure pseudo-random generator (PRG), tree PRG, collision-resistant hash function, (hiding and binding) commitment scheme, (honest verifier) zero-knowledge proof of knowledge and secure multiparty computation protocols (in the semi-honest model). Those notions are formally recalled in the full version [FR22]. We recall hereafter the definition of (quasi-)threshold linear secret sharing.

Along the paper, the sharing of a value s is denoted $[\![s]\!] := ([\![s]\!]_1, \ldots, [\![s]\!]_N)$ with $[\![s]\!]_i$ denoting the share of index i for every $i \in [N]$. For any subset of indices $J \subseteq [N]$, we shall further denote $[\![s]\!]_J := ([\![s]\!]_i)_{i \in J}$.

Definition 1 (Threshold LSSS). *Let $\mathbb{F}$ be a finite field and let $\mathbb{V}_1$ and $\mathbb{V}_2$ be two vector spaces over $\mathbb{F}$. Let t and N be integers such that $1 < t \leq N$. A (t, N)-threshold linear secret sharing scheme is a method to share a secret $s \in \mathbb{V}_1$ into N shares $[\![s]\!] := ([\![s]\!]_1, \ldots, [\![s]\!]_N) \in \mathbb{V}_2^N$ such that the secret can be reconstructed from any t shares while no information is revealed on the secret from the knowledge of $t - 1$ shares.*

Formally, an (t, N)-threshold LSSS consists of a pair of algorithms:

$$\begin{cases} \textsf{Share} : \mathbb{V}_1 \times R \mapsto \mathbb{V}_2^N \\ \textsf{Reconstruct}_J : \mathbb{V}_2^t \mapsto \mathbb{V}_1 \end{cases}$$

where $R \subseteq \{0,1\}^*$ denotes some randomness space and where $\textsf{Reconstruct}_J$ is indexed by a set (and defined for every) $J \subset [N]$ such that $|J| = t$. This pair of algorithms satisfies the three following properties:

1. **Correctness:** *for every $s \in \mathbb{V}_1$, $r \in R$, and $J \subset [N]$ s.t. $|J| = t$, and for $[\![s]\!] \leftarrow \textsf{Share}(s; r)$, we have:*

$$\textsf{Reconstruct}_J([\![s]\!]_J) = s.$$

2. **Perfect $(t-1)$-privacy:** *for every $s_0, s_1 \in \mathbb{V}_1$ and $I \subset [N]$ s.t. $|I| = t - 1$, the two distributions*

$$\left\{ [\![s_0]\!]_I \;\middle|\; \begin{matrix} r \leftarrow R \\ [\![s_0]\!] \leftarrow \textsf{Share}(s_0; r) \end{matrix} \right\} \quad and \quad \left\{ [\![s_1]\!]_I \;\middle|\; \begin{matrix} r \leftarrow R \\ [\![s_1]\!] \leftarrow \textsf{Share}(s_1; r) \end{matrix} \right\}$$

   are perfectly indistinguishable.

3. **Linearity:** *for every $v_0, v_1 \in \mathbb{V}_2^t$, $\alpha \in \mathbb{F}$, and $J \subset [N]$ s.t. $|J| = t$,*

$$\textsf{Reconstruct}_J(\alpha \cdot v_0 + v_1) = \alpha \cdot \textsf{Reconstruct}_J(v_0) + \textsf{Reconstruct}_J(v_1).$$

Definition 2 (Quasi-Threshold LSSS). *Let $\mathbb{F}$ be a finite field and let $\mathbb{V}_1$ and $\mathbb{V}_2$ be two vector spaces over $\mathbb{F}$. Let t_1, t_2 and N be integers such that $1 \le t_1 < t_2 \le N$. A (t_1, t_2, N)-quasi-threshold linear secret sharing scheme is a method to share a secret $s \in \mathbb{V}_1$ into N shares $[\![s]\!] := ([\![s]\!]_1, \dots, [\![s]\!]_N) \in \mathbb{V}_2^N$ such that the secret can be reconstructed from any t_2 shares while no information is revealed on the secret from the knowledge of t_1 shares.*

The formal definition of (t_1, t_2, N)-quasi-threshold LSSS is similar to Definition 1 with the $\textsf{Reconstruct}_J$ function defined over $\mathbb{V}_2^{t_2}$ (instead of $\mathbb{V}_2^t$) with cardinalities $|I| = t_1$ and $|J| = t_2$ (instead of $|I| = t-1$ and $|J| = t$). In particular an $(t-1, t, N)$-quasi-threshold LSSS is an (t, N)-threshold LSSS.

Definition 3 (Additive Secret Sharing). *An additive secret sharing scheme over $\mathbb{F}$ is an (N, N)-threshold LSSS for which the Share algorithm is defined as*

$$\textsf{Share} : (s ; (r_1, \dots, r_{N-1})) \mapsto [\![s]\!] := \left(r_1, \dots r_{N-1}, s - \sum_{i=1}^{N-1} r_i \right),$$

with randomness space $R = \mathbb{F}^{N-1}$, and the $\textsf{Reconstruct}_{[N]}$ algorithm simply outputs the sum of all the input shares.

Definition 4 (Shamir's Secret Sharing). *The Shamir's Secret Sharing over $\mathbb{F}$ is an $(\ell+1, N)$-threshold LSSS for which the Share algorithm builds a sharing $[\![s]\!]$ of $s \in \mathbb{F}$ as follows:*

- *sample $r_1, \ldots, r_\ell$ uniformly in $\mathbb{F}$,*
- *build the polynomial P as $P(X) := s + \sum_{i=1}^{\ell} r_i X^i$,*
- *build the shares $[\![s]\!]_i$ as evaluations $P(e_i)$ of P for each $i \in \{1, \ldots, N\}$, where $e_1, \ldots, e_N$ are public non-zero distinct points of $\mathbb{F}$.*

For any subset $J \subseteq [N]$, s.t. $|J| = \ell + 1$, the Reconstruct$_J$ algorithm interpolates the polynomial P from the input $\ell + 1$ evaluation points $[\![s]\!]_J = (P(e_i))_{i \in J}$ and outputs the constant term s.

3   The MPC-in-the-Head Paradigm

The MPC-in-the-Head (MPCitH) paradigm is a framework introduced by Ishai, Kushilevitz, Ostrovsky and Sahai in [IKOS07] to build zero-knowledge proofs using techniques from secure multi-party computation (MPC). We first recall the general principle of this paradigm before introducing a formal model for the underlying MPC protocols and their transformation into zero-knowledge proofs.

Assume we want to build a zero-knowledge proof of knowledge of a witness w for a statement x such that $(x, w) \in \mathcal{R}$ for some relation $\mathcal{R}$. To proceed, we shall use an MPC protocol in which N parties $\mathcal{P}_1, \ldots, \mathcal{P}_N$ securely and correctly evaluate a function f on a secret witness w with the following properties:

- each party $\mathcal{P}_i$ takes a share $[\![w]\!]_i$ as input, where $[\![w]\!]$ is a sharing of w;
- the function f outputs ACCEPT when $(x, w) \in \mathcal{R}$ and REJECT otherwise;
- the protocol is ℓ-private in the semi-honest model, meaning that the views of any ℓ parties leak no information about the secret witness.

We can use this MPC protocol to build a zero-knowledge proof of knowledge of a witness w satisfying $(x, w) \in \mathcal{R}$. The prover proceeds as follows:

- she builds a random sharing $[\![w]\!]$ of w;
- she simulates locally ("in her head") all the parties of the MPC protocol;
- she sends a commitment of each party's view to the verifier, where such a view includes the party's input share, its random tape, and its received messages (the sent messages can further be deterministically derived from those elements);
- she sends the output shares $[\![f(w)]\!]$ of the parties, which should correspond to a sharing of ACCEPT.

Then the verifier randomly chooses ℓ parties and asks the prover to reveal their views. After receiving them, the verifier checks that they are consistent with an honest execution of the MPC protocol and with the commitments. Since only ℓ parties are opened, the revealed views leak no information about the secret witness w, which ensures the zero-knowledge property. On the other hand, the random choice of the opened parties makes the cheating probability upper bounded[1] by $1 - \binom{N-2}{\ell-2}/\binom{N}{\ell}$, which ensures the soundness of the proof.

---

[1] The optimal strategy for a malicious prover is to have an inconsistency only between two parties. The soundness error is thus the probability that these two parties are not simultaneously in the set of the ℓ opened views.

The MPCitH paradigm simply requires the underlying MPC protocol to be secure in the semi-honest model (and not in the malicious model), meaning that the parties are assumed to be honest but curious: they follow honestly the MPC protocol while trying to learn secret information from the received messages.

Several simple MPC protocols have been proposed that yield fairly efficient zero-knowledge proofs and signature schemes in the MPCitH paradigm, see for instance [KZ20b,BD20,BDK+21,FJR22]. These protocols lie in a specific sub-class of MPC protocols in the semi-honest model which we formalize hereafter.

3.1   General Model of MPC Protocol with Additive Sharing

We consider a passively-secure MPC protocol that performs its computation on a base finite field $\mathbb{F}$ so that all the manipulated variables (including the witness w) are tuples of elements from $\mathbb{F}$. In what follows, the sizes of the different tuples involved in the protocol are kept implicit for the sake of simplicity. The parties take as input an additive sharing $[\![w]\!]$ of the witness w (one share per party). Then the parties compute one or several rounds in which they perform three types of actions:

Receiving randomness: the parties receive a random value (or random tuple) ε from a randomness oracle $\mathcal{O}_R$. When calling this oracle, all the parties get the same random value ε. This might not be convenient in a standard multi-party computation setting (since such an oracle would require a trusted third party or a possibly complex coin-tossing protocol), but in the MPCitH context, these random values are provided by the verifier as challenges.

Receiving hint: the parties can receive a sharing $[\![\beta]\!]$ (one share per party) from a hint oracle $\mathcal{O}_H$. The hint β can depend on the witness w and the previous random values sampled from $\mathcal{O}_R$. Formally, for some function ψ, the hint is sampled as $\beta \leftarrow \psi(w, \varepsilon^1, \varepsilon^2, \ldots; r)$ where $\varepsilon^1, \varepsilon^2, \ldots$ are the previous outputs of $\mathcal{O}_R$ and where r is a fresh random tape.

Computing & broadcasting: the parties can locally compute $[\![\alpha]\!] := [\![\varphi(v)]\!]$ from a sharing $[\![v]\!]$ where φ is an $\mathbb{F}$-linear function, then broadcast all the shares $[\![\alpha]\!]_1, \ldots, [\![\alpha]\!]_N$ to publicly reconstruct $\alpha := \varphi(v)$. If φ is in the form $v \mapsto Av + b$, then the parties can compute $[\![\varphi(v)]\!]$ from $[\![v]\!]$ by letting

$$[\![\varphi(v)]\!]_i := A[\![v]\!]_i + [\![b]\!]_i \text{ for each party } i$$

where $[\![b]\!]$ is a publicly-known sharing of b.[2] This process is usually denoted $[\![\varphi(v)]\!] = \varphi([\![v]\!])$. The function φ can depend on the previous random values $\{\varepsilon^i\}_i$ from $\mathcal{O}_R$ and on the previous broadcasted values.

After t rounds of the above actions, the parties finally output ACCEPT if and only if the publicly reconstructed values $\alpha^1, \ldots, \alpha^t$ satisfy the relation

$$g(\alpha^1, \ldots, \alpha^t) = 0$$

---

[2] Usually, $[\![b]\!]$ is chosen as $(b, 0, \ldots, 0)$ in the case of the additive sharing.

for a given function g.

Protocol 1 gives a general description of an MPC protocol in this paradigm, which we shall use as a model in the rest of the paper. In general, the computing & broadcasting step can be composed of several iterations, which is further depicted in Protocol 2. For the sake of simplicity, we shall consider a single iteration in our presentation (as in Protocol 1) but we stress that the considered techniques and proofs equally apply to the multi-iteration setting (*i.e.* while replacing step (c) of Protocol 1 by Protocol 2).

---

1. The parties take as input a sharing $[\![w]\!]$.

2. For $j = 1$ to t, the parties:

   (a) get a sharing $[\![\beta^j]\!]$ from the hint oracle $\mathcal{O}_H$, such that

   $$\beta^j \leftarrow \psi^j(w, \varepsilon^1, \dots, \varepsilon^{j-1}; r^j)$$

   for a uniform random tape r^j;

   (b) get a common random ε^j from the oracle $\mathcal{O}_R$;

   (c) for some $\mathbb{F}$-linear function $\varphi^j_{(\varepsilon^i)_{i \leq j}, (\alpha^i)_{i < j}}$, compute

   $$[\![\alpha^j]\!] := \varphi^j_{(\varepsilon^i)_{i \leq j}, (\alpha^i)_{i < j}}\left([\![w]\!], ([\![\beta^i]\!])_{i \leq j}\right),$$

   broadcast $[\![\alpha^j]\!]$, and then publicly reconstruct α^j.
   Note: This step can be composed of several iterations as described in Protocol 2.

3. The parties finally accept if $g(\alpha^1, \dots, \alpha^t) = 0$ and reject otherwise.

Note: In the above description w, β^j, ε^j, α^j are elements from the field $\mathbb{F}$ or tuples with coordinates in $\mathbb{F}$ (whose size is not made explicit to keep the presentation simple).

Protocol 1: General MPC protocol Π_{add}.

Output Distribution. In the following, we shall denote $\vec{\varepsilon} := (\varepsilon^1, \dots, \varepsilon^t)$, $\vec{\beta} := (\beta^1, \dots, \beta^t)$, $\vec{\alpha} := (\alpha^1, \dots, \alpha^t)$ and $\vec{r} := (r^1, \dots, r^t)$. From the above description, we have that the output of the protocol deterministically depends on the broadcasted values $\vec{\alpha}$ (through the function g), which in turn deterministically depend on the input witness w, the sampled random values $\vec{\varepsilon}$, and the hints $\vec{\beta}$ (through the functions φ's). It results that the functionality computed by the protocol can be expressed as:

$$f(w, \vec{\varepsilon}, \vec{\beta}) = \begin{cases} \text{ACCEPT} & \text{if } g(\vec{\alpha}) = 0, \\ \text{REJECT} & \text{otherwise,} \end{cases} \quad \text{with } \vec{\alpha} = \Phi(w, \vec{\varepsilon}, \vec{\beta}), \qquad (1)$$

(c) for $k = 1$ to η_j:

- compute a sharing

$$[\![\alpha^{j,k}]\!] := \varphi^{j,k}_{(\varepsilon^i)_{i \leq j},(\alpha^i)_{i < j},(\alpha^{j,i})_{i < k}}\left([\![w]\!],([\![\beta^i]\!])_{i \leq j}\right),$$

for some $\mathbb{F}$-linear function $\varphi^{j,k}_{(\varepsilon^i)_{i \leq j},(\alpha^i)_{i < j},(\alpha^{j,i})_{i < k}}$;

- broadcast their shares $[\![\alpha^{j,k}]\!]$;
- publicly reconstruct $\alpha^{j,k}$;

We denote $\alpha^j := (\alpha^{j,1}, \ldots, \alpha^{j,\eta_j})$.

Protocol 2: General MPC protocol Π_{add} – Iterative computing & broadcasting step for iteration j (with η_j denoting the number of inner iterations).

where Φ is the deterministic function mapping $(w, \vec{\varepsilon}, \vec{\beta})$ to $\vec{\alpha}$ (defined by the coordinate functions $\varphi^1, \ldots, \varphi^t$). We shall restrict our model to MPC protocols for which the function f satisfies the following properties:

- If w is a *good witness*, namely w is such that $(x, w) \in \mathcal{R}$, and if the hints $\vec{\beta}$ are genuinely sampled as $\beta^j \leftarrow \psi^j(w, (\varepsilon^i)_{i<j}; r^j)$ for every j, then the protocol always accepts. More formally:

$$\Pr_{\vec{\varepsilon}, \vec{r}}\left[f(w, \vec{\varepsilon}, \vec{\beta}) = \textsc{Accept} \;\middle|\; \begin{array}{c} (x, w) \in \mathcal{R} \\ \forall j, \beta^j \leftarrow \psi^j(w, (\varepsilon^i)_{i<j}; r^j) \end{array}\right] = 1.$$

- If w is a *bad witness*, namely w is such that $(x, w) \notin \mathcal{R}$, then the protocol rejects with probability at least $1 - p$, for some constant probability p. The latter holds even if the hints $\vec{\beta}$ are not genuinely computed. More formally, for any (adversarially chosen) deterministic functions $\chi^1, \ldots, \chi^t$, we have:

$$\Pr_{\vec{\varepsilon}, \vec{r}}\left[f(w, \vec{\varepsilon}, \vec{\beta}) = \textsc{Accept} \;\middle|\; \begin{array}{c} (x, w) \notin \mathcal{R} \\ \forall j, \beta^j \leftarrow \chi^j(w, (\varepsilon^i)_{i<j}; r^j) \end{array}\right] \leq p.$$

We say that a *false positive* occurs whenever the MPC protocol outputs $\textsc{Accept}$ on input a bad witness w, and we call p the *false positive rate*.

The general MPC model introduced above captures a wide majority of the protocols used in the MPCitH context, such as [KKW18, DDOS19, KZ20b, BFH+20, BN20, BD20, DOT21, BDK+21, DKR+21, KZ22, FJR22, FMRV22]. To the best of our knowledge, our model applies to all the MPCitH schemes in the literature except those derived from the ZKBoo [GMO16] and Ligero [AHIV17] proof systems. An example of protocol fitting this model is the [BN20] protocol where the random multiplication (Beaver) triples to sacrifice are given by the hint oracle. Another example is Limbo [DOT21] for which the hint oracle $\mathcal{O}_H$ corresponds to the untrusted subroutines $\Pi_{\mathsf{InnerProd}}$ and Π_{Rand} while the randomness oracle $\mathcal{O}_R$ is RandomCoin.

3.2   Application of the MPCitH Principle

Any MPC protocol complying with the above description gives rise to a practical short-communication zero-knowledge protocol in the MPCitH paradigm. The resulting zero-knowledge protocol is described in Protocol 3: after sharing the witness w, the prover emulates the MPC protocol "in her head", commits the parties' inputs, and sends a hash digest of the broadcast communications; finally, the prover reveals the requested parties' inputs as well as the broadcast messages of the unopened party, thus enabling the verifier to emulate the computation of the opened parties and to check the overall consistency.

Soundness. Assuming that the underlying MPC protocol follows the model of Sect. 3.1 with a false positive rate p, the soundness error of Protocol 3 is

$$\frac{1}{N} + \left(1 - \frac{1}{N}\right) \cdot p.$$

The above formula results from the fact that a malicious prover might successfully cheat with probability $1/N$ by corrupting the computation of one party or with probability p by making the MPC protocol produce a false positive. This soundness has been formally proven in some previous works, see *e.g.* [DOT21,BN20,FJR22]. In the present article, we provide a general proof for any protocol complying with the format of Protocol 1 in the more general context of any (threshold) linear secret sharing (see Theorem 2).

Performances. The communication of Protocol 3 includes:

- the input shares $(\llbracket w \rrbracket_i, \llbracket \beta^1 \rrbracket_i, \dots, \llbracket \beta^t \rrbracket_i)$ of the opened parties. In practice, a seed $\mathsf{seed}_i \in \{0,1\}^\lambda$ is associated to each party so that for each committed variable v (among the witness w and the hints $\beta^1, \dots, \beta^t$) the additive sharing $\llbracket v \rrbracket$ is built as
$$\begin{cases} \llbracket v \rrbracket_i \leftarrow \mathrm{PRG}(\mathsf{seed}_i) \text{ for } i \neq N \\ \llbracket v \rrbracket_N = v - \sum_{i=1}^{N-1} \llbracket v \rrbracket_i. \end{cases}$$

Thus, instead of committing $(\llbracket w \rrbracket_i, \llbracket \beta^1 \rrbracket_i)$, the initial commitments simply include the seeds for $i \neq N$, and com_i^j becomes useless for $j \geq 2$ and $i \neq N$. Formally, we have:

$$\mathsf{com}_i^j = \begin{cases} \mathrm{Com}(\mathsf{seed}_i; \rho_i^1) & \text{for } j = 1 \text{ and } i \neq N \\ \mathrm{Com}(\llbracket w \rrbracket_N, \llbracket \beta^1 \rrbracket_N; \rho_N^1) & \text{for } j = 1 \text{ and } i = N \\ \emptyset & \text{for } j > 1 \text{ and } i \neq N \\ \mathrm{Com}(\llbracket \beta^j \rrbracket_N; \rho_N^j) & \text{for } j > 1 \text{ and } i = N \end{cases}$$

Some coordinates of the β^j might be uniformly distributed over $\mathbb{F}$ (remember that the β^j are tuples of $\mathbb{F}$ elements). We denote β^{unif} the sub-tuple composed of those uniform coordinates. In this context, the last share $\llbracket \beta^{\mathrm{unif}} \rrbracket_N$ can be built as $\llbracket \beta^{\mathrm{unif}} \rrbracket_N \leftarrow \mathrm{PRG}(\mathsf{seed}_N)$ so that a seed seed_N can be committed

1. The prover shares the witness w into a sharing $[\![w]\!]$.

2. The prover emulates "in her head" the N parties of the MPC protocol.
   For $j = 1$ to t:

   (a) the prover computes
   $$\beta^j = \psi^j(w, (\varepsilon^i)_{i<j}),$$
   shares it into a sharing $[\![\beta^j]\!]$;

   (b) the prover computes the commitments
   $$\mathsf{com}_i^j := \begin{cases} \mathsf{Com}([\![w]\!]_i, [\![\beta^1]\!]_i; \rho_i^1) & \text{if } j = 1 \\ \mathsf{Com}([\![\beta^j]\!]_i; \rho_i^j) & \text{if } j > 1 \end{cases}$$
   for all $i \in \{1, \ldots, N\}$, for some commitment randomness ρ_i^j;

   (c) the prover sends
   $$h_j := \begin{cases} \mathsf{Hash}(\mathsf{com}_1^1, \ldots, \mathsf{com}_N^1) & \text{if } j = 1 \\ \mathsf{Hash}(\mathsf{com}_1^j, \ldots, \mathsf{com}_N^j, [\![\alpha^{j-1}]\!]) & \text{if } j > 1 \end{cases}$$
   to the verifier;

   (d) the verifier picks at random a challenge ε^j and sends it to the prover;

   (e) the prover computes
   $$[\![\alpha^j]\!] := \varphi^j_{(\varepsilon^i)_{i \le j}, (\alpha^i)_{i < j}}([\![w]\!], ([\![\beta^i]\!])_{i \le j})$$
   and recomposes α^j.
   Note: This step is computed according to Protocol 2 in case of an iterative computing & broadcasting step.

   The prover further computes $h_{t+1} := \mathsf{Hash}([\![\alpha^t]\!])$ and sends it to the verifier.

3. The verifier picks at random a party index $i^* \in [N]$ and sends it to the prover.

4. The prover opens the commitments of all the parties except party i^* and further reveals the commitments and broadcast messages of the unopened party i^*. Namely, the prover sends $([\![w]\!]_i, ([\![\beta^j]\!]_i, \rho_i^j)_{j \in [t]})_{i \ne i^*}, \mathsf{com}_{i^*}^1, \ldots, \mathsf{com}_{i^*}^t, [\![\alpha^1]\!]_{i^*}, \ldots, [\![\alpha^t]\!]_{i^*}$ to the verifier.

5. The verifier recomputes the commitments com_i^j and the broadcast values $[\![\alpha^j]\!]_i$ for $i \in [N] \setminus \{i^*\}$ and $j \in [t]$ from $([\![w]\!]_i, ([\![\beta^j]\!]_i, \rho_i^j)_{j \in [t]})_{i \ne i^*}$ in the same way as the prover.

6. The verifier accepts if and only if:

   (a) the views of the opened parties are consistent with each other, with the committed input shares and with the hash digest of the broadcast messages, *i.e.* for $j = 1$ to $t+1$,
   $$h_j \stackrel{?}{=} \begin{cases} \mathsf{Hash}(\mathsf{com}_1^1, \ldots, \mathsf{com}_N^1) & \text{if } j = 1 \\ \mathsf{Hash}(\mathsf{com}_1^j, \ldots, \mathsf{com}_N^j, [\![\alpha^{j-1}]\!]) & \text{if } j > 1 \\ \mathsf{Hash}([\![\alpha^t]\!]) & \text{if } j = t+1 \end{cases}$$

   (b) the output of the MPC protocol is ACCEPT, *i.e.*
   $$g(\alpha^1, \ldots, \alpha^t) \stackrel{?}{=} 0.$$

Protocol 3: Zero-knowledge protocol - Application of the MPCitH principle to Protocol 1.

in com_N^1 (instead of committing $[\![\beta^{\text{unif}}]\!]_N$). This way the prover can save communication by revealing seed_N instead of $[\![\beta^{\text{unif}}]\!]_N$ whenever the latter is larger;

- the messages $[\![\alpha^1]\!]_{i^*}, \ldots, [\![\alpha^t]\!]_{i^*}$ broadcasted by the unopened party. Let us stress that one can sometimes save communication by sending only some elements of $[\![\alpha^1]\!]_{i^*}, \ldots, [\![\alpha^t]\!]_{i^*}$ and use the relation $g(\alpha^1, \ldots, \alpha^t) = 0$ to recover the missing ones;
- the hash digests $h_1, \ldots, h_{t+1}$ and the unopened commitments $\text{com}_{i^*}^1, \ldots,$ $\text{com}_{i^*}^t$ (as explained above, we have $\text{com}_{i^*}^j = \emptyset$ for $j > 1$ if $i^* \neq N$).

Moreover, instead of revealing the $(N-1)$ seeds of the opened parties, one can generate them from a generation tree as suggested in [KKW18]. One then only needs to reveal $\log_2 N$ λ-bit seeds. We finally obtain a total communication cost for Protocol 3 of

- when $i^* \neq N$,

$$\text{Cost} = \underbrace{(t+1) \cdot 2\lambda}_{h_1, h_2, \ldots, h_{t+1}} + (\ \underbrace{\text{inputs}}_{[\![w]\!]_N, [\![\beta^1]\!]_N, \ldots,} + \underbrace{\text{comm}}_{[\![\alpha^1]\!]_{i^*}, \ldots, [\![\alpha^t]\!]_{i^*}} + \underbrace{\lambda \cdot \log_2 N}_{\text{seed}_i \text{ for } i \neq i^*} + \underbrace{2\lambda}_{\text{com}_{i^*}^1}\ ).$$

- when $i^* = N$,

$$\text{Cost} = \underbrace{(t+1) \cdot 2\lambda}_{h_1, h_2, \ldots, h_{t+1}} + (\ \underbrace{\text{comm}}_{[\![\alpha^1]\!]_{i^*}, \ldots, [\![\alpha^t]\!]_{i^*}} + \underbrace{\lambda \cdot \log_2 N}_{\text{seed}_i \text{ for } i \neq i^*} + \underbrace{t \cdot 2\lambda}_{\text{com}_{i^*}^1, \ldots, \text{com}_{i^*}^t}\ ).$$

where inputs denote the bitsize of $(w, \beta^1, \ldots, \beta^t)$ excluding the uniformly distributed elements β^{unif}, and where comm denotes the bitsize of $(\alpha^1, \ldots, \alpha^t)$ excluding the elements which can be recovered from $g(\alpha^1, \ldots, \alpha^t) = 0$.

To achieve a soundness error of $2^{-\lambda}$, one must repeat the protocol $\tau = \frac{\lambda}{\log_2 N}$ times. The resulting averaged cost is the following:

$$\text{Cost} = (t+1) \cdot 2\lambda + \tau \cdot \left(\frac{N-1}{N} \cdot \text{inputs} + \text{comm} + \lambda \cdot \log_2 N + \frac{N-1+t}{N} \cdot 2\lambda \right).$$

Several recent works based on the MPCitH paradigm [BD20,KZ21,FJR22] provides zero-knowledge identification protocols with communication cost below 10 KB for a 128-bit security level. Unfortunately, to obtain a small communication cost, one must take a large number of parties N, which induces an important computational overhead compared to other approaches to build zero-knowledge proofs. Indeed, the prover must emulate N parties in her head for each of the τ repetitions of the protocol, which makes a total of $\frac{\lambda N}{\log_2 N}$ party emulations to achieve a soundness error of $2^{-\lambda}$. Thus, increasing N has a direct impact on the performances. For instance, scaling from $N = 16$ to $N = 256$ roughly halves the communication but increases the computation by a factor of eight. Given this state of affairs, a natural question is the following:

Can we build zero-knowledge proofs in the MPC-in-the-head paradigm while avoiding this computational overhead?

In what follows, we show how applying (low-threshold) linear secret sharing to the MPCitH paradigm provides a positive answer to this question.

4   MPC-in-the-Head with Threshold LSS

4.1   General Principle

Let ℓ and N be integers such that $1 \leq \ell < N$. We consider an $(\ell+1, N)$-threshold linear secret sharing scheme (LSSS), as formally introduced in Definition 1, which shares a secret $s \in \mathbb{F}$ into N shares $[\![s]\!] \in \mathbb{F}^N$. In particular, the vector spaces of Definition 1 are simply defined as $\mathbb{V}_1 = \mathbb{V}_2 = \mathbb{F}$ hereafter (other definitions of these sets will be considered in Sect. 5). We recall that such a scheme implies that the secret can be reconstructed from any $\ell + 1$ shares while no information is revealed on the secret from the knowledge of ℓ shares. The following lemmas shall be useful to our purpose (see proofs in the full version [FR22]). The first lemma holds assuming the MDS conjecture [MS10] while the second one comes from the equivalence between threshold LSSS and interpolation codes [CDN15, Theorem 11.103].

Lemma 1. *Let $\mathbb{F}$ be a finite field and let ℓ, N be integers such that $1 \leq \ell < N-1$. If an $(\ell + 1, N)$-threshold LSSS exists for $\mathbb{F}$, and assuming the MDS conjecture, then $N \leq |\mathbb{F}|$ with the following exception: if $|\mathbb{F}|$ is a power of 2 and $\ell \in \{2, |\mathbb{F}|-2\}$ then $N \leq |\mathbb{F}| + 1$.*

Lemma 2. *Let (Share, Reconstruct) be an $(\ell + 1, N)$-threshold LSSS. For every tuple $v_0 \in \mathbb{V}_2^{\ell+1}$ and every subset $J_0 \subseteq [N]$ with $|J_0| = \ell+1$, there exists a unique sharing $[\![s]\!] \in \mathbb{V}_2^N$ such that $[\![s]\!]_{J_0} = v_0$ and such that*

$$\forall J \ s.t. \ |J| = \ell + 1, \mathsf{Reconstruct}_J([\![s]\!]_J) = s,$$

where $s := \mathsf{Reconstruct}_{J_0}(v_0)$. Moreover, there exists an efficient algorithm Expand_{J_0} which returns this unique sharing from $[\![s]\!]_{J_0}$.

In the rest of the paper we shall frequently use the following notions:

- **Sharing of a tuple.** If v is a tuple, a secret sharing $[\![v]\!]$ is defined coordinate-wise. The algorithms Share, Reconstruct and Expand (from Lemma 2) further apply coordinate-wise.
- **Valid sharing.** We say that a sharing $[\![v]\!]$ is *valid* when there exists v such that

$$\forall J \ s.t. \ |J| = \ell + 1, \mathsf{Reconstruct}_J([\![v]\!]_J) = v,$$

or equivalently[3], when there exists J such that $[\![v]\!] = \mathsf{Expand}_J([\![v]\!]_J)$.

---

[3] This second formulation is true only for threshold schemes (and not for quasi-threshold schemes that we will introduce latter).

– **Consistent shares.** We say that shares $[\![v]\!]_{i_1}, \ldots, [\![v]\!]_{i_z}$ are *consistent* when there exist other shares $[\![v]\!]_{[N]\backslash\{i_1,\ldots,i_z\}}$ such that $[\![v]\!]$ is a valid sharing.

Application to the MPCitH Paradigm. We suggest applying a threshold LSSS to the MPCitH paradigm instead of a simple additive sharing scheme. Let us consider a protocol Π_{add} complying with the MPC model introduced in the previous section (Protocol 1). We can define a protocol Π_{LSSS} similar to Π_{add} with the following differences:

– the parties initially receive an $(\ell+1, N)$-threshold linear secret sharing of the witness w,
– when invoked for a hint β_j, the oracle $\mathcal{O}_H$ returns an $(\ell + 1, N)$-threshold linear secret sharing of β^j,
– when the shares of α^j are broadcasted, the value α^j is reconstructed using the algorithm Reconstruct. Namely, the parties arbitrarily choose $\ell+1$ shares $([\![\alpha^j]\!]_i)_{i \in J_0}$, run the algorithm Reconstruct$_{J_0}$ to get α^j, and check that all the broadcast shares are consistent with the output of Expand$_{J_0}$. If the check fails, the protocol returns REJECT.

The resulting MPC protocol, formally described in Protocol 4, is well-defined and ℓ-private in the semi-honest model (meaning that the views of any ℓ parties leak no information about the secret). This is formalized in the following theorem (see proof in the full version [FR22]).

Theorem 1. *Let us consider an MPC protocol Π_{add} complying with the protocol format described in Protocol 1. If Π_{add} is well-defined and $(N-1)$-private, then the protocol Π_{LSSS} corresponding to Π_{add} with an $(\ell+1, N)$-threshold linear secret sharing scheme (see Protocol 4) is well-defined and ℓ-private.*

4.2 Conversion to Zero-Knowledge Proofs

We can convert the MPC protocol using threshold linear secret sharings into a zero-knowledge protocol using the MPC-in-the-Head paradigm. Instead of requesting the views of $N-1$ parties, the verifier only asks for the views of ℓ parties. Since the MPC protocol is ℓ-private, we directly get the zero-knowledge property. One key advantage of using a threshold LSSS is that only $\ell+1$ parties out of N need to be computed by the prover, which we explain further hereafter.

Besides the commitments on the input sharing $[\![w]\!]$, and the hints' sharings $[\![\beta^1]\!], \ldots, [\![\beta^t]\!]$, the prover must send to the verifier the communication between the parties, which for the considered MPC model (see Protocol 4) consists of the broadcast sharings $[\![\alpha^1]\!], \ldots, [\![\alpha^t]\!]$. Observe that such a sharing $[\![\alpha^j]\!]$ is also an LSSS sharing of the underlying value α^j since it is computed as

$$[\![\alpha^j]\!] := \varphi^j_{(\varepsilon^i, \alpha^i)_{i \leq j}}([\![w]\!], ([\![\beta^i]\!])_{i \leq j})$$

where $[\![w]\!], [\![\beta^1]\!], \ldots, [\![\beta^t]\!]$ are LSSS sharings and φ^j is an affine function. This notably implies that, for all i, the broadcast sharing $[\![\alpha^j]\!] = ([\![\alpha^j]\!]_1, \ldots, [\![\alpha^j]\!]_N)$

---

1. The parties take as input an $(\ell+1, N)$-threshold linear sharing $[\![w]\!]$.

2. For $j = 1$ to t, the parties:
   (a) get an $(\ell+1, N)$-threshold linear sharing $[\![\beta^j]\!]$ from the hint oracle $\mathcal{O}_H$, such that

   $$\beta^j \leftarrow \psi^j(w, \varepsilon^1, \ldots, \varepsilon^{j-1}; r^j)$$

   for a uniform random tape r^j;
   (b) get a common random ε^j from the oracle $\mathcal{O}_R$;
   (c) for some $\mathbb{F}$-linear function $\varphi^j_{(\varepsilon^i)_{i \leq j}, (\alpha^i)_{i < j}}$,
       - compute

       $$[\![\alpha^j]\!] := \varphi^j_{(\varepsilon^i)_{i \leq j}, (\alpha^i)_{i < j}}\big([\![w]\!], ([\![\beta^i]\!])_{i \leq j}\big),$$

       - broadcast $[\![\alpha^j]\!]$,
       - compute

       $$\alpha^j := \mathsf{Reconstruct}_{J_0}([\![\alpha^j]\!]_{J_0})$$

       for some J_0 of size $\ell+1$,
       - verify that $\mathsf{Expand}_{J_0}([\![\alpha]\!]_{J_0})$ is consistent with $[\![\alpha^j]\!]$ (*i.e.* that $[\![\alpha^j]\!]$ forms a valid sharing) and reject otherwise.

       Note: This step can be composed of several iterations as described in Protocol 2.

3. The parties finally accept if $g(\alpha^1, \ldots, \alpha^t) = 0$ and reject otherwise.

Note: In the above description w, β^j, ε^j, α^j are elements from the field $\mathbb{F}$ or tuples with coordinates in $\mathbb{F}$ (whose size is not made explicit to keep the presentation simple).

Protocol 4: General MPC protocol Π_{LSSS} with LSSS.

contains redundancy. According to Lemma 2, in order to uniquely define such a sharing, one only needs to commit $\ell + 1$ shares of $[\![\alpha^j]\!]$. In other words, we can choose a fixed subset S of $\ell + 1$ parties and only commit the broadcast shares from these parties, which then acts as a commitment of the full sharing $[\![\alpha^j]\!]$. For all $j \in [t]$, the prover needs to send the broadcast share $[\![\alpha^j]\!]_{i^*}$ of an arbitrary unopened party i^*. To verify the computation of the ℓ opened parties $I = \{i_1, \ldots, i_\ell\} \subseteq [N]$, the verifier can recompute the shares $[\![\alpha^j]\!]_{i_1}, \ldots, [\![\alpha^j]\!]_{i_\ell}$. Then, from these ℓ shares together with $[\![\alpha^j]\!]_{i^*}$, the verifier can reconstruct the shares $[\![\alpha^j]\!]_S$ using $\mathsf{Expand}_{\{i^*, i_1, \ldots, i_\ell\}}$ and check their commitments.

By committing the broadcast messages of only a subset S of parties, the proof becomes independent of the computation of the other parties. It means that the prover must commit the input shares of all the parties but only need to emulate $\ell + 1$ parties to commit their broadcast shares. When ℓ is small with respect to N, this has a great impact on the computational performance of the prover. The resulting zero-knowledge protocol is described in Protocol 5.

4.3 Soundness

Consider a malicious prover $\tilde{\mathcal{P}}$ who does not know a correct witness w for the statement x but still tries to convince the verifier that she does. We shall say that such a malicious prover cheats for some party $i \in [N]$ if the broadcast shares $[\![\alpha^1]\!]_i, \ldots, [\![\alpha^t]\!]_i$ recomputed from the committed input/hint shares $[\![w]\!]_i, [\![\beta^1]\!]_i, \ldots, [\![\beta^t]\!]_i$ are not consistent with the committed broadcast shares $([\![\alpha^1]\!]_S, \ldots, [\![\alpha^t]\!]_S)$.

Let us first consider the simple case of false positive rate $p = 0$. If a malicious prover cheats on less than $N - \ell$ parties, then at least $\ell + 1$ parties have broadcast shares which are consistent with $([\![\alpha^1]\!]_i, \ldots, [\![\alpha^t]\!]_i)_{i \in S}$ and give rise to broadcast values $\alpha^1, \ldots, \alpha^t$ for which the protocol accepts, i.e. $g(\alpha^1, \ldots, \alpha^t) = 0$. Since $p = 0$, the input shares of those $\ell + 1$ parties necessarily define a good witness w (i.e. satisfying $(x, w) \in \mathcal{R}$), which is in contradiction with the definition of a malicious prover. We deduce that in such a zero-false-positive scenario, a malicious prover (who does not know a good witness) has to cheat for at least $N - \ell$ parties. Then, if the malicious prover cheats on more than $N - \ell$ parties, the verifier shall always discover the cheat since she shall necessarily ask for the opening of a cheating party. We deduce that a malicious prover must necessarily cheat on exactly $N - \ell$ parties, and the only way for the verifier to be convinced is to ask for the opening of the exact ℓ parties which have been honestly emulated. The probability of this event to happen is

$$\frac{1}{\binom{N}{N-\ell}} = \frac{1}{\binom{N}{\ell}},$$

which corresponds to the soundness error of the protocol, assuming $p = 0$.

Let us now consider a false positive rate p which is not zero. A malicious prover can then rely on a false positive to get a higher probability to convince the verifier. In case the committed input shares $[\![w]\!]_1, \ldots, [\![w]\!]_N$ were consistent (i.e. they formed a valid secret sharing), the soundness error would be

$$\frac{1}{\binom{N}{\ell}} + \left(1 - \frac{1}{\binom{N}{\ell}}\right) \cdot p.$$

However, we cannot enforce a malicious prover to commit a valid secret sharing $[\![w]\!]$ since the verifier never sees more than the shares of ℓ parties. More precisely, let us denote

$$\mathcal{J} := \{J \subset [N] : |J| = \ell + 1\}$$

and let $w^{(J)}$ be the witness corresponding to the shares $[\![w]\!]_J$ for some subset $J \in \mathcal{J}$, formally $w^{(J)} := \mathsf{Reconstruct}_J([\![w]\!]_J)$. Then we could have

$$w^{(J_1)} \neq w^{(J_2)}$$

1. The prover shares the witness w into an $(\ell+1, N)$-threshold linear secret sharing $[\![w]\!]$.

2. The prover emulates "in her head" a (public) subset S of $\ell+1$ parties of the MPC protocol. For $j = 1$ to t:

   (a) the prover computes
   $$\beta^j = \psi^j(w, (\varepsilon^i)_{i<j}),$$
   shares it into an $(\ell+1, N)$-threshold linear secret sharing $[\![\beta^j]\!]$;

   (b) the prover computes the commitments
   $$\mathsf{com}_i^j := \begin{cases} \mathsf{Com}([\![w]\!]_i, [\![\beta^j]\!]_i; \rho_i^j) & \text{if } j = 1 \\ \mathsf{Com}([\![\beta^j]\!]_i; \rho_i^j) & \text{if } j > 1 \end{cases}$$

   for all $i \in [N]$, for some commitment randomness ρ_i^j, and computes the Merkle root
   $$\tilde{h}_j := \mathsf{MerkleTree}(\mathsf{com}_1^j, \ldots, \mathsf{com}_N^j).$$

   (c) the prover sends
   $$h_j := \begin{cases} \tilde{h}_j & \text{if } j = 1 \\ \mathsf{Hash}(\tilde{h}_j, [\![\alpha^{j-1}]\!]_S) & \text{if } j > 1 \end{cases}$$
   to the verifier;

   (d) the verifier picks at random a challenge ε^j and sends it to the prover;

   (e) the prover computes, for $i \in S$,
   $$[\![\alpha^j]\!]_i := \varphi^j_{(\varepsilon^k)_{k \le j}, (\alpha^k)_{k < j}}\left([\![w]\!]_i, ([\![\beta^k]\!]_i)_{k \le j}\right)$$

   and recomposes α^j. This step is repeated as many times as in the MPC protocol (cf Protocol 2).

   The prover further computes $h_{t+1} := \mathsf{Hash}([\![\alpha^t]\!]_S)$ and sends it to the verifier.

3. The verifier picks at random a subset $I \subset [N]$ of ℓ parties (i.e. $|I| = \ell$) and sends it to the prover.

4. The prover opens the commitments of all the parties in I, namely she sends $([\![w]\!]_i, ([\![\beta^j]\!]_i, \rho_i^j)_{j \in [t]})_{i \in I}$ to the verifier. The prover further sends the authentication paths $\mathsf{auth}_1, \ldots, \mathsf{auth}_t$ to these commitments, i.e. auth_j is the authentication path for $\{\mathsf{com}_i^j\}_{i \in I}$ w.r.t. Merkle root $\tilde{h}_j$ for every $j \in [t]$. Additionally, the prover sends broadcast shares $[\![\alpha^1]\!]_{i^*}, \ldots, [\![\alpha^t]\!]_{i^*}$ of an unopened party $i^* \in S \setminus I$.

5. The verifier recomputes the commitments com_i^j and the broadcast values $[\![\alpha^j]\!]_i$ for $i \in I$ and $j \in [t]$ from $([\![w]\!]_i, ([\![\beta^j]\!]_i, \rho_i^j)_{j \in [t]})_{i \in I}$. Then she recovers $\alpha^1, \ldots, \alpha^t$, by
   $$\alpha^j = \mathsf{Reconstruct}_{I \cup \{i^*\}}([\![\alpha^j]\!]_{I \cup \{i^*\}})$$
   for every $j \in [t]$.

6. The verifier accepts if and only if:

   (a) the views of the opened parties are consistent with each other, with the committed input shares and with the hash digest of the broadcast messages, i.e. for $j = 1$ to $t+1$,
   $$h_j \overset{?}{=} \begin{cases} \tilde{h}_j & \text{if } j = 1 \\ \mathsf{Hash}(\tilde{h}_j, [\![\alpha^{j-1}]\!]_S) & \text{if } 2 \le j \le t \\ \mathsf{Hash}([\![\alpha^{j-1}]\!]_S) & \text{if } j = t+1 \end{cases}$$
   where $\tilde{h}_j$ is the Merkle root deduced from $(\{\mathsf{com}_i^j\}_{i \in I}, \mathsf{auth}_j)$ and $[\![\alpha^{j-1}]\!]_S$ are the shares in subset S deduced from $[\![\alpha^{j-1}]\!] = \mathsf{Expand}_{I \cup \{i^*\}}([\![\alpha^{j-1}]\!]_{I \cup \{i^*\}})$;

   (b) the output of the opened parties are ACCEPT, i.e.
   $$g(\alpha^1, \ldots, \alpha^t) \overset{?}{=} 0 .$$

Protocol 5: Zero-knowledge protocol: application of the MPCitH principle to Protocol 4 with an $(\ell+1, N)$-threshold linear secret sharing scheme.

for distinct subsets $J_1, J_2 \in \mathcal{J}$. A malicious prover can exploit this degree of freedom to increase the soundness error.

Soundness Attack. Let us take the example of the [BN20] protocol on a field $\mathbb{F}$. In this protocol, the MPC functionality f outputs ACCEPT for a bad witness w (*i.e.* such that $(x, w) \notin \mathcal{R}$) with probability $p = \frac{1}{|\mathbb{F}|}$, *i.e.* if and only if the oracle $\mathcal{O}_R$ samples a specific element ε_w of $\mathbb{F}$. In this context, a possible strategy for the malicious prover is the following:

1. Build the shares $[\![w]\!]_1, \dots, [\![w]\!]_N$ such that

$$\forall J_1, J_2 \in \mathcal{J}, \ \varepsilon_{w^{(J_1)}} \neq \varepsilon_{w^{(J_2)}}.$$

   We implicitly assume here that $\binom{N}{\ell+1} \leq |\mathbb{F}|$ and that constructing such collision-free input sharing is possible. We assume that $(x, w^{(J)}) \notin \mathcal{R}$ for every J (otherwise the malicious prover can recover a good witness by enumerating the $w^{(J)}$'s).
2. After receiving the initial commitments, the verifier sends the challenge ε.
3. If there exists $J_0 \in \mathcal{J}$ such that $\varepsilon = w^{(J_0)}$, which occurs with probability $\binom{N}{\ell+1} \cdot p$ since all the $\varepsilon^{(J)}$ are distinct, then the malicious prover defines the broadcast values $\alpha^1, \dots, \alpha^t$ (and the broadcast shares in the set S) according to the broadcast shares of the parties in J_0. It results that the computation of the parties in J_0 is correct and the prover will be able to convince the verifier if the set I of opened parties is a subset of J_0 ($I \subset J_0$).
4. Otherwise, if no subset $J_0 \in \mathcal{J}$ is such that $\varepsilon = w^{(J_0)}$, the malicious prover is left with the option of guessing the set I. Namely, she (randomly) chooses a set I_0 of ℓ parties as well as broadcast values $\alpha^1, \dots, \alpha^t$ such that $g(\alpha^1, \dots, \alpha^t) = 0$, and then she deduces and commits the broadcast shares $[\![\alpha^j]\!]_S$ from the $[\![\alpha^j]\!]_{I_0}$ (computed from the committed input shares) and the chosen α^j's. The malicious prover will be able to convince the verifier if and only if the challenge set I matches the guess I_0.

The probability p_{attack} that the malicious prover convinces the verifier using the above strategy satisfies

$$p_{\text{attack}} := \overbrace{\binom{N}{\ell+1} p}^{\Pr[\exists J_0 : \varepsilon = w^{(J_0)}]} \cdot \overbrace{\frac{\binom{\ell+1}{\ell}}{\binom{N}{\ell}}}^{\Pr[I \subset J_0]} + \overbrace{\left(1 - \binom{N}{\ell+1} p\right)}^{\Pr[\forall J, \varepsilon \neq w^{(J)}]} \cdot \overbrace{\frac{1}{\binom{N}{\ell}}}^{\Pr[I = I_0]}$$

$$= \frac{1}{\binom{N}{\ell}} + p \cdot \frac{\ell \cdot (N - \ell)}{\ell + 1} \geq \underbrace{\frac{1}{\binom{N}{\ell}} + \left(1 - \frac{1}{\binom{N}{\ell}}\right) \cdot p.}$$

Soundness error if the
committed sharing is well-formed.

Soundness Proof. We can prove that the above strategy to forge successful transcripts for the [BN20] protocol is actually optimal and that it further applies to other protocols complying with our model. This is formalized in the following theorem (together with the completeness and HVZK property of the protocol).

Theorem 2. *Let us consider an MPC protocol Π_{LSSS} complying with the protocol format described in Protocol 4 using an $(\ell + 1, N)$-threshold LSSS, such that Π_{LSSS} is ℓ-private in the semi-honest model and of false positive rate p. Then, Protocol 5 built from Π_{LSSS} is complete, sound and honest-verifier zero-knowledge, with a soundness error ϵ defined as*

$$\epsilon := \frac{1}{\binom{N}{\ell}} + p \cdot \frac{\ell \cdot (N - \ell)}{\ell + 1}.$$

Proof. The completeness holds from the completeness property of the underlying MPC protocol. The zero-knowledge property directly comes from the ℓ-privacy property of the MPC protocol with an $(\ell + 1, N)$-threshold linear secret sharing scheme. See the full version [FR22] for the soundness proof.

Remark 1. Let us remark that the above theorem includes the MPCitH setting with additive sharing as a particular case. Indeed, when $\ell = N - 1$, we obtain the usual formula for the soundness error, that is:

$$\ell = N - 1 \quad \Longrightarrow \quad \epsilon = \frac{1}{N} + p \cdot \left(1 - \frac{1}{N}\right).$$

Remark 2. When $\ell = 1$, we have $\epsilon \approx \frac{1}{N}$ (assuming p is small). It can look as surprising that we can have such soundness error by revealing a single party's view. Since the communication is only broadcast, a verifier does not need to check for inconsistency between several parties, she just needs to check that the revealed views are consistent with the committed broadcast messages. Moreover, the verifier has the guarantee that the shares broadcast by all the parties form *a valid sharing of the open value*. It means that even if the prover reveals only one party's view, the latter can be inconsistent with the committed broadcast. Assuming we use Shamir's secret sharing, committing to a valid broadcast sharing consists in committing a degree-ℓ polynomial such that evaluations are the broadcast shares. By interpolating the broadcast shares of ℓ honest parties (and given the plain value of the broadcast message), one shall entirely fix the corresponding Shamir's polynomial, and the other parties can not be consistent with this polynomial without being consistent with the honest parties (and the latter can only occur if there is a false positive).

4.4   Performances

The advantage of using a threshold LSSS over a standard additive sharing mainly resides in a much faster computation time, for both the prover and the verifier. Indeed, according to the above description, the prover only emulates $\ell + 1$ parties while the verifier only emulates ℓ parties, which is particularly efficient for a small ℓ. For example, assuming that p is negligible and taking $\ell = 1$, the soundness error is $1/N$ (which is similar to standard MPCitH with additive sharing) and the prover only needs to emulate $\ell + 1 = 2$ parties (instead of N) while the verifier only needs to emulate $\ell = 1$ party (instead of $N - 1$).

When targeting a soundness error of λ bits, one needs to repeat the protocol $\tau := \frac{-\lambda}{\log_2 \epsilon}$ times and thus the number of times that a prover emulates a party is multiplied by τ. Table 2 summarizes the number of party emulations for the prover and the verifier for the standard case (additive sharing) and for the case of an $(\ell + 1, N)$-threshold LSSS. Interestingly, we observe that the emulation phase is more expensive when increasing N for the additive sharing case while it becomes cheaper for the threshold LSSS case (with some constant ℓ). For the sake of comparison, we also give in Table 2 the numbers corresponding to the hypercube optimization from the concurrent work [AGH+23].

The computational bottleneck for the prover when using an LSSS with low threshold ℓ and possibly high N becomes the generation and commitment of all the parties' input shares, which is still linear in N. Moreover the sharing generation for a threshold LSSS might be more expensive than for a simple additive sharing. On the other hand, the verifier does not suffer from this bottleneck since she only has to verify ℓ opened commitments (per repetition). One trade-off to reduce the prover commitment bottleneck is to increase ℓ, which implies a smaller τ (for the same N) and hence decreases the number of commitments.

Table 2. Number of party emulations to achieve a soundness error of $2^{-\lambda}$ (assuming a negligible false positive rate p).

	With additive sharing		With threshold LSSS	
	Traditional	Hypercube	$\ell = 1$	Any ℓ
Prover	$\approx \lambda \frac{N}{\log_2 N}$	$\approx \lambda \frac{\log_2 N + 1}{\log_2 N}$	$\approx \lambda \frac{2}{\log_2 N}$	$\approx \lambda \frac{\ell+1}{\log_2 \binom{N}{\ell}}$
Verifier	$\approx \lambda \frac{N-1}{\log_2 N}$	$\approx \lambda \frac{\log_2 N}{\log_2 N}$	$\approx \lambda \frac{1}{\log_2 N}$	$\approx \lambda \frac{\ell}{\log_2 \binom{N}{\ell}}$

In terms of communication, using a threshold LSSS implies a slight overhead. In particular, since only ℓ parties out of N are opened, we use Merkle tree for the commitments and include the authentication paths in the communication.

Let us recall the notations defined in Sect. 3.2:

– inputs: the bitsize of $(w, \beta^1, \ldots, \beta^t)$ excluding the uniformly-distributed elements β^{unif}, and
– comm: the bitsize of $(\llbracket \alpha^1 \rrbracket_{i*}, \ldots, \llbracket \alpha^t \rrbracket_{i*})$ excluding the elements which can be recovered from $g(\alpha^1, \ldots, \alpha^t) = 0$.

We denote unif the bitsize of the uniformly-distributed elements β^{unif}. Then, the proof size (in bits) when repeating the protocol τ times is

$$\text{Cost} = \underbrace{(t+1) \cdot 2\lambda}_{h_1, h_2, \dots, h_{t+1}} + \tau \cdot (\underbrace{\ell \cdot (\text{inputs} + \text{unif})}_{\{[\![w]\!]_i, [\![\beta^1]\!]_i, \dots, [\![\beta^t]\!]_i\}_{i \in I}} + \underbrace{\text{comm}}_{[\![\alpha^1]\!]_{i*}, \dots, [\![\alpha^t]\!]_{i*}} + \underbrace{2\lambda \cdot t \cdot \ell \cdot \log_2 \frac{N}{\ell}}_{\text{auth}_1, \dots, \text{auth}_t}).$$

Let us remark that the bitsize unif appears here while it was not the case for additive sharings. This comes from the fact that, even if β^{unif} is uniformly sampled, $[\![\beta^{\text{unif}}]\!]$ has some structure (*i.e.* some redundancy) when using an arbitrary linear secret sharing scheme.

5   Further Improvements

In this section, we suggest potential ways to further improve and generalize our approach.

5.1   Using Linearly Homomorphic Commitments

As explained previously, one of the bottlenecks of this construction is that the prover must realize N commitments. Although we decrease the cost of emulating the MPC protocol (from N parties to a constant number), we still need to commit the inputs of all the parties which is still linear in N. For this reason, we cannot arbitrarily increase the number of parties N even while working on large fields (*e.g.* $\mathbb{F}_{2^{32}}$ or larger). One natural strategy to improve this state of affairs and get rid of those N commitments is to use a linearly homomorphic commitment scheme. When relying on such a scheme, the prover can just commit the input shares for the $\ell + 1$ parties in S, instead of committing all the parties' input shares. Then the commitment of any party can be expressed as a linear combination of these commitments. For applications to the post-quantum setting (which is a context of choice for MPCitH schemes), one could rely on lattice-based homomorphic commitment schemes. To the best of our knowledge, most of these schemes are only additively homomorphic (not linearly) and they support a bounded number of additions which makes their application to our context not straightforward. This is yet an interesting question for future research.

5.2   Using Quasi-Threshold Linear Secret Sharing

Theorem 2 only considers linear secret sharing schemes, but we can generalize the result to any quasi-threshold linear secret sharing scheme. In such schemes, ℓ shares leak no information about the secret and $\ell + 1 + \Delta$ shares are necessary to reconstruct the secret, with $\Delta > 0$, namely we have a gap between the two thresholds. In our context, this gap shall impact the soundness of the protocol. Indeed, the prover just needs to cheat for $N - \ell - \Delta$ parties (such that there is less than $\ell + \Delta$ honest parties), but the verifier asks to open only ℓ parties.

Considering quasi-threshold schemes bring more versatility to our approach and opens the door to techniques that are not possible with tight threshold schemes (*e.g.* batching such as proposed below).

Let us remark that the set S of emulated parties in Protocol 5 must be chosen such that $[\![v]\!]_S$ enables to deduce all the shares $[\![v]\!]_{[N]}$. In the tight threshold case, such a set S is always of size $\ell+1$ (see Lemma 2), but in the case of quasi-threshold LSSS, this set S might be larger than $\ell + \Delta + 1$. Moreover, sending shares $[\![\alpha^1]\!]_{i^*}, \ldots, [\![\alpha^t]\!]_{i^*}$ for one non-opened party $i^* \in S$ might not be enough to enable the verifier to recompute $[\![\alpha^j]\!]_S$ for all j. Therefore the size of S and the number of additional shares $[\![\alpha^j]\!]_i$ to be revealed depend on the underlying quasi-threshold linear secret sharing, which impacts the communication cost. On the other hand, the soundness error of the obtained proof of knowledge is not impacted.

Theorem 3. *Let us consider an MPC protocol $\Pi_{QT\text{-}LSSS}$ complying with the protocol format described in Protocol 4, but using an $(\ell, \ell + \Delta + 1, N)$-quasi-threshold LSSS in place of an $(\ell+1, N)$-threshold LSSS, and such that $\Pi_{QT\text{-}LSSS}$ is ℓ-private in the semi-honest model and of false positive rate p. Then, Protocol 5 built from $\Pi_{QT\text{-}LSSS}$ is complete, sound and honest-verifier zero-knowledge, with a soundness error ϵ defined as*

$$\epsilon := \frac{\binom{\ell+\Delta}{\ell}}{\binom{N}{\ell}} + p \cdot \frac{\ell}{\ell+\Delta+1} \cdot \binom{N-\ell}{\Delta+1}.$$

Proof. The completeness holds from the completeness property of the underlying MPC protocol. The zero-knowledge property directly comes from the ℓ-privacy property of the MPC protocol with an $(\ell, \ell + \Delta + 1, N)$-threshold linear secret sharing scheme. See the full version [FR22] for the proof of the soundness.

Using Algebraic Geometric Secret Sharing? One drawback while using a tight threshold LSSS is that the number N of parties is limited by the size of the underlying field $\mathbb{F}$, specifically we have $N \leq |\mathbb{F}|$ (see Lemma 1). In the full version [FR22], we investigate whether quasi-threshold LSSS based on algebraic geometry [CC06] can improve this state of affairs. Our result is negative: we show that we cannot tackle this issue by using such schemes. We also show that the soundness error (with $\ell = 1$) is at least $1/(2|\mathbb{F}| - 1)$ for any quasi-threshold LSSS. This implies that such sharing schemes could only have a limited interest to achieve smaller sizes, since it could decrease the soundness error by a factor at most *two* compared to the case with the Shamir's secret sharing scheme.

We show hereafter that the above generalization to quasi-threshold LSSS is useful for another purpose, namely an efficient batching technique in our framework.

5.3   Batching Proofs with Shamir's Secret Sharing

Principle. Shamir's secret sharing is traditionally used to share a single element of the underlying field, but it can be extended to share several elements simultaneously. To share $v_1, v_2, \ldots, v_u \in \mathbb{F}$, we can sample ℓ random elements $r_1, \ldots, r_\ell$ of $\mathbb{F}$ and build the polynomial P of degree $\ell + u - 1$ such that, given distinct fixed field elements $e_1, \ldots, e_{u+\ell}$,

$$
\begin{cases}
P(e_1) = v_1 \\
P(e_2) = v_2 \\
\quad \vdots \\
P(e_u) = v_u
\end{cases}
\quad \text{and} \quad
\begin{cases}
P(e_{u+1}) = r_1 \\
\quad \vdots \\
P(e_{u+\ell}) = r_\ell
\end{cases}
$$

The shares are then defined as evaluations of P on fixed points of $\mathbb{F} \backslash \{e_1, \ldots, e_u\}$. Revealing at most ℓ shares does not leak any information about the shared values $v_1, \ldots, v_u$, while one needs at least $\ell + u$ shares to reconstruct all of them. In other words, this is an $(\ell, \ell + u, N)$-quasi-threshold linear secret sharing scheme for the tuple $(v_1, \ldots, v_u)$. Thus, while applying such a sharing to our context, the soundness error is given by (see Theorem 3)

$$
\frac{\binom{\ell+u-1}{\ell}}{\binom{N}{\ell}} + p \cdot \frac{\ell}{\ell+u} \cdot \binom{N-\ell}{u}.
$$

When running an MPC protocol on such batch sharing, the operations are simultaneously performed on all the shared secrets $v_1, \ldots, v_u$. It means that we can batch the proof of knowledge of several witnesses which have the same verification circuit (*i.e.* the same functions φ^j in our MPC model – see Protocol 1). Using this strategy, the soundness error is slightly larger, but we can save a lot of communication by using the same sharing for several witnesses.

Specifically, the proof size while batching u witnesses is impacted as follows. The parties' input shares are not more expensive, but to open the communication, the prover now needs to send u field elements by broadcasting (instead of a single one). Thus the communication cost for τ executions is given by

$$
\text{Cost} = \underbrace{(t+1) \cdot 2\lambda}_{h_1, h_2, \ldots, h_{t+1}} + \tau \cdot (\underbrace{\ell \cdot (\text{inputs} + \text{rtapes})}_{\{[\![w]\!]_i, [\![\beta^1]\!]_i, \ldots, [\![\beta^t]\!]_i\}_{i \in I}} + \underbrace{u \cdot \text{comm}}_{\alpha^1, \ldots, \alpha^t} + \underbrace{2\lambda \cdot t \cdot \ell \cdot \log_2 \frac{N}{\ell}}_{\text{auth}_1, \ldots, \text{auth}_t}).
$$

Unfortunately, the scope of application of this batching technique is limited. In particular, while we can multiply the batched shared secrets by the same scalar, with

$$
[\![\begin{pmatrix} \gamma \cdot v_1 \\ \vdots \\ \gamma \cdot v_u \end{pmatrix}]\!] := \gamma \cdot [\![\begin{pmatrix} v_1 \\ \vdots \\ v_u \end{pmatrix}]\!]
$$

for some $\gamma \in \mathbb{F}$, we cannot compute

$$
[\![\begin{pmatrix} \gamma_1 \cdot v_1 \\ \vdots \\ \gamma_u \cdot v_u \end{pmatrix}]\!] \quad \text{from} \quad [\![\begin{pmatrix} v_1 \\ \vdots \\ v_u \end{pmatrix}]\!]
$$

for distinct scalars $\gamma_1, \ldots, \gamma_u$ (whenever at least two scalars are distinct). This restriction implies that the scalar factors used in the verification circuit must be independent of the different witnesses which are batched together. More precisely, it implies that the functions φ^j in our MPC model (see Protocol 1) must be of the form

$$\varphi^j_{(\varepsilon^i)_{i \leq j},(\alpha^i)_{i<j}}(\,\cdot\,) \quad = \quad \underbrace{\bar{\varphi}^j_{(\varepsilon^i)_{i \leq j}}(\,\cdot\,)}_{\substack{\text{Linear function with} \\ \varepsilon^i\text{-dependent coefficients}}} \quad + \quad \underbrace{b^j_{(\varepsilon^i)_{i \leq j},(\alpha^i)_{i<j}}}_{\substack{\text{Constant offset which} \\ \text{depends on the } \varepsilon^i \text{ 's and } \alpha^i\text{'s}}}$$

This restriction prevents the use of this batching strategy for several MPCitH protocols. For example, all the protocols using the multiplication checking protocol from [BN20] as a subroutine cannot use this batching strategy. To the best of our knowledge, the only protocols in the current state of the art which support this batching strategy are Banquet [BDK+21] and Limbo [DOT21].

Batching Strategies. In what follows, we propose three strategies to batch MPCitH proofs relying on the same verification circuit:

Naive strategy: The naive way to batch u MPCitH proofs is to emulate u independent instances of MPC protocol, one for each input witness. Compared to sending u independent proofs, one can save communication by using the same seed trees and the same commitments for the u instances. This strategy can be applied for standard MPCitH schemes based on additive sharing as well as for our framework of threshold LSSS-based MPCitH. When using additive sharings, the main drawback of this strategy is that the prover and the verifier need to emulate the party computation a large number of times, *i.e.* N times (or $N-1$ times for the verifier) per iteration and per statement. When batching $u \geq 25$ statements with $N = 256$, the prover and the verifier must emulate more than $100\,000$ parties to achieve a security of 128 bits. When using a low-threshold LSSS, the emulation cost is much cheaper, but the proof transcript is larger. While batching u statements, the emulation cost and the soundness error are given by the following table:

	# Emulations	Soundness Error
Prover	$\tau \cdot (\ell + 1) \cdot u$	$\frac{1}{\binom{N}{\ell}} + p \cdot \frac{(N-\ell)\cdot\ell}{\ell+1}$
Verifier	$\tau \cdot \ell \cdot u$	

SSS-based strategy: We can use the batching strategy based on Shamir's secret sharing (SSS) described above. Instead of having u independent input sharings (one per witness), we have a single input sharing batching the u witnesses. The number of MPC emulations is lower than for the naive strategy. The proof size is also smaller and (mostly) below that of the standard setting for small u, but it grows exponentially when considering a small field $\mathbb{F}$. Each batched statement consumes one evaluation point (in $\mathbb{F}$), the number N of parties is hence limited by $N \leq |\mathbb{F}| + 1 - u$. Because of this limitation together with the security loss due to the use of a quasi-threshold sharing scheme, the soundness error of this batched protocol degrades rapidly as u grows. While batching u statements using Shamir's secret sharings, the emulation cost and the soundness error are given by the following table:

	# Emulations	Soundness Error
Prover	$\tau \cdot (\ell + u)$	$\frac{\binom{\ell+u-1}{\ell}}{\binom{N}{\ell}} + p \cdot \frac{\ell}{\ell+u} \cdot \binom{N-\ell}{u}$
Verifier	$\tau \cdot \ell$	

Hybrid strategy: In the previous strategy, the proof size is convex w.r.t. the number u of batched proofs and, for small some u, the curve slope is flatter than the slope in the additive case. It means that using a hybrid approach can achieve smaller proof sizes (as well as better performances) than with the two above strategies. Specifically, instead of having one input sharing encoding the u witnesses (one per batched statement) and a single emulation of the MPC protocol, we can use ν input sharings each of them encoding $\frac{u}{\nu}$ witnesses and have then ν emulations of the MPC protocol. Using this hybrid strategy, the emulation cost and the soundness error are given by the following table:

	# Emulations	Soundness Error
Prover	$\tau \cdot (\ell + \frac{u}{\nu}) \cdot \nu$	$\frac{\binom{\ell+u/\nu-1}{\ell}}{\binom{N}{\ell}} + p \cdot \frac{\ell}{\ell+u/\nu} \cdot \binom{N-\ell}{u/\nu}$
Verifier	$\tau \cdot \ell \cdot \nu$	

Section 6.2 presents some application results for these batching strategies. In particular the full version [FR22] compares the three strategies for batched proofs of the SDitH scheme [FJR22].

6   Applications

In the past few years, many proof systems relying on the MPC-in-the-Head paradigm have been published. Table 3 provides a tentatively exhaustive list of these schemes while indicating for each scheme:

- the base field (or ring) of the function computed by the underlying MPC protocol,
- whether the underlying MPC protocol fits our general model (see Sect. 3.1),

- the hard problem (or one-way function) for which the witness knowledge is proved.

In column *Base Ring*, the notation "$\mathbb{F}$ ($\mathbb{K}$)" means that the function computed by the underlying MPC protocol is composed of $\mathbb{F}$-linear functions and multiplications over $\mathbb{K}$. For example, the schemes for AES use $\mathbb{F}_2$-linear functions and $\mathbb{F}_{256}$-multiplications.

Applying our framework with an arbitrary (low-)threshold linear secret sharing scheme instead of an additive sharing scheme is possible whenever

- the underlying MPC protocol fits the model introduced in Sect. 3.1,
- the underlying MPC protocol is defined over a field (and not only a ring),
- this base field is large enough (since the number of parties N is limited by the size of the field).

Because of this last condition, all the proof systems for Boolean circuits and/or one-way functions with $\mathbb{F}_2$ operations (*e.g.* AES, Rain, SDitH over $\mathbb{F}_2$) do not support our framework of MPCitH based on (low-)threshold LSSS. Same for the scheme recently proposed in [FMRV22] and which achieves short communication using secret sharing over the integers: this idea is not compatible with our approach.

6.1 Application to the SDitH Signature Scheme

We can transform the zero-knowledge proofs of knowledge described in Sect. 4 into signature schemes using the Fiat-Shamir's heuristic [FS87].

In the following, we focus on the signature scheme obtained when applying this approach to the SDitH protocol (SDitH for "Syndrome Decoding in the Head") [FJR22]on the base field $\mathbb{F}_{SD}$. We apply the ideas of Sect. 4 to this scheme using Shamir's secret sharing. Since the number N of parties is limited by the field size, $N \le |\mathbb{F}_{SD}|,$[4] we consider the instance with $\mathbb{F}_{SD} := \mathbb{F}_{256}$ as base field. As explained previously, our MPCitH strategy with $(\ell + 1, N)$-threshold LSSS does not make the signature smaller but substantially improves the signing and verification times. According to Sect. 4.4, we obtain signatures of size (in bits):

$$\text{SIZE} = 6\lambda + \tau \cdot \left(\ell \cdot (\text{inputs} + \text{unif}) + \text{comm} + 2\lambda \cdot \ell \cdot \log_2 \frac{N}{\ell} \right)$$

where inputs, unif, and comm are such as defined in Sect. 3 (see the full version [FR22] for explicit values for the SDitH scheme).

In [FJR22], the authors choose p a bit lower than 2^{-64} which implies that the number of executions τ just needs to be increased by one while turning to the

---

[4] The Shamir's secret sharing over a field $\mathbb{F}$ can have at most $|\mathbb{F}| - 1$ shares (one share by non-zero evaluation point), but we can have an additional share by defining it as the leading coefficient of the underlying polynomial (*i.e.* using the point at infinity as evaluation point).

Table 3. Generic MPC-in-the-Head Techniques and Signature Schemes from MPC-in-the-Head Techniques. All the signature sizes are in kilobytes and target a security of 128 bits. The *original* signature sizes correspond to values given by the underlying articles. The *normalized* signature sizes are given for a range of $8 - 32$ parties (in the underlying MPC protocol) when there is a preprocessing phase and for a range of $32 - 256$ parties otherwise. The column "Model" indicates whether the underlying MPC protocol fits our general model.

Scheme Name	Year	Base Ring	Model	#Rounds	Helper	Hard Problem	Signature Size	
							Original	Normalized
ZKBoo [GMO16]	2016	Any ring	✗	3	✗	Any $(2,3)$-decomposition circuit	–	–
ZKB++ [CDG+17]	2017	Any ring	✗	3	✗		–	–
Ligero [AHIV17]	2017	Any field	✗	5	✗	Any arithmetic circuit C (additions and multiplications)	–	–
Ligero++ [BFH+20]	2020	Any field	✗	5	✗		–	–
KKW [KKW18]	2018	Any ring	✓	3 or 5	✓		–	–
BN [BN20]	2020	Any field	✓	5	✗		–	–
Limbo [DOT21]	2021	Any field	✓	$\log|C|$	✗		–	–
BN++ [KZ22]	2021	Any field	✓	5	✗		–	–
Helium [KZ22]	2021	Any field	✓	7	✗		–	–
Picnic1 [CDG+17]	2016	$\mathbb{F}_2$	✗	3	✗	LowMC (partial)	32.1	–
Picnic2 [KKW18]	2018	$\mathbb{F}_2$	✓	3	✓		12.1	$12.1 - 15.4$
Picnic3 [KZ20b]	2019	$\mathbb{F}_2$	✓	3	✓	LowMC (full)	12.3	$11.1 - 13.7$
Helium+LowMC [KZ22]	2022	$\mathbb{F}_2$ ($\mathbb{F}_8$)	✓	7	✗		$5.4 - 12.1$	$6.4 - 9.2$
BBQ [DDOS19]	2020	$\mathbb{F}_2$ ($\mathbb{F}_{256}$)	✓	3	✓	AES	30.9	$31.8 - 48.6$
Banquet [BDK+21]	2021	$\mathbb{F}_2$ ($\mathbb{F}_{256}$)	✓	7	✗		$13.0 - 19.3$	$13.0 - 17.1$
Limbo-Sign [DOT21]	2021	$\mathbb{F}_2$ ($\mathbb{F}_{256}$)	✓	13	✗		$14.2 - 17.9$	$14.2 - 17.9$
Helium+AES [KZ22]	2022	$\mathbb{F}_2$ ($\mathbb{F}_{256}$)	✓	7	✗		$9.7 - 17.2$	$9.7 - 14.4$
LegRoast [BD20]	2020	$\mathbb{F}_{2^{127}-1}$	✓	7	✗	Legendre PRF	$12.2 - 16.0$	$12.2 - 14.8$
PorcRoast [BD20]	2020	$\mathbb{F}_{2^{127}-1}$	✓	7	✗	Higher-Power Residue Characters	$6.3 - 8.6$	$6.3 - 7.8$
Rainier-128 [DKR+21]	2021	$\mathbb{F}_2$ ($\mathbb{F}_{128}$)	✓	5	✗	Rain [DKR+21]	$5.1 - 9.4$	$5.9 - 8.1$
BN++Rain [KZ22]	2022	$\mathbb{F}_2$ ($\mathbb{F}_{128}$)	✓	5	✗		$4.4 - 5.8$	$4.9 - 6.4$
SDitH [FJR22]	2022	$\mathbb{F}_2$	✓	5	✗	Syndrome Decoding over $\mathbb{F}_2$	$11.8 - 17.0$	$10.9 - 15.6$
	2022	$\mathbb{F}_{256}$	✓	5	✗	Syndrome Decoding over $\mathbb{F}_{256}$	$8.3 - 11.5$	$8.3 - 11.5$
[FMRV22]	2022	$\mathbb{Z}$	✓	5	✓/✗	Subset-Sum Problem	$21.1 - 33.2$	$24.3 - 34.8$
	2022	$\mathbb{Z}$	✓	5	✗	BHH PRF [BHH01]	4.8	$4.8 - 6.5$

non-interactive case. Here, by taking $\ell > 1$, we decrease τ and each execution has more impact on the communication cost. Therefore we take p negligible in order to avoid to increase τ while turning to the non-interactive setting. At the same time, it means that we can apply an idea from Limbo [DOT21] which consists in using the same first challenge for all parallel executions of the underlying MPC protocol.

As explained in Sect. 4.3, in case of a non-negligible false positive rate, an adversary can try to forge a proof of knowledge by committing an invalid sharing of the witness (which is not possible in the case of additive sharing). This ability is also exploitable in the non-interactive setting while considering the attack of [KZ20a]. In order to thwart this type of attack on our variant of the SDitH scheme, we make the conservative choice of taking a false positive rate p satisfying

$$\tau \cdot \binom{N}{\ell+1} \cdot p \leq 2^{-128}.$$

This way, the probability that a single witness encoded by a subset of $\ell + 1$ shares among N leads to a false positive (in at least one of the τ iterations) is upper bounded by 2^{-128} so that any attack strategy which consists to guess (even partially) the first challenge shall cost at least 2^{128} operations. Then, we simply need to take τ such that $\binom{N}{\ell}^\tau \geq 2^{128}$ in order to achieve a 128-bit security in the non-interactive setting. We propose four possible instances of our scheme for $\ell \in \{1, 3, 7, 12\}$ and $N = 256$ (the maximal number of parties).

We have implemented our variant of the SDitH signature scheme in C. In our implementation, the pseudo-randomness is generated using AES in counter mode and the hash function is instantiated with SHAKE. We have benchmarked our implementation on a 3.8 GHz Intel Core i7 CPU with support of AVX2 and AES instructions. All the reported timings were measured on this CPU while disabling Intel Turbo Boost.

Table 4 summarizes the obtained performances for the different sets of parameters. We observe that the verification time is significantly smaller –between one and two orders of magnitude– than for the original scheme. This was expected since the verifier only emulates the views of ℓ parties instead of $N - 1$. The gain in signing time is more mitigated: even if the signer emulates only few parties, she must still commit the input shares of N parties. Nevertheless, the number of executions τ decreases while increasing the threshold ℓ, which further improves the signing time. The resulting signatures are slightly larger than for the original scheme with the same number of parties (the short version), but our scheme gains a factor 10 in signing and verification time. Compared to the fast version of the original signature scheme (which uses a lower number of parties $N = 32$) and for similar signature size, our scheme gains a factor 3 in signing time and a factor 10 in verification time.

Table 4 further compares our scheme with recent MPCitH schemes based on AES (both AES and SD for random linear codes being deemed as a conservative assumption) as well as with SPHINCS$^+$ [ABB+22] as a baseline conservative scheme. We can observe that our scheme outperforms AES-based candidates for comparable signature sizes (around 10 KB). In particular, compared to Helium+AES [KZ22], signing is 5 times faster with our scheme while verification is 40 times faster. Fast versions of those schemes have signatures about twice larger, while being still slower than ours in signing and verification. Compared to SPHINCS$^+$, our scheme achieves slightly better verification time and much better trade-offs for signature size vs. signing time. Some other MPCitH signature schemes reported in Table 3 achieve smaller signature sizes (down to 5KB) but they are based on less conservative assumptions (LowMC, Rain, BHH PRF). Yet none of these schemes achieve fast verification as SPHINCS$^+$ or our scheme.

6.2   Application of the Batching Strategy

We apply in the full version [FR22] our batching technique to two different contexts:

- We batch non-interactive proofs of knowledge for the syndrome decoding problem using the SDitH scheme [FJR22]. Since SDitH is not compatible

Table 4. Parameters, performances and comparison. The parameters for [FJR22] and our scheme are $(m, k, w) = (256, 128, 80)$ and $\mathbb{F}_{SD} = \mathbb{F}_{poly} = \mathbb{F}_{256}$. Timings for [FJR22] and our scheme have been benchmarked on a 3.8 Ghz Intel Core i7. Timings for Banquet, Helium and SPHINCS$^+$ have been benchmarked on a 3.6 GHz Intel Xeon W-2133 CPU [BDK+21, KZ22]. Timings for Limbo have been benchmarked on a 3.1 GHz Intel i9-9900 CPU [DOT21].

Scheme	N	τ	ℓ	t'	$\|\mathbb{F}_{points}\|$	$\log_2 p$	$\|sgn\|$	t_{sgn}	t_{verif}
Our scheme	256	16	1	3	2^{64}	-167	10.47 KB	7.1 ms	0.46 ms
	256	6	3	3	2^{64}	-167	**9.97 KB**	3.2 ms	**0.38 ms**
	256	3	7	4	2^{64}	-222	11.10 KB	2.5 ms	0.47 ms
	256	2	12	4	2^{64}	-222	11.99 KB	**2.2 ms**	0.51 ms
[FJR22] - Var3f	32	27	–	5	2^{24}	-78	11.5 KB	6.4 ms	5.9 ms
[FJR22] - Var3s	256	17	–	5	2^{24}	-78	8.26 KB	30 ms	27 ms
Banquet (AES)	16	41	–	1	2^{32}	$(-32, -27)$	19.3 KB	6.4 ms	4.9 ms
	255	21	–	1	2^{48}	$(-48, -43)$	13.0 KB	44 ms	40 ms
Limbo-Sign (AES)	16	40	–	–	2^{48}	-40	21.0 KB	2.7 ms	2.0 ms
	255	24	–	–	2^{48}	-40	14.2 KB	29 ms	27 ms
Helium+AES	17	31	–	1	2^{144}	$(-136, -144)$	17.2 KB	6.4 ms	5.8 ms
	256	16	–	1	2^{144}	$(-136, -144)$	9.7 KB	16 ms	16 ms
SPHINCS$^+$-128f	–	–	–	–	–	–	16.7 KB	14 ms	1.7 ms
SPHINCS$^+$-128 s	–	–	–	–	–	–	7.7 KB	239 ms	0.7 ms

with our batching strategy, we propose a tweak of it. We achieve an amortized proof size around 2.3 KB using $\ell = 1$ and around 0.83 KB using $\ell = 8$, instead of around 8 KB (proof size when non batched).

– We batch proofs for general arithmetic circuits using the Limbo proof system [DOT21]. We obtain an amortized proof size lower than $1/10$ of the baseline scheme when batching, while the amortized performances are also significantly improved (in particular for the verifier).

References

[ABB+22] Aumasson, J.-P., et al.: SPHINCS+ - Submission to the 3rd round of the NIST post-quantum project. v3.1 (2022)

[AGH+23] Aguilar-Melchor, C., Gama, N., Howe, J., Hülsing, A., Joseph, D., Yue, D.: The return of the SDitH. In: Hazay, C., Stam, M. (eds.) EUROCRYPT 2023. LNCS, vol. 14008, pp. 564–596. Springer, Cham (2023). https://doi.org/10.1007/978-3-031-30589-4_20

[AHIV17] Ames, S., Hazay, C., Ishai, Y., Venkitasubramaniam, M.: Ligero: lightweight sublinear arguments without a trusted setup. In: ACM CCS 2017, pp. 2087–2104. ACM Press (2017)

[BBHR19] Ben-Sasson, E., Bentov, I., Horesh, Y., Riabzev, M.: Scalable zero knowledge with no trusted setup. In: Boldyreva, A., Micciancio, D. (eds.) CRYPTO 2019. LNCS, vol. 11694, pp. 701–732. Springer, Cham (2019). https://doi.org/10.1007/978-3-030-26954-8_23

[BCR+19] Ben-Sasson, E., Chiesa, A., Riabzev, M., Spooner, N., Virza, M., Ward, N.P.: Aurora: transparent succinct arguments for R1CS. In: Ishai, Y., Rijmen, V. (eds.) EUROCRYPT 2019. LNCS, vol. 11476, pp. 103–128. Springer, Cham (2019). https://doi.org/10.1007/978-3-030-17653-2_4

[BD20] Beullens, W., Delpech de Saint Guilhem, C.: LegRoast: efficient post-quantum signatures from the Legendre PRF. In: Ding, J., Tillich, J.-P. (eds.) PQCrypto 2020. LNCS, vol. 12100, pp. 130–150. Springer, Cham (2020). https://doi.org/10.1007/978-3-030-44223-1_8

[BDK+21] Baum, C., de Saint Guilhem, C.D., Kales, D., Orsini, E., Scholl, P., Zaverucha, G.: Banquet: short and fast signatures from AES. In: Garay, J.A. (ed.) PKC 2021. LNCS, vol. 12710, pp. 266–297. Springer, Cham (2021). https://doi.org/10.1007/978-3-030-75245-3_11

[BFH+20] Bhadauria, R., Fang, Z., Hazay, C., Venkitasubramaniam, M., Xie, T., Zhang, Y.: Ligero++: a new optimized sublinear IOP. In: ACM CCS 2020, pp. 2025–2038. ACM Press (2020)

[BHH01] Boneh, D., Halevi, S., Howgrave-Graham, N.: The modular inversion hidden number problem. In: Boyd, C. (ed.) ASIACRYPT 2001. LNCS, vol. 2248, pp. 36–51. Springer, Heidelberg (2001). https://doi.org/10.1007/3-540-45682-1_3

[BN20] Baum, C., Nof, A.: Concretely-efficient zero-knowledge arguments for arithmetic circuits and their application to lattice-based cryptography. In: Kiayias, A., Kohlweiss, M., Wallden, P., Zikas, V. (eds.) PKC 2020. LNCS, vol. 12110, pp. 495–526. Springer, Cham (2020). https://doi.org/10.1007/978-3-030-45374-9_17

[CC06] Chen, H., Cramer, R.: Algebraic geometric secret sharing schemes and secure multi-party computations over small fields. In: Dwork, C. (ed.) CRYPTO 2006. LNCS, vol. 4117, pp. 521–536. Springer, Heidelberg (2006). https://doi.org/10.1007/11818175_31

[CDG+17] Chase, M., et al.: Post-quantum zero-knowledge and signatures from symmetric-key primitives. In: ACM CCS 2017, pp. 1825–1842. ACM Press (2017)

[CDN15] Cramer, R., Damgård, I.B., Nielsen, J.B.: Secure Multiparty Computation and Secret Sharing. Cambridge University Press, Cambridge (2015)

[DDOS19] de Saint Guilhem, C.D., De Meyer, L., Orsini, E., Smart, N.P.: BBQ: using AES in picnic signatures. In: Paterson, K.G., Stebila, D. (eds.) SAC 2019. LNCS, vol. 11959, pp. 669–692. Springer, Cham (2020). https://doi.org/10.1007/978-3-030-38471-5_27

[DKR+21] Dobraunig, C., Kales, D., Rechberger, C., Schofnegger, M., Zaverucha, G.: Shorter signatures based on tailor-made minimalist symmetric-key crypto. Cryptology ePrint Archive, Report 2021/692 (2021)

[DOT21] de Saint Guilhem, C.D., Orsini, E., Tanguy, T.: Limbo: efficient zero-knowledge MPCitH-based arguments. In: ACM CCS 2021, pp. 3022–3036. ACM Press (2021)

[FJR22] Feneuil, T., Joux, A., Rivain, M.: Syndrome decoding in the head: Shorter signatures from zero-knowledge proofs. In: Dodis, Y., Shrimpton, T. (eds.) CRYPTO 2022. LNCS, vol. 13508, pp. 541–572. Springer, Heidelberg (2022). https://doi.org/10.1007/978-3-031-15979-4_19

[FMRV22] Feneuil, T., Maire, J., Rivain, M., Vergnaud, D.: Zero-knowledge protocols for the subset sum problem from MPC-in-the-head with rejection. In: Agrawal, S., Lin, D. (eds.) ASIACRYPT 2022. LNCS, vol. 13792, pp. 371–402. Springer, Cham (2022). https://doi.org/10.1007/978-3-031-22966-4_13

[FR22] Feneuil, T., Rivain, M.: Threshold linear secret sharing to the rescue of MPC-in-the-head. Cryptology ePrint Archive, Report 2022/1407 (2022)

[FS87] Fiat, A., Shamir, A.: How to prove yourself: practical solutions to identification and signature problems. In: Odlyzko, A.M. (ed.) CRYPTO 1986. LNCS, vol. 263, pp. 186–194. Springer, Heidelberg (1987). https://doi.org/10.1007/3-540-47721-7_12

[GMO16] Giacomelli, I., Madsen, J., Orlandi, C.: ZKBoo: faster zero-knowledge for Boolean circuits. In: USENIX Security 2016, pp. 1069–1083. USENIX Association (2016)

[GSV21] Gvili, Y., Scheffler, S., Varia, M.: BooLigero: improved sublinear zero knowledge proofs for Boolean circuits. In: Borisov, N., Diaz, C. (eds.) FC 2021. LNCS, vol. 12674, pp. 476–496. Springer, Heidelberg (2021). https://doi.org/10.1007/978-3-662-64322-8_23

[IKOS07] Ishai, Y., Kushilevitz, E., Ostrovsky, R., Sahai, A.: Zero-knowledge from secure multiparty computation. In: 39th ACM STOC, pp. 21–30. ACM Press (2007)

[KKW18] Katz, J., Kolesnikov, V., Wang, X.: Improved non-interactive zero knowledge with applications to post-quantum signatures. In: ACM CCS 2018, pp. 525–537. ACM Press (2018)

[KZ20a] Kales, D., Zaverucha, G.: An attack on some signature schemes constructed from five-pass identification schemes. In: Krenn, S., Shulman, H., Vaudenay, S. (eds.) CANS 2020. LNCS, vol. 12579, pp. 3–22. Springer, Cham (2020). https://doi.org/10.1007/978-3-030-65411-5_1

[KZ20b] Kales, D., Zaverucha, G.: Improving the performance of the Picnic signature scheme. IACR TCHES **2020**(4), 154–188 (2020)

[KZ21] Kales, D., Zaverucha, G.: Efficient lifting for shorter zero-knowledge proofs and post-quantum signatures. Preliminary Draft, 29 October 2021

[KZ22] Kales, D., Zaverucha, G.: Efficient lifting for shorter zero-knowledge proofs and post-quantum signatures. Cryptology ePrint Archive, Report 2022/588 (2022)

[MS10] MacWilliams, F.J., Sloane, N.J.A.: The Theory of Error-Correcting Codes, 9th edn. Discrete Mathematics and its Applications. Elsevier Science (1978/2010)

[Sha79] Shamir, A.: How to share a secret. Commun. Assoc. Compu. Mach. **22**(11), 612–613 (1979)

Author Index

J. Guo and R. Steinfeld (Eds.): ASIACRYPT 2023, LNCS 14438, pp. 475–476, 2023.
https://doi.org/10.1007/978-981-99-8721-4

Printed in the United States
by Baker & Taylor Publisher Services